July 11–13, 2016
Arequipa, Peru

I0028880

**Association for
Computing Machinery**

Advancing Computing as a Science & Profession

ITiCSE'16

Proceedings of the 2016 ACM Conference on
Innovation and Technology in Computer
Science Education

Sponsored by:
ACM SIGCSE

Supported by:
Universidad Católica San Pablo & Eastern Institute of Technology

Association for
Computing Machinery

Advancing Computing as a Science & Profession

The Association for Computing Machinery
2 Penn Plaza, Suite 701
New York, New York 10121-0701

Notice to Past Authors of ACM-Published Articles

ISBN: 978-1-4503-4231-5 (Digital)

ISBN: 978-1-4503-4610-8 (Print)

Additional copies may be ordered prepaid from:

ACM Order Department
PO Box 30777
New York, NY 10087-0777, USA

Phone: 1-800-342-6626 (USA and Canada)
+1-212-626-0500 (Global)
Fax: +1-212-944-1318
E-mail: acmhelp@acm.org
Hours of Operation: 8:30 am – 4:30 pm ET

Printed in the USA

Foreword

Bienvenido!

Welcome to ITiCSE 2016 in Arequipa.

In Peru, Arequipa is called the "The independent Republic of Arequipa." Our city is a UNESCO World Heritage Site. Its historic heritage, natural scenery and cultural sites make the city a major tourist destination. Its religious, colonial, and republican architectural styles blend European and native characteristics into a unique style. During the last years, Arequipa has been recognized as the best place to study computing programs in Peru. It is probably one of the reasons we have ITiCSE this year here!

The conference continues to be a truly international conference with 147 submissions from 35 countries on six continents (Africa - 5, Asia - 13, Europe - 36, North America - 55, Oceania - 18, and South America - 20); and that is only considering the first author. These submissions consisted of 134 papers, 3 panels, and 10 working group proposals. Additionally, there were 43 posters and the tips & techniques submissions spanning 13 countries.

All research papers were double blind reviewed by at least three reviewers, though most papers received between four and six reviews. This year 38% were selected for presentation and inclusion in the proceedings. The first authors of the papers are distributed over 22 different countries on six continents.

All posters and tips & techniques submissions were also reviewed by members of the program committee. Twenty six Poster papers and nine Tips and Techniques papers were accepted, representing 12 countries.

There are seven working groups including gender equity, game development, academic integrity, teaching specific issues and internationalization. Participating in a working group is probably one of the most efficient ways to become part of the ITiCSE community. It provides participants a unique opportunity to work with people from different countries who are interested and knowledgeable in the area of the working group.

This conference will have two keynote speakers. Mehran Sahami from Stanford University, under the title "Statistical Modeling to Better Understand CS Students" will present some statistical models trying to explain specific behavior for CS students. Mats Daniels will talk about "Professional Competencies for Real? A Question about Identity!" will talk about how to meet competences for real problems.

The conference dinner will be held at the Santa Catalina Monastery. It was built in 1579 and was enlarged in the 17th century. The over 20,000-square-meter monastery was built predominantly in the Mudéjar style, and is characterized by its vividly painted walls. There are approximately 20 nuns currently living in the northern corner of the complex; the rest of the monastery is open to the public. Attendees will also have the opportunity to enjoy one of two local excursions and one or two post conference tours, the first to the famous Colca Canyon and also the world famous Inca ruins of Machu Picchu.

Le damos la bienvenida a Arequipa, to enjoy ITiCSE in Peru.

Alison Clear and Ernesto Cuadros   **Janet Carter and Yvan Tupac**
ITiCSE 2016 Conference Chairs   *ITiCSE 2016 Program Co-Chairs*

Table of Contents

Keynote Talks

Session 1A: Panel Session

Session 1B: Mobile Computing

Session 1C: Active Learning

Session 2B: Automated Feedback

Session 4C: Exam Issues

Session 5A: Panel Session

Session 5B: Software Engineering

Session 5C: CS Education Research

Session 6A: Panel Session

Session 6B: Motivational Issues

Session 6C: Tools

Session 7A: Tips, Techniques & Courseware

Session 7B: Data Driven Automation

Session 7C: Introductory Programming

Session 8A: Skills & Misconceptions

Session 8B: Pedagogical Issues

Session 8C: Curriculum Issues

Poster Session

ITiCSE 2016 Conference Organization

Conference Co-Chairs: Alison Clear *(Eastern Institute of Technology, New Zealand)*
Ernesto Cuadros-Vargas *(San Pablo Catholic University, Peru)*

Program Co-Chairs: Janet Carter *(University of Kent, UK)*
Yvan Tupac *(San Pablo Catholic University, Peru)*

Treasurer & Registration Chair: Cary Laxer *(Rose-Hulman Institute of Technology, USA)*

Working Groups: Tony Clear *(Auckland University of Technology, New Zealand)*
Dennis Barrios *(San Pablo Catholic University, Peru)*
John Barr *(Ithaca College, USA)*

Panels: Simon *(University of Newcastle, Australia)*

Tips, Techniques & Courseware: Dennis J Bouvier *(Southern Illinois University Edwardsville, USA)*

Proceedings: Stan Kurkovsky *(Central Connecticut State University, USA)*
Michael Goldweber *(Xavier University, USA)*

Posters: Amruth Kumar *(Ramapo College of New Jersey, USA)*

Database Coordinators: Brad Miller *(Luther College, USA)*

International liaison: Diana Cukierman *(Simon Fraser University, Canada)*

Publicity: Michelle Craig *(University of Toronto, Canada)*

Evaluations: Renzo Davoli *(University of Bologna, Italy)*

Student Volunteers: Luisa Nuñez *(San Pablo Catholic University, Peru)*
Barbara Chicata *(San Pablo Catholic University, Peru)*
Angela Talavera *(San Pablo Catholic University, Peru)*

Website: Luisa Nuñez Villagomez *(San Pablo Catholic University, Peru)*

Local Committee: Yessenia Yari *(San Pablo Catholic University, Peru)*
Julio Santisteban *(San Pablo Catholic University, Peru)*

ITiCSE 2016 Reviewers

Name	Affiliation
Raman Adaikkalavan	Indiana University South Bend
Rajeev Agrawal	North Carolina A & T State University
Hend Al-Khalifa	King Saud University
Barbara Anthony	Southwestern University
Michal Armoni	Weizmann Institute of Science
John Aycock	University of Calgary
Doug Baldwin	SUNY Geneseo
Dennis Barrios Aranibar	Universidad Católica San Pablo
Tim Bell	University of Canterbury
Mordechai Ben-Ari	Weizmann Institute of Science
Marie Bienkowski	SRI International
David Bunde	Knox College
Barry Burd	Drew University
Kevin Burger	Arizona State University
Andre Paul Calitz	Nelson Mandela Metropolitan University
Jennifer Campbell	University of Toronto
Janet Carter	University of Kent
Tim Chamillard	University of Colorado at Colorado Springs
Wei Kian Chen	Champlain College
Peng-Wen Chen	Oriental Institute of Technology
Li-hsiang Cheo	William Paterson University of New Jersey
John Cigas	Park University
Dawn Cizmar	St. Edward's University
Alison Clear	Eastern Institute of Technology
Joe Clifton	University of Wisconsin, Platteville
Randy Connolly	Mount Royal University
Stephen Cooper	Stanford University
Michelle Craig	University of Toronto
Joyce Blair Crowell	Belmont University
Lawrence D'Antonio	Ramapo College of New Jersey
Renzo Davoli	University of Bologna
Katherine Deibel	University of Washington-Seattle
Barbara Demo	University Torino
Martin Dick	RMIT University
Zachary Dodds	Harvey Mudd College
J. Philip East	University of Northern Iowa
Alec Engebretson	Doane College

Sergio F. Lopes	University of Minho
Alan Fekete	University of Sydney
Georgios Fesakis	University of the Aegean
Paul Gestwicki	Ball State University
Don Goelman	Villanova University
Jean Goulet	Universite de Sherbrooke
Brian Hanks	Redfin
Stuart Hansen	University of Wisconsin - Parkside
Sarah Heckman	North Carolina State University
Michael Helmick	Google
Tyson Henry	California State University, Chico
Matthew Hertz	Canisius College
Curtis Hill	Valley City State University
Hoda Hosny	The American University in Cairo
Brian Howard	DePauw University
James Huggins	Kettering University
Steven Huss-Lederman	Beloit College
Colin Johnson	University of Kent at Canterbury
Anthony Joseph	Pace University
Mike Joy	University of Warwick
Daniel Joyce	Villanova University
Viggo Kann	KTH
Jennifer Kay	Rowan University
David G. Kay	University of California, Irvine
Petros Kefalas	The University of Sheffield International Faculty
Nancy Kinnersley	University of Kansas
David Klappholz	Stevens Institute of Technology
Carsten Kleiner	University of Applied Sciences & Arts Hannover
Ari Korhonen	Aalto University
Jan Kruger	Unisa school for business leadership
Amruth Kumar	Ramapo College of New Jersey
Benjamin Kuperman	Oberlin College
Stan Kurkovsky	Central Connecticut State University
Zachary Kurmas	Grand Valley State University
Clif Kussmaul	Muhlenberg College
Joan Langdon	Bowie State University
David Largent	Ball State University
Eric Larson	Seattle University
Robert Law	Glasgow Caledonian University
Alina Lazar	Youngstown State University
Arthur Lee	Claremont McKenna College

Gilliean Lee	Lander University
Cynthia Lee	Stanford University
Byong Lee	Bennett College
Chi Un Lei	University of Hong Kong
Andrew Luxton-Reilly	The University of Auckland
Lester McCann	The University of Arizona
O. William McClung	Nebraska Wesleyan University
Sean McCulloch	Ohio Wesleyan University
Susan Mengel	Texas Tech University
Jose Carlos Metrolho	Polytechnic Institute of Castelo Branco
Joe Miro	Universitat de les Illes Balears
Briana Morrison	Southern Polytechnic State University
Srikanth Mudigonda	Saint Louis University
Michael Murphy	Concordia University Texas
Robert Noonan	College of William and Mary
Keith O'Hara	Bard College
Lawrence Osborne	Lamar University
James Paterson	Glasgow Caledonian University
Eileen Peluso	Lycoming College
Teresa Peterman	Grand Valley State University
Andrew Petersen	University of Toronto Mississauga
Vreda Pieterse	University of Pretoria
Wayne Pollock	Hillsborough Community College
Jon Preston	Southern Polytechnic State Unviersity
Sarah Monisha Pulimood	The College of New Jersey
Ricardo Queirós	University of Porto
John Rager	Amherst College
Noa Ragonis	Beit Berl and Technion IIT
Michael Redmond	La Salle University
Charles Riedesel	University of Nebraska - Lincoln
Suzanne Rivoire	Sonoma State University
Christian Roberson	Plymouth State University
Susan H. Rodger	Duke University
Dr. Guido Rößling	TU Darmstadt
Martin Ruckert	Munich University of Applied Sciences
Rebecca Rutherfoord	Southern Polytechnic State University
Roberta Evans Sabin	Loyola College
Mehran Sahami	Stanford University
Ian Sanders	University of South Africa
André Santos	ISCTE-IUL
Otto Seppälä	Aalto University

Amber Settle	DePaul University
Cliff Shaffer	Virginia Tech
Ching-Kuang Shene	Michigan Technological University
Mark Sherriff	University of Virginia
Yasuto Shirai	Shizuoka University
Simon	University of Newcastle
Peter Smith	California State University - Channel Islands
Jaime Spacco	Knox College
Ben Stephenson	University of Calgary
Fred Strickland	South University
Kazunari Sugiyama	National University of SIngapore
Valerie Summet	Emory University
Megan Thomas	California State University Stanislaus
Rebecca Thomas	Bard College
William Turner	Wabash College
Hakan Tuzun	Hacettepe University
Ian Utting	University of Kent at Canterbury
Jan Vahrenhold	Westfälische Wilhelms-Universität Münster
Tammy VanDeGrift	University of Portland
Brad Vander Zanden	University of Tennessee
Yaakov Varol	University of Nevada Reno
Jorge Vasconcelos	Johns Hopkins University
Troy Vasiga	University of Waterloo
Steven Vegdahl	University of Portland
David Voorhees	Le Moyne College
Sally Wahba	Clemson University
Henry Walker	Grinnell College
Thomas Way	Villanova University
Linda Werner	University of California, Santa Cruz
Howard Whitston	University of South Alabama
Linda Wilkens	Providence College
Steven Wolfman	University of British Columbia
Arthur Yanushka	Christian Brothers University
Duane Yoder	University of West Georgia
Daniel Zingaro	University of Toronto

ITiCSE 2016 Working Groups

Working Group 1: Latin American Perspectives to Internationalize Undergraduate Information Technology Education

Co-Leaders: Mihaela Sabin *(University of New Hampshire, USA)*
Barbara Viola *(Viotech Solutions, Inc., USA)*
John Impagliazzo *(Hofstra University, USA)*

Participants: Renzo Angles *(University of Talca, Chile)*
Mariela Curiel *(Pontificia Universidad Javeriana, Colombia)*
Paul Leger *(Universidad Católica del Norte, Chile)*
Jorge Murillo *(IEEE Computer Society, Costa Rica)*
Nina Hernan *(Universidad Nacional de San Antonio Abad del Cusco, Peru)*
Jose Antonio Pow-Sang *(Pontificia Universidad Católica del Perú, Peru)*
Cara Tang *(Portland Community College, USA)*
Ignacio Trejos *(Universidad Cenfotec, Costa Rica)*

Working Group 2: Game Development for Computer Science Education

Co-Leaders: Chris Johnson *(University of Wisconsin, USA)*
Monica McGill *(Bradley University, USA)*

Participants: Z. Sweedyk *(Harvey Mudd College, USA)*
Michael Adrir Scott *(Falmouth University, UK)*
Larry Merkel *(Air Force Institute of Technology, USA)*
Durell Bouchard *(Roanoke College, USA)*
Michael Bradshaw *(Centre College, USA)*
Mohammed Fouad *(Winston-Salem University, USA)*
Randy Kaplan *(Kuztown University, USA)*
J. Angel Velazquez Iturbide *(Universidad Rey Juan Carlos, Spain)*

Working Group 3: Teaching Model-Driven Software Development

Co-Leaders: Ludwik Kuzniarz *(Blekinge Institute of Technology, Sweden)*
Luiz Eduardo G. Martins *(Federal University of São Paulo, Brazil)*
Plínio R. S. Vilela *(D2S, Brazil)*

Working Group 4: Ground Rules for Academic Integrity in Computing

Co-Leaders: Simon *(University of Newcastle, Australia)*
Judy Sheard *(Monash University, Australia)*

Participants: Amber Settle *(DePaul University, USA)*
Andrew Petersen *(University of Toronto, Canada)*
Charles Riedesel *(University of Nebraska – Lincoln, USA)*
Gerry Cross *(Mount Royal University, Canada)*
Jane Sinclair *(University of Warwick, UK)*
Michael Morgan *(Monash University, Australia)*

Working Group 5: Gender Equity in Computing Programs

Co-Leaders: Margaret Hamilton *(RMIT University, Melbourne, Australia)*
Andrew Luxton-Reilly *(University of Auckland, New Zealand)*

Participants: Shoba Ittyipe *(Mount Royal University, Canada)*
Lecia Barker *(University of Texas, USA)*
Helen Hu *(Westminster College, USA)*
Vanea Chiprianov *(University of Pau & the Adour Region, France)*
Naomi Augar *(RMIT University, Australia)*
Michael Oudshoorn *(Wentworth Institute of Technology, USA)*
Eveling Gloria Castro Gutierrez *(Catholic University of Santa Maria, Arequipa, Peru)*
Elizabeth Vidal Duarte *(La Salle University, Arequipa, Peru)*
Emma Wong *(Carmel Institute, USA)*

Working Group 6: Novice Programmers and the Problem Description Effect

Co-Leaders: Dennis Bouvier *(Southern Illinois University, USA)*
John Matta *(Southern Illinois University, USA)*
Ellie Lovellette *(Southern Illinois University, USA)*

Participants: Brett Becker *(University College Dublin, Ireland)*
Mark Zarb *(Robert Gordon University, UK)*
Jana Jackova *(Matej Bel University, Slovakia)*
Kate Sanders *(Rhode Island College, USA)*
Michelle Craig *(University of Toronto, Canada)*
Robert McCartney *(University of Connecticut, USA)*
Bedour Alshaigy *(Oxford Brookes University, UK)*

Working Group 7: Game Jam Junior Working Group

Co-Leaders: Allan Fowler *(Kennesaw State University, USA)*
Johanna Pirker *(Graz University of Technology, Austria)*

Participants: Bruno Campagnola de Paula *(Pontifical Catholic University of Paraná, Brazil)*
Marco Lopez *(San Agustin University of Arequipa, Peru)*
Emilia Echeveste *(National University of Córdoba, Argentina)*
Marcos J. Gómez *(National University of Córdoba, Argentina)*
Ian Pollock *(California State University (East Bay), USA)*

ITiCSE 2016 Sponsor & Supporters

Sponsor:

Supporters:

 Universidad Católica **San Pablo**

Statistical Modeling to Better Understand CS Students

Mehran Sahami
Stanford University
Stanford, CA, USA
sahami@cs.stanford.edu

Abstract

While educational data mining has often focused on modeling behavior at the level of individual students, we consider developing statistical models to give us insight into the dynamics of student populations. In this talk, we consider two case studies in this vein. The first involves analyzing the evolution of gender balance in a college computer science program, showing that focusing on percentages of underrepresented groups in the overall population may not always provide an accurate portrayal of the impact of various program changes. We propose a new statistical model based on Fisher's Noncentral Hypergeometric Distribution that better captures how program changes are impacting the dynamics of gender balance in a population, especially in the case where the overall population is rapidly increasing (as has been the case in CS in recent years).

Our second study looks at the performance of student populations in an introductory college programming course during the past eight years to better understand the evolving mix of students' abilities given the rapid growth in the number of students taking CS courses. Often accompanying such growth is a concern from faculty that the additional students choosing to pursue computing may not have the same aptitude for the subject as was seen in prior student populations. To directly address this question, we present a statistical analysis of students' performance using mixture modeling. Importantly, in this setting many variables that would normally confound such a study are directly controlled for. We find that the distribution of student performance during this period, as reflected in their programming assignment scores, remains remarkably stable despite the large growth in course enrollments. The results of this analysis also show how conflicting perceptions of students' abilities among faculty can be consistently explained.

The presentation includes work done jointly with Sarah Evans, Chris Piech, and Katie Redmond.

Keywords

Educational data mining; Gender balance; Student Performance; Introductory courses

Bio

Mehran Sahami is a Professor and Associate Chair for Education in the Computer Science department at Stanford University. He is also the Robert and Ruth Halperin University Fellow in Undergraduate Education at Stanford. In 2014, he received the ACM Presidential Award for his work on the CS2013 curricular guidelines in computer science. He also co-founded the ACM Conference on Learning at Scale, which has become an annual meeting focused on interdisciplinary research at the intersection of the learning sciences and computer science. In addition to his work in CS education, Mehran has published over 50 technical papers and has over 20 patent filings on a variety of topics including machine learning, web search, recommendation engines in social networks, and email spam filtering that have been deployed in several commercial applications.

Permission to make digital or hard copies of part or all of this work for personal or classroom use is granted without fee provided that copies are not made or distributed for profit or commercial advantage and that copies bear this notice and the full citation on the first page. Copyrights for third-party components of this work must be honored. For all other uses, contact the Owner/Author.
Copyright is held by the owner/author(s).
ITiCSE '16, July 09-13, 2016, Arequipa, Peru
ACM 978-1-4503-4231-5/16/07.
http://dx.doi.org/10.1145/2899415.2925470

Professional Competencies for Real?
A Question about Identity!

Mats Daniels

Uppsala University,
Uppsala, Sweden
Mats.Daniels@it.uu.se

Abstract

How students develop professional competencies has been an interest for me for decades. There are several aspects to this issue that I have addressed, e.g. what are professional competencies, how can their development of them be supported in educational settings, what motivates a student to put in an effort towards developing a competency, how can they be assessed, how can progression of professional competencies be handled in education curricula, and how can development of professional competencies be specified in a course description. These are among the more prominent issues that have been on my mind. In this work I have noticed a huge "gap" between how professional competencies are expressed as important learning outcomes of degree programs and the almost zero link to how this development should be done at the course instance level. This "gap" is frustrating for me and a source for thoughts regarding how to bridge that "gap".

Work in our research group UpCERG (Uppsala Computing Education Research Group, www.it.uu.se/research/group/upcerg) has lately included studying issues related to identity, initially mostly the identity of different student cohorts, but now also that of teachers and education leaders. This research provides valuable insights towards causes for the "gap". That is, the slow closing of the "gap" can be understood by placing this in the context of the identity of the teachers (especially) and the students. It is how professional competencies are valued in relation to "pure" subject knowledge among these identities that provides severe obstacles to inclusion of development of professional competencies in a meaningful way at the course instance level. This is despite much of the previous work regarding issues related to developing professional competencies in educational settings, as those mentioned above.

I will address how I view the identities of teachers and students interfering with integration of development of professional competencies in degree programs. I will give examples from our research and my experience that illustrates the difficulties and outline some potential interventions that might lead to changes. My hope is that this talk will result in many fruitful discussions, both at the talk and afterwards.

Keywords

Student competencies; Student and teacher identities

Bio

Mats Daniels is Associate Professor and director of undergraduate studies at the Department of Information Technology, Uppsala University, Sweden. Mats is also director of the national centre for pedagogical development in technology education in a societal and student oriented context (CeTUSS, www.cetuss.se) and future site coordinator for the ACM ITiCSE conference. He is a founder and member of the Uppsala Computing Education Research Group (UpCERG, http://www.it.uu.se/research/group/upcerg). He has published over 100 journal and conference papers. His ambition when it comes to education is to find new formats and especially such where the students will experience a holistic learning environment, e.g. in Open Ended Group Projects.

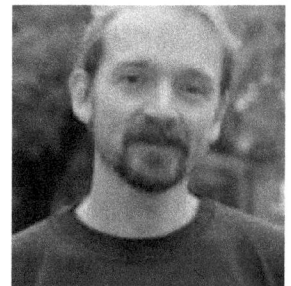

ITiCSE '16, July 09-13, 2016, Arequipa, Peru
ACM 978-1-4503-4231-5/16/07.
http://dx.doi.org/10.1145/2899415.2925471

The Best Way to Unblock the Pipeline in CS is by Getting Everyone to Code in Schools. A Debate.

Annemieke Craig	Catherine Lang	MaryAnne Egan	Reyyan Ayfer
Deakin University	La Trobe University	Siena College	Bilkent University
Victoria	Victoria	New York	Ankara
Australia	Australia	United States	Turkey
+61352272152	+61394791858	1+518-782-6546	+903122905065
a.craig@deakin.edu.au	c.lang@latrobe.edu.au	maegan@siena.edu	ayfer@bilkent.edu.tr

ABSTRACT

Many believe that the push to increase the number of skilled computer scientists must be a multi-pronged approach and be institutionalized at all levels of education. Some federal and local governments are requiring that all students become proficient in technical areas in primary and secondary schooling. Will the call for all schools to teach every student coding be the magic bullet that unblocks the computing pipeline? Is adding another core subject to an already crowded curricula the answer? Are schools ready? It is noted that there is no universal computer science/coding curriculum for teachers to follow, some teachers don't have the skills or the enthusiasm to do this, not all students can think logically so why try to force them? In the words of Einstein "Everybody is a genius. But if you judge a fish by its ability to climb a tree, it will live its whole life believing that it is stupid".

Keywords

Gender diversity; computing curricula; teacher technical self-efficacy

Debate Facilitator

Barbara Boucher Owens, Ph.D., Southwestern University

1. Speakers For:

Dr Annemieke Craig is an Associate Professor in the Business School at Deakin University. Annemieke researches in the field of Information Systems with particular emphasis on trying to increase the involvement and representation of women in the computing professions. Annemieke has contributed to building the Women in Computing community, nationally and internationally.

ITiCSE '16, July 09-13, 2016, Arequipa, Peru
ACM 978-1-4503-4231-5/16/07.
http://dx.doi.org/10.1145/2899415.2899418

On an international scale Annemieke was a council member of ACM-W, the Australian Ambassador for the ACM's Committee for Women and then led the ambassador program. She has chaired the Global Advisory Committee for two Grace Hopper Conferences as well as organising international panels at three Grace Hopper Conferences. Annemieke has been on the organising committee for the Go Girl- Go for IT program and a chief investigator in the ARC Funded research project Digital Divas.

Dr MaryAnne Egan is a Professor of Computer Science at Siena College. MaryAnne is involved in various aspects of computer science education including the recruitment and retention of underrepresented groups. In addition to presenting on these topics, she is co-PI on an NSF IUSE grant and regularly participates on the conference committees for Grace Hopper Celebration of Women in Computing, SIGCSE, ACM's Conference for Innovation and Technology in Computer Science Education (ITiCSE), Consortium for Computing Sciences in Colleges — Northeastern Region (CCSCNE) and NYCWiC. She is a member of the international Association of Computing Machinery Committee on Women in Computing, co-founder of the regional New York Celebration of Women in Computing (NYCWiC), and an active member of ACM Special Interest Group for Computer Science Education (SIGCSE).

2. For argument:

Some of the points that will be addressed by the FOR speakers include but are not limited to:

- Currently, many students are not exposed to coding, so they are unsure about careers in the field.
- If coding is compulsory, underrepresented groups in lower socio-economic schools would have access to the classes that are typically offered in the more affluent schools.
- Students who want to code now need to pay for lessons or seek out these schools.
- There will be 1.4 million new jobs created in the future in computing [1] and we aren't producing enough graduates to fill these jobs [2]
- We are currently missing large groups of young people who could help to mitigate the deficit of qualified tech employees
- While there may be a lack of teacher skills this is not insurmountable - students can turn to each other-- which could further encourage some students to not only work in CS, but possibly teach.
- Currently there is insufficient exposure at school to computational/algorithmic thinking – coding is a necessary

way for students to understand the concepts of data, information and knowledge. Once students develop these computational skills, the idea of a major or career in CS is less daunting.

- Getting everyone to code in school takes away the stigma that is often associated with students who take CS classes in high school and eventually, computer scientists, in general.

- Students who go on to study other majors can take the knowledge learned in CS to enhance other career areas. Our world is much more interdisciplinary and most careers require some kind of technical knowledge. So, not only could we unblock the pipeline, we could even expand it!

3. Speakers Against:

Dr Catherine Lang is an Associate Professor in the School of Education, La Trobe University. Her research focus since 1996 has been on the under-representation of women in computing, which resulted in an Australian Research Council grant "Digital Divas" developing a curriculum based initiative for secondary school girls. She has published on the topics of student transition to higher education, computing education and pedagogy, as well as social networking in education. She was a founding board member of the Victorian ICT for Women Network, the ACM-W Australian Ambassador from 2005-2011 and the International Committee Liaison for the ACM's Special Interest Group for Computer Science Education (SIGCSE) for 2012 and 2013. She was the recipient of several competitive national and university grant and awards in recognition of her research strengths including Google CS4HS grants in 2013, 2014 and 2015.

Reyyan Ayfer decided to pursue a role in the field of education. after working for various organizations as a computer engineer for more than a decade and noting the increasing demand for expertise in programming, In 1988 she began working at Bilkent University in Ankara, Turkey and held a multitude of titles including: Department Chair of Computer Technology and Programming and Vice Chair of Computer and Instructional Technology Teacher Education where she also teaches, and the Director of the Institutional Relations and History Unit and Coordinator of BETS Bilkent Educational Technology Services. She also contributes her time to international committees, most notably as a council member of ACM Europe and as the Chair of ACM Women in Computing Europe Committee as well as leading a community of students who have formed the first international ACM-W Student Chapter.

4. Against Argument:

The against team will present a position that questions both the merit and feasibility of this proposal before questioning the effectiveness of compulsory computer science subjects in schools to unblock the pipeline.

The against argument will address, but are not limited to these points:

- There are many disciplines competing for space in the curriculum in schools. Education is a very competitive field - unfortunately it is driven by politics [3].

- Currently the political conversations are around STEM [with or without the A for Arts] Consider each of these subjects. Science is core in most curricula to Year 10. Technology is used in schools, 1:1 devices are the norm in western nations. Engineering is about creativity and hands on activities in the tech block and in most schools Maths is core to Year 10 [4].

- These disciplines also lack diversity and popularity despite being compulsory in the curriculum. Compulsory subjects do not create desire for further education in the discipline.

- The issue is not a lack of awareness of computer science. The issue is who influences students in their course and career choices: parents, teachers [5,6].

- The issue is also the schizophrenic nature of the discipline – computer science, information systems, information technology, media computation.

- The issue is the continued gender stereotypes and poor behaviors that get much media – young pale males, brogrammers, ageist, sexist, racist [7,8].

- Introducing compulsory coding will have a minimal influence on parents and may turn teachers away too - The two major course and career choice influencers.

5. References

[1]   Department of Labor Bureau of Labor, Employment by Detailed Occupation 2014 (Occupational Category: 15-1100)

[2]   New York Times: De Blasio to Announce 10-Year Deadline to Offer Computer Science to All Students, 9/15/15.
(http://www.nytimes.com/2015/09/16/nyregion/de-blasio-to-announce-10-year-deadline-to-offer-computer-science-to-all-students.html)

[3]   Teacher Magazine Stem Subjects Open Up Diverse Career Paths 5 April 2016
https://www.teachermagazine.com.au/article/stem-subjects-open-up-diverse-career-paths

[4]   Report: Australia's STEM Workforce
http://www.chiefscientist.gov.au/2016/03/report-australias-stem-workforce/ March 2016

[5]   Lang, C. (2010). Happenstance and Compromise: a gendered analysis of students computing degree course selection. Computer Science Education, 20(4), 317-345.

[6]   Lang, C. (2012). Sequential Attrition of Secondary School Student Interest in IT Courses and Careers. Information Technology and People, 25(3), 281-299.

[7]   Lyons, D. Congratulations! You've been fired. April 9 2016
http://www.nytimes.com/2016/04/10/opinion/sunday/congratulations-youve-been-fired.html?_r=0

[8]   Wong, A. The Australian tech industry will only close the skills gap if it addresses diversity. 26 April 2016
http://www.startupsmart.com.au/advice/growth/the-australia-it-industry-will-only-close-the-skills-gap-when-it-addresses-diversity/

Seven Semesters of Android Game Programming in CS2

Michael Black
Bridgewater State University
131 Summer St
Bridgewater, MA 02325
micheal.black@bridge.edu

ABSTRACT

Mobile game development is a topic that interests many computer science students. The author included an open-ended Android game development project as the final project in a CS2 course for four years. Over 7 semesters, 141 students produced 87 different mobile games, of which 29 were published on the Google Play store. This paper discusses the experience of how this Android project was integrated with the course, as well as the projects themselves, and examines the factors that led to successful student submissions.

Keywords
CS2; Android

1. INTRODUCTION

Over seven semesters, from 2011 until 2015, the author included an Android development component in CSC-281, "Introduction to Computer Science II", the second required course for computer science majors at a small computer science department at American University. This component primarily consisted of a three week open-ended project where students, mostly working in teams, developed an Android game of their choosing. Students were required to write a proposal describing their intended game, were given two weeks of development time, and demonstrated their game to the class during the final lecture period. Bonus points were awarded if the students published their game to the Google Play Store.

Introduction to Computer Science II is a typical second course, introducing objects and classes, inheritance, event-driven programming, GUIs, threads, and elementary data structures. Students are exposed to the Java language for the first time. Two major projects were assigned: the first, Chess, was completed using Java Swing, and the second was a game of the students' choosing. Additionally students completed 3 to 5 smaller programming assignments, which, combined with the two projects, made up the bulk of the course grade.

ITiCSE '16, July 09-13, 2016, Arequipa, Peru
© 2016 ACM. ISBN 978-1-4503-4231-5/16/07...$15.00
DOI: http://dx.doi.org/10.1145/2899415.2899470

The Android project, when introduced to the course as a one-off experiment, took the place of the second project. Inserting Android into the course resulted in several challenges and

tradeoffs, as discussed below, however student surveys, evaluations, and word-of-mouth were consistently positive and the experiment was continued. This has resulted in an archive of 61 unique student submissions, completed by 89 students total (26 projects were unfortunately not uploaded to Blackboard and are consequently lost). This archive of games is examined in this paper, which seeks to determine which projects were successful and what factors made for a successful project.

2. Integrating Android into CS2

Mobile development courses are becoming common in the computer science curriculum. It was not the objective of this experiment to transform CS2 into such a course; rather we sought to include Android programming with a minimum of disruption to the schedule. On the other hand we did not provide students with toolkits to simplify the experience, as was done in other studies [7]. All student work was done in Eclipse or Android Studio using the standard Android SDK and the Android emulator. The goals of the project were: 1) to engage students by offering them a "real world" platform, 2) to show students that they were able to do mobile development (students widely believed that this was an arcane skill far beyond their ability), 3) to reward students by publishing their work, and 4) to give them a marketable skill that could lead to internships.

Android programming, in its basic form, is not much different than Swing. The primary challenges were setting up the software on the students' own computers and teaching students who did not own Android phones to use the emulator. This tended to be a lengthy and frustrating process, not least due to the variety of operating systems students used and the quirkiness of the Android development software. For this reason we found that Android was best introduced in the 8th or 9th week of the semester when the students were comfortable with Swing and less likely to translate their difficulties with Android into frustration with the course in general.

Approximately two to three weeks of lecture time on Android was needed to prepare students for the project, meaning that sorting algorithms and data structures were given less coverage. This lecture time was spent as follows:

1 or 2 lessons: installing the software and translating a previous Swing class exercise to Android

2 lessons: writing a small game in Android as a class exercise. Two games chosen by the students and developed in class included "Flying Pandas": tapping a Panda bear as it flies around the screen, and "Robotachi": a Tamagatchi-like game of caring for a robot.

1 lesson (optionally): learning a mobile-specific feature, such as sound, accelerometer, or SMS texting

1   lesson: introducing and explaining a homework assignment.

2.1 DC-Locator

DC-Locator" is a homework assignment given to the students to help them get comfortable with Android before assigning the larger project.

"Your objective is to create an Android GPS tracker utility for the DC area. Your program should display a map of DC. Every ten seconds it should read the latitude and longitude from the Android GPS system and store it into an arraylist. It should then draw lines between the readings, thus plotting your movement on the map."

The assignment was written as a tutorial and provided detailed step-by-step instructions. Students would: 1) Create the "Hello world" default app; 2) make a nested *View* class that would display a map image given with the assignment; 3) make an ArrayList of latitude/longitude coordinates; 4) scale coordinates to the screen so that, for example, a latitude of 38.99 (the northernmost point in DC) would map to pixel 0; 5) iterate through the coordinate list and draw lines over the map image showing the paths taken; 6) call a read GPS function, given to the students, to read coordinates from the phone's GPS and save them in the list, 7) instantiate a thread to call that function every ten seconds. On completing the assignment students would learn Thread instantiation, ArrayLists, the Android GPS interface, and linear scaling, and finally how to build a simple app and deploy it to an Android phone.

3. The Project

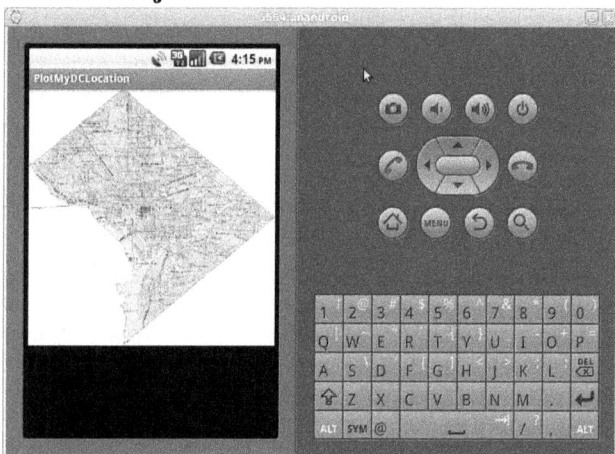

The creative design project required students to implement a board game in teams of two. The project statement provided examples of 12 board games such as *Sorry, Monopoly, Settlers of Catan,* gave examples of previous student projects, and explained how ambitious the students' work should be. It was emphasized that the final submission need not be a exact reproduction of the game, but rather model the game's core functionality. Students were also explicitly allowed to choose a game other than the ones listed, a non-board game, or a novel game; however, the game had to be of similar complexity to the listed examples.

At the end of the first week students had to submit a design proposal that included a description of the game, UI mockups, class hierarchy, data structures to be used, team members and roles, and a timeline. Students were expected to meet with the instructor in individual groups after preparing this document.

Two weeks later, each group demonstrated their final project to the class. Grades were assigned based on the following criteria: 1) Did the game compile and run?, 2) Was the game ambitious or use data structures, threads, or other course material?, 3) Was the game complete, achieved the goals in the proposal, and generally bug-free?, 4) Is the game attractive and intuitive to play? Bonus points were awarded if the students uploaded their finished game to the Google Play Store.

For this paper we revisit the archive of student submissions and reevaluate them. In addition to the above criteria we also examine whether the project: demonstrates independent learning of concepts not covered in class, uses interdisciplinary knowledge, demonstrates creativity (is substantially different than class examples or suggested projects), has wide or narrow appeal, was published (or publishable, meaning that it avoided using copyrighted graphics, sound, and trademarks).

Table 1: Projects by semester

	F2011	S2012	F2012	S2013	S2014	F2014	S2015
projects	7	18	12	10	17	13	14
%teams	0.28	0.5	0.33	0.2	0.8	0.66	0.3
in study	7	15	10	8	10	12	3

We also look at external factors. Was the project completed in a team? Was the student a CS major? Was the student, in the instructor's memory, particularly enthusiastic or motivated by the project? Did the team seek the instructor's aid or complete the project independently? Did the team include female, minority, international, or nontraditional students? Did any of the students involved subsequently do further mobile development as a capstone project, internship, or career?

Each project was rated on the following factors, with scores ranging from 0=lowest and 4=highest.

1. Did the project achieve the objectives in the design proposal?

2. Did the project work correctly or was it buggy?

3. Does the project reflect student effort? Was it ambitious?

4. Was the project creative?

5. Did the project have an attractive user interface? Was it clear how to use it?

We also ask whether the project motivated the students:

6. Did the team publish it?

7. Did the students do more mobile design projects afterwards? Or take a job developing mobile apps?

8. Did the students subsequently become active in the computer science student community?   (Although this can't be necessarily credited to the project, it is intriguing to ask.)

Additionally:

9. Was the project completed in a team or solo?

10. Did the project include women, minority, or nontraditional students?

4. Student and Project Characteristics

During the period from 2011 to 2015 the computer science department experienced rapid growth, reflecting nation-wide trends. Prior to 2011 CSC281 was offered only in the spring semester, but starting that fall it was offered every semester. The total enrollment in the course, the population of majors, and the percentage of female students is shown in Table 2.

Table 2: Enrollment by semester

	F2011	S2012	F2012	S2013	S2014	F2014	S2015
students	9	24	19	12	23	22	25
majors	8	8	7	8	10	10	
female	4	6	4	3	11	7	11

Students who dropped the course or did not complete the project are not included. Table 2 shows the number of project submissions by semester and the percentage of project that were teams of two, or on rare occasions, three, as opposed to solo efforts. Also shown are the number of projects that are evaluated in this study. Only 61 projects out of 87 total were uploaded to Blackboard; the remainder were unfortunately not archived. In most of these cases the student demonstrated the project to the instructor, received a grade, and subsequently forgot to upload it.

Table 3 shows an intriguing trend: the student's choice of genre of game, which varies dramatically by semester. The project assignment listed a set of example games, nearly all board games, and in the first semester of the project nearly all students chose a game from that list. Although these example games did not change, student preferences did. In Fall 2012, half of the class chose to implement variants of Monopoly, while in Fall 2014 three groups created falling object games. The actual games, however, were very dissimilar. For example, of the three falling object games, one had the user controlled a dinosaur with buttons to avoid meteors, another had a basket moved with screen swipes to catch falling bread, and the third had the user move a dog to catch bones and avoid excrement, with the position of the finger controlling the dog's motion. Likewise the Monopoly games varied not only in appearance but in the particular features of the game the students chose to implement. In general, over the four years, the games tended to become more mobile friendly as students became more experienced with smartphones. The first semester only two students owned smartphones - both of them Blackberrys - and the games tended to rely on text and buttons. In Fall 2014, however, there was only one student who did not have a smartphone (most students had iPhones, however, not Androids), and only one of the games used text anywhere in its interface.

	F2011	S2012	F2012	S2013	S2014	F2014	S2015
board	7	4	2	2	0	5	2
arcade	0	5	0	2	3	3	1
mobile	0	1	1	1	2	1	0
card	0	2	1	1	1	2	0
puzzle	0	2	4	1	1	1	0
simulation	0	1	1	0	3	0	0
rpg	0	1	0	1	0	0	0
gag	0	0	1	0	0	0	0

Table 3: Game genre by semester

5. Exemplary Projects

A framework for evaluating a course project is provided by the EngageCSEdu initiative, sponsored by the NCWIT [4], which lists a set of factors that have been proven to motivate and engage students, especially female students. Some specifically relevant factors include: "Student-Faculty Interaction", "Student-Student Interaction", "Incorporating Student Choice", "Make Interdisciplinary Connections to CS", and "Problem-based Learning". What were the projects that exemplified these, and how did they score?

5.1 "BitBounce": Student-Student Interaction

BitBounce is a novel project starring a girl jumping on a trampoline. Objects, such as umbrellas, wrenches, t-shirts, and bombs move along clothesline overhead. If the girl makes contact with a "good" object, such as an umbrella, she scores points. Touching a "bad" object, however, will lose lives or end the game. A random "wind" will occasionally push the girl off, forcing the user to swipe the screen to keep her on. BitBounce has custom drawn graphics, realistic physics, and is stable and fun to play. The team creating BitBounce was an almost perfect example of synergy. Two students collaborated: a graphics design major who now professionally designs software user interfaces, and a crack coder with strong analytic skills.

Figure 1: BitBounce

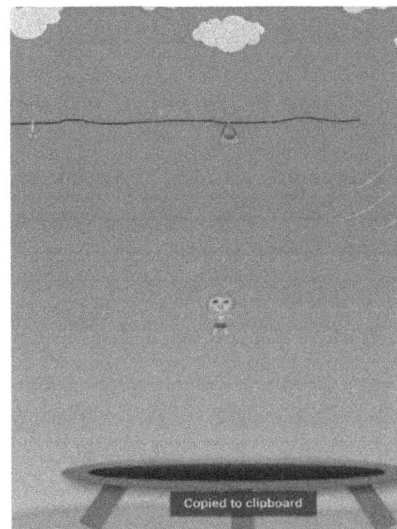

Table 4: Projects with good team collaboration

	complete	correct	effort	creative	usable
Penguin Crossing	3	2	2	2	3
Bomberdude	3	2	3	2	1
Bitbounce	4	3	4	4	4

5.2 "Tetris" and "Settlers of Catan": Professor-Student Interaction

The students who completed Tetris and Settlers of Catan were neither the most confident nor most prepared students, but were the most dogged about seeking help from the instructor. Neither game was fully realized: Settlers of Catan used scans of the board-game graphics (making it unpublishable) and an untuitive interface, while Tetris was scaled down to a game of one-square blocks. However in both projects the students were pushed to achieve far more than they expected. Three of the four students on these projects subsequently did Android and iPhone development as capstone projects, which in two cases led directly to jobs after graduating.

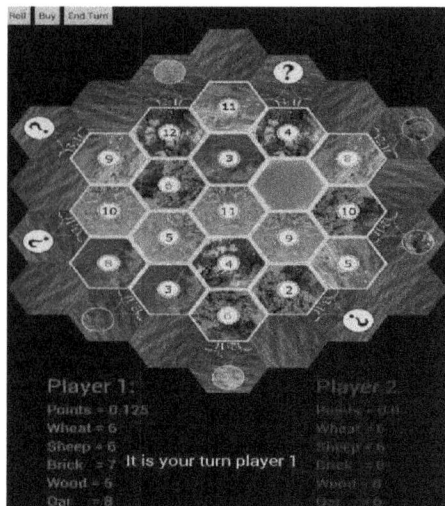

Figure 2: Settlers of Catan

Projects where students worked closely with the instructor included:

- Candy Crunch: A faithful implementation

- Helicopter: A flappy-bird like game from before Flappy Bird was popular

- Tilty-Ball (described below)

Table 4: Projects where students met with the professor

	complete	correct	effort	creative	usable
Tetris	2	2	1	1	2
Catan	3	2	3	1	1
Candy	3	2	3	1	2
Tilty-Ball	4	3	4	2	3
Helicopter	3	2	3	2	2

5.3 "Tilty-Ball": Problem-based learning

In several projects, students were forced to teach themselves new concepts, study external code, and learn independently. Tilty-Ball was a collaboration between a nontraditional student and a foreign student where neither fully grasped the challenges of the project when they proposed it. Tilty-Ball simulates a ball trapped in a randomly-generated maze that rolls downhill as the user tilts the phone. The objective is to roll the ball through the maze to a target square. The students studied and incorporated a minimum-spanning tree maze generator program provided by the instructor, retaught themselves trigonometry to handle the collision detection between the ball and the walls (including corners and edges), and learned how to read from the phone's accelerometer. The result was a polished and intuitive game, which led directly to a job offer for one of the students.

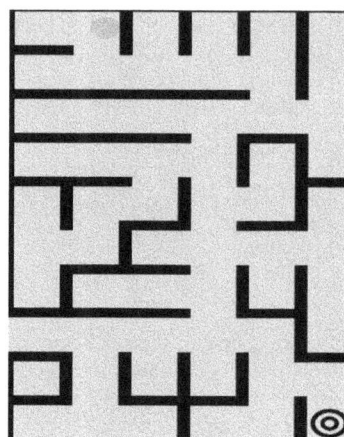

Figure 3: Tilty-Ball

Other projects where the students learned independently included:

- Reversi   Student learned the minimax algorithm and implemented an AI

- Puzzle Maker   Makes jigsaw puzzles from camera. Student learned to use the camera, import images, and make intents.

- Invaders   A faithful implementation of space invaders. Possibly the most technically impressive of all the projects. Student learned networking to store high scores, accelerometer, and hardware buttons

Table 5: Submissions showing independent learning

	complete	correct	effort	creative	usable
Reversi	3	3	3	1	2
Puzzle	2	3	2	2	2
Invaders	4	4	4	3	4
Tilty-Ball	4	3	4	2	3

figure 4: Space Invaders

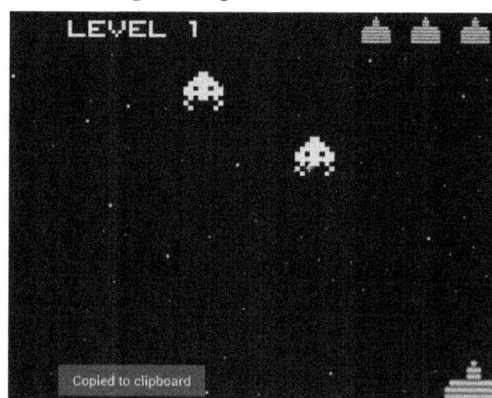

5.4 "OwningDCEducation": Interdisciplinary Connections

53% of the students surveyed were non-computer science majors. Of these, the majority were from Mathematics and

Audio Technology, with smaller populations of Graphics Design and Physics. Relatively few students, however, applied interdisciplinary knowledge or interests.

OwningDCEducation is a Monopoly game that uses local social services in place of the properties. Of the various Monopoly submissions it is the most complete, aesthetically appealing, and intuitive. The game was a collaboration between a sociology student and a computer science student; however, both students had strong coding skills.

- Drumpad   A drum playing program written by Audio Technology students

- Drum Machine Similar to Drumpad, also written by Audio Technology majors

- Wack-a-mole Graphics design students; very polished

- BitBounce

Table 6: Interdisciplinary projects

	complete	correct	effort	creative	usable
Drumpad	3	1	3	2	1
DrumMachine	2	1	2	2	1
Wack-a-mole	4	3	3	2	4
Bitbounce	4	3	4	4	4
OwningEd	3	3	4	3	3

Figure 5: OwningDCEducation

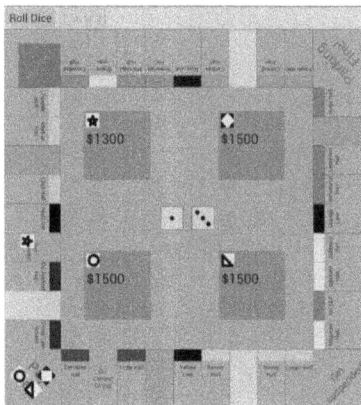

Figure 6: Wack-a-mole

5.5 Incorporating Student Choice

EngageCSEdu recommends that projects provide students a wide-range of topics or allow students to choose a topic. While the recommendations in the project assignment only included board games, many students nevertheless opted for a different genre. The following table shows how different genres of games scored:

Table 7: Scores by category

	complete	correct	effort	creative	usable
average	**2.62**	**2.22**	**2.29**	**1.38**	**1.76**
arcade	2.93	2.36	2.43	1.57	2.00
board	2.55	2.20	2.30	0.75	1.45
card	3.00	2.25	2.75	1.25	1.75
mobile	3.20	2.40	2.60	2.20	2.20
puzzle	2.33	2.44	2.00	1.67	1.89
other	1.57	1.29	1.57	1.71	1.43

In general, board games score below average in every category, implying that students who choose the follow the suggested games produced weaker projects. Mobile games, which tend to be more innovative, generally score the highest.

5.6 Other High Scoring Projects

When taking the sum of the individual scores as a rating for the project, 7 projects earn a total of 14 or better. Of these, nearly all have been covered in one of the above categories. The exceptions are:

- Blocks: A tile matching game

- Landlord: A card game popular in Asia. One of the most ambitious projects submitted.

Table 8: Other superlative projects

	complete	correct	effort	creative	usable
Blocks	4	3	3	2	3
Landlord	4	3	4	2	1

Figure 7: Blocks

6. Impact on Students

As the objective of the project was to engage students, motivate them to study computer science, and give them practical experience, what was the impact?

- 20 of the students from Fall 2014 or before told the author that they subsequently pursued mobile-design as a capstone or independent project, or got an internship or job related to mobile-design

- 29 of the projects (33%) were published to the Google Play Store.

- 20 students told the author that they got an internship or a job related to mobile-design.

One of the key missions of the EngageCSEdu project is to motivate women, minority, and underrepresented students. The table below shows how students of different demographics performed on the project as compared to the class average. For the purpose of this analysis, "underrepresented" includes African-American, Latino, openly gay, transgender, and physically disabled students, while "nontraditional" includes students older than 25. The score is based on projects where the team has at least one student belonging to the corresponding group.

Table 9: Breakdown by student demographics

	complete	correct	effort	creative	usable
average	2.63	2.24	2.31	1.37	1.78
women	2.43	1.93	2.13	1.43	1.87
nontraditional	3.20	2.60	3.20	1.80	2.60
minority	2.50	2.00	1.67	1.33	1.83
international	2.91	2.18	2.82	1.27	1.82

7. REFERENCES

[1]   Jennifer Campbell and Anya Tafliovich. 2015. An Experience Report: Using Mobile Development To Teach Software Design. In *Proceedings of the 46th ACM Technical Symposium on Computer Science Education* (SIGCSE '15). ACM, New York, NY, USA, 506-511.

[2]   James B. Fenwick, Jr., Barry L. Kurtz, and Joel Hollingsworth. 2011. Teaching mobile computing and developing software to support computer science education. In *Proceedings of the 42nd ACM technical symposium on Computer science education* (SIGCSE '11). ACM, New York, NY, USA, 589-594.

[3]   Jeff Gray, Hal Abelson, David Wolber, and Michelle Friend. 2012. Teaching CS principles with app inventor. In *Proceedings of the 50th Annual Southeast Regional Conference* (ACM-SE '12). ACM, New York, NY, USA, 405-406.

[4]   National Center for Women & Information Technology and Google, Inc. EngageCSEdu: Engagement Practices; http://www.engage-csedu.org/engagement.

[5]   Stephen H. Edwards and Anthony Allevato. 2014. Re-imagining CS1/CS2 with Android using the Sofia framework. *J. Comput. Sci. Coll.* 29, 3 (January 2014), 101-101.

[6]   Mark Goadrich, Jacob Jennings, and Matthew Jadud. 2011. Exploring the Use of Android OS in CS2. In *Proceedings of the First International SMArtphones in the Curriculum workshop* (SMACK 2011).

[7]   Ivaylo Ilinkin. 2014. Opportunities for android projects in a CS1 course. In *Proceedings of the 45th ACM technical symposium on Computer science education* (SIGCSE '14). ACM, New York, NY, USA, 615-620.

[8]   Leo Porter and Beth Simon. 2013. Retaining nearly one-third more majors with a trio of instructional best practices in CS1. In *Proceeding of the 44th ACM technical symposium on Computer science education* (SIGCSE '13). ACM, New York, NY, USA, 165-170.

[9]   Anya Tafliovich, Andrew Petersen, and Jennifer Campbell. 2015. On the Evaluation of Student Team Software Development Projects. In *Proceedings of the 46th ACM Technical Symposium on Computer Science Education* (SIGCSE '15). ACM, New York, NY, USA, 494-499.
NY, USA, 494-499.

Using Interactive Exercise in Mobile Devices to Support Evidence-based Teaching and Learning

M. Muztaba Fuad
Dept. of Computer Science
Winston-Salem State Uni.
Winston-Salem, NC, USA
+1-336-7503325
fuadmo@wssu.edu

Debzani Deb
Dept. of Computer Science
Winston-Salem State Uni.
Winston-Salem, NC, USA
+1-336-7502496
debd@wssu.edu

James Etim
Dept. of Education
Winston-Salem State Uni.
Winston-Salem, NC, USA
+1-336-7502382
etimj@wssu.edu

Clay Gloster
Dept. of CST
NC A&T State Uni.
Greensboro, NC, USA
+1-336-3347717
cgloster@ncat.edu

ABSTRACT

To improve student's class experience, the use of mobile devices has been steadily increasing. However, such use of mobile learning environments in the class is mostly static in nature through content delivery or multiple choice and true/false quiz taking. In CS courses, we need learning environments where students can interact with the problem in a hands-on-approach and instructor can assess their learning skills in real-time with problems having different degree of difficulty. To facilitate such interactive problem solving and real-time assessment using mobile devices, a comprehensive backend system is necessary. This paper presents one such system, named Mobile Response System (MRS) software, associated interactive problem-solving activities, and lessons learned by using it in the CS classrooms. MRS provides instructor with the opportunity of evidence-based teaching by allowing students to perform interactive exercises in their mobile devices with different learning outcomes and by getting an instant feedback on their performance and mental models. MRS is easy-to-use, extensible and can render interactive exercises developed by third-party developers. The student performance data shows its effectiveness in increasing student understanding of difficult concepts and the overall perception of using the software was very positive.

Keywords

Interactive learning environments; educational technology system; improving classroom teaching; STEM learning; mobile technology.

1. INTRODUCTION

Studies [1]-[2] have shown that in order to improve student learning in CS, traditional pedagogical approaches are not enough to transfer critical knowledge to students. More interactive teaching and learning strategies are necessary to make learning more productive. In CS courses, students need to actively solve problems by interacting with the problem in a hands-on approach.

ITiCSE '16, July 09-13, 2016, Arequipa, Peru
© 2016 ACM. ISBN 978-1-4503-4231-5/16/07...$15.00
DOI: http://dx.doi.org/10.1145/2899415.2899467

Students cannot develop skills such as problem solving and critical thinking only by using traditional question types, such as multiple-choice or true-false questions. Since exams and quizzes are the dominant form of assessing student learning, we need to make such assessment tools more interactive and involving to gaze student learning, mental models and engagement better. We argue that by presenting the problems as interactive entities, where students can actively participate in different steps of the problem; student's critical thinking and problem solving skills can be improved. Mobile technology has brought incredible opportunities for educators to enable and deliver learning in ways that could not have been accomplished before. There have been an increasing number of studies [3]-[7] related to the research and development of learning environments intended for mobile computing devices. This study proposes having interactive exercises (IE) in the form of mobile App quizzes rather than traditional paper-based quizzes where the goal is to make the problem-solving exercises more visual and appealing to the students and allow them to realize the effect of their interactions at the different stages of the exercise. We expect the students to fully comprehend a concept and clarify any confusion through visual presentation, active interaction and hands-on nature of the mobile-based approach. As it is possible to automate the question generation, delivery, time keeping and grading in the proposed approach, we anticipate that the instructors would be able to offer more quizzes and students could have more opportunity to practice concepts where they receive immediate feedback.

Having IE activities as mobile Apps encourage evidence-based teaching practices as well. Research has shown that immediate feedback has positive effect on students' success [8]-[9] and by utilizing the proposed mobile-based approach, an instructor could provide immediate and context sensitive feedback to the students. Additionally, instructor would have the ability to identify and correct common misconceptions and reinforce specific topics immediately which students have not shown mastery of. By monitoring and analyzing student device usage data (button clicks, time spent, navigation behavior etc.) through these Apps, instructors have better understanding of their attitude, mental model, and barriers that they faced during problem solving.

To facilitate such interactive problem solving and real-time assessment and tracking using mobile devices, a comprehensive backend system is necessary. This paper presents details of Mobile Response System (MRS) software [10]-[12] and its usage and evaluation in the classroom. MRS facilitates anonymous communication, interaction and evaluation of in-class interactive problem solving activities using mobile devices. MRS enables a feedback-driven and evidence-based teaching methodology, which is important to enhance student learning. MRS is a client-server software that allows the instructor to dynamically prompt the students with interactive exercises, synchronized with the lecture material in their mobile devices. Students are able to actively interact with the problem and send their answers back to the server computer. MRS then facilitates grading of the exercises automatically, by comparing the student made sequence of steps with the correct sequence of steps. After grading, MRS also makes the grading statistics and student submissions available for the instructor to view and share with the students.

This formative assessment allows the instructor to have real-time evidence of students' comprehension of covered lecture materials on a particular class and also helps instructor to identify the concepts that need to be repeated or reinforced. With MRS, instructor can also capture screens from student submissions and generate immediate discussion on those screens if context-sensitive feedback is needed. This approach allows the students to obtain faster and frequent feedbacks that reinforce their learning and help them to identify misconceptions and problem areas. The visual and active interaction with a problem via multiple steps while going back and forth and seeing the consequence of their choices at each step is expected to enhance students' analytical and problem solving capabilities. The other important feature supported by MRS is the ability to submit feedback/question anonymously during the class. Several studies [13]-[14] identifies the benefits of remaining anonymous during social interaction and the proposed approach leverages that in the mobile learning environment. The software allows students to send anonymous feedback/questions to the instructor and to vote on existing pool of questions that instructor may choose to review and answer at the end of the class. This encourages more class interaction and in-depth discussion between students and instructor. Finally, MRS is extensible to other disciplines than CS and can render interactive exercise Apps developed by third-party developers.

The rest of the paper is organized as follows: section two details the MRS system and interactive exercises, section three presents the evaluation data that is gathered when MRS is deployed in CS classrooms, section four discusses the related researches and section five concludes the paper.

2. MRS SYSTEM

The MRS software is designed as a client-server application. The instructor computer runs the server component of the software, which hosts questions, manages users, and maintain communication and synchronization. The client component executes in student's mobile devices and allows students to login to the system, to submit anonymous feedbacks/questions, and facilitates interactive exercise solving. The server has been developed in Java and the client has been developed in Android.

2.1 MRS Client

The client is a light-weight mobile application that provides essential functionality to deploy IE apps. It allows verification of student credentials and once logged in, the client shows a home screen where student can either submit anonymous feedback/question or exit from the system. When the client receives a new IE problem from the server, the corresponding App that renders the given problem into IE is located by the client and then executed. The MRS client and an IE activity App communicates using standard API calls and therefore is completely separated in application logic. This separation allows MRS's features to be extended to any domains with different IE Apps. More information about extensibility is provided in Section

2.4. Every IE activity has a set amount of time to answer (assigned by the instructor) and a visible timer starts counting for students to see how much time they have left to answer the question. Once the student answer is received, the client will capture that and will send it to the server for grading. At any time during the class, students can initiate a session from the home screen to post a feedback/question or vote on an existing one anonymously.

2.2 MRS Server

The MRS server is designed as a multi-process, multi-threaded entity to satisfy simultaneous invocation from users and to provide real time responses to in-class activities. Instructor running the MRS server can import student credentials, which will allow students to login to the sever. When a student logs in to the system, the server validates the identity and sets privileges accordingly. Once all students are logged in, instructor can import the IE question and broadcast them to the client devices. When the server receives answers back from all the clients, it uses runtime reflection to find the corresponding server-side grading component of the IE and loads and executes the corresponding method in that component dynamically in order to grade student submissions. As soon as grading is completed, MRS sends each student an email with the correct answer, their answer and their score in that exercise. This happens instantaneously and students receive the email with the feedback and their score in real time. Separate thread of the server constantly monitors whether a student using the client App wants to initiate a feedback/question session. In that case, it sends the current pool of feedback/questions to the corresponding client. Once a response from the client is received, if it is a new entry, then it is added to the existing list. Otherwise a vote on an existing entry is increased by matching it with the list of entries.

2.3 Interactive Exercises (IE)

The most important aspect of the MRS software is the facilitation of interactive problem solving. An interactive problem solving activity is defined as an Interactive Exercise (IE) with corresponding grading components and associated rubrics. In an IE, students require to directly work on a visual representation of a problem and develop the answer following a set of steps guided by a particular algorithm or process. In each step, students make key choices (for example clicking the table or array indices for selection or swap, selecting from a drop-down menu, selecting a tree node or an edge of a graph etc.) that will impact their next step of interaction. During these interaction steps, students can go back and forth (by utilizing "Back" and "Next" button) and see the impact of their different choices. Interactive exercises can be offered as solving a whole problem from bottom-up or top-down fashion or solving certain steps of a particular problem in order to give students different perspective on the problem and to assess their problem solving skills. Only after the student traverse each of the steps or the allotted time to answer a problem runs out, the results of their interactions performed at each step are then sent back to the server. The MRS software automatically handles the grading of the exercises, by comparing the student made sequence of interactions with the model sequence of interactions for a particular problem. Each problem has a rubric that grade partially correct answers to gauge student's problem solving skills and cognitive models.

In this research, the interactive exercises are designed as dynamic entities rather than static entities to support greater diversity and to allow students to practice the same problem solving activity with different question parameters. The exercises are therefore parameterized, where parameters can be populated with either randomly generated values or instructor generated values to create different instances of a problem. An IE definition is stored as an XML file and contains exercise parameters such as problem components, time to answer, special instructions etc., which are used to render the corresponding IE App in the client device. The file additionally contains different rubric and grading parameters such as correct answers, step-wise grading weights, etc. to support server-side automated grading. Student device usage during interactive problem solving can also be tracked by setting the correct parameters in the IE definition file such as how often they utilize the "Back" button, how much time they spend in individual stages of a problem, how often they navigate to other Apps (such as browsers, Tweeter, Facebook etc.). The data gathered on these aspects of the system shows some interesting insight into student learning and engagements. For instance, students barely switch to other Apps during problem solving sessions, which shows that they are completely engaged into problem solving and that they are not looking for answers in the internet. Also the more time a student presses back button, her grade is better on that problem compared to a student who did not utilizes back button frequently. This validates that the ability to go back-and-forth during problem solving enable students to check their actions better. To date, seven interactive exercise Apps have been developed as listed in Table 1.

Table 1. Developed Interactive Exercise (IE) Apps

App	Where can be deployed?
Interactive matching	Any course, Any discipline
Analytical answering	Any course, Any discipline
Truth Table formation	Freshman/sophomore CS/EE course
K-map simplification	Freshman/sophomore CS/EE course
Bubble Sorting	Sophomore/Junior CS course
Selection Sorting	Sophomore/Junior CS course
Prim's Minimum Spanning Tree	Sophomore/Junior CS course

Figure 1(a), (b) and (c) shows intermediate screens of an IE App that was developed for assessing the student's understanding of K-map simplification algorithm. At first, students can select cells corresponding to the given Sum of Minterm expression (Figure 1(a)). Correct execution of this step verifies whether students learned how the map is laid out and what every cell points to. Students then make groups with the cells following the minimization algorithm (Figure 1(b)) in the next screen. Students can select any cell and each group made will take a different color (with the group number as superscript) to distinguish it from other groups. This step validates whether students comprehend different attributes of making groups. Next, students interact with each group and select common literal from each group (Figure 1(c)) following the minimization algorithm. During these steps, student can traverse back and forth and change their answer. However, since the IE App cannot verify whether the student devised answer is correct or not; students can not heuristically figure out the answer of a question. Therefore, what the student come up as the answer of a problem, represents student's own understanding and learning levels.

The MRS server automatically grades student submitted exercises, summarizes them, and displays grading and tracking statistics for instructor to gain further insight and to share them with the class. Figure 2(a) captures the "Grade Summary" screen that instructor can immediately share with the class. The "Grade Details" tab presents student performance data for individual problem steps, so that instructor can reinforce some particular step of the problem

immediately if majority students struggle on that step instead of repeating the whole process. The "Time Taken" tab displays step-

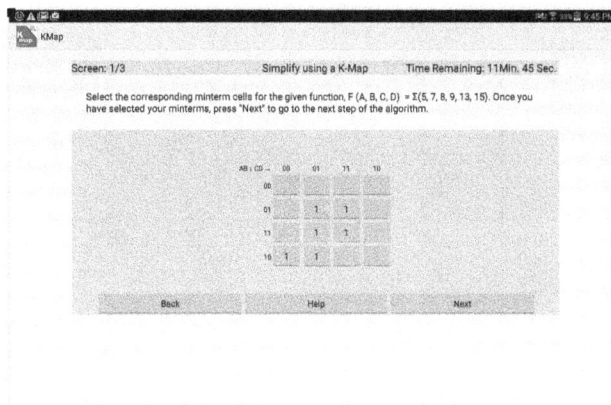

(a)

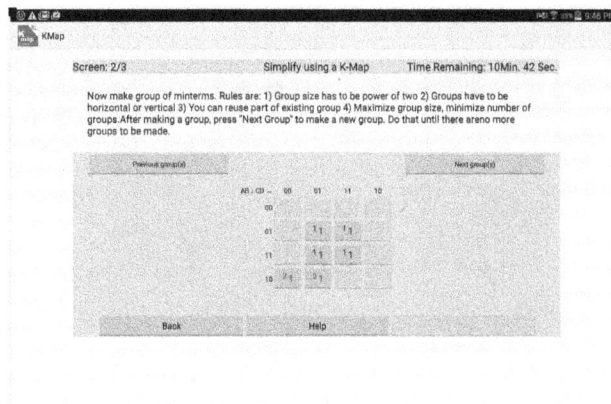

(b)

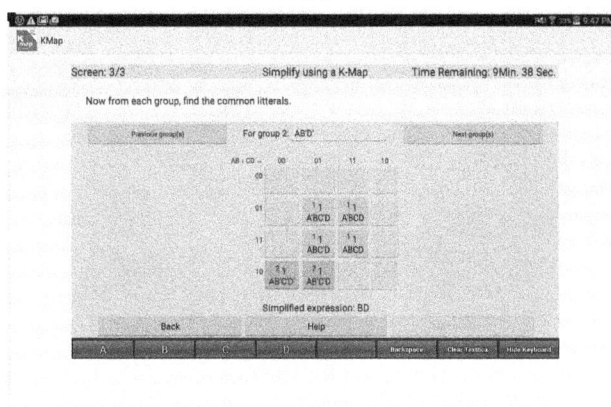

(c)

Figure 1. Intermediate screens of k-map App.

wise student timing data to understand the steps that students spend most time on. The "App Swap" tab tracks "Back" button usage and "Navigation" tab tracks how often student navigates away to other Apps during problem solving. Instructor can share the correct answer with the class by utilizing the "Correct Answer" tab. Moreover, each student receives an email instantly with an attachment (Figure 2(b)) that notifies them of their score with the correct answer and their answer of the exercise for future review. Immediate availability of this step-wise assessment and tracking information allows instructor to gain better understanding of student learning of a concept and allows students to assess their own progress toward the concept and to compare it with the rest of the class.

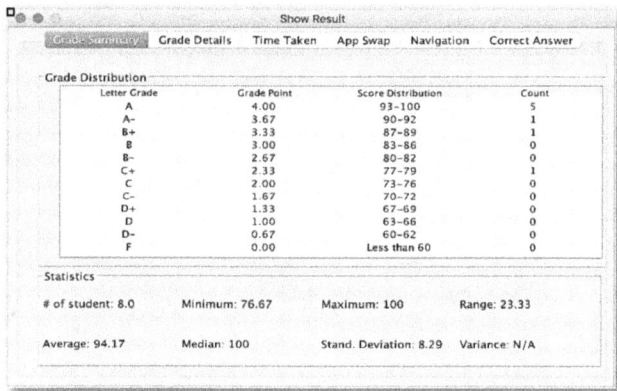

(a)

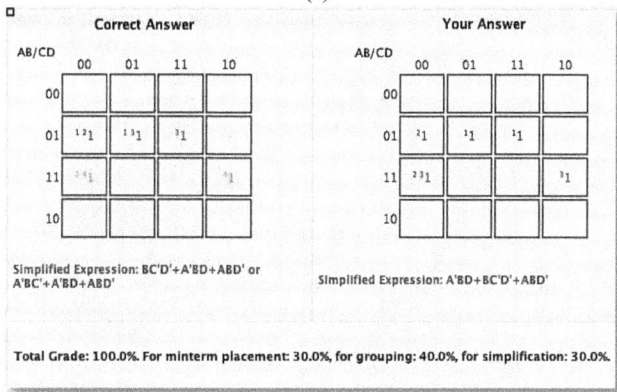

(b)

Figure 2. Grading statistics and grade notification email.

2.4 MRS Extensibility

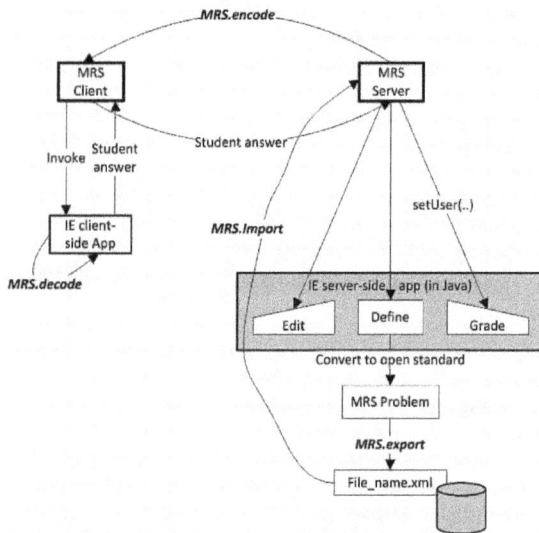

Figure 3. MRS components, interfaces, and interactions.

In order to encourage broader adoption and dissemination, MRS is designed to be extensible and therefore has the ability to render IE Apps created by third-party developers. To build a problem-solving interactive exercise App, the third-party developer needs to design the nature of interactions and implement Android's activity life cycle accordingly for their App. In order to incorporate that App to MRS environment, additionally they need to create the corresponding IE definition file and server-side grading component. Then by following a set of well-specified requirement and APIs (Figure 3), one can integrate and execute any IE App into MRS learning environment with minimal effort.

3. EVALUATION

The MRS software and associated interactive exercises were deployed in a sophomore course (traditional face-to-face classroom setting) titled as "Introduction to Computer Hardware Organization" during the period of Fall 2014, Spring 2015, and Fall 2015. In each class, students were given Android tablets to use during the class for interactive exercise solving and anonymous questions/feedback submission or for performing other class related works. Students are allowed to utilize their own tablet or mobile device as long as they have installed the MRS client. The current version of MRS only support Android clients, however the system is built in a way that accommodates client from any platforms. The evaluation of the impact of the MRS learning environment is determined using the data collected from an experience survey, from a focus group, and from a comparison of the grades received by students when completing targeted exercises with or without using the software. During Fall 2014, the deployment was carried out as a Pilot study for recognizing and correcting errors and to fine-tune the implementations. Therefore, the data gathered during this term is excluded from the evaluation. Table 2 shows some important class related attributes. In both intervened semesters, instructors were able to administer similar or more graded exercises compared to the non-intervened semesters. However, since the process of grading and management was automated, instructor could spend more time on answering student questions and encourage class discussions. The same exercises were offered in the class in a pen- and-paper based setting without MRS and in the mobile IE App setting with MRS. IEs related to two separate concepts, truth–table and k-Maps were used before and after MRS. For the sake of comparison, same weighted grade calculation was utilized in all semesters.

Table 2. Class related Information

	Without MRS		With MRS	
	Fall 2013	Spring 2014	Spring 2015	Fall 2015
# of students	11	17	14	8
# of graded exercise	11	10	11	13
# of anonymous questions/feedbacks	N/A	N/A	3	34
# of votes on questions/feedbacks	N/A	N/A	4	53

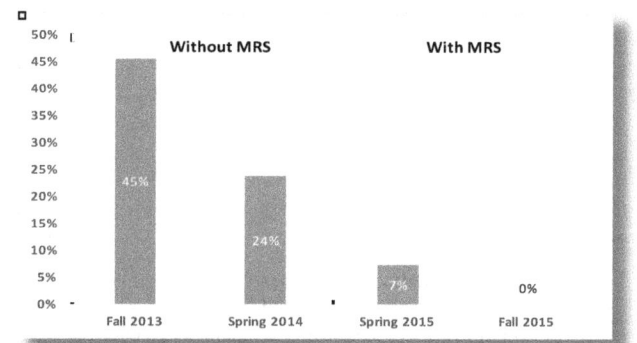

Figure 4. % of D's and F's with and without MRS.

Figure 4 presents the percentage of failure (D & F grades) in the class with and without MRS intervention. The figure reveals significant decline in course failing when using the MRS software along with interactive exercises. The data also reveals that, on average the number of A's in the class increased by 10% with intervention. Hence, in the case of students who had difficulty understanding concepts such as Truth Table and K-Map, the use of MRS software significantly enhances student learning.

Figure 5 and 6 shows the student performance data for K-Map and truth table exercises with and without using MRS. The figures represent the performance data averaged over the number of exercises and clearly represents the improvement when MRS is deployed in classroom. The data verifies that the use of the MRS software is effective in increasing student understanding of concepts that are typically difficult for students to comprehend.

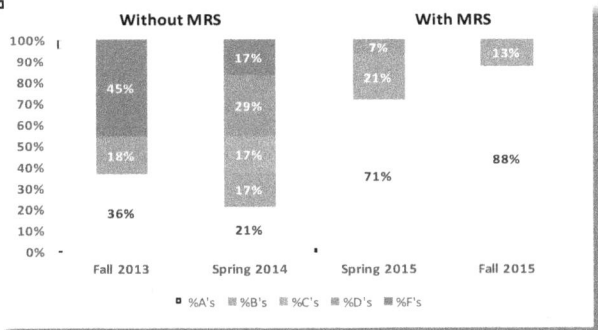

Figure 5. Grade distribution of k-map exercises.

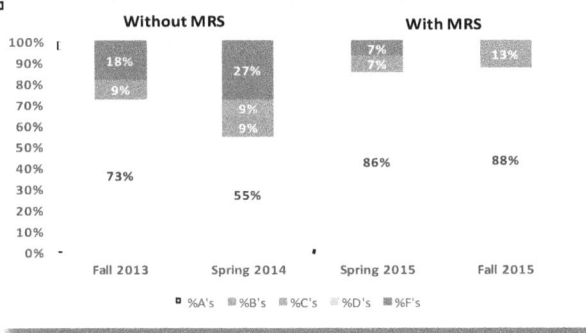

Figure 6. Grade distribution of truth table exercises.

In order to assess student perception of the MRS environment and its overall effectiveness, an experience survey was offered to the students during both intervened semesters. The survey results are shown in Table 3. This survey also reveals the impact of continuous improvement and fine-tuning of the proposed effort which is evident from notable increase in learner's positive impression from Spring 2015 to Fall 2015 in most cases.

A focus group was formed including a small number of students to further assess the effectiveness of the proposed approach. The participating students were asked specific questions about their experiences with the software and the improvements could be made to the system. All students positively attested that hands-on activities enhanced learning and MRS software was very effective in this regard. Anonymous question and immediate grading were appreciated most during the conversation. One focus group member mentioned that the anonymous question/vote feature should be utilized in each and every day of class and in other courses throughout the university. By using this feature of the MRS software, students feel they can let the instructor know whether he/she is going too fast or whether some concepts need more explanation without revealing their identity. Some students feel that making comments to the instructor about their teaching

could potentially have an adverse impact on their grades. However, with the software, this fear can be alleviated. When asked what improvements could be made to the system, students

Table 3. Data on student perception about MRS.

Question	Semester	Strongly agree	Agree	Disagree	Strongly disagree
Q1	Spring 2015	55%	45%		
	Fall 2015	100%			
Q2	Spring 2015	55%	45%		
	Fall 2015	100%			
Q3	Spring 2015	73%	27%		
	Fall 2015	86%	14%		
Q4	Spring 2015	55%	45%		
	Fall 2015	100%			
Q5	Spring 2015	45%	55%		
	Fall 2015	86%	14%		
Q6	Spring 2015	64%	36%		
	Fall 2015	100%			
Q7	Spring 2015		9%	73%	18%
	Fall 2015	14%		43%	43%
Q8	Spring 2015			27%	73%
	Fall 2015	14%		14%	71%

Q1. MRS is helpful in understanding k-map and truth table.
Q2. MRS helps in visualizing the steps in k-map and truth table.
Q3. Seeing my grades immediately after taking the exercises is really helpful.
Q4. The k-map and truth table Apps are intuitive and easy to use.
Q5. I feel competent and confident to solve problems in MRS than in a pen- and paper-based setting.
Q6. I am enjoying this experience.
Q7. Using MRS did not improve my understanding of k-map and truth table problems.
Q8. Learning to use MRS software and related Apps is additional work beyond the normal course work.

requested that a) the software be used more often; b) it be made available for download onto their smartphones including iPhones; and c) more interactive exercises be developed to cover other concepts.

4. RELATED WORK

To facilitate interactive teaching and learning, 'clickers' were utilized in various ways [15]-[17], however, they are not suitable for assessing multi-step exercises which limits its applicability to only certain assessments. There is a plethora of research [3]-[7] which shows that mobile learning engages students more and improve student learning. For instance, Researchers at Rochester Institute of Technology reported that their use of a technology-rich learning environment in several undergraduate engineering-technology courses has improved learning and decreased withdrawals from, or failing grades in, the courses [3]. Boston University adopted tablet-based problem solving exercises in their freshman mathematics class and reported noticeable increase in student attendance and course completion [4]. Many other approaches [5]-[7] also reported enhanced educational experiences when technology such as mobile and tablet devices has been adopted in the classroom. However, the abovementioned efforts neither provide support for interactive exercises nor its assessment. Few researches support integrated assessment of interactive exercises. TRAKLA2 [18] is the pioneering learning environment that supports algorithm simulation exercises, automatic assessment and visual feedback. JHAVÉ [19] is a java application that renders algorithm visualizations and allows student explorations by pop-up questions. JSAV [20] is a JavaScript based algorithm visualization library that supports proficiency exercises. However, all of them support content delivery via web browser and therefore utilized technologies such as HTML, Java, JavaSript etc. but none to our knowledge do so via mobile App like MRS. The novelty of MRS is represented by its support for interactive problem solving, evidence-based teaching, anonymous classroom interaction and easier extendibility to other areas.

5. CONCLUSION

This paper presents details of MRS software, associated pedagogy, and lessons learned from using it in class. MRS provides instructors with the opportunity of evidence-based teaching by offering students with exercises having different learning outcomes and by receiving an immediate feedback on their performance. MRS is easy-to-use, extensible and can render interactive exercise developed by third party developer. The MRS software, associated interactive exercise Apps along with documentation and installation information are available for download from [21]. The assessment data verified that the MRS software is a really helpful intervention. Data collected on the distribution of the grades on specific assignments indicated that the use of the MRS software was very effective in increasing student understanding of concepts that are typically difficult for students to comprehend. Moreover, the students really enjoyed using the anonymous question feature as it allowed them to ask question without raising their hands. Additionally, these students were pleased that the software was able to provide immediate grading and feedback. Overall, student experiences with the system was positive and students enjoyed using it. Starting from Spring 2016, MRS will be deployed in two of the CS courses, where all of the seven developed interactive exercise Apps will be administered and in Fall 2016, MRS will also be used in 3 other disciplines alongside Computer Science. It would be interesting to see results obtained when using the software for additional courses, particularly those outside of the Department of Computer Science. With the advent of the MRS software, there is a tremendous opportunity to enhance the learning of hundreds, even thousands of students.

6. ACKNOWLEDGMENTS

This research was supported by National Science Foundation Award # 1332531.

7. REFERENCES

1. D. Perry, How The Brain Learns Best, *Instructor Magazine*, 11: 34-37, 2000.
2. T. L. Naps, G. Roˋßling, V. Almstrum, W. Dann, R. Fleischer, C. Hundhausen, A. Korhonen, L. Malmi, M. McNally, S. Rodger, and J. A. Velaˊzquez-Iturbide. Exploring the role of visualization and engagement in computer science education. In Working group reports from ITiCSE'02 on Innovation and technology in computer science education, 131–152, 2002.
3. M. Cometa, Use of Technology-Rich Learning Environment Reveals Improved Retention Rates, Rochester University of Technology, Nov 16, 2011 http://www.rit.edu/news/story.php?id=48699.
4. C. A. Romney, Tablet PC use in freshman mathematics classes promotes STEM retention, *Frontiers in Education Conference (FIE)*, F1J-1 - F1J-7, 2011.
5. Z. Avery, M. Castillo, H. Guo, J. Guo, N. Warter-Perez, D. S. Won, J. Dong, Implementing Collaborative Project-Based Learning using the Tablet PC to enhance student learning in engineering and computer science courses, *Frontiers in Education Conference*, F1E-1-F1E-7, 2010.
6. R. J. Young, Mobile College App: Turning iPhones Into 'Super-Clickers' for Classroom Feedback, *Chronicle of higher education*, 2008.
7. D. Berque, An evaluation of a broad deployment of DyKnow software to support note taking and interaction using pen-based computers. *Journal of Computing Sciences in Colleges*, 21(6): 204-216, 2006.
8. J. Hattie, Visible learning: A synthesis of over 800 meta-analyses relating to achievement. Routledge, 2000.
9. G. Wiggins, Seven keys to effective feedback. *Educational Leadership*, 70: 10–16, 2012.
10. M. M. Fuad, D. Deb, J. Etim, and C. Gloster, Mobile Response System: A Novel Approach to Deliver Interactive and Hands-on Activity in the Classroom, *Journal of Educational Technology Research and Development, Springer*, Under revision, 2016.
11. D. Deb, M. M. Fuad and W. Farag, Developing Interactive Classroom Exercises for use with Mobile Devices to Enhance Class Engagement and Problem-solving Skills, *IEEE Frontier's of Education Conference*, IEEE Press, 343-346, Madrid, Spain, October 22-25, 2014.
12. M. M. Fuad, D. Deb. and J. Etim, An Evidence Based Learning and Teaching Strategy for Computer Science Classrooms and its Extension into a Mobile Classroom Response System, Proceedings of the 14th IEEE International Conference on Advanced Learning Technologies (ICALT), IEEE Press, 149-153, Athens, Greece, July 7-9, 2014.
13. T. Postmes, R. Spears, K. Sakhel, and D.De Groot, Social influence in computer-mediated communication: The effects of anonymity on group behavior, *Personality and Social Psychology Bulletin*, 27: 1243–1254, 2001.
14. M.-T. Félix, C.-O. Jesús, G.-J. Luis, Anonymity effects in computer-mediated communication in the case of minority influence, *Computers in Human Behavior*, 23:1660–1674, 2007.
15. J. E. Caldwell, Clickers in the Large Classroom: Current Research and Best-Practice Tips, *CBE— Life Sciences Education*, 6(1): 9–20, 2007.
16. J. K. Knight and W. B. Wood, Teaching more by lecturing less, *Cell biology education*, 4(4): 298-310, 2005.
17. E. E. Fredericksen and M. Ames, Can a $30 Piece of Plastic Improve Learning? An Evaluation of Personal Responses Systems in Large Classroom Settings, *EDUCAUSE, 2009*.
18. L. Malmi, V. Karavirta, A. Korhonen, J. Nikander, O. Seppaˊlaˋ, and P. Silvasti. Visual algorithm simulation exercise system with automatic assessment: TRAKLA2. *Informatics in Education*, 3(2):267–288, 2004.
19. T. L. Naps, Jhavé: Supporting algorithm visualization, *Computer Graphics and Applications*, IEEE, 25(5):49-55, 2005.
20. V. Karavirta and C. A. Shaffer, Creating Engaging Online Learning Material with the JSAV JavaScript Algorithm Visualization Library, in *Learning Technologies, IEEE Transactions on*, PP(99): 1-1, 2015.
21. Mobile Response System, http://compsci.wssu.edu/MRS, 2016.

Student Concerns Regarding Transition into Higher Education CS

Angela A. Siegel
School of Computing Science and Digital Media
Robert Gordon University
Aberdeen
+44 (0)1224 262201
a.a.siegel@rgu.ac.uk

Mark Zarb
School of Computing Science and Digital Media
Robert Gordon University
Aberdeen
+44 (0)1224 262768
m.zarb@rgu.ac.uk

ABSTRACT

This paper discusses a study where 249 students from 18 secondary schools around Scotland who were on the verge of applying to study Computing Science at a higher education institution were surveyed on their concerns about the upcoming transition. Preliminary conclusions from this work point to the fact that this transition process is one that seems to evolve with the student as they progress through their education, and as such, should be treated differently at various stages within that process.

Keywords

Student transitions; student concerns; student issues; quantitative survey; computer science education; secondary schools; higher education.

1. INTRODUCTION

Typically, the literature deals with transitions into higher education from the perspective of early undergraduates. This paper presents a case study with data collected from over 200 secondary school students around rural Scotland in order to better understand the issues and concerns that arise when transitioning from secondary school into higher education.

2. RELATED WORK

The experience of transitioning to and starting university is a very individual one, with some students viewing higher education as an unknown entity; an 'alien environment' [1]. This is especially true of students who are the 'first generation' in their family to go to university. Thus, these students are found to lack the cultural capital needed to access teaching and learning within higher education [4].

Across STEM subjects, there is an acknowledgement of the importance of understanding and tackling transition from pre-tertiary education into higher education [2]. The transition issue is seen as strategically important for higher education providers, as new students face similar issues surrounding this transition with every new intake.

The issues faced by these students have been discussed in a wide number of publications: Yorke [7] presents case studies of students who have problems associated with gender, class, age

and financial management. In these cases, students started their higher education experience blind to these issues, and were only subject to them once they had started their studies. Ozga and Sukhnandan [6] discuss the fact that the surveyed students found difficulty with managing their lives in their 'new' environment, both in terms of having moved to a new locality, usually far away from what they had previously considered to be 'home', and also due to the the amount of independence that has suddenly been afforded to them.

Transitioning into higher education also presents issues for staff, particularly those with pastoral care roles (e.g. staff with roles such as personal tutors and guidance counsellors). There is currently concern about whether students are adequately equipped with appropriate study skills for higher education (e.g. time-keeping and independent learning), and whether students might find difficulty in adjusting to the different teaching environments across the two contexts (e.g. due to a large difference in class sizes) [2].

While there are a number of studies (e.g. [3, 5]) which survey first year undergraduates about these transitions, this paper considers the secondary school students who (at the time of the study) were still considering the transition to higher in order to better understand their concerns, and how they can be supported in future.

2.1 Expectations

Based on the literature referenced above, the authors had started this work with a number of expectations about student issues. These expectations will be compared and contrasted with the findings in this work in the discussion below (section 5.3).

It should be noted that these expectations have been driven by personal experience along with a literature survey that focussed on the issues seen within early higher education.

From the literature, it can be seen that 'environment' is a strong theme amongst transition concerns [1, 2, 6]. Other themes encountered include the following: expectation of academic work [4] and financial management and part-time work [7]. Due to personal, pastoral experience, there was also an expectation of finding concerns regarding accessibility, distance from home, and homesickness in general.

3. INSTITUTIONAL CONTEXT

Robert Gordon University (RGU) is a public research university based in the North East of Scotland, with over 17000 students. Due to its location, it is one of the most northern universities in the UK, and as such, attracts a number of students from more rural communities. Within the School of Computing Science and Digital Media at RGU, students typically take four modules of

ITiCSE '16, July 09-13, 2016, Arequipa, Peru
© 2016 ACM. ISBN 978-1-4503-4231-5/16/07…$15.00
DOI: http://dx.doi.org/10.1145/2899415.2909581

study per semester (with two semesters across one academic year).

It is important to note that within Scottish higher education institutions, home students (a classification that includes both students from Scotland as well as the EU) are typically eligible to have their tuition subsidised by the Students Awards Agency Scotland (SAAS), effectively allowing them to undertake a fee-free degree programme.

In order to gain an offer to study at undergraduate levels, students in Scotland are required to complete a set of national exams (at the most basic level, these are known as 'Highers' and are taken by students during their fifth year of secondary school studies, typically at age 16).

During the year leading up to the national exams, teachers not only prepare students for the upcoming qualification, but often also discuss future career options, and highlight potential universities that could be applied to. This is often aided by university academics, who organize outreach activities for interested parties. These activities would nominally be tailored to the secondary school audience, and showcase key items from the degree programmes on offer. Within an academic body, there is mixture of concern about whether these students are appropriately equipped with the skills required by that of a higher education environment [2].

3.1 Participants

As part of RGU's outreach strategy for the academic year of 2015-16, contact was made with a number of schools across Scotland, requesting participation. It is estimated that the average distance of these schools to the nearest higher education institution was 55 miles. All schools that replied to the initial invite were given a more detailed explanation of the aims and objectives of the study. Academics from RGU arranged to visit each school to discuss the transition process with the relevant students: at this stage, it was requested that access be given to students studying for a Computing-related Higher exam, or who had expressed an interest in studying a Computing-related subject at Higher Education. The participant pool was limited to students in their final year of high school.

A total of 249 students from 18 secondary schools around Scotland agreed to participate in the data collection exercise, which was carried out over the course of a couple of months. Each school was visited by an RGU academic, who led a discussion on university life. As part of this discussion, students were asked to anonymously fill in a survey which aimed to gather student concerns.

3.2 Survey

The aim of the survey was to gather anonymous responses from high school students regarding their concerns in relation to their upcoming transition into Higher Education. The questions within the survey was loosely based on the issues discussed within the literature, and comprised mainly of two sections: a set of 28 questions asking students to rank their concerns about the upcoming transition using a four-point Likert scale (ranging from 'no concern' to 'this is a major concern for me'), as well as an additional 'does not apply to me' tick-box.

These questions were grouped into larger topic areas drawn from experiences and expectations discussed in section 2.1 above, as follows:

- Academic environment;

- Academic staff;
- Academic work;
- Accessibility;
- Homesickness;
- Housing;
- Job-related concerns;
- Money; and
- Social.

These were followed by a set of free-text questions which aimed to collect outlying qualitative data and generate further discussion. For the purposes of this paper, the quantitative data will be analysed and discussed, while the qualitative data will be considered in a future paper.

The survey was validated with three groups prior to its release: pastoral tutors within the university ('foundation year coordinators'), CS1 students (asked to think about concerns they had prior to their transition) and school teachers.

At the point of data collection, the survey was kept anonymous: the only data gathered was the name of the students' school for analytic purposes related to geographical proximity to a Higher Education provider. Students were told to fill in as many questions as they felt were necessary to adequately describe their concerns. For the purpose of data evaluation, the authors have filtered out data which was deemed to be non-applicable by the students (i.e. where students ticked the 'does not apply' box).

4. DATA ANALYSIS

The data collected from the surveys was initially compiled by topic area in order to direct further investigation.

Table 1: Concerns compiled by Topic Area

Topic Area	Percentage of Students expressing Some or Major Concern
Money	64%
Job-related	61%
Academic Work	55%
Housing	51%
Academic Staff	42%
Homesickness	38%
Social	31%
Accessibility	30%
Academic Environment	25%

Table 1 gives a percentage of results where students have selected either 'some concern' or 'major concern' for questions within that topic area. This allows a visualisation of the topic areas, arranged by most concerning to least concerning.

Initial inspection of the data was surprising in that concerns related to more traditional views about transitions (e.g. Family life, friends, etc.) scored quite low in comparison to other topics. In Scotland, the majority of home students get fee-free tuition, and thus when considering 'transitions', minimal effort is normally placed in these areas.

The following sections will consider the 'top three' and 'bottom three' issues in further detail. While it is recognised that other data is equally as important, the focus of this paper is very much about what students perceive to be concerns and issues with their forthcoming transition.

4.1 Top Concerns

The preliminary analysis (as well as Table 2 below, which depicts the top ten concerns expressed by students) shows that when considering the data by topic area, 64% of students showed concern about items related to money, with 61% of students showing concern about job-related questions. Second to these financial concerns, it is perhaps not surprising to see that students were most concerned about their academic work (55%).

Table 2: The top ten ranked student concerns

Rank	Topic	Concern
1	Job-related	Job after graduating
2	Academic Work	Will I fail? (What happens if I do?)
3	Money	General money concerns
4	Money	Housing fees
5	Academic Work	Course choice (Have I chosen the right course?)
6	Money	Course fees
7	Academic Work	Preparedness (Am I prepared?)
8	Academic Work	Will I be good at it?
9	Money	Applying for SAAS (tuition) funding
10	Academic Work	Workload amount (What will the workload be?)

4.1.1 Money

This topic area included questions about general money concerns, housing fees, course fees, and applying for SAAS (tuition) funding (Figure 1).

These issues were all highly rated by students in terms of concern, and ranked in the top 10 concerns (out of 28). Notably, few people selected the 'no concern' option, highlighting the questions within this topic area as being generally important.

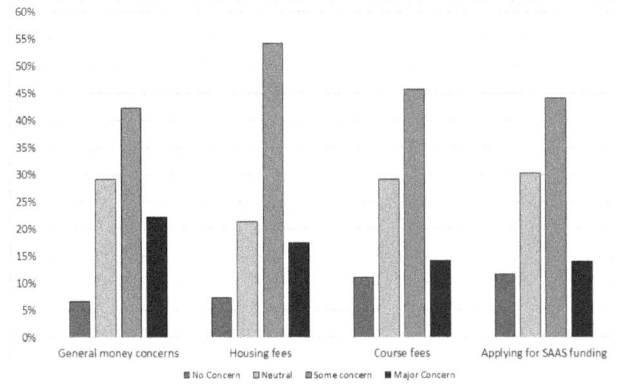

Figure 1: Concerns related to individual questions from the Money topic. Each question shows responses ranked from 'no concern' to 'major concern'.

In the first three cases depicted in Figure 2, at least 60% of students had at least some concern on these issues. In the case of housing fees, 71% of students showed concern (some concern: 54%; major concern: 17%). This is likely due to the fact that while SAAS funding in Scotland covers the students' tuition, housing fees typically are paid for by the student themselves. At the stage during which these students were surveyed, they would likely not have considered how they would be paying for these fees, nor would they have been likely to be exposed to the amount that these fees would end up being.

4.1.2 Job-Related

This topic area included questions about obtaining a full-time job after graduation, as well as their ability to find a part-time job that would support them throughout their studies (Figure 2).

These issues were all highly rated by students in terms of concern, and ranked in the top 10 concerns (out of 28).

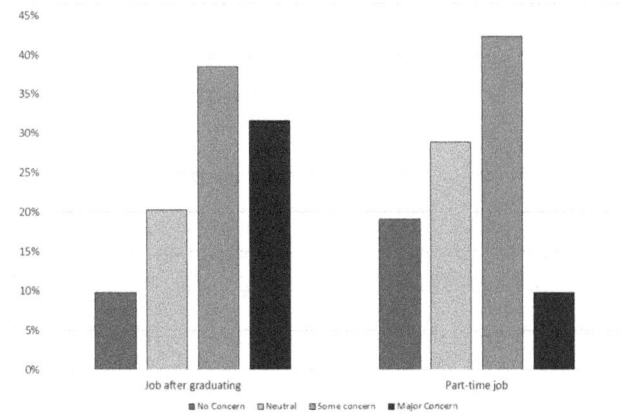

Figure 2: Concerns related to individual questions from the Job-Related topic. Each question shows responses ranked from 'no concern' to 'major concern'.

The issue of obtaining a job after graduation was of greatest concern to the students: this ranked as the top concern when compared to all 28 questions. Notably, 32% of respondents considered this to be a major concern (with a total of 70% of students having shown at least some concern).

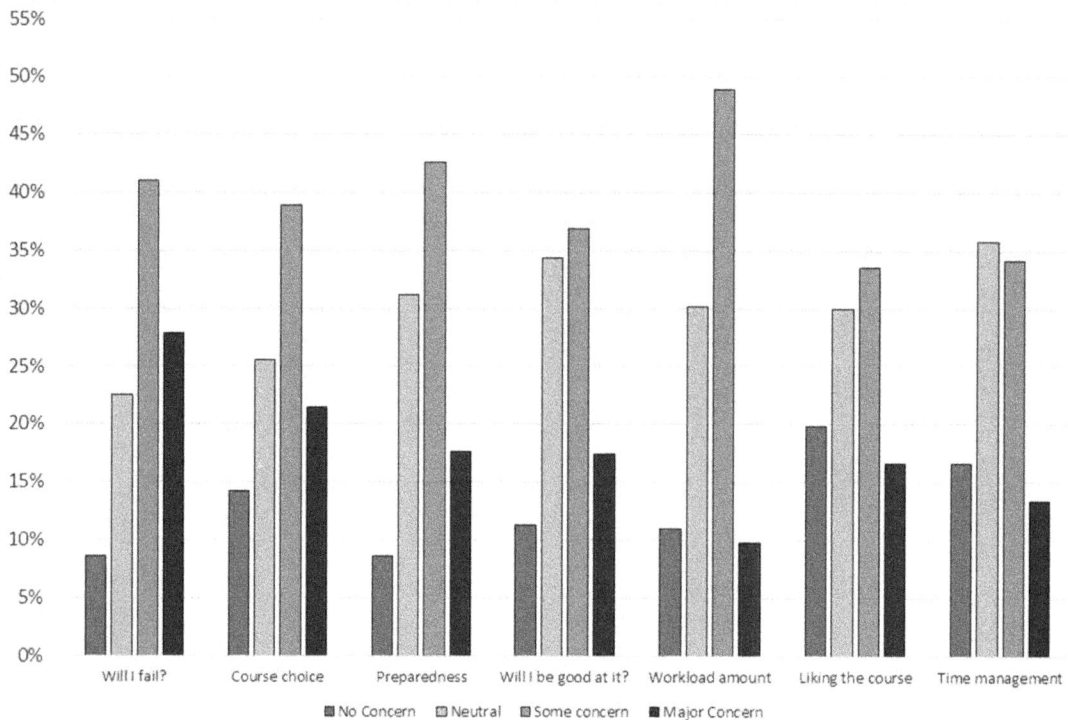

Figure 3: Concerns related to individual questions from the Academic Work topic. Each question shows responses ranked from 'no concern' to 'major concern'.

It is surprising, however, that 48% of students showed little concern (19%: no concern; 29%: neutral) about obtaining a part-time job during their studies. This may suggest that this survey was either delivered too early to them in this transitioning process, that it would be easy for them to find a part-time job, or that (at this stage) they do not plan on being employed during their studies.

4.1.3 Academic Work

This topic area included questions about potential failure, choosing the right course, being prepared for their chosen course, being good at it, the amount of expected workload, whether the course would be liked, and time management (Figure 3).

Out of these issues, all were highly rated by students in terms of concern (at least 48% of students rated each issue as being of at least some concern to them), and ranked in the top 10 concerns (out of 28), apart from 'liking the course' and 'time management'. For the purposes of this section, the latter two will be discounted.

Of these issues, it is clear that students are concerned about failing a course on which they have not yet embarked. This is worrying, as it is a fear which is difficult to counteract at this stage in their education.

As money has proven to be of a high concern, it is the authors' conjecture that the high concern with success in academic work is likely also linked to the financial ramifications of failure (e.g. cost of starting a new course following the failure of a first one).

4.2 Lowest Concerns

While many of the top concerns were not issues that could be under the direct control of the students, it is interesting to note that those items amongst the lowest concerns are issues which the students have a certain degree of control over.

The three topics which students identified as being the least concerned about were their new academic environment (25%), accessibility services at the new institution (30%) and their social life (31%).

4.2.1 Academic Environment

This topic area included questions about the classroom environment for lectures and labs, class sizes (in terms of the number of students) and the university city size (Figure 4).

For each of these issues, at least 70% of students had no concern or were neutral. No more than 5% of students have expressed major concerns for any of these issues.

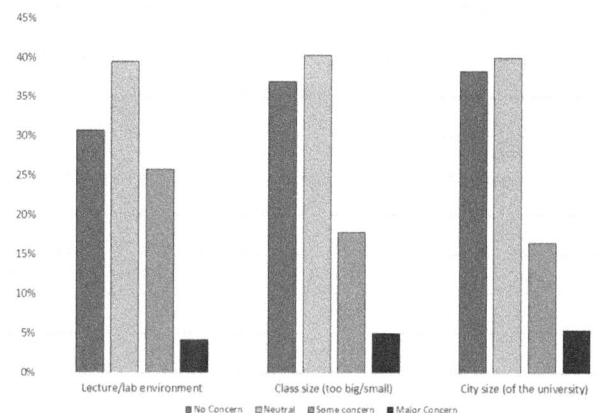

Figure 4: Concerns related to individual questions from the Academic Environment topic. Each question shows responses ranked from 'no concern' to 'major concern'.

The authors find this very interesting: as a university, much effort is placed into assuring that support is provided in terms of an environment for the students to learn in. One could postulate that

26

either universities have succeeded in meeting this need, or that students among the ages of those surveyed are not concerned with these issues.

4.2.2 Accessibility

This topic area only included one question: that of whether the transition to higher education would come with adequate accessibility support (Figure 5). The term 'accessibility' is used here to indicate access to adequate disability support.

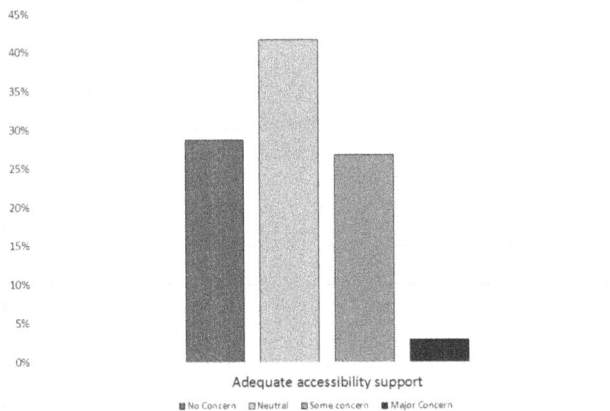

Figure 5: Concerns related to individual questions from the Accessibility topic. Each question shows responses ranked from 'no concern' to 'major concern'.

It is notable that 15% of all students that took the survey chose instead to not answer this question and tick the 'does not apply' box. Of those that responded, a high number of students (70%) rated this as one of minimal or neutral concern. It is important to note that whilst this number ranks 'accessibility' as one of the lowest concerns, it was not expected that this would be a concern for all students.

Through informal interviews with both teachers and students, it is posited at this point that most students marked this question as minor because up until this point in their education, these students would largely fall into one of two categories: a) they did not require accessibility services and therefore were unaware of them; b) they did require accessibility services, but were used to their parent/legal guardian being in control of the situation, and had not considered that this might change when they transitioned to Higher Education. Furthermore, students who required accessibility services reported considering an institution that they knew would be able to support their needs, therefore expressing little concern in this area.

4.2.3 Social

This topic area included questions about being able to make friends, as well as concerns about being subject to peer pressure (Figure 6).

It is of note that among concerns that arise with students (in higher education), many of those seen by the authors have fallen under the umbrella of pastoral care and typically involve social issues. The fact that both social issues ranked in the bottom concerns was surprising.

One might conjecture that in their final years of secondary school, students are typically part of an established peer group that has been cultivated over a number of years. As such, these specific concerns might be once that students are not giving weight to.

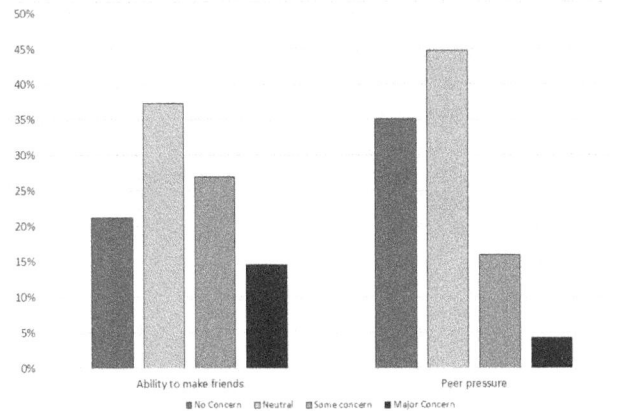

Figure 6: Concerns related to individual questions from the Social topic. Each question shows responses ranked from 'no concern' to 'major concern'.

5. RESULTS AND DISCUSSION

In the top ten questions, the concerns all relate to financial and job-related issues. The bottom concerns were primarily issues related to social life, academic environment and accessibility.

5.1 Discussion of Top Concerns

From the more detailed analyses reported in section 4.1 above, certain conclusions can start to be drawn. It is interesting to note that the top two concerns rated by students ('job after graduation' and 'what happens if I fail') were items that the students have little or no control over.

It was surprising to see that finance was rated so highly as a topic of concern for students, considering the fact that students would typically not need to worry about paying their tuition fees (at least in universities within Scotland).

5.2 Discussion of Lowest Concerns

From the analyses reported in section 4.2 above, it is clear that in order to better support this transition into higher education, it is important to understand the issues that students are facing while still in secondary school.

It should also be noted that the topic of 'homesickness' (with questions about distance to home, missing relatives and friends, and visiting their home), which is one that is typically most associated with transitioning concerns was ranked in the bottom four. Moreover, out of the 28 questions, those related to 'homesickness' were ranked 20 (at most).

5.3 Overall Discussion

While the literature review focused on transition into higher education from the standpoint of undergraduates, the survey data collected was from the perspective of secondary students. The distinction is an important one to make because it can be seen that the issues/concerns experienced by these students are different from those reported by early undergraduates.

While the works within the literature (e.g. [1, 2, 6]) focus on environment, it is notable that for those secondary students surveyed, this topic did not rank highly amongst the overall list of concerns, directly opposing the initial expectations of this survey.

It should be noted, that while Yorke [7] discussed problems associated with financial management amongst other topics, he notes that the students began their university careers unaware of these issues. However, within Scotland, it appears that secondary students, at least among those surveyed, are very aware of the financial implications of higher education and, indeed, this is a top concern to them, with both money-related and job-related concerns ranking in the top ten.

In terms of other expectations, that of academic work was a valid one, and was seen to be, in most cases, a top ten concern. However, lower concern than expected was placed by students in the areas of accessibility, distance from home, and homesickness in general.

6. CONCLUSIONS

The results in this paper indicate an agreement with a major point resulting from the studies reported by Yorke, that "some issues relating to the student experience only unfold after enrolment" [7]. Due to the variance in pre- and post-enrolment concerns, the student transition is one that must be treated appropriately according to each stage.

It is clear from the gathered data within this paper that certain topics such as the academic environment and social issues are not of great concern to these students. While anecdotally, these issues have been seen to evolve into the ones more typically seen in early undergraduate students, it is important that the issues that are of actual concern to these students are addressed at the appropriate time in their education.

There are a number of limitations to this study. First, whilst the surveyed students subscribed to a number of different ethnicities, all schools surveyed were mainly based in North-East Scotland. Second, a number of the schools surveyed were based in more rural areas. These may introduce location bias into the reported results. Finally, although academics were careful not to introduce bias into their pre-survey talk on transitions, student opinions may have been affected by that discussion, or the opinions of their classmates.

6.1 Future Work

When analysing the data, the authors were surprised to find that there was no significant concern for more 'traditional' transition issues, such as being apart from friends and family. It is conjectured that these concerns are absent based on the fact that university choice (in terms of location) is within the students' control, thereby mitigating potential issues that arise from longer distances.

However, it is felt that these distance-related issues may be among those that arise even at smaller scales than expected by the students. Based on informal pastoral care discussions with university students, it is felt that these issues can also arise when the distance between university and home is not significantly large. It may benefit from being looked at in further detail: future analysis plans to consider the data geographically, to understand whether the physical distance from the nearest higher education

provider could uncover any correlation between 'rurality' and these issues.

The work and results discussed in this paper have been used to inform the creation of a process of extended induction which has been used with CS1 students at RGU. This induction aims to address most of the concerns reported by students, and acts as a buffer between their secondary school studies and their new university life. The preliminary work carried out for this induction is being prepared for submission as a workshop, and is currently being authored for a follow-up paper.

7. ACKNOWLEDGMENTS

The authors would like to thank all of the secondary school teachers around Scotland who have allowed us access into their classrooms, and to all of the students that participated in the survey. In particular, we would like to thank AW for his tireless work in analysing the initial data set as a student research project funded by the Nuffield Research Foundation. This research, and the follow-up extended induction, were funded by the Higher Education Academy.

8. REFERENCES

[1] Askham, P. 2008. Context and identity: exploring adult learners' experiences of higher education. *Journal of Further and Higher Education.*

[2] Hulme, J.A. and De Wilde, J. 2014. *Tackling transition in STEM disciplines: Supporting the Science, Technology, Engineering and Mathematics (STEM) student journey into higher education in England and Wales.*

[3] Krause, K.-L. and Coates, H. 2008. Students' engagement in first-year university. *Assessment & Evaluation in Higher Education.* 33, 5 (2008), 493–505.

[4] Leese, M. 2010. Bridging the gap: supporting student transitions into higher education. *Journal of Further and Higher Education.*

[5] Lowe, H. and Cook, A. 2003. Mind the Gap: Are students prepared for higher education? *Journal of Further and Higher Education.* 27, 1 (Feb. 2003), 53–76.

[6] Ozga, J. and Sukhnandan, L. 1998. Undergraduate Non-Completion: Developing an Explanatory Model. *Higher Education Quarterly.* 52, 3 (1998), 316–333.

[7] Yorke, M. 2000. Smoothing the transition into higher education: What can be learned from student non-completion. *Journal of Institutional research.* 9, 1 (2000), 35–47.

Interdisciplinary and International Game Projects for Creative Learning

Johanna Pirker
Graz University of Technology
IICM - Inffelgasse 16c
8010 Graz, Austria
jpirker@iicm.edu

Daphne Economou
Computer Science
University of Westminster
W1W 6UW, United Kingdom
D.Economou@wmin.ac.uk

Christian Gütl
Graz University of Technology, Austria
& Curtin University, Perth, Western
Australia, Australia
cguetl@iicm.edu

ABSTRACT

In traditional computer science courses, students do not often get the chance to experience an entire project cycle, starting from the idea development stage and ending with the final release of a product together with collaborators from different disciplines. Developing a game gives learners the possibility to experience an entire development cycle, to learn how to work in a team, and to learn new skillsets required to create games. Students can profit even more from an interdisciplinary and international setup. In this paper, we describe a first pilot of an interdisciplinary and international student game project, during which students from different backgrounds, and with different nationalities and different learning expectations can work together to develop games. We report on a first pilot with 24 students studying different subjects, such as computer science, law, or biology, in two different countries. First results show that such programs are highly engaging for students, can boost their employability, have a high learning outcome, and raise their interest in international collaborations.

Categories and Subject Descriptors

K.3.2 [**Computer and Education**]: Computer and Information Science Education – *computer science education*.

General Terms

Design, Experimentation, Human Factors,

Keywords

Computer science education; game development; creative learning; collaborative learning

1. INTRODUCTION

The power of making games to encourage students to learn basic programming concepts is already well known. Creating their own games, parts of games,

or mods for games can encourage school pupils and university students to develop an interest in learning programming, also appealing to female students [1][2][3].

For computer science students, developing games is an attractive and also engaging field, since they can learn programming and software engineering by developing real applications with clear goals and visible outcomes [6]. Additionally, computer games challenge computer science (CS) students in a variety of specific CS areas, such as HCI, networking, computer graphics, or AI.

Developing games, however, also requires expertise in many other fields, such as art, 3d modeling, sound design, audio engineering, program management, design, and many more. Thus, to create a successful game, CS students have to team up and learn how to collaborate with students from different disciplines to create art and audio assets, to manage the development process, to design and test the game, and also to promote and present the outcomes. Due to these aspects, game development projects teach participants how to work as a team and allow students to experience an entire project cycle [3].

But not only computer science students, art students, or students from other creative disciplines are interested in developing games. Including experts from different fields, which appear not to be relevant for the game development process, can add interesting new topics, new educational aspects, and innovative ideas. In industry too, more game studios include experts from different disciplines in the development process. For example, in Assassin's Creed, historians were involved in the development process to create a more interesting and realistic historic environment and story [5].

When offering a course on game design and development for our CS students, we wanted to create a similar creative and innovative environment, where they would be able to work together in teams with other disciplines to develop games. To promote internationalization and teach students how to optimize collaboration and communication with remote teams, we have set up the course activities as an international student project. In a first pilot, we ran a program for computer science students at an Austrian university to develop games together with students from an UK university open to all different disciplines such as law, biology, and design.

In this paper, we present course design and experiences of a pilot with 12 Austrian computer science students, who teamed up with 12 British students from different disciplines to develop games together. Developing a game from scratch allows the students to experience an entire project cycle, from the idea finding stage, to the final release and the presentation of a first build. Also, developing a project together with "strangers" and students from different cultures is an entirely new situation for most students. The overall project experience is very close to a development situation in industry and can increase their career potential. The experience of working together with people from other countries should raise their interest in exchange programs, in international collaborations, and prepare them for the global job market.

Our goals in this paper are threefold. First, we want to illustrate our attempt to design an international and interdisciplinary game development program. Second, we want to identify benefits of international and interdisciplinary game development projects from a student's perspective. Finally, we want to report remaining gaps and problems identified to be able to enhance this program in future iterations.

The remainder of this paper is organized as follows. In section 2, we discuss related work. In section 3, we describe interdisciplinary game projects and the proposed process of the course design. Section 4 describes findings and results from our first showcase course and section 5 concludes with overall findings and future work.

2. BACKGROUND AND RELATED WORK
Game development projects have already been shown to be successful tools in the promotion of learning, creative and innovative thinking, and independent problem-solving strategies. In the next section, we discuss project-based learning with a focus on game development projects and game jams.

2.1 Project-Based Learning
Project-based learning, i.e. engaging students in solving and working on authentic problems, is, in particular in computer science (CS), a well-known and important way to teach programming and software development skills. Blumenfeld et al. describe projects, *"in which students pursue long-term investigations of a significant question and produce artifacts that represent answers to those questions have the potential to motivate students and help them better understand subject matter content"* [7]. Students can foster their theoretical knowledge by applying it to real cases [10]. Different studies in programming courses and CS courses show that students achieve a better understanding of the course's objectives [8].

To make use of the above-mentioned benefits, however, the projects for the students have to be compelling and interesting to motivate students and to maximize the learning outcomes. One way to make such projects more interesting is to involve game projects. In particular in the CS curriculum, many students are interested in digital games and their development process. And it is not only men who are interested in games. According to the ESA Fact 2015, 44% of game players are female [19]. The genre and type of games the students are interested in can differ, so it is important to let students make such decisions.

2.2 Game Development in CS curriculum
Different authors have discussed and evaluated the potential of game development for computer science students.

Kurkovsky discusses an approach where they use mobile game development early in their CS curriculum to challenge students at the beginning of the educational program with basics of different CS topics, such as Java programming, mobile development, computer graphics, HCI, algorithms, networking, AI, and database management [4]. Focusing on school education, Robertons and Howells also discuss the potential of game authoring as an opportunity for children to learn in an encouraging and exploratory environment. They also discuss the potential of such a pedagogical model to embrace the possibility for pupils to help and teach each other [11]. Bayliss and Strout discuss the potential of computer games in introductory programming courses with a focus on teaching simple programming concepts, software engineering processes, and ethical implications [6]. El-Nasr and Smith describe their experience with modding (modification of specific parts) existing games in a CS classroom and find that game modding can enhance student performance and that applying CS concepts in such a visual way is highly motivating for students [3].

Many of these approaches are very promising in their ability to raise school pupils' interest in CS, and encourage computer science students to enhance their programming skills and learn different CS concepts as well as allowing them to experience an entire project cycle. However, due to the interdisciplinary character of game development projects, incorporating such a program with interdisciplinary teams (programmers, artists, sound engineers, business experts) in a CS curriculum is a challenge. One way to promote such development projects is the organization of extra-curricular game jam events. In the next section we describe game jam events and their potential for learners.

2.3 Game Jams for Learning
Game jams are events, where people meet for a short time (typically 48 hours) and develop a game together under different constraints (e.g. a specific topic, in a specific style). Game jams have great potential to teach participants prototyping, collaboration, and creative and independent developing [14]. Such events are collaborative opportunities to work and learn in a creative and interdisciplinary environment [12]. Such events and development processes can foster creative thinking, innovation-driven development, and demonstrate the power of rapid prototyping techniques [15][16].

Game jams have a strong learning component and different studies suggest a positive correlation between students' performance and jam participation [12][13].

Most participants join game jam events to develop games in a group, and to meet people with similar interests and different skillsets [18]. However, due to the nature of game development projects, most participants have a background either in programming, design, art, or sound engineering [17]. Only a few participants with a background in fields such as history, law, or other fields, which are not directly related to the development process, participate in game jams.

In the next section, we propose a project-based learning approach, which brings together computer science students with students from all different disciplines in a jam-like environment to develop games together.

3. INTERDISCIPLINARY AND INTERNATIONAL GAME PROJECTS
Inspired by the interdisciplinary character of game development projects and the reported benefit of engaging students to work on projects, we developed an international and interdisciplinary learning design model to bring together students from different disciplines and nationalities to collaboratively develop games and learn how to work together in teams, both remotely and on-site.

3.1 Objective

The goals of the international interdisciplinary game project were:

- To design a project-based learning experience, which has interdisciplinary and international collaboration involved

- Increase the students' experience of (remote) team collaboration and supporting collaboration, and communication tools

- Encourage students to learn and master a variety of CS topics by developing games

- Expose students to an entire project cycle, from the idea finding stage to the final release presentation

- Increase students' interest in international collaborations and exchange

The project-based learning experience was organized into three main stages. (1) The team formation stage, (2) the idea and design developing stage in a remote collaboration setup, and (3) the development stage in an on-site jam environment. The single stages of the program are illustrated in figure 1.

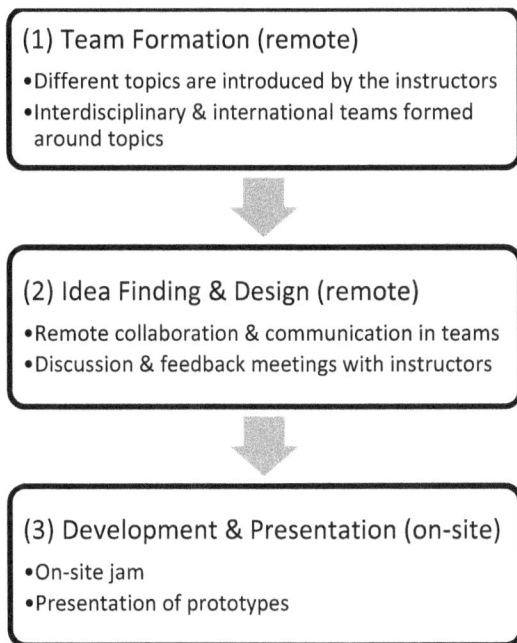

(1) Team Formation (remote)
- Different topics are introduced by the instructors
- Interdisciplinary & international teams formed around topics

(2) Idea Finding & Design (remote)
- Remote collaboration & communication in teams
- Discussion & feedback meetings with instructors

(3) Development & Presentation (on-site)
- On-site jam
- Presentation of prototypes

Figure 1. Stages of the interdisciplinary international learning experience on project-based game development

The next sections describe the setup of the interdisciplinary & international game project in an international cooperation between an Austrian University and UK-based university.

3.2 The Setting

In the course "Game Design and Development", Austrian computer science students learn the basics of how to develop games, basics of the development environment Unity, and software project management basics with a focus on iterative development processes. In previous iterations of this course, students worked on game projects together with other students in the same course at the same university. For this iteration, students from this course were able to apply for the international interdisciplinary project-based learning activity as part of this course. Students from the UK were able to apply for the games program as an extracurricular activity.

Following the model depicted in Fig. 1, two introductory sessions were held as part of the team forming stage, to introduce the participating students to each other, introduce the game topics, and suggest collaboration and communication tools. In addition, a Google group for questions and communication was set up. We introduced different subjects for games to be built, such as biology, law, holidays, or similar. The students were then able to choose a topic they found interesting. After that, they were asked to form international groups with group sizes 5-6 (2-3 from each country).

This was the starting point for stage 2, the idea finding & design stage. After forming groups, they started working on an initial game idea and a first game design. Two meetings with the instructors were organized, who supervised the design phase and commented on the ideas.

Stage 3 was organized as an on-site game jam event in London. The students were finally able to meet in person and to develop their games in a three-day on-site jam event. On the last day, they presented their games to a jury. The starting point of the game jam was an initial introduction of the jamming infrastructure. Next, every group of students (who already knew each other due to the remote collaboration) could choose a working space at the UK University. During the jam days, students had the possibility to work together on their projects from 09:00 to 21:00. Every day, the instructors paid a brief visit to each group to discuss the current stage and potential design and development issues. On the final day of the jam, all student groups presented their outcomes.

3.3 Material and Methods

To evaluate this learning design model, we conducted an initial small-scale trail of the proposed learning experience with 12 computer science students from an Austrian University and 12 students from a UK university, all from different disciplines (such as law, biology, or design). In order to learn from and improve our first attempt, the research scope has been defined broadly:

- Evaluate students' attitudes towards the international setup and the collaboration
- Evaluate students' experience with the group forming process
- Evaluate students' communication and collaboration methods
- Evaluate students' opinion on how such an activity contributes to their career
- Analyze their learning progress and their engagement

Thus, after the experience, we organized a final survey consisting of 19 open-ended questions, which included organizational aspects, and questions focusing on answering the research scope mentioned above. The survey took approximately 15-20 minutes to complete. The survey questions are listed in Appendix A.

4. FINDINGS

22 students, 12 students from an Austrian university and 10 from a UK university, participated in the final survey. In the following section, we will discuss the outcomes of the survey, focusing on the main objectives.

4.1 The Experience

In the following section we describe the students' experiences with the format based on their answers from the survey.

Experiences with the international student collaboration program

All 22 students participating in the survey would recommend such a learning experience format and 21 (95.95%) would participate in a similar course again. Asking the students what they liked in this format, many mentioned the international and collaborative format: *"Collaborating with international students was very interesting and stimulating"*, *"It was wonderful to learn about communicating and working with people from a different culture as a team."*

Experiences with the group forming process

Students had different experiences with the group forming process. While students were satisfied with the topics (*"Convenient, because broad categories were suggested and it was easy to find a team with similar interests"*) some students mentioned that it could be improved by adding further selection aspects to the process: *"the group forming was fine; could be better divided for number, specialization and student-year"*

Experiencing the remote communication & collaboration

Many teams had minor issues with remote communication and collaboration in the beginning phase, while other teams had a very good experience with their tools: *"It's pretty difficult to have proper online communication if the boundaries aren't set"*, *"Communication was pretty good considering the geographical element and people's own commitments"*. For communication tools, students recommend using Google+ groups, newsgroups, Facebook groups, or instant messaging with videos or audio (skype, WhatsApp). For collaboration students mainly recommend Git, SVN, Google Drive, and/or Dropbox. For project management, some groups used Asana.

Experiencing the importance to their career

Asking the students how they would judge the importance of this program for their future career 15/21 (71.43%) fully agreed and mentioned different skills they learned, which they find important for their careers. Many comments included the collaboration in an international team as such a skill: *"Yes, because you learn about the difficulties of international collaboration and how to get over them"*, *"Yes, as in this industry this is the kind of collaboration that would be carried out professionally"*, *"Yes, working with a diverse team (different study programs) and remote communication was interesting"*, *"Yes, building a project like this will be useful for the future, working in a team, online communication[...]"*, *"It was fun, educational and important for developing a range of skills to boost employability"*. Students also mentioned the potential of this course to raise their awareness of career possibilities in other countries. *"You learn about opportunities and chances in other countries"*.

Learning progress

Most students mentioned their improved skills in working as a team, in remote collaboration, game development, and also new technical skills such as coding, or the use of different tools. Most students groups used Unity3D as a game engine. Thus, the CS students were able to improve their programming skills in C#, but also their 3D modeling skills in Blender. The outcomes are discussed in the next section.

4.2 Outcomes

Five games were developed during this program. From the instructors' perspective, the outcomes were extraordinary innovative and interesting. Many groups picked topics for games from their specific field (e.g. law or biology) and added new and interesting design aspects to the game. Figure 2 displays a puzzle element added by a group to their game inspired by the design of BioBrick (DNA sequences) structures, which influence the player and his abilities. Figure 3 illustrates a stealth game where the goal is to steal specific objects. Every crime is recorded and, if the player is caught, all the crimes and the time the player has to spend in prison are listed according to real UK law.

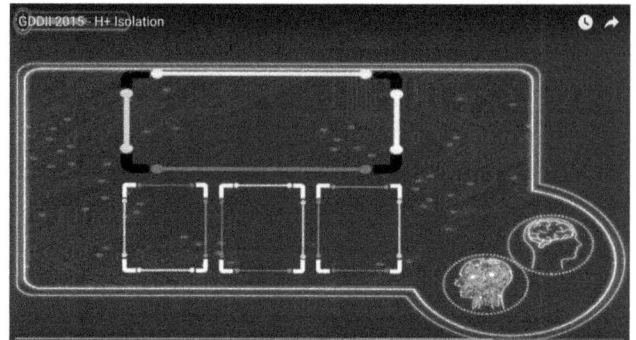

Figure 2. Puzzle game with bioengineering context inspired by DNA sequences

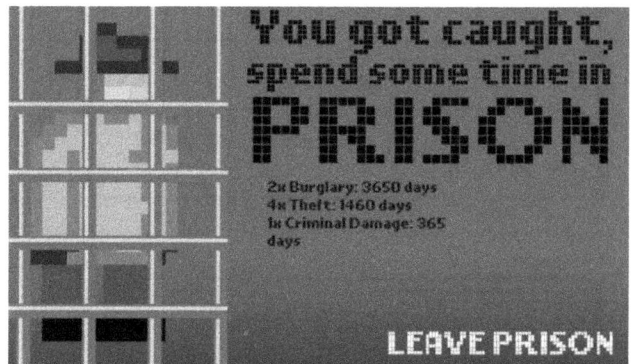

Figure 3. Game with law input summarizing the crimes committed in the game referring to real UK law

4.3 Challenges and Solutions

While the program was extremely well received, there is room for many aspects to be improved. Several students mentioned that they would like to get more support, tips, and feedback during the on-site jam event. One student suggested inter-team testing and feedback rounds to improve their game: *"More support to point out weaknesses and giving tips for improving the project"*. Some students mentioned time issues and would suggest longer on-site jams (4-5 days).

Based on the recommendations of the students, we are currently developing an updated version of this program. We are planning to add two on-site jams. So students would meet in the beginning phase of the program to find teams, create first ideas and a first design. After that, they can work remotely on their projects. In a final jam, they can finalize their game projects, again on-site. This also gives all students the possibility to get to know the two different universities and cities. This is a valuable point, which can make the entire experience more attractive to both student groups.

Another point and potential obstacle to consider when implementing similar programs is definitely the budget necessary to support such an exchange. This exchange was partly supported by the international office at the university in order to provide students with grants to travel to the UK. Costs would be even higher, when implementing a program with two travelling partner universities. In a future experiment, it would be interesting to design a similar program using remote collaboration only and to compare the results with this study to see if similar positive results can be reached.

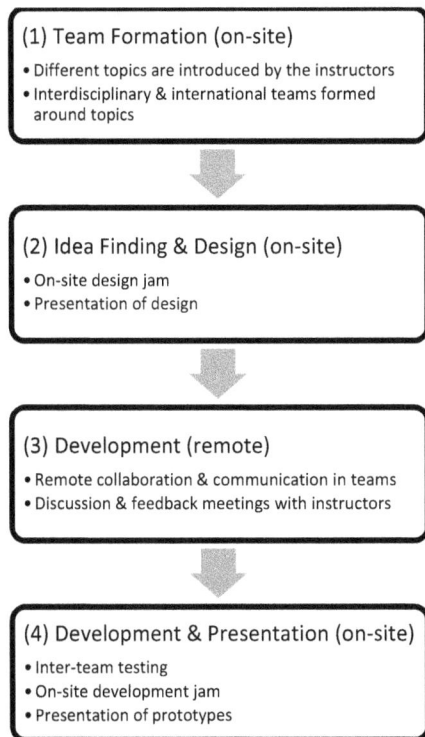

Figure 4 –Updated stages of the interdisciplinary and international game program

5. CONCLUSION

In this paper, we have presented an international and interdisciplinary project-based game development learning experience with the aim of creating a learning format to engage students studying different subjects, developing games together in an international setting. In an initial pilot we evaluated the students' experience with this program and their learning progress. Findings revealed that students are highly engaged by this program, and experience this program as a possibility to "boost employability". In addition to game development skills, they also learned how to work in international and interdisciplinary teams as well as how to work remotely in such teams.

Based on the results of our pilot, we were able to make several recommendations for future similar courses; in particular, the on-site jams should be longer. In a next iteration, we will design the program to have two on-site jams, one for the initial team-building and design phase and a second for the final game development. This gives students more time to work on their games, makes the meeting and group building more personal and gives all students the possibility to visit the two different countries.

ACKNOWLEDGMENTS.

We would like to thank Graz University of Technology and Westminster University to support this student exchange. We would also like to thank the anonymous reviewers for their valuable suggestions to improve the quality of this paper. Special thanks also to all students involved in this program. Details and credits to the games as seen in the screenshots can be found: gamelabgraz.com/london/

6. REFERENCES

[1] Overmars, M. 2004. Teaching computer science through game design. *Computer*, *37*(4), 81-83.

[2] Feldgen, M., and Clúa, O. 2004. Games as a motivation for freshman students learn programming. In *Frontiers in Education, 2004. FIE 2004. 34th Annual* (pp. S1H-11). IEEE.

[3] El-Nasr, M. S., and Smith, B. K. 2006. Learning through game modding. *Computers in Entertainment (CIE)*, *4*(1), 7.

[4] Kurkovsky, S. 2009. Engaging students through mobile game development. In *ACM SIGCSE Bulletin* (Vol. 41, No. 1, pp. 44-48). ACM.

[5] Kamen, M., 2014. Assasin's Creed historian on merging the past with fiction. In Wired.co.uk. Retrieved January 17, 2016. http://www.wired.co.uk/news/archive/2014-10/23/assassins-creed-unity-interview-maxime-durand

[6] Bayliss, J. D., and Strout, S. 2006. *Games as a Flavor of CS1* (Vol. 38, No. 1, pp. 500-504). ACM.

[7] Blumenfeld, P. C., Soloway, E., Marx, R. W., Krajcik, J. S., Guzdial, M., and Palincsar, A. 1991. Motivating project-based learning: Sustaining the doing, supporting the learning. *Educational psychologist*, *26*(3-4), 369-398.

[8] Davenport, D. 2000. Experience using a project-based approach in an introductory programming course. *Education, IEEE Transactions on*, *43*(4), 443-448.

[9] Leutenegger, S., and Edgington, J. 2007. A games first approach to teaching introductory programming. *ACM SIGCSE Bulletin*, *39*(1), 115-118.

[10] Köse, U. 2010. A web based system for project-based learning activities in "web design and programming" course. *Procedia-Social and Behavioral Sciences*, *2*(2), 1174-1184.

[11] Robertson, J., and Howells, C. 2008. Computer game design: Opportunities for successful learning. *Computers & Education*, *50*(2), 559-578.

[12] Preston, J. A., Chastine, J., O'Donnell, C., Tseng, T., and MacIntyre, B. 2012. Game jams: Community, motivations, and learning among jammers. *International Journal of Game-Based Learning (IJGBL)*, *2*(3), 51-70.

[13] Arya, A., Chastine, J., Preston, J., and Fowler, A. 2013. An international study on learning and process choices in the global game jam. *International Journal of Game-Based Learning (IJGBL)*, *3*(4), 27-46.

[14] Fowler, A., Khosmood, F., and Arya, A. 2013. The evolution and significance of the Global Game Jam. In *Proc. of the Foundations of Digital Games Conference 2013*.

[15] Fowler, A., Khosmood, F., Arya, A., and Lai, G. 2013. The global game jam for teaching and learning. In *Proceedings of the 4th Annual Conference on Computing and Information Technology Research and Education New Zealand* (pp. 28-34).

[16] Pirker, J., Kulima AK., Gütl, C. 2016. The Value of Game Prototyping for Students and Industry. In *Proceedings of the*

International Conference on Game Jams, Hackathons, and Game Creation Events (pp. 54-57). ACM.

[17] Reng, L., Schoenau-Fog, H., and Kofoed, L. B. (2013). The motivational power of game communities-engaged through game jamming. In *Proceedings of the 8th International Conference on the Foundations of Digital Games.*

[18] Pirker, J. and Voll, K. 2015. Group Forming Processes – Experiences and Best Practice from Different Game Jams. Proceedings of the 2015 Workshop on Game Jams, Hackathons and Game Creation Events (Co-located with FDG2015).

[19] Entertainment Software Association. (2015). 2015 - Essential facts about the computer and video game industry. *Retrieved January, 17,* 2016. http://www.theesa.com/wp-content/uploads/2015/04/ESA-Essential-Facts-2015.pdf

APPENDIX A

The questionnaire consists of three main parts: (1) organizational aspects, (2) studying abroad and international awareness, and (3) educational aspects. Following, all 19 questions of the open-ended questionnaire are listed. The term Hackathon was used in this context for the on-site game jam event.

1. How did you find the preparation of the program?

2. Did you feel you have been provided enough information about the international student collaboration program?

3. How did you find the group forming process?

4. How did you find the choosing topic process?

5. How did you find the communication and collaboration with your team before the game jam?

6. How did you find the communication and collaboration with the instructors before the Hackathon?

7. Can you suggest tools that would be better for communication?

8. Can you suggest that would be better for collaboration and file sharing?

9. Suggestions for improving the organization of the program.

10. Did the international student collaboration program raised interest in studying abroad and would you consider getting involved in further international programs?

11. Do you think that the experience of being involved in this international student collaboration program is import for a future career and why?

12. Did you find the learning approach used in this international student collaboration engaging and motivating and how else could it be improved?

13. State the most important things that you learned/gained from this international student collaboration program.

14. Do you feel that the support/guidance during the Hackathon was satisfactory and how could it be improved?

15. What other activities would you expect from the Hackathon?

16. Did you find the facilities satisfactory during the Hackathon; what else would you expect?

17. Would you take part in this or a similar program next year?

18. Would you recommend the program to others next year; why?

19. Other suggestions for improvements.

Teaching Programming - Understanding Lecture Capture YouTube Analytics

Aidan McGowan
Queen's University Belfast
1 Elmwood Avenue Belfast,
Northern Ireland
+44 (0)28 9097 1185
aidan.mcgowan@qub.ac.uk

Philip Hanna
Queen's University Belfast
13 Stranmillis Road, Belfast,
Northern Ireland
+44 (0)28 9097 4634
p.hanna@qub.ac.uk

Neil Anderson
Queen's University Belfast
1 Elmwood Avenue Belfast,
Northern Ireland
+44 (0)28 9097 1190
n.anderson@qub.ac.uk

ABSTRACT

The proliferation in the use of video lecture capture in universities worldwide presents an opportunity to analyse video watching patterns in an attempt to quantify and qualify how students engage and learn with the videos. It also presents an opportunity to investigate if there are similar student learning patterns during the equivalent physical lecture. The goal of this action based research project was to capture and quantitatively analyse the viewing behaviours and patterns of a series of video lecture captures across several university Java programming modules. It sought to study if a quantitative analysis of viewing behaviours of Lecture Capture videos coupled with a qualitative evaluation from the students and lecturers could be correlated to provide generalised patterns that could then be used to understand the learning experience of students during videos and potentially face to face lectures and, thereby, present opportunities to reflectively enhance lecturer performance and the students' overall learning experience. The report establishes a baseline understanding of the analytics of videos of several commonly used pedagogical teaching methods used in the delivery of programming courses. It reflects on possible concurrences within live lecture delivery with the potential to inform and improve lecturing performance.

Keywords

Video lecture Capture; Programming; YouTube analytics; Java;

1. INTRODUCTION

The use of video lecture capture in Higher Education is becoming increasing commonplace in universities worldwide [9]. There have been a large number of studies dedicated to the effects of videoing lectures with most concentrating on attitudinal surveys of staff and students and the effects on student attendance and engagement (e.g. [2],[4], [16]). Generally the body of research in the area points to positive benefits to the use Lecture Capture (LC).

ITiCSE '16, July 09-13, 2016, Arequipa, Peru

© 2016 ACM. ISBN 978-1-4503-4231-5/16/07...$15.00

DOI: http://dx.doi.org/10.1145/2899415.2899421

These include the argument that videoing lectures provides an extra resource that may complement students' studies [11]. Flexibility of learning is also a stated benefit with Prodanov arguing "the commonly held benefit (for the students) is the ability to review material and catch up with missed lectures" [17].

The potential negative effects of video lecture capture have also examined [6]. One of the main concerns stated by lecturers is a potential impact on student attendance ([5], [8]). The concern from faculty appears to be based largely on the link between attendance and academic success. Nyamapfene argues that, "class attendance is highly correlated to academic performance" [14]. This apprehension is reflected in the large volume of research into attendance on video lectured programmes. Other research has concluded that videoed lectures can make the lectures uninteresting [10]. The same authors also contend that "videoed lectures may hinder the development of students as independent learners on the basis that the students view the lecturer via the video as the only important source of knowledge in the area", an argument which is accepted by Davis [6].

Increasing student demand and technical infrastructure improvements have seen an increase in its usage in third level education worldwide [15]. However the effects of lecture capture in the area of computer programming is a relatively under researched area with Watkins offering one of a few studies [19]. Video delivery of programming solutions may be particularly useful in enabling a lecturer to illustrate the complex decision making processes and incremental nature of the actual code development process.

Additionally in the past five years there has been a significant increase in the popularity of online learning, specifically via Massive Open Online Courses (MOOCs) [18]. One of the key aspects of a MOOC is the simulated recording of lecture like activities. There is an increasing body of research into the analysis of the video engagement performance of MOOCs, (e.g. [2], [7], [12]). Studies of MOOC video engagement and LC have shown that students regularly stop, start and rewind recorded lectures to enable them to revisit points of the lecture they perhaps did not understand [10], [13], [20]. Typically, video viewing patterns exhibit a varied peak and drop-off playback graph that can be analyzed to provide an insight of overall engagement within the video. The spikes in the graph may indicate student confusion, introduction of important concepts or engaging demonstrations [8]. The drop-offs can also reveal if important sections are skipped over. Knowledge gained from research into MOOC video performance coupled with easily accessible YouTube LC video analytics offers a potentially rich source of information that is currently largely untapped. For example, an analysis of the LC viewings could offer a quick response formative feedback mechanism for a lecturer on the engagement performance of the video and perhaps the corresponding physical lecture. If there is significant tail off in the viewing of the video does this indicate that the same disconnect occurred in the lecture? Does a rewind and replay spike suggest that the students found the related point difficult to comprehend and thereby highlight an area that should be readdressed in the next lecture?

2. RESEARCH OBJECTIVES

This research was conducted across two full Java programming modules within a computing degree in Queen's University, Belfast. The modules employed a series of video lecture captures in which the audio of lectures and video of on-screen projected content were recorded and made available to the students via a closed YouTube channel. This study concentrates on establishing a baseline understanding of viewing behaviors of several common teaching methods and investigating the potential teaching and learning performance feedback that may be generated from an analysis of the video engagement behaviors using YouTube Analytics. Given that the videos used in this study were a faithful representation of the physical lecture, they offered a potential means of linking the performance analysis of the videos into areas of in-lecture improvement that could help significantly improve the quality of learning. To the best of our knowledge this is an area that has not been researched before.

The Implications for practice and/or policy

- If a videoed lecture is a true reflection of the actual lecture then it follows that an analysis of the viewing patterns for the video may reveal trends that correspond with the live delivery.
- The analysis of the readily accessible YouTube analytics of Lecture Capture videos provides a low-cost, easily implemented and rich source of information that could be used to improve overall quality of teaching and learning performance.

3. METHOLOGY

The study was conducted with a cohort of 80 post graduate students taking two compulsory modules in Java programming (Programming 1 & Programming 2) over two semesters in a one year MSc. Software Development course in 2014-2015. The video capture of lecture was presented as 10 – 30 minutes snippets that consisted of the audio of the lecturer and video of on-screen projected content. The on-screen projected content of the LC videos utilized four pedagogically different formats: Slides with predominant text (Figure 1), Slides with predominant code (Figure 2), Code walkthroughs (Figure 3) and Code development (Figure 4).

A total of 55% of the students in the study stated that with first time views of Lecture Capture videos they watched the whole way through without stopping regardless if they had attended the lecture or not. This is consistent with Kim who states "first time views tend to be more sequential" [10]. However with subsequent views only 14% of the students in the survey watched the complete video. The targeted viewing of sections of the video was the predominant viewing pattern for re-watched videos. As such the first time views are more representative of and reveal a closer student experience to the physical lecture and are considered in this study.

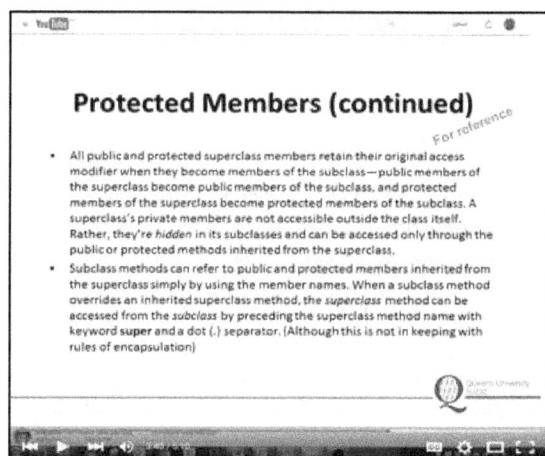

Figure 1 : PowerPoint slides with majority theory text based content.

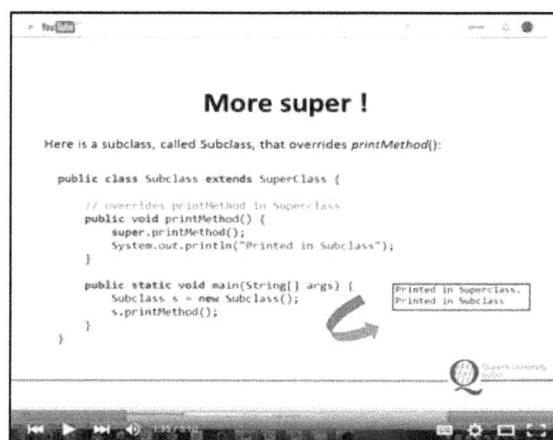

Figure 2 : PowerPoint slides with majority programming code based content.

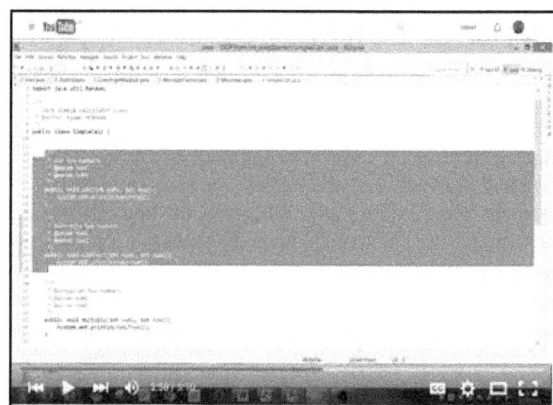

Figure 3 : Programming code walkthroughs, with the lecturer highlighting and explaining code.

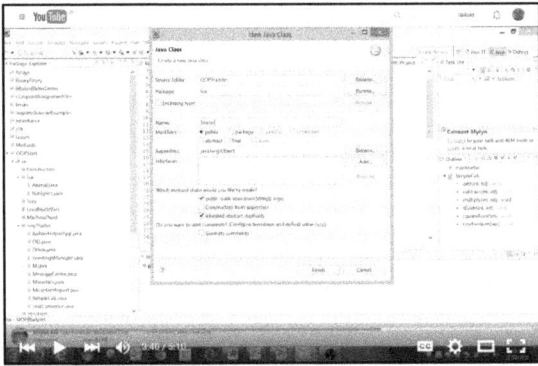

Figure 4 : Real time programming and code development. With the lecturer manually entering and explaining the development of code in an Integrated Development Environment (IDE).

3.1 Lecture Capture video analysis

The Lecture Capture videos were hosted on a closed YouTube channel only available to the students in the modules. The channel had analytics which offered engagement reports for the videos. A comparative study of the general performance of the videos was made using viewing (hits) figures. Additionally an analysis of each of the pedagogically different teaching formats enabled a study of the comparative performance of each section of the video.

3.2 In-video dropout rate and audience retention

A dropout rate is defined as the percentage of students who start watching a video but leave before the video finishes. The audience retention (AR) rate is a cumulative measurement of the average percentage of the video that was watched. The analysis of the dropout rate and AR can reveal factors that affect why a student leaves or skips over content in a video [10]. Consideration of these factors would likely improve the LC video performance but may also in turn be extrapolated to performance improvements within the physical lecture. An analysis of the dropout and AR rates suggests that when the student no longer perceives the material in the video as relevant then the video is skipped forward or stopped. Considering this study is limited to the first time views of the videos it is may not be unreasonable to conclude that a similar topic and delivery within a physical lecture would also result in a similar outcome, with the student's active engagement switching off.

3.3 Interaction peaks and drop offs

When a significant number of students repeatedly interact with a section of a video a peak in the viewing profile will occur. Conversely when the students repeatedly fail to interact with part of a video a drop-off in the profile is observable. The peaks and drop-offs are of significance to the analysis of the engagement with the video and potentially within the related lecture.

3.4 Student and lecturer views – a qualitative study

All students were surveyed about their viewing behaviors and several students were selected randomly and interviewed in respect to their viewing habits. The lecturers where also interviewed to help qualify and relate their experience of the content being taught in the video.

4. RESULTS

4.1 In-video dropout rate and Audience Retention (AR)

From the student interviews and surveys the factors concerning In-video dropout are many and varied but generally relate to length, structure or content relevance. Generally the AR decreases with video length (Figure 5). The observed AR suggests that an optimum time for a video would be no more than 10 minutes. Relating the engagement performance of Lecture Capture videos in this study to the physical lecture would suggest that a lecturer presenting narrative based delivery that lacks student interaction beyond 10 minutes in length runs the risk of losing the attention of a significant number of the students.

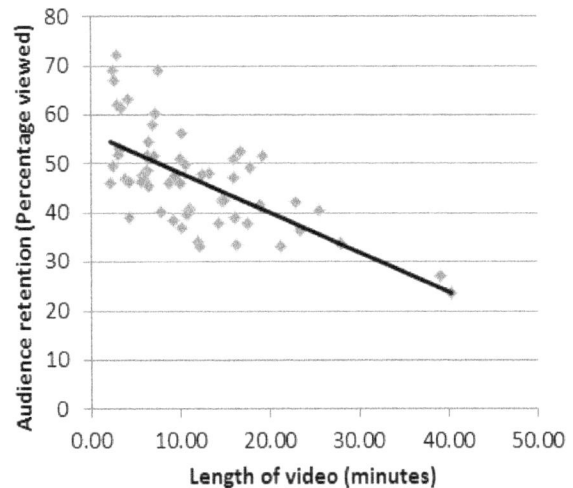

Figure 5 : Audience Retention of each video shown with the length of the video.

4.2 Viewing engagement profiles

As illustrated in Figure 6 video viewing graphs generally consist of three stages.

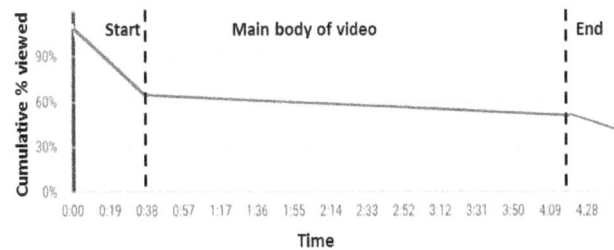

Figure 6 : Typical video engagement graph

A start-up period during which there is usually a sharp decline in views. Following this period is the main body of the video which generally shows a gradual decline followed by a tail which normally shows a sharp decline. However the viewing engagement graphs of video lecture capture rarely have a smooth curve with the majority tending to have a similar appearance to figure 7. Normally there are many peaks and troughs evidenced in the engagement graphs.

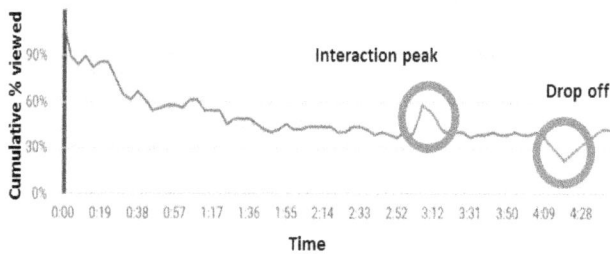

Figure 7 : Typical engagement graph with peaks and drop offs

Skip forward activities show on the graphs as down turns (Drop-offs) and rewind and replay activities are shown as upturns (Interaction Peaks). The smoother the graph or section of the graph suggests that the students were able to watch without the need to stop and replay and were engaged enough not to skip forward. A lack of rewind and replay activity suggests that students understood the content and the cadence of the video was correct.

A lack of drop-off is consistent with the students being engaged with the section. It would follow that a similar delivery in a lecture should have similar outcomes. It is therefore the interaction peaks and drop-offs that are of particular interest in video engagement analysis and may possibly be further related to the student learning engagement in the lecture theatre.

4.2 General trends, Interaction peaks and drop-offs

An analysis of the video engagement graphs suggest some general patterns, however the context of the video is important.

General trends:

The same activity over time causes a gradual decline.

The same activity over a prolonged time period will generally cause a gradual disengagement regardless of the pedagogical format.

Drop-offs at the end, are summaries a good idea?

Most videos display a gradual decline over time but many present a significant drop-off towards the end (Figure 8, Section D). On

analysis these areas correspond to a summary or an advertisement for the next topic. Taken at face value this decline would suggest that few students watch the summaries and have little immediate interest in the next topic. This would go against commonly recommended teaching practice to "summarise the key points and direct students toward further learning", [3]. To further qualify this phenomenon the students were surveyed with 98% reporting that they continued to watch the summaries. The physical lectures also generally have a summary at the end with 95% of the students stating that they found these to be "really necessary". Neither of these student-stated opinions corresponds with the observed viewing patterns on the video or indeed within the lectures. The students suggested that the lecturer should avoid recapping at the end of the video as they could simply rewind to the part they wanted to review. Additionally it was noted that on videos when the lecturer started a summary with phrase like "in summary,", "to finish off," or "to wrap things up" there was a sharp decline in viewing. The students felt that it was an indicator that the "good information is over" and they simply switched off.

Base lining performance

The videos consisted of pedagogically different formats, slides (with majority text or code based content), code walkthroughs and active code development. Based on the collected evidence, there are differences in the viewing patterns among these formats. In order to differentiate unexpected peaks and drop-offs in the graphs it was important to establish a baseline understanding of the general performance of these sections. To illustrate this, a case study of an actual video engagement graph is presented (Figure 8) which is representative of many of the other videos in the study.

Slides (theory)

Typically the slides with predmoninant text and accompanying narrative description are initially well engaged with, however they soon suffer a sharp decline in engagement resulting from skip forward activity. This is especially evidenced when the slide remains on screen for longer than 30 seconds. This teaching format performs worst in terms of holding the students' attention on video and is likely to have the same affect during the live lecture.

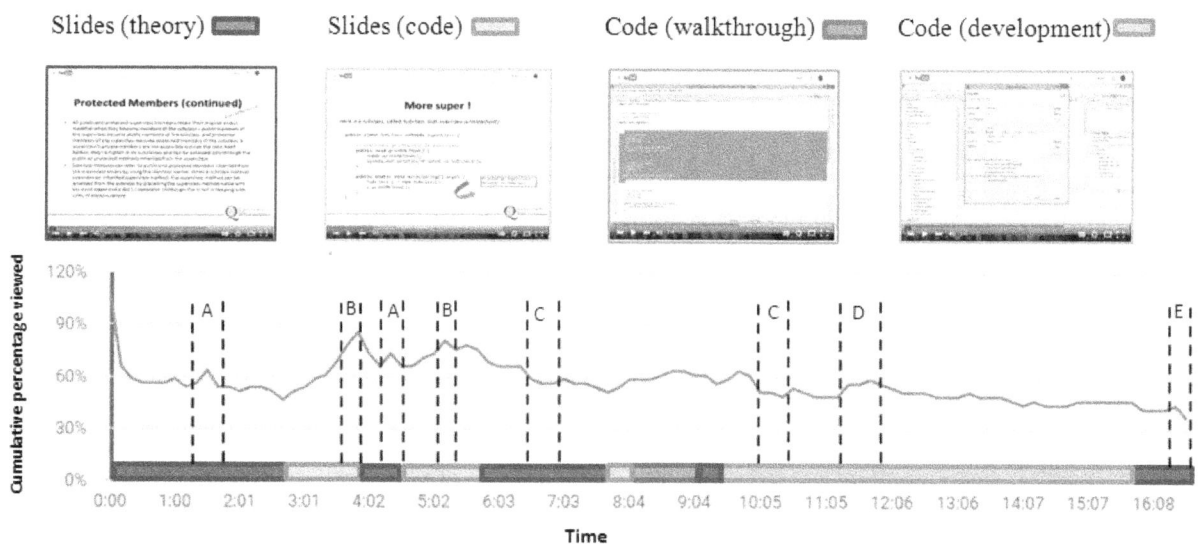

Figure 8: Case study of video that contained the common delivery formats of PowerPoint slides, Code walk through and Active code development and points of interest marked A to E.

Slides (code)

This format performs better than theory limited slides. From interviews the students explained that the code helps actualise the theory and the health of the engagement is due to students pausing and also rewinding to make notes.

Code walkthrough and code development

Generally a sustained upturn in the engagement graphs will relate to some form of coding, either a static walkthrough explanation or active coding. The students report that when watching the video they either actively take notes or follow along by entering the code in their own IDE. The students report that it is the code related sections that they were most likely to rewind and replay; again due to the active nature they are using it for i.e. following along.

The students stated that they use the code walkthroughs primarily to watch and listen rather than follow along on their own IDE. There is a difference in the viewing engagement between these coding formats. The walkthroughs tend to have a higher engagement than the active coding sections. Typically this can be attributed to the pace of the walkthroughs which are generally quicker than the active coding and this was the main reason given by the students for the replay activity and consequently a higher engagement as seen on the graphs. Commonly this was the highest sustained engagement evidenced across all formats.

The active code development engagement profile also performs well and was reported by the students to be their most accessed section of the videos. Yet this was not always evidenced in the engagement graphs. It has a slower pace compared to the walkthroughs and the students tend to pause the video rather than needing to rewind as the code stays on the screen longer. Subsequently even though the students spend more time in these areas the graph remains unaffected. Additionally some students report they nudge the video ahead as they do not feel the need to wait and watch the lecturer type every line of code.

Areas of concern

Given this baseline understanding of the teaching format performances and general trends it is the unexpected peaks or drop-offs that are areas of interest with engagement analysis and could help indicate potential performance improvements.

Spikes during theory or code explanations

As shown in Figure 8 Sections A, there were unexpected peaks within the areas involving Slides with theory. On review with the students and the lecturers it was discovered the peaks corresponded to complex areas and so required a replay. In addition it was commonly acknowledged by the lecturers in these areas that the explanations may not have been sufficiently clear and could have benefited from a code example.

Peaks in slides with code (Figure 8, Sections B) were related to detailed explanations that associated theory to code. Students primarily replayed these sections to rehear the lecturer's explanation. In the video in the case study the lecturer felt that the explanation was reasonably comprehensible. However with the retrospective analysis of the video engagement and student feedback indicating that the students found it difficult to follow, he indicated he would change the future delivery format to a slower paced active code presentation.

In Section D the lecturer provided a set of multiple instructions which the students stated were too quick to follow and therefore stopped and replayed. Interestingly some of the students related the same occurrence in the physical lecture with some recalling they missed the instructions and were unable to actively follow the remaining demonstration. Crucially this appeared to have affected a significant number of the students yet none of students asked the lecturer to repeat the steps during the lecture. The lecturer was unaware that many students were unable to follow the demonstration until it was highlighted in the video analysis and indicated if he had known this he would have readdressed it in the next lecture.

Drop-offs

Figure 8 Sections C illustrate drop-offs indicating that the students nudged the video forward. On reflection the students felt that the pace of delivery was too slow. On review the lecturer accepted this and suggested that the pace could have been quickened but significantly he had been unaware of this student perception at the time of the physical lecture.

4.4 Design implications for videos and lecture delivery

The review of the analytics of the engagement reports across all the videos has identified common patterns which provides performance improvement recommendations for video capture and consequently for lecture delivery.

1. Longer videos attract less views and an increase in-video drop out. The recommendation is to limit narrative delivery to no more than 10 minutes.

2. Code based practical demonstrations associating theory are more highly valued by students than theory only explanations.

3. Summaries are important but need to be addressed as conclusions (careful use of language required).

4. Slides with code are typically more engaging than sides with textual only descriptions.

5. Taking into consideration the baseline performance of any particular presentation format then a relatively smooth line of viewing engagement is good; it suggests a good delivery pace.

6. All formats exhibit a decline in viewership over a prolonged length of time, variation in format is important.

5. FUTURE WORK AND CONCLUSIONS

We believe that this study has shown that knowledge of the baseline performance profiles of various common teaching formats in programming LC videos coupled with identification and analysis of the causes of peaks and drop-offs represents a feedback mechanism to identify short comings in video and related lecture delivery. The limitation of the study to programming lectures is also an opportunity for further study in that there may be other applications of the findings in other fields. It is likely that other STEM subjects especially with similar technical and practical subject content and delivery may exhibit similar patterns. For future work we plan to analyse more courses and interaction patterns including other academic disciplines.

The reconsideration of accepted practice in providing a summary at the end of lectures is an interesting finding and we feel it makes sense as the control is very much in the hands of the student to formulate their own recap if this were necessary. It is of interest that the data contrasted with what the students reported and may also be a worthy area of further exploration.

The increase of LC and the accessibility of YouTube analytics could well mean that video analytics could become a widely adapted performance review practice potentially leading to an improved delivery and learning experience.

6. LIMITATIONS

The study is limited to the two Java programming modules over a one year period and as such is representative only of that sample. It is also limited to a study of the lecture capture of programming code development lectures. The optimum time for a video lecture in this course was concluded to be around 10 minutes however it may be that in more narrative based subjects this target may vary in length and that further studies in other discipline would be beneficial.

7. REFERENCES

[1] Bennett, E., and Maniar, N., 2007. Are videoed lectures an effective teaching tool? Available at: http://citeseerx.ist.psu.edu/viewdoc/summary?doi=10.1.1.105.6020

[2] Breslow, L., Pritchard, D. E., DeBoer, J., Stump, G. S., Ho, A. D., & Seaton, D. T. (2013). Studying learning in the worldwide classroom: Research into edX's first MOOC. *Research & Practice in Assessment*, *8*(1), 13-25.

[3] Cantillon P., (2003). Teaching large groups. British Medical Journal. 2003;326(7386):437

[4] Chandra, S. ACM., (2007) SIGCSE Bulletin - Proceedings of the 12th annual SIGCSE conference. Volume 39 Issue 3, September 2007

[5] Chang, S., (2007). Academic perceptions of the use of Lectopia: Available at: http://www.ascilite.org.au/conferences/singapore07/procs/chang.pdf

[6] Davis S, Connolly A, Linfield E, Lecture capture (2009) Making the most of face-to-face learning. Engineering Education vol.4 issue 2Guo, P., (2013). Available at: https://www.edx.org/blog/optimal-video-length-student-engagement

[7] Guo, P., (2013). Available at: https://www.edx.org/blog/optimal-video-length-student-engagement

[8] Guo, Philip J., Juho Kim, and Rob Rubin. "How video production affects student engagement: An empirical study of mooc videos." Proceedings of the first ACM conference on Learning@ scale conference. ACM, 2014.

[9] Holliman, R., Scanlon, E., (2004). Mediating Science Learning Through Information and Communications Technology. Routledge Falmer, London, 301p

[10] Kim, J., Guo, P., Seaton., D (2014) Understanding In-Video Dropouts and Interaction Peaks in Online Lecture Videos. Proceeding L@S '14 Proceedings of the first ACM conference on Learning @ scale conference Pages 31-40 ACM New York, NY, USA 2014 ISBN: 978-1-4503-2669-8

[11] Krüger, M. and Nickolaus, R., (2005). Self-directed and cooperative learning with lecture recording. Available at http://stadium.open.ac.uk/prolearn/summer05/documents/marc_krueger_abstrakt_of_dissertation.pdf

[12] Li, N., Kidzinski, L., Jermann, P., (2015). Proceedings of the European MOOCs Stakeholder Summit 2015, p. 112-121, P.A.U. Education, 2015

[13] Le A., Joordens S., Chrysostomou S. and Grinnell R., (2010). Online lecture accessibility and its influence on performance in skills-based courses. Computers & Education 55 (2010) 313–319

[14] Nyamapfene, A., 2010. Does class attendance still matter? Engineering Education, volume 5, no.1 pp 64-74

[15] Olson, J., Codde, J., (2011). Available at http://cas.msu.edu/wp-content/uploads/2013/09/E-Learning-White-Paper_oct-2011.pdf

[16] Pinder-Grover, T., Millunchick, J.M., (2008) Work in progress - using screencasts to enhance student learning. Frontiers in Education Conference, 2008. FIE 2008. 38th Annual. DOI:10.1109/FIE.2008.4720446

[17] Prodanov, V., (2010). In-Class Lecture Recording: Available at http://digitalcommons.calpoly.edu/cgi/viewcontent.cgi?article=1339&context=eeng_fac

[18] Vardi, M., 2014. Will MOOCs Destroy Academia? Commun ACM, 2012, 55, 11, 5-5, Association for Computing Machinery Kim, J., Guo, P., Seaton, D., Mitros, P., Gajos, K., Miller R., 2014.

[19] Watkins, A. Hufnagel, E., 2007. Video Vignettes: Teaching Computer Programming to the MTV Generation. Decision Sciences Journal of Innovative Education Volume 5 Number 2. May, 2007

[20] Zupancic, B. and Horz, H., 2002. Lecture Recording and Its Use in a Traditional University Course. ACM SIGCSE Bulletin Homepage Volume 34 Issue 3, September 2002. Pages 24-28

Towards a Systematic Review of Automated Feedback Generation for Programming Exercises

Hieke Keuning
Open University of the
Netherlands and Windesheim
University of Applied Sciences
hw.keuning@windesheim.nl

Johan Jeuring
Utrecht University and Open
University of the Netherlands
j.t.jeuring@uu.nl

Bastiaan Heeren
Open University of the
Netherlands
bastiaan.heeren@ou.nl

ABSTRACT

Formative feedback, aimed at helping students to improve their work, is an important factor in learning. Many tools that offer programming exercises provide automated feedback on student solutions. We are performing a systematic literature review to find out what kind of feedback is provided, which techniques are used to generate the feedback, how adaptable the feedback is, and how these tools are evaluated. We have designed a labelling to classify the tools, and use Narciss' feedback content categories to classify feedback messages. We report on the results of the first iteration of our search in which we coded 69 tools. We have found that tools do not often give feedback on fixing problems and taking a next step, and that teachers cannot easily adapt tools to their own needs.

Keywords

systematic literature review; automated feedback; programming tools; learning programming

1. INTRODUCTION

Tools that support students in learning programming have been developed since the 1960s [6]. Such tools provide a simplified development environment, use visualisation or animation to give better insight in running a program, guide students towards a correct program by means of hints and feedback messages, or automatically grade student solutions [11].

Two important reasons to develop tools that support learning programming are: (1) learning programming is hard, and students need help to make progress, and (2) programming courses are taken by many thousands of students all over the world, and helping students individually with their problems requires a huge time investment of teachers.

Feedback is an important factor in learning [22]. Boud and Molloy define feedback as 'the process whereby learners obtain information about their work in order to appreciate the similarities and differences between the appropriate standards for any given work, and the qualities of the

work itself, in order to generate improved work' [2]. Thus defined, feedback is formative: it consists of 'information communicated to the learner with the intention to modify his or her thinking or behavior for the purpose of improving learning' [22]. Summative feedback in the form of grades or percentages for assessments also provides some information about the work of a learner. However, the information a grade gives about similarities and differences between the appropriate standards for any given work, and the qualities of the learner's work, is usually only superficial. In this paper we focus on the formative kind of feedback as defined above. Formative feedback comes in many variants, and the kind of formative feedback together with student characteristics greatly influences the effect of feedback [15].

Given the role of feedback in learning, we want to find out what kind of feedback is provided by tools that support learning programming. What is the nature of the feedback, how is it generated, can a teacher adapt it, and what can we say about its quality and effect? To answer these questions, we are performing a systematic literature review of automated feedback generation for programming exercises.

A systematic literature review (SLR) is a research method that identifies and investigates all relevant publications on a particular topic. A research plan is designed in advance, and the execution of this plan is documented in detail, allowing insight into the rigorousness of the research.

This paper reports on the results found in the first iteration of our search for relevant papers.[1] We searched for related overviews on tools for learning programming and executed the first step of 'backward snowballing' by selecting relevant references from the papers we found. Our search until now has resulted in a set of 102 papers, describing 69 different tools. We have designed a labelling to classify the tools and provide answers to our research questions. Although not yet complete, this collection is representative and large enough to report some findings.

This review makes the following contributions:

- We analyse what kind of feedback is used in tools that support a student in learning programming. Although quite a few reviews analyse such tools, none of them looks at the feedback provided by these tools.
- We relate the feedback content to its technology, and to the adaptability of the tool and the feedback.

Section 2 discusses related reviews of tools for learning

ITiCSE '16, July 11–13, 2016, Arequipa, Peru.

---

[1]This is a short version of our work. We have published a Technical Report containing detailed information and the complete reference list [12].

programming. Section 3 gives our research questions and research method. Section 4 shows and discusses the results. Section 5 concludes the paper.

2. RELATED WORK

We have found almost twenty reviews of tools for learning programming, mostly on automated assessment (AA) tools [1, 3, 6, 10, 20, 21, 23] or learning environments for programming [4, 5, 7, 9, 11, 13, 14, 18, 19, 24]. Generating feedback is important for both kinds of tools. Most AA tools only grade student solutions, but some tools also provide elaborated feedback, and can be used to support learning [1].

Most reviews describe the features and characteristics of a number of tools, identify challenges, and direct future research. Except for Ihantola et al. [10] and the review in progress by Nesbit et al. [17], authors select papers and tools using unknown criteria, some mention qualitative factors such as impact (citations) or the thoroughness of the evaluation of the tool. Most studies do not strive for completeness. The scope of the tools that are described varies greatly. Tools are usually categorised, but there is no agreement on the naming of the different categories. Very few papers discuss technical aspects.

Our review distinguishes itself from the above reviews by focusing on the aspect of generating feedback in learning tools for programming. Furthermore, we employ a more systematic approach than almost all of the above papers.

3. METHOD

Performing an SLR requires an in depth description of the research method. This section describes our research questions, the criteria and the search process.

3.1 Research questions

The following four research questions guide our review:

RQ1. What is the nature of the feedback that is generated?

RQ2. Which techniques are used to generate the feedback?

RQ3. How can the tool be adapted by teachers, to create exercises and to influence the feedback?

RQ4. What is known about the quality and effectiveness of the feedback or tool?

3.2 Criteria

We have defined a set of inclusion and exclusion criteria that direct our research and target the characteristics of the papers and the tools described therein.

General. We include journal and conference papers in English, and Master or PhD theses, or technical reports only if a journal or conference paper is available on the same topic. The publication describes a tool of which at least a prototype has been constructed. We exclude papers shorter than four pages.

Functionality. Developing a program that solves a particular problem is an important learning objective for learning programming. We include tools in which students work on programming exercises of class 2 or higher from the classification of Le and Pinkwart [13]. Class 1 exercises have a single solution, and are often quiz-like questions. Class 2 exercises can be solved by different implementation variants. Usually a program skeleton or other information

about the solution strategy is provided, but variations in the implementation are allowed. Finally, class 3 exercises can be solved by applying alternative solution strategies, which we interpret as allowing different algorithms as well as different steps to arrive at a solution. The type of exercises that a learning tool supports determines to a large extent how difficult it is to generate feedback. Tools provide automated, textual feedback on (partial) solutions, targeted at the student. We exclude tools that only produce a final grade.

Domain. We include tools that support a high-level, general purpose, textual programming language used in the industry and/or taught at universities, including pseudocode. We exclude visual programming tools (block programming, flowcharts), and tools that focus on one aspect of programming, such as recursion or multi-threading.

We select papers and tools that satisfy all inclusion criteria and none of the exclusion criteria. We have included some theses because they have been cited often.

3.3 Search process

The starting point of our search for papers was the collection of 17 review papers given in Section 2. Two authors of this SLR independently selected relevant references from these reviews. Then two authors independently looked at the full text of the papers in the union of these selections, to exclude papers not meeting the criteria. After discussing the differences, we assembled a final list of papers. We had to exclude a small number of papers that we could not find after an extensive search and, in some cases, contacting the authors. Some excluded papers point to a potentially interesting tool. We checked if these papers mention a better reference that we could add to our selection.

Often multiple papers have been written on (versions of) a single tool. We searched for all publications on a tool by looking at references from and to papers already found, and searching for other relevant publications by the authors. We selected the most recent and complete papers about a tool.

Starting with an initial selection of 197 papers, we ended up with a total of 102 papers describing 69 different tools.

4. RESULTS AND DISCUSSION

To systematically encode the information in the papers, we use a labelling based on the answers to the research questions we expected to get, refined by encoding a small set of randomly selected papers. One of the authors encoded the complete set of papers. Whenever there were questions about the coding of a paper, another author checked. In total, 28% of the codings were handled by two authors. A third author joined the general discussions about the coding. When necessary, we made adjustments to the labelling.

The results we have found so far in our SLR are shown in the table, sorted by exercise class. We record the highest exercise class a tool supports. A majority of the tools supports imperative languages, including object-oriented languages (Java, C and C++, and earlier FORTRAN, Ada). Fewer tools support a functional language (Lisp, Haskell) or logic programming (Prolog). Three recent tools focus on web scripting languages (PHP, JavaScript). The remaining tools support multiple languages, and are often test-based AA systems. Tools often only support a subset of the features of a programming language.

The remainder of this section describes the labelling for the research questions, provides examples and concludes with some observations. We refer to the tools in the table by their name in a SMALL CAPS font, or the first author and year of the most recent paper (AUTHOR00) on the tool we have used.

4.1 RQ1 Feedback type

Narciss [16] describes a 'content-related classification of feedback components' for computer-based learning environments, in which the categories target different aspects of the instructional context, such as task rules, errors and procedural knowledge. We use these categories and extend them with representative subcategories identified in the selected papers. Narciss also considers the *functions* and *presentation* of feedback, which are related to the effectiveness of tutoring. We do not include these aspects in our review because it is often unclear how a tool or technique is used in practice (e.g. formative as well as summative).

Narciss first gives *simple* feedback components: 'Knowledge of performance for a set of tasks', 'Knowledge of result/response' and 'Knowledge of the correct results'. These types of feedback are not intended to 'generate improved work', a requirement in the feedback definition by Boud and Molloy. Because we focus on formative feedback on a single exercise, we do not identify these types in our coding.

The next five types are *elaborated* feedback components. Each type addresses an element of the instructional context. We provide several examples to illustrate how the different types are instantiated in learning tools for programming. We have also identified a few examples of feedback messages that do not fit into our classification, such as motivating feedback.

Knowledge about task constraints (KTC)

- Hints on task requirements (TR). A task requirement for a programming exercise can be to use a particular language construct or to not use a particular library method. An example can be found in the BASIC INSTRUCTIONAL PROGRAM (BIP): '*Wait. Something is missing. For this task, your program should also include the following basic statement(s): FOR*'
- Hints on task-processing rules (TPR). These hints provide general information on how to approach the exercise and do not consider the current work of a student.

Knowledge about concepts (KC)

- Explanations on subject matter (EXP), generated while a student is working on an exercise. The ASK-ELLE programming tutor refers to relevant internet sources when a student encounters certain language constructs.
- Examples illustrating concepts (EXA). THE LISP TUTOR uses examples in its tutoring dialogue. For example, after a student has made a mistake, the tutor responds with: '*Since you seem to be having trouble with the recursive cases, let us work through some examples and figure out the conditions and actions for each of these cases.*'

Knowledge about mistakes (KM)

KM feedback messages have a type and a level of detail. A level of detail can be basic ($\bigcirc$), which can be a numerical value (total number of mistakes, grade, percentage), a location (line number code fragment), or a short type identifier such as 'compiler error'; or detailed ($\bullet$), which is a de-

scription of the mistake, possibly combined with some basic elements. We distinguish five different mistake types.

- Test failures (TF). A failed test indicates that a program does not produce the expected output. COFFMAN10, an AA tool for web programming, provides detailed feedback on test results, showing the informative name of the test cases (such as 'checkInvalidLogin'), a colour indicating their success and the reason why a particular test case failed. We found this type of feedback, which resembles the output of professional testing tools, in many AA tools.
- Compiler errors (CE) are syntactic errors (incorrect spelling, missing brackets) or semantic errors (type mismatches, unknown variables) that can be detected by a compiler and are not specific for an exercise. Feedback on compiler errors might be the output of a compiler that is passed on to the student. Test-based AA systems often provide compiler output as feedback, because successful compilation is a prerequisite for executing tests.
- Solution errors (SE) can be found in programs that do not show the behaviour that a particular exercise requires, and can be runtime errors (the program crashes) or logic errors (the program does not do what is required), or the program uses an alternative algorithm that is not accepted. AUTOLEP describes the results of matching the student program with several model programs, comparing aspects such as size, structure, and statements.
- Style issues (SI), such as untidy formatting, inconsistent naming or lack of comments, are not serious mistakes that affect the behaviour of a program. However, many teachers consider learning a good programming style important for novice programmers. The feedback generated by the tool of JACKSON00 shows a list of style metrics such as '4.0% comment lines' and '20.9% indentation'.
- Performance issues (PI). A student program takes too long to run or uses more resources than required. NAUR64, one of the earliest systems, checks one particular exercise that lets students write an algorithm for finding the root of a given function. The system gives performance feedback for each test case, such as '*No convergence after 100 calls.*'

Knowledge about how to proceed (KH)

- Bug-related hints for error correction (EC). Sometimes it is difficult to see the difference between KM feedback and EC. We identify feedback as EC if the feedback clearly focuses on what the student should do to correct a mistake. JITS gives feedback on typing errors, such as '*Would you like to replace smu with sum?*'
- Task-processing steps (TPS). A TPS hint contains information about the next step a student has to take to come closer to a solution. The Prolog tutor (HONG04) provides a guided programming phase. If a student asks for help in this phase, the tutor will respond with a hint on how to proceed and generates a template for the student to fill out: '*You can use a programming technique that processes a list until it is empty by splitting it into the head and the tail, making a recursive call with the tail.*'

Each of these types of feedback has a level of detail: a hint ($\leftmoon$) that may be a in the form of a suggestion, a question, or an example; a solution ($\rightmoon$) that directly shows what needs to be done to correct an error or to execute the next step; or both hints and solutions ($\bullet$).

The following is a large data matrix (reviewed programming assessment tools). Columns are grouped under RQ1 Feedback type (KTC: TR, TPR; KC: EXP, EXA; KM: TF, CE, SE, SI, PI; KH: EC, TPS; KMC), RQ2 Technique (MT, CBM, AT, BSA, PT, IBD, EX, Other), RQ3 Adaptability (ST, MS, TD, ED, SM, Other), and RQ4 Evaluation (ANC, ANL, EM-LO, EM-SU, EM-TA). (● = filled, ○ = open, ◐ = half.)

Name, reference	Language	Ex. class	TR	TPR	EXP	EXA	TF	CE	SE	SI	PI	EC	TPS	KMC	MT	CBM	AT	BSA	PT	IBD	EX	Other	ST	MS	TD	ED	SM	Other	ANC	ANL	EM-LO	EM-SU	EM-TA
ACT Programming Tutor (APT)	Multi	C2	●				○		●						●		●								●						●	●	●	
Bridge	Imp/OO	C2						●	●			◐	◐		●						●		●		●				●		●		●	●	●
(Chang00)	Imp/OO	C2							●			◐											●		●				●					●	●	
DISCOVER	Imp/OO	C2				●	●		●			●	◐								●				●								●	●	●
ELP	Imp/OO	C2		●			●		●			●												●	●										●
HabiPro	Imp/OO	C2				●			●			●												●	●										●
InSTEP	Imp/OO	C2					●	●	●			◐	●		●		●		●					●	●							●			●
INTELLITUTOR (II)	Imp/OO	C2					●	●				●	●				●		●					●	●							●			●
JITS	Imp/OO	C2					○	○				◐					●		●						●										●
LAURA	Imp/OO	C2		●			●		●			●																							
PASS	Imp/OO	C2	●						●			●	●				●			●				●	●								●		
ProPL	Imp/OO	C2							●				●																				●		
RoboProf	Imp/OO	C2		●					●			●	●				●								●									●	
The LISP tutor	Fun	C2					●					◐					●		●					●	●								●		●
ADAPT	Log	C3		●	●							●			●		●			●					●									●	●
AnalyseC	Imp/OO	C3					●					○					●								●									●	●
APOGEE	Web	C3															●		●					●	●	●							●	●	
APROPOS2	Log	C3			●		●		●								●		●	●					●								●	●	
ASAP	Imp/OO	C3					●	●	●			●	●				●								●				●				●	●	
Ask-Elle	Fun	C3			●		●	●					●				●							●	●								●	●	●
ASSYST	Imp/OO	C3					●	●	●	●	●						●	●							●					●		●	●	
AutoGrader	Imp/OO	C3	●				●	●									●	●							●				●	●		●	●	
autograder	Imp/OO	C3					●	●									●								●								●	●	
AutoLEP	Imp/OO	C3					●	●	●								●	●					●	●								●	●	
Automatic Marker for Sakai	Imp/OO	C3					●										●								●							●		
(Bettini04)	Imp/OO	C3		●	●		●		●	●	●	●	●				●					●		●	●				●			●		
BIP	Imp/OO	C3		●	●		●	●	●		●	●	●				●							●	●	●			●			●	●	●
BOSS	Multi	C3					●				○	◐					●							●	●						●	●	●	
Ceilidh	Multi	C3			●		●	●		○							●								●			●				●	●	
(Chen04)	Imp/OO	C3					●										●							●	●			●					●	
(Coffman10)	Web	C3					●		●		●	●					●	●						●	●					●			●	
CourseMarker/CourseMaster	Multi	C3			●		●	●	●	●	●		●		●		●			●			●		●				●			●	●	●
datlab	Imp/OO	C3	●	●													●							●	●								●	
EduComponents	Multi	C3	●	●			●										●								●								●	
ELM-PE/ELM-ART (II)	Fun	C3					●	●	●	●		●	●		●		●							●	●			●				●	●	●
(Fischer06)	Imp/OO	C3	●				●	○		○	○	◐					●			●					●				●			●	●	
GAME (2, 2+)	Multi	C3					○	●	●								●								●					●		●	●	●
(Harris04)	Imp/OO	C3					●	●		○							●								●				●	●			●	
HOGG	Log	C3					●					◐	●				●			●			●		●								●	
INCOM	Log	C3		●			●	●	●	●	●	●	●				●						●		●								●	●
(Isaacson89)	Imp/OO	C3			●		●	○			○	◐					●								●								●	
ITEM/IP	Imp/OO	C3					●	●				◐	●				●								●			●				●	●	
JACK	Imp/OO	C3		●			●		●								●								●								●	
Kassandra	Imp/OO	C3					●										●								●					●	●		●	
Ludwig	Imp/OO	C3			●		●	●									●	●							●					●	●		●	
MarmoSet	Multi	C3					●	●				◐					●								●					●	●			
Mooshak	Imp/OO	C3					●		●	●							●								●				●	●		●	●	
(Naur64)	Imp/OO	C3					○	○	●	○	○						●								●									●
Online Judge	Imp/OO	C3	●		●		●	●	●		●	◐					●			●					●			●	●				●	●
PASS	Imp/OO	C3					●		●								●								●					●		●	●	
PATTIE	Imp/OO	C3					●	●								●	●								●					●			●	●
Praktomat	Multi	C3					●	●	●								●								●					●			●	
PROUST	Imp/OO	C3					●		●			●					●	●			●		●											●
Quiver	Imp/OO	C3			●		●	●				●					●							●	●				●				●	
RoboLIFT	Imp/OO	C3					●	●	●								●								●					●	●	●		●
SAC	Imp/OO	C3					●		●	●		◐	●				●								●					●			●	
(Sant09)	Fun	C3					○	●		○							●				●		●	●	●			●				●	●	●
Scheme-robo	Fun	C3					●										●								●					●			●	
SiPLeS-II	Multi	C3					●	●	●	●						●	●	●				●			●					●		●	●	●
submit	Imp/OO	C3					●										●								●						●		●	●
(Sztipanovits08)	Web	C3					○										●								●							●		
TRY	Multi	C3					●										●								●					●			●	
Virtual Programming Lab	Multi	C3					●										●								●				●				●	
Web-CAT	Multi	C3	●				●	●									●								●	●					●		●	●
WebToTeach	Imp/OO	C3					●	●	●								●								●								●	●
WebWork-JAG	Imp/OO	C3		●			●	●									●			●					●			●				●	●	●
xLx	Imp/OO	C3					●	●	●								●								●					●				●

Knowledge about meta-cognition (KMC)

We have only found one example of KMC so far. HABIPRO provides a 'simulated student' that responds to a solution by checking if a student really knows why an answer is correct.

4.2 RQ2 Technique

General ITS techniques

- Tools that use model tracing (MT) generate feedback on the process that the student is following. Student steps are compared to production rules and buggy rules.
- Constraint-based modelling (CBM). A constraint-based tool checks a student program against predefined solution constraints, such as the presence of a for-loop or the calling of a method with certain parameters, and generates error messages for violated constraints.

Domain-specific techniques for programming

- Dynamic code analysis using automated testing (AT). The most basic form of AT is running a program and comparing the output to the expected output. More advanced techniques are unit testing and property-based testing, often implemented using existing test frameworks (e.g. JUnit). Most tools that use automated testing support C3 exercises, because black-box testing does not require using a specific algorithm or design process.
- Basic static analysis (BSA) analyses a program (source code or byte code) without running it, and can be used to detect misunderstood concepts, the absence or presence of certain code structures, and to give hints on fixing these mistakes [23]. Some tools use BSA for calculating metrics, such as cyclomatic complexity or number of comments.
- Program transformations (PT) transform a program into another program in the same language (e.g. normalisation) or a different language (e.g. to bytecode). Transformations are often used together with static code analysis to match a student program with a model program.
- Intention-based diagnosis (IBD) uses a knowledge base of programming goals, plans or (buggy) rules to match with a student program to find out which strategy the student uses to solve an exercise.
- External tools (EX) other than testing tools, for example CheckStyle for checking code conventions and FindBugs for finding bugs, and standard compilers. These tools are not the work of the authors themselves and papers do not usually elaborate on the inner workings of the external tools used. If a tool uses automated testing, for which compilation is a prerequisite, we do not use this label.

Other techniques

Tools use various A.I. techniques, such as natural language processing (PROPL) or machine learning (DATLAB). We expect that some of the techniques in this category will develop into their own category. For example, we have noticed the use of data analysis in quite a number of recent publications: large data sets with student solutions to exercises are used to generate feedback.

4.3 RQ3 Adaptability

Which input to a tool can be adapted by teachers without recompiling the tool? Using such input a teacher constructs a new exercise or influences the generated feedback, without too much effort or specialised knowledge.

- Solution templates (ST) (e.g. skeleton programs and projects) presented to students for didactic or practical purposes.
- Model solutions (MS): correct solutions to a programming exercise.
- Test data (TD), such as expected output and test cases.
- Error data (ED), such as bug libraries, buggy solutions, buggy rules and correction rules. Error data usually specify common mistakes for an exercise, and may include corresponding solutions.
- Other. Some tools let a teacher define feedback messages (ASK-ELLE), or configure how much feedback should be given (COURSEMARKER).

Another aspect we consider is the adaptability of the feedback generation based on a student model (SM). A student model contains information on the capabilities and level of the student, and may be used to personalise the feedback.

4.4 RQ4 Quality

Tools have been evaluated using a large variety of methods. We use the three main types for the assessment of tools distinguished by Gross and Powers [8].

- Anecdotal (ANC) assessment is based on the experiences and observations of researchers or teachers with using the tool. We will not attach this label if another type has been applied as well, because we consider anecdotal assessment to be inferior to the other types.
- Analytical (ANL) assessment compares the characteristics of a tool to a set of criteria related to usability or a learning theory. For example, THE LISP TUTOR and JITS are based on ACT-R.
- Empirical assessment analyses qualitative or quantitative data. We distinguish three types of empirical assessment: looking at the learning outcome (EM-LO) (mistakes, grades, pass rates) after students have used the tool, and observing tool use; student and teacher surveys (EM-SU) and interviews on experiences with the tool; and technical analysis (EM-TA) to verify whether a tool can correctly recognise (in)correct solutions and generate appropriate hints. Tool output for a set of student submissions is compared to an analysis by a human tutor.

4.5 Discussion

Feedback about mistakes is the most common type of feedback, with information on test failures as the largest subcategory. Generating feedback based on tests is a useful way to point out errors, emphasizes the importance of testing, and is relatively easy to implement. We have found feedback on solution errors in fewer tools, and with varying depth and detail. Most tools that support C3 exercises give no 'knowledge on how to proceed (KH)' feedback. According to Boud and Molloy's definition, these tools lack the means to really help a student. In general, the feedback that tools generate is not that diverse, and mainly focused on identifying mistakes. Exceptions are tools that only offer C2 exercises. These tools more often provide KH feedback. However, these tools do not support alternative solution strategies, and may restrict students in their problem solving process.

We have found that tools use various dynamic and static analysis techniques. More sophisticated techniques, such as model tracing and intention-based diagnosis, appear to complicate adding new exercises and adjusting the tool.

Whether or not a tool can be adapted easily depends on the amount and complexity of the input. Very few papers explicitly describe this, or even address the role of the teacher, so we assume that the tool can only be adjusted by developers. When a publication does describe how an exercise can be added, it is sometimes not clear how difficult this is. We conclude that teachers cannot easily adapt tools to their own needs, except for test-based AA systems.

Most tools provide some form of evaluation, although for 23% of the tools we could only find anecdotal evidence, or none at all. The evaluation of a tool may not be directly related to the quality of the feedback, so the results only give a general idea of how much attention was spent on evaluation. The many different evaluation methods make it difficult to assess the effectiveness of the feedback. Moreover, the quality (e.g. the presence of control groups, pre- and post-tests, group size) of empirical assessment varies greatly. Finally, the description of the evaluation method and results often lacks clarity and detail.

5. CONCLUSIONS AND FUTURE WORK

We have analysed and categorised the feedback generation in 69 tools for learning programming, selected from 17 earlier reviews. Although our search is not yet complete, our take-home message is that tools for learning programming should offer more diverse feedback, and better support teachers in specifying exercises. To complete this SLR, we continue our 'backward snowballing' approach by searching the papers we have found so far for relevant references, and we will conduct a search on multiple databases. Lastly, we will further analyse the results by relating them to programming concepts that students find difficult, common novice programming errors, and human tutoring strategies.

Acknowledgements

This research is supported by the Netherlands Organisation for Scientific Research (NWO), grant number 023.005.063.

6. REFERENCES

[1] K. M. Ala-Mutka. A survey of automated assessment approaches for programming assignments. *Computer Science Education*, 15(2):83–102, 2005.

[2] D. Boud and E. Molloy, editors. *Feedback in higher and professional education: understanding it and doing it well.* 2012.

[3] J. C. Caiza and J. M. Del Alamo. Programming assignments automatic grading: review of tools and implementations. In *INTED*, pages 5691–5700, 2013.

[4] F. P. Deek, K.-W. Ho, and H. Ramadhan. A critical analysis and evaluation of web-based environments for program development. *The Internet and Higher Education*, 3(4):223–269, 2000.

[5] F. P. Deek and J. A. McHugh. A survey and critical analysis of tools for learning programming. *Computer Science Education*, 8(2):130–178, 1998.

[6] C. Douce, D. Livingstone, and J. Orwell. Automatic test-based assessment of programming: A review. *Journal on Educational Resources in Computing (JERIC)*, 5(3), 2005.

[7] M. Gómez-Albarrán. The Teaching and Learning of Programming: A Survey of Supporting Software Tools. *The Computer Journal*, 48(2):130–144, 2005.

[8] P. Gross and K. Powers. Evaluating assessments of novice programming environments. In *ICER*, pages 99–110, 2005.

[9] M. Guzdial. Programming environments for novices. In *Computer Science Education Research*, pages 127–154. 2004.

[10] P. Ihantola, T. Ahoniemi, V. Karavirta, and O. Seppälä. Review of recent systems for automatic assessment of programming assignments. In *Koli Calling*, pages 86–93, 2010.

[11] C. Kelleher and R. Pausch. Lowering the barriers to programming: A taxonomy of programming environments and languages for novice programmers. *ACM Computing Surveys*, 37(2):83–137, 2005.

[12] H. Keuning, J. Jeuring, and B. Heeren. Towards a systematic review of automated feedback generation for programming exercises – extended version. Technical Report UU-CS-2016-001, 2016.

[13] N.-T. Le and N. Pinkwart. Towards a classification for programming exercises. In *Workshop on AI-supported Education for Computer Science*, pages 51–60, 2014.

[14] N.-T. Le, S. Strickroth, S. Gross, and N. Pinkwart. A review of ai-supported tutoring approaches for learning programming. In *Advanced Computational Methods for Knowledge Engineering*, pages 267–279. 2013.

[15] D. C. Merrill, B. J. Reiser, M. Ranney, and J. G. Trafton. Effective tutoring techniques: A comparison of human tutors and intelligent tutoring systems. *Journal of the Learning Sciences*, 2(3):277–305, 1992.

[16] S. Narciss. Feedback strategies for interactive learning tasks. *Handbook of research on educational communications and technology*, pages 125–144, 2008.

[17] J. C. Nesbit, L. Liu, Q. Liu, and O. O. Adesope. Work in Progress: Intelligent Tutoring Systems in Computer Science and Software Engineering. In *ASEE Annual Conference & Exposition*, pages 1–12, 2015.

[18] A. Pears, S. Seidman, L. Malmi, L. Mannila, E. Adams, J. Bennedsen, M. Devlin, and J. Paterson. A survey of literature on the teaching of introductory programming. *SIGCSE Bull.*, 39(4):204–223, 2007.

[19] N. Pillay. Developing intelligent programming tutors for novice programmers. *SIGCSE Bull.*, 35(2):78–82, 2003.

[20] K. A. Rahman and M. J. Nordin. A review on the static analysis approach in the automated programming assessment systems. In *National conference on programming*, 2007.

[21] R. Romli, S. Sulaiman, and K. Z. Zamli. Automatic programming assessment and test data generation: a review on its approaches. In *Int. Symp. in Information Technology*, pages 1186–1192, 2010.

[22] V. J. Shute. Focus on formative feedback. *Review of Educational Research*, 78(1):153–189, 2008.

[23] M. Striewe and M. Goedicke. A review of static analysis approaches for programming exercises. In *Computer Assisted Assessment. Research into E-Assessment*, pages 100–113. 2014.

[24] M. Ulloa. Teaching and learning computer programming: a survey of student problems, teaching methods, and automated instructional tools. *SIGCSE Bull.*, 12(2):48–64, 1980.

Automatic Grading of Programming Exercises using Property-Based Testing

Clara Benac Earle*
Universidad Politécnica de
Madrid, Spain
cbenac@fi.upm.es

Lars-Åke Fredlund
Universidad Politécnica de
Madrid, Spain
lfredlund@fi.upm.es

John Hughes
Chalmers University of
Technology and Quviq AB,
Göteborg, Sweden
rjmh@chalmers.se

ABSTRACT

We present a framework for automatic grading of programming exercises using property-based testing, a form of model-based black-box testing. Models are developed to assess both the functional behaviour of programs and their algorithmic complexity. From the functional correctness model a large number of test cases are derived automatically. Executing them on the body of exercises gives rise to a (partial) ranking of programs, so that a program A is ranked higher than program B if it fails a strict subset of the test cases failed by B. The model for algorithmic complexity is used to compute worst-case complexity bounds. The framework moreover considers code structural metrics, such as McCabe's cyclomatic complexity, giving rise to a composite program grade that includes both functional, non-functional, and code structural aspects. The framework is evaluated in a course teaching algorithms and data structures using Java.

Keywords

Automated assessment; Testing; Java

1. INTRODUCTION

We consider an approach to automate the grading of programming exercises based on testing. Test models for the exercises are developed using property-based black-box testing [5], and from testing student programs against the models a *ranking* of the programs is derived, based on the observation of which programs have fewer bugs than others. However, teachers typically consider far more factors when correcting programming exercises, e.g., whether the code is well written, whether the implementation of an algorithm has the right algorithmic complexity, etc.

*Work partially funded by European Comission FP7 project ICT-2011-317820 (*PROWESS*), Comunidad de Madrid grant S2013/ICE-2731 (*N-Greens Software*) and by Spanish MINECO Project TIN2012-39391-C04-03 (*StrongSoft*).

In our approach, property-based testing is reused for computing the algorithmic complexity of a program (e.g., whether the execution time of a program for sorting an array is quadratic in the size of the array). However, such models do not specify the behaviour of the program, but rather guide the testing process into computing the best and worst case complexity. At present this approach is semi-automatic; complexity bounds are computed automatically, but the grading of a program with regards to complexity is the decision of a teacher.

Sect. 2 discusses related work, while Sect. 3 presents the techniques used for grading. Thus, Sect. 3.1 describes how testing is used to evaluate functional behaviour (i.e., find bugs), leading to a ranking of different implementations with regards to their bugs. Sect. 3.2 describes how programs are ranked with regards to algorithmic complexity.

Note that our approach to evaluating functional correctness and algorithmic complexity is largely programming language agnostic. In the article the analysis is applied to Java programs. However, with only small changes to the test models, programs written in other languages are analysable. Sect. 3.3 and Sect. 3.4 show how to combine these analyses with language specific code metrics, such as counting source code statements, and measuring the branching structure of a program (McCabe's cyclomatic complexity).

The resulting framework has been validated in an experiment at the School of Computer Engineering at the Technical University of Madrid, Spain. The setting was a course on algorithms and data structures attended by second year undergraduate students, taught using Java. The course has a heavy emphasis on using practical exercises to improve programming skills, including ten supervised sessions where students are given a simple programming task which they are supposed to complete during a two hour session. Although teachers provide assistance to the students during the programming sessions, the students are graded on how well they complete the programming exercises. On average 100 programs were handed in for each exercise, resulting in a total of around 1000 programming exercises to correct.

The last few years, a single associate professor has been responsible for grading exercises, and has spent, on average, 20 hours per exercise, which amounts to using 12 minutes grading a program. Although having a single teacher do the correction ensures consistent grading, there are several drawbacks too, e.g., students do not receive their exercise grades until three weeks after the hand-in date, and receive little feedback regarding problems with their programs.

In view of these difficulties, the course on algorithms and data structures presents a setting where introducing automated grading of exercises might lead to an improved course, and this paper reports on an evaluation of this potential. In parallel with the normal running of the algorithms and data structures course, where student programming exercises where graded manually as usual, we developed test models and used structural analysis tools to calculate an automatic grading of exercises. To contrast the different approaches to grading we estimated how *efficient* automatic correction is, by comparing the time spent on developing models for testing programs with the time spent for manual correction. Secondly, we try to estimate the *quality* of automatic correction, i.e., whether the calculated grades accurately reflect the differences in quality of the programs being graded. To answer the second research question, we assumed that the results of the manual grading was perfect, and calculated the average error introduced by using the automatic grading framework. Note that in this article we do not attempt to quantify other expected benefits of introducing automatic grading, i.e., quicker and better feedback to students, which are likely to be at least as important as the grading itself.

As the course focuses on algorithms and efficient implementations of data structures, rather than object-orientation, the evaluation criteria for programs do not include analyses for Java-specific concerns. However, such analyses can be combined with the main results from this work in the same manner as e.g. the McCabe cyclomatic complexity metric was taken into account into a final program grade.

Further details regarding the course, and the evaluation procedure, are described in Sect. 4. The final section 5 summarises the work, and discusses items for future work.

2. RELATED WORK

Continuous assessment during a programming course is key to ensure that students get enough practice as well as early feedback on the quality of their solutions, and many automated assessment tools have been developed. A comprehensive survey can be found in [8]. One notable recent system is ASys [9], which mainly focuses on correctness properties orthogonal and thus complementary to the ones considered in this article. ASys is mainly used to check that the students source code fulfills some syntactical properties desired by the teacher (e.g., compiles correctly, correct implementation of interfaces, etc.). In our framework, the focus is on behavioural properties of the code. Web-CAT [6] is a very interesting testing based grading system, but in contrast to our system, it grades students on how well *they* have tested their code.

An example of a widely used random testing tool for Java is Randoop [11]. Randoop can be used to generate a *suite* of independent failing tests, for one implementation. Our approach, in contrast, generates a suite of tests from *all* the implementations, where each test represents a different bug.

For estimating the algorithmic complexity of a program essentially two methods are used: static analysis of the program [1], and testing-based empirical computation of complexity [3]. As static analysis based tools for estimating complexity bounds are often quite limited in the types of programs for which it is possible to compute complexity bounds automatically, we opted for a testing-based approach.

3. GRADING

This section describes the various techniques used to grade programs with respect to functional correctness (bugs), algorithmic complexity, and structural complexity.

3.1 Functional Correctness

To grade programs with respect to how functionally correct they are, the property-based testing tool QuviQ Erlang QuickCheck [2] (henceforth abbreviated QuickCheck) is used. QuickCheck is part of a by now rather large family of property-based testing tools for different programming languages, inspired by the original Haskell tool [4].

The basic functionality of QuickCheck is simple: when supplied with a data term that encodes a boolean property, which may contain universally quantified variables, QuickCheck generates a random instantiation of the variables, and checks that the resulting boolean property is true. This procedure is by default repeated at most 100 times. If for some instantiation the property returns false, or a runtime exception occurs, an error has been found and testing terminates. Although QuickCheck uses random test case generation instead of coverage directed test generation, this does not mean that the the tool is inferior (see [7] for a thorough comparison on the different methods of test case generation).

QuickCheck moreover provides a state machine based library for testing API's with side effects. The goal of the library is to enable a tester to easily generate randomly sequences of sensible calls to the API, and to decide if the execution of such a call sequence was successful (i.e., the API returned the expected results) or not. Technically the tester, with help from the library, builds a state machine that serves as a model of the behaviour of the API, *and* is used to generate the sequences of calls used to test the API.

A state machine is invariably used as the basic test model to detect problems of functional correctness, even if the API implemented by the program is stateless. The reason is that we want to be able to detect errors caused by the implementation of stateful solutions for pure functional API's (e.g., using static class attributes inappropriately).

Ranking Algorithm.

Perhaps the most obvious method to grade programs depending on how functionally correct they are is to count the number of bugs they have, i.e., a program A is worse than a program B if it has more bugs than program B.

Unfortunately using random black-box testing it is quite difficult to identify multiple program bugs. Repeated testing using the QuickCheck state machine library of a buggy program will yield a set of test cases, such that each test case is a sequence of API calls which when executed by the program under test causes the program to behave incorrectly. The difficulty is in determining when two such (not trivially identical) test cases really exhibit the same underlying bug.

The ranking procedure [5] which is used in this article does not attempt to count the number of bugs a program has, but rather decides that a program A is worse than program B, if, when a large number of test cases have been run, the set of test cases which program B fails is a strict subset of the set of test cases which program A fails. That is, $failed(B) \subset failed(A)$ where $failed(P)$ is the set of test cases failed by program P.

An open source tool (available at https://github.com/fredlund/Ranker.git) implements the ranking procedure as a partition refinement algorithm, where initially all programs are in the same set. A partition is split when an "interesting" test case is found, i.e., a test case for which the set of failing programs splits an earlier set. To find a new "interesting" test case QuickCheck generates a random new test case, and runs it against all implementations. If the test case does not cause any new split, the process is repeated, until 100 random test cases have been generated without causing a split.

An example of an analysis result is depicted in Fig. 1. Nodes correspond to sets of students whose programs behave identically. Edges are labelled by test cases, such that all students in the nodes located below the edge (transitively) fails the test cases, and all students above the edge executed the tests successfully. For example, the top node contains 63 students; test cases t3 and t6 causes the students 901 and 187 to fail, and moreover student 187 also fails test case t0 which student 901 does not fail.

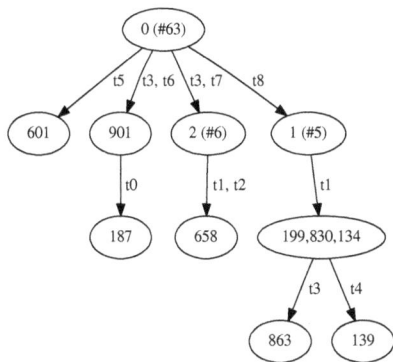

Figure 1: A ranking tree

Using the Ranking for Grading.

We can use such a ranking tree for grading by observing that it defines a partial order: implementations on a higher level (e.g., all the top implementations in Fig.1), which are connected to implementations on a lower level, either directly (e.g., 601) or transitively (e.g., 187), behave strictly better than the lower-level implementations. Implementations that are not hierarchically linked (e.g., 901 and 601) are in a sense not comparable, since there are test cases (t3, t5, t6) that one implementation fails, and the other executes successfully, and vice versa. However, we can convert the partial order into a total one using various heuristics. The heuristic used in the framework uses the maximum path length to an implementation in the ranking tree as the ranking measure for that implementation.

A Derived Test Suite.

The set of test cases labelling the ranking tree forms a test suite, which is used to inform students of the bugs in their programs.

3.2 Algorithmic Complexity

To compute the algorithmic complexity of a program the "Complexity" tool (open source, available at https://github.com/prowessproject/complexity) is used. The tool empirically calculates the best case and worst case algorithmic complexity of a program, e.g., that the complexity of a method to sort an array in Java has the worst case complexity $O(n \ log \ n)$ in terms of the size of the array. The calculation of such complexity measures is accomplished using property-based testing.

To calculate the parameters for a Java method call which yield the worst (or best) performance, the Complexity tool follows a search procedure, guided by the test model. Beginning with a parameter of a small size, parameters of a somewhat larger size are randomly generated guided by the test model, and the method is executed. Next the tool selects a subset of these parameters which are deemed promising (e.g., having worse execution times than calls with other parameters), and repeats the above procedure, generating larger and larger parameters.

When the search procedure terminates, the parameter yielding the worst (or best) execution time for a given parameter size is selected as a data point. The Complexity tool then tries to fit different curves to the resulting data points, and the best fitting curve (e.g., logarithmic or linear) is reported as the result of the complexity estimation.

Developing Performance models.

To use the Complexity tool it is concretely required to (i) define a "complexity model", i.e., a recipe for how to extend a test case of size N to an (interesting) test case of size $N + M$ (where M is usually 1), and (ii) provide a means for running the test case and to measure its execution time (or some other relevant metric). Note that developing such complexity models is not a trivial task, as usually there are too many possible tests to run given the available time for estimating the algorithm complexity, and thus the model must carefully prioritise some test cases which are thought to contribute most to best-case or worst-case behaviour.

Obtaining performance results.

Due to the difficulties of accurately measuring the execution time of method calls in Java (due to caches, just-in time compilation, etc.) we instead measure the number of Java virtual machine instructions executed for a method call, using a debugging build of a normal Java runtime. Such a measure will be invariant over different executions, but the performance predicted may not reflect real-world performance. Nevertheless, for comparing programs in a course on algorithms and data structures, the measure is surely relevant.

Best-case or worst-case.

However, even given repeatable experimental results, we still have no direct way to compare two implementations. What should be compared, best-cases, worst-cases, or both? And how relevant are the figures, really? A truly bad implementation that raises an exception for every combination of arguments will have a very good best- and worst-case complexity, for the simple reason that nothing is computed. We could compute the best and worst behaviour for correct computations only (using the functional correctness model too), but it might well be that the parameter combinations that would then be omitted are exactly the ones with the worst-case behaviour. So we decided not to do this, and to use the worst-case performance figures only, to avoid penalising implementations with bugs twice; whether this is a good decision is left for a future evaluation.

Comparing implementations.

Next, how exactly do we compare such performance figures? We could compare the computed algorithmic complexity, such that a program A is better than a program B if A has a "better" complexity (e.g., $O(n\ log\ n)$ instead of $O(n^2)$), or if they are the same, if the constant factors for A are better than the ones for B. However, one can argue against such a ranking too. If the constant factors for the $O(n\ log\ n)$ program are large, and the ones for the $O(n^2)$ program are small, it is conceivable that the supposedly inferior program has a better performance than the superior program, *for the test parameters used in the experiment.* Moreover, strictly speaking we cannot really say anything about the performance of the programs on bigger examples, as a program may actually contain different algorithms for handling parameters of different sizes. Another option is to compare the performance of two programs based on the size of the areas defined by the measured data points.

However, humans are quite good at interpreting performance data in diagrams. To explore this, we designed a simple tool for manual ranking, permitting to display and interact with plots depicting simultaneously the performance of all measured programs, utilising the gnuplot tool (http: //www.gnuplot.info/). Upon invoking the plotting tool the upper figure in Fig. 2 is shown, which displays the worst-case performance graphs for the 83 programs analyzed. Already it is possible to draw conclusions about the relative performance of the implementations. Essentially there are three "performance segments"; the top one having what looks like quadratic complexity, the middle one probably also quadratic, and the lower one looks linear. Using the tool we can select the upper segment, and move it into its own window shown in the lower figure in Fig. 2.

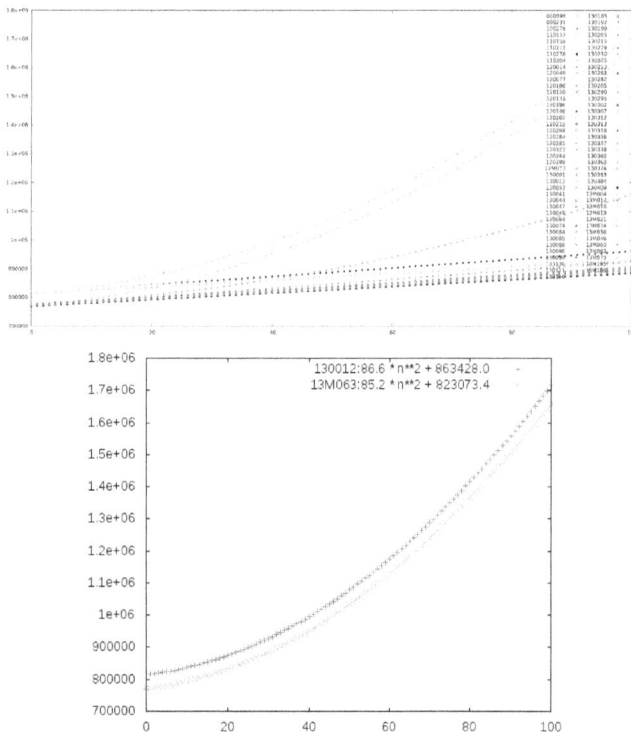

Figure 2: Grading Complexity

We can see that as expected both programs indeed have quadratic complexity (we used an option in the tool to display the complexity measures; this would just have cluttered the first plot). The procedure of partitioning the implementations into different windows is repeated, until we are satisfied. The remaining task is to assign a numeric grade to the different windows, corresponding to a subjective valuation of the performance of the implementations in a window.

The experience from grading the student exercises using the plotting tool is that grading with respect to algorithmic complexity is rapid, and generally without any controversy with regards to how to separate programs into different segments (for all six sets of exercises). Given the performance data for around 100 programs, the task of grading could normally be completed in less than five minutes. The difficulty in this approach seems to lie in how to obtain the performance data, rather than how to interpret it, and here the use of the Complexity tool was very helpful.

3.3 Measuring Source Code Complexity

This section considers code metrics to measure the structural complexity of code. We consider two such metrics: non-commenting source statements (NCSS), and McCabe's cyclomatic complexity metric [10]. Both metrics were computed by the JavaNCSS utility (http://www.kclee.de/ clemens/java/javancss/). Informally, NCSS counts the number of ";" and "{" characters in a Java program.

It might be surprising that we do *not* measure a number of other common code metrics, e.g. the number of comments in the code, or checking for common Java anti-patterns. The reason is that the course used to evaluate the framework (see Sect. 4) did not penalise students for a lack of comments – earlier programming courses that students must attend *do* focus on such concerns, but in this course the focus is mainly on penalising *behavioural* defects of the program, rather than structural ones. The only exception is that teachers *do* penalise students who write overly complex or long programs to solve a task, leading to a focus on metrics such as the NCSS and the McCabe ones. For a different course, integrating other code metrics into grading is an easy task, following the methodology described in this article.

The grade of a program with regards to the NCSS metric, then, is computed, somewhat arbitrarily, as the absolute value v of dividing its NCSS metric with the average NCSS metric for the 7 implementations with the lowest NCSS figures (and with no detected functional bugs). If the resulting value v is less than 1.75, the NCSS grade is considered perfect (0), and otherwise its grade is penalised according to the computed value. The McCabe cyclomatic complexity metric is computed analogously.

3.4 Calculating a Composite Program Grade

The combined automatic grade g_{auto} for a program i is:

$$g_{auto} = 10 - p_{fc} * fc - p_{ncss} * ncss - p_{mc} * mc - p_{ac} * ac$$

where 10 is the perfect grade, and $fc, ncss, mc, ac$ are the "penalties" resulting from grading with respect to functional correctness, NCSS (source code complexity), McCabe Cyclomatic complexity, and algorithmic complexity. The constants p_x are weights, which should be tailored to account for the relative importance of the different grades.

4. EVALUATION

Our framework was evaluated in a course on algorithms and data structures using Java, taken by second-year undergraduate students in a four-year software engineering programme. Students participate in ten two hour laboratory sessions where they solve, in groups of two, a simple programming assignment.

Students submit solutions using a web-based system which checks the program against a fixed test suite, to enforce a minimum level of functionality on programs to be considered for grading. The system reports the test results to the student, and accepts the program if it passed the tests.

To evaluate the composite grading scheme, we focused on the first six assignments: counting the number of consecutive elements in an array (nG), removing the first occurrence of a sublist from a list (rm), merge two sorted lists using three variants: with loops (ml), obligatory use of recursion (mr), and use of iterators (mi), and finally sorting a list using the insertion sort algorithm (is).

4.1 Development and Grading Time

The time and effort to develop functional correctness models for these six assignments are summarised below:

	nG	rm	ml	is	mr	mi
model loc.	151	227	251	230	251	251
new loc.	151	124	61	43	0	0
% change	100%	54%	24%	19%	0%	0%
time (h)	4	3	1	1	0	0

The "model loc." row counts the number of lines in the functional correctness model, and the row "new loc." counts the number of new lines compared to the most similar earlier model[1], and "% change" is the change percentage. Note that the measure of change is a rather coarse over-approximation of the difference between the models, as even a very tiny change in a line counts as model change. Finally time (h) counts in hours the time needed for developing the correctness model; note that the merge models (ml, mr and mi) are identical. For completeness we also report on the results of the functional correctness analysis:

	nG	rm	ml	is	mr	mi
# programs	103	91	102	96	93	83
comp. time (s)	129	1055	662	259	503	885
# tests	4	13	14	7	14	21

The "# programs" row indicates the number of programs considered, while the "comp. time" row reports the number of seconds it took to run the ranking algorithm implementation, on a workstation with a six core Intel Xeon E5-1650 CPU (at 3.20GHz) with 32GB RAM installed. The time to run the algorithm depends heavily on a number of factors, e.g., the execution speed of the programs being compared[2], and the test harness used. For the harness the options are to either always create a new Java runtime for each combination of test case and program, or try to reuse an already existing Java runtime. Non-reuse is obviously the safest option, but leads to ranking times at least on an order of a magnitude worse than the figures reported here, and with substantial memory re-

---

[1]computed using the UNIX command
```
diff --suppress-common-lines --speed-large-files
     -y best_old_model new_model | wc -l
```
[2]Very slow, or non-terminating implementations, are automatically removed from consideration by the ranking algorithm implementation

quirements. Full reuse is obviously unsafe, as students frequently use static attributes. Instead, the Javassist (http://jboss-javassist.github.io/javassist/) byte code manipulation library is used to create a new class for each test run against an implementation, while reusing the runtime itself. This is safe, as long as programs do not modify the state of other objects and classes.

The time required to develop an algorithmic complexity model was 4 hours on average. Note that a good algorithmic complexity model is more costly to develop than a functional correctness model. The maximum time permitted for the algorithm complexity analysis was set to 3 hours per sets of exercises. However, this figure is somewhat arbitrary, as investing more time can yield a more precise worst-case complexity bound. Computing the structural complexity metrics for a program was essentially instantaneous.

Finally, recall that on average manual grading took around 20 hours per exercise set, whereas the first (and by far the most time consuming) exercise required around 4 hours to develop the correctness model, and around 6 additional hours for the complexity model. In addition, the automatic grading tools had to be run. The functional correctness of a small percentage of programs (on average 2%) could not be determined automatically, so these had to be corrected manually. A conservative estimate is that the automatic grading took around 6 teacher hours on average, leading to a total figure of around 16 hours, which compares favourably with the average manual grading time of 20 hours. Both these estimates depend on the resources available: the teacher responsible for manual grading had at least 3–4 years of prior experience, and was very efficient at the task. The automatic grading was done by a teacher assisting the students during the laboratory exercises, and with substantial prior experience in developing models for functional correctness.

The row "# tests" reports the size of the test suite derived from functional correctness analysis. These are the test cases that were useful for distinguishing differently behaving programs, i.e., test cases which at least one program fails, and another program correctly executes. As an example, consider the method $nGroup(numOfOccs, elem, list)$ in the first exercise nG, which counts the number of times $elem$ occurs $numOfOccs$ times consecutively in $list$. The following four test cases were generated by the ranking algorithm: $nGroup(2, 0, null)$, $nGroup(1, 1, [1, 0, 1])$, $nGroup(2, 2, [2, 0, 2])$ and $nGroup(1, 0, null)$. The first and last test cases both check whether a program handles a null argument correctly. However, it is surprising that both test cases were necessary for computing a ranking. Manual inspection revealed that there was indeed one program that behaved correctly for $numOfOccs \equiv 2$ and $list \equiv null$, and failed for $numOfOccs \equiv 1$. This is one example where random testing arguably improves on black-box boundary condition testing, as the letter test case would probably never have been generated using boundary condition testing.

4.2 Adequacy of Automatic Grading

To judge how faithful the automatic ranking is to the manual ranking, the mean squared error (MSE) and the root mean squared error ($RMSE$), for n students, are:

$$
\begin{aligned}
MSE &= \frac{1}{n} * \sum_{i=1}^{n} \left(g_{manual_i} - g_{auto_i} \right)^2 \\
RMSE &= \sqrt{MSE}
\end{aligned}
$$

where g_{manual_i} is the manual grade for student i, and g_{auto_i} is the grade computed by the framework.

To find out how useful automatic ranking can be we *minimise* the root mean squared error *RMSE*, finding *optimal* weights p_x. To minimise the error, the weights were varied from 0 to 3, with an increment of 0.25. The weights can be calculated more exactly. However, for a practical application of the automatic grading framework, we considered it beneficial having well-understood weights. The optimal weights for the six exercises, and the resulting errors, are:

	nG	rm	ml	is	mr	mi
p_{fc}	1.0	2.0	2.5	0.75	2.75	2.25
p_{ncss}	0	1.75	0	0.75	1.5	0.5
p_{mc}	0,75	0	0	0	0	0.25
p_{ac}	0.5	0.5	1.0	2.0	0	0.5
MSE	0.41	0.83	1.1	0.61	0.75	0.68
$RMSE$	0.64	0.91	1.0	0.78	0.86	0.83

The average difference in the manually assigned grades, compared to the automatically assigned grades, ranges from 0.64 (nG) to 1.0 (ml); for a range of grades 0-10. Note that adding additional code metrics, apart from just functional correctness, is beneficial, as the "best" solutions invariably take into account more factors than just functional correctness. On the other hand, functional correctness is vital; there is no exercise which has weight 0 for functional correctness. Moreover a popular criticism against the McCabe cyclomatic complexity metric is that it essentially just measures the number of lines of code, or, as here, the NCSS metric. The results mostly confirm this, as there is just a single exercise (mi) where both p_{ncss} and p_{mc} are nonzero.

The weights used for different exercises vary substantially. In part this is because the manual grading was not consistent during the course, as for instance more emphasis was put on structural complexity code metrics in later parts of the course. Moreover, we can see that the weight for functional correctness is comparatively low (1.0 and 0.75) for the exercises where the students made comparatively few different mistakes (as evidenced by the table showing the number of test cases in the derived test suite), hence probably requiring the grading teacher to emphasise other grading criteria such as algorithmic and structural complexity.

The set of weights which give the lowest errors for all exercises is $p_{fc} = 2.25$, $p_{ac} = 0.5$, $p_{ncss} = 0.5$, $p_{mc} = 0.25$, with MSE 0.89 and $RMSE$ 0.94. The maximum average error MSE is 1.3 for exercise ml; for other exercises the error using the fixed weights is below 1.

5. CONCLUSIONS AND FUTURE WORK

Is the automatic grading framework presented here good enough to replace an experienced teacher's manual grading? The results reported in this article suggest that they are. However, grades should only be a small part of the feedback students receive; more important is to communicate to students *why* their programs are unsatisfactory. In this respect, our framework makes a number of valuable contributions: feedback can be quicker (days instead of weeks), and feedback will include unit tests that the program fails. Detailed feedback can be given on performance, with calculated complexity bounds, and, perhaps more importantly, including a graph relating the performance of the students' program to other implementations of the same API, quickly highlighting bad performance.

Designing test models for functional correctness and algorithmic complexity is, unfortunately, not a common skill. Nevertheless, writing such models, for simple API's, is not so hard. Moreover, unlike manual grading, test model artifacts for automatic grading are highly *reusable*. In our experience exercises usually change little from year to year, and the resulting model changes are often trivial. Moreover, universities could collaborate to develop shared model libraries to support automatic grading for courses on the same topic.

What remains to be done? One missing grading factor vital for a course on algorithms and data structures is memory usage. It should be possible to calculate and illustrate memory usage using the Complexity tool. Unfortunately, at this time we were unable to find a good (open source) solution for calculating the exact memory usage of a Java program.

6. REFERENCES

[1] E. Albert, P. Arenas, S. Genaim, G. Puebla, and D. Zanardini. COSTA: design and implementation of a cost and termination analyzer for Java bytecode. In *FMCO 2007, Amsterdam, LNCS 5382*, 2007.

[2] T. Arts, J. Hughes, J. Johansson, and U. T. Wiger. Testing telecoms software with QuviQ QuickCheck. In *Proceedings of the 2006 ACM SIGPLAN Workshop on Erlang*, pages 2–10, Portland, Oregon, USA, 2006.

[3] J. Burnim, S. Juvekar, and K. Sen. WISE: Automated test generation for worst-case complexity. In *Proceedings of the 31st International Conference on Software Engineering*, ICSE '09. IEEE, 2009.

[4] K. Claessen and J. Hughes. QuickCheck: A lightweight tool for random testing of Haskell programs. *SIGPLAN Not.*, 35(9):268–279, Sept. 2000.

[5] K. Claessen, J. Hughes, M. Palka, N. Smallbone, and H. Svensson. Ranking programs using black box testing. In *Proceedings of the 5th Workshop on Automation of Software Test*, 2010.

[6] S. H. Edwards. Improving student performance by evaluating how well students test their own programs. *J. Educ. Resour. Comput.*, 3(3), Sept. 2003.

[7] G. Gay, M. Staats, M. W. Whalen, and M. P. E. Heimdahl. The risks of coverage-directed test case generation. *IEEE Trans. Software Eng.*, 2015.

[8] P. Ihantola, T. Ahoniemi, V. Karavirta, and O. Seppälä. Review of recent systems for automatic assessment of programming assignments. In *Proceedings of the 10th Koli Calling International Conference on Computing Education Research*, 2010.

[9] D. Insa and J. Silva. Semi-automatic assessment of unrestrained Java code: A library, a DSL, and a workbench to assess exams and exercises. In *Proc. of the 2015 ACM Conference on Innovation and Technology in Computer Science Education*, 2015.

[10] T. J. McCabe. A complexity measure. *IEEE Trans. Softw. Eng.*, 2(4):308–320, July 1976.

[11] C. Pacheco, S. K. Lahiri, M. D. Ernst, and T. Ball. Feedback-directed random test generation. In *Proceedings of the 29th International Conference on Software Engineering*, ICSE '07. IEEE, 2007.

Automated Feedback Framework for Introductory Programming Courses

Jianxiong Gao
University of Illinois at
Urbana-Champaign
1308 W Main St
Urbana, USA
gao2@illinois.edu

Bei Pang
University of Illinois at
Urbana-Champaign
1308 W Main St
Urbana, USA
beipang2@illinois.edu

Steven S. Lumetta
University of Illinois at
Urbana-Champaign
1308 W Main St
Urbana, USA
lumetta@illinois.edu

ABSTRACT

Using automated grading tools to provide feedback to students is common in Computer Science education. The first step of automated grading is to find defects in the student program. However, finding bugs in code has never been easy. Comparing computation results using a fixed set of test cases is still the most common way to determine correctness among current automated grading tools. It takes time and effort to design a good set of test cases that can test the student code thoroughly. In practice, tests used for grading are often insufficient for accurate diagnosis.

In this paper, we present our utilization of industrial automated testing on student assignments in an introductory programming course. We implemented a framework to collect student codes and apply industrial automated testing to their codes. Then we interpreted the results obtained from testing in a way that students can understand easily. We deployed our framework on five different introductory C programming assignments here at the University of Illinois at Urbana-Champaign. The results show that the automated feedback generation framework can discover more errors inside student submissions and can provide timely and useful feedback to both instructors and students. A total of 142 missed bugs were found within 446 submissions. More than 50% of students received their feedback within 3 minutes of submission. We believe that based on the current automated testing tools, an automated feedback framework for the classroom can benefit both students and instructors, thus improving Computer Science education.

Keywords

Computer Science Education; Concolic Testing; Auto Grader

1. INTRODUCTION

The ability to program has become increasingly important in recent years. As a result, more people are trying to learn programming. Becoming a good programmer requires

ITiCSE '16, July 09 - 13, 2016, Arequipa, Peru

ⓒ 2016 Copyright held by the owner/author(s). Publication rights licensed to ACM.
ISBN 978-1-4503-4231-5/16/07...$15.00

DOI: http://dx.doi.org/10.1145/2899415.2899440

both practice and feedback. The rate at which a novice programmer makes progress depends heavily on how much instructive feedback the programmer receives from qualified instructors. However, skilled programmers who can provide such feedback are a limited resource.

In practice, basic input-output testing is the most common way of assessing student programs. Student programs are executed with a set of test inputs, and the results are compared with correct outputs. However, it takes time and effort to design an adequate set of test cases. Designing test cases that can cover most of the possible bugs is hard, especially for introductory level programming classes. Novice programmers are not as predictable as experienced programmers. The behavior of novice programmers' code is more unpredictable. Thus the task of designing test cases is never as trivial as it sounds. For each of the programming assignments examined in this paper, there were unexposed bugs in student code that were not caught by the normal grading procedure.

This paper describes a framework that uses automated testing tools to detect defects in student code and to provide feedback on those defects in the form of specific examples of incorrect behavior. During the development process, students can submit their code for review by the framework. Feedback is generated within minutes of student code submission.

The technique that our framework uses to identify defects is called concolic testing [8]. Concolic testing executes a program both concretely and symbolically. The aim is to maximize code coverage. In other words, to create tests that execute all parts of a program. The result of concolic testing is a set of inputs that covers different parts of the code. Concolic testing has been successfully commercialized and adopted by the software industry. For example, Microsoft utilizes concolic testing heavily in its Sage tool [3].

We deployed our framework as an automatic feedback generation tool in ECE220, one of the introductory programming courses at the University of Illinois at Urbana-Champaign. All Electrical and Computer Engineering (ECE) students take this course, which thus has roughly 350 students every semester. Our results show that we can identify more defects in student code than can traditional automated grading. Students can learn from the failed test cases generated and can improve their code. Experiments show that the mean processing time for a recursive maze solver is 260 seconds, meaning that one can scale this solution to provide directed and specific feedback based on a particular student's code within a few minutes.

Compared to current tools, the automated grading tool proposed in this paper has several benefits:

- Improves ability to identify code defects.

- Generates test cases leading to defects as feedback.

- Improves grading fairness.

- Has Comparable processing time to current methods.

We provide an overview of the sections of this paper. Section 2 gives additional detail on our motivation for building a framework based on industrial tools. Section 3 gives background information on concolic testing. Section 4 describes our framework and workflow for applying concolic testing to automated grading. Section 5 describes our experiment with student assignments. Section 6 discusses the results. We conclude in Section 7.

2. MOTIVATION

Teaching programming is hard. The dropout rate of introductory programming courses can be as high as 50% [9]. Because more students tend to take such class, the number of students enrolled in introductory programming courses has been growing in recent years. Outside of universities, people are also in massive online open courses (MOOC) to learn programming. Due to the large number of students, these introductory programming courses are usually taught in a lecture+laboratory structure [4]. Lectures are important for students to learn concepts, language definitions, and common mistakes. However, the most important part of learning engineering is to practice.

For programming courses, students practice by doing programming assignments. When students finish their programming assignments, they need to know whether their programs are correct. However identifying defects in code is not an easy task. Even experienced programmers in industry produce programs that have bugs in them. In industry, code review helps programmers to get feedback about their work. In programming courses, students are supposed to get feedback about their work from instructors. Human inspection is yet still heavily used as a way of code review. Ganssle [2] and Kemerer and Pavik [6] reported that an ideal rate of 150-200 lines per hour is most effective for manual inspection. For student code, the efficiency may be even less. However, manual inspection can only be done by experienced programmers. With large class sizes, the process requires hiring more teaching assistants, who cost less than instructors, but are more variable in the quality of their code review. The increasing number of students learning programming and the limited time of instructors are causing problems in programming education.

3. CONCOLIC TESTING

Concolic testing [7] is a software verification technique that combines symbolic execution with concrete values. The goal of concolic testing is to generate test cases that can achieve high code coverage. Concolic testing starts with a set of variables that are marked as symbolic. Then random concrete values are generated for these variables. The program executes using the concrete values, and the control

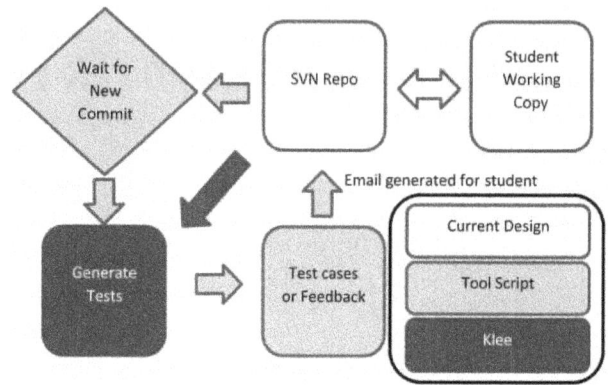

Figure 1: Collect Student Code/Generate Feedback: We implemented tool scripts to react to student commits. When a student commits a new version, we generate tests and send feedback to the student.

flow is recorded. Code that has been executed as part of the program execution is marked as covered. In order to expand the covered part of the program, one symbolic constraint in the path is negated and solved using SMT solvers. A new set of concrete values is thus generated that directs the program into a different execution path. The process continues until no more execution paths can be explored.

Concolic testing combines random testing and symbolic execution. Concrete values are used to overcome some limitations of fully symbolic execution, while symbolic execution is used to generate better coverage than random testing.

4. FRAMEWORK SETUP

The framework developed in this paper consists of two main parts. The frontend collects student-submitted code, initiates the grading process on the backend, distributes graded code back to students and notifies students. The backend first compiles student code into LLVM byte code, then executes the student code using KLEE [1], a concolic testing tool. If there is any defect inside student code, a test case leading to that defect is generated.

4.1 Frontend

The system implemented for students to submit their code for feedback revolves around the flow diagram in Figure 1. The framework implements a system that assesses the student code and distributes feedback to students. When new submissions are detected, the system pulls the latest commit of student work from the Subversion server. The student work is passed to the backend for assessment. The backend assesses student work and generates test input sets. After test inputs are generated, we collect the test input sets that lead to errors in student code. We analyze the test input sets and generate a feedback message to the corresponding Subversion repository. After the grading process is finished, we generate an email to the student to notify the student that the auto-grading process has finished. On receiving the email, the student can collect generated feedback from Subversion. The whole frontend system is written in Ruby.

4.2 Backend System: KLEE

The work flow of the backend system is shown in Figure 2. The backend system takes two inputs: a student solution

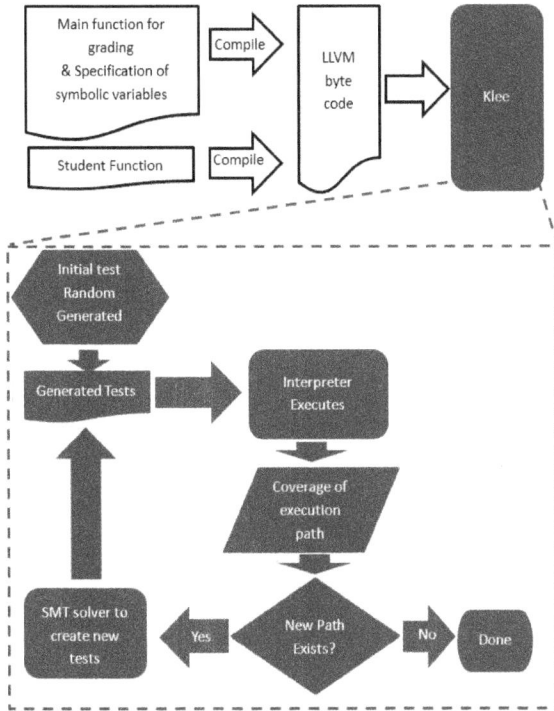

Figure 2: Workflow: Main function (contribution of paper) and student function are compiled into Llvm byte code. The KLEE is applied to generate tests that can cover the most execution paths.

```c
#include "stdio.h"
#include "assert.h"
int gold_calculate(a,b,operator){
  if(operator=='+'){
    return a+b;
  }
  else if(operator=='-'){
    return a-b;
  }
  return 0;
}

int main(){
  int a,b;
  char operator;
  klee_make_symbolic(&a,sizeof(a),"a");
  klee_make_symbolic(&operator,
      sizeof(operator),"operator");
  klee_make_symbolic(&b,sizeof(b),"b");
  if(stu_calculate(a,b,operator) !=
      gold_calculate(a,b,operator)){
    assert("Student Calculate Function Error.\n");
  }
  return 0;
}
```

Figure 3: Symbolic Variable Marked: Selected variables are marked as symbolic using the *klee_make_symbolic* function. Different sets of values are generated and assigned to these variables to explore all the possible execution paths. Each set of values forms a test case.

and a wrapper main function. Both input files are compiled into LLVM byte code. This LLVM code is then passed to KLEE for assessment.

In order for KLEE to work, some setup work needs to be done. The setup work is divided into two parts: marking symbolic variables and checking functional correctness. Symbolic variables are used to generate test inputs and are also the key to achieving maximum coverage. To check functional correctness, we need to verify that the program can achieve the desired goal. KLEE by itself only tries to achieve high code coverage. The testing of functional correctness of the program is not the aim of KLEE, but is supported by our wrappers and checking code.

4.2.1 Selecting Symbolic Variables

The symbolic variables are usually chosen from inputs to the student program. Figure 3 is an example calculator program. The inputs are two numbers and an operand. To use KLEE to find maximal coverage, we need to mark the two numbers and the operand as symbolic. Marking these variables as symbolic can be done by calling a function call *klee_make_symbolic*. All the initialization of a,b and operator is now done by KLEE.

4.2.2 Functional Correctness Checking

KLEE was designed to achieve high code coverage, so by default KLEE only generates test cases that can cover most of the code. To verify that the program under test has the desired behavior, we add post-condition checking with the *assert* function. A predicate that checks the result of the

student function can be used. An assert function can be done on the predicate. KLEE will try to a find path that leads to an assert failure (to cover that code). In Figure 3, the return value of student function *stu_calculate* is checked against the return value from the reference implementation *gold_calculate*. Because KLEE uses an SMT solver to find new execution paths, the SMT solver tries to solve for a set of values that can lead the execution to the *assert* function. These assertions are effectively branches under the execution of KLEE. The SMT solvers effectively checks for functional correctness by trying to maximize code coverage. If any execution path that leads to an assertion failure exists, the student program has functionality bugs. Assertions are usually added at the end of the wrapper code, after the execution of student code.

5. EXPERIMENTS

The automated feedback framework has been applied to five different assignments here at the University of Illinois at Urbana-Champaign. All five assignments are for an introductory level programming class, ECE220. The framework has successfully done the job of providing quick and accurate feedback to students. Here in this section, some background information about the assignments and the feedback framework is provided.

5.1 Design of Assignments

These programming assignments are designed by the instructors of the course without considering any aspect of our framework. Thus, these assignments are not designed specially for the automated feedback framework. The automated feedback framework works in parallel with the normal grading process, which forms the basis against which we compare our results. Student grades are not affected by the feedback and are solely decided by the normal grading procedure. Even if additional bugs are identified inside student code, this information is reported to the student only, but not to the instructors.

Also, the normal grading procedure is mostly kept unknown to us. The only access that we have is to the test cases released to students. Any additional grading test cases used at the time of final grading are not released.

5.2 Assignments

There are 5 different assignments in total, each of which is now explained in detail:

Code Breaker The Code Breaker assignment requires students to implement the logic for a code-breaking game. A code sequence of four numbers from 1 to 8 is first chosen at random. These four numbers are the solution code, and are also referred to as pegs. The player guesses a sequence of four numbers and is given feedback on each guess, including the number of correct values that appear in the same place in the solution code (these are called perfect matches). The user is also told the number of values that appear in a different place in the solution code (these are called misplaced matches). Values guessed are matched pairwise with the solution, so a given guess value can count either as a perfect match or as a single mismatch, but cannot count as both types, nor as multiple mismatches. Similarly, a given solution value can only count as one match of one type. Functions to implement: set_seed, start_game, and make_guess.

Learning objectives: if statement, logical operators, function calls. Typical student code length: 100 lines.

Image Editor An image is represented as four 1-D arrays, one for each channel (Red, Green, Blue, and Alpha). Each array has the same number of elements as there are pixels in the image. In student functions, these arrays are passed as pointers (for example uint8_t *inRed, uint8_t *inBlue, uint8_t *inGreen, uint8_t *inAlpha). Students are required to implement five functions that modify the image: calculate_cosine_filter, invert_image, convolve_image, convert_to_gray, color_thr-eshold.

Learning objectives: for loops, arrays. Typical student code length: 100 lines.

Sudoku Game The Sudoku assignment is to implement a C program that solves a standard Sudoku puzzle using recursive backtracking. Functions to implement: is_val_in_row, is_val_in_col, is_val_in_3x3_zone, int is_val_valid, solve_sudoku.

Learning objective: recursion. Typical student code length: 150 lines.

2048 Game Students are required to implement the 2048 game with an arbitrarily-sized game board. The game 2048 is played on a grid, with numbered tiles that slide smoothly when a player moves them using the four arrow keys. Every turn, a new tile appears randomly in an empty spot on the board with a value of either 2 or 4. Tiles slide as far as possible in the chosen direction until they are stopped by either another tile or the edge of the grid. If two tiles of the same number collide while moving, they merge into a tile with the summation of the two tiles that collided. The resulting tile cannot merge with another tile again in the same move.

Functions to implement: make_game, destroy_game, get_cell, move_up, move_down, move_left, move_right, legal_move_check, remake_game.

Learning objectives: structures, dynamic allocation (malloc and free). Typical student code length: 200 lines.

Maze Solver Students are required to find a solution for a maze game. An acyclic map of the maze is given to them. The starting location is marked as "S", and the ending location is marked as "E". If the maze is solvable, any point along the solution path has to be marked as ".". Other locations that have been searched but are not on the solution path have to be marked as "∼". The starting and ending location symbols "S" and "E" cannot be overwritten.

Functions to implement: find_start, print_maze, solve_maze_DFS.

Learning objective: recursion. Typical student code length: 250 lines.

Automated feedback generation for Maze Solver was applied in both Spring and Fall semesters of 2015, while the rest were applied to the Fall 2015 semester only. For both semesters, students were asked to volunteer to allow us to provide real-time feedback depending on their code. The process is totally voluntarily and does not affect the normal grading procedure at all. Participating students do not need to do any extra work. For Spring 2015 semester, 82 out of 349 students volunteered; for Fall 2015, 91 out of 393 students volunteered to participate in the experiment.

6. RESULTS

In this section, the quality of the generated feedback is discussed. Because students are allowed to use the automated feedback framework multiple times before the deadline, multiple versions of feedback may exist. Only the last submission by each student, the versions that are actually graded, are considered in this section.

Functional correctness is the most important aspect of a program. Missed bugs inside student code may leave students with misunderstood concepts. The quality of the generated feedback is assessed based on the ability to find defects inside student codes. The results show that the automated feedback framework does a better job than the original grading procedure at discovering defects.

With regard to the time required for creating grading scripts and processing student submissions, space allows only a few brief comments. An undergraduate teaching assistant was able to produce a grading script for an assignment in less than eight hours. And more than half of student submissions received feedback in less than three minutes. See [5] for more detail.

solution peg	1	2	3	4
guesses	1	1	5	6

Table 1: Example for Code Breaker

6.1 Code Breaker

For the Code Breaker assignment, every student submission with defects reported was human-inspected to assess the quality of auto-generated feedback. Among 91 total submissions, three pairs of duplicate code were found, thus only one copy for each pair is considered in the discussion.

6.1.1 Failed to Generate Feedback

The framework failed to generate feedback for 5 out of the 88 valid submissions. Following is a list of failure reasons:

Over time The processing time limit was 3 minutes. Two functionally correct but unnecessarily complex submissions timed out.

Printf Two students used *printf* with the wrong number of arguments.

Set Seed The *set_seed* function should be called only once to set the game up. One submission called *set_seed* multiple times, causing the *rand* function to return erroneous results.

6.1.2 Bugs Missed by Normal Grading

Sixteen student submissions containing bugs passed all tests in the normal grading procedure. Ten of these exhibited the Multiple Mismatch Peg bug, three failed to write back to the output variables, one accessed out-of-bounds pointers, one failed to check negative input values, and two used uninitialized values.

The most common bug was the Multiple Mismatch Peg bug, in which multiple input pegs are counted as mismatches with a single solution peg. As a result the code reports an inflated mismatch value. For the example in Table 1, the correct output should be 0 perfect matches and 1 mismatch. With the Multiple Mismatch Peg bug, the number of mismatches is calculated as 2.

The cause of the bug is usually that when student submissions match an input guess to a solution peg, the solution peg is not marked as being paired with one of the input guesses. In the example, the solution peg with value 1 did not get marked when pairing with any of the 1s in the guesses, so the other guess could be matched with the same solution peg, which results in 2 mismatches instead of 1.

The multiple mismatch peg is also the most common bug missed by the class' normal grading procedure. Ten student submissions, or 63% of the submissions that had this bug, passed the normal grading procedure. Six more student submissions with this bug were caught because of other bugs, while this bug was never exposed by the normal grading procedure.

6.2 Image Editor

Among the student submissions that were determined to be correct by the normal grading procedure, the checking of index bounds for array accesses alone identified 30 buggy submissions. The normal grading procedure only compared the end result, which led to the failure to detect this kind of bug.

```
if (...) {
    if (...) {
        return 1;
    }
}
else {
    return 0;
}
```

Figure 4: Example Code for Sudoku Game

6.3 Sudoku Game

6.3.1 Compile Failure

Five student submissions failed to compile, of which one failed to compile with the normal grading procedure as well. The main reason for compilation failure is compiler differences. The normal grading procedure used g++ as the default compiler, while the auto-grading framework used llvm-gcc. All five students used C++ syntax supported only by g++.

6.3.2 Time Limit

Because the Sudoku game assignment is a recursion assignment, the number of execution paths may become extremely large with erroneous student submissions. Though the execution time limit was set for 5 minutes, 17 student submissions failed to finish. However, for 4 of the timed-out submissions, bugs were identified within the student code before timing out.

6.3.3 Bugs Missed by Normal Grading

The most frequently missed-bug for the Sudoku game assignment was implementation of a challenge problem (not required for full credit). The specification clearly stated that the check for number uniqueness on diagonals should only be done outside of the *is_val_valid* function. However, 37 student submissions had the diagonal check included inside the *is_val_valid* function. The normal grading procedure did not test if the diagonal check was implemented outside the *is_val_valid* function. There was no individual test for the *is_val_valid* function at all.

Another two missed bugs were related to the problem of misplaced return values. One example is given in Figure 4. Depending on calling convention, if the return value of a function happens to be 0, the functionality of the buggy code is still correct. It is assumed that the normal grading procedure used a compiler that happens to have the return value as 0, as the student submissions passed the test.

6.4 2048 game

6.4.1 Compile Failure

There were two compilation failures; both student submissions failed the class' grading procedure as well.

6.4.2 Out of Time

There were 28 student submissions that ran out of time for automated feedback. Of these, 18 were determined to have errors by the normal grading procedure. With human inspection, all the 10 correct student submissions had unnecessarily complex algorithms for the *move_* functions.

6.4.3 Bugs Missed by Normal Grading

The most obvious missed bug was the a lack of test cases for invalid moves. When a move is invalid, the *move_* functions should return 0. By default, the *move_* functions return 1 in the given code. Missing test cases on invalid moves caused two students, with their *move_up* function empty except for the "return 1" statement, to pass the return value test for the normal grading procedure. One other student submission, which was checked with invalid moves but failed to return 0, also passed the normal grading procedure.

Two more student submissions containing logic errors were found to pass the normal grading procedure. The test cases for the normal grading procedure simply failed to discover these logic errors.

Fourteen student submissions were determined to have out-of-bounds pointer errors.

6.5 Maze Solver

The automated feedback framework tested *find_start* and *solve_maze_DFS* successfully. However for *check_maze*, even though most of the defects were identified, some bugs were still missed. By inspection, the reason that these bugs were missed is that the precondition was set to test valid solutions only. In other words, our choice of symbolic variables only generated solvable mazes to test student functions. A solvable maze is not enough to identify all of the defects in the *check_maze* function. To identify all the defects, both solvable and unsolvable mazes need to be generated.

6.5.1 Defects

For the Spring 2015 semester, with 82 students volunteering, a total of 241 submissions were graded, 141 of which contained test cases leading to errors generated. Only 16 students have no generated test cases for all of their submitted code. More than 80% of the students had defects in their submissions. After we provided feedback to them, 50 out of 82 students passed our grading tool, a 42% increase in correction rate. Among the 32 buggy submissions, 17 passed the normal grading procedure.

6.6 Summary

The traditional way of grading relies on developing a comprehensive set of test inputs. When test inputs do not cover defective code, the grade does not reflect the defects. For all of the five assignments tested, student submissions with bugs that the normal grading tests did not cover have been identified. A list of the most important missed bugs follows:

Code Breaker Multiple Mismatch Peg.
Image Editor Out of Bound Array Accesses.
Sudoku Game Return Value not set.
2048 Game General logic error.
Maze Game Adjacent Starting and Ending location.

The normal grading procedure also failed to test some aspects of the student submissions according to the specification.

Code Breaker Write back to the output variables.
Sudoku Game Diagonal test should be implemented outside the *is_val_valid* function.
Maze Solver Maze map with no outside wall.

The feedback is for instructors as well. By monitoring the feedback generated, instructors can learn about common errors and address these errors in lecture. Instructors can provide more detailed explanation about the common errors than the default generated message from the framework.

7. CONCLUSION

The use of industrial automatic testing tools on automated grading has been limited. With the implemented framework that utilizes concolic testing tools to identify defects in student code, and that generates feedback to students, students get a better understanding of the course material. The result shows that industrial automated testing tools can identify defects in student code.

With the framework, students can get timely feedback on their submissions. The mean processing times for five assignments in an introductory course are all under 5 minutes. There is also more coverage of student submissions than with the traditional automated grading tool. Results show that more than half of defective student code submissions passed the traditional automated grading tool. Thus, further exploration into the application of an industrial automated testing tool in computer science education should be conducted.

In the future, it would be beneficial to tune these tools toward a better fit for automated assessment. Also, because concolic testing is based on an interpreter, some of the common library calls can be replaced with an instructor-provided versions. More implementations for system calls such as malloc and free are desired in the future.

8. ACKNOWLEDGEMENTS

This project was supported by the Strategic Instructional Innovations Program of the College of Engineering at the University of Illinois at Urbana-Champaign.

9. REFERENCES

[1] C. Cadar, D. Dunbar, and D. R. Engler. Klee: Unassisted and automatic generation of high-coverage tests for complex systems programs. In *OSDI*, volume 8, pages 209–224, 2008.

[2] J. G. Ganssle. A guide to code inspections, 2001.

[3] P. Godefroid, M. Y. Levin, and D. Molnar. Sage: whitebox fuzzing for security testing. *Queue*, 10(1):20, 2012.

[4] I. Huet, O. R. Pacheco, J. Tavares, and G. Weir. New challenges in teaching introductory programming courses: a case study. In *Frontiers in Education, 2004. FIE 2004. 34th Annual*, pages T2H–5. IEEE, 2004.

[5] G. Jianxiong. Auto grading tool for introductory programming courses. Master's thesis, University of Illinois, Champaign, 2015.

[6] C. F. Kemerer and M. C. Paulk. The impact of design and code reviews on software quality: An empirical study based on PSP data. *Software Engineering, IEEE Transactions on*, 35(4):534–550, 2009.

[7] K. Sen. Concolic testing. In *Proceedings of the twenty-second IEEE/ACM International Conference on Automated Software Engineering*, pages 571–572. ACM, 2007.

[8] K. Sen and G. Agha. Cute and jcute: Concolic unit testing and explicit path model-checking tools. In *Computer Aided Verification*, pages 419–423. Springer, 2006.

[9] A. Yadin. Reducing the dropout rate in an introductory programming course. *ACM Inroads*, 2(4):71–76, Dec. 2011.

A "Multiple Executions" Technique of Visualization

J. Ángel Velázquez-Iturbide
ETS Ingeniería Informática
Universidad Rey Juan Carlos
28933 Móstoles, Madrid, España
angel.velazquez@urjc.es

Isidoro Hernán-Losada
ETS Ingeniería Informática
Universidad Rey Juan Carlos
28933 Móstoles, Madrid, España
isidoro.hernan@urjc.es

Antonio Pérez-Carrasco
ETS Ingeniería Informática
Universidad Rey Juan Carlos
28933 Móstoles, Madrid, España
antonio.perez.carrasco@urjc.es

ABSTRACT

Algorithm visualizations can be structured or presented in different ways: animation, multiple algorithms, etc. In this paper, we present a presentation format that has hardly been explored, namely to display simultaneously visualizations of a given algorithm for several test cases. By similarity with other presentation formats, we call it the "multiple executions" technique. We illustrate this presentation format with a history-preserving graphical representation, namely recursion trees. Multiple executions composed of recursion trees provide at a glance a view of the behavior of an algorithm in different situations. We illustrate their application to a number of issues in algorithm courses. We also report on two evaluations conducted on the effects of structured multiple executions on students' comprehension of complex recursive algorithms. The results show some statistically significant differences on students' skills for some design tasks.

General Terms

Algorithms, Design.

Keywords

Program visualization; SRec system; multiple executions.

1. INTRODUCTION

Teaching computer programming has been a challenge for university instructors for about forty years [10]. A remarkable approach advocates for the use of algorithm visualizations [6]. During the eighties and first nineties of the last century, most contributions to the field of algorithm visualization were technical. Then, the emphasis shifted to pedagogical issues, such as educational effectiveness [4], student engagement [8], or system dissemination [9].

An algorithm is often illustrated with more than one single, static visualization. More elaborated presentations are:

- Use of time. A sequence of states is displayed, corresponding to steps in the algorithm execution for given input data. The sequence is often displayed dynamically as an animation.

- Several algorithms. The simultaneous display of several algorithms is the "multiple algorithms" technique.

ITiCSE'16, July 09–13, 2016, Arequipa, Peru.
© 2016 ACM. ISBN 978-1-4503-4231-5/16/07...$15.00.
DOI: http://dx.doi.org/10.1145/2899415.2899451

- Several graphical formats. Data of an algorithm are displayed in different formats, typically with different abstraction levels. The simultaneous and coordinated animation of several graphical representations is called "multiple views".

Another form of structuring visualizations, which has hardly been used in algorithm visualization, is to display simultaneously the executions of a given algorithm for several test cases [14]. Note that if the graphical representation is history-preserving, the display provides at a glance a view of the behavior of an algorithm in different situations. We explore this presentation format in this paper. By similarity to the names cited above, we call "multiple executions" to this visualization format.

The use of figures corresponding to several cases is a common recourse used by textbook authors [15] with several purposes:

- Cases that are important for some step of an algorithm, for instance two cases for the split operation of quicksort.

- An optimal and a suboptimal (but valid) solution for an optimization problem. For combinatorial problems, a non-valid solution is sometimes shown.

In this paper, we focus on multiple executions generated by program visualization systems. By program visualization we mean the automatic display of program source code or data [11], either dynamically (as a side effect of the program execution) or statically. Note that the automatic nature of program visualizations limits their capabilities compared to the freedom of textbook authors. For instance, try to generate automatically a non-valid output from a given combinatorial algorithm.

We illustrate the issues addressed in the paper with the system SRec [17][18]. SRec is a program visualization system that visualizes recursion in Java methods. Recursion is a programming construct used in many algorithm design techniques or algorithms, therefore its selection does not limit significantly the issues here addressed. SRec supports several graphical representations, being recursion trees the most versatile and useful. Please, refer to [3] for a definition of recursion trees, and to [17] for the mechanics of their animation in SRec.

The user typically interacts with SRec by iteratively performing the following process: load a file – select a method – launch an execution – interact with the visualizations generated. Active interactions [16] are necessary to engage students and to successfully perform understanding or analysis tasks. One of the simplest interactions is (manual) animation of an algorithm execution, which displays how the algorithm visualization varies as the execution advances (forward or backward). SRec also provides other ways of interacting with a visualization: change the graphical properties of the visualization components, filter the amount of data to display, adjust the zoom scale, change the relative order of data, browse a large visualization, look for specific data in a visualization, and give statistics about a visualization.

The contributions of the paper are twofold. Firstly, we advocate for the multiple executions technique, illustrating it with a number of uses in algorithm courses. Secondly, we present two evaluations of the use of structured multiple executions to understand the complex, recursive algorithms used in a first stage of development of dynamic programming algorithms.

The paper is structured as follows. In Section 2, we present a number of cases where the multiple executions technique fit well, and in Section 3 se sketch its implementation in SRec. In Section 4, we describe the evaluations conducted. The two last sections include, respectively, related work and our conclusions.

2. USES OF MULTIPLE EXECUTIONS

In this section, we present several cases for which we have found multiple executions useful. Two caveats are in place here. Firstly, we do not mean that the list of uses is exhaustive. Secondly, we cannot include visualizations at larger size. However, the reader should not be too worried about this: they can be zoomed but, for most examples, watching the shape and size of the trees suffices to understand the issues addressed.

2.1 Analysis of Algorithm Efficiency

We may distinguish three interesting cases.

2.1.1 Best, Worst and Average Cases

The running time of some algorithms does not only depends on the size of their parameters but also on their contents. For these algorithms, we must differentiate several performance cases.

For instance, the worst-case of quicksort has asymptotic complexity $O(n^2)$, while the best and average cases have complexity $O(n\log n)$. See two worst cases and one best case for an array of length eight in Fig. 1. Note that these three recursion trees have the same number of nodes. However, the computation performed at each row of the tree has lineal complexity. Consequently, the overall algorithm complexity depends on the different height of the trees [2, Section 7.3].

However, running time of mergesort only depends on the array size. If we generate different recursion trees for mergesort with arrays of length eight, all of them will have the same shape as Fig. 1(b).

2.1.2 Asymptotic Behavior of Algorithms

A good way of understanding the huge differences among different asymptotic orders is to watch them. For example, Fig. 2 illustrates exponential growth in time of the direct recursive version of the Fibonacci series. The figure shows the recursion trees for n ranging from 2 to 6. Their number of recursive calls is: 3, 5, 9, 15, and 25. (We do not include more cases because of lack of space.)

An optimized algorithm should have better asymptotic behavior. Fig. 3 illustrates the lineal behavior of a memoized version [1, Section 8.8] of the same algorithm. In this case, the number of recursive calls grows lineally: 4, 6, 8, 10, and 12. (Nodes are large because the state of the table used for memoizing also is displayed.)

2.1.3 Redundancy Check

Although some multiple recursive algorithms are asymptotically very efficient (e.g. mergesort or quicksort), multiple recursive algorithms whose recursive calls represent overlapping subproblems are extremely inefficient. Many calls are invoked more than once, recomputing their value in each invocation. Recursive algorithms designed for dynamic programming belong to this class.

The first step in removing redundancy is to check its presence. We must first obtain a representative recursion tree and then find repeated nodes (only for recursive cases!). This is a simple but laborious task that is typically done by trial-and-error. We generate a recursion tree for a relatively small case. If we do not find evidence of redundancy, we must generate more complex recursion trees. We will probably succeed in very few attempts, but there always is uncertainty about when we will find an adequate and illustrative case.

If we have several recursion trees available simultaneously, the task is easier to perform. Consider Fig. 2 again. If we examine *fib*(4), we only find one redundant node (for n=2), thus it does not provide evidence enough of redundancy. By inspection of the immediately greater cases, we notice that *fib*(6) is not too complex and provides higher evidence: there are redundant nodes for n=2, 3 and 4.

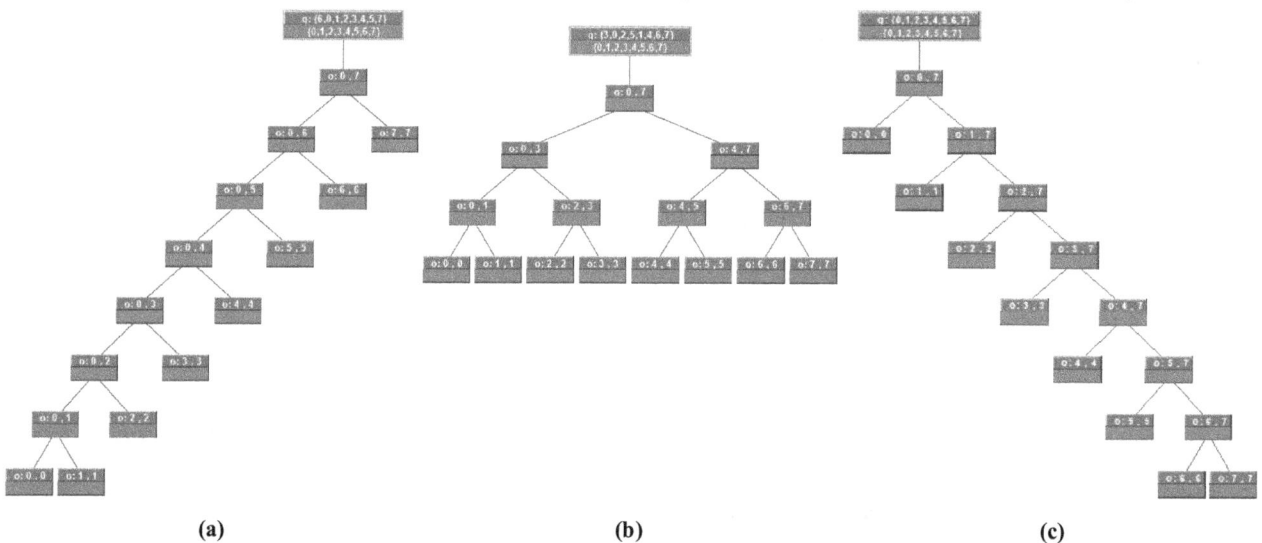

(a)   (b)   (c)

Figure 1. Recursion trees showing different cases for quicksort: (a) a worst case, (b) a best case, and (c) another worst case.

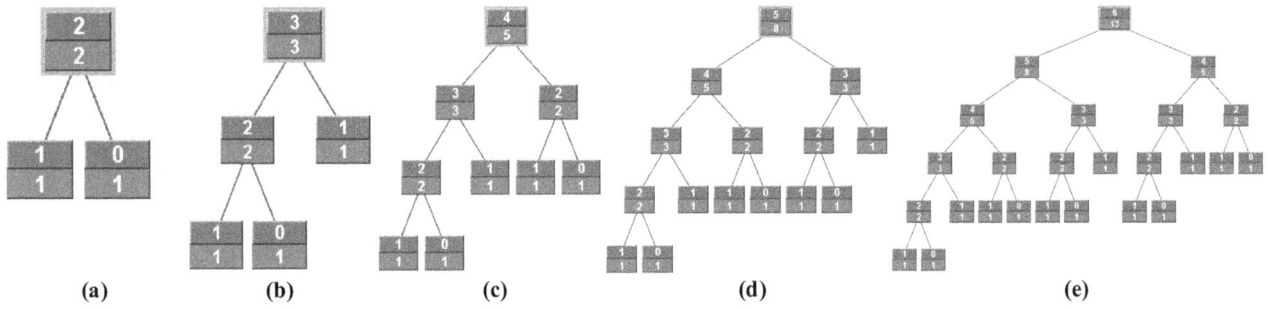

Figure 2. Recursion trees of the recursive algorithm that computes the Fibonacci series for *n*=2, 3, 4, 5, and 6.

Figure 3. Recursion trees of a memoized algorithm that computes the Fibonacci series for *n*=2, 3, 4, 5, and 6.

2.2 Understanding Complex Algorithms

For many recursive algorithms, a single recursion tree is enough to illustrate its behavior. However, some algorithms are difficult to understand by students, for instance, recursive algorithms designed in a first step of the development of dynamic programming algorithms. Students have difficulties in understanding their two major design decisions: organization of the construction of the solution in stages, and identification of the alternatives that must be considered at each stage.

In a structured collection of multiple executions, the visualizations displayed change gradually so that the student may compare their similarities and differences. This may be achieved by invoking a sequence of calls with increasingly complex input data, so that two consecutive visualizations allow illustrating incremental differences in the algorithm behavior.

For example, consider the weighted activity selection problem [5, Section 6.1]. Given a set of *n* activities, each one characterized by a start time s_i, a finish time f_i, and a profit p_i, we want to determine a subset of non-overlapping activities whose accomplishment yields maximum profit. For instance, given the set of six activities displayed in Fig. 4, with associated profits {2,4,4,7,2,2}, an optimal solution is formed by activities 3 and 5 (using Java indices), with profit equal to 9.

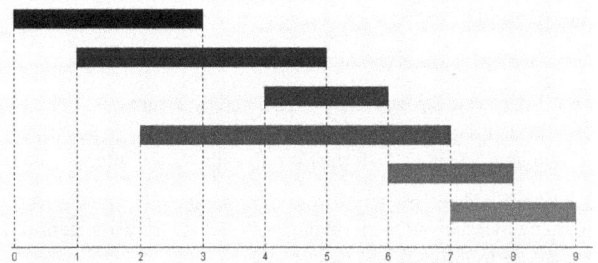

Figure 4. A set of six (partially) overlapping activities.

Let us sketch the rationale of a recursive solution and then we show a corresponding structured, multiple executions visualization. Assume that activities are sorted in non-decreasing order of finish time. We define $p(i)$, for an arbitrary activity *i*, as the activity *j* compatible with *i* that is closest to *i* from its left. If such an activity does not exist, $p(i)$=-1. For this example, the set of values $p(i)$ is equal to {-1,-1,0,-1,2,3}.

We define *sel(i)* as the generalized problem for activities ranging from 0 to *i*, included, $0 \leq i \leq n$. The complete problem is solved with an initial call *sel(n)*. The problem can then be solved by the following recursive algorithm:

$$sel(-1) = 0$$

$$sel(i) = \max(sel(i-1), b_i + sel(p(i))) \quad for \ i \geq 0$$

There is a potentially huge number of combinations of an arbitrary number of activities. A useful structured collection of multiple executions must be relatively simple. In addition, it must show the effect of incremental changes in input data on the algorithm behavior.

Fig. 5 shows a structured collection of five multiple executions. Our choice is based on the following rationale:

- We used a small set of activities (i.e. three activities) with small values for their start and finish times (instants 1, 2 or 3).

- The three activities have different finish times.

- Recursion trees differ in the total number of overlaps among activities. Three activities may add together 3, 2, 1 or 0 overlaps. In addition, there are two ways of obtaining one overlap under the previous restriction. Therefore, we have five cases.

At the left of each recursion tree, the activities are displayed to enhance the tree readability. Each recursion tree contains calls to three methods:

- The main method, with three arrays containing start times, finish times, and profits of the activities.

- The recursive method *sel* defined above.

- An auxiliary method *c* that computes, from the sorted activities, the array *p* used by *sel*.

The visualizations of *sel* illustrate that the solution is constructed in a maximum of $n+1$ stages, being n the number of activities. At each stage i, two choices are possible: either taking activity i or discarding it. Notice that test cases with fewer overlaps allow a higher number of valid solutions and, therefore, larger trees.

3. IMPLEMENTATION

We have implemented multiple executions in SRec [17]. The dialog to launch one execution was modified so that several test cases can be specified. Consequently, several executions of the algorithm are launched and a visualization is displayed for each test case.

There are two ways of giving several values for a parameter:

- Specifying several values, separated by commas.
- Specifying a range of values, using the syntax 'lower value .. higher value'. This format is only allowed for integer values.

If multiple values are given to several parameters, the Cartesian product of all the values is computed, launching as many algorithm executions as different test cases result.

As a result of launching multiple executions, a set of visualizations is generated, similar to but smaller than those presented here. One of the two visualization panels of SRec was modified to host such a set of visualizations. Then, the user may select any visualization. Consequently, the visualization is displayed at larger scale in the second panel and the user may interact with it (animating, zooming, filtering, etc.)

The system also provides a complementary function. The user may export, in a single action, all the visualizations resulting from a multiple executions action. It a mundane but very useful function to instructors and students for documentation purposes.

4. EVALUATION

We conducted two evaluations of students' performance and acceptance of multiple executions of complex recursive algorithms. The evaluations were conducted in November 2013 and November 2014 in the elective fourth-year course "Advanced Algorithms" offered at our University to Computer Science students.

The evaluations were conducted as a part of an assignment aimed at implementing an efficient dynamic programming algorithm. As a first task, students were given in a lab session the recursive algorithm specified above for the weighted activity selection problem [6, Section 6.1] and they had to analyze its redundancy. The number of students who attended the lab session in both years was 27 and 16, respectively. In both cases, they were divided into two homogeneous groups receiving different treatments:

- Control group. They were given a previous version of SRec as a tool to generate individual recursion trees.

- Experimental group. They were given the multiple executions visualizations displayed in Fig. 5.

Close to the end of the session, students were given two questionnaires to be filled before leaving the lab:

- A knowledge questionnaire composed of five open questions about the problem and the recursive algorithm.

- (Only the experimental group.) A satisfaction questionnaire composed of five multiple-choice questions with a Likert scale ranging from 1 (completely disagree) to 5 (completely agree).

The knowledge questions were intended to measure different goals. We summarize the results:

1. Understanding the problem statement. Almost all students in both groups understood it properly.
2. Understanding the information encoded in recursion trees. Most students in both groups understood it properly.
3. Understanding the effects of input data on the size of recursion trees (design test cases of length 4). In the first evaluation, students in the experimental group performed better than the control group (p=.002, bilateral Fisher test using a 95% confidence interval), but not in the second evaluation.
4. Understanding the effects of input data on the size of recursion trees (design general test cases). The results were similar to the previous question in both evaluations (p=.016).
5. Design a table adequate to remove redundancy. The main difference between both groups was that many more students in the control group left this question in blank than in the experimental group (p=.04 and .02, respectively.)

The results are not conclusive. The evaluations were conducted on samples with few students, but we did not have a chance to access more populated courses that included dynamic programing in their syllabus. Nevertheless, we may summarize the findings. In both evaluations, students had similar performance regarding understanding tasks. However, more students in the experimental group designed tables than in the control group. Finally, students in the experimental group performed better for some design tasks based on prediction.

The results of the satisfaction questionnaire were successful in both evaluations. They asked to rate the collection with respect to ease of understanding and utility. Four questions were rated with mean above 4. In particular, ease of understanding was rated 4.38 in both evaluations. A fifth question asked students if they preferred constructing their own trees with SRec (means 2.15 and 2.75, respectively), thus they preferred to have the collection given.

(a)

(b)

(c)

(d)

(e)

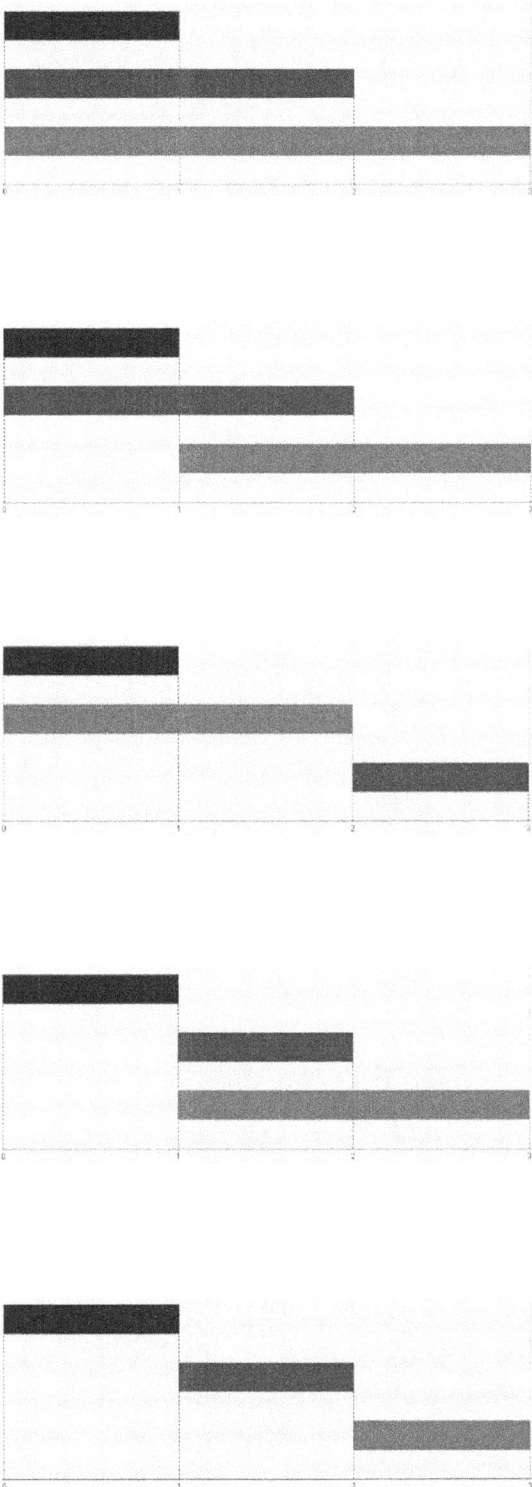

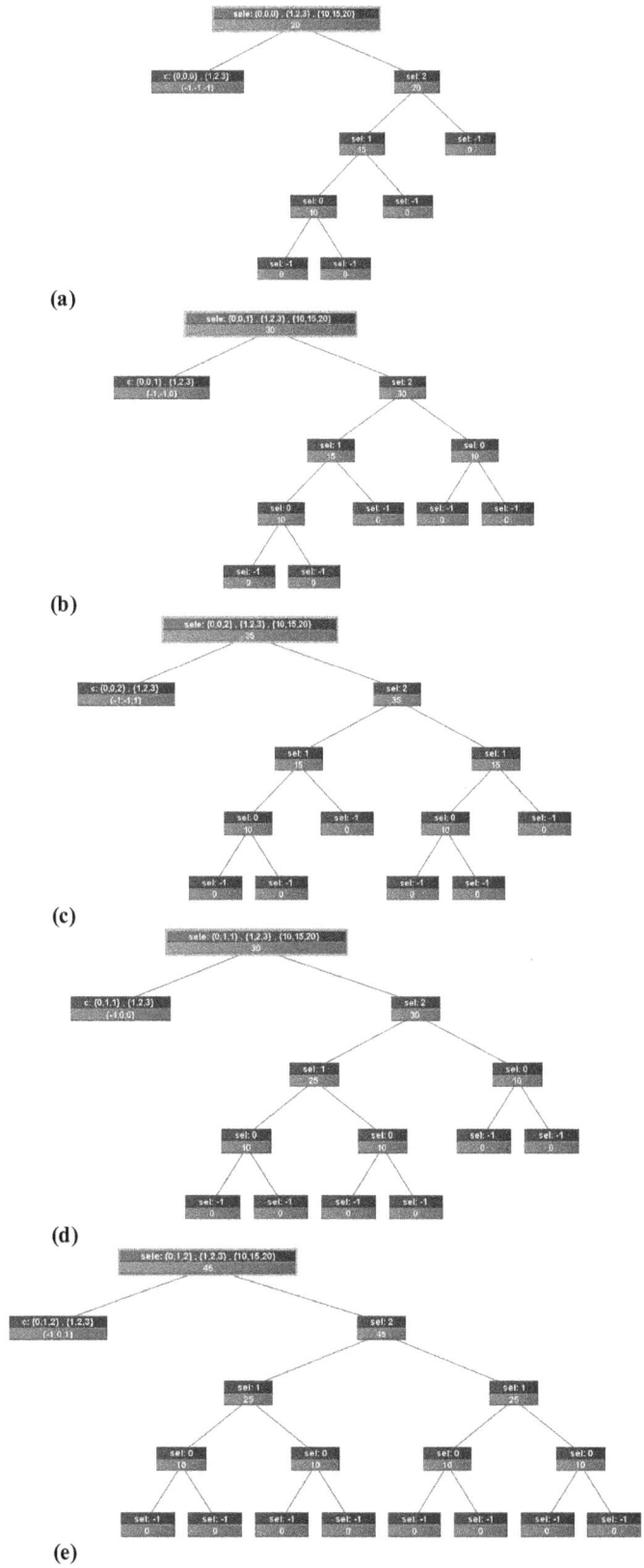

Figure 5. A set of five executions for the weighted activity selection problem involving three activities with varying degree of overlap.

5. RELATED WORK

A trivial antecedent of multiple executions in software visualization is the availability of several input cases in "canned" animations. However, visualizations are typically not displayed simultaneously.

The more elaborated collections proposed to understand complex algorithms are related to other works in information visualization or pedagogy. Multiple executions is a particular case of the "small multiples" technique proposed by Edward Tufte [13]. The technique is frequently used in visual explanations, e.g. continental drift or movements of the crawl style. According to Tufte [13, p. 105], "Multiple images reveal repetition and change, pattern and surprise", "Multiples directly depict comparisons".

The value of repetition and change also is appreciated in education. Variation theory [7] claims that people become aware of a phenomenon through the way that it varies from its environment or the way in which its internal parts vary in relation to one another. Multiple executions of a multiple recursive algorithm show both kinds of variations. Incremental changes in parameter values produce incremental changes in visualizations. Depending on the algorithm, these changes are small or big, but they are the smallest possible ones according to the algorithm logic. Students can compare adjacent visualizations to better appreciate similarities and differences and thus better understand the key algorithm decisions.

The theory of cognitive load [12] provides a number of tested principles for effective instruction. A worked example provides a step-by-step solution to a problem. A "worked example effect" occurs when learners presented worked examples to study perform better on subsequent test problems than learners asked to solve the equivalent problem. Given the maturity needed to design a structured collection of multiple executions, it should be a part of a worked example of complex algorithms.

6. CONCLUSIONS

We have presented a way of structuring visualizations that has hardly been explored, namely to display simultaneously visualizations of a given algorithm for several test cases. We called it the "multiple executions" technique. We used this presentation format jointly with a history-preserving graphical representation, namely recursion trees. Multiple executions of recursion trees provide at a glance a view of the behavior of an algorithm in different situations. We illustrated our proposal with a number of issues of algorithm courses, emphasizing structured collections of multiple executions. We also reported on two evaluations conducted on the effects of these structured collections on students' comprehension of complex recursive algorithms. The results show some statistically significant differences on students' skills for some design tasks. However, it is recommended to replicate the evaluations with more populated samples, as well as deepen into the reasons why many students in the control group left answers in blank.

For next academic year, we plan to prepare a comprehensive set of "worked examples" of dynamic programing algorithms based on collections of multiple executions, and to evaluate their effects on students' learning outcomes.

7. ACKNOWLEDGMENTS

This work was supported by research grants TIN2011-29542-C02-01 and TIN2015-66731-C2-1-R of the Ministry of Economy and Competitiveness, S2013/ICE-2715 of the Regional Government of Madrid, and 30VCPIGI15 of the Universidad Rey Juan Carlos.

8. REFERENCES

[1] Brassard, G., and Bratley, P. 1996. *Fundamentals of Algorithmics*. Prentice-Hall, Englewood Cliffs, NJ.

[2] Cormen, T.H., Leiserson, C.E., Rivest, R.L., and Stein, C. 2009. *Introduction to Algorithms*, 3rd ed. MIT Press, Cambridge, MA.

[3] Haynes, S.M. 1995. Explaining recursion to the unsophisticated. *SIGCSE Bulletin* 27, 3 (Sept.), 3-6 and 14.

[4] Hundhausen, C., Douglas, S., and Stasko, J. 2002. A meta-study of algorithm visualization effectiveness. *Journal of Visual Languages and Computing* 13, 3 (2002) 259–290.

[5] Kleinberg, J., and Tardos, É. 2006. *Algorithm Design*. Pearson Addison-Wesley, Boston, MA.

[6] Lister, R. The naughties in CSEd research: A retrospective. 2010. *Inroads* 1, 1 (Mar. 2010) 22-24.

[7] Marton F., and Tsui, A. B. M. 2004. *Classroom Discourse and the Space of Learning*. Routledge, New York, NY.

[8] Naps, T., Roessling, G., Almstrum, V., Dann, W., Fleischer, R., Hundhausen, C., Korhonen, A., Malmi, L., McNally, M., Rodger, S., and Velázquez-Iturbide, J.Á. 2003. Exploring the role of visualization and engagement in computer science education. *SIGCSE Bulletin* 35, 2 (June 2003) 131-152.

[9] Naps, T., Roessling, G., Anderson, J., Cooper. S., Dann, W., Fleischer, R., Koldehofe, B., Korhonen, A., Kuittinen, M., Leska, C., Malmi, L., McNally, M., Rantakokko, J., and Ross, R. J. 2003. Evaluating the educational impact of visualization. *SIGCSE Bulletin* 35, 4 (Dec. 2003) 124-136.

[10] Robin, A., Roundtree, J., and Roundtree, N. 2003. Learning and teaching programming: A review and discussion. *Computer Science Education* 13, 2 (2003) 137-172.

[11] Stasko, J., Domingue, J., Brown, M.H., and Price, B.A. Eds. 1998. *Software Visualization*. MIT Press, Cambridge, MA.

[12] Sweller, J., Ayres, P., and Kalyuga, S. Eds. 2011.*Cognitive Load Theory*. Springer.

[13] Tufte, E. 1997.*Visual Explanations*. Graphics Press, Cheshire, CT.

[14] Velázquez-Iturbide, J.Á. 2011. Characterizing time and interaction in a space of software visualizations. In *Proceedings of the 6th Program Visualization Workshop*. PVW'11. Technical Report TUD-CS-2011-0153, Technische Universität Darmstadt, Germany, 43-51.

[15] Velázquez-Iturbide, J.Á. 2013. 2013). Using textbook illustrations to extract design principles for algorithm visualizations. In *Handbook of Human Centric Visualization*, W. Huang, Ed. Springer Science+Business Media, 227-249.

[16] Velázquez-Iturbide, J.Á., and Pérez-Carrasco, A. 2010. InfoVis interaction techniques in animation of recursive programs. *Algorithms* 3, 1 (Mar. 2010) 76-91.

[17] Velázquez-Iturbide, J.Á., Pérez-Carrasco, A., and Urquiza-Fuentes, J. 2008. SRec: An animation system of recursion for algorithm courses. In *Proceedings of the 13th Annual Conference on Innovation and Technology in Computer Science Education*. ITiCSE 2008, 225-229.

[18] Velázquez-Iturbide, J.Á., Pérez-Carrasco, A., and Urquiza-Fuentes, J. 2009. A design of automatic visualizations for divide-and-conquer algorithms. *Electronic Notes in Theoretical Computer Science*, 224 (2009), 159-167.

Algorithms + Organization = Systems

Ali Erkan[*]
Ithaca College
953 Danby Rd
Ithaca, New York 14850
aerkan@ithaca.edu

John Barr[†]
Ithaca College
953 Danby Rd
Ithaca, New York 14850
barr@ithaca.edu

ABSTRACT

Even though a computer science or computing-oriented degree is unavoidably broken into semesters and courses, we always hope that our students form a holistic picture of the discipline by the time they graduate. Yet we do not have too many opportunities to make this point in a convincing manner. This paper reports our efforts to point out the connections between a seemingly (in the eyes of students) disconnected subset of courses in our degree requirements. In particular, we report on how we have used research papers as the glue between topics covered in our algorithms and systems oriented courses (such as Organization and Computer Networks). Our assessment of the course has shown that students have not only made gains in their understanding and appreciation of meaningful intra-disciplinary connections, but have also advanced in designing empirical experiments (mimicking the methodologies observed in the chosen papers) and reading/writing technical papers.

CCS Concepts

•Networks → Control path algorithms; •Theory of computation → Data structures design and analysis; •Applied computing → Education;

Keywords

Education, Operating Systems, Networks, Algorithms

1. INTRODUCTION

Computer science curricula has been well defined for many years through the publication of the Computer Science Curricula document developed by the two major professional societies, the Association for Computing Machinery (ACM) and the IEEE Computer Society. This document defines computer science curricula by providing knowledge areas and *course exemplars*. The most recent version of this document, the Computer Science Curricula 2013 (CSC13 [1]), provides 18 knowledge areas including "Algorithms" (AL) and at least three systems areas, "Networking and Communications" (NC), "Operating Systems" (OS) and "Systems Fundamentals" (SF). Courses that cover *Algorithm* knowledge area topics and courses that cover system (NC, OS, and SF) area topics have traditionally been seen by most computer science departments as separate courses even though computer systems employ many sophisticated algorithms. The CSC13, for example, lists three algorithm *course exemplars* none of which contain NC, OS, or SF knowledge area topics. Similarly, there are three network *course exemplars*, five operating system *course exemplars*, and two system programming *course exemplars* none of which contain AL knowledge area topics. However, as the report states, knowledge areas are not meant to correspond to courses [1, page 27].

This separation of concepts into courses introduces a number of deficiencies in a student's education. In particular, fields within computer science end up appearing to be siloed and students lack an understanding of interrelationship between sub-fields. For example, without a comprehension of interrelationships, students may fail to find or modify algorithms to meet efficiency constraints in real-world software.

We can say that this deficiency is likely to be addressed after years of experience (or graduate school) but as educators, it is important for us address it in a more deliberate and timely fashion. In particular, we may be able to make use of a particular type of artifact (one that is far less concerned about conceptual partitions) to create a context for this endeavor: a research paper. That is, we may be able to use papers as agents to pull together whatever it takes to resolve an open ended question or design a system or advance a theoretical boundary.

What does it mean for a paper to be "far less concerned about conceptual partitions?" It means that for conceptual prerequisites on which they rest, papers do not typically align well with our course-based divisions in the curriculum. And nor do they care to. For example, figure 1 illustrates the topics needed by the paper *Survey and Taxonomy of IP Address Lookup Algorithms* [23], arranged in terms of the related courses we offer. Reading the paper, it becomes clear that understanding the design of efficient systems to optimize the operation of IP address lookups connect with our Organization, Computer Networks, Algorithms, and (as the provider of prerequisites of prerequisites) Discrete Math.

[*]Associate Professor
[†]Associate Professor

ITiCSE '16, July 09–13, 2016, Arequipa, Peru.

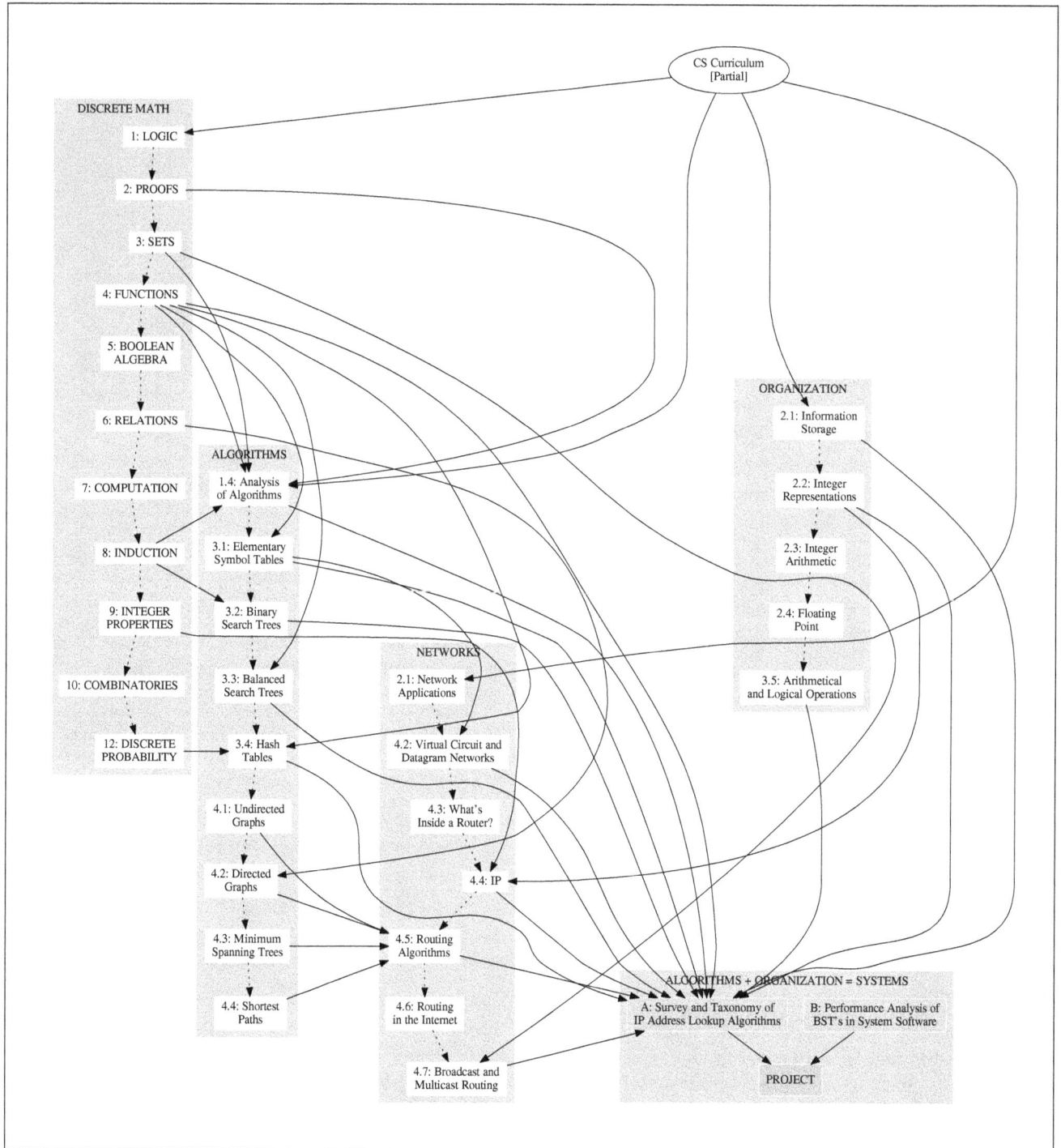

Figure 1: **A visual representation (based on GraphViz) of the direct and indirect dependencies between our Discrete Math, Algorithms, Organization, Computer Networks courses and one of the 18 selected papers**: *To minimize clutter, the topics listed in each box is only an order-preserved subset of the content covered in the associated course. The project shown at the bottom right corner is what students attempt once they have read and thoroughly discussed a particular paper. In the view above, this project is shown to be based on [23] because that paper led to a more visually appealing (i.e. readable) layout for this figure. However, in our trial course, the project was based on [19] because it was a more accessible starting point for that particular set of students.*

The idea that led to the design of a new course at our institution as well as the writing of this paper is based on generalizing this idea. That is, could we come up with a set of (mostly seminal) papers, each of which directly or indirectly depends on topics covered in our courses, while illustrating how algorithms and organizational topics come together to create systems?

2. PREVIOUS WORK

The authors were not able to identify work that directly addresses the driving question of their inquiry. There is rich literature, however, addressing the integration of research into undergraduate courses [20, 11]. Koppleman, in particular, acknowledges one of the problems that we raise here (i.e., determining the contextual knowledge for the paper) and proposes that students be given structure for their research without providing any details. Fong [4] and Keshav [10] discuss how to read a computer science research paper, but do not address how the reader would have to "backtrack" down to the courses where particular prerequisite concepts are covered. Musicant et.al. [18], address the slightly more general matter on the challenges associated with involving students in research. Holtz et.al. [7] provide a taxonomy of research methods and skills necessary to carry out the associated work, but do not connect their suggestions to holistic curricular appreciations.

3. THE AOS COURSE

The *Algorithms + Organization = Systems* (AOS)[1] course was designed to use research papers as the glue between topics covered in our algorithms and systems oriented courses (such as Organization and Computer Networks). We chose to focus on the following goals:

- Understanding the basic concepts of operating systems and networks.
- Understanding the interconnection of systems and algorithm concepts.
- Understanding how algorithms can be modified to affect performance.
- Performing empirical testing of algorithms for specific system contexts.
- Selecting the most appropriate algorithm for a given task by doing literature searches and through empirical testing.
- Reading research papers and determining what concepts are necessary to understand the papers.

The selected papers were made available to students in digital format at least a week before class and students were required to read them prior to our discussions. References to appropriate systems concepts were also made available electronically.

---

[1]The name of the pilot offering of the course was "Complex Systems" since we wanted to focus on the holistic picture of what it takes to build a computer. However, since then, the course focused on two particularly fundamental pillars of building computers: Algorithms and Organization. We thus renamed the course to "Algorithms + Organization = Systems,", also to pay homage to one of our favorite textbooks of the discipline: "Algorithms + Data Structures = Programs" [27]

Classes were two hours long and met twice a week and one to three papers were covered each week. As expected, students had problems mastering certain system concepts and thus the instructor led students backtrack to course materials to patch any missing information. This was the context in which the structure of the paper became the guide to connect sets of topics distributed in multiple courses.

One would wish to have a set of papers that are arranged in a natural thematic progression but, in reality, we found ourselves making decisions based on three factors: (i) the accessibility of the paper to a typical undergraduate, (ii) the coverage of the paper by our courses, and (iii) by the significance of the paper for the field to which it belonged. Our final selection fell into the following four groups:

1. **Networks**: IP addressing [23, 19, 25], routing & forwarding [23, 19, 24, 23], peer-to-peer networks [25], DNS [25].
2. **Operating Systems**: Virtual memory [19], garbage collection [2, 28, 16, 15], dynamic memory allocation [13, 22], deadlocks [6], load balancing [17], scheduling [9, 8, 14], file systems [21, 5].
3. **Architecture**: Pipelining [19], interrupts [6], caches [21].
4. **System Tools**: Version control [12, 26, 3].

There were two forms of assessment in the course: exams and projects. Two take-home exams were given that required students to explain aspects of the papers that they had read. This was where we tested for conceptual comprehension and made sure that all students (i.e. not just the presenter) spent sufficient time on the reading.

Of the two projects, the first had students conduct empirical testing of a sophisticated algorithm in a systems environment. In particular, this project required students to find an application, identify a key data structure, figure out its typical use, create a test harness for the data structure, perform an analysis of variations of the data structure measured against the captured data, and describe their findings in a technical paper. The applications chosen by students included DNS lookups, an application to capture star data, and data compression. This project was successful but also daunting for the students. Though they had gone through several technical papers that described empirical testing, students realized that they had not yet mastered the process. We therefore plan to have a warm-up project in future iterations course to avoid this issue.

For the second project, students were required to do a literature search on a data structure bottleneck in a systems environment of their choice. Through this search, students determined the most optimal data structure to use in their chosen systems environment, and presented their findings.

4. SURVEY RESULTS AND DISCUSSION

At the end of semester, we had students fill out an anonymous two-part survey to get information for evaluating and fine-tuning the course. The first part of this survey captured students' opinions and perceptions with the degree to which they agreed with 10 cross-cutting departmental curricular goals (e.g. "*Algorithms are important in the design of computer systems*"). In addition, to get a sense of *change*, we asked students to respond to each assertion first as how they would have thought at the beginning of the semester v.s. the

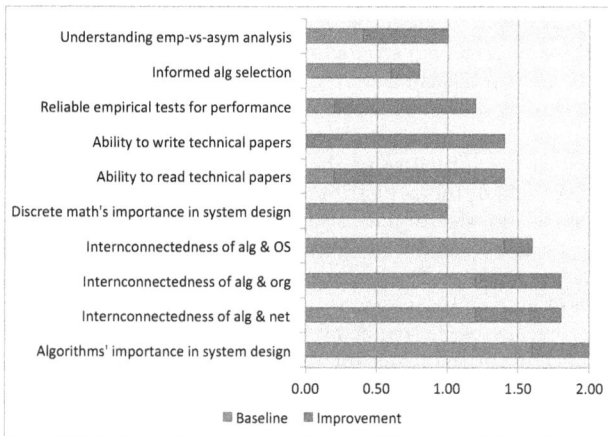

Figure 2: **Gains in cross-cutting curricular goals**: *Student responses to express the degree to which their opinions had changed for 10 cross-cutting curricular goals of our department. The responses were based on a five-point Likert scale that ranged from "Strongly disagree" (-2) to "Strongly agree" (2) and thus class averages were expected to be real numbers between -2 to 2. However, since none of "baseline" responses dipped below zero, the range of the x-axis of the above plot is from 0 to 2.*

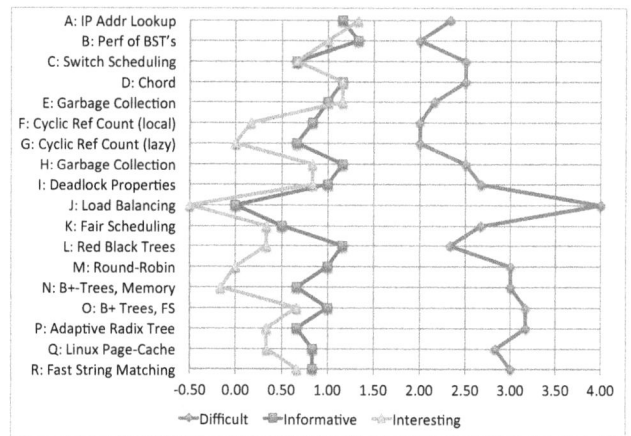

Figure 3: **Comparison of student responses to the 18 papers read in the course**: *For the "Informative" and "Interesting" prompt, the five-point Likert scale we used ranged from "Extremely uninformative/uninteresting" (-2) to "Extremely informative/interesting" (2); for the "Difficulty" prompt, on the other hand, the five-point Likert scale ranged from "Extremely easy" (0) to "Extremely difficult" (4). To compare these three measures, a numeric range of (-2) to (4) appears to be needed. However, since the class average for "Informative" and "Interesting" never went under -0.5, the above plot focuses on the range of -0.5 to 4.*

end; this gave us a pre- and a post- data set[2]. To encourage a thoughtful process in making their choices, we also asked students to provide qualitative comments any time their pre-vs post- responses differed for a particular assertion (due to space constraints, qualitative statements are not included in this paper). The average of the pre- responses formed our *baseline* and the average of the post- responses minus the baseline formed our measure of *gain*. The results are shown in figure 2.

None of the baseline values were negative; that is, none of the students reported to have started the course in a way that conflicted with our departmental goals (at least the ones captured in the assertions). Furthermore, the gain was positive for all but one assertion; that is, regardless of their interests within computer science, exposing students to 18 research papers did not lead to any unintended consequences (at least in the way we could measure). The biggest gain was in students' increased confidence in reading and writing papers but they also registered non-trivial (even significant) increases in their appreciation/recognition of inter-course connections (e.g. "Algorithms" and "Organization" as well as "Algorithms" and "Computer Networks").

In the second part of the survey, we asked students to rate the papers by the three distinct measures of "how *difficult* was this paper?", "how *informative* was this paper?", and "how *interesting* was this paper?" Looking at the results shown in figure 3, two things are immediately visible.

First, when a paper is considered to be particularly difficult, students consider that paper not to be interesting or informative; this is an understandable reaction that can be attributed to frustration. Second, there is a visible correlation between the lines for "Interesting" and "Informative"; in fact, the Pearson product-moment coefficient (which is referred to as the "correlation factor" from here on) between them is 0.74. Furthermore, the line for "Informative" never dips under "Interesting", exceeding it for all but four papers. We were particularly pleased with this since it implies that students consider research papers to be informative even when they focus on fields outside the students' area of interest.

Finally, with respect to the "Difficult", "Informative", and "Interesting" measures, we were interested in seeing the consistency between students and the instructor (one of the authors). But this was not just a matter of curiosity; as we assess the virtues of a paper, we are unavoidably using a lens that's been trained for a longer time (and under different circumstances) than those of our students. Consequently, it's easy for us to be "off". And since papers are not vetted for readability at the same level as books, a disconnect between the instructor and the students can be a stealth obstacle in reaching the goals of the course.

As shown in figure 4a, the student and instructor plots are almost parallel when it comes to assessing the difficulty of the papers; and with a correlation coefficient of 0.51, we can even claim significance. However, the instructor is on average one whole Likert-scale level lower than the students. This reveals the extent to which papers contain nuances that require the general knowledge we have acquired through the years and the attention we should pay in processing the difficulties of these papers through the eyes of out students. With a correlation coefficient of 0.49 and the trends visi-

---

[2]We could have gathered this information from a true pair of pre-/post- semester surveys. However, we preferred a reflective end-of-semester exercise for students to self-report the change they experienced. The primary reason for this decision was that the students' definition of "technical paper" was destined to change rather drastically throughout the course because most of them had not previously read a rigorous research paper.

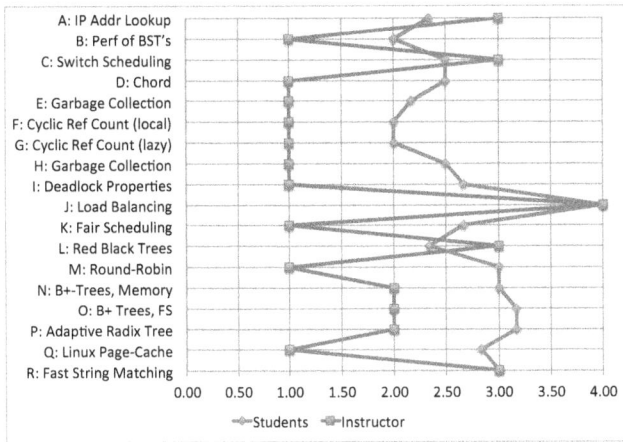

(a) Difficult

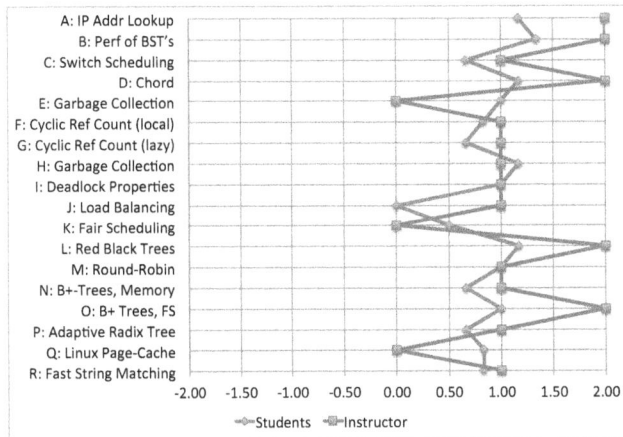

(b) Informative

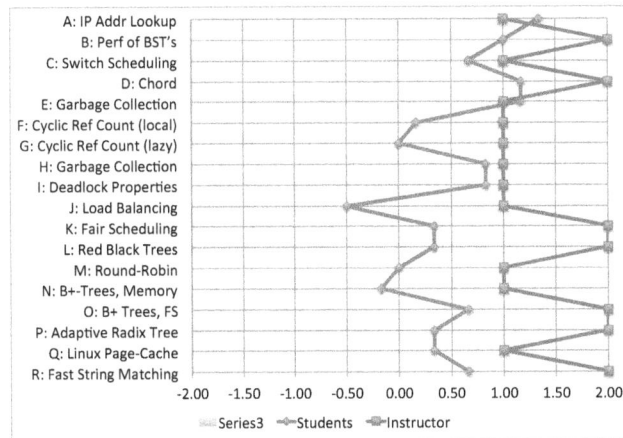

(c) Interesting

Figure 4: **Comparison of the results of the students and the instructor for the second part of the survey**: *The y-axis for all three are paper names. The x-axis for figure 4a ranges from 0 (extremely easy) to 4 (extremely difficult); the x-axis for figure 4b and 4c, on the other hand range from -2 (extremely uninformative/uninteresting) to 2 (extremely informative/interesting). However, our primary focus is on the trends displayed by these plots rather than their details.*

ble in figure 4b (but without the systematic displacement present in figure 4a), the instructor and the students are in greater agreement regarding the extent to which the selected papers are informative. When it comes to assessing how interesting these paper are, the correlation coefficient drops to 0.21 and the plot lines in figure 4c do not offer a more revealing interpretation.

5. CONCLUSION

The conclusions drawn in earlier sections were limited to assessing the first iteration of the course but we do have a number of concrete changes planned for future. Here we outline two.

A not-so-positive take-away from the results in figure 2 was the zero gain for the assertion *"Discrete Math is important in the design of computer systems."*. The importance of discrete math is self-evident to CS faculty members since it provides the mathematical language/thinking/facilities for the ideas expressed in Algorithms (and in any other course with non-trivial levels of theory). Therefore, if (in the context of papers that squarely depend on these two topics) students have increased their appreciation of Algorithms but not that of Discrete Math, then we (the authors of this paper who also teach Discrete Math) have not been sufficiently successful in forming an important curricular connection. This realization has already led to changes in how we teach Discrete Math in subsequent semesters. In addition, as an example of vertical assessments in the degree, we will repeat this inquiry during the next offering of our AOS course to confirm that our Discrete Math changes have indeed led to an improvement.

We also need to create assignments/exercises that emphasize the primary goal of the course (i.e. forming a holistic view of the discipline). We therefore plan to make the production of detailed conceptual dependency representations (as shown in figure 1) to be a student activity. That is, using a simple visualization system such as GraphViz[3], we will ask students to connect the papers with the prerequisite topics covered in courses. A textual representation will also allow us to quantitatively compare these artifacts and review particularly diverging ones in class to create moments of reflection and big-picture inquiry.

6. APPENDIX

A thematic breakdown of the papers selected for our course was provided in section 3. The following is the weekly order for a 14 week semester along with the particular systems topic covered by the chosen paper(s):

- Week 1: IP addressing [23].
- Week 2: VM, IP addressing, switching [19].
- Week 3: Networks, switching [24].
- Week 4: Network, distributed IP [25].
- Week 5: Garbage collection [2, 16, 15].
- Week 6: Garbage collection [2, 28].
- Week 7: PROJECT AND MIDTERM EXAM.
- Week 8: Deadlocks [6].
- Week 9: Load balancing [17].

---

[3]GraphViz allows dependencies to be expressed in textual form which are then automatically rendered as directed acyclic graphs.

- Week 10: Scheduling [9, 8, 14].
- Week 11: File Systems [21, 5].
- Week 12: Memory Management [13, 22].
- Week 13: Diff, version control [12, 26, 3].
- Week 14: REVIEW.

7. REFERENCES

[1] ACM and A. f. C. M. IEEE Computer Society Joint Task Force on Computing Curricula. *Computer Science Curricula 2013: Curriculum Guidelines for Undergraduate Degree Programs in Computer Science*. ACM, New York, NY, USA, 2013. 999133.

[2] H.-J. Boehm and M. Weiser. Garbage collection in an uncooperative environment. *Softw. Pract. Exper.*, 18(9):807–820, Sept. 1988.

[3] T. Cormen, C. E. Leiserson, R. L. Rivest, and C. Stein. *Introduction to Algorithms, 3rd ed.* MIT Press, Cambridge, MA, USA, 2009.

[4] P. W. Fong. Reading a computer science research paper. *SIGCSE Bull.*, 41(2):138–140, June 2009.

[5] F. Havasi. An improved b+ tree for flash file systems. In I. ÄŇernÃ¡, T. GyimÃ§thy, J. HromkoviÄ, K. Jefferey, R. KrÃ¡loviÄ, M. VukoliÄ, and S. Wolf, editors, *SOFSEM 2011: Theory and Practice of Computer Science*, volume 6543 of *Lecture Notes in Computer Science*, pages 297–307. Springer Berlin Heidelberg, 2011.

[6] R. C. Holt. Some deadlock properties of computer systems. *ACM Comput. Surv.*, 4(3):179–196, Sept. 1972.

[7] H. J. Holz, A. Applin, B. Haberman, D. Joyce, H. Purchase, and C. Reed. Research methods in computing: What are they, and how should we teach them? *SIGCSE Bull.*, 38(4):96–114, June 2006.

[8] P. W. Howard and J. Walpole. Relativistic red-black trees. Technical report, Portland State University, 1900 SW 4th Ave., Suite 120, Portland, OR 97201, Feb. 2010. http://www.pdx.edu/sites/www.pdx.edu.computer-science/files/tr1006.pdf.

[9] T. M. Jones. Inside the Linux 2.6 completely fair scheduler. Technical report, IBM, IBM developerWorks, 2009. http://www.ibm.com/developerworks/library/l-completely-fair-scheduler/.

[10] S. Keshav. How to read a paper. *SIGCOMM Comput. Commun. Rev.*, 37(3):83–84, July 2007.

[11] H. Koppelman, B. van Dijk, and G. van der Hoeven. Undergraduate research: A case study. In *Proceedings of the 16th Annual Joint Conference on Innovation and Technology in Computer Science Education*, ITiCSE '11, pages 288–292, New York, NY, USA, 2011. ACM.

[12] G. M. Landau and U. Vishkin. Fast string matching with k-differences. *J. Comput. Syst. Sci.*, 37(1):63–78, Aug. 1988.

[13] V. Leis, A. Kemper, and T. Neumann. The adaptive radix tree: Artful indexing for main-memory databases. In *Proceedings of the 2013 IEEE International Conference on Data Engineering (ICDE 2013)*, ICDE '13, pages 38–49, Washington, DC, USA, 2013. IEEE Computer Society.

[14] T. Li, D. Baumberger, and S. Hahn. Efficient and scalable multiprocessor fair scheduling using distributed weighted round-robin. *SIGPLAN Not.*, 44(4):65–74, Feb. 2009.

[15] R. D. Lins. Cyclic reference counting with lazy mark-scan. *Inf. Process. Lett.*, 44(4):215–220, Dec. 1992.

[16] A. D. Martínez, R. Wachenchauzer, and R. D. Lins. Cyclic reference counting with local mark-scan. *Inf. Process. Lett.*, 34(1):31–35, Feb. 1990.

[17] M. Mitzenmacher. The power of two choices in randomized load balancing. *IEEE Trans. Parallel Distrib. Syst.*, 12(10):1094–1104, Oct. 2001.

[18] D. Musicant, A. Kumar, D. Baldwin, and E. Walker. Mechanics of undergraduate research at liberal arts colleges: Lessons learned. *SIGCSE Bull.*, 39(1):65–66, Mar. 2007.

[19] B. Pfaff. Performance analysis of BSTs in system software. In *Proceedings of the Joint International Conference on Measurement and Modeling of Computer Systems*, SIGMETRICS '04/Performance '04, pages 410–411, New York, NY, USA, 2004. ACM.

[20] A. M. Quade. Promoting undergraduate research: A classroom model. In *Proceedings of the 9th Annual SIGCSE Conference on Innovation and Technology in Computer Science Education*, ITiCSE '04, pages 235–235, New York, NY, USA, 2004. ACM.

[21] J. Rao and K. A. Ross. Making b+-trees cache conscious in main memory. *SIGMOD Rec.*, 29(2):475–486, May 2000.

[22] S. Rao, D. Heger, and S. Pratt. Examining Linux 2.6 page-cache performance. In *Proceedings of the Linux Symposium (2005)*, pages 79–90, https://www.kernel.org/doc/ols/2005/ols2005v2-pages-87-98.pdf, 2005. IBM.

[23] M. A. Ruiz-Sanchez, E. W. Biersack, and W. Dabbous. Survey and taxonomy of ip address lookup algorithms. *Netwrk. Mag. of Global Internetwkg.*, 15(2):8–23, Mar. 2001.

[24] D. Shah, P. Giaccone, and B. Prabhakar. Efficient randomized algorithms for input-queued switch scheduling. *Micro, IEEE*, 22(1):10–18, Jan 2002.

[25] I. Stoica, R. Morris, D. Karger, M. F. Kaashoek, and H. Balakrishnan. Chord: A scalable peer-to-peer lookup service for internet applications. *SIGCOMM Comput. Commun. Rev.*, 31(4):149–160, Aug. 2001.

[26] R. A. Wagner and M. J. Fischer. The string-to-string correction problem. *J. ACM*, 21(1):168–173, Jan. 1974.

[27] N. Wirth. *Algorithms + Data Structures = Programs*. Prentice Hall PTR, Upper Saddle River, NJ, USA, 1978.

[28] B. Zorn. The measured cost of conservative garbage collection. *Softw. Pract. Exper.*, 23(7):733–756, July 1993.

Systematic Development of Dynamic Programming Algorithms Assisted by Interactive Visualization

J. Ángel Velázquez-Iturbide

ETS Ingeniería Informática
Universidad Rey Juan Carlos
28933 Móstoles, Madrid, España
angel.velazquez@urjc.es

Antonio Pérez-Carrasco

ETS Ingeniería Informática
Universidad Rey Juan Carlos
28933 Móstoles, Madrid, España
antonio.perez.carrasco@urjc.es

ABSTRACT

Dynamic programming is an algorithm design technique that is very difficult to learn. In this paper, we introduce an extension of the recursion visualization system SRec, intended to support some phases of the systematic development of dynamic programming algorithms: generation of recursion trees, checking redundancy in an adequate recursion tree, generation of the dependency graph associated to that recursion tree, and matching the graph to a table. These facilities require high degree of interactivity to be effective. We have successfully applied the new version of SRec to a number of dynamic programming algorithms in an algorithm course. We have also evaluated the performance of two groups of students in a recursion removal task: an experimental group using SRec and a control group using traditional means. Many of the results were similar for both groups. However, the experimental group did the task with higher confidence and was more efficient in some issues, while the control group was more persistent in one task.

General Terms

Algorithms, Design.

Keywords

Program visualization; SRec; recursion; dynamic programming.

1. INTRODUCTION

Algorithm courses are often structured around algorithm design techniques. A *de facto* consensus exists about the most important design techniques. If we browse well-known textbooks (e.g. [3][5][7][9][13]), they unanimously include chapters on divide and conquer, greedy algorithms, and dynamic programming, as well as chapters on other common techniques. Dynamic programming is a technique to solve optimization problems and is the most complex of the abovementioned techniques.

The paper presents an extension of the recursion visualization system SRec [17][18], intended to support the construction of dynamic programming algorithms. This extension is based on a graphical representation of recursion, namely recursion trees. Technically, SRec is a program visualization system [14], since it automatically generates visualizations as a side effect of running

Java methods. Note that the visualizations generated by the system often are not the most adequate to the user needs, thus the system must support user interaction with visualizations to produce more useful representations [16].

Studies on educational uses of software visualization have shown that a key issue in its success is students' engagement [8]. A number of generic recommendations have been given about how to make engagement concrete [11] but no definitive results have been established [15]. The extension of SRec described here comprises a number of functions. Some functions support understanding and analysis tasks (using terminology of the revised Bloom's taxonomy [1]). Moreover, the most interesting functions support application or creation tasks.

The contributions of the paper are threefold. Firstly, the extension of SRec capabilities to support several steps in the systematic development of dynamic programming algorithms (and, more generally, of optimization of redundant, multiple recursive algorithms). Secondly, the system gives support to application or creation tasks, which is an uncommon feature in program visualization tools. Thirdly, adequacy of SRec to these tasks is supported by an evaluation of students in a recursion removal task. Many of the results were similar for two groups of students, but students who used SRec did the task with higher confidence and were more efficient in some issues.

The paper is structured as follows. In Section 2, we present the background of the work presented here: the SRec system and dynamic programming. Section 3 and Section 4 describe the extensions included in SRec, and its generality and limitations, respectively. In Section 5, we describe the evaluation conducted. Finally, we present our conclusions.

2. BACKGROUND

We first introduce the system SRec and we then summarize how to design dynamic programming algorithms in a systematic way.

2.1 The SRec System

SRec is a program visualization system aimed at displaying recursive processes coded in Java [17][18]. The system provides several graphical representations: traces, the control stack and, above all, recursion trees. The user typically interacts with SRec by iteratively performing the following process: load a file – select a method – launch an execution – interact with the visualizations generated.

Interaction with visualizations is a key element of SRec to support understanding or analysis tasks [16]. The simplest interaction is the (manual) animation of an algorithm execution, which displays how the algorithm visualization varies as the execution advances (forward or backward). SRec also provides other ways of interacting with a visualization: change the graphical properties of

ITiCSE'16, July 09–13, 2016, Arequipa, Peru.
© 2016 ACM. ISBN 978-1-4503-4231-5/16/07...$15.00.
DOI: http://dx.doi.org/10.1145/2899415.2899450

the visualization components, filter the amount of data to display, adjust the zoom scale, change the relative order of data, browse a large visualization, look for specific data in a visualization, and give additional statistics about a visualization. In the rest of the paper, we include several figures that illustrate the results of these interactions.

SRec also provides several educational facilities, including the exportation of a visualization to a graphical file. Most figures contained in the paper were obtained using this function.

2.2 Dynamic Programming

Dynamic programming algorithms are obscure algorithms, very difficult to understand. They are not too complex, as they are iterative algorithms that compute values and store them in tables. However, their rationale is often difficult to grasp. Misconceptions about this technique have been studied elsewhere [6].

One approach to reduce difficulty in the learning of concepts or procedures is to decompose it into parts (for instance, advocated by the variation theory [10]). In particular, the development of dynamic programming algorithms may be simplified by decomposing it into a series of phases. We may follow a methodology formed by four phases [5, chap. 15][13, chap. 20]:

1. Characterize the structure of an optimal solution.
2. Develop a recursive algorithm that computes an optimal value in a top-down fashion.
3. Develop an equivalent, iterative algorithm that computes an optimal value in a bottom-up fashion. In turn, this phase may be decomposed into several steps:
   a. Check the redundancy of the recursive algorithm using a recursion tree.
   b. Analyze the redundancy pattern after converting the recursion tree into a dependency graph.
   c. Design a table capable to store the value of all the subproblems (that is, the results of the different recursive calls).
   d. Design an iterative algorithm that computes all the subproblems without redundancy, preserving their dependencies and using a table to store their results.
4. Extend the iterative algorithm to determine the decisions associated to the optimal value computed.

Steps of phase 3 are typically presented in intuitive terms in textbooks, but the interested reader may find them explained in full detail in technical publications [2][12]. We focus here on support to steps 3(a-c), where a recursive algorithm with redundancy is handled.

We illustrate the different issues addressed in this paper with the matrix-chain multiplication problem [3, chap. 8][5, chap. 15][13, chap. 20]. Two matrices can be multiplied if they have compatible dimensions $p \times q$ and $q \times r$, where p denotes the number of rows in the first matrix and q, the number of columns. Two important properties of matrix multiplication are: the product of two matrices with dimensions $p \times q$ and $q \times r$ requires $p \times q \times r$ scalar multiplications, and it is an associative operation. In the matrix-chain multiplication problem, n matrices of compatible dimensions are available and we want to determine an optimal multiplication ordering so that the number of scalar multiplications is minimum.

For example, consider four matrices A, B, C and D, of dimensions 5×2, 2×4, 4×1, and 1×7. An optimal multiplication order is (A(BC))D, that is, matrices B and C must be multiplied in the first place, then the resulting matrix must be multiplied by A and finally, by D. The required number of scalar multiplications is

$2 \cdot 4 \cdot 1 + 5 \cdot 2 \cdot 1 + 5 \cdot 1 \cdot 7 = 8 + 10 + 35 = 53$. Any other multiplication order of the four matrices requires more scalar multiplications.

The number of columns of any of the matrices to multiply (but the last one) must be equal to the number of rows of the following matrix. Consequently, the dimensions of n matrices may be represented in an array dim of $n+1$ cells.

A recursive solution to the problem first requires defining the more general problem of the optimal multiplication of matrices ranging from i to j. We may denote this generalized problem as $mult(i,j)$, Obviously, $mult(1,n)$ solves the complete problem of multiplying n matrices. Given this definition, the following recursive algorithm solves the original problem:

$$mult(i,i) = 0$$
$$mult(i,j) = \min_{i \leq k < j} \left\{ mult(i,k) + mult(k+1,j) + \dim_{i-1} \cdot \dim_k \cdot \dim_j \right\}$$
$$for\ 1 \leq i < j \leq n$$

Coded in Java:

```java
public static int chainedMult (int[] dim) {
    return mult(dim,1,dim.length-1);
}

private static int mult (int[] dim,
                         int i, int j) {
    if (i==j)
        return 0;
    else {
        int smallest = Integer.MAX_VALUE;
        for (int k=i; k<j; k++) {
            int result = mult(dim,i,k)
                       + mult(dim,k+1,j)
                       + dim[i-1]*dim[k]*dim[j];
            if (result < smallest)
                smallest = result;
        }
        return smallest;
    }
}
```

where *chainedMult* is the main method and *mult* is the auxiliary recursive method.

3. EXTENSION OF SREC

In this section, we present the new functions implemented in SRec. They are presented in temporal order of their use to develop a dynamic programming algorithm that solves the matrix-chain multiplication problem.

3.1 Redundancy Analysis

Some multiple recursive algorithms are asymptotically very efficient, such as divide-and-conquer sorting algorithms, but other multiple recursive algorithms are very inefficient. This behavior occurs when recursive calls do not represent independent subproblems but overlapping subproblems. Consequently, many calls are invoked more than once, recomputing their value in each invocation. Recursive algorithms designed for dynamic programming belong to this class of redundant algorithms.

In step 3(a) of the methodology outlined above, we must make sure that the recursive algorithm developed in step 2 is redundant. Note that this is the ultimate rationale of constructing efficient, dynamic programming algorithms: otherwise, we would use the recursive algorithms designed in step 2. As instructors, we often skip this step or we perform it intuitively, especially when the dynamic programming technique already is familiar to students. However, if we are rigorous, we should always check redundancy. Furthermore, it is very important to check it for the first dynamic programming algorithms presented to students.

We check redundancy on a particular recursion tree of the algorithm. Therefore, we must first generate a recursion tree and then check its redundancy. Although it is not difficult to select an adequate recursion tree, we often generate either a too small or a too large tree, and then we need to generate other trees before obtaining a good one.

In order to make easier the generation and selection of an adequate recursion tree, SRec was extended to allow generating several recursion trees in an atomic operation. The dialog to launch an execution was modified so that several test cases can be specified. As a consequence, several executions of the algorithm are launched and a visualization is displayed for each test case.

There are two ways of giving several values for a parameter:

- Specifying several values, separated by commas.
- Specifying a range of values, using the syntax 'lower value .. higher value'. This format is only allowed for integer values.

If multiple values are given to several parameters, the Cartesian product of all the values is computed, launching as many algorithm executions as different test cases result.

Consider again the matrix-chain multiplication problem. The size and shape of a recursion tree for this algorithm only depends on the number of matrices to multiply, not on their dimensions. Therefore,

we may specify a set of five executions of increasing complexity by entering in the dialog the dimensions of a set of 1, 2, 3, 4 and 5 arbitrary matrices to multiply (see Fig. 1).

Fig. 2 shows the user interface of SRec, where the editor panel was hidden in order to leave more room for the two visualization panels. The lower panel contains the five recursion trees generated using the dialog displayed in Fig. 1. The tree corresponding to the multiplication of five matrices was selected and framed in blue. It is also displayed in the upper panel on a larger scale, so that the user may interact with it.

The upper panel displays a recursion tree through a global+detail interface [4]. This interface is composed of two views, global and detail, which occupy the lower and the higher part of the panel, respectively. The contents of the global view of the tree are unreadable but its shape can be distinguished. The part of the tree displayed in the global view is framed (in black) and is displayed in the detail view at larger resolution. The resulting interface allows both navigating through the whole visualization and examining selected parts in detail.

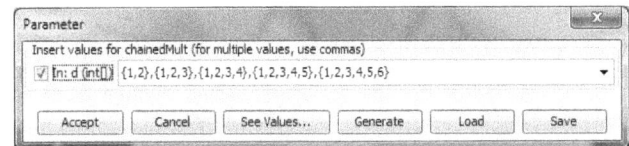

Figure 1. Dialog where five test cases are specified for the matrix-chain multiplication problem.

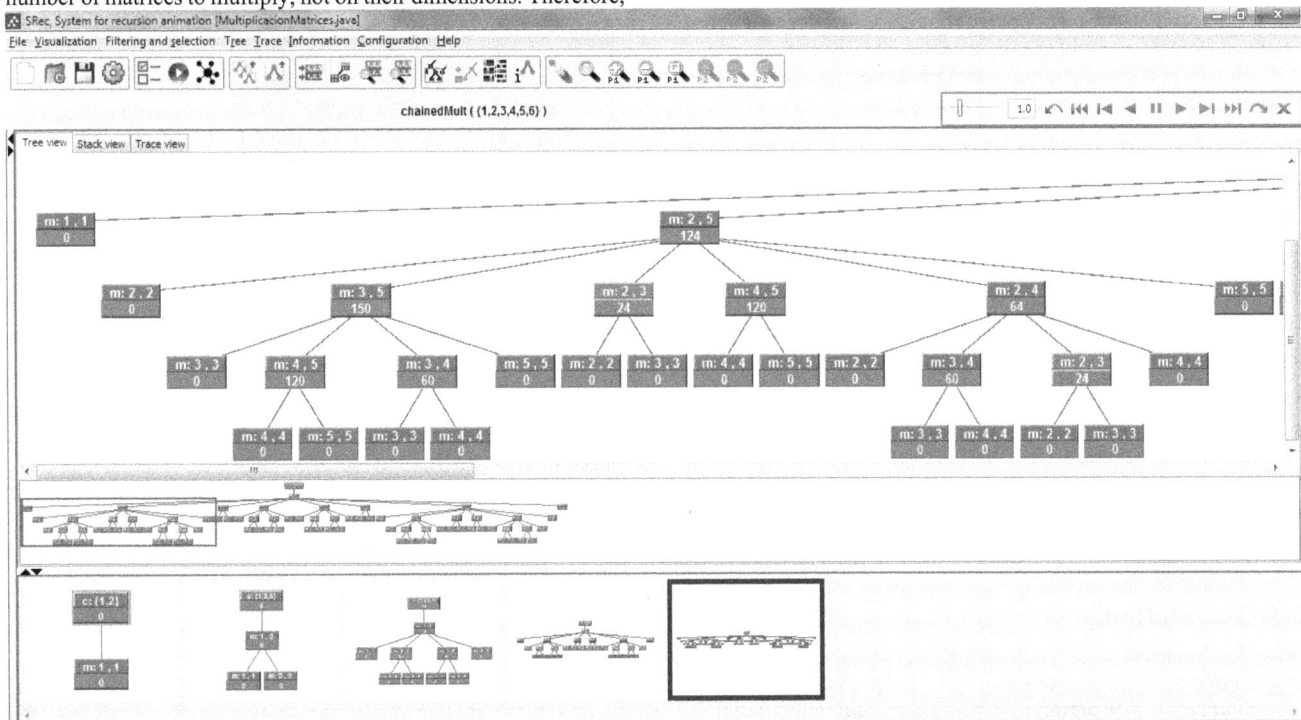

Figure 2. Capture of the SRec user interface, showing five recursion trees for the matrix-chain multiplication problem.

We want to remark that the visualization shown in Fig. 2 is the result of first generating automatically a visualization and then performing several interactions on the visualization. The first interaction operation was to filter some parameters. In particular, the array *dim* was filtered because it does not change from call to call of the method *m*. Therefore, the array is only displayed in the initial call to the main method *chainedMult*, yielding a more compact and readable visualization.

The second interaction with the resulting visualization was zooming to make it fit better the panel.

The third interaction performed was to check redundancy, resulting in the visualization displayed in Fig. 2. (Note that the lower part of the panel already provided a hint on the algorithm redundancy, as the growth rate of the recursion tree seems to be exponential.) SRec supports the visual analysis of redundancy with a function to search recursive calls. The user specifies concrete values and SRec highlights in a different color all the nodes in the recursion tree that match the search criterion. In Fig. 2, we looked for all the occurrences of recursive call *mult*(2,3), and the corresponding nodes were highlighted in light brown. These nodes can be seen in both the global view (5 nodes) and the detailed view (2 nodes).

The search function is flexible: it allows only specifying the value of some parameters, but also the output value. A complementary function restores the original color to the nodes highlighted.

3.2 Dependency Graphs

After checking that a recursive call is redundant, redundancy must be removed. A number of techniques exist for this goal, being tabulation the most common in dynamic programming algorithms. The resulting algorithms are iterative algorithms that store the value of the different subproblems in a table. The algorithm solves subproblems in a sequential order that preserves the dependencies existing in the original algorithm.

Dependencies among subproblems can be more easily determined by first generating a dependency graph [2][12], i.e. an acyclic directed graph. The dependency graph associated to a recursion tree is built by joining all the occurrences of each call in a single node, preserving arcs between calls.

Fig. 3(a) shows the dependency graph automatically generated by SRec from the recursion tree displayed in Fig. 2. Note that the nodes are distributed in a (relatively) arbitrary way.

SRec allows the programmer to relocate freely the nodes while trying to identify any redundancy pattern. Fig. 3(b) shows the result of distributing the nodes so that calls that have the same value for the first parameter are placed on the same row, and calls with the same value for the second parameter are placed on the same column. Careful inspection of the resulting graph shows that each node depends on all the nodes placed at its left or below.

3.3 Tabulation

Once the dependency pattern among recursive calls is known, the programmer must determine a sequential order of computation of the subproblems that preserves dependencies, and must design a table capable to store the values of all the subproblems. SRec also gives support to this task.

The programmer may let SRec distribute automatically the dependency graph in a one- or bi-dimensional table, where he/she must only specify its dimensions. However, the result is often poorly constructive (similarly to the previous automatic distribution of nodes of the dependency graph).

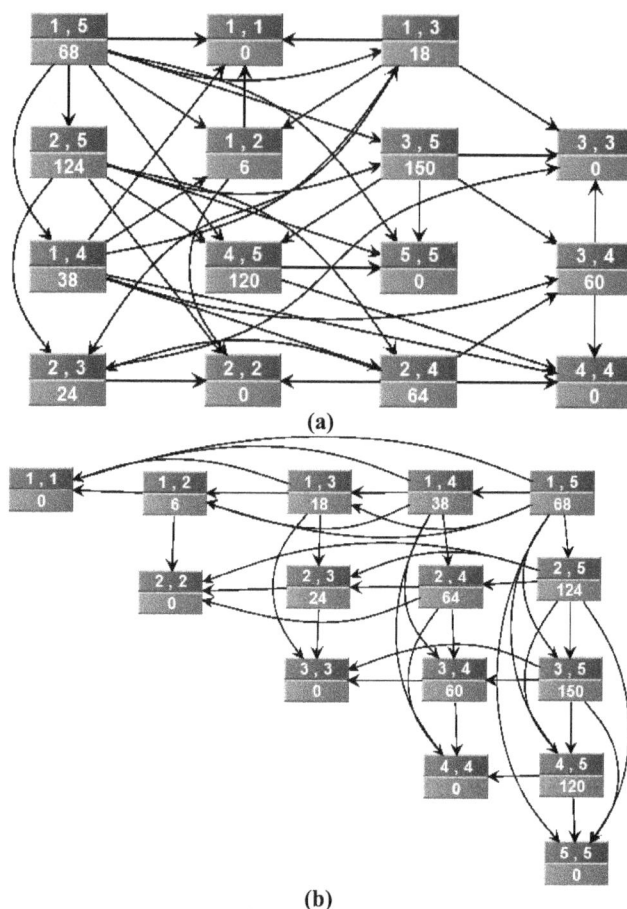

(a)

(b)

Figure 3. Dependency graphs for the matrix-chain multiplication problem obtained from the previous recursion tree (a) automatically, and (b) after manually rearranging the nodes.

SRec provides a function that allows the user to specify with expressions how to determine the recursive call corresponding to each cell in the table. Fig. 4 shows the dialog for this function, where the expression *i*-1 is associated to each row *y* of the table, and expression *j*-1 is associated to each column *x*.

Fig. 5 shows the result of specifying different mapping expressions. The table resulting from the mapping given above is displayed in Fig. 5(b), being a minimum-size square table with as many rows and columns as matrices to multiply. However, in a first approach, the programmer would probably enter the simpler expressions *y=i*, *x=j*. In this case, the table has one row and one column in excess that will host no useful value (see Fig. 5(a)). Analyzing the table, it is easy to deduce that the optimal expressions are *y=i*-1, *x=j*-1.

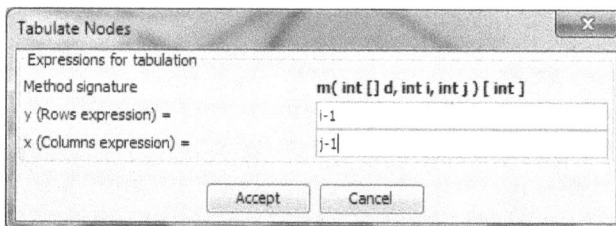

Figure 4. Dialog to specify expressions mapping parameters into table cells for the matrix-chain multiplication problem.

(a)

(b)

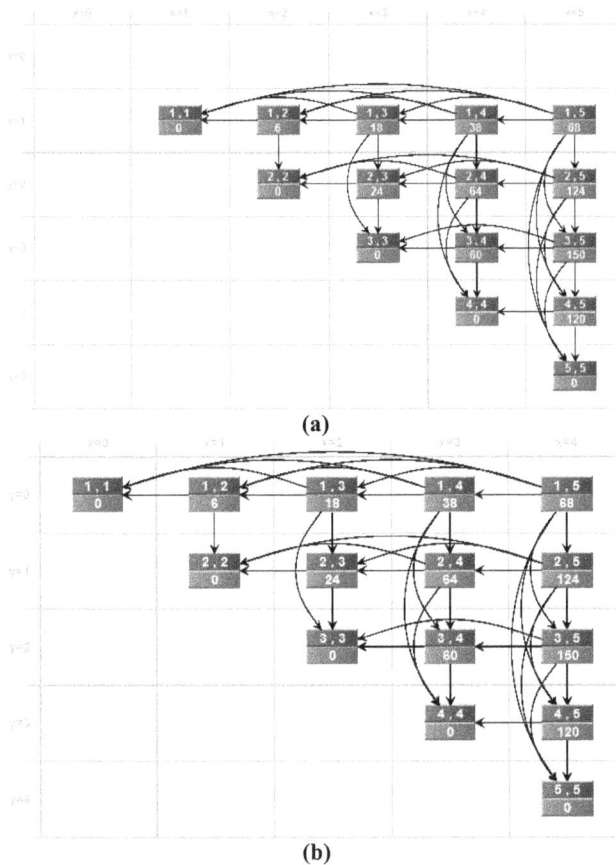

Figure 3. Tables generated for the matrix-chain multiplication problem by means of mappings (a) $y=i$, $x=j$, and (b) $y= i$-1, $x = j$-1.

Next, the programmer will determine a sequential computation order that preserves dependencies. Finally, an iterative algorithm will be constructed from the following elements: the sequential computation order, the original equations (which describe the numeric dependency among values) and the table. This task is often trivial and can be done using any programming tool.

For our example, there are several valid orders: by rows bottom-up, by columns from left to right, or even by diagonals. If we choose the computation order by rows bottom-up (and left to right within each row), the corresponding iterative algorithm can be coded as follows:

```
public static int chainedMult (int[] dim) {
    int[][] table
            = new int[dim.length-1][dim.length-1];
    for (int y=table.length-1; y>=0; y--) {
        table[y][y] = 0;
        for (int x=y+1; x<table.length; x++) {
            table[y][x] = Integer.MAX_VALUE;
            for (int k=y; k<x; k++) {
                int cost = table[y][k] + table[k+1][x]
                        + dim[y]*dim[k+1]*dim[x+1];
                if (cost<table[y][x])
                    table[y][x] = cost;
            }
        }
    }
    return table[0][table.length-1];
}
```

4. GENERALITY AND LIMITATIONS

We have tested the extension of SRec with a number of recursive versions of dynamic programming algorithms, including the most common in algorithm textbooks. A non-exhaustive list follows:

- Matrix-chain multiplication (the problem used in this paper).
- 0/1 knapsack [3 chap. 8][9, chap. 6][13, chap. 20].
- Longest common subsequence [5, chap. 15].
- Edit distance [9, chap. 6].
- Multistage graph [7, chap. 5].
- Single-source shortest path (Bellman-Ford's algorithm [5, chap. 24][9, chap. 6][13, chap. 20]).

The SRec extension presented here has some limitations for tabulation. It allows handling any dynamic programming algorithm provided the following constraints are satisfied:

- Mapping expressions only depend on the current values of parameters, not on their initial values.
- The number of varying parameters in the recursive algorithm must be one or two. For algorithms with three or more varying parameters, a 2D visualization cannot represent adequately any table. For instance, the recursive algorithm for the all-pairs shortest paths problem (Floyd's algorithm [3, chap. 8][5, chap. 25] [13, chap. 20]) has three varying parameters. (Afterwards, an analysis of dependencies and invariant computations in the tri-dimensional array allows deducing that a matrix is enough.)

5. EXPERIENCE

Last autumn we used the new version of SRec in the elective fourth-year course "Advanced Algorithms" offered at our University to Computer Science students. The dynamic programming technique was addressed in two steps:

1. A first chapter on removal of redundant recursion. The methodology outlined in Section 2.2 is presented in detail and exercised. It is adapted to derive either tabulated or memoized algorithms. Algorithms are numeric, for instance, recursive declarations of Fibonacci or combinatorial numbers.
2. A second chapter on the dynamic programming technique. The emphasis is put on the design of recursive algorithms, a non-trivial task. Recursion removal is exclusively accomplished using tabulation.

Students must solve one assignment per chapter. We made use of the assignment on recursion removal to evaluate the effectiveness of the extension of SRec. Students attended a laboratory session, which was two hours long. They were given a redundant algorithm, and were asked to convert it into two efficient algorithms (a tabulated algorithm and a memoized one). Students were given a report outline, and had one week to complete the work and submit it to the instructor through the virtual campus. In addition, they had to submit a (partial) report at the end of the laboratory session.

Students were evenly divided into two groups (an experimental group using SRec and a control group) by using their grades in previous assignments. We gathered 13 reports from students in the experimental group and 20 from students in the control group.

Both groups had similar performance and behavior in many regards. We summarize the main differences found:

- Results about redundancy check are mixed. Redundancy was checked by a higher percentage of students in the experimental group than in the control group (92% vs. 74%). However, only one third of students in the experiment group used the search function provided by SRec. Within students who checked redundancy manually, students in the control group searched redundant nodes more exhaustively (86% vs. 43%).

- About 25% of the reports from the control group contain errors in the dependency graph derived from a recursion tree.
- Students of the experimental group delivered more table declarations in Java (92% vs. 55% of students). However, only one student from the experimental group used mapping expressions to design his/her table.
- The same percentage of students in both groups contributed with optimized algorithms, but the experimental group was more productive: being fewer students, they elaborated 13 algorithms vs. 9 algorithms by the control group.
- Students in the experimental group were more efficient, submitting their partial report an average of 7 minutes before their colleagues of the control group.

6. CONCLUSIONS

We have presented an extension of the system SRec intended to support the design of dynamic programing algorithms. Some functions enrich the set of operations defined over recursion trees, whereas other extensions involve new graphical representations (namely, dependency graphs and tables). A key issue for the effectiveness of this extension is the high interactivity of SRec. In the paper, we have shown the need for operations to, at least, filter data, adjust the zoom, navigate very large visualizations, search nodes, and rearrange nodes.

We have also presented the main results of an evaluation of this new version of SRec in an algorithm course. In many issues, there were no relevant differences between the experimental and the control group. We may highlight that reports from the experimental group contained fewer mistakes, checked redundancy more often, elaborated more software products (table declarations, tabulated or memoized algorithms), and submitted their reports in shorter time. However, only one third of students in the experimental group checked redundancy using the function provided by SRec, and only one student used the function to design a table using expressions. Within students who checked redundancy, the control group checked it more exhaustively than the experimental group.

In summary, SRec assists adequately students in the systematic removal of recursion in redundant, multiple recursive algorithms. Students who used SRec had the expected benefits of a software tool, such as higher reliability and productivity. However, we also detected the need to reconsider the approach used to implement one task (to check redundancy), and the need to train students in advanced features (table design based on expressions).

It is remarkable to note that students used SRec in a subsequent assignment aimed at developing a dynamic programming algorithm. The major difficulty was in the design of the recursive algorithm, not in the steps supported by SRec. Finally, there is room for additional enhancements or extensions of SRec, e.g. supporting the semiautomatic generation of iterative algorithms from tables.

7. ACKNOWLEDGMENTS

This work was supported by research grants TIN2011-29542-C02-01 and TIN2015-66731-C2-1-R of the Ministry of Economy and Competitiveness, S2013/ICE-2715 of the Regional Government of Madrid, and 30VCPIGI15 of the Universidad Rey Juan Carlos.

8. REFERENCES

[1] Anderson, L. W., Krathwohl, D. R., Airasian, P. W., Cruikshank, K. A, Mayer, R. E., Pintrich, P. R., Raths, J. and Wittrock, M. C. 2001. *A Taxonomy for Learning, Teaching, and Assessing: A Revision of Bloom's Taxonomy of Educational Objectives*. Longman, New York, NY.

[2] Bird, R. S. Tabulation techniques for recursive programs. *ACM Computing Surveys* 12, 4 (Dec. 1980) 403-417.

[3] Brassard, G., and Bratley, P. 1996. *Fundamentals of Algorithmics*. Prentice-Hall, Englewood Cliffs, NJ.

[4] Cockburn, A., Karlson, A., and Bederson, B. B. 2008. A review of overview+detail, zooming, and focus+context interfaces. *ACM Computing Surveys* 41, 1 (Dec.) article 2.

[5] Cormen, T. H., Leiserson, C. E., Rivest, R. L., and Stein, C. 2009. *Introduction to Algorithms*, 3rd ed. MIT Press, Cambridge, MA.

[6] Danielsiek, H., Paul, W., and Vahrenhold, J. 2012. Detecting and understanding students' misconceptions related to algorithms and data structures. In *Proceedings of the 43rd Technical Symposium on Computer Science Education*. SIGCSE 2012. ACM, New York, NY, 21-26.

[7] Horowitz, E., and Sahni, S. 1978. *Fundamentals of Computer Algorithms*. Pitman.

[8] Hundhausen, C., Douglas, S., and Stasko, J. 2002. A meta-study of algorithm visualization effectiveness. *Journal of Visual Languages and Computing* 13, 3 (2002) 259–290.

[9] Kleinberg, J., and Tardos, É. 2006. *Algorithm Design*. Pearson Addison-Wesley, Boston, MA.

[10] Marton F., and Tsui, A. B. M. 2004. *Classroom Discourse and the Space of Learning*. Routledge, New York, NY.

[11] Naps, T., Roessling, G., Almstrum, V., Dann, W., Fleischer, R., Hundhausen, C., Korhonen, A., Malmi, L., McNally, M., Rodger, S., and Velázquez-Iturbide, J. Á. 2003. Exploring the role of visualization and engagement in computer science education. *SIGCSE Bulletin* 35, 2 (June 2003) 131-152.

[12] Pettorossi, A. 1984. A powerful strategy for deriving efficient programs by transformation. In *Proceedings of the ACM Symposium on Lisp and Functional Programming*. ACM, New York, NY, 273-281.

[13] Sahni, S. 2005. *Data Structures, Algorithms and Applications in Java*. Silicon Press Summit, NJ.

[14] Stasko, J., Domingue, J., Brown, M. H., and Price, B. A. Eds. 1998. *Software Visualization*. MIT Press, Cambridge, MA.

[15] Urquiza-Fuentes, J., and Velázquez-Iturbide, J. Á. 2009. A survey of successful evaluations of program visualization and algorithm animation systems. *ACM Transactions on Computing Education* 9, 2 (Jun. 2009) article 9.

[16] Velázquez-Iturbide, J. Á., and Pérez-Carrasco, A. 2010. InfoVis interaction techniques in animation of recursive programs. *Algorithms* 3, 1 (Mar. 2010) 76-91.

[17] Velázquez-Iturbide, J. Á., Pérez-Carrasco, A., and Urquiza-Fuentes, J. 2008. SRec: An animation system of recursion for algorithm courses. In *Proceedings of the 13th Annual Conference on Innovation and Technology in Computer Science Education*. ITiCSE 2008. ACM, New York, NY, 225-229.

[18] Velázquez-Iturbide, J. Á., Pérez-Carrasco, A., and Urquiza-Fuentes, J. 2009. A design of automatic visualizations for divide-and-conquer algorithms. *Electronic Notes in Theoretical Computer Science*, 224 (2009), 159-167.

Lessons Learned on Computer Science Teachers Professional Development

M. Cecilia Martínez
Centro de Investigaciones
FFyH/CONICET, Universidad
Nacional de Córdoba
Córdoba, Argentina
cecimart@gmail.com

Marcos J. Gómez
Logic, Interaction and
Intelligent Systems Group
FAMAF, Universidad Nacional
de Córdoba
Córdoba, Argentina
mgomez4@famaf.unc.edu.ar

Marco Moresi
Computer Science Section
FAMAF, Universidad Nacional
de Córdoba
Córdoba, Argentina
mrc.moresi@gmail.com

Luciana Benotti
Logic, Interaction and
Intelligent Systems Group
FAMAF, Universidad Nacional
de Córdoba/CONICET
Córdoba, Argentina
benotti@famaf.unc.edu.ar

ABSTRACT

This paper describes an introductory Computer Science (CS) Professional Development (PD) course for K-12 teachers in Argentina that integrates pedagogical content knowledge and teacher classroom practice. We analyzed teachers' learning of what CS entails and the implementation of inquiry-based programming lessons in their schools. Based on pre and post teachers surveys and classroom observations, we found that most teachers learned about the CS object of study and about fundamental programming concepts such as conditionals, loops, variables, etc. Teachers were more likely to replicate the same activities they experienced during PD workshops in their classrooms than to produce their own. Teachers who had a previous background on CS provided in-depth explanations of CS concepts to their students while other teachers superficially introduced the content knowledge. We describe PD activities and characteristics that could explain teachers' learning and incorporation of programming lessons. Findings imply that a PD program that integrates pedagogical content knowledge and teachers classroom practice can effectively improve inquiry-based CS teaching, but may be insufficient preparation for teachers with no previous background on CS.

CCS Concepts

•Social and professional topics → K-12 education;

ITiCSE '16, July 09-13, 2016, Arequipa, Peru

ⓒ 2016 ACM. ISBN 978-1-4503-4231-5/16/07. . . $15.00

DOI: http://dx.doi.org/10.1145/2899415.2899460

Keywords

Computer science K-12 outreach, experimental evaluation, Computer Science (CS) Professional Development (PD)

1. INTRODUCTION

As many countries are moving forward in their efforts to introduce Computer Science (CS) massively into the mandatory school curriculum, one topic of debate between academics, policy makers and the whole educational community is who is going to teach CS in schools and how are teachers going to be prepared. Currently, one of the major challenges for teaching CS is the lack of teacher subject knowledge [8].

While most researchers and policymakers agree that teacher certification degrees offered by Universities are the best option to prepare highly qualified teachers [13], some countries are considering training teachers "on the job" (such as the UK, New Zealand, the US and Germany) [14, 7, 11, 4]. These countries face the dilemma to move forward with their CS curriculum reform whit a shortage of CS professionals willing to move into a teaching path. Hence, they opt for in service training or short term Professional Development (PD). In Argentina, for the last five years members of the National Secretary of Science and Productive Innovation together with National Universities have been promoting the teaching of CS, and in particular CS programming, in mandatory education.

Researchers have documented that effective PD programs, that include an explicit focus on the subject matter and analyze student thinking, can promote teacher learning [6]. Requiring teacher active learning through workshops or study groups within a coherent program where learning goals, content and activities are aligned, has significant effects on positively changing teacher learning [6]. When it comes to teacher PD in technology, first hand experiences with technology, combined with observation and analysis of other teachers using technology are effective strategies to change teachers beliefs and practices about technology [15]. While research on effective PD and on introducing technology into teachers practices is vast, little is known about teacher pedagogical and conceptual learning during CS PD programs. Also, we ignore how teaching practice can change as a result of these programs. With the purpose of studying both teacher CS learning and contributing to promote best CS education PD practices, we designed an exploratory study to analyze how the PD learning experiences impacted teaching practices in CS, and how teachers changed their beliefs about the subject area. We offered a 50 hours introductory course on teaching programming at the Universidad Nacional de Córdoba, in Argentina for K-12 teachers. The course required 10 hours of teaching classroom practice at their schools. Advanced CS college students provided coaching. In this paper, we describe the innovative characteristics of our PD course and show how teachers implemented CS programming lessons learned at our workshops. Our findings can inform the design of effective CS PD programs. In the next section, we describe previous studies that analyzed CS PD events. Then, we present the design of our PD plan supported by theoretical foundations. The section that follows, explains the methodology of the study. In a fifth section, we present our findings. Finally we draw some conclusions and discuss implications.

2. PREVIOUS WORK

The current literature on CS teacher development, whether it is on teacher preparation or in-service training, points out at two major structural issues. First, there is no consensus on what CS education involves and what the minimum requirements should be [8]. Second, it is not clear which higher education institutions should offer teacher preparation programs. CS teachers preparation programs in Argentina and other countries do not have a clear definition of the field and confuse CS with other subject areas such as Technology Education/Educational Technology (TE/ET), Industrial or Instructional Technology (IT), Management Information Systems (MIS), or even the use of computers to support learning in other subject areas (CSTA)[1].

Second, current CS or informatics teachers (in the few schools where the subject is taught) do not necessarily have CS backgrounds with many being from "ICT", which focuses more on training computer users rather than software developers [14, 7, 4]. Most CS teachers are science or math teachers who register on in-service programs, online courses or short PD offers to teach CS [7, 11, 12] .

A third issue that is not particular to our country is that Argentina can not currently cover the demand of programmers and CS engineers the industry requires, thus is it very difficult to attract the workforce towards a traditionally lower pay sector such as education.

Given these structural conditions (lack of coherence among CS preparation programs, current CS teachers with heterogeneous CS backgrounds, lack of CS professionals interested in teaching) many countries have considered preparing teachers through short-term PD. However, there are no enough documented experiences that can provide some information about how these initiatives resulted. Previous work showed that a short training experience in the format

of summer workshops could not modify the teaching of CS. Moreover, teachers with no previous knowledge of CS are more likely to drop out of these training courses [4]. During an experience in Los Angeles School District where teachers had two weeks of summer course on Advance Placement in Computer Sciences (APCS) teachers reported successfully engaging their students in introductory CS ideas. Moreover, in a few years, the program doubled the amount of schools offering APCS courses in the district [7], not a minor milestone when many CS courses are closing in the US because so few students register [3]. However, teachers expressed a concern on their ability to teach more advanced APCS concepts and advocated for further training opportunities especially teachers with the least prior CS knowledge [7]. In theses experiences, teachers expressed confidence in launching the course, but reported trying "to stay one step ahead of students" as the course progressed and they had to present more difficult concepts to the class.

Thompson and Bell [14] reported that teachers self reported programming experience and confidence on teaching CS has improved in New Zealand after two years of the CS curriculum implementation in the country. Surveyed teachers took a variety of PD training offered by non governmental organizations. While overall studies seemed to show that teachers gained confidence in CS education, the research literature is not clear on how teachers incorporated what they learned in their classrooms and what relation can be established between PD activities and teaching practices.

In the next section we describe the design of our PD program to explain possible links between PD activities, teacher learning and classroom implementation.

3. A COMPREHENSIVE APPROACH TO TEACHER PD IN COMPUTER SCIENCE

For the last three years we have organized an introductory CS programming teaching PD course for K to 12 educators at the Universidad Nacional de Córdoba in Argentina. In 2015 the National Ministry of Science decided to replicate our course in 10 other national universities in the country in order to engage more public universities in a national effort to increase the number of CS teachers.

We offered a 50 hours long course with classes distributed across one academic semester. 40 of these hours were taught at the University. We hold 4 to 6 hours workshops every three weeks for the teachers. In addition, teachers had to complete 10 hours of "teaching classroom practice" in their own schools delivering CS lessons to their students. That is, teachers had to teach one hour of CS per every 4 hours of PD. Advanced CS college students, who we call "coaches", worked with each teacher individually for 4 extra hours reviewing lesson plans and providing in class support. Coaches help teachers pick the programming platform that teachers prefer and propose them different strategies for focusing their lessons on programming concepts instead of doing it on the selected programming platform.

We require teachers to register with another teacher from their school to reduce teacher isolation in implementing innovations. Research suggests that the most important predictor of teachers using computers in their schools is the computer use of their peers [5]. We offer teachers a vast array of curricular resources including CS inquiry based lessons plans specially developed for this course.

---

[1]CSTA National Secondary School Computer Science Survey: Comparison of Results from 2005, 2007, 2009, 2011, and 2013 Surveys

Three modules: Robot, Chatbot, and Animations; purposely address fundamental programming concepts such as sequence, event, conditional, cycle, variable, method, parameter, among others. Technological content knowledge is also present in our course as we promote the use of different computer platforms specifically designed to teach programming such as the well known Alice, Code.org tutorials, and our own developed open sources teaching CS platforms: Chatbot which allows programming chat automatons [2], and UNC++Duino, a multi programming language platform for Arduino robot programming [1]. We repeatedly teach the same CS concepts in all platforms, thus focusing on a conceptual approach to learning CS, with the goal that teachers do not become platform dependent. We strongly convey the message that teaching programming is not about using a platform or learning a particular programming language, but about learning CS concepts and computational thinking skills.

Each of the teacher meetings follow an inquiry based approach. In a short first 5 minutes segment of the meeting, we introduce the particularities of the selected platform. Before introducing any CS concept, we give teachers a programming challenge. For example, developing an obstacle dodger robot using the robot programming software, UNC++Duino. We require teachers to solve the challenge in groups of 4 to 5 people promoting teacher collaboration. Coaches walk around the room to assist teachers and prevent anxiety and frustration. Intentionally, we train coaches to avoid giving teachers the solutions but rather to guide them with questions. Based on the literature, we know that most teachers have a tendency to teach with the same teaching strategies they were taught, and that learning pedagogical theories can not compete with what teachers experienced as students.We also know that most teachers did not have previous experiences in learning CS in their schools, thus, we want to create an inquiry based and meaningful first time, first hand programming learning experience [15] that can have impact in their future teaching. In addition, to encourage teachers implementing programming lessons into their classrooms, we invite teachers and their students to an end of the year programming fair at the University. In this fair, students of participant schools bring their programming productions (video games, animations, chat automata or robots). The fair has proven to be an important incentive for teachers and students to bring programming projects into their schools. Teaching teachers through programming challenges allows the integration of CS concepts, inquiry based pedagogy and technology. University coaches support these complex learning process enriched with in classroom practical experience. This format permits preparing teachers in pedagogical technological content knowledge [10] necessary to provide high quality CS teaching.

4. STUDY DESIGN

We wanted to know what teachers with different CS backgrounds were learning in our introductory CS programming teaching PD course offered in 2014 and 2015. Specifically we wanted to document what CS concepts and teaching strategies teachers were selecting to teach their lessons and how these strategies relate to the activities we offered in the PD hours. An exploratory research was best to answer these open ended questions.

4.1 Sample

Our course was open to all primary and secondary school teachers who were willing to teach CS in their classrooms. We advertised it in social networks, the university web page and local news TV channel. Therefore, our sample included self selected teachers who had access to these channels of communication. The course was free of charge for teachers and financed by Google in Education in 2014 and by the National Ministry of Science in 2015. All the requirements to complete the course were informed up front. Google, the National Ministry of Science and National University endorsement provided strong legitimacy for the course.

46 teachers completed the course in 2014 and 60 did in 2015. For several reasons (personal, institutional, and cognitive), about 10% of the registered teachers could not fulfill all the requirements to complete the course. Teachers' background and profile was heterogeneous. Table 1 summarizes the profile of the teachers who registered for our course. Primary school teachers in Argentina have a general preparation in pedagogy and primary school content knowledge. Most primary school teacher preparation programs include one course called "technology" and another course called "audiovisual media". But none include formal CS programming content. Among the secondary schools teachers, 22% of them held a degree in a CS related field such as programming technician, informatics technician, or bachelors degree in CS systems or alike. 20% of the teachers held a tertiary degree on educational technology. Most educational technology programs prepare teachers to integrate ICT in schools, but do not address CS subject matter. The rest of the teachers held degrees in math, language arts, arts, and chemistry education. Many of the teachers who held a degree on educational technology were teaching subjects such as computers labs or informatics. In a previous study [9] we documented that some CS high school courses offered general ICT preparation, most likely because of lack of teachers' CS content and pedagogical knowledge.

Teachers general profile	%
Public School Teachers	75%
Secondary school teachers	60%
Primary school teachers	20%
Secondary and tertiary school teachers	20%
Teachers with a degree in CS related fields	22%
Teachers with a degree in educational technology	20%
Teachers teaching technology courses	13%
Teachers teaching CS related courses	25%
Teachers teaching Mathematics	20%

Table 1: Summary of sample profile (N=106)

4.2 Data Collection and Analysis

Teachers completed three online surveys that included 27 open ended and multiple choice questions. The first survey, completed upon registering for the course, gathered teachers information on previous preparation and current position.

After reviewing the literature on variables and conditions that affect teachers appropriation of curriculum and pedagogical innovation; we designed the second and third questionnaires that were used as teachers pre and post survey. The survey gathered information on teaching styles, use of computers, and teachers representations about CS.

All teachers responded to the mandatory first and second questionnaires. However, in spite of emphasizing to teachers that completing the end of the course questionnaire was important, only half of them did so. Besides the questionnaires, the coaches wrote semi structured classroom observations after every lesson they participated. The observations included items such as students and school demographics, CS content knowledge selected for the lesson, description of teachers expertise delivering the content, description of teaching strategies, best moment of the lesson, and things that could have been done differently. In all, we gathered 73 coaches observations for both the 2014 and 2015 editions. Because teachers registered in pairs, some of them also decided to deliver the lessons in pairs, in those cases, the coaches wrote only one observation for both teachers. Teachers questionnaires and coaches observations were the main source of data for this paper.

We created frequency tables for the multiple choice responses and analyzed qualitative data inductively. We identified emerging themes upon reading teachers and coaches discourses and from these themes we constructed analytic categories. 9 members of our team, including the coaches and research assistants, coded coaches observations. To ensure reliability, each observation was coded more than one time by another researcher rather than the coach who wrote the reflection.

Teachers questionnaires were analyzed in a spreadsheet also inductively assigning emerging codes to the teachers responses. We compared pre and post survey responses only among teachers who responded both questionnaires. Peer and multiple coding of data and triangulation of teachers questionnaires with the coaches observation contributed to the validity of our study as we could contrast and compare our emerging themes with different sources of data. As a result of this analysis, we developed broad emerging themes that helped us answers some of our research questions.

5. FINDINGS

In this section we describe our findings with respect to what the teachers learned during the PD training and how they were able to apply it in their classrooms.

5.1 Teachers learning Computer Science

A comparison of pre and and post teacher survey responses showed that teachers changed their definition about the discipline CS and increased the number of CS concepts they reported to know.

Because teacher understanding of the discipline is central to teach CS, we asked teachers with an open ended question in the pre and post survey what CS was for them. We classified teachers responses and grouped answers in 6 emerging themes. Table 2 compares teachers answers.

Emerging theme	Pre-test	Post-test
Imprecise definition of CS	18.5%	0%
Theory in informatics	33%	35%
Computer programming	22%	15%
Information processing	15%	8%
ICT	11%	0%
Discipline to solve problems	0%	38%

Table 2: What teachers think CS is (N=54)

About 30% of the teachers answered in both pre and post survey that CS included the theories, disciplines and sciences that study informatics. About 20% mentioned that CS was related to programming. 18% of teachers gave broad and unclear definitions of CS in the pre survey. For example, teachers mentioned: "CS is about electronics", "CS is about the computer", "CS is a broad discipline". None of the teachers answered in such broad and unclear terms in the post survey. 11% of the teachers answered in the pre survey only that CS was related to ICT. Answers coded in this category included for example: "CS is related to ICT use", "CS is the science that study technology". Again, no teachers provided such answers in the post survey. Teachers viewing CS as a discipline that solve problems through technology, automation of tasks, and informatics systems, was an emerging answer exclusively in the post survey (38%). The wording "solves problems" was present in all of the answers coded in this category. For example some teachers mentioned: "CS is the discipline that helps solving all kinds of complex problems with computers in the areas of health, education, and security".

During our teachers meetings we emphasized repeatedly that CS was not ICT and contrasted programming with ICT cognitive demands evidencing the logical thinking of programming vs the mechanical use of ICT. We believe that such emphasis resulted in teachers dissociating CS with ICT. Our approach to teaching programming through inquiry based programming challenges might have contributed to teachers perception of CS as a problem solving discipline.

Teachers also increased the reported number of CS topics they were familiar with between the pre and post survey. In the pre survey, half the teachers reported having no previous knowledge on any CS topics or having office automation skills (ex: I am a savvy internet and word processor user). In the post survey all teachers recalled PD content such as basic programming, basic algorithms, animation techniques with Alice, etc. They also mentioned specific concepts such as variables, conditionals, loops, parameter, attributes, etc.; all concepts learned along the PD course.

Survey responses indicate that teachers are gaining some understanding of CS subject matter, specially among teachers who had little or no previous knowledge on computer programming. Besides teachers learning of the subject, we also wanted to know how teachers brought what they learned into their classroom.

5.2 Bringing programming into the classroom

Teachers reported using more programming platforms in their classroom in the post survey than in the pre survey. Table 3 shows responses to the multiple choice question "What computer platforms do you use during your classes?" Teachers could choose more than one option.

Options	Pre-test	Post-test
My students do not use the computers	26%	16%
Word, spreadsheet, slide processors	71%	64%
Audiovisual production software	51.5%	48%
Spreadsheets or database programs	29%	40%
Programming languages platforms	27%	64%
Internet search	65%	78%

Table 3: Programs used in the classrooms (N=54)

We also asked teachers what percentage of what they usually learn in PD courses they bring into the classroom. Two times more teachers reported bringing between 90% and 100% of what they learned in "this" PD course into the classroom, suggesting that the characteristics of this PD course had effect in their teaching.

Besides teachers' self reported data on the survey, we want to describe different situations that contributed to our qualitative analysis. Every year about 300 students from participating schools come to our end of the year fair to show their animations and video games. Students' work is an important evidence showing that teachers are bringing programming into their classroom.

Teachers analysis of school CS curriculum required in our workshops plus supplying several CS teaching materials might have contributed to encourage teachers, and specially teachers with CS background who were not teaching programming, to change their practice. During our workshops teachers engaged in heated conversations when we asked what CS content knowledge schools should be teaching. Some teachers defended teaching to use commercial software, or preparing the workforce in one industrial programming language. Others advocated for teaching open source resources or teaching the basics of programming.

Because many teachers thought that teaching programming was not possible, this course represented a hinge moment in their professional career. One teacher expressed in the last survey:

"I started this course in a very particular moment regarding my profession: I am a System Analyst graduated in 1993, but started to "play" with computers in 1981-1982. I became proficient with Logo, Basic, Cobol, Pascal, Clipper, dBase, Fox. I was "disappointed" and a little frustrated, tired and "stuck" in my knowledge. This course made me fall in love again with my profession, I discovered that you can always start over and that that old knowledge can be dusted and rescued to support new content. I have much to thank the people of the National University of Cordoba because they literally changed my line of work and professional life."

Many other teachers have also told us similar stories. A great amount of teachers holding a CS background are not teaching CS because of curriculum mandates for ICT integration or for being unaware of pedagogical strategies for teaching CS in an engaging way.

5.3 Teachers implementation of the lessons

Coaches observations analysis showed differences in the way teachers brought CS into their classrooms. While most teachers selected the educational platform Alice to program animations or video games, 30% of the teachers taught CS concepts through robot programming and the rest used Chatbot or unplugged activities. Sometimes, teachers used more than one resource.

48% of the teachers used the same inquiry based programming challenges we used during our workshops. Teachers reproduction of the teaching practices they experienced as students is consistent with previous teacher learning theories. In this case, because a big part of the PD activities was devoted to solving challenges, could explain why a large percentage of teachers took these challenges to their classrooms However, 15% of the teachers presented students with open challenges that did little to develop understanding of CS concepts. For example, some teachers simply asked their

students to make an animation using Alice, or a dialogue using Chatbot. In these lessons, the teachers did not design the tasks to focus on specific CS concepts. Lack of subject matter domain could explain why these teachers posed such broad challenges.

We did showed teachers other teaching platforms such as a Code.org and told them about the step-by-step lesson plans offered by them. However, it is clear that these strategies we "told" teachers did not compete with the strategies teachers experienced first hand. Only 30% of the teachers used strategies we showed but not experienced in the workshops, and 20% used unplugged activities we practiced during PD hours.

Two high school teachers at different schools decided to assemble and program their own robots using Arduino boards creating a "Programming Club" at their school. In this case teachers' previous technical knowledge combined with the new initiative resulted in a school based innovation.

5.4 Teachers explanations of CS concepts

Analyzing classroom observations we identified that in 75% of the lessons teachers tried to incorporate and explain fundamental CS concepts learned in the workshops. Analyzing each of the observed lessons we identified different levels of expertise explaining the concepts. Table 4 summarizes these levels in the 73 classroom observations.

Teacher could not explain the concept	5%
Teacher explained the concept by memory	3%
Teacher explained the concept correctly but commits a simple mistake	17%
Teacher explained the concept correctly	35%
Teacher explained the concept using analogies, examples and practical situations	23%
Other	13%

Table 4: Teachers explainations of CS concepts

58% of teachers explained CS concepts effectively. As an example of teachers explanation we cite one of the coaches reflections

"This is the first time that I see a teacher explaining the concept of methods and parameters. And he did it perfectly. Based on tutorial videos, but without using the video in class, he explained students how to make characters walk in Alice. He used method "pose" to capture all necessary movements. First, he explained how to create a method and asked how they thought they should do for a character to walk towards an object..."

The most frequent CS concepts that teachers were conditionals, loops, variable, sequence, methods, random numbers, objects and events. Teachers taught at least three of these concepts in about 70% of the lessons we observed. Parameters, constant, binary numbers, networks and other topics were less frequent and presented in about 30% of the lessons we observed. The inquiry based approach allowed to integrate more than one concept in a lesson. Almost 20% of the teachers confused CS concepts with platform commands. For example one of the teachers who decided to work with the Alice platform, confused the command of moving gallery objects, and choosing a scene as CS concepts. Out of 10 teachers who could not teach CS concepts correctly, 7 of them had no previous CS background, but 3 of them did, including one primary school teacher with a certification in Educational Informatics. We are positive that this certification prepares teachers to use educational software in schools but do not address CS concepts. This finding suggest that teachers with no previous background on CS need longer teacher preparation than a 50 hours course.

6. CONCLUSIONS

Conducting a PD course for two consecutive years we have learned important lessons about teacher CS learning and classroom implementation of CS programming. Most teachers who come to our course have wrong or weak ideas about what CS is. For the last twenty years educational authorities and curriculum experts have conveyed the message that teaching CS is teaching office automation and ICT. Some teachers have CS background, but because of this curricular orientation they strongly believe do not have to teach CS. In many cases, because teachers had difficult CS learning experiences themselves and are unaware of newly developed teaching resources, they simply cannot imagine how to teach programming to primary and high school students. Understanding teachers beliefs and needs is necessary to design effective PD programs. Learning about the discipline CS and the importance of teaching it to promote both cognitive development and digital literacy, is our first challenge as trainers. Reflection and debates on teachers' practices contributed to change teachers pre notions about teaching CS. Teachers also learned about pedagogical content knowledge with first hand experiences on inquiry based programming teaching. Learning the pedagogy is as important as learning CS concepts because simply teaching algorithms and definitions can not promote meaningful learning of the discipline. Solving programming challenges during PD hours, and having a coach at their schools for their teaching practice, provided teachers with pedagogical resources to bring programming into their classroom. Requiring teacher classroom practices as part of the PD hours, was essential to promote classroom implementation. However, this training was insufficient to prepare teachers with no previous background on CS as they weakly addressed CS concepts in their classrooms. While we observed that teachers with previous CS background were better at explaining CS concepts in their classroom, it is unclear to us what specific CS background would be best to become an effective CS teacher. One strong limitation of this study is that we only observed lessons where the teachers were required to teach programming as part of the PD hours. In addition, all observed lessons were conducted in the presence of coaches who supported teachers and could have influence teachers' practices. Thus, we do not know about long term effects of our course beyond PD requirements. Nevertheless, the evidence presented here shows that a CS PD course that includes first hand programming experiences, curricular debates among teachers, and classroom practice with coaches support, contributed to increase teacher learning of CS and implementation of inquiry based programming lessons in schools.

Acknowledgments

This work was partially funded by the grants PICT-2014-1833, PICT-2012-712, PDTS-CIN-CONICET-2015-172, and PID-2012-2013-R18.

7. REFERENCES

[1] L. Benotti, M. J. Gomez, and C. Martinez. UNC++Duino: Learning to program in Python and C++ starting from blocks. In *Proceedings of the Conference on Robotics in Education*, 2016.

[2] L. Benotti, M. C. Martínez, and F. Schapachnik. Engaging high school students using chatbots. In *Proceedings of the 2014 Conference on Innovation and Technology in Computer Science Education*, pages 63–68, New York, NY, USA, 2014. ACM.

[3] J. Cuny. Finding 10,000 teachers. *CSTA Voice*, 5(6):1–2, 2010.

[4] B. Ericson, M. Guzdial, and M. Biggers. Improving secondary CS education: progress and problems. In *SIGCSE Bulletin*, volume 39, pages 298–301, 2007.

[5] P. A. Ertmer. Teacher pedagogical beliefs: The final frontier in our quest for technology integration? *Educational technology research and development*, 53(4):25–39, 2005.

[6] M. S. Garet, A. C. Porter, L. Desimone, B. F. Birman, and K. S. Yoon. What makes PD effective? Results from a national sample of teachers. *American educational research journal*, 38(4):915–945, 2001.

[7] J. Goode. If you build teachers, will students come? the role of teachers in broadening computer science learning for urban youth. *Journal of Educational Computing Research*, 36(1):65–88, 2007.

[8] K. Lang, R. Galanos, J. Goode, D. Seehorn, F. Trees, P. Phillips, and C. Stephenson. Bugs in the system: CS teacher certification in the US. *The CSTA and The ACM*, 2013.

[9] M. C. Martinez and M. E. Echeveste. Representaciones de estudiantes de primaria y secundaria sobre las ciencias de la computación y su oficio. *Revista de Educación a Distancia*, (46), 2015.

[10] P. Mishra and M. Koehler. Technological pedagogical content knowledge: A framework for teacher knowledge. *The Teachers College Record*, 108(6):1017–1054, 2006.

[11] A. Mühling, P. Hubwieser, and T. Brinda. Exploring teachers' attitudes towards object oriented modelling and programming in secondary schools. In *Proc of the Sixth international workshop on Computing education research*, pages 59–68. ACM, 2010.

[12] L. Ni and M. Guzdial. Who am I?: understanding high school CS teachers' professional identity. In *Proc of the Technical Symposium on Computer Science Education*, pages 499–504. ACM, 2012.

[13] N. Ragonis, O. Hazzan, and J. Gal-Ezer. A survey of CS teacher preparation programs in Israel tells us: CS deserves a designated high school teacher preparation! In *Proceedings of the 41st Symposium on Computer Science Education*, pages 401–405. ACM, 2010.

[14] D. Thompson and T. Bell. Adoption of new CS high school standards by New Zealand teachers. In *Proc of the Workshop in Primary and Secondary Computing Education*, pages 87–90. ACM, 2013.

[15] M. Windschitl and K. Sahl. Tracing teachers' use of technology in a laptop computer school: The interplay of teacher beliefs, social dynamics, and institutional culture. *American educational research journal*, 39(1):165–205, 2002.

Out of the Comfort Zone: Embedding Entrepreneurship in a Cohort of Computer Science Doctoral Students

Oonagh McGee, Matthew Forshaw,
Barry Hodgson
Newcastle University, Newcastle upon Tyne, UK
{first.last}@newcastle.ac.uk

Steve Caughey
Arjuna Technologies Ltd
Newcastle upon Tyne, UK
steve.caughey@arjuna.com

ABSTRACT

The study of entrepreneurship, and widening debate on providing Computer Science (CS) students with skills for employment, has led to a rise in programmes offering additional skills including entrepreneurship, presentation skills and communication skills. This paper provides an early stage reflection of the design, development and delivery of a bespoke entrepreneurship module, designed to empower students and provide them with skills to build successful startup businesses. This course was designed specifically for Computer Science and Mathematics students, within a cohort-learning environment. Students were guided through the principles of the Ostervalder Business Model Canvas, allocated into groups and asked to devise a business idea, iterating this throughout an eight week period. Students were provided with support from teaching staff alongside weekly coaching from successful entrepreneurs and flipped classroom tuition. The teaching methods employed in the Professional Skills course are not traditionally used in Computer Science education and students reported a number of challenges in completing the module. These included team dynamics, time and investment required and the requirement for engagement with stakeholders. All of these issues highlight the unique nature and practical application of the course material, presenting the opportunity for reflection of the success and impact of the module. In addition, the tutors of the course reflect on their experience of delivering the course for the first time, and their response to student feedback. We also provide advice on reproducing the course.

CCS Concepts

•Social and professional topics → Computing education programs; Employment issues;

Keywords

Entrepreneurship; startups; industry engagement

ITiCSE '16, July 09 - 13, 2016, Arequipa, Peru

© 2016 Copyright held by the owner/author(s). Publication rights licensed to ACM.
ISBN 978-1-4503-4231-5/16/07...$15.00

DOI: http://dx.doi.org/10.1145/2899415.2899469

1. INTRODUCTION

The importance of entrepreneurship as a basis for business growth, economic activity and employability are well understood [10]. The efficacy of entrepreneurship education has been widely debated, with scholars arguing that some traits cannot be taught within a classroom environment [14]. However, it is acknowledged that certain skills and processes valuable to business creation, can be embedded within educational programs, if correct methods are employed.

There exists widespread support in the literature advocating action-based and experiential approaches to entrepreneurship education [11, 8]. Williams-Middleton *et al* argue; *"In order to provide the conditions for experience-based learning, entrepreneurship education needs to provide possibilities for both entrepreneurial experience and reflection"* [15]. Despite increased interest in the area, a lack of integrated experience-based approaches in CS education are observed [9, 8].

Within this paper we outline the development and delivery of a bespoke entrepreneurship module, Professional Skills, which aims to develop entrepreneurial skills within a cohort of doctoral students from Computer Science and Mathematics backgrounds. Our students are brought together in a Centre for Doctoral Training (CDT) in Cloud Computing for Big Data, established to meet significant and growing demand for skilled graduates in an area we will term the 'Big Data Economy' [4]. Furthermore, the contribution of micro firms to the economy is huge and the introduction of entrepreneurial skills into the curriculum could be critical to the success of graduates' future careers [16].

In the paper we seek to analyse the impact of our course, considering student feedback, assessing our current teaching methods, and providing details of future curriculum adaptations. Issues which arose throughout the course are discussed, including stakeholder engagement, group dynamics and investment of time. We also discuss the potential challenges of reproducibility and provide suggestions for educators wishing to replicate this course in their own institutions.

The remainder of this paper is organised as follows. Section 2 considers relevant literature relating to entrepreneurship, employability and the integration of industry partners within CS education. In Section 3 we provide a description of the course structure and assessment. Section 4 comprises of student feedback and key areas for consideration. This is followed by reflections from industry partners in Section 5, and staff reflections in Section 6. We consider issues of reproducibility in Section 7, offering guidelines for course delivery at other institutions. Finally, we conclude and outline areas of future work in Section 8.

2. RELATED WORK

A number of initiatives have sought to equip Computer Science students with employability [5] and entrepreneurship skills. These initiatives vary in the following dimensions; *a)* authenticity of business environment – ranging from simulated environments to those incubating real businesses, *b)* emphasis on entrepreneurial versus software engineering activities, *c)* extent of industry involvement.

Hickey *et al* [6] document three years of a web and mobile development ten-week summer school in the context of entrepreneurship, combining both entrepreneurial and software development activities. Our work differs in its insessional and compulsory delivery, depth of industry collaboration, and focus on entrepreneurial processes, e.g. business model iteration and stakeholder engagement.

Venture Creation Programs (VCPs) [8] are a class of entrepreneurship programme characterised by a longer programme duration (typically 1-2 years) with an emphasis on the creation of a viable business from University research.

Whilst other initiatives seek to fast-track and equip students with skills for more immediate employment, our students are enrolled on a four-year doctoral programme. By fostering entrepreneurial thinking and providing students with the necessary tools to set up and develop their business ideas at an early stage within their education, we hope to enable and empower the students to consider research commercialisation opportunities throughout their studies, and entrepreneurship as a viable future employment option.

There are a number of challenges in integrating entrepreneurship within the curriculum [3], which we consider within this paper. In addition, issues around group work are further compounded by different learning styles [7].

3. COURSE DESCRIPTION

The aim of the Professional Skills course (or *'module'*) is to develop students' knowledge, understanding and practical expertise around enterprise culture. Students learn the key fundamentals of entrepreneurial thinking, by gaining the key tools required in forming a successful startup business.

Crucially, students are expected to step out of the classroom (and their comfort zone) in order to engage with external stakeholders, including industry experts, finance specialists, local businesses and potential customers. This is a key component of the module and critical to their understanding of the importance of communication skills and relationship forming, outside of academia. These interactions inform the iterations of the business canvas and support students in forming a robust business plan, providing evidence for their idea, which is crucial for pitches to investors.

The course employs the techniques of the flipped classroom model, combining interactive, hands-on workshops and weekly iterations of the Business Model Canvas [12, 2].

Another unique aspect of the module is the formation of the teaching team. Two members of staff have been involved in a successful software spin-out company, one a current entrepreneur. This unique blend of expertise and skills affords the students to be exposed to individuals with a wide knowledge base to create a simulated incubator environment.

3.1 Industry experts

The students are exposed to industry experts each week, who provide a vital role in being a *critical friend* and mentor for the groups. In order for the sessions to be of maximum benefit to the students, they begin with the industry expert describing their own entrepreneurial journey, highlighting the challenges they faced and how they combatted these. Giving the students this insight enables them to consider a number of issues, previously unexplored within their academic education programs. Although other programs involve industry partners and feature guest seminars, ours is unique in that the industry experts are integral to the learning experience.

3.2 Structure

The Professional Skills module runs for eight weeks, with a four-hour scheduled lectured slot in each week. Assessment for the course is 100% project based. Students are allocated a further ten hours of guided independent study within which they may conduct stakeholder engagement, hold group meetings, prepare for weekly presentations, etc.

The introductory session aims to familiarise the students with the business model canvas. It exposes the students to basic principles of startup formation, guides them through the Business Model Canvas and begins to develop their entrepreneurial thinking.

Following this initial introduction, the students are required to develop their business idea, having undertaken market analysis with external and internal stakeholders. During subsequent weekly sessions, the students present their current business model iteration, receive feedback, and gain insight from an industry expert. The final week's session comprises of a student pitch to a panel of industrial partners, posing as potential investors.

3.3 Assessment

Students are assessed through a combination of individual and group exercises.

Group Report: A substantial group written report represents 60% of the overall course mark. Within this report, students should document their process iterating around their business idea, culminating in a concrete business plan.

Individual Reflective Log: Acknowledging the importance of reflection in developing entrepreneurship [15], we assess students on a reflective log document contributing 20% of the overall course mark. This is a reflective written piece charting a student's personal learning in the course, and identifying particular issues that have affected them.

Each week, students are expected to reflect on the process, and use this to inform subsequent iterations. These reflective reports are contributed to a Virtual Learning Environment (VLE) monitored by each member of the teaching team. The Individual Reflective Log exercise is introduced as a mechanism to provide students with formative feedback throughout the course, as well as providing teaching staff with insights into the running the course. This in turn inform the focus of subsequent sessions.

Reflections from each week of the course are collated, and supplemented with additional discussion to summarise the student's experience across the whole course.

The Final Pitch: In the final week of the course, each group delivers their final pitch to the teaching team and a panel of industry guests. Each team is assessed on the presentation of their idea, articulation of market research, consideration of finance and future plans, contributing 20% of the course mark.

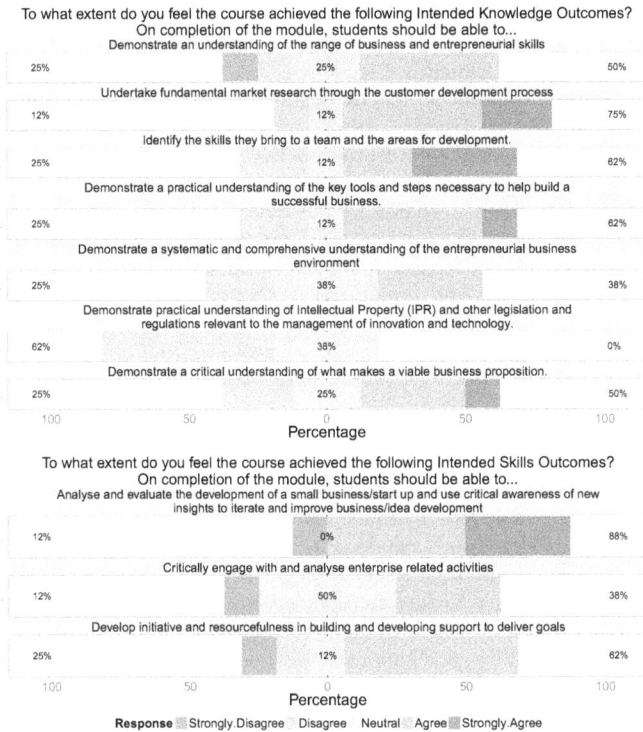

Figure 1: Student feedback on Intended Knowledge and Skills Outcomes

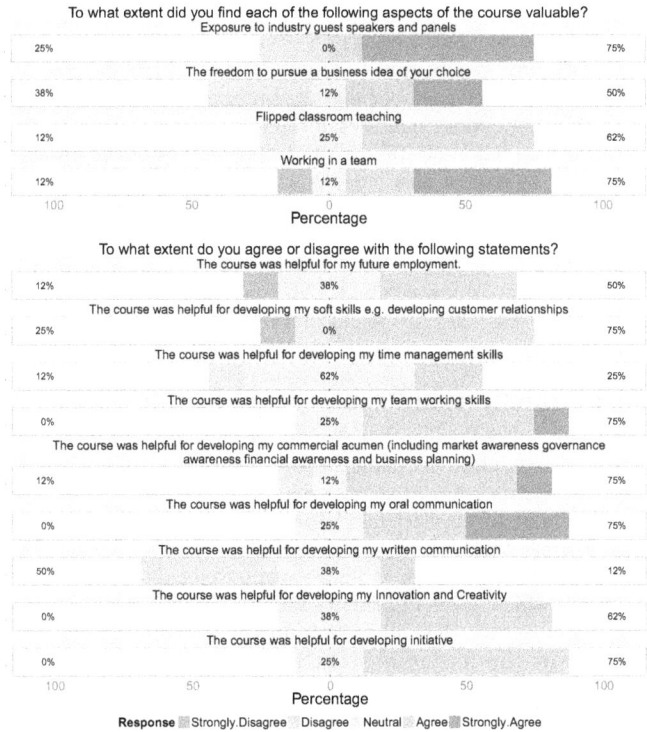

Figure 2: Follow-up Questionnaire Results

4. EVALUATING COURSE IMPACT USING STUDENT FEEDBACK

Within this section we examine free-text responses to the University-administered student module questionnaire. In order to substantiate our initial findings, and afford the students the additional opportunity to reflect on their learning experience, we also administered a follow-on survey to students six months after course completion. Results from the follow-on survey, on a five-point Likert scale, with eight out of ten students responding, are presented in Figures 1 and 2.

For the purpose of discussion, we have included quotes from the module survey, and follow-on survey responses below. A number of issues, initially revealed by the module feedback, are explored in light of the follow-on feedback. We draw inferences on the impact of the module and select areas for future research, including; group dynamics and teamwork, Intellectual Property; investment of time and exposure to industry experts.

4.1 Group Dynamics

Group dynamics featured heavily in the module feedback, demonstrating the need for further exploration of this area. The results identified that some students felt that they were unable to identify the skills they brought to a team and their own areas for development. This could be as a result of being in a task-driven environment, affecting their overall learning experience of group work. This echoes previous research on task-driven cohorts [13], where individuals take on the role required to enable the task to be completed, rather than one which would challenge them or allow them to develop. However, the follow-on survey identified that

the students had found the teamwork aspect of the module valuable, stating that they found the course useful for developing teamworking skills. This suggests that, despite the challenges, teamwork is an essential and important component of the module.

The students also commented on the fact that they had not been able to select their own teams:

"We should be able to choose who is in our group, and there should be a procedure if someone isn't willing to work with you in the group."

As the course leader allocated the students into teams, the typical behaviours of organically formed teams might not have been able to come to the surface. Bains [1] highlights that within the startup environment, *"team efficiency is the key to success"* as close working and flexibility are critical within the formation stages of a business.

In response to this feedback the following change has now been implemented for future years. The groups will now be selected five months in advance of the course start date and communicated to students, to enable them to develop ideas and relationships in advance. The students were working within groups on two parallel modules; one which required them to utilise their technical skills by applying them to a research problem, the other a research skills module which reinforced important research techniques and presentation skills. The issue of group fatigue may have been a contributing factor to their discontent with group work overall, rather than being an issue specific to this module. By communicating group selection in advance, this will streamline, and create synergy, across the curriculum to improve the student experience.

After a year, we will review the group selection process

in light of additional student feedback. In addition we will set weekly review meetings to review individual logs and identify any group issues earlier, working with groups to ensure that each member is contributing.

Previously, some members of the team presented the business ideas each week, taking the responsibility of the group. In order to redress this balance we will now ask each group to identify the contribution of team members. Where a team member does not take part in the presentation of the business idea or the pitch, they will be asked to answer questions on e.g. finance, stakeholder engagement. We hope that this will alleviate some of the issues around fairness within groups and perceived levels of effort.

4.2 Intellectual Property and Business Law

"I think that the incorporation of law into the module would be really useful. [...] whether it be in industry or in academia where patents arise from research."

The issue of Intellectual Property Rights was reported as a key area, which we had failed to explicitly cover within the taught course sessions. We have acknowledged this as a limitation, which needs immediate attention, if the students are able to progress their ideas beyond the initial design stage. To rectify this for future years, and provide a valuable and rounded learning experience, we will seek the support of a business law expert and a member of the University's Business Development team to give an overview of the patent process and issues surrounding academic spin-outs. This will afford us to strengthen the student's knowledge of an area of critical importance within business formation. This is especially relevant in a fast-paced technology environment.

4.3 Idea Selection and Buy-in

"I feel that while the module was very fun, a lot of time was spent on the business cycle for a product that we all knew was never going to materialise; and this was a big demotivator"

As the course was delivered in a simulated environment, some students felt that their ideas were not going to be developed into a viable product. In the first year we asked students to formulate business ideas approximately four weeks in advance, but stressed the importance of the learning experience and knowledge acquisition, rather than a focus on developing a real and successful business. In addition, as the students were already assigned to groups there was a limit to the formation of ideas in some groups.

In future years we plan to implement the following: Students will be asked to asked to formulate ideas during induction week in September and bring these to a workshop in January. During this workshop the students will vote on three ideas to develop as a business and select which group they would like to join. This enables students to join a team and develop an idea which they have chosen. We will also provide further examples of successful academic spin-out companies and explain that there would be support available, for students who wished to pursue their business outside of the course structure.

4.4 Investment of time

"The true entrepreneur is a doer, not a dreamer."

The Professional Skills module is designed to simulate a real business environment, and this includes a significant investment of time and effort, on behalf of the students.

This level of dedication is expected within small busi-

nesses, but the students saw this as a disproportionate level of work in relation to the number of credits they received for the module. Educating students, on the challenges and investment required in the early stages of business formation, was reinforced by each guest speaker from industry. The industry experts commented on this during their feedback to the students, cementing the importance of passion, belief and investment in making a business a success.

"The time and effort required for this module is not proportional to the credits available. I spend 2-3 days a week meeting people and organising presentations. I don't think that I need to be as long as it was; with an ever fractured group motivation was very low towards the final weeks. This certainly was not a reflection of the quality of teaching that we received."

The above quote also highlights the issue of motivation, which is explored further in the 'Buy-In' Section 4.3.

"This module ended up taking an disproportionate amount of time out of my schedule. It may benefit from a slightly different structure - maybe a 2-3 week intensive course."

Whilst some organisations do operate their business formation courses in an intensive setting, we elected to construct a course which allowed the students additional time for stakeholder development, iteration of ideas and reflection. We feel these are key aspects which would be lost in a shorter, intensive environment. In addition we are restricted by the semester system within the University and an intensive first year programme, designed to equip the students with a multitude of skills, before they are able to progress to the research stage of their doctorate.

4.5 Exposure to industry experts

One area of importance, in light of both formal University course evaluation and the follow on survey, is the integration of industry partners. 75% of respondents identified this as being an important part of the course and felt that the module had succeeded in attaining this learning outcome. This highlights the importance of industry collaboration, exposure to entrepreneurs and the involvement of experts in delivering this important set of skills.

In light of this feedback, we are seeking to develop and embed industry panels further. We will do this by selecting a core team of entrepreneurs to support the students throughout the iterations of their ideas; strengthening the simulated incubator environment.

Whilst many of the entrepreneurs were sourced through local and existing collaborative relationships this involvement could be realised by an outreach programme.

4.6 Stakeholder Engagement

"Pity that we need to go out and speak with people - I think the fact that we are all mathematicians and computer scientists means that by our very nature, we are introverts."

A number of the students reported that they had difficulties in meeting the requirements of weekly stakeholder engagement, a key component of the module, citing that the expectation was too much.

"The recommendation of speaking to at least 10 potential customers/clients per week was too much."

A key issue, as identified from the initial feedback, was communication with external stakeholders; a critical aspect of forming a successful business and meeting the market research aspect of the course. This is a central component and will not be changed, although the tutors have acknowledged that in forthcoming years, there will be further support offered to combat these issues. One potential way to support this would be for the staff members to provide accompaniment on the initial customer visits, in order to enable the students to observe and practice conducting this essential part of the module. The rationale behind this is that once students gain confidence in speaking to stakeholders, they should then feel empowered to continue this activity without further guidance. We followed up on this, and asked students if the course had met the intended outcome of developing soft skills e.g. developing customer relationships.

Within the responses some students felt that the course had not met these needs. However, a possible limitation should be acknowledged here. The inclusion of the example of customer relationships may have unintentionally linked the notion of soft skills with their previous negative experience of having to engage with external stakeholders; one of their main perceived difficulties. Upon reflection of this further feedback, we compared the results of this question with one related to the development of oral communication skills. Conversely the students reported that the course had improved their oral communication skills, suggesting a positive impact of the focus of the course outcomes and the requirement for students to present their business ideas to both internal and external stakeholders. This skill, in combination with teamwork and an understanding of business formation are undoubtedly beneficial for future employment.

4.7 Skills for Employment

The Professional Skills course aims to teach students the skills required to start a business, but the underlying skills and attributes are applicable to all areas of employment. Within the follow-on feedback students reported that the course was useful for developing their commercial acumen, team working and oral communication; skills valued by prospective employers. This was a positive impact of the course, demonstrating the importance of embedding these skills within a CS curriculum. Traditionally these skills are not adequately integrated within CS education programmes [5], and students are often expected to gain these from additional programmes provided by other university departments, such as the Careers Service.

5. INDUSTRY REFLECTIONS

During the evaluation of the impact of our course, we contacted industry partners and asked them to provide a reflection of the course and their involvement.

"As an IT service provider to business it is essential that our staff can understand and identify organisations' needs and then architect and deliver the technology to enable them. All too often we are having to educate our (post) graduate starters from a very low level of understanding about how to make this connection between business/entrepreneurial need and technology so it was a breath of fresh air to be involved in a project that provided this perspective on a technology course. The enthusiasm of the students was clear and the progress they made on their concepts from initial thoughts to final presentation was great to see. Their appreciation of the business & entrepreneurial aspects of technology projects should be of great benefit to their future careers.", Andrew Robson, Perfect Image Ltd.

This reflection supports our argument that the course is

able to provide students with the necessary skills to work within industry, saving organisations time and investment.

"I was invited to take part in the professional skills course as part of the CDT overall course and was great to see real business input into the CDT course rather than being treat as an academic only exercise. Using the latest lean startup ideas and helping students link their research to real-world problems and understand how to incorporate this into a potential business will stand them in good stead as they embark on their PhD studies and I'm sure will enable them all to make a real impact on the local economy.", Dominic Murphy, CEO, Geek Talent

Our partners highlight the importance of the link between business and academic knowledge for developing industry-ready graduates, able to contribute to the economy.

6. STAFF REFLECTIONS

Following the delivery of the first year of the course, we asked the course leader to reflect, taking in account student feedback. The following quote identifies that some of the issues raised by the students, could have been directly influenced by their engagement with the course.

"Given the background and motivation of students on the CDT for Cloud Computing for Big Data, the feedback for this module illustrates how many students found the course content outside of their comfort zone. Students found it challenging to gather data from real stakeholders (to go out and talk to potential customers, etc.) They found group work difficult in a context where the focus was not on technical issues but on business issues. Some students thought the course lacked intellectual stimulation – although, as well as offering a general grounding in business thinking the course offered experiential benefits (building relationships and networks) which are directly aligned to the participation and contribution of the student. Without real engagement with the business idea and willingness to participate and contribute, the intellectual reward will undoubtedly be less rich."

A core member of the teaching staff is an alumni of the institution, who participates on a part-time basis to support entrepreneurship within the University. He highlights the importance of developing skills within graduates, drawing on the difference between UK and US educational structures.

"As a UK entrepreneur who has spent quite a lot of time visiting the US and talking to entrepreneurs there, it has frequently struck me that in the UK PhD students are being trained for academic careers whilst in the US they are being trained for business careers. Yet in both cases the majority end up in business. In addition in the US, PhD students in tech mix frequently with people of their own generation who have succeeded as entrepreneurs. This instills an attitude of "well, if they can do it, so can I". The Professional Skills program at Newcastle University addresses both of these issues. It encourages students to consider their business opportunities (and provides them with some fundamental business skills) and exposes them to people from a similar background to their own who have created successful companies."

7. CHALLENGES TO REPRODUCIBILITY

In developing this curriculum, we seek to provide guidance to other practitioners seeking to replicate the course within their institutions. Whilst we acknowledge there are a number of unique factors which contributed to the success of the module within our institution, we support and encourage the adoption of the methods at other institutions, arguing that the course can be reproduced.

Investment of time: The most significant challenge for reproducing the course, is the significant investment of time required by tutors at both the planning stages and during classroom sessions. Whilst the course is advertised as employing a 'flipped classroom' technique, the amount of contact time should not be underestimated. Within the initial business canvas mapping and idea selection, we utilised the skills of two external consultants alongside four tutors. Whilst we appreciate that not all institutions have the resources to enable this level of interaction, we believe that the skills required to deliver this session could be acquired by tutors and enthusiastic postgraduate students. By holding an initial skills training session, guided by additional reading and an understanding of the Business Model Canvas, the course could be delivered by one tutor with the support of graduate assistants. In addition, the tutors could offer the opportunity as a learning experience for business law/MBA students within another faculty, strengthening cross-faculty relationships and providing the opportunity for inter-disciplinary student collaboration.

Access to Industry Experts: One limitation, which should be acknowledged, is that access to industry experts could be a potential barrier for some smaller institutions willing to run a similar course. One suggestion, to assist in making these connections, would be to use your institution's business development unit, Careers service or alumni organisation. Each of these departments have mechanisms for engaging with external organisations. Alternatively, small business organisations such as the Federation of Small Businesses, or in the US, the Small Business Administration, have local contacts and access points. Whilst smaller businesses do not always have the resources to invest significant time, they can benefit from involvement with the course by developing networks with the academic institution.

8. CONCLUSIONS

Embedding entrepreneurship into the curriculum, within any subject area, is challenging. However, introducing these concepts to students from a Computer Science and Mathematics background, brought a fresh set of challenges. Taking into account issues of group cohesion and the introduction of a new subject area, there was also an underlying issue around communication skills and stakeholder engagement which arose during the delivery of the module. Student feedback has afforded us with the opportunity to make amendments to the curriculum to benefit future cohorts.

Concerns around engagement and commitment were raised by the students and in future years we will seek to investigate alternative practices, e.g. task rotation within groups. This will provide opportunities for each student to experience different roles within the business, enhancing their skill set and exposing them to new experiences.

The involvement of industry is critical to the success of this course and we seek to embed this further in future years, examining the effects of a single, dedicated, panel throughout the course. This was supported by reflection from a member of teaching staff, a current entrepreneur, who highlighted that there is a disparity between the UK and US educational programmes for doctoral students. This is something we are keen to investigate further, and we plan to

further our understanding of industry integration, in order to learn from best practice within the US.

Acknowledgment

This work was supported by the Engineering and Physical Sciences Research Council [grant number EP/L015358/1].

9. REFERENCES

[1] W. Bains. What makes a happy team? data from 5 years' entrepreneurship teaching suggests that working style is a major determinant of team contentment. *J. Commerc Biotechnol*, 20(3):12–22, 2014.

[2] S. G. Blank and B. Dorf. *The startup owner's manual.* "K&S Ranch, Inc.", 2012.

[3] G. Curri. Introducing entrepreneurship teaching at select german universities. *Higher Education Management and Policy*, 20(3):1–20, 2008.

[4] e-Skills UK. Big data analytics: Assessment of demand for labout and skills 2013-2020, 2014.

[5] M. Forshaw, E. Solaiman, O. McGee, H. Firth, P. Robinson, and R. Emerson. Meeting graduate employability needs through open-source collaboration with industry. In *SIGCSE*. ACM, 2016.

[6] T. J. Hickey and P. Salas. The entrepreneur's bootcamp: a new model for teaching web/mobile development and software entrepreneurship. In *SIGCSE*, pages 549–554. ACM, 2013.

[7] P. Honey, A. Mumford, et al. The manual of learning styles. 1992.

[8] M. Lackéus and K. Williams Middleton. Venture creation programs: bridging entrepreneurship education and technology transfer. *Education+ Training*, 57(1):48–73, 2015.

[9] G. Lang and J. S. Babb. Addressing the 21st century paradox: Integrating entrepreneurship in the computer information systems curriculum. *Information Systems Education Journal*, 13(4):81, 2015.

[10] A. Maritz and J. Donovan. Entrepreneurship and innovation: Setting an agenda for greater discipline contextualisation. *Education+ Training*, 57(1):74–87, 2015.

[11] E. Mwasalwiba. Entrepreneurship education: a review of its objectives, teaching methods, and impact indicators. *Education+ Training*, 52(1):20–47, 2010.

[12] A. Osterwalder and Y. Pigneur. *Business model generation: a handbook for visionaries, game changers, and challengers.* John Wiley & Sons, 2010.

[13] J. P. Scribner and J. F. Donaldson. The dynamics of group learning in a cohort: From nonlearning to transformative learning. *Educational Administration Quarterly*, 37(5):605–636, 2001.

[14] A. Valerio, B. Parton, and A. Robb. *Entrepreneurship education and training programs around the world: dimensions for success.* World Bank, 2014.

[15] K. Williams Middleton, S. Mueller, P. Blenker, H. Neergaard, and R. Tunstall. Experience-based learning in entrepreneurship education-a comparative study of four programmes in europe. In *RENT XXVIII*, pages 1–15, 2014.

[16] L. Young. Growing your business: a report on growing micro businesses. *London: Lord*, 2013.

Using a Student Consultant in a Computer Science Course: An Experience Report

Eli Rose
Department of Computer Science
Oberlin College
Oberlin, Ohio
really.eli@gmail.com

Cynthia Taylor
Department of Computer Science
University of Illinois at Chicago
Chicago, Illinois
cynthiat@uic.edu

ABSTRACT

This paper describes the experience of using a student consultant in a sophomore level computer science course. A *student consultant* is a student who is not enrolled in the course, but attends selected class sessions and provides feedback on the in-class experience to the instructor, with the goal of improving some aspect of the course. In this paper we describe our experience with such a program from the point of view of both the instructor and the student consultant. We provide our views of the experience with the dual goals of making student consultant programs better known within the computer science education community, and to provide guidance and insight to those who may wish to use such a program themselves.

Keywords

student consultant; instructor feedback

1. INTRODUCTION

In this paper, we describe the experience of using a *student consultant* in a computer science course. A student consultant is a student who is not enrolled in the course, who attends at least one class session a week and provides the instructor with feedback on the course, focusing on student responses to the material. The student consultant and instructor work together in order to explore and improve some aspect of the course.

Unlike a TA, the student consultant's job is not to help students with the homework. It is to observe the atmosphere and dynamics of the class and to record these observations in detailed notes. Meetings with the instructor serve to communicate the student's observations and to provide space for the instructor to talk out their thoughts about the class. Just as the act of explaining a software bug to someone can illuminate the fix, simply talking about how this week's class went with the student consultant can help the instructor debug their class.

ITiCSE '16, July 09 - 13, 2016, Arequipa, Peru

© 2016 Copyright held by the owner/author(s). Publication rights licensed to ACM.
ISBN 978-1-4503-4231-5/16/07... $15.00

DOI: http://dx.doi.org/10.1145/2899415.2899434

Both the instructor and student consultant found this experience to be both useful and rewarding. We report on it here in order to make the greater computer science education community aware of student consultants in general, and to report what we learned from the experience. As the use of student consultants is relatively new within the computer science community, this paper is not a rigorous study of student consultant use within computer science, but rather a subjective report of our experiences as both instructor and student.

In this paper, we describe student consultant programs in general, and then describe the specifics of how we adapted the idea for this particular course. This is followed by an in depth discussion by both the instructor and student consultant of the benefits and difficulties of the program, and recommendations for those who wish to implement such a program in their own courses.

2. RELATED WORK AND BACKGROUND

Student consultants have been used by a variety of disciplines, at a variety of institutions. Our program was modeled after the student consultant program developed by Alison Cook-Sather at Bryn Mawr College, which has been running there as the Students as Learners and Teachers (SaLT) program since 2006 [3]. Similar programs include the Students Consulting on Teaching Program (SCOT) at Brigham Young University [12], the Students Consulting on Teaching Program at the University of Lincoln [4], and the Student Observer Program at Carleton College [2].

The SaLT program matches instructors who are interested in exploring the in-class experience of a course with student consultants for a semester. The student consultant attends and observes one class a week, taking detailed notes on what is happening in the class. They record both what the instructor is doing, and how the students are responding. The instructor and student consultant meet weekly to discuss the class session the consultant observed. These discussions include both a factual recounting of what the student consultant observed, and their subjective assessment of how the students reacted or any issues with the lesson.

Cook-Sather describes the goals of the program at the institution level as supporting faculty and students in exploring pedagogical questions and improving classroom dynamics, but also to foster constructive dialogue between students and faculty, and to encourage general dialogue between students and faculty about teaching and learning [3]. At the instructor and course level, the goals may vary widely within the general framework of course and pedagogical improvement. Given this, the details of what the student consultant records during class, and the focus of their discussions with the instructor may vary widely, and must be defined by the instructor and consultant themselves.

3. THE SETTING

In this section, we describe the basics of the course that the student consultant observed, as well as the goals the instructor and consultant had going into the program.

3.1 The Course

Our course was an Introduction to Computer Architecture course, covering MIPS assembly, digital logic, the data and control path, pipelining and the memory hierarchy. This course is a required course for the Computer Science major at the institution at which it was taught, and is usually taken by sophomore and junior level students. Thirty-seven students were enrolled in the course (a fairly large course size for this institution). The course was taught at a small liberal arts college.

The course was taught using peer instruction. Peer instruction is an active learning technique that has been well documented to increase student's conceptual understanding of topics [5], and has been increasingly used in computer science [11, 10, 9, 6, 13, 8]. Using peer instruction, throughout the lecture the instructor displays a multiple-choice question, with one correct answer and two to four distractor answers. Students first vote individually on an answer, using an electronic clicker device [1]. They then discuss the question in small, assigned groups, and after a brief discussion, the group votes on a single answer.

During most class periods in this course, the instructor would lecture for a short amount of time to introduce a concept, and then put up a clicker question on the material she had just covered. Students would vote individually, discuss, and revote in their groups. After this, a single discussion group would be responsible for telling the class about their discussion, what answer they selected, and why. The instructor would discuss the answer, and answer any student questions. When the discussion was resolved, the instructor would continue to the next mini-lecture. This would generally repeat around five to eight times per fifty minute class.

3.2 Instructor Goals

The instructor had previously taught this course twice before. She was particularly interested in trying to improve student engagement with the material, as feedback on the course previously had indicated some students found the material dry or uninteresting. She also wanted to know what material was particularly confusing to the students, and how to make material more comprehensible in general. After discussion with the student consultant, they decided to focus on how students responded to clicker questions, as this would give a concrete opportunity for the student consultant to observe student reactions to material.

3.3 Student Consultant Goals

The student consultant took on this job in his last undergraduate semester.

Since the student consultant was and is interested in pursuing teaching as a career, he saw the job as a way of getting a behind-the-scenes-look at the process of teaching. Being able to participate in the running of a real class was a major draw for this student consultant.

Another hope was that he could, by working with the instructor, improve the classroom experience for students. This student consultant had worked a variety of campus jobs tutoring for similar classes in the CS department, and took on this role with a similar perspective and set of goals.

At the outset of the program, the student consultant had goals that were, in part, activist. Though he overall had an excellent, encouraging introductory CS experience, he recalled certain things about it that he had found frustrating, confusing, or discouraging. He wanted to prevent other students from encountering the same difficulties.

4. THE EXPERIENCE

In this section, we discuss the details of our use of the student consultant program within this course.

4.1 Selecting the Student Consultant

In selecting the student consultant, we were looking for an upper level computer science major who was not currently taking any other courses with the instructor. Since one of the instructor's goals was to explore student understanding of the course material, she felt it was important to have a student consultant who had either taken the course, or who had enough other computer science experience to understand the material in context. This differed from the original SaLT program, in which students were frequently consultants for subject areas they had no prior experience with.

Following the SaLT model, we selected a student who was not taking any other courses with the instructor, as we did not want any situations in which the student consultant might feel that providing negative feedback on the course could have potential repercussions.

In order to find students, we put out an open call advertising the position to all computer science majors. We selected a student consultant who was a senior computer science major, and who expressed an interested in pedagogy and teaching as a future career. The student consultant had previously taken this course from the instructor.

The student consultant was paid an hourly wage similar to that of other student workers (tutors, graders, etc.) in the CS department.

4.2 Training and External Support

This took place as part of a pilot program using student consultants at our institution. As a result, the role of the student consultant may have been less clearcut than if this was a more established program.

At the beginning of the semester and several times throughout the semester, the student consultant and the instructor had meetings with the other instructor and student consultant in the student consultant program, as well as the head of their institution's Teaching Center (who was responsible for starting the program). Usually these meetings had breakout sessions with just instructors or just student consultants, as well as meeting with the entire group.

At the beginning of the semester, these meetings had more of a training aspect, with an external expert training the student consultants on note taking, and meeting with both instructors and consultants to discuss their goals for the semester, and how best to achieve those goals. Later meetings offered instructors and consultants an opportunity to reflect on how the process was going, and offer each other suggestions for improvements.

4.3 Classroom Observation and Weekly Discussions

The student consultant attended one of the three classes each week. At the beginning of the course, the instructor introduced him to the students, along with a brief description of his role as student consultant. Because one of our goals was to focus on student discussion, the student consultant sat in a different place in the classroom in each class he attended, in order to observe different groups of students.

During class, the student consultant took detailed notes, with the time, what was happening in the lecture, and his thoughts, recording what was happening in class every three to five minutes. These notes included specifics of the small group student discussions that he observed, including approaches students took to solving problems, how difficult they found particular problems, and general reactions to material and group dynamics. He also recorded aspects of classroom discussion, including questions asked of the instructor, and student reactions to her answers (sample notes pictured in Table 1).

After class, the student consultant typed up and clarified his notes, and then shared them with the instructor before their weekly meeting, so they both had a written record of the class. In their weekly meeting, they went over the notes together, and discussed what had happened in the class and student reactions, as well as the student consultant's subjective assessments of class comprehension and engagement. During these meetings, the instructor usually had both her lecture slides and the student consultant's notes up on her computer screen, to get as comprehensive a picture as possible of what was happening at a specific point in class. The instructor would frequently take notes in relevant places in her slides, or revise slides during the meeting based on their discussion.

These meetings generally lasted about an hour, and the topics discussed varied widely in specificity, from comments like "I noticed that some of the students seemed confused at this point" or "I felt this was a very engaging class overall", to in depth discussion of what distractor answers would best illustrate common student misconceptions in a peer instruction question. The student consultant would also frequently ask the instructor what her perception of something that had occurred in class was, or the instructor would ask the student consultant what his personal experience learning specific material had been. Discussions tended to be grounded in specific lecture slides or course materials, but also touched on student reactions to the course as a whole, and occasionally touched on what could be added to materials like labs or problem sets in order to aid student understanding of specific points.

4.4 Midterm Feedback

Following the SaLT model, halfway through the course, the student consultant lead a class discussion on how students felt about the course, as well as having the students fill out a standard, anonymous questionnaire on the course. The instructor was not present for this discussion, but the student consultant wrote up and conveyed the key points.

Since the student consultant made it clear that all feedback was welcome, that no one's name would be shared if they didn't want it to be, and because he was not the instructor, the discussion ended up being quite frank. Even students who were often quiet in class spoke up – if they were less comfortable participating in the group discussion, they approached the student consultant immediately afterwards. While the discussion was frank, it was not largely negative. When one student complained about some aspect of the class, another would pipe up just to say how much they enjoyed that aspect. For example, the coursework included written problem sets as well as lab assignments: some students felt some of these problem sets were too easy, and had "busy work" qualities, while an equal number found them to be useful practice for the tests.

It's common for students to have different opinions about a course, but what the midterm discussion did was get them talking to each other about it. It's not likely that any such conversation would have happened independently. We feel that having the opportunity to engage with view contrary to their own made students more aware that others found value in parts of the course that they did not. Additionally, having a structured discussion instead of an anonymous survey enabled the student consultant to ask specific follow-up questions, and also got students to give higher-quality feedback, not just noting problems but talking about solutions.

Student response to the midterm class discussion was overwhelmingly positive. Students said that merely setting aside time for the discussion made them feel that the instructor cared about their experience of the course, and also that they felt more ownership over the course. Some found it cathartic to be able to address issues that they had not had a forum for before. One student expressed surprise that this was not standard practice in every class.

4.5 Student Consultant as Intermediary

An unexpected outcome of having a student consultant who was known to the students was that he became a course representative who may have seemed more approachable than the instructor to some students. One significant outcome of this was that at one point a student who wished to remain anonymous to the instructor approached the student consultant to report observing cheating on an in-class exam. Students also took the initiative to approach the student consultant with feedback about the course.

5. DISCUSSION AND RECOMMENDATIONS

What follows is a subjective assessment by both the instructor and the student consultant about their experience with the student consultant program.

5.1 Benefits

Both the instructor and student consultant had a very positive experience with the program. Below they discuss specific aspects which they found especially beneficial.

5.1.1 Instructor

- **In depth discussion of lecture/course activities.** Typically, instructors develop lectures on their own, and get very little feedback on the granularity of individual lectures, examples, or discussion questions. The instructor gets feedback on the course as a whole from students at the end of the course, and individual students may ask questions or comment on a specific aspect of a lecture, but it is rare to get a chance to

Time	Observation	Reflection
2:43	More slides on how MIPS translates to machine code – shamt, funct, etc. You do a demo translation. You emphasize that the order of the operands is switched in machine code. Someone in front of me (S) is shaking her head.	I think she was intimidated by the amount of information on the slide.
2:45	G asks "What is SA". You answer "shift amount" and explain shifts.	I wonder about whether people have seen shifts before. I don't think it's all that hard to pick up; a short visual explanation like yours seemed to work.
2:49	You complete the demo, emphasizing labor-saving tricks when converting numbers to binary (17 = 16 + 1, 18 = 17 + 1). You note that the hex value in funct is bounded by available space.	I really like these sorts of tricks – I think they can create engagement by being a way to save time through understanding. I wonder if that's just me?
2:51	Clicker Question: Now you do the reverse! (translate from machine code to MIPS). Some banter while everyone crunches the numbers. People are whispering about the problem.	Interesting how everyone collaborated on this.
2:54	Discussion. Guy in S's group is mostly explaining; S is asking "but why?" a lot. Other student in their group is mostly silent.	Discussion was sort of a continuation of working on the problem, since people were doing it collaboratively to start with. But there was a lot more talking once it was official.

analyze how effective an individual class period was in terms of student engagement and understanding. Getting a chance to discuss this was very rewarding, and lead to more in depth analysis of how to convey specific information.

The instructor is a relatively new instructor, and was in her third year of teaching when participating in this program. As such, she found getting in depth feedback on her teaching to be especially useful.

- **Immediate reflection and revision of course materials.** Instructors are constantly revising course content based on its prior success or lack thereof. However, given busy schedules, this revision frequently does not occur until the next time the course is taught, which may be a semester, a year, or even multiple years later. Having a dedicated weekly time to go over a recently taught class, reflect on it, and make changes to the materials meant that changes were made while the experience of teaching the content was still recent.

- **Insight from a novice perspective.** A common issue in teaching is that novices and experts simply conceptualize material differently [7]. Since the student consultant had learned the information himself only a year prior, he was able to offer an opinion that combined a basic knowledge of the material with a recent memory of what about it had been difficult or confusing to learn.

- **Records of individual group discussion.** The observed course heavily featured student discussion in small groups, as well as full class discussion. As the course was taught in a lecture hall, it was difficult for the instructor to observe what individual student groups were discussing in class, especially those towards the back of the classroom. Having the student consultant observe and record individual group discussion meant that the instructor got a window into how students were approaching and solving the posed problems.

The instructor found this information very enlightening. Some questions that the instructor felt were too "plug and chug" (and was thinking of cutting) were actually leading to interesting discussions on how to solve problems, while other questions were too easy or had distractor answers that gave the answer away. Not only did this allow the instructor to improve individual questions (and give her fodder for good distractor answers based on actual student misconceptions), but it also gave her valuable insight into how students were actually approaching problem solving, and what they found misleading or confusing.

- **Records of full classroom discussion.** It was surprisingly helpful for the instructor to have a written record of all class discussion from a class period. Being able to review student comments and questions while reviewing and revising the lecture allowed for reflection on discussion details that the instructor otherwise would likely not have remembered. It also meant that over the course of the semester, there was a clear record of who talked in class: which students were more likely to ask questions or spearhead discussions. Working purely as an observer allowed the student consultant to record details of classroom interaction that the instructor missed, allowing for a much clearer picture of classroom activity.

5.1.2 Student Consultant

- **Reflection on content and one's own learning process.** Seeing a fresh round of students get exposed to concepts he was already familiar with, the student consultant realized that he wasn't actually so familiar with them. Specifically, though he remembered big ideas, he had forgotten some of the glue that held them together. Discussing students' reactions to concepts with the instructor, he discovered new approaches and understood subtleties that he missed the first time around.

- **Reflection on others' learning processes.** As noted in the 'Goals' section, at the outset of the program one of this student consultant's goals was to use his input into the class to guide its students around certain obstacles and help them avoid making certain mistakes. This goal turned out to be fairly misguided, because (as this student consultant realized) his experience with Computer Science classes was hardly universal. Listening to the students, especially at midterm review time, he found that the range of difficulties they had and the range of triumphs they experienced didn't match his preconceptions very well. He found that the student consultant note-taking process – sitting in the lecture hall, being as attentive as possible to the atmosphere of the room, recording it in detail, trying to think from the perspective of 37 other people – quickly expanded his ideas about students' experiences of Computer Science classes.

5.2 Difficulties

While this experience was positive overall, certain aspects of it were difficult or uncomfortable at times. We describe these below.

5.2.1 Instructor

- **Facing classroom failures.** There are many reasons a particular class session may not have gone as well as possible. Working with a student consultant means spending time dwelling on those failures. It is not pleasant to be reminded that the back row of your class was reading their phones instead of paying attention. There were times when a lesson didn't work and there was no clear reason why or how to fix it.

- **Perceptions of instructor competence.** On the first day of class, we introduced the student consultant to the class, and explained a little bit about the program. Overall, this was a positive. Students reacted well to the idea that the instructor wanted their feedback on the course, and was receptive to their ideas. However, there is the danger of students questioning the instructor's competence because they are asking for this kind of feedback. This is especially relevant to instructors who are women or part of other underrepresented groups in computer science.

- **Students wanting too much ownership.** Students may interpret asking for feedback as a guarantee that the instructor will implement their specific proposed changes, or feel upset or ignored if the instructor does not make specific changes.

5.2.2 Student Consultant

- **Bringing up subjects in meetings with the instructor.** Since this student consultant wasn't used to having a partner-to-partner, as opposed to mentor-to-student, relationship with his professors, he initially had some difficulty taking the initiative to bring up topics on his own during the weekly meetings with the instructor. Even though the instructor was committed to discussion and examining her pedagogy, a good discussion partner needs to bring in material from their own point of view. The rigorous note-taking format

helped with this, since putting what you noticed in writing forces you to talk about it.

- **Dealing with bad stuff that can't be helped.** No class will be perfect, or maybe even good, for every student. Doing the midterm review exposed this student consultant to a wide range of feedback, including students who were unhappy with the course for very different reasons, some of which were things we could change, some of which weren't, some of which were hard to tell.

5.3 Recommendations

We provide recommendations for both instructors and student consultants interested in implementing a similar program in their own courses below.

5.3.1 Instructor

- **Have a specific thing to talk about, but don't be afraid to discuss other things as well.** Having a specific aspect of the course to focus on (in this case, clicker questions), gave the initial discussions between the instructor and student consultant a natural focus. As the student consultant and instructor became more used to these discussions and their partnership, they were able to move on to discuss other aspects of the course as well.

- **Be open to whatever form feedback takes.** Going into this experience, the instructor pictured making drastic changes to the course based on the student consultant's feedback. While this did not happen, the instructor felt she left the experience with a much clearer, in depth picture of what was happening in the course and what students struggled with. Instead of large, sweeping changes she ended up making a large number of small changes to course materials, based on this detailed information of how students were reacting in class.

5.3.2 Student Consultant

- **Listen when meeting with the instructor.** You're there to provide your viewpoint, but also to get an actual conversation going. In order to do that, you need to be responsive. Don't just deliver a list of facts, or read off your notes blow-by-blow.

- **Spy in class.** When the class isn't in lecture mode (working in small groups, in pairs, etc.) walk around and see what's going on. Even when it is, take notice of how and when students seem engaged, whether a whispered conversation is actually confused student asking their friend for help, who's raising their hand to ask questions and who's not. This student consultant found that he sometimes got stuck just recording what was happening on the slides (leading to notes reading "3:55 – Covered topic A. 4:00 – Covered topic B") but it's more important to record stuff the instructor isn't focusing on, since that's what they know the least about.

- **Have the student consultant be a paid position.** The student consultant needed to work a certain number of hours every week in order to meet his financial plans (He was completing his last semester as a part-time student for financial reasons). If the job weren't paid, the student consultant might not have been able to take it on.

5.4 Customization to Computer Science

There were a couple of key issues in using this program within the computer science domain. We reflect on these below.

- **Having a student consultant who was familiar with the course material.** Since one of the instructor's main goal for this project was to try to make material more accessible to students, she felt it was important to have a student consultant who already understood the material. Having a consultant who had taken the course already allowed the instructor and consultant to engage in a close reading of lecture materials such as slides and clicker questions, and discuss details as minute as wording of slides and examples used in class. While instructors who are less focused on student comprehension issues in the course may find consultant understanding of the material less important, the student consultant having a basic knowledge of computer science concepts was critical to giving informed, detailed feedback on the course.

  The student consultant we selected had previously taken the course with the same instructor - this was unavoidable as no other instructor had taught the class in the previous two years. This may mean the student consultant was more likely to think about concepts in similar ways as the instructor. Since the student consultant had already taken the course, he could also provide insight on the outside of lecture aspects of the course such as lab assignments and problem sets.

- **Emphasizing the student consultant and instructor were on the same team.** As a relatively young, female instructor in Computer Science, the instructor was especially aware of the possibility of students questioning her competence. She discussed this with the student consultant before the midterm feedback session, instructing him to be aware of it in the discussion, and letting him know that while she solicited critical feedback from students on the course, she wanted to make sure her basic competence as an instructor and computer scientist was respected during the discussion.

6. CONCLUSION

Our participation in the student consultant program was a valuable experience for both the student consultant and instructor. While difficult at times, the program had many benefits, including a reflection on pedagogy in general, in computer science, and in this specific course. The program resulted in an improvement in course materials for future offerings of the course, and had a positive response from students in the course.

We provide this experience report in order to make computer science instructors aware of the benefits offered by using a student consultant in their courses, and to provide information on our experience to those who may wish to try.

7. ACKNOWLEDGEMENTS

Thanks to Steven Volk of Oberlin College and Alison Cook-Sather at Bryn Mawr College for their guidance throughout the student consultant experience. Thanks to Dean Timothy Elgren of Oberlin College for funding this program.

8. REFERENCES

[1] J. E. Caldwell. Clickers in the large classroom: Current research and best-practice tips. *CBE Life Sciences Education*, 6(1):9–20, Mar. 2007.

[2] Carleton College. Student observer program. Online at https://apps.carleton.edu/campus/ltc/faculty-services/observers/, 2015. Last accessed January 6, 2016.

[3] A. Cook-Sather, C. Bovill, and P. Felten. *Engaging students as partners in learning and teaching: A guide for faculty.* John Wiley & Sons, 2014.

[4] K. Crawford. Rethinking the student/teacher nexus: students as consultants on teaching in higher education. *2012) Towards teaching in public reshaping the modern university*, pages 52–67, 2012.

[5] C. H. Crouch and E. Mazur. Peer Instruction: Ten years of experience and results. *American Journal of Physics*, 69(9):970–77, Sept. 2001.

[6] Q. Cutts, A. Carbone, and K. van Haaster. Using an electronic voting system to promote active reflection on coursework feedback. In *Proceedings of ICCE 2004*. APSCE, Nov. 2004.

[7] Z. Hrepic, D. A. Zollman, and N. S. Rebello. Comparing students' and experts' understanding of the content of a lecture. *Journal of Science Education and Technology*, 16(3):213–24, June 2007.

[8] R. P. Pargas and D. M. Shah. Things are clicking in computer science courses. In S. Haller and I. Russell, editors, *Proceedings of SIGCSE 2006*, pages 474–78. ACM Press, Mar. 2006.

[9] L. Porter, C. B. Lee, B. Simon, Q. Cutts, and D. Zingaro. Experience report: A multi-classroom report on the value of Peer Instruction. In T. L. Naps and C. Spannagel, editors, *Proceedings of ITiCSE 2011*, pages 138–42. ACM Press, June 2011.

[10] L. Porter, C. B. Lee, B. Simon, and D. Zingaro. Peer Instruction: Do students really learn from peer discussion in computing? In M. E. Caspersen, A. Clear, and K. Sanders, editors, *Proceedings of ICER 2011*, pages 45–52. ACM Press, Aug. 2011.

[11] B. Simon, M. Kohanfars, J. Lee, K. Tamayo, and Q. Cutts. Experience report: Peer Instruction in introductory computing. In T. Cortina and E. Walker, editors, *Proceedings of SIGCSE 2010*, pages 341–45. ACM Press, Mar. 2010.

[12] L. Sorenson. College teachers and student consultants: Collaborating about teaching and learning. *Student-assisted teaching: A guide to faculty-student teamwork*, pages 179–183, 2001.

[13] D. Zingaro. Experience report: Peer Instruction in remedial computer science. In J. Herrinton and B. Hunger, editors, *Proceedings of Ed-Media 2010*, pages 5030–35. AACE, June 2010.

Using Student Performance to Assess CS Unplugged Activities in a Classroom Environment

Brandon Rodriguez, Cyndi Rader, and Tracy Camp
Dept. of Electrical Engineering and Computer Science
Colorado School of Mines, Golden, CO, USA
brandonrrodriguez@gmail.com, crader@mines.edu, tcamp@mines.edu

ABSTRACT

Computer Science Unplugged activities have been shown to be successful in increasing student interest in computer science when used in outreach and after school events. There is less research available on adapting these extra-curricular activities for use in a classroom setting, where there are more students and the activities must support educational goals, not just changes in attitude. We describe our work in updating several existing CS Unplugged activities as well as introducing some new activities for use in an American middle school classroom. One challenge when using CS Unplugged activities is to determine what, if anything, students are learning. In this paper we detail one approach that links the updated activities to computational thinking skills, then incorporates worksheets where students illustrate their understanding.

CCS Concepts

•Applied computing → Interactive learning environments;

Keywords

CS Unplugged, Classroom Assessment, Computational Thinking

1. INTRODUCTION

In 2006, Jeannette Wing (Carnegie Mellon University) coined the term Computational Thinking (CT) as a way that humans conceptualize computable problems [12]. Computational thinking is a process for solving or interpreting unstructured problems such that a computer could output an answer. Computational thinking is important when there are many solutions that can lead to a correct answer, and where some solutions may offer a computational advantage when using a machine to calculate the result. Since computers are pervasive in our society, teaching CT concepts at the middle school level will give students tools for effectively solving a variety of problems in different disciplinary areas.

Computational thinking encompasses much more than learning how to program. Following several years of discussion within the CS education community, the five CT skills that are commonly accepted are [2]:

- Data Representation: the act of representing information so that it may be effectively processed by a computer.

- Decomposition: breaking a problem into several smaller problems that, when solved, will answer the original problem.

- Abstraction: generalizing a problem to see if techniques from similar problems can be used to solve the current task.

- Algorithmic Thinking: designing step-by-step processes or applying known algorithms to obtain a solution.

- Pattern Recognition: identifying trends or discovering the cause of patterns in data.

Now that skills have been identified, the next challenge is to determine how to teach and assess CT in the classroom. Computer Science Unplugged (CS Unplugged) activities are a set of lesson plans made available for free on the internet [3]. The aim of these lesson plans is to convey fundamental computer science concepts to students without any computer skills and to help bridge the gap for K-12 teachers who may not have a technical background but are expected to teach technical ideas. CS Unplugged activities are kinesthetic, engaging, and above all emphasize that computer science is about problem solving, and not synonymous with programming. A number of studies have explored the impact of CS Unplugged on students' attitudes [7, 9]. In this paper we are primarily concerned with what students are learning. We explore two questions. First, what CT skills might we expect students to acquire from various activities? And second, can we devise instruments that integrate into the activities so that the assessments are both engaging and provide insight into what students are learning? We provide results from deploying our modified versions of CS Unplugged activities in two American middle schools.

2. RELATED WORK

Numerous research projects have presented methods for teaching computer science without the use of computers or

ITiCSE '16, July 09-13, 2016, Arequipa, Peru

© 2016 ACM. ISBN 978-1-4503-4231-5/16/07. . . $15.00

DOI: http://dx.doi.org/10.1145/2899415.2899465

programming languages. CS Unplugged and "computer science magic shows" have been successful examples of teaching computer science through highly engaging activities for students [6]. CS Unplugged activities have been adopted by a variety of educational outreach programs such as after-school workshops and summer camps [3], and have even been incorporated into the Exploring CS Curriculum [5].

The majority of the studies conducted using these types of activities have been concerned primarily with increasing interest in computer science, and not necessarily about using the lessons in classroom environments or assessing what the students are learning by completing the activities.

Renate Thies and Jan Vahrenhold from the Technical University of Dortmund in Germany investigated the suitability of CS Unplugged activities for use in a classroom (instead of an after-school program) by using the activities with a group of students. They used CS Unplugged activities to teach half the students, and used alternative tools for the other half of the students. Their findings showed CS Unplugged activities were equally effective in transferring knowledge as there was no significant difference in achievement between the group who learned with CS Unplugged activities and the group who learned with alternative materials [11]. Additionally, the researchers studied the impact of using CS Unplugged activities in different grade levels, and found that the activities had a significant positive impact when used with middle school classes. Thies and Vahrenhold have also mapped CS Unplugged lessons to Bloom's Taxonomy to determine what level of cognitive processes are prompted by various activities [10].

Thies and Vahrenhold's research examined all unmodified CS Unplugged activities. CS Unplugged activities were originally designed to be used in outreach scenarios, and therefore do not explicitly list learning objectives. The researchers' extrapolation of learning objectives suggests that the CS Unplugged curriculum lies in the lower end of the Bloom's Taxonomy spectrum. The authors noted that higher level learning objectives are needed for middle school audiences [11]. Thies and Vahrenhold's research is of particular significance because they bridge the gap between entertaining outreach programs and measurable student outcomes that can be used in a traditional classroom. The extensions and new activities our group has developed specifically address higher learning objectives in order to make CS Unplugged materials better suited for secondary education.

Quintin Cutts of the University of Glasgow detailed how group exercises in classroom environments can be just as effective as one-on-one tutors. Group work can also increase confidence and encourage students to become personally interested in the material [4]. Cutts' work supports what we have observed while deploying CS Unplugged activities. Namely, students prefer working in groups, and students who otherwise would not have asked questions to the teacher are comfortable asking their peers for help.

Lynn Lambert of Christopher Newport University published an article in 2009 that deployed pre- and post-surveys to evaluate CS Unplugged activities [7]. Lambert's results found students showed an increase in confidence in computing topics, but failed to gain knowledge about computing careers. The conclusions from Lambert's study were the basis for our development of career related and real world extensions and lecture material for CS Unplugged activities. See our career extensions on our website for details [1].

3. THE STUDY

The focus of our study is assessing the use of CS Unplugged in middle school classrooms. Based on interviews with teachers and pilot tests in after school settings, we selected a subset of the CS Unplugged activities that seemed age appropriate. Since classroom time is valuable, we limited our deployments to approximately six activities (i.e., there are more than six activities that are suitable for middle school, but we studied only six in detail). For each activity, we developed a detailed lesson plan that would fill a 50-minute class period. All of the lesson plans have a similar structure that includes whole class discussions, collaborative group work, and individual work. As part of each activity, students completed worksheets that were collected by the researchers. Unless otherwise noted, worksheets were completed individually by each student. To remain true to the spirit of CS Unplugged [8], we strove to incorporate game-like challenges or stories into the worksheets. This is also consistent with CT goals, which represent a process or approach to problem solving rather than a set of facts that can easily be assessed using, for example, multiple choice questions. We should note that CT is not currently required material for middle school students in our state, so the purpose of these assessments was for us to measure the impact of the activities, not for the teachers to assign a grade.

We partnered with two local middle schools to deploy and assess activities in 7th-grade classrooms. Both schools place extra emphasis on science and technology. Six CS Unplugged activities were deployed to students as part of their normal classroom work during the school day. Our first deployment was during fall 2015, with approximately 130 students. The results from that deployment highlighted a few issues with some of the activities and/or assessments. A second deployment during spring 2016 showed improved results, but we again identified issues with a few of the activities (e.g., insufficient coverage of some topics) and assessments (e.g., confusing instructions on worksheets). Results are presented below from our third deployment, which also occurred during spring 2016.

Table 1 shows a mapping of the Unplugged activities to CT, along with a brief list of any modifications we made to the original activities. A description of these extensions is beyond the scope of this paper, but lesson plans and worksheets for all revised Unplugged activities, including four that are not mentioned in this paper, are available on our website [1].This paper will focus on six activities (Finite State Automata, Binary Numbers, Cryptology, Error Detection, Minimal Spanning Trees, and Searching) with worksheets that assess computational thinking. The worksheet from the Searching activity included pairs of students; all other worksheets were done individually. The number of students varies from 64 to 122 and will be reported for each activity.

4. METHOD

After the classroom deployment, a rubric was created for each worksheet. The rubrics provided guidelines on how to score worksheet answers as either *Proficient*, *Partially Proficient*, or *Unsatisfactory*. Every worksheet was individually scored by two researchers to ensure consensus. Disagreements on any score were resolved by having both researchers score the question together and then editing the rubrics to

Table 1: Classification of CS Unplugged activities and their CT skills.

Activity Name	CT Skills	Our Contributions
Binary Numbers	Data Representation Pattern Recognition Abstraction	Check Your Understanding worksheet Bit Ranges worksheet Binary Go Fish activity
Cryptology	Decomposition Pattern Recognition Abstraction Algorithmic Thinking	New activity using Caesar cipher Encode/Decode worksheet Surprise party activity
Finite State Automata	Data Representation Abstraction	Lesson plan using fruit vendor rather than Treasure Hunt Robot Dog worksheet Chores Robot worksheet
Parity Bits and Error Detection	Data Representation Decomposition Algorithmic Thinking	ASCII and Parity worksheet
Searching	Algorithmic Thinking	Raffle ticket activity Guess My Number lecture Dragons and Cows worksheet
Minimal Spanning Trees	Algorithmic Thinking	Halloween Candy worksheet

better document any edge cases. Student scores were used to determine whether there was evidence that students could apply the concepts from the activities and, in some cases, to identify revisions to the activities and/or assessments.

As mentioned, the worksheets were designed to be integrated into the activity, rather than a "quiz" to be completed after the activity is done. Worksheets also needed to be straightforward enough to be completed within the time frame of a typical 50-minute class period. One consequence of this constraint is that the worksheets do not ask students to provide reasoning or show how they arrived at an answer. In determining the proficiency levels, students who scored *Proficient* arrived at the correct answer, *Partially Proficient* arrived at an incorrect answer, but one which the evaluators could understand (i.e., student was on the right track but had a clear misconception or made a computational error), and *Unsatisfactory* included responses where the student did not attempt the problem or where the answer was blatantly incorrect.

For brevity, only the Finite State Automata activity will be discussed in detail. Results are presented, however, for all six activities.

5. FINITE STATE AUTOMATA (FSA)

The FSA lesson plan explores problems and situations that can be represented with a set of states, and the transitions required to move between states. In this activity, students begin by playing a game without any introduction to FSA terminology or concepts. In groups of four or five, one student is designated as a fruit vendor and the other students as fruit buyers. In the game, the fruit vendor sells apples and bananas, but may not always sell what he/she is asked for. The buyers are tasked with finding a sequence of fruit purchases that will result in the vendor selling three apples in a row.

After groups realize the pattern, the entire class reassembles. The syntax for states, transitions, start state and stop state are introduced on the whiteboard, and a FSA diagram of the fruit vendor's selling pattern is constructed (with fruits as possible states, and purchase requests as transi-

tions). Vendors are then given new instructions (a different pattern), and the buyers are again tasked with receiving three apples in a row. This time, however, they can represent their findings as an FSA to assist in articulating the vendor's pattern. An optional third set of vendor instructions allows for flexibility in timing and provides an additional fun activity for students who quickly identified the second pattern.

Once students have finished the fruit vendor activity, they are given two worksheets to apply their new FSA knowledge to different problems. In the first worksheet, students are given a complete FSA diagram that depicts a robotic dog's various states. They are asked to evaluate transition paths to determine what state the robot dog would be in after completing the transitions. In the second worksheet, students are given a list of rules for a chores robot. The rules explain the robot's functions, and clearly identify the different states the robot can take, as well as the different transitions the robot recognizes. Students must then take the list of rules and convert it into a well formed FSA diagram.

Results from the FSA worksheets are given in Figure 1. Because student performance on the worksheets was generally good, the scale on each figure is from 50 to 100%. A total of 103 students completed worksheets for this lesson. Students generally did well, with over 65% achieving *Proficient* scores on all questions. The results indicate that students struggled most with using an FSA diagram to generate a sequence of transitions that end at a specified state (specifically, they were asked to identify two different paths that would result in the robot performing all the chores). However, they were able to evaluate given paths of transitions with much higher success.

6. RESULTS FOR THE REMAINING ACTIVITIES

Brief summaries of the results for the other five activities are included in the following sections. Each section lists the number of students who turned in worksheets for that activity. Mapping the activities to CT skills has allowed for

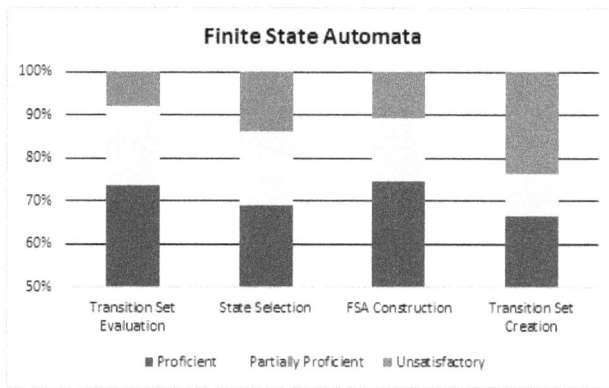

Figure 1: Results from our deployment of the FSA lesson plan in spring 2016.

our research team to measure what students are learning; thus, the results are more detailed than an attitude survey alone.

6.1 Binary Numbers

In the binary numbers activity, students learn that data is stored in computers as ones and zeros and they use binary flip cards to learn how to count in base two. As part of that discussion, students practice converting between number systems, and they use the flip cards to understand the range of values that can be represented by a 5-bit number. After the discussion, students complete a worksheet with six questions. Results are given in Figure 2. In general students performed well on this worksheet, with greater than 80% of the 79 students achieving *Proficient* scores on all questions.

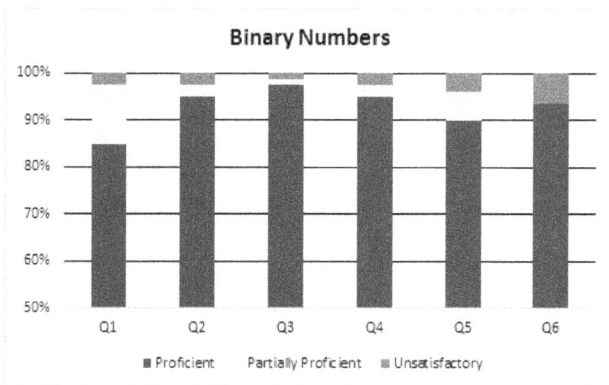

Figure 2: Results from our deployment of the Binary Numbers lesson plan in spring 2016.

The first question on the worksheet addresses the CT area of *Pattern Recognition*, as students are given a sequence of four binary numbers and asked what number would be next. The following two questions deal with *Data Representation*, as students are asked to convert a binary number to decimal and then a decimal number to binary. The final three questions incorporate several CT areas, including *Abstraction*, as students are asked about the largest number that can be represented with five bits (covered during whole class discussion) and then need to generalize this to three bits and six bits.

6.2 Cryptology

In the cryptology activity, students practice encryption and decryption using Caesar ciphers. As part of this activity, students create a cipher using a given key (e.g., offset by two letters) and then encode a message. Then, they analyze how many possible keys a Caesar cipher could have before using a given cipher to decode a message. To make the discussion more concrete, students explore why cryptology is important and what types of data they consider important to protect. The results from the cryptology assessments are shown in Figure 3, with 122 students being represented.

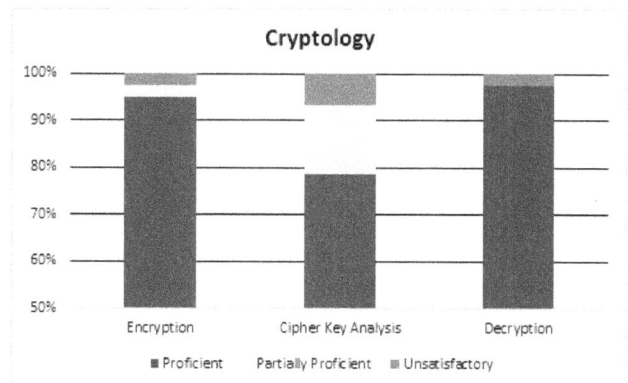

Figure 3: Results from our deployment of the Cryptology lesson plan in spring 2016.

Students showed overwhelming comfort with using Caesar ciphers to encrypt messages, with over 95% of students correctly encrypting a given message. They also did very well using a known Caesar cipher to decrypt an encrypted message, with 98% of students retrieving the original plaintext message. A few students struggled with using the Caesar cipher in reverse, and instead of decrypting the message, they re-encrypted it. A majority of students were also able to think about Caesar ciphers abstractly and determine how many possible cipher keys could exist using a simple cipher.

6.3 Parity Bits and Error Detection

The Parity Bits and Error Detection activity is an expanded version of the existing "Card Flip Magic" lesson from CS Unplugged [3]. Students start the lesson by seeing the magic trick. A classroom discussion introducing ASCII follows, and students learn that computers can sometimes make mistakes while transmitting data. Students then practice error detection on ASCII messages before realizing the same concept can be applied to explain the magic trick from the beginning of the class. Results from the ASCII worksheet are presented in Figure 4. A total of 118 students participated in this activity.

The results show that over 80% of students answered all questions at the Proficient level. In the first question, students were given a 7-bit ASCII chart and asked to convert binary patterns to letters. Almost all of the students were able to do this successfully. The second question asked students to compute the parity bit for four letters (they were given the first 22 letters as an example). In the final question, students were given a binary message and asked to identify the error. The questions related to parity were challenging for about 15% of the students.

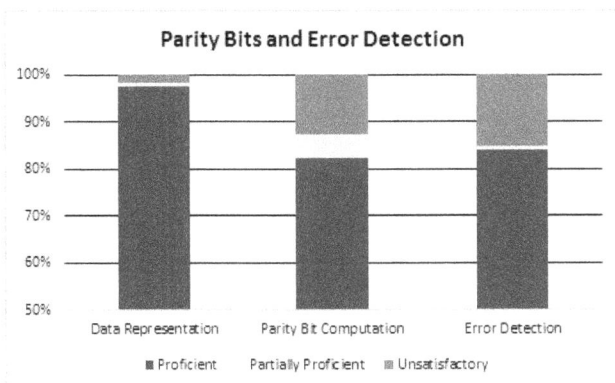

Figure 4: Results from our deployment of the Parity Bits and Error Detection lesson plan in spring 2016.

6.4 Minimal Spanning Trees

The Minimal Spanning Tree activity is an extension of the "Muddy City"activity from CS Unplugged [3]. Students first find a MST in the Muddy City worksheet using a brute force approach. After, students are introduced to Kruskal's algorithm for finding a minimal spanning tree (without any mention of proofs, graphs, edges, or nodes). They are then given another worksheet with a different graph to practice using Kruskal's algorithm. A classroom discussion helps identify where MSTs exist in the real world and how what they've learned can help solve certain types of problems. Finally (time permitting), students build their own graphs using pennies and toothpicks before rotating and finding the minimal spanning tree on their classmate's graph.

Results for the second MST worksheet (after students have learned Kruskal's algorithm) are given in Figure 5. Worksheets were collected from 121 students.

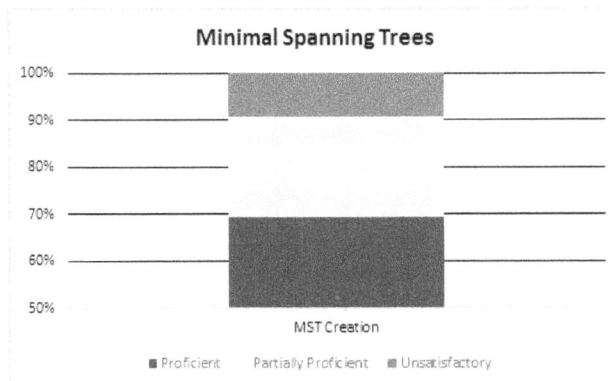

Figure 5: Results from our deployment of the Minimal Spanning Tree lesson plan in spring 2016.

A majority of students were able to correctly identify the minimal spanning tree by applying a given algorithm to the graph. When considering the students who scored *Partially Proficient* (where the MST was off by one or two edges), over 90% of students reached a solution.

6.5 Searching

The searching activity begins with a raffle ticket activity in which students try to locate a winning ticket. The optimal approach would be to use a binary search, but for this introduction students typically search in some random order. Next the ping pong demo, as described on the CS Unplugged website [3], is used to introduce binary search. An additional "guess my number" lecture is done via whole class discussion, to reinforce the concept. Finally students work in pairs on a worksheet in which students must search effectively (i.e., using binary search) to find the desired cow and save the entire herd from the attacking dragon. Figure 6 shows the results from the Dragons and Cows worksheet with 64 students.

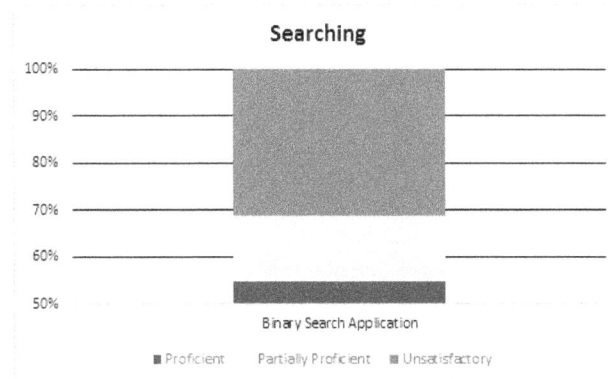

Figure 6: Results from our deployment of the Searching lesson plan in spring 2016.

As Figure 6 shows, only 53% of the students performed a correct binary search. Another 14% were on the right track but made a mistake in applying the algorithm. The remaining 31% did not apply a binary search. It's not clear whether the lack of performance is due to students not understanding binary search or due to the structure of the activity. The worksheet included 26 cows labeled A-Z, and students needed to find the specified cow (by weight) within five guesses. The students were not required to use binary search, but we hoped that they would choose to do so in order to find the cow quickly. The majority of students did choose one of the middle cows (M or N) for their first guess. But with only 12 or 13 cows remaining at that point, a number of students did not continue doing a strict binary search. Despite this, most students were able to locate the desired cow within five guesses. In this case, the activity was engaging, but not an adequate assessment of students' understanding.

7. EXTENDING CS UNPLUGGED

This paper presents results from six CS Unplugged activities. For the binary number activity, we followed the "Count the Dots" lesson plan from the CS Unplugged website [3] but developed our own worksheet to assess students' understanding. We also added an activity to reinforce the number of bits needed for a given number and a fun game (Go Fish) for students to practice binary conversions. The error detection activity uses the "Card Flip Magic" activity but with additional worksheets to more directly focus students' attention on parity bits. The lesson plan includes time for students to practice the magic trick with a partner. The cryptology activity was developed from scratch at Colorado School of Mines. The fruit vendor FSA activity is included on the CS

Unplugged website as an alternative to the "Treasure Hunt" activity. We added the assessment worksheets. The minimal spanning tree activity uses the "Muddy City" activity but with an additional worksheet for students to attempt after learning about Kruskal's algorithm. The searching activity replaces the "Battleship" exercise with two similarly structured activities, one dealing with raffle tickets and one with a dragon attacking cows.

In addition to these activities, we have deployed five others: Image Representation (added an assessment worksheet), Artificial Intelligence (added a career extension), Computer Vision (developed from scratch), Routing (developed from scratch) and Sorting (added more whole-class discussion and an assessment worksheet). See [1] for details.

8. CONCLUSIONS

Using CS Unplugged activities for after school groups or other demonstrations have been shown to be sufficiently engaging to keep kids' attention in the lesson. When being deployed in classrooms, however, the activities need more structure and content. Since computational thinking is fairly new, and not understood well by those outside of computer science, the activities need to provide methods to measure and convey what students are learning so that teachers and school administrators can better justify supporting these topics.

In this paper we have presented an approach that supplements CS Unplugged activities with worksheets that relate specifically to CT skills and are designed to capture students' understanding. Our first pilot test with these activities and worksheets helped us identify a number of issues. The second pilot showed improvement, but the results were not as high as we would have liked. After a final round of revisions, we achieved results greater than 50% on all questions, with many results greater than 80% and some approaching 100%.

A few lessons that we learned from our pilot tests:

- A priming activity, in which students attempt to solve a problem in a naïve fashion (e.g., attempting Muddy City before knowing Kruskal's algorithm), is often useful to focus students' attention.

- Students need individual practice to fully grasp a concept. Whole class demonstrations help to engage students and introduce material, but are not sufficient for producing desired results on assessment worksheets.

- Instructions on worksheets must be kept to a minimum and edited carefully so that students can quickly attempt the exercise. Any confusion about what they need to do will result in many students not even attempting the activity. Logistics must be carefully considered to ensure all students have a role to play (any amount of down time potentially results in bored, disengaged students and lower assessment results).

- Vocabulary on worksheets must be consistent with how topics are presented.

- Real world connections help to engage students' interest, but examples must be relevant to the audience (i.e., middle school students).

The results from the spring 2016 deployment are promising. Much remains to be done, however, to a) determine the range of topics that are appropriate for middle school students, b) design additional worksheets that are both engaging for the students and map well to CT concepts, and c) incorporate these worksheets and assessments into lesson plans that can be used by middle school teachers with limited knowledge of CT.

9. ACKNOWLEDGMENTS

The authors would like to thank the CS Unplugged team at Mines (Stephen Kennicutt, Nicholas Dyer, Shelly Konopka, Mykel Allen, Vy Ta and Martin Kuchta) for their assistance in refining, deploying and assessing the CS Unplugged activities. This material is based upon work supported by the National Science Foundation under Grant Numbers CNS-1240964 and DGE-0801692. Any opinions, findings, and conclusions or recommendations expressed in this material are those of the author(s) and do not necessarily reflect the views of the National Science Foundation.

10. REFERENCES

[1] CS Unplugged at Mines. http://toilers.mines.edu/CS-Unplugged. Retrieved 28 April 2016.

[2] Computer Science Teachers Association. Operational definition of computational thinking. http://csta.acm.org, 2011. Retrieved 28 April 2016.

[3] CS Unplugged. About CS Unplugged. http://csunplugged.org, 2015. Retrieved 28 April 2016.

[4] Q. Cutts, S. Esper, and B. Simon. Computing as the 4th "R": A general education approach to computing education. In *International Workshop on Computing Education Research*, Rhode Island, 2011.

[5] Exploring Computer Science. http://exploringcs.org. Retrieved 28 April 2016.

[6] D. D. Garcia and D. Ginat. Demystifying computing with magic. In *Special Interest Group on Computer Science Education*, Raleigh, 2012.

[7] L. Lambert and H. Guiffre. Computer science outreach in an elementary school. *Journal of Computing Sciences in Colleges*, 24(3):118–124, 2009.

[8] T. Nishida, S. Kanemune, Y. Idosaka, M. Namiki, T. Bell, and Y. Kuno. A CS Unplugged design pattern. In *Special Interest Group on Computer Science Education*, Chattanooga, 2009.

[9] R. Taub, M. Ben-Ari, and M. Armoni. The effect of CS Unplugged on middle-school students' view of CS. In *Conference on Innovation and Technology in Computer Science Education*, Paris, 2009.

[10] R. Thies and J. Vahrenhold. Reflections on outreach programs in CS classes: Learning objectives for "unplugged" activities. In *Special Interest Group on Computer Science Education*, Raleigh, 2012.

[11] R. Thies and J. Vahrenhold. On plugging "unplugged" into CS classes. In *Special Interest Group on Computer Science Education*, Denver, 2013.

[12] J. M. Wing. Computational thinking. *Communications of the ACM*, 49(3):33–35, 2006.

Interactive Exercises for Teaching Logic Circuits

Ville Karavirta
University of Turku,
Department of Information
Technology
Vesilinnantie 4
Turku, Finland
visaka@utu.fi

Rolf Lindén
University of Turku,
Department of Information
Technology
Vesilinnantie 4
Turku, Finland
rolind@utu.fi

Einari Kurvinen
University of Turku,
Department of Information
Technology
Vesilinnantie 4
Turku, Finland
emakur@utu.fi

Mikko-Jussi Laakso
University of Turku,
Department of Information
Technology
Vesilinnantie 4
Turku, Finland
milaak@utu.fi

ABSTRACT

Logic circuits are a central concept in understanding how computers and electronics work underneath. While there are educational, web-based systems for visualizing and building circuits, few systems exist which are capable of providing automatically assessed exercises with visual feedback on the topic. In this paper, we describe the lechef library for providing exercises on logic circuits. The library supports two types of exercises: 1) giving students a logic circuit and the input to the circuit asking them to give the input and output values for each gate in the circuit, and 2) giving students a truth table of the wanted circuit and requiring them to construct a circuit fulfilling the requirements. Furthermore, we explain how we integrated it into the ViLLE learning environment and used it on our introductory computer science course. We also report on our initial findings on student experiences on using the exercises as well as their results. We believe the system and our experiences provide valuable feedback to other members of the community on how and why to use such exercises.

CCS Concepts

•Theory of computation → Logic and verification; •Applied computing → Interactive learning environments; •Hardware → Logic circuits;

Keywords

logic circuits; educational technology; automatic assessment

ITiCSE '16, July 9 – 13, 2016, Arequipa, Peru

1. INTRODUCTION

Logic circuits are a central concept in understanding how computers and electronics work underneath. Understanding how logic gates work provides the necessary background on understanding how more complex circuits can be composed of them, and, ultimately, how computers can execute the instructions given to them.

Several educational systems to help learning and understanding logic circuits already exist. However, they typically aim for understanding more complex circuits, or for visualizing values of the circuit. Relatively few systems are able to offer exercises for students, especially with guiding feedback.

We are strong believers in *active learning* [1], that is, that students learn best when they are actively working on the topic. Furthermore, as we are used to classes with hundreds of students, *automatic assessment* is essential in our online education. When using automatic assessment, learners can work on online exercises whenever it suits them best. Moreover, the timely feedback – guiding and visual – can help their learning. For the teachers, automatic assessment can provide a way to reduce the time and resources needed to grade student work. This also makes it possible to give more coursework for students, as well as allow teachers a better use of their time. In programming education, there is an ever-growing number of automatic assessment systems [2, 3]. However, there is a lack of systems with logic circuits.

To overcome the lack of a suitable system for logic circuits, we built the lechef library[1]. It is an open-source[2] JavaScript library for providing automatically assessed exercises on logic circuits with visual and immediate feedback. Furthermore, we integrated lechef into the ViLLE learning environment. Our initial experiences with students indicate that they find the exercises useful.

The rest of this paper is organized as follows. In Section 2, we introduce the lechef library and in Section 3 we describe how we integrated it into the ViLLE environment. In Section 4 we describe our use of the tool on a course as well as initial student results and feedback. We go through related

---

[1]https://vkaravir.github.io/lechef/
[2]https://github.com/vkaravir/lechef/

work and other tools in Section 5 and discuss and conclude our contribution in Section 6.

2. THE LECHEF LIBRARY

The lechef library is a JavaScript library which supports exercises for initially understanding logic circuits. Here, we start by describing the components and utilities provided by the library and then describe the types of exercises which can be built with the system.

2.1 Library Overview

The lechef library supports the basic logic gates NOT, AND, OR, NAND, NOR, XOR, and EQV, as well as input and output from the circuit. These components are shown in Figure 1. The current version also includes the half-adder and the half-subtractor, but these have not been used with students yet.

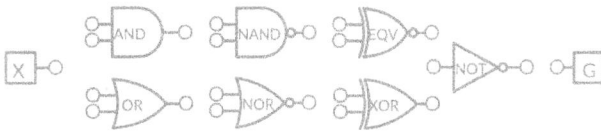

Figure 1: Components supported the library.

The components, when used, are always part of a logic circuit. A circuit editor provides an interactive way to edit circuits with drag-and-drop operations. With the editor, components can be added or removed from the circuit, and connected to other components by dragging connections from one component's output into another component's input. On the other hand, the logic circuit also provides a JavaScript API that can be used to specify a circuit. Thus, a logic circuit can be defined by writing code or with the editor.

On top of the logic circuit visualization and the editor, we have built interactive exercises with automatic and immediate feedback. There are two types of exercises, both of which will be introduced in the next subsections.

2.2 Simulation exercises

In the circuit simulation exercise, the learner is given a logic circuit and the input values are fixed and given. The exercise requires the learner to set the values of all the inputs and outputs of the components in the circuit to the correct values. This is done by toggling the values with mouse clicks. An example of a circuit simulation exercise is shown in Figure 2. Note, that while the "Reset" and "Feedback" buttons are often used when giving such exercises to students, the buttons are not added by lechef. Instead, they should be created with whatever learning environment is eventually used. The library does include the functionality to reset the exercises and to create the feedback, though.

The visual feedback is shown for each input and output of every component whether it was correct or not. An example of such feedback is shown in Figure 3. Every input/output is colored either green or red based on whether it is correct or incorrect, respectively. In addition to showing the feedback, it is possible to, for example, calculate a grade based on how many of the inputs/outputs were correct.

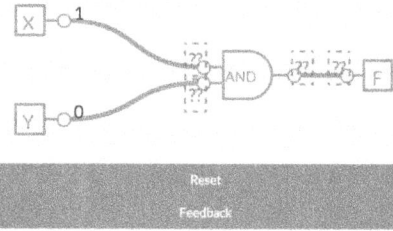

Figure 2: Example of a simulation exercise.

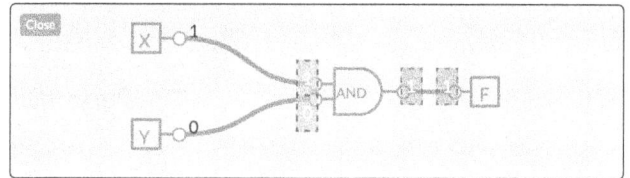

Figure 3: Example of a simulation exercise feedback.

2.3 Design exercises

The circuit design exercise requires the learner to build a logic circuit matching the assignment description. Typically, this would be the truth table or Boolean expression describing the circuit. An example of a circuit design exercise is shown in Figure 4. In the example exercise, the student is instructed to design a circuit which has the given truth table. Note, that the gates available in the example are AND, NOT, and OR. The available gates can be specified for each exercise, thus essentially preventing learners to use certain gates, or forcing them to use the gates wanted by the instructor.

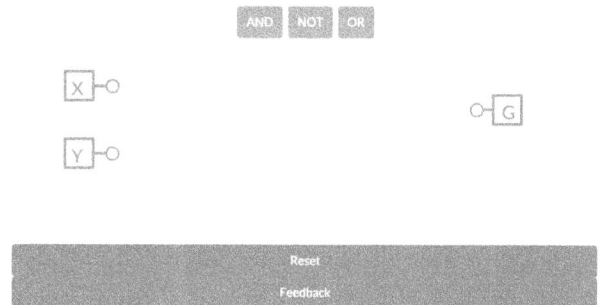

Figure 4: Example of a design exercise.

The correct solution for a design exercise is always specified as an input→output mapping. An example of the feedback generated by comparing the correct solution to the learner's circuit is shown in Figure 5. The feedback shows the correctness of the output for each input. Each line in the feedback table is interactive, and by clicking the row a learner can see how his/her circuit behaved with the input of the row. Again, based on the number of correct outputs, a correctness for the solution can be calculated when a grade is needed.

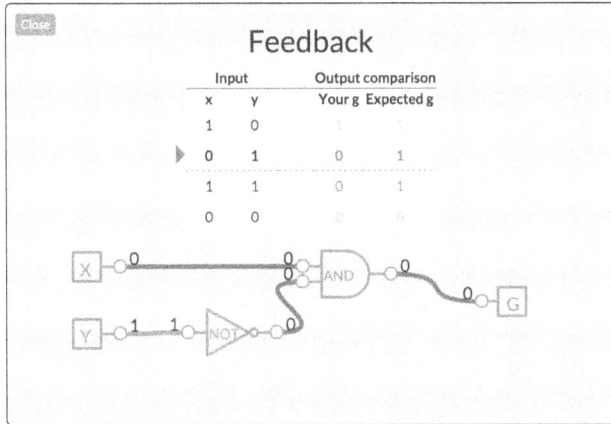

Figure 5: Example of a design exercise feedback. The circuit for input x=0, y=1 is shown, like it is shown when the learner clicks that row in the feedback table.

3. VILLE EXERCISE TYPE

The lechef library itself is a stand-alone library and can be used on any web page with the limitation of not being able to store the student answer and grade. To overcome this issue, we integrated it into the ViLLE learning environment [4] using the ViLLE exercise framework [5]. The effectiveness of the framework has been previously evaluated in various studies (see for example [6], [7]).

ViLLE is a learning environment with support for numerous types of exercises with automatic assessment and feedback. The exercise types include math exercises for elementary school and high school levels, programming exercises, databases and language learning. The environment includes a framework for creating new types of exercises without modifying or knowing the whole environment [5].

Using the exercise framework, we created an exercise type for learning logic circuits using the lechef library. An exercise type in ViLLE needs to provide an editor for creating new instances of the exercise used by teachers when creating their course content. The logic circuit exercise type includes an editor where both types of circuit exercises – simulation and design – can be created. In the simulation exercise, the teacher needs to create the circuit using the lechef editor as well as provide the input values. In the design exercise, the teacher only needs to provide the truth table of the correct circuit as well as specify the gates available for the learner.

For the learner, the exercises in ViLLE look a lot like those in Figures 2 and 4. Feedback is shown in another part of the ViLLE UI, after the learner requests for his/her solution to be submitted for grading. The shown feedback looks like the examples in Figures 3 and 5.

Like all exercise types in ViLLE, the logic circuit exercise collects every student submission for later use. The teacher can view every student submission at any time. The sub-

mission viewer shows the teacher the grade received by the student, and the same feedback the student was shown.

4. FIRST EXPERIENCES AND DATA ANALYSIS

Our first experience with using the lechef exercises was in the Fall of 2014, when several of the exercises were used on the course Introduction to Computer Science II at the University of Turku. The course covers the execution of a program from the level of logic gates all the way to the parsing and execution of a program written in a high-level programming language. Logic gates were covered for one week of the seven-week course.

The course was organized using a tutorial-based approach, where each week consisted of a lecture on the topic, followed by a two-hour tutorial where students worked in pairs reading and solving exercises on the topic of the week. Furthermore, each topic had a set of individually solved online assignments. On the course, there were lechef exercises in the tutorial and home assignments, as well as in the course exam. Both simulation exercises and design exercises were used.

After the tutorial, and as part of the same week's home assignments, there was a feedback questionnaire about the exercise type. The questionnaire included four claims which students had to answer on a scale of 1 ("Totally disagree") to 4 ("Totally agree"). The claims were the following: 1) The exercises helped my learning, 2) The exercises were easy to use, 3) The feedback of the exercise helped my learning, and 4) The exercises should be used in the future. The results are shown in Figure 6.

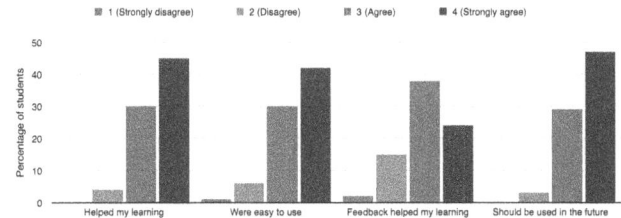

Figure 6: Student opinions of the exercise type.

In the feedback questionnaire, we also asked general, free-form feedback about the exercise type. The most often mentioned feedback was a complaint about not being able to remove gates and connections, and thus students were forced to reset their solution when they made a mistake. Furthermore, a bug causing connections to disappear when creating a tall circuit was mentioned by multiple students. Both issues were quickly fixed, and the improved version was already used in the exam. As for the positive feedback, the most often mentioned thing was that the exercise helped understand and learn logic circuits. Other comments included *"connection of the circuits [sic] was surprisingly smooth"*, *"exercises . . . worked and felt nice"*, *"logic circuit exercises were awesome"* and *"intuitive"*. Overall, a majority of the feedback was positive.

5. RELATED WORK

There have been many tools built for learning different aspects of logic circuits. The tools can be roughly divided to systems teaching digital logic design and systems focusing on simulation of circuits. As lechef includes both design and simulation features, we introduce systems in both categories.

HADES [8] is one of the early systems. It is a Java-based tool for simulating and visualizing digital circuits on the gate level. Yosof and Hassan have presented a Flash-based tool for learning digital logic design [9]. They presented interactive animations for exploring a wide range of topics, including logic gates, flip-flops, counters, electric components, etc. DLD-VISU [10] is a web-based animation and visualization tool for learning digital logic design. While the tool is aimed at students, it can also be used by instructors to generate examples. WinLogiLab [11] is a Windows application for learning digital logic design. It consists of several smaller modules including gate-level circuit diagrams, Boolean equations, and flip-flop circuits. SDLDS [12] is another tool for designing and simulating circuits.

Logisim [13] is a Java tool for creating and exploring the behavior of logic circuits. The tool supports basic gates, flip-flops, and custom components. LoGen [14] is another tool for gate-level and logic level generation and functional simulation of circuits. LoGen is a web-based tool implemented in PHP and HTML. The SmartSim[3] application (Window, Linux, and Raspberry Pi) can be used to create complex circuits and interactively simulate them. EasySim[4] is another commercial Windows application for creating and simulating circuits. DLSim3 [15] is a system for studying both low-level digital circuits as well as complete CPU designs.

Finally, VISUAL-VHDL [16] is a platform for visualizing digital circuits written in the VHDL language. It is an extension to the Java-based ANIMAL [17] educational animation system.

Many of the existing systems include much more advanced topics than lechef, which focuses on the basic logic gates. The biggest advantage of lechef is that it is open source and based on standard web technologies. Furthermore, unlike any of the other systems, lechef can be easily embedded into any online learning material.

6. DISCUSSION AND CONCLUSIONS

The redesign of our course required us to have interactive exercises on logic circuits. After reviewing the currently available options, it became clear that none of them fitted well with our requirements. We needed a system with interactive exercises, automatic assessment, immediate feedback, and the possibility to integrate with our ViLLE learning environment. Thus, we were forced to implement our own system.

The system we implemented is lechef, which supports the kind of interactive exercises we were after. Furthermore, it can be used in other contexts where logic circuit visualizations and editors are needed.

Our first experience with assigning lechef-based exercises to students was mostly positive. The negative feedback was related to bugs and missing features, which we fixed promptly. The anecdotal evidence we gathered from students suggests that majority of them felt the exercises helped their learning, were easy to use, and should be used in the future.

There is still room for improvement, though. First, we would like for the library to support more complex circuits. Moreover, we would like to do a proper evaluation of the effectiveness of the exercises in a controlled experiment. In addition, we will analyze the student solutions in order to understand the common mistakes they have on the behavior of the logic gates and circuits. Finally, we would like to create an open collection of exercises available to all educators. Hopefully, this collection could be created in collaboration with other teachers.

7. REFERENCES

[1] S. Grissom. Introduction to special issue on alternatives to lecture in the computer science classroom. *ACM Transactions on Computing Education (TOCE)*, 13.3(9), 2013.

[2] P. Ihantola, T. Ahoniemi, V. Karavirta, and O. Seppälä. Review of recent systems for automatic assessment of programming assignments. In *Proceedings of the 10th Koli Calling International Conference on Computing Education Research*, Koli Calling '10, pages 86–93, New York, NY, USA, 2010. ACM.

[3] K. Ala-Mutka. A survey of automated assessment approaches for programming assignments. *Computer Science Education*, 15(2):83–102, 2005.

[4] M.-J. Laakso, E. Kaila, and T. Rajala. Ville - collaborative education tool: Designing and implementing an exercise-based learning platform. *IEEE Transactions on Educational Technologies*, 2016, Submitted.

[5] V. Karavirta, R. Haavisto, E. Kaila, M.-J. Laakso, T. Rajala, and T. Salakoski. Interactive learning content for introductory computer science course using the ville learning environment. In *Proceedings of Learning and Teaching in Computing and Engineering*, 2015, Accepted.

[6] E. Kaila, T. Rajala, M.-J. Laakso, R. Lindén, E. Kurvinen, V. Karavirta, and Salakoski T. Comparing student performance between traditional and technologically enhanced programming course. In *Proceedings of the Seventeenth Australasian Computing Education Conference ACE2016*, 2016, Accepted.

[7] E. Kaila, E. Kurvinen, E. Lokkila, and M.-J. Laakso. Redesigning an object-oriented programming course. *IEEE Transactions on Educational Technologies*, 2016, Submitted.

[8] N. Hendrich. A java-based framework for simulation and teaching: Hades âĂŤ the hamburg design system. In B. Courtois, N. Guillemot, G. Kamarinos, and G. Stéhelin, editors, *Microelectronics Education*, pages 285–288. Springer Netherlands, 2000.

[9] N.H. Yusof and R. Hassan. Flash notes and easy electronic software (ees): New technique to improve digital logic design learning. In *Electrical Engineering and Informatics (ICEEI), 2011 International Conference on*, pages 1–6, July 2011.

[10] A. Shoufan, Z. Lu, and S. Huss. A web-based visualization and animation platform for digital logic design. *Learning Technologies, IEEE Transactions on*, PP(99):1–1, 2014.

---

[3]http://smartsim.org.uk/
[4]http://www.research-systems.com/easysim/easysim.htm

[11] C. Hacker and R. Sitte. Interactive teaching of elementary digital logic design with WinLogiLab. *Education, IEEE Transactions on*, 47(2):196–203, May 2004.

[12] Z. Stanisavljevic, V. Pavlovic, B. Nikolic, and J. Djordjevic. Sdlds – system for digital logic design and simulation. *Education, IEEE Transactions on*, 56(2):235–245, May 2013.

[13] C. Burch. Logisim: A graphical system for logic circuit design and simulation. *J. Educ. Resour. Comput.*, 2(1):5–16, March 2002.

[14] S. Kubisch, R. Rennert, H. Pfueller, and D. Timmermann. Logen – generation and simulation of digital logic on the gate-level via internet. In *E-Learning in Industrial Electronics, 2006 1ST IEEE International Conference on*, pages 46–51, Dec 2006.

[15] R. M. Salter and J. L. Donaldson. Using dlsim 3: A scalable, extensible, multi-level logic simulator. In *Proceedings of the 13th Annual Conference on Innovation and Technology in Computer Science Education*, ITiCSE '08, pages 315–315, New York, NY, USA, 2008. ACM.

[16] A. Shoufan, Z. Lu, and G. Rößling. A platform for visualizing digital circuit synthesis with vhdl. In *Proceedings of the Fifteenth Annual Conference on Innovation and Technology in Computer Science Education*, ITiCSE '10, pages 294–298, New York, NY, USA, 2010. ACM.

[17] G. Rößling and B. Freisleben. ANIMAL: A system for supporting multiple roles in algorithm animation. *Journal of Visual Languages & Computing*, 13(3):341–354, 2002.

An Empirical Analysis of Video Viewing Behaviors in Flipped CS1 Courses

Suzanne L. Dazo, Nicholas R. Stepanek, Robert Fulkerson, and Brian Dorn
University of Nebraska at Omaha
Omaha, NE 68182
{sdazo, nstepanek, rfulkerson, bdorn}@unomaha.edu

ABSTRACT

Video-enabled education is becoming increasingly popular in support of active learning in CS education. Although present work on both video based learning and flipped classrooms emphasize the necessity for students to view the materials, there is a lack of detailed, objective data on student viewing behaviors. This article aims to use fine grain student log data from TrACE, an asynchronous media platform, to understand student viewing behaviors in three sections of a flipped CS1 course taught by the same instructor. We find that students often have low compliance with video viewing expectations in one section, and that re-watching course content does not often occur. Watching course content earlier has a significant correlation to course performance, and other behaviours correlate when compliance is not enforced via course requirements. These findings highlight concerns for flipped classroom researchers and suggest methods instructors can use to improve student viewing behaviors.

CCS Concepts

•Social and professional topics → Computing education; *CS1;*

Keywords

flipped courses, online video usage

1. INTRODUCTION

The flipped classroom model continues to garner significant interest among both computing educators and STEM educators more generally. Put simply, a flipped class is one where students complete direct initial instruction tasks independently prior to course sessions, with face-to-face class time being reserved for hands-on activities related to the course material for which students have prepared [2, 8]. Discipline-based education conferences, like SIGCSE in computer science and ASEE in engineering, now regularly include multiple reports on practical experiences with flipping (see, e.g. [1, 5, 6, 7, 11]), and entire conferences on the

ITiCSE '16, July 09 - 13, 2016, Arequipa, Peru

© 2016 Copyright held by the owner/author(s). Publication rights licensed to ACM.
ISBN 978-1-4503-4231-5/16/07. . . $15.00

DOI: http://dx.doi.org/10.1145/2899415.2899468

flipped classroom have been formed in recent years. In the majority of both classroom reports and research studies on flipping, students' preparatory work takes the form of viewing web-based video lectures that contain similar content to more traditional face-to-face settings. While we acknowledge that not all flipped courses rely on video viewing as preparatory work, its prevalence motivates our focus here.

Most users of flipping undergird their work with theoretical arguments about active and constructivist learning and/or the practical benefits of time-shifting lecture through video-based instruction. Bishop and Verleger [2] summarize much of the common literature on student-centered learning theories and note the importance of them in the intentional design of the classroom activities. They caution against conceptualizing "the flipped classroom based only on the presence (or absence) of computer technology such as video lectures" [2]. Nonetheless, many authors are quick to highlight intuitive benefits of video lectures like students' ability to work through material at their own pace and review content at a later time [5, 12].

Yet, reports on increased learning gains in flipped classrooms are mixed, and published studies often suffer from multiple confounds which makes interpreting and comparing results difficult [2]. Early work by Day and Foley [3] showed promising gains in computing courses, but recent controlled studies in several STEM disciplines at one institution showed no significant differences between courses utilizing or not-utilizing videos [9, 13].

Studies of flipped classrooms commonly examine artifacts of student performance and attitudinal survey data, but the current literature suffers from a significant missing variable— objective behavioral data about how students actually interact with the online course content. Instructors generally assume that students watch videos as assigned and may use entrance quizzes at the start of class to further incentivize this behavior [7], but instructors are often left wondering to what degree students interacted with the materials.

In this paper, we seek to address this gap by providing empirical evidence related to common assumptions about students' viewing behaviors during a flipped CS1 class over the course of a full semester. Further, we examine how instructional and technological changes introduced over three iterations of the course impact student viewing behaviors. Specifically, we address the following research questions:

RQ1 To what extent do students actually prepare for class by viewing videos in advance?

RQ2 To what extent do students revisit course content?

RQ3 Which viewing behaviors correlate with course performance metrics?

RQ4 How do student viewing behaviors vary with sociotechnical changes in the class?

In the remainder of this paper we first provide a brief overview of recent reports of flipping in CS classrooms (section 2). In section 3 we then detail specific aspects of the course and study methodology used here. Section 4 outlines the results of our data collection over three semesters, followed by a broader discussion of our findings relative to instructional changes in section 5. We conclude by examining implications of our work for both classroom practice and research on flipping.

2. RELATED WORK

Research on implementations of flipped classrooms is plentiful, but student viewership trends and their potential effects on flipped classroom success is still relatively unexplored. Due to the nature of many flipped classrooms, watching videos prior to class is necessary to effectively learn the material and be prepared for the assigned tasks [11]. If a significant portion of students come unprepared for class, the instructor may be forced to spend more time reviewing the lecture material, taking away activity time [7]. Otherwise group work will be less productive as some students will not have the requisite knowledge. Gannod et al. [5] pose a number of implementation strategies for maintaining student viewership, as this is considered a precursor to productive flipped classes.

Even though student preparation is widely recognized as being essential to student success in flipped classrooms, studies generally rely on student self-reports or do not consider the possibility of students not preparing for class in their research. Gehringer, in an implementation of a flipped classroom [6], reported that instructors thought students generally came to class prepared, likely due to a pre-quiz forcing students to keep up with material. However, students self-reported that they watched on average 11.6 out of 25 total videos (46%). Lacher and Lewis attempted to measure the legitimacy of quizzes as a measure of preparedness [7], but ultimately did not find evidence that entry quizzes improved learning outcomes. Lockwood and Esselstein, in another flipped class implementation, were worried that students' tendency to not complete assigned reading before class may carry over to lecture videos in the flipped setting [10]. They found that 70% of students reported having "almost always" watched the assigned videos before class, though students needed to get used to coming prepared.

Not only do students in several of these studies report low compliance to viewing videos, but self-reported measurements often suffer from recollection biases. This leaves one wondering if at least some of the conflicting findings in studies of learning gains in flipped classes stem from a lack of consistent data about student preparation. Not only is this an important variable for research, but it also would serve as a key piece of formative data for instructors prior to the start of in-class activities. In this study we aim to provide such objective data and examine its relationship to student performance indicators.

3. METHOD AND DATA COLLECTION

3.1 Course Structure

The course studied in this paper is a typical 15-week, objects-late CS1 course covering introductory Java concepts

Table 1: Descriptive Information on Course Videos

Number of Videos	25
Minimum Length	26:49
Max Length	1:13:36
Average Length	47:53
Std. Deviation	11:42

and syntax for data-types, conditionals, loops, methods, etc. At the time data collection began, the instructor (the third author) had flipped the course for 1.5 years, and we examined data from three consecutive semesters (Fall 2014, Spring 2015, and Fall 2015 in North American vernacular). Students in this course come from a variety of majors. Basic college algebra is a prerequisite for the course, and students enrolled in the flipped section were required to own laptops which they had to bring to class for programming activities.

Across all semesters, the structure of the course remained largely the same and video lectures were unchanged. Students were assigned 25 videos to watch via the Web prior to coming to class during the semester; see Table 1 for summary data about the videos used. The 75-minute course period was divided between a brief summary lecture at the beginning of class ($\approx$ 20 minutes), in-class activities ($\approx$ 40 minutes), and a daily quiz distributed at the end of class ($\approx$ 15 minutes). Summary lectures highlighted key takeaways from the video and were used to provide additional examples motivating the day's activities. The in-class activities included a mixture of reviewing the previous class's quiz, working through small programs as a class, in groups or individually, and taking time to explain concepts of the next programming assignment.

3.2 TrACE and Class Integration

In course offerings prior this study, students enrolled in the flipped CS1 course were instructed to prepare for class by viewing video lectures through the university's learning management system. During the study period, students used a new collaborative streaming platform called TrACE for this purpose. TrACE provides basic video playback functionality alongside affordances for students (and instructors) to add asynchronous discussions within a video at given times and physical locations [4]. Students are thus able to ask and answer questions or engage in other sensemaking activities while completing their class preparations. Additionally TrACE collects fine-grained log data about students' interactions with the system. This allows for examining viewing patterns at both the individual and class level.

Instructors using TrACE can take advantage of additional features to further integrate the system into their course. Due dates can be assigned to each video, which then allows TrACE to remind students of which videos to watch upon logging in. Instructors can insert special discussion types that automatically pause the playback interface for students and pose a free-response question. Lastly, the system also includes a basic analytics dashboard that allows instructors to investigate student viewing and posting behaviors on videos.

TrACE integration with the CS1 class evolved over the study period. During the Fall'14 term, it was used primarily as a delivery mechanism for the lecture videos instead of the LMS, with the intent that the instructor would be able to gain some insight into viewing behaviors via the analytics. There were no graded requirements for watching or otherwise interacting with the videos. For the following term (Spring'15), the instructor placed the following self-reflection question near the end of videos to encourage

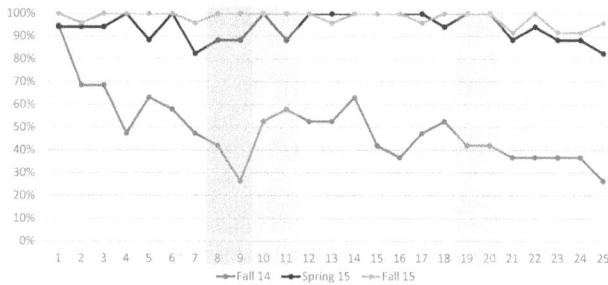

(a) Percentage of students accessing course videos

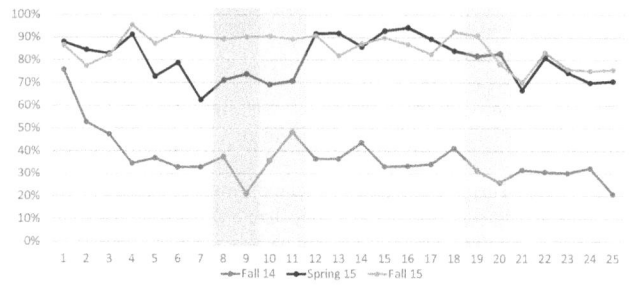

(b) Average percent of content of videos viewed by students

Figure 1: Viewing and Coverage Metrics by Video (X-axis)

more student engagement, but interaction was not graded initially:

> "Do you feel you have a good understanding of the material in this lecture? If not, what topic specifically would you like more information about? If yes, what would you feel comfortable explaining to someone else?"

Around mid-term (ie., week 6, video 13), the instructor instituted a new policy that required students to add at least one post or reply to each video as part of a course participation grade. This policy was in place for the full duration of the Fall'15 academic term, and grading weights were adjusted to increase the emphasis on in-class work over quiz marks. This was intended to force the students to use the material they had watched, thus encouraging them to make sure to watch and interact with the lectures before coming to class. We will revisit these course changes in section 5 as they relate to research question four.

3.3 Data Collection and Processing

At the beginning of each semester, students enrolled in each of the three courses were given the opportunity to participate in this research study. For those consenting to participate, we analyzed two primary data sources: naturally occurring course performance metrics collected during the term (homework, exam, and course grades) and behavioral traces captured during their use of TrACE. Students enrolled in the course but who did not grant consent still had access to all system features, but their data was excluded from the analysis here. Out of the 30, 20, and 28 students in the Fall '14, Spring '15, and Fall '15 semesters respectively, 23, 19, and 24 students opted to participate in the study.

Fine-grained log data for each student was parsed into sessions, wherein an individual session represents an instance of a student opening a particular video in a course. A session thus encapsulates all actions from that point until the student left the video page or the browser connection timed out. In order to account for misclicks leading to seconds-long sessions on an unintended video, we then filtered out all empty sessions where no student actions were recorded beyond opening and closing the video. Further, as we were interested in the behaviors of students who would watch every lecture video, only those who completed the full course were included. We filtered out data from those who dropped the course early or failed the course due to academic dishonesty. 4, 2, and 1 students were left out for these reasons in the Fall '14, Spring '15, and Fall '15 semesters respectively. After removing data from those who opted out of the study and those who were filtered out, our dataset included data from 75.6% of students from all semesters.

The filtered set of sessions was then used to calculate various metrics for student interactions on videos in the course including data about content coverage and viewing punctuality. We will discuss the details of each of these metrics alongside the data in the following section.

4. RESULTS

Results in this section are structured around the first three research questions (RQ1–RQ3) posed in the introduction.

4.1 Student Preparation (RQ1)

We examine students' preparation for the flipped class sessions using three primary metrics: videos viewed, coverage, and punctuality. Videos viewed examines the tendency of students to open videos at all. Coverage statistics measure the percentage of each video played by a student. Punctuality deals with the time at which students accessed the content for the first time, with the hope being that students accessed content prior to the assigned class period. Table 2 compares differences between averages for these values in each course. We present results of these analyses in turn.

The first of these metrics, *videos viewed*, is the percentage of videos accessed by students out of the 25 videos in the course. This is a common measure of compliance reported in several other studies [6, 10], but here it is computed from objective log file data rather than self-reports. Figure 1a presents this viewing percentage over time for each video in the term. Shaded regions represent pairs of videos due on a single class day. For every class, the first video is very high, with over 90% of the class watching it. A pronounced decreasing trend in viewing is apparent in Fall'14, though Spring'15 and Fall'15 remain fairly high throughout the semester, with some videos having a 100% access rate.

A one-way ANOVA showed statistically significant differences in video viewing between the groups ($F(2, 56) = 36.40, p < 0.001$) (see Table 2). Post-hoc, pair-wise analysis with Bonferroni correction identified Fall'14 students as accessing significantly fewer videos than either Spring'15 ($p < 0.001$) or Fall'15 ($p < 0.001$). However, there was not a significant difference between Spring'15 and Fall'15.

Table 2: Mean Viewing Statistics with Std. Deviations (σ)

Term	N	Videos Viewed % (σ)	Content Coverage % (σ)	Punctuality in Hours (σ)
Fa'14	19	49.3 (33.7)	36.7 (33.2)	-88.0 (217.7)
Spr'15	17	94.1 (9.2)	80.1 (18.7)	0.6 (33.8)
Fa'15	23	98.3 (4.8)	85.3 (20.1)	34.6 (33.3)

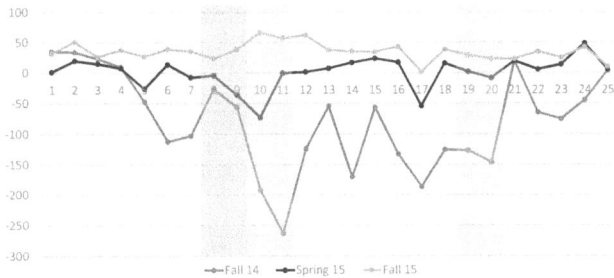

Figure 2: Average student punctuality in hours (Y) per lecture video (X)

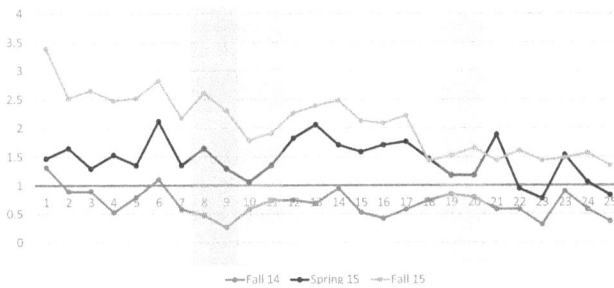

Figure 3: Average student visits (Y) per video (X)

An obvious limitation of the videos viewed metric is that it simply provides a binary measure of whether a student has accessed a video, and does not account for how much of a video was actually watched during a session. Thus we define *content coverage* as the proportion of each video actually played by the student. It is computed using data about play-head positioning when various actions take place within a session (e.g., play, pause, seek, etc.).[1] For each student we computed the average coverage across all 25 videos and then a class average from these partial averages, which can be seen in Table 2.

As shown in Figure 1b, coverage is uniformly lower than the simple videos viewed values, as might be expected. Coverage for Fall'14 roughly mirrors trends in video viewing percentage with a steady decline in coverage over the semester. However, there seem to be differences between Spring'15 and Fall'15 that were not as noticeable when looking at video viewing alone. Spring'15 has lower coverage in the first half of the term but jumps up at video 12, one video before the introduction of the new course requirement to contribute one post per video.

A one-way ANOVA showed statistically significant differences in coverage between the groups ($F(2,56) = 22.78, p < 0.001$) (see Table 2). In post-hoc analysis, Fall'14 had significantly lower coverage values in comparison to both Spring'15 ($p < 0.001$) and Fall'15 ($p < 0.001$). However, there was no statistically significant difference between Spring'15 and Fall'15, despite an apparent visual distinction for the early videos in the courses in Figure 1b.

Looking at the data from a different perspective, we define *punctuality* as a measure of the first time a student viewed or interacted with some portion of a video relative to the start of class.[2] Figure 2 shows average student punctuality in hours for each lecture video in each course. Zero hours on

---

[1] Videos not viewed by a student have a coverage of 0.

[2] The punctuality metric excludes students who never watched the video, as it cannot be computed for them.

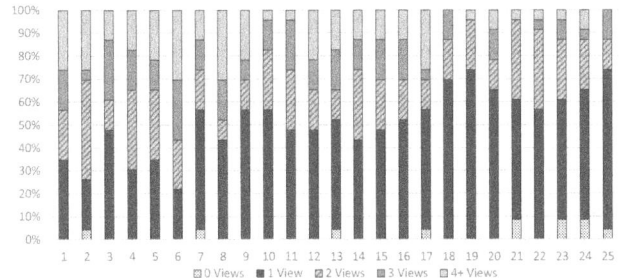

Figure 4: Visiting proportions for Fall 2015 students

the y-axis represents the start of class, with positive values indicating the video was watched before class, and negative values after class. Students in the Fall'14 semester almost exclusively viewed each video *after* class beyond the first four videos. This is drastically different compared to the average punctuality of Spring'15 and Fall'15. Students in the Spring'15 semester viewed all but three videos prior to class on average, and average punctuality for Fall'15 students was always positive even when considering one standard deviation from the mean.

A one-way ANOVA analysis showed statistically significant differences in average punctuality between the groups ($F(2,55) = 5.074, p = 0.009$) (see Table 2). A post-hoc pair-wise analysis using Bonferroni correction showed that Fall'15 students viewed videos significantly earlier than Fall'14 (p=0.008). Although there appears to be modest differences between Spring'15 and the other two semesters in Figure 2, these differences are not statistically significant.

At a high level, there were clear differences in students' compliance with course expectations to view video content prior to the start of face-to-face class sessions, and Fall'15 students exhibited behaviors closest to the ideal. We revisit possible reasons for these differences relative to sociotechnical changes in the course in Section 5.

4.2 Revisiting Course Content (RQ2)

A commonly cited benefit of using videos in the flipped environment is that students can revisit the material as needed. To investigate the extent to which students actually revisit content, we analyzed the number of non-empty sessions generated by each student for each video. There were statistically significant differences between the courses ($F(2,56) = 13.27, p < 0.001$) where, on average, Fall'14 students viewed videos 0.70 ($\sigma = 0.61$) times, Spring'15 students viewed videos 1.47 ($\sigma = 1.03$) times, and Fall'15 students viewed videos 2.11 ($\sigma = 0.93$) times.

To visualize revisiting trends, Figure 3 shows the mean number of visits per student for each video and course. The ranges of averages in the Fall'14 and Spring'15 semesters are smaller than that of Fall'15, where a downward trend is apparent over the term. All videos except two in the Fall'14 semester have means below 1, also demonstrating the low compliance that term. Spring'15 has averages mostly between 1 and 2, and Fall'15 has higher averages than both courses for most of the term until around video 18. We posit that the large drop off of viewing at video 18 in Fall'15 may be from students re-watching less due to the freshness of material from the end of the course, though the further exploration of this is beyond the scope of this analysis.

Limiting our analysis to the latter two terms, where students were markedly more compliant with course viewing policies, we were still surprised to observe that the proportion of students revisiting videos was lower than expected. Figure 4 shows the distribution of students visiting each video 0, 1, 2, 3, and 4 or more times during Fall'15. In Fall'15, only 11 of 25 videos were multiply accessed by a majority of students, and in Spring'15 only 2 of the 25 videos were multiply accessed by a majority of students. In other words, most students tend to access most videos 0 or 1 time, even when they exhibit positive behaviors with respect to content viewing deadlines.

Overall, students do not appear to be revisiting content with great regularity even in instances where they view content initially on time. However, there were clear cases of individual students who accessed videos many times and may thus skew class averages significantly. For example in Fall'15, the maximum revisits on a video for a single student was 20, and the maximum average across all videos for a single student was 5.08. Admittedly, one limitation of our analysis here is that we do not attempt to evaluate the quality of the revisit interaction nor the time lapse between visits to a video, but we see these as potential future extensions that could shed additional light on these behaviors.

4.3 Correlations with Performance (RQ3)

To investigate the relationship between students' behaviors and their course performance, we employ non-parametric statistics due to the non-normality of grade distributions. Despite clear differences in viewing behaviors, a preliminary Kruskal-Wallis test found no statistically significant differences in grade distributions between the courses.

Table 3 shows the Spearman correlation coefficients between the various student behavior metrics and final course grades for each course separately. In Fall'14, videos viewed, coverage, punctuality and revisiting all positively correlated significantly with course grade, while only punctuality exhibited a statistically significant positive relationship across all semesters.

It is interesting to note that the course with the lowest overall compliance (Fall'14) with video watching had the largest number of significant indicators of performance. Put another way, when students are not adhering to course preparation, those that do voluntarily engage with content are likely to also perform well in the class. However, when students are more uniformly compliant with viewing (as in Spring'15 and Fall'15), many of these co-variates fall away. At the very least, this suggests that there is a strong need to quantitatively control for differences in viewing behaviors when conducting analyses of students' performance in flipped courses.

5. DISCUSSION

Per the research questions posed, there are a number of important takeaways about student viewing behaviors in flipped classes:

- With regard to the question of student preparation in flipped classes (RQ1), we saw marked differences between courses. While Fall'15 students' behaviors closely approximated an instructor ideal—viewing all videos well in advance of class—students from Fall'14 were highly sporadic in viewing and generally watched videos after the class period where they were assigned. Viewing is not guaranteed and should not be assumed.
- Although a common benefit of using web-based video is the persistence of lecture material for later review, we found that students infrequently did so even when

Table 3: Spearman correlation coefficients for behavioral data and course grade

Metric	Fall'14	Spring'15	Fall'15
% Videos Viewed	0.499*	0.349	0.289
Avg % Coverage	0.608*	0.310	0.164
Avg Punctuality	0.533*	0.596*	0.475*
Avg Visits/Video	0.461*	-0.393	-0.215
Total Posts	0.228	0.305	0.187

* denotes significant correlations at the $\alpha = 0.05$ level

initial viewing compliance was high (RQ2). The reality is that students may not give persistence of videos the same value that instructors believe they do.

- Students who voluntarily watch all videos (and do so earlier and more completely) tend to perform better in the course (RQ3). However, when compliance with viewing prior to class is generally high in a course, only the punctuality measure significantly correlates with student performance.

Given that we observed such stark differences between the three terms under study, it is natural to ask whether these differences were just due to changes in the students enrolled each term or whether there was something different about the course design that might explain things (and thus be adopted by other flipped course instructors).

5.1 Examining Course Differences (RQ4)

In examining the differences between courses, we first consider Fall'14. During that term, the instructor simply transferred his earlier videos into the TrACE system, but did not alter course expectations despite having greater abilities to monitor student interactions. In this sense, Fall'14 is a more typical flipped class, and viewing rates of less than 50% resemble self-reported data from earlier studies [6, 10].

Fall'15 students demonstrated considerably more desirable behaviors and watched the vast majority of video content early. We noted three key differences as compared to the course a year earlier:

1. The instructor uniformly required students to post at least one video-related comment in each video as part of the participation grade, and he gave students a structured reflection prompt at the end of each video if they had not already posted something earlier.
2. The playback interface in TrACE actively provided unobtrusive feedback to students about which video segments had (and had not) been viewed. This feature had previously not been available.
3. Starting about 1 month into the course, TrACE began automatically reminding students to view content due in the next 48 hours along with overdue content if it had not been previously accessed.

While it is hard to say exactly which of these changes had the most influence, there are indications that the sociotechnical system made a difference. For example, the first major shift in student behaviors seemed to occur midway through Spring'15 around video 12. This nearly coincides with video 13 where the instructor instituted the new posting policy that term. Following the change in Spring'15, students were even more compliant with viewing requirements.

Evidence in support of the TrACE changes also was present. On average, students in Fall'15 were watching videos 34.6 hours in advance of class, which roughly falls within the 48 hour email reminder threshold introduced that term. Taken together, we see significant potential for these features to encourage advance preparation among students in flipped courses, but more evidence is needed to quantitatively examine these impacts in other courses and qualitatively understand their role on student attitudes.

5.2 Limitations and Future Work

While the results of this study provide new empirical evidence that raises questions about common instructor intuitions, we recognize some inherent limitations of our data that suggest new opportunities for further work. First, our statistical analyses are somewhat limited by relatively small sample sizes as a result of the course sizes at this institution. At this point it would be tenuous to attempt generalizing findings from this study broadly to all instances of flipped courses in STEM disciplines. Our findings related to objective student behaviors should be taken as suggestive, and further replication studies with larger classes in other contexts would help tease out nuanced variations. In addition, we did not have access to demographic data given the nature of our human subjects approval, and future studies with larger sample sizes may also be interested in exploring claims about demographic data and student behaviors.

Further, we acknowledge there is a fundamental limitation with log-file data, such as that provided by TrACE. It is easy to compute accesses to videos and proportions of content played in the browser, but it is non-trivial to determine whether a student actually paid attention to the video as it played. Our use of "viewing" and "coverage" is thus necessarily coarse and errs on the side of inclusion. In follow-up work, there is an opportunity to model student interactions within a video to classify different forms of engagement during viewing. This may provide more detailed knowledge about which types of interactions matter most.

Lastly, a finer grained analysis of revisiting behaviors that accounts for elapsed time and the specific nature of the revisit is necessary. Coupling this type of log-data with interview data from students may also give us new insight into why students choose to revisit (or not).

6. CONCLUSION

The flipped course pedagogy continues to be a popular topic of discussion among educators, however many of our intuitions about how students prepare for face-to-face class periods are not tied to objective evidence. This paper contributes to our understanding of flipped classes by providing empirical log data about student interactions with videos in a CS1 course. Further, it helps us understand how subtle changes in instructor expectations within a flipped course can have dramatic changes in student behaviors.

As educators, the data presented makes it clear that simply expecting students to prepare for class by watching videos is unlikely to yield compliance, and the majority of students do not often take advantage of the potential to review video content in flipped classes. However, adding something as small as a reflection prompt to each video and requiring students to complete it prior to class seems to increase both content coverage and punctuality metrics. Further, viewing rates here appeared higher than in previously reported studies utilizing entrance quizzes to encourage preparation. Put simply, students need an integrated reason to engage with the material and instructors may benefit from being more aware of their actions.

Our results also suggest that the research community investigating the efficacy of flipped classrooms is missing an important variable. The need to capture objective data about student preparation and control for its effect on student performance is clear. By incorporating such multivariate data into the analysis of flipped classes we may be able to better understand contextual factors leading to success and better transfer one educator's findings to new courses.

ACKNOWLEDGMENTS

This work is funded in part by the National Science Foundation under grant IIS-1318345. Any opinions, findings, and conclusions, or recommendations expressed in this material are those of the authors and do not necessarily reflect the views of the NSF.

References

[1] A. Amresh, A. R. Carberry, and J. Femiani. Evaluating the effectiveness of flipped classrooms for teaching CS1. In *IEEE Frontiers in Education 2013*, pages 733–735, 2013.

[2] J. L. Bishop and M. A. Verleger. The flipped classroom: A survey of the research. In *ASEE National Conference Proceedings, Atlanta, GA*, 2013.

[3] J. A. Day and J. D. Foley. Evaluating a web lecture intervention in a human–computer interaction course. *IEEE Trans. on Education*, 49(4):420–431, 2006.

[4] B. Dorn, L. B. Schroeder, and A. Stankiewicz. Piloting trace: Exploring spatiotemporal anchored collaboration in asynchronous learning. In *Proc. CSCW'15*, pages 393–403. ACM, 2015.

[5] G. C. Gannod, J. E. Burge, and M. T. Helmick. Using the inverted classroom to teach software engineering. In *Proc. ICSE'08*, pages 777–786, 2008.

[6] E. F. Gehringer and B. W. Peddycord III. The inverted-lecture model: a case study in computer architecture. In *Proc. SIGCSE'13*, pages 489–494, 2013.

[7] L. L. Lacher and M. C. Lewis. The effectiveness of video quizzes in a flipped class. In *Proc. SIGCSE'15*, pages 224–228, 2015.

[8] M. J. Lage, G. J. Platt, and M. Treglia. Inverting the classroom: A gateway to creating an inclusive learning environment. *J. Economic Education*, 31(1):30–43, 2000.

[9] N. Lape, R. Levy, D. Yong, K. Haushalter, R. Eddy, and N. Hankel. Probing the inverted classroom: A controlled study of teaching and learning outcomes in undergraduate engineering and mathematics. In *ASEE National Conference Proceedings*, 2014.

[10] K. Lockwood and R. Esselstein. The inverted classroom and the CS curriculum. In *Proc. SIGCSE'13*, pages 113–118. ACM, 2013.

[11] M. L. Maher, C. Latulipe, H. Lipford, and A. Rorrer. Flipped classroom strategies for cs education. In *Proc. SIGCSE'15*, pages 218–223, 2015.

[12] M. Ronchetti. Video-lectures over Internet. In G. Magoulas, editor, *E-Infrastructures and Technologies for Lifelong Learning: Next Generation Environments*, pages 253–270. Information Science Reference, Hersey, PA, 2011.

[13] D. Yong, R. Levy, and N. Lape. Why no difference? a controlled flipped classroom study for an introductory differential equations course. *PRIMUS*, 25(9-10):907–921, 2015.

Introducing Computational Thinking to K-5 in a French Context

Vanea Chiprianov
University of Pau & Pays Adour
Mont de Marsan, France
vanea.chiprianov@univ-pau.fr

Laurent Gallon
University of Pau & Pays Adour
Mont de Marsan, France
laurent.gallon@univ-pau.fr

ABSTRACT

Computational Thinking (CT) is beginning to be accepted as one of the fundamental 21st century skills for everyone. Curricula and environments are being developed for different group ages, from kindergarten to university, in several countries. As part of this global tendency, France has recently taken political decisions to integrate CT Education (CTE) in the mandatory national curriculum. However, many challenges remain until a full implementation is achieved. In this paper we report on a partnership between a university, local elementary schools and the county Ministry of Education (MoE), and on an exploratory project of introducing CT to K-5 students. This project has provided us with valuable feedback on the specifics of integrating CT in a national curriculum and the creation of a partnership and a community. These lessons will be used in the following stage of scaling up to more elementary schools in the entire county, but also addressing other school levels such as kindergarten, middle school and high school.

Keywords

Computer Science Education, Elementary School, Curriculum, Community of practice, Teacher training

1. INTRODUCTION

Computational Thinking (CT), while still being debated on its exact definition, deals mainly with a generalization of Computer Science (CS) concepts, skills and principles for a larger demographic. It involves [23], [16], [11]: solving problems; designing systems; conditional logic; iterative, recursive and parallel thinking; using abstraction and pattern generalizations; problem decomposition and remixing; critical thinking; creativity; systematic processing of information and algorithmic notions of flow of control; symbol systems and representations; thinking in terms of prevention, protection, and recovery from worst-case scenarios; debugging and systematic error detection; efficiency and performance constraints; using heuristic reasoning to discover a solution;

ITiCSE '16, July 09 - 13, 2016, Arequipa, Peru

© 2016 Copyright held by the owner/author(s). Publication rights licensed to ACM.
ISBN 978-1-4503-4231-5/16/07...$15.00

DOI: http://dx.doi.org/10.1145/2899415.2899439

teamwork, communication, leadership; seeing programming as a collaborative, distributed effort - computational participation; assessment.

In practice, CT comprises [4] *concepts* such as: sequences, loops, parallelism, events, conditionals, operators, data; *practices* such as: being incremental and iterative, testing and debugging, reusing and remixing, and abstracting and modularizing; and *perspectives* such as: expressing (oneself, with a creative tool), connecting (by creating *with* others and *for* others), questioning (interrogating the taken for granted).

CT has been argued to be a fundamental skill for everyone, not only computer scientists [23], [16], [11]. Due to the pervasiveness of computers, many of the advances in numerous fields nowadays involve CS. Moreover, many of the current problems require diverse teams with backgrounds in multiple domains, and an understanding of the fundamentals of CS by most team members may help enhance critical elements of proposed solutions.

In many countries there is an important change towards promoting CT as a standard subject, e.g., UK [5], USA and Israel [9], New Zealand [2]. Moreover, the focus is from teaching how to *use* computers - digital literacy, to how to *program* - informatics, empowering children.

While it appears the value of learning CT has been established, some **big questions** still remain [12], among which: *At what age should CT Education (CTE) start? Which content, learning objectives, methods, and environments are suitable to learn CT concepts at each developmental stage? How to integrate CT teaching time with other important learning fields? How to best prepare and sustain teachers in acquiring the necessary CT skills? How to take into account national/local curriculum specificities?*

In this paper we report on a *partnership* between a university, local elementary schools (ES) and the departmental French Ministry of Education (MoE). This produced an exploratory project of introducing CT to K-5 students, in the 2014-2015 school year. Such intervention studies in the regular classroom are the next step to evaluate proposed curricula, environments and computational practices, as recommended e.g., by [16]. In the remainder of the paper *we describe how we answered in this exploratory project to the big research questions on introducing CT in French ES.*

2. PRESENT STATE OF CTE IN THE FRENCH SCHOOL SYSTEM

A good synthetic and up-to-date presentation of the French Education System can be found in [1]. We focus here on presenting only the aspects pertinent to our work. The school system in French starts around age 6 with the ES, which lasts for 5 years until about age 11. Children are organized in groups of about 20-30. One teacher takes care of the group, teaching most subjects.

Most ES teachers are trained mainly by Superior Schools of Teaching and Education - SSTE (*Ecoles supérieures du professorat et de l'éducation*) which deliver them a masters. They are than recruited through a national yearly contest and are then tenured civil servants. They are organized in educational districts (*académies*), under the responsibility of a regional pedagogical inspector.

The curriculum is established by groups of experts - the Superior Curricula Council (*Conseil supérieur des programmes*), appointed by the MoE.

In France [1], like in many other countries [10], [2], [5] until recently, the curriculum included CS only from the *user* point of view. The general public, including teachers and students, had little to no awareness of the difference between *using* (digital literacy) and *programming* (informatics) a computer. For example, in France, even at high school level, the tests for CS required just elementary usage and office skills[1]. However, this is changing.

On 7th May 2015, the French president announced[2] one billion euros dedicated to initiating all children, from ES to high school, to both *programming* and digital literacy, as part of a larger plan for the digitalization of schools, from the start of the 2016 school year. He also promised an exceptional program to prepare the teachers and school personnel on the next three years, 2016, 2017, and 2018. While the SSTE will take care of the initial training of teachers, additionally there will also be an exceptional effort for the ongoing education / lifelong learning.

In September 2015, the Superior Curricula Council proposed new curricula for kindergarten, elementary and middle school [6]. It explicitly includes programming for ES: "Ils décrivent un système technique par ses composants et leurs relations. Les élèves découvrent l'algorithme en utilisant des logiciels d'applications visuelles et ludiques. Ils exploitent les moyens informatiques en pratiquant le travail collaboratif." Roughly translated as: "They (pupils) describe a technical system through their components and relations. The pupils discover the concept of algorithm by using graphical and playful software. They explore computing tools collaboratively."

To help implement these objectives in 2016, the French Education Minister announced[3] that in ES, an introduction to coding will be proposed, on a optional basis, in the extracurricular time. Moreover, to help teachers, all SSTE have included CS in their curriculum, starting 2014. However, it should be noted that until now, this mainly consisted in digital literacy, and not programming.

To conclude, the French education system is undergoing a major change, at all levels, to introduce and develop CT. This raises many challenges, from developing suitable curriculum that weave informatics in a multidisciplinary manner, to training the teachers. Weaving CS with existing curriculum subjects comes to meet the very concept of CT

as a multidisciplinary and fundamental skill that helps developing cognitive aptitudes of students.

3. CHILD COGNITIVE AND AFFECTIVE DEVELOPMENT

As discussed earlier, one of the big questions of CT research is related to *the age at which CTE should start*. Many aspects need to be taken into account. We will focus here on affective and cognitive ones.

Research from educational and cognitive psychology [15] suggests that both affect and cognitive attributes develop easier and are easier to change in the early years, while they are much more stable and therefore harder to influence later in the student's life. This suggests that student exposure to CT and STEM in general, earlier in their life, may create and maintain their affect towards these subjects, thus students being more likely to integrate them in their later education. It is therefore *critical to include CT integrated learning at the earlier elementary levels*. Another reason is related to equity - presenting the fundamentals of CT at a young age gives students of all backgrounds the possibility to absorb and practice these principles as a life-long way of thinking.

The influence of CS on cognitive aspects such as the development of thinking skills (e.g., causal reasoning, metacognition) has been studied since the 1980s [11], [16]. Such studies underline the manner in which teaching happens, for example by remarking the importance of group collaborative activities which reinforce interaction, teachers offering suggestions during difficulties, or designing learning activities that are meaningful and challenging - thus engaging - while also being achievable so as to avoid discouragement [8].

As it is still an important reference, we remind here Piaget's cognitive development stages [20], which for ages 7-11, comprise the concrete operational stage. This stage is characterized by the fact that abstract, hypothetical thinking is not yet developed, and children can only solve problems that apply to concrete events or objects. They are also able to use inductive reasoning, but they struggle with deductive reasoning. Children also begin to think in more scientific and trial-and-error fashion, using hypothetical-deductive reasoning, making plans which they test in a systematic manner.

Of course, any curriculum, activities, tools as well as social organization of teaching need to take into consideration the cognitive development of children, so as to propose appropriate activities and content.

4. THE PROJECT: THEORETICAL CONSIDERATIONS

To answer the objectives of introducing CT in French ESs, the University of Pau partnered in 2014 initially with departmental MoE services and two local schools to launch an exploratory project in the department of Landes. The persons directly involved comprised initially: 2 researchers, 4 teachers, 3 classes, and a MoE counselor. The project finally involved many more persons, among which most notably the directors and the technical teachers of the local schools, as discussed further.

In choosing the education objectives, content, activities, tools and in planning their order, we looked at existing curricula in the world and analyzed them in light of specifics of the French education system.

---

[1] http://www.legifrance.gouv.fr/affichTexte.do;jsessionid= ?cidTexte=JORFTEXT000027811513&dateTexte= &oldAction=dernierJO&categorieLien=id

[2] http://www.elysee.fr/chronologie/#e9309,2015-05-07, d-placement-l-cole-change-avec-le-num-rique-

[3] http://www.gouvernement.fr/action/l-ecole-numerique

4.1 CT in World Curricula

Several curricula are being proposed worldwide to teach CS/CT/Informatics, including the Computer Science: Principles site[4], the Computing at Schools Initiative[5], national curricula like those of New Zealand[6], UK[7]and finally the Computer Science Teachers Association (CSTA) standards [21]. Not all of these address teaching CS/CT from the ES level. One that does is for example the CSTA, which recommends at Level 1 (grades 3-6), in the CT and Computing Practice and Programming strands, among others, that pupils:

1. Understand and use the basic steps in algorithmic problem-solving.
2. Develop a simple understanding of an algorithm (e.g., sequence of events) using computer-free exercises.
3. Demonstrate how a string of bits can be used to represent alphanumeric information.
4. Describe how simulation can be used to solve problems.
5. Make a list of sub-problems to consider while addressing a larger problem.
6. Understand the connections between CS and other fields.
7. Construct a program as a set of step-by-step instructions to be acted out (e.g., make a sandwich activity).
8. Implement problem solutions using a block-based visual programming language.

A lot of emphasis is put on *the concept of algorithm and the flow of control*, using both computer-free activities and block-based visual programming languages.

4.2 Specificity of CT in French Curriculum

In France, the new curriculum [6] explicitly includes programming. It is noteworthy that it is well aligned with the CSTA standard, though an exploration in detail of this alignment is out of the scope of this paper.

However, the curriculum for the year 2014-2015, did not explicitly include CS. This could have been a problem for our project, as there seems to be no place for it. However, that curriculum does include a STEM section, which recommends acquiring a scientific awareness and approach - to be noted the concordance with Piaget's concrete operational development stage at this age. An important aspect in our project was then *the presentation of CT in the light of a scientific, systematic investigation, discovery-based approach*.

Therefore, *our exploratory project has been introduced as a project of Support on Science and Technology in ES* - in French *Accompagnement en science et technologie à l'école primaire (ASTEP)*[8]. ASTEP is an initiative that brings together scientists and school teachers, so as to facilitate getting started with new subjects.

4.3 Theoretical Framework: Constructionism

Based on Piaget's *constructivism* [20]: the child actively builds knowledge through experience, and the related "learn-by-doing" approach to education, Papert proposed [18] the *constructionism*: children learn deeply when they build their own meaningful projects in group and reflect on the process.

Based on such theoretical frameworks, many learning environments have been proposed. For example, [16] proposed that a constructionism-based problem-solving learning environment, with information processing, scaffolding and reflection activities, could be designed to foster computational practices and computational perspectives.

4.4 Educational Games, Computer Programming Environments and Robots

In the previous subsections we gave elements towards answering the big question of which content, learning objectives and methods may be suitable to teach CT to ES in France. In this subsection we investigate which environments and tools are suitable to support them.

Many different educational tools and games, activities that use or not the computer, and programming environments specially designed for teaching CT to young children have been proposed. For a short history from Logo to Scratch, cf. e.g., [16]; a review can be found in e.g., [11]; also many resources are grouped in [17].Most of them are based on constructionism principles.

Choosing among so many environments is not obvious. However, one approach that seems particularly well adapted and is one of the few that propose a full K-12 pathway [19], is that proposed by Code.org[9]. The site is structured as a series of puzzle-based games. To play them, children have to give instructions in a visual programming language of a Blockly type, in which they drag and drop command symbols to compose programs. Key concepts that are taught include, among others: CS, computer scientist, applications of CS, algorithm, decomposing, abstracting, debugging and programming concepts such as: sequence, loops, conditionals, functions with and without parameters, variables. It mixes unplugged, computer-free activities, based on real-life knowledge children already have, with online ones, thus facilitating transfer, connection and abstraction of knowledge. One can *notice the good, if not total accordance between the proposals of Code.org and the definition of CT and aspects of various curricula proposed worldwide, such as that of CSTA*.

Code.org has many valuable aspects, such as pedagogical materials and well organized activities, from simple to complex. It proposes a learning-management system, in which teachers can monitor the activities of their entire class, the progress of each pupil, at their own pace, in terms of completed levels and time spent, which makes it easier to provide guidance and feedback. Individual child progress can be followed by parents as well, thus enabling a deeper implication of children, teachers and parents in the learning process.

More recently, Code.org has partnered with CS: Principles and Exploring CS[10], which have developed cohesive well-designed CS programs [19]. As of summer 2015, Code.org had prepared more than 10.000 teachers; 2 million girls - 43% of their students - are learning introductory CS [19]. A study [14] teaching programming to 32 ES pupils with the Code.org site found that students developed a positive attitude towards programming and that programming could be part of their future plans.

Another category of tools that have been investigated for education are robots. A systematic review [3] presents a synthesis of the available quantitative empirical evidence on

---

[4]http://www.csprinciples.org/, http://apcsprinciples.org/
[5]https://www.computingatschool.org.uk/
[6]http://nzcurriculum.tki.org.nz/Curriculum-documents/The-New-Zealand-Curriculum
[7]https://www.gov.uk/government/collections/national-curriculum
[8]http://www.fondation-lamap.org/fr/astep

[9]https://code.org/
[10]http://www.exploringcs.org/

the effectiveness of robotics as an educational tool in schools. It concludes that educational robotics usually act as an element enhancing learning. It notes that robotics help emphasize skills in problem solving, logic and scientific inquiry.

The robots we selected are Dash[11] and Thymio[12]. Dash can be programmed using a Blockly-like environment, which is very similar to that used by Code.org. Thymio has a programming environment which combines visual and textual programming, which makes it a potential good candidate to ease the transition towards textual programming languages.

5. THE PROJECT: PUTTING IT INTO PRACTICE

In parallel with addressing questions related to content, methods and tools of teaching, partnerships had to be established and decisions taken.

5.1 Organization, Preparation and Developing a Community of Practice

Several meetings and informal discussions took place during the school year 2013-2014, to prepare the project for the year 2014-2015. It was decided 2 schools be part of the project. One is in Mont de Marsan, the county town, and the other in a nearby village. One of them has a good internet connection, and access to 10 laptops; their class size is around 30; 2 classes from this school would participate in the project. The other school has a weak internet connection, one computer in the classroom, and class size is around 20 pupils; one class would participate.

All teachers were motivated and had inclinations towards digital literacy, but none had previous knowledge of programming. A training session of 3 hours was organized, in which the project was officially kick-started in the presence of the MoE inspector and then presentations and discussions of the proposed curriculum and tools took place. This training session was a good start, but had to be completed by informal discussions and sometimes live decisions in the classroom. Also, teachers shared between them by mail or by discussion their decisions and adaptations. Moreover, a site enabling exchange of such information was put in place.

The material consisted in 10 tablets, 5 Dash robots and 10 Thymio robots. This meant that during lessons using Code.org, when tablets were used, depending on the schools and their own computers, pupils worked either individually or in pairs. For lessons involving robots, pupils were organised in groups of 4 to 6 for Dash, and 2 to 3 for Thymios.

5.2 Lesson Plan

In the context of ASTEP, 10 lessons were dedicated to the project. Our curriculum is primarily inspired from the one proposed by Code.org, Course 2. We selected and adapted activities from it. For example, we selected the lessons dealing with CT concepts such as algorithm, programming, variable, loop and conditional. These seem essential concepts, as recommended by worldwide curricula, and in particular the CSTA standards. We alternated unplugged activities with computer ones. Due to French specific curriculum, some activities could not be used. For example, the puzzles involving an "artist" use trigonometry concepts which

are not taught in the French ES. Most teachers thus decided to exclude them. Among the unplugged activities, the dance introducing the concept of loop was replaced with other repetitive activities that involved less rearranging of class furniture.

The curriculum encourages active learning. The unplugged activities are based on pupils' previous knowledge, such as introducing the concept of algorithm based on routine activities like teeth brushing. This scaffolding process eases the acquisition of CT concepts and skills. Based on the concepts thus introduced, the computer-based puzzles invite pupils to search solutions, first individually and then collaboratively, and ultimately search the advice of the teacher. In this way, CT concepts and problem-solving skills, are actively acquired, using an inquiry-based pedagogy.

To these lessons we added an introductory lesson in which programming was introduced as an objective to program behaviors like robots finding their way on a carpet on which a labyrinth inspired from Code.org puzzles has been drawn. After this, the Code.org activities followed. At the end, two more sessions used the acquired concepts to program the robots, one for Dash and one for Thymio.

The Blockly-based programming environment for Dash resembles the one used by Code.org. Moreover, it can be installed on tablets, therefore the transition was quite straightforward for pupils. For Thymio, at the moment we used it for this project, the programming environment existed only for computers, which posed additional constraints, as the tablets could not be used. Also, the programming paradigm for Thymio is an event-based one, with no graphical entities for concepts such as iteration. Therefore, while using Dash seems well suited at this stage, Thymio seems better suited at a later stage.

5.3 Strategies of Teaching

The classroom delivery involved several methods. Co-teaching between the class teacher and a researcher was frequently employed. While the teacher conducted the lesson, they would solicitate the researcher for specific points, usually more technical or unclear content. Similar to other case studies [13], a typical lesson would start with whole-class directions and demonstrations, thus enabling learning by example, after which independent and collaborative work followed. Depending on the available material, pupils worked either individually, or in pairs, or in groups of 4 to 6, thus enabling collaborative learning and peer instruction.

Although reflection time for sharing solutions with the entire class and reviewing comments on examples, were included in the curriculum for each lesson, in practice this was not always possible. This was sometimes due to technical problems, or to incorrect estimates of the time necessary to organize the pupils into groups, or because of the teacher to pupil ratio. In some cases, for classes of about 30 pupils, in which each worked individually, the teacher and researcher were over-solicited. In some cases, a third university staff or student had to participate for additional support.

6. LESSONS LEARNED

One of the major benefits of this project have been the multiple lessons related to the various actors involved.

6.1 The Teachers

Teachers play an essential role for multiple reasons. They

---

stimulate pupils and give them positive attitudes [3]. They also implement the curriculum change [2] and adapt it to their environment, pupils, material. For example, some teachers chose to eliminate certain lessons from the proposed curriculum (e.g. to teach the concept of iteration, they estimated the second lesson using planes was not necessary). It is thus *essential they have a degree of autonomy in implementing the curriculum*. It is them who ensure the pedagogical presentation of the material. Their main motivation is providing better opportunities for pupils.

The teachers involved in our project were enthusiastic about integrating CT. However, coaching on how to use the material, the software and on how to solve the puzzle-based content was essential. This brings us to a possible major barrier [13], [2]: *professional development of teachers*. In the beginning of our project, teachers had only one 3-hour training session. Additional training happened during the lessons, or in informal discussions beforehand. While this was feasible for a reduced number of motivated teachers, it is of course not feasible for the long term.

To tackle this issue, in the current year starting September 2015, in partnership with the French MoE, 3 more hours have been allocated. This is a step in the right direction, and a considerable effort on the part of the MoE. However, to extend this training for the entire department or region, more time and tools like MOOCs [7] would be needed.

Feedback from teachers allowed us to identify strong and weak points in our curriculum. For example, groups of 4 (especially in robotics classes, as in other studies [3]) was estimated as too big a number. Teachers also evoked the need for more time being allotted for activities that allow them to observe and evaluate how and where each pupil is on their path of acquiring the concepts and to share with the entire class different solutions and discuss them.

Many of these comments have been integrated in the curriculum version for the current year. To ensure smaller groups, in some cases we will experiment with dividing the class in two. Another solution is to have more material (e.g., a bigger number of robots). This will allow for teams of 3 or even pairs. However, we expect having a bigger number of groups (10 to 15!) to put a bigger strain on the teacher.

To allow for more sharing time, all lessons have been allotted 15 minutes at the end (but which can be used anytime the teacher decides) to share solutions and discuss them. To enable discussions, solutions with comments on advantages and disadvantages have been provided.

6.2 The Children

A typical robotics lesson sequence consists in children programming the robot, either at the tables of their group or a little aside from the labyrinth carpet, then coming on the carpet, sitting down the robot and themselves on it, and testing the program. In the lessons dedicated to puzzle-based games, on the hand-held tablets, we observed more interaction between the children when they were seated at tables in groups of 4-5, than when seated at tables by 2.

An important note is related to *discovering the material*: robots, but also tablets; this may probably be applied to desktops or laptops or any other material as well. The first sessions, mainly because of time limitations, the teacher presented different visible components, naming them and explaining their function. While this was very time-efficient, and many pupils retained well and afterwards used the ma-

terial correctly, pupils were mostly inactive during this period. In the current iteration of the project we changed this. We dedicate more time, give the material to the pupils, let them look, touch and explore it, and then the teacher asks questions about what they have seen. In this way, children co-construct in an active manner their knowledge.

The introduction to programming and robotics also *activated the use of other skills* by pupils. The current versions of robot programming environments are in English - foreign language. Pupils worked in groups, so their social and language skills were activated.

One skill that deserves special mentioning is *space location*. In the initial curriculum, we started with computer-based puzzles and finished with applying learned CT concepts to robot programming. In the puzzles, pupils need to guide an on-screen character through a labyrinth. They give it commands to advance or rotate left, or right. To determine the right instruction, children would often role play, positioning themselves in place of the character. This seems harder to do when the environment has only 2 dimensions and is much more abstract - the screen, than in the case of robots, with 3 dimensions and which are more concrete, tangible. Therefore, in the current iteration, we are experimenting with introducing spatial relations through robots, in the first lesson, and then transferring it to puzzles. Preliminary observations seem to indicate that children still role-play in the case of puzzles, at least in the first lesson, but that this seems to almost completely disappear in later puzzle lessons.

While we did not have the opportunity to perform extensive evaluation, other studies [14] found that children using Code.org stated learning programming, improving their mathematical knowledge, computer literacy, and cognition, finding solutions through less steps, creating love of mathematics, learning to think logically and to find directions.

6.3 The Administrators of Learning

This category includes school directors, but also personnel of the MoE. Their support was instrumental in realizing our project. It is them that gave us permission to enter the schools, and helped us find the right type of administrative form into which we could experiment - the ASTEP project.

They are instrumental in passing at a larger scale. While during the 2014-2015 year the project was deployed around one town, during the year 2015-2016 it is being deployed in schools all over the county. It is the personnel of the MoE who found the teachers interested in being part of our project and who will probably manage the shared material.

Due to their intervention, we can address a larger diversity of pupils, from urban and rural schools, girls and boys, of various ethnic and social background. This will allow for a more representative population on which the project will be experimented and evaluated. It is also instrumental into ensuring equity and equal access to opportunities.

6.4 The Researchers and the Universities

One of the main and selfish! reasons for which we, as CS university teachers, are interested in promoting the importance of pupils having a good CS level at pre-university levels, is related to the CS level of students starting courses at universities. The better their CS level, the easier for us, and the further we can go in our courses!

One of the main actions was to begin constructing a community of practice - as advised by example in [5] - , involving local schools, departmental personnel of the MoE, the local SSTE. This community reinforces connections, enables further research actions, as well as rapid transfer of ideas from research into practice, and mutual support.

As advised also by [2], we are looking into involving selected university students. This may be done in pairs: one CS and one SSTE student. This would enable having both technical and pedagogical skills and knowledge and better assisting the teacher. It would provide further experience for the 2 students and a direct link for pupils to the university.

7. CONCLUSION AND PERSPECTIVES

In this paper we presented the first phase of a project introducing CT to ES in a French context. We focused on the kick-start of the project, creating the local community, adapting a curriculum to French specifics, teacher implementation and first feedbacks. In this first phase, formal feedback and validation from pupils was not a main focus.

In the second phase, which started September 2015, our experimental community has expanded to include 3 ESs with 5 classes. Two classes are from urban area, the other 3 from rural. The local SSTE has manifested interest in our project and will very likely join us next year 2016-2017. This will enable pairing of CS students with their students.

Another dimension into which our project is expanding is assuring a continuation from ES through middle and high school. We currently have a partnership with 2 high schools, into which CT is present as an all year long project to prepare Mindstorm robots compete in a local olympics. There is also one middle school interested in joining the robotics olympics. Such partnerships will enable us to test a complete curriculum. We are also considering tackling CT in kindergarten using approaches such as [22].

8. ACKNOWLEDGMENTS

We would like to thank especially the primary school teachers: Mélisa Devaux, Sophie Evangelista, Florence Rassinier and Sandra Saint-German and the French MoE counselor, Frederic Carrincazeaux.

9. REFERENCES

[1] G.-L. Baron, B. Drot-Delange, M. Grandbastien, and F. Tort. Computer Science Education in French Secondary Schools: Historical and Didactical Perspectives. *Trans. Comput. Educ.*, 14(2):11:1–11:27, 2014.

[2] T. Bell, P. Andreae, and A. Robins. A Case Study of the Introduction of Computer Science in NZ Schools. *Trans. Comput. Educ.*, 14(2):10:1–10:31, 2014.

[3] F. B. V. Benitti. Exploring the educational potential of robotics in schools: A systematic review. *Computers & Education*, 58(3):978 – 988, 2012.

[4] K. Brennan and M. Resnick. New frameworks for studying and assessing the development of computational thinking. In *American Educational Research Association, Vancouver, Canada*, 2012.

[5] N. C. C. Brown, S. Sentance, T. Crick, and S. Humphreys. Restart: The Resurgence of Computer Science in UK Schools. *Trans. Comput. Educ.*, 14(2):9:1–9:22, 2014.

[6] Conseil Supérieur des Programmes. Projet de programmes pour les cycles 2,3,4 (French), 2015.

[7] K. Falkner, R. Vivian, and N. Falkner. Teaching Computational Thinking in K-6: The CSER Digital Technologies MOOC. In *17th Australasian Computing Education Conference*, 2015.

[8] G. Fessakis, E. Gouli, and E. Mavroudi. Problem solving by 5-6 years old kindergarten children in a computer programming environment: A case study. *Computers & Education*, 63:87 – 97, 2013.

[9] J. Gal-Ezer and C. Stephenson. A Tale of Two Countries: Successes and Challenges in K-12 Computer Science Education in Israel and the United States. *Trans. Comput. Educ.*, 14(2):8:1–8:18, 2014.

[10] W. Gander, A. Petit, G. Berry, B. Demo, J. Vahrenhold, A. McGettrick, R. Boyle, A. Mendelson, C. Stephenson, C. Ghezzi, et al. Informatics education: Europe cannot afford to miss the boat. *ACM [online] Available at: http://europe.acm.org/iereport/ie.html*, 2013.

[11] S. Grover and R. Pea. Computational Thinking in K-12: A Review of the State of the Field. *Educational Researcher*, 42:38–43., 2013.

[12] P. Hubwieser, M. Armoni, and M. N. Giannakos. How to Implement Rigorous Computer Science Education in K-12 Schools? Some Answers and Many Questions. *Trans. Comput. Educ.*, 15(2):5:1–5:12, 2015.

[13] M. Israel, J. N. Pearson, T. Tapia, Q. M. Wherfel, and G. Reese. Supporting all learners in school-wide computational thinking. *Comput. Educ.*, 82(C):263–279, Mar. 2015.

[14] F. Kalelioglu. A new way of teaching programming skills to K-12 students: Code.org . *Computers in Human Behavior*, 52:200 – 210, 2015.

[15] R. Lamb, T. Akmal, and K. Petrie. Development of a cognition-priming model describing learning in a STEM classroom. *Journal of Research in Science Teaching*, 52(3):410–437, 2015.

[16] S. Y. Lye and J. H. L. Koh. Review on teaching and learning of computational thinking through programming: What is next for k-12? *Computers in Human Behavior*, 41:51 – 61, 2014.

[17] L. Mannila, V. Dagiene, B. Demo, N. Grgurina, C. Mirolo, L. Rolandsson, and A. Settle. Computational Thinking in K-9 Education. In *ITiCSE*, pages 1–29, 2014.

[18] S. Papert. *Mindstorms: Children, Computers, and Powerful Ideas*. Basic Books, Inc., 1980.

[19] H. Partovi. A Comprehensive Effort to Expand Access and Diversity in Computer Science. *ACM Inroads*, 6(3):67–72, 2015.

[20] J. Piaget. *The construction of reality in the child*. Routledge, 2013.

[21] D. Seehorn, S. Carey, B. Fuschetto, I. Lee, D. Moix, D. O'Grady-Cunniff, B. B. Owens, C. Stephenson, and A. Verno. CSTA K–12 Computer Science Standards: Revised 2011. 2011.

[22] D. Wang, T. Wang, and Z. Liu. A Tangible Programming Tool for Children to Cultivate Computational Thinking. *The Scientific World Journal*, 2014.

[23] J. M. Wing. Computational thinking. *Commun. ACM*, 49(3):33–35, Mar. 2006.

Back to School: Computer Science Unplugged in the Wild

Renate Thies
Cusanus-Gymnasium Erkelenz
Schulring 6
41812 Erkelenz, Germany
th@cusanus-gymnasium.eu

Jan Vahrenhold
Westfälische Wilhelms-Universität Münster
Department of Computer Science
48149 Münster, Germany
jan.vahrenhold@uni-muenster.de

ABSTRACT

We report on case studies of using *Computer Science Unplugged* material as an alternative teaching method for computer science. The scope and target audiences for these studies were determined based upon reported classroom use of "unplugged" material by teachers. Our studies revalidate previous findings across multiple institutions and a broader student population and shows that, at least for the scenarios studied, "unplugged" activities are equally efficient compared to teaching using textbooks or interactive methods.

CCS Concepts

•Social and professional topics → K-12 education;

Keywords

Computer Science Unplugged; Teaching Methodology

1. INTRODUCTION

Computer Science Unplugged (CSU) [1] is a series of kinesthetic activities designed to promote computer science concepts without the use of a computer. CSU has been used successfully for outreach; see [2] and the references therein.

While not initially designed as teaching material, CSU activities have made their way into several curricula. For example, the *CSTA K-12 Computer Science Standards* [9] lists 21 example activities for classroom use. Of these, 6 activities are directly taken from CSU. In a recent CACM *viewpoint* article, Cortina strongly suggests that *"as computing professionals, we should encourage the addition of unplugged activities in our schools [. . .]. We should help to create, study, and evaluate new unplugged activities for teachers to use to reach a more diverse population of children."* [5, p. 27].

There is little literature [6, 8, 11, 13] on the (evaluated) use of CSU in schools. In contrast to [8, 13], Feaster et al. [6] and Taub et al. [11] shed a rather negative light on the effectiveness of teaching using CSU. However, both studies focus primarily on the impact CSU has on attitudes and views.

ITiCSE '16, July 11–13, 2016, Arequipa, Peru.

© 2016 Copyright held by the owner/author(s). Publication rights licensed to ACM.
ISBN 978-1-4503-4231-5/16/07. . . $15.00

DOI: http://dx.doi.org/10.1145/2899415.2899442

Even though Feaster et al. [6] mention a control group, no results other than self-perceived proficiency and change in attitude are reported. Taub et al. [11] suggest to rework the activities to tie into computer science curricula more explicitly and conclude that "further research is needed to clarify the influence of the teacher and the classroom environment on the effectiveness of CS Unplugged" [11, p. 26].

In previous work [12], we derived a set of learning objectives from the CSU material. We subsequently showed in a controlled experiment that for the factual, procedural, and contextual understanding resulting from single lessons no statistically significant differences between groups taught with "unplugged" and "alternative" methodology could be found [13]. Our study was controlled in the sense that there was only one student population that was taught by one of the authors. In contrast to the study by Feaster et al., who investigated a group of students that was taught using CSU for a full term, our focus was on single lessons.

The research question of the present study was which of the above findings could be revalidated across multiple teachers at different institutions, thus enlarging the size and diversity of the population studied. In the design of our study, we incorporated feedback from teachers using CSU "in the wild", i.e., in their classroom: which modules did they use at which point of their classes, and for how long?

2. TEACHER FEEDBACK

Preceding our study, we ran a series of 90-minutes CSU workshops during regional computer science teachers' conferences. Our workshops were based on the original material [1] but also included a discussion of the learning objectives as identified in our previous work [12] and of the setup of our previous case study [13]. At the end of the academic year following the workshops, we sent out surveys to over 90 participants and asked them whether they had used CSU in class since the workshop. Of the 42 respondents, 17 had not done so. They stated that they felt uncomfortable teaching kinesthetically (3 respondents) or that preparing "unplugged" lessons would take too much time relative to their perceived effectiveness (2 respondents). The other teachers stated that they their students were either "too young" or "too old" or that the classrooms were too small or otherwise inappropriate for kinesthetic activities.

The 25 teachers that had used CSU in their classroom were presented with a number of statements regarding CSU and asked to indicate how much they agreed with them based upon their teaching experiences. Their classroom experiences (see Table 1) can be summarized as follows:

Statement	--	-	+	++	N/A	Average
Compared to other teaching methods, students taught using CSU material learn more subject matter.	1	5	18	0	1	2.71 ± 0.54
Students taught using CSU get curious to learn more about computer science.	0	3	10	12	0	3.36 ± 0.69
Students are subchallenged by CSU material.	14	9	0	0	2	1.39 ± 0.49
Students identify CSU with playfulness and miss the scientific contents.	10	13	2	0	0	1.68 ± 0.61
CSU activities do not readily fit into regular classes.	18	2	4	0	1	1.42 ± 0.76
CSU cannot be used in higher secondary education.	19	0	1	0	5	3.71 ± 0.68
I would recommend CSU to a fellow teacher or have done so already.	0	0	6	18	1	3.75 ± 0.43

Table 1: Responses of $N = 25$ teachers who have used CSU in their classroom. Agreement with each statement is on a scale from 1 ("--", strongly disagree) to 4 ("++", strongly agree).

- CSU makes students more curious to learn more about computer science.
- CSU does not subchallenge students.
- Students recognize the scientific content behind CSU.
- CSU modules can integrated into regular classes.
- CSU modules can be used across a variety of ages, i.e., from lower secondary (or even primary) to higher secondary education.

Of course, the strong agreement with the last two items can be traced back to the self-selection bias: all respondents had used "unplugged" material in class. It should be seen, however, in the light of the fact that many of the teachers that had decided not to use CSU in class quoted exactly these issues as major obstacles. Consequently, more outreach among teachers and the dissemination of "unplugged" material and best-practice reports seems to be a promising way of furthering the use of CSU in schools; see [5].

When asked which modules were used at which point of a teaching unit, teachers most frequently cited the modules "Count the Dots" [1, Activity 1] (binary numbers, 24 respondents), "Treasure Hunt" [1, Activity 11] (finite-state automata, 19 respondents), and "Battleships" [1, Activity 6] (binary search, 13 respondents). Almost all teachers used these modules to introduce longer, traditional teaching units.

3. CASE STUDIES

We selected the three above-mentioned modules most frequently cited and included the module on sorting networks as well to cover all three modules reported upon in the previous study. We then reached out to workshop and survey participants asking for help with carrying out the case studies with classes that had not been exposed to CSU material before. Our goal was to investigate whether our previous results [13] are independent of the teacher and study group.

Teaching and assessment replicated the methodologies used in the previous study: The instructors were asked to split their classes into two groups of approximately the same size and abilities. They then used the two halves of a 90-minute class session to teach each group according to one methodology. The assessment covered factual, procedural, and conceptual knowledge and was performed for all students on the day following instruction ("Round 1"). Two to three weeks later, the teacher repeated the technical content of the module in a neutral way for the whole class. Another two to three weeks later, the assessment was repeated ("Round 2"); see [13]. The fourth CSU module investigated by us ("Treasure Hunt") was not covered in our previous study.

For all statistical analyses, i.e., significance tests, we used Fisher's exact test (R, version 3.2.3) at the 0.05-level.

3.1 Case Study 1: Binary Numbers

The CSU module reported most often to be used in school was the module "Count the dots" [1, Activity 1] addressing binary numbers. This module requires only very basic counting, matching, and sequencing abilities and is recommended at ages "7 and up" [1, p. 3]. Since binary numbers are often covered in mathematics classes, teachers can use this module also in grades where no computer science classes are offered.

Subjects and Methodology.

The participants in our study were 78 grade-5 students at three different institutions and 30 grade-6 students taught by one of the teachers as well. One grade-5 class (27 students) was a class at a grammar school (just as the students in our previous study [13]), while the remaining 81 students attended two different intermediate secondary schools. Intermediate secondary schools provide career-oriented education on lower secondary level with slightly lower academic standards than grammar schools. Due to fluctuations in attendance, not all students participated in all assessments. All participating courses were mathematics courses offered by teachers also formally qualified to teach computer science. Binary numbers had not been covered before and were not covered other than as part of the intervention until the second assessment had been conducted.

For assessing the factual and procedural knowledge related to binary numbers, we followed our previous study [13] and asked the students to convert two numbers (10101_2 and 11_2) from binary representation to decimal and vice versa (16_{10} and 112_{10}). The results (details omitted due to space constraints) are consistent with the previous study: for none of the items, a statistically significant difference between the students taught using the "unplugged" material and the students taught using the alternative material could be detected. This consistency holds true also on teacher level.

For assessing the conceptual knowledge, we followed the approach of our previous study and asked the students to write down "what they had learned in the respective lesson [...] [and] how the topic taught related to Computer Science" [13, p. 368]. We then analyzed their answers using the SOLO taxonomy [3]; see [13] for more details.

Interpretation of the Results.

The results of our analysis are summarized in Figure 1. First of all, we observe that the aggregated results for all students confirm the previous findings: Fisher's exact test shows that there is no statistically significant difference between either the methodologies in the same round or the rounds for the same methodologies. Comparing the average

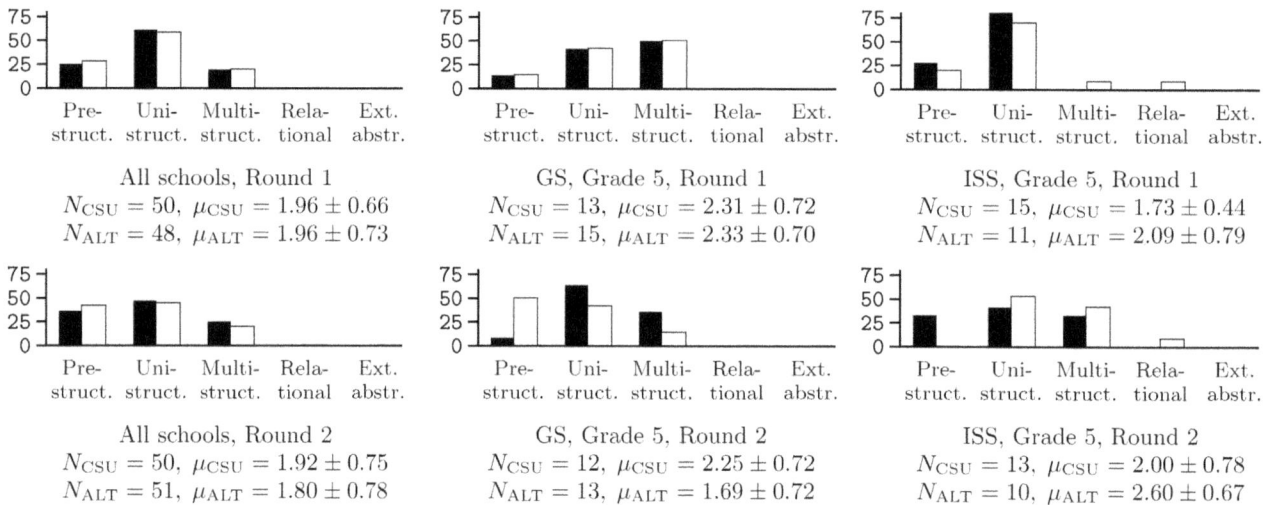

Figure 1: Classification according to SOLO (in percent). Black: Unplugged (CSU), white: Alternative (ALT). Percentages are shown for all schools (left), grade 5 of a grammar school (GS, middle), and grade 5 of an intermediate secondary school (ISS, right) with a large percentage of non-native speakers.

ratings, however, to the ratings reported upon in our previous study [13, Fig. 1], we found our ratings to be shifted down by roughly one level of the SOLO taxonomy.

There are three possible explanations for this. First, the rating scheme could have been different. While this would pose a threat to validity in general, we consider the description of the SOLO categories (at least) on the three lowest levels most frequently encountered in the students' responses to be sufficiently clear-cut to rule out this explanation. Second, the person teaching both groups in the previous study was one of the authors who had formalized the learning objectives and constructed the teaching material. It can be reasonably assumed that this positively influenced the presentation in class; the fact that the ratings are consistently higher for both groups corroborates this explanation. Finally, the participants in the previous study attended a special STEM class in a grammar school. No such classes participated in our study. Instead, roughly two-thirds of our participants attended intermediate secondary schools.

A break-down of the results by class showed that the answers of the participating grammar-school students were indeed rated higher than average; see Figure 1 (middle). For the part of this class taught using the "alternative" material, we could actually observe a significant decrease ($p < 0.045$) in the ratings; no such significance was found for the "unplugged" group. So far, we have been unable to explain this.

We also observed that the answers of students at one of the participating intermediate secondary schools were rated much lower that the answers of the students at the participating grammar school; see Figure 1 (middle and right). Furthermore, a striking, but not statistically significant, disadvantage for the students taught using the "unplugged" material could be seen at least in Round 1.

When we followed up on this, the teacher for this class informed us that almost all of the students came from families in which the language of instruction was not the first language.[1] Owing to this, almost twice the allocated class

time was reported to have been used for the CSU module. In contrast, teaching using the "alternative", i.e., textbook material went smoothly. The teacher observed, however, that, irrespective of the teaching method, all students "should have understood how to convert numbers" (this is consistent with our statistical analysis). Furthermore, the teacher commented that students appeared to have had "much more fun" with the CSU material and perceived the CSU material as more "adequate for that age group". Our subsequent break-down of the analysis to this particular group revealed that this teachers' students who were taught using the "unplugged" material were the only of our groups for which a statistically significant increase ($p < 0.038$) could be shown from Round 1 to Round 2 (see Figure 1, right). Put differently, this group appeared to need just a little more time than others to consolidate the contextual knowledge.

In summary, this case study was able to confirm previous findings regarding the relative effectiveness of "unplugged" and "alternative" material: there is no statistically significant difference between "unplugged" and "alternative" material. For the factual and procedural knowledge tested, previous findings could be replicated on a larger scale and across different teachers and target groups. For conceptual knowledge, we seem to have found evidence that students for which the language of instruction is not their first language need extra time for "unplugged" material and that the consolidation of the conceptual knowledge apparently needs more time. A more detailed analysis of this conjecture, however, is beyond the scope of this report and is left for future research. Unsurprisingly, the academic standards required by the type of secondary school have been found affect the absolute level of conceptual understanding. They do not affect, however, the relative effectiveness of the teaching methodology used.

3.2 Case Study 2: Searching and Sorting

One of the teachers responding to our survey volunteered to teach using both the "Battleships" [1, Activity 6] module addressing binary search and the "Beat the Clock" [1, Activity 8] module addressing sorting networks. Both modules had been subject of our previous study [13]. We followed

---

[1]In all of the other study groups, almost all of the students had the language of instruction as their first language.

Binary Search, Round 1
$N_{CSU} = 12$, $\mu_{CSU} = 2.75 \pm 0.43$
$N_{ALT} = 9$, $\mu_{ALT} = 2.00 \pm 0.67$

	Correct
CSU	12
ALT	9
p-value	1.000

Binary Search, Round 1, executing and explaining.

Sorting Networks, Round 1
$N_{CSU} = 9$, $\mu_{CSU} = 1.89 \pm 0.87$
$N_{ALT} = 12$, $\mu_{ALT} = 1.11 \pm 0.31$

	Correct
CSU	7
ALT	8
p-value	0.659

Sorting Networks, Round 1, executing the algorithm.

Binary Search, Round 2
$N_{CSU} = 9$, $\mu_{CSU} = 2.33 \pm 0.47$
$N_{ALT} = 10$, $\mu_{ALT} = 1.20 \pm 0.40$

	Correct
CSU	0
ALT	2
p-value	0.211

Binary Search, Round 2, executing and explaining

Sorting Networks, Round 2
$N_{CSU} = 9$, $\mu_{CSU} = 1.44 \pm 0.50$
$N_{ALT} = 10$, $\mu_{ALT} = 1.30 \pm 0.46$

	Correct
CSU	6
ALT	9
p-value	0.303

Sorting Networks, Round 2, executing the algorithm.

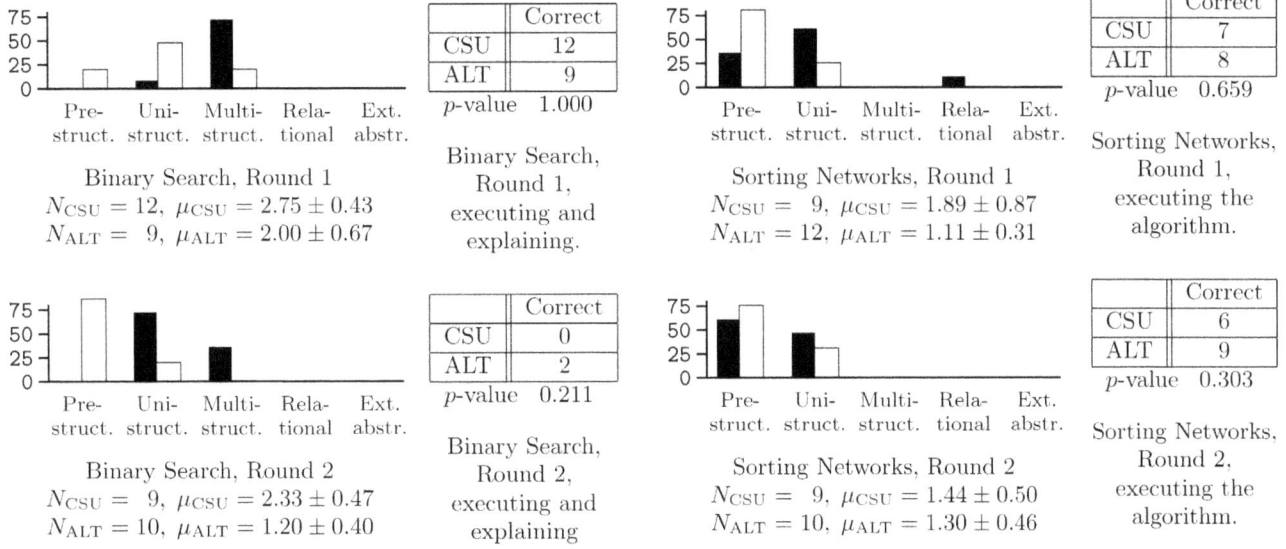

Figure 2: Classification according to SOLO (in percent). Black: Unplugged (CSU), white: Alternative (ALT). There was a seven-week summer vacation between Round 1 and Round 2. "Binary Search" ratings are significantly better for the CSU group in both Round 1 ($p < 0.020$) and Round 2 ($p < 0.001$).

the same methods and procedures. The session on binary searching was taught using "unplugged" material and, alternatively, using *think-pair-share* methodology based upon a textbook [10]. The session on sorting networks alternatively used an edited version of the "unplugged" video, leaving out – as in [13] – all scenes showing kinesthetic activities, plus extra paper-based material.

The subjects were 21 grade-8 students at an intermediate secondary school. Due to administrative constraints, however, the teacher could run only the first round of evaluations immediately after the instruction. The second round could only be run after a seven-week summer vacation that immediately followed the first round of evaluations. Instead of discarding the data because of incompatibility with the previous study design, we decided to use it for a preliminary investigation of the longer-time retention of the concepts.

The results for the "Binary Search" module, summarized in Figure 2 (left) show that both groups can correctly execute and explain the algorithm for a given input. The conceptual knowledge was found to be significantly better ($p < 0.020$) for the group taught using the "unplugged" material. Consistent with findings regarding performance over extended periods of vacation [4], we found a significant drop in the ability to correctly execute and explain the algorithm ($p_{CSU} < 0.001$, $p_{ALT} < 0.002$) and in the conceptual understanding ($p_{CSU} < 0.050$, $p_{ALT} < 0.034$) for both groups.

In contrast, the results for the "Sorting Networks" module are consistent across methodologies and evaluations. Just as in the previous study, no significant difference between the two groups could be found in either round. Moreover, the summer break did not cause any statistically significant decrease in either the ability to correctly execute and explain algorithm or in the observed conceptual understanding for both groups; see Figure 2 (right). We attribute this to the visual representation of the sorting network on the evaluation sheet that is likely have served as a subconscious reminder and reactivation of the learned procedure.

These observations, even when reported for only a small number of students, seem to indicate that relative difficulty of the two modules is the overarching influential factor. While the concept of a sorting network apparently can be recalled with no difficulty given a visual representation of such a network, recalling how to perform binary search and to explain the concepts behind it is far more challenging over a longer period of (vacation) time. Neither for our study group nor for the group in the previous study using CSU material was detrimental. In fact, the students in the "Binary Search" study performed significantly better when having been taught with "unplugged" material. Whether this might be attributed to the particular teacher or group of students cannot be answered conclusively given the data available.

3.3 Case Study 3: Finite-State Automata

The fourth CSU module frequently used in practice and, hence, investigated in a case study is the "Treasure Hunt" module [1, Activity 11]. This module uses a kinesthetic game to introduce finite-state automata: students enact a treasure hunt that takes pirates from one island (state) to another according to certain transition rules. The goal is to reconstruct the whole map of (state) transitions and to ultimately arrive at Treasure Island, i.e., the final state.

While this module is recommended for students at ages "9 and up" [1, p. 86], almost all teachers who responded to our survey stated that they had used it in grade 10 and up. In alignment with the reasons cited for (not) using CSU modules in class, the module was always used to start a class section devoted to finite-state automata which is part of the mandatory curriculum for grades 10–12 in grammar school. Our study thus focused on this age group and context.

Subjects and Methodology.

The participants in our study were $N_{FSA} = 64$ students in introductory grade-10 computer science classes of four teachers at three different institutions in three different cities. Because computer science is an elective subject that cannot be substituted for other science subjects, the number of students in these classes (8, 15, 15, and 26, respectively) was smaller than in other STEM classes.

The study was conducted at the beginning of the academic year. Since the courses were prerequisite-free introductory computer science courses, the students did not have any prior exposure to finite-state automata or graphs.

In accordance with the other case studies reported upon, teachers were asked to first split their classes into groups of roughly the same size and abilities. They then taught each group for 45 mins. using the material and lecture plan given to them by the first author. The material was distributed to the students as well. All students then were given a homework assignment (see below). To follow-up, the first author visited each school one week after the intervention had taken place. For each class, three students taught using the "unplugged" material and three students taught using the "alternative" material were interviewed in a semi-structured manner. Interview participation was voluntary and participants were not compensated for it. Conducting interviews instead of free-form responses aimed at acknowledging both the higher maturity of the students and the more challenging content of the topic, e.g., the number of technical terms.

Material and Lesson Plan.

The CSU material was taken from the CSU book [1, Activity 11]. The teacher was asked to first introduce the rules for the kinesthetic game and then to play the game with up to seven students while the others were observing. For small groups, the teacher simultaneously enacted multiple islands to allow more students to actively explore the game. After the game, the class discussed it and the abstract concept behind it. At this point, the proper terminology and the graph-based representation was introduced. Also, the lengths different transition sequences and loops were discussed. Students then worked on Task 3 [1, p. 97] which asked to construct words of a language accepted by a given automaton by traversing its graph representation. For consolidation, students were then asked to also work on a short assignment (see below) in class. The solutions obtained were then discussed before the class ended.

For the groups not working with CSU material, the *think-pair-share* approach [7] already employed in our previous study [13] was used. After a brief introduction by the teacher, students studied an except from a computer science textbook approved for grades 10–12 (*think*). They then teamed up in groups of two to work on two assignments from this textbook (*pair*). These assignments asked to construct the representation of finite-state automata for two simple examples and to derive the set of accepted words for one of these automata. The teacher then worked with the class to summarize the concepts and notations touched upon in the textbook excerpt. Only then students were asked to present and discuss their solutions (*share*). To synchronize the consolidation with the "unplugged" group, the class session ended by working on the same short assignment and by discussing the solutions obtained.

Immediate Assessment.

The assessment of this teaching unit was done with parts of a test item on finite-state automata used in a recent high-school leaving exam. In the federal state where the study

was conducted, the test items used in high-school leaving exams are the same for each high school and are created by a state board. Thus, curricula and assessment are aligned across high schools. As students had been taught for only one lesson, we could only use the very basic parts of this test item. Students were given the following representation and told that the automaton shown could be used to find out whether a sequence of characters contained the string "007".

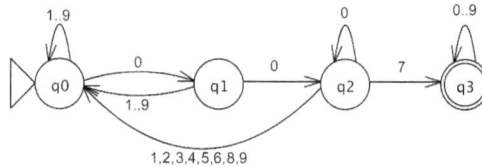

- Item 1 asked to name the automaton's initial state.
- Item 2 asked whether this automaton had more than one final state and indicate the final state(s).
- Item 3 asked to write down the input alphabet.
- Item 4 asked to come up with three words accepted by the given automaton. Not all of these words should end with the character '7'.
- Item 5 asked to trace the input "120006007006" through the automaton by listing all intermediate states.

Given the moderate number of students in some of the groups and our goal to investigate the modules independent of the teachers, we discuss the results in aggregate form.

Table 2 presents the results for all $N_{\text{FSA}} = 64$ homework assignments. As the items were targeted at a very basic level of understanding of the concepts, each answer was graded for correctness on a $\{0, 1\}$-scale. Obvious typographic errors did not count as errors. The results summarized in Table 2 show that students taught using the "unplugged" material seem to perform slightly better, with the exception of Item 2 ($p < 0.038$), however, none of these differences is significant.

	N	Item 1	Item 2	Item 3	Item 4	Item 5
CSU	30	28	27	28	26	27
ALT	34	32	23	26	23	25
p-value		1.000	0.038	0.089	0.086	0.117

Table 2: Number of correct answers on the homework assignment for finite-state automata.

Performing the analysis on teacher level yields the same results for Items 1, 3, 4, and 5. For one class, Item 2 shows a significant advantage for the group working with CSU material; this class was the largest (26 students), so the significance carried over to the global analysis. For all other classes, the difference is not significant for Item 2, either.

Follow-Up Interviews.

The participants were first asked to recapitulate the session on finite-state automata. If they did not come up with the proper technical terms, the interviewer presented these. In any case, participants were then asked to explain the technical terms addressed in class. In next part of the interview, the automaton used in the homework assignment was presented again. Participants were asked to explain the technical terms while referring to this automaton. To investigate the limits of understanding finite-state automata from just one session, participants then were asked to come up with an automaton for the input alphabet $\{a, b, c\}$ that would

	N	Remembers terminology on his/her own			Explains topic referring to context only			Can explain terminology when presented with			Can explain terminology using given automaton		
		-	○	+	-	○	+	-	○	+	-	○	+
CSU	12	6	6	0	5	5	2	0	10	2	3	3	6
ALT	12	7	4	1	6	3	3	0	7	5	0	2	10
p-value		0.680			0.761			0.371			0.160		

Table 3: Analysis of the follow-up "Treasure Hunt" interviews ("-": Does not apply/no or incorrect response; "○": Partially applies/partially incorrect response; "+": Fully applies/(almost) fully correct response).

accept all words in which each 'a' was followed by exactly one 'b'. The interview concluded by asking for opinions on the teaching material and its perceived effectiveness.

Given the very brief exposure of the students to the topic addressed in the module, the follow-up interviews were coded on a rather coarse scale. For each of the criteria investigated, we recorded whether the criterion was fulfilled (almost) completely, fulfilled partially, or not fulfilled at all. In case of doubt, we consistently erred on the positive side.

The results of this analysis are summarized in Table 3. While Fisher's exact test could not detect any statistical significance, the students taught using the alternative, i.e., *think-pair-share* methodology seem to perform slightly better on average (the second criterion is inverted as it measures how little a student can abstract away from a given context).

Even though all students were eager to construct an automaton for the task described, no one was able to solve this problem. We conclude that asking for such an active understanding given only 45 minutes of exposure to the topic plus one simple homework assignment is simply too much irrespective of the teaching methodology. We leave the detailed analysis of the students' artifacts for future research.

When asked for comments on the methodology experienced and the self-perceived understanding, students positively highlighted both the playful character of the CSU material and the self-study opportunity offered by *think-pair-share*. Two out of the twelve students taught using the CSU material perceived it as "unnecessarily playful". On the other hand, four out of the other twelve students considered the reading assignment as "dull" and "hard to understand".

4. CONCLUSIONS

Our study could revalidate our previous results across multiple teachers and institutions and extends the scope to finite-state automata taught in higher grades. We found no statistically significant difference between the effectiveness of teaching single lessons using CSU modules compared to alternative methods. For the introductory scenario most frequently reported by teachers, CSU modules thus have been confirmed to be equally effective. Hence, teachers can teach using CSU with good conscience if their personal style of teaching and the students' mindset permits.

The extension of previous studies to a broader student population raised new issues to be studied in future work: how much does the students' first language influence the short-term effectiveness of non-textbook based teaching, i.e., do we need more recitation material for CSU? Also, it would be interesting to study the long-term retention of concepts taught using CSU versus non-kinesthetic methods.

Acknowledgments.
We thank all teachers who participated in our workshops and provided feedback. We are indebted to those who helped to evaluate teaching CSU more broadly and on a larger scale.

5. REFERENCES

[1] T. Bell, I. H. Witten, and M. Fellows. Computer Science Unplugged: An enrichment and extension programme for primary-aged children. http://www.google.com/educators/activities/unpluggedTeachersDec2006.pdf, 2002.

[2] T. C. Bell, J. Alexander, I. Freeman, and M. Grimley. Computer Science Unplugged: School students doing real computing without computers. *The New Zealand Journal of Applied Computing and Information Technology*, 13(1):20–29, 2009.

[3] J. Biggs and K. Collis. *Evaluating the quality of learning: the SOLO taxonomy*. New York, 1982.

[4] H. Cooper, B. Nye, K. Charlton, J. Lindsay, and S. Greathouse. The effects of summer vacation on achievement test scores: A narrative and meta-analytic review. *Review of Educational Research*, 66(3):227–268, 1996.

[5] T. J. Cortina. Broadening participation: Reaching a broader population of students through "unplugged" activities. *Comm. ACM*, 58(3):25–27, Mar. 2015.

[6] Y. Feaster, L. Segars, S. K. Wahba, and J. O. Hallstrom. Teaching CS Unplugged in the high school (with limited success). In ITiCSE '11, pp. 248–252, 2011.

[7] F. T. Lyman. The responsive classroom discussion: The inclusion of all students. In *Mainstreaming Digest*, pp. 109–113. College Park, 1981.

[8] T. Nishida, Y. Idosaka, Y. Hofuku, S. Kanemune, and Y. Kuno. New methodology of information education with "computer science unplugged". In ISSEP 2008, LNCS 5090, pp. 241–252, Springer, 2008.

[9] D. Seehorn, S. Carey, B. Fuschetto, I. Lee, D. Moix, D. O'Grady-Cunniff, B. B. Owens, C. Stephenson, and A. Verno. *K-12 Computer Science Standards (Revised 2011)*. ACM/CSTA, New York, 2011.

[10] T. Seidl and J. Enderle. Binary search. In *Algorithms Unplugged*, chapter 1, pp. 5–11. Springer, 2011.

[11] R. Taub, M. Armoni, and M. Ben-Ari. CS Unplugged and middle-school students' views, attitudes, and intentions regarding CS. *ACM Trans. Computing Education*, 12(2), Apr. 2012. Article 8, 29 pages.

[12] R. Thies and J. Vahrenhold. Reflections on outreach programs in CS classes: Learning objectives for "Unplugged" activities. In SICGSE 2012, pp. 487–492, 2012.

[13] R. Thies and J. Vahrenhold. On plugging "Unplugged" into CS classes. In SICGSE 2013, pp. 365–370, 2013.

From Alice to Python. Introducing Text-based Programming in Middle Schools.

Nour Tabet
Al-Arqam Academy for Girls
Doha, Qatar
nour.t@al-
arqamacademy.com

Huda Gedawy
Computer Science
Carnegie Mellon University
Doha, Qatar
hgedawy@cmu.edu

Hanan Alshikhabobakr
Computer Science
Carnegie Mellon University
Doha, Qatar
halshikh@cmu.edu

Saquib Razak
Computer Science
Carnegie Mellon University
Doha, Qatar
srazak@cmu.edu

ABSTRACT

In this paper, we present our experience in designing computing curriculum for Middle School students. Computing education is becoming an important part of STEM education and several national curriculums are incorporating computing education in their core curriculums. We design a curriculum that uses Alice – an interactive drag-and-drop interface that provides a simple interface to learn programming concepts. Once the students are comfortable in these concepts, they take Python in higher classes to learn computing concepts in the context of a text-based programming language. This study attempts to provide "mediated transfer" for applying concepts learned in Alice, to programming in Python. We present the results of our study in applying this curriculum in a local school.

CCS Concepts

• **Social and professional topics-- Computing education--K-12 education**

•**Applied computing--Education--Interactive learning environments**

Keywords

Alice; Computing Curriculum; K-12; Computational Thinking; Python.

1. INTRODUCTION

Several educational institutions and policy makers across the globe are realizing the importance of computing literacy and computational thinking for students in K-12. Trends in professions indicate that the future holds a special place for those with computing skills and are able to create technological innovations that meet the growing needs of people. In addition, computing education will prepare students for success in the workplace as well as in higher education pursuits; it equips them with skills that'll enable them to use computational thinking to solve problems in different aspects of life. This thought is aptly described in Code.org's mission statement where they say that: "We believe computer science and computer programming should be part of the core curriculum in education, alongside other science, technology, engineering, and mathematics (STEM) courses, such as biology, physics, chemistry and algebra" [3].

Seventeen states in the US have policies in place to count computer science as one of the science and mathematics electives [10]. In Singapore, the governmental agency responsible for country's Internet policy is working together with the Ministry of Education to introduce computer science courses in schools to boost the economy of the country [15]. The ministry of education in UK is considering a new curriculum for the ICT (information and communication technology) subject that focuses on computing. The new National Curriculum in UK requires schools to teach computing from K-12 [13]. The ministry of education in Qatar (MoE) is making an effort towards having computing as a core subject in K-12.

This growing trend in introducing computing to K-12 curriculum has created a need to study the best-practices and techniques that make teaching computer science useful in schools. Over the last decade, several tools and applications have been created that introduce complex concepts in a more accessible way for students.

Over the past three years, we have worked on developing instructional and curricula materials that were used by teachers of math and ICT in secondary schools. The curricular material focuses on concepts of analytic, logical thinking, and problem solving skills in the context of creating animations that tell stories of local culture. We use Alice as the tool for teaching these concepts. We work closely with local English schools – majority of which follow the National Curriculum from UK [13]. Due to the recent changes introduced by the UK curriculum in teaching Computing for K-12 students, we felt a need for developing courses that take concepts learned in visual interactive development environments and apply these concepts in more text-based programming languages.

The concept of "mediated transfer", where concepts learned in one context are applied in a different context are popular in education research and developing methodologies that make this transfer explicit and easy are active areas of education research [1, 8, 9, 17]. One of the first works in this area by Perkins and Salomon [17], categorizes "mediating transfer" techniques as "bridging" and "hugging". In "bridging" techniques, students learn how to apply a concept learnt in one context, to different contexts. On the other hand "hugging" techniques allow the students to engage in an activity to embrace a new skill rather than theoretically learn about it. Researchers develop teaching techniques that allow the teachers to ease this transfer process. In our previous work, we exploited "hugging" by teaching algorithmic thinking through Alice programming. However in this work, we use "bridging" techniques to explicitly highlight concepts learned in Alice as they are applied to programming text-based Python language.

In this paper, we present our experience in designing an Alice based curriculum for teaching computing to middle school students. The curriculum emphasizes computing concepts like algorithm design and programming blocks like sequential and conditional execution, repetition, variable, etc. Alice provides an interactive drag-drop environment that reduces cognitive load on the students as they don't have to deal with syntax. This curriculum is implemented in grade seven. Once students are comfortable with programming concepts through Alice, we present our design of a computing curriculum that uses Python programming language. Students take this course in grade eight. The design of Python curriculum draws several lessons from Alice curriculum and builds on top of programming concepts that students are already familiar with. This Alice to Python approach, which borrows from the concepts of "mediated transfer" mentioned earlier, enables students and instructors to transfer concepts learned in the context of Alice animations to programming in Python. Alice teaches fundamental concepts that can be translated into any text-based programming language, thus we believed that students with Alice background can quickly and easily learn other text-based programming languages. Our hypothesis was that using explicit mediated transfer with Alice would improve students' achievement in learning Python in higher grades.

2. RELATED WORK
2.1 Introductory CS tools
Recently many tools were developed to promote computing education to the young generation.

Alice is a software tool that introduces computational thinking and programming concepts in the context of creating 3D animations [6, 22]. In Alice, 3D models of objects (e.g., people, animals and vehicles) populate a virtual world and students use a drag and drop editor to manipulate different actions of these objects. Scratch, developed at MIT media labs, is a tool that allows users to create interactive 2D games and animations. Scratch encourages students to work collaboratively and learn creative thinking and logical reasoning [22]. Green foot is an integrated development environment that uses interactive games to teach students programming in Java [13]. The use of program visualization with educational software tools such as Alice, Scratch, and Green foot is gaining acceptance as an educational approach, particularly in K-12 classrooms. Moreover, one of the most popular initiatives to encourage early computer science education is Code.org, a nonprofit organization that aims to bring computer science to K-12 classes in the United States through providing online curriculum and short tutorials.

2.2 Visual vs. Textual tools
New approaches to promote computational thinking lean towards using code blocks, which are often called Visual Programming Languages (VPL). Such tools are recommended for the young learners as they contribute to maintaining a positive impression of programming in the long run compared to Textual Programming Languages (TPL) [12]. Although not considered as a professional programming language, it is believed that VPL's make the initial experience an intuitive and personal process [11]. Alice is one of the most successful VPLs and was distinguished as the only 3D environment therefore most suitable for storytelling and virtual world's creation [26].

A study compared the user experience of students using VPL verses TPL while learning to program Arduino. The study found that the participants not only felt more confident to modify VPL code, they also had a more positive experience than when using the TPL [5]. More generally, of the various curricula that were designed in alignment with the Advanced Placement Computer Science Principles framework [7], notably one curriculum started the course with a drag-and-drop language then switched to a text-based language. The study reported that the students utilized their understanding of logic from VPL and applied it in the TPL [2].

Furthermore, a recent study had experimented teaching VPL in middle school level then teaching TPL in high school found that the students' relational thinking significantly improved when they had the VPL background [4]. In addition the motivation and self-confidence were much higher for this group.

2.3 Alice
Alice is a visual programming environment designed to enable novice programmers to create 3D virtual worlds including animations and games. Alice proposed to use the context of animation to introduce computing, logic, and communication skills and the fundamental programming concepts to students in secondary schools. Although the original intent of Alice was to increase student retention in computer science and to attract females and under-represented minorities, several studies have shown the effectiveness of using Alice to teach computational thinking to middle school students [14, 18, 21, 27]. We developed a curriculum for middle school students that encourage students to develop analytic, logical, computational thinking, and problem solving skills as well as enable creativity and innovation, using Alice.

Alice project recently developed Alice 3 that can be transferred to Java IDE. "Alice 3 to Java" approach was used in an undergraduate introductory computer science course [8]. The overall experience of introducing Alice 3 before Java resulted in at least one letter grade increase. However during the course, the students faced difficulty dealing with irrelevant and complex Java code during the transfer phase. Hence we decide to avoid Java and use a simpler programming language, Python, which is getting widely used in introductory programming courses [19, 23, 25, 28].

3. THE COMPUTING CURRICULUM
We present seventh and eighth grade computing curriculum with the Alice and Python approaches respectively. We highlight that the topics covered in each curriculum overlap so that bridging is applied in the learning process. However, a few topics such as concurrency and event handling are only covered in the Alice curriculum due to its complexity level in Python that would not suit the target learner level.

Each of the two curriculums is designed for one semester of the academic year. In the following subsections, we present the methodology for presenting each concept in Alice and Python along with examples. The concepts presented here are based on the computing program of study in the National curriculum in England [16].

3.1 ALICE APPROACH

This introductory curriculum builds a computing foundation for seventh grade students. Following this curriculum, students are expected to understand and develop algorithms; in addition, they are expected to write simple programs using building blocks like sequence, selection and repetition. Building on this experience, students will learn to decompose real world problems and model it using computational abstractions and logical thinking. This approach is based on "hugging" technique, where the students learn computing concepts by practice while creating Alice programs, rather than studying theoretically studying concepts. Alice curriculum and implementation results was previously presented by the authors in details [20].

3.1.1 Algorithms and Design

The first two weeks of the semester are mainly spent learning the Alice environment and playing around with the tool until students are familiar with different controls in Alice. The first computation concept we cover is the concept of algorithms and sequential statements. Students work on animations where character move around the screen to act out a story. We encourage students to work on a storyboard, drawing out each scene of the story on paper and then implementing the scenes in Alice. We formally introduce the concepts of storyboarding during weeks three and four, and give student templates to build their stories using rough drawing of each scene they want to create.

Learning to use Alice as a tool helps students with the concept of computational abstraction. Storyboard design supports the computational thinking aspects.

3.1.2 Sequential and Concurrent Execution

We start implementing these storyboards by using only sequential execution. Students very quickly realize the deficiency of sequential execution when they want to illustrate a man walking while moving his hands at the same time. This would seem very unnatural in case we illustrate a sequential movement of the arms and then the motion of legs. At this point we introduce the concept of concurrent execution that is made easy in Alice using a "Do Together" block. In this block, all instructions are executed concurrently. Hence now the students know how to animate a man walking forward while moving his arms and legs at the same time. At this point students are able to distinguish between actions that must occur in sequence and those that should happen simultaneously. We spend weeks five and six practicing storyboarding and implementing these storyboards.

As an overarching principle, we encourage the students to adapt incremental development and test approach. Alice makes is convenient to do that since the instantaneous visual feedback helps the students determine the validity and correctness of their implementations. Building these habits in Alice at the very beginning not only help later when Alice animations become more complex, but also help when learning any text-based programming in the future.

3.1.3 Repetition

A major theme in our approach is to make the student feel the need for a programming construct and then introduce that construct. This helps motivate the students to learn the new concept while understanding the context in which the concept should be used. After the students are taught how to make an object (ex. a rabbit) jump, the first comment they usually give is "It is only jumping once!" and "Can I repeat the jumping?". Most students would duplicate the jumping line of code by copying and pasting the initial

jump several times. That is when loops come in and they appreciate when repetition comes handy. Figures 1 and 2 present the implementation of loops in the code. The concept of loops is covered during weeks seven and eight.

3.1.4 Methods and Parameters

One of the most important aspects of solving a complex problem is the ability to decompose it into smaller sub-problems or modules, solve each sub-problem individually and then implement the complex solution as a sequence of these modules. Program decomposition is often a difficult concept to master for most novice programmers. In Alice, we teach modularity as natural consequences of using objects. In the example about a bunny jumping, it makes sense to create a method that modularizes a method for the bunny jumping motion. This approach teaches them the three stages of creating methods and functions in any other programming language; define, declare, then call. Due to instant visual feedback, students learn that a method can never be processed unless it is called.

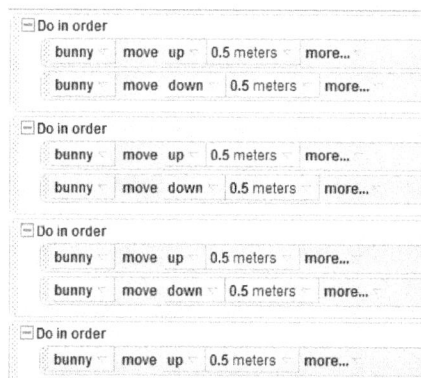

Figure 1: Bunny jumping before Loops are introduced

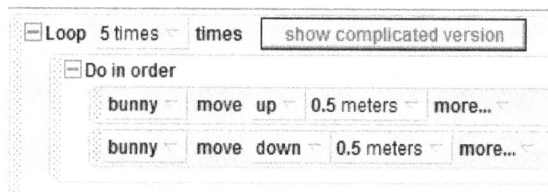

Figure 2: Bunny jumping with Loops

3.1.5 Events and Conditional Execution

By the tenth weeks, the students are eager to have some more dynamic control over their animations. In the remaining four weeks of the semester, we introduce event driven programming where objects behave based on certain events or input from the user. We also introduce the idea of conditional (if-else) statements at this point since dynamic movement of objects creates unpredictable circumstances that are best tested by using conditional statements.

A good use of if-else is when creating a game that makes something happen as a result of an action performed by the user. Figure 3, shows the following example: the bunny is the first player; as long as the bunny is more than a meter away from the beach ball it says "where is my ball?". Once it gets near to the ball it says "oh, that is my ball!" then the ball disappears. This example helps the student to visualize the effect conditional flow and their response to new events.

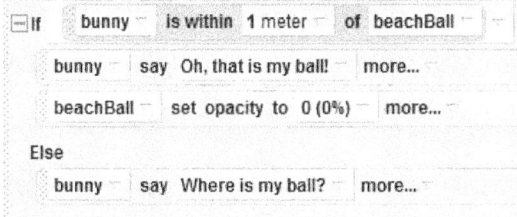

Figure 3: using if-else construct to check for proximity between objects

3.1.6   Math and Boolean Logic

Throughout the examples used in Alice curriculum, we introduce arithmetic operations like addition, subtraction, division – for example; move an object half a distance from another object. We also cover topics like Boolean logic in the context of expressing conditions for selection structures. Moreover, in the context of games, we introduce the idea of random number generation to add uncertainty and help create exciting games.

3.2   PYTHON APPROACH

We designed Python curriculum for eighth grade. The first implementation of the curriculum was applied to students that had very little programming experience with Alice. During the same academic year, our Alice curriculum was implemented in seventh grade. Hence, in the following year, eighth grade students had substantial experience with programming concepts in Alice. We modified our existing Python curriculum to consider this background and use bridging techniques to explicitly transfer concepts from Alice to Python. Here we present the concepts we covered in Python and the links established with Alice curriculum. Some concepts in Alice like event driven programming and concurrent execution require a lot of background in terms of Object Oriented Programming and threading. We believe that these topics are too advanced for middle school and hence we do not cover them in our coverage of Python.

3.2.1   Variables

Traditionally when teaching Python to students who did not learn Alice, or any other programming languages, we start with basic concepts such as definition of variable, data type, printing out a result, etc. As for students who have learnt Alice, this phase can be accelerated since they covered most of these topics. Students already have a previous background about variables, so the only new part would be to learn the syntax difference in Python.

3.2.2   Sequential Execution

Students have understood the implications of sequential execution in Alice. In our proposed Python curriculum, we introduce the turtle library to emphasize these concepts in the context of a text-based programming language. Turtle graphics were first developed as part of the Logo programming language where users can write code to move an imaginary turtle around a drawing canvas [24]. As the turtle moves, it draws a line along its movement path. We teach the students to use the primitives provided by the library to draw a house – which is a combination of several rectangles. Figure 4

shows Python code that draws a rectangle using turtle graphics. The right side of figure 4 shows the output of the code.

```
from turtle import *

forward(200)
left(90)
forward(100)
left(90)
forward(200)
left(90)
forward(100)
left(90)
```

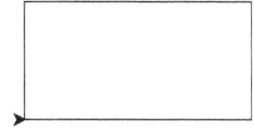

Figure 4: Python code to draw a rectangle using turtle graphics

3.2.3   Repetition

A *for loop* in Python can be directly translated from a *loop* in Alice. A *loop* in Alice is used to repeat an action for a given number of times; similarly, a *for loop* in Python will repeat the action requested according to the number of times specified. The examples below reflect how similarities are drawn with loops presented in Alice as well as Python.

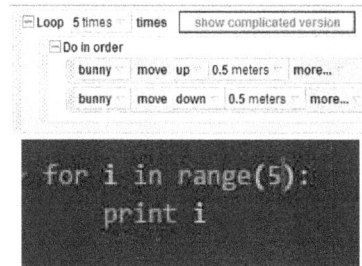

```
for i in range(5):
    print i
```

Figure 5: Python and Alice codes for loops

A concrete example of using a *loop* in Python is also demonstrated in turtle graphics. As shown in Figure 6, loops are used to help us draw the brick wall for the house we wish to draw. Since otherwise it would be very tedious to do so with a sequential code:

```
for i in range(10):
    for j in range(10):
        drawRectangle(20,10)
        forward(20)
    backward(200)
    left(90)
    forward(10)
    right(90)
```

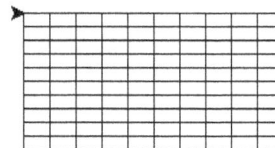

Figure 6: Brick wall illustration using nested loops in Python

3.2.4   Functions and parameters

Students with Alice background already experienced defining and calling functions. Building on our Alice example of creating a function that commands the bunny to jump several times, we motivate the same approach when drawing rectangles to make a house. Since the house needs many rectangles, it is convenient to have one method that takes care of drawing the rectangle. Moreover, we motivate function's parameters to make each rectangle have different width and height. Figure 5 shows the resulting function definition and two calls to the function along with its output.

```
from turtle import *

def drawRectangle(width, height):
    forward(width)
    left(90)
    forward(height)
    left(90)
    forward(width)
    left(90)
    forward(height)
    left(90)

drawRectangle(200,100)
forward(250)
drawRectangle(200,100)
```

Figure 7: Python code that defines a function and calls is twice

3.2.5 Nesting and Conditional flow

This concept focuses on conditional statements which are already covered in Alice. The background that the students acquire help the teacher to only emphasize on the structure and syntax used in Python. This approach is again applicable to all the concepts that are common between Alice and Python.

```
if 3%1 <= 2 and 4**2==16:
    print "The first condition is True"
elif 4>1 and not (4==0) or (0>-1):
    print "The second condition is True"
else:
    print "None of your conditions are true"
```

Figure 8: Example of using nested if-else statements in Python

In the example above, students learn how to construct a nested if-else; using if statement to check more than one condition. In the same time, student experience the effect of mathematical operators and logic gates. Again, it is important to emphasize that these students already had knowledge on how mathematical operators and logic statements are used, as they learnt their meaning and implications in Alice. The example in Figures 8 and 9 present how students used logic operations within an if-else statement.

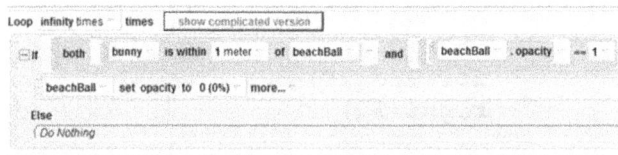

Figure 9: Example of using nested if statement with Boolean logic using Alice

4. EXPERIMENT

We implemented presented curriculum in a local private school over two years. It is worthy of notice that the teacher who reported and ran this experiment is a member of our research team.

4.1 Method

During the first year of the study, the Alice curriculum was implemented in grade seven and Python curriculum was implemented in grade eight. During this year, students in grade eight had minimal experience in Alice programming. We refer to

this group that consisted of 70 students as "group A". The following year Python curriculum was implemented for the eighth grade students who already studied Alice programming extensively in grade seven. We refer to this group of 71 students as "group B". During each year, classes meet twice a week and grade seven had a total of 15 weeks, whereas for grade eight students got a worth of 12 weeks of study.

Table 1. Summary of the Research Setting

Group	Year	Students	7th Grade curriculum
Group A	2014	70	Python
Group B	2015	71	Alice

4.2 Quantitative Analysis

Both groups were given the same assessment in grade eight final exam. For group A, the highest grade was 23 out of 25; only one student was able to score that. The average grade was 15.67 and standard deviation was 5.3. For group B, four students were able to score the full mark, and four scored 24 out of 25. The average grade was is 19.94 with a standard deviation of 3.2.

It is also important to mention that in group A, no student was able to structure complete code. The last question of the test given asked the students to create a simple code with user input and a conditional statement to check the input, and then produce output accordingly. Only one student from group A was able to script part of the code. In group B, 10% of the students wrote the code completely with no syntax errors. About 25% of the students were able to construct the code with small syntax errors, 7% of the students did not answer the question, and the rest 58% constructed part of the code.

4.3 Qualitative Analysis

Qualitatively, the teacher observed a big difference between students attitude towards programming in Python. Group B had much easier time understanding the structure of Python in comparison to group A students. Group A was struggling with understanding the concepts as well as learning the syntax, as a result, each time the students try to understand Python, its syntax and the computational idea behind it, it was a confusing process. Group A students in general lacked debugging and analysis skills while in group B, a greater number of students demonstrate code debugging skills. Accordingly, group B students were able to fix their code independently from the teacher.

Based on teacher's observation of the students, while teaching Python to group A, topics such as variables, control flow, logic expression, and other topics were hard to understand. This resulted in more lessons required to cover each topic. Students' energy toward learning Python was not always positive, many found it confusing, and as a result their grades dropped. However, some aspects were positive, as the students understood the programming concept, and what is code, how to execute it, and other basic programming concepts.

Students in group B had a deeper coverage on programming concepts using Alice as it helped them understand various aspects of programming in an easier and enjoyable way. While teaching Python to this group, students understood most of the concepts and programming fundamentals, hence it was easy to relate the topics to Alice. Students did not need to understand the concept anew; instead, they just had to learn how to structure their code in Python.

5. CONCLUSIONS

In this work we shared some results from teaching Python with a cohort of eighth grade students with extensive background in Alice programming gained during seventh grade and compared them with students with very little Alice background. Qualitative assessment determines that students with Alice background found programming in Python easier and more enjoyable. Our quantitative results show in final assessment of students in Python programming, the performance of students with Alice background was superior to those without.

Furthermore, we found that using similar examples in both Alice and Python effectively helped students better mediate transferring concepts. The 3D animation nature of Alice made it easier and an enjoyable experience for students to learn fundamental programming concepts.

6. ACKNOWLEDGMENTS

This paper was made possible by NPRP grant # 5-1070-2-451 from the Qatar National Research Fund (a member of Qatar Foundation). The statements made herein are solely the responsibility of the authors.

7. REFERENCES

[1] Alex, I. 2002. Learning Theories: Transfer of Learning. Retrieved January 18, 2016, from http://otec.uoregon.edu/learning_theory.htm

[2] Arpaci-Dusseau, A., Astrachan, O., Barnett, D., Bauer, M., Carrell, M., Dovi, R., Franke, B., Gardner, C., Gray, J., Griffin, J. and Kick, R. 2013. Computer science principles: analysis of a proposed advanced placement course. *In Proceeding of the 44th ACM technical symposium on Computer science education*, (March 2013), 251-256.

[3] Anybody can learn. 2013. Retrieved January 17, 2016, from https://code.org/about

[4] Armoni, M., Meerbaum-Salant, O., & Ben-Ari, M. 2015. From scratch to "real" programming. *ACM Transactions on Computing Education (TOCE), 4*(25), 14.

[5] Booth, T., & Stumpf, S. 2013. End-user experiences of visual and textual programming environments for Arduino. In *End-User Development*. Berlin Heidelberg: Springer. 25-39.

[6] Conway, M. J. *Alice: Easy-to-learn 3D scripting for novices.* School of Engineering and Applied Science, University of Virginia, Charlottesville, VA. 1997.

[7] Cuny, J. 2015. Transforming K-12 computing education: AP® computer science principles. *ACM Inroads, 6*(4), 58-59.

[8] Dann, W., Cosgrove, D., Slater, D., Culyba, D., & Cooper, S. 2012. Mediated transfer: Alice 3 to java. I*n Proceedings of the 43rd ACM technical symposium on Computer Science Education*, ACM, 141-146.

[9] Forgarty, R., Perkins, D., & Barell, J. *The mindful school: How to teach for transfer.* Palatine, IL: IRI/Skylight Publishing, 1991.

[10] Heitin, L. 2014. Computer Science: Not Just an Elective Anymore. *Education Week, 3*, 22.

[11] Kafai, Y. B., & Burke, Q. 2015. Computer programming goes back to school. *Education Week*, 61-65.

[12] Kaucic, B., & Asic, T. 2011. Improving introductory programming with Scratch? *MIPRO, 2011 Proceedings of the 34th International Convention*, 1095-1100.

[13] Kölling, M. 2010. The greenfoot programming environment. *ACM Transactions on Computing Education, 10* (4), 14.

[14] Lee, I., Martin, F., Denner, J., Coulter, B., Allan, W., Erickson, J., Malyn-Smith, J. and Werner, L. 2011. Computational thinking for youth in practice. *ACM Inroads*, 32-37.

[15] Lee, T. 2014. Singapore plans to introduce programming lessons in public schools to boost the economy, *Techinasia*. Retrieved January 18, 2016, from https://www.techinasia.com/singapore-introduce-programming-lessons-schools-boost-economy

[16] *National curriculum in England: computing programmes of study*. 2013. (GOV.UK) Retrieved January 18, 2016, from https://www.gov.uk/government/publications/national-curriculum-in-england-computing-programmes-of-study

[17] Perkins, D. N., & Salomon, G. 1988. Teaching for Transfer. *Educational Leadership, 46*(1), 22-32.

[18] Qualls, J. A., & Sherrell, L. B. 2010. Why computational thinking should be integrated into the curriculum. *Journal of Computing Sciences in Colleges, 25*(5), 66-71.

[19] Radenski, A. 2006. Python First: A lab-based digital introduction to computer science. *ACM SIGCSE Bulletin., 38*(3), 197-201.

[20] Razak, S. G. 2015. Alice in UK An Alice Based Implementation of UK National Computing Curriculum. *Computer Science Education Innovation & Technology (CSEIT).* Singapore.

[21] Razak, S. H. 2016. Alice in the Middle East: An experience report from the. *Proceedings of the 47th ACM Technical Symposium on Computing Science Education.* Memphis, TN, USA.

[22] Resnick, M., Maloney, J., Monroy-Hernández, A., Rusk, N., Eastmond, E., Brennan, K., Millner, A., Rosenbaum, E., Silver, J., Silverman, B. and Kafai, Y. 2009. Scratch: programming for all. *Communications of the ACM, 52*(11), 60-67.

[23] Shannon, C. 2003. Another breadth-first approach to CS I using python. *ACM SIGCSE Bulletin, 35*(1), 248-251.

[24] Solomon, C. J., & Papert, S. 1976. A case study of a young child doing Turtle Graphics in LOGO. *In Proceedings of the national computer conference and exposition,*, 1049-1056.

[25] Tsukamoto, H., Takemura, Y., Nagumo, H., Ikeda, I., Monden, A., & Matsumoto, K. I. 2015. Programming education for primary school children using a textual programming language. *IEEE Frontiers in Education Conference (FIE)*, 1-7.

[26] Utting, I., Cooper, S., Kölling, M., Maloney, J., & Resnick, M. 2010. Alice, greenfoot, and scratch--a discussion. *ACM Transactions on Computing Education (TOCE) , 10*(4), 17.

[27] Werner, L., Denner, J., Campe, S., & Kawamoto, D. C. 2012. The fairy performance assessment: measuring computational thinking in middle school. *In Proceedings of the 43rd ACM technical symposium on Computer Science Education (SIGCSE '12)*, 215-220.

[28] Zelle, J. M. 1999. Python as a first language. *Proceedings of 13th Annual Midwest Computer Conference, 2*, 145.

Competition and Feedback through Automated Assessment in a Data Structures and Algorithms Course

Tommy Färnqvist and Fredrik Heintz
Linköping University
SE-581 83, Linköping, Sweden
tommy.farnqvist@liu.se, fredrik.heintz@liu.se

ABSTRACT

We have investigated competitive elements and different forms of feedback through automated assessment in a Data Structures and Algorithms course. It is given at the start of the second year and has about 140 students. In 2011 we investigated the effects of introducing competitive elements utilizing automated assessment. In 2012 we investigated how feedback through automated assessment on the labs influences student's ways of working, their performance, and their relations to the examining staff. The students get immediate feedback concerning correctness and efficiency. When judged correct the assistants make sure the program also fulfill requirements such as being well structured. After the course, we investigated the students attitudes to, and experiences from, using automated assessment via a questionnaire. 80% of the students are positive and it positively influenced their ways of working. 50% said they put in more effort because of automated judging. Moreover, assessment is seen as more objective as it is executed in the exact same manner for everyone. Both of these statements are confirmed by assessing the labs from 2011 using the same automated tool as was used in 2012. Our conclusions are that feedback through automated assessment gives wanted positive effects and is perceived as positive by the students.

Keywords

competition; feedback; automated assessment; data structures and algorithms

1. INTRODUCTION

Feedback is fundamental to all learning situations [7]. Feedback gives information concerning what one is doing right and what one is doing wrong and gives the possibility of correcting or improving one's behavior. Our goal is to give students better, faster, and more individualized feedback. Automated feedback cannot replace all other forms of feedback but can be an important complement. Advantages of automated assessment are that it is impartial, consistent,

ITiCSE '16, July 09-13, 2016, Arequipa, Peru
© 2016 ACM. ISBN 978-1-4503-4231-5/16/07...$15.00
DOI: http://dx.doi.org/10.1145/2899415.2899454

immediate, can handle large groups of students, and can be individualized. The interest for using automated assessment has increased steadily as an effect of both better systems for automated judging as well as the fact that the increasingly popular online courses, attended by thousands of students, require the use of automated feedback.

In this paper, we describe our experiments with introducing automated assessment in a Data Structures and Algorithms course (DALG) at Linköping University during 2011 and 2012. The DALG course is given at the start of the second year for about 140 students from the main Computer Science curricula. The 6 ECTS credit course is organized in traditional monolithic form with weekly lectures, class room sized tutorials, laboratory sessions, and a written final exam.

From a learning perspective, the hope is that the automated assessment can move students from a passive stance to an active position of tracking their own comprehension through the immediate feedback that the automated system provides. We want to engage the students and involve them in the loop of assessment as active participants. According to Bandura's cognitive theory of self efficacy [1], it is possible to impact student motivation positively by providing instruction that allows for checking one's progress at a designated level of proficiency. Constructivist theory says that giving timely feedback can encourage students to modify their work [8]. Furthermore, Lovett and Greenhouse [6] have shown that getting comments and feedback on learning steps have significant influence on learning compared to receiving feedback from the instructor on performance only.

There have been a considerable number of attempts in higher education institutions to build applications for automated assessment for different types of assignments. Due to the specific nature of programming assignments, automated evaluation of user submitted programs is fairly natural and was first used over fifty years ago [4]. In particular, such use both saves valuable instructor time and ensures impartial and immediate feedback on programs submitted. We refer the reader interested in more background to the survey by Ihantola et al. [5], and the many references therein.

2. DALG 2011

In the 2011 edition of the DALG course, we investigated two different ways of using competitive elements to support students' deliberate practice in programming, which are activities that are designed to lead to improvements of specific aspects of performance [3]. These activities should stretch an individual just beyond his or her current abilities, provide immediate feedback, be repeated multiple times, and require

	All	Group 1	Group 2	Group 3
Number of students	140	32	33	35
Total credits	42.4	43.6	43.4	40.0
Programming credits	11.0	10.9	11.1	11.0
Programming grade	3.73	3.75	3.84	3.58
Math credits	15.0	16.2	16.1	12.4
Math grade	3.61	3.57	3.65	3.60
CS credits	15.1	14.6	14.8	16.0
CS grade	3.78	3.75	3.84	3.74

Table 1: Background data groups, DALG 2011.

sufficient effort and full concentration. The voluntary contest was wholly dependent on automated assessment, while the programming assignments were mainly graded manually.

2.1 Lab Assignment Contests

To compare different designs for the lab assignment contest we divided the students into four different groups. The first group competed based on speed (days from the start of the course) and correctness (+3 penalty days for incorrect submissions). The second group competed based on quality (cyclomatic complexity and instruction count) and efficiency (runtime and memory consumption). The third and fourth groups were control groups and did not compete. Table 1 gives various background statistics about the groups at the start of the course. We have performed extensive statistical testing and found that the only significant difference (at the 5% level) between any groupings in Table 1 concerns math credits taken for Group 1 and Group 3, where both the means as well as the entire populations are significantly different. Group 4 consisted of students from our IT programme, while the other groups contained a mixture of students from our two other main CS programmes.

All groups had to submit their labs to an online system as soon as they thought they were ready. We found that both competing groups were influenced by our competitions, with the strongest effect being that the submission pattern for the groups differs dramatically. This is shown in Fig. 1, where Group 1 worked very fast and Group 2 slightly faster than the control groups (Group 3 and Group 4).

In particular, the lectures did not cover the material for the first lab assignment until week two of the course, so the submission pattern of Group 4 is more like what you would expect during a year with no competitions. We believe that since Group 3 consisted of students from the same programmes as the competing groups the thrill of competition more easily spilled over to Group 3 than to Group 4. There were also large variations in the quality of the code between and in the groups, as evidenced by Table 2.

A few things stand out in Table 2. Apparently the contest concerning minimizing instruction count and cyclomatic complexity number (CCN) that Group 2 participated in did not have any significant effect when compared to the other groups. We see that in Lab 2, where students implement deletion in binary search trees and are inclined to write complicated methods with a lot of unnecessary special cases, the CCN value is generally higher than for the rest of the assignments. Competing based on memory consumption, however, seemed to be a more concrete task. In Lab 4, where you are given a working program and are supposed to optimize it by clever choices of algorithm and data structures, the best

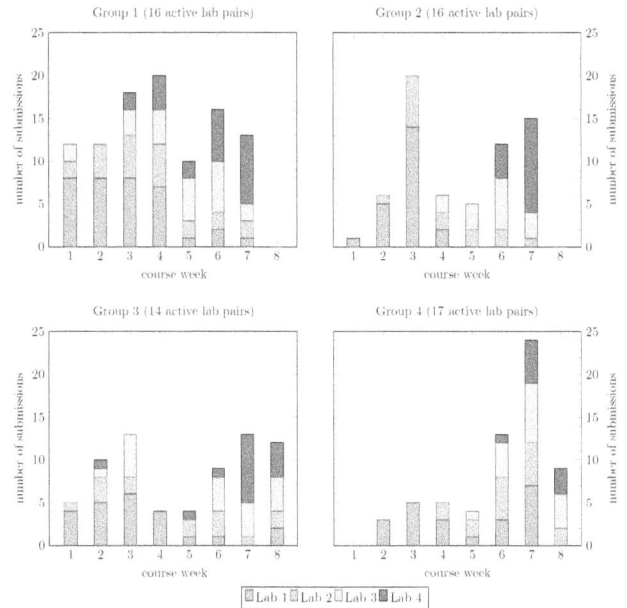

Figure 1: Submission activity, DALG 2011.

students in Group 2 use a factor 30 less memory than the average and a factor 100 less than the worst. Also, running time could be cut in half by the better students compared to the worst. The running times of the quick-sort implementations in Lab 3 do not show the same amount of variation, which is probably due to its more constrained nature.

2.2 Voluntary Contest

To provide further motivation for deliberate practice we also provided a voluntary contest based on problems from the automated judging system at Universidad de Valladolid. After each lecture the students enrolled in the contest received a challenge with a programming problem to solve. The problems were selected to either reinforce and repeat a topic just addressed in the lecture or to stretch the students' abilities by demanding use of deeper knowledge. The online judge used provides immediate feedback and since the contest requires students to solve challenges as quickly as possible due to time penalties otherwise incurred, it should prove to be an intensive experience. All together, this contest also satisfies the conditions for deliberate practice.

Table 3 shows that 30 students registered for the voluntary contest and that 15 solved at least one task. The tendency that the average grade rises with rising commitment to our extra activities is not strong enough to be significant if we only look at the averages. However, the distribution of grades for students enrolled in the voluntary contest and/or solving at least one task in the contest is significantly different (at the 10% level) from the distribution for all students.

Inspecting Table 4, it would seem that a possible explanation for students enrolled in the voluntary contest performing better on the final exam could be that they are already stronger students, based on their past performance. Indeed, the average number of total credits taken by students solving at least one task is significantly larger (at the 5% level) than the average number of total credits over all students. The same holds for credits from programming courses for

Category	Instructions min/avg/max	CCN min/avg/max	Memory (MB) min/avg/max	Running time min/avg/max
Group 1	215/492/948	4/8/15	n/a	n/a
Group 2	208/492/1218	4/7/18	n/a	n/a
Group 3	217/458/842	4/8/21	n/a	n/a
Group 4	157/490/733	3/9/23	n/a	n/a
Group 1 Lab 1	345/464/627	4/7/10	n/a	n/a
Group 2 Lab 1	368/451/570	4/6/9	n/a	n/a
Group 3 Lab 1	365/452/573	4/6/11	n/a	n/a
Group 4 Lab 1	157/446/578	3/7/12	n/a	n/a
Group 1 Lab 2	434/498/640	4/9/15	n/a	n/a
Group 2 Lab 2	426/532/733	5/10/18	n/a	n/a
Group 3 Lab 2	419/521/669	6/11/21	n/a	n/a
Group 4 Lab 2	558/625/733	7/15/23	n/a	n/a
Group 1 Lab 3	215/272/312	4/9/13	n/a	10/11/13
Group 2 Lab 3	208/259/384	4/6/9	n/a	10/12/17
Group 3 Lab 3	217/250/329	4/8/12	n/a	9/11/12
Group 4 Lab 3	184/274/359	4/9/15	n/a	10/12/22
Group 1 Lab 4	564/720/948	6/7/9	3/16/21	84/124/150
Group 2 Lab 4	620/704/1218	5/7/9	0.6/20/62	80/129/196
Group 3 Lab 4	357/609/842	5/6/8	3/23/66	110/135/194
Group 4 Lab 4	506/641/727	4/6/7	13/22/28	110/130/148

Table 2: Quality measures, DALG 2011.

Student group	Total number	Took exam	Passed exam	Average grade
All	140	118	95	3.36
Answered questionnaire	79	74	62	3.47
Completed all labs	76	73	62	3.47
Registered for voluntary contest	30	29	27	3.56
Solved at least one task in contest	15	15	15	3.6

Table 3: Exam results, DALG 2011.

	All	Answered questionnaire	Completed all labs	Reg. for contest	Solved at least one task
No. students	140	79	76	30	15
Total credits	42.4	45.7	46.2	45.4	50.0
Prog. credits	11.0	11.4	12.1	12.6	13.5
Prog. grade	3.73	4.00	3.83	4.00	4.27
Math credits	15.0	16.5	16.1	15.8	16.9
Math grade	3.61	3.68	3.70	3.68	3.89
CS credits	15.1	15.6	16.4	16.9	18.4
CS grade	3.78	4.06	3.89	4.04	4.26

Table 4: Background data activities, DALG 2011.

same time, only 3% and 11% said they gave the course much higher or a bit higher priority because of the contests, respectively. Also, only 3% and 16% of the respondents said that the contests had any conscious effect on their effort in the course. It might seem strange that so many students were positive towards the competitive elements in the course while relatively few of them actually participated actively in the activities proffered. The explanation for this can be found in the answers to the free text questions, where students cite lack of time and/or lack of incentive in the form of credits or points on the exam as the main reason for not participating actively. We also want to mention that general student satisfaction with the course, as evaluated by university central instruments as well as the questionnaire, remained at the same (high) level as previous years.

3. DALG 2012

For the 2012 edition of the DALG course we made two important changes. First, we introduced automated assessment of lab assignments, which means employing feedback through automated assessment when assessing the learning objectives of the course. Second, the voluntary contest gave bonus points on the final exam to students solving enough tasks. The course had 138 active students.

For each lab assignment the students get immediate feedback from the automated judging system. To be accepted, a program has to be both fast enough and give the correct answer to all test data. When the program is correct and resource efficient, the course assistants make sure that the program also fulfill requirements such as being well written and well structured. We used the exact same assignments as the year before, which means that we can compare the results with those from the previous year. The automated judging system employed is Kattis [2].

3.1 Lab Assignments

To investigate and compare different feedback models we divided the students into four different groups. The first group only received the default feedback from the automated judge, which means that they are told if their program crashes, if it takes too long time to execute, if it gives the wrong answer, or if it gives the right answer. The three other groups were provided with some information concerning the type of test case they failed on and were also given access to all output from their submitted program. Table 5 gives various background statistics about the groups.

We have performed extensive statistical testing and found that: the number of programming credits for Group 2 differs significantly (at the 10% level) from Group 1 when compar-

students registered for the contest and/or solving at least one task when compared to all students, as well as for CS credits for students solving at least one task. The average programming grade for students solving at least one task is significantly different from the average programming grade of all students (at the 10% level). No other such explanatory significant differences were found. It would seem that, statistically, the whole effect of students performing better on the final exam if they were enrolled on the voluntary contest cannot be explained by their stronger backgrounds (but perhaps it could with a larger sample size).

2.3 Questionnaire

At the end of the course we asked the students to fill out a questionnaire with differing questions depending on their involvement in different course activities. 79 out of 140 students responded. With respect to the background variables in Table 4, the only difference between students answering the questionnaire and all students was that they have significantly different CS grades (at the 10% level).

We posed both multiple choice questions as well as questions allowing free text answers. Here, we choose to only relate a few of the more important ones. On the question "What is your general attitude towards the DALG contests?", 22% answered very positive, 35% fairly positive, 30% neutral, 11% fairly negative, and 0% very negative, reinforcing the feeling of the course assistants and the authors that our experiments were received well in general. At the

	Group 1	Group 2	Group 3
Total credits	46.3	46.2	46.0
Programming credits	13.6	12.8	13.3
Programming grade	4.3	4.0	4.2
Math credits	15.2	14.9	11.9
Math grade	3.6	3.5	3.5
CS credits	17.5	16.3	19.5
CS grade	4.3	4.0	4.0

Table 5: Background data groups, DALG 2012.

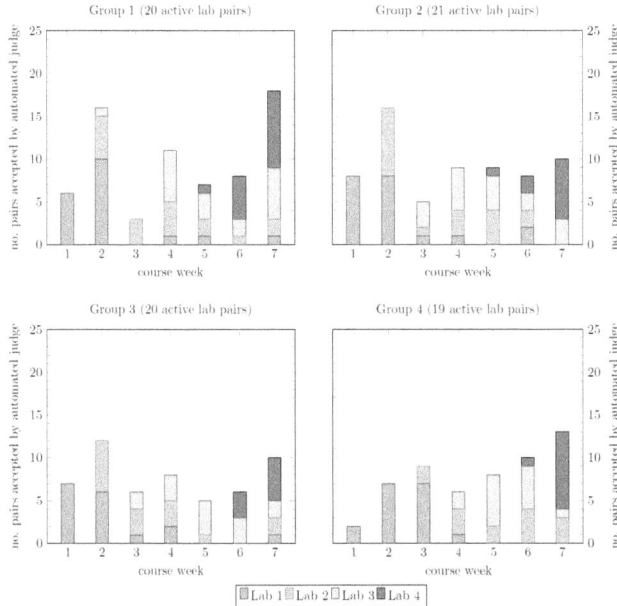

Figure 2: Finished assignments, DALG 2012.

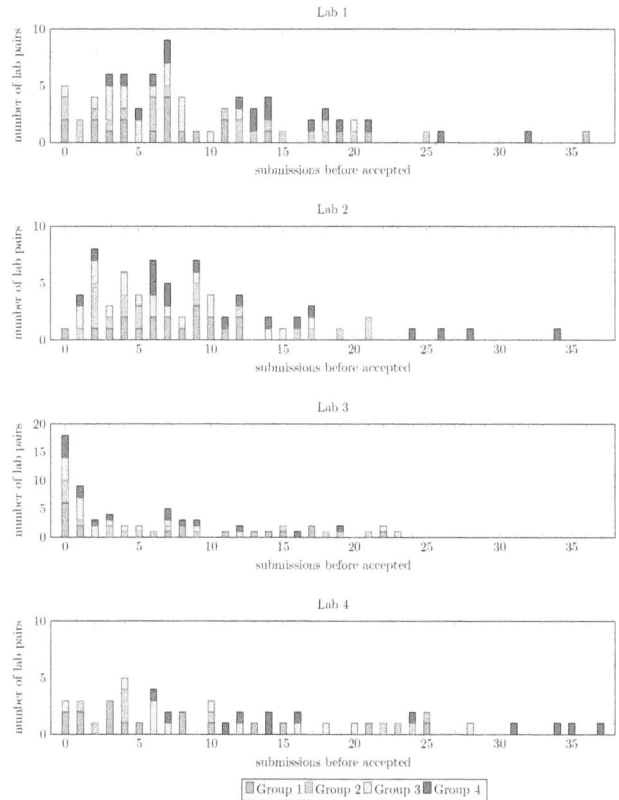

Figure 3: Submissions before AC, DALG 2012.

ing averages (but not when comparing the distributions), the number of math credits for Group 3 is significantly different (at the 5% level) from Group 1 and Group 2 both when comparing averages as well as distributions, the number of CS credits differs significantly (at the 1% level) from Group 1 and Group 2 when it comes to averages and differs significantly (at the 5% level) from Group 1 and Group 2 when comparing distributions. Group 1 and Group 2 consisted of students from the same educational programme, while Group 3 had students from two different programmes. Group 4 consisted of students from our IT programme, so (like 2011) their results are not included in the comparison.

Fig. 2 shows how many lab pairs (the students work in pairs) from each group finished the different assignments per course week. The only significant difference is that the distribution for Group 4 differs for some assignments. The same observation holds for Fig. 3, the number of submissions before Kattis accepted the assignment.

In Fig. 4 we can see how many accepted submissions the lab pairs have made per assignment and group. One of the criteria the automated judge uses to accept an assignment is that the code is efficient enough. This means that Fig. 4 gauges how long different pairs have chosen to continue working on an assignment to optimize running time even though they have already passed. Judging from the figure, you would perhaps expect that Lab 3 and Lab 4, but

also Lab 1, have a clear focus on running time issues, while Lab 2 probably has its focus on functionality rather than efficiency. This is also the case — Lab 3 involves implementation of a certain quick-sort variant, while the task in Lab 4 is to speed up a given program so that it goes from taking days to tenths of a second to execute.

In conclusion, we see that, even though Group 1 only got Kattis' default feedback, while the other groups were given hints concerning types of test cases as well as all output from their submitted programs we cannot observe any differences with regards to when students finished the assignments. We know from the answers to our questionnaire that a few students exploited the fact that they had access to all their submission output, but in the majority of the cases we cannot observe any difference between the feedback types.

3.2 Improved Quality of Assessment of Labs

One major benefit of introducing automated assessment is that the quality of the assessment is significantly increased. To quantify the improvement we submitted labs 1, 2 and 3 from DALG 2011 to Kattis, see Table 6. We did not include Lab 4 since it requires manual work for each submission.

A number of interesting observations can be made. First, about 60% of all labs that passed the human assessment was not accepted (AC) by Kattis. We can also see that there is a large variation among the groups. For Group 1 and 2 at least 50% of the labs were accepted both by the lab assistant and Kattis while for Group 3 and 4 only about 25% of the labs were accepted by both. If we look at the individual lab assignments we see that Lab 2, which revolves around a bi-

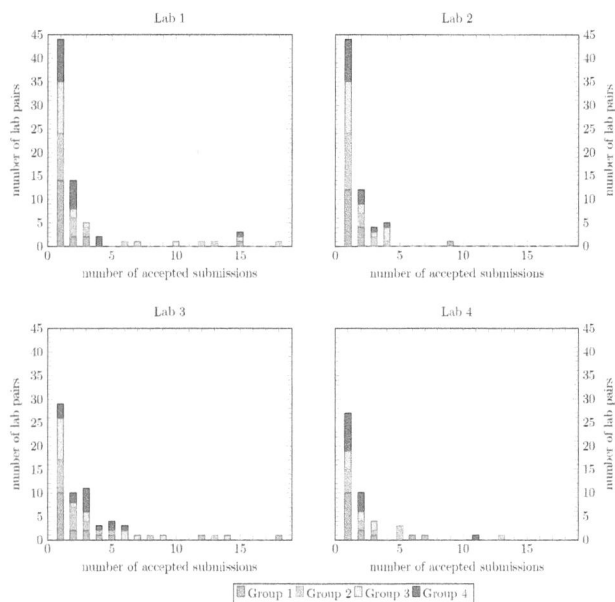

Figure 4: Accepted submissions, DALG 2012.

Category	Submissions	Passed and AC	Passed and not AC	Not passed and AC	Not passed and not AC
All	254	59	95	27	73
Group 1	85	19	19	9	38
Group 2	54	22	17	6	9
Group 3	59	11	28	4	16
Group 4	56	7	31	8	10
Lab 1	106	27	31	18	30
Lab 2	73	14	36	4	19
Lab 3	75	18	28	5	24
Group 1 Lab 1	35	8	6	5	16
Group 2 Lab 1	23	9	5	4	5
Group 3 Lab 1	26	4	11	3	8
Group 4 Lab 1	22	6	9	6	1
Group 1 Lab 2	24	4	9	3	8
Group 2 Lab 2	16	6	7	0	3
Group 3 Lab 2	16	4	8	1	3
Group 4 Lab 2	17	0	12	0	5
Group 1 Lab 3	26	7	4	1	14
Group 2 Lab 3	15	7	5	2	1
Group 3 Lab 3	17	3	9	0	5
Group 4 Lab 3	17	1	10	2	4

Table 6: Kattis applied to DALG 2011 labs 1–3.

Student group	Total number	Took exam	Passed exam	Average grade
All	138	128	51	3.27
Answered questionnaire	57	51	27	3.37
Completed all labs	68	64	35	3.34
Registered for voluntary contest	65	63	36	3.31
Solved at least one task in contest	50	49	28	3.36
Received bonus points on exam	5	5	4	4.00

Table 7: Results final exam, DALG 2012.

nary search tree implementation, is the hardest for a human to assess correctly in some sense.

As expected, it is not enough for a submission to be accepted by Kattis to be accepted by the lab assistants. Each group and each lab has submissions that are accepted by Kattis but not by the assistant. We note that Lab 1 has the most of these. A potential explanation is that it takes a while for the students to realize the level of quality required by the assistants. It could also be the case that assistants are a bit harder in the beginning to set the bar.

Another interesting observation is that the lab assignment contest influenced the quality of submissions. Group 1 should solve the labs as quickly as possible, which has resulted in that they submit too early and need more submissions to get it right. Group 2 focused on quality, which resulted in both the fewest submissions and the highest share of submissions accepted by both the assistant and Kattis.

When we look into the detailed results of the Kattis assessment we find that most submissions fail on only one or two test cases for each lab assignment. For Lab 1, involving implementation of a simple symbol table by hashing, there are two difficult test cases. The first test case checks whether the code can handle multiple key, value pairs with the same hash value. The second test case checks whether the code is efficient enough on large hash tables when the load factor is relatively high. For Lab 2 the difficult test case is the first test case where explicit examples are not provided in the lab instructions. This means that the students need to read the course book to find out what to do. For Lab 3 the difficult test case is the final test case where a large number of elements should be sorted. This checks whether the students have correctly implemented an appropriate method for selecting the pivot element in quick-sort. This also shows that it is especially hard for the assistants to determine if the code is efficient enough by only looking at it.

From the results it is clear that the quality of assessment is greatly improved by having the students first submit the code to Kattis and then, when it is correct and efficient, the assistants can give feedback on coding style and structure.

3.3 Voluntary Contest

Also for the 2012 edition of the course a voluntary contest was arranged, but now wholly based on the Kattis automated judging system. Most of the problems used were the same both years, the big difference was that in 2012 we did not hand out any (cash) prizes, which we did in 2011. However, students solving enough problems were given bonus points on the final exam.

From Table 7[1], we see that 65 students took part in the contest and that 50 solved at least one problem, compared to 2011, when 30 students were active in the contest and 15 solved at least one problem. The absence of cash prizes thus did not have any negative impact on the interest for the competition. However, the effort required to achieve bonus point on the exam was too high. This was corrected for the 2013 edition of the course, when a bonus point ladder was implemented and about 25 students earned some bonus points.

The tendency that increasing commitment to different activities in the course correlates with a higher grade on the final exam is not strong enough to be statistically significant except if we compare the average grade for all students with

---

[1]We want to remark that the exam results for all students was very poor. The amount of students failing the exam is usually between 20% to 30%. Still, 90% of the students were fairly satisfied or very satisfied with the course in general.

those receiving bonus points on the exam — then both the averages and the distributions are significantly different (at the 10% level and the 5% level, respectively). This has a natural explanation in the fact that the four students with bonus points are strong students overall.

3.4 Questionnaire

After the course, we asked the students to fill out a questionnaire asking questions about their commitment to different activities in the course. 57 out of 138 students did.

On the question of whether the students think they were able to work more independently when compared to other lab courses (thanks to automated assessment), 36% answered yes, a lot, and 50% yes, to some extent. Earlier, there have been complaints that grading of lab assignments have taken too long time and that the assistants have not been able to cope with all questions from students during lab sessions.

On the question if the students felt that the role of the assistant in the course differs from other similar courses with no automated assessment, about half of them said Yes. Among those answering Yes, there are free text comments stating that the assistants role as examiner of programming assignments has evolved to be less about demonstrating code and more about demonstrating problem solving. This is in complete agreement with the findings in Enström et. al. [2].

We also asked what the students would like to change about the feedback Kattis gives. Among the answers we can see that students from Group 1 would like to have more information about what went wrong with their submission, e.g. by telling what type of test case failed — i.e. exactly the type of information the other groups were given. At the same time it does not seem that students who got this information used it in any systematic way.

On the question "What is your general attitude towards automated assessment", 33% answered very positive and 51% fairly positive. On the question "Has the automated assessment had any conscious effect on your effort in the course", 9% answered yes, very positive, 47% answered yes, fairly positive, and 29% answered no, none. On the question "Have you spent more time on the course as a result of automated assessment than you think you would have otherwise", 11% replied yes, a lot more, 56% yes, a bit more, and 29% no, the same amount. Altogether, this indicates that the students are positive towards automated assessment and that more than half of them thinks that it both has a positive influence and that they put in more effort when automated assessment is used. It is our hope that they also can work more efficiently since they get immediate feedback.

We also asked if the students believe that grading is more fair when using automated assessment. To this question 27% answered yes, a lot and 46% yes, to some extent. Additionally, 50% of the students felt that they had to try harder to pass the assignments compared to manually graded labs.

Both of these statements, concerning fairness and perceived effort, are confirmed by assessing the labs from DALG 2011 using Kattis. In total, only about 40% of the labs accepted by the assistants were also accepted by Kattis. The variation among the groups was also large with two groups having about 50% accepted both by Kattis and the assistant compared to about 25% for the other two groups.

On the question of whether the students prefer automated assessment over manually graded assignments 80% said Yes, which shows that the students, like us, are positive.

4. CONCLUSIONS

Our goal is to use automated assessment to give students faster, higher quality, and better adapted feedback. Automated feedback cannot replace all other forms of feedback but is an important complement. Some key advantages are that it is impartial, consistent, immediate, can handle large groups, and can be individualized. Our experiments and investigations in a Data Structures and Algorithms course in 2011 and 2012 indicate that students are positive towards using automated assessment (80% of all respondents in 2012) and that it influences student work in a mainly positive fashion. For example, 50% in 2012 said that they put in more effort in the course thanks to automated assessment. Furthermore, grading is more objective since it is performed in the exact same manner for everyone. The fact that grading is perceived as fair is also plain from the 2012 questionnaire, where 73% of the students replied that they think automated grading is more fair than manual grading. Both of these statements are confirmed by assessing the labs from DALG 2011 using the same automated tool as in DALG 2012.

Student behavior is affected positively by contests, as evidenced by our 2011 and 2012 experiments. We now routinely employ voluntary contests of the same type as in the 2012 edition of the DALG course where no other reward than bonus points on the final exam is given. Typically, 20–30% of the students in a given course earn bonus points and, in that way, practice more on solving problems relevant for the course goals. We have also continued to see that having the automated judge report back a timing result and keeping a highscore list spur certain students to continue working on and improving already acceptable solutions.

Our conclusions are that feedback through automated assessment gives wanted positive effects and is perceived as positive by the students and the teachers.

5. ACKNOWLEDGMENTS

This study was partially financed by the pedagogical development group at the Institute of Technology at LiU.

6. REFERENCES

[1] A. Bandura. *Social Foundations of Thought and Action.* Prentice Hall, 1986.

[2] Enström et.al. Five years with Kattis - Using an automated assessment system in teaching. In *Proc. FIE*, 2011.

[3] A. Ericsson, K. Nandagopal, and R. Roring. Toward a science of exceptional achievement: Attaining superior performance through deliberate practice. *Annals of New York Academy of Science*, 2009.

[4] J. Hollingsworth. Automatic graders for programming classes. *Comm. of the ACM*, 3(10):528–529, 1960.

[5] Ihantola et.al. Review of recent systems for automatic assessment of programming assignments. In *Proc. Koli Calling Int. Conf. on Computing Ed. Research*, 2010.

[6] M. Lovett and J. Greenhouse. Applying cognitive theory to statistics instruction. *The American Statistician*, 54(3):196–211, 2000.

[7] P. Ramsden. *Learning to Teach in Higher Education.* Routledge, 1992.

[8] K. Swan. *Elements of quality online education: Engaging communities*, chapter A Constructivist model for thinking about learning online. 2005.

A Generic Framework for Engaging Online Data Sources in Introductory Programming Courses

Nadeem Abdul Hamid
Berry College
Mount Berry, GA 30149
nadeem@acm.org

ABSTRACT

This paper presents work on a code framework and methodology to facilitate the introduction of large, real-time, online data sources into introductory (or advanced) Computer Science courses. The framework is generic in the sense that no prior scaffolding or template specification is needed to make the data accessible, as long as the source uses a standard format such as XML, CSV, or JSON. The implementation described here maintains minimal syntactic overhead while relieving novice programmers from low-level issues of parsing raw data from a web-based data source. It interfaces directly with data structures and representations defined by the students themselves, rather than predefined and supplied by the library. Together, these features allow students and instructors to focus on algorithmic aspects of processing a wide variety of live and large data sources, without having to deal with low-level connection, parsing, extraction, and data binding. The library, available at http://cs.berry.edu/big-data, has been used in an introductory programming course based on Processing.

Keywords

open data; XML; introductory CS; library; web services

1. INTRODUCTION

The average student in an introductory programming course today has grown up interacting with large and real-time sources of data from the Internet on a daily basis. Programming exercises and projects they encounter in a traditional CS1/2 course, however, are often limited to contrived input data, often student-generated and supplied through "standard input" or a simple GUI mechanism. This dichotomy, in terms of the data that students interact with, may contribute to a disconnect between students' experience with mainstream computing and their perception of Computer Science as they work through their first programming course.

As Bart et al. discuss in [5], there are a couple of compelling reasons for instructors to consider incorporating the use of real-time web-based data in courses early in the Com-

ITiCSE '16, July 09 - 13, 2016, Arequipa, Peru

© 2016 Copyright held by the owner/author(s). Publication rights licensed to ACM.
ISBN 978-1-4503-4231-5/16/07... $15.00

DOI: http://dx.doi.org/10.1145/2899415.2899437

puter Science (CS) curriculum. Primarily, this might contribute to meeting students' expectations of a CS1/2 experience that is engaging and relevant and through which they can draw some connection to the web services and mobile apps that they are used to interacting with every day.

Instances may be found of exercises for introductory courses (e.g. [3]) involving, for example, social media, weather, or financial data, but the frameworks developed for such assignments is often ad hoc. Instructors usually prepare a code module ahead of time that carries out the tasks of connecting to a web service and parsing data (into an instructor-defined data structure), or they provide pre-processed downloaded sets of data for students to use in an assignment.[1] When attempting to incorporate "live," online data sources into an assignment there are a few major difficulties that an instructor may face. In particular, every web service provides a different API for accessing data. Furthermore, the raw data, whether directly accessed through a web service API or read from locally downloaded data files, must be parsed, and often only a subset of the information associated with each record in the data is of interest.

In the project described here, we develop a code framework and methodology to facilitate the incorporation of real, online data sets into traditional introductory programming courses. The framework is generic in the sense that (in most instances) no prior scaffolding or template specification is needed to make the data accessible. Our implementation aims to maintain minimal syntactic overhead while relieving novice programmers from issues of parsing and extracting raw data from a web-based data source. This allows students and instructors to focus on algorithmic aspects of engaging with arbitrary data sources, without having to deal with low-level issues related to accessing the data.

Our motivation and approach is similar to that of [5] with a couple of significantly novel features, highlighted in Section 2. In the sections that follow, we detail the particular requirements and rationale for our framework followed by concrete examples of its use. We discuss our initial implementation of a library in Java and its use (limited so far) in an introductory programming course. Finally, we wrap up with an evaluation of the current implementation, future directions and related work.

2. REQUIREMENTS AND RATIONALE

The overarching motivation for this project (like [5]) is to provide an interface to a wide variety of web-based data

---

[1] The Nifty Assignments archive, nifty.stanford.edu, has multiple examples of these approaches.

sources suitable for use by novice programmers. This leads to a set of requirements between which some tension exists.

Firstly, we seek to access data directly through a web URL (though locally-downloaded files are also supported) and relieve the programmer (i.e. student) from low-level issues of reading and parsing raw data formats like CSV, JSON, or XML. Simultaneously, we would like to require minimal syntactic overhead for use of the framework. Loading and parsing primitive or simple structured data should not involve much more than what is involved in reading from standard or file input (e.g. using a `Scanner` object in Java). The library should incorporate a cache to reduce load on data services and improve local runtime performance.

Another key requirement we aim to support (and that is a significant difference from the work of Bart et al. [5], discussed further in Section 6) is the ability to instantiate data objects based on student-defined data structures and representations. In Java, for example, students should be able to develop their own `class` definitions for the data of interest, independently of the data source or the library. Data accessed through our framework should then use the student-supplied definitions to construct objects in the program when it is run. Our anecdotal experience is that this enhances students' feeling of achievement. They see that they are really defining the structure and organization of the data that is eventually fetched, rather that having data structures already defined and fixed for them in the black box provided by some library. This serves as an active and motivating context to practice developing and defining data representations, rather than passively dealing with pre-defined structures.

Most of the time, data sets will contain many more fields of information than are of interest to the student, who should be able to identify and select data fields of interest in a straightforward manner. Additionally, the framework should enable retrieval of entire lists or arrays of objects (again, based on student-defined classes/structures) from the data source whenever appropriate. Missing data should be handled elegantly, e.g. by filling in with sensible default values.

In addition to having data binding occur dynamically at runtime, as described in the preceding paragraphs, we would also like to eliminate the need (as much as possible) for pre-supplied data schemas or templates to parse and process the data. This is another significant novelty with respect to [5]. We anticipate that this will make it even more feasible and attractive for instructors and students to engage with a wide variety of data sources since, as long as a service supplies data in a standard format, there is no need for prior generation of a client library or preprocessing template. While carrying out automated structure inference of data in common formats like XML, the framework should nonetheless provide mechanisms to specify a schema for the data, as well as enable custom extensions for connecting to and parsing additional data formats.

Finally, to enhance usability by novice programmers, the framework should incorporate built-in help/usage functionality and robust error-handling and reporting.

3. EXAMPLES OF USE

3.1 Basic Usage

To access any data source using our framework, there are three basic steps to be carried out: *connect* to the data source via URL or filename (includes setting options/parameters), *load* the data, and *fetch* elements of interest. The following complete, minimal example connects to the WorldCat online library catalog and fetches the title of a particular book.

```
import easy.data.*;

public class WorldCatSimple {
  public static void main(String[] args) {
    DataSource ds = DataSource.connect("http://xisbn.worldcat.org"
        + "/webservices/xid/isbn/9780201038019"
        + "?method=getMetadata&fl=*");          // step 1
    ds.load();                                    // step 2
    String title = ds.fetchString("isbn/title");  // step 3
    System.out.println(title);
  }
}
```

Note that other than downloading the JAR file for the library and including it in one's classpath, no other prior setup specific to the WorldCat data source is required. The `connect` method automatically infers the data format (XML in this case) and prepares to download it or access a cached copy. (If necessary, connection methods to force a specific format, such as `connectXML`, `connectJSON`, etc., can be used.) The `load` method carries out some simple structure inference on the raw data and exposes a set of labeled fields and structures that can be accessed. The actual XML returned by the URL in this example is:

```
<?xml version="1.0" encoding="UTF-8"?>
<rsp xmlns="http://worldcat.org/xid/isbn/" stat="ok">
    <isbn  oclcnum="311084141 ..." form="BA" year="1975"
    lang="eng" ed="2. ed., 1. print." author="Donald E. Knuth."
    title="The art of computer programming"
    ...>9780201038019</isbn>
 </rsp>
```

The set of inferred data fields is available by invoking the method `ds.printUsageString()`. It is up to the user to fetch the data as an appropriate type (`String`, `int`, etc.).

Our framework requires dealing with URLs of web services, as may be observed in the example above. This requires some discussion of concepts such as URL paths and query parameters. To obviate the need to construct raw query strings, i.e. `"?method=..."`, one may use `set` methods on the `DataSource` object, as shown in the left half of Figure 1. The nature of the exposed data also needs to be explained since it often involves nested structures. As in this example, the fields are accessed by paths like `"isbn/author"`. (The examples in Figure 1 compose, or chain, method calls for brevity of presentation.)

3.2 Structured Data and Collections

In the `APStatus` program on the right side of Figure 1, the student has defined their own class, `AP`, with several fields to represent airport information. The data source is loaded and the `fetch` method is provided the name of the class along with the paths of fields to extract from the data, in the order they should be provided to the `AP` constructor.

If the data source provides a list of data elements (e.g. a list of airport statuses), one could simply use a `fetchList` (or `fetchArray`) method instead of `fetch`. The library intelligently unifies the available data with the requested object type(s). Again, no prior preparation is required to access this particular data source using the `easy.data` library. Thus, in a few statements of code, a student is able to load, parse, and instantiate hundreds or thousands of objects (of a user-defined class) from the data.

```
import easy.data.*;

public class WorldCat {
    public static void main(String[] args) {
        String isbn = "9780201038019";   // could be user input
        DataSource ds = DataSource.connect(
            "http://xisbn.worldcat.org/webservices/xid/isbn/"
            + isbn);
        ds.set("method", "getMetadata").set("fl", "*");
        ds.set("format", "xml").load();
        String title = ds.fetchString("isbn/title");
        String author = ds.fetchString("isbn/author");
        int year = ds.fetchInt("isbn/year");
        System.out.printf("%s, %s, %d.", title, author, year);
    }
}
// OUTPUT:
// The art of computer programming, Donald E. Knuth., 1975.


public class APStatus {
    public static void main(String[] args) {
        DataSource ds = DataSource
            .connect("http://services.faa.gov/airport/status/BOS")
            .set("format", "application/xml").load();
        AP x = ds.fetch("AP", "Name", "State", "Delay",
                        "Weather/Weather");
        System.out.println(x);
    }
}

class AP {
    ...
    public AP(String name, String place,
              boolean delay, String weather) { ... }
    ...
}
```

Figure 1: Sample Java programs.

3.3 Data Source Specifications

While having an automated framework is convenient in many instances, there are times when it might be more practical for an instructor to provide a data schema ahead of time and/or be able to set various options or parameters for a particular data source. Our framework provides a facility to do so in the form of *specification files*. These are XML format files that may contain the data source URL and format, a human-friendly description and data schema with annotations, pre-supplied and user-supplied (required and optional) query parameters or path parameters, options specific to a particular type of data source, cache settings, etc. Details and examples are omitted here for lack of space.

4. DESIGN AND IMPLEMENTATION

As demonstrated in the preceding section, we have currently implemented a Java library to satisfy the requirements of the framework envisioned in Section 2. A call to `connect()` prepares the URL (or filename) path, accumulating parameters and options via the `set()` methods, and attempts to infer the data format based on the path extension and potentially the data itself. When `load()` is invoked, the library actually accesses the data source, downloads the data, and analyzes it to infer its structure, producing a *field schema*. A call to `fetch*()` provides the library with the type of object that the programmer wishes to have data instantiated as - either as a primitive, using an arbitrary class constructor with an ordered list of fields names of interest, or as a list of either of the previous. The library uses the lightweight annotation provided by `fetch*()` to build a *type signature* for the desired object(s) to be produced from the data. It then instantiates it by unifying the signature against the field schema to determine how exactly to extract the data and produce an object(s) to be returned to the programmer.

The initial version of our library uses XML as its internal format for data representation. A field schema is either a primitive field, or a list or structure of arbitrarily nested field schemas. Structure inference is performed by a fairly straightforward function that recursively analyzes the XML document node. A node with no tagged sub-nodes is inferred to be a primitive field. In the event sub-tags occur, each tag name may occur once or multiple times. The entire node is then mapped to a structure field schema with each child tag associated with the field schema inferred for the subnode.

The inferred field schema for tags that occur multiple times is wrapped as a list. Throughout this process, field schema elements are annotated with XML tag names (or paths, in general) to enable navigating through the data later based on the schema. To account for XML attributes, the data is preprocessed to turn all attributes of elements into child nodes (as in the example of Section 3.1).

Type signatures are similar to field schemas except the signature for a structure is annotated with a Java `Class` object, and primitive signatures are associated with a specific Java base type (`int`, `String`, etc.). While signatures may be arbitrarily nested internally, the library's `fetch` methods currently only enable specification of flat objects (i.e. objects with primitive type fields, or lists of those).

The process of instantiating a type signature against a field schema and associated raw data is more complicated. In effect, the supplied signature must be unified against the field schema while simultaneously extracting data and constructing Java objects. The simplest case is when the shape of the signature precisely matches that of the schema. However, the library also attempts to handle other cases as well. For example, if the field schema is that of a list, but a primitive or structure type signature is supplied, then the sub-schema of the list elements is unified against the first element in the actual data and returned as a Java object. On the other hand, if the field schema is that of a structure, but a list type signature is provided, then the library attempts to unify the structure against the sub-signature of the list, and wraps the result as a one-element `ArrayList`.

For brevity, the complete details of structure inference and object instantiation are omitted here. It bears mentioning, however, that use of the Java Reflection library (`java.lang.reflect`) is critical to achieve tasks such as reifying a `Class` object from a name (a `String` such as `"AP"`) and invoking arbitrary Java constructors at runtime. As this library has been initially used in a course based on the Processing [2] development environment, some additional management of runtime configuration had to be implemented. Processing allows developers to write *sketches*, using a subset of Java, which are then embedded into a hidden Java applet template that does various behind-the-scenes manipulation (e.g. of environment and directory paths).

The library handles other standard data formats (currently, comma-separated and tab-separated values, and JSON)[2]

---

[2]An extension to scrape tables or other arbitrary data from HTML pages via regular expressions is also in development.

by converting them to an XML object before processing them, but future work involves developing more direct methods of parsing and binding the data, to improve performance on large data sets.

5. EVALUATION

We evaluate the library of this paper from two perspectives: one in terms of its use in an introductory programming course, and secondly in terms of how well its current implementation meets the requirements and goals described earlier in the paper.

5.1 In the Classroom

No formal study has been performed on the library's use in a course, but the author has used this library for two years in an introductory programming course based on Processing [2], a Java-based IDE and set of libraries geared towards programming in a visual arts context. In the most recent offering of the course (Fall 2014), the library was introduced in the last month of the semester. (In the future, we anticipate integrating the material earlier on.)

Students were provided a set of tutorial-style labs to work through (available on the project GitHub site). The tutorials gradually progress through a hierarchy of data complexity from accessing primitive data, to simple objects, then lists of primitive types, and finally lists of objects. They introduce concepts such as URLs, the nature of data schemas, caching, and dealing with incomplete data (many real-world data sets have records that are missing fields). For the final project in the course, students were asked to find a data source on their own and develop an interactive GUI visualization of the data. Figure 2 lists some data sources that were presented in lecture and chosen by students for their projects. (A large list of sites to browse for data sources was provided by the instructor.) Almost all the sources were automatically processed by the library directly via the data source URL. In a couple of cases, students manually created a CSV file from an HTML table on a web site.

One issue that arose in some instances was finding a link to the raw data provided by a service. The primary URL for many web services often provides an interactive interface or visualization of the data. It takes some digging around to find a direct URL to the underlying XML data or a JSON rendering. Related to this, some students had initial difficulty understanding the distinction between data rendered in a human-friendly form (such as is visible when a web page is viewed in a browser), and the raw data in a format amenable to machine-processing by their program. When they found a web page that displayed a set of data in tabular form, they would attempt to use that page's URL to `connect` to the data source. Nonetheless, this serves an opportunity for a "learning moment."

Another concern that did not seem to be a major problem, but may have limited the choice of data sources, was that some sites require "developer" registration and an API key to be obtained in order to access data. Some students were hesitant to register for such. Also, this required various query parameters to be `set` on the `DataSource` object before it is loaded. Determining the necessary parameters involved reading into the developer documentation of a particular web service, an experience which varies in pleasantness from site to site.

Overall, insofar as operation of the library itself was concerned, things seemed to go fairly smoothly. As noted earlier, introducing the library earlier on in the course, and integrating it more thoroughly with the course content would make the students more comfortable with it and allow them a better sense of how to access data for the purpose of analysis or visualization. And, of course, more extensive field studies, using the library in other courses and institutions, are necessary to formally gauge its true usefulness.

5.2 Technical Challenges

Based on the limited testing and use so far, our current implementation appears to meet many of the goals laid out in Section 2. However, there are a few areas where improvement is clearly needed. One is to provide a more robust approach to error handling and reporting. Currently, exceptions are raised when things do not match up as expected at various stages of loading and instantiating data but the error messages can be improved. This could be achieved partly by providing a high-level description of the source of a problem, rather than just a line number in a file, to help a novice programmer understand what happened.

As alluded to in the previous section, one complication in accessing data sources is providing a user-specific API key or access token. While this can be achieved using the existing `set` methods, it can be frustrating for students to figure out how to specify the necessary parameters. Also, rather than having user API tokens exposed directly in source code of a program, which might be shared with others, it would be better to have private user data stored in a separate file. We need to investigate a mechanism for doing this in a simple manner, combined with a curated set of data source specifications for common APIs (Ebay, Twitter, etc.) that require special parameters, to make it easier for students to access these. Also, a GUI tool for managing data source-related parameters, as mentioned in the next section, might be very helpful.

In terms of performance, the library handles many small to medium-size data sets well. However, the current implementation loads the entire data set into memory. Along with the adoption of XML as a common intermediate format, this results in significant delays when loading large data sets (tens of thousands of records). Even with caching, there is at least a two-fold delay loading a CSV file, for example. First the data must be loaded and converted to XML; then the entire converted data is scanned again to infer its schema. Depending on the `fetch` operation that is then executed, there may be further delay in processing. Even with intelligent caching, XML is not the most efficient representation of data and in many cases it would be much more efficient (time and space) to access CSV data, for example, using a data structure other than an XML object.

A complete reorganization of the internals of the library is currently in progress. It abandons XML as the common intermediate format and adopts more abstract mechanisms to encapsulate arbitrary data format objects, allowing them to be traversed using a uniform interface. The initial focus of our project was on dealing with XML-based data, as it seemed the most general and challenging representation to handle. Now that we have established the viability of the approach presented in this paper, we are in the process of refining the architecture of our initial implementation. A

Name (Asterisk * indicates data set discovered and/or used by students)	Source	Type	Records
*1000 songs to hear before you die	opendata.socrata.com	XML	1,000
Abalone data set	UCI Machine Learning Repository	CSV	4,177
*Airport Weather Mashup	NWS + FAA	XML	fixed
*Chicago life expectancy by community	data.cityofchicago.org	XML	~80
Earthquake feeds	US Geological Survey	JSON	variable
*Fuel economy data	US EPA	XML	35,430
*Jeopardy! question archive	reddit	JSON	216,930
Live auction data	Ebay	XML	100/page
Magic the Gathering card data	mtgjson.com	JSON	variable
Microfinance loan data	Kiva	XML	variable
*SEC Rushing Leaders 2014	ESPN	CSV (manual)	variable

Figure 2: Examples of data sources used in lecture examples and student final projects.

complementary feature that also remains to be explored is to provide methods for streaming and/or paginating data.

5.3 Additional Future Directions

In addition to addressing the more immediate technical challenges of the previous section, there are some other ideas for future development that would improve the library's usefulness. One is the ability to invoke a GUI interface to configure various settings for the library and parameters for a particular data source. Upon loading a data source, it could also allow the user to view usage info (as an alternative to `printUsageInfo`), preview the available data, provide help for invoking methods of the library, and perhaps even generate code snippets.

As mentioned in Section 4, the `fetch()` methods currently only support the specification of flat signatures. It is possible to directly construct and provide a type signature object to the library that involves, for example, lists of structures with nested lists or structures. Providing a simplified way to supply such signatures via `fetch()` remains future work, and the process of data instantiation against completely general signatures is an interesting challenge that needs to be studied further.

We chose Java as the initial language in which to implement the ideas of this paper. Since Java is widely used in introductory programming courses, this should make the library accessible to a large number of instructors if they are interested in trying it out. Nonetheless, we hope to also provide realizations of the framework in other languages, such as Racket [9] and Python. The initial inspiration for our work came from the author's reimplementation [11] of a Racket "teachpack" (initially developed by Shriram Krishnamurthi and Kathi Fisler) to access Kiva data through its XML API. In Racket, a language derived from Scheme, macro facilities were used, instead of reflection, to realize "dynamic" binding of data to user-defined structures. Macros allow expansion of code prior to execution. The details of the implementation thus have a different flavor than that of the Java version, and even allow some compile-time checks (such as ensuring, for example, that the number of fields specified in a `fetch()` expression match the number of parameters of a constructor). Another interesting feature of the Kiva library was that it provided a small, fixed subset of the data for testing purposes. This would be a useful feature to incorporate in our Java implementation– a way to cache a small portion of data and make it available for development

and testing, eliminating the need to load the entire data set for large sources of data until the final run of the program.

6. RELATED WORK

As cited in the Introduction, our motivation mirrors that of RealTimeWeb [5], a framework that makes real-time web data accessible for introductory programming projects, although the approach differs substantially. RealTimeWeb (now renamed the CORGIS [4] project) utilizes a JSON-formatted "client library specification" to generate specialized code in one of several languages - Java, Python, and Racket. The generated library code (which requires additional manual tweaking) can then be packaged, imported into a student program, and used to access data from web sources. This approach is similar to that of mainstream tools, discussed later in this section, in that a schema of the data source as well as the client language API (what methods the generated code will provide to access selected information) must be manually specified (e.g. by an instructor) and then compiled to produce actual code for the target language. While the CORGIS project envisions development of a curated gallery where many client libraries may be shared (and a number have indeed been produced to date), we believe this approach limits the flexibility of the framework because a new data source cannot be accessed until a specification is defined and a client library generated and tested.

While our framework also supports use of a data source specification file to provide a simple schema for accessing a data source, our primary motivation and ideal is to develop a library that dynamically and automatically infers the structure of data simply upon connection to the data source. We believe this improves the usability and applicability of such a library because instructors can choose to access any online data source, not just ones for which a client library exists. Furthermore, students are able to access data sources of their own choosing if they so wish, for example, if working on a project idea developed by themselves. At the same time, the syntactic complexity of invoking our library remains barely more than that of a CORGIS library. For example, to implement the same example as in Figure 2 of [5], we replace the first two statements of the `main` method with:

```
DataSource ds = DataSource.connectJSON("http://earthquake.usgs"
    + ".gov/earthquakes/feed/v1.0/summary/all_hour.geojson");
```

and replace the statement containing the `getEarthquakes` method call with:

```
ds.load();
List<Q> qs = ds.fetchList("Q", "features/properties/title", ...);
// Q is a user-defined class with fields of interest for a quake...
```

The only arguable complexity introduced here is the exposure of the underlying URL for the data source and the paths to the fields of interest. We do not believe this is excessively burdensome on students, and in fact it may increase the sense of "realness" of their engagement with the data.

Beyond the pedagogical context, the approach this paper takes towards interfacing between (primarily) XML and Java falls in the category of *vocabulary-specific data access interfaces* (DAIs) [13]. These tools map data from XML to application-specific data structures. Such an approach enables developers to work with data in a concise manner that fits into the semantics of their particular application and language. Among the most popular "real world" tools of this nature for Java currently are the Java Architecture for XML Binding (JAXB) [1] and Castor [8]. These and all similar libraries currently available, to our knowledge, provide an automated way to generate Java class definitions from an XML schema and/or vice versa, and then facilities for serializing/deserializing Java objects to/from XML data. By design, the data binding in these libraries is two-way, and they all incorporate both static (compile-time) as well as dynamic (run-time) aspects. In particular, there is a very tight correspondence between the automatically-generated Java or XML schema definitions, and customization involves adding various types of annotations, which can become complex.

In contrast to such frameworks, the work presented in this paper focuses on a constrained, one-way flow of data: from XML to Java objects. Also, we relax the tight coupling between the Java and XML representations, allowing the developer (student) to define Java classes more or less as they wish, and then later specify how to bind XML data to them. Furthermore, our process is entirely dynamic - we do not require any static generation of class or schema definitions prior to binding data.

As the framework of this paper purposefully avoids the necessity of a predefined schema or XML data type definition, it must perform inference of XML data structure at runtime. There has been much prior work on inference and extraction of XML document structure and schema, e.g. [10, 6, 7], and there are mature commercial tools for doing so, e.g. [12]. Again, however, for our context we do not need to support the full generality of inference of arbitrary structure and properties of XML data. It is sufficient to determine only enough structure to be able to bind data to programmer-defined object types based on some simple hints.

7. CONCLUSION

A number of contextualized approaches to teaching introductory Computer Science courses have been developed in the past decade, catering to students with different interests and backgrounds. For instance, entire courses have been developed around media computation or robots (real and virtual). There is, however, one context which, to our knowledge, has not been exploited in a systematic fashion – that of "live data," or widely available, large and live online datasets from a wide variety of sources. Engaging novice programming students with such data sources may be a powerfully engaging experience that adds relevance to their introductory experience in Computer Science. In order to develop a course centered around this idea, however, a software toolbox is needed that enables instructors and students to rapidly access data of interest from a web service without becoming bogged down in low-level details of I/O, parsing, etc. We hope that the ideas of the framework described in this paper, and the implementation presented, are a further step towards achieving this vision. In addition to the interesting software architecture challenges that remain open, the next step is to develop a complete set of materials (lecture examples, labs, programming projects, etc.) to support such a course.

8. REFERENCES

[1] Java architecture for XML binding (JAXB). https://jaxb.java.net. September 2014.

[2] Processing. http://processing.org/overview/. June 2015.

[3] R. E. Anderson, M. D. Ernst, R. Ordóñez, P. Pham, and B. Tribelhorn. A data programming CS1 course. In *Proceedings of the 46th ACM Technical Symposium on Computer Science Education*, SIGCSE '15, pages 150–155, New York, NY, USA, 2015. ACM.

[4] A. C. Bart. Situating computational thinking with big data: Pedagogy and technology (abstract only). In *Proceedings of the 46th ACM Technical Symposium on Computer Science Education*, SIGCSE '15, pages 719–719, New York, NY, USA, 2015. ACM.

[5] A. C. Bart, E. Tilevich, S. Hall, T. Allevato, and C. A. Shaffer. Transforming introductory computer science projects via real-time web data. In *Proceedings of the 45th ACM Technical Symposium on Computer Science Education*, SIGCSE '14, pages 289–294, New York, NY, USA, 2014. ACM.

[6] G. J. Bex, F. Neven, T. Schwentick, and K. Tuyls. Inference of concise DTDs from XML data. In *Proceedings of the 32Nd International Conference on Very Large Data Bases*, VLDB '06, pages 115–126. VLDB Endowment, 2006.

[7] G. J. Bex, F. Neven, and S. Vansummeren. Inferring XML schema definitions from XML data. In *Proceedings of the 33rd International Conference on Very Large Data Bases*, VLDB '07, pages 998–1009. VLDB Endowment, 2007.

[8] ExoLab Group. The castor project. http://castor.codehaus.org. September 2014.

[9] M. Flatt and PLT. Reference: Racket. Technical Report PLT-TR-2010-1, PLT Design Inc., 2010. http://racket-lang.org/tr1/.

[10] M. Garofalakis, A. Gionis, R. Rastogi, S. Seshadri, and K. Shim. Xtract: Learning document type descriptors from xml document collections. *Data Min. Knowl. Discov.*, 7(1):23–56, Jan. 2003.

[11] N. A. Hamid. Kiva teachpack for DrRacket. http://github.com/nadeemabdulhamid/Kiva-Teachpack. June 2015.

[12] Microsoft Corporation. Inferring an XML schema. http://msdn.microsoft.com/en-us/library/b6kwb7fd(v=vs.110).aspx. September 2014.

[13] J. White, B. Kolpackov, B. Natarajan, and D. C. Schmidt. Reducing application code complexity with vocabulary-specific XML language bindings. In *Proceedings of the 43rd Annual Southeast Regional Conference - Volume 2*, ACM-SE 43, pages 281–287, New York, NY, USA, 2005. ACM.

A STEM Incubator to Engage Students in Hands-on, Relevant Learning: A Report from the Field

Jennifer Burg
Dept. of Comp. Sci.
Wake Forest University
Winston-Salem, NC 27109
+1 (336) 758-4982
burg@wfu.edu

V. Paúl Pauca
Dept. of Comp. Sci.
Wake Forest University
Winston-Salem, NC 27109
+1 (336) 758-4982
paucavp@wfu.edu

William Turkett
Dept. of Comp. Sci.
Wake Forest University
Winston-Salem, NC 27109
+1 (336) 758-4982
turketwh@wfu.edu

Pete Santago
Dept. of Comp. Sci.
Wake Forest University
Winston-Salem, NC 27109
+1 (336) 758-4982
ps@wfu.edu

ABSTRACT

This paper describes the development of a STEM Incubator program to engage students in hand-on, relevant projects that draw student interest toward computer science and other STEM fields. The program is implemented via one-credit courses allowing students to collaborate on projects in various areas (such as digital sound and music, 3D design, robotics, digital image processing, bioinformatics, and mobile and pervasive computing) and around multiple application domains (e.g. internet of things and security, apps for college campus life, 3D printing and art, wearable sensors for disabilities, and sensors and unmanned vehicles for conservation). An apprentice/leader learning environment is created to sustain student involvement in ongoing projects. The evolution of the program is reviewed, including successes and challenges. We report on the demographics of students who have participated in the program so far, and on the success in attracting enthusiastic interest, notably among female students. The STEM Incubator program, like other similar programs described in this paper, attempts to put into practice the evidence-based teaching practices in active learning that have gained credence over the past decade. The paper is of interest to those considering a similar program or wishing to compare other programs to their own.

Keywords

hands-on learning; situated learning; collaboration

1. BACKGROUND

The value of engaging students in hands-on, relevant projects has largely been agreed upon in education of the 21st century. An overview of keywords in SIGCSE and ITiCSE conference papers of the past ten years gives evidence of this (Table 1). Hands-on STEM learning also has strong federal support, demonstrated in a 2014 conference, co-organized by The White House Office of Science and Technology Policy. In the conference report, "early experiential learning" and "active learning methods" are promoted, and STEM educators are urged to realize the "evidence-based teaching practices" that have emerged out of research [1].

It falls to educators now to create the best hands-on experiences for their students, and to integrate the experiences into the computer

ITiCSE '16, July 09-13, 2016, Arequipa, Peru
© 2016 ACM. ISBN 978-1-4503-4231-5/16/07…$15.00
DOI: http://dx.doi.org/10.1145/2899415.2899461

science curriculum in a way that not only attracts students but also retains them in the program and teaches useful concepts, skills, and ways of solving problems. Our STEM Incubator program, which vertically integrates participating students in small teams through a leader/apprentice model, is an effort in this direction.

Table 1 Common keywords in SIGCSE and ITiCSE papers of the past decade

	SIGCSE	ITiCSE
active learning	100	32
situated learning	4	0
computational thinking	79	31
problem-based learning	9	11
SIGCSE: Conference Proceedings of Special Interest Group on Computer Science Education		
ITiCSE: Conference Proceedings of Innovation and Technology in Computer Science Education		

To our knowledge, among the first to create robust active learning programs were the University of Texas and Georgia Tech. UT's Freshman Research Initiative involves students in research with faculty and graduate students in integrated course and lab work over a period of three semesters. This program involves chemistry, biochemistry, nanotechnology, molecular biology and computer science. Georgia Tech's Vertically-Integrated Projects Program also spans three years and engages teams of 30 cohorts. The "vertical" movement arises as entry-level students learn from more experienced student leaders and then progress to leadership positions themselves [2]. Both UT's and Georgia Tech's programs have engendered other initiatives. UT's model appears to have been adopted by Iowa State and SUNY Binghamton. Georgia Tech's program has grown into a Vertically Integrated Programs Consortium that includes approximately 14 schools (by our recent count) and has strong private funding. Other similar programs have sprung up, including the University of Central Florida's LEARN (Learning Environment and Academic Research Network), which has a 12 week apprenticeship; and the University of Wisconsin's STEM Innovation Pipeline Project, which extends to pre-college students.

Our STEM Incubator program has similarities to and differences from those just mentioned, in particular with Georgia Tech's VIP program. However, the environment in which it is implemented is fundamentally different as our institution is a small liberal arts university without the benefit of an engineering program.

2. METHODOLOGY

2.1 Motivation

The initial motivation of our STEM Incubator program was to attract more students into STEM disciplines, particularly women, and specifically into computer science. This was at a time when the number of computer science majors had greatly declined (pre-2013). However, as the demand for workers educated in science and technology has grown in the past four years, computer science enrollments have surged, and attracting students is no longer a unique focus. The value of hands-on, relevant projects as an important component not only of attracting but also of retaining computer science students and providing them with an up-to-date education has increasingly been recognized.

Students of the current generation have grown up in the midst of a head-spinning digital revolution that has popularized things that were only imagined a few short years ago – voice recognizers that actually understand us and answer our far-flung questions, truly immersive virtual reality goggles, ubiquitous and wearable sensors that seek to anticipate our needs, wristbands that monitor our every move, smart phones, smart prostheses, constant worldwide connectivity, and an app for everything. It seems that computer science education has had to scramble to keep up. While we, with admirable deliberation, have taught our data structures and theory of computation courses, the world has raced forward with transformative, game-changing, even disruptive innovations. Students who grew up in the digital world are likely to be uninspired by computer science programs that don't give them a tangible, visible connection with today's digital innovations, and a sense that they can contribute something of their own. Thus we have embraced relevance, applications, collaboration, and hands-on learning.

Another aspect of our vision for the STEM Incubator was related to social relevance, a theme which has received attention in the computer science education literature [2] [3] [4] [5]. Thematically, we initially described our vision for the STEM Incubator program as *socially-inspired learning* – learning *in* and *for* a community, motivated by collaboration, caring, creativity, and competition [6]. These elements have remained integral to the program as it has developed. In practical terms, the theme has been manifested in team-work; relevant applications, particularly for those with special needs; interdisciplinary project efforts that extend to music and the visual arts; and light-hearted competitions that help to make the projects more fun.

2.2 The STEM Incubator Courses

The centerpiece of our STEM Incubator program is a continuing series of one-hour courses on a wide range of topics, as described in the abstract. The topics may vary each semester according to the interests of the professors who teach them. Professors are allowed a great deal of flexibility in how they conduct their individual courses. The shared concept is that the courses offer students an interesting, non-threatening introduction to STEM and, in particular, computer science, by means of hands-on projects that seem timely and relevant to today's students.

Some course topics – robotics and drone development, for example – are more hardware oriented. Others – like digital image processing, bioinformatics, and app invention – may involve more software (application programs) or introductory level programming. While the courses have clearly defined learning goals, the outcomes are specified by the professor, constrained so that the projects can realistically be completed in a one-hour, one semester course. Some courses are more open-ended, allowing the

students to discover the outcomes and to specify milestones around a significant challenge set by the instructor. The students set about on an exploratory path to prototype and test along the direction of their final goal.

2.3 Leader/Apprentice Model and Vertical Integration

The STEM Incubator courses implement a leader/apprentice model, with entry level students (apprentices) learning from more advanced students (leaders) in small teams and in projects that can progress in successive semesters. A student can take the course three times if the topic varies, twice as an apprentice and once as a leader, or vice versa. The courses are graded pass/fail. The three STEM Incubator credits can count toward a minor or BA in computer science degree. To receive a pass, the students must have shown participation in all activities, including teamwork, oral presentations and demonstrations, as well as kept track of their work in electronic or paper-based journals.

Significantly, it is the students rather than the professors who serve as primary project leaders to their teammates. Leaders are expected to have some experience in a previous STEM course similar to the one they are currently taking, or relevant knowledge (like programming ability) from another computer science course. The professor's role as the academic mentor is to inspire, guide, facilitate, and provide additional information and instruction when required.

The leader/apprentice model has proliferated both in academia and business/industry and it is a key component of the type of vertical integration proposed by Parslow [7]. Similarly, the "cognitive apprenticeship model" emphasizes mentoring of abstract thinking and problem solving skills [8]. The thrust of our program is to integrate computational and algorithmic problem-solving with hands-on skills.

2.4 Project Continuity

An outgrowth of the apprentice/leader model is an effort towards continuity – i.e., fostering projects that can evolve and grow in successive semesters. Our goal is to foster projects that continue from one semester to the next, with apprentices graduating to leader level and then bringing entry-level students up-to-speed with on-going projects.

2.5 Space and Resources

We began our STEM Incubator program with some departmental resources and no support in the form of grants or university funding. We had to use our already-limited space in the Computer Science Department to make room for the additional number of students attracted by the program and by the type of hands-on projects involved. With this "can do" attitude, we developed our course structure and passed it through university approval, reconfigured a classroom as our STEM Incubator Lab, and spent some of our departmental budget on equipment such as drone components, Raspberry Pis, Arduinos, Makey-Makeys, Kinect Cameras, a 3D printer, and so forth. Some faculty members were able to use grant money when their STEM courses related to their research.

We discovered that lack of resources was not a bar to the initial success of the program. The STEM courses themselves and the excitement and buzz about our program circulating among the student population is helping raise awareness and recognition of our efforts in our institution.

2.6 Faculty Participation

Seventy percent of our full-time faculty in computer science have offered STEM courses since its inception, all of them more than once. This is in spite of the fact that the course is a one-hour addition to their usual teaching load. There appear to be three motivations for teaching the STEM courses. First, the department as a whole is always looking to update and enhance the students' learning experience. The attraction of hands-on, relevant projects – the ability to build something or "make something happen" – is clear among our students. Second, faculty can be equally interested in doing hands-on work to update their knowledge and supplement their more abstract research. A third motivation is that STEM projects sometimes relate to or evolve into the faculty member's ongoing research. We have excellent, high-achieving undergraduate students at our university, some of whom end up collaborating on publications by their senior year. A good number of our undergraduate students continue in our Master's program as well. Thus, the STEM Incubator gives faculty an opportunity to prepare students for increasingly advanced research.

2.7 Participation of Other Disciplines

From its inception, we planned for the STEM Incubator program to involve collaboration with other STEM departments and even art and music at our university. The Biology Department and the Center for Innovation, Creativity and Entrepreneurship have been our primary collaborators thus far. Two professors from the Biology department have participated for the last two years as faculty mentors, bringing their expertise as well as their own students to the program. We have also had conversations with Physics and Art Departments, and they have expressed interest in developing one-hour hands-on type courses of their own. We continue to pursue these collaborations.

3. EXAMPLE COURSES AND OUTCOMES

Out of the various topics initially offered by participating faculty, the following four STEM courses and their outcomes, through various semesters of instruction, are described. These courses offer project continuity and maturation, and students indicate high enthusiasm and a high level of perceived learning according to our survey data (presented in Section 4).

3.1 Bioinformatics and Game-Like Algorithmic Problem-Solving

The most successful version of the Bioinformatics STEM course provided students the opportunity to gain insight into how computer algorithms are being used to solve complicated biological problems, while also getting the students to exercise creativity in determining how to teach others how to think about algorithms. This version, held in Fall 2015, started by exposing the students to the complex problem of whole genome DNA sequence assembly. Students examined this problem as if it was a complex combinatorial puzzle to be solved. The concept of algorithms was then introduced, with examples provided of algorithms that can be used for sequence assembly. In the second half of the course, the students focused on creative activities – designing a game to teach young students, in a fun way, the ideas behind sequence assembly. The students examined aspects of game play and mobile app creation, as well as exercised creativity in assembling a physical version of the game. The course concluded with the students leading their peers through the motivation for and actual play of the physical version of the game.

3.2 Robotics and Fun Competition

The challenge of the Robotics STEM section (roboSTEM) is to enable a robot to navigate autonomously through an obstacle course. Students learn about simple robots, controls, sensors, algorithm development, simple machine learning and AI, and basic Python. Since programming

Figure 1 Working with robots

experience is not required, the emphasis is on algorithmic development. Apprentices are placed in teams of two, each team equipped with all the necessary hardware. Leader students assist with programming, and apprentices learn some basic Python in the process, some becoming reasonably proficient in the fundamentals. Students learn about sensors and must design and execute experiments to calibrate an ultrasonic range sensor. A competition is held at the end of the semester for fastest navigation through the obstacle course.

Students have generally been very enthusiastic about this section, enjoying the fact that programming results in a physical manifestation of their algorithm. Interviews with female students after the course revealed that they particularly enjoyed the "freedom to fail," the hands-on, experimental nature of the work, the collaboration, and the fun of the final competition.

3.3 STEM and Artistic Experimentation

Some STEM courses have sought a relationship between computation and the arts. One course challenged the students to strip the sound track off a silent movie (without listening to it first), choose a dramatic portion of the movie, and create their own sound track for it. Another section introduced students to 2D image processing, particularly filters and convolutions. The students were challenged to apply filters at the application program level, and learn the basics of how these filters operate as mathematical convolutions. Their project was to apply their knowledge creatively by creating an illustration for Roald Dahl's BFG ("Big Friendly Giant") in which the giant captures dreams in a jar. More recent art-related STEM courses involve creative 3D modeling and printing.

3.4 STEM Pro Humanitate

Following the motto of our University (For Humanity), one sequence of STEM courses since our Incubator program inception has focused on problems and projects with high social relevance [4], namely focusing on people with special needs as well as the environment. In particular, a number of student teams in this STEM course have focused on design and development of Arduino-based wearable sensors and the exploration of related pervasive

Figure 2 H.E.L.P device to inform user of obstacles

technology for people who are visually or hearing impaired. A watch-like device, dubbed H.E.L.P. by the students (Human Echo

Location Partner), uses sonar and vibration on the skin to inform the user of obstacles in the scene [9]. The device has been tested with over 25 people and a second version is currently under development. Similar STEM work is being done for the hearing impaired and other conditions, such as Guillain-Barré syndrome. Another group of student teams has been focusing on the development of unmanned aerial and underwater vehicles for the collection of data related to ecology and conservation. A prototype developed by students last Fall 2015 will be taken to the field in 2016 for observation of coral life in Belize. A Senior Honors project that explored visualization of sound for the hearing impaired was also born out of STEM incubator course. Faculty mentors for these STEM courses include professors from the Computer Science as well as Biology Departments.

4. ASSESSMENT

4.1 Enrollment and Demographics, and Assessment

We have been collecting demographic information about our course and major/minor enrollments since the inception of our STEM Incubator program, Fall 2013. To date, 205 students have enrolled in the courses, as indicated in Table 2. The percentage of female students has grown, and in the most recent semester, more than 50% of the students are female. The number of female computer science majors and minors has also grown. In our first report on the program, the percentage of female majors or minors was 26%. It is now 32%.

Among the students who have taken a STEM Incubator course since Fall 2013, 76 took a computer science course (other than STEM) before or during the same semester as the STEM Incubator course. Importantly, 14 students have gone on to take CS1 after the STEM course. Twenty-two students have taken two or three STEM Incubator courses.

Table 2 Demographics of STEM Incubator course

Semes-ter	# stu-dents	African-Amer	Hisp	2 or more races	M	F	Fresh-men
Fall 2013	30	3 10%	3 10%	NR**	18 60%	12 40%	
Spr 2014	46	1 2%	4 9%	NR	27 59%	19 41%	19 41%
Fall 2014	47	2 4%	3 6%	NR	30 64%	17 36%	25 53%
Spr 2015	23	1 4.5%	2 9%	NR	11 48%	12 52%	2 9%
Fall 2015	30	2 7%	2 7%	NR	15 50%	15 50%	19 63%
Spr 2016	26	2 7.7%	0	2 7.7%	12 46%	14 54%	3 12%
total*	177						

*In each row but the last, the totals are total course enrollments. Students may take the course multiple semesters. In the last row, the total is the total number of individuals who took a STEM course.
**Not reported
The totals in the last row are not the sum of the columns above because students who took more than one STEM course are counted only once in the last row.

Table 3 Demographics of computer science majors and minors at our university

	# stu-dents	African-Amer	Hisp	2 or more races	M	F
CS Major	89	2 2%	7 8%	5 6%	66 74%	23 26%
CS Minor	52	3 6%	2 4%	2 4%	30 58%	22 42%
Total	141	5 3.5%	9 6.3%	7 5%	96 68%	45 32%

4.2 Pre- and Post-Course Surveys

We have conducted pre- and post-course surveys since the inception of the program, measuring students' changing interest in a STEM or computer science major and the extent to which the course had an influence. We reported on the period from Fall 2013 to Fall 2014 in a previous paper [6]. In 2015 (Spring and Fall), out of 56 students who took the courses, 37 completed post-course surveys. The tables below show the results of two questions in the post-course survey. (The "increased interest" numbers may be deceiving because some students already had a high level of interest going in, resulting perhaps in "not much increase.") The "increased confidence" results – where 54% of the students responded with a 4 or 5 – show good results regarding the effect of the STEM courses on student perceptions.

Table 4 Answers to the question "To what extent has the STEM course increased your interest in a major in STEM?"

Increased interest	5	4	3	2	1
Spring 2015	4	2	4	0	1
Fall 2015	13	6	2	5	0

Table 5 Answers to the question "To what extent has the STEM course increased your confidence in your logical problem-solving ability?"

Increased confidence	5	4	3	2	1
Spring 2015	3	3	5	0	0
Fall 2015	7	13	3	2	0

The 2015 survey results also showed that nine students – seven of whom were freshmen – settled on computer science as their major in the post-course survey, where that was not their first choice in the pre-course survey.

These data suggests that we have had success in attracting entry-level students, retaining their interest, and giving them confidence in their problem-solving ability. The surveys, along with interviews that have been conducted with five recent female students, give a strong indication that female students are enjoying and benefiting from the program. This is attributable in large part to the type of hands-on projects that we offer in the STEM courses, conducted in the apprentice/leader learning model.

5. CHALLENGES AND FUTURE WORK

5.1 Interdisciplinary Collaboration

Involvement of other disciplines in an overarching STEM initiative can be challenging, given the constraints, existing faculty commitments, and cultures across other departments. We already have an active relationship with members of the Biology Department as well as with faculty in the Program for Innovation, Creativity, and Entrepreneurship. The Physics and Chemistry Departments are open to course collaborations, and possible collaborations with the Art Department are currently being explored. This may entail the creation of a STEM course in other departments with the ability to cross-list interdisciplinary courses. Some departments, such as Biology, are able to use existing courses for handling students who wish to participate in our STEM incubator program but receive credit from Biology. Though challenging, interdisciplinary participation and collaboration can be key to the growth of vertically integrated programs such as our STEM Incubator.

5.2 Space

As noted earlier in the paper, we have had to "make do" with the existing space in our department as we initiated our STEM program. We have refurbished one of our labs (larger than our initial STEM space) and dedicated it as the STEM lab, to be used by students in any of the STEM courses. This gives us an opportunity to see if having groups of students working on different projects in the lab at the same time creates synergy and excitement or distraction and mayhem.

As hands-on learning has gained popularity, maker spaces have been popping up everywhere, on university campuses and within business and industry. Generally these spaces serve multiple disciplines, envisioned as a place where scientists and artists can meet to experiment and collaborate. One of the authors of this paper has attended a workshop in which a variety of designs for open, fluid, interdisciplinary maker spaces were presented [10]. Buildings and spaces such as these are something to aspire to with adequate funding, but the practical situation is that we often have to use the space we have.

As we have explored the creation of a maker space with other departments on our campus, we find that our STEM Incubator lends itself quite well to the implementation of a distributed or hub-and-spokes maker space model. The idea is to engage students in more interdisciplinary projects and make them aware of the many resources and spaces available to them across campus. This takes cooperation, planning, awareness, and deliberateness on our part.

5.3 Pedagogical Challenges

One of the challenges of our STEM courses is to have continuity from one semester to another and cross-fertilization among projects. Centering our program on a one-credit P/F course has the advantage of creating a non-threatening environment for students to be introduced to STEM learning. However, practically speaking, students are not going to spend enough on a one-hour course to be able to produce very impressive results – even given their enthusiasm for the work.

Our vision is to have on-going projects that evolve from one semester to the next, with students advancing from apprentice to leader positions. We have had some success with this, especially as students sometimes move forward from STEM course projects to more complex Senior Honors projects or summer research fellowships (funded by our university). This has happened with 2D imaging and 3D printing projects, among others [11].

Another pedagogical challenge is in the relatively open, experimental nature of our STEM course projects. In the more open-ended, experimental courses, where students have some freedom to follow their curiosity, professors have to be prepared to answer questions about areas that may not be within their expertise. The hands-on nature of the courses leads professors into electronics, Bluetooth communication, Arduino programming, innovative goggles, drone assembly, and all kinds of things that require more than a soldering iron. Our experience is that the projects can turn out to be almost as fun for professors as for students, and they help us to be more in touch with the fast-changing world of digital devices.

5.4 Conclusions

In this paper, we describe the key elements of our STEM Incubator initiative, a vertically integrated approach for engaging underclassmen and upperclassmen students interested in science applications. The data we have collected, as well as anecdotal data provided by students, suggests that our approach based on the leader/apprentice model is increasing interaction among students and furthermore, the work is found to be enjoyable. We base this on the data we have collected as well as the very visible enthusiasm that students communicate to us about the courses and projects that they have been involved in. Interviews with some of the female students have revealed that they came into the STEM course with little understanding of computer science, and emerged from the course thinking it was something they actually liked and could be good at. This was exactly what we hoped for. The hands-on projects have the added benefit of reinvigorating our own interest in our discipline and making us feel more in step with the digital world.

Though we are pleased with the current results achieved by our STEM Incubator, we realize that there are still many challenges that need to be addressed in order to make our effort sustainable. We are striving to refine the STEM Incubator program, to improve our own teaching within the courses, to find more and better ways to assess the program's impact, and to seek collaborations with other units within the university.

6. REFERENCES

[1] D. L. Reinholz and K. Perkins, "Improving Access for STEM: Challenges and Commitments. Report on a Conference Held September 22, 2014," University of Colorado at Boulder and The White House Office of Science and Technology Policy, Sep. 2014.

[2] M. Buckley, H. Kershner, K. Schindler, C. Alphonce, and J. Braswell, "Benefits of Using Socially-relevant Projects in Computer Science and Engineering Education," in *Proceedings of the 35th SIGCSE Technical Symposium on Computer Science Education*, New York, NY, USA, 2004, pp. 482–486.

[3] C. Rader, D. Hakkarinen, B. M. Moskal, and K. Hellman, "Exploring the Appeal of Socially Relevant Computing: Are Students Interested in Socially Relevant Problems?," in *Proceedings of the 42Nd ACM Technical Symposium on Computer Science Education*, New York, NY, USA, 2011, pp. 423–428.

[4] V. P. Pauca and R. T. Guy, "Mobile Apps for the Greater Good: A Socially Relevant Approach to Software Engineering," in *Proceedings of the 43rd ACM Technical Symposium on Computer Science Education*, New York, NY, USA, 2012, pp. 535–540.

[5]   M. Buckley, J. Nordlinger, and D. Subramanian, "Socially Relevant Computing," in *Proceedings of the 39th SIGCSE Technical Symposium on Computer Science Education*, New York, NY, USA, 2008, pp. 347–351.

[6]   J. Burg, V. P. Pauca, W. Turkett, E. Fulp, S. S. Cho, P. Santago, D. Cañas, and H. D. Gage, "Engaging Non-Traditional Students in Computer Science Through Socially-Inspired Learning and Sustained Mentoring," in *Proceedings of the 46th ACM Technical Symposium on Computer Science Education*, New York, NY, USA, 2015, pp. 639–644.

[7]   "Vertically Integrated Projects Program | VIP." [Online]. Available: http://www.vip.gatech.edu/. [Accessed: 16-Jan-2016].

[8]   D. Vanessa P. and Kerry J. Burger, "The Cognitive Apprenticeship Model in Educational Practice," in *Handbook Of Research on Educational Communications and Technology*, 3rd ed., Routledge, 2008, pp. 426–439.

[9]   Bonnie Davis, "Sonar-assisted human navigation | News Center | Wake Forest University," 14-Nov-2014. [Online]. Available: http://news.wfu.edu/2014/11/14/sonar-assisted-human-navigation/. [Accessed: 19-Jan-2016].

[10]   "Designing STEM Facilities to Meet 21st Century Needs." Conference material distributed on Feb. 23, 2015, Orlando, FL. Denver, CO: Academic Impressions.

[11]   Cyrus Xiyuan Liu, "3D-Printed Animatronic Hand with Wireless Mirroring Glove and Precision Control," presented at the Proceedings of the 47th ACM Technical Symposium on Computer Science Education, Memphis, TN, 2016.

ERSP: A Structured CS Research Program for Early-College Students

Michael Barrow
UC San Diego
mbarrow@eng.ucsd.edu

Shelby Thomas
UC San Diego
sht005@eng.ucsd.edu

Christine Alvarado
UC San Diego
cjalvarado@eng.ucsd.edu

ABSTRACT

Research experiences for undergraduates (REUs) have many positive outcomes on students' perception of and retention in Computer Science (CS). Yet nearly all REUs are aimed at late-college students, well into a CS program. We present the Early Research Scholars Program (ERSP), a 4 quarter program designed to engage early-college (first or second year) CS students in high-quality research experiences in active research groups at a large research university. ERSP's *structured course-supported group-apprentice model* and its unique *dual advising structure* make it possible to vastly increase number of early-career CS students who participate in high-quality research experiences with little additional burden on individual faculty mentors. ERSP's focus on *community building and support* makes it particularly appropriate for students from groups who are traditionally underrepresented in CS. This paper reports the structure of the program and observations and learning thus-far with ERSP, with the goal of enabling others to implement this program at other large research-focused universities.

CCS Concepts

•Social and professional topics → Model curricula; *Computer science education;*

Keywords

diversity; undergraduate research

1. INTRODUCTION

Research experiences for undergraduates (REUs) have been shown to increase retention for students in computer science, particularly for women and underrepresented minorities (URMs) [7, 6]. Unfortunately, at many large schools research experiences are usually ad hoc. Undergraduates must seek out individual research positions, and they usually can only get these positions late in their undergraduate careers. Most REUs are not appropriate for high-potential

ITiCSE '16, July 09 - 13, 2016, Arequipa, Peru

© 2016 Copyright held by the owner/author(s). Publication rights licensed to ACM.
ISBN 978-1-4503-4231-5/16/07... $15.00

DOI: http://dx.doi.org/10.1145/2899415.2899436

students early in the major because REUs usually assume at least some advanced CS knowledge. Additionally, most faculty do not have the resources for the "hand-holding" needed to take on early-college students.

We developed the Early Research Scholars Program (ERSP) with the goal of providing a structured research experience for first and second-year CS students that would impose a minimal additional burden on the faculty supervising the research. ERSP is a 4-quarter[1] program in which students learn fundamentals of CS research in a classroom setting, and apply this knowledge to a group-based research project within an active research group in the department.

The central components of ERSP are:

1. A **course-supported apprentice model** in which students work on real research problems within an active research group as they learn the fundamentals of CS research in a structured class setting.

2. A **dual mentoring framework** in which students are co-advised by a central team of ERSP mentors and a faculty or grad student research mentor.

3. A **team-based structure** that builds community and student-to-student support.

Although ERSP is likely appropriate for all early-college CS students, we designed it explicitly as a retention program for women and URMs in CS. We found that these students were leaving the major at disproportionately high rates compared to White and Asian men, particularly in the second year of the major. Our hypothesis is that by exposing students to research—with all of its struggles, applications of classroom knowledge, and community—students would feel more connected to the department, have a better idea of the applications they were learning in their classes, and be more willing to persist when they struggled in their classes.

ERSP has been running for almost two years. Its novel structure has allowed us to increase the participation of first and second year CS students in research from just a couple per year to up to 36 students per year, so far. Almost all ERSP participants have been women or URMs and the majority of participants have completed or are on track to complete all four quarters of the program.

Although the program is still new, our initial results have been so positive that we are eager to share it with others. This paper describes ERSP's novel structure and components with the goal of allowing others to replicate our successes. We conclude with some early results from cohort 1 and some future directions for this program.

---

[1]Our university uses a quarter-system in which there are three quarters (fall, winter, spring) in an academic year

2. BACKGROUND AND RELATED WORK

REU programs exist at many levels, from nationally coordinated programs (e.g. the NSF REUs), to programs on individual campuses. REUs are widely acknowledged to have many positive benefits for students including increased confidence, increased interest and retention in STEM, and increased likelihood of pursuing graduate study [14, 1, 15].

Evidence also suggests that structured research increases STEM program retention of URMs [10]. Women and URMs face particular challenges early in a college CS career due to feelings of isolation due to a poor cultural fit compounded with an initial lack of experience. This creates an exclusionary feeling for students and a negatively skewed view on the nature of CS. [2, 13, 5, 11, 12]. A structured research experience can help students develop their "science identity" [4] whereby a student displays competence and performance in science that is affirmed by others, and this recognition is acknowledged by both the individual and their peers.

Several existing research programs share our goal of attracting and retaining women and URMs in STEM. Large multi-institutional programs like the Louis Stokes Alliances for Minority Participation (LSAMP) Program at the University of Maryland [8] incorporate research experiences in addition to broader community-building activities and support mechanisms which have been proven effective in retaining minorities in STEM fields. While extremely effective, these programs are also expensive to set up and run successfully.

ERSP is more directly comparable with institutional programs such as the UR STEM program at the University of Northern Kentucky. UR STEM engages students from rising sophomores to rising seniors in research projects across the STEM disciplines, with an emphasis on targeting students at risk for leaving the major at the lower end of the academic spectrum [3]. The major difference between that program and ours is while UR STEM focuses broadly on STEM, ERSP focuses strictly on early-career CS students. This focus on CS is important because the challenges faced by students engaged in CS research may be greater than in other disciplines. Barker finds that when CS students have less experience or are not well-prepared for research, some faculty mentors attribute their struggles to their gender and/or their race [1]. ERSP's focus on CS allows it to address these issues directly within its mentoring structure.

ERSP takes some of its inspiration from the Affinity Research Group (ARG) model [16], which incorporates the deliberate design of research groups, student apprenticeship structure and aspects of broader community building. While the ARG model is rich, it requires that individual faculty mentors have a a deep understanding of and strict commitment to the model. In a large-scale setting, this overhead can make it difficult to implement. In contrast ERSP's dual-mentoring model eases this burden on the research mentors by centralizing the support and community building mentorship to a central ERSP mentoring team.

3. PROGRAM OVERVIEW

We aimed to create a program that would be able to sustain the involvement of a large number of first and second-year CS students in a productive, positive CS research experience without imposing undue work on individual research advisers. This program needed to have sufficient structure and support for the students to build their skills, confidence

and feeling of belonging in CS while keeping the administrative overhead low. To achieve these goals, ERSP is a dual-mentored, team-based program where students are supported and trained by a central mentoring team but also complete a research project under the direct supervision of a faculty member with an active research group.

Each ERSP cohort begins in the spring quarter and runs through the following academic year (Figure 1). Upon entry to the program, students are grouped into ERSP teams of four and then matched with a research group. In the first quarter (spring), ERSP students receive research training through a 2-unit academic course, while attending their research group's meetings or seminars to begin to acclimate themselves to the context of research. In the fall, they continue their training with a second 2-unit academic course, but also begin to transition to freeform research by meeting weekly with their research adviser to propose a project to complete in the winter and spring. In the winter and spring they complete their research project under the dual supervision of the ERSP mentor and their research mentor. Finally, students conclude their ERSP experience with a poster presentation at a department-wide undergraduate research poster session at the end of the academic year.

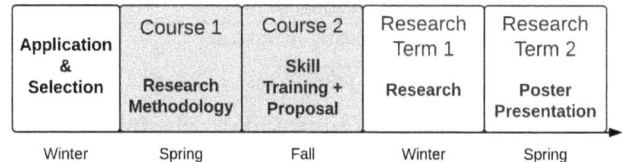

Application & Selection	Course 1 Research Methodology	Course 2 Skill Training + Proposal	Research Term 1 Research	Research Term 2 Poster Presentation
Winter	Spring	Fall	Winter	Spring

Figure 1: ERSP general timeline. See Table 1 for a detailed timeline of the highlighted course blocks

We developed ERSP to match our quarter-based academic year, but we discuss in Section 9 how this timeline, including the coursework, can be adapted to a semester-based year.

4. COURSEWORK+APPRENTICESHIP

A lack of consensus prevails on the nature of Computing Research Method [9]. As noted by [9], research training is often done via apprenticeship, with little formal structure. However, that same report argues that there are specific skills and knowledge that can be formally taught via structured coursework. ERSP combines the benefits of a formal course with an apprenticeship via a 2-phase training+application structure. In the training phase, students take a course in which they learn necessary skills and knowledge in the context of an apprenticeship experience with a research group. In the application phase, the coursework is phased out in favor of freeform research.

4.1 ERSP Support Courses

During the training phase of the program (spring 1 and fall) ERSP participants take a research methodology and skills course that is grounded in the context of the research lab they will be working with. The rough content and timeline for these courses are given in Table 1.

The first course centers on developing a research mindset, focusing on a range of skills from communication and teamwork to familiarity with the research cycle. At the end of this course, students orally present an overview of their lab's work and the related literature, along with an initial proposal for how they might contribute to this work.

	ERSP Quarter 1: Course 1 topics
1	Effective group work
2	Research problem identification and refinement
3	Reading CS research papers
4	Effective literature search methods
5	Independent learning methods
6	Effective technical oral communication
7	Grad student life
8	**Final Presentation: Oral** Research Problem Overview
	ERSP Quarter 2: Course 2 topics
1	Research proposal writing
2	General CS research method
3	Experimental design
4	Interpreting results
5	Analysis and visualization of data
6	Research ethics & opportunities beyond ERSP
7	Research project management
8	**Final Presentation: Written** Written Project Proposal

Table 1: ERSP course topics. We schedule 8 of 10 weeks to accommodate holiday and reflection time. See: https://sites.google.com/a/eng.ucsd.edu/ersp-course-2015-2016/ for more details and updates

The second course focuses more on specific skills required for success in a research group. First and second year students generally have limited or no experience with statistics, data analysis and the programming languages that support these. In this second course we teach students just enough to understand the importance of these skills, guide them in applying these basic skills to problems specific to their research group and lay the groundwork for further developing these skills outside of the course. The second course also revolves around its final deliverable: the written project proposal. Students produce and refine several drafts of this proposal until at the end of the quarter they have a document that details the research they will carry out in the last two quarters of the program.

The novel aspect of these courses is that every activity is grounded in the student's specific research area, thus the courses begin to bridge the gap from structured assignments to open research practice. For example, when students learn to read a research paper in class, each group of students reads a different paper which is directly related to their own research group's work.

4.2 Research Apprenticeship

The ERSP research apprenticeship begins even in the training phase of ERSP. During this training phase in addition to attending class, students attend their research group's weekly meetings. They are not expected to participate in these meetings, but rather simply to observe to get used to the structure and culture of their research group and of research in general. During the second quarter, the course-

work gradually gives way to focusing more on the group's research proposals, preparing students for independent work in the second phase of the program.

The second half of ERSP, the application phase, focuses on applying all of the skills taught in the first half in a real-world research scenario. During this phase students work in their ERSP groups to complete their proposed research under the dual mentoring of the ERSP staff and their research advisor. This unique dual-mentoring model is discussed in more detail in the next section.

The work in this phase is highly dependent on the specific research project, but some common requirements are shared across all participants. Students maintain weekly online logs in which they record their goals, activities, questions, and results. These logs not only provide a record for the student's own use, but are also open for the group members and lab mentors to see. In this way all knowledge and concerns are openly discussed and fosters a sense of teamwork and collaboration. Students also produce two concrete deliverables at the end of this phase: a poster presentation at a department-wide undergraduate research poster session, and a written report that details their problem, approach, results, and information on the state of the project that would allow another student to quickly get up to speed to continue their work.

5. DUAL MENTORING STRUCTURE

ERSP employs a dual-mentoring structure that provides the high-touch guidance early-career students require without undue burden on technical research faculty. ERSP students have two research mentors (or mentoring teams): a lab mentor from the assigned research group and an ERSP mentor who oversees all the research groups. The lab mentor is a graduate student or faculty member (or combination) from the assigned research lab; there is one lab mentor for each ERSP team. In contrast the ERSP mentorship team comprises a single lead faculty member (the ERSP course instructor and program director) and an advanced graduate student with experience in leadership, research, and a variety of CS areas. The ERSP mentor[2] focuses on general research and personal guidance, leaving the lab mentors free to provide technical mentorship, more similar to the interactions they would have with graduate students.

The time costs for a fully scaled ERSP program are:
- ERSP graduate student mentor: 10-15 hours per week.
- ERSP faculty mentor: 1 full time or 2 half-courses per year plus 6-8 hours per week in non-course quarters.
- Lab mentors: 0.5-1 hour per week.

5.1 ERSP Mentor

The role of the ERSP mentor is to bridge the gap between the predictable and well-defined nature of classroom projects and the fluid and open-ended nature of academic research. The responsibilities of the ERSP mentor include: helping groups set personal and research goals, assisting with time management and communication issues, addressing research issues, and providing emotional support and encouragement.

During the application phase of ERSP (winter and spring), the ERSP mentor meets weekly with each group. During these meetings the mentor may address personnel or com-

---
[2]We will use the singular term "ERSP mentor" to refer to the ERSP mentoring team.

munication issues, set weekly goals, help students formulate technical questions to ask their lab mentors, provide general computer science or tool support, provide general support or coaching, or some combination of these. In short, ERSP mentors try to take on as much of the mentoring duties as they can, stopping only when they lack specific technical knowledge required for a particular project.

The workload of the ERSP mentor is significant, requiring 1-2 hours per ERSP group per week. While it is possible for a single faculty member, or even an advanced graduate student, to serve as ERSP mentor, we have found that this position works best when it is split between a faculty member who provides very high-level guidance and an advanced graduate student who provides the majority of the lower-level mentoring support. While faculty tend to have more management experience, graduate students are more deeply engaged in the department's culture and are closer in age and experience to the ERSP participants. However, this graduate student must be chosen carefully. Ideally he or she is an advanced PhD candidate with a broad research background and mentorship experience.

5.2 Lab Mentor

The role of lab mentor is to provide expertly informed research direction to the students and to provide a research environment into which ERSP students can be immersed.

During the fall, winter and spring lab mentors meet weekly with their ERSP group. In the fall in consultation with the ERSP mentor, lab mentors help ERSP groups identify and refine their research project. They also provide the computational resources and tools needed to work on these projects. Lab mentors are expected to include their ERSP students in lab-wide events as much as possible.

Only occasional coordination between the ERSP mentor and lab mentors is required; we recommend quarterly synchronization either in person or over email, except in extraordinary circumstances such as long standing lack of progress in student groups.

Many faculty are suitable lab mentors, provided they meet the following criteria. First, mentors must have an active research group and weekly lab or student meetings that they are willing to let ERSP students observe. Second, mentors must be willing to devote a minimum of 30-minutes per week to meeting with their ERSP group in addition to providing their group offline channels such as email or a discussion board to get their technical questions answered. Finally, we require that mentors express an interest in the program's goals of engaging more early-college students, women and URMs in particular, in computer science research. We find that mentors who embrace ERSP's goals are more likely to provide a working environment that emphasizes building students' research experience and students' self-perception as scientists rather than scientific results.

We find that when faculty lab mentors engage or delegate to their graduate students it often produces the most productive lab mentor relationship. Graduate students tend to be more closely involved in the technical details that will trip up ERSP students, and ERSP students can more easily relate to a student who is just a few years ahead of them in their careers than they can to a faculty member, no matter how well-intentioned.

6. RESEARCH PROJECTS

The selection of an appropriate research project is one of the most difficult, yet most critical, aspects of ERSP. The projects must be real enough that students feel they are making a real contribution, but not so critical that they will derail a lab's progress if unsuccessful. Every lab is different but we identify several key properties the projects must possess to be suitable for ERSP.

1. **Low Research Risk:** The lab mentors should be familiar enough with the research involved in the project that they know what outcomes to expect. Optimization projects or repeated experiments are examples that fit this criteria.
2. **Clearly Defined Milestones:** The project should be composed of sequential steps that are defined before the investigation starts.
3. **Accessible Topic:** The project should not rely heavily on specialized CS knowledge. If it is required, students must have either demonstrated knowledge in the area ahead of project assignment or else be trained in the domain specific prerequisites by their lab ahead of the main investigation.

In terms of scope, a general rule of thumb is that the ERSP group research project should be broadly equivalent to a lab orientation research project that a PI would assign to a first year PhD or as a one-semester Master's thesis project.

We illustrate an application of our project criteria with a successful ERSP project from cohort 1.

Project context: The structure from motion (SFM) algorithm allows archaeologists studying remote or hard to reach areas to construct 3D models from 2D surveillance images. However, the algorithm cannot yet be performed in real-time. The Embedded Systems group at UCSD is working to optimize SFM towards real time performance.

Specific ERSP Project: The ERSP project involved profiling an existing implementation of SFM on a particular hardware platform. The group then experimented with replacing high-level instructions with machine-level instructions specific to the hardware platform, and measured the speedup obtained.

Project Suitability Discussion: This example project was suitable for ERSP for the following reasons:

1. **Low Research Risk:** The SFM algorithm was well known in the literature and had been explored by the Embedded Systems research group previously. Students were given a SFM implementation built from commonly used open source libraries. As such, the students had a ready-made research environment, working example of the research problem and community support on their research tools.
2. **Clearly Defined Milestones:** At a high level, project milestones were software profiling, software optimization and software validation. These milestones could be worked on sequentially.
3. **Accessible Topic:** SFM is a complex algorithm, and hardware-level optimization required the students to acquire domain specific knowledge. With guidance from the Embedded lab graduate student who met with the students and coordinated with the ERSP mentor, students were able to map what they were learning in the computer organization and systems programming course they were taking to the knowledge and skills they needed for their project.

Group Results: Although this ERSP group experienced above average attrition throughout the program, the research project was completed successfully. The baseline SFM implementation was accelerated 50%. Additionally, one team member continued researching with the Embedded lab after the end of the ERSP program.

7. STUDENT SELECTION AND GROUPING

ERSP targets high-performing students early in their CS careers. Because of the fluidity of student standing at UCSD, we use time in the major instead of their freshman or sophomore standing. Students who apply to the program must not yet have completed any upper division courses in the major at the time of application.

Students are selected based on academic performance, interest in CS research and the ERSP program, and potential contribution to diversity in CS. The application consists of their grades in CS courses they have taken so far and their answers three questions that elicit answers related to the criteria on which they will be judged. More details of the application can be found on the ERSP website[3].

A committee of faculty and grad students numerically rate each applicant on their academic potential, their specific interest in the ERSP and their potential to contribute to the diversity of the CS major. Based on the results of these reviews, a threshold is determined above which an applicant is deemed "worthy of selection." The details of how this threshold is determined are beyond the scope of this paper. This threshold produces a set that is larger than the number of students that the program can accommodate, and from this set the participants are randomly selected.

This process of thresholding and random selection was chosen for two reasons. First, because the applicants are so early in their careers it is difficult to make fine distinctions between applicants. Second, this process gives us a built-in control group to which we can compare in our evaluation.

We are currently still ramping up to the target size of the program: 40 students matched with 10 research groups, our target for cohort 3. Our first two cohorts have comprised 23 students with 6 research groups, and 36 students with 9 research groups, respectively.

ERSP group formation and research group assignment is done based on a combination of students' expressed interests and, most importantly, scheduling concerns. During the application process students are asked to rate their interest in a number of sub-fields of CS. After they are selected, they are polled about whether they would be free to attend the group meeting times for each of the research groups involved in ERSP. We then manually match students by assigning students who are free to meet at a group's meeting time, attempting to take into account students' research interests.

8. INITIAL OUTCOMES

It is too early to assess the long-term retention impacts of ERSP on its participants, but initial results and student feedback have been encouraging. Cohort 1 engaged 23 students (18 women, 6 URMs) and cohort 2 engaged 36 students (29 women, 6 URMs), all in their first or second year of the CS major when the program began. 17 of the cohort 1 students finished the 4-quarter program, while 28 of the cohort 2 students are still in the program.

---

[3]https://sites.google.com/a/eng.ucsd.edu/cse-ersp/

Students' qualitative feedback after completion of the program gathered through focus groups and interviews illustrate some of ERSP's strengths and areas for improvement. Because the focus of this paper is the program itself and the evaluation of the program is still in its early stages, we present only a few piece of feedback from cohort 1, and save a more complete discussion of these results, and further statistical analysis, for future work.

Students completing the program left with a greater appreciation for the diversity of research available with the CSE community and how different fields connect.

Student A: *I was working on a computer vision thing and you could apply that – I want to do machine learning or artificial intelligence in the future – you can connect the two... Yes, I could bridge them. My mentor knows that I'm interested in AI so what he's trying to help me to do now is find aspects of the project that I could apply machine learning to so I could still work on this project and have experience in machine learning.*

We also find evidence that ERSP contributes to developing students' science identity. While said in different ways, students reported being more confident, less intimidated, and leaving the program with a sense of accomplishment.

Student B: *Like I said before, a sense of accomplishment I think. Just saying oh, we did this whole year's worth of program. We stuck to it; we got our work done. We just did the piece by piece, all the work that we needed to do to be able to present at that conference... So that's something that I think is really cool.*

Of course, not all feedback was positive, and student feedback helps us shape future changes to the program, discussed in the next section. Most suggestions for improvement centered on an earlier introduction to research, and to some extent a compression of the coursework associated with ERSP.

9. DISCUSSION AND FUTURE WORK

We hope that our experience inspires others to implement ERSP at other large universities. Here we include a discussion of the most challenging aspects of running ERSP to help others avoid potential pitfalls in implementing the program.

Student Motivation The long length and fluid requirements of ERSP in comparison to typical CS courses means extra effort must be made to keep students motivated and focused on the program each quarter. Students are likely to prioritize specific course assignments and course grades over self-driven research, especially when they feel like they are not making progress in their research. Our approach to keeping students engaged and motivated is to frame activities in a 'big picture' that spans the entire duration while emphasizing support that will be provided to them in helping them reach their next milestone. Additionally, we emphasize the positive differentiation factor that ERSP provides their resume over their coursework.

Student Support The scale of ERSP requires support from multiple professors and labs. While we have not had trouble recruiting lab mentors, we note a occasional significant disparity in student support from lab mentors. In the typical case, the dual mentor framework can compensate with ad-hoc support. In the worst case, groups may have to re-deploy to another lab, which requires careful management to maintain student morale.

Scheduling Logistics The large size of the program creates difficulty for scheduling meetings with all student group members. These time conflicts can make management of teams a difficult task. We have three strategies for combating this problem. First, we use student schedule as a factor in selecting groups, matching students with the most compatible schedules. Second, we insist students determine contact hours as a priority when scheduling their other commitments at the start of each quarter. Finally, we plan to shorten ERSP to three quarters to reduce the frequency of schedule changes, as discussed below.

As ERSP enters its third cohort, we continue to revise the program. The most significant planned revision for cohort 3 involves shortening the program's duration from 4-quarters to a single academic year. Based on student and mentor feedback, and our own experience, the first quarter does not seem to provide a gain that is worth the added work. Although many students appreciate this first (spring) quarter as a time to slowly acclimate to research and their research group, others find the start of the program frustratingly slow. Additionally, students forget most of what they learned in the spring over the summer, and the transition between spring and fall provides an additional challenge of keeping groups together in their research group meetings in the face of completely new academic schedules. Beginning in 2016, students will apply and be accepted to the program in the spring quarter, but will not begin until the fall quarter. We will keep the application and acceptance in spring rather than summer to combat the potential attrition that can start to occur over the summer after students' first year.

The transition from 4-quarters to a single academic year will also make it clearer how this program can be adapted to a semester-based academic calendar. We will condense the ERSP support course into a single quarter carrying 4 units instead of 2 so that students can devote more time to research training and project proposal development. However, in a semester-based calendar, our two current courses could be merged into a single semester-long course, so that the fall semester comprises the training phase and the spring semester the application phase where students complete and present their research projects.

10. CONCLUSION

We will continue our long term tracking and surveying of students both in the program and in our control group to understand ERSP's success as a retention program. However, even with our current data we are convinced of the value of ERSP. It has already proven itself a relatively low-overhead way to engage dozens of early-college students in meaningful and successful research experiences, and we believe that through ERSP these same outcomes can be achieved at other large research universities.

11. ACKNOWLEDGMENTS

We would like to thank the lab mentors who have participated in ERSP so far. This material is based upon work supported by the National Science Foundation under Grant No. CNS-1339335.

12. REFERENCES

[1] L. Barker. Student and faculty perceptions of undergraduate research experiences in computing. *Trans. Comput. Educ.*, 9(1):5:1–5:28, Mar. 2009.

[2] S. Beyer, K. Rynes, J. Perrault, K. Hay, and S. Haller. Gender differences in computer science students. In *Proc. SIGCSE '03*, pages 49–53, 2003.

[3] B. Bowling, H. Bullen, M. Doyle, and J. Filaseta. Retention of STEM majors using early undergraduate research experiences. In *Proc. SIGCSE '13*.

[4] H. B. Carlone and A. Johnson. Understanding the science experiences of successful women of color: Science identity as an analytic lens. *Journal of research in science teaching*, 44(8):1187–1218, 2007.

[5] J. M. Cohoon. Toward improving female retention in the computer science major. *CACM*, 44(5):108–114, 2001.

[6] S. R. Gregerman, J. S. Lerner, W. v. Hippel, J. Jonides, and B. A. Nagda. Undergraduate student-faculty research partnerships affect student retention. *The Review of Higher Education*, 22(1):55–72, 1998.

[7] C. G. Gutierrez, L. M. Tunstad, A. Fratiello, and S. L. Nickolaisen. Undergraduate research participation increases minority retention and success in chemistry. In *Abstracts of Papers, 225th ACS Nat'l Mtg*, 2003.

[8] T. Hamilton and R. Parker. UMCP LSAMP: 15 years of successful retention and graduation of underrepresented minority students. *Women in Engineering ProActive Network*, 2011.

[9] H. J. Holz, A. Applin, B. Haberman, D. Joyce, H. Purchase, and C. Reed. Research methods in computing: What are they, and how should we teach them? In *ACM SIGCSE Bulletin*, volume 38, pages 96–114. ACM, 2006.

[10] S. Hurtado, N. L. Cabrera, M. H. Lin, L. Arellano, and L. L. Espinosa. Diversifying science: Underrepresented student experiences in structured research programs. *Research in Higher Education*, 50(2):189–214, 2009.

[11] S. Katz, D. Allbritton, J. Aronis, C. Wilson, and M. L. Soffa. Gender, achievement, and persistence in an undergraduate computer science program. *SIGMIS Database*, 37(4):42–57, 2006.

[12] M. Klawe, T. Whitney, and C. Simard. Women in computing—take 2. *Commun. ACM*, 52(2):68–76, 2009.

[13] J. Margolis. *Stuck in the Shallow End: Education, Race, and Computing*. The MIT Press, 2008.

[14] S. H. Russell, M. P. Hancock, and J. McCullough. The pipeline: Benefits of undergraduate research experiences. *Science*, 316(5824):548–549, 2007.

[15] E. Seymour, A.-B. Hunter, S. L. Laursen, and T. Deantoni. Establishing the benefits of research experiences for undergraduates in the sciences: First findings from a three-year study. *Science Education*, 88:493–534, 2004.

[16] P. Teller and A. Gates. Applying the affinity research group model to computer science research projects. In *Proceedings 30th ASEE/IEEE Frontiers in Education Conference*, October 2000.

Benchmarking Introductory Programming Exams: How and Why

Simon
University of Newcastle
Australia
simon@newcastle.edu.au

Judy Sheard
Monash University
Australia
judy.sheard@monash.edu

Daryl D'Souza
RMIT University
Australia
daryl.dsouza@rmit.edu.au

Peter Klemperer
Mount Holyoke College
United States of America
pklemper@mtholyoke.edu

Leo Porter
University of California, San Diego
United States of America
leporter@eng.ucsd.edu

Juha Sorva
Aalto University
Finland
juha.sorva@aalto.fi

Martijn Stegeman
University of Amsterdam / Open University of the Netherlands
Netherlands
martijn@stgm.nl

Daniel Zingaro
University of Toronto Mississauga
Canada
daniel.zingaro@utoronto.ca

ABSTRACT
Ten selected questions have been included in 13 introductory programming exams at seven institutions in five countries. The students' results on these questions, and on the exams as a whole, lead to the development of a benchmark against which the exams in other introductory programming courses can be assessed. We illustrate some potential benefits of comparing exam performance against this benchmark, and show other uses to which it can be put, for example to assess the size and the overall difficulty of an exam. We invite others to apply the benchmark to their own courses and to share the results with us.

Keywords
Introductory programming; examination; benchmarking.

1. INTRODUCTION
It is widely accepted that learning to program is hard for some students [2, 4]. It has been established that around the world, pass rates in introductory programming courses are worse than their instructors would like [1, 14]. But one thing that remains unknown is whether the 75% of students who pass an introductory programming course at one institution are performing at about the same level as the 65% who pass a different introductory programming course at another institution.

One way to establish this would be to undertake a detailed analysis of the exams at different institutions, and indeed this has been done for exams in data structures [13] and programming [6, 7, 10], but not in conjunction with an analysis of student performance on those exams.

Another approach is to seed identical questions into the exams at a number of institutions and compare the students' performance on those identical questions. That is what we have done in this project, and in this paper we present our method and some indications of how it might be used.

2. BACKGROUND
Benchmarking is essentially comparing items against a published standard of some sort, to determine whether the items meet the standard, exceed it, or fall short of it. Benchmarking is used in many contexts, such as to compare the performance of software packages [9] or the fuel economy of diesel vehicles. In the context of education, benchmarking might be used to assess cognate degrees or individual courses from different institutions, and thus perhaps to compare those degrees or courses. Within the broad area of computing education, a benchmarking approach has been proposed for courses in computer literacy [5].

Within programming education, one of the express goals of the BABELnot project [3] was "to include some common questions in exams … and to benchmark student performance on those questions". As part of that project, we initially derived a set of four questions that could be used in such a benchmarking exercise [8]. We subsequently expanded that set to ten questions [11] and invited others to include the questions in their own exams. The work reported in this paper is a consequence of that invitation. The ten questions, which are given as an appendix to this paper, were used by a number of examiners around the world.

ITICSE'16, July 09-13, 2016, Arequipa, Peru
© 2016 ACM. ISBN 978-1-4503-4231-5/16/07…$15.00
DOI: http://dx.doi.org/10.1145/2899415.2899473

3. METHOD AND CONTEXTS

The ten benchmarking questions were incorporated into 13 final written examinations at seven institutions in five countries. At two institutions there were three identical exams for the same course: a course taught in three sections, and a course offered on three different campuses of a university in two countries. At each of two other institutions the questions were used in the exams for two different introductory programming courses. The remaining three institutions used the questions in one exam each.

The questions are currently available in five procedural/object-oriented programming languages, but the exams analysed in this paper used only Python, Java, and C.

No constraints were imposed on how much of the exam the benchmarking questions should make up, and on the exams represented here they constituted between 16% and 47% of the complete exam. Furthermore, the final exams contribute differently to the overall marks in the courses: as much as 60% and as little as zero, the latter in a course where the exam is a hurdle that students must clear but that does not contribute to their final mark.

We specified a precise marking scheme for the ten benchmarking questions, but this pertained only to the data collection for this project. Examiners were free to mark the questions in an entirely different manner for the purposes of their assessment, but were constrained to use our marking scheme for the benchmarking analysis. Of course there is an advantage to using the same scheme for both purposes, so that the questions do not need to be marked twice; but this was not a requirement of participation in the project.

4. A SAMPLE OF THE ANALYSIS

In this section we present a sample of the results of our benchmarking, not to illustrate the results themselves, but to illustrate how the benchmarking questions might be used by others. Instructors can use the questions in their own exams (we will provide our marking scheme), examine their students' results in the manner outlined here, and draw their own conclusions about their courses.

Throughout this section and its subsections, any differences observed on the graphs and discussed have been confirmed as significant by applying chi-square tests in the case of questions with binary responses or Kruskal-Wallis tests in the case of questions allocated marks in a range.

4.1 The big picture

After determining the score for each student on each of the benchmarking questions, we calculated a score for each question for each course. For the four multiple-choice questions and the two fixed-answer questions, this score is the proportion of students who chose or wrote the correct answer. For the remaining questions, it is the students' average mark on the question, represented as a percentage. Figure 1 shows the average performance on each question for all 13 courses. This graph gives only a broad overview of performance on all of the courses, and is not intended for detailed analysis; the subsequent plots will prove more informative in this regard.

Figure 1: performance in all 13 exams on the ten benchmarking questions

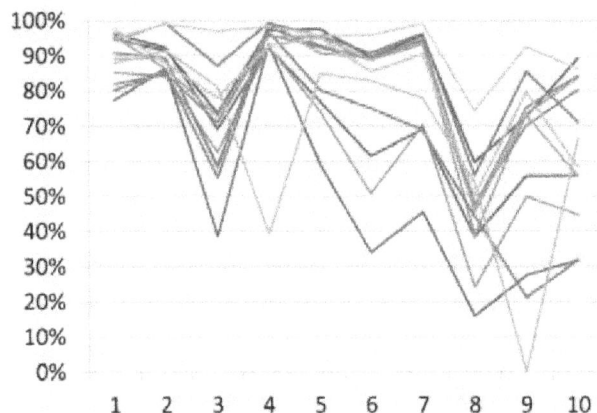

4.2 Comparison with average

One useful technique involves taking an average of the 13 courses for each question and comparing individual courses with the average. The more courses that contribute to the average, the closer it should come to representing the average of all introductory programming courses. We hope that the 13 courses represented here are just the beginning, with results from more courses to be added in the future. At present the average is formed on the basis of these courses – with one exception. Even in the confusion of lines in figure 1, something appears to have gone dramatically wrong with questions 4 and 9 in one course. This will be explained in the next subsection, and that course has been omitted from the average.

Figure 2 shows the performance at two institutions as compared with the average. It is easier to interpret these plots, and it is clear that at one of the institutions the performance is better than the average and at the other the performance is worse than the average.

Figure 2: performance at two institutions (dotted and dashed lines) compared with average over six institutions (solid line)

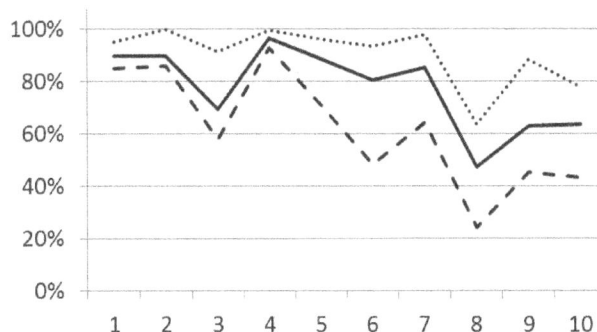

4.3 Identification of anomalies

Comparison with the average can quickly draw attention to anomalies that might require individual attention. Figure 3 shows the performance on two courses compared with the average, in the manner of figure 2. Both courses showed somewhat worse performance than the average, but of most interest are the performance in one course (the dotted line) on questions 4 and 9, and in the other (the dashed line) on question 9.

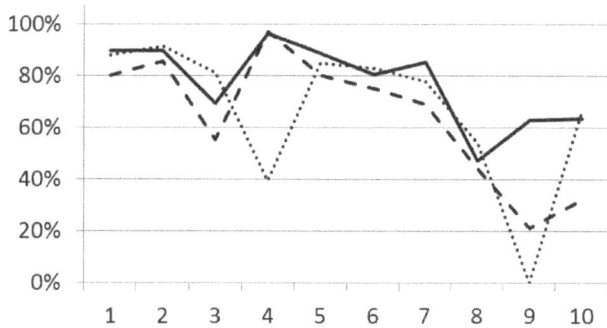

The question 9 anomaly shown by the dotted line was known in advance. The examiner for that course had declined to include question 9 on the exam, feeling that it would be too difficult for the students in that course. Therefore marks of zero were reported for that question for all students in that course.

The question 4 anomaly was entirely unexpected, and indeed it can be discerned from figure 1 that with the exception of this exam, question 4 was the most tightly bunched of the questions. Once the anomaly had been identified from this analysis, the examination paper was rechecked. At this point it was discovered that the code in the question had been edited slightly before use, removing unnecessary braces; but that the indentation had also been adjusted, and no longer reflected the structure of the code. This is a tracing question, asking students to determine the value of a particular variable once the code has been executed; and the misleading indentation appears to have led about half of the students to an incorrect answer.

The remaining anomaly, for question 9 in the exam represented by the dashed line in figure 3, has not yet been investigated. It remains an interesting question for the examiner in that course.

4.4 Comparison within a course

Some of our data comprises separate but identical exams within the same course. At one university the introductory programming course is taught in three sections, each with a different teacher and not necessarily using the same pedagogical approach. Student performance was fairly uniform across the sections, suggesting that the students' learning, at least at the level of this benchmarking, is independent of the teacher or the approach.

At another university a single course is taught at three different campuses, with three different teachers all using the same teaching

Figure 4: a single course offered at three different campuses of a single institution

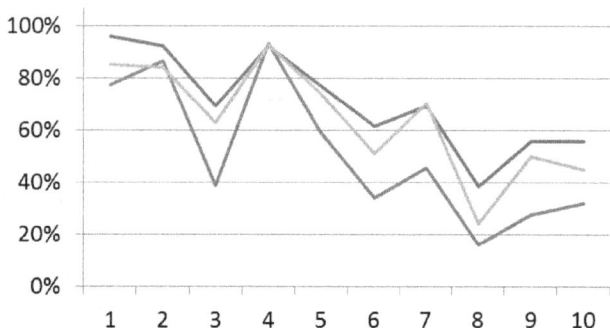

materials and assessment items. As shown in figure 4, performance is distinctly worse at one campus than at the other two. The worst-performing campus is in a different country, and the coordinator of the three offerings believes it is possible that the worse performance is due in part to the distinctly different student cohort at that campus.

At another university a single course is taught in two different modes, one taking half the weekly time and twice as many weeks as the other. At that university the benchmarking performance was almost identical for the two exams, suggesting that the speed of delivery had no substantial impact on student learning.

4.5 Comparison within an institution

At one university in our study the introductory computing course is taught as a two-quarter sequence, with the second course in the sequence described as being more like CS1.5 than CS1. The benchmarking questions were used in the final exams of both courses. Figure 5 shows that students in both courses performed well on the benchmarking questions, but in one course, the second in the sequence, they performed better than in the other. If the two courses were expected to be comparable at the level of these questions, the instructors could now focus on the questions that displayed most difference (3, 8, 9, and 10) and try to determine what aspects of the teaching and learning might have led to those differences.

Figure 5: a two-course sequence at a single institution

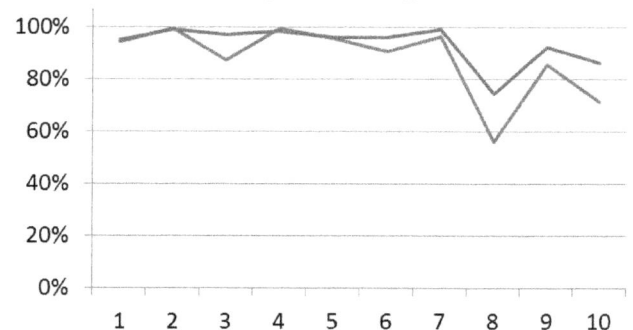

4.6 Comparison with exam performance

Any single exam can be analysed by comparing the students' marks on the benchmarking questions with their marks on the exam as a whole. Ideally, we would compare their marks on the benchmarking questions with their marks on the *remaining* exam questions; however, we did not collect this data. Furthermore, some participants devised their own exam marking schemes for the benchmarking questions. The marks given to their students for these questions in the exam are not the same as the marks given to the same students for benchmarking purposes; therefore we cannot reconstruct the students' marks for the rest of the exam by subtracting their benchmarking mark from their exam mark.

Figure 6 plots, for two different courses, students' marks on the benchmarking questions (out of 27) against their marks on the whole exam (out of 100). Points on the diagonal represent comparable performance on the benchmarking questions and on the whole exam. If the points tend to lie above the diagonal, as in the first exam shown, students tended to perform better on the benchmarking questions than on the exam as a whole, suggesting that this is a challenging exam. If the points tend to lie below the diagonal, as in the second example, students tended to perform

Figure 6: for two different exams, students' benchmarking marks (vertical, out of 27) vs their exam marks (horizontal, out of 100), with the diagonal shown as a dashed line and the trendline as a solid line

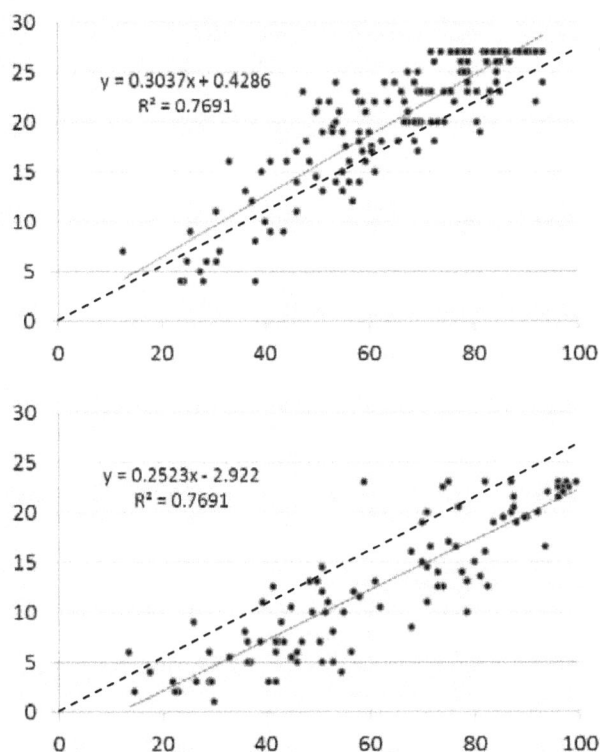

$$y = 0.3037x + 0.4286$$
$$R^2 = 0.7691$$

$$y = 0.2523x - 2.922$$
$$R^2 = 0.7691$$

better on the exam as a whole than on the benchmarking questions, suggesting that this is a less challenging exam.

4.7 Size of exam

It is possible to form an idea of the 'size' of an exam from the part played in it by the benchmarking questions. Assuming that an exam question has a 'size', which might be some sort of composite of its difficulty and the time a student would take to answer it, the size of the exam would be the sum of the sizes of its questions. Assuming further that the marks allocated to questions are more or less proportional to their sizes, the size of an exam can be computed as a multiple of the size of the benchmarking questions. By this measure, the biggest exam in our sample is 6.25 times the size of the benchmarking questions (ie those questions make up 16% of the whole exam), while the smallest is 2.1 times the size of the benchmarking questions. One might expect that students would be permitted more time for exams that are bigger in this sense.

4.8 Importance of uniformity

When combining the data for analysis we encountered a number of potential problems. As discussed in section 4.3, one question was intentionally omitted from one exam. Question-by-question analysis is still possible on the remaining questions, but it is not meaningful to compare the overall performance on that exam with the average overall performance.

A second issue was the marking scheme. The multiple-choice and fixed-answer questions are trivial to mark, each having a single correct answer. But the code-writing questions, 3, 9, and 10, and

the code-explaining question, 8, were allocated marks according to a specified scheme. For example, one of the six marks for question 10 was for "a complete and correct method definition", and another was for "correctly specifying a loop with the correct bounds". The intention was that these marks be given as 0 or 1. However, some of our data included non-integer totals for these questions, suggesting that some participants chose to give marks of 0.5 for partial correctness. This clearly has the potential to boost their students' marks, confounding the benchmarking effect.

Finally, one exam included bonus marks. While this is not an uncommon practice, it led to some students being given final exam marks of more than 100%, making it difficult to compare that exam with the others in the sample.

4.9 Language dependence

When starting this project we assumed that simple questions such as these would be effectively independent of the programming language being used. This assumption proved to be flawed.

Questions 9 and 10 were clearly intended to test students' skill at writing iterative code. But some languages, such as Python and Visual Basic, offer higher-level methods or constructs that permit trivial solutions to those questions, solutions in which the iteration is implicit. A trivial solution to question 9 would simply extract the first element from the list/array and append it to the end. A trivial solution to question 10 would simply call the inbuilt averaging method or function. As well as failing to demonstrate the intended knowledge, trivial solutions make it impossible to apply the detailed marking scheme.

Referring back to figure 1, we see that while most of the lines follow more or less the same shape, there appears to be more variation at the end. In particular, some lines drop from question 9 to question 10, while others rise. The higher marks on either question might be due in part to students' use of trivial solutions.

On a smaller scale, one mark for question 10 was for ensuring that the value returned is a double, not an integer. This is meaningful only in programming languages that give an integer result when dividing two integers. In other languages the mark is awarded for nothing.

Another potential issue concerns the language coverage rather than the language itself. One prospective participant, who taught a course using C, covered the *while* statement but not the *for* statement, so for that course the questions involving iteration were reworded accordingly. Unfortunately, that participant was unable to continue with the project, so we are unable to look for possible effects of the change.

5. DISCUSSION AND CONCLUSION

Having deployed the ten benchmarking questions in 13 introductory programming exams at seven institutions in five countries, we can affirm the potential usefulness of this measure. We have established a preliminary average against which individual courses can be benchmarked, and have shown that courses can consistently exceed this average or fall short of it. Independently of this, we have shown how the benchmarking questions can be used to assess the difficulty of an exam (section 4.6) and the size of the exam (section 4.7). Instructors wishing to use the benchmarking questions will be given the questions in other programming languages if appropriate, our marking scheme, and the current average for each question.

Instructors using the benchmarking questions on their own exams should ensure that their students are familiar in advance with all of the question types. In particular, there is evidence [12, 15] that students struggle with code-explaining questions (questions 7 and 8) when they first encounter them.

Instructors will also need to work to understand the outcomes of any benchmarking they carry out. A poor benchmarking performance does not necessarily mean poor teaching, and a good performance does not necessarily mean good teaching. There are many other factors to consider, such as the pedagogical approach used in a course, the programming language, the coverage in the course of the concepts tested by the questions, the quality of student intake, the level of scaffolding provided, and more. In section 4 we have suggested some possible inferences from the analysis; but in each case further work is necessary to turn those suggestions into plausible conclusions.

6. FUTURE WORK

As indicated in section 4.9, the questions in the current set are not entirely independent of the programming language in which they are set. We hope to refine the questions to overcome any language dependencies, but not at the expense of making all of the questions trivial. Our goal is to find a set of questions, not all of them trivial, that are as close as possible to agnostic regarding programming language and teaching approach.

This work will be more useful if other educators now apply the same benchmark to their own courses, and we will assist in this regard. If they are then willing to share their results with us, we can incorporate them in a new and more representative average.

If we are able to collect more metadata about the introductory programming courses, such as what degree or major students are in when they take the courses, and in what year of their university study they typically take the courses, this will help us to look for explanations of the benchmarking findings.

Finally, we would like to develop a single numeric measure of a class's performance on the benchmark, to make it easier to compare student performances in different courses.

7. ACKNOWLEDGEMENTS

We are grateful to Kerttu Pollari-Malmi and Andy Cheng for expanding our dataset by including the benchmarking questions in their introductory programming examinations.

8. REFERENCES

[1] Bennedsen, J. and Caspersen, M.E. (2007). Failure rates in introductory programming. SIGCSE Bulletin, 39:2, 32-36.

[2] Lister, R., Adams, E. S., Fitzgerald, S., Fone, W., Hamer, J., Lindholm, M., McCartney, R., Moström, E., Sanders, K., Seppälä, O., Simon, B. and Thomas, L. (2004). A multi-national study of reading and tracing skills in novice programmers. SIGCSE Bulletin, 36:4, 119-150.

[3] Lister, R., Corney, M., Curran, J., D'Souza, D., Fidge, C., Gluga, R., Hamilton, M., Harland, J., Hogan, J., Kay, J., Murphy, T., Roggenkamp, M., Sheard, J., Simon and Teague, D. (2012). Toward a shared understanding of competency in programming: An invitation to the BABELnot project. 14th Australasian Computing Education Conference (ACE 2012), 53-60.

[4] McCracken, M., Almstrum, V., Diaz, D., Guzdial, M., Hagan, D., Ben-David Kolikant, Y., Laxer, C., Thomas, L., Utting, I. and Wilusz, T. (2001). A multi-national, multi-institutional study assessment of programming skills of first-year CS students. SIGCSE Bulletin - Working Group reports: Making inroads to improve computing education, 33:4, 125-140.

[5] Oliver, R. and Towers, S. (2000). Benchmarking ICT literacy in tertiary learning settings. 17th Annual Conference of the Australian Society for Computers in Learning in Tertiary Education (ASCILITE 2000), 381-390.

[6] Petersen, A., Craig, M. and Zingaro, D. (2011). Reviewing CS1 exam question content. 42nd ACM Technical Symposium on Computer Science Education (SIGCSE'11), 631-636.

[7] Sheard, J., Simon, Carbone, A., Chinn, D., Clear, T., Corney, M., D'Souza, D., Fenwick, J., Harland, J., Laakso, M.-J. and Teague, D. (2013). How difficult are exams? A framework for assessing the complexity of introductory programming exams. 15th Australasian Computing Education Conference (ACE 2013), 145-154.

[8] Sheard, J., Simon, Dermoudy, J., D'Souza, D., Hu, M., and Parsons, D. (2014). Benchmarking a set of exam questions for introductory programming. 16th Australasian Computing Education Conference (ACE 2014), 113-121.

[9] Sim, S.E., Easterbrook, S. and Holt, R. (2003). Using benchmarking to advance research: a challenge to software engineering. 25th International Conference on Software Engineering, 74-83.

[10] Simon, Sheard, J., Carbone, A., D'Souza, D., Harland, J. and Laakso, M.-J. (2012). Can computing academics assess the difficulty of programming examination questions? 11th Koli Calling International Conference on Computing Education Research, 160-163.

[11] Simon, Sheard, J., D'Souza, D., Lopez, M., Luxton-Reilly, A., Putro I.H., Robbins, P., Teague, D., and Whalley, J. (2015). How (not) to write an introductory programming exam. 17th Australasian Computing Education Conference (ACE 2015), 137-146.

[12] Simon and Snowdon, S. (2011). Explaining program code: giving students the answer helps – but only just. Seventh International Computing Education Research Workshop (ICER 2011), 93-99.

[13] Simon, B., Clancy, M., McCartney, R., Morrison, B., Richards, B., and Sanders, K. (2010). Making sense of data structures exams. Sixth International Computing Education Research workshop (ICER 2010), 97-105.

[14] Watson, C. and Li, F.W. (2014). Failure rates in introductory programming revisited. 19th ACM Conference on Innovation and Technology in Computer Science Education (ITiCSE '14), 39-44.

[15] Whalley, J., Lister, R., Thompson, E., Clear, T., Robbins, P., Kumar, P.K.A. and Prasad, C. (2006). An Australasian study of reading and comprehension skills in novice programmers, using the Bloom and SOLO taxonomies. Eighth Australasian Computing Education conference (ACE 2006), 243-251.

Appendix: Ten benchmarking questions, Java version (Simon et al [11]; used with permission)

Q1. If a dependent child is a person under 18 years of age who does not earn $10,000 or more a year, which expression would define a dependent child?

(a) `age < 18 && salary < 10000`
(b) `age < 18 || salary < 10000`
(c) `age <= 18 && salary <= 10000`
(d) `age <= 18 || salary <= 10000`

Q2. What are the values of *girls*, *boys*, and *children* after the following code has been executed?

```
int girls = 0;
int boys = 0;
int children = 0;
children = girls + boys;
girls = 15;
boys = 12;
```

(a) 0, 0, 0
(b) 0, 0, 27
(c) 15, 12, 0
(d) 15, 12, 27

Q3. There are three integer variables, *a*, *b* and *c*, which have been initialised. Write code to shift the values in these variables around so that *a* is given *b*'s original value, *b* is given *c*'s original value, and *c* is given *a*'s original value. The following diagram illustrates the direction of the shifts:

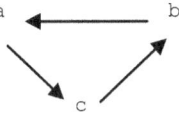

Q4. What will be the value of the variable *z* after the following code is executed?

```
int x = 1; int y = 2; int z = 3;
if (x < y) {
    if (y > 4) {
        z = 5;
    } else {
        z = 6;
    }
}
```

Q5. Consider the following block of code, where variables *a*, *b*, *c*, and *answer* each store integer values:

```
if (a > b) {
    if (b > c) {
        answer = c;
    } else {
        answer = b;
    }
} else if (a > c) {
    answer = c;
} else {
    answer = a;
}
```

Which of the following sets of values for *a*, *b*, and *c* will cause *answer* to be assigned the value in variable *b*?

(a) a = 1, b = 2, c = 3
(b) a = 1, b = 3, c = 2
(c) a = 2, b = 1, c = 3
(d) a = 3, b = 2, c = 1

Q6. What will be the value of *result* after the following code statements are executed?

```
int[] nums1 = { 1, -5, 2, 0, 4, 2, -3 };
int[] nums2 = { 1, -5, 2, 4, 4, 2, 7 };
int result = 0;
int j = 0;
while (j < nums1.length)
{
    if (nums1[j] != nums2[j])
    {
        result = result + 1;
    }
    j = j + 1;
}
```

Q7. What is the outcome or likely purpose of the following piece of code?

```
int result = 0;
for (int j = 0; j < number.length; j++)
{
    if (number[j] < 0)
    {
        result = result + 1;
    }
}
```

(a) to find the smallest number in the array
(b) to count the negative numbers in the array
(c) to sum the negative numbers in the array
(d) to add 1 to each of the negative numbers in the array
(e) to find the index of the first negative number in the array

Q8. What is the outcome or likely purpose of the following piece of code? Express your answer as a short phrase, like the phrases provided as possible answers in question 7.

```
int result = 0;
for (int count = 1; count <= num; count++)
{
    result = result + count;
}
```

Q9. We can represent an array of integers as a sequence of elements arranged from left to right, with the first element at the left and the last element at the right. Using this representation, a programmer wishes to move all elements of an array one place to the right, with the rightmost element being 'wrapped around' to the leftmost position, as shown in this diagram.

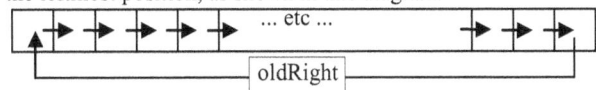

Here is the code that performs that shift for an array referred to by the name *values*:

```
int oldRight = values[values.length - 1];
for (int j = values.length - 1; j > 0; j--)
    values[j] = values[j - 1];
values[0] = oldRight;
```

For example, if *values* initially contains the integers [1, 2, 3, 4, 5], once the code has executed it would contain [5, 1, 2, 3, 4].
Write code that will undo the effect of the above code. That is, write code that will move all the elements of the array one place to the left, with the leftmost element being wrapped around to the rightmost position.

Q10. Write a method that will be given an array of integers and will calculate and return (as a double) the mean (average) of all the integers in the array.

Typing Patterns and Authentication in Practical Programming Exams

Juho Leinonen
University of Helsinki
Finland
juho.leinonen@helsinki.fi

Krista Longi
University of Helsinki
Finland
krista.longi@helsinki.fi

Arto Klami
University of Helsinki
Finland
aklami@cs.helsinki.fi

Alireza Ahadi
University of Technology
Sydney
Australia
alireza.ahadi@uts.edu.au

Arto Vihavainen
University of Helsinki
Finland
avihavai@cs.helsinki.fi

ABSTRACT

In traditional programming courses, students have usually been at least partly graded using pen and paper exams. One of the problems related to such exams is that they only partially connect to the practice conducted within such courses. Testing students in a more practical environment has been constrained due to the limited resources that are needed, for example, for authentication.

In this work, we study whether students in a programming course can be identified in an exam setting based solely on their typing patterns. We replicate an earlier study that indicated that keystroke analysis can be used for identifying programmers. Then, we examine how a controlled machine examination setting affects the identification accuracy, i.e. if students can be identified reliably in a machine exam based on typing profiles built with data from students' programming assignments from a course. Finally, we investigate the identification accuracy in an uncontrolled machine exam, where students can complete the exam at any time using any computer they want.

Our results indicate that even though the identification accuracy deteriorates when identifying students in an exam, the accuracy is high enough to reliably identify students if the identification is not required to be exact, but top k closest matches are regarded as correct.

CCS Concepts

•Information systems → Data mining; •Social and professional topics → Computer science education; CS1; •Computing methodologies → Supervised learning by classification; •Security and privacy → Biometrics;

ITiCSE '16, July 09 - 13, 2016, Arequipa, Peru

© 2016 Copyright held by the owner/author(s). Publication rights licensed to ACM.
ISBN 978-1-4503-4231-5/16/07. . . $15.00

DOI: http://dx.doi.org/10.1145/2899415.2899472

Keywords

authentication, machine exam, programmer identification, source code snapshots

1. INTRODUCTION

Hundreds of thousands of students around the world attend an introductory programming course each year, and at the end of the course, many of them take part in an exam. The exam may for example be a traditional written exam, where students answer questions using pen and paper, or, it may be a more practical laboratory exam, where students are expected to construct programs in a lab setting [2,20]. In both cases, students typically take the exams at their own educational institution, where their identity is determined by administrators or course staff.

With the trend towards blended and online course offerings, it is meaningful to consider taking at least parts of the exam by telecommute. Naturally, when such an option is considered, concerns related to e.g. plagiarism [5, 19] and authentication are involved. Plagiarism detection is about determining whether the student is the author of the proposed solution, while authentication is related to determining whether the student is who he or she poses to be.

Our work explores the possibility of automatically authenticating students taking an exam by telecommute using their typing patterns as the authentication mechanism. If authentication using such means is possible, it could lead to reducing costs related to the facilitation of local examinations, increase the flexibility in when the exam is given, and also provide the students with the chance to take the exam at a location where they feel comfortable, possibly helping them perform better during the exam.

While authentication of students based on typing speed and keystroke durations has been previously explored outside the programming domain [11, 18], the task was only recently considered within the domain of programming by Longi et al. [14]. They used programming course data to learn students' typing profiles, and then sought to identify the students in two separate situations: during a future session on the same course and during a future course. With the best approach, over 90% of the students in the dataset were correctly identified.

In this work, we (1) replicate the work previously reported by [14] with separate data sets, (2) explore to which extent the method can be applied to distinguish students with data from a shorter period, i.e. an exam, and (3) study how the accuracy of the method changes when students work using machines that they are accustomed to when compared to machines in a laboratory setting. The main goal of these experiments is to study the robustness of the approach in practical settings.

This article is organized as follows. We provide a brief overview of identification of users using keystroke data in Section 2, after which we outline our research methodology and data in Section 3. The description of results and experiments is given in Section 4, followed by a discussion of the results in Section 5. Finally, in Section 6, we conclude the article and outline future work.

2. RELATED WORK

Various characteristics can be calculated from typing data. These characteristics include duration of keystrokes, pressure of keystrokes, and keystroke latencies [11], which may vary depending on the situation – typing patterns can be affected by different keyboards, for example, or different types of texts [8]. Out of these characteristics the keystroke latencies, especially *digraph* latencies – the time it takes to move between a pair of keys – have been widely used [6,7,12,17,24]. Generally, digraphs are any two adjacent characters, for example, the word *word* includes three digraphs: *wo, or* and *rd*. If the word is mistyped, additional digraphs are also observed – it also is possible to include events such as deletions.

Much of the previous work on typing analysis has been based on transcribed or pre-determined text, such as usernames and passwords [3,4,9,10,25], but there are studies where the input has been free text instead [3,8,15]. The results vary significantly based on the data used. For example, in a study by Monrose and Rubin with 46 participants, the identification accuracy decreased significantly from 79% with transcribed text to 21% with free text [17]. They suggested that this result could be partially explained by the writer having to think about something to write rather than being just able to type in whatever is given.

There are positive results from using free text as well. For example, in an experiment with 20 participants, Killourhy and Maxion found no significant difference in classification results when using transcribed or free text [12]. In their experiment, the participants were given comparable transcription and free composition tasks, and they used lowercase digraph and key-hold times with two separate classification algorithms. Although the results were not exactly the same, they were very close and neither one was always better [12].

Typing patterns can be affected by different conditions such as the keyboard [24]. In a study by Villani et al. [24], where participants had either only freely typed or transcribed text, identification accuracies of over 98% were achieved when when the subjects only used one type of keyboard. However, when the keyboard was switched between the session that produced the data from which the typing profile was learned and the session where the participant was being identified, the identification accuracy dropped to about 60%. However, at the same time, using both desktop and laptop keyboards in both sessions did not noticeably decrease the accuracy [24].

Keystroke analysis has also been successfully applied in identifying students in online exams [16, 21]. Using data from 30 students taking examinations in a business school, Monaco et al. were able to correctly identify all the students [16]. Similarly, Coursera is collecting typing samples from students who want to acquire a verified certificate [1].

In a programming context, keystroke analysis has been used to infer programming performance [13, 22]. Thomas et al. [22] found that there exist some digraphs that have a moderate negative correlation with course scores. They argue that more knowledgeable programmers type certain digraphs faster than novice programmers.

3. METHODOLOGY

3.1 Context

The data for the experiments has been collected from four programming courses held at the University of Helsinki in 2015 spanning both spring and autumn semesters. Both semesters had a beginner and an advanced course in Java. All four courses had a machine examination. The machine exams consisted of Java programming assignments and the students were allowed to use the Internet, but not communicate with anyone. The machine exams in spring 2015 were conducted at university facilities in a computer lab, where students' identities were verified by course personnel. In autumn 2015, the students were allowed to complete the examination at any location using any computer they wished to use, and their identities were only verified by the system used to submit the solutions to the programming assignments. The students had two and a half hours to complete the exam in both the controlled and the uncontrolled machine exams.

All four courses lasted 7 weeks each. In the beginner courses, the students practice basic programming concepts such as variables, inputs and outputs, loops, and objects, and in the advanced courses, the students learn to use interfaces, inheritance, file handling, and user interfaces. The students complete multiple programming exercises every week. Keystroke data from the exercises is collected using the Test My Code -system, which provides an IDE integration for the purposes of data gathering as well as providing feedback to students as they work on the course assignments [23].

For each keystroke conducted within the environment that changes the code, timestamp, exercise information, course information, student information and the diff-information of the change is collected. As the system only records visible differences in the code, the data does not include special keys like the Shift- and Ctrl-keys. The students can also opt-out of data collection during the weekly exercises, but not in the machine exam.

3.2 Research Questions

Our research questions for this study are as follows:

RQ 1. How does the identification accuracy vary between data sets?

RQ 2. How does a controlled machine examination situation affect the identification accuracy?

RQ 3. How does an uncontrolled machine examination situation affect the identification accuracy?

To answer the first research question, we replicate the study by Longi et al. [14] to determine how identification accuracy varies between data sets. To answer the second and third research questions, we study how the exam situation affects identification accuracy using two different experiments.

In the first experiment, the students complete a mandatory machine examination at university facilities in a computer lab and their identity is verified. In the second experiment, the students were allowed to complete a similar mandatory machine examination at any location using any computer they wish to use and their identity is not verified.

3.3 Preprocessing

In the first experiment where we replicate the study by Longi et al. [14], we used the same filters as outlined in the original study to achieve as reliable replication as possible in Section 4.1. This means that students who typed less than 2000 characters during the first week of the course were not included in the experiments. For the machine exam experiments we only included data from the students who participated in the machine exam.

Following the process described in [14], we filtered out keystroke events that added more than one character to eliminate refactoring and copy-paste events. We used the same limitation on the typing event time; only typing events where the duration from the previous event was in the range of 10ms – 750ms were included.

3.4 Feature selection

In the original study by Longi et al. [14], the typing profiles were constructed using three different types of features: 1. the average latency between any two keys, i.e. the typing speed of the student, 2. single character latencies, i.e. the average latency from any key to a specific key, and 3. digraph latencies, i.e. the average latency from a specific key to a specific key. Since digraph latencies have been shown to work better than the other two types or a combined feature vector that includes all three types [14], we only use digraph latencies in our experiments.

In the replication experiments, we used the 100 most common digraphs for building the typing profiles similar to Longi et al. [14]. The most common digraphs were determined by sorting the digraphs by the median amount of times the students had used them in both the training and the test set. One digraph corresponds to one feature, and for a feature to be included from a specific student, the student had to have at least five instances of the digraph in the data. In the machine exam experiments, we calculated the differences in identification accuracy if the amount of features used to build the typing profile is varied. The results for one data set are presented in Figure 1. The figures for other data sets show similar diminishing returns in the increase of accuracy after around 25 features. The 25 most common digraphs for the same set are presented in Table 1. Since the digraphs are from a programming context, the most common ones include programming-related digraphs such as $i \rightarrow n$ and $n \rightarrow t$ from writing int, and the digraph used in creation of Java's code blocks { -> }.

3.5 Identification

The identification is based on comparing typing profiles estimated during the test context against personal typing profiles learned for each student during the course, using Eu-

clidean distance between the profiles for finding the nearest ones. A simple nearest-neighbor classifier would give the best estimate for the identity of the student, but for the purpose of verifying whether the student is who he or she claims to be it is not necessary to solve this full classification problem. Instead, it is sufficient that the correct training profile is within top k closest profiles (Longi et al. [14] called this *acceptance threshold*). The parameter k controls the balance between two types of error: Large k increases the accuracy for recognizing the true identities, but also makes it easier for false identities to pass the identification test. The probability for that is k/N, where N is the number of students. In the following experiments we will vary the choice of k, searching for the smallest k that has sufficiently high accuracy.

4. EXPERIMENTS AND RESULTS

In this section, we present the experiments we conducted to answer our research questions and their results.

4.1 Replication

To answer the question *"How does the identification accuracy vary between data sets?"*, we test identification accuracy with four data sets from different courses. Previous work has tested identification using data sets with around 200 students [14]. We include data sets with fewer students in our replication experiment to see how the accuracy of identification changes when there are fewer students.

The results of our replication experiments are shown in Table 2. There, data set 1 is from an introductory programming course in spring 2015. Data set 2 is from an advanced programming course in spring 2015. Data sets 3 and 4 are from an introductory and an advanced programming courses held during the autumn semester of 2015. In each data set, we used the first six weeks of the course for building the training set typing profiles and the last week of the course for building the test set typing profile. We achieve similar results having above 90% accuracy with every data set regardless of the acceptance threshold. The results indicate that identification can be conducted reliably even with smaller data sets.

4.2 Controlled Machine Exam Identification Accuracy

Next, we answer the question *"How does a controlled machine examination situation affect the identification accuracy?"*. Here, we use data from the spring of 2015 courses at the University of Helsinki, where the students had to complete a mandatory machine examination in a controlled environment at university premises. The results are presented in Table 3.

The students can be identified with quite high accuracy, even though the identification accuracy is significantly lower than the accuracy achieved in Section 4.1. Especially precise identification, i.e. identifying a student with a threshold of one, does not work as well in the exam as it does for a larger data set that consists of one week's worth of programming.

In addition to studying the identification accuracy in a controlled machine examination, we study the effect of feature quantity on identification accuracy to see how the feature count influences the identification accuracy. The results show that for identifying students precisely, i.e. with an acceptance threshold of one, 50 features seem to be enough as the increase in accuracy with 100 features is not signi-

Table 1: The 25 most common digraphs in a programming course which were used in building the typing profiles for that course.

from key	space	t	n	l	a	a	=	r	j	t	{	l	h	i	s	o	backspace	k	i	t	v	u	t	e	u
to key	=	u	t	u	r	t	space	i	a	h	}	i	i	n	t	u	backspace	u	s	a	a	k	space	t	t

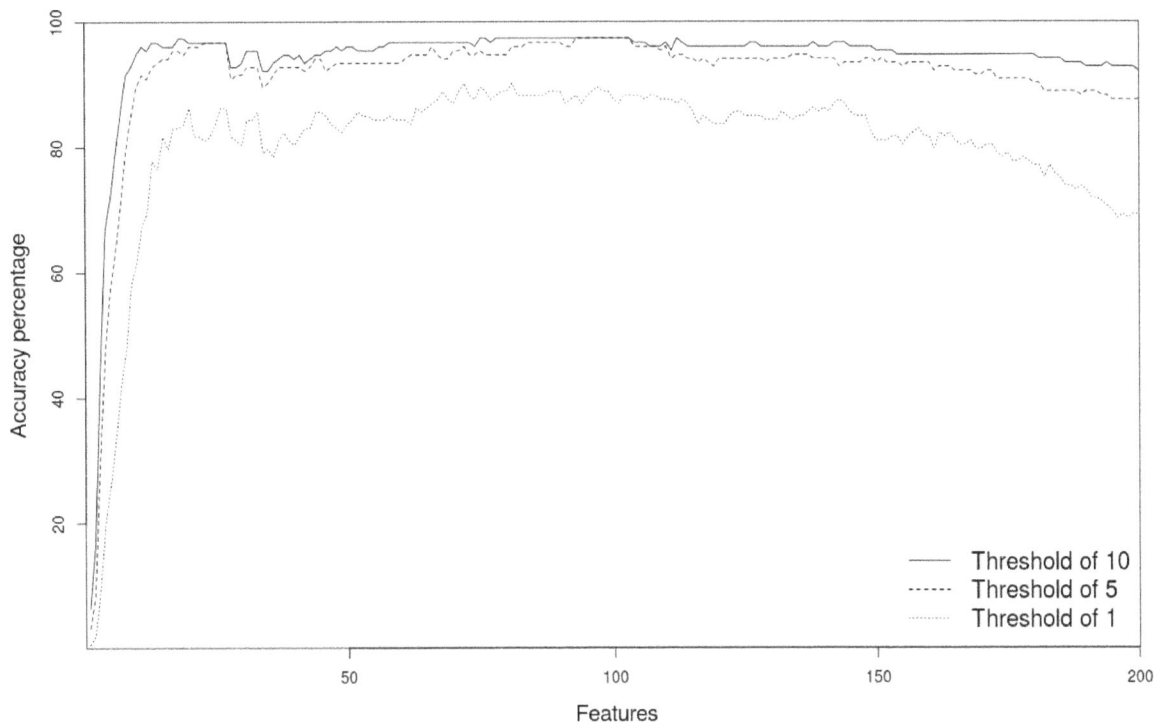

Figure 1: Smoothed identification accuracy plotted against the number of features. The threshold specifies the number of students that are considered to be correct for identification purposes. The figure shows that using around 25 features provides a good identification accuracy with all three thresholds and that the accuracy starts to deteriorate after around 150 features.

Table 2: Identification Accuracy with Different Data Sets

Data set	Students	Threshold 1	Threshold 5	Threshold 10
1	69	94.03%	97.02%	97.02%
2	61	93.22%	100%	100%
3	153	91.37%	97.84%	99.28%
4	128	94.64%	100%	100%

ficant enough to warrant increased complexity. If we allow the student to be within an acceptance threshold of 5 or 10, 25 features seem to suffice. In the advanced course, using 10 features seems to achieve a quite reliable identification accuracy of 95% with an acceptance threshold of five.

4.3 Uncontrolled Machine Exam Identification Accuracy

Last, we answer the question *How does an uncontrolled machine examination situation affect the identification ac-*

curacy?. In this experiment, we use data from the programming courses held at the University of Helsinki in the autumn of 2015. The results are presented in Table 4.

The results show that identification accuracy in an uncontrolled machine exam is slightly worse than in a controlled one. Regardless, the identification accuracy is still sufficiently high especially if we allow for an acceptance threshold of 10 and use at least 25 features.

Contrary to the results in 4.2, increasing the feature amount from 25 to 50 does not improve the identification accuracy significantly when the acceptance threshold is one. 25 features seem to suffice with any threshold to achieve a high identification accuracy. In the beginner course, having 50 features instead of 25 has a detrimental effect on accuracy, which is lower with all three threshold levels when using 50 features compared to using 25.

5. DISCUSSION

Previous work by Bennedsen and Caspersen [2] argues strongly for having machine examination on introductory

Table 3: Identification Accuracy in a Controlled Machine Exam

Beginner course with 69 students

Features	Threshold 1	Threshold 5	Threshold 10
10	44.93%	78.26%	89.86%
25	75.36%	92.75%	97.10%
50	86.89%	100%	100%
100	86.89%	100%	100%

Advanced course with 61 students

Features	Threshold 1	Threshold 5	Threshold 10
10	73.77%	95.08%	98.36%
25	85.25%	96.72%	98.36%
50	91.37%	97.84%	99.28%
100	94.64%	100%	100%

Table 4: Identification Accuracy in an Uncontrolled Machine Exam

Beginner course with 153 students

Features	Threshold 1	Threshold 5	Threshold 10
10	67.32%	91.50%	96.08%
25	86.28%	96.73%	96.73%
50	84.31%	93.46%	96.08%
100	86.93%	97.39%	97.39%

Advanced course with 128 students

Features	Threshold 1	Threshold 5	Threshold 10
10	68.75%	86.72%	91.41%
25	86.72%	92.97%	96.09%
50	87.50%	94.53%	96.09%
100	89.06%	94.53%	96.09%

programming courses. However, a big limitation for having machine examinations is the cost of overseeing students taking the exam. Our experiments show that it is possible to identify students in a machine examination based on their typing profiles, which means that the cost of machine examinations could be alleviated by having the students complete the exam remotely on their own devices, since cheating students could be identified based on their typing patterns. However, condemning a student for cheating solely based on their typing profile is not advisable, since there could be other factors that affect typing such as exam stress or a broken arm. Nevertheless, what could be done is that a flag could be raised in situations where the student is suspected of cheating based on their typing, and further analysis is performed manually. A limitation of our approach is that keystroke analysis can only identify cases where a student has someone else complete the exam for them, but not cases where the whole course is taken by someone else than the student. Since we can only observe typing, a student could cheat by having a friend help them during the exam, but do all the typing himself. However, at the same time, such behavior might likely also influence the typing patterns in the same way as changing from transcribed to free-text does [17].

In most of our experiments, an acceptance threshold of 5 seems to have about as good performance as a threshold of

10, and both perform significantly better than exact identification, i.e. using a threshold of one. There are a few exceptions though, which suggests that to be certain, a threshold of 10 should be used. With only 25 features and a threshold of 10, we can get over 95% identification accuracy with all data sets in our experiments. This means that in a real-world scenario, only 5% of the cases would be false positives, i.e. identifying a "cheating" student where there is no cheating. The acceptance threshold is still small enough to guarantee reasonably low false negative rate; for all contexts the probability of an impostor passing the identification test is below 10%.

The fact that no major difference in the identification accuracies between the uncontrolled examination and the controlled examination could indicate that there is some cheating, since hypothetically, the results should be better if the students are allowed to complete the exam on the same computer that they have used during the exercises – previous work has shown that changing keyboards had an adverse effect on identification [8]. However, there could be other unknown factors that influence the results. For example, the fairly low-dimensional typing profiles and relatively high acceptance threshold might make the identification algorithm robust for such changes.

To achieve optimal identification accuracy, at least 25 features should be used. This is less than used by Longi et al. [14], who used 100 features. In our experiments the accuracy gain for going from 25 to 50 features was only marginal, and that around 150 to 200 features the accuracy already drops visibly (see Figure 1). This discrepancy compared to the earlier study is to be expected since the training and test context differ more in our setup; the most frequent features are likely to be more robust against changes caused by different keyboard or other external factors. For highly controlled setups one could use also features that would be too fragile for the less controlled test situations in our experiments.

6. CONCLUSIONS AND FUTURE WORK

In this work, we explored how students' typing patterns could be used to authenticate them in a computer-based examination. We were able to identify programmers from their typing patterns. This replicates the study by Longi et al. [14] as well as shows that identification is possible with data sets containing a smaller number of students. We also showed that it is possible to identify students in a machine exam based on typing profiles built with exercise data. Identification in an exam setting does not work as well as identification of students on the last week of introductory programming courses, but shows promise that even though the accuracy is lower, it might be enough to catch cheaters in computerized exams.

We also observed that in all of our data sets, the optimal amount of features was around 25. After 25 features, identification accuracy did not improve significantly, and even deteriorated when more than about 150 features were included in the typing profiles. We therefore argue that should keystroke analysis be used in identifying students in a machine examination, the typing profiles should be built considering the 25 most common digraphs to avoid considering features that are too fragile to work in different test settings. To get reliable identification accuracy, we furthermore suggest that students should be identified using the acceptance threshold method [14] and that the acceptance threshold should be 10, i.e. a student is not considered to have cheated if his or her profile is in the top ten closest samples in the training set. This suggestion is valid for student populations of roughly 50-150 students; for smaller courses the threshold needs to be lowered.

For future work, we are interested in researching in more detail how participant and feature quantities affect identification. Here, we only showed that identification is possible in data sets with fewer than a hundred students. We hope to examine how identification accuracy changes when there are hundreds or thousands of students. We are also hopeful that keystroke analysis is included in cheating prevention in machine exams since the results presented here indicate that it is possible to identify students in a machine examination situation. We are also looking for approaches to anonymize the data so that datasets such as ours could be published without privacy concerns.

Acknowledgements

The research was supported in part by the Academy of Finland (project 1266969 and COIN Centre of Excellence) and the Finnish Funding Agency for Innovation (under project Re:Know).

7. REFERENCES

[1] Coursera signature track. https://www.coursera.org/signature/. Accessed: 2015-07-31.

[2] J. Bennedsen and M. E. Caspersen. Assessing process and product: A practical lab exam for an introductory programming course 1. *Innovation in Teaching and Learning in Information and Computer Sciences*, 6(4):183–202, 2007.

[3] F. Bergadano, D. Gunetti, and C. Picardi. User authentication through keystroke dynamics. *ACM Trans. Inf. Syst. Secur.*, 5(4):367–397, Nov. 2002.

[4] S. Cho, C. Han, D. H. Han, and H.-I. Kim. Web-based keystroke dynamics identity verification using neural network. *Journal of organizational computing and electronic commerce*, 10(4):295–307, 2000.

[5] M. Dick, J. Sheard, C. Bareiss, J. Carter, D. Joyce, T. Harding, and C. Laxer. Addressing student cheating: Definitions and solutions. *SIGCSE Bull.*, 35(2):172–184, June 2002.

[6] P. Dowland and S. Furnell. A long-term trial of keystroke profiling using digraph, trigraph and keyword latencies. In Y. Deswarte, F. Cuppens, S. Jajodia, and L. Wang, editors, *Security and Protection in Information Processing Systems*, volume 147 of *IFIP - The International Federation for Information Processing*, pages 275–289. Springer, 2004.

[7] R. S. Gaines, W. Lisowski, S. J. Press, and N. Shapiro. Authentication by keystroke timing: Some preliminary results. Technical report, 1980.

[8] D. Gunetti and C. Picardi. Keystroke analysis of free text. *ACM Trans. Inf. Syst. Secur.*, 8(3):312–347, Aug. 2005.

[9] S. Haider, A. Abbas, and A. Zaidi. A multi-technique approach for user identification through keystroke dynamics. In *Systems, Man, and Cybernetics, 2000 IEEE International Conference on*, volume 2, pages 1336–1341 vol.2, 2000.

[10] R. Joyce and G. Gupta. Identity authentication based on keystroke latencies. *Communications of the ACM*, 33(2):168–176, 1990.

[11] M. Karnan, M. Akila, and N. Krishnaraj. Biometric personal authentication using keystroke dynamics: A review. *Applied Soft Computing*, 11(2):1565 – 1573, 2011. The Impact of Soft Computing for the Progress of Artificial Intelligence.

[12] K. S. Killourhy and R. A. Maxion. Free vs. transcribed text for keystroke-dynamics evaluations. In *Proceedings of the 2012 Workshop on Learning from Authoritative Security Experiment Results*, LASER '12, pages 1–8, New York, NY, USA, 2012. ACM.

[13] J. Leinonen, K. Longi, A. Klami, and A. Vihavainen. Automatic inference of programming performance and experience from typing patterns. In *Proceedings of the 47th ACM Technical Symposium on Computing Science Education*, SIGCSE '16, pages 132–137, New York, NY, USA, 2016. ACM.

[14] K. Longi, J. Leinonen, H. Nygren, J. Salmi, A. Klami, and A. Vihavainen. Identification of programmers from typing patterns. In *Proceedings of the 15th Koli Calling Conference on Computing Education Research*, pages 60–67. ACM, 2015.

[15] J. Monaco, N. Bakelman, S.-H. Cha, and C. Tappert. Recent advances in the development of a long-text-input keystroke biometric authentication system for arbitrary text input. In *Intelligence and Security Informatics Conference (EISIC), 2013 European*, pages 60–66, Aug 2013.

[16] J. Monaco, J. Stewart, S.-H. Cha, and C. Tappert. Behavioral biometric verification of student identity in online course assessment and authentication of authors in literary works. In *Biometrics: Theory, Applications and Systems (BTAS), 2013 IEEE Sixth International Conference on*, pages 1–8, Sept 2013.

[17] F. Monrose and A. Rubin. Authentication via keystroke dynamics. In *Proceedings of the 4th ACM Conference on Computer and Communications Security*, CCS '97, pages 48–56, New York, NY, USA, 1997. ACM.

[18] A. Peacock, X. Ke, and M. Wilkerson. Typing patterns: A key to user identification. *IEEE Security & Privacy*, 2(5):40–47, 2004.

[19] J. Sheard, M. Dick, S. Markham, I. Macdonald, and M. Walsh. Cheating and plagiarism: perceptions and practices of first year it students. In *ACM SIGCSE Bulletin*, volume 34, pages 183–187. ACM, 2002.

[20] J. Sheard, Simon, A. Carbone, D. D'Souza, and M. Hamilton. Assessment of programming: Pedagogical foundations of exams. In *Proceedings of the 18th ACM Conference on Innovation and Technology in Computer Science Education*, ITiCSE '13, pages 141–146, New York, NY, USA, 2013. ACM.

[21] J. Stewart, J. Monaco, S.-H. Cha, and C. Tappert. An investigation of keystroke and stylometry traits for authenticating online test takers. In *Biometrics (IJCB), 2011 International Joint Conference on*, pages 1–7, Oct 2011.

[22] R. C. Thomas, A. Karahasanovic, and G. E. Kennedy. An investigation into keystroke latency metrics as an indicator of programming performance. In *Proceedings of the 7th Australasian Conference on Computing Education - Volume 42*, ACE '05, pages 127–134, Darlinghurst, Australia, Australia, 2005. Australian Computer Society, Inc.

[23] A. Vihavainen, T. Vikberg, M. Luukkainen, and M. Pärtel. Scaffolding students' learning using test my code. In *Proceedings of the 18th ACM Conference on Innovation and Technology in Computer Science Education*, ITiCSE '13, pages 117–122, New York, NY, USA, 2013. ACM.

[24] M. Villani, C. Tappert, G. Ngo, J. Simone, H. Fort, and S.-H. Cha. Keystroke biometric recognition studies on long-text input under ideal and application-oriented conditions. In *Computer Vision and Pattern Recognition Workshop, 2006. CVPRW '06. Conference on*, pages 39–39, June 2006.

[25] E. Yu and S. Cho. Ga-svm wrapper approach for feature subset selection in keystroke dynamics identity verification. In *Neural Networks, 2003. Proceedings of the International Joint Conference on*, volume 3, pages 2253–2257, July 2003.

Latin American Perspectives and the IT2017 Curricular Guidelines

John Impagliazzo
Panel Moderator
Engineering and Applied Sciences
Hofstra University
Hempstead, New York 11549 USA
+1.631.513.2833
John.Impagliazzo@hofstra.edu

Ernesto Cuadros-Vargas
Latin American Center
on Computing (CLEI)
San Pablo Catholic Univ,
Arequipa, Perú
+51.958.339.127
ecuadros@spc.org.pe

Gonzalo Begazo Escobedo
Chazki Corporation
Av del Sur 213 Dpt 102
Chacarilla, Surco
Lima 33, Perú
+51.971.505.759
gonzalo@chazki.com

Juan José Miranda del Solar
APESOFT/Magia.Digital
Calle General Borgoño 1189
Miraflores, Lima, Perú
+ 51.1.441.7197
jjmiranda@magia.digital

Mihaela Sabin
Computing Technology
Department
University of New Hampshire
Manchester, New Hampshire
03101 USA
+1.603.641.4144
mihaela.sabin@unh.edu

Barbara Viola
Assoc. of Information Technology
Professionals (AITP)
Viotech Solutions Inc.
1111 Route 110, Suite 362
Farmingdale, New York 11735 USA
+1.631.630.4640
bviola@viotechsolutions.com

ABSTRACT

The term 'information technology' has many meanings for various stakeholders and continues to evolve. This discussion presents an overview of the developing curricular guidelines for rigorous, high quality, bachelor's degree programs in information technology (IT), called IT2017. Panel participants will focus on Latin American academic and industry perspectives on IT undergraduate education. Discussion will seek to ascertain commonalities and differences between the current draft IT2017 report and perspectives from Latino/a professional and academic communities. It also addresses ways in which this endeavor contrasts with current practices in Latin America industry and academia.

1. BACKGROUND

The ACM/IEEE-CS effort to update the IT2008 Curriculum Guidelines for Undergraduate Degree Programs in Information Technology [3], currently tagged as the IT2017 report, focuses on being a forward thinking document to capture both the current and future changes in information technology (IT). The report is in draft form and is accessible for public review and comment [5].

Information technology means different things for different stakeholders. These stakeholders include industry and business sectors, academic institutions, professional and scientific societies, and students graduating from high school or technical schools interested in pursuing undergraduate degrees in IT. The academia

and industry dimensions are compounded by geographic factors. High-tech professional organizations have international membership and IT degree programs are becoming omnipresent as IT industry advances continue at a fast pace worldwide.

2. PRESENTATION

This panel discussion addresses the content of the pending IT2017 report and the ways it reflects industry needs within the context of academia. It is based on research results addressed in a paper titled "Multinational Perspectives on Information Technology from Academia and Industry" [6]. The paper addressed issues such as the commonalities and differences in IT curricular frameworks, pathways into and through IT education programs, and the future of IT.

This paper also addressed the global context of information technology by providing several meanings of information technology. The definition from the 2008 IT Model Curriculum states,

> "Information Technology (IT) in its broadest sense encompasses all aspects of computing technology. IT, as an academic discipline, is concerned with issues related to advocating for users and meeting their needs within an organizational and societal context through the selection, creation, application, integration and administration of computing technologies." [3]

This and other definitions convey the all-inclusive, ever-expanding and integrative role of IT by organizations in our society. This presentation discusses the IT2017 report within the context of IT education in Latin America.

3. GLOBAL PERSPECTIVES

The notion of IT could mean different things around the world. In terms of business, research into various technology hubs worldwide seems to confirm these basic definitions. Europe, for example, tends to use the term information and communication technologies (ICT). In the Far East, information technology covers a broad spectrum of industries such as hardware, software, electronics, semiconductors, internet, telecom equipment, e-commerce, and unlimited computing services.

Some Latin American countries such as Mexico view IT as a vehicle or driver for a technological and communications revolution [4]. In Brazil, IT becomes a way to create a competitive and innovative environment to promote economic development of the country [1]. Chile has already created a Ministry of Science and Technology to "lay the foundations to compete as a country on an equal footing with the rest of the world" [2].

4. PRESENTERS
The following individuals constitute the presenters for this panel discussion. A brief biography accompanies their listing.

John Impagliazzo is Professor Emeritus from Hofstra University in New York. John is a member of the executive committee of the IT2017 task group; he also is the chair of the computer engineering curriculum project CE2016. John has a long history devoted to computing education including former editor-in-chief of the publication *ACM Inroads* as well as an active member of the Computing Curricula Overview Report (CC2005) and the 2004 computer engineering report. John has published eighteen books and has evaluated over seventy-five computing programs worldwide.

Ernesto Cuadros-Vargas is full time professor and Head of the School of Computer Science at the San Pablo Catholic University in Arequipa, Perú. He was also a member of the ACM/IEEE-CS Computing Curricula for Computer Science (CS2013). He is now executive secretary of the Latin American Center on Computing (CLEI). Since 2001, Cuadros-Vargas has been the initiator and most active contributor of the initiative led by a number of professionals in Perú, to bring international standards, especially the ACM/IEEE-CS computing curricula into the higher education in computing in the country.

Juan José Miranda is founder and current project director and international business director of Magia Comunicaciones S.A., a Magia.Digital company. He has over nineteen years of experience by providing consulting and business solutions using information technologies, owns successful brands such as Aurix Software Solutions, Pariwana Studios, and Inka Madness. He is president of the Peruvian Association of Software and Technologies - APESOFT. He is professor of Digital Projects, Digital Media and Technology and the Internet at the Universidad de Lima and the University of Science and Arts of Latin America (UCAL). He is the director of First Tuesday, a startup of the Peruvian initiative to support entrepreneurship. He is a member of the Technical Standards in Software Engineering and Information Systems Committee of INDECOPI.

Gonzalo Begazo Escobedo received a business administration and accounting degree from the Universidad del Pacifico in Lima, Peru and a MBA from Cornell University in New York. He is a member of advisory boards for several universities throughout Peru. Gonzalo brings an industry, investor, and startup perspectives to the discussion. He is the co-founder of Chazki, an urban logistics technology startup; previously, he was finance director at Google by managing the global financial aspects of the company at its headquarters in Mountain View, California. He also worked for Microsoft, Goldman Sachs, IBM and Digeo, a company of Paul Allen - co-founder of Microsoft. Included in the 2010 and 2011 lists of the 100 most influential Hispanics in technology in the United States released by HITEC and the top 100 most influential Hispanics published by Hispanic Magazine's Technology Engineering in 2011. He is an angel investor and advisor of cognicor.com, plazapoints.com, Yump.com, cinepapaya.com, pick1.com and Altodot.com, and mentor of Wayra Peru (Telefonica's Incubator).

Mihaela Sabin is the Chair of the ACM/IEEE-CS IT2017 Task Group. She has been a long-standing member of ACM SIGITE and currently serves as its Vice-Chair for Education. Mihaela is an associate professor of computer science at the University of New Hampshire (UNH), and has been involved in curriculum development and revision of undergraduate and graduate programs in computer science and information technology at UNH. Her research is in computing education, open source content and development, and teacher professional learning.

Barbara Viola is President and Chief Executive Officer of Viotech Solutions, a successful information technology placement company in New York. Barbara is a member of the IT2017 task group and coordinates the group's work as its project manager. As immediate past president of the Association of Information Technology Professionals (AITP), Barbara has bridged the gap between industry profession practitioners and members from academic communities. She also leads a vibrant AITP chapter for Long Island in New York and she is the chair of the newly formed New York Metro chapter of ACM.

5. ACKNOWLEDGEMENTS
The presenters extend their thanks to the ACM Education Board for its support for this important project.

6. REFERENCES
[1] Brazilian Association for Information and Communications Technology. 2014. Associations unite "For a Digital and Competitive Brazil" (August 20114). http://www.brasscom.com.br/brasscom/Ingles/detNoticia.php?codArea=2&codCategoria=54&codNoticia=794. Accessed 2016 Jan 15.

[2] How does a ministry ICT change the map? 2015. ACTI - Chilean Association of Information Technology (June 2015). http://www.acti.cl/. Accessed 2016 Jan 55.

[3] Lunt, B.M., Ekstrom, J.J., Gorka, S., Hislop, G., Kamali, R., Lawson, E., LeBlanc, R., Miller, J. and Reichgelt, H. 2008. IT 2008: Curriculum Guidelines for Undergraduate Degree Programs in Information Technology; https://www.acm.org//education/curricula/IT2008%20Curriculum.pdf. Accessed 2016 Jan 15.

[4] Mexico is an Information Technology Powerhouse. 2011. The Catalyst (October 2011). http://thecatalist.org/2011/10/mexico-is-an-information-technology-powerhouse/; Accessed 2016 Jan 16.

[5] Sabin, M. et al. 2016. "Information Technology Curricula 2017" draft report; http://it2017.acm.org/. Accessed 2016 Jan 18.

[6] Sabin, M. et al. 2016. "Multinational Perspectives on Information Technology from Academia and Industry." Working Group 6, Proceedings of the ITiCSE Conference 2015, Vilnius, Lithuania.

Using Fast Model-Based Fault Localisation to Aid Students in Self-Guided Program Repair and to Improve Assessment

Geoff Birch
University of Southampton
gb2g10@ecs.soton.ac.uk

Bernd Fischer
Stellenbosch University
bfischer@cs.sun.ac.za

Michael Poppleton
University of Southampton
mrp@ecs.soton.ac.uk

ABSTRACT

Computer science instructors need to manage the rapid improvement of novice programmers through teaching, self-guided learning, and assessment. Appropriate feedback, both generic and personalised, is essential to facilitate student progress. Automated feedback tools can also accelerate the marking process and allow instructors to dedicate more time to other forms of tuition and students to progress more rapidly. Massive Open Online Courses rely on automated tools for both self-guided learning and assessment.

Fault localisation takes a significant part of debugging time. Popular spectrum-based methods do not narrow the potential fault locations sufficiently to assist novices. We therefore use a fast and precise model-based fault localisation method and show how it can be used to improve self-guided learning and accelerate assessment. We apply this to a large selection of actual student coursework submissions, providing more precise localisation within a sub-second response time. We show this using small test suites, already provided in the coursework management system, and on expanded test suites, demonstrating scaling. We also show compliance with test suites does not predictably score a class of "almost correct" submissions, which our tool highlights.

Keywords

Debugging; Model-Based Fault Localisation; Student Code Submissions; Assessment; Self-Training

1. INTRODUCTION

Introductory programming courses typically require instructors to assess a large number of small programs by novice programmers. Many of these programs contain errors, ranging from small mistakes to complete design and implementation failures, reflecting the students' misunderstanding of the task or their solution attempt. With limited resources the best learning outcomes are achieved if students are (in the former case) automatically directed towards the locations of their mistakes to allow self-guided repairs, so that the instructors can focus (in the latter case) on addressing fundamental misunderstandings. However, existing basic assessment tools (such as Ceilidh [2], ASSYST [14], and BOSS [16]) based on simple

ITiCSE '16, July 09 - 13, 2016, Arequipa, Peru

© 2016 Copyright held by the owner/author(s). Publication rights licensed to ACM.
ISBN 978-1-4503-4231-5/16/07...$15.00

DOI: http://dx.doi.org/10.1145/2899415.2899433

compilation tests, test suites, or model solutions do not provide the detailed feedback necessary for self-guided repairs and do not support instructors in quickly separating solutions with small mistakes from complete failures. Compilation tests do not give any feedback for syntactically correct programs, test suites can give misleading results if programs contain simple errors that affect a large number of test cases, and model solutions cannot account for the variability of student programs.

In this paper we address these issues and describe a fast and accurate fully automated fault localisation tool for C programs and demonstrate its application to a corpus of student programs. Our tool assumes that the programs are specified only by test suites and returns a list of source code locations where a single assignment fault can be repaired to bring the program into compliance with the entire test suite. Such weak specifications make accurate localisation challenging: spectrum-based fault localisation methods [37] are unable to sufficiently narrow down the list of possible fault locations [24], while more precise model-based methods [10] suffer from high run-times. We have recently presented [3] an intelligent search algorithm to scale up model-based fault localisation, but demonstrated it only on a single localisation benchmark. It is thus an open question whether model-based fault localisation can be exploited in aiding novice programmers, in particular with debugging, and in improving the assessment of their solutions; more precisely, we investigate the following research questions:

RQ1 Does model-based fault localisation scale to large submission databases of real-world student code? Is it fast enough, and does it accurately pin-point fault locations, given typical test suites?

RQ2 Does model-based fault localisation improve over the more common spectrum-based methods?

RQ3 Can model-based fault localisation improve automated grading based on functional correctness over test suites?

Our experiments with real-world student code from an existing submissions database are encouraging. Our tool can indeed accurately pin-point fault locations and so allow students to surmount the final hurdle to completing writing of source code that fully complies with a test suite without requiring advanced debugging skills. The short list of locations where an assignment repair is possible, provided by our tool, can aid students in pinpointing improvements before they resubmit their code. The run-times of our tool are competitive with the common, fast spectrum-based localisation techniques while providing significantly more accurate fault localisation, which is of high value to novice programmers. This also allows our tool to work with existing coursework submission systems and workflows, for both self-training and grading, even at the scale required by Massive Open Online Courses (MOOCs).

Our tool also provides instructors with automated assistance detecting submissions which would provide perfect compliance with a single assignment edit (e.g. incrementing a counter before returning it as the final value) but fail the test suite. This will allow test suite-based automated graders to identify submissions whose quality is being underestimated by this functional assessment method; repair information also provided by our tool can help instructors manually grading the submission. We show that real-world student submissions which are a single assignment edit away from full compliance with a test suite are not provided with a fair mark by grading against that test suite.

2. RELATED WORK

Novice programmers can be divided into three classes [23, 35]: *stoppers*, who give up; *tinkerers*, who appear to modify their code at random; and *movers*, who are already able to engage with feedback to make progress. Even though the movers already demonstrate debugging skills beyond the average of their cohort, all three classes still need high-quality, novice-friendly debugging feedback to allow a self-guided refinement of their solutions towards a correct answer. Enhanced (syntax) error messages appear to be ineffectual in this respect [8], but when students are given hints regarding failures over a test suite, their effort increases compared to students not given hints [6]. On-demand programming feedback provides students the motivation to iterate on submissions [20]. Moreover, a correlation has been found between sessions where students were provided with feedback from a test suite and sessions that improved the student's score [31], indicating this assisted self-training. However, despite its benefits, students are somewhat resistant to a pure test-driven development (TDD) approach [5], as for example embodied in the Web-CAT [9] submission system, partly because TDD also requires expertise in developing test suites as a prerequisite to demonstrating programming ability.

A significant part of the debugging process is finding the location where the file needs to be changed to repair the fault [34]. Tools like AskIgor [38] provide cause chains to assist programmers in localising faults from test failures. While this lowers the threshold, it still requires too much debugging expertise for novices. Our tool instead provides a list of locations where a single assignment fault can be repaired to bring the program into compliance with the entire test suite. Giving tinkerers viable repair locations massively reduces the mutation space they are exploring. Giving movers viable repair locations directs their effort, allowing faster debugging times [22]. This should increase the chance that both will realise the repair and convert a program failure into a learning event.

For programmers to retain their status of movers, they must be provided with feedback in terms of suitable scaffolding to overcome progress stalls and achieve an otherwise unattainable goal [36]. Tinkerers who are unable to be scaffolded into movers will eventually become stoppers due to lack of progress [35]. Since the absolute number of locations shown before the actual repair site is critical to allowing progress before programmer interest drop-off generates stoppers [22], the provided list of locations to investigate must be short. Unfortunately, widespread spectrum-based fault localisation methods are unable to provide sufficiently short candidate lists. Pham et al. [24] tested Tarantula and Ochiai tools and on three variants of an algorithm, with an average length of 13 statements, they found over 9 statements shared the same top suspiciousness ranking. Localisation thus becomes a function of luck.

However, the feedback cannot be too prescriptive or too detailed. Complete program synthesis repair tools such as Auto Grader [29]

remove all debugging or repair self-training from the process, trivialising the contribution and so learning of the student. Our tool bridges the gap between standard error reports, which many students lack the expertise to use, and fully automated repair suites.

Automated submission and assessment systems deliver immediate feedback to students for self-training, which is enjoyed by students and feeds into improvements throughout courses that use it [17]. They include tools to help accelerate grading of final submissions, providing both self-training and grading benefits [32]. Such assessment tools take many forms. Ceilidh [2] uses regular expressions to specify the test output of compiled student code, providing more freedom to define the expected answers than traditional test suites. ASSYST [14] contains style and complexity analysis tools that provide metrics beyond test suite correctness, and evaluate non-functional aspects such as code quality and efficiency. FrenchPress [4] focuses on analysis of code style and design, attempting to isolate errors only made by novices in Java programming. AutoGrader [12] requires students to program to a public interface, allowing whitebox testing at the cost of restricting the form of the code submissions. Pex4Fun [33] uses automated test case generation to guide student submissions and to scale to MOOC capacities. This approach requires students to demonstrate advanced debugging skills. Scheme-Robo [28] compares the program source to a model answer, assuming that Scheme's functional design limits the variability of meaningfully different programs that correctly answer the question.

Student code exhibits a wide range of program forms and performance characteristics [30, 21, 18, 26] and students do not necessarily work towards solutions that are similar to an instructor-authored model answer. It is thus inadvisable to only provide feedback directing students towards model answers. Vujošević-Janičić et al. [15] use a static verifier as well as test suites when student solutions do not match the control flow of the model answer. A weighting system then mixes these feedback components to guide students to repair code errors and transform the structure towards that of the model answer or to grade the submission. ASys [13] attempts to overcome the limitation of functional testing using test suites with a customisable semi-automated grading system. Marking templates describe extensions to the test suite for a question, generating new tests specific to the student submission that verify each assessment property defined in the template. In their use on campus, 48% of the grading work was automatically handled by the tools. Interestingly, most of the marks difference between the group using ASys and the control group going through traditional grading was accountable to errors made in the manual marking process. Similarly, our tool provides added feedback beyond functional grading using test suites, identifying student programs which "almost" conform to the question requirements and can be fixed with a single assignment edit. Our tool can also enrich existing systems like ASys, providing this alternative test of closeness to compliance when using test suites in other contexts.

Instructors spending several minutes per student per submission for feedback [19] cannot scale to MOOC environments with thousands of students per course. To test the scaling of an automated hint system to these environments, AutoTeach [1] provides students with access to a hint system which uncovers partial model answers to assist with learning. Such systems, while scaling very well, strictly constrain students to working towards a single model answer. However, the deployment of test suite grading for MOOCs is gaining traction [25] with the drawbacks of formatting issues (3.2% of submissions were awarded zero marks due to formatting issues, not functional failures) and failure to detect almost-correct submissions weighed against the benefits of providing some form

```
                          int t = symbolic();                    int t = symbolic();
/* ... */                 /* ... */                              /* ... */
int v = a*b;              int v = (t==5) ? symbolic() : a*b;     int v = (t==5) ? symbolic() : a*b;
/* ... */                 /* ... */                              /* ... */
assert(o==d); //added spec  assert(o==d);                        assume(o==d);
exit(0);                   exit(0);                              assert(0); exit(0);
```

Figure 1: Program Transform Process: (a) Code with Test Case Spec; (b) Model of Code; (c) Inverted Model

of code assessment, as manual grading is not viable. Such issues can be reduced via importing more advanced tools into the grading system, assuming their run-time cost can be kept low enough for MOOC execution.

3. DATA SET

We use a data set of around 30k passing and 150k failing Java and Python programs collected by the automated assessment system of the University of Auckland [26]. These programs were written by students to answer 1693 different Computer Science coursework questions. We translated the programs into a C-representation using a simple converter that was designed to retain the style and functionality of programs without translating any detailed differences between the languages, such as language-specific handling of integer overflows. This translation would allow the mapping back of locations to the original Java or Python source code, although our model-based downstream components currently only reason within the specifications of the C programming language they have been translated into. We consider the translated programs in C to be the corpus on which we are testing the efficacy of our tool. Our methods are more directly applicable for native reasoning on Java or Python programs by using suitable downstream components designed for those languages.

We rejected programs that produced translation failures (typically due to unsupported standard library calls), that use floating-point arithmetic (which is not yet supported for symbolic exploration by our downstream components), that comprise less than three assignments (to avoid trivial localisation tasks), or that Klee or GCov (which we use as downstream components) could not process. We then analysed the data set to identify pairs where a student had submitted a failing program which, after a single assignment edit, was later found in the database passing the full test suite. This yielded 304 pairs. These programs contain an average of 5 assignments in 11 statements (as counted by GCov).

We ran a script to analyse each provided test suite (averaging 7.8 tests per pair) and generated new test suites that randomly picked inputs within an order of magnitude of the existing values. The passing program from the code pair was used as oracle to establish desired output values. These large test suites average 154 tests per pair, with 80 failing.

4. METHOD

Model-based fault localisation [27] is the application of model-based diagnosis methods [7] to programs. It involves three main steps: (i) the construction of a logical model from the original program; (ii) the symbolic analysis of this model; and (iii) mapping any faults found in the model back to program locations. The approach to model-based fault localisation used by our tool is to transform the program so that a symbolic program verification tool can be reused for all three steps.

Our tool is fed a C program and a set of failing test cases written in the form of an input and a desired output. The worked example of Figure 1 gives excerpts from a C program that, for the fifth as-

signment, declares an int v equal to a*b and eventually assigns the final value to int o.

Each test case is taken as a search branch to be explored for potential assignment locations. The input and desired output are encoded into the program via an expanded argv/stdin. In this encoding the desired output is assigned to d (not shown). String input and output is also possible by iterating over an output char array, checking it against the chars that would be created by stdout commands before they were transformed into these checks. Every assignment in the encoded C program is modified to allow the symbolic program verification tool to exhaustively explore different assignment values when that location is activated, creating the program model. In the example this is done with a toggle variable t which selects the location to explore with the symbolic call in Figure 1b. Finally, this model is "inverted" [10] which forces the verifier to suppress any assertion failures in the original model but generate new counter-examples if the program can terminate normally without violating these assertions. This is achieved by converting assertions to assumptions in the model and replacing any point where the program ends successfully with a new failing assertion, shown in Figure 1c.

This complete transformation effectively searches the model to find assignments which are possible repair locations. That is, every such assignment can be edited to a symbolic value which corrects the flow of *one* failing test case and results in the desired output being generated, i.e. not violating the assume(o==d) statement in the worked example's inverted model. Assignments where a symbolic value is found for *every* failing test case are returned as repair locations.

The localisation process effectively generates a look-up table at each returned location that will repair all failing test cases. For each failing test case, the alternative value of the assignments will be reported (via a counter-example) for each location flagged by this process. The flagging process means the chosen assignment values lead to the end of the program without failure of the original specification. All passing test cases define their own correct values for the assignments (they already execute within the test suite specification). So this look-up table is a genuine repair for the full test suite, albeit repairing only from the test cases provided as specification.

A multiprocess design that takes advantage of modern consumer processor architectures is used to accelerate the process [3]. Each test case is dispatched as a task to a worker pool with any pruning percolated to future tasks. The symbolic execution load is minimised by two features. Firstly, intelligent pruning of the search space, i.e. not searching known-unrepairable assignments in subsequent test cases after the search has started. Secondly, minimising the disruption of an intractable (a risk of model-checking programs) or slow search branch by monitoring and evicting tasks to be retried later after the search space has been pruned.

The end result of this method is that we generate a genuine list of repair locations as specified by test cases for any repair that could be expressed as a look-up table for the right-hand side of an assignment, within the limits of symbolic analyser accuracy.

5. EXPERIMENTS AND DISCUSSION

5.1 Experimental Setup

We generated all results on a 3.1GHz Core i5-2400. Our tool, using the Klee 1.1 symbolic analyser, operates as described in section 4. Spectrum-based fault localisation results using Ochiai and Tarantula formulas [37] are provided by Hawk-Eye [11]. As the rank of the fault location did not vary between formulas with this data set, both are referred to simply as the Hawk-Eye result.

5.2 Evaluation Strategy

Localisation tools typically produce a ranked list of locations, based on the generated suspiciousness value of each location. The rank is calculated using Hawk-Eye's middle-line strategy, ranking equally suspicious statements with the mid-point rank. For example, statements with suspiciousness (0.1, 0.4, 0.8, 0.4, 0.4) are ranked (5th, 3rd, 1st, 3rd, 3rd). Results from our model-based tool have been converted from an unranked list using the same middle-line strategy (where all locations returned are given a suspiciousness of 1.0 and all others a suspiciousness of 0.0).

Localisation performance is reported in the average percentage of other locations that will be searched before the fault is found when iterating over the locations in rank order. So in the above example, if the second statement is the fault location then the ranked localisation scores 50%. If the first statement (which is ranked last) was the fault then this would score 100%, the worst possible score, indicating every other returned statement would be searched before the fault was reached. A score near 0%, indicating very few locations ranked above the location used by the student to repair the submission in the database, means fewer instances of the debugging process stalling before repair synthesis can begin. Spectrum-based methods have been shown to provide rankings insufficient for novices [22] or even be unable to discriminate between most locations [24].

5.3 Results for Original Test Suites

On the 304 failing student submissions and the instructor-authored test suites, our tool returns the faulty assignment after, on average, only 16% of other assignments. In Figure 2a the p.p. difference to the spectrum-based results (i.e. percentage points closer to a perfect 0% localisation) is plotted for every student submission, ordered by relative advantage. Positive differences indicate our tool's advantage. Hawk-Eye, on this data set, ranks the statement the student later used to repair the program after an average of 63% of other statements, 47 percentage points adrift (dashed line). No correlation was found between the program size and the comparative performance of our tool compared with Hawk-Eye.

On average, Hawk-Eye is provided eight test cases for each submission which are used to rank eleven statements. Our tool is provided with an average of four failing test cases, due to the small test suite size, and localises over the average of five assignments in each submission. These localisations are produced in an average of 0.3 seconds per submission by both our tool and Hawk-Eye. 254 times our tool was a fraction of a second ahead, 48 times Hawk-Eye was a fraction of a second ahead, and twice our tool hit too many pathological cases to adapt and only provided results at the tool's ten second time-out.

Our tool regularly pin-pointed the assignment later used by the student to bring the submission into compliance with the test suite. 125 of the 304 student submissions were returned from our tool with only that assignment flagged, the ideal result [22]. All other assignments were eliminated as viable repair candidates for the test suite specification. The limited number of failing test cases did not hinder our tool on this sample of short, real-world student programs.

When looking at those 125 submissions, Hawk-Eye ranked the repair statement after an average of 65% of other statements. Only 15 of those submissions provided the repair in the first third of the ranked list. The best ranking from Hawk-Eye for the statement the student used to repair the program was after 25% of other statements.

This comparison strongly supports the use of our tool for assisting students in repairing single-assignment faults in small program submissions, even when only specified by a very small test suite. When a student has made a mistake on constructing an assignment in an otherwise solid submission, an expensive debugging process may be averted by use of this feedback.

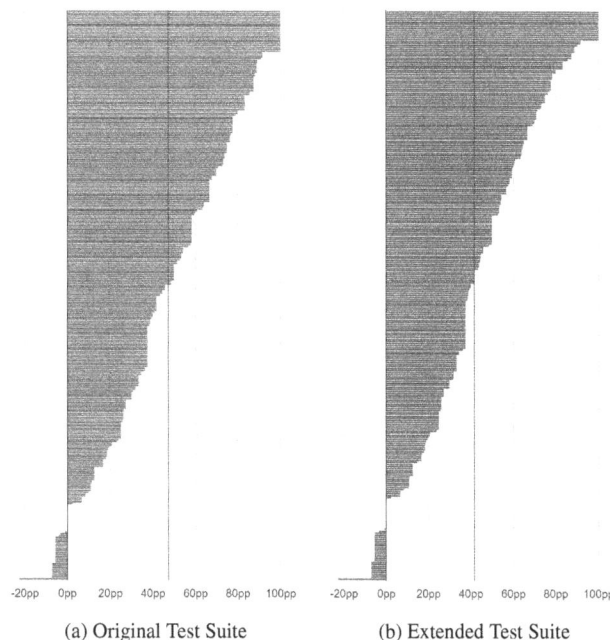

(a) Original Test Suite   (b) Extended Test Suite

Figure 2: Comparison of Results: Our Tool vs Hawk-Eye

5.4 Results for Extended Test Suites

When the large test suite was used, Hawk-Eye showed a modest improvement. Although Figure 2b shows it continued to lag our tool significantly, at a 42 percentage point deficit (dashed line). Running an average of 154 test cases through each submission resulted in localisation of the repair statement to rank below 58% of other statements. Our tool, provided with an average of 80 failing test cases, did not improve from the 16% localisation score achieved previously. This lack of further improvement is due to a combination of different factors. Over a third of these submissions, with the smaller test suite, already provided perfect results using our tool; some programs will contain several assignments where a genuine repair is possible so there is no more compact list of repair locations; and some programs are resistant to analysis by symbolic analysis, which does not change with test suite size. This may have provided very little room for improvement by our tool.

However, the run-time on these much larger test suites confirm the scalability of our tool, an area where model-based fault localisation has traditionally suffered [10]. Our tool averaged 0.9 seconds per submission while Hawk-Eye lagged behind, averaging 1.1 seconds. Included in that average, three times our tool hit too many pathological cases to adapt and only completed at the time-out.

Hawk-Eye never ranked the statement that was used to repair the program as the most suspicious when localising on the data set, with either the original or extended test suite.

5.5 Effects of Programming Language

Comparing data for submissions originally written in Java to those in Python showed no significant skew to the data points explored. Translating a simple subset of each language into C syntax generated comparable subsets.

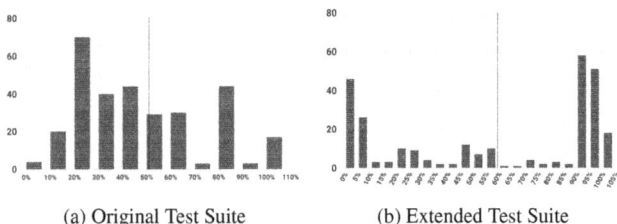

(a) Original Test Suite   (b) Extended Test Suite

Figure 3: Histogram of Test Suite Failure Percentage

5.6 Grading Support

To confirm the value of this localisation data for detecting "almost correct" student submissions that test suites do not highlight, we extracted the test suite results for the data set. As each of these student submissions was selected because there exists a single edit to an assignment which brings it into compliance with the complete instructor-authored test suite, they should be graded within a generally narrow distribution, reasonably close to a fully compliant solution. However, as Figure 3a shows in a histogram of the test suite compliance score of these programs, this is not the case. The average submission fails for 51% of the test cases (dashed line) and the distribution of scores is very uneven, not clustering around a single value. As there are so few test cases per submission, the histogram buckets have been set to best show the distribution curve.

When expanding out to the much larger test suite in Figure 3b, the average submission fails for 59% of the test cases (dashed line). Here the distribution of grades is less flat, with clumping at both poles. Half of the "almost correct" submissions are scored with 80% or more of the test suite failing. Our tool will accelerate automation-assisted marking by flagging nearly-good code with the likely location of a repair that will radically increase a test suite-based grading.

5.7 Threats to Validity

Our tool and the slice used on the database of student programs to generate the pairs for analysis makes a single-fault assumption. This is a common assumption in the fault localisation field but does not reflect real world debugging, although the existence of many code pairs in this data set does confirm real-world applicability.

The slicing of the student programs via a simple language translation stage, without any translation of library calls, and rejection of unparseable code restricts the form of programs explored. This slice assumes a repair possible via assignment modification. The choice of symbolic analyser (with an integer solver) also restricts the type of programs processed. Some programs are not suitable for automated localisation, such as those that never terminate on some inputs, and these would not make it through the database slice. These restrictions could add a bias to the student programs explored which could unfairly advantage one tool or call the generalisability of these results into question.

The open-source script used to execute the spectrum-based localisation was written in Java. Executing Java scripts is known to come with a high initialisation time cost to start the JVM. Due to the short run-times involved, this may have inflated the run-time costs of this technique beyond some competing implementations based on the same GCov underlying tool.

6. CONCLUSIONS AND FUTURE WORK

Novice programmers are unlikely to be capable of advanced debugging techniques. Coursework and charettes provide an opportunity for fast, accurate fault localisation to assist in educational institutions, which have already built up databases and workflows around test suite specified exercises. We have demonstrated a fast, model-based fault localisation tool on a collection of single-fault, real-world student submissions. The high quality localisation information reduces the search space for novice debuggers working down a list of potential repair locations when compared to the results from spectrum-based techniques (cf. RQ2). In over a third of the sampled failing student programs, our tool used the test suite to provide a localisation result that uniquely identified the location later used by the student to repair the program and rejected all other locations. This reinforces the qualitative difference between model-based fault localisation that reasons over a model of the student program to derive a list of feasible repair locations compared to a spectrum-based ranking process that infers suspiciousness of each program statement (cf. RQ1). These short, often exact, lists of potential assignment repair locations can direct students to the site of improvement, assisting in the construction of a final submission that fully complies with the test suite.

Spectrum-based techniques showed marginal location ranking improvements with much larger test suites than found in the provided data set. This was, however, still vastly inferior to our tool's output (which did not significantly vary with test suite size) and came with an increased run-time cost. The run-time cost of our high quality localisation matches that of fast spectrum-based fault localisation, even with large test suites, ensuring that our approach is viable even at the scale required by MOOCs (cf. RQ1).

We have demonstrated that these submissions, which are a single assignment edit away from full compliance with a test suite, would not be scored predictably if scoring were based on compliance with the test suite only. This confirms the need for tools which can isolate such "almost correct" student submissions (cf. RQ3).

Future studies into this tool can survey the real world performance of tool-assisted learning in classroom environments and the effect on student progress when one group is provided with this high quality localisation information in typical student programming tasks. Such studies can validate this feedback as valuable for novices, improving total debugging time and reducing the number of students who stop before completing a source code submission fully conforming to the provided test suite. The integration of this localisation feedback into student integrated development environments must be managed to maximise and quantify student comfort and views on the ease-of-use of this additional information. Future studies could be done with direct interaction tracking, surveys, or analysis of achievement changes when this tool is introduced to an existing course.

The underlying methods used by this tool are programming language and symbolic analyser agnostic. This will allow future tests using other programming languages and beyond the restrictions of the currently selected downstream components.

7. ACKNOWLEDGEMENTS

We would like to thank Ewan Tempero and Paul Denny at the University of Auckland for access to an anonymised copy of their student exercises and submissions to those exercises, from which we generated our data set. We would also like to thank Eli Bendersky, author of the PyCParser; the Automated Software Testing Group at Beihang University for Hawk-Eye; all the contributors to the KLEE symbolic virtual machine project; and contributors to all downstream components of these tools and Linux Mint.

This academic research was funded by the Engineering and Physical Sciences Research Council, UK. Funding number 1239954.

8. REFERENCES

[1] P. Antonucci et al. An Incremental Hint System For Automated Programming Assignments. *ITiCSE '15*, pp. 320–325, 2015.

[2] S. D. Benford et al. The Ceilidh System for the Automatic Grading of Students on Programming Courses. *ACM Southeast Regional Conf.*, pp. 176–182, 1995.

[3] G. Birch, B. Fischer, and M. R. Poppleton. Fast Model-Based Fault Localisation with Test Suites. *TAP '15, LNCS 9154*, pp. 38–57, 2015.

[4] H. Blau and J. Eliot. FrenchPress Gives Students Automated Feedback on Java Program Flaws. *ITiCSE '15*, pp. 15–20, 2015.

[5] K. Buffardi and S. H. Edwards. Exploring Influences on Student Adherence to Test-Driven Development. *ITiCSE '12*, pp. 105–110, 2012.

[6] K. Buffardi and S. H. Edwards. Responses to Adaptive Feedback for Software Testing. *ITiCSE '14*, pp. 165–170, 2014.

[7] J. deKleer and B. Williams. Diagnosing Multiple Faults. *J. Artificial Intelligence*, 32(1):97–130, 1987.

[8] P. Denny, A. L. Reilly, and D. Carpenter. Enhancing Syntax Error Messages Appears Ineffectual. *ITiCSE '14*, pp. 273–278, 2014.

[9] S. H. Edwards. Using Software Testing to Move Students from Trial-and-Error to Reflection-in-Action. *SIGCSE '04*, pp. 26–30, 2004.

[10] A. Griesmayer, S. Staber, and R. Bloem. Automated Fault Localization for C Programs. *Electronic Notes in Theoretical Computer Science*, pp. 95–111, 2007.

[11] Hawk-Eye: 2010. *http://code.google.com/p/hawk-eye/*.

[12] M. T. Helmick. Interface-based Programming Assignments and Automatic Grading of Java Programs. *ITiCSE '07*, pp. 63–67, 2007.

[13] D. Insa and J. Silva. Semi-Automatic Assessment of Unrestrained Java Code: A Library, a DSL, and a Workbench to Assess Exams and Exercises. *ITiCSE '15*, pp. 39–44, 2015.

[14] D. Jackson and M. Usher. Grading Student Programs Using ASSYST. *SIGCSE '97*, pp. 335–339, 1997.

[15] M. Vujošević-Janičić et al. Software Verification and Graph Similarity for Automated Evaluation of Students' Assignments. *Inf. Softw. Technol.*, 55(6):1004–1016, 2013.

[16] M. Joy, N. Griffiths, and R. Boyatt. The Boss Online Submission and Assessment System. *J. Educational Resources in Computing*, 5(3):2A, 2005.

[17] M-J. Laakso et al. Automatic Assessment of Exercises for Algorithms and Data Structures - a Case Study with TRAKLA2. In *Finnish/Baltic Sea Conf. on Comp. Sci. Edu.*, pp. 28–36, 2004.

[18] R. Lister et al. Naturally Occurring Data As Research Instrument: Analyzing Examination Responses to Study the Novice Programmer. *SIGCSE Bull.*, 41(4):156–173, 2010.

[19] T. MacWilliam and D. J. Malan. Streamlining Grading Toward Better Feedback. *ITiCSE '13*, pp. 147–152, 2013.

[20] L. Malmi, A. Korhonen, and R. Saikkonen. Experiences in Automatic Assessment on Mass Courses and Issues for Designing Virtual Courses. *ITiCSE '02*, pp. 55–59, 2002.

[21] M. McCracken et al. A Multi-National, Multi-Institutional Study of Assessment of Programming Skills of First-year CS Students. *ITiCSE-WGR '01*, pp. 125–180, 2001.

[22] C. Parnin and A. Orso. Are Automated Debugging Techniques Actually Helping Programmers? *ISSTA '11*, pp. 199–209, 2011.

[23] D. N. Perkins et al. Conditions of Learning in Novice Programmers. *J. Educational Computing Research*, 2(1):37–55, 1986.

[24] L. H. Pham et al. Assisting Students in Finding Bugs and their Locations in Programming Solutions. *Int. J. Quality Ass. in Eng. and Tech. Edu.*, 3(2):12–27, 2014.

[25] V. Pieterse. Automated Assessment of Programming Assignments. *Comp. Sci. Edu. Research Conf.*, CSERC '13, pp. 45–56, 2013.

[26] A. L. Reilly et al. On the Differences Between Correct Student Solutions. *ITiCSE '13*, pp. 177–182, 2013.

[27] R. Reiter. A Theory of Diagnosis from First Principles. *J. Artificial Intelligence*, 32(1):57–95, 1987.

[28] R. Saikkonen, L. Malmi, and A. Korhonen. Fully Automatic Assessment of Programming Exercises. *ITiCSE '01*, pp. 133–136, 2001.

[29] R. Singh, S. Gulwani, and A. S. Lezama. Automated Feedback Generation for Introductory Programming Assignments. *PLDI '13*, pp. 15–26, 2013.

[30] E. Soloway and J. C. Spohrer. Studying the Novice Programmer. 1988.

[31] J. Spacco et al. Towards Improving Programming Habits to Create Better Computer Science Course Outcomes. *ITiCSE '15*, pp. 320–325, 2015.

[32] M. Striewe, M. Balz, and M. Goedicke. A Flexible and Modular Software Architecture for Computer Aided Assessments and Automated Marking. *CSEDU '09*, pp. 54–61, 2009.

[33] N. Tillmann et al. Teaching and Learning Programming and Software Engineering via Interactive Gaming. *ICSE '13*, pp. 1117–1126, 2013.

[34] Q. Wang, C. Parnin, and A. Orso. Evaluating the Usefulness of IR-Based Fault Localization Techniques. *ISSTA '15*, pp. 1–11, 2015.

[35] J. Whalley and N. Kasto. A Qualitative Think-Aloud Study of Novice Programmers' Code Writing Strategies. *ITiCSE '15*, pp. 320–325, 2015.

[36] D. Wood, J. S. Bruner, and G. Ross. The Role of Tutoring in Problem Solving. *J. Child Psychology and Psychiatry*, 17(2):89–100, 1976.

[37] X. Xie et al. A Theoretical Analysis of the Risk Evaluation Formulas for Spectrum-based Fault Localization. In *TOSEM '13*, 22(4):31A, 2013.

[38] A. Zeller. Isolating Cause-Effect Chains with AskIgor. *IWPC '03*, pp. 296–297, 2003.

Teaching DevOps and Cloud Computing using a Cognitive Apprenticeship and Story-Telling Approach

Henrik Bærbak Christensen
Computer Science / Aarhus University
8200 Aarhus N - Denmark
hbc@cs.au.dk

ABSTRACT

DevOps is a new way of developing software that is challenging from a teaching perspective. In this paper, we outline these challenges and propose teaching methods that focus on skill acquisition and technical practices that focus on performant virtualization to overcome them. We describe central elements from our course *Cloud Computing and Architecture* that has been designed and executed upon these methods and practices and report our experiences and lessons learned.

Keywords

DevOps, Cloud Computing, Programming Education, Course Design, Virtualization

1. INTRODUCTION

Technology has once again changed the way we live over the last decade. Google has changed the way we find information; FaceBook the way people connect and interact; AirBnB the way people find accommodation on their holidays; NetFlix the way people watch TV; and Uber the way people transport in many big cities. These companies have defined new business models but their success also relies heavily on the way they produce software and their technical platform that must maintain high availability and scale at an unprecedented speed, as the number of users increases by orders of magnitude over short time intervals.

To cope with these demands on scalability, performance, and availability, a novel way of doing software development has emerged termed *DevOps* (from the merging of *Dev*elopment and *Op*erations.) This new paradigm can be viewed as the natural next step of the agile movement, which emphasized working software, collaboration, speed, and responding to change [2]. However, DevOps introduces new elements namely the strong focus on *operations*: features, bug fixes, and increments are developed, tested, integrated, and deployed to end users in matter of hours, and the devel-

ITiCSE '16, July 09 - 13, 2016, Arequipa, Peru

© 2016 Copyright held by the owner/author(s). Publication rights licensed to ACM.
ISBN 978-1-4503-4231-5/16/07... $15.00

DOI: http://dx.doi.org/10.1145/2899415.2899426

opment team is responsible for *the full stack*: requirements, development, testing, deployment, and monitoring.

From an educational perspective, this new software development paradigm is challenging. It emphasizes *hybrid skills* [14], i.e. skills that crosscut the classical boundaries between the courses we typical offer at universities; it emphasizes *operations skills* which is not a core area of expertise for the average university teacher; it requires highly complex execution architectures consisting of 5-10-20 servers which both pose a challenge on setting up the execution context for exercises and even more so on how to evaluate the systems developed and submitted by our students.

In this paper, we will outline what DevOps is, and analyses its core challenges from a teaching perspective. We identify key aspects to emphasize in a course: learning hybrid skills and providing as performant execution and virtualization environment, and outline how we have addressed these aspects in a master level course on cloud computing and DevOps. We have drawn upon constructive alignment, cognitive apprenticeship, and story-telling in designing the learning context, with heavy emphasis on a concrete project as main learning vehicle; and have analyzed and selected Docker[1] as a strong virtualization environment. We present the project used, example exercises, outline our assessment process, and finally discuss lessons learned from teaching our course for 130 students.

2. WHAT IS DEVOPS?

DevOps can be summarized as *a practice that [...] aims at establishing an environment where building, testing, and releasing software, can happen rapidly, frequently, and more reliably* [15]. DevOps appeared as a direct response to the challenges of large-scale software platforms that are rapidly updated, as outlined by Anderson [3]: *The DevOps movement, for example, emerged from one of the classic stumbling blocks in a lot of organizations. Developers build code and applications and ship them to the operations people, only to discover that the code and applications don't run in production. This is the classic "it works on my machine; it's operations' problem now."* With such systems, manual operations do not scale, and the response was to "move infrastructure into code" [11]. At the programming skills level, DevOps require three types of programming skills that we classify as:

- *Coding application logic*: The programming of logic for the core business functionality under the assumption

---

[1] www.docker.io

that all services work correctly. Example: Developing application server code to access an external inventory service and retrieve the price and stock availability of an item.

- *Coding quality attribute logic*: The programming of logic for architectural quality attributes [4] (nonfunctional requirements) like availability or performance, such as to handle the situations where one or several services fail, are slow, or produce unexpected results. Example: Developing code that implements graceful failure modes in case the inventory service is too slow to respond due to a peak load or simply unavailable due to network failure.

- *Coding infrastructure logic*: The programming of logic for the deployment of services. Traditionally handled by manual procedures (installing, configuring, and linking services), but in face of large-scale deployments, this too must be coded. Example: Developing scripts that start the application server, inventory service and associated database, initialize them, and connect them correctly—i.e. create a *staging environment*.

Moreover, DevOps focuses strongly on testing skills, automated testing, and continuous integration.

3. CHALLENGES IN TEACHING DEVOPS

Traditional software engineering (SE) curriculum typically emphasizes early and middle phases of the software lifecycle (requirements, design, programming, testing, and tooling) while late phases are ignored or only treated in theory (deployment, maintenance). The 2013 ACM curriculum [1] do mention "deployment; and operation and maintenance" in the introduction of the SE chapter, but these terms do not reappear in any of the following course descriptions. Browsing the course offerings of universities that provide degrees in SE generally show the same picture. Relating to our proposed three types of programming, traditional curriculum put much emphasis on *application logic*, less on *quality attribute logic*, and almost nothing on *infrastructure logic*. We teach "Dev" but not "Ops".

From a teaching perspective, DevOps is challenging for a number of reasons, and we identify at least the following:

- *Teachers' experience*: Operations is an area where few university teachers have much experience. A university teacher may train by designing and programming a few large system, however, operations experience requires a (large) number of users over an extended period of time—not a core duty of most university teachers.

- *Hybrid skills*: University courses tend to be named after specific topics: "Databases", "Programming", "OO Analysis and design", "Testing", etc. DevOps crosscuts them all as well as requires a few seldom mentioned in any course curriculum.

- *Emphasize skills*: Expertise relies on knowledge and skills, but DevOps is essentially a skill-focused competence: the ability to apply your knowledge in a concrete context to develop a working solution. Drawing the UML of the architecture of a passive replicating database on the whiteboard is the easy part—configuring and setting up the database cluster, and coding the infrastructure logic in your application

server that correctly handles the exceptions thrown during the master election phase, is the tricky part.

- *Realistic environment*: DevOps is the response to the challenge of speed, scale, and availability: more users than a single server can handle, software updates in production every few hours, providing end user services even in the face of failing subsystems and overloaded databases. Creating a (semi) realistic environment for students to practice within is not trivial.

- *Assessment and marking*: The challenge of creating a realistic environment is even more important when it comes to evaluating students' work: How can we verify that the developed quality attribute logic by a student correctly handles a database failure? Alternatively, that the latency is not too high even when 10.000 users are submitting two requests per second?

Of these, the first challenge, teachers' experience, is a training issue and outside the scope of the present paper. The remaining challenges falls in two broad categories, skills acquisition and technical environment, which we have actively tried to address. In the next section, we will describe how we have designed and executed a course that has tried to cope with these challenges: The skills challenge through the course pedagogy and teaching focus, the technical environment through careful selection of a strong virtualization platform.

4. COURSE DESCRIPTION

Our course, *Cloud Computing and Architecture*, is a 5 ECTS quarter length (7-week) course taught for computer science master level students, at Computer Science, Aarhus University, Denmark. The course had around 130 student organized in around 60 groups of 1–3 students. Each week consisted of a three-hour lecture and a three-hour lab. The author and two teaching assistants staffed it.

The main intended learning outcomes of the course were i) Designing and implementing highly distributed, cloud-based, systems; ii) Architectural patterns to achieve the quality attributes [4] of primarily *availability*, and secondary *scalability* and *performance*; and iii) Deployment and testing distributed systems in virtualized environments.

4.1 Pedagogical Considerations

DevOps is a skill-oriented practice and we therefore used teaching theories and practices that emphasize skill acquisition. We combined elements from constructive alignment [5], cognitive apprenticeship [7] with a story-telling approach [8]. Constructive alignment is based on constructivist theory that learners must use their *own activity* to construct knowledge and skills, that teachers must state the intended learning outcome clearly, and that the activities students engage in, must be aligned so they directly aim at the learning outcome. Cognitive apprenticeship aims primarily at teaching the *processes* that experts use to handle complex tasks through scaffolding, fading, and coaching, typically by supplying exemplary programs and solution templates that students base their increasingly complex system upon. Finally, story-telling aims at providing a scaled-down but *realistic context* in which learning topics are introduced as response to realistic requirements in a number of iterations of evolving and increasing complexity.

The main terms of these theories: *own activity, processes, realistic context*; match core aspects of DevOps. This led us to design our course on the following premises:

- Learning activities were primarily quality attribute and infrastructure logic programming assignments on a large DevOps project in which students evolve a functionally correct but simple distributed system (called *SkyCave*) into a cloud based, highly available and fault tolerant, scalable massive multi-user system. Each exercise added increments of complexity over the previous ones, focusing on enhancing availability, scalability, or performance to the SkyCave system; and testing, deploying, and monitoring it.

- Submissions were primarily in the form of their developed programs and systems. We avoided requesting written reports—time should be spent in Eclipse, not in Word.

- The final course grade was directly based on the amount and quality of exercises solved. Each exercise has a point score, each solved exercise increased the total score, and this was the foundation for the final grade.

- Unlimited attempts—students were free to submit a given exercise multiple times to achieve a better score by refactoring/recoding their submission based upon the feedback from course instructors.

- No set deadlines—except for a final deadline at the end of the course, students were free to submit at any time.

- Agile feedback on exercises. The instructors took turns to assess submitted exercises to ensure that they were marked and returned within 24 hours during normal working days.

We argue that this structure and process aligns well with DevOps. The students' activities are skill oriented: programming quality attribute and infrastructure logic to enhance SkyCave, and to test and deploy it. The unlimited attempts and agile feedback are designed to create a positive feedback loop in which the students improve poor or less viable submissions iteratively based on advice and hints from instructors. That the learning activities and processes are on a single, large, project also aligns well with a typical industrial DevOps situation. Finally, the course grade is directly aligned with the work invested in the SkyCave exercise set, rather than in a separate written or oral exam at the end of the course.

4.2 SkyCave

The central learning vehicle in our course is student groups' continued work on an evolving project *SkyCave*. SkyCave is a massive, multi-user, online exploration experience, in which users explore, modify, and extend a cave consisting of numerous rooms, navigated by standard compass directions. SkyCave is inspired by the first adventure game, Colossal Cave Adventure [9]; however, game elements have been removed and replaced by social networking and massive multi-user aspects: Friends can log into the SkyCave, meet in specific rooms, post and read messages on that room's wall, and extend the cave by creating new rooms. Furthermore, SkyCave connects to several external services, notably a centralized subscription server, handling all user login.

At the onset of the course, the students are given high quality source code of a fully operational SkyCave system, using simple socket-based client-server communication, and a JSON based protocol [anonymized link to source code].As such, it represents a "worked example" [7] that provides the scaffolding for their learning activities. SkyCave is imple-

mented in Java, uses Ant as build system, JUnit for testing, and Ivy for dependency management. Furthermore, JaCoCo was included for measuring test code coverage. The code base handed out to students is about 2300 SLOC implementation and 1900 SLOC JUnit test code in 78/29 files.

To keep focus on the architectural and "server-room" flavor of DevOps, the SkyCave client was a crude textual 'real-evaluate-print' interface (user commands after the > prompt):

```
== Welcome to SkyCave, player Joe ==
Entering command loop, type "q" to quit, "h" for help.
> look
You are standing at the end of a road before a
   small brick building.
There are exits in directions:
   NORTH  EAST  WEST  UP
You see other players in this room:
   [0] Joe [1] Carla [2] Peter
> north
You moved NORTH
You are in open forest, with a deep valley to one side.
```

The provided SkyCave contained most of the application logic, but no quality attribute or infrastructure logic. Thus "it functionally works" but fails in case of internal failures, network issues, high load, high latency, etc. It only implements a single server, and many central interfaces are only provided by fake-object implementations [12]: for instance, the database interface is implemented by in-memory data structures—not a real database; the subscription service interface is implemented by a hard coded table of only four fixed users; etc.

At the end of the course, the best solutions have enhanced SkyCave to handle more than 10.000 concurrent users, fully horizontal scalable with session management, redundant NoSQL databases across geographically disjoint server farms, tolerating network loss or latency in any servers, and deployed at commercial cloud providers. These 'best solutions' required more than 20 interconnected servers to operate correctly.

4.3 Technical Environment

To teach the infrastructure logic coding aspects as well as testing and deployment skills, the choice of technical environment is essential. The final exercises in the course require a large set of running servers to test and operate, and even the exercises around the fourth week require five servers. The challenges for the students to create a staging environment must not be prohibitively difficult.

Virtual machine (VM) systems are essential but they vary greatly in ease of use and performance. During the course development phase we considered VMWare[2], Vagrant[3], and Docker[4] and a few others, but settled on Docker. Docker was an almost ideal fit for our purpose, primarily for three reasons:

- *Small image size*: Docker VMs (called "images") are typically in the size region of a few hundred megabytes in contrast to full-fledge virtualization platforms like VMWare that are measured in 5-10 GBytes. This is vital in a process where images for around 60 groups need to be downloaded, instantiated, and assessed every day.

---

[2]www.vmware.com
[3]www.vagrantup.com
[4]www.docker.com

- *Docker hub*: Docker provides a free-to-use cloud based repository that allows one private repository per student. This way, students "pushed" their VMs to their private repository, and gave the instructors read-access. Our evaluation framework could then download images and start them in order to evaluate and mark. Thus, the aspects that makes Docker appealing in operations (easy deployment and fast start-up) makes it appealing for assessment as well.

- *Docker scripting*: Docker VMs are operated through command line arguments in the Linux shell: `docker run group7/skycave` will download 'group7's VM named 'skycave' from docker hub and power it up. Most other virtualization tools come with graphical UIs that are nice but less suitable for automatization and scripting.

These aspects allowed us to develop a small set of scripts that automated much of the chores of fetching, executing and assessing submissions.

4.4 Learning Goals and Week plan

Our teaching plan encompassed the following learning goals, and associated tools/techniques.
– Week 1: Cloud Computing overview and the architecture of SkyCave.
– Week 2: Virtualization and Docker.
– Week 3: Availability through Nygard's stability patterns [13].
– Week 4: Availability through Redundancy, exemplified by MongoDB's replica set[5].
– Week 5: Scalability and messaging, exemplified by RabbitMQ's queueing system[6].
– Week 6: Performance through database sharding and concurrency.
– Week 7: Perspectives and invited talks.

4.5 Exercise Examples

Below we present some examples of exercises. The complete list of all 40+ exercises of which about one third are mandatory can be found at [anonymized link to exercise set].

Week 1: *operations-socket (Max 32 points):*

Create a node with fixed IP on your favorite cloud computing IaaS provider, and install Docker version 1.6+. Deploy your socket based server as a Docker container on it, so clients can contact it at '(IP):37123'.

Evaluation: Your server will be logged in every hour around the clock using from our evaluation server that acts as a user.

This exercise emphasizes infrastructure logic, deployment and operations in the cloud. While there is no application logic implementation involved, the students have to learn the Docker VM, and write scripts to 'containerize' the SkyCave server code into a Docker image, and make it run in the cloud. They simply submit the IP address of their running server, and we gave a score from 0 to 32 depending upon their server's uptime.

---

[5]www.mongodb.org
[6]www.rabbitmq.com

Week 3: *weather-circuit-breaker (40 points):*

Increase availability by implementing Nygard's "Circuit Breaker" [13] pattern on the weather service integration point in your SkyCave server.

Evaluation: Review and execution of your staging environment.

Here the emphasis is on implementing quality attribute logic for a safe failure mode in case the SkyCave server cannot contact an associated external service.

Our final exercise example builds upon a previous one in which the students have made a production implementation of the SkyCave's persistent storage interface, CaveStorage, using the MongoDB API.

Week 4: *mongo-replica-set (40 points):*

Increase availability of storage by introducing MongoDB replica sets of three servers.

Evaluation: Review and execution of your staging environment.

This exercise emphasizes the operations aspect. The focus is on setting up a master/slave passive replication using MongoDB's replica set, which involves starting three database servers and defining their configuration. We review and mark their configuration scripts and process descriptions embedded in their Docker images.

4.6 Exercise Assessment

The requirement of agile feedback required a special assessment process. The course was assigned four teaching assistant (TA) units, covered by two Ph.D. students. Combined with the course instructor there were thus five units, which were allocated on the week's five working days: The instructor covered Tuesday, one TA covered Monday and Wednesday, etc. Thus, a student group was not associated with a particular teaching assistant, instead, submissions were simply queued once handed in, and instructors worked on their assigned days to empty the queue.

Docker suited the submission format perfectly for submitting source code and executing systems. To solve a given exercise, the process for both students and TAs were simple: The students work on the code for a given assignment and once they feel they fulfill the learning objectives, they push their Docker image with their source code to their repository at Docker hub. This is just a one-liner in the shell: `docker push group7/skycave`. A push simply overwrites any previous version of their image at Docker hub—as all exercises always extend SkyCave, this is a perfect, incremental, solution.

The TA will note the submission in the queue, and can then pull the image, and can simply instantiate it: `docker run group7/skycave`—and connect it to other services, like MongoDB databases, etc. As this VM linking process is under the control of the TA, it was also possible to link their systems to ill-behaving versions that we had crafted, like slow responding services, to test whether their quality attribute logic code behaved correctly.

5. DISCUSSION

The viability of the course topics and teaching methods were assessed through formal questionnaires, and through

Question	Agree
Learning topics are relevant	99.9%
'Agile feedback' supports learning	94.3%
'Unlimited submissions' supports learning	88.6%
'No deadline' supports workload control	84.1 %
Exam format introduces stress	25.0 %

Table 1: Summary of responses.

informal communication and discussion with students and teaching assistants.

The formal course evaluation executed by our faculty only had 35 respondents, but of these 94.3% answered "Agree" (37.1%) or "Strongly agree" (57.2%) on the question "The course activities have in the best manner helped me to achieve the learning outcomes".

We also did an internal questionnaire, focusing on aspects of the course design. This questionnaire was also formulated as a set of statements to be evaluated on a five point Likert scale from "Strongly agree" to "Strong disagree". Here 88 students responded. Table 1 summarizes the answers, with the percentage in the second column showing the combination of "Strongly agree" and "Agree".

In conclusion, the topics were considered highly relevant, the combination of agile feedback and the possibility of re-submitting an exercise were considered helpful in the learning process, and lack of weekly deadlines generally appreciated. The last question regarding stress was included as several students expressed a frustration regarding the notion of "gathering points by solving exercises": As a student noted in the comment field of the questionnaire: *"I feel like everybody else want to collect full points for the exercises. This is a stress factor, since I have to put more work load into the course if I do not want to be placed in the lower end of the grading scale.".* Thus, some students felt that they had to work harder to "keep up." While we did some adjustment of the translation from a score to a final grade due to the point distribution, it had much less impact than students feared, but we unfortunately failed to communicate this clearly.

The final distribution of grades, see Figure 1, supports findings by others, namely that multiple/unlimited submissions of exercises lead to better performance. In the figure, 85 out of 113, that is, more than 75 %, have a grade A or B. The failed group of 13 students with grade F represents students that enrolled but never showed up—so everybody that invested some effort in the course passed it. As the passing grade equals solving all mandatory SkyCave exercises, it is also easy for a student to ensure a passing grade.

Seen from the teacher's perspective there are also some important lessons learned. The exam grading based upon accumulated scores on exercises was initially also envisioned in order to avoid spending much time on a final oral or written exam. In addition it was envisioned that we would have time to build some kind of automated assessment, partly inspired by [6], that could save time. In the end, however, the assessment process turned out to be somewhat frustrating, due to a number of factors. First, we did not have time to make anything but the most rudimentary automated testing of submissions, leaving most of it to manual processes. Second, as mentioned earlier it is daunting to setup a proper

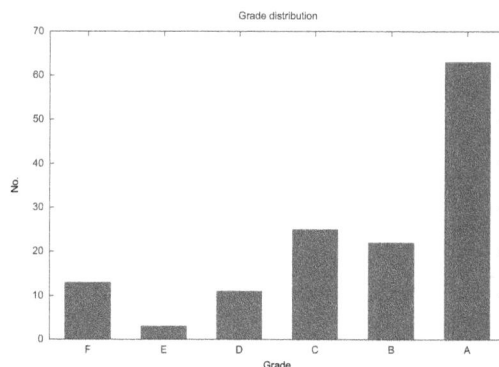

Figure 1: Grade distribution.

testing environment of 5-10-20 servers, which meant that some of the evaluation (especially the later and more complex exercises) was done by code review instead of by system execution. Third, the 'unlimited submission' strategy had the unfortunate consequence of many groups being sloppy with their submission—thus we wasted quite a lot of time on retrieving Docker images only to find that the submitted code could not even compile. Forth, the 'no deadline' meant that the in-coming queue late in the course contained submissions from all iterations, so you would review one submission solving an exercise from week 6 while the next was an exercise from week 1—thus you had to have the full spectrum of exercises in fresh mind to assess consistently. Finally there was a clear element of psychology involved: you started your assessment work at 9 AM with a queue of 55 submissions, would then work for six hours of hard work handling 45 submissions—only to find that the queue contains 45 submissions. Students obviously submit to the queue while you are working on it!

We monitored the time used exclusively to assess and mark submissions and spent 148.5 hours totally over the course. Thus, the total amount of time spent per student on the course is less than 1.2 hours (or 2.5 hours per group) which in hindsight seems very reasonable.

The analysis that led to choosing Docker as virtualization engine turned out to be correct. Docker hub is a built-in repository that facilitates easy and efficient access to the VMs produced. The design choices made in Docker suits a teaching context perfectly: the "copy-on-write" file system means only the delta between the image on Docker hub and the image on the TAs local machine has to be downloaded. Thus getting the code snapshot for a group is downloads in the range of kilo or megabytes, and not gigabytes. With around 60 groups, this is a major time saver.

The ability to fast handle the complete student virtual machine with all source code and execution scripts in an image, and control it using the command line and ultimately through scripting was pivotal in a DevOps context, and a major time saver in a teaching context as well.

On the downside, Docker is also a bleeding edge technology: At the start of the design phase of our course, it was in version 1.4. When the course started, it was 1.7 and changed to 1.8 during the course. Moreover, at the time of writing, several of the key features we required students to use during the course have been marked as deprecated starting from release 1.9. More severe, however, was the constant updating of the tutorial material on Docker's webpages, which meant that our course material and links, only one month old, was already becoming outdated.

Regarding future work, we are working on automated prechecking of students' submissions, that is, ensuring that submitted code in the Docker images can compile and will pass some simple validation checks. As outlined above, the TAs wasted much time pulling images only to find that the contents failed in some trivial way unrelated to the actual exercise solution. This will be a major time saver. We are also looking into automated assessment of the actual exercises, but as argued, it is not trivial to setup a correct multi-server staging environment, and influence it to detect errors in the students' submissions.

Very few papers have been published about teaching DevOps. The most relevant we have found is Pengxiang et al. [14] that present a gap analysis between current curriculum and the skill set demanded by DevOps companies. They arrive at similar conclusions as we do, outlining a course focusing on hybrid skills and hands-on experience. Jiang et al. [10] discuss benefits and liabilities in using Docker in student laboratories, and value the performance benefits similar to our evaluation, but do not reflect on the teaching of DevOps per se.

6. CONCLUSION

We have described DevOps as a novel software development and deployment process, and outlined why it is challenging from a teaching perspective. As DevOps is highly skills oriented and have strong requirements on bringing up complex deployment architectures fast, we have argued in favor of teaching methods that emphasize programing process and realistic context as well as using performant virtualization environments. We have described our course that is based upon these methods and outlined learning topics, concrete project examples of exercises, as well as exam and assessment structure. Finally, we have discussed lessons learned and argued that our approach is a viable and well-received way of teaching DevOps.

Acknowledgements

We would like to acknowledge the valuable contributions by the teaching assistants Kasper S. R. Eenberg and Matus Tomlein.

7. REFERENCES

[1] ACM. Computer science curricula 2013. Technical report, IEEE Computer Society, 2013. http://www.acm.org/education/CS2013-final-report.pdf.

[2] Manifesto for agile software development. http://www.agilemanifesto.org/.

[3] C. Anderson. Docker. *IEEE Software*, pages 102–105, May/June 2015.

[4] L. Bass, P. Clements, and R. Kazman. *Software Architecture in Practice, 3rd Edition*. Addison-Wesley, 2012.

[5] J. Biggs and C. Tang. *Teaching for Quality Learning at University*. Open University Press, McGraw-Hill, 2007.

[6] R. Cardell-Oliver, L. Zhang, R. Barady, Y. H. Lim, A. Naveed, and T. Woodings. Automated Feedback for Quality Assurance in Software Engineering Education. In *Proceedings of 21th Australian Software Engineering Conference (ASWEC)*, pages 157–164. IEEE, Apr. 2010.

[7] M. E. Caspersen and J. Bennedsen. Instructional Design of a Programming Course: A Learning Theoretic Approach. In *Proceedings of the Third International Workshop on Computing Education Research*, ICER '07, pages 111–122, New York, NY, USA, 2007. ACM.

[8] H. B. Christensen. A Story-Telling Approach for a Software Engineering Course Design. In *Proceedings of the 14th annual ACM SIGCSE conference on Innovation and technology in computer science education*, ITiCSE '09, pages 60–64, New York, NY, USA, 2009. ACM.

[9] D. G. Jerz. Somewhere Nearby is Colossal Cave: Examining Will Crowther's Original "Adventure" in Code and in Kentucky. *Digital Humanities Quarterly*, 1(2), 2007.

[10] K. Jiang and Q. Song. A Preliminary Investigation of Container-Based Virtualization in Information Technology Education. In *Proceedings of the 16th Annual Conference on Information Technology Education*, SIGITE '15, pages 149–152, New York, NY, USA, 2015. ACM.

[11] M. Loukides. What is DevOps? http://radar.oreilly.com/2012/06/what-is-devops.html, June 2012.

[12] G. Meszaros. *xUnit Test Patterns: Refactoring Test Code*. Addison-Wesley, 2007.

[13] M. T. Nygard. *Release It! Design and Deploy Production-Ready Software*. Pragmatic Bookshelf, 2007.

[14] J. Pengxiang and P. Leong. Teaching Work-Ready Cloud Computing using the DevOps Approach. In *Proceedings of International Symposium on Advances in Technology Education (ISATE)*, Sept. 2014.

[15] Wikipedia. Devops. www.wikipedia.org. Accessed January 2016.

Software Engineering Education in Chile - Status Report

Maíra Marques
CS Department
Universidad de Chile
Santiago, Chile
mmarques@dcc.uchile.cl

Sergio F. Ochoa
CS Department
Universidad de Chile
Santiago, Chile
sochoa@dcc.uchile.cl

María Cecilia Bastarrica
CS Department
Universidad de Chile
Santiago, Chile
cecilia@dcc.uchile.cl

ABSTRACT

Although most computer science graduates develop their professional careers as software engineers, there are no academic program with a specific focus on software engineering in Chile. Considering ACM/IEEE Software Engineering 2014 Curriculum Guidelines as a starting point, we analyzed the curricula of the CS Engineering and CS Technology programs offered by the most traditional Chilean universities, in order to establish to what extent they address the knowledge areas included in that recommendation. We also gathered information about theoretical and/or practical approaches of their courses, their types of evaluations and temporality. The results of this status report indicate that most knowledge areas of the ACM/IEEE curricula are covered but not all with the same emphasis. Programs count on three or four mandatory software engineering courses, most of them have a practical approach, are evaluated through exams and projects and start between the seventh and eight semesters. These results let us learn that some knowledge areas are not emphasized as they deserve. For example, *Software Quality* or *Software Process* are skills that industry often requires but academia does not seem to take into account. Similarly, it might be necessary to have students learn about software engineering earlier during their career. Knowing the actual status, actions can be taken.

CCS Concepts

•Social and professional topics → Software engineering education;

Keywords

Software engineering education; Chile

1. INTRODUCTION

In Chile there are two types of computer science programs: Computer Science Engineering[1] (CS Engineering) and Com-

---

[1]Ingeniería Civil en Computación.

ITiCSE '16, July 09-13, 2016, Arequipa, Peru

© 2016 ACM. ISBN 978-1-4503-4231-5/16/07...$15.00

DOI: http://dx.doi.org/10.1145/2899415.2899459

puter Science Technology[2] (CS Technology). The former lasts six years and the latter five. These programs cannot be classified according to the ACM-Curricula [5] as Software Engineering, Computer Science, Computer Engineering, Information Systems or Information Technology. Chilean programs are generic and intend to cover all areas, probably in detriment of their depth. In particular these programs include only a few courses in software engineering. Students in Chile have 12 years of education without any special technical training before entering the University. It is known that most students in Computer Science develop their professional careers as software engineers, and this situation is not different in Chile. So having only a few courses could not be enough to train a skilled software engineer.

The ACM/IEEE Software Engineering Curriculum Guidelines (SE2014) [6] represents the most widely adopted software engineering education body of knowledge for undergraduate programs. The last version of this recommendation considers ten knowledge areas: three basic ones (*Computing Essentials*, *Mathematical & Engineering Fundamentals* and *Professional Practice*) and seven specific areas about software engineering (shown in Tab. 1). Each knowledge area is divided into knowledge units and each unit describes the topics that should be taught.

In this study we want to know what is the state of education in SE in Chile. In order to make a diagnosis of the SE education in Chile, we analyzed the CS programs of 20 of the most traditional universities [2]. Following a similar approach as that in [1, 3, 4], the SE body of knowledge delivered to the students was compared with the ACM/IEEE Software Engineering 2014 Curriculum Guidelines [6] in order to determine: What knowledge areas recommended by ACM/IEEE are taught in these programs? What knowledge areas are not taught? We also wondered: How many software engineering courses are included in these programs? When are the students introduced to SE? Is SE education addressed in a theoretical, practical or a mix of both ways? In order to answer these questions, we analyzed the programs' curricula and the course contents of 20 CS Engineering and 9 CS Technology programs. The courses contents where retrieved from the courses Web page, and the instructors were contacted when extra information was required.

The study results indicate that most ACM/IEEE Software Engineering knowledge areas are taught, although with several levels of depth. The most frequently taught knowledge areas were *Software Modeling and Analysis*, *Requirements Analysis and Specification* and *Software Design* and

---

[2]Ingeniería en Ejecución con mención en Informática.

Table 1: Knowledge Areas and Units of Knowledge of the ACM-IEEE SE 2014 Curriculum Guidelines

Knowledge Area	Units of Knowledge
Software Modeling and Analysis.	Modeling foundations, Types of models, Analysis fundamentals.
Requirements Analysis and Specification.	Requirements fundamentals, Eliciting requirements, Requirements specification and documentation, Requirements validation.
Software Design.	Design concepts, Design strategies, Architectural design, Human computer interaction design, Detailed design, Design evaluation.
Software Verification and Validation.	Verification and Validation terminology and foundations, Review and static analysis, Testing, Problem analysis and reporting.
Software Process.	Process concepts, Process implementation, Project planning and tracking, Software configuration management, Evolution process and activities.
Software Quality.	Software quality concepts and culture, Process assurance, Product assurance.
Security.	Security fundamentals, Computer network security, Developing secure software.

Table 2: Number of computer-related programs offered by Chilean universities in 2015

University	CS Engineering	CS Technology
Universidad Austral de Chile	1	-
Universidad del Bío-Bío	1	1
Pontificia Universidad Católica de Valparaíso	1	1
Pontificia Universidad Católica de Chile	1	-
Universidad de Tarapacá	1	-
Universidad Andrés Bello	1	1
Universidad Católica Santísima Concepción	1	-
Universidad Católica de Temuco	1	-
Universidad Católica del Maule	1	-
Universidad Católica del Norte	1	1
Universidad de Atacama	1	-
Universidad de Chile	1	-
Universidad de Concepción	1	-
Universidad de La Frontera	1	1
Universidad de Playa Ancha	1	-
Universidad de Santiago de Chile	1	1
Universidad de Talca	1	-
Universidad de Valparaíso	1	2
Universidad Técnica Federico Santa María	1	-
Universidad Tecnológica Metropolitana	1	1

in a lesser extent *Software Process* and *Software Verification and Validation*. *Software Quality*, and *Security* are scarcely taught. Programs usually include between three and four software engineering-related courses; most of them are delivered using a practical rather than theoretical approach. The first SE courses are generally introduced between the seventh and eight semesters, and most of the SE knowledge is included in courses between the seventh and tenth semesters. Preliminary results of this study were presented in WASE'2015 [7].

The rest of the paper is structured as follows. Next section presents the research settings and methodology. The study results are reported and discussed in Sec. 3. Threats to validity are discussed in Sec. 4. Finally, conclusions of this study and the future work are presented in Sec. 5.

2. STUDY SETTING

In order to evaluate the software engineering education in Chile, we compare the ACM-IEEE Software Engineering Curriculum Guidelines with the curricula of CS Engineering and CS Technology programs. To this end we analyzed courses contents to find out:

- Number of software engineering courses in Chilean CS programs and their characterization.
- The knowledge units of SE2014 that are covered in these programs.
- The type of evaluation that is used in SE courses.
- When, during the program, each knowledge area is addressed.

2.1 Sample of CS Programs

There are 43 universities accredited by the Chilean government, where 25 of them belong to CRUCH[3] [2], the organization that groups the most traditional universities. Two of them do not have computer-related programs and other four were not available to answer questions. Therefore, we considered 19 universities and we also included the information about Universidad Andrés Bello that, even though is

[3]Board of Presidents of Chilean Universities (in Spanish)

not part of CRUCH, it is also a well-recognized university (see Tab. 2). This means that from the 24 universities that were part of our sample, we managed to contact 20 universities, which represent 83% of the sample. As a first step in this study, we wanted to know which type of computer-related programs each university offers: CS Engineering or CS Technology. Table 2 shows that all universities offer CS Engineering and only eight of them deliver CS Technology.

2.2 Information Gathering

The data collection was conducted between October and November, 2015. This procedure followed the next five steps:

1. Identification of CS programs and curriculum gathering from Web pages or contacting the programs.
2. Curriculum analysis to identify software engineering (mandatory) courses.
3. Identification of the course instructor searching in the Web or contacting the program.
4. Obtaining course information from the Web site or contacting the instructor.
5. Clarification of doubts interacting with the course instructor (when needed).

This information allowed us to characterize the SE courses included in these programs.

2.3 SE Courses Characterization

After identifying at least one software engineering instructor per university, we contacted them by mail to know if they were available to participate in a phone interview to talk about the software engineering courses of their respective universities. In the interview we asked basic questions about programs and courses, e.g.:

- Are these courses (identified by the authors) the only ones related to SE in this program?
- Can you briefly describe the units included in each of these courses?
- How are the students of these courses evaluated?
- Do these courses have student projects? And, in the

case of a positive answer, What is the project size? Which relevance does the project score have in the final grade?

- What is the students perception about their software engineering courses?

In some cases we asked them to provide courses contents because they were not available on Internet. We conducted 25 phone interviews to SE instructors, and in some cases we interviewed more than one instructor per program. In average each interview lasted 25 minutes (the longest was 75 minutes and the shortest 15 minutes long). All the interviews were recorded.

Considering the existence or not of a project as part the course, as well as the project size and impact of the project score in the final grades, we defined four courses categories:

- **Theoretical** - Courses that mainly deliver theoretical knowledge through lectures, and students are usually evaluated with exams, readings and homework.
- **Theoretical-Practical** - Courses with an important theoretical component that also include students small projects or case studies whose score has some impact on the course final grade (less than 50%).
- **Practical-Theoretical** - Courses focused on projects that also include theoretical lectures that support the project work. Typically, the project score represents more than 50% of the final grade.
- **Practical** - Courses that are focused almost exclusively on students projects.

3. OBTAINED RESULTS

3.1 Computer Science Courses

Analyzing programs curricula we found that CS Engineering has an average of 3.4 SE courses and CS Technology has 2.8 (Tab. 3). Provided that CS Engineering programs involve (in average) 46 courses, the SE courses represent only 7.4%; in case of CS Technology programs the average number of courses is 30, therefore the SE courses stand for 9.3%. Other courses in the curricula are mostly mathematics and physics.

We then classified the courses of each program according to the characterization presented in Sec. 2.3. Figure 1a shows the course characterization in CS Engineering programs, where we can see that Theoretical-Practical courses account for more than half of the courses (51%), and Practical-Theoretical courses account for 25%. Only 15% of the courses are Practical and 9% are Theoretical. Figure 1b shows the same characterization but for CS Technology programs. Here Theoretical-Practical courses have an even larger relevance (61%) and there are no Theoretical courses. These number show the high relevance that the practice has in the instructional approaches used to teach software engineering. Although those approaches are fine, they are usually focused more on operative aspects of software development than on concepts behind the software engineering. The first one is short-term knowledge and the second one represents mid-term or long term knowledge.

3.2 Courses Evaluations

Another point of interest of this study was to determine how students are being evaluated in SE courses. The review of the courses contents allowed us to identify six types of evaluations: exams, readings, homework, case-studies,

Table 3: Number of Software Engineering Courses in each Program in 2015

University	CS Engineering	CS Technology
Universidad Austral de Chile	4	-
Universidad del Bío-Bío	2	3
Pontificia Universidad Católica de Valparaíso	4	2
Pontificia Universidad Católica de Chile	2	-
Universidad de Tarapacá	3	-
Universidad Andrés Bello	2	3
Universidad Católica Santísima Concepción	3	-
Universidad Católica de Temuco	3	-
Universidad Católica del Maule	6	-
Universidad Católica del Norte	5	3
Universidad de Atacama	3	-
Universidad de Chile	3	-
Universidad de Concepción	2	-
Universidad de La Frontera	4	2
Universidad de Playa Ancha	3	-
Universidad de Santiago de Chile	5	4
Universidad de Talca	3	-
Universidad de Valparaíso	3	3
Universidad Técnica Federico Santa María	4	-
Universidad Tecnológica Metropolitana	3	2
Average	3.4	2.8
Median	3	3

projects and peer-assessments. We found certain relationships between course characterization and evaluations. For instance, there are no exams on practical courses, and there were peer-assessment only in practical and practical-theoretical courses, as expected. Figure 2a shows the courses evaluations for the CS Engineering and in Figure 2b for the CS Technology programs.

In both cases the projects and exams are the most frequent instruments of evaluation; however, homework is significant for CS Engineering and not for CS Technology. CS Engineering theoretical courses are evaluated mainly with exams and homework, and also with readings and case-studies to a lower extent.

3.3 SE Knowledge Areas Coverage

After reviewing the knowledge areas and their associated units (Tab. 1), which are being taught as part of CS programs in Chile, we built a list of units indicating the number of times that each one was taught as part of mandatory SE courses.

The teaching frequency was calculated as the average number of courses that cover that unit in each program. Table 4 and Tab. 5 shows the SE units most frequently and least frequently taught respectively in the CS Engineering programs. Similarly, Tab. 6 and 7 present the results for CS Technology programs.

We then aggregated the number of units considering their corresponding knowledge areas and taking into account the courses characterizations. Figs. 3 and 4 show that *Software Design* and *Requirements Analysis and Specification* are the most emphasized areas. The rest of the knowledge areas, except *Security* and *Software Quality*, have also a relevant representativeness in the software engineering education.

3.4 Temporality

In order to determine when the students are introduced to the different knowledge areas, we counted the number of times that units of each knowledge area was mentioned to be

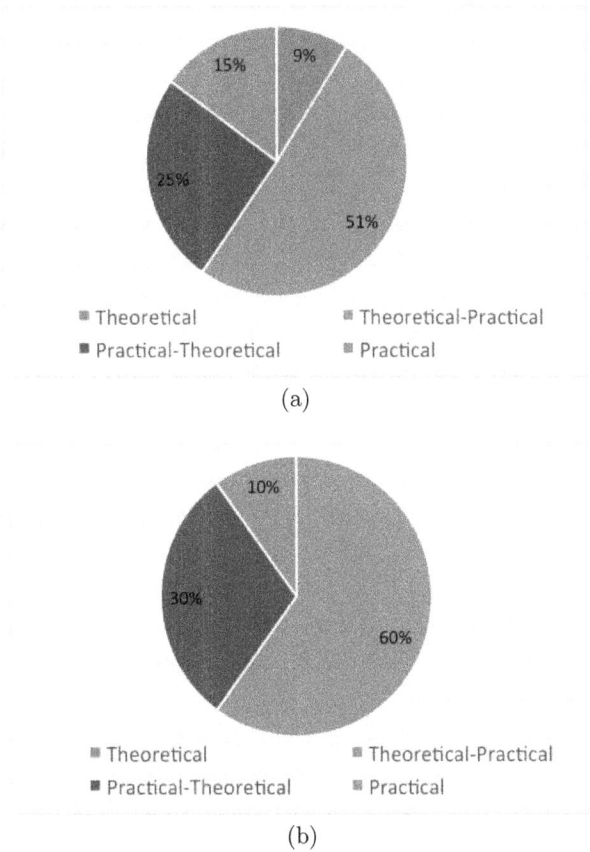

Figure 1: Course Characterization in (a) CS Engineering and (b) CS Technology Programs

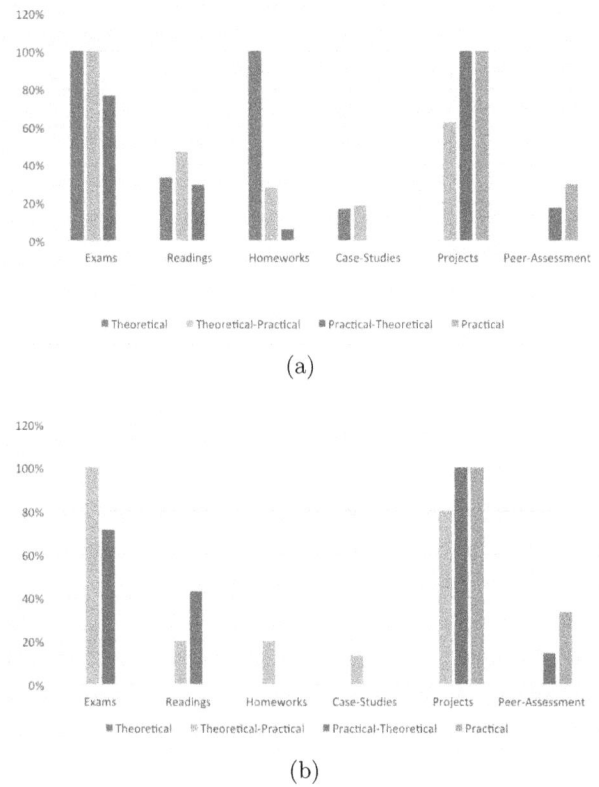

Figure 2: Courses Evaluation of (a) CS Engineering and (b) CS Technology Programs

Table 4: Most Frequent Knowledge Units in CS Engineering Programs

Units	Courses
Design Concepts	2.45
Design Strategies	2.40
Analysis Fundamentals	2.20
Types of Models	2.15
Requirements Fundamentals	1.95
Architectural Design	1.75
V&V Terminology and Foundations	1.75
Eliciting Requirements	1.70
Project Planning and Tracking	1.55
Requirements Specification & Documentation	1.50
Human Computer Interaction Design	1.50
Process Concepts	1.50

Table 6: Most Frequent Knowledge Units in CS Technology Programs

Units	Courses
Types of Models	2.25
Analysis Fundamentals	2.20
Design Concepts	2.25
Design Strategies	2.13
Requirements Fundamentals	2.00
Requirements Specification & Documentation	1.75
Eliciting Requirements	1.63
Architectural Design	1.50
Human Computer Interaction Design	1.50
V&V Terminology and Foundations	1.50

Table 5: Least Frequent Knowledge Units in CS Engineering Programs

Units	Courses
Communication Skills	0.90
Computer and Network Security	0.60
Problem Analysis and Reporting	0.60
Developing Secure Software	0.50
Evolution Process and Activities	0.50
Software Configuration Management	0.40
Product Assurance	0.30
Process Assurance	0.25
Modeling Foundations	0.05
Professionalism	0.05

Table 7: Least Frequent Knowledge Units in CS Technology Programs

Units	Courses
Reviews and Static Analysis	0.87
Testing	0.87
Software Quality Concepts and Culture	0.62
Software Quality Process	0.62
Developing Secure Software	0.50
Software Configuration Management	0.50
Problem Analysis and Reporting	0.37
Process Evolution and Activities	0.37
Product Assurance	0.25
Process Assurance	0.12
Professionalism	-
Modeling Foundations	-
Evolution Activities	-

183

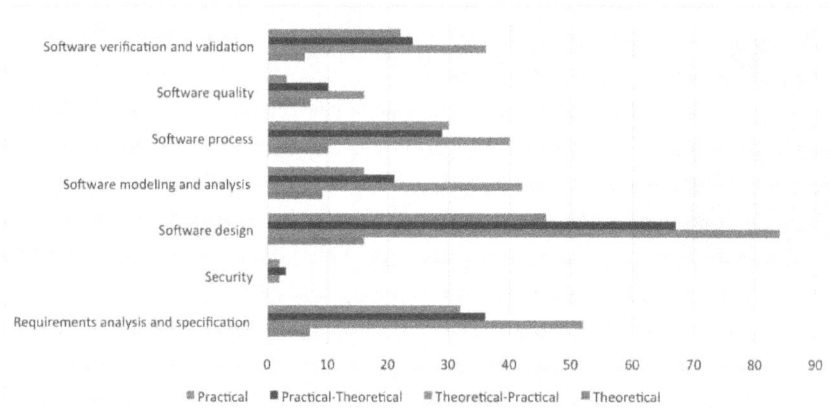

Figure 3: Knowledge Areas Characterization of CS Engineering Programs

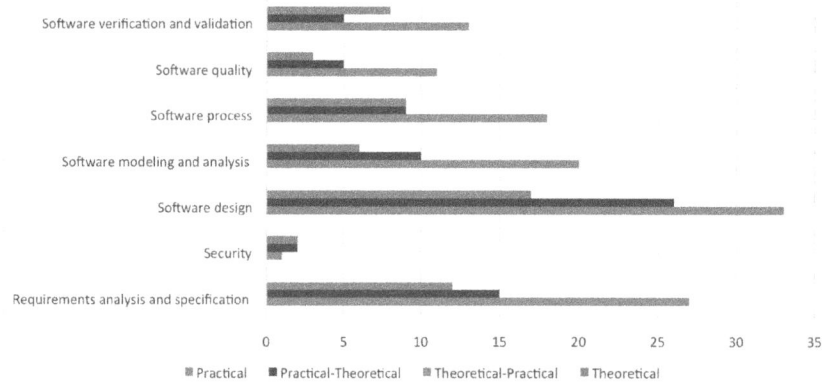

Figure 4: Knowledge Areas Characterization of CS Technology Programs

addressed in each semester for the considered programs. In Fig. 5 we show when the knowledge of each is introduced for CS Engineering programs, while the Fig. 6 present the data for CS Technology programs. These results indicate that the latter introduce software engineering knowledge earlier than the former; this may be due to the more technical orientation of the program type.

4. THREATS TO VALIDITY

The sample considered in this study involves the most traditional universities in the country, however, it does not describe all of Chilean universities, since our sample represents 42.4% of them. Moreover, we are only considering universities that are part of CRUCH. Nevertheless, we believe that programs of other universities are not very different since, even though they are generally newer, their CS programs were created by people from CRUCH universities replicating their experience.

Construct validity relates to what is being investigated, i.e., if it actually answers the research questions. This study has two major sources of information: the course contents and the phone interviews. The interviews were designed to gather the information required to answer the research questions whenever it was not available in the course content.

Data reliability focuses on repeatability: if other people follow the same procedure they would obtain the same results. Courses contents were confidential in various cases, therefore they cannot be published without aggregation. How-

ever, as we publish the questions included in the interviews, anybody interviewing the same instructors should get the same information.

5. CONCLUSIONS AND FUTURE WORK

In this work we analyzed the curricula of CS Engineering and Technology programs, in order to infer how well we are teaching software engineering in Chile. Particularly, we identified the number of SE courses in both types of programs and which knowledge areas and units are covered by them. Both types of programs include around three SE courses that cover most of the knowledge areas included in the ACM/IEEE Software Engineering 2014 Curriculum Guidelines. The results of this work allow us to eventually reformulate programs in the future based on actual information, but this is out of the scope of this work.

The study results also show that most courses follow a practical or practical-theoretical approach in both kinds of programs; however, the CS Technology programs do not include any purely theoretical courses at all, which could be indicating that the knowledge delivered to students is the minimum required to run software projects and not to be life-long learners. Exams and projects are the most frequent types of evaluations for software engineering courses, but homework also play a relevant role in CS Engineering.

We found that both programs teach few software engineering courses in their first half. Most courses concentrate in the middle. As CS Technology is a shorter program, soft-

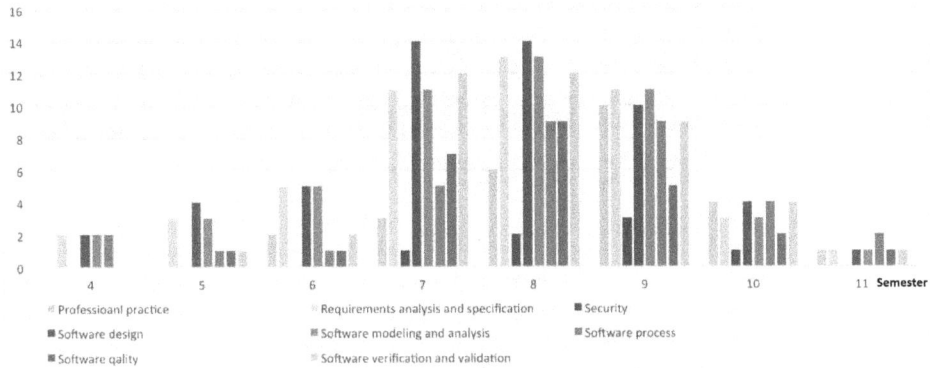

Figure 5: Courses Temporality in CS Engineering Programs

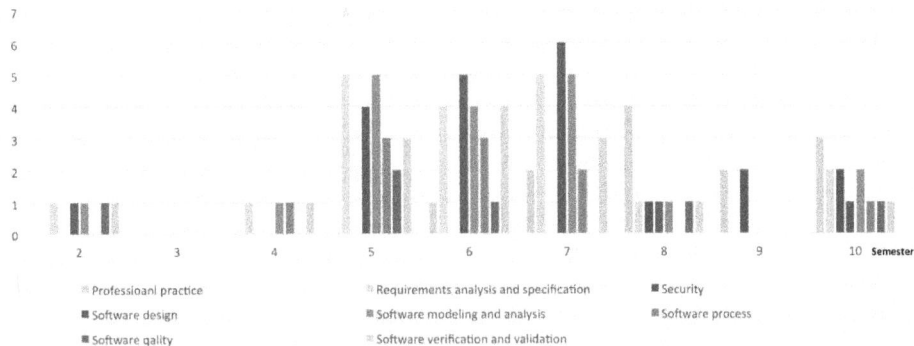

Figure 6: Courses Temporality in CS Technology Programs

ware engineering courses start in fifth semester while in CS Engineering in seventh. Even though we believe that students should learn software engineering earlier in their programs, they need to count on knowledge provided by other courses such as programming or databases before software engineering shows to be useful and meaningful for them.

The results suggest that the number of software engineering courses is quite low. However, is still to be proved if this is enough for students to perform satisfactorily in industry once graduated. Analyzing professional performance is part of our current work; we will use this information as a feedback for curriculum design taking into account the starting point reported in this work.

6. ACKNOWLEDGMENTS

The work of Maíra Marques Samary was supported by the PhD Scholarship Program of Conicyt Chile (CONICYT-PCHA/Doctorado Nacional/2012-21120544). This work was also partly supported by the Project Fondef IDeA IT13I20010.

7. REFERENCES

[1] Amin Khodabandeh Amiri, Maria Banari, and Narges Yousefnezhad. An investigation of undergraduate software engineering curriculum: Iranian universities case study. In *Computer Science & Education (ICCSE), 2011 6th International Conference on*, pages 638–644. IEEE, 2011.

[2] CRUCH. Consejo de Rectores de Chile. http://www.consejoderectores.cl/web/, January 2015.

[3] Samer Hanna, Hayat Jaber, Fawze Abu Jaber, Tarek Al Shalaby, and Ayad Almasalmeh. Enhancing the software engineering curriculums: A case study of the Jordanian Universities. In *Software Engineering Education and Training (CSEE&T), 2014 IEEE 27th Conference on*, pages 84–93. IEEE, 2014.

[4] Alok Mishra and Ali Yazici. An assessment of the software engineering curriculum in Turkish Universities: IEEE/ACM guidelines perspective. *Hrvatski časopis za odgoj i obrazovanje*, 13(1):188–219, 2011.

[5] The Joint Task Force on Computing Curricula Association for Computing Machinery (ACM) IEEE Computer Society. *Computer Science Curricula 2013*. 2013.

[6] Joint Task Force on Computing Curricula Association for Computing Machinery/IEEE Computer Society. Curriculum guidelines for undergraduate degree programs in software engineering. http://www.acm.org/binaries/content/assets/education/se2014.pdf, February 2015.

[7] WASE. Workshop on Advanced Software Engineering. http://jcc.stationdomain.com/files/WASE-2015.pdf, November 2015.

Results from a Survey of Faculty Adoption of Process Oriented Guided Inquiry Learning (POGIL) in Computer Science

Helen H. Hu
Westminster College
Salt Lake City, Utah, USA
hhu@westminstercollege.edu

Clifton Kussmaul
Muhlenberg College
Allentown, Pennsylvania, USA
kussmaul@muhlenberg.edu

Brian Knaeble
Westminster College
Salt Lake City, Utah, USA
bknaeble@westminstercollege.edu

Chris Mayfield
James Madison University
Harrisonburg, Virginia, USA
mayfiecs@jmu.edu

Aman Yadav
Michigan State University
East Lansing, Michigan, USA
ayadav@msu.edu

ABSTRACT

This paper presents an analysis of CS faculty perceptions of the benefits of POGIL, the obstacles to POGIL adoption, and opportunities for professional development. Participants strongly agreed that with POGIL, students are more engaged and active, develop communication and teamwork skills, and have better learning outcomes. The largest perceived obstacle was lack of preparation time; other obstacles included availability of relevant POGIL activities and pressure to cover more content. Participants expressed a desire for further training and mentoring beyond workshops. Our data analysis also considers bivariate associations and interactions. The results should help to improve professional development for CS faculty adopting evidence-based strategies, and thereby help more CS students to be successful.

1. INTRODUCTION

Process Oriented Guided Inquiry Learning (POGIL) is an evidence-based, student-centered pedagogy that focuses on the simultaneous development of *content knowledge* and *process skills* (such as critical thinking, problem solving, teamwork, and written/oral communication). Students work in learning teams on carefully designed activities that guide them to construct course concepts. POGIL incorporates techniques that have been shown to retain students from underrepresented groups, and it has been shown to be highly effective in chemistry, biology, and many other disciplines. This paper presents results and analysis from a survey of CS faculty who have attended POGIL training and/or adopted POGIL in their classrooms. The survey is intended to explore CS faculty perceptions of the benefits of POGIL, the obstacles to POGIL adoption, and options for professional development and support.

ITiCSE '16, July 11–13, 2016, Arequipa, Peru.

© 2016 Copyright held by the owner/author(s). Publication rights licensed to ACM.
ISBN 978-1-4503-4231-5/16/07. . . $15.00

DOI: http://dx.doi.org/10.1145/2899415.2899471

The ICAP framework [5] describes how learning outcomes tend to improve as student engagement progresses from *Passive* (read, watch) to *Active* (copy, rehearse) to *Constructive* (explain, generate, reflect) to *Interactive* (discuss, debate). Thus, in more effective strategies, students tend to work together to construct understanding. A variety of evidence-based strategies have been explored recently in CS education, including *Cooperative Learning* [1], *Pair Programming* [27], *Pedagogical Code Reviews* [18], *Peer Instruction* [22, 28], *Peer-Led Team Learning* [9, 15] and *Studio-Based Learning* [19]. Many of these strategies include elements that help close the achievement gap for students from underrepresented groups (e.g., [4]).

Unfortunately, very few faculty seek out and consistently adopt evidence-based strategies. CS faculty rarely (<10%) search methodically in the literature; most changes occur without outside sources, or via personal interactions [8]. Professional development often increases knowledge about innovations, but it rarely provides incentives or ongoing support [3]. A survey of 700 physics faculty found that only 23% currently used 3+ evidence-based strategies, 12% were unfamiliar with any, 16% had some knowledge but had never tried one, and 23% had tried one and stopped [13]. A survey of 400 US engineering faculty found that fidelity of implementation ranged from 11-80% [2]; i.e., faculty are likely to omit critical components.

Henderson et al. [13] conclude that: "... current change strategies seem to do a reasonably good job of helping faculty develop knowledge and motivation to try [evidence-based strategies]... It may be more fruitful to focus on those who discontinue use..." Thus, we need to better understand how to encourage and support faculty to adopt and persist with evidence-based strategies. Effective approaches for doing so are aligned with or seek to change beliefs, involve long-term interventions (at least one semester), and approach education as a complex system [12]. In many cases, evidence-based strategies cannot be adopted directly; they must be adapted and customized for particular institutions, student populations, and faculty [20].

Compared to other strategies, POGIL is more explicitly constructive and interactive because of the ways its activities are designed and facilitated. POGIL activities incorporate **models** (e.g., figures, tables, equations, sample code) and a sequence of **critical thinking questions** that guide students to *explore* the models, *invent* key concepts, and *apply* their new understanding [10]. The models and critical thinking questions must be robust and well-aligned, and they distinguish POGIL from simply having students complete worksheets in small groups [24]. In a POGIL classroom, self-managed teams of 3-4 students work together and discuss problems to improve understanding for all team members. At the same time, instructors purposefully help students to develop process skills such as critical thinking, problem solving, and teamwork. The instructor's role shifts from disseminator of information ("sage on the stage") to facilitator of learning ("guide on the side"), who continually assesses how and when to offer additional guidance as the teams work [10].

For example, instructors may use the following POGIL activity on the first day of CS 1 to show students that CS is about analyzing problems and solutions, not just programming. The first model lists instructions for a two-player game where Player A picks a number from 0 to 100 and then answers "too high" or "too low" in response to Player B's guesses. Critical thinking questions prompt the student teams to play the game (explore), and then to identify a set of strategies (algorithms) for player B, such as "guess at random", "count up by 1s", or "split the range in half". As the teams work, the instructor listens, answers questions, and prompts teams to improve their descriptions. After a few minutes, the instructor has each team describe a strategy to the class. Next, teams rank their strategies by number of guesses and how hard they are to describe, and compare the rankings to discover the common tradeoff between speed and difficulty (invent). Teams then identify other situations with similar tradeoffs, and share them with the class (apply). In the next cycle, the strategies are the model, which teams explore to find the maximum (worst case) and average number of guesses for each strategy, leading them to invent O()-style complexity analysis, which they then apply in homework.

POGIL was originally studied in college general chemistry courses, where it was found both to improve student performance and significantly decrease DFW grades (e.g., [7, 24, 25]). Hanson [10] summarizes the student outcomes for POGIL generally described in the literature: (1) attrition is lower; (2) content mastery is greater; (3) students prefer POGIL; (4) students have more positive attitudes about the course and the instructors; and (5) learning skills appear to improve. POGIL has been used across STEM disciplines including engineering [6, 26], mathematics [23], and physiology [29]; and at a variety of institutions including minority-serving and community colleges (e.g., [11, 14]).

POGIL is especially appropriate for CS, because it shifts student attention away from issues like language syntax and towards conceptual understanding. After converting a CS1 course to POGIL, one author saw pass rates increase for female students but not males [17]. A POGIL CS Principles course increased student interest in taking additional CS courses [16]. In a software project course, POGIL activities helped students to understand the importance of communication in real software projects [21]. A CS1 course with 29 POGIL-like cooperative activities yielded exam scores that were significantly higher overall and by major, ethnicity, and gender, compared to a traditional course [1].

However even for experienced faculty, POGIL requires significant effort to develop or adapt materials and to implement effective classroom facilitation techniques. Founded in 2005, the POGIL Project (https://pogil.org) is a nonprofit 501(c)3 that organizes regional workshops and develops classroom resources. The Project offers a curriculum of sixteen 90-minute sessions and a pool of trained workshop facilitators, using evidence-based propagation practices. Half- and full-day workshops offered throughout the year introduce basic concepts and practices to help instructors decide how to implement POGIL. Each summer, the Project organizes interdisciplinary, three-day POGIL regional meetings.

In the computer science education community, POGIL is relatively new but growing quickly. The CS-POGIL Project (see http://cspogil.org) has fostered a community of practice within CS through conference sessions and workshops, financial support for CS faculty to attend summer workshops on POGIL (25 faculty, including 4 at community colleges), and online discussions. At the time of writing, CS faculty have authored over 200 POGIL activities for a variety of CS undergraduate courses. These sets of activities make it easier for other CS faculty to adopt POGIL.

2. METHODS

The authors' personal experiences adopting POGIL and training and supporting other faculty, as well as the literature on effective propagation and professional development, has suggested that existing POGIL workshop experiences are valuable but often insufficient, and that faculty could benefit from additional support, such as advanced or discipline-specific workshops, enhanced classroom materials, and a community of practice. In order to accurately gauge faculty perceptions, we surveyed CS faculty involved in POGIL to explore their views about the benefits of POGIL, the obstacles to POGIL adoption, and options for professional development and support.

In December 2015, we invited 65 CS faculty from the United States (including both college and secondary teachers) to complete an online survey. Note that this is not a representative sample of all CS faculty, since we only invited faculty who had participated in POGIL training and/or taught using POGIL. Our survey (see https://goo.gl/forms/yov406fywh) was adapted from a national survey of science faculty's perceptions of implementing case-based instruction in undergraduate science courses [30]. Specifically, our survey asked about (a) demographics for the instructor and institution, (b) perceptions of POGIL's effect on students' experiences, (c) perceptions of potential obstacles to adopting POGIL, and (d) perceptions of what support would be helpful for CS faculty to adopt POGIL.

2.1 Demographics

The study participants were 32 CS instructors (49% response rate) from junior high (1), high schools (3), community colleges (3), and 4-year institutions (25). A majority of respondents (n=22) had attended a three-day POGIL Regional Meeting; these were referred to below as high training. Those who had not (n=10) were referred to as low training; of them, five had attended a one-day introductory POGIL workshop, and five had less than one day of training. Of the 32 respondents, 9 used POGIL at least biweekly, and another 11 used POGIL 3-6 times per semester. In the analyses below, high use refers to those who used POGIL at least 3 times per semester (n=20). Those who used POGIL fewer than three times per semester (n=12) are classified as low use, and this group includes those who had never used POGIL, and one user who had discontinued use of POGIL. In their classrooms, instructors used POGIL activities from multiple sources; 15 used activities shared directly by another CS instructor, 16 used activities from the CS-POGIL website (http://cspogil.org), and 23 developed their own activities.

2.2 Data Analysis

There were ten survey questions relating to POGIL's effectiveness, six survey questions relating to obstacles to adoption, and five survey questions relating to the helpfulness of additional support for instructors adopting POGIL. The effectiveness questions had five response options (5:strongly agree, 4:agree, 3:neutral, 2:disagree, and 1:strongly disagree), and also an N/A option for those who had not used POGIL. The obstacle questions had five response options (5:very strong, 4:strong, 3:middle, 2:somewhat, and 1:not at all) for the strength of each obstacle. The support questions had five response options (5:extremely helpful, 4:very helpful, 3:somewhat helpful, 2:slightly helpful, and 1:not at all). We performed an exploratory, descriptive analysis on the resulting data using R.

When describing data for a single variable, we report proportions without specifying confidence intervals, as we were not inferring to any well-defined population. We occasionally use the numerical correspondences from the previous paragraph to compute means. When describing data for pairs of variables we utilized the Wilcoxon rank-sum test for independent samples and the Wilcoxon signed-rank test for paired samples, as the response options were naturally ordered but not naturally spaced. The test statistics for the Wilcoxon rank-sum test and signed-rank test are denoted with W and V, respectively. In both cases we considered p values less than .05 as statistically significant.

Our stated statistics should be interpreted with caution. The Wilcoxon p values were not exact because we had repeated values, and small sample size may be to blame for lack of significance in some cases, especially when we restricted our attention to demographic subsamples. Concern about multiple comparisons is more valid with our stated W statistics than with our V statistics. Also, a small group of respondents may be responsible for a statistically significant result, and we recommend viewing graphs in addition to stated statistics. Interpretation of observed associations is provided in the text of Section 3.

3. RESULTS

3.1 Perceived Effectiveness

Figure 1 shows how strongly participants agreed with each statement, sorted by agreement. The x-axis of all figures is the number of respondents. There is strong agreement that students were more engaged (92%) and more active (88%). One respondent wrote "the most noticeable change is the increased engagement."

With regard to process skills, participants also agreed that students develop stronger skills in communication (84%) and teamwork (85%). One respondent wrote "students enjoy showing each other the concepts and how to understand them", while another noted "My students develop peer-to-peer relationships that lead to more learning opportunities, very important on a campus with 90% commuter students. In addition, their communication skills improve and this teaching method opens a dialog between professor and students."

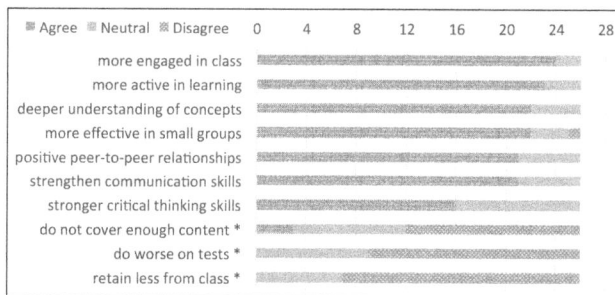

Figure 1: Perceptions of POGIL effectiveness measured by 26 POGIL instructors' agreement with 7 positive statements and 3 negative(*) statements.

A third respondent highlighted that the better peer-to-peer relationships affect other assignments: "The students form stronger relationships with their peers and I see more collaboration outside of the POGIL assignments."

Faculty also perceived an increase in student learning outcomes. Participants agreed that students developed deeper understanding (85%). There was also strong agreement that students did not retain less (73%), students did not do worse on tests (65%), and students did not feel they were covering too little content (54%). Some faculty appeared to tie this increase in student learning outcomes to increased engagement and collaboration: "Students are better able to make sense of the more confusing topics by being active in their own discovery and having ownership in what they are learning." Other free response answers suggest additional possible reasons: "POGIL activities helps to focus effort on the material that needs it", "students are developing conclusions instead of me telling them the conclusions", and "Students retain more, develop a vocabulary for discussing CS".

While we did not ask directly whether students perceived the same positive effect on learning outcomes, some faculty shared their experiences. One faculty wrote: "While I think students are learning more, they don't seem to think so." Another respondent found the reverse: "Student feedback from my CS 1 class was that they enjoyed the POGIL activities, and that they helped them better understand the content. They also felt the somewhat more conceptual approach helped them when they did the actual programming."

3.2 Obstacles to Adoption

In the next part of the survey, participants were asked to respond to six items to "indicate the degree to which you experienced these potential obstacles". Figure 2 summarizes participant responses, ordered by increasing percentage experiencing the obstacle. Of the six obstacles surveyed, the most frequently perceived obstacle was lack of preparation time (94% experiencing some difficulty, including 19% experiencing very strong difficulty). Availability of relevant POGIL activities (88%, including 6% very strong) and pressure to cover content (78%, including 6% very strong) were also obstacles for many instructors. 68% respondents experienced resistance from students (none very strong), whereas only a quarter experienced resistance from colleagues and administrators (3% very strong) as obstacles to adopting POGIL. 72% experienced difficulty adapting to teaching style (3% very strong).

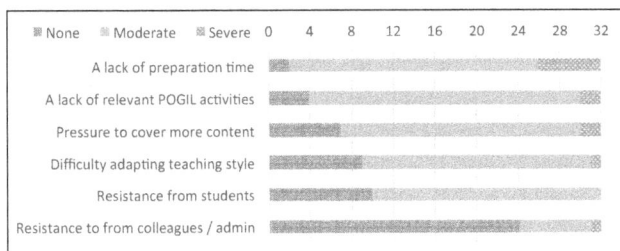

Figure 2: Obstacles to POGIL adoption (n=32)

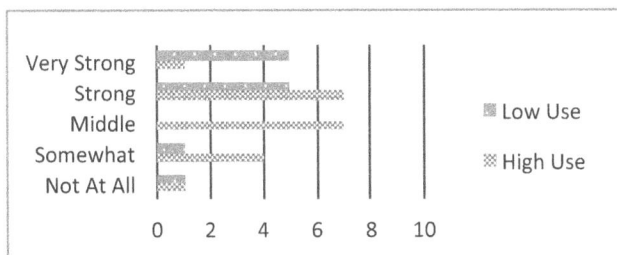

Figure 3: Lack of preparation time as a perceived obstacle to POGIL adoption (n=32). Low use may be due to a perceived lack of preparation time.

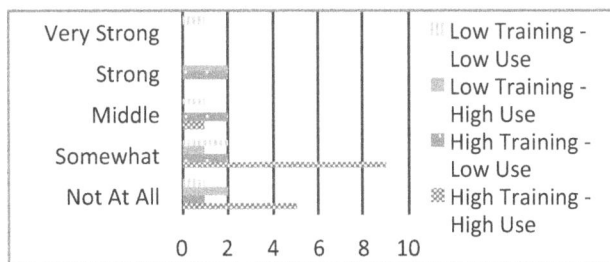

Figure 4: Difficulty adapting teaching style as a perceived obstacle to POGIL adoption (n=32). Highly-trained instructors may refrain from adoption due to perceived difficulty in adapting their teaching style.

For the "lack of preparation time", we found a significant association with POGIL use (W=61.5, p=.019), shown in Figure 3. Specifically, low use respondents (n=12, mean=4.0) experienced this obstacle more strongly than high use (n=20, mean=3.15). This suggests that low use respondents overestimate the preparation time required, or that there were economies of scale as the level of use increases. 44% of the respondents mentioned time in their answers to the free-response question about their main obstacles in adopting or implementing POGIL. While many were vague (e.g., "time") or cited lack of time to prepare, others seemed to be more concerned with classroom time, specifically "balancing lab time with POGIL time". Similarly, another instructor explained "It is challenging to provide enough coding practice time in-class, and POGIL takes time, some of which is coding." While the survey asked about "pressure to cover more content", some faculty may not have interpreted this pressure equivalent to lack of classroom time. Future surveys should include an additional question about classroom time.

88% of the respondents cited "a lack of relevant POGIL activities" as an obstacle to POGIL adoption, which seems connected to lack of preparation time. One respondent pointed out "Finding, selecting, and integrating existing activities may take as much time as authoring a custom activity. The advantage of using an existing activity is that it may be better designed than one I wrote just in time for class." Some people's concern about a lack of relevant POGIL activities may lessen with more POGIL use (W=85, p=.164).

In Figure 4, we observed a significant association (W=24.5, p=.036) between POGIL use and "difficulty adapting teaching style" among highly trained individuals (n=22). With regards to "difficulty adapting teaching style", the mean score for fifteen highly trained, high-use respondents was 1.73, and the mean score for seven highly trained, low-use respondents was 2.71. This difference suggests that some highly trained individuals may refrain from using POGIL because of difficulties associated with adapting their teaching style.

Six respondents mentioned classroom facilitation issues in their free-response answers about their main obstacles to implementing POGIL, including pacing the classroom experience, meeting the needs of students with prior knowledge, dealing with difficult students (both difficult personalities and difficult group dynamics), and "selling" POGIL to students ("hard to sell both Pair Programming and POGIL to the same group of students").

3.3 Forms of Support

In the last part of the survey, we asked faculty to estimate how "helpful would each of the following have been as you began to adopt POGIL, or if you have not tried POGIL, which do you think would be the most helpful if you decided to try it". Independent of prior training and current POGIL implementation, we observed interest in additional training and support. In free response questions, several suggested additional forms of support that were not mentioned in our survey (e.g., "videos of POGIL classes, to see more examples of facilitation", "more generic activities", and "a POGILized CS textbook").

72% of respondents believed that "face-to-face meetings with other POGIL practitioners" would be somewhat, very, or extremely helpful, while 66% said the same for virtual meetings. For each respondent we looked at the difference between their response for face-to-face meetings and their response for virtual meetings, and recorded their comparative preference (face-to-face more helpful, virtual more helpful, or neutral). Figure 5 shows how the distribution is skewed (V=107, p=.006). 44% prefer face-to-face, so the overall statistical significance is due to the opinions of a minority group. In free response questions, multiple respondents expressed an interest in mentorship and/or community, e.g., " a mentor to rely on for informal conversations" and "definitely more people to talk with regularly and share ideas for exercises."

Depending on the workshop topic, 59% to 75% of the respondents believed workshops would be somewhat, very, or extremely helpful. Some respondents preferred specialized workshops on POGIL classroom facilitation over general workshop training (V=110, p=.102), and preferred specialized workshops on authoring POGIL activities over general workshop training (V=92, p=.067). This could represent an overall desire for advanced training or two different areas of specific interest. High-use instructors were significantly more interested in facilitation over general workshops (W=170,

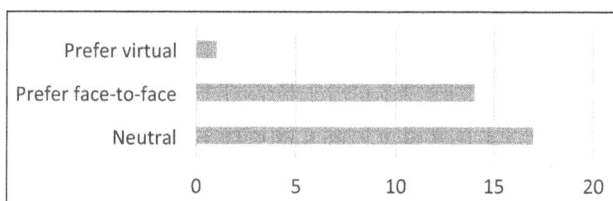

Figure 5: Regarding support, those with a preference desire face-to-face meetings over virtual meetings (14:1), but a majority (n=17) lack a preference.

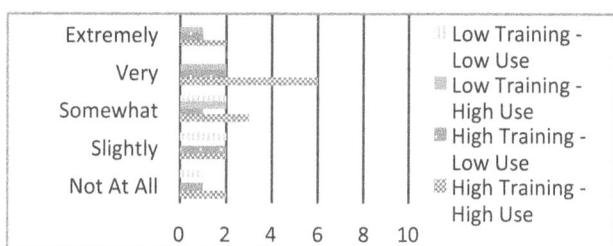

Figure 6: There is likely more interest in classroom observation among instructors with little training and high use of POGIL.

p=.038), perhaps because they are more aware of the importance and difficulty of effective facilitation.

69% of respondents believed classroom observations would be somewhat, very, or extremely helpful. Among the ten respondents with Low Training (see Section 2.1 for definitions, Figure 6 for graph), High Use instructors were significantly more interested in classroom observations (W=23, p=.030). The authors have viewed this effect personally: instructors are hesitant about classroom observations until after they start to teach with POGIL and suddenly have more questions about classroom facilitation. The effect is less for respondents with High Training, perhaps because the three-day POGIL Regional Meeting includes a workshop that demonstrates the value of classroom observations.

4. DISCUSSION

Survey respondents generally agreed that POGIL had a positive effect on students in the classroom, especially by keeping them more engaged and active in learning (see Figure 1). We examined each of the 10 measures of POGIL effectiveness and found no associations for high versus low training or for high versus low use of POGIL. These findings support prior research showing that people do not adopt new instructional strategies because those strategies are effective [8, 13]. Also, more training and more use did not appear to artificially inflate one's opinion of POGIL.

The greatest perceived obstacles included in the survey were lack of preparation time, availability of POGIL activities and pressure to cover more content. The results corroborate prior research that suggests that implementing active learning approaches faces similar barriers [30, 31]. Based on free responses, it seems possible that classroom time would rank high but this was not included in our survey. Most survey respondents did not perceive resistance to POGIL from colleagues or administrators to be an obstacle for adopting POGIL. The CS POGIL community could address these

obstacles by improving the number of CS POGIL activities and standardizing them to make them easier to adopt by different instructors, possibly reducing the prep time.

Highly trained individuals with low POGIL use in their classrooms are a subpopulation of particular interest when considering barriers to faculty adoption. Based on Figure 4, we hypothesize that perceived time constraints are the major obstacle. Data for highly trained instructors is consistent with this hypothesis that it is a perceived lack of time that prevents some highly trained instructors from using POGIL. We compared time concerns among highly trained individuals and found an association with use (W=26.5, p=.053), statistically insignificant possibly because of a smaller sample size (n=22), but nonetheless indicative of a possible mechanism for workshop organizers to be aware of.

In addition to addressing perceived obstacles in future POGIL workshops, we can use the survey results to help shape additional support for faculty adopting POGIL. Most respondents were interested in additional workshops (especially classroom facilitation and activity writing workshops), meetings with other POGIL practitioners, and even classroom observations. Faculty unsurprisingly preferred face-to-face meetings to virtual meetings, but 53% exhibited no preference for the type of meeting, suggesting that some number of faculty would benefit from even less-costly, virtual meetings. Given the increased interest in classroom observations with POGIL use, we hypothesize that classroom observations should occur after new POGIL adopters have had the opportunity to use POGIL a few times in the classroom, when they have more experience to form questions.

Because the effectiveness and obstacle statements were adapted from a survey of faculty adopting case studies to teach undergraduate science [30], it is possible to compare our results with those from the original study of science faculty (n=101). Responses from both studies had similar percentages for the effects on student engagement, peer-to-peer relationships, and test performance. POGIL was perceived by the CS POGIL faculty as being more effective for communication skills, whereas case-studies were perceived by science faculty as being more effective for active learning and deeper understanding of concepts. On the other hand, more CS POGIL faculty than science faculty reported some difficulty with the obstacles listed in the survey.

In the future, we will continue surveying the CS POGIL community to expand on our results. We will extend the list of questions to address other process skills, obstacles, and forms of support. It would be useful to replicate this survey with other (larger) populations in POGIL and other evidence-based strategies, to be able to compare benefits, obstacles, and support options across disciplines and strategies.

From a practical perspective, the results of this survey suggest ways to help more instructors adopt POGIL. Since preparation time, classroom time, and availability of activities are perceived barriers, POGIL workshops should be revised to more explicitly address these concerns. Similarly, additional sets of POGIL activities should be developed and enhanced to facilitate adoption and reduce the time required for adaptation. At least some instructors new to POGIL would benefit from more post-workshop support, such as classroom observations and other mentoring.

5. ACKNOWLEDGMENTS

This material is based upon work supported by National Science Foundation Grant DUE-1044679, a Google CS4HS grant, multiple Google CS Engagement grants, and a grant from the AAC&U TIDES Institute and the Leona M. and Harry B. Helmsley Charitable Trust.

6. REFERENCES

[1] L. Beck and A. Chizhik. Cooperative Learning Instructional Methods for CS1: Design, Implementation, and Evaluation. *ACM Transactions on Computing Education*, 13(3):10:1–10:21, 2013.

[2] M. Borrego, S. Cutler, M. Prince, C. Henderson, and J. E. Froyd. Fidelity of Implementation of Research-Based Instructional Strategies (RBIS) in Engineering Science Courses. *Journal of Engineering Education*, 102(3):394–425, 2013.

[3] S. E. Brownell and K. D. Tanner. Barriers to Faculty Pedagogical Change: Lack of Training, Time, Incentives, and...Tensions with Professional Identity? *CBE-Life Sciences Education*, 11(4):339–346, 2012.

[4] A. F. Chávez. Toward a Multicultural Ecology of Teaching and Learning: A Critical Review of Theory and Research. *Journal on Excellence in College Teaching*, 21(4):49–74, 2011.

[5] M. T. H. Chi and R. Wylie. The ICAP Framework: Linking Cognitive Engagement to Active Learning Outcomes. *Edu. Psychologist*, 49(4):219–243, 2014.

[6] E. P. Douglas and C.-C. Chiu. Implementation of Process Oriented Guided Inquiry Learning (POGIL) in Engineering. *Adv. in Eng. Edu.*, 3(3):1–15, 2013.

[7] J. J. Farrell, R. S. Moog, and J. N. Spencer. A Guided-Inquiry General Chemistry Course. *Journal of Chemical Education*, 76(4):570–574, 1999.

[8] S. Fincher, B. Richards, J. Finlay, H. Sharp, and I. Falconer. Stories of Change: How Educators Change Their Practice. In *Frontiers in Edu. Conf.*, 2012.

[9] L. Gafney and P. Varma-Nelson. *Peer-Led Team Learning: Evaluation, Dissemination, and Institutionalization of a College Level Initiative.* Springer Science & Business Media, 2008.

[10] D. M. Hanson. *Instructor's Guide to Process-Oriented Guided-Inquiry Learning.* Pacific Crest, 2006.

[11] T. Hemraj-Benny and I. Beckford. Cooperative and Inquiry-Based Learning Utilizing Art-Related Topics: Teaching Chemistry to Community College Nonscience Majors. *Journal of Chemical Education*, 91(10):1618–1622, 2014.

[12] C. Henderson, A. Beach, and N. Finkelstein. Facilitating Change in Undergraduate STEM Instructional Practices: An Analytic Review of the Literature. *Journal of Research in Science Teaching*, 48(8):952–984, 2011.

[13] C. Henderson, M. Dancy, and M. Niewiadomska-Bugaj. Use of Research-Based Instructional Strategies in Introductory Physics: Where Do Faculty Leave the Innovation-Decision Process? *Phys. Rev. ST Phys. Educ. Res.*, 8(2):020104, 2012.

[14] T. B. Higgins. Teaching Chemistry with POGIL at an Urban, Minority-Serving Community College. In *Abs. of Papers of The American Chemical Society*, 2013.

[15] S. Horwitz, S. H. Rodger, et al. Using Peer-Led Team Learning to Increase Participation and Success of Under-Represented Groups in Introductory Computer Science. *ACM SIGCSE Bulletin*, 41(1):163–167, 2009.

[16] H. Hu and B. Avery. CS Principles with POGIL Activities As a Learning Community. *Journal of Computing Sciences in Colleges*, 31(2):79–86, 2015.

[17] H. H. Hu and T. D. Shepherd. Teaching CS 1 with POGIL Activities and Roles. In *Proceedings of the 45th ACM Tech. Sym. on CS Education*, 2014.

[18] C. D. Hundhausen, A. Agrawal, and P. Agarwal. Talking About Code: Integrating Pedagogical Code Reviews into Early Computing Courses. *ACM Trans. on Computing Education*, 13(3):14:1–14:28, 2013.

[19] C. D. Hundhausen, N. H. Narayanan, and M. E. Crosby. Exploring Studio-Based Instructional Models for Computing Education. *SIGCSE Bulletin*, 40(1):392–396, 2008.

[20] A. Kezar. What Is the Best Way to Achieve Broader Reach of Improved Practices in Higher Education? *Innovative Higher Education*, 36(4):235–247, 2011.

[21] S. Kumar and C. Wallace. Instruction in Software Project Communication through Guided Inquiry and Reflection. In *IEEE Frontiers in Edu. Conf.*, 2014.

[22] C. B. Lee, S. Garcia, and L. Porter. Can Peer Instruction Be Effective in Upper-division Computer Science Courses? *ACM Transactions on Computing Education*, 13(3):12:1–12:22, 2013.

[23] L. Lenz. Active Learning in a Math for Liberal Arts Classroom. *PRIMUS*, 25(3):279–296, 2015.

[24] R. Moog. *Integrating Cognitive Science with Innovative Teaching in STEM Disciplines*, chapter Process Oriented Guided Inquiry Learning, pages 147–166. Washington University Open Scholarship, 2014.

[25] R. S. Moog and J. N. Spencer, editors. *Process-Oriented Guided Inquiry Learning (POGIL).* American Chemical Society, 2008.

[26] M. Rutten. A POGIL Approach to Teaching Engineering Hydrology. In *American Geophysical Union Fall Meeting Abstracts*, 2012.

[27] N. Salleh, E. Mendes, and J. Grundy. Empirical Studies of Pair Programming for CS/SE Teaching in Higher Education: A Systematic Literature Review. *IEEE Trans. on Software Eng.*, 37(4):509–525, 2011.

[28] B. Simon and Q. Cutts. Peer Instruction: A Teaching Method to Foster Deep Understanding. *Communications of the ACM*, 55(2):27–29, 2012.

[29] T. Vanags, K. Pammer, and J. Brinker. Process-Oriented Guided-Inquiry Learning Improves Long-Term Retention of Information. *Advances in Physiology Education*, 37(3):233–241, 2013.

[30] A. Yadav, M. Lundeberg, et al. Teaching Science with Case Studies: A National Survey of Faculty Perceptions of the Benefits and Challenges of Using Cases. *Journal of College Science Teaching*, 37(1):34–38, 2007.

[31] A. Yadav, G. M. Shaver, and P. Meckl. Lessons Learned: Implementing the Case Teaching Method in a Mechanical Engineering Course. *Journal of Engineering Education*, 99(1):55–69, 2010.

The Effectiveness of Visualization for Learning Expression Evaluation: A Reproducibility Study

Amruth N. Kumar
Ramapo College of New Jersey
Mahwah, NJ 07430, USA
1 201 684 7712
amruth@ramapo.edu

ABSTRACT

A study was conducted to reproduce the results of an earlier study on the effectiveness of visualization for learning expression evaluation in a problem-solving software tutor on arithmetic expressions. In the current reproducibility study, data was collected from a software tutor on assignment expressions over six semesters. ANOVA analysis of the amount and speed of learning was conducted with treatment, sex and racial groups as fixed factors. Results include that visualization helped the students learn significantly more concepts, whether the students needed to use the tutor or benefited from using the tutor. However, it only benefited the less-prepared students. It did not help the students learn faster. It benefited both the sexes and traditionally represented as well as underrepresented groups. The current study confirmed almost all the results from the previous study, albeit for a harder topic. One reason why visualization was found to be effective in both these studies may be that the same visualization scheme was used by the students to both view feedback and construct their answers.

1. INTRODUCTION

Program visualization deals with visualizing programs at lower levels of abstraction [10]. It may be static or dynamic, the latter also referred to as program animation. Program visualization systems may be specialized or generic: the former visualize specific programming constructs, whereas the latter visualize entire programming languages [10]. The subject of the current study is static program visualization, specialized for expression evaluation.

A systematic review of generic program visualization and animation systems cataloged a mix of systems that were never evaluated, those that did not yield positive results, those whose results were not statistically significant and those with significant positive results [10]. Another survey of successful evaluations of visualization systems found that about half of the evaluations were only about usability; and a third were informal, "with little contribution to future improvements" [11]. A meta-

study of algorithm visualization, the other type of software visualization found similarly equivocal results [2].

Few of the specialized visualization systems, i.e., those built for specific programming constructs, have been evaluated. Among those that have been evaluated, one study found that animation was no more effective than text explanation for learning the semantics of C++ pointers [3]. Another study found that graphic visualization with text explanation was better than graphic visualization alone when learning expression evaluation [4].

A recent large-scale study of a specialized visualization system for arithmetic expression evaluation found that visualization indeed helped students learn more concepts, but that the "benefits primarily accrued to less-prepared students." [6]. Arithmetic expressions, the subject of the reported study, are arguably one of the easiest topics in introductory programming. Could the results of the study be **reproduced** with assignment expressions, arguably one of the harder expressions in programming languages thanks to prefix, postfix, and compound assignment operators? This was the question addressed by the current study.

Reproducibility is a core principle of scientific research. A recent study of reproducibility of 100 results published in 2008 in three top Psychology journals highlights its importance: It found that only 35 of the 100 results could be reproduced at a statistically significant level [8]. The reproduced results were weaker than the claims made in the original paper for *all* 100 studies, although no claim was disproven. A hyper-competitive scientific culture that prizes novelty, and provides little incentive to reproduce earlier findings or publish results of such studies was found partly to blame for this state of affairs. Reproducibility as an issue is increasingly being addressed by numerous Computer Science research communities, as revealed by a search of the ACM digital library (e.g., Human Computer Interaction, Software Engineering, Recommender Systems, Databases, Simulation, Systems Research, Data Mining), but Computer Science Education research is not one of them.

Reproducibility is not replicability. Whereas reproducibility refers to the ability to draw the same results using different instruments, methods, protocols and/or participants, replicability refers to repeating the original experiment with exactly the same instruments, methods, protocols and participants to see if the same results can be obtained. Reproducibility is desirable, whereas replicability is not even "good science" [1].

Being able to reproduce the results of the earlier study on arithmetic expressions [6] would not only provide additional support to the results of the earlier study, but also extend the results to harder topics such as assignment expressions. In this

ITiCSE '16, July 09 -13, 2016, Arequipa, Peru
© 2016 ACM. ISBN 978-1-4503-4231-5/16/07...$15.00
DOI: http://dx.doi.org/10.1145/2899415.2899427

context, the current study was conducted to evaluate the effectiveness of visualization in a software tutor on assignment expressions and possibly reproduce or refute results from the earlier study [6].

2. METHODOLOGY
2.1 Participants
The participants of the study were students in introductory programming courses from 41 institutions: 1721 students from baccalaureate institutions, 154 from community colleges and 104 from high schools over six semesters: Fall 2011-Spring 2014. Students were given the option to identify their sex and race. 1348 students identified themselves as male, and 487 as female. 1275 students identified themselves as Caucasians or Asians, the traditionally represented groups in Computer Science, and 256 identified themselves as belonging to underrepresented racial groups. Since this was a controlled study, institutions were randomly assigned to control or experimental group each semester.

2.2 Instrument – The Software Tutor
The instrument used for this study was a software tutor on assignment expression evaluation. The tutor presents expressions to the student, has the student evaluate each expression one operator at a time, grades the student's answer and provides feedback. The student evaluates each operator by dragging the mouse across the operator and appropriate operands to draw an underbrace across them, and entering the intermediate result in the dialog box presented for the underbrace. The feedback includes whether the student's answer is correct and step-by-step explanation of the correct answer, which has been shown to help students learn [5].

The tutor covers the following concepts: simple assignment, compound assignment, prefix and postfix increment and decrement operators, precedence and associativity of assignment operators, and narrowing and widening coercion during assignment. The tutor is accessible over the web – students can use it on their own time, and at their own convenience. It is part of a suite of problem-solving tutors for introductory programming topics, available for free for educational use called problets (problets.org).

The feedback provided by the tutor is in two forms:

- **Text explanation** feedback explaining each step in the evaluation of the expression. For example, the text explanation provided for the expression -- weight is:

```
The value of weight is 14
weight is decremented to 13
-- weight returns 13
Prefix -- operator returns the value of
the variable after decrementing it
```
- **Graphic visualization** feedback in the form of an underbrace spanning the operator (-- in the above example) and operands (weight above), with the intermediate result (13 above) drawn centered underneath the underbrace.

Figure 1 shows a snapshot of the two forms of feedback.

Graphic visualization explains the order of evaluation of operators, but not concepts such as coercion. So, it was provided in addition to rather than instead of text explanation. The benefits of simultaneous presentation of the same information in text and visual forms is explained by dual coding theory [9], which postulates that visual and verbal information are processed differently, in separate channels, to organize the information and create separate mental representations, either of which can be used later to recall the information.

2.3 Protocol
The software tutor administered pre-test-practice-post-test protocol as follows:

Pretest – During the pretest, the tutor presented one problem per concept. If a student solved a problem correctly, no feedback was provided to the student, and no more problems were presented to the student on the concept. On the other hand, if the student solved a problem incorrectly, or opted to skip the problem because the student did not know the answer, feedback was presented to the student and additional problems on the concept were scheduled to be presented during the subsequent stages.

Adaptive practice – Once a student had solved *all* the pretest problems, practice problems were presented to the student on only the concepts on which the student had solved problems incorrectly during the pre-test. For each such concept, the student was presented multiple problems until the student mastered the concept. After solving each problem, the student received feedback explaining the correct answer. Since this was a controlled study, students in the control group received only text explanation whereas those in the experimental group received both text explanation and graphic visualization.

Post-test - During this stage, the student was presented test problems on the concepts that the student had mastered during the adaptive practice.

Demographics - Students were provided the option to identify their demographic information, including sex and race.

The entire protocol was limited to 30 minutes and was administered back-to-back, entirely over the web. A concept was considered to have been learned during this session if the student solved the problem on that concept incorrectly during the pre-test, solved enough problems during the adaptive practice to master the concept, and proceeded to solve the problem on the concept correctly during the post-test.

2.4 Design
The dependent variables of this study were all between-groups:
- Pre-test mean score per problem, calculated as the total pre-test score divided by the number of pre-test problems solved – this normalized the variation in the number of problems solved by the students (10-17). Since the students used the tutor after classroom instruction on assignment expressions, pre-test score was a measure of their *prior knowledge*;
- Number of concepts learned;
- Number of practice problems solved per learned concept, calculated as the number of problems solved during practice, divided by the number of concepts learned, once again, to normalize the variation in the number of concepts learned by the students. Since the tutor was adaptive, and presented practice problems on a concept until the student had mastered the concept, the more the practice problems a

student needed to learn a concept, the slower *the pace of learning*.

The independent variables of this study were:

- Treatment – text explanation only versus text explanation with graphic visualization.
- Sex: male or female.
- Representation – traditionally represented (Caucasians and Asians) versus underrepresented (the other racial groups, viz., Black/African American, Hispanic/Latino, Native American, Native Hawaiian/Pacific Islander and Other races)

2.5 Data Collection

The pre-test contained 17 problems for C++ and 16 problems for Java. Since students could use the tutor as often as they pleased, if a student used the tutor multiple times, only the first attempt when the student solved all the pre-test problems was considered. If the student never solved all the pre-test problems, the attempt with the most number of pre-test problems solved was considered. In order to eliminate trial or frivolous attempts by students, only those sessions were considered where students solved at least 10 pre-test problems. After this sifting, the control group contained 1112 students and experimental group, 867 students – this was the group for which statistics were reported earlier in Section 2.1.

Although students from high schools, community colleges and undergraduate institutions used the tutor, in order to maintain homogeneity of participant population, we considered only students from undergraduate institutions.

2.6 Data Analysis

A typical expression contains one or more operators. The grade awarded for a problem was calculated by the software tutor as the number of operators correctly evaluated, divided by the total number of operators in the expression. Therefore, the score on each problem was normalized to $0 \rightarrow 1.0$ regardless of the number of operators in the expression.

Univariate ANOVA analysis was conducted for the dependent variables listed in Section 2.4, with treatment, sex and representation as the fixed factors.

3. RESULTS

We first analyze the data of all the students. Thereafter, we consider subsets of students based on programming language, need, benefit and preparation to see if we can localize the results obtained for the entire population. We list only significant results (i.e., main effects), except for treatment.

3.1 All the undergraduate students

The results of analyzing the pre-test score per problem were:

- *No difference in the prior knowledge of the control (N=751) and test (N=565) groups.* So, any subsequent difference between the groups can be attributed to the use of the tutor.

- Male students scored significantly higher than female students and traditionally represented students scored significantly higher than students from under-represented groups as shown in the table below. *So, male students and students from traditionally represented groups had*

significantly greater prior knowledge than their counterparts.

Pre-test Score	N	Mean
Sex [F(1,1315) = 8.845, p = 0.003]		
Male	965	0.872 ± 0.013
Female	351	0.835 ± 0.021
Representation [F(1,1315) = 13.601, p < 0.001]		
Traditional	1121	0.877 ± 0.01
Underrepresented	195	0.83 ± 0.023

Analysis of the number of concepts learned found that the experimental group learned significantly more concepts than the control group [F(1,787) = 3.831, p = 0.051] as shown in the table below, i.e., *students learned more with visualization than without.*

Concepts Learned	N	Mean
Control	446	2.679 ± .288
Test	342	3.104 ± .314

Analysis of the number of practice problems solved per learned concept yielded no significant results.

3.2 C++ Students

We considered C++ students who had solved all 17 pre-test problems (N=352). The results of analyzing the pre-test score per problem, summarized in the table below, were that the control group students scored significantly *more* than the experimental group students; male students scored significantly higher than female students; and traditionally represented students scored significantly higher than students from under-represented groups. In other words, the control group students, male students and students from traditionally represented groups had significantly greater prior knowledge than their counterparts.

Pretest Score	N	Mean
Treatment [F(1,351) = 9.778, p = 0.002]		
Control	275	0.882 ± 0.027
Test	77	0.800 ± 0.043
Sex [F(1,351) = 13.222, p < 0.001]		
Male	285	0.889 ± 0.026
Female	67	0.794 ± 0.044
Representation [F(1,351) = 27.607, p < 0.001]		
Traditional	296	0.91 ± 0.023
Underrepresented	56	0.773 ± 0.046

The results of analyzing the number of concepts learned, as summarized in the table below, were that the experimental group learned significantly more concepts than the control group, i.e., *students learned significantly more with visualization than without;* and female students learned significantly more concepts than male students.

Concepts Learned	N	Mean
Treatment [F(1,160) = 5.233, p = 0.024]		
Control	127	2.456 ± .471
Test	34	3.621 ± .889
Sex [F(1,160) = 4.932, p = 0.028]		
Male	128	2.473 ± 0.709
Female	33	3.604 ± 0.715

The results of analyzing the number of practice problems solved per learned concept, as summarized in the table below, were that the experimental group solved significantly more problems per learned concept than the control group, and female students solved significantly more problems per learned concept than male students. In other words, *the pace of learning was significantly slower with visualization than without, and for female students as compared to male students.* .

Practice Problems	N	Mean
Treatment [F(1,160 = 4.118, p = 0.044]		
Control	127	3.105 ± 0.276
Test	34	3.71 ± 0.52
Sex [F(1,160) = 9.787, p = 0.002]		
Male	128	2.941 ± 0.415
Female	33	3.874 ± 0.418

3.3 Java Students

We considered Java students who had solved all 16 pre-test problems (N=730). The results of analyzing the pre-test score per problem were:

- *There was no difference in the prior knowledge of the control (N=346) and test (N=384) groups.*

- Male students scored marginally higher than female students, and traditionally represented students scored significantly higher than students from under-represented groups, as shown in the table below.

Pretest Score	N	Mean
Sex [F(1,729) = 2.996, p = 0.084]		
Male	517	0.875 ± 0.017
Female	213	0.845 ± 0.029
Representation [F(1,729) = 5.259, p = 0.022]		
Traditional	629	0.88 ± 0.012
Underrepresented	101	0.84 ± 0.031

Analysis of the concepts learned and the number of practice problems solved per learned concept yielded no significant results.

3.4 Students who needed to use the Tutor

A normalized score of 1.0 represented ceiling effect. The students who scored less than 1.0 stood to benefit from using the tutor, since they had incorrectly solved one or more problems during the pretest. For our next analysis, we considered all the students whose normalized score was 0.95 or less – this included even those who had incorrectly solved exactly one problem.

The results of analyzing the pre-test score per problem were:

- *There was no difference in the prior knowledge of the control (N=438) and test (N=327) groups.*

- Traditionally represented students scored significantly higher than students from under-represented groups [F(1,764) = 7.34, p = 0.007] as shown in the table below.

Pretest Score	N	Mean
Traditional	636	0.799 ± 0.012
Underrepresented	129	0.759 ± 0.026

Analysis of the concepts learned found that the experimental group learned significantly more concepts than the control group [F(1,619) = 4.973, p = 0.026] as shown in the table below,

i.e., *students learned significantly more with visualization than without.*

Concepts Learned	N	Mean
Control	264	3.019 ± .316
Test	356	3.547 ± .342

Analysis of the number of practice problems solved per learned concept yielded no significant results.

3.5 Students who benefited from the Tutor

The students who benefited from using the tutor were those who learned at least one concept. For our next analysis, we considered all the undergraduate students who had learned at least one concept.

The results of analyzing the pre-test score per problem were:

- *There was no difference in the prior knowledge of the control (N=446) and test (N=342) groups.*

- Male students scored marginally more than female students, and traditionally represented students ˙ scored significantly higher than students from under-represented groups, as shown in the table below.

Pretest Score	N	Mean
Sex [F(1,787) = 2.769, p = 0.097]		
Male	559	0.83 ± 0.16
Female	229	0.806 ± 0.23
Representation [F(1,787) = 8.7, p = 0.003]		
Traditional	677	0.84 ± 0.011
Underrepresented	111	0.797 ± 0.027

Analysis of the concepts learned found that the experimental group learned significantly more concepts than the control group [F(1,787) = 3.831, p = 0.051] as shown in the table below, i.e., *students learned significantly more with visualization than without.*

Concepts Learned	N	Mean
Control	342	2.679 ± .288
Test	446	3.104 ± .314

Analysis of the number of practice problems solved per learned concept yielded no significant results.

3.6 Less-prepared Students

The mean of normalized pre-test scores for the entire undergraduate cohort was 0.853. The students who scored 0.853 or lower on the pre-test were less-prepared as compared to those who scored more than 0.853. We next considered the less-prepared undergraduate students.

Analysis of the pre-test score per problem found *no difference in the prior knowledge of the control (N=281) and test (N=177) groups.*

Analysis of the concepts learned found that the experimental group learned significantly more concepts than the control group [F(1,379) = 6.859, p = 0.009] as shown in the table below, i.e., *students learned significantly more with visualization than without.*

Concepts Learned	N	Mean
Control	233	3.568 ± .377
Test	147	4.326 ± .427

Analysis of the number of practice problems solved per learned concept yielded no significant results.

3.7 Better-prepared Students

Finally, we considered the better-prepared students: those whose normalized score was over the cohort average of 0.853, but under 1.0. We excluded the students who had scored 1.0 since they knew all the concepts, and could not benefit from using the tutor.

Analysis of the pre-test score per problem found that *there was no difference in the prior knowledge of the control (N=249) and test (N=246) groups*.

Analysis of the concepts learned and the number of practice problems solved per learned concept yielded no significant results.

4. DISCUSSION

The following table summarizes the results of the various cases that we analyzed in the previous section. The rows correspond to the 7 cases we considered: **All** the students, **C++** students, **Java** students, the students who **need**ed the tutor, the students who **benefit**ed from using the tutor, the **less**-prepared students and the **better**-prepared students. For each of **Pretest Score**, **Concepts Learned** and **Problems per Learned concept**, the columns list Treatment (**T**), Sex (**S**) and Representation (**R**). A cell contains a check mark if a statistically significant result was found for it, e.g., when **all** the students were considered, a significant difference was found between the sexes (**S**) on the **Pretest Sore**.

	Pretest Score			Concepts Learned			Problems per Concept		
	T	S	R	T	S	R	T	S	R
All		√	√	√					
C++	√	√	√	√	√		√	√	
Java		√	√						
Need				√					
Benefit				√	√				
Less				√					
Better									

From the **Pretest Score (T)** column of the table, it is clear that the prior preparation of the control and experimental groups was statistically comparable in all but one case. Yet, from the **Concepts Learned (T)** column of the table, it is clear that *visualization helped the students learn significantly more concepts in most cases. It helped the students learn more concepts, whether the students needed to use the tutor or benefited from using the tutor. However, it only benefited the less-prepared students, not the better-prepared ones.*

From the **Problems per Concept (T)** column of the table, it is clear that *visualization did not help the students learn faster, as measured by the number of practice problems solved per learned concept.* In the one instance when a significant

difference was found for treatment (C++), learning was slower with visualization than without!

Considering the lack of significant differences in **S** and **R** columns of **Concepts Learned** and **Problems per Concept**, we can state that 1) the tutor was not biased towards either sex or racial group; and 2) *both the sexes and racial groups benefited the same from using the tutor.* In the one case (C++) when a significant difference was found for sex, female students learned *more* concepts, although at a *slower* pace than male students.

From (**S**) and (**R**) columns of **Pretest Score**, we can summarize that regrettably, *female students were often less-prepared before using the tutor than male students and underrepresented students were often less-prepared than traditionally represented students.* In the prior study, arithmetic expressions were used [6]. Since many of the concepts covered as arithmetic expressions in programming languages are typically also covered in K-12 math, it is harder to localize the reason for the differences in the prior preparation of the sexes and racial groups, if any. Assignment expressions on the other hand are concepts unique to programming languages – it is safe to assume that they are not covered in K-12 math. Any prior knowledge of assignment expressions is acquired by the students in class or through programming activity. This leads to one of two explanations for the lower prior-preparation of female and underrepresented students:

- Although introductory programming courses typically assume that students will not have had any prior programming experience, this may not be entirely accurate. Male and traditionally represented students may be entering the introductory programming course with more exposure to programming concepts than their counterparts. If so, providing additional encouragement to female and underrepresented students in high school to engage in programming activities may redress this difference.

- Somehow, male and traditionally represented students learn better from classroom instruction of introductory programming concepts than their counterparts. If so, Computer Science educators and education researchers may want to isolate the instructional strategies for introductory programming that are effective across sexes and races and propagate them.

Since this is a reproducibility study, comparison of the results from this study with those from the previous study [6] are in order. Primary results of the prior study were that "visualization helped students learn more concepts; visualization did not increase the speed of learning; the benefits of visualization accrued primarily to less-prepared students; and visualization may affect different demographic subgroups differently". All the results were reproduced in the current study except the last one – the population size of the current study was not large enough to confirm/refute whether visualization affected different demographic subgroups (e.g., underrepresented female students) differently. Students find the subject of this study, viz., assignment expressions to be harder than arithmetic expressions, the subject of the prior study. So, in addition to confirming the results of the earlier study, this study extended those results to harder topics.

So, why was visualization found to be effective in both the studies, especially for the less-prepared students, when the form of visualization was "viewing", one of the least effective forms of engagement [7]? It could be because students also "constructed" their answer using the same visualization scheme before submitting it, and "constructing" is considered to be one of the highest levels of engagement [7]. Using the same visualization scheme to both view feedback and construct answers may hold the key to improving the effectiveness of visualization in software tutors. For instance, just as drawing underbraces was found to be effective for evaluating expressions, the following student-constructed visualization techniques might turn out to be effective for other program comprehension tasks: drawing boxes around code segments to clarify scope; drawing arrows across code to trace the flow of control and data; and superimposing state diagram on the code to track and debug the lifecycle of variables. Future work includes evaluating the effectiveness of these student-constructed visualization techniques in online tutors.

5. ACKNOWLEDGMENTS

Partial support for this work was provided by the National Science Foundation under grant DUE 1432190.

6. REFERENCES

[1] Drummond, C. Replicability is not Reproducibility: Nor is it Good Science. Proc. Evaluation Methods for Machine Learning Workshop, 26th ICML, Montreal, Canada, 2009.

[2] Hundhausen, C.D., S.A. Douglas, and J.T. Stasko, A meta-study of algorithm visualization effectiveness. Journal of Visual Languages and Computing, 2002. 13(3): p. 259-290.

[3] Kumar, A.N., Data Space Animation for Learning the Semantics of C++ Pointers, in SIGCSE Technical Symposium2009: Chattanooga, TN. p. 499-503.

[4] Kumar, A.N., Results from the Evaluation of the Effectiveness of an Online Tutor on Expression Evaluation, in 36th SIGCSE Technical Symposium2005: St. Louis, MO. p. 216-220.

[5] Kumar, A.N., Explanation of step-by-step execution as feedback for problems on program analysis, and its generation in model-based problem-solving tutors. Technology, Instruction, Cognition and Learning (TICL) Journal, 2006. 4(1).

[6] Kumar, A.N. The Effectiveness of Visualization for Learning Expression Evaluation. Proc. 40th SIGCSE Technical Symposium on Computer Science Education. SIGCSE 2015. Kansas City, KS. 362-367.

[7] Naps, T.L., et al., Exploring the role of visualization and engagement in computer science education, in SIGCSE Bulletin 2003. p. 131-152.

[8] Open Science Collaboration, Estimating the reproducibility of psychological science, Science, Vol. 349(6251), 28 August 2015

[9] Paivio, A., Mental representations: A dual coding approach, 1990, New York: Oxford University Press.

[10] Sorva, J., V. Karavirta, and L. Malmi, A Review of Generic Program Visualization Systems for Introductory Programming Education. Transactions on Computing Education, 2013. 13(4): p. 1-64.

[11] Urquiza-Fuentes, J. and J.Á. Velázquez-Iturbide, A Survey of Successful Evaluations of Program Visualization and Algorithm Animation Systems. Transactions of Computing Education, 2009. 9(2): p. 1-21.

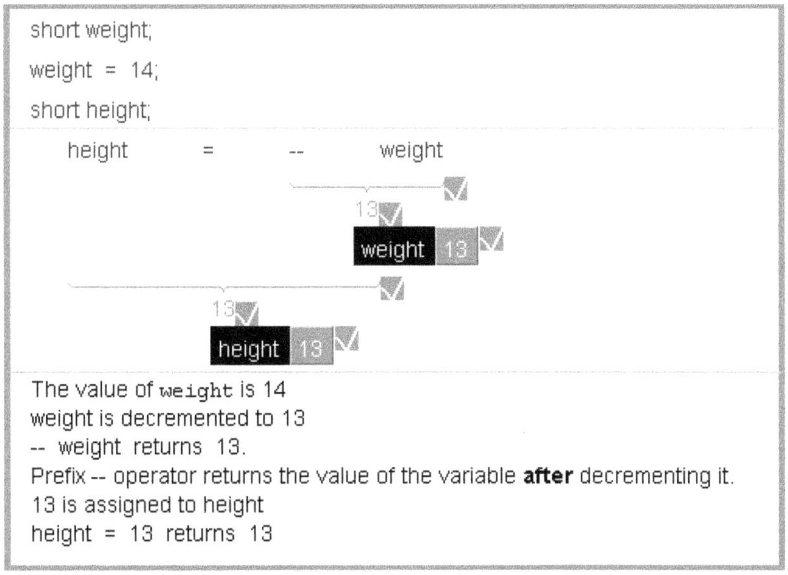

Figure 1 (© Amruth N. Kumar): Screen shot of the feedback provided by Assignment Expression Tutor. Both graphic visualization (between the two pink lines) and text explanation (after the second pink line) are shown. Courtesy: problets.org.

Investigating Factors Influencing Students' Intention to Dropout Computer Science Studies

Ilias O. Pappas, Michail N. Giannakos and Letizia Jaccheri

Department of Computer & Information Science Norwegian University of Science and Technology (NTNU)

Sem Saelands vei 9, Trondheim, NO-7491, Norway

+47 73 59 34 88, +47 73 59 07 31, +47 73 59 34 69

{ ilpappas, michailg, letizia.jaccheri } idi.ntnu.no

ABSTRACT

Research in the area of Computer Science (CS) education, has focused on identifying the reasons that students do not finish their studies in CS. Although there is increasing demand for CS professionals, there is not enough knowledge to explain the high dropout rates in CS education. This study aims to empirically examine how students' intention to complete their studies (retention) in CS is affected by variables playing a key role in higher education. By identifying which variables contribute to dropout in CS studies, we will be able to focus on how to improve aspects related with them in order to reduce dropout rates. To do so we identified the following variables: Year of studies, Gender, Age, Students' Effort, Absence from Classes, Expected Grade point average (GPA), and Current GPA, and tested their effect on retention, based on the responses collected from 241 CS student. Year of studies and Effort have positive effects on students' intention to finish their studies in CS. Interestingly, the expected GPA has a negative effect on students' intentions to finish their studies. The findings contribute to theory and practice, as they offer CS educators and policy makers insights that may aid towards increased student retention and reduced dropout rates.

Categories and Subject Descriptors

[Computing Education]: Computing Education Programs, Computer Science Education.

General Terms

Measurement, Experimentation, Human Factors.

Keywords

Computer Science Education; Retention; Dropout; Higher Education.

ITiCSE '16, July 09 - 13, 2016, Arequipa, Peru
Copyright is held by the owner/author(s). Publication rights licensed to ACM.
ACM 978-1-4503-4231-5/16/07 $15.00
DOI: http://dx.doi.org/10.1145/2899415.2899455

1. INTRODUCTION

In the past decade, an increase started to occur in the degrees in Computer, Information Science and Technology [1] a field which has received increased attention as there is an expanding need for CS professionals [2; 3]. In this study, the term Computer Science (CS) is used.

Based on employment projections from the Bureau of Labor of Statistics (see: US Bureau of Labor Statistics) [4], students in CS have second thoughts on completing their studies, obtaining their degree and finding a job in the field of CS. To this end, based on a 2015 report from European Commission [5], a shortage of over than 800.000 CS professional is expected by the year 2020 in Europe (see also: ICT Skills Action Plan 2014-2018) [6].

Extant literature in the area has examined students' retention and suggests that students with high levels of academic and social integration are likely to experience higher levels of retention and graduation odds [7-11]. Previous studies indicate that student dropout rates may be reduced [12], suggesting that there is a need to identify the reasons that may aid students in completing their studies in CS. To this end, it is important to better understand and explain how, during their studies, CS students choose to stay and complete their studies or to dropout from them [13].

Previous studies in CS, regarding student dropout and retention, suggest that the first two years are critical for the students as they present the higher dropout point [14]. The findings indicate an almost 40% dropout rate for these years, which may vary from 30%-40% based on the institution [15]. Poor quality of teaching, increased demands, poor performance have been identified as critical factors in students' decision to dropout from STEM related disciplines (Science, Technology, Engineering, and Mathematics) and choose to major on a different one [16].

This research aims to investigate students' intention to complete their studies in CS education. Specifically, variables playing a key role in higher education were identified and empirically tested as per their contribution to dropout in CS studies. In particular, we tested how Year of studies, Students' Effort, Expected GPA, Current GPA, Absence from Classes, Gender, and Age effect students' intention to finish their studies in CS. Our hypotheses were tested on 241 CS students' responses.

This study is organized into six sections. The second section presents the background and the hypotheses. Next, the methodology followed is described. Section four presents the data analysis, while section five describes the findings of the study. Finally, the last section presents the discussion of the findings along with implications, limitations and suggestions for future research.

2. BACKGROUND AND HYPOTHESES

2.1 Background

Students in CS need to gain many competences and skills that are necessary for them to pursue a career in the industry, such as software, hardware, communications, electronics, networks, and so on. Such competences and skills include software estimation, project management, communication, and progress management which all may be acquired through CS education as it offers a great range of knowledge (e.g., programming, software design, information retrieval etc.) [17]. CS education is able to help students with creative thinking that will help them offer solutions to the various problems of the industry. CS students may gain the opportunity to identify technical innovations, innovate themselves and create a career in the best sectors of the industry, such high tech companies or work for government agencies. CS education is based on competences and skills, such as computation thinking, problem solving, human behavior. Such skills are among the most important skill in the 21st century because they offer the students the opportunity to build artifacts by using computers.

Regardless of how important are the skills acquired in CS education, the dropout rates remain considerably high while in the mean time there is an increasing demand for CS professionals. Previous studies have identified that almost 40% of the students who enroll on a CS degree program dropout from their studies [15]. The decreased number of CS graduates will lead to a smaller workforce in the IT industry. Hence, it is critical to identify factors that influence students' intention to complete their studies and investigate how they affect their behavior, in order to reduce the dropout rates in CS education.

2.2 Hypotheses

2.2.1 Year of studies and demographics

Various aspects have been found to influence students' behavior in their studies and their intentions towards majoring in CS (e.g., [10; 18], including demographic characteristics (e.g., gender) as well as factors that describe students' status of their studies (e.g., year of studies). Thus, in this study, we examine the *year of studies and demographics* of the CS students, which include their Year of studies, age, and gender. Students' perceptions regarding their future in CS are expected to evolve, and sometimes change, during their studies. Students that have limited knowledge about CS are likely to be less interested to continue studying in CS [19], as would be the case for students in their first year of studies compared, for example, to older students being in their second or third year. The year of studies and demographics are likely to affect student intention to complete their studies in CS, thus we propose the following hypotheses:

> H1. Students' retention is significantly related with their Year of studies.
>
> H2. Students' retention is significantly related with their Age.
>
> H3. Students' retention is significantly related with their Gender.

2.2.2 Effort and Performance

Previous research in the area has identified the importance of the difficult learning material, along with the demanding exams as factors that may influence students' behavior in CS and STEM studies [20]. This suggests that the effort and time the students put in their studies and courses is related with their performance and behavior, because course difficulty is likely to influence CS persistence [21]. Thus, in this study we examine students' *Effort*

and Performance, which include Effort, Absence, Expected GPA, and Current GPA. Furthermore, academic preparation, which can be obtained by high efforts, is considered as an important antecedent of persistence regarding students' intention to continue studying in CS [22]. For successful academic preparation, it is expected from students to be present in the courses, since absence from class has been found to influence student performance in higher education [23]. When students put more effort in their studies their performance will be affected, thus leading to a different learning outcome [24]. Students create high expectations to themselves regarding their performance, when they compare to their peers or their excellent performance in high school [7]. Thus, it is likely for students that have accomplished performance in their studies, to present high intentions to complete their studies.

> H4. Students' retention is significantly related with the effort they put in their studies.
>
> H5. Students' retention is significantly related with their absence from the courses.
>
> H6. Students' retention is significantly related with their expected GPA.
>
> H7. Students' retention is significantly related with their current GPA.

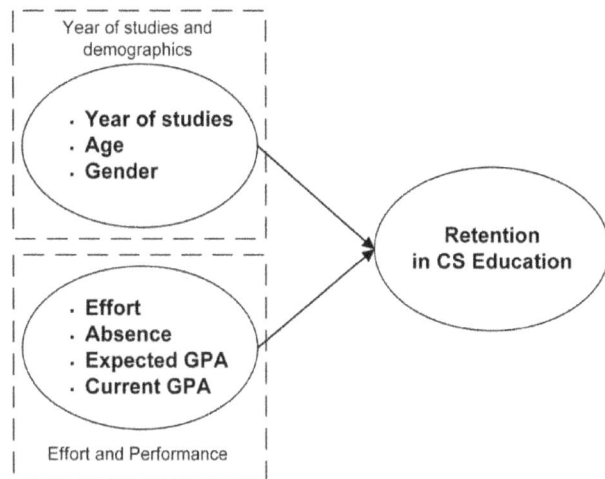

Figure 1. Conceptual Model for students' intention to complete their studies (retention) in CS education

3. METHODOLOGY

3.1 Sampling

The data was obtained through a survey delivered to about 1050 Norwegian CS students. From the 1050 CS students, 438 responded. Reponses with over 5% of missing variables were removed from the sample. The respondents were students from the Bachelor in Informatics, the 5-year Master in CS and from 2-year Master programs. For this study, the sample is created based on the class level of the CS students. In order to be consistent, we include students that are in the first, second, or third year of their studies, thus the sample consists only of students from the Bachelor in Informatics and from the 5-year Master in CS.

Eventually, 241 students are used for the analysis, out of which almost half (52.3%) are enrolled on the Bachelor in Informatics and the rest (47.7%) are enrolled on the 5-year Master in CS. The vast majority of the respondents (78.8%) were males. Regarding the age of the sample, 41% were 21 or 22 years old, 23% were 20 years old, 12% were 19 years old, and the rest (24%) are 23 years old or older. Finally, almost 43% were in their first year of studies, and the rest (57%) being in their second or third year of studies.

3.2 Measures

The questionnaire that was handed out to the students aimed to measure their intention to complete their studies in CS. First, it included questions regarding the demographics of the sample (e.g., gender, age). Further, it included measures that may affect students' decision to leave studies in CS (e.g., GPA, effort, expected progress) Finally, a question regarding students' intention to complete their studies in CS was asked. A 7-point Likert scale was used to measure the amount of effort students' put in their studies, and their intentions' to finish their studies. Their overall grade point average (GPA) was measured from A to E, and their absence from class was measured as the times they missed a course (i.e., 0-1,2-3,4-5,6-7,8+).

4. Data Analysis

In order to examine how intention to complete studies in CS differs based on the aforementioned factors, independent sample t-tests are performed for each factor separately. We used the unequal variance t-test, also referred in the literature as the Welch test, which is not affected by unequal sample sizes [25], which is the case in this study. To this end, the data were separated into two groups by performing median split on Effort, Expected GPA, Current GPA, Absence, and Age, thus creating the low and high groups respectively. For Year of studies the students were divided into two groups, comprising of those in their 1st year of studies and those in their 2nd or 3rd year of studies. In order to be consistent, we chose only the students in their first three year of studies, thus removing from the sample those on the 4th or 5th year of the 5-year study program. Consequently, the students from the two study programs may be studied together as they are expected to present similar characteristics. Gender was divided in males and females. Further, the construct of Intention to complete your studies was evaluated in terms of reliability and validity.

In order, to test for reliability the Cronbach alpha indicator was used, which requires to be higher than 0.7 for the factor [26]. Also, the item validity was assessed by measuring the loading of every item on the construct. The loadings are suggested to be higher than 0.7 [27]. Next, establishing construct validity requires that average variance extracted (AVE) is greater than 0.50 and that the correlation between the different variables in the confirmatory models does not exceed 0.8 points, as this suggests low discrimination [27]. The analysis was performed with the use of the SPSS Version 19.0 software.

5. Findings

Reliability testing, based on the Cronbach alpha indicator, suggests acceptable indices of internal consistency, as the constructs of retention is above the cut-off threshold of .70. Further, the loading of items into the construct, should be over .7 [27] suggesting validity at the item level. The AVE for retention is .80, above the cut-off threshold of .50. The findings are presented in Table 1.

Further, the correlation among the constructs is examined, and as indicated in Table 2, all correlations are significant and lower than .80. The opposite would suggest that there is low discrimination among the constructs.

Table 1. Measurements for Student Retention

	Items	Mean (SD)	CR	AVE	Loading
Retention	I plan to continue to work towards my degree	6.45 (1.2)	.92	.8	.843
	It is likely to finish my studies	6.48 (1.12)			.89
	I plan to complete my degree	6.58 (1.07)			.94

Table 2. Measurements and Spearman correlations of the constructs

Construct	Mean (SD)	\multicolumn{8}{c}{Construct}								
		1	2	3	4	5	6	7	8
1.Year of studies	1.8 (0.79)	1							
2.Age	21.6 (2.53)	.49	1						
3.Gender	1.79 (0.41)	-.04	.02	1					
4.Effort	4.83 (1.11)	-.1	-.05	-.09	1				
5.Absence	3.12 (1.44)	.18	.21	.01	-.18	1			
6.Expected GPA	2.4 (0.70)	.02	-.06	-.13	.32	.05	1		
7.Current GPA	2.78 (0.81)	.13	.07	-.14	-.28	-.02	.58	1	
8.Retention	6.42 (1.18)	.08	-.06	.01	.26	.02	-.2	-.13	1

Correlations of .1 or higher are significant, p< 0.01. All constructs are single item factors except Retention.

To examine the hypotheses regarding the effect of Effort, Expected GPA, Current GPA, Absence, Gender, and Age on student Retention, first we divided all variables into two categories (i.e., low and high) by performing a median split. For the Year of studies, we divided the students in two categories, that is students in the first year of studies and students in the second or third year of studies. Next, we performed t-tests including student Retention as a dependent variable, and the other factors (Year of studies, Effort, Expected GPA, Current GPA, Absence, Gender, Age) as independent variables. The reported analysis was conducted with a .05 level of significance. Table 3 presents the findings from the independent samples t-test.

By observing Table 3, we notice that three out of seven examined factors affect significant students' retention. For Year of studies, Effort, and Expected GPA there is a significant difference between the two groups regarding students' intention to finish their studies in CS.

Table 3. Testing the effect of the selected variables on students' intention to complete their studies in CS

Dependent Variable	Mean (S.D.)		T
	Low	**High**	
	Effort		
	6.09 (1.49)	6.60 (0.91)	**-2.88***
	Expected GPA		
	6.56 (1.00)	6.23 (1.26)	**2.04***
	Current GPA		
Retention	6.42 (1.27)	6.41 (1.14)	0.04
	Absence		
	6.42 (1.13)	6.41 (1.25)	0.11
	Age *(median split to 21)*		
	6.44 (1.22)	6.34(1.04)	0.60
	Year of studies *($1^{st}/2^{nd}$-3rd)*		
	6.21 (1.45)	6.57 (0.91)	**-2.14***
	Gender *(Male – Female)*		
	6.60 (0.71)	6.38 (1.27)	0.11

*p< 0.05

In detail, there is a positive difference between 1st year students and those in their 2nd and 3rd year. The latter have higher intentions to complete their studies in CS, indicating a positive effect of Year of studies on students' retention. Next, there is a difference between the students that put low effort on their studies and those that put high effort, with the latter having higher intentions to continue their studies, suggesting a positive effect of effort on students' retention. Further, the students that expect low GPA, have higher intentions to continue their studies in CS that those that expect high GPA, indicating a negative effect of the Expected GPA on students' retention.

On the other hand, the level of Current GPA does not affect significantly students' intention to complete their studies with the levels of low and high Current GPA being almost equal. Similarly, the absence from the courses has no significant effect on students' intentions as both low and high absence have nearly the same level of retention. Finally, regarding the two demographic variables that we examined, neither made a significant difference on student retention. Specifically, male students had higher intentions to complete their studies than female students. Finally, younger students, 21 years old or younger had higher intention to complete their studies from older students, 22 years old or older.

Observing Table 3, we notice that only effort, expected GPA and year of studies have significant effect on students' intention to complete their studies, and from Figure 2, we can observe that expected GPA is the only one with a negative effect on retention. In other words, the higher are the expectations the more likely is to dropout. In addition, age and gender seem to have an influence which is insignificant based on the t-test. Although insignificant, we must acknowledge the negative effect of age; figure 2 exhibits that the influence of age is reversed compared to the year of studies, this is strange since age and year of studies are very much related (i.e., in most of the cases the higher the age the higher is the year of studies). Overall, Figure x clearly exhibits the significant (based on the t-test) influence of students' efforts, expected GPA and year of studies on students' intention to complete their studies (retention).

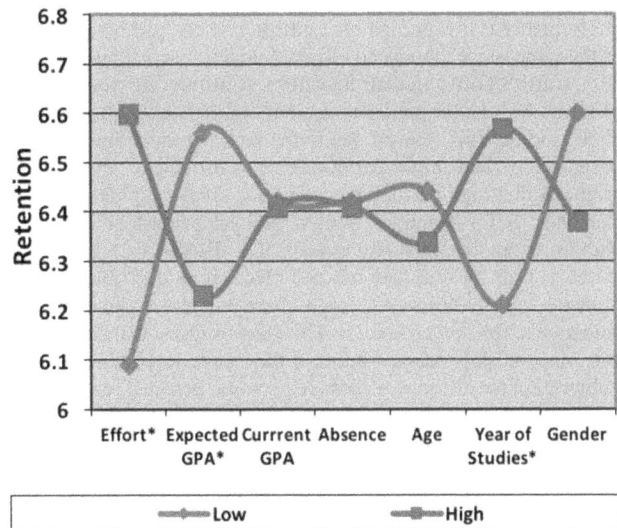

Figure 2 The influence of students' studies status, demographics and expectations in their intention to complete their studies

6. DISCUSSION AND CONCLUSION

Previous studies in the area of CS have explored various reasons and strategies on how to retain students that major in CS (e.g., [7; 10]) or reasons that students choose to major in CS (e.g., [18]). This study attempts to provide insights on why students may choose to leave their studies in CS. The main objective of this work is to empirically investigate the relationship among CS students' intention to finish their studies and various factors related with students' efforts, expectations and stage of their studies.

The findings indicate that three factors may affect students' intentions regarding their decision to finish their studies in CS; those are Year of studies, Effort, and Expected GPA. Firstly, the results demonstrate that students in their 2nd or 3rd year of studies have higher intention to finish their studies in CS, which may be explained by the fact that after finishing successfully the first year they have already adopted the philosophy (and difficulties) of CS education, in addition the students who think of changing major or dropping out – it is most likely to do so during the first year of their studies; hence these students will not be surveyed in the second or third year. Further, our findings regarding the lower intention to complete studies in CS are consistent with previous studies who have found that the largest dropout occurs in the first year of studies [14]. Next, the findings indicate a positive relationship between Effort and Retention, an expected outcome, since when students decide to put more effort in their studies is because they have higher intentions to finish them. This finding may be related with the Year of studies of the students, since complete each year suggests also putting more effort into studying. Finally, the results demonstrate a negative relationship between students' expected performance (i.e., Expected GPA) and their intentions to finish their studies, indicating that expectations for high performance lead to reduced retention. A quite interesting result, which may be explained by the fact that students who have set their expectations very high, might not be able to fulfil them, especially in the CS field which is a challenging one, with many departments with high competition. Previous studies have found that (female) students are likely to lose their confidence in their studies when they compare their excellent high school performance [13], thus creating high expectations.

On the other hand, the findings suggest that either students' performance is low or high their intention to complete their studies is the same, since there is no effect of students' actual performance (i.e., Current GPA) on their intentions. However, we would expect students with better grades to present higher intention to compete their studies. This may be due to the fact that the majority of the respondents had high performance. Nonetheless, the finding suggests that high performance may not always explain students' behavior, as for example students may achieve a high GPA, but they may not be fully interested in CS. Further, we found that absence from the courses has no effect on student retention, as students with either low or high absence had the same level of intention to finish their studies. This might suggest that students do not miss or skip courses because they have lost interest in the subject, but for different reasons (e.g., work, personal reasons) that do not affect their decisions about finishing their studies.

Finally, both gender and age do not affect students' intention to finish their studies in CS, partially in contradiction to previous studies that found gender to influence students' decisions in their CS majors [18]. Male students' exhibit higher intentions finish their studies, but the difference is not significant, probably due to the fact that the vast majority of CS students are males and the few females are interested in the subject; another explanation can be the high gender equality of the Norwegian context of the study (Norway has been described as a "haven for Gender Equality" by CEDAW[1]). Although age has no significant effect on retention, it is interesting to note that younger students have higher intention to complete their studies than older students. Since, all students are either on their first, second or third year of studies, the findings suggest that the older someone start studies in CS, the more likely is that he or she will drop out.

The findings may aid professors, administrators and CS policy makers, as this study makes a step towards the better understanding and encountering of students' dropout behavior by identifying the high dropping out risk groups or groups that are sensitive to some specific important factors influencing CS students' to dropout from their studies. It is crucial to identify dropout reasons in order to be able to reduce the dropout rates, because the need for CS students in IT industry is rising in the 21st century. The faculties should focus on treating differently freshmen students since they have low rates of retention and higher dropout rates, for example by offering courses with clear relation between the expected work and the grade as well as avoiding very difficult courses (e.g., sophisticated math courses) which might disappoint students and drop their expectations brutally. Further, it may be helpful redesign faculty interventions to evoke students' interest in the subject, and lead them to put more effort in their studies, which was found to increase their intention to finish their studies.

Although the present study offers evidence on why students choose to complete their studies in CS, it is exploratory and has some limitations. The sample consists only of Norwegian CS students; thus the generalization of the results should be performed with caution. However, the CS study programs that were used in this study, conforms to the international standards as they have been defined by the ACM/IEEE Computer Science 2013 curriculum guidelines for undergraduate programs in computer science [17]. Further, we should note that the sample of this study was collected from a single survey, thus limiting the generalization and interpretation of the findings.

Further research is needed to replicate and verify our findings, and to determine if these results characterize students who have left their studies (dropout) or others who have graduated and now work in the industry (e.g., via an alumni survey). In particular, future studies with larger sample from different countries and universities (i.e., United States) and educational systems' using wide variety of measures (i.e., observations, interviews) would valuable contribute on the understanding of factors influencing students' intentions to dropout their studies in CS. In addition, we propose further work in examining the effect of additional factors (e.g., analytics from LMSs explaining learning styles and habits) on students' intention to dropout.

7. Acknowledgements

The authors would like to thank all the students that took part and responded in this study. Also the authors want to thank the Norwegian Research Council for its financial support under the project FUTURE LEARNING (number: 255129/H20).

8. References

[1] Zweben, S. and Bizot, B., 2015. CRA Taulbee Survey Report 2014: Relentless Growth in Undergraduate CS Enrollment; Doctoral Degree Production Remains Strong but No New Record. *Computing Research News.*

[2] Giannakos, M.N., Doukakis, S., Pappas, I.O., Adamopoulos, N., and Giannopoulou, P., 2015. Investigating teachers' confidence on technological pedagogical and content knowledge: an initial validation of TPACK scales in K-12 computing education context. *Journal of Computers in Education 2*, 1, 43-59.

[3] Wilson, Z.S., Holmes, L., Sylvain, M.R., Batiste, L., Johnson, M., McGuire, S.Y., Pang, S.S., and Warner, I.M., 2012. Hierarchical mentoring: A transformative strategy for improving diversity and retention in undergraduate STEM disciplines. *Journal of Science Education and Technology 21*, 1, 148-156.

[4] U.S. Bureau of Labor Statistics (BLS), 2010. *Employment Projections 2010-2020*, available at http://www.bls.gov/emp/

[5] European Commission, 2015. *Skills & Jobs*. Retrieved 23 Dec. by: http://ec.europa.eu/digital-agenda/en/skills-jobs

[6] ICT Skills Action Plan 2014-2018, 2014. *Government, Education and Industry working together to make Ireland a global leader in ICT talent*, retrieved 19 Feb. by: http://cork.etb.ie/wpcontent/uploads/sites/20/2014/08/1404201 4-ICT_Skills_Action_Plan-Publication.pdf

[7] Cohoon, J., 2006. Just get over it or just get on with it. *Retaining women in undergraduate computing. In J. Cohoon & W. Aspray (Eds.), Women and information technology: Research on underrepresentation*, 205-238.

[8] Doll, J.J., Eslami, Z., and Walters, L., 2013. Understanding why students drop out of high school, according to their own reports. *Sage Open 3*, 4, 2158244013503834.

[9] Gramling, T., 2013. How five student characteristics accurately predict for-profit university graduation odds. *SAGE Open 3*, 3, 2158244013497026.

---

[1] http://www.un.org/press/en/2003/wom1377.doc.htm

[10] Rosson, M.B., Carroll, J.M., and Sinha, H., 2011. Orientation of undergraduates toward careers in the computer and information sciences: Gender, self-efficacy and social support. *ACM Transactions on Computing Education (TOCE) 11*, 3, 14.

[11] Xenos, M., Pierrakeas, C., and Pintelas, P., 2002. A survey on student dropout rates and dropout causes concerning the students in the Course of Informatics of the Hellenic Open University. *Computers & Education 39*, 4, 361-377.

[12] Barker, L., Hovey, C.L., and Thompson, L.D., 2014. Results of a large-scale, multi-institutional study of undergraduate retention in computing. In *Frontiers in Education Conference (FIE), 2014 IEEE* IEEE, 1-8.

[13] Biggers, M., Brauer, A., and Yilmaz, T., 2008. Student perceptions of computer science: a retention study comparing graduating seniors with cs leavers. In *ACM SIGCSE Bulletin* ACM, 402-406.

[14] Huang, P.M. and Brainard, S.G., 2001. Identifying determinants of academic selfconfidence among science, math, engineering, and technology students. *Journal of women and minorities in science and engineering 7*, 4.

[15] Ohland, M.W., Sheppard, S.D., Lichtenstein, G., Eris, O., Chachra, D., and Layton, R.A., 2008. Persistence, engagement, and migration in engineering programs. *Journal of Engineering Education 97*, 3, 259-278.

[16] Seymour, E., 2000. *Talking about leaving: Why undergraduates leave the sciences*. Westview Press.

[17] ACM/IEEE Computing Curricula Task Force, 2013. *Computer science curricula 2013: Curriculum guidelines for undergraduate degree programs in computer science*. Technical report, Association for Computing Machinery (ACM) IEEE Computer Society.

[18] Barker, L.J., McDowell, C., and Kalahar, K., 2009. Exploring factors that influence computer science introductory course students to persist in the major. In *ACM SIGCSE Bulletin* ACM, 153-157.

[19] Carter, L., 2006. Why students with an apparent aptitude for computer science don't choose to major in computer science. *ACM SIGCSE Bulletin 38*, 1, 27-31.

[20] Jacobs, J.E., 2005. Twenty-five years of research on gender and ethnic differences in math and science career choices: What have we learned? *New directions for child and adolescent development 2005*, 110, 85-94.

[21] Araque, F., Roldán, C., and Salguero, A., 2009. Factors influencing university drop out rates. *Computers & Education 53*, 3, 563-574.

[22] Mau, W.C., 2003. Factors that influence persistence in science and engineering career aspirations. *The Career Development Quarterly 51*, 3, 234-243.

[23] Arulampalam, W., Naylor, R.A., and Smith, J., 2012. Am I missing something? The effects of absence from class on student performance. *Economics of Education Review 31*, 4, 363-375.

[24] Yu, T. and Jo, I.-H., 2014. Educational technology approach toward learning analytics: Relationship between student online behavior and learning performance in higher education. In *Proceedings of the Fourth International Conference on Learning Analytics and Knowledge* ACM, 269-270.

[25] Ruxton, G.D., 2006. The unequal variance t-test is an underused alternative to Student's t-test and the Mann-Whitney U test. *Behavioral Ecology 17*, 4, 688-690.

[26] Cronbach, L.J., 1951. Coefficient alpha and the internal structure of tests. *psychometrika 16*, 3, 297-334.

[27] Hair, J., Tatham, R., Anderson, R., and Black, W., 2006. Multivariate data analysis (Vol. 6): Pearson Prentice Hall Upper Saddle River NJ.

Global Perspectives on the Role of Two-Year/Technical /Junior Colleges in Computing Education

Cara Tang
Portland Community College
Portland, OR, USA
cara.tang@pcc.edu

Elizabeth K. Hawthorne
Union County College
Cranford, NJ, USA
hawthorne@ucc.edu

Cindy S. Tucker
Bluegrass Community and Technical College
Lexington, KY, USA
cindy.tucker@kctcs.edu

Ernesto Cuadros-Vargas
San Pablo Catholic University
Arequipa, Peru
ecuadros@spc.org.pe

Diana Cukierman
Simon Fraser University
Burnaby, BC, Canada
diana@sfu.ca

Simon
University of Newcastle
Australia
simon@newcastle.edu.au

Ming Zhang
Peking University
Beijing, China
mzhang@net.pku.edu.cn

ABSTRACT

This panel presents varying global perspectives on the role of community colleges and 2- or 3-year technical schools (collectively called junior colleges here) in computing education. In some countries, students interested in a career in computing can obtain a 2- or 3-year degree instead of, or as a precursor to, a traditional Bachelor's degree. With representatives from five different countries and four different continents, the panel discusses the variety of pathways in computing education around the world, and in particular the role of community colleges and 2- or 3-year technical schools in these pathways.

1. INTRODUCTION

The landscape of higher education institutions includes, in addition to traditional universities (which may or may not have graduate programs as well as undergraduate programs), colleges and technical schools that offer shorter-term degrees and programs, usually 2 or 3 years. These schools go by varying names in different countries and for ease of reference we use the term junior college to refer to them collectively.

Junior colleges play an important role in computing education. They may be a source of students transferring into traditional university programs; they may provide terminal degrees for technician or entry level roles in computing; they may provide computing education courses in non-degree formats and to non-traditional students. The panel will discuss the purpose and role these varying institutions from around the world play in providing computing education.

ITiCSE '16, July 09-13, 2016, Arequipa, Peru
ACM 978-1-4503-4231-5/16/07.
DOI: http://dx.doi.org/10.1145/2899415.2899420

2. DISCUSSION

The members of the panel represent five different countries in which junior colleges play an important role in computing education.

2.1 Australia

In Australia the 'two-year degrees' are called diplomas, and have traditionally been offered by state-based TAFEs, government-subsidized institutes of Technical And Further Education, which generally offer technical and vocational qualifications. Progression to a diploma is typically by way of a number of certificates, which would each take one or two semesters to complete.

A two-year TAFE diploma often offers a deeper coverage of core topics than a three-year university degree, as the former is tightly focused while the latter is a broader education.

Linkages between TAFEs and universities are varied. In some cases, where a TAFE and a university share the same campus, university entrants with TAFE diplomas are given close to full credit for their TAFE study; in other cases the credit is minimal.

In recent years the Australian government has extended its subsidies to private education providers, with two unfortunate effects: the TAFEs are struggling, unable to compete across a very broad spectrum with providers targeting highly specific programs such as computing; and a number of those providers have been operating questionably: inducing students with the offer of a free laptop, regardless of their academic capability; making it exceedingly difficult to withdraw from courses; and even granting diplomas after a fixed time despite never having taught the students.

2.2 Canada

In Canada, education is a provincial jurisdiction, and so the country has a distinct higher education system in each province, and the vast majority of students study at publicly funded, non-profit schools. In general, Canadian higher education offers government regulated 1- and 2-year academic, pre-professional and trades credentials at institutes of technology, technical colleges, and regional colleges. These credentials are known as certificates (6 months to 1 year), diplomas (2 years), associate degrees (2 years) and advanced diplomas (2+ years) in technical and career programs. In some provinces Colleges and Institutes of Technology also offer 4-year degrees, usually in career-oriented fields, and, in some provinces, technically-oriented master's degrees [3].

These institutions are not lesser versions of universities, but rather serve to provide institutional specialization within a larger education ecosystem. In some provinces, such as British Columbia and Alberta, significant effort is made to ensure that there is a seamless transition between colleges and universities to support articulation and student mobility between institutions.

2.3 China

Junior college education in China began around 1950 when a model similar to the U.S. community college system was explored and adopted [2]. The Chinese community colleges which only admitted local students now faced an awkward situation where they had trouble enrolling students, so that most of the institutions transformed into delivering community training services.

Currently, there are two types of vocational education systems in China: the secondary vocational schools and the junior colleges. No longer limiting enrollments to the community, both types enroll students city wide, province wide, or nation wide. The secondary vocational schools provide 2- to 4-year programs in parallel with high schools. The junior colleges provides 2- and 3-year programs with lower requirements than higher colleges.

In 2014, about 5.8 million students graduated from Chinese secondary vocational schools (including general secondary specialized schools, vocational high schools, adult secondary specialized schools, and technical schools), and about 5.6 million of them successfully got jobs, which puts the employment rate at 96.68%. Very few graduates take the National College Entrance Exam (Gaokao) along with high school students and pursue higher education.

The national higher education gross enrollment rate reached 37.5%, including both junior and higher college education in 2014. About 7.3 million students graduated from national colleges, and junior and higher colleges had 3.9 million and 3.4 million graduates, respectively. Among all the graduates, nearly one million students were from computer related majors. The students whose Gaokao scores are not high enough for higher colleges can be admitted to junior colleges. Higher colleges owned by local municipal governments such as Beijing are required to reserve up to 15% of enrollments for the graduates from junior colleges. These students can have 2 to 3 years of further study to get their Bachelor's degrees. The employment rate after graduation from junior colleges is 83.7%, as compared to 66% from higher colleges.

2.4 Peru

Peru offers tertiary education which includes both higher education (including universities, technical colleges, and pedagogical colleges) and vocational education. Technical colleges offer 3-year academic courses focusing on technical professions such as computer technician, nursing technician, accounting technician, among others, with titles endorsed by the Peruvian government. Technical colleges also offer 1-year and 2-year academic courses, focusing on technical and vocational education. The titles of these certificates and diplomas are only endorsed by the technical colleges themselves. Finally, technical colleges also offer several short courses, to meet a particular niche market such as Cisco, Oracle, or computer assembly, among others.

Academic institutions focusing in technical-productive areas aim to satisfy the demand of a particular niche market at the technical level or technical assistant level. These courses generally last 1 year or 6 months, resulting in "technical-productive" diplomas and certificates which are endorsed by the academic institution.

For the case of training educators, there is a specialized pedagogical college that works similarly to a technical college, but with a focus in education.

All educational institutions are governed and authorized by the Peruvian Ministry of Education. Students who want to pursue higher education such as a Bachelor's degree at a university, are able to get recognition of their previous studies.

2.5 USA

Community colleges in the United States enroll almost half of all undergraduate students [1], and play a significant role in U.S. educational pathways. The wide variety of computing programs offered at these junior colleges includes Computer Science transfer programs that allow students to transfer to a university to complete a Bachelor's degree, as well as applied associate degree programs (usually with names like Information Technology, Computer Information Systems, or Network Security) that offer a 2-year degree leading to entry-level employment.

In addition to offering degrees, community and technical colleges in the U.S. offer a variety of shorter-term certificate programs, usually with a narrower focus. Students may pursue certificates in conjunction with a degree, or sometimes stack them toward an associate degree. Some of the students pursuing certificates are working professionals returning to college to learn a new technology or improve their chances of promotion. Some community colleges engage in contracts with local businesses to offer certificates or degrees to a targeted audience for computing education.

3. CONCLUSION

There are differences in educational systems across the world, with varying institutions, purposes, length of study, terminology, and types of certificate or diploma awarded. In computing education there is often a distinction made between programs that prepare for further study and those geared toward career-ready skills. At the same time, students moving between programs occurs. The five countries represented in this panel gave only a sampling of the role junior colleges play in computing education around the world, but a rich variety of perspectives were shared.

4. REFERENCES

[1] American Association of Community Colleges. *Community College Fast Facts.* http://www.aacc.nche.edu/AboutCC/Pages/fastfactsfactsheet.aspx. Accessed April 2016.

[2] Postiglione, G. Community Colleges in China's Two Systems. In Raby, R. L. and Valeau, E., *Community College Models: Globalization and Higher Education Reform,* Amsterdam, Springer Press, 2009.

[3] Schools in Canada. *Community Colleges in Canada.* http://www.schoolsincanada.com/Community-Colleges-In-Canada.cfm. Accessed January 2016

Motivation, Optimal Experience and Flow in First Year Computing Science

Roger McDermott,
Mark Zarb
School of Computer Science and
Digital Media
Robert Gordon University
Scotland, United Kingdom
+44 1224 262717
roger.mcdermott@rgu.ac.uk
m.zarb@rgu.ac.uk

Mats Daniels,
Åsa Cajander
Dept. of Information Technology
Uppsala University
Uppsala, Sweden
+46 18 4713160
mats.daniels@it.uu.se
asa.cajander@it.uu.se

Tony Clear
School of Computing and
Mathematical Sciences
AUT University
Auckland, New Zealand
+64 9 921 9999
tony.clear@aut.ac.nz

ABSTRACT

We examine the concept of motivation from the perspective of Self Determination Theory and give a brief overview of relevant results. We also consider the optimal state known as "Flow" and give an account of its conceptualisation in the theory due to Csikszentmihalyi. After discussion of ways in which these concepts can be measured, we describe a set of preliminary studies that investigate motivation and flow in the context of a first year computing class. We analyse student responses to enquiries about perceptions of motivation and flow experiences and look at links between them. We also discuss intrinsic motivation within the subject.

Keywords

motivation; self determination theory; optimal experience; flow

1. INTRODUCTION

The factors that affect how an individual student engages with a course of study are often complex and multifaceted, dependent upon a range of cognitive, affective and social considerations [38]. However, there is good evidence that students are much more likely to persist in higher education if they are psychologically invested in the experience of learning than if not [29, 35]. This seems intuitively obvious, and providing opportunities for learning that are both academically meaningful and cognitively rewarding is a fundamental part of professional teaching activity. The concept of motivation, viewed as the aspect of intentionality that focuses on direction and reasons to accomplish a task, is understood to play a foundational role in such concepts as self-efficacy [4, 41] and self-regulation [34]. Students themselves report that enhanced learning may follow from a variety of states characterised by high levels of engagement and increased motivation, but educational psychology

ITiCSE'16, July 09–13, 2016, Arequipa, Peru.
© 2016 ACM. ISBN 978-1-4503-4231-5/16/07…$15.00.
DOI: http://dx.doi.org/10.1145/2899415.2899474

research is particularly strong when considering those in which motivation is, to a greater extent, generated from within the task itself and not forced by external constraints [14].

This result is clearly important from a pedagogical perspective and has implications for the way educators develop, deliver and assess learning activities. Given that these modalities can often vary quite considerably from discipline to discipline, it is natural to try to learn more about this in the specific context of computer science education [6].

This paper draws on two main theories from educational psychology to investigate the experience of optimal states described by some students when learning aspects of computer science. Our aim is to try to situate the experience of a student who reports such a state within the broader theoretical context of those reported in other academic disciplines, and more widely in other individual or social activities. To do this, we draw on the concepts and terminology of Self Determination Theory (SDT) [13, 14, 33] to describe various levels of motivation experienced by a student when undertaking an activity. This approach proposes that the degree of motivation depends on the individual's "locus of control" [32] i.e. the extent to which that person believes that they can control the events affecting them. It is a well-established theory which evolved out of attempts to account for the effects of extrinsic rewards on intrinsic motivation, specifically the "Overjustification Effect", i.e. the observation that, somewhat counter-intuitively, such rewards do not always motivate persistence in challenging tasks, and in some cases may serve to undermine it [12].

Since motivation is a psychological construct and therefore not directly observable, factors associated with engagement such as activation, persistence and intensity, are generally taken as proxies and assumed to correlate with it. An increase in the likelihood that a person will initiate an action, greater effort to persist in the face of challenges, and more intense activity in pursuit of goals all contribute to an operational definition of motivation. Given this, the analysis provided by self determination theory suggests that increases in these observable factors are generally correlated with increased levels of intrinsic motivation, i.e. when an individual finds a task rewarding for its own sake.

One such state is that of "optimal experience" or, to use the terminology of Csikszentmihalyi [8], "Flow". This phenomenon, in which the person feels simultaneously cognitively efficient, highly-motivated, and happy" [10], has been studied by researchers for over forty years and the concept has been found to be useful in a range of subject areas, especially in sport, music and art, where there is some degree of physical activity or performance. Flow states are characterised, within the execution of a task, by a merging of action and awareness, a centering of attention, and the loss of self-consciousness. Subjects speak of an immersive experience in which the person experiences a strong feeling of control and where requirements are clear and unambiguous. Such experiences are "autotelic" in nature, i.e. rewarding in themselves, without the need for external motivation.

Within the broad field of computing, autotelic states such as flow have been studied in a range of contexts such as immersive gaming [17, 37], game-based learning [18], instructional design [5], Information Systems adoption [23] and HCI [19, 20, 3].

We believe that the concepts of flow, and autotelic behaviour in general, are illustrated in a range of CS education contexts. These range from the programmer who becomes completely absorbed in the coding exercise, to the student working on an open-ended project. The purpose of this paper is twofold. Firstly we seek to give a general and accessible account of some of the basic results associated with Self Determination Theory and Flow Theory, and secondly we report on an initial study into these concepts in the context of first year computing science students. We analyse student responses to enquiries about perceptions of flow experiences and look at links between these reports and intrinsic motivation within the subject. We also investigate links with student perceptions of confidence and self-identity.

2. BACKGROUND

From the standpoint of practical pedagogy, understanding the basis for student motivation, and its expression in course engagement, is a key task that impacts critically on most aspects of teaching and learning. In what follows, we use the perspective of Self Determination Theory to describe motivational states, while eventually focussing on Flow-states. We therefore give a brief, general account of both of these theories before looking at how these concepts are measured.

2.1 Motivation and Self Determination Theory

Early theories of motivation focused on a classification of motives in terms of needs and how these are fulfilled. So, for example, the theory proposed by Maslow [25] as well as later developments such as such as ERG theory [1] sought to describe motivation in terms of a hierarchy of needs, with the satisfaction of its lower levels (physiological, safety) being a prerequisite for engagement with the higher levels, culminating in the need for what Maslow termed self-actualisation and self-transcendence.

While these general theories have proved useful in some fields such as sociology, they generally treat motivation as a unitary concept and this does not conform to experience within an educational context. One influential psychological theory that does attempt to consider different types of motivation is Self Determination Theory [13, 14, 33]. The theory attempts to give an account of the concept of motivation from both a social and a cognitive perspective using the degree of self-determination to characterise it along a continuum from least to most self-determined. It posits a broad distinction between extrinsic and intrinsic forms: the former referring to initiation of activities in order to fulfil some external goal whereas the latter is characterised by engagement in tasks for their own sake, regardless of any external reward structure.

Deci and Ryan visualised this as a "motivation continuum" based upon increasing levels of self-determination. At the lowest end is what they term "*amotivation*", an absence of motivation characterised by a feeling of lack of control over actions and an absence of value derived from completion of tasks. This is followed by an intermediate level of extrinsic motivation, which itself can be differentiated into a number of sub-categories. At the lowest end of this intermediate scale is *external regulation*, where motivation is caused solely by external rewards and punishments. Above this is *introjection* in which individuals begin to internalise the reasons for their own behaviour and impose their own reward structures in terms of what they perceive they ought to do. *Identification* takes place when the individual identifies with the reason for behaving in a certain way and moves from normative to volitional justification. Finally, *integrated regulation* is said to occur when the extrinsic motivation is fully assimilated and accepted into the sense of self. The distinction between the first two extrinsic categories and the latter two was also stated using the terms *non-self-determined extrinsic motivation* for behaviour completely controlled by external factors and contrasted with *self-determined extrinsic motivation* which occurs when the individual engages in an activity because of a personal choice and an attribution of socially determined values to the task.

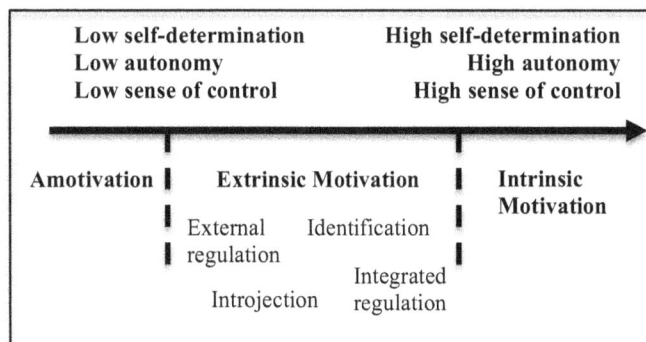

Figure 1. The Motivation Continuum (adapted from Deci & Ryan, [32])

The highest form of self-determination occurs with intrinsic motivation where participation in some task is done for its own sake, because of personal interest or the satisfaction derived from the experience. Later development within the framework of SDT investigated the effect of contextual factors on intrinsic motivation and proposed a direct correlation between high intrinsic motivation and features that promote feelings of personal autonomy and competence. Personal growth and psychological well-being are enhanced when individuals try to gain as much autonomy over their own behaviour as possible and this occurs through the development of competence in both actions and the decision-making processes that lead to them [33]. Since high-quality learning and creativity are often the result of the more self-determined form of motivation, a pedagogical priority would be to provide an environment that promotes this. Both intrinsic and the self-determined forms of extrinsic motivation have been found to be associated with positive educational outcomes such as greater engagement in learning [7], better performance [27], and greater psychological well-being [36].

The dual need for autonomy and competence is accompanied by a further motivational factor, that of the desire for relatedness. This is a contextual factor in which individuals seek to establish a psychological connection with others and is especially important in the setting of social interactions, such as those that occur in learning environments. SDT proposes that people have an innate tendency to internalise new knowledge and the practices that are acquired through socialisation, and that satisfaction of the need for relatedness facilitates this process of internalisation. In particular, external motivators derived from the values and practices of other people with whom an individual feels (or desires to feel) some kind of connection, are accepted as his or her own and transformed into intrinsic motives. This would, for example, be important in an educational context where academic maturation is seen as a process by which the learner is inducted into a community of practice, taking on the norms and values of that community. In the context of secondary school, such relatedness has been shown to be associated with student perceptions of value and respect from teachers and parents, and this understanding fosters intrinsic motivation [21]. SDT therefore maintains that, when students' basic psychological needs for autonomy, competence, and relatedness are supported in the classroom, they are more likely to internalize their motivation to learn and to be more autonomously engaged in their studies.

Later elaboration of the theory [40] proposed a multidimensional picture of motivation and suggested that different motivational impulses needed to be incorporated in any comprehensive account of the concept. In sport science research, for example, more autonomous motivational factors such as self-determined extrinsic motivation have been linked to enhanced performance and more effective coping strategies in the face of set-backs [2], greater levels of persistence and higher levels of time investment in activities [30].

2.2 The Concept of Flow

While Deci, Ryan and their co-workers were investigating these concepts of motivation in the context of Self Determination Theory, other aspects of intrinsic motivation were being developed by other researchers. One such motivational theory was that elaborated by Csikszentmihalyi based on the concept of "Flow". Csikszentmihalyi [8] defined flow as "the holistic sensation that people feel when they act with total involvement". Following interviews with individuals pursuing a variety of different activities - artists, dancers, chess players, rock-climbers, surgeons – Csikszentmihalyi noticed common elements in their description of feelings of optimal performance. In particular, expressions such as "being in the midst of flow" or "flowing from one moment to the next" were often used to describe such experiences

Flow states are states of heightened experience in the sense that the person involved in the activity feels "simultaneously cognitively efficient, motivated, and happy" [9, 28]. Moreover, Csikszentmihalyi and others found that these states correlated with enhanced performance in a variety of creative and sporting activities, as well as learning [31, 16]. The conditions of flow include a sense that one is engaging in challenges at a level which is appropriate to one's capacities, having clear, proximal goals with immediate, accessible feedback about progress that is being made. The enjoyable nature of flow promotes learning and engagement with more complicated activities since, to maintain the state, the subject of the experience has to maintain the balance between challenge and skills, resulting in a synchronized increase in task difficulty as proficiency develops. It was this unfolding "virtuous circle" of self-actualisation, in which an individual continually seeks out new tasks by setting, and ultimately

surpassing, increasingly challenging problems, that Csikszentmihalyi saw as the key not only to a rewarding and productive life for the individual [11] but also for the flourishing of whole communities and cultures [26].

Csikszentmihalyi early work on flow describes a number of elements that characterise the state. The first is a "merging of action and awareness" in which a person is aware of the actions being performed but not the state of awareness itself. There is a focusing or centering of attention on the specific details of the problem at hand and a loss of self-consciousness so that individual considerations become irrelevant to the task. This is accompanied by feeling of control or mastery over the performance of the task together with clear, unambiguous knowledge of the course of action, clarified by immediate and plain feedback. Objectives are perceived as logically connected with a clear order of operation and reaction to subtasks is automatic. Finally, the state has an "autotelic" nature, that is, there is no need for external goals or rewards as the experience of participation is its own reward.

In subsequent elaboration of the theory, Csikszentmihalyi [11] and others also suggested that further characteristics of flow included a sense of "the distortion of temporal experience of time", i.e. that time seemed to go faster when the individual engaged in the activity in the flow-like state. In addition he looked at precursors or conditions that are required to exist before a flow-like state develops. The most important of these is that a person should have a feeling of control over the process with a balance between the challenge involved and the skills required to complete a task.

The challenge-skill requirement has led a number of researchers to try to develop a model of flow based on these components. One developed by Csikszentmihalyi and LeFevre [9] is the Quadrant model.

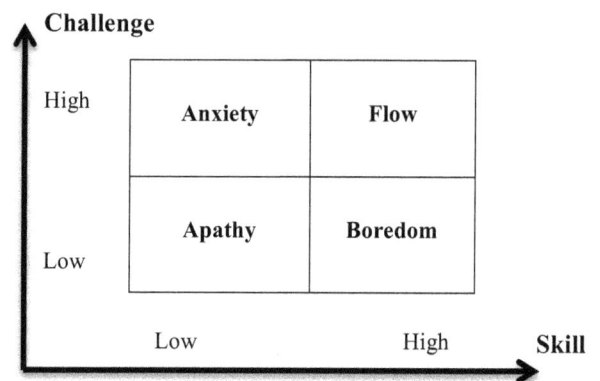

Figure 2. The quadrant model of the flow state (Adapted from Csikszentmihalyi & LeFevre 1989, [9])

An expanded version, the Octal, or Experience Fluctuation model, was developed in Massimini et al. [26] which kept the two-component axes of the model but included a finer classification of sectors in the diagram. It retained the apathy-flow characterisation of the low-to-high diagonal but included more nuanced states surrounding these corresponding to medium-level values of challenge and skill, e.g. "control" (high skill/medium challenge) and "worry" (low skill/medium challenge).

Whatever the precise details of the particular model, there seems to be agreement in the literature that flow is associated with high skill/high challenge situations and that the cognitive and affective reward experienced by the individual is such that they are more likely to engage in the activity again. This has implications for learning akin to the previous discussion about optimal states in the context of intrinsic motivation.

3. METHOD

We wished to investigate concepts such as intrinsic motivation and flow in the context of first year computing students. The question we wished to answer was whether the states described by students were similar to those found elsewhere in the literature and whether they exhibited the same structure as those found in flow questionnaires in other situations. Previous discussion with the individual members of the student cohort had attested to a general feeling that many of them had had prior experience of optimal states, which they themselves interpreted as flow, although not necessarily in a computing education context. Many of these had been in the more reported setting of computer gaming, music or other artistic performance, or in sport. We wished to investigate whether they perceived being in such states in the context of their university computing education. In this initial study, we were not trying to check the veracity of the claims themselves, but simply trying to compare the characteristics of the states reported with those described elsewhere in the literature. Consequently, although we collected data from a general population of first year computing students, the data analysis was restricted to those students who reported that they did have some flow-like experience. This reduced the sample size somewhat but we still feel the quantitative results obtained are useful for this initial study especially when taken in conjunction with more qualitative text-based data that was subsequently sought from individual students.

3.1 The Participants

Our study used data obtained from a group of forty first-year undergraduate students in Robert Gordon University. The students in the investigation were aged between 17 and 30 with the majority having entered university directly from secondary school. They were registered on four degrees within the School: the largest group was studying Computer Science, with the remainder studying Business Information Technology, Graphics and Animation and Digital Media degrees. The first three of these courses undertook identical course units in the first year while the Digital Media students took the same subjects but with a programming course unit more tailored to their specific subject. The students had completed the first semester course when the questionnaires were distributed. Results from 64 students were collected, of which 40 completed the two questionnaires and reported some experience of a state similar to flow.

3.2 The Questionnaires

The students were asked to complete two questionnaires. The first was a 24-item motivation survey based on a subject-specific version of the Sports Motivation Scale-6 (SMS-6) [24], which was itself an adaptation of the academic motivation scale (AMS) [39]. It was decided to use the SMS-6 rather than the original AMS because the latter did not specifically address the most autonomous form of extrinsic motivation: integrated regulation. Since our main interests were precisely in the more self-determined forms of motivation, this was not appropriate for us. In addition, SMS-6 had previously reported high levels of convergent validity with measures of flow. The use of the SMS-6 outside its original domain of application (sports science) required some slight alteration of the text to refer to computing rather than sporting activity but this was fairly straightforward as the original had been developed from the more general AMS and many of the

questions reflected this, e.g. in most case it was possible to substitute "computing activity" for "sporting activity".

The questionnaire itself comprised twenty-four statements and was constructed to track 6 factors associated with types of motivation in self determination theory, namely amotivation, the four subcomponents of extrinsic motivation, and intrinsic motivation. The data collected consisted of responses to the question "Why are you studying computing?". These responses comprised a set of statements, agreement with which was rated on a seven-point Likert scale from 1 ("Does not correspond at all") to 7 ("Corresponds exactly"). The statements included in the questionnaire were divided into groups corresponding to the motivational typology described by SDT. So, for example, those corresponding to amotivation (lack of perceived control) include "*I have the impression of being incapable of succeeding in this subject*", and "*I don't seem to be enjoying computing as much as I did*" while those for identified regulation (where the person starts to internalise the externally motivated reasons for doing something) include "*Because it is a good way for me to learn lots of things that would be useful to me in other areas of my life*" and "*Because it is one of the best ways to maintain good relationships with my friends*". Also, intrinsic motivation is addressed with statements such as "*For the excitement I feel when I am really involved in the activity*" and "*For the satisfaction I experience when perfecting my abilities*".

The second questionnaire was the Flow-State Scale (FSS) [22]. This is a well-established survey instrument that attempts to measure flow in the context of sport or physical exercise. As with the SMS-6, this FSS required some textual change in order to refer to a computing context rather than a sporting one but this was straightforward to accomplish. The questionnaire is made up of 36 items divided into 9 components that track elements described by flow research. These consist of autotelic experience, clarity of goals, the balance between challenge and skill, concentration on task, feeling of control, unambiguous feedback, the merging of action and awareness, the loss of self-consciousness and the transformation of time. Students were asked to recall one specific instance that occurred while participating in the programming module that they believed constituted an optimal experience in the sense described previously. Response was then given to the items in the flow questionnaire using a 5-point Likert scale where 1 indicated "Strongly disagree" and 5 indicated "Strongly agree". For example, one statement tracking autotelic experience was "*the experience was really rewarding*", one for challenge-skill balance was "*I was challenged but believed my skills would allow me to meet the challenge*", while an example of a statement tracking concentration on task was "*My attention was focussed entirely on what I was doing*".

4. RESULTS AND DISCUSSION

Factor analysis of the questionnaires yielded results that were generally in line with those reported in other research. For the Motivation questionnaire, both the scree plot of the principal components and Kaiser's criterion (eigenvalue > 1) indicate a 6-factor model in agreement with the claims for SMS-6. Examination of the model structure with 5 and 7 factors did not appear to facilitate greater identification of the factors themselves.

Internal consistency of the responses to the components within the questionnaire was acceptable with Cronbach alpha scores in the range 0.68 – 0.87. Given the rotated factor loadings and the questionnaire rubric, attempts to identify the factors suggested strong evidence for the components of Introjection and Amotivation. There was less definitive (although still reasonable) evidence for Integrated Regulation and Intrinsic Motivation and some for External Regulation. The last factor was difficult to identify but appears to be a mixture of Identified Regulation with Integrated Regulation, and therefore would represent the initial stages of self-determined extrinsic regulation according to the classifications used in self determination theory.

Turning to the Flow State Scale questionnaire, we again saw broad agreement with results from other fields, although there is more variation with this questionnaire. Factor analysis yields a scree plot of the principal components that has one large eigenvalue with a number of smaller ones. Kaiser's criterion gives 9 factors although visual inspection of the plot did not reveal any significant points of inflection beyond the first eigenvalue. This suggests that identification of the subsequent factors is difficult and this is indeed what is found.

The first factor is a mixture of components associated with the "Challenge-Skill Balance" and "Merging of Action and Awareness". The second factor appears to be associated with "Clarity of Goals" and "Unambiguous Feedback" while the third factor is "Concentration on the Task at Hand". The fourth factor has a mixture of responses about "Transformation of Time" and "Loss of Self-Consciousness". The identity of factors after this becomes difficult as the loadings become smaller and no set of value tends to dominate. It should be noted however that a similar factor analysis carried out with 8 factors also gave rise to identification of these factor groupings although not in the same order. It is therefore reasonable to infer that the states described by students could be characterised, at least in a first approximation, by categories such as the balance between challenge and skills and a merging of action and awareness, clear objectives provided by unambiguous feedback they were receiving from the task, a high degree of concentration on the narrow remit of the task in hand, and some kind of absorption factor associated with not being conscious that time was passing more quickly.

While not reproducing the full set of factors associated with the Flow-State Scale, the results do provide some insight into the experiences reported by students. Furthermore, although, due to space limitations, we do not report here on the information gained from the more qualitative data obtained from student, this tends to corroborate the perception of flow states in terms of the variables described above.

The validity of the results reported here can of course be challenged on a number of grounds. The sample size (N = 40) is small. Nevertheless, the results are broadly comparable, at least qualitatively, with those found in in more extensive studies on the subject in areas such as sports science. It is also recognised that this initial study says nothing about those students who claim not to have such optimal experiences at any point in their educational journey through computing.

5. CONCLUSION
While the results discussed above are only an initial foray into the study of optimal experience in computer science education, we do believe that the subject is deserving of further, more systematic investigation. The link between engagement and intrinsic types of motivation appears to be both intuitively reasonable and fairly well-documented in the educational psychology research literature. Furthermore students do appear to report these states in other areas such as leisure activities, performance arts and sport.

Of course, the fact that a student reports some degree of absorption and loss of self-consciousness in one particular activity, e.g. playing an immersive video game, does not necessarily imply that this state is the same as one that occurs in a learning context, say, a particularly engaging coding exercise. Nor, by itself, does it signify the existence of an optimal state such as flow. It may also be that, even if such states do exist in a non-educational situation, their benefits are not transferable to a pedagogical context.

Nevertheless, even if they only serve to motivate students to engage with an activity in order to recapture affective aspects of the optimal experience, this would enhance engagement, and so there may well be merit in further investigation. The idea that a significant aim of education is to promote intrinsic, or at least self-determined extrinsic motivation for activities is an attractive one. States of intrinsic motivation, such as flow, purport to set up a virtuous circle in which students themselves desire to perform well in challenging situations that push the limits of their skills, which then prompts them to develop greater expertise. This approach is paradigmatic in post-university education and is something that finds support in the discussion of cognitive skills necessary for lifelong learning. Nevertheless, while computer science education is necessarily concerned with the development of the technical skills and professional competencies that allow students to gain employment in the computing industry, it is surely also about allowing students to develop insights into the aesthetic and, perhaps, transcendental nature of the subject. We would wish to facilitate and indeed, where genuine, validate the experiences that some students have while studying the subject and it does appear that they are often associated with cognitive states such as flow. Such considerations also appear to be relevant to questions concerning student identity. Students who report flow-like experiences are more likely to identify as a member of the practising community and some of the questions on the Flow-State Scale questionnaire are directed to the investigation of the self-attribution of subject- or discipline-based identity, e.g. "I do this because I am a computer scientist" as well as that of learning identity in the sense of Dweck's Self-theory [15]. Trying to understand the nature and implications of identity in learning is an important issue and we therefore believe that the concept outlined in this paper will be of use in the future, and that further work in this area is warranted.

6. REFERENCES

[1] Alderfer, C. P. 1969. An empirical test of a new theory of human needs. Organizational behavior and human performance. 4. 2, 142-175.

[2] Amiot, C.E., Gaudreau, P. and Blanchard, C.M., 2004. Self-determination, coping, and goal attainment in sport. Journal of Sport and Exercise Psychology, 26. 3, 396.

[3] Bahador, S., Scheidegger, C. and Kobourov. S. 2015. Towards Understanding Enjoyment and Flow in Information Visualization. arXiv preprint: 1503.00582.

[4] Bandura, A. 1977. Self-efficacy: toward a unifying theory of behavioral change. Psychological review 84. 2, 191.

[5] Chan, T.S. and Ahern, T.C., 1999. Targeting motivation—adapting flow theory to instructional design. Journal of Educational computing research, 21. 2, 151-163.

[6] Clear, T. and Kassabova, D., 2005. Motivational patterns in virtual team collaboration. In Proc. 7th Australasian

conference on Computing education. 42. 51-58. Australian Computer Society, Inc.

[7] Connell, J. P., and Wellborn, J. G. 1991. Competence, autonomy, and relatedness: A motivational analysis of self-system processes. in Gunnar, M. R. (Ed), Sroufe, L. A. (Ed), Self processes and development. The Minnesota symposia on child psychology, Vol. 23., (43-77). Hillsdale, NJ, England: Lawrence Erlbaum Associates, Inc.

[8] Csikszentmihalyi, M., 1975. Play and intrinsic rewards. Journal of humanistic psychology, 15. 3, 41-63.

[9] Csikszentmihalyi, M. and LeFevre, J., 1989. Optimal experience in work and leisure. Journal of personality and social psychology, 56. 5, 815.

[10] Csikszentmihalyi, M. 1990. Flow: The psychology of optimal experience. New York: Harper & Row.

[11] Csikszentmihalyi, M., 1996. The creative personality. Psychology Today, 29. 4, 36-40.

[12] Deci, E., 1971. Effects Of Externally Mediated Rewards On Intrinsic Motivation. Journal of Personality and Social Psychology, 18. 1, 105-115.

[13] Deci, E. L., & Ryan, R. M., 1985. Intrinsic motivation and self-determination in human behavior. New York: Plenum.

[14] Deci, E., & Ryan, R. 2008. Self-determination Theory: A Macrotheory Of Human Motivation, Development, and Health. Canadian Psych./Psych. Canadienne, 49. 3, 182-185.

[15] Dweck, C. S. 2000. Self-theories: Their role in motivation, personality, and development. Psychology Press.

[16] Engeser, S. and Rheinberg, F., 2008. Flow, performance and moderators of challenge-skill balance. Motivation and Emotion, 32. 3, 158-172.

[17] Faiola, A. and Voiskounsky, A.E., 2007. Flow experience of MUD players: Investigating multi-user dimension gamers from the USA. In Online Communities and Social Computing, 324-333. Springer Berlin Heidelberg

[18] Faiola, A., Newlon, C., Pfaff, M. and Smyslova, O., 2013. Correlating the effects of flow and telepresence in virtual worlds: Enhancing our understanding of user behavior in game-based learning. Comp. Human Behavior, 29. 3, 1113..

[19] Finneran, C. and Zhang, P., 2002. The challenges of studying flow within a computer-mediated environment. *AMCIS 2002 Proceedings*, 146.

[20] Ghani, J.A. and Deshpande, S.P., 1994. Task characteristics and the experience of optimal flow in human—computer interaction. The Journal of psychology, 128. 4, 381-391.

[21] Grolnick, W.S. and Ryan, R.M., 1989. Parent styles associated with children's self-regulation and competence in school. Journal of educational psychology, 81. 2, 143.

[22] Jackson, S.A. and Marsh, H.W., 1996. Development and validation of a scale to measure optimal experience: The Flow State Scale. J. Sport & Exercise Psychology, 18, 17-35.

[23] Lowry, P.B., Gaskin, J., Twyman, N., Hammer, B. and Roberts, T., 2012. Taking 'Fun and Games' Seriously: Proposing the Hedonic-Motivation System Adoption Model (HMSAM). *Journal of the Association for Information Systems*, 14. 11, 617-671.

[24] Mallett, C., Kawabata, M., Newcombe, P., Otero-Forero, A. and Jackson, S., 2007. Sport motivation scale-6 (SMS-6): A revised six-factor sport motivation scale. Psychology of Sport and Exercise, 8. 5, 600-614.

[25] Maslow, A. H. 1943. A theory of human motivation." Psychological review 50. 4, 370.

[26] Massimini, F., Csikszentmihalyi, M. and Fave, A.D., 1988. Flow and biocultural evolution. In Csikszentmihalyi, M. , Csikszentmihalyi, I. S. (Ed), Optimal experience: Psychological studies of flow in consciousness. , 60-81. NY,

[27] Miserandino, M. 1996. Children who do well in school: Individual differences in perceived competence and autonomy in above-average children. Journal of Educational Psychology, 88. 2, 203.

[28] Moneta, G.B. and Csikszentmihalyi, M., 1996. The effect of perceived challenges and skills on the quality of subjective experience. Journal of personality, 64. 2, 275-310.

[29] Moxley, D., Najor-Durack, A., and Dumbrigue. C., 2001. Keeping Students in Higher Education: Successful Practices & Strategies for Retention.

[30] Pelletier, L.G., Fortier, M.S., Vallerand, R.J. and Briere, N.M., 2001. Associations among perceived autonomy support, forms of self-regulation, and persistence: A prospective study. Motivation and emotion, 25. 4, 279-306.

[31] Rathunde, K. and Csikszentmihalyi, M., 2005. Middle school students' motivation and quality of experience: A comparison of Montessori and traditional school environments. American Journal of Education, 111. 3, 341-371.

[32] Rotter, J. B. 1954 Social Learning and Clinical Psychology. Englewood Cliffs, NJ: Prentice Hall.

[33] Ryan, R., & Deci, E., 2000. Intrinsic and extrinsic motivations: Classic definitions and new directions. Contemporary educational psychology, 25. 1, 54–67.

[34] Schunk, Dale H., and Barry J. Zimmerman. 2003. Self-regulation and learning. Handbook of Psychology.

[35] Quaye, S. R., and Harper J. S., 2014. Student Engagement in Higher Education: Theoretical Perspectives and Practical Approaches for Diverse Populations. Routledge.

[36] Sheldon, K. M., and Kasser, T. 1995. Coherence and congruence: two aspects of personality integration." Journal of personality and social psychology. 68. 3, 531.

[37] Sweetser, P., and Wyeth, P. 2005. Gameflow: A model for evaluating player enjoyment in games. Computers in Entertainment, 3. 3, 3–3.

[38] Trowler, Vicki. 2010. Student engagement literature review. *York: Higher Education Academy.* 11, 1 – 15.

[39] Vallerand, R. J., Pelletier, L. G., Blais, M. R., Briere, N. M., Senecal, C., & Vallieres, E. F. 1992. The academic motivation scale: A measure of intrinsic, extrinsic, and amotivation in education. Education and Psychological Measurement, 52, 1003–1017.

[40] Vallerand, R. J. 1997. Toward a hierarchical model of intrinsic and extrinsic motivation". In Zanna, Mark P. (Ed), (1997). Advances in experimental social psychology, 29. 271-360. San Diego, CA, US: Academic Press.

[41] Zimmerman, B. J., 2000. Self-efficacy: An essential motive to learn." Contemporary educational psychology, 25. 1, 82-9

Where You Sit Matters
How Classroom Seating Might Affect Marks

David Insa   Josep Silva   Salvador Tamarit
Departament de Sistemes Informàtics i Computació
Universitat Politècnica de València
Camí de Vera, s/n
46022 València, Spain

ABSTRACT

In this article we perform a detailed statistical analysis of a large experiment that was carried out in two engineering schools at Universitat Politècnica de València. The goal of the study is to quantify how the distance of students to the professor affects their marks. In the experiment, we collected and processed data about the exact students' position in the lecture hall and in the computer lab for two academic years, their changes of position along the course, and their marks in various degrees, courses, and terms, for both lectures and practicals. Our experiments provide quantitative data that is analyzed using advanced statistical methods such as ANOVA, the TukeyHSD post-hoc test, and the Mantel test based on Pearson product-moment correlation coefficient.

Categories and Subject Descriptors

K.3.2 [**Computer and Information Science Education**]: Computer science education, Information systems education

Keywords

Mark; classroom; seat

1. INTRODUCTION

Many professors often say that their best students use to sit in the first rows of the classroom while those students less interested in the course use to sit in the last rows or in those closer to the exit door. In this paper we validate these ideas with quantitative statistically-supported data. We want to answer questions such as: How much does the distance between the students and the professor affect the students' marks? As an average, what is the difference between the marks of the students seated in the first row and those seated in the, e.g., third row?

The way in which students sit in the lecture hall has been often ignored, even in methodologies for active learning. This is somehow surprising, because there already exist

ITiCSE '16, July 09 - 13, 2016, Arequipa, Peru

© 2016 Copyright held by the owner/author(s). Publication rights licensed to ACM.
ISBN 978-1-4503-4231-5/16/07. . . $15.00

DOI: http://dx.doi.org/10.1145/2899415.2899444

studies that show a clear relation between the position in the lecture hall and the final mark. Most of these studies have been done in the context of primary and secondary schools (see, e.g., [1, 9], or more recently [13]), but there are also studies applied to the university with the same results [10, 12, 3].

For instance, Giles et al. [4] studied the students' recall in relation with their position in the lecture hall, and they concluded that the student's seating position in the lecture hall is associated with the level of immediate recall. In educational psychology the potential learning advantages of being close to the teacher have been already studied:

1. better vision of the blackboard,

2. better hearing of what is being said by the teacher,

3. better attention to what is being said because there are fewer (or no) people between them and the teacher to distract them, and

4. greater eye contact with the teacher, which may increase their sense of personal responsibility to listen to, and take notes on, what their teacher is saying.

One could think that the relation between the seating position and the marks is not causal, because this relation may well be a reflection of motivational factors which determine where students choose to sit rather than of seating position *per se* [4]. However, some studies were conducted with the teacher selecting the students' position: students in the front, middle, and back rows of the class scored 80%, 71.6%, and 68.1% respectively on the course exams [10]. This is a clear indication that it is not simply due to the fact that more motivated students tend to sit in the front and centre of the classroom. Instead, the higher academic performance of students sitting in the front and centre is most likely due to the fact that there are learning advantages provided by these seating positions.

Obviously, not all the students are equal. Some of them are shy or just afraid of the questions that the teacher could ask them. This feeling makes them sit far away from the teacher in order to avoid questions. For other students, however, sitting far away from the teacher is an opportunity to chat with classmates when they cannot follow or they are not interested in a particular lesson. This is also usual among students who cannot keep their attention over a long period of time. Other students, contrarily, try to sit as close as possible to the teacher to avoid the noise and to have, in this way, a better understanding.

Table 1: Data from the groups of the analyzed courses

	Name	Year	Degree	Groups	Students	Sessions
Lectures	DSA	2°	ACE	2	66	23
	AC	2°	IDE	1	38	24
	PRG	1°	BCE	1	23	28
Practicals	DRQS	1°	MSEFMIS	1	5	12
	ATSD	5°	MCE	1	20	12
	GUI	3°	MCE	2	28	12
	AC	2°	IDE	1	36	12
	PRG	1°	BCE	2	39	10

This paper presents a wide experiment performed over two academic years in two engineering schools at Universitat Politècnica de València (UPV). The experiment studied the relationship between the position of all the students in the classrooms (both the lecture hall and the computer laboratory) and their marks. To the best of our knowledge, this is the widest study of this kind performed at university schools, and it analyzes relations not studied before. In particular, we introduce a novel methodology, which roughly consists in studying the marks associated to chairs (instead of to students). The analysis of the collected data, as described below, proves the fact that a student's position really influences their marks. Similar studies can be found in [7, 14] for primary and secondary schools; and in [11, 12, 6] for the university, although with a reduced sample of students.

The rest of the paper describes the experiment and its results. Section 2 presents the experiment and its context. Concretely, in Section 2.1 we explain how the data was collected, and the methodology used to normalize them. Then, in Section 2.2 we present the statistical results obtained. Finally, the conclusions and future work are discussed in Section 3, where we provide an interpretation of the data and ideas about how to use this information.

2. THE EXPERIMENT

The experiment has been conducted at the School of Engineering Design and at the School of Computer Science, both at UPV. It was supported by the Institute of Education Sciences of UPV. Specific details about the experiment are the following:

- Data Size: 255 students (2160 attendances).

- *Programs*: Bachelor in Industrial Design Engineering (IDE), Master in Computer Science Engineering (MCE), Associate degree in Computer Engineering (ACE), Bachelor in Computer Engineering (BCE), and Master of Software Engineering, Formal Methods, and Information Systems (MSEFMIS).

- *Courses*: Development of Reliable and Quality Software (DRQS), Data Structures and Algorithms (DSA), Advanced Tools for Software Development (ATSD), Graphical User Interfaces (GUI), Applied Computing (AC), and Programming (PRG). Table 1 provides additional information about the courses, including whether each course corresponds to lectures or practicals, mark, degree, number of groups and students involved in the experiment, and number of sessions.

- Null Hypothesis: There is no relation between the students' position in the lecture hall and their marks.

In order to ensure the replicability of our study and analyses, and to make public our information to other researchers for other possible analyses, all the source data, together with the intermediate and final processed data have been made publicly available at:

http://www.dsic.upv.es/~jsilva/sitsandmarks/

2.1 Data collection

Prior to the experiment, we developed a software tool called AWAD [5]. AWAD allows for automatic data collection and processing as well as performing online exams. This tool stores the row and column where each student is sat when logged in. In those lecture halls without computers, the row and column were taken manually by the professor. These data were collected in all lectures and practicals in all sessions. Moreover, at least one official exam was registered for each course. AWAD combined the final marks with the other available data to generate a number of reports with statistics and other calculations that are the basis of more advanced statistics shown in Section 2.2. One of the biggest challenges was to obtain statistics not related to individual students but, on the contrary, associated with the different physical positions that can be occupied inside classrooms. To achieve this goal, we designed the experiment in a novel way (we are not aware of any other experiment, neither in universities nor in primary or secondary schools, that processes the data in this way): we collected the data linked to each individual chair of each classroom instead of analyzing the students. Therefore, the data linked to each chair have been produced by combining the data collected every time a student (not necessarily the same one) sat in this particular chair. All data were later combined to produce extrapolative results. The data provided by AWAD are the following:

Average mark of a chair: It represents the average mark a specific chair got in a particular exam. It was obtained by adding up the marks of all students that occupied that chair (if the same student occupied the chair several times, their mark was also counted several times) and then dividing the result by the number of times this chair was occupied (hence, we get the average mark of the individual occupation of this chair).[1] We can see specific examples of this in Figure 1. Observe that each

---

[1] Our statistical analysis considers the fact that the sample is not distributed homogeneously, i.e., one chair could be occupied many times, while other chair could be occupied only a

from 1 to 3
from 3 to 5
from 5 to 6
from 6 to 7
from 7 to 8
from 8 to +

Classroom: DSIC - Laboratory 0 [Laboratory]
Exam: 23
Blackboard

5.97 4.75 5.18 4.75 8.08   4.75 4.75

5.85 5.5   6.57 5.63 7.61   7.37 8.08

5.74 5.03 4.08 4.17

8.08   4.25 7.33

7.33

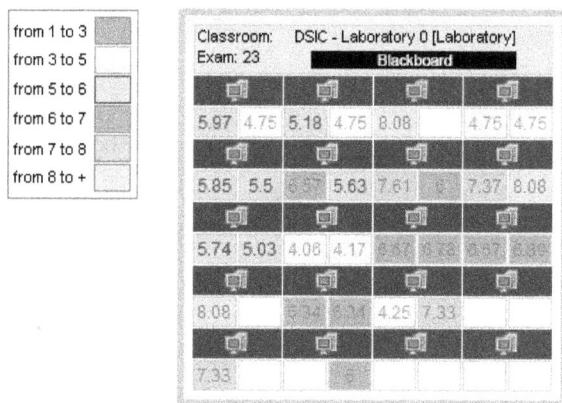

(a) Course: PRG - Group: PL1

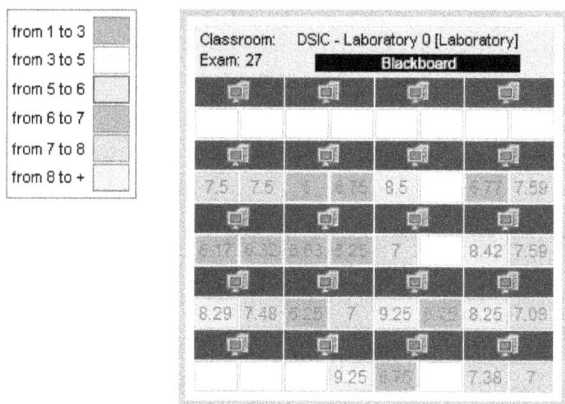

from 1 to 3
from 3 to 5
from 5 to 6
from 6 to 7
from 7 to 8
from 8 to +

Classroom: DSIC - Laboratory 0 [Laboratory]
Exam: 27
Blackboard

7.5   7.5   8.5   7.59

                7   8.42 7.59

8.29 7.48   7   9.25   8.25 7.09

                9.25   7.38 7

(b) Course: GUI - Group: PL5

Figure 1: Two (real) examples of average marks of chairs in a group

chair (not each student) is labelled with a mark. Observe also that each computer is shared by two students in the labs. The blank chairs were never occupied by any student in any session. Lecture halls and labs have a symmetric and proportional distribution of chairs, thus, row $2i$ is twice as far to the professor as it is row i. The reader should not extract conclusions from these figures, because they just show unprocessed data from two examples of courses. These data (together with the rest of courses) are mixed and statistically analyzed in Section 2.2.

Times a chair was used: It counts the number of times that (possibly different) students occupied the chair during the course. Figure 2 contains examples of these counters.

Times a chair was used by students who gave up the course: It represents the total amount of times a chair was used by a student who gave up the course (those that did not take the exam).

---

few times. As a consequence, our results are presented with confidence intervals (see Table 2, Figure 3, and Figure 4).

2.2 Results

The data collected and processed by AWAD have been further analyzed to extract statistically valid results. In all cases, we have computed 95% symmetric confidence intervals and we show the centre of the interval. We have analyzed the data in two phases. In the first phase, we obtained individual results for each group. In the second phase, we combined the data from all groups to obtain global results.

Phase 1: The data collected by AWAD were stored in a database that was later processed using R.[2] For each group we produced a table as those shown in Table 2. These tables summarize information for each row of chairs in a classroom, in such a way that the first row in the table corresponds to the first row in the classroom, the second with the second, and so on. Column *Attendance* shows the number of times that the chairs in each row were used by students that finally took the exam. Column *Mean* shows the average mark associated with each row. Column *Norm. Mean* (*Normalized*

Table 2: Results obtained by group
(a) Course: PRG Group: PL1

Row	Attendance	Mean	Norm. Mean
1	22	$[_{4.76}\ 5.18\ _{5.61}]$	$[_{0.82}\ 0.89\ _{0.97}]$
2	34	$[_{5.85}\ 6.33\ _{6.80}]$	$[_{1.01}\ 1.09\ _{1.17}]$
3	39	$[_{4.96}\ 5.48\ _{6.00}]$	$[_{0.85}\ 0.94\ _{1.03}]$
4	8	$[_{5.76}\ 6.63\ _{7.51}]$	$[_{0.99}\ 1.14\ _{1.29}]$
5	3	$[_{5.57}\ 6.44\ _{7.31}]$	$[_{0.96}\ 1.11\ _{1.26}]$

Total Mean $= [_{5.52}\ 5.80\ _{6.09}]$

(b) Course: GUI Group: PL5

Row	Attendance	Mean	Norm. Mean
1	0	–	–
2	68	$[_{6.92}\ 7.17\ _{7.43}]$	$[_{0.95}\ 0.98\ _{1.02}]$
3	63	$[_{6.80}\ 7.05\ _{7.29}]$	$[_{0.93}\ 0.96\ _{1.00}]$
4	46	$[_{7.56}\ 7.84\ _{8.12}]$	$[_{1.04}\ 1.07\ _{1.11}]$
5	10	$[_{6.73}\ 7.35\ _{7.97}]$	$[_{0.92}\ 1.01\ _{1.09}]$

Total Mean $= [_{7.15}\ 7.30\ _{7.46}]$

Mean) represents the average mark of the row with regard to the average mark of the group. The average mark of the group is represented with the value 1.0 and it is calculated adding up the marks of all chairs (regardless of in which row they are). For instance, in the second row of Table 2(a) we see that the normalized mean is 1.09 and thus, those students who sat in the second row got marks 9% higher than the average mark of the group.

Phase 2: In the second phase of the analysis we combined the information of all individual groups, separately in lecture and practical groups, to obtain global results that can be generalized to all groups. In order to obtain statistically valid global results, we needed to introduce another process

---

[2]R is a programming language for statistical computing. See https://www.r-project.org/ for details.

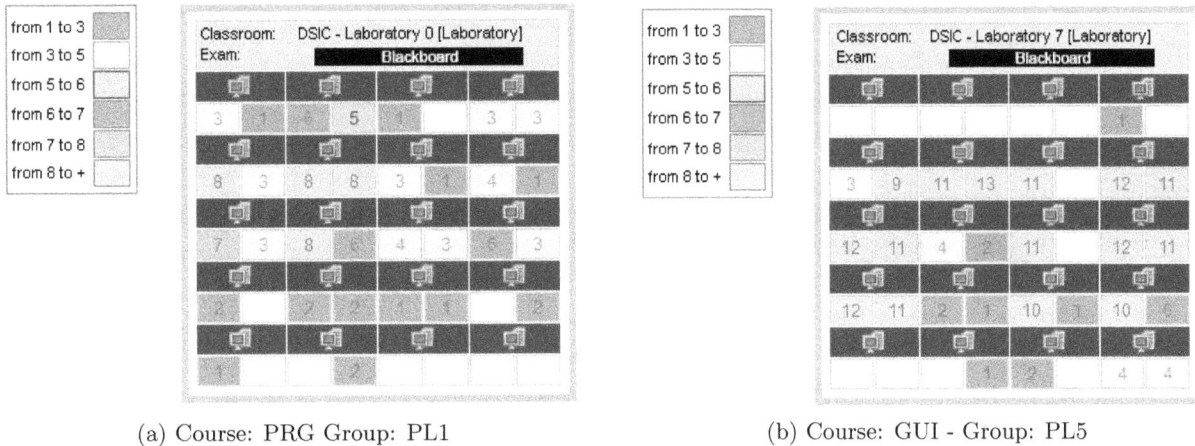

(a) Course: PRG Group: PL1   (b) Course: GUI - Group: PL5

Figure 2: Two (real) examples of number of times each chair has been occupied

of normalization because we cannot mix data obtained from different groups for three fundamental reasons:

1. All marks must use the same scale (e.g., from 1 to 10). In this way, a mark of 7 would mean the same in all groups. Hence, we changed all the marks to a mark out of 10.

2. The marks of different groups cannot be combined or averaged out if these groups have a different average mark. For instance, groups PRG PL1 and GUI PL5 (Table 2(a) and Table 2(b)) have, respectively, average marks of 5.80 and 7.30. This means that a mark of 7 points in the second group is a bad—below the average—mark, whereas in the first group, it is a good mark (far above the average). In order to combine marks from different groups we normalized the marks regarding to the average marks of the groups. This is shown in column *Norm. Mean* of Table 2, which can be already combined with other groups.

3. In each group, each mark associated with a chair has a different confidence level. For instance, the marks from the chair in row 2, column 8, in the two groups shown in Figure 1 (PL1 and PL5) are very similar (8.08 and 7.59 respectively). However, if we observe the associated tables of attendance in Figure 2 we see that 7.59 was obtained from a sample of 11 attendances (that is, it is a high confidence data, which has been probably obtained from several students who sat repeatedly in that chair). On the opposite side, the mark of 8.08 comes from a student that sat in that chair only once (and probably this student sat in another chair the rest of the times). In consequence, this last figure has a very low confidence level. In order to compare data with different confidence levels the computed marks take into account the number of attendances associated with each mark.

We elaborated two tables that summarize the information from all groups to obtain conclusions for lecture and practical groups. This division is interesting because in lectures the interaction with the professor is mainly passive, therefore being close to the professor and the blackboard seems

to be more important than in practical sessions, where autonomous work predominates. This information is shown in Table 3 and Table 4.

Table 3: Total attendance and normalized marks for lectures

Row	Attendance	Normalized Mean	Volume
1	127	1.16	19.75%
2	163	1.05	25.35%
3	218	0.88	33.90%
4	135	0.99	21.00%

Total Attendance = 643

Table 4: Total attendance and normalized marks for practicals

Row	Attendance	Normalized Mean	Volume
1	108	1.14	16.80%
2	226	0.97	35.15%
3	230	0.96	35.77%
4	106	1.06	16.49%
5	51	0.99	7.93%

Total Attendance = 721

These tables show combined information from several groups for each row of chairs in the classrooms. Here again, the first row of the table corresponds to the first row in the classroom, the second corresponds to the second, etc. Column *Attendance* shows the summation of attendances in each row for all groups. Column *Normalized Mean* represents the normalized mean combining the normalized means of all groups. Column *Volume* shows the percentage of attendances of students sat in each row with respect to the total amount of attendances. We only considered representative those rows with a percentage higher than 5%. We can

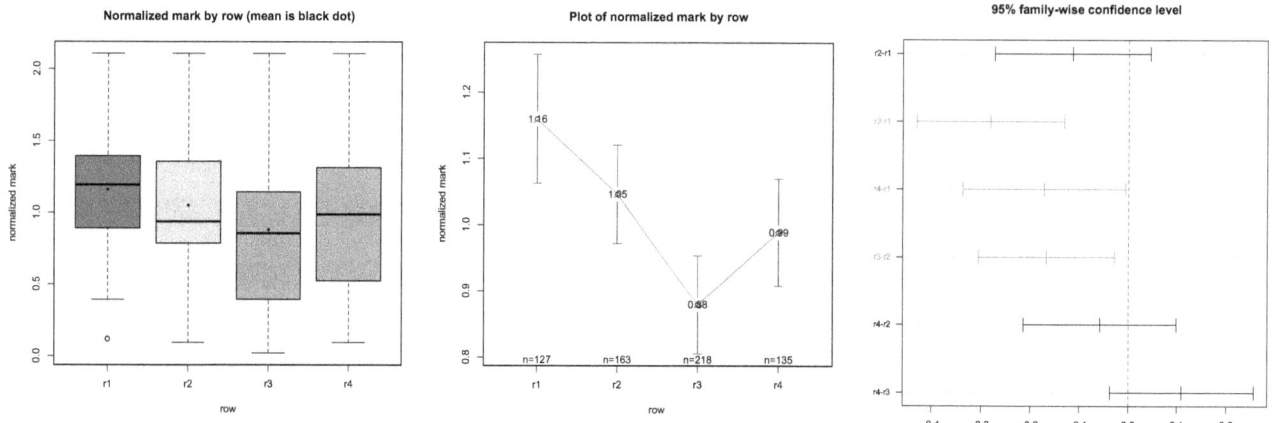

Figure 3: Statistical analysis of the relation position-mark in lectures

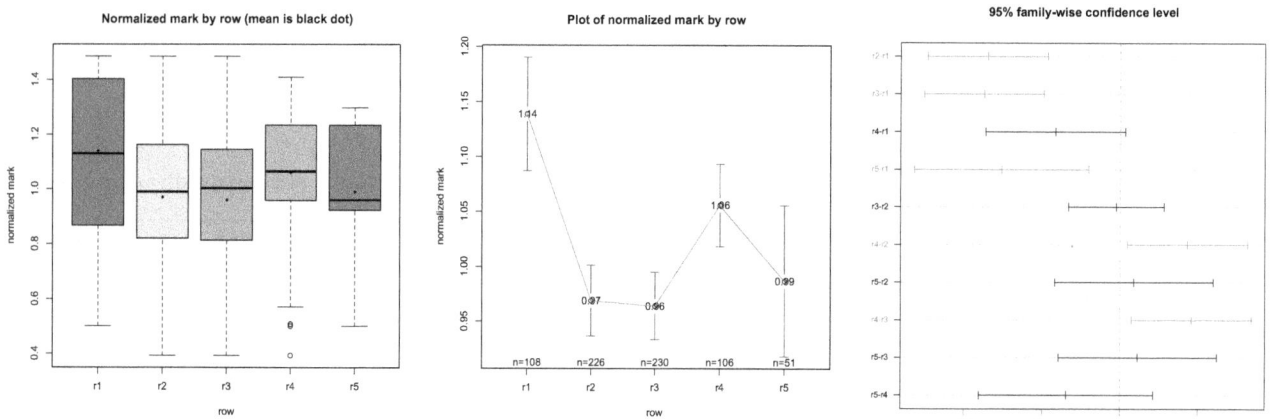

Figure 4: Statistical analysis of the relation position-mark in practicals

see that the students in the first row obtain, as an average, a 16% higher mark than the mean. Similarly, in the laboratory, the students in the first row obtain, as an average, a 14% higher mark than the mean. Clearly, marks are more uniform in the laboratory, which means that the position is not so influential.

With the collected data shown in these tables, we can perform an analysis with a huge sample (more than 1300 attendances) obtained from different groups, courses, students, professors, exams, classrooms, academic years, terms, and degrees (all of them from engineering schools). This sample is big and heterogeneous enough to obtain conclusions (or at least indicators) free from being affected by local factors of a given subsample.

We processed all the data to extract statistically supported conclusions. Firstly, we considered lecture groups. We can observe a standard boxplot showing the distribution of data in Figure 3 (left). It shows the Q1, Q2 (median), and Q3 quartiles for each row. The white point in row 1 is an outlier. We performed the Mantel test based on Pearson product-moment correlation coefficient with 999 replicates, and we got a p-value of 0,069. This value indicates that the null hypothesis may be rejected. Therefore, we performed an analysis of variance (ANOVA) using R, and got the following result:

	Df	$Sum\ Sq$	$Mean\ Sq$	$F\ value$	$Pr(> F)$
row	3	6.78	2.2611	8.348	$1.89e-05$

With this result, and assuming a significance level of 0.05, we can reject the null hypothesis because the significance probability value associated with the F Value, $Pr(> F) = 1.89e - 05$, is three orders of magnitude bellow the significance level. Hence, the first important conclusion is that the position in a classroom actually influences the students' marks. Figure 3 (centre) shows the plot with the relation row-mark.

To complement the ANOVA and study the differences between each row, we used the TukeyHSD post-hoc test. It produced the plot in Figure 3 (right), where significant differences are the ones which do not cross the zero value. Hence, this plot provides evidences that rows (r4-r1), (r3-r1), (r3-r2) have different influence on the mark. The influence is the expected one: the closer to the professor (and to the blackboard) the better mark is obtained.

We repeated the analysis for practical groups. The standard boxplot with the distribution of data is shown in Figure 4 (left). We also performed the Mantel test based on Pearson product-moment correlation coefficient with 999 replicates, and we got a p-value of 0,013. Again, this value indicates that the null hypothesis may be rejected. Therefore, we performed an analysis of variance (ANOVA) using R, and got the following result:

	Df	$Sum\ Sq$	$Mean\ Sq$	$F\ value$	$Pr(>F)$
row	4	2.90	0.7243	12.57	$6.9e-10$

A value of $6.9e-10$ for the probability $Pr(>F)$ clearly indicates that the position in the lab does influence the students' marks. Figure 4 (centre) shows the plot with the row-mark relation. The TukeyHSD post-hoc test produced the plot in Figure 4 (right), which provides evidence that row $r1$ has a positive influence on marks w.r.t. rows $r2$, $r3$, and $r5$; and row $r4$ also has a positive influence on marks w.r.t. rows $r2$ and $r3$.

After having analyzed the data, our (subjective) interpretation of this phenomenon is that central rows in the lab concentrated the largest number of students, leading them to share computer and to have classmates by their sides, front and back, which certainly influenced negatively their academic achievement.

3. CONCLUSIONS

We believe that this experiment is an excellent starting point for a debate about how to handle the students' location in a classroom. An advanced knowledge would allow the professor to know where the students who need more help should be placed, or it could allow a software tool to recommend laboratory partners in order to form pairs of students who help each other in their learning.

This experiment provides a lot of useful information for professors, but it has generated new questions that must be further investigated. In particular, we would like to analyze the influence of the student's gender in the results, and the behavior of repeaters (students). Another interesting study would be to repeat the experiment in another area not related to engineering to compare the results. All this information may be useful in the future to define recommendations or methodologies for student distributions inside classrooms as it is studied in [2, 8].

4. ACKNOWLEDGEMENTS

This work has been partially supported by the European Union (FEDER) and the Spanish *Ministerio de Economía y Competitividad* under grant TIN2013-44742-C4-1-R and by the *Generalitat Valenciana* under grant PROMETEO-II/2015/013 (SmartLogic). Salvador Tamarit was partially supported by Madrid regional projects N-GREENS Software-CM (S2013/ICE-2731), and by the European Union project POLCA (STREP FP7-ICT-2013.3.4 610686). The authors acknowledge a partial support of COST Action IC1405 on Reversible Computation. The authors thank the colleagues who helped them to carry out the experiment and all the students who participated in it.

5. REFERENCES

[1] M. Benedict and J. Hoag. Seating Location in Large Lectures: Are Seating Preferences or Location Related to Course Performance? *Journal of Economic Education*, 35(3):215–231, 2004.

[2] A. Capwell-Burns. Exploring the Formation of Groups: Students Choose Their Own Fate. In *Annual meeting of the NCA 93rd Annual Convention*. TBA, Chicago, IL, 2007.

[3] P. Ganowsky. Effect of classroom seating on student academic performance. Dixie State College, 2003.

[4] R. M. Giles, M. R. Johnson, K. E. Knight, S. Zammett, and J. Weinman. Recall of lecture information: a question of what, when and where. *Medical Education*, 16(5):264–268, 1982.

[5] V. Mateo. *Diseño e implementación de un sistema de evaluación docente*. Master's Thesis, Universitat Politècnica de València, 2011.

[6] M. Meeks, T. Knotts, K. James, F. Williams, J. Vassar, and A. Wren. The impact of seating location and seating type on student performance. *Education Sciences*, 3(4):375–386, 2013.

[7] D. Montello. Classroom Seating Location and its Effect on Course Achievement, Participation, and Attitudes. *Journal of Environmental Psychology*, 8(2):149–157, 1988.

[8] N. E. A. (NWEA). Guidelines for Placing Students. http://www.nwea.org, 2012.

[9] K. Perkins and C. Wieman. The Surprising Impact of Seat Location on Student Performance. *The Physics Teacher*, 43(1):30–33, 2005.

[10] M. Rennels and R. Chaudhari. Eye-Contact and Grade Distribution. *Perceptual and Motor Skills*, 67(October):627–632, 1988.

[11] J. Silva. ¿Influye en la nota de los estudiantes su posición en el aula? In *II Jornadas de Innovación Docente de la Universidad Politécnica de Valencia*, 2009.

[12] J. Silva. Are Marks Related to Chairs? In *34th ATEE International Conference of the Association for Teacher Education in Europe*, pages 78–87, 2010.

[13] R. Szparagowski. Effects of altering student seating position on student learning in an 8th grade mathematics classroom. *Honors Projects*, paper 115, 2014.

[14] I. Çinar. Classroom Geography: Who Sit Where in the Traditional Classrooms? *Journal of International Social Research*, 3(10):200–212, 2010.

On the Number of Attempts Students Made on Some Online Programming Exercises During Semester and their Subsequent Performance on Final Exam Questions

Alireza Ahadi and Raymond Lister
University of Technology, Sydney
Australia
alireza.ahadi@uts.edu.au
raymond.lister@uts.edu.au

Arto Vihavainen
Department of Computer Science
University of Helsinki
Finland
arto.vihavainen@cs.helsinki.fi

ABSTRACT

This paper explores the relationship between student performance on online programming exercises completed during semester with subsequent student performance on a final exam. We introduce an approach that combines whether or not a student produced a correct solution to an online exercise with information on the number of attempts at the exercise submitted by the student. We use data collected from students in an introductory Java course to assess the value of this approach. We compare the approach that utilizes the number of attempts to an approach that simply considers whether or not a student produced a correct solution to each exercise. We found that the results for the method that utilizes the number of attempts correlates better with performance on a final exam.

Keywords

Programming; educational data mining; learning analytics

1. INTRODUCTION

For decades, students who were learning to program submitted their assignments on paper. Thus, the only artifact available for analysis was a student's final program. But in recent years, with the advent of web-based systems for teaching programming, it is now possible to study the student behaviour that culminates in the final program.

Jadud [2] studied the sequence of source code *snapshots* generated by students, where a snapshot is collected each time a student compiles their code. Jadud introduced a metric that quantifies how students fix errors, which he called the *error quotient*. Using a version of the error quotient, Rodrigo et al. [4] found a strong correlation between error quotient and midterm score in an introductory programming course. Watson et al. [5] proposed an improvement to the error quotient called *Watwin*. Watson et al. also noted that a simple measure, the average amount of time that a student

ITiCSE '16, July 09-13, 2016, Arequipa, Peru
© 2016 ACM. ISBN 978-1-4503-4231-5/16/07. . . $15.00
DOI: http://dx.doi.org/10.1145/2899415.2899452

spends on a programming error, is strongly correlated with final course score.

1.1 Motivation for this Study

While the aforementioned research work on the error quotient and other measures is very promising, in this paper the authors study students in a simpler way, without directly analyzing student code, for the following reasons:

1. As practising teachers, we often find ourselves focusing on two simpler aspects of a student's performance on practical programming tasks, before we look at the student's code: (1) whether or not the student provided a piece of code that generates correct answers, and (2) how long it took the student to write the code.

2. As practising teachers, we also want ways of assessing the quality of the exercises we are giving the students.

3. As education researchers, we feel the work on the error quotient and other measures currently lacks a suitable benchmark, a simpler approach, upon which those more complicated approaches are incumbent to improve.

In the next section, we describe our simpler approach, which does not directly analyze student code. We then present and discuss results generated with this approach.

2. METHOD AND DATA

2.1 Educational Context and Data

The data for this study was collected from students enrolled in a 6 week introductory Java programming course at the University of Helsinki. In the course, 50% of the overall mark comes from completing online exercises during the 6 week semester, while the other 50% comes from a final exam. Furthermore, to pass the course, students must achieve at least half of the available marks in both the exercises and the final exam.

There are 106 online exercises available for inspection at http://mooc.fi/courses/2013/programming-part-1/material.html but only 77 of those exercises are used in the course. Students were allowed to make multiple submissions of an exercise, henceforth referred to as "attempts". Attempts could fail for both syntactic and semantic reasons, and the online system provides feedback to students. There were lab sessions where students could seek assistance with the exercises from teaching staff, but students were also allowed to work on and submit the exercises at any other time and place of their choosing. More information about the educational context and the data could be found in [1]. As data for this paper, each student's performance on each exercise was recorded as two values:

1. A dichotomous variable; 0 if the student did not succeed in answering the exercise correctly, or 1 if the student did provide a correct answer.

2. An integer; the number of attempts a student submitted for the exercise (irrespective of whether or not the student provided a correct answer).

The three final exam questions analyzed in this paper are provided in an appendix to this paper. As data for this paper, a student's performance on each of those three questions was recorded as a dichotomous variable; 0 if the student's mark for the question was below the class median mark for that question, or 1 if it was above the median.

2.2 Construction of Contingency Tables

A 2×2 contingency table is illustrated in Figure 1. The four variables in Figure 1, "a", "b", "c" and "d" represent the number of students who satisfy each of the four possible combinations of the two dichotomous variables, for exercise X and final exam question Y. The simplest example of a criterion for an exercise X is that students answered the exercise correctly. Given that criterion, then according to the example value in Figure 1 for "a", 32 students answered exercise X correctly and also scored above the class median mark on final exam question Y.

		Scored above the class median mark on final exam question Y ?	
		Yes	No
Meets criteria for exercise x ?	Yes	a (e.g. 32)	b (e.g. 6)
	No	c (e.g. 18)	d (e.g. 16)

Figure 1: A 2×2 Contingency Table for Exercise X and Final Exam Question Y.

2.2.1 Number of Student Attempts

More complicated criteria for exercise X in Figure 1 were constructed by combining whether or not students answered an exercise correctly with the number of attempts. That is, for each combination of exercise X and final exam question Y, a number of contingency tables were generated, where the dichotomous criteria for exercise X was that students answered the exercise ...

1. Correctly

2. Correctly, and in $< 2^n$ attempts

3. Correctly, and in $\geq 2^n$ attempts

4. Incorrectly, and in $< 2^n$ attempts

5. Incorrectly, and in $\geq 2^n$ attempts

6. In $< 2^n$ attempts

7. In $\geq 2^n$ attempts

The largest number of attempts by a student on any exercise was 513, so "n" in each of the list items takes on all values from 0 to 10.

2.3 Measures of Performance

We use two measures to describe the relationship between an exercise and a final exam question, in terms of the values within the contingency table, which are described below.

2.3.1 Accuracy

Accuracy, which ranges from 0 to 1, is the fraction of occasions when a student either (1) meets the criteria on exercise X and is in the upper half of the class on final exam question Y, or (2) did not meet the criteria on exercise X and is in the lower half on exam question Y. Formally, in terms of the contingency table values shown in Figure 1, accuracy is defined as:

$$acc = \frac{a + d}{a + b + c + d} \quad (1)$$

2.3.2 Phi Correlation Coefficient

The phi correlation coefficient is a standard measure of the correlation of two binary variables. The Pearson correlation coefficient for two binary variables is equivalent to the phi coefficient. The phi coefficient ranges from 1 (where the two binary variables are always equal), through zero (where the two binary variables are not related), to -1 (where the two binary variables are never equal). The phi coefficient is computed for a 2 by 2 contingency table as follows:

$$phi = \frac{ad - bc}{\sqrt[2]{(a + b)\,(c + d)\,(a + c)\,(b + d)}} \quad (2)$$

2.4 Contingency Table Pruning Rules

To select the statistically significant and most useful contingency tables, the following pruning rules were used to eliminate some contingency tables. In these pruning rules, where a rule refers to two contingency tables, the two contingency tables are for the same exercise and same final exam question. Also, of those two contingency tables, the table with a wider range of student attempts is the more general table (e.g. ≥ 8 attempts is more general than ≥ 16 attempts).

1. Contingency tables with any cell value of less than 5 were pruned. This is a well known and widely used criterion for ignoring a contingency table, which reduces the likelihood of over-fitting a model to data, for the reasons explained in [6].

2. Contingency tables with a negative phi were pruned. Such contingency tables always have "mirror image" contingency table with a positive phi.

3. Contingency tables with p > 0.01 (χ^2 test) were pruned.

4. If the phi values of two contingency tables differed by less than 0.01, then the less general bin was pruned.

5. If the phi values of two contingency tables differed by more than 0.01, and the phi value of the more general contingency table was higher than the phi value of less general table, then the less general table was pruned.

6. If the phi value of a more general contingency table was lower than the phi value of another table, but a statistical test for significant difference (z score transformation [3]) revealed no significant difference (p<0.05), then the less general bin was pruned.

3. RESULTS

3.1 When number of attempts is ignored

Table 1 shows the exercises with the highest correlation to final exam questions 2, 3 and 4, when the number of attempts by students is ignored. The final exam question numbers are designated in the table's second column, the column headed "ExamQ". Questions 2, 3 and 4 from the final exam are provided as an appendix to this paper.

For final exam question 2, the three highest correlating exercises are 59, 70 and 61, as shown in the third column, headed "Ex". These three exercises (and all other exercises) are available for inspection at http://mooc.fi/courses/2013/programming-part-1/material.html. The column with the heading "Week" indicates that all the exercises are from weeks 3 and 4 of the 6 week semester.

The columns headed "Q1", "Q2" and "Q3" show the quartile boundaries for the number of attempts made by students. For example, row 1.1 of the table shows that 25% of the students made 10 attempts or less on the exercise, 50% of the students made 15 attempts or less, and 50% of the students made between 10 and 20 attempts. Note that these quartile boundaries are for all students, irrespective of whether or not they answered the exercise correctly.

The values in the column headed "Correct" indicate that, for the contingency table used to construct each row of this table, answering each exercise correctly is the sole "criteria on exercise X" in Figure 1.

The columns headed "Phi" and "Accuracy" show the measures of performance as defined earlier. For each exam question, the rows of Table 1 are ordered on "Phi", from highest to lowest. Both "Phi" and "Accuracy" in each row are calculated using a contingency table as shown in Figure 1. In Table 1, the columns headed "a", "b", "c" and "d" show the values for each of these contingency tables. For each row of Table 1, "Meet criterion on exercise x" in Figure 1 is "yes" if a student answered the exercise correctly. For example, column "a" in row 1.1 of Table 1 shows that 32 students answered exercise 59 correctly and also scored above the median mark on final exam question 2. The values recorded for "a", "b", "c" and "d" in that row of Table 1 are the four example values shown in Figure 1. The column "sum" is simply the sum of the values in columns "a", "b", "c" and "d", which show that this table used data from approximately 70 students. The sum values in that column vary as sometimes a student did not attempt an exercise. The column headed "p" shows the statistical significance of the contingency table for each exercise, using the standard χ^2 test. All exercises shown in this table easily meet the traditional p<0.05 criteria for statistical significance.

3.2 When number of attempts is considered

Table 2 shows the exercises with the highest correlation to final exam questions 2, 3 and 4, when the number of attempts made by students on an exercise is considered. Most of the columns in this table contain the same type of infor-

mation as the previous table. The differences between the previous table and this table are:

- The column headed "Attempts" describes the range of the number of attempts a student must have made on an exercise as part of meeting the criteria on exercise X (as shown in Figure 1). For example, the "≥8" in row 2.1 indicates that a student needed to make at least 8 attempts at the exercise to be counted within either cell "a" or "b" of the contingency table. In rows 2.6 and 2.7, "<16" indicates that a student needed to make less than 16 attempts to meet the criteria.

- Some rows in the column headed "Correct" contain an asterisk. Each of those asterisks indicates that whether a student answered the exercise correctly is irrelevant; the sole criterion for including a student in cell "a" or "b" of the contingency table is the number of attempts the student made on the exercise.

- Rows 2.8 and 2.9 contain "correct" in the column headed "Correct", indicating there are two criteria that need to be met for a student to be counted in either cell "a" or "b" of the contingency table: (1) the student must have answered the exercise correctly, and (2) the student must have done so in the number of attempts specified in the "Attempts" column.

4. DISCUSSION

There are differences between Tables 1 and 2, which illustrate the utility of considering the number of attempts students make, rather than focusing on correctness alone:

- Table 1 shows no exercise correlated significantly with final exam question 3, but Table 2 shows several exercises correlated with that question.

- For final exam question 2, the phi correlation and accuracy of each exercise is much higher in Table 2 than in Table 1.

- In Table 1, all the exercises listed are from weeks 3 and 4 of the 6 week semester. The authors believe that it is counter-intuitive that exercises from mid-semester would always correlate better with a final exam question than exercises done late in semester. That intuition is supported by Table 2, where 6 out of 10 exercises listed in Table 2 are from weeks 5 and 6.

Before generating the results in the tables, the authors had thought that the column "Attempts" in Table 2 would be dominated by criteria that placed an upper bound on the number of attempts, not a lower bound (i.e. we thought there would have been more "<" symbols in the "Attempts" column, not the "≥" symbols that actually dominate). Our intuition was that stronger students would consistently complete exercises in fewer attempts than weaker students. Our explanation as to why "≥" symbols dominate is three-fold:

1. Students do the exercises at any time or place of their choosing. Students who complete some exercises in an unusually small number of attempts may be receiving too much assistance from someone else.

2. The reader may recall one of the pruning rules for contingency tables; that the smallest value in any cell of

Table 1: The exercises with the highest correlation to final exam questions 2, 3 and 4, where the sole criterion is whether a student answered the exercise successfully; the number of attempts prior to success is ignored. No exercises correlated significantly ($p < 0.05$) with final exam question 3.

Row No.	ExamQ	Ex	Week	Q1	Q2	Q3	Correct	Phi	Acc	a	b	c	d	sum	p
1.1	2	59	3	10	15	20	correct	0.33	0.66	32	6	18	16	72	0.004
1.2	2	70	4	15	40	70	correct	0.32	0.63	29	5	21	17	72	0.005
1.3	2	61	3	11	14	20	correct	0.28	0.61	27	5	23	17	72	0.01
1.4	3	—	—	—	—	—	———	—	—	—	—	—	—	—	——
1.5	4	52	3	16	24	35	correct	0.34	0.66	30	6	18	17	71	0.004
1.6	4	59	3	10	15	20	correct	0.33	0.66	31	7	17	17	72	0.004
1.7	4	55	3	19	26	35	correct	0.31	0.65	30	7	18	17	72	0.007

Table 2: The exercises with the highest correlation to final exam questions 2, 3 and 4, when the number of attempts by students is considered.

Row No.	ExamQ	Ex	Week	Q1	Q2	Q3	Correct	Attempts	Phi	Acc	a	b	c	d	sum	p
2.1	2	92	5	4	53	91	*	≥ 8	0.57	0.82	43	7	6	15	71	<0.001
2.2	2	102	6	2	113	199	*	≥ 16	0.48	0.77	38	6	10	15	69	<0.001
2.3	2	103	6	1	86	190	*	≥ 4	0.46	0.76	38	6	11	15	70	<0.001
2.4	3	92	5	4	53	91	*	≥ 4	0.43	0.77	44	10	6	11	71	<0.001
2.5	3	93	5	2	40	69	*	≥ 16	0.36	0.72	38	8	12	13	71	0.002
2.6	3	28	2	7	9	14	*	< 16	0.35	0.75	46	12	6	9	73	0.003
2.7	3	49	3	12	14	18	*	< 16	0.34	0.70	37	8	13	13	71	0.004
2.8	4	52	3	16	24	35	correct	≥ 8	0.38	0.68	30	5	18	18	71	0.001
2.9	4	59	3	10	15	20	correct	≥ 8	0.37	0.68	31	6	17	18	72	0.002
2.10	4	103	6	1	86	190	*	≥ 16	0.37	0.70	34	7	14	15	70	0.002

the contingency table must be at least 5. Given that the data is only from approximately 70 students, many contingency tables that place an upper bound on the number of attempts are pruned.

3. The occurrence of a "$\geq$" symbol in the "Attempts" column is an indication that an exercise is non-trivial. We note that in rows 2.6 and 2.7, where "<" symbols appear, the values in columns "Q1", "Q2" and "Q3" indicate that most students required relatively few attempts to complete the exercise. If the desire of the instructor is to provide students with a set of exercise in which the level of difficulty increases slowly, then the dominance of "$\geq$" symbols may be an indication that some exercises need to be added to the pool to reduce sudden jumps in difficulty.

On initial consideration, the many asterisks in the "Correct" column of Table 2 might be thought to indicate that the value for students in doing the exercises resides in the effort of doing the exercises, more so than getting the exercises right. However, there is also a more prosaic explanation, which is related to the contingency table pruning rule that the smallest value in any cell of the contingency table must be at least 5. For example, consider column "b" in row 2.1 of Table 2. The value in that column is 7, so the associated contingency table only narrowly avoided being pruned. Adding the extra criterion that students must also get exercise 92 right would shift some of the students from cells "a"

and "b" to cells "c" and "d". In doing so, the value in cell "b" is likely to drop from 7 to below 5. We note that in rows 2.8 and 2.9 of Table 2, where the selection criteria includes getting the exercise right, the values in the "b" column are 5 and 6, so the associated contingency tables only narrowly avoided being pruned. If data became available from many more students, it is the authors' suspicion that fewer asterisks would appear in the "Correct" column of Table 2.

Our method can identify gaps in a set of exercises. For example, the relatively low values of phi and accuracy for question 4, for all six exercises in both Tables 1 and 2, may indicate that the exercises did not prepare students well for this exam question – perhaps the exercises do not cover Object-Oriented concepts adequately.

Note that neither Table 1 or Table 2 show all the exercises that correlate significantly with each final exam question. Only the highest correlating exercises are shown.

4.1 Over-fitting

With data from only 70 students, a natural concern for any analysis is the danger of over-fitting. That is, there is a danger that the exercises selected for Table 2 exploit unrepresentative patterns in the relatively small data set; patterns that would not be present in a much larger data set. The specific problem with our method is that, for each pair of final exam question and exercise, there is only one contingency table that ignores the number of attempts, but there are several contingency tables that consider the number of attempts. For example, consider row 2.2 of Table 2. The column "Q3" indicates that a quarter of the students made 199 attempts or more at this exercise. If we assume that the highest number of attempts by any student was less than 512, there are 9 attempt ranges to consider: 1 attempt, 2-3 attempts, 4-7 attempts, 8-15 attempts ... 256-511 attempts. Furthermore, for each of those attempt ranges, there are two contingency tables: one that considers correctness and another that ignores correctness. It might therefore be argued that the reason why the exercises selected for Table 2 have higher phi and accuracy values is simply because there are more contingency tables to choose from when constructing Table 2. There are at least two reasons to discount that argument, which we describe in the remainder of this section.

The primary reason for discounting the danger of over-fitting is the pruning rule that all values in a contingency table must be ≥ 5. Table 3 shows the number of contingency tables after pruning for each of the final exam questions, across all exercises, for both when the number of attempts at each exercise are ignored and when the number of attempts are considered. For final exam questions 2 and 4, the small ratio between contingency tables when attempts are considered and contingency tables when attempts are ignored (as shown in the final column of Table 3) is unlikely to be large enough to explain the consistent superiority of phi and accuracy values in Table 2 over Table 1.

The second reason for discounting the above argument about over-fitting is that the argument incorrectly assumes statistical independence among all contingency tables. Consider two contingency tables for a given exercise and final exam question, where both contingency tables either ignore correctness or both consider it. Furthermore, assume that one of the contingency tables is for the case where the number of attempts is $\geq 2^n$ and the other contingency table is for the case where the number of attempts is $\geq 2^{n+1}$. The students who meet the criteria for the latter contingency table also meet the criteria for the former contingency table, so the two tables are not statistically independent.

Table 3: The number of contingency tables after pruning for final exam questions 2, 3 and 4, across all exercises, when the number of attempts at each exercise are ignored and considered.

Row No.	ExamQ	Attempts Ignored	Attempts Considered	Ratio
3.1	2	10	35	3.5
3.2	3	0	16	—
3.3	4	15	34	2.3

5. CONCLUSION

Our method can be used to benchmark more sophisticated methods for analyzing student performance on coding exercises. But practising teachers can also use this approach to identify weaknesses in a set of exercises, and identify students who may need help. Furthermore, the information that emerges from our method is simple enough to provide to students, as a guide to how many attempts it might take them to complete an exercise. Doing so might calm some students who are slow to understand that programming is an iterative process. It might also act as an indication to

other students that they either need to become more systematic in their approach, or they need to seek help from teaching staff.

6. REFERENCES

[1] A. Ahadi, R. Lister, H. Haapala, and A. Vihavainen. Exploring machine learning methods to automatically identify students in need of assistance. In *Proceedings of the Eleventh Annual International Conference on International Computing Education Research*, ICER '15, pages 121–130, New York, NY, USA, 2015. ACM.

[2] M. C. Jadud. Methods and tools for exploring novice compilation behaviour. In *Proceedings of the second international workshop on Computing education research*, pages 73–84. ACM, 2006.

[3] A. Papoulis. *Probability and Statistics*. Prentence-Hall International Editions, 1990.

[4] M. M. T. Rodrigo, E. Tabanao, M. B. E. Lahoz, and M. C. Jadud. Analyzing online protocols to characterize novice Java programmers. *Philippine Journal of Science*, 138(2):177–190, 2009.

[5] C. Watson, F. W. Li, and J. L. Godwin. Predicting performance in an introductory programming course by logging and analyzing student programming behavior. In *Advanced Learning Technologies (ICALT), 2013 IEEE 13th International Conference on*, pages 319–323. IEEE, 2013.

[6] F. Yates. Contingency tables involving small numbers and the Ĭ Ǧ2 test. *Supplement to the Journal of the Royal Statistical Society*, 1(2):217–235, 1934.

7. APPENDIX

The exam questions discussed in detail in this paper:

Question 2, part a
Create a program that outputs (using a loop statement such as while or for) all integers divisible 2, starting with 1000 and ending in 2. The output must occur so that 5 integers are printed on each row, and that each column must be aligned. The program output should look like this:

```
1000 998 996 994 992
 990 988 986 984 982
 980 978 976 974 972
    (lots of rows)
  10   8   6   4   2
```

Question 2, part b
Create a program where the input is integers representing the exam points gained by students. The program starts by reading the numbers of points from the user. The reading of the points stops when the user enters the integer -1.

The number of points must be an integer between 0 and 30. If some other integer is input (besides -1 that ends the program), the program ignores it.

After reading the numbers of points, the program states which number of points (between 0 and 30) is the greatest. Out of the number of points, the integers under 15 are equivalent to the grade *failed*, and the rest are *passed*. The program announces the number of passed and failed grades.

Example:

```
Enter numbers of exam points, -1 ends the program:
20
12
29
15
-1
best number of points: 29
passed: 3
failed: 1
```

In the above example, 12 points failed and the points 20, 29 and 15 passed exams. Thus, the program announces that 3 students passed and 1 student failed.

Please note that the program must ignore all integers outside 0-30. An example of a case where there are integers that have to be ignored among the input numbers:

```
Enter numbers of exam points, -1 ends the program:
10
100
20
-4
30
-1
best number of points: 30
passed: 2
failed: 1
```

As shown, the points -4 and 100 are ignored.

Question 3, part a
Create the method `public static void printInterval(int edge1, edge2)` that prints, in ascending order, each integer in the interval defined by its parameters.

If we call `printInterval(3, 7)`, it prints

```
3 4 5 6 7
```

The methods also works if the first parameter is greater than the second one, i.e. if we call `printInterval(10, 8)`, it prints

```
8 9 10
```

Thus, the integers are always printed in ascending order, regardless of which method parameter is greater, the first one or the second one.

Question 3, part b
Create the method `public static boolean bothFound(int[] integers, int integer1, integer2)`, which is given an integer array and two integers as parameters. The method returns true if both integers given as parameters (`integer1` and `integer2`) are in the array given as method parameter. In other cases the method returns false.

If the method receives as parameters for example the array [1,5,3,7,5,4], and the integers 5 and 7, it returns true. If the method received the array [1,5,3,2] and the integers 7 and 3 as parameters, it would return false.

Create a main program, as well, which demonstrates how to use the method.

Note! If you don't know how to use arrays, you can create `public static boolean bothFound(ArrayList <Integer> integers, int integer1, int integer2)`, where the method is given as parameters an ArrayList containing the integers and the integers to be found.

Question 4.
Create the class Warehouse. The warehouse has a capacity, which is an integer, and the amount of wares stored in the warehouse is also stored as an integer. The warehouse capacity if specified with the constructor parameter (you can assume that the value of the parameter is positive). The class has the following methods:

- `void add(int amount)`, that adds the amount of wares given in the parameter to the warehouse. If the amount is negative, the status of the warehouse does not change. When adding wares, the amount of wares in the warehouse cannot grow larger than the capacity. If the amount to be added does not fit into the warehouse completely, the warehouse is filled and the rest of the wares are 'wasted."

- `int space()`, that returns the amount of empty space in the warehouse.

- `void empty()`, that empties the warehouse.

- `toString()`, which returns a text representation of the warehouse status, formulated as in the example below; observe the status when the warehouse is empty!

Next is an example that demonstrates the operations of a warehouse that has been implemented correctly:

```
public static void main(String[] args) {
  Warehouse warehouse = new Warehouse(24);
  warehouse.add(10);
  System.out.println(warehouse);
  System.out.println("space in warehouse "
    + warehouse.space());
  warehouse.add(-2);
  System.out.println(warehouse);
  warehouse.add(50);
  System.out.println(warehouse);
  warehouse.empty();
  System.out.println(warehouse);\\
```

if the class has been implemented correctly, the output is
capacity: 24 items 10
space in warehouse 14
capacity: 24 items 10
capacity: 24 items 24
capacity: 24 empty

Making Formal Methods More Relevant to Software Engineering Students via Automated Test Generation

Gene Fisher
Department of Computer Science
California Polytechnic State University
San Luis Obispo, CA 93407
gfisher@calpoly.edu

Corrigan Johnson
Department of Computer Science
California Polytechnic State University
San Luis Obispo, CA 93407
johnsoncorrigan@gmail.com

ABSTRACT

The use of formal methods in software engineering has been advocated for a long time, by a lot of people. Unfortunately, advocates of formal methods remain a distinct minority among software engineering educators, as well as industrial practitioners. A number of reasons have been cited for the lack of acceptance of formal methods. Popular among these reasons is that formal methods lack relevance and utility to the everyday work of software engineers.

This paper presents a tool intended to increase the practical value of formal methods for software engineering students. The tool, called "Spest", generates unit testing code from a formal program specification. There have been other such tools developed in the past, but all have been difficult for us to use in our educational setting. With Spest, we hope to overcome some of the difficulties with a tool that is easy to use and which generates readable and extendible testing code. Initial results of using Spest in our classes are promising and we are planning continued development.

Keywords

Formal methods; software testing; automated test generation; software engineering education

1. INTRODUCTION

Simply put, a "formal method" is one based on formal mathematical principles. In general, formal methods are an integral part of computer science education. They are of course used in theoretical computer science classes, where mathematical concepts are at the center of the curricula. Formal methods are also used in many other courses where mathematically-based concepts can be applied to various aspects of the course subject matter. In software engineering courses, formal methods can be used in all phases of software development, to provide benefits that include:

- precise specification of software requirements
- precise definitions of design and implementation

- formal basis for generating program tests
- basis for formal verification of program correctness
- clearer understanding overall of what software is supposed to do and how it does it

Despite such benefits being compelling to formal method devotees, the methods remain a hard sell to students.

Resistance to formal methods is by no means unique to software engineering courses. Computer science students often have difficulty in courses that employ formal mathematical reasoning. A number of educational studies have confirmed this. In [22] for example, Pillay puts it bluntly and succinctly in saying that students find mathematically-oriented course content "boring and difficult".

We have observed the same student opinions in our software engineering courses. Furthermore, in addition to finding formal methods boring and difficult, our students also find them irrelevant to the software development work they need to do. Given such dismal student opinions, those of us who seek broader acceptance of formal methods clearly have our work cut out for us.

1.1 Our Experience with Formal Methods

For nearly three decades, we have tried a variety of approaches to teach formal methods in software engineering courses. We have prepared detailed course materials on the use of formal methods. We have designed course assignments to integrate formal methods into the work that students do. We have continually updated the tools we use for formal methods support, to keep them as up to date as possible. In graduate courses, we have had students read the literature on formal methods usage, including practical applications [20] , educational benefits [23] , and the "myth buster" papers that debunk popular misconceptions about formal methods [11, 4, 14]. For undergraduates, we have discussed the ideas presented in the literature and provided detailed examples for them to use in their course work.

Despite our best efforts, what students have taken away from our courses is that formal methods may have some *potential* benefits, but this potential remains unmet in the day-to-day work they do to engineer software. Outside of academia, it appears that many industrial practitioners have reached similar conclusions [25]. As educators, the industrial view does indeed figure into our work. This is because one of the factors cited for lack of industrial acceptance of formal methods is that students are not well trained in the methods. Hence, if we can succeed in improving student acceptance and use of formal methods, that may well have a positive effect on industrial use.

ITiCSE '16, July 09-13, 2016, Arequipa, Peru

© 2016 ACM. ISBN 978-1-4503-4231-5/16/07. . . $15.00

DOI: http://dx.doi.org/10.1145/2899415.2899424

1.2 An Opportunity

In response to our lack of success, we have searched continuously for tools and techniques that could make formal methods of direct tangible benefit to our students. One particular technology has stood out in this regard – *automated generation of program tests from formal specifications*. There have been a number of tools developed for this purpose, but none has been realistically usable in our classes.

In the absence of a usable test generation tool, we have told our students of the promising research in this area, and said we have high expectations that such tools should soon be available. Alas, we have been waiting twenty years for this to happen. In the meantime, we have asked the following question in many student surveys: *"Suppose there were a tool that could generate usable tests from a formal software specification, alleviating a good deal of manual test implementation. Would the existence of such a tool make it worthwhile for you to write the specifications?"* The answer to this question has consistently been a clear "yes".

In our experience, we have observed that our software engineering students believe these things:

- software testing is necessary, but writing tests by hand is tedious, boring, and difficult to do thoroughly

- formal software specification is unnecessary, but we could change our mind about this if there were a tool to generate genuinely usable tests from the specifications

We see from the second observation a clear opportunity to improve acceptance of formal methods. The test-generation system we are developing, named *Spest*, is designed to address this opportunity. Spest has two components:

- a simple specification language, based on well-established concepts of behavioral program specification

- a test generation component, that produces readable testing code, using testing techniques that are part of the software engineering course curriculum

2. BACKGROUND AND RELATED WORK

2.1 Specification Languages

A formal specification language is used to express abstractly the desired behavior of software. For the interested reader, an excellent in-depth survey of behavioral specification languages is provided by Hatcliff et al in [12].

Throughout the long history of formal specification, the key constructs have remained surprisingly stable. A widely used form of specification is based on *preconditions* and *postconditions*, dating back to the seminal 1967 paper by Robert Floyd [8]. This style of specification is reasonably well known in computer science, even appearing in a number of introductory computer science textbooks e.g., [13], as well as the 2013 ACM curriculum guidelines [15].

In an elementary form, preconditions and postconditions can appear as English-language comments associated with program functions, defining respectively what must be true before and after the function runs. In fully formal specification languages, preconditions and postconditions are compilable logic expressions, used for a number of purposes including runtime checks, as formulae for test-case generation, and as the basis of formal program verification.

Our earliest use of preconditions and postconditions was in the form of natural language program comments. Our

use of compilable specification languages began in the late 1980s with Larch [10] and Z [24]. In promoting the use of Larch and Z to students, we described them as a means to understand fully and unambiguously what a program does. While the students had some begrudging appreciation for why this is important, there were at least two significant practical problems with these languages:

1. their syntax and semantics were entirely separate from the programming languages used to implement the specifications

2. the tools available for the languages allowed the specifications to be checked for syntactic and type correctness, but the compiled specifications could be put to no other useful purpose by the students

An early language that addressed both of these problems was ADL – the Assertion Definition Language [5]. The ADL language itself was tailored for use with C programs. More importantly, the ADL environment provided one of the earliest practical tools to generate program tests from specifications. We discuss further details of the ADL test-generation strategy in the next subsection of the paper.

As promising as ADL was, it suffered from a somewhat common problem for formal specification languages – it went extinct. Even though ADL was backed by Sun Microsystems in the form of "SunTest", it was a hard sell to a math-phobic software engineering community. Compounding the problem was the fact that software testing was also a bit of a hard sell to developers, in the pre-JUnit era.

To address the issues of language stability and lack of tools, we had a go at developing our own requirements specification language (RSL), initially under contract to NASA [9], and then extended for use in our software engineering courses. While the RSL toolset proved useful, the language still had the problem of being syntactically and semantically distinct from any implementation language.

With the advent of Java as a widely-used instructional language, an evolutionary step in formal specification was the introduction of several Java-specific notations. These include iContract, J@va, JASS, jContractor, and JML [17, 3, 1, 16, 18]. These notations were implemented using Java annotations and solved the problem of RSL and earlier languages being divorced from the concrete implementation language. Of these particular Java-based notations, all but JML have gone effectively extinct.

JML is alive and well; we had used it in our classes until last year, when we began to use Spest. JML has much to recommend it, including very active user and developer communities, as well as a number of useful tools. Further discussion of the JML test generation tools follows in the next subsection, followed after that with a discussion of why we have moved from JML to Spest.

While we have never used the Eiffel programming language [21] in any of our classes, it is certainly worth noting in this discussion of related work. Eiffel is one of the few procedural programming languages in which formal specification constructs are built in to the language. The design of Eiffel has clearly been influential, having been cited explicitly for example by the designers of iContract, JASS, jContractor, and JML. Also of note is that the Eiffel development environment includes functionality for test generation [19], about which we say more in the next subsection.

2.2 Test Generation from Specifications

As noted above, the ADL system was an early example of a practical tool for the automated generation of unit tests from formal specifications. The ADL test generator was based on the highly-influential research of Elaine Weyuker, who formulated the *meaningful impact* strategy for test generation [26]. The Spest test generator itself employs a variant of meaningful impact. A detailed technical discussion of this and other test generation techniques is beyond the scope of this paper. Suffice it to say that the early work of Weyuker and others made it clear that automated specification-based test generation can be practical and effective.

The test generation tools that are most directly related to Spest are those that have been developed for JML. These are JMLUnit [6] and JMLUnitNG [27]. JMLUnitNG was designed expressly as an upgrade to the earlier JMLUnit. With respect to Spest, one or both of these tools have the following significant shortcomings:

- an excessive number of tests are generated
- tests take an excessive amount of time to run
- generated test code is not as readable or extendible by students as it could be
- there is little to no active support for the tools

Among non-Java languages, the test generation tool provided in the Eiffel environment is definitely noteworthy [19]. It uses a different generation technique than ADL, JMLUnitNG, or Spest, but it does use formal program specifications. From a pedagogical standpoint, the goals for Eiffel test generation are in substantial alignment with our goals for Spest. In [19], the authors make the following observation, with which we completely agree:

"Our experience is that students who are less inclined towards mathematical techniques are more amenable to their study, use, and description if they are couched in terms of accepted engineering tasks, particularly testing, with which they have some experience."

3. THE SPEST NOTATION

There are two over-arching goals for the Spest formal specification notation:

1. keep it as simple as possible
2. provide support for multiple programming languages

We have established these goals based on the reasons that we and others have observed for lack of acceptance of formal specification languages. We note also that these goals motivate our move from JML to Spest.

To achieve the first goal we have included in Spest a very small number of core constructs. To achieve the second goal, we have designed the core constructs so they can be readily incorporated into common programming languages.

The idea for the second goal stems from two separate but potentially conflicting language features. One feature is implementation-independent specification. While this can be desirable to allow flexibility in selecting an implementation language, we have noted its difficulties. Hence some have chosen the feature of a programming-language-specific specification notation. To support both these features, we have designed Spest so it can be incorporated into different "host" programming languages by absorbing as much as possible the standard syntax and semantics of that host.

```
abstract class UserDB {

  Collection<UserRecord> data;

  /** Add a new UserRecord to this.data.

  pre:
    // No existing record in the input data has
    // the same ID as the new record.
    !exists (UserRecord other_rec ;
        data.contains(other_rec) ;
          other_rec.id.equals(rec.id));

  post:
    // A record is in the output data if and
    // only if it's the new record to be added
    // or it's already in the input data.
    forall (UserRecord any_rec ;
        (data'.contains(any_rec)) iff
          any_rec.equals(rec) ||
            data.contains(any_rec));
  */
  abstract void add(UserRecord rec);
}
```

Figure 1: A Spest example.

At present, we have implemented the Java version of Spest. We have near-term plans for C, C++, and Python versions. We believe this multi-language agenda is realistic given our previous experience developing multi-language programming environments [7] and the wide availability of open-source compilation tools.

Figure 1 shows an excerpt of a Spest specification. The example illustrates important Spest features:

- Spest keywords: `pre`, `post`, `forall`, `exists`, `iff`
- quantifier expressions
- the apostrophe character (read "prime"), used to distinguish pre versus post (primed) identifier values

Constructs not shown in Figure 1 are the `except` clause for exceptional behavior and the use of standard Java keywords `return`, `throw`, and `if-else` in expression contexts.

At first glance, one might say of Figure 1 that we have failed to meet our goal of notational simplicity. Indeed, the notation in Figure 1 is rather dense, which is one of the red flags raised in Wassyng's critique of formal notations [25]. In or own defense, we can say that the example in Figure 1 was chosen purposely to show a non-trivial specification, with notation that is admittedly dense. In many cases, preconditions and postconditions are much simpler than this, particularly ones that do not use quantifiers.

Many students do reel at the notational density of examples like Figure 1. However, we have seen very similar perplexed reactions with other difficult subject matter, such as students' first look at the density of a triple-deference operator in ANSI C (e.g., `***ptr`). The point is that students accept complexity when they see its ultimate benefits.

Pedagogically, we use common techniques to discuss the dense notation. We give the English transliteration and describe how it is used as inline comments. We tell students

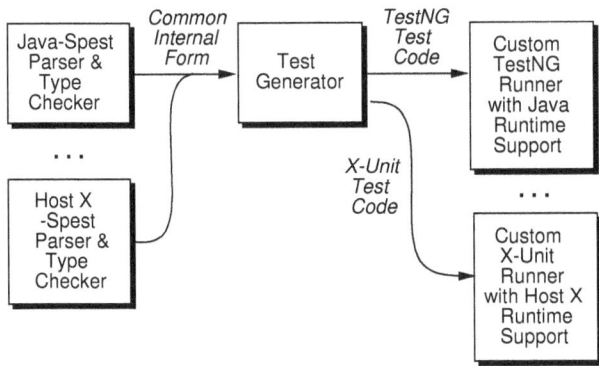

Figure 2: Components of the Spest system.

about reusable specification idioms. For example, the add method precondition uses an idiom for ensuring item uniqueness in a collection, and the postcondition uses an idiom for the precisely correct addition of an item into a collection. Such idioms can be used like design patterns, to characterize and categorize common idiomatic forms.

Our class materials also include detailed discussion of specification-based test generation techniques:

- provide input values that fully exercise the boolean logic of the preconditions, including data range conditions, collection-size ranges, and pairwise combinations of multiple input values

- use the postcondition as the testing oracle to define the expected output of the method

- use a coverage tool to measure test adequacy, writing additional white-box tests when necessary

Despite our best efforts to encourage use of these techniques, the testing practices actually employed by many of our students go something like this:

- do a half-hearted job of writing specifications

- use one's own familiarity with the code, together with an ad hoc application of black-box and white-box testing techniques to develop a substandard set of tests

- be satisfied with a low grade on project testing

Given these observations about students' testing practices, our goal for Spest is not to have students simply *accept* the utility of formal specification. Rather, the goal is to provide tool support that shows the concrete utility of specifications and help students achieve better testing results.

4. GENERATING TESTS WITH SPEST

Figure 2 is a high-level flow diagram of the Spest system. The first step in the test generation process is to parse and type check the specification. As new parser/type-checker components are added, they will produce the same internal form as currently produced by the Java-based component. This internal form is comprised of an abstract syntax tree and symbol table, sent to the test generation component.

The test generation component uses the same black-box test generation techniques we discuss in class. The generated testing code is in a readable form, so that students can (a)

```
public class UserDBTest {
  @Before
  public void setUp() {
    UserDB testObj = (UserDB)javaTestUtility.
      getSampleObject(classUnderTest);
  }
  @Test
  public void testAdd() throws Exception {
    // Clone pre-execution collection values
    java.util.Collection<UserRecord> data =
      cloner.deepClone(getFieldValues(...));

    // Generate basic test inputs
    List<UserRecord> testValues =
      javaTestUtility.getSampleObjects(...);

    // Generate inputs to exercise quantifiers
    List<UserRecord> quantTestValues =
      javaTestUtility.getUniversalValues(...);

    // Generate pairwise input combinations
    int[][] combos =
      CombinationSupport.getCombinations(...);

    // Loop through each test case
    for (int i = 0; i < combos.length; i++) {

      // Invoke the method under test
      javaTestUtility.invokeMethod(...);

      // Validate method postcondition
      Assert.assertTrue(javaTestUtility.
        validatePostcondition(...));
    }
  }
}
```

Figure 3: Spest-generated testing code.

understand it as an example of applied testing techniques, and (b) extend it when it achieves inadequate test coverage. The generator can produce inadequate tests due either to an inadequate specification or the inherit limitations of its less-than artificially intelligent algorithms.

The Spest system has a simple stand-alone GUI. It allows users to select code files to be tested, validate the specifications in that code, and generate the tests. The generated test code uses the TestNG library [2]. Users employ their preferred IDE to compile the tests with the application files under test. Part of the compilation process is the inclusion of a Spest runtime jar file. The pre-compiled runtime support has mnemonically-named methods that are called from the testing code. The support methods encapsulate lower-level aspects of test execution, so when students view the generated test code, higher-level testing concepts are more clearly evident. Also, the generated test code is clearly commented to indicate where students can add testing extensions.

Figure 3 has an excerpt of the testing class that Spest generates for the UserDB class shown in Figure 1. The excerpt is essentially as-generated, but with some elisions for brevity. It shows the major aspects of a generated test for a specification that uses unbounded quantification over a collection class, which is one of the more challenging aspects

Please rate your level of agreement with the following statements on a scale from 1 (disagree strongly) to 5 (agree strongly).

1. Using **L** for formal specification helped me understand the programs I developed, better than if **L** had not been used.
2. The **L** specifications written by my teammates helped me understand the intended behavior of their code.
3. When using **L**, I had to write additional support code that I would not have written if **L** had not been used.
4. Using **L** helped with the development of unit tests for the programs I wrote.
5. As a language, **L** was easy to understand.
6. The **L** compilation tools were easy to use.
7. The **L** documentation was useful.

Please describe your experience and any problems you encountered while using **L**. (Response here is optional free-form text.)

Figure 4: Survey questions.

of test generation. A detailed discussion of the generated testing code is beyond the scope of this paper. The inline comments explain the major functionality.

5. USING SPEST IN CLASSES

In the Fall and Winter quarters of the 2014-15 academic year, we used JML in a two-quarter software engineering sequence taken by junior and senior students. In the Winter and Spring quarters of that same academic year, we ran exactly the same course sequence using Spest. All course materials in the JML and Spest versions of the courses were the same, except for the use of JML versus Spest.

Our initial plan was to compare the test generation capabilities of JMLUnitNG and Spest. However, we were unable to use JMLUnitNG with student projects due to our use of Java 8, as well as other usage problems with JMLUnitNG. Given these problems, we chose to compare JML and Spest without having the students use the Spest test generator. Hence the studied comparison of JML and Spest is of their use as specification languages. We did perform a post hoc quantitative analysis, as described in Section 5.2.

5.1 Qualitative Student Survey

Figure 4 shows the survey questions we asked students at the end of the two-quarter sequences for JML and Spest. The letter "**L**" was substituted with "JML" or "Spest".

Table 1 shows the statistical results of the survey. The survey population size was 25 students for the JML class and 22 for the Spest class. For all questions, the data show no statistically significant difference between JML and Spest. This is an important result for future usage studies. Namely, since we see no significant difference between using Spest and its best alternative, we can use Spest alone in further studies that assess the effectiveness of Spest's specification-based test generation.

Overall, the results of our qualitative survey are consistent with many past surveys. That is, student attitudes are neutral at best towards formal methods in and of themselves, without something to make them more relevant.

5.2 Quantitative Analysis of Test Generation

As noted above, we were unable to compare tests gen-

Table 1: Statistical summary of survey results.

Ques:	1	2	3	4	5	6	7
JML:							
Mean	2.68	2.72	2.52	2.84	2.96	2.92	2.64
Std Dev	1.22	1.4	1.29	1.43	1.17	1.15	1.19
Spest:							
Mean	2.45	2.77	2.91	2.77	2.86	2.59	2.77
Std Dev	0.96	1.11	1.15	1.07	1.17	0.85	0.92
Stats:							
T-Test:	0.47	0.89	0.28	0.85	0.82	0.27	0.68
Sig?	No	No	No	No	No	No	No

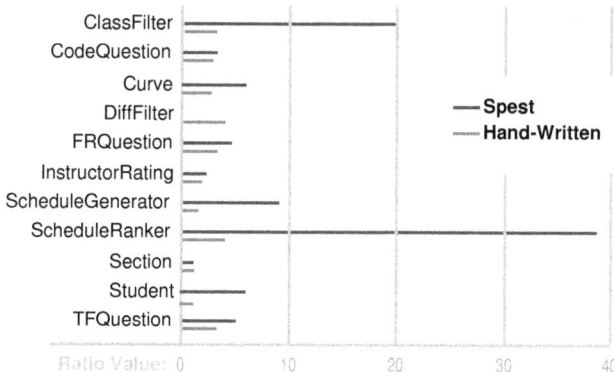

Figure 5: Efficiency of Spest vs. hand-written tests.

erated from JML versus Spest. The 2014-15 data do provide the basis for comparing hand-written tests to Spest-generated tests. Since the quality of Spest-generated tests is based on the quality of the specification, we chose student-written Java classes that met both of the following criteria:

1. they were well specified, based on human inspection
2. they were well tested, based on code coverage

For all classes that met these criteria, we generated Spest tests to compare to the student-written tests.

Given the observations made earlier about student testing practices, the number of student-written classes that met both of these criteria was relatively small. Furthermore, code coverage alone was not a useful distinguishing metric for hand-written versus Spest-generated, since coverage was high for both categories. Hence, we formulated a metric we believe provides a useful quantitative comparison.

The metric we used is a *test efficiency ratio*. This is defined as the ratio of line coverage to the number of lines of testing code to obtain that coverage. While this is a non-standard metric, it is a useful way to perform quantitative analysis of the data on hand. Figure 5 shows the results of the analysis. The left column in the figure has the names of Java classes that met the preceding two criteria. The red and blue lines compare efficiency ratios. The data show that Spest-generated tests have a higher efficiency ratio in all but one case, being statistically significant in four cases.

6. CONCLUSIONS AND FUTURE WORK

Our results so far are encouraging. For the 2015-16 academic year we are planning a controlled study using Spest with and without automated test generation, in two large sections of software engineering.

We also have a large body of archived student projects from past software engineering courses. We plan to mechanically translate formal specifications written in past specification languages into Spest, generate tests from those specifications, and then compare the Spest-generated tests with student-written tests. We will use well-accepted test comparison metrics including code coverage and mutation.

Outside of classes, we plan to use Spest to generate tests for suitable open source projects that are well tested and for which specifications exist or could be feasibly written by us. Open-source projects using JML are good candidates. With hand-written and Spest-generated tests for the same code base, we will compare their quality using standard metrics.

In the way of tools, an Eclipse plug-in is also planned, to replace the stand-alone GUI.

7. REFERENCES

[1] D. Bartetzko, C. Fischer, M. Möller, and H. Wehrheim. Jass – java with assertions. *Electronic Notes in Theoretical Comp. Sci*, 55(2):103–117, 2001.

[2] C. Beust and H. Suleiman. *Next Generation Java Testing: TestNG and Advanced Concepts*. Addison-Wesley Professional, 2007.

[3] I. B. Bourdonov, A. V. Demakov, A. A. Jarov, A. Kossatchev, V. V. Kuliamin, A. Petrenko, and S. V. Zelenov. Java specification extension for automated test development. In *Revised Papers from the 4th Intl. Andrei Ershov Memorial Conference on Perspectives of System Informatics: Akademgorodok, Novosibirsk, Russia*, PSI '02, pages 301–307, London, UK, UK, 2001. Springer-Verlag.

[4] J. P. Bowen and M. G. Hinchey. Seven more myths of formal methods. *IEEE Software*, 12(4):34–41, 1995.

[5] J. Chang, D. J. Richardson, and S. Sankar. Structural specification-based testing with adl. In *Proc. of the 1996 ACM SIGSOFT Intl. Symposium on Software Testing and Analysis*, ISSTA '96, pages 62–70, New York, NY, USA, 1996. ACM.

[6] Y. Cheon and G. T. Leavens. A simple and practical approach to unit testing: The jml and junit way. In *Proc. of the 16th European Conference on Object-Oriented Programming*, ECOOP '02, pages 231–255, London, UK, UK, 2002. Springer-Verlag.

[7] G. Fisher. An overview of a graphical multilanguage applications environment. *IEEE Transactions on Software Engineering*, 14(6):774–786, 1988.

[8] R. W. Floyd. Assigning meanings to programs. *Proc. of Symposium on Applied Mathematics*, 19:19–32, 1967.

[9] D. Frincke, D. Wolber, G. Fisher, and G. C. Cohen. Requirements specification language (rsl) and supporting tools. NASA Contractor Report 189700, NASA Langley Research Center, 1992.

[10] J. V. Guttag, J. J. Horning, and J. M. Wing. The larch family of specification languages. *IEEE Software*, 2(5):24–36, Sept 1985.

[11] A. Hall. Seven myths of formal methods. *IEEE Software*, 12:11–19, 1990.

[12] J. Hatcliff, G. T. Leavens, K. R. M. Leino, P. Müller, and M. Parkinson. Behavioral interface specification languages. *ACM Comput. Surv.*, 44(3):16:1–16:58, June 2012.

[13] C. S. Horstmann. *Big Java*. Wiley Publishing, 4th edition, 2010.

[14] C. Jaspan, M. Keeling, L. Maccherone, G. L. Zenarosa, and M. Shaw. Software mythbusters explore formal methods. *IEEE Software*, 26(6):60–63, 2009.

[15] A. f. C. M. A. Joint Task Force on Computing Curricula and I. C. Society. *Computer Science Curricula 2013: Curriculum Guidelines for Undergraduate Degree Programs in Computer Science*. ACM, New York, NY, USA, 2013. 999133.

[16] M. Karaorman and P. Abercrombie. jcontractor: Introducing design-by-contract to java using reflective bytecode instrumentation. *Formal Methods in System Design*, 27:275–312, 2005.

[17] R. Kramer. icontract - the java(tm) design by contract(tm) tool. *Technology of Object-Oriented Languages, Intl. Conference on*, 0:295–308, 1998.

[18] G. T. Leavens, A. L. Baker, and C. Ruby. Preliminary design of jml: A behavioral interface specification language for java. *SIGSOFT Softw. Eng. Notes*, 31(3):1–38, May 2006.

[19] A. Leitner, I. Ciupa, M. Oriol, B. Meyer, and A. Fiva. Contract driven development = test driven development - writing test cases. In *Proc. of the the 6th Joint Meeting of the European Software Engineering Conference and the ACM SIGSOFT Symposium on The Foundations of Software Engineering*, ESEC-FSE '07, pages 425–434, New York, NY, USA, 2007. ACM.

[20] T. Margaria and B. Steffen, editors. *ISoLA'12: Proc. of the 5th Intl. Conference on Leveraging Applications of Formal Methods, Verification and Validation: Applications and Case Studies - Volume Part II*, Berlin, Heidelberg, 2012. Springer-Verlag.

[21] B. Meyer. *Eiffel: the Language*. Prentice-Hall, 1st edition, 1992.

[22] N. Pillay. Learning difficulties experienced by students in a course on formal languages and automata theory. *SIGCSE Bull.*, 41(4):48–52, Jan. 2010.

[23] A. K. Sobel and M. Clarkson. Formal methods application: An empirical tale of software development. *IEEE Transactions on Software Engineering*, 28(3):308–320, 2002.

[24] J. Spivey. *Understanding Z, A Specification Language and its Formal Semantics*. Cambridge University Press., 1st edition, 1998.

[25] A. Wassyng. Though this be madness, yet there is method in it? (keynote). In *1st FME Workshop on Formal Methods in Software Engineering (FormaliSE)*, ICSE '13, pages 1–7, Piscataway, NJ, USA, 2013. IEEE Press.

[26] E. Weyuker, T. Goradia, and A. Singh. Automatically generating test data from a boolean specification. *IEEE Transactions on Software Engineering*, 20(5):353–363, 1994.

[27] D. M. Zimmerman and R. Nagmoti. Jmlunit: The next generation. In *Proc. of the 2010 Intl. Conference on Formal Verification of Object-oriented Software*, FoVeOOS'10, pages 183–197, Berlin, Heidelberg, 2011. Springer-Verlag.

AESvisual: A Visualization Tool for the AES Cipher

Jun Ma, Jun Tao,
Jean Mayo,
Ching-Kuang Shene
Department of Computer
Science
Michigan Technological
University
Houghton, MI
{junm,junt,jmayo,shene}@mtu.edu

Melissa Keranen
Department of Mathematical
Sciences
Michigan Technological
University
Houghton, MI
msjukuri@mtu.edu

Chaoli Wang
Department of Computer
Science & Engineering
University of Notre Dame
Notre Dame, IN
chaoli.wang@nd.edu

ABSTRACT

This paper describes a visualization tool AESvisual that helps students learn and instructors teach the AES cipher. The software allows the user to visualize all the major steps of AES encryption and decryption. The demo mode is useful and efficient for classroom presentation and the practice mode provides the user with an environment to practice AES encryption with error checking. AESvisual is quite versatile, providing support for both beginners learning how to encrypt and decrypt, and also for the more advanced users wishing to see all the details, including the $GF(2^8)$ addition and multiplication operations. Classroom evaluation of the tool was positive.

Keywords

Cryptography, visualization

1. INTRODUCTION

In 1997, the National Institute of Standards and Technology asked for potential candidates to replace the Data Encryption Standard (DES) as the official data encryption standard. In 1998, there were five finalists, and eventually from this list Rijndael was chosen to be the winner. It was developed by two Belgian cryptographers, Joan Daemen and Vincent Rijmen [3]. The Advanced Encryption Standard (AES) is based upon Rijndael. It has been a federal government standard since 2002 and is now used worldwide.

AES is a type of block cipher. It consists of 10 rounds; each round has an input of 128 bits and produces an output of 128 bits. The algorithm has four basic steps, or layers, that when put together form the rounds. When studying this cipher, it is sometimes easier to focus on each step of the algorithm separately. Although each step is straightforward, students often have difficulties putting all of the pieces together. Therefore, when asked to complete one round of

the algorithm, they may find that they do not understand it in its entirety. We have created a visualization tool, AESvisual, to aid in the process of learning the cipher.

AES appears in nearly every cryptography and computer security textbook [6, 7]. Many tools are available ranging from some simple ones [2, 4] to publicly available and more sophisticated systems [1] such as applets directly accessible on the web. However, many pedagogical tools available now only provide an animation of the algorithm. The one that is closely related to our goal [5] uses hardware visualization. AESvisual is different in that it allows for the user to both view the process and practice using the cipher. Users can work through, in detail, each of the four layers: Substitute Bytes Transformation, Shift Rows Transformation, Mix Columns Transformation, and Add Round Key. The software also leads the user through the Key Expansion process, which is used to generate the key for the cryptosystem.

In the following, Section 2 provides the background of our cryptography course, Section 3 presents our visualization tool, Section 4 provides a detailed study of our findings from a survey, and Section 5 is our conclusion.

2. COURSE INFORMATION

AESvisual was used in a cryptography course, MA3203 Introduction to Cryptography, that is offered out of the Department of Mathematical Sciences at Michigan Technological University. It is a junior level course that gives a basic introduction to the field of cryptography. This course covers classical cryptography, the Data Encryption Standard (DES), the Advanced Encryption Standard (AES), the RSA algorithm, discrete logarithms, hash functions, and elliptic curve cryptography. For each cryptosystem, we study how it was designed, why it works, how one may attack the system, and how it has been used in practice.

The widespread use of AES makes it an essential algorithm for any introductory cryptography student to understand. Therefore, it is an important piece of our cryptography course, and we pay great attention to it. AESvisual was used in the classroom to demonstrate an entire round of the algorithm throughly and efficiently. It was also used by students for self-study to learn and practice both the encryption and decryption processes.

ITiCSE '16, July 09-13, 2016, Arequipa, Peru

© 2016 ACM. ISBN 978-1-4503-4231-5/16/07...$15.00

DOI: http://dx.doi.org/10.1145/2899415.2899425

3. SOFTWARE DESCRIPTION

AESvisual supports Windows, MacOS and Linux. It consists of two major components: the Demo mode and the Practice mode. The Demo mode displays both the encryption and decryption operations of the AES algorithm, and each operation has multiple pages to demonstrate the major steps. The Practice mode helps the user learn the detailed computations step-by-step and perform self-study. Only encryption is available in this mode since decryption follows the same workflow in a reversed order. A test report system helps the instructor verify student learning effectiveness.

3.1 The Demo Mode

AESvisual always starts from the Demo mode. It has four subpages: Overview, Encryption, Decryption and Key Expansion. The Overview subpage is used to demonstrate the workflow of the encryption and decryption operations and their relationship (Figure 1). Encryption and decryption involve ten rounds, but only the first round (highlighted in red) is shown. Clicking the Go button below the Round 1 marking brings the user to the Encryption subpage or Decryption subpage. The user may also click the Expand Key button to advance to the Key Expansion subpage.

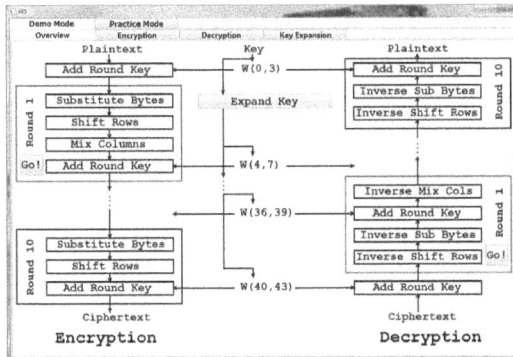

Figure 1: Overview of the AES Algorithm

3.1.1 Encryption

This subpage demonstrates the four major steps of the first round (i.e., Round 1) for encryption: Substitute Bytes, Shift Rows, Mix Columns and Add Round Key. Each of these four steps has its own subpage.

Substitute Bytes. This subpage shows how the 128-bit original plaintext is processed using Add Round Key and the S-box transformation (Figure 2). The user may generate a new random plaintext-key pair with the Random button. The generated key is then expanded in the Key Expansion subpage to create 44 32-bit words. Clicking the Expand Key button brings the user to the corresponding subpage. The user may click the Add Round Key button to see how the plaintext is added with the first four words W(0, 3). The output is then transformed with the S-box Transformation. The user may select an element (in red) in the output matrix of the Add Round Key subpage and then click the Check S-box button to see the details of the transformation (Figure 3). The corresponding element in the result is highlighted and the selected row and column are also shown above the Check S-box button. The result from this transformation is then used as the input matrix to the Shift Rows subpage.

Shift Rows. This subpage demonstrates how the input ma-

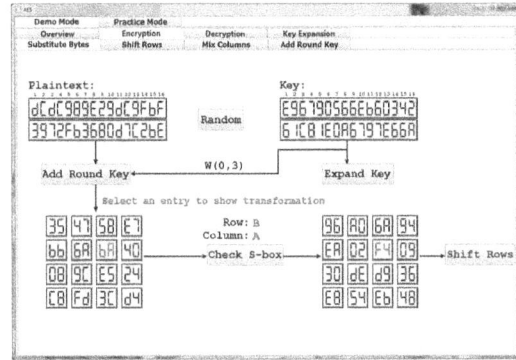

Figure 2: Substitute Bytes of Encryption

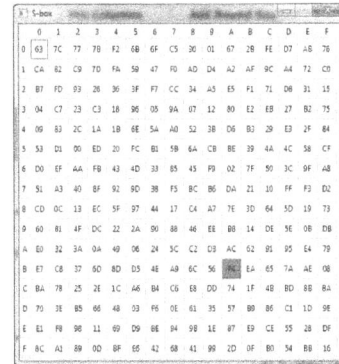

Figure 3: SBox for the S-Box transformation

trix is transformed by performing row-based byte rotation (Figure 4). The result goes to the Mix Columns subpage.

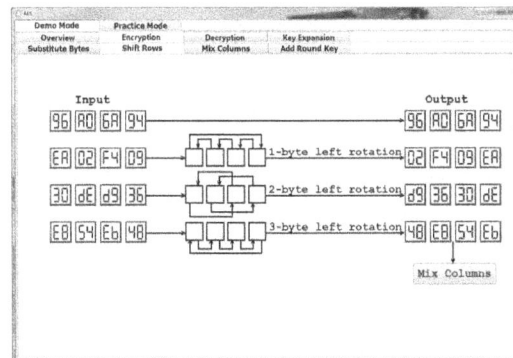

Figure 4: Shift Rows of Encryption

Mix Columns. This subpage shows how the output matrix is obtained by multiplying the input matrix with a given matrix in $GF(2^8)$ (Figure 5). If the user selects a column (in red) of the input matrix, the corresponding column of the output matrix will be highlighted (in green). The lower half of this subpage has the details of the matrix multiplication for the selected column. The user may click $\times$ and $+$ to explore the corresponding $GF(2^8)$ multiplication (Figure 6) and addition (Figure 7) operations in detail. The numbers in these windows are in binary format. The output matrix is then used as the input for the Add Round Key subpage.

Add Round Key. This subpage shows how the input matrix is XORed ($\oplus$) with the word matrix element-by-element (Figure 8). The user may select an element of the input

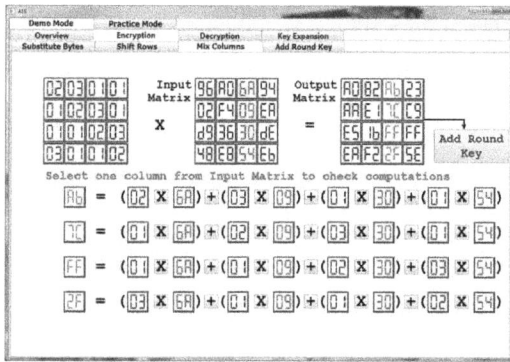

Figure 5: Mix Columns **of Encryption**

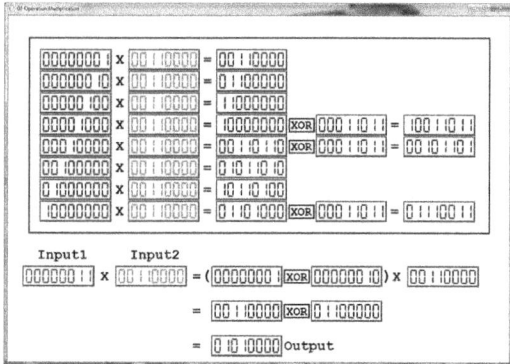

Figure 6: $\mathbf{GF}(2^8)$ **Multiplication**

matrix (in red) or the word matrix (in blue) and the corresponding element in the output matrix will be highlighted (in green). The lower half of this subpage shows the corresponding exclusive disjunction operation in binary format. The final ciphertext after the ten rounds of the encryption process is shown in the lower right corner of this page.

3.1.2 Decryption

The Decryption subpage also has four subpages showing the four major steps of the first round of decryption. It starts with the Shift Rows subpage (Figure 9), followed by Substitute Bytes, Add Round Key, and Mix Columns. The ciphertext in Shift Rows is taken from encryption and the user may click the Add Round Key and Substitute Bytes buttons to advance to the corresponding subpages. The decrypted plaintext after ten rounds is shown at the lower right corner of the Mix Columns subpage (Figure 10). The Sub-

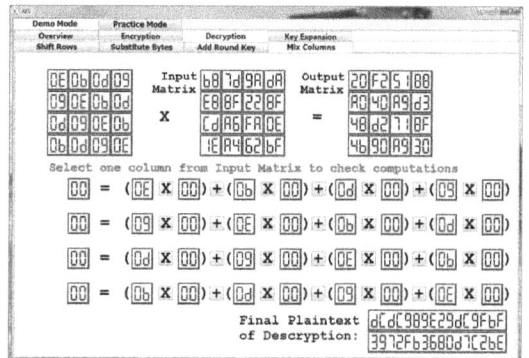

Figure 7: $\mathbf{GF}(2^8)$ **Add**

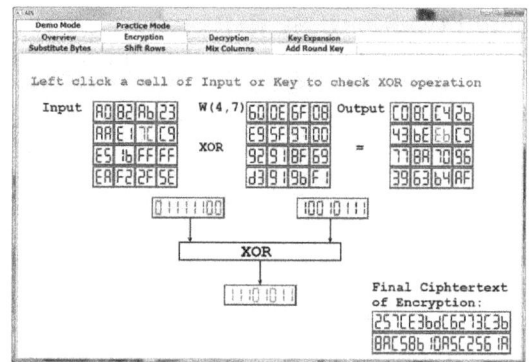

Figure 8: Add Round Key of Encryption

stitute Bytes and Add Round Key subpages are the same as in the Encryption subpage.

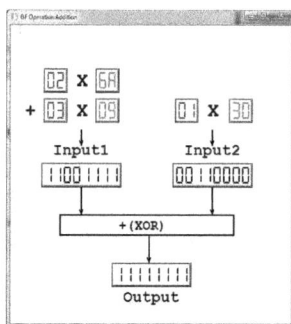

Figure 9: Shift Rows **of Decryption**

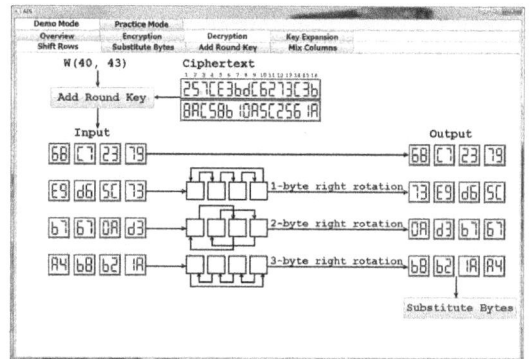

Figure 10: Mix Columns **of Decryption**

3.1.3 Key Expansion

This subpage demonstrates how the original 128-bit key is expanded to 44 32-bit words (Figure 11). These words are used in the ten rounds (four words per round) and one initial step for both encryption and decryption (Figure 1). The first four words (in black) are directly derived from the input and all other words (in red) are generated from them. The user may right drag the mouse to move words back and forth horizontally and click a single word (in blue) to check the word generation procedure. The lower portion of this subpage shows how the four output words with the selected word in blue are obtained using the four input words. Clicking the G button brings up the OperationG window (Figure 12). The user may also check the XOR ($\oplus$) operations using the XOR buttons (Figure 13).

232

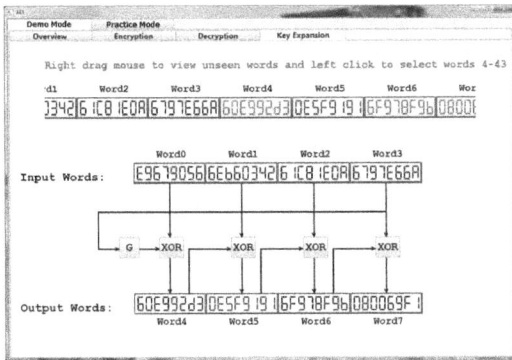

Figure 11: The Key Expansion Subpage

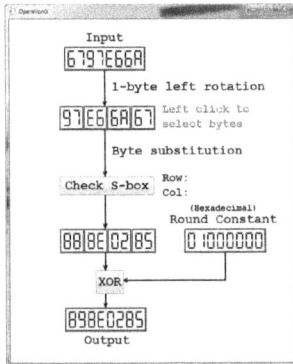

Figure 12: The OperationG Window

3.2 The Practice Mode

The Practice mode follows the same structure of the Demo mode (Figure 14), but only supports encryption. The user may step through each computation step; however, all results are hidden and a correct answer is required to advance to the next. The user may click the Start button to start a new session by generating a new plaintext-key pair. A dialogue window will pop up to briefly describe the current question and ask the user to enter the answer. The user clicks the Check Ans button to verify if the answer is correct and may enter a new answer if the current one is wrong. The Show Ans button is provided to show the correct answer and let the user skip the current question. A simple hexadecimal-binary converter is also provided. After the user finishes all questions, a Completion Report window will pop up to show the answer to each question with Correct, Wrong or Show Ans if the answer was correct, incorrect or skipped. This report may be sent to the instructor to check the student's completion rate and evaluate the learning effectiveness.

4. EVALUATION AND ASSESSMENT

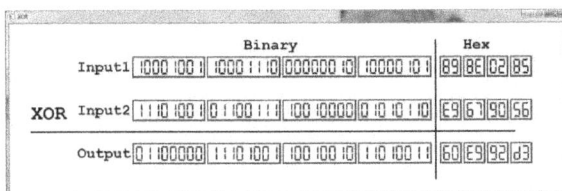

Figure 13: The XOR Window

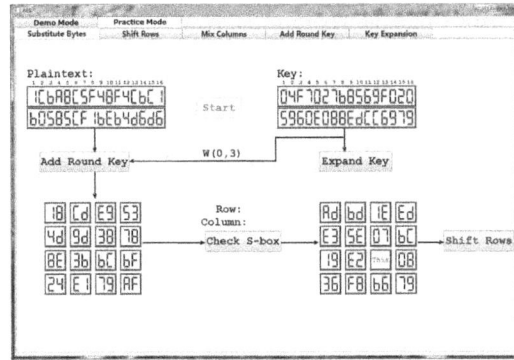

Figure 14: Practice Mode of AESvisual

Our survey consists of two parts: a set of 12 questions and 11 write-in comments. Choices available are 5: strongly agree, 4: agree, 3: neutral, 2: disagree, and 1: strongly disagree. We collected 23 valid forms. The distribution of majors was as follows: 1 in computer network and system administration, 8 in electrical and computer engineering, 9 in computer science, 2 in mathematics, 1 in chemical engineering, and 2 undeclared.

4.1 General Discussion

This paper uses $\alpha = 0.05$ as the level of significance for all statistical decisions. Our survey shows that the students used AESvisual 2.6 times on average during the period of evaluation and the average time they spent on the software was 34.3 minutes with standard deviation and confidence interval 18.9 and $(26.4, 41.0)$.

Table 1: Survey Questions

Q1	The Demo mode helped better understand encryption workflow
Q2	The Demo mode helped better understand decryption workflow
Q3	The Demo mode was helpful for self-study
Q4	The "Mix Columns" module helped understand multiplication and addition in GF(2^8)
Q5	The Practice mode helped remember how to encrypt and decrypt
Q6	AESvisual helped identify the parts of AES that I did not understand
Q7	AESvisual helped better understand AES
Q8	AESvisual enhanced the course
Q9	Is AESvisual easy to use?

A summary of the remaining questions is in Table 1. The first three questions Q1, Q2 and Q3 received means 4.04, 4.09 and 3.83, standard deviations 0.64, 0.67 and 0.98, and confidence intervals $(3.79, 4.30)$, $(3.82, 4.35)$ and $(3.45, 4.20)$. This suggested that AESvisual helped students better learn the encryption and decryption flow. On the other hand, the Practice mode (Q5) was rated slightly lower with mean, standard deviation and confidence interval 3.70, 0.97 and $(3.31, 4.09)$. The Mix Columns module (Q4) rating was low with mean, standard deviation and confidence interval 3.26, 1.32 and $(2.73, 3.79)$. Questions Q6, Q7 and Q8 received good ratings with means 3.87, 3.91 and 3.78, standard deviations 0.97, 0.79 and 0.90, and confidence intervals $(3.48, 4.26)$, $(3.60, 4.23)$ and $(3.42, 4.23)$. Thus, AESvisual helped students better understand the AES algorithm and did enhance the course. Finally, the easy to use question Q9 was rated with mean 3.48, standard deviation 0.95 and confidence interval $(3.10, 3.86)$.

The Mix Columns component requires the students to have a deeper understanding of GF(2^8) arithmetic to completely comprehend the workflow. This may not be very easy for some students. On the other hand, the low rating of Q4 (3.26) also indicated that we need to improve the AESvisual design and material presentation. A few students were not satisfied with the diagram-based design and preferred to have an algorithmic view. In our opinion, the complexity of the GF(2^8) arithmetic and many subpages/steps could have introduced some issues for the students to rate the "easy to use" question (Q9) lower at 3.48. However, the remaining ratings were reasonably high, especially for the Demo mode.

4.2 Further Statistical Analysis

The ratings of questions are loosely related to each other. The correlation between every pair of questions was positive. The lowest correlation was 0.18 between Q8 and Q9, which indicated "whether AESvisual enhanced the course" is mostly independent of "whether AESvisual is easy to use". The highest correlation was 0.77 between Q3 and Q7, which suggested that the helpfulness of the Demo mode for self-study and the helpfulness of AESvisual to better understand AES were closely related. The correlation between Q1 and Q2 was 0.63, indicating the ratings for the Demo mode to better understand encryption workflow and decryption workflow were moderately related to each other.

We also investigated the reaction from different disciplines. We grouped students into three groups: computer science (CS), electrical and computer engineering (ECE), and students from other departments (non-CS). Since the questions may correlate with each other, the questions were also grouped into three groups: (1) Q1, Q2, Q3: the Demo mode was helpful, (2) Q6, Q7, Q8: AESvisual was helpful, and (3) all other questions in a single group. We applied MANOVA (multivariate ANOVA) to study the differences among the three student groups on each of the three questions groups. We also applied ANOVA to investigate the difference among all three student groups on each single question.

The p-values for the three groups were 0.72, 0.75 and 0.87. This indicated that the ratings from students in different groups did not vary significantly. The ANOVA result on each single question did not suggest any significant difference either, with the smallest p-value being 0.45 for Q7. In addition, we investigated the difference between CS and ECE using MANOVA on the same question groups and ANOVA on each question. The p-values for the three groups were 0.49, 0.31 and 0.78, indicating that the ratings from CS and ECE did not vary significantly. We did not find significant difference on any single question either. The smallest p-value from the ANOVA results was 0.21 for Q7.

4.3 A Test Score Comparison

A quiz of six problems that address all aspects of the AES cipher was given after the classroom lecture. Then, we discussed AESvisual and made the software available. One week later a second quiz was given. The quiz problems were similar to those of the first. The problems covered Substitute Bytes, Shift Rows, Mix Columns, Add Round Key and Key Expansion. Both quizzes had a full score of 6 points (*i.e.*, one point per problem). We collected 37 and 36 papers from the first quiz and second quiz, and the results are shown in Table 2. The t-values of comparing the means obtained in various t-tests were all larger than 3 with p-values

around 0.003, and Cohen's d is 0.73. Thus, the difference between the means is significant and the effect size is reasonably large. As a result, we concluded that the software contributed to student learning significantly.

Table 2: Test Scores

	Quiz 1	Quiz 2
Mean	3.32	4.17
St. Dev	1.23	1.13
CI	(2.93, 3.72)	(3.80, 4.54)

4.4 Student Comments

There are 11 write-in questions asking students to make suggestions for further development. We focused on the following issues: whether only doing the first round of the AES algorithm would be sufficient, whether the Substitute Bytes, Shift Rows, Mix Columns, Add Round Key and Key Expansion modules are helpful, the usefulness of the Practice mode, whether the Demo mode is more useful than blackboard work, whether new features should be added, and software installation issues.

Students uniformly indicated that only doing the first round of the AES algorithm is sufficient. Of the five modules, only the Mix Columns module received some negative comments. Students indicated that the Substitute Bytes, Shift Rows, Add Round Key and Key Expansion modules were straightforward. Typical comments were "*It [Substitute Bytes] was explanatory and did enhance my learning*", "*The diagrams [of Shift Rows] made it very easy to learn*", "*It [Add Round Key] did not enhance my learning as much as other modules but it was still helpful*", and "*This section greatly enhanced my learning by visually showing the full key expansion procedure and operation*".

The Mix Column module was rated the lowest at 3.26. Thus, student comments may provide more information of the possible problems. In general, students felt that the Mix Columns component is the most difficult part of the AES algorithm. Reactions were mixed. Typical positive comments were: "*Helped me understand what I was doing wrong the first time I did the assignment*", "*The Mix Columns module does a great job demonstrating the operation*", and "*Allowing the user to select individual columns and see how the output was calculated is very helpful*". Typical negative comments were "*The multiplication steps are still complicated*" and "*This is really the only hard part of AES, and the program did not help. (Neither the book nor the program explain multiplication in GF(2^8) field.)*". In general, those who provided negative comments indicated that AESvisual did not help step through and did not explain the multiplication and addition over GF(2^8). The textbook [7] explains GF(2^8) arithmetic with polynomials and provides several examples step-by-step. Some students perhaps expected AESvisual to follow these steps closely.

Some students believed that the Demo mode would be sufficient and they did not use the Practice mode. The following has some typical comments: "*I think it is a useful way for some people to visualize it, but I don't learn that way*", "*Pretty great. It has a nice step-by-step implementation*" and "*I enjoyed it. It made studying easy*".

As for the question "if the Demo version helped the students follow the AES algorithm better than the use of the blackboard", most students believed it was useful with typical comments like: "*The demo version is quicker than the blackboard and is more organized*", "*The most effective is the* step-by-step action of the software. It allowed me to follow along better", "I think it did because I learn better visually, which is what this tool provided. Watching values change instantaneously helped", and "The Demo mode version did help me more than the use of the blackboard". A few students suggested that the use of blackboard would help them take notes: "The blackboard is more helpful to me. It is easier to take notes that way", and "I feel you couldn't have one without the other. A basic intro is needed before demoing the software".

Students did not offer many suggestions for new features. The most needed one was allowing to use user input in the Demo mode and in some modules. One student disliked the 7-segment-display font, another suggested to add binary and decimal base notation options, and yet another would prefer to have a web-based version. No significant installation issues were reported.

4.5 Self-Study Investigation

We invited students who did not take our course for a self-study. This small scale survey was used to determine if there was a difference between classroom and self-study with our tool. There were two stages, each stage took one week. In Stage 1, volunteers were asked to find resources to learn the AES, and at the end they were required to evaluate their progress and complete six quiz problems. In Stage 2, students were provided with AESvisual, and at the end they filled in an evaluation form and completed another six problems. The Stage 2 evaluation form and all quiz problems were identical to those used in class.

We collected five complete survey forms from 10 volunteers. Volunteers were usually highly motivated, and, as a result, students received nearly perfect scores in both quizzes. They used the tool 2.8 times on average, and spent on average 43.5 minutes using the software. Both numbers are higher than the classroom averages. Table 3 shows both the classroom and self-study results. Note that question Q3 is omitted because it is not needed for self-study survey. It is clear from the table that the two sets of ratings were not very different because the p-values were all larger than $\alpha = 0.05$.

Table 3: Self-Study Survey Results

	Q1	Q2	Q4	Q5	Q6	Q7	Q8	Q9
Class μ	4.04	4.09	3.26	3.70	3.87	3.91	3.78	3.48
Class σ	0.64	0.67	1.32	0.97	0.97	0.79	0.90	0.95
μ	4.40	4.20	4.00	3.80	4.00	4.20	4.20	3.50
σ	0.55	0.84	1.00	1.10	1.22	0.84	0.84	1.29
p-value	0.43	0.79	0.31	0.69	0.79	0.63	0.50	0.83

μ: mean σ: standard deviation

Stage 1 evaluation indicated that the Mix Columns is the most difficult part to understand. Other components are usually considered being straightforward. As a result, they did not have problems in using AESvisual except for the Mix Columns module. However, they did feel that the use of AESvisual was helpful although they still believed that the $GF(2^8)$ arithmetic presentation requires improvement.

Suggestions for further development were not very different from those classroom ones, namely: resizable windows, more colors to distinguish different items, and more pop-up hint windows for explanation and simple exercises.

5. CONCLUSIONS

This paper presented a visualization tool AESvisual for teaching and learning the AES cipher. With this tool, instructors are able to present all the details of AES encryption and decryption, and all complex computation steps, including $GF(2^8)$ addition and multiplication. The Demo mode helps students see the flow of the cipher and learn the concepts, and Practice mode offers the students an environment to practice the AES encryption. Evaluation results showed that AESvisual was effective in the classroom presentation and for student self-study.

Based on the student comments, the most needed extensions are (1) resizable windows, (2) allowing the user to enter his input, (3) making decimal and hexadecimal input and output possible, (4) a better organized and clearer view of the $G(2^8)$ addition and multiplication with explanations, and (5) developing a web-based version so that the system would be more "portable" as suggested by some students.

AESvisual is a part of larger development of cryptography visualization tools supported by the National Science Foundation. In addition to AESvisual, VIGvisual for the Vigenère cipher, DESvisual for the DES cipher, RSAvisual for the RSA cipher, ECvisual for the elliptic curve based ciphers, and SHAvisual for the Secure Hash Algorithm are available. We hope to complete this development with Diffie-Hellman key exchange, discrete logarithm and digital signature. Tools, evaluation forms, and installation and user guides for Linux, MacOS and Windows can be found at the following link:

www.cs.mtu.edu/~shene/NSF-4.

6. REFERENCES

[1] Cryptool. http://www.cryptool.org.

[2] O.-S. Chok and S. Herath. Computer Security Learning Laboratory: Implementation of DES and AES Algorithms using Spreadsheets. In *Proceedings of the 37th Midwest Instruction and Computing Symposium*, 2004.

[3] J. Daemen and V. Rijmen. *The Design of Rijndael*. Springer, 2002.

[4] A. McAndrew. Teaching Cryptography with Open-Source Software. In *Proceedings of the 39th ACM SIGCSE Technical Symposium on Computer Science Education*, pages 325–329, 2008.

[5] M. I. Soliman and G. Y. Abozaid. Hardware Visualization of the Advanced Encryption Standard (AES) Algorithm. In *Proceedings of the 18th International Conference on Computer Theory and Applications*, pages 85–93, 2008.

[6] W. Stallings. *Cryptography and Network Security*. Prentice-Hall, third edition, 2003.

[7] W. Trappe and L. C. Washington. *Introduction to Cryptography with Code Theory*. Prentice-Hall, 2002.

Acknowledgements

The authors are supported by the National Science Foundation under grants DUE-1140512, DUE-1245310 and IIS-1456763.

Can Interaction Patterns with Supplemental Study Tools Predict Outcomes in CS1?

Anthony Estey
Department of Computer Science
University of Victoria
aestey@uvic.ca

Yvonne Coady
Department of Computer Science
University of Victoria
ycoady@uvic.ca

ABSTRACT

Recent research suggests that one-third of the students enrolled in CS1 courses typically end up failing. Several studies have demonstrated how learning tools can assist struggling students. This work presents the evolution of a practice tool co-designed with student input. *BitFit* was developed to (1) provide students with an environment to practice weekly material and receive support when needed; and (2) collect student usage data as students progress through programming exercises. Our analysis of 652 students over three semesters highlights a number of predictors for success. Our findings support recent studies that suggest that at-risk students can be identified as early as two weeks into the semester; this group accounted for almost 30% of the students who failed the course in our study. Our results also reveal that interaction patterns with BitFit, in particular with hint features requested by students, allow the identification of another 52% of students who eventually fail. Throughout the semester, students who failed the course used hint features four times as often as top students, while only attempting to compile code one-third as often. The combination of early indicators and interaction patterns identify 81% of students who failed the course during our study.

Keywords

CS1; programming practice tool; student study behavior; educational data mining; predictors of success

1. INTRODUCTION

The average failure rate in CS1 is high—estimated at nearly 33% worldwide [4]. Inspired by studies showing students at-risk of failure can be identified early in the semester [1, 2, 14, 15], we designed and implemented a prototype programming practice tool called *BitFit*. Given recent research showing how programming behavior [1, 7, 10, 12] and workflow patterns [9, 13, 17] can differentiate between successful and unsuccessful students, our goal was to use BitFit to uncover subtle indicators of productive learning behavior.

ITiCSE '16, July 09-13, 2016, Arequipa, Peru

© 2016 ACM. ISBN 978-1-4503-4231-5/16/07... $15.00

DOI: http://dx.doi.org/10.1145/2899415.2899428

Based on early feedback from student groups, BitFit was extended to allow students to optionally reveal a progressive series of *hints* about programming problems, as shown in Figure 1. In response to student demand, the final hint provides a complete sample solution. The key results of our study reveal that at-risk students not only attempted fewer questions and compiled less frequently, but also had distinctly different workflow patterns regarding their consumption, and repeated consumption, of hints.

The contributions of the study presented here build on previous work by offering (1) a novel co-design of a practice programming tool instrumented with telemetry to identify at-risk students; and (2) an analysis of the collected data, revealing that compilation rates and repeated hint consumption differentiate perceived success from effective learning practices in our CS1 course.

2. BACKGROUND AND RELATED WORK

Our work explores the intersection of early at-risk student detection with tools used to identify learning behavior. A number of studies have established that performance on early coursework correlates with final exam scores [2, 6, 14]. Recent studies suggest that students can be identified as early as the first two weeks of the course [1]. Grades have also been shown to correlate positively with the amount of help students receive beyond office hours and email [5], as well as through peer instruction [18].

Large-scale studies of compilation errors from hundreds of thousands of students hold promise to identify at-risk patterns in types and frequencies of errors [3, 11]. Similarly, workflow behavior, such as starting work earlier [9], and submitting work frequently [17], have been confirmed as highly effective markers for success. A study on student behavior during lab periods found that confusion and boredom are two affective states associated with lower achievement [16]. Both code generation and debugging activities within an IDE have also been shown to correlate with final grades [8].

Our findings support the notion that students who do not successfully complete early work tend not to recover. In our case this accounted for almost 30% of the students who failed. We can identify this group as early as two weeks into the semester with high accuracy due to their lack of overall engagement. Beyond this group, we demonstrate how subtle patterns of interaction with BitFit indicate that students may be actively engaging in what they perceive to be successful study practices, but are ultimately ineffective ways of learning CS1 material. In our case, these patterns were identified in over 50% of the students who failed the course.

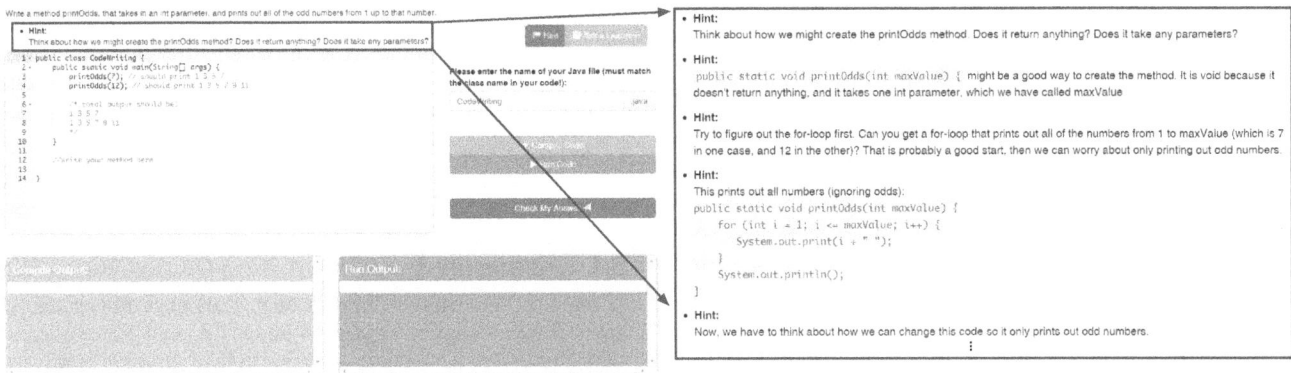

Figure 1: A screenshot of BitFit, our practice programming tool, and an example of the first few hints it provides. Hints are shown one at time, when requested by the user.

3. COURSE AND TOOL CONTEXT

The data in this study was collected from three semesters of a 13-week CS1 course taught in Java. Topics covered include variables, control flow, methods, conditionals, loops, I/O, arrays, searching and sorting algorithms, and objects. The course consists of 2.5 hours of lecture a week, with 10 two-hour computer labs where students are provided with problem-based learning activities and weekly programming assignments. Midterm exams take place during the fifth and ninth weeks, and there is a final exam at the end of term.

Activity on BitFit, shown in Figure 1, is completely voluntary, and does not affect student grades in any way. BitFit was introduced as a supplemental practice resource offering exercises similar to those presented during weekly labs. Bit-Fit is an online, open-source[1], practice programming tool where students write code in the browser. Buttons to compile code, run code, submit a solution (labeled "Check My Answer"), get a hint, and ask a question are all instrumented to collect student interaction patterns.

Compilation and execution results are displayed to the user as they work through the current problem. Submitting a solution runs the current code through a number of test cases, visible to the user, and displays the results. A solution is considered correct if all of the test cases pass. There is no restriction on the number of times a student is allowed to compile, run, or submit a question.

Each semester BitFit was used, there were over 80 questions distributed over the course's topic areas. Within each topic there are six to ten questions, ordered by difficulty. Students are not required to correctly solve "easy" questions before visiting more difficult questions within a given topic area, and are able to start on any topic area they choose.

Similar to Khan Academy[2], hints progressively lead students to a correct solution of the problem. BitFit was first designed with hints that provided high level guidance, but when students were consulted about the design of additional features, they requested sample code solutions.

The data considered for this study includes the number of questions, hints, compiles, runs, submissions, and correct solutions. Number of revisited questions and repeated hints were also recorded. The ratio of correct versus overall submissions, compiles versus executions, and error-free compiles versus overall compiles were also computed. All of this collected data was measured against final exam grades.

[1] https://github.com/ModSquad-AVA/BitFit
[2] https://www.khanacademy.org/

4. METHODOLOGY

For the purposes of this study, a grade of 50% or higher is a pass, and less than 50% or unsubmitted is a fail. Three semesters are considered, involving four different instructors, as Semester 3 was broken into two sections, each taught by a different instructor. An effort was made to cover the same concepts, and the assignments, exams, and grade boundaries were designed to be consistent between offerings. BitFit was introduced a few weeks into Semester 1 and was used all throughout Semesters 2 and 3.

We used a mixed-method approach, involving both quantitative and qualitative results. Surveys distributed every four weeks throughout each semester collected feedback on BitFit features and student progress. This feedback was used to refine features in BitFit, and compare student perception of success with usage data and course performance.

4.1 Objectives

The staged objectives of our study were to (1) determine how opting out of the tool was correlated to at-risk behavior; and (2) investigate whether interaction patterns with different features of the tool can be used to differentiate between successful and unsuccessful efforts to learn the material.

Previous studies show that performance on early coursework correlates with final exam scores [2, 6, 14]. We first investigated whether similar predictors could be used in our study to account for students who chose not to use BitFit.

Our remaining objective was to investigate whether unsuccessful students can be identified through BitFit interaction behavior. To reach this objective, we combined quantitative BitFit data with qualitative feedback collected from monthly surveys. Features in BitFit were refined each semester. The refinements were largely driven according to students perceptions of success.

4.2 Threats to Validity

In terms of external validity, the limited number of semesters may not be representative of the general population. Those conducting the qualitative surveys identified themselves to the students throughout the semester, which may have introduced bias into survey responses and BitFit usage. Internal threats include behavior patterns such as students initially exploring features of the tool to familiarize themselves with it, skewing early usage patterns. Students sometimes studied in groups, affecting each individual's usage data for the questions solved together. Some questions were refined be-

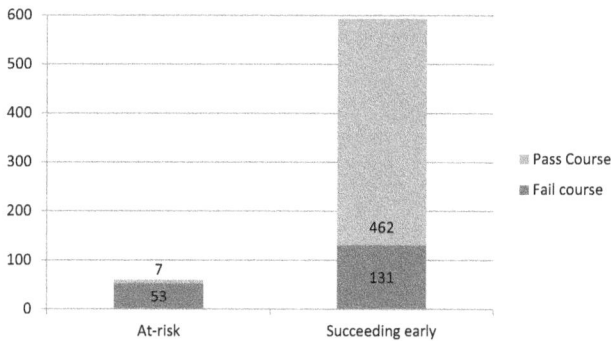

Figure 2: Course pass rates grouped by our "at-risk" identification metric two weeks into the course.

tween semesters, and the hint system was restructured between Semesters 1 and 2. Students' previous computer and programming experience were not taken into account for this study. Students who had previously failed the course were able to retake the course, and would have some familiarity with the questions on BitFit.

5. RESULTS

First, we wanted a metric to classify students as at-risk as early as possible in the semester that accounted for students who did not use BitFit. We investigated the 106 students who failed one of the first two assignments, and found that 84 of them eventually failed the course (79%). From this group, there were 60 students who also did not use BitFit, with an 88% fail rate. We define this group "At-risk", satisfying our first objective to accurately identify students who are unsuccessful early, potentially due to a late start.

Next, we wanted to better classify the 593 students in the group labeled "Succeeding Early" in Figure 2 based on their BitFit behavior. Although only 131 out of these students failed the course (22%), these 131 students make up 71% of the overall number of course fails. Our experiment is designed to investigate whether it is possible to differentiate successful students from unsuccessful students in this group based on interaction patterns found in BitFit usage data.

Radar plots are used to show the differences in BitFit usage between student groups. The axes represent the standardized average number of unique questions attempted, compile attempts, solution submissions, hints, and the number of times previously viewed hints were requested when revisiting a question. Each axes ranges from -1 to +1 standard deviations from the mean (0).

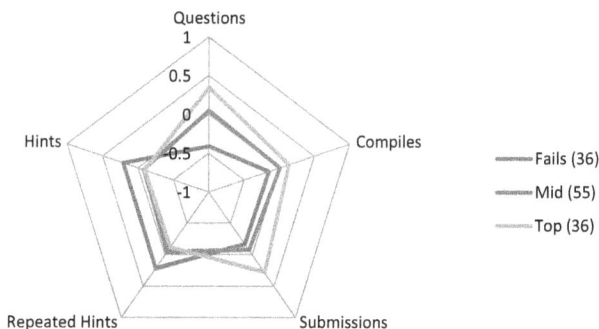

Figure 3: Standardized usage trends for the 127 students who used BitFit during Semester 1. Units for each axis are denoted by standard deviations from the mean (0).

Unsuccessful students are compared with the same number of students performing at the top of the class, the third group is composed of the remaining students. Using this breakdown, Figures 3 through 6 compare three groups:

- **Fails:** the n students who failed the final exam
- **Top:** the top n students based on final exam scores
- **Mid:** the remaining students *(total BitFit users - 2n)*

5.1 Semester 1

The first semester BitFit was used, 156 out of 199 students attempted at least one question on BitFit, and 126 students participated in the study. A multiple regression analysis revealed that the number of questions attempted ($p < 0.01$) and questions answered correctly ($p < 0.05$) positively and significantly correlated with final exam grades. As shown in Figure 3, top students attempted more questions, compiled more code, and submitted more solutions. Hints were not used very often by any student group.

5.1.1 Qualitative Feedback

During Semester 1, hints provided high-level guidance on how to solve problems, but did not include code. We learned the following from surveys distributed throughout the semester:

- The most common *Suggestion for improvement* was to provide a full solution to each problem (47%).
- Students also commonly requested more questions (18%), and a larger variety of difficulty (11%).
- When asked where students went for help when stuck, the most common responses were: the Internet (66%), friends (58%), the Assistance Centre (12%), and instructor office hours (10%).

BitFit's hint features were restructured between semesters to allow access to a full solution to each problem. This change was made to accommodate the factors students perceived to be necessary for success. The question repository was also updated, to provide a more comprehensive coverage of all course topics and a wider range of exercise difficulties.

5.2 Semesters 2 and 3

In Semester 2, 53 out of 64 students attempted at least one question on BitFit, and 42 students participated in the study. Figure 4 shows BitFit usage trends for the full semester. Although many students did utilize the hint features during Semester 2, 25% of the total hint requests were made by the five students who failed. This group of students also frequently requested the same hints previously seen when revisiting a question, as denoted by the *Repeated Hints* axis.

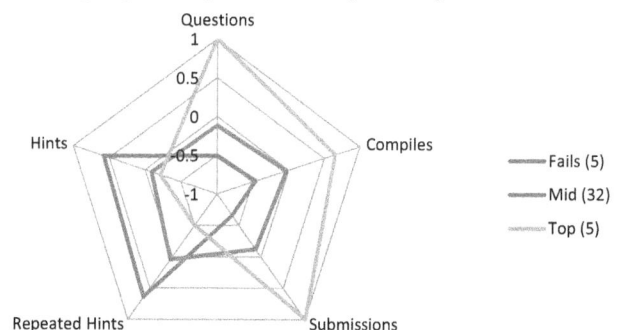

Figure 4: Usage trends for the 42 students who used BitFit during Semester 2.

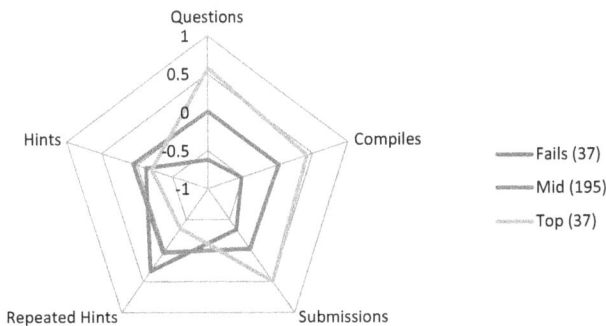

Figure 5: Usage trends for the 269 students who used BitFit during Semester 3.

Programming trends were very similar to those found in Semester 1, with top students attempting more questions, and compiling and submitting more code. No changes were made to the hint features between semesters 2 and 3.

In Semester 3, 319 out of 389 students attempted at least one question on BitFit, and 269 students participated in the study. Questions attempted (p < 0.01), solutions submitted (p < 0.01), and correct solutions (p < 0.05) were positively and significantly correlated with final exam grades, while the number of repeated hints requested (p < 0.05) was negatively and significantly correlated with final exam grades.

Figure 5 shows student usage trends for Semester 3. Similar to Semester 2, some well-established trends can be seen with respect to compilation numbers and hint usage. Looking at BitFit usage on a per-question basis, these trends are even more pronounced, as shown in Figure 7. Failing students compiled 3 times less per question, but requested 4 times as many previously viewed hints as top students.

If we look at the BitFit usage patterns of students with the biggest rise or drop in performance on the midterm versus final, their interaction patterns with tool features align with our established successful/unsuccessful trends. Figure 8 shows that the 12 students with the biggest drop in exam scores exhibit behavior associated with unsuccessful students, whereas students whose grades increased the most exhibit patterns similar to top performing students.

5.2.1 Qualitative Feedback

Student survey feedback about hint features was positive in Semesters 2 and 3. All students selected either "Helpful" or "Extremely Helpful" on a 5-point Likert scale. Students in the failing group most commonly reported that they used hints to initially learn the material as well as when they were stuck. Students in the top group most commonly re-

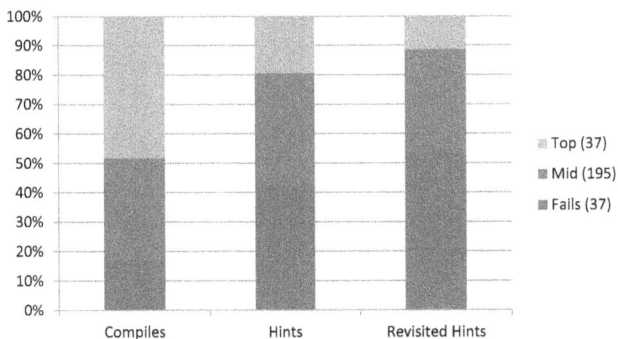

Figure 7: Average values for number of compiles and hint usage per question during Semester 3.

ported that they used hints to compare their solution with "an instructor's solution". At five weeks into the semester, 36 of the participants had not yet attempted a question on BitFit. Of these 36, 14 students reported they did not know the tool existed, 11 that they did not have time to use it, 8 did not feel like they needed any help, 2 found the material on BitFit too easy, and 1 student found it too difficult.

6. ANALYSIS

Semester 3 had the highest number of participants, so we took a closer look at some of the aforementioned results to further analyze BitFit usage trends. First, we highlight how our findings support the notion that at-risk students can be identified as early as two weeks into the semester, and how we can decrease false positives by sharpening a metric for engagement. Then, semester-long trends are discussed, with particular focus on the effectiveness of using interaction patterns collected in BitFit to identify unsuccessful students who were not identified early. Given that these students demonstrate engagement, the disparity between their perception of successful behavior and actual learning can be identified in their patterns of interaction with BitFit.

6.1 Early Identification

Figure 6 shows standardized BitFit usage over the first two weeks of Semester 3. Compared to the semester-long data (Figure 5), differences between failing and passing students are not as pronounced, but trends are already beginning to develop with respect to the number of question attempts, compilation rates, and hint usage. Only 22 of the 77 students (29%) that failed one of the first assignments used BitFit during the first two weeks of the semester, compared to 211 of the 313 students (67%) that passed both assignments. Figure 11 shows the usage trends between these two groups two weeks into the semester. The at-risk group attempted 13% fewer questions, compiled 33% less often, and requested

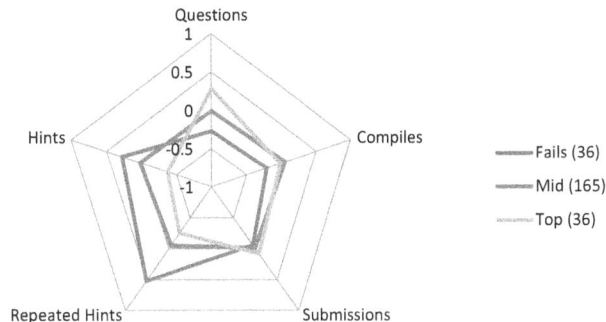

Figure 6: First two weeks of Semester 3 BitFit data.

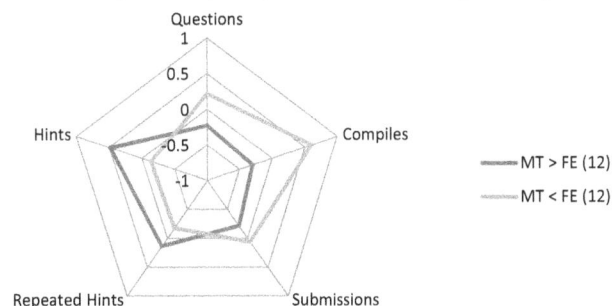

Figure 8: Semester 3 BitFit data for the 12 students with the biggest score differences between the first midterm (MT), and final exam (FE).

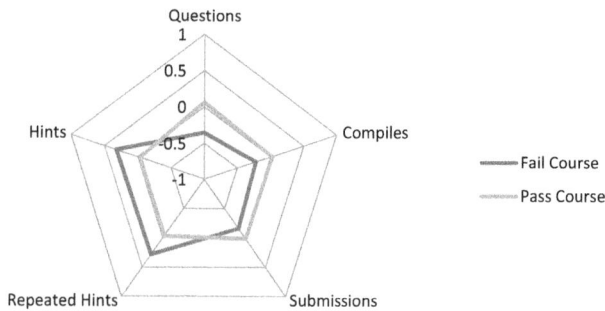

Figure 9: BitFit data from the first two weeks for students who pass the first two assignments.

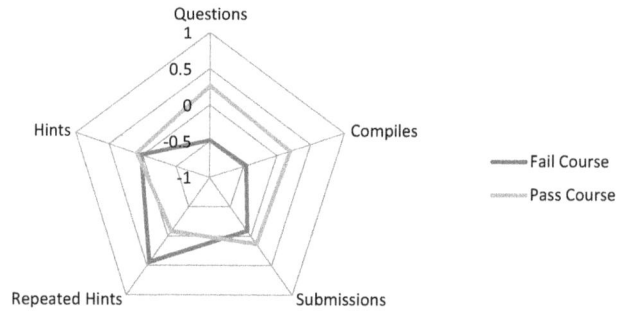

Figure 10: Semester-long BitFit data for students who pass the first two assignments.

71% more previously viewed hints than passing students. Even early in the semester, the at-risk group engaged in activity that our qualitative results suggest align with what students *incorrectly* perceive as successful behavior.

Focusing only on students who passed the first two assignments, Figure 9 shows BitFit usage trends over the first two weeks of the course. Although students who ended up failing the course did request more hints and compiled slightly less than students who passed, usage trends are similar enough that it would be very difficult to identify students individually. At this point in the semester, these students had passed all graded work, so it is possible that they did not yet exhibit study habits associated with students at-risk of failure.

Figure 10 shows semester-long data for the same sets of students. Throughout the semester, the differences between students who pass and those who fail become increasingly pronounced. This suggests that although it may be difficult to identify potentially unsuccessful students after two weeks, certain trends develop as the semester progresses. Students who succeed with early material but end up failing increasingly exhibit trends associated with at-risk behavior.

6.2 Overall Trends

Based on our analysis of data collected over three semesters of our CS1 course, the overall trends are as follows:

- Many at-risk students can be identified with high certainty as early as two weeks into the semester.
- Low compile rates combined with high, repeated hint usage are behaviors associated with at-risk students.
- At-risk students exhibit this behavior early, and continue to exhibit such behavior throughout the semester.
- Successful students attempt more questions, and their behavior is characterized by a high number of code compilations and submissions.
- Workflow patterns of students who succeed with early material but struggle later become increasingly similar to at-risk behavior.

Over the three semesters BitFit was used, 184 out of 652 (28%) students failed our CS1 course. Figure 12 shows the distribution of at-risk students identified throughout this study. Overall, our proposed metrics identify 149 out of the 184 (81%) students who failed over the three semesters.

7. DISCUSSION

Our study shows that interaction patterns students may have perceived to be associated with success (accessing a solution) did not always result in effective strategies for learning. A number of students frequently requested all of the hints on a question, but never compiled any code. This behavior was exhibited most commonly by students who ended up failing the final exam. Currently, we are unable to tell if such students had written any code, just that they did not choose to compile any code before leaving the question.

In response to student surveys, full solutions were added to BitFit. Although many at-risk students repeatedly failed graded coursework throughout Semesters 2 and 3, 100% of survey participants reported that the hints were helpful. Based on qualitative results from survey data, students believe that solutions assist their success. This might be true for students who use solutions to check their answers, but does not appear to be true for students who keep revisiting solutions without compiling any code.

This mismatch between perception of success and course performance warrants further investigation. Perhaps some students believe that they can learn more efficiently by memorizing a solution to a problem instead of working through a question to understand the problem-solving process. Students who were successful early but who went on to fail the course increasingly exhibited these ineffective study habits.

For upcoming semesters, we plan to refine our hint system to restrict users from accessing a full solution without first writing and compiling code. From a pedagogical perspective, it is not helpful to provide a full solution that accounts for edge cases to students who do not yet understand how to

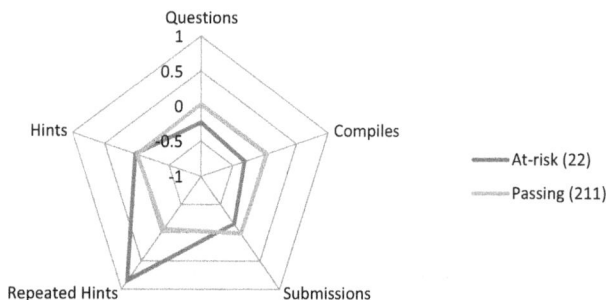

Figure 11: At-risk behavior patterns in Semester 3.

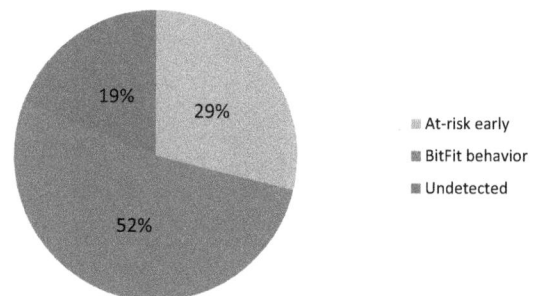

Figure 12: Proportion of failing students identified.

240

begin to solve a problem. BitFit must allow struggling students to be supported, but also must convince all students that writing and exploring their own code enhances learning more than viewing a solution to a problem does.

8. CONCLUSIONS AND FUTURE WORK

Our analysis of 652 students over three semesters of our CS1 course provides evidence that almost 30% of our at-risk students can be identified within the first two weeks of the semester. Perhaps more importantly, our results reveal that students who succeed on early topics but end up failing the course exhibit identifiable patterns of interaction with BitFit based on their compilation to hints-viewed ratios. Overall, our metrics identify 81% of the students who end up failing.

Looking into the BitFit data, at first glance it may seem that failing students simply work less than successful students. To a certain extent this may be true, but many failing students use BitFit heavily—an *ungraded* practice resource. The fact that these students are using BitFit suggests they want to succeed with the material. One possibility is that some students think that their study habits and methods of learning are correct, and are unaware that memorizing a solution is not an effective way to learn CS1 material.

Our future research plans include an analysis of questions split by topic and difficulty, as all questions were treated equally for this study. In addition, we plan to collect feedback from students about their own progress, and link this with BitFit data collected throughout the semester.

It is critical to understand precisely why students engage in ineffective learning behavior to be able to determine how to best guide at-risk students towards habits that better enable success. We have shown that tools like BitFit are able to identify at-risk students early in the semester, but many questions still remain about how to best provide intervention to support all students. Beyond this, it is difficult to evaluate the effectiveness interventions aimed at improving study habits have on overall student success rates.

We plan to continue research focused on better understanding where, when, and why students exhibit different workflow patterns. As we as educators continue to learn more about why certain students do not engage with learning opportunities effectively, we can continue to improve support initiatives to reach an increasingly broad population of students. We hope that such efforts will result in a more diverse set of strong, empowered programmers, and better success rates in our computer science programs.

9. REFERENCES

[1] A. Ahadi, R. Lister, H. Haapala, and A. Vihavainen. Exploring machine learning methods to automatically identify students in need of assistance. In *Proceedings of the Eleventh Annual International Conference on International Computing Education Research*, 2015.

[2] A. Ahadi, R. Lister, and D. Teague. Falling behind early and staying behind when learning to program. In *25th Anniversary Psychology of Programming Annual Conference*, 2014.

[3] A. Altadmri and N. C. Brown. 37 million compilations: Investigating novice programming mistakes in large-scale student data. In *Proceedings of the 46th ACM Technical Symposium on Computer Science Education*, SIGCSE '15, 2015.

[4] J. Bennedsen and M. E. Caspersen. Failure rates in introductory programming. *SIGCSE Bull.*, 39, 2007.

[5] J. Carter, P. Dewan, and M. Pichiliani. Towards incremental separation of surmountable and insurmountable programming difficulties. In *Proceedings of the 46th ACM Technical Symposium on Computer Science Education*, SIGCSE '15, 2015.

[6] L. F. Dame. *Student readiness, engagement and success in entry level undergraduate mathematics courses*. PhD thesis, University of Victoria, 2012.

[7] P. Denny, A. Luxton-Reilly, and E. Tempero. All syntax errors are not equal. In *Proceedings of the 17th ACM Annual Conference on Innovation and Technology in Computer Science Education*, 2012.

[8] G. Dyke. Which aspects of novice programmers' usage of an ide predict learning outcomes. In *Proceedings of the 42Nd ACM Technical Symposium on Computer Science Education*, 2011.

[9] S. H. Edwards, J. Snyder, M. A. Pérez-Quiñones, A. Allevato, D. Kim, and B. Tretola. Comparing effective and ineffective behaviors of student programmers. In *Proceedings of the Fifth International Workshop on Computing Education Research Workshop*, 2009.

[10] M. C. Jadud. Methods and tools for exploring novice compilation behaviour. In *Proceedings of the Second International Workshop on Computing Education Research*, 2006.

[11] M. C. Jadud and B. Dorn. Aggregate compilation behavior: Findings and implications from 27,698 users. In *Proceedings of the Eleventh Annual International Conference on International Computing Education Research*, 2015.

[12] J. P. Munson and E. A. Schilling. Analyzing novice programmers' response to compiler error messages. *J. Comput. Sci. Coll.*, 31, 2016.

[13] C. Murphy, G. Kaiser, K. Loveland, and S. Hasan. Retina: Helping students and instructors based on observed programming activities. *SIGCSE Bull.*, 41, 2009.

[14] L. Porter and D. Zingaro. Importance of early performance in cs1: Two conflicting assessment stories. In *Proceedings of the 45th ACM Technical Symposium on Computer Science Education*, 2014.

[15] L. Porter, D. Zingaro, and R. Lister. Predicting student success using fine grain clicker data. In *Proceedings of the Tenth Annual Conference on International Computing Education Research*, 2014.

[16] M. Rodrigo, R. Baker, M. Jadud, A. Amarra, T. Dy, M. Espejo-Lahoz, S. Lim, S. Pascua, J. Sugay, and E. Tabanao. Affective and behavioral predictors of novice programmer achievement. In *Proceedings of the 14th Annual ACM SIGCSE Conference on Innovation and Technology in Computer Science Education*, 2009.

[17] J. Spacco, P. Denny, B. Richards, D. Babcock, D. Hovemeyer, J. Moscola, and R. Duvall. Analyzing student work patterns using programming exercise data. In *Proceedings of the 46th ACM Technical Symposium on Computer Science Education*, 2015.

[18] D. Zingaro and L. Porter. Peer instruction in computing: The value of instructor intervention. *Comput. Educ.*, 71, 2014.

Evidence-based Teaching with the Help of Mobile Response System (MRS)

Mohammad Muztaba Fuad
Department of Computer Science
Winston-Salem State University
Winston-Salem, NC 27110, USA
+1-3367503325
fuadmo@wssu.edu

Debzani Deb
Department of Computer Science
Winston-Salem State University
Winston-Salem, NC 27110, USA
+1-3367502496
debd@wssu.edu

ABSTRACT

Over the past couple of years, evidence-based teaching and learning methods are brought into focus from the experience gained in clinical psychology and their use of Evidence-Based Practices. Different authors have discussed the advantages of using such evidence-based methods for teaching and learning in academia. Measuring real-time impact of traditional pedagogical approaches used in STEM disciplines are not easy and do not provide faculty an instant evidence about student learning. This paper will present Mobile Response System (MRS) software, which facilitate anonymous communication, interaction and evaluation of in-class interactive problem solving activities using mobile devices. MRS facilitates a feedback-driven and evidence-based teaching methodology, which is important to enhance student learning.

CCS Concepts

•Applied computing →Computer-assisted instruction •Applied computing →Interactive learning environments

Keywords

Interactive problem solving; mobile technology; active learning.

1. INTRODUCTION

Active learning is an educational approach where learners become engaged in interactive learning activities in the classroom. Studies [1]-[2] reveal strong empirical evidence that active involvement in the learning process is crucially important for the mastery of skills, such as critical thinking. Specifically in STEM disciplines, it is important for learners to actively study a problem and explore possible solutions by interacting with the problem in a hands-on approach. In such situations, traditional pedagogical approaches are not enough and more interactive teaching and learning strategy is necessary to make learning more productive. This research explores whether by presenting the in-class exercises as visual interactive entities (where students can actively play with the problem), student's critical thinking and problem solving

ITiCSE '16, July 09-13, 2016, Arequipa, Peru
ACM 978-1-4503-4231-5/16/07.
http://dx.doi.org/10.1145/2899415.2925498

skills can be improved. In recent years, mobile technology has brought incredible opportunities for educators to enable and deliver learning in ways that could not have been accomplished before. There have been an increasing number of studies [3-4] related to the research and development of learning software intended for mobile computing devices. By having interactive mobile App quizzes rather than traditional pen-and-paper quizzes, the goal of this research is to make the quizzes more appealing to students and to allow them to realize the effect of their interactions at the different stage of the exercise. The presented approach allows the student to fully comprehend a concept and clarify any confusion through active interaction and hands-on nature of the system. This also allows students to practice the concept outside the class using these interactive quiz applications and allows faculty to administer more of it in class without the stress of manual grading.

2. Mobile Response System

This paper presents the Mobile Response System (MRS) [5] software, which facilitate anonymous communication, interaction and evaluation of in-class interactive problem solving activities using mobile devices. MRS facilitates a feedback-driven and evidence-based teaching methodology, which is important to enhance student learning. By allowing interactive problem solving using mobile devices and by being extensible to other disciplines, MRS makes itself distinctive than similar systems. MRS is a client-server software that allows the faculty to dynamically prompt the students with interactive exercises synchronized with the lecture material in their mobile devices. Students are able to actively interact with the problem and send their answers back to the faculty computer. MRS then grades the exercise by comparing the student made sequence of steps with the correct sequence of steps. After grading, MRS also makes the grading statistics and student submissions available for the faculty to view and share with the students.

This formative assessment information allows the faculty to have real-time evidence of students' comprehension of covered lecture materials on a particular class and also helps faculty to identify the concepts that need to be repeated or reinforced. By utilizing MRS software, faculty is also able to capture screens from student submissions and discuss on those screens if context-sensitive feedback is needed. Additionally, this approach allows the students to obtain faster and frequent feedback that reinforce their learning and help them to identify problem areas. The active interaction with a problem via multiple steps while going back and forth and seeing the consequence of their choices at each step is expected to enhance students' analytical and problem solving capabilities. The other important feature supported by MRS is the ability to submit feedback/question anonymously during the class. The software allows students to send anonymous feedback/questions to faculty and vote on feedback/questions that faculty will choose to review and answer at the end of the class.

2.1 Software Architecture

The MRS software is designed as a client-server application as shown in Figure 1. The faculty computer runs the server component of the software, which hosts questions, manages users and maintain communication and synchronization. The client component executes in student's mobile device, which allows students to login to the system, to submit anonymous feedback/questions and facilitates interactive exercise solving.

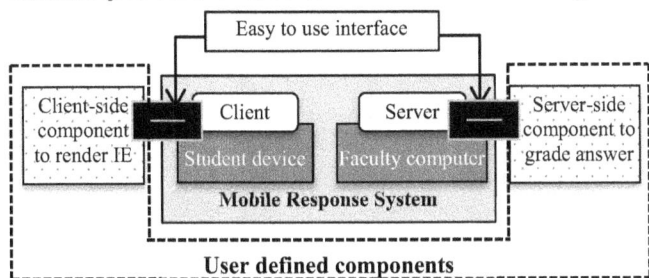

Figure 1. MRS Software Architecture

Building each possible problem type within the MRS client is impossible and will make it domain dependent and overly bulky to run on mobile platforms. To overcome this, the interactive activity is designed to be separated from the application logic of the MRS client software. Similarly on the server side, the grading component is also separated from the application logic, so that faculty can use any statistical or grading instrument on the student responses. Both the server and the client provides easy to use application programmer interface for users to develop their own interactive problem solving apps and corresponding grading modules to be used within MRS environment.

2.2 Interactive Problems

An Interactive Problem in MRS allows students to devise the answer by following a set of steps and by using a particular algorithm/process. In each step, students have to make key choices that will have impact on the next step of the interaction. During these interaction steps, students can go back and forth and change their answer. This will allow them to see what is the effect of different selection on the result and how every piece fits together. Problems can be started bottom up or at the middle to give students different perspective on the problem and assess their problem solving skills. Only after the student traverses each of the steps or the allotted time to answer a problem runs out, the result of their interaction is sent back to the server as the answer of that student. The rubric for each problem supports partial grading along with grading correct answers.

2.3 MRS at work

MRS environment provides an intuitive and easy to use interface for learners and instructors to utilize the software. The faculty can use server-side user interface (Figure 2(a)) to import student information, initiate the system, import questions, broadcast question to students, process results, monitor student's feedback/question etc. On the client-side, student can use the client interface (Figure 2(b)) to login to the system, submit

anonymous feedback/question or vote on an existing feedback/question. Once the client receives a question, it locates the app that will render the question into interactive activity. After student submit their answer, the client sends it back to the faculty computer for result processing.

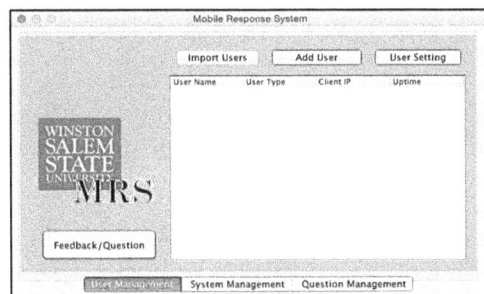

(a)

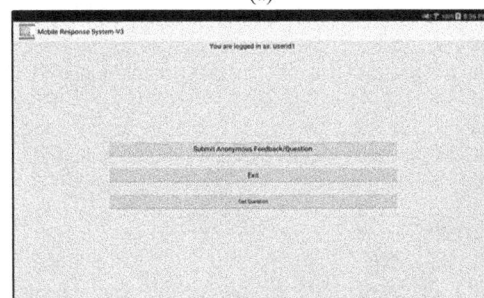

(b)

Figure 2. MRS User Interfaces.

2.4 Current status

Currently, the developed MRS software and corresponding course modules are being deployed in one sophomore and one junior Computer Science course. The data obtained from the survey, focus group and student grade distribution supports the effectiveness of the software. For both intervened classes, students positively attested that MRS and related apps helped them to learn through hands-on activities that they enjoyed.

3. ACKNOWLEDGMENTS

This research is supported by National Science Foundation grant #1332531.

4. REFERENCES

[1] J. M. Braxton, W. A. Jones, A. S. Hirschy, & H. V. Hartley, The role of active learning in college persistence. *New Directions for Teaching and Learning*, 115:71–83, 2008.

[2] M. Prince, Does active learning work? A review of the research. *Journal of Engineering Education*, 93(3): 223–231, 2004.

[3] R. J. Young, Mobile College App: Turning iPhones Into 'Super-Clickers' for Classroom Feedback, *Chronicle of higher education*, 2008.

[4] K. Whattananarong, An Experiment in the Use of Mobile Phones for Testing at King Mongkut's Institute of Technology North Bangkok, Thailand. *Proc. International Conference on Making Education Reform Happen: Learning from the Asian Experience & Comparative Perspectives*, 2004.

[5] Mobile Response System, http://compsci.wssu.edu/MRS.

Teaching the First Programming Course with Python's Turtle Graphic Library

Elizabeth Vidal Duarte
Universidad La Salle
Av. Alfonso Ugarte 517
Arequipa - Perú
evidal@ulasalle.edu.pe

ABSTRACT

How to keep students interested in a programming course is not new to those who teach the subject. This work describes our experience in the use of Python with its Turtle Graphic Library in a game-oriented approach that seeks to increase the interest and motivation of students. We present the main assignments used in our course. Our experience has shown us that students get engaged and motivate themselves with the graphical component. We have found an improvement in students grades.

Keywords

First Programming Course; Teaching; Motivation; Game-Oriented; Specific Assignments, Pedagogical Tool.

1. BACKGROUND

There are experiences that have shown that the visual nature of games is suitable for learning, since it is fairly easy for students to see how a loop or branch is used in a game and check the logical errors of implementation [1,2,3,4,5,6]. In this work we present our experience using Python's Turtle Graphic Library [7] in a game-oriented approach. We highlight the assignment related to branch, loops and functions.

2. COURSE DESIGN

2.1 Overview

The course has 17 weeks. It has 8 hours a week (4 theoretical hours and 4 laboratory hours). Python is used as a programming language since 2012, but only since 2015 we are using Python's Turtle graphic library under a game-oriented approach. Python's Turtle library has a simple syntax, it is easy to use and its methods are quite intuitive. The detailed documentation is available at [7].

2.2 Branch, Loop and Function

Assignment for branch, loops and functions is the simulation of a basic game with three elements (Figure 1). The spaceship (triangle) moves horizontally at the bottom of the screen and is

ITiCSE '16, July 09-13, 2016, Arequipa, Peru

ACM 978-1-4503-4231-5/16/07.

http://dx.doi.org/10.1145/2899415.2925499

Figure 1. Branch, Loop and Function Assignment

```
1    import turtle
2    import random
3
4    window = turtle.Screen()
5    window.bgpic('fondo.gif')
6
7    enemy = turtle.Turtle()
8    enemy.color("red")
9    enemy.shape("square")
10   enemy.penup()
11   enemy.setposition(-250,250)
12
13   ship = turtle.Turtle()
14   ship.color("blue")
15   ship.shape("triangle")
16   ship.penup()
17   ship.setposition(-250,-250)
18
19   def moveLeft():
20       ship.backward(10)
21
22   def moveRight():
23       ship.right(10)
24
25   def shoot():
26       bullet = turtle.Turtle()
27       bullet.hideTurtle()
28       bullet.color('green')
29       bullet.shape('circle')
30       bullet.penup()
31       bullet.setposition(ship.xcor(), -230)
```

```
32      bullet.showturtle()
33      bullet.left(90)
34      while bullet.ycor()<300:
35          bullet.forward(10)
36
37          #Collision Detection using euclidian distance
38          difXs = abs(bullet.xcor() - enemy.xcord())**2
39          difYs = abs(bullet.ycor() - enemy.ycord())**2
40          if (difXs + difYs)**0.5 <= 20:
41              enemy.hideturtle()
42
43      turtle.onkey(moveLeft, 'Left')
44      turtle.onkey(moveRight, 'Right')
45      turtle.onkey(shoot, 'Up')
46
47      listen()
48
49  while True:
50      enemy.forward(5)
51      if enemy.xcord()>280 or enemy.xcor()<-280:
52          enemy.right(180)
```

Figure 2. Branch, Loop and Function Assignment Code

controlled by using the arrow keys. The spaceship can shoot a bullet (circle) to the enemy (square) that moves horizontally at the top of the screen. If the bullet touches the enemy, the enemy disappears from the screen. The detailed code is shown in Figure 2. One of the tasks performed by the students is the implementation of the function shoot() (lines 25 to 41). Part of the challenge that students face is getting the bullet out of the spaceship every time they press the up arrow key (line 31). The other challenge is to make the enemy disappear when it is struck by the bullet. This is done by calculating the distance of the two objects (lines 38 to 41).

3. RESULTS

Our experience has shown us that students get engaged and motivate themselves with the graphical component and later with the implementation of a little game where students implement score, lives and levels. Some examples are shown in Figure 3. The use of Turtle has shown us an improvement in students' grades. We show in Table 1 the global average of grades in 2014 I, 2014 II, 2015 I and 2015 II regarding to the first exam where the topics of branch, loops and functions are evaluated. Turtle has been used since 2015. It is important to mention that our grade range goes from 0 to 20.

Table 1. Global Grade Average – First Exam

Academic Year	2014 I First Exam	2014 II First Exam	2015 I First Exam	2015 II First Exam
Total of students	34 students	33 students	39 students	35 students
Global average grade	10.55	10.17	13.69	14.17

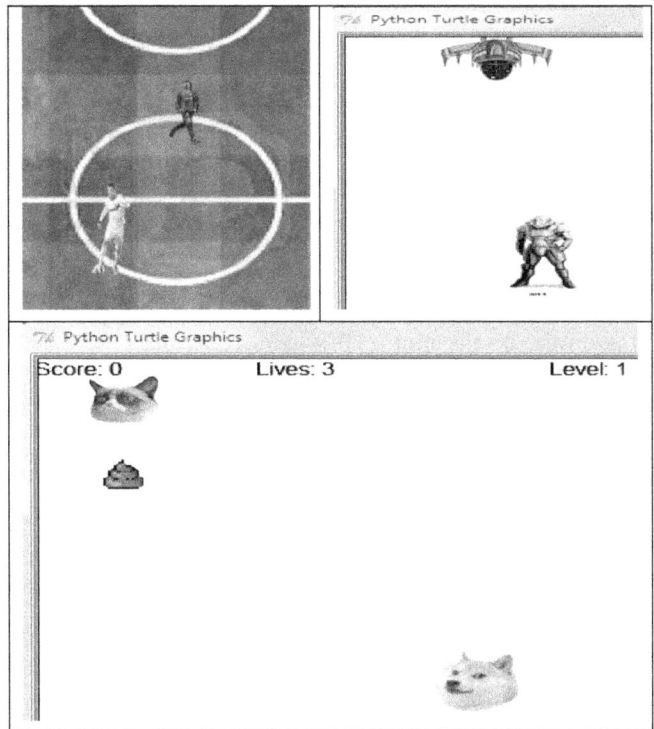

Figure 3. Student's games 2015

4. REFERENCES

[1] H. Wang, Engaging Students with Game Programming in Python. InProceedings of the World Congress on Engineering and Computer Science, Vol 1. 2009.

[2] H. Wang, "Teaching CS1 with Python GUI Game Programming." In IAENG TRANSACTIONS ON ENGINEERING TECHNOLOGIES: Volume 4: Special Edition of the World Congress on Engineering and Computer Science-2009, vol. 1247, no. 1, pp. 253-260. AIP Publishing, 2010.

[3] E. Sweedyk, M. deLaet, M. C. Slattery, and J. Kuffner, "Computer games and CS education: why and how," in Proceedings of the 36th SIGCSE technical symposium on Computer science education , St. Louis, Missouri, USA , 2005, pp. 256-257.

[4] U. Wolz, T. Barnes, I. Parberry, and M. Wick, "Digital gaming as a vehicle for learning," ACM SIGCSE Bulletin, vol. 38, no. 1, pp. 394-395, 2006.

[5] J. D. Bayliss and S. Strout, "Games as a "flavor" of CS1," ACM SIGCSE Bulletin, vol. 38, no. 1, pp. 500-504, Mar. 2006.

[6] T. Lorenzen, W. Heilman , Cs1 and cs2: write computer games in java! SIGCSE Bull., 34(4), 99-100, 2002.

[7] Turtle. https://docs.python.org/2/library/turtle.html, last visited August 2015.

A LEGO-based Approach
to Introducing Test-Driven Development

Stan Kurkovsky
Central Connecticut State University
kurkovsky@ccsu.edu

ABSTRACT

Test-driven development (TDD) is an important software engineering technique that requires writing tests before writing the code to be tested. We describe an approach to introduce the main ideas and practices of TDD using an engaging hands-on activity where students write test cases and construct testable tangible objects with LEGO bricks.

Keywords

Test-driven development, refactoring, software engineering, active learning, LEGO.

1. INTRODUCTION

TDD is a software development strategy that requires writing test cases for every functional unit of the program before it is created. Typical units are the smallest testable components; usually these are individual functions, procedures, or class methods. Automated unit testing frameworks, such as JUnit for Java, help streamline the testing process and minimize the required amount of effort. The main emphasis of TDD is that the developer needs to write the tests before the code that will be tested. Consequently, the *test-driven* aspect of TDD has a significant impact on how software engineers approach their analysis, design, and programming decisions [8]. TDD aligns well with agile methods, which assume that the product requirements are incomplete or will be changing soon.

Refactoring is an integral part of TDD, which promotes testing as an integral part of the analysis and design steps. Refactoring aims to modify the existing internal structure of the code without modifying its external behavior. As the new tests are written and new features are implemented by adding new code, the resulting program structure may become too complex or inflexible. Refactoring aims to reduce that complexity without affecting the outcomes of the corresponding unit tests.

Recent studies indicate that TDD can improve code quality and productivity [2]. Writing tests before writing code forces developers to make better design decisions because they must be able to "distinguish between the functionality to implement and the base conditions under which the implementation has to work" [11]. From the educational perspective, using TDD in the curriculum may help improve students' analytical skills, increase their confidence levels [5], and offer them a practical experience that can become very useful in their professional careers.

For many students, as well as for seasoned developers, it may be a radical departure from their existing practices to have a test case written before the code that is to be tested. It is the opposite of the traditional test-last software development approach where code is written to design specifications, and most of test cases are written after the bulk of the code has been produced. Consequently, to minimize the amount of confusion that students may have with conflicting testing and development practices, many educators choose to introduce TDD very early in the curriculum and continue using it for an extended period of time, at least throughout a single semester [10]. In a survey of 18 studies, Desai et al [5] describe the applications of TDD at various points in academic programs (from freshmen, to upper level, to graduate courses) and suggests that in order to be most effective, TDD should be introduced sooner in the curriculum. Although many studies report overall positive experiences, some concerns remain. In particular, TDD places a high cognitive and technical load, especially on novice programmers, which may serve as a significant deterrent to making it a persisting practice [8,9].

TDD is very simple to describe, but is rather difficult to utilize as a sustained practice, which requires the programmer to be well-disciplined and methodical in applying the technique [6]. Furthermore, TDD cannot be adequately covered in a typical standalone lecture [12]. For novice programmers, additional hurdles include the difficulty of learning a new framework, which can be overcome using student-friendly tools like WebCAT [3] and Marmoset [12]. Although using these tools forces students to use TDD, they may still not be convinced from the outset about the value of the test-first approach. Some reports indicate that students may not view writing tests as a relevant or helpful task [7]. In fact, students may prefer debugging or just running the program to writing test cases. Some researchers link poor students attitudes towards testing as a reason for not adhering to TDD practices [3], which may have far reaching effects. Furthermore, a systematic literature review of industrial practices found that adoption of TDD is hindered by the insufficient adherence to TDD protocol and inadequate testing skills [4].

2. Learning TDD with LEGO

In courses where instructors want to have coverage of TDD, but may not want to use a dedicated software tool, it is important to have an active learning technique to demonstrate and engage students in TDD. Since 2014, the author has been using a hands-on activity where students are introduced to the main ideas and practices of TDD by building LEGO models. It was inspired by the presentations by the work of Beecham and Bowler [1] who conducted numerous training workshops for professional software developers. The technique presented here retains the playful elements of LEGO construction, but offers a number of substantial differences: it is more *student-centric* with a focus on a tangible product; it demonstrates that *refactoring* is an integral activity of TDD; it allows students to build *functional models* that provide a rich foundation for experimenting with the models and writing test cases; it helps students learn from the *collective effort* and refine their unit tests based on the experience of the entire class.

Below is a detailed description of this activity focusing on building a functional model of a catapult using the TDD approach. It has been piloted in several offerings of an upper level software engineering course with several teams consisting of 4-5 students.

Materials and supplies. Each team needs one or two LEGO sets with some long plates to build the arm of the catapult and axles to allow the arm to swing. Useful LEGO sets include many of the larger LEGO Classic boxes or LEGO Serious Play Starter Kit. Ping pong balls are useful as projectiles. Rubber bands can be used to spring-load the catapult's arm.

Introduction. Typically, a the basics of TDD are covered during the previous class. Each student receives a one-page worksheet that includes a simple diagram summarizing TDD as a refresher. Students are told that they will be building a catapult, but no specific details are given except that it will have a base platform, a frame, and a moving arm.

Building. Student teams are asked to build one element/feature of the catapult at a time. Teams are asked to create the catapult elements following this sequence of steps: build the main platform on a large LEGO baseplate; build a frame on the platform; build and attach an arm to the frame; build and attach a payload bucket to the arm; use a rubber band to spring load the arm; launch a ping pong ball at least 10 feet forward. Before building the element of each step, the teams are asked to formulate and write down the test cases that they would use to verify the correctness of their construction. Typical test cases may refer to minimal/maximal or relative sizes (e.g., the frame must be three times taller than the base) of the catapult elements or about their functional properties (e.g., the arm must be able to swing). Once the test cases are written for the given step, teams build the corresponding element of the catapult and apply the tests. If one or more tests fail, teams would need to adjust their models and run the tests again. Following each step, teams are asked to refactor their entire models by reviewing and, if necessary, modifying what has been constructed so far to make sure that the element added at the last step is well-integrated well and that *all* of the test cases written thus far are satisfied.

Review. Once the teams finish all construction steps, they are asked to revisit the test cases they wrote. The teams are asked whether they would write some tests differently for each step given the experience with TDD they have gained by completing this exercise. If the team decides to make changes, students are asked to write down the revised tests for each step in a separate column of the worksheet. By verifying the meaningfulness of the test cases, the instructor can see how well students understand the principles of TDD. Comparing the original tests with the revised ones would enable the instructor to determine whether this exercise helped students understand TDD better. Finally, if time permits, it's always fun to have teams compete against each other to launch a projectile the farthest distance or at a specific target.

3. REFERENCES

[1] Beecham, B. and Bowler, M. 2014. *TDD and Refactoring with LEGO*. http://www.infoq.com/presentations/tdd-lego.

[2] Bissi, W., Neto, A., Emer, M. 2016. The effects of test driven development on internal quality, external quality and productivity: A systematic review. *Information and Software Technology* 74, (2016), 45-54.

[3] Buffardi, K. and Edwards, S. 2012. Exploring influences on student adherence to test-driven development. In *Proceedings of the 17th ACM annual conference on Innovation and technology in computer science education* (ITiCSE '12), 105-110.

[4] Causevic, A., Sundmark, D. and Punnekkat, S. 2011. Factors Limiting industrial adoption of test driven development: a systematic review. In *Proceedings of the 4th IEEE International Conference on Software Testing, Verification and Validation (ICST)*, 337-346.

[5] Desai, C., Janzen, D. and Savage, K. 2008. A survey of evidence for test-driven development in academia. *SIGCSE Bull.* 40, 2 (June 2008), 97-101.

[6] Hammond, H. and Umphress, D. 2012. Test driven development: the state of the practice. In *Proceedings of the 50th Annual Southeast Regional Conference* (ACM-SE '12), 158-163.

[7] Isomöttönen, V. and Lappalainen, V. 2012. CSI with games and an emphasis on TDD and unit testing: piling a trend upon a trend. *ACM Inroads* 3, 3 (Sep. 2012), 62-68.

[8] Janzen, D. and Saiedian, H. 2005. Test-driven development: concepts, taxonomy, and future direction. *Computer* 38, 9 (Sep. 2005), 43-50.

[9] Kollanus, S. and Isomöttönen, V. 2008. Test-driven development in education: experiences with critical viewpoints. In *Proceedings of the 13th annual conference on Innovation and technology in computer science education* (ITiCSE '08), 124-127.

[10] Marrero, W. and Settle, A. 2005. Testing first: emphasizing testing in early programming courses. In *Proceedings of the 10th annual SIGCSE conference on Innovation and technology in computer science education* (ITiCSE '05), 4-8.

[11] Müller, M.M. and Tichy, W.F. 2001. Case study: extreme programming in a university environment. *Proceedings of the 23rd International Conference on Software Engineering (ICSE 2001)*, 537-544.

[12] Spacco. J. and Pugh, W. 2006. Helping students appreciate test-driven development (TDD). In *Companion to the 21st ACM SIGPLAN symposium on Object-oriented programming systems, languages, and applications* (OOPSLA '06), 907-913.

An Improved Approach for Interactive Ebooks

Thomas Way
Villanova University
800 Lancaster Avenue
Villanova, PA 19803, USA
+1 610-519-7307
thomas.way@villanova.edu

ABSTRACT

Motivated by widespread changes to how technology is used in education, perceived high costs of traditional textbooks, and a desire to incorporate interactivity into materials, the fundamental nature of the textbook is changing. We present our ebook approach in the form of an interactive Java resource that can fully replace a course textbook or be used as a supplementary resource. We will demonstrate a platform and approach to the interactive textbook that improves on the significant and ongoing efforts by others in this area and that uses higher degrees of interactivity to increase student engagement while maintaining the pedagogical value of a textbook as both a learning tool and a trusted reference.

CCS Concepts

• Applied Computing→ Education→ Interactive learning environments • Applied Computing→ Education→ E-learning.

Keywords

Electronic textbook; interactive pedagogy; textbook replacement; online exercises; multimedia content; animations.

1. INTRODUCTION

For many years, our students and colleagues have expressed frustration with the cost and short shelf-life of traditional textbooks for our discipline, particularly those involving concepts that include the latest techniques for learning to program. As a result, we have developed our own ebook approach and platform. We surveyed the literature related to interactive approaches to computer science education and assessed current online tutorials and electronic textbooks before starting our work. The result is a highly flexible and interactive ebook platform and approach.

2. PRESENTATION ELEMENTS

The proposed aspects of the presentation of our interactive, electronic textbook approach and results are as follows:

2.1 Motivation and Validity

Significant work in the area of interactive, online learning material has been done for this project and by others. There appears to be long-standing consensus that the learning benefits are considerable for the use of dynamic content, such as:

ITiCSE'16, July 09-13, 2016, Arequipa, Peru
ACM 978-1-4503-4231-5/16/07.
http://dx.doi.org/10.1145/2899415.2925502

animations of algorithms, tools for exploring various CS concepts, online code learning tutorials, and even some interactive textbooks [1]. In the past, students expressed a preference for traditional textbooks over ebooks [4], though this result pre-dates fully interactive ebooks and recent studies indicate a trend toward ebook preference when interactivity is well-realized [2]. Such interactivity engages students, leading them to more deeply engage with the material, thus learning at a higher level in Bloom's Taxonomy [3]. In our presentation, we plan to very briefly summarize supporting research results and recent similar resources in this area to inform comparison with our current work.

2.2 Demonstration of Interactive Elements

To support our approach, we will demonstrate the following innovative and interactive elements that comprise our ebook:

Hypertext Topic Content

We applied accepted good practices of graphic design and layout for the textual content of our ebook, which is managed in a custom, content-management system. The existing content is flexibly organized as approximately 150 "topics" (with more planned) with each topic representing a chapter section or subsection of a traditional, paper-based textbook. The content uses a hypertext approach to appropriately link coordinating content, font faces and sizes chosen for readability, and use of color, whitespace, embedded graphics, and callouts for things like common programmer errors to helping coding tips. The quantity of content provided supports both effective and efficient learning and use as a future and thorough reference on the subject matter.

Interactive "Try This" Elements

Also embedded within the content of a topic are "Try This" elements that enable students to directly interact with code in a variety of unique ways. For example, a "Try This" element in the "Representing Color" topic enables a student to explore RGB color spaces while instantly visualizing the corresponding Java code that represents the selected color.

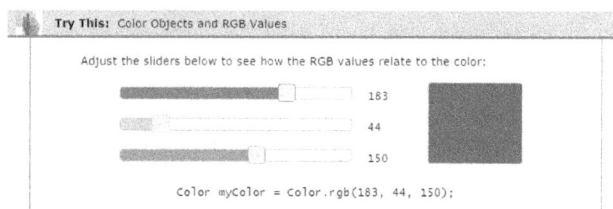

Flipped Classroom Videos

Most topics contain videos that present each topic's content in an engaging and supporting way. We have used these videos in our own teaching as part of a flipped classroom approach, though they easily can serve as complementary learning material for a standard lecturer-driven approach.

Use of Humor and Context

The writing style used, including primary content and examples, incorporates a light touch of humor when it fits. This use of humor is a side-effect of the primary author's prior experience in Hollywood as a comedy writer for television and film, with the use of humor widely accepted as a way to facilitate communication of all forms. Quotations from famous and infamous people from history initiate each topic and are used to lend context beyond the technical content being explored.

> He that would perfect his work must first sharpen his tools.
> - Confucius
>
> Computer Science is no more about computers than Astronomy is about telescopes.
> - Edsger Dijkstra

Animations

Topics also may contain animations of algorithms or other concepts that benefit from a step-by-step demonstration.

Watch This: Binary Search

Binary Search

Search for 38   Search for 88   Search for 69

0	1	2	3	4	5	6	7	8	9	10	11	12	13	14	15	16	17	18	19
12	17	22	26	27	30	33	38	41	48	55	59	64	70	75	77	81	88	93	97

Feedback

An important aspect of our ebook approach is that of feedback and our response to it. We have had success with quickly responding to feedback, including updates to content that can happen within minutes of receiving feedback. Using this approach, the ebook can be continually updated and improved.

Quick Checks

Each topic concludes with three to five interactive true/false, multiple choice and matching exercises that test the students understanding of the material. While these Quick Checks are tracked for right and wrong answers, including attempts, our goal for them is not as part of calculating a grade but as motivation for students to complete the assigned reading. We have used them to verify student completion of reading, in as much as successful completion of a topic's Quick Checks provides some level of assurance that the material was understood by the student.

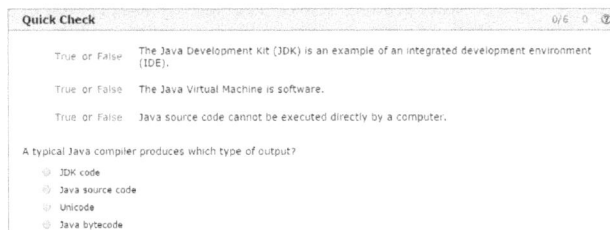

Quick Check

True or False   The Java Development Kit (JDK) is an example of an integrated development environment (IDE).

True or False   The Java Virtual Machine is software.

True or False   Java source code cannot be executed directly by a computer.

A typical Java compiler produces which type of output?
- JDK code
- Java source code
- Unicode
- Java bytecode

Toolkits for Instructors and Students

Tools are provided for instructors to learn more about features, create and manage courses, and create and manage syllabi. For both students and instructors tools are available to measure progress, update passwords and provide feedback.

Syllabus Design Interface

The most noteworthy tool in the instructor toolkit is the syllabus design interface. Because the content is organized by topic, an instructor using the ebook has the flexibility to create a unique syllabus, organized by week, to provide a topic flow that guides student reading and learning. In contract to a chapter-oriented approach, this provides an instructor with the ability to completely customize the organization of content to match his or her specific course. The instructor and students still have access to the complete topic content, as with a traditional textbook, with the syllabus serving as an organized view of the course-specific content.

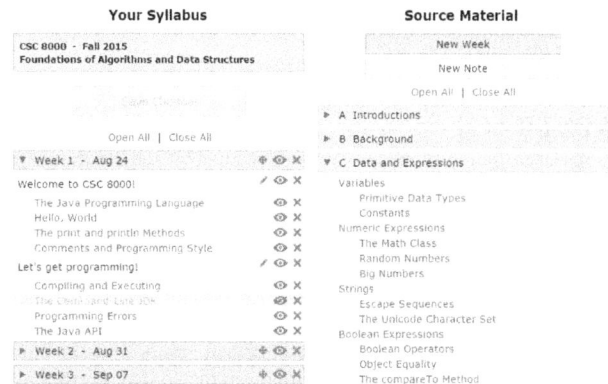

Interactive "Run & Revise" Code Examples

Embedded within the content of a topic can be runnable example code that a student can review, compile, run and edit and run again. These examples provide immediate learning support to topics as they are explored in the form of a concrete example.

```
public class HelloWorld
{
    public static void main(String[] args)
    {
        System.out.println("Hello, World!");
    }
}
```

2.3 Providing Access
We plan to provide access to attendees to our ebook, and hope to encourage feedback that could help us improve the approach

3. ACKNOWLEDGMENTS
Thanks go to my students and faculty colleagues who encouraged my work on this project and provided invaluable feedback that has made it much better than it otherwise would be.

4. REFERENCES

[1] Edgcomb, Alex, and Frank Vahid. "Effectiveness of online textbooks vs. interactive web-native content." 2014 ASEE Annual Conference. 2014.

[2] Gu, Xiaoqing, Bian Wu, and Xiaojuan Xu. "Design, development, and learning in e-Textbooks: What we learned and where we are going." *Journal of Computers in Education* 2.1 (2015): 25-41.

[3] Shaffer, Clifford A., Thomas L. Naps, and Eric Fouh. "Truly interactive textbooks for computer science education." Proceedings of the Sixth Program Visualization Workshop. 2011.

[4] Woody, William Douglas, David B. Daniel, and Crystal A. Baker. "E-books or textbooks: Students prefer textbooks." *Computers & Education* 55.3 (2010): 945-948.

Collaborative Content Creation among All Students in a Class through a Literature Review Activity (and an Informal Introduction to Machine Learning)

Diana Cukierman
Simon Fraser University
Burnaby, BC.
Canada
diana@cs.sfu.ca

ABSTRACT

A research literature review activity leading to the creation of a word cloud is described. The word cloud is an emergent result from submissions from all students in the class, and it is used as further learning material. The collaborative nature of this exercise, and in particular considering that all the students in the class participate adds a sense of ownership and belonging to the class and also expectation and enthusiasm to discover the emergent result. The process to obtain the emergent result is at the same time an example illustrating later topics in the course. Further, the activity includes reflection discussions providing further opportunities to learn from both, the process and the result itself. While the activity was developed for an Artificial Intelligence course, it can be used in other courses where research and exploration is encouraged, as well as in classes or varied sizes.

Keywords

computer science education; collaborative content creation; wikis; student engagement; word cloud; machine learning introduction

1. INTRODUCTION

It is widely recognized by educators that student engagement is highly beneficial or even essential for their learning [3]. If additionally students are direct contributors of class material through a collaborative non-competitive exercise involving the whole class, the engagement is further powerful as an educational tool. Creating educational material among all the students in the class empowers the class as a whole and provides a sense of ownership and belonging; each individual takes part and pride of an emergent result which is beneficial for all in the class. Collaborative learning is usually referred to apply to a learning pedagogy involving small groups work [1]. In the present case the proposal is to involve the whole class in the content creation, facilitated by the instructor. If the creation process additionally requires individual exploration then the educational activity is even richer. On top of the previous characteristics, adding discussion and reflection about the resulting material and about the process itself makes the activity truly worthwhile [3]. The

ITiCSE '16, July 09-13, 2016, Arequipa, Peru
ACM 978-1-4503-4231-5/16/07.

http://dx.doi.org/10.1145/2899415.2925501

activity presented here includes elements of all of these aspects: there is individual exploration, there is a collaborative creation of a word cloud, (which has been used successfully as an educational research tool e.g. [2]); the emergent result becomes class material and provides new, emergent learning content, and depending on the course context it also constitutes an illustration of further topics in the course. Further, the learning is increased by incorporating reflective discussions about the result itself and about the process. The activity is also current and attractive to the students as it is conceived to rely on internet exploration and easily available on line tools.

This activity was conceived for an Artificial Intelligence (AI) introductory course, which among others explicitly aims to expose students to doing some research literature review and exploration; however it could well be adapted to other courses. The additional connection of this activity to an AI course (or possibly also a Machine Learning or Data Science course) is that this activity shows an example of a very coarse machine learning algorithm in action, and thus illustrates that better machine learning algorithms are desirable. Even if machine learning is not part of the course topics, the activity adapts well to any course where there is the expectation that students do some literature review.

The context and the activity are described in detail next. A discussion concludes this paper.

2. THE ACTIVITY

The activity described here took place in a third year university undergraduate course, Introduction to Artificial Intelligence, in a research Canadian University, in the Fall 2015 semester. There were 85 students in the class. The requirements for this activity are that students have internet access and the possibility to simultaneously work with some document (for example using Google Docs or other wiki systems). The activity adapts well to a large or a small class.

The first component of the activity is an assignment. The assignment was named "Initial explorations word cloud". The directives for the assignment consisted on asking students to individually do a very initial exploration of AI articles, published in recognized AI journals or conferences. A list of suggested publications was offered, all electronically accessible to students through the university library. The assignment description informed that the objectives of the assignment were to construct, among the whole class, a "word cloud", and at the same time to encourage individual initial exploration of AI literature. This exercise was also described to serve as an individual exploration leading to selecting a topic for a later course project and at the same time to learn from the emergent result: this word cloud would represent in some way the current AI research interests as selected by everyone in the class.

The instructor initialized a common document (a wiki page) containing the names of all the students in the class. Students were asked to each select one article of their interest and incorporate its abstract in the common document, verbatim. Students were also required to include the selected complete article bibliographic reference together with the abstract. Thus in passing, students were reminded about bibliographic referencing and importantly the need to acknowledge authors. Students were to include their contribution immediately below their name. The instructor and the teaching assistant names were also initialized in the document, and they also each included a contribution to exemplify what was expected. Grading was done just taking into account the completion of the assignment, and taking into account that the proper components and bibliographic reference were submitted. After the assignment deadline, the instructor processed the document. A file was created containing the abstracts and eliminating the bibliographic references and the students' names. This file was input to a word cloud generator [4] and the emergent result was born. See Figure 1.

Figure 1. The resulting word cloud

The word cloud was shared the class immediately after the assignment deadline. Clearly this made apparent some major words and themes, but as expected it produced a very coarse classification. A discussion in class included observing the quality of the result obtained and also extract from there some common themes. It was apparent that the classification was not the most appropriate. For example, the word "paper" has a significant importance in the cloud, but such does not correspond to the AI topics that the students selected. On the other hand, the word "game" is very clearly emerging, not surprisingly suggesting that many students specifically chose articles related to AI games. A valuable characteristic of this exercise is that the word cloud emerged exclusively based on the abstracts that the students selected, and one could view the result as coarsely representing the interests of the whole class, adding an important ownership flavour to the exercise.

3. DISCUSSION

The activity fulfilled the learning experience expectations. The first time this activity was run there was an implementation problem that should be taken into account; the wiki page that was used was part of the course management system which ensured privacy, however, it had some concurrency problems. This caused that some of the students' contributions were not present in the final version of the document, although they were traceable through the document editing history. After some initial student anxiety, students were assured that their materials were not lost, however this increased (although minimally) the processing needed to be done by the instructor. Students were encouraged to individually initially browse some research articles relevant to the course and at the same time being reminded of the importance of acknowledging authors for their publications, a useful preamble to literature review activities for novel researchers. The collaboration was not threatening in any way to students, all had to contribute similarly, and all would be graded similarly; thus the way the activity was conceived motivated students to see the emergent result with no reservations about sharing. There was excitement and expectation to see what the emergent word cloud would look like, and this excitement and expectations applied to both, the students and the instructor. Showing the resulting word cloud was a sort of revelation and the associated discussion created an enjoyable and worthwhile learning moment.

Certainly there are several possibly extensions to this activity. Depending on when in the course this activity takes place other elements could be included in the common document, for example, annotated references could be part of the assignment as well, making the processing and learning of the material deeper. Should the class be very large and the common document become too long, several word clouds could be created. In the case of having several word clouds, the preferences of different subgroups in the class could result in an interesting discussion. As an epilogue of this activity, in a later test, students could be asked to reflect about their selected article and/or about the emergent result. If the activity is done early in the course it could be clarified that questions in a test would not imply deep understanding of the article. Even if the questions in the test are basic, including such in a test encourages students to review the material, adding to the learning experience. Current work includes the evaluation of this activity including the investigation of how students perceive this kind of activity based on anonymous surveying.

4. REFERENCES

[1] Johnson, D.W. and R.T. Johnson. 1993. Learning together and alone. Prentice Hall, Englewood Cliffs, N.J.

[2] McNaught, C., & Lam, P. 2010. Using Wordle as a supplementary research tool. The Qualitative Report, 15(3), 630-643. Retrieved from http://www.nova.edu/ssss/QR/QR15-3/mcnaught.pdf

[3] Taylor, L. & Parsons, J. 2011. Improving Student Engagement. Current Issues in Education, 14(1). Retrieved from http://cie.asu.edu/

[4] Wordle. http://www.wordle.net/create

Employing Multiple-Answer Multiple Choice Questions

Andrew Petersen
Univ. of Toronto Mississauga
Mississauga, Canada
petersen@cs.toronto.edu

Michelle Craig
Univ. of Toronto
Toronto, Canada
mcraig@cs.toronto.edu

Paul Denny
Univ. of Auckland
Auckland, New Zealand
paul@cs.auckland.ac.nz

ABSTRACT

Increasing enrollments and adoption of online resources have encouraged the use of multiple choice questions as a means of providing scalable assessment. However, in contexts where formative feedback is desired, standard multiple choice questions may lead students to a false sense of confidence – a result of their small solution space and the temptation to guess. We propose the use of multiple-answer multiple choice questions in situations where formative feedback is desired and present evidence that these questions are well suited for that role.

Keywords

assessment; formative feedback; multiple choice

1. INTRODUCTION

Multiple choice questions (MCQs) are an effective means of evaluation, and several papers describing effective use of MCQs in computer science contexts are available [8, 4, 6]. There are multiple reasons to consider using MCQs: to reduce grading and marking time, to provide multiple modalities in a test, and even to increase objectivity [5].

However, in situations where students are receiving formative feedback, traditional MCQs may simply be too easy. With a limited number of answer choices, students should be able to select the correct answer quickly, even when guessing. Particularly in online learning situations, where feedback is provided immediately and the instructor is not available to encourage reflection on misunderstandings, this may lead to a student developing a false sense of confidence.

In response, we propose the adoption of an uncommon form of MCQ, the multiple-answer multiple choice question (MAMCQ), to provide formative feedback to students in programming courses. In our experience, the larger solution space provided by MAMCQs discourages guessing and provides better discrimination of student understanding, and with care, MAMCQs can be designed that provide effective feedback on a broad topic area.

ITiCSE '16 July 09-13, 2016, Arequipa, Peru

© 2016 Copyright held by the owner/author(s).

ACM ISBN 978-1-4503-4231-5/16/07.

DOI: http://dx.doi.org/10.1145/2899415.2925503

2. CONTEXT

There are two broad categories of multiple choice questions: single-best answer, where only one option is correct, and multiple-answer, where the respondent must select all correct options. MAMCQ were proposed as early as 1928 [2], and were used extensively in medicine in the 1980's to provide validated assessments to large numbers of test-takers. They have since been largely replaced by other multiple choice formats, including single-best answer.

The move away from MAMCQ was driven by two factors [7]. The first, clueing, has become less significant due to advances in technology that allow multiple options to be selected. Early versions of MAMCQ used single-best answer MCQ tools, so the options had to be encoded in a form like "A and B but not C". Because only four or five of these encodings could be presented on most scantron sheets, this implementation provided unintentional clues to the student.

Clueing remains a problem in both MAMCQ and standard MCQ questions, as badly written multiple choice options may easily be eliminated by students. This connects to the second factor contributing to a decline in MAMCQ usage: the difficulty of writing questions that test more than the recall of specific facts. Since more than one option may be correct, respondents must determine when an option becomes "true enough" if it is ambiguous or not completely true. To resolve this issue, the test writer must ensure that prompts, or stems, are clear, and that options are unambiguously true or false, which often leads to questions that target recall [1]. In programming courses, this issue is mitigated by the content. For MCQs involving code, fragments in the prompts and options can simply be executed.

3. DISCUSSION

We used MAMCQs in two distinct programming courses at a research-intensive North American university. Both of these courses were taught in a flipped format, where the students were introduced to content online, through videos and practice questions, and then worked in teams to solve coding problems in face-to-face class meetings. Students were expected to view videos and complete comprehension questions before each class meeting, and to complete review questions and coding problems at the end of each week.

The questions were primarily intended to provide formative feedback. Students were allowed to submit answers as many times as necessary, and the system that hosted the videos and questions marked each submission immediately, providing the students with instant feedback on the correctness of their submission. The system hosting the content logged all actions taken by students, including submissions to questions and video views, and informed consent was obtained to analyze and present the collected data.

```
Assuming that city_temp refers to {'Toronto' : 7,
'Sydney' : 11, 'Algiers' : 19}, select the expression(s)
that evaluate to True.

  1. len(city_temp) == 6

  2. city_temp['Toronto'] < city_temp['Sydney']

  3. 19 in city_temp

  4. 'Algiers' in city_temp
```

Figure 1: An Example MAMCQ

The first course was an introduction to programming (CS1) taught in Python, and MAMCQs were used to provide a more robust check of student comprehension of the material. Figure 1 presents a MAMCQ used toward the end of this course. If it were written as a standard MCQ, a student would need at most four submissions to solve the question. However, as an MAMCQ, there are 2^4 possible solutions, and other questions featured up to seven options, which dramatically increases the solution space.

Over the term, 147 students each completed 109 standard MCQs, 50 MAMCQs, and 39 online coding problems. As expected, the MAMCQs required more submissions to complete (mean 5.4 attempts) than standard MCQs (mean 2.1 attempts). In addition, we believe students guessed randomly less often, as students took more than the expected number of attempts (if guessing randomly) to solve a question on 30% of MCQs and only 17% of MAMCQs.

We calculated a variation of the *facility index* as evidence of whether the questions were providing effective feedback. Facility measures how easy a question is to answer, with values ranging from 0 (no one answered the question completely correctly) to 1 (everyone answered it completely correctly). For summative assessment, higher facilities (around 0.8) are desirable, and for formative feedback, lower facilities (between 0.4 and 0.6) are preferred [3]. Since students received immediate feedback and could submit multiple times, most students eventually answered all questions correctly, so we used the first submission each student made to calculate the facility index. On average, standard MCQs had a facility index of 0.73 – higher than recommended – and MAMCQs had an index of 0.44, which is more appropriate for the purpose of formative feedback. For comparison, the average facility of the coding problems was 0.37.

We also investigated whether performance on MCQs and MAMCQs was correlated with performance in the course. We applied Spearman's rank correlation and detected a low, negative correlation between the average number of submissions a student needed to solve both standard (r=-0.43, p<0.001) and multiple-answer (r=-0.36, p<0.001) MCQs and the final exam. This indicates that for both MCQs and MAMCQs, needing more attempts to solve a problem correctly (on average, over all such problems) is weakly correlated with lower performance in the course.

Standard MCQs require a limited number of attempts to solve (usually 1 to 5), and any single measurement is susceptible to noise. As such, we expected little to no correlation between the number of attempts needed to solve any individual question and the exam mark. However, unlike any of the MCQs, we noticed that several individual MAMCQs exhibited moderate correlations with the exam. To explore if this phenomenon might be caused by the broader topic coverage afforded by MAMCQs, we analyzed four MAMCQs from a second-year systems programming course taught in C. Two of these questions were carefully designed to cover the major concepts relating to pointers (a range that would be infeasible for a single standard MCQ). The other two MAMCQs were written to test simple comprehension of a single video. 93 students completed all four questions. For the two designed to provide broad topic coverage, the average number of submissions required was moderately correlated with exam performance (r=-0.52, p<0.001), and no correlation was detected for the other two questions (p>0.05).

4. CONCLUSION

We have explored the use of an alternate form of MCQ, the MAMCQ, to provide formative feedback in an online context. The increased size of the solution space of MAMCQs provides a deterrent to guessing and provides better discrimination between levels of understanding than standard MCQs. While the difficulty of writing unambiguous options is a drawback in some domains, these questions are well suited for programming courses, where stems and options can often be executed and shown to be unambiguous.

We are also intrigued by the possibility that these questions, if carefully constructed, may be better correlated with overall performance in the course than standard MCQs. This suggests added utility in a formative role and the possibility that these questions could be employed effectively in summative assessments.

5. REFERENCES

[1] S. M. Case and D. B. Swanson. Constructing written test questions for the basic and clinical sciences. http://www.nbme.org/publications/item-writing-manual.html. Accessed: 2016-03-04.

[2] G. T. Duncan and E. O. Milton. Multiple-answer multiple-choice test items: Responding and scoring through bayes and minimax strategies. *Psychometrika*, 43(1):43–57.

[3] G. Isaacs. *Multiple choice testing*. HERDSA Green Guide No 16. Higher Education Research and Development Society of Australasia, Australia, 1994.

[4] R. Lister. On blooming first year programming, and its blooming assessment. In *Proc. of the Australasian Conf. on Computing Education*, pages 158–162, 2000.

[5] R. Lister. Objectives and objective assessment in CS1. *SIGCSE Bull.*, 33(1):292–296, Feb. 2001.

[6] R. Lister. One small step toward a culture of peer review and multi-institutional sharing of educational resources: A multiple choice exam for first semester programming students. In *Proc. of the 7th Australasian Conf. on Computing Education*, pages 155–164, 2005.

[7] P. McCoubrie and L. McKnight. Single best answer MCQs: a new format for the FRCR part 2a exam. *Clinical Radiology*, 63(5):506–510, 2008.

[8] K. Woodford and P. Bancroft. Multiple choice questions not considered harmful. In *Proc. of the 7th Australasian Conf. on Computing Education*, pages 109–116, 2005.

Learning Computer Science Languages in Enki

José Carlos Paiva
CRACS & INESC-Porto LA &
DCC - Faculty of Sciences,
University of Porto
Porto, Portugal
up201200272@fc.up.pt

José Paulo Leal
CRACS & INESC-Porto LA &
DCC - Faculty of Sciences,
University of Porto
Porto, Portugal
zp@dcc.fc.up.pt

Ricardo Queirós
CRACS & INESC-Porto LA &
DI/ESEIG/IPP
Porto, Portugal
ricardoqueiros@eseig.ipp.pt

ABSTRACT

This paper presents an overview and main features of Enki, a web-based learning environment for computer science languages. Enki was designed to be a sort of entry level IDE, aggregating tools for navigating and viewing course materials, for solving exercises and receiving automated feedback, as well as promoting the learning process. Enki uses services from several other systems, namely for content sequencing and recommendation, exercise assessment, and gamification.

Keywords

Learning; Integration; Gamification; Educational Resources; Sequencing; Exercises; Programming Languages

General Terms

Languages, Design, Experimentation

1. INTRODUCTION

Enki is a web integrated environment for learning computer science languages, such as programming languages or diagrammatic languages. This environment is one of the GUIs of Mooshak 2.0 (the new version of Mooshak [2]), a framework for automated assessment of computer science languages. Enki was designed for a wide range of use cases, from introductory high school or college courses, to massive online open courses. It assumes that the students may have little or no help from a teaching assistant and that they may not have the necessary tools installed on their computers. In fact, students may be accessing the Internet through a tablet rather than a computer, where these tools would be virtually impossible to install. In spite of these constraints, it aims to prepare students to the development environments typically used in computer, namely IDEs.

Enki can be described as an entry level IDE, a scaffolding to support the progress of students towards more complex environments and tools. It has simplified versions of common IDE tools, such as editors or launchers, and new

ITiCSE '16 July 09-13, 2016, Arequipa, Peru

© 2016 Copyright held by the owner/author(s).

ACM ISBN 978-1-4503-4231-5/16/07.

DOI: http://dx.doi.org/10.1145/2899415.2925504

tools required by a learning environment, such as a resource browser or a content recommender. Enki borrows from IDEs both the role of a tool integrator and the characteristic graphic user interface (GUI).

A typical IDE, such as Eclipse or NetBeans, organizes its GUI in *regions*, each one containing several overlapping windows organized using tabs. The layout scheme for these regions locates them roughly in the main directions. Regions are resizeable and the windows they contain can be moved among regions, according to the needs and preferences of students. The remainder presents the main regions and tools as shown on the screen shot in Figure 1.

2. LEFT REGION

The left region of the GUI, with a purple highlight in Figure 1, contains a *resource browser*. In reference IDEs this region usually contains browsers that provide different views of the workspace, either organized in projects, packages and classes, or organized in directories and files. In Enki this region is used for browsing pedagogical resources using a tree widget that mimics those used by IDE browsers.

The resource browser is a particularly important part of Enki's GUI as it drives student interaction by presenting both the course structure and content. The view of course unfolds as the student progresses throughout the course. This view is mediated by Seqins [3], a learning content sequencing engine. Tree leaves may hold educational resources of different types: text (HTML or PDF), multimedia and activities (exercises). They are presented in the tree with an icon reflecting its type and a color depending on its state relative to the student: available, solved/seen, unavailable or recommended.

3. CENTER REGION

The center region, highlighted in magenta in Figure 1, is the main region of Enki's GUI. By default, the expository and evaluative resources selected in the browser will be open here in one or more tabs.

Expository resources are presented in specialized viewers. For instance, a sequence of steps can be illustrated by an embed video hosted in YouTube, and reference material can be presented in PDF or HTML formatted pages.

Evaluative resources open several windows: to show the exercise statement, to edit a solution and to evaluate it. Currently Enki supports two editors for different kinds of computer science languages: a code editor for programming languages such as Java or C#, and a diagram editor for diagrammatic languages such as EER or UML.

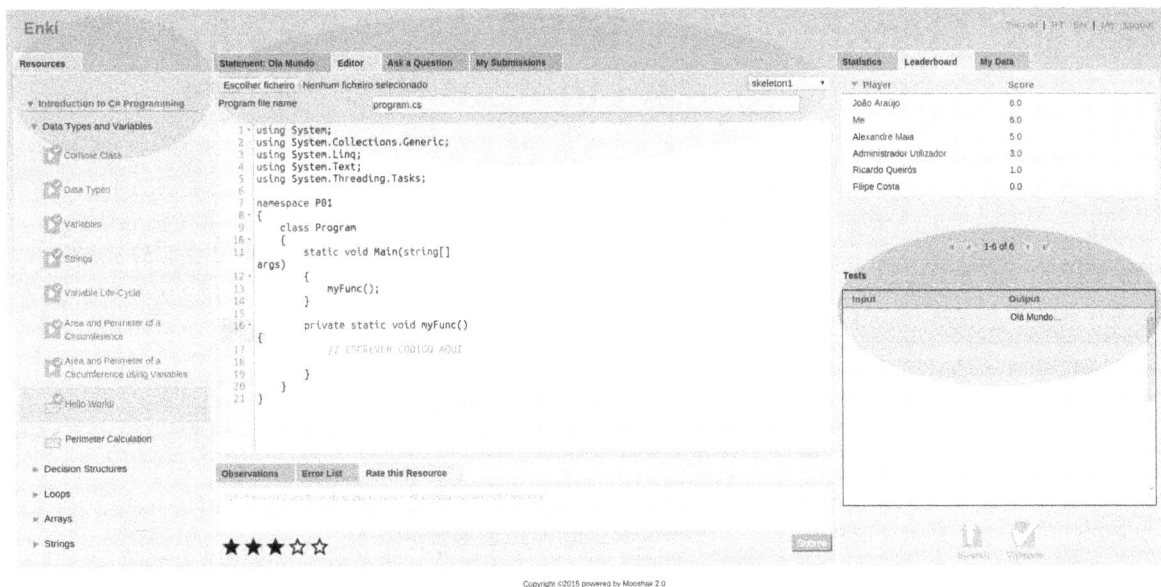

Figure 1: Interface of Enki for students with different regions highlighted in different colors

4. UPPER RIGHT REGION

The upper right region is highlighted in yellow in Figure 1. It aggregates gamification related windows, such as the leaderboard and the achievements, and windows that summarize global or personal progress, such as problem statistics and profile data. These windows are not always present, it depends on the selected resource type.

The gamification related windows use the gamification features provided by Odin [1], a gamification service inspired in the Google Play Game Service (GPGS) which authenticates institutions rather than end-users, and the others may use services provided by Seqins [3], a sequencing tool of digital educational resources which includes a flexible sequencing model that fosters students to learn at different paces.

5. BOTTOM RIGHT REGION

By default, the bottom right region is just available, in exercises and activities. In this case, it contains the window to write input test cases to execute with the exercise, where corresponding outputs are later on presented, and buttons to validate or submit the solution.

The validation of an exercise consists in taking the inputs provided by the student, and/or public inputs (written by the exercise author), and running the program with these inputs. This kind of evaluation is not graded. If the test case is public, it will be highlighted in green (if the output matches) or red (if it does not match). If the input is provided by the student, the output obtained with the program with that input is written in the grid.

A submission follows a similar process but uses a complete set of test cases provided by the exercise author. It sends the program for assessment and returns the a grade and a feedback. Unlike a validation, a submission is considered for statistics and can unlock new resources of the course.

6. BOTTOM REGION

The windows presented in this region (highlighted in green

in Figure 1) depend on the selected resource type. In exercises and activities, three windows are shown in different tabs: the observations window which contains automated feedback on an exercise, the error list window that summarizes the compilation/syntax errors and warnings, and a window that allows the student to rate and/or comment a resource. This last window is also shown on educational resources, as well as one with links to related resources.

7. ACKNOWLEDGMENTS

Work funded by the ERDF and FCT Project NORTE-01-0145-FEDER-000020 and POCI-01-0145-FEDER-006961; and by IPP trough Project BInt-ICD/IPP-BST/KMILT/01/2015.

8. REFERENCES

[1] J. P. Leal, J. C. Paiva, and R. Queirós. Odin: A service for gamification of learning activities. In *to appear*, page to appear. Springer, 2015.

[2] J. P. Leal and F. Silva. Mooshak: a web-based multi-site programming contest system. *Software: Practice and Experience*, 33(6):567–581, 2003.

[3] R. Queirós, J. P. Leal, and J. Campos. Sequencing educational resources with seqins. 2014.

Teaching Abstraction, Function and Reuse in the First Class of CS1 – A Lightbot Experience

Marco Aedo López
Universidad Nacional San Agustín
Arequipa - Perú
maedol@unsa.edu.pe

Elizabeth Vidal Duarte
Universidad Nacional San Agustín
Universidad La Salle
Arequipa - Perú
evidal@ulasalle.edu.pe

Eveling Castro Gutierrez
Universidad Nacional San Agustín
Arequipa - Perú
ecastro@unsa.edu.pe

Alfredo Paz Valderrama
Universidad Nacional San Agustín
Arequipa - Perú
apazv@unsa.edu.pe

ABSTRACT

Educators have long been trying to motivate students in their introductory programming courses. There are key concepts that are not easy to teach like abstraction, function and reuse. We believe that the visual nature of game-oriented approach to teaching anything is more effective for students. This work describes our experience in the use of Lightbot to introduce students to these concepts. This approach has been implemented in two Universities in CS1: Universidad Nacional de San Agustín and Universidad La Salle, from Arequipa – Perú. One of them uses Java and the other one uses Python as first programming languages. Lightbot has been used in both of them since 2015 in the first laboratory session. Results were measured by student's grades in comparison with previous years when Lightbot was not used.

Keywords
CS1; Teaching; Motivation; Game-Oriented, Pedagogical Tool; Specific Assignments.

1. BACKGROUND

There are experiences that have shown that the visual nature of games is suitable for learning since it is fairly easy for students to see how a loop or branch is used in a game and check the logical errors of implementation [1],[2],[3],[4]. An special implementation of this approach is Karel the robot [5] that uses predefined classes to introduce the fundamentals of object-oriented programming followed by fundamentals of iteration and selection. Following the robot idea, we used Lightbot [6] for teaching an introductory idea of abstraction, functions and reuse. The main advantage of Lighbot is that it is independent from the programming language.

2. LIGHTBOT

Lightbot is a programming puzzle game. Its properties lead themselves to have a relationship with programming concepts.

ITiCSE '16, July 09-13, 2016, Arequipa, Peru
ACM 978-1-4503-4231-5/16/07.
http://dx.doi.org/10.1145/2899415.2925505

The goal of the game is to guide a robot to light up the blue tiles. We must tell it how to do that by using a set of instructions: forward(), turnRight(), turnLeft(), jump(), light(), funct1(), and funct2(). The instructions are shown in Figure 1.

Figure 1: Lightbot instructions

3. COURSE DESIGN
3.1 Overview

This approach has been implemented in two Universities in CS1. One of them uses Java and the other one uses Python as programming languages. CS1 has 8 hours a week (4 theoretical hours and 4 laboratory hours). Lightbot has been used in both of them since 2015 as a tool to introduce three programming concepts: abstraction, function and reuse. Lightbot is used in the first laboratory session. The game has eleven levels. We have divided the session in two assignments. The first assignment covers levels 1 to 5 and the second assignment covers levels 6 to 11.

3.2 Assignment 1: Lightbot Basics

The first assignment explains Lightbot's world (Figure 2). We focus on the main method that can only hold twelve instructions. In this assignment students only use the forward(), jump(), turnLeft(), turnRight() and light() instructions. Motivation comes automatically and levels 1 to 5 are solved quickly.

3.3 Assignment 2: More Lightbot

The next assignment is when students discover that they can not continue with the next level because of the limited number of instructions in the main method.

Here students get a hint. They can group instructions in functions using f1 and f2. Then they can be called in the main method. Students discover by themselves that they can call the same function more than once when they abstract a pattern. (Figure 3).

Also some students found that it was also possible that one function (f1) can call another function (f2) (Figure 4).

Figure 2 : Lightbot Level 1

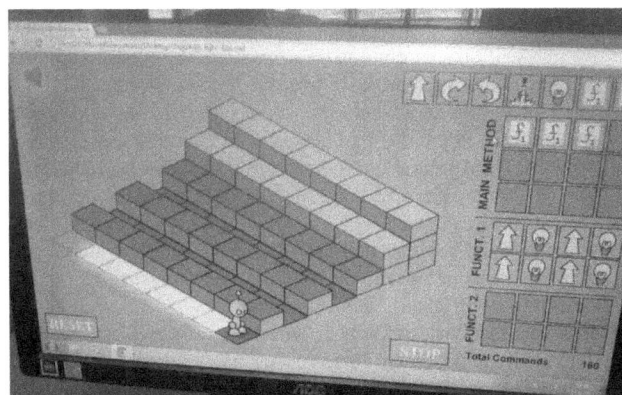

Figure 3: Lightbot calling a function f1

Figure 4: Lightbot f1 calling function f2

Part of the challenge that students face is to continue until level eleven is completed. By the end of the class, professors show different kinds of solutions to solve level eleven. Students can see that they can call f1 and f2 in the main method or that f1 could call f2 as it is shown in Figure 4.

4. RESULTS

The overall feedback received from students was very positive. Students seemed to enjoy Lightbot and the challenge to finish the game. In the second class we gave them a quiz with five questions: (1) What is an instruction? (2) What is a function? (3) Why are functions useful?, (4) Can we call a function inside another function? and (5) Describe by giving an example what is abstraction? From the answers we found that students got a clear idea of abstractions, functions and reuse.

Later in the course the same concepts are taught but in the respective programming language: Java and Python. In order to measure the impact of Lightbot we show in Table 1 and Table 2 the global average of grades in 2013, 2014 and 2015 regarding the second exam where the topic of functions (including abstraction and reuse) is evaluated. It is important to mention that our grade range goes from 0 to 20.

Table 1. Global Grade Average – Universidad Nacional de San Agustín

Year	2013	2014	2015
Total of students	115	120	111
Global average grade	12.50	11.9	14.50

Table 2. Global Grade Average – Universidad La Salle

Year	2013	2014	2015
Total of students	25	34	39
Global average grade	11.2	10.55	13.69

5. REFERENCES

[1] E. Sweedyk, M. deLaet, M. C. Slattery, and J. Kuffner, "Computer games and CS education: why and how," in Proceedings of the 36th SIGCSE technical symposium on Computer science education , St. Louis, Missouri, USA , 2005, pp. 256-257.

[2] U. Wolz, T. Barnes, I. Parberry, and M. Wick, "Digital gaming as a vehicle for learning," ACM SIGCSE Bulletin, vol. 38, no. 1, pp. 394-395, 2006.

[3] J. D. Bayliss and S. Strout, "Games as a "flavor" of CS1," ACM SIGCSE Bulletin, vol. 38, no. 1, pp. 500-504, Mar. 2006.

[4] T. Lorenzen, W. Heilman , Cs1 and cs2: write computer games in java! SIGCSE Bull., 34(4), 99-100, 2002.

[5] B. W. Becker. "Teaching CS1 with karel the robot in Java." ACM SIGCSE Bulletin. Vol. 33. No. 1. ACM, 2001.

[6] Lightbot. https://lightbot.com/

Instructional Module Development System (IMODS)

Srividya K. Bansal
Arizona State University
School of Computing, Informatics, Decision Systems
Engineering, Mesa, AZ 85212 USA
srividya.bansal@asu.edu

Odesma Dalrymple
University of San Diego
Shiley-Marcos School of Engineering
San Diego, CA USA
odesma@sandiego.edu

ABSTRACT

To ensure that future generations of engineering, science, and other technological practitioners are equipped with the required knowledge and skills to continue to innovate solutions to solve societal challenges, effective courses or instructional modules that incorporate best pedagogical and assessment practices must be designed and delivered. Science, technology, engineering and mathematics (STEM) educators typically come from STEM backgrounds and have little or no formal STEM education training. Their approaches to learning, instruction, and assessment mimic the experiences they were exposed to as students and are not necessarily informed by scholarship in the area of how people learn. The road to effective STEM instruction starts with a well-conceived and constructed plan or curriculum that includes the tight alignment of content, pedagogical approaches and assessments, around the learning objectives, and draws upon best-practices in each of these areas. An information technology (IT) tool that can guide STEM educators through the complex task of course design development, ensure tight alignment between various components of an instructional module, and provide relevant information about research-based pedagogical and assessment strategies will be of great value. This demonstration presents a Web-based software tool called the Instructional Module Development System (IMODS) that supports these ventures and broadens the impact and reach of professional development in the scholarship of teaching and learning, particularly to STEM faculty.

Keywords

Instruction design; Semantic web-based tool; Outcome-based education; Assessment techniques; Instructional techniques.

1. INTRODUCTION

At many colleges and universities, engagement in scholarly teaching is becoming a minimum expectation of faculty who are held accountable for the quality of the learning experienced by students enrolled in their course(s). These expectations are even greater for STEM faculty given the national demands for a well-trained STEM workforce [1]. Since education training is not typically included in the plan of study of most STEM programs, faculty who graduate with STEM degrees gain their teaching expertise post-appointment and "on-the-job". In the absence of formal training, most faculty can take as much as five years to truly become proficient teachers, and during that period, it is the students who are most affected [2]. There is a growing demand and interest in faculty professional development in areas such as outcome-based education [3], curriculum design, and pedagogical and assessment strategies. In response to this demand, a number of universities have established teaching and learning centers to provide institution-wide, and sometimes program specific support. Instructional Module Development System (IMODS) supports these ventures and broaden the impact and reach of professional development in the scholarship of teaching and learning, particularly to STEM faculty. The IMODS is a web-based course design software that:

1. Guides individual or collaborating users, step-by-step, through an outcome-based education process as they define learning objectives, select content to be covered, develop an instruction and assessment plan, and define the learning environment and context for their course(s).
2. Contains a repository of current best pedagogical and assessment practices, and based on selections the user makes when defining the learning objectives of the course, the system will present options for assessment and instruction that align with the type/level of student learning desired.
3. Generates documentation of course design. In the same manner that an architect's blue-print articulates the plans for a structure, the IMODS course design documentation will present an unequivocal statement as to what to expect when the course is delivered.
4. Provides just-in-time help to the user. The system will provide explanations to the user on how to perform course design tasks efficiently and accurately.
5. Provides feedback to the user on fidelity of the course design. This will be assessed in terms of the cohesiveness of the alignment of the course design components (i.e., content, assessment, and pedagogy) around the defined objectives.

2. IMODS FRAMEWORK

Outcome-based education (OBE) is an approach where the product defines the process, i.e., the outcomes that specify what students should be able to demonstrate upon leaving the system are defined first, and drive decisions about the content and how it is organized, the educational strategies, the teaching methods, the assessment procedures and the educational environment [4], [5]. This is a contrast to the preceding "input-based" model that placed emphasis on the means as opposed to the end of instruction. OBE was used as the principal guide for the development of the IMODS framework. It was chosen for the following reasons: 1) win-for-all solution – OBE is shown to improve student success, provides a structure to educators for designing instruction, and facilitates reporting to external stakeholders in an accountability education climate; 2) it supports the How People Learn framework for designing learning environments [6]; 3) growing adoption of outcome-based program accreditation – Accreditation boards such as ABET, have moved to an outcome focused model (what students learned) to assess the quality of programs in Applied Science, Computing, Engineering, and Engineering Technology; 4) alignment with other models that are meant to increase innovation in STEM education – OBE dictates the end and not the means thereby allowing innovation in instruction. It also provides an empirical structure to track impact and identify shortcomings. The IMODS framework adheres strongly to the OBE approach and treats the course objective as the spine of the structure. New constructs (not included in the models previously discussed) are incorporated to add further definition to the objective. The work of Robert Mager [7, 8)] informs the IMOD definition of the objective. Mager identifies three defining characteristics of a learning objective: Performance – description of what the learner is expected to be able to do; Conditions – description of the conditions under which the performance is expected to occur; and the Criterion – a description of the level of competence that must be reached or surpassed. For use in the IMODS framework an additional characteristic was included, i.e., the Content – description of the disciplinary knowledge, skill, or behavior to be attained. The resulting IMODS definition of the objective is referred to as the PC^3 model.

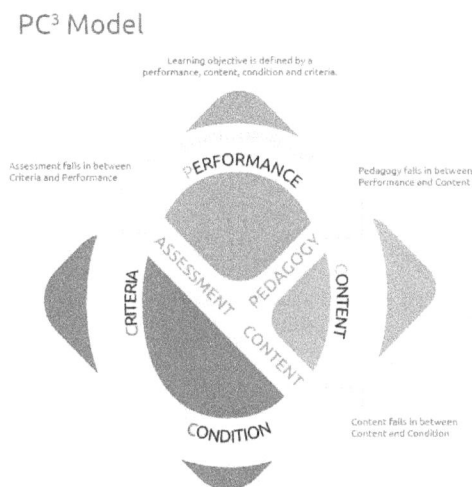

Figure 1: IMODS PC^3 Model

The other course design elements (i.e., Content, Pedagogy, and Assessment) are incorporated into the IMODS framework through interactions with two of the PC3 characteristics. Course-Content is linked to the content and condition components of the objective. The condition component is often stated in terms of pre-cursor disciplinary knowledge, skills or behaviors. This information, together with the content defined in the objective, can be used to generate or validate the list of course topics. Course-Pedagogy is linked to the performance and content components of the objective. The types of instructional approaches or learning activities used in a course should correspond to the level of learning expected and the disciplinary knowledge, skills or behaviors to be learned. The content and performance can be used to validate pedagogical choices. Course-Assessment is linked to the performance and criteria components of the objective. This affiliation can be used to test the suitability of the assessment strategies since an effective assessment, at the very least, must be able to determine whether the learner's performance constitutes competency. Figure 1 shows PC3 model of a learning objective.

3. IMPLEMENTATION OF IMODS

Different programming platforms and technology options were considered and appropriate technologies were identified for the development of the IMODS web application, design of the back-end database schema, installation and configuration of the server-side and client-side technologies, and development of the user interface screens for login, registration, index, and creation of an instructional module and the connectivity of these web pages with the backend database. An Agile software development methodology called Scrum is being used for the development of

this project. Scrum is an iterative and incremental framework for managing product development. A sprint (or iteration) is the basic unit of development in Scrum. The sprint is restricted to a specific duration, two weeks in case of the IMODS project. Each sprint is started with a planning meeting. The aim is to define a sprint backlog where the tasks for the sprint are identified and an estimated commitment for the sprint goal is made. Each sprint ends with a sprint review-and-retrospective meeting, where the progress is reviewed and shown to stakeholders and improvements for the next sprints are identified. Groovy on Grails is an open source, full stack, web application framework for the Java Virtual Machine. It takes advantage of the Groovy programming language and convention over configuration to provide a productive and streamlined development experience. The Groovy/Grails Tool Suite™ (GGTS) provides the best Eclipse-powered development environment for building Groovy and Grails applications. Git is a distributed revision control and source code management (SCM) system with an emphasis on speed. Grails uses Spring Model–View–Controller (MVC) architecture as the underlying web application framework. MVC is a software architecture pattern that separates the representation of information from the user's interaction with it.

The IMODS framework was applied to design introductory software engineering courses titled "Software Enterprise I: Personal Software Process" and "Software Enterprise II: Testing and Quality" in B.S. in Software Engineering program. Using the IMODS framework ensured the alignment between various course elements and thereby ensuring high-quality course design. The framework supports the checking of alignment between course assessments and learning objectives. The course assessments are linked to the performance and criteria elements of the learning. The framework supports the checking of alignment between course instructional activities and learning objectives. Course pedagogical activities are linked to performance and content of the learning objective as shown in Figure 1.

4. ACKNOWLEDGMENTS

The authors gratefully acknowledge the support for this project under the National Science Foundation's Transforming Undergraduate Education in Science, Technology, Engineering and Mathematics (TUES) program Award No. DUE-1246139

5. REFERENCES

[1] M. T. Huber and S. P. Morreale, Eds., *Disciplinary Styles in the Scholarship of Teaching and Learning: Exploring Common Ground.* AAHE Publications, 2002.

[2] R. Boice, *Advice for new faculty members.* Allyn & Bacon, 2000.

[3] G. C. Furman, "Outcome-Based Education and Accountability.," *Educ. Urban Soc.*, vol. 26, no. 4, pp. 417–437, 1994.

[4] R. M. Harden, J. R. Crosby, M. H. Davis, and M. Friedman, "AMEE Guide No. 14: Outcome-based Education: Part 5--From Competency to Meta-Competency: A Model for the Specification of Learning Outcomes.," *Med. Teach.*, vol. 21, no. 6, pp. 546–552, 1999.

[5] W. G. Spady, "Organizing for Results: The Basis of Authentic Restructuring and Reform.," *Educ. Leadersh.*, vol. 46, no. 2, pp. 4–8, 1988.

[6] J. D. Bransford, A. L. Brown, and R. R. Cocking, *How people learn.* National Academy Press Washington, DC, 2000.

[7] R. F. Mager, *Measuring instructional results, or, Got a match?*, 2nd ed. Belmont, Calif: Pitman Management and Training, 1984.

[8] R. F. Mager, *Preparing instructional objectives: a critical tool in the development of effective instruction*, 3rd ed. Atlanta, GA: Center for Effective Performance, 1997.

Data-Driven Test Case Generation for Automated Programming Assessment

Terry Tang
Rice University
terry.tang@rice.edu

Rebecca Smith
Rice University
rjs@rice.edu

Scott Rixner
Rice University
rixner@rice.edu

Joe Warren
Rice University
jwarren@rice.edu

ABSTRACT

Building high-quality test cases for programming problems is an important part of any well-built Automated Programming Assessment System. Traditionally, test cases are created by human experts or using machine auto-generation methods based on the problem definition and sample solutions. Unfortunately, the human approach can not anticipate the numerous ways that programmers can construct erroneous solutions. The machine auto-generation methods are complex, problem-specific, and time-consuming.

This paper proposes a fast, simple method for generating high-quality test sets for a programming problem from an existing collection of student solutions for that problem. This paper demonstrates the effectiveness of the proposed method in online programming course assessments. The experiments showed that, when applied to large collections of such programs, the method produces concise, human-understandable test sets that provide better coverage than test sets built by experts with rich teaching experience.

Categories and Subject Descriptors

K.3.2 [**Computers and Education**]: Computer and Information Science Education—*Computer science education*

General Terms

Reliability, Verification

Keywords

Automated Programming Assessment System; Automatic Test Case Generation; Data-Driven; MOOC

1. INTRODUCTION

Automated Programming Assessment (APA) systems have been widely used in many areas to evaluate program

ITiCSE '16, July 09-13, 2016, Arequipa, Peru

© 2016 ACM. ISBN 978-1-4503-4231-5/16/07. . . $15.00

DOI: http://dx.doi.org/10.1145/2899415.2899423

correctness and efficiency. Universities and companies have built automated systems for judging programming competitions, such as UVa [7], PC^2 [3], TopCoder [6], and Google Code Jam [1]. Educators have created Leetcode [2], Rosalind [5], and Project Euler [4] to teach programming skills and algorithms through problem-solving exercises. Recently, many massive open online courses (MOOCs) have relied heavily on automated assessment systems for grading programming assignments [18].

The effectiveness and efficiency of an APA system is largely determined by the quality of its test cases. Manually building test cases is tedious and time-consuming, and makes it difficult to guarantee a high level of error detection. Thus, researchers have put a great deal of effort into test case auto-generation to reduce human effort and increase test quality [10, 16, 21].

Traditional software testing systems target a single existing piece of software, and are typically used to validate software that is already believed to be largely correct. In contrast, APA systems target a broad spectrum of programs implementing a single specification, and are typically used as a step in the incremental feedback-debugging cycle. As a result, they face additional requirements. First, they demand fast execution to provide a rapid feedback cycle. Therefore, they typically employ test suite reduction strategies [11] to minimize the number of tests while retaining quality. Second, they should be capable of assessing yet-to-come implementations based on a problem description and a few correct sample solutions. Third, APA systems often benefit from presenting test cases in a logical order, *e.g.*, increasing complexity, particularly in the context of offering feedback and partial credit to students in programming courses.

Shayma *et al.* [16], categorized traditional test case auto-generation techniques into random-based, search-based, and data mining-based methods. Random-based methods randomly generate a large number of tests within a constrained search space [8]. Given an existing piece of code, techniques like mutation-driven selection [12] can be applied in random-based methods to eliminate unimportant test cases. However, future submissions are hard to predict, and thus cannot guide test selection in this way.

Search-based methods [15] use more advanced algorithms such as genetic algorithms [14] and particle swarm optimization [18] to directly search for high quality test cases. However, these methods are complex and computation intensive. Moreover, they are not easily generalizable, requiring problem-specific fitness function selection and tuning.

Data mining-based approaches have been proposed to reduce the number of test cases without losing coverage [17, 20, 22] by identifying hidden input-output (I/O) relations. However, these methods are typically more complex, requiring a large number of training samples and significant tuning in order to achieve accurate predictions.

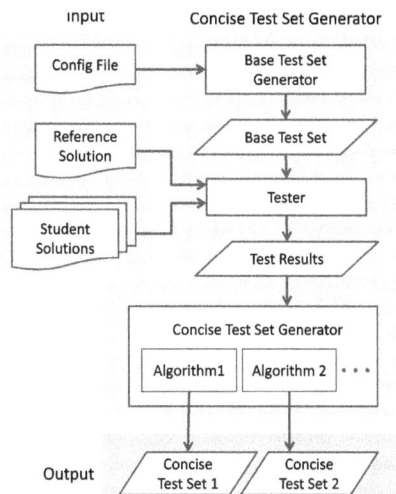

Figure 1: FEAT Structure and Workflow

This paper describes a simple and easy-to-use toolchain for creating high-quality test sets for automated assessment systems, Feedback and Evaluation via Auto-generated Tests (FEAT). It utilizes a collection of previously-submitted student solutions to guide the test generation process, under the assumption that no error is unique in a crowd-sourcing scenario [13].

FEAT consists of three modules (Figure 1): the base test set generator, the tester, and the concise test set generator. The first module auto-generates a large pool of test cases for a particular programming assignment, based on an instructor-provided problem specification. This pool is referred to as the *base test set*. The second module uses the base test set to check the correctness of a training set of student solutions against an instructor-provided reference solution. The third module uses the testing results to construct *concise test sets* that are small subsets of the base test set. These concise test sets are carefully chosen such that they detect every erroneous solution that could be found using the much larger base test set, while providing the efficiency needed for use in an APA system.

The effectiveness of FEAT was tested in a series of assignments from massive open online courses [19]. The test sets for these assignments were manually built by the authors in the first course session, but were reported as incomplete by students. Evaluation demonstrated that FEAT generates superior test sets, providing students with higher-quality feedback while freeing instructors from the tedious, time-consuming work needed to use APA systems.

This paper presents three key contributions:

- **Base test set generation:** This paper proposes a simple specification for the inputs to a programming problem and describes an algorithm for creating a large set of test cases based on this specification.

- **Concise test set generation:** Given a collection of previous solutions to a programming problem, this paper describes test reduction methods for selecting concise subsets of the base test set with the property that all programs that fail on the base test set also fail on the concise test sets. Two types of concise test sets are presented: approximately minimal and gradated.

- **Comparison with expert test sets:** Finally, this paper compares the test coverage of these auto-generated concise test sets to that of expert-generated test sets, showing that the concise test sets provide greater test coverage.

2. BASE TEST SET

This section presents the first module of the FEAT toolchain: a generic, automated approach to generating an expansive set of test cases based on a simple yet powerful means of inductively defining the inputs of the function being tested. The resultant base test set B serves as the pool of candidate tests from which the two concise test sets are ultimately drawn (see Section 4). Further, this section presents a method for assigning a complexity heuristic to each test case. These heuristics enable the construction of gradated test sets, designed to give students actionable feedback (see Section 4.2).

FEAT employs a hybrid approach to base test set generation. A fully-exhaustive test set — *i.e.*, all valid combinations of arguments — is guaranteed to catch all incorrect programs, but generating such a test set is often impossible and nearly always computationally prohibitive. In contrast, generating a random test set is tractable, but has a high probability of missing edge cases. Thus, B is the union of two disjoint test sets: an exhaustive set covering a manageable subset of the input domain, and a random set providing partial coverage of the remaining portion of the domain.

2.1 Specifying the Domain for Test Cases

To generate the base test set, the user must specify four pieces of information in a config file: parameter types, argument domains for both exhaustive and random generation, and the desired number of random test cases.

Valid parameter types include all built-in Python types, such as lists, dictionaries, strings, and integers, nested arbitrarily deeply. Further, types may be classes, specified as composites of built-in types. Argument domains bound the values that FEAT will use as arguments for each parameter, and may be continuous or discrete.

FEAT also provides three optional means of further constraining the arguments, to facilitate testing functions with arbitrarily complex specifications. First, the config file language includes keywords, such as `sorted`, for constraining a single parameter. Second, dependencies may exist between parameters. The user can express such dependencies by defining and using variables; Section 2.4 presents an example of such a dependency.

Keywords and dependencies are lightweight, intuitive means of expressing constraints, but they do not always suffice. Thus, the user may provide a validation function with parameters identical to those of the function being tested. This function returns `True` if the arguments are valid, and `False` otherwise. FEAT uses this function to post-process its tentative base test set, discarding invalid cases.

Table 1: Base Test Set Results on Student Solutions

Prob. Index	Problem Module	Problem Function	Base Test Set Size Exhaustive	Base Test Set Size Random	Base Test Set Size Total	Num Student Solutions	Num Incorrect Solutions	Runtime (hours)
1	2048 Game	merge	781	219	1000	55523	39617	12:16
2	Graph Theory	compute_in_degrees	285	215	500	5145	1577	0:16
3	Graph Theory	in_degree_distribution	285	215	500	5109	2805	0:15
4	Graph Theory	make_complete_graph	30	20	50	5120	1094	4:27
5	DNA Alignment	build_scoring_matrix	864	136	1000	3374	1090	12:59
6	Yahtzee	expected_value	627	373	1000	65217	37733	14:52
7	Yahtzee	gen_all_holds	462	538	1000	57758	35597	51:15
8	Yahtzee	score	461	539	1000	65652	26336	4:45

2.2 Auto-Generating Test Cases

Base test set generation has two phases: exhaustive generation and random generation. Exhaustive generation operates as follows. First, for each individual parameter, FEAT recursively generates all possible arguments. During generation, FEAT maintains metadata for each argument: a set of values for each variable that are compatible with that argument. FEAT uses this metadata to prune the search tree when it encounters disjoint sets of compatible values for the same variable across nested layers of the argument.

Once FEAT has amassed a set of consistent arguments for each parameter, it takes the cross product of these sets to generate all possible test cases, again pruning the search upon incompatibility. Last, if a validation function was provided, it uses this function to filter the set of test cases.

Random generation is simpler. While the size of the random test set is less than the target, FEAT randomly selects a value for each variable. It then randomly selects each argument subject to these variable constraints. If the resultant test case is not yet in B, it is added to the random test set.

2.3 Assigning Test Case Complexity

After generating B, FEAT assigns a floating point complexity $C[t]$ to each individual test case t. Complexity is defined as $C[t] = \prod C[t_i]$, where $C[t_i]$ is the complexity of the ith argument and $C[t_i]$ is the product of the average complexity of each nested component. Component complexity is the length for sequences and value for primitives. By default, each component of each argument is incorporated into this heuristic. However, the user may optionally specify a subset of arguments and/or components to use.

As an example, consider the list [1, 2, 3]. The complexity of the list itself is its length (3.0), and the complexity of its contents is the average value (2.0), for a default complexity of 6.0. Imagine that the user declares the contents irrelevant; in this case, the complexity will be 3.0.

2.4 Configuration Example

In the dice game Yahtzee, a player rolls a set of dice and then holds some subset of the dice while re-rolling the remaining dice. Consider a function expected_value with three inputs — the dice held (a sorted tuple of integers), the number of sides on each die (an integer), and the number of dice to be re-rolled (an integer) — and computes the expected value after the roll. Naturally, the values of the held dice may not exceed the number of sides on the dice.

Figure 2 shows a sample config file for this function, with syntax slightly condensed for brevity. Parameter types are expressed under the [types] header using a combination of keywords (sorted) and Python types (tuple, int), with parentheses indicating nesting. For instance, sorted tuple

```
[types]        sorted tuple (int); int; int
[e domain]     0-3 (1-m); m; 1-3
[r domain]     2-8 (0-n); n; 0-3
[variables]    m 1-6; n 6-10
[complexity]   True (False); True; True
[num random]   545
```

Figure 2: Sample Config File

(int) denotes a tuple of integers sorted in ascending order.

Exhaustive and random domains ([e domain] and [r domain]) for each parameter are expressed as inclusive ranges, representing lengths for sequences and values for primitive types. For instance, the first exhaustive domain (0-3 (1-m)) stipulates that the tuple of held dice has a length on $[0, 3]$, where each element in the tuple is an integer on $[1, m]$.

Dependencies between parameters — in this example, the fact that values representing rolled dice may not exceed the number of sides — are captured using variables. Consider the exhaustive case. The domain for the number of sides is m, defined under the [variables] header as $[1, 6]$, and the upper bound on the values of the rolled dice is likewise m, ensuring that no die's value exceeds the number of sides.

Finally, the [complexity] header specifies which features of the input define its complexity. Here, True (False); True; True indicates that increasing the number of dice held, number of sides, and number of dice rolled increases the complexity of the test case, but changing the particular values of the held dice does not affect the complexity.

3. TESTING STUDENT SOLUTIONS

Once the base test set has been created, student solutions can be tested. Tests are first run on a reference solution to acquire the expected results, and then run on a corpus of student solutions, S, to ascertain correctness.

Recall that the goal of running the base test set on S is not merely to check these particular solutions. Rather, these solutions serve as a training set to identify high-quality test cases — those that trip up many erroneous solutions — and to derive the concise test sets (see Section 4). The concise test sets can then be used to efficiently test future solutions.

The tester maintains a mapping D of each solution, S_i, to the set of test cases that it failed on, B_i (i.e., $B_i = D[S_i]$). This data enables selection of a concise subset of B without sacrificing coverage of any known incorrect solutions.

FEAT was used to generate and run base test sets for eight problems from four different programming assignments. Table 1 shows the inputs ($|B|$, $|S|$) and outputs (number of incorrect solutions identified, runtime) of the tester.

The number of student solutions tested ranged from 3639–73156; between 20–78% of those solutions proved incorrect. The size of the base test set was typically configured to 500–1000 test cases, with one exception: `generate_complete_graph`, which takes as its input an integer and generates a complete graph with that many nodes. In this case, the simplicity of the parameter types led to diminishing returns as the size of B was increased.

Using such an extensive training set leads to strong coverage, but demands tradeoffs in time. Runtime varied greatly, influenced by $|B|$ and $|S|$; the minimum was 15 minutes, and the maximum was 51 hours. This non-trivial runtime motivates the use of a data-driven approach like FEAT, as performing semantic analysis on each training solution would likely prove computationally prohibitive. Further, Section 5 will show that $|S|$ can be reduced substantially while maintaining over 95% of the original coverage.

4. CONCISE TEST SETS

The base test set is designed to provide broad coverage, but is ill-suited for direct use in APA systems as its large size would slow the feedback cycle. This section describes two algorithms for extracting concise test sets from B. The first algorithm constructs an approximately minimal test set M with the property that every solution in S which fails on some element in B also fails on some element in M. The second algorithm generates a gradated test set G that is similar in size to M, but favors lower complexity.

4.1 Approximately Minimal Test Sets

As stated in Section 3, the tester computes a subset B_i of B for which the solution S_i disagrees with the reference solution. The goal of concise test set generation is to compute a subset M of B that contains at least one test case from each non-empty B_i. In other words, M has the property that $B_i \cap M \neq \emptyset$ over all B_i.

This problem corresponds to the classical hitting set problem, which is known to be NP-hard. Fortunately, there exists a simple greedy methods utilizing GRE heuristics [21] for computing a hitting set whose size is guaranteed to be within $\log(|B|)$ of the optimal size.

FEAT maintains a family F of the sets B_i that is dynamically updated as the algorithm proceeds. The GRE heuristic is *coverage*, where the coverage of a test case t with respect to F is defined as the number of sets in F that contain t. M is then constructed using a three-step iterative strategy:

1. Compute the test case t that has maximal coverage;
2. Add this test case t to M;
3. Remove those sets in F that contain t.

This process continues until F is empty. Since each entry in F corresponds to one student solution, this guarantees that M has the same coverage as B. The pseudo-code for this algorithm is as follows:

Algorithm 4.1: APPROXMINIMALTESTSET(D, B, S)

$M \leftarrow \emptyset$, $F \leftarrow \emptyset$
for each $S_i \in S$
  do $\begin{cases} B_i \leftarrow D[S_i] \\ F \leftarrow F \cup \{B_i\} \end{cases}$
while $F \neq \emptyset$
  do $\begin{cases} t \leftarrow \arg\max_{t \in B} |\{B_i \in F | t \in B_i\}| \\ M \leftarrow M \cup \{t\} \\ F \leftarrow F \setminus \{B_i \in F | t \in B_i\} \end{cases}$
return (M)

Table 2: Test Set Size Comparison

Function	Base Test Set	Concise Test Set	
		Minimal	Gradated
`merge`	1000	31	39
`compute_in_degrees`	500	4	5
`in_degree_distribution`	500	5	7
`make_complete_graph`	50	3	3
`build_scoring_matrix`	1000	2	3
`expected_value`	1000	12	19
`gen_all_holds`	1000	6	9
`score`	1000	9	14

4.2 Gradated Complexity Test Sets

Since Algorithm 4.1 repeatedly chooses test cases with maximal coverage, the resultant M is significantly smaller than B. However, it has one major drawback: the test cases in M tend to have high complexity, which is inconsistent with good testing practice. If used in an APA system, it may cause the system to report that a user failed a complex test case when a simpler example would be more valuable to the learning process.

One possible solution to this problem is to run the test cases in M in order of their complexity to ensure that a user solution fails on the simplest test in M first. However, this approach can fall victim to the situation where Algorithm 4.1 selects few simple tests.

A better solution is to balance the coverage of a test case versus its complexity when choosing a new test case. Algorithm 4.2 computes the gradated test set G by assigning a score to each test case: the ratio of its current coverage to the square of its complexity. In each iteration, Algorithm 4.2 selects the test case t with the highest score. Ties are broken by choosing the test case with lower complexity. After selecting t, the algorithm updates set family F by removing those test cases sets that have been covered by t. The pseudo-code below outlines the process:

Algorithm 4.2: GRADATEDTESTSET(D, B, S, C)

$G \leftarrow \emptyset$, $F \leftarrow \emptyset$
for each $S_i \in S$
  do $\begin{cases} B_i \leftarrow D[S_i] \\ F \leftarrow F \cup \{B_i\} \end{cases}$
while $F \neq \emptyset$
  do $\begin{cases} t \leftarrow \arg\max_{t \in B}(|\{B_i \in F | t \in B_i\}| / (C[t])^2) \\ G \leftarrow G \cup \{t\} \\ F \leftarrow F \setminus \{B_i \in F | t \in B_i\} \end{cases}$
return (G)

Table 2 shows the size of M and G for the same eight problems introduced in Section 3; in each case, both concise test sets are substantially smaller than the corresponding base test set. While each $|G|$ is greater than or equal to the corresponding $|M|$, the gradated test sets benefit from gradual growth in complexity. Figure 3 compares the complexities of the tests in M and G for the problem `expected_value`. M contains complex test cases with random ordering, shown as *M-Original* and sorted as *M-Sorted*. In contrast, G achieves the same coverage as M with notably less complexity.

The auto-generated gradated test sets were deployed in a programming MOOC. The APA system for that MOOC tests student' programs against sorted tests cases in G from

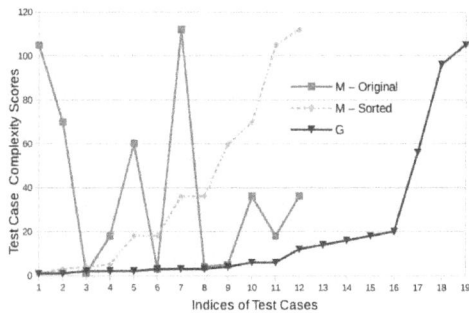

Figure 3: Comparison of test case complexities in two concise test sets for the problem `expected_value`

easy to complex. The system provides partial credit to erroneous programs based on which tests in G that they fail, rather than making a binary correct/incorrect judgment. Following the test-driven development principle [9], the system also returns the first — and therefore simplest — failed test case to the student, aiding the student in debugging their code. Students repeat this practice until they are satisfied with their scores, practicing their coding and debugging skills in the meanwhile.

5. METHOD SENSITIVITY ANALYSIS

Since FEAT selects test cases based on their results on the training set, the error detection ability of the resultant concise test sets on future programs is driven by the number and quality of programs in this training set. Too few or too similar programs can bias the test selection, leading to false positive verdicts on future submissions. On the other hand, a large training set will slow the testing phase, and may be difficult to come by. Thus, it is necessary to study the relationship between training set size and test set coverage in order to navigate these tradeoffs.

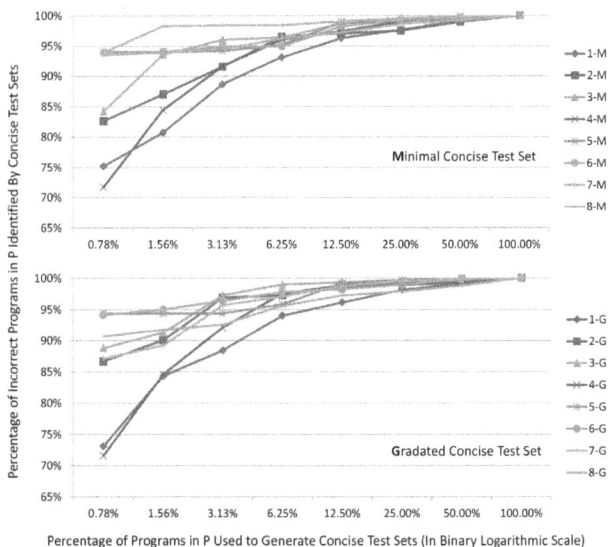

Figure 4: FEAT's coverage with respect to $|S|$

FEAT's sensitivity to training set size was evaluated on the same eight problems analyzed in Sections 3 and 4. For each problem, 1000 solutions were randomly selected to serve

as the test pool P. From this pool, the percentage of programs randomly selected to serve as the training set S was gradually increased from 0.78125% – 100%. The resultant concise test sets were then used to evaluate all programs in P. To account for the randomness in the selection of S, this process was repeated five times for each problem. Figure 4 shows the average coverage for each training set size.

Intuitively, the percentage of incorrect programs in P identified by FEAT's concise test sets increases with $|S|$. More surprisingly, for all eight problems, using a mere 12.5% of the programs in P achieved over 95% test coverage of P. In other words, the test coverage of the generated concise test sets does not increase linearly with respect to the number of training programs. Rather, it increases quickly when $|S|$ is small and then plateaus. This suggests that FEAT can generate concise test sets with good coverage even using a reasonably small number of training programs.

These results also shows that more challenging problems, such as `merge` (1-M, 1-G) — for which 71% of student solutions were identified as incorrect (see Table 1) — tend to require a larger training set in order achieve high coverage, as there is a wider variety of ways in which students may err. As shown in Figure 4, the coverage of `merge` increases more gradually than that of easier problems. Yet, coverage still increases nonlinearly and eventually reaches a plateau.

6. COMPARISON WITH EXPERT TESTS

The gradated concise test sets computed by Algorithm 4.2 were deployed in the second session of the authors' programming MOOC. Student response was positive, with no reports of incorrect solutions passing the machine grader's tests. Additionally, this section presents a more methodological analysis of the coverage of the concise test sets versus the instructor-created test sets used in the first session of the MOOC. All student solutions for the eight problems studied in previous sections were analyzed.

Table 3 reports the results of comparing the coverage of the expert test sets and the auto-generated concise test sets. Recall that both M and G have the same coverage as their common base test set B. Thus, the "C" in the headings of this table simultaneously represents the results from B, M, and G. The four columns in the table indicate, respectively, the number of student solutions that pass both test sets, fail both test sets, pass the expert and fail the concise, and fail the expert and pass the concise.

Most importantly, note that the entries in Column 4 are very small — often zero — compared to those of the other columns. This reflects the fact that the concise test set caught almost all of the errors that the expert test caught. The expert test set occasionally caught a few incorrect solutions that were not identified by the concise test sets; however, this was rare, as this situation only occurs when a solution does not fail *any* of the tests in the base set. In this situation, the expert test set usually included tests that exploited problem knowledge that was not encoded in the configuration file provided to FEAT.

Another important observation is that, for many problems, the values in column three were large in comparison to column two. This indicates that the expert test set failed to detect a non-trivial fraction of the programs marked incorrect by the concise test set. For example, the expert test set for `score` allowed almost two-thirds of the solutions marked incorrect by the concise test set to pass. This indicates that the expert test set had substantial deficiencies, correlating with the student complaints from the first session.

Table 3: Test Result Comparison

Function	✓ E * ✓ C	× E × C	✓ E × C	× E ✓ C
merge	15860	37776	1838	25
compute_in_degrees	3562	1555	21	6
in_degree_distribution	2301	2742	61	3
make_complete_graph	4025	865	229	0
build_scoring_matrix	2283	1030	60	0
expected_value	27256	34573	2923	3
gen_all_holds	11424	31576	669	0
score	39316	9320	17016	0

* Note: ✓ E means "correct on expert test set" and × C means "incorrect on concise test set" and so on so forth

7. CONCLUSION AND FUTURE WORK

This paper introduced a data-driven approach to generating high-quality concise test sets for feedback and assessment in programming courses, as well as an implementation of this method in the FEAT toolchain. FEAT incorporates concise test set generation algorithms for producing near minimal test sets and slightly larger gradated test sets with simpler cases. The gradated test sets are designed to be student-friendly for feedback and evaluation. With simpler tests, the students can more easily understand and debug problems with their programs. Both algorithms take advantage of a diverse pool of student solutions, resulting in superior coverage as compared to expert-generated tests.

For the problems studied, 1.3–64.6% of the known incorrect programs were identified as incorrect by the auto-generated test sets, but erroneously deemed correct by the expert test set. Moreover, only 0–0.4% of the known incorrect programs were identified as incorrect by the expert test set, but erroneously deemed correct by the generated test sets. This highlights the advantages of utilizing student submissions to generate tests.

FEAT exploits a relatively large base test set in order to find incorrect programs. The fact that a few programs were identified as incorrect by the expert tests but not the auto-generated concise tests means that students made errors that were not exercised by any tests in the base test set. To increase coverage, the base test set could be expanded, either by adding more random test cases or by more targeted selection of additional test cases. One method to identify valuable additional test cases would be to incorporate semantic analysis of the reference solution or student solutions. The challenge would be to optimize the analysis so that it is feasible to apply to a large collection of solutions.

Another interesting question for future study is the relationship between the problem specification and the size of the resulting concise test set. For some problems, only a small number of tests were needed; for others, the size of the size of the concise test set was larger, indicating that there were more ways for a student to err. Quantifying this relationship may shed some light on the "difficulty" of various programming problems.

8. ACKNOWLEDGEMENTS

This material is based upon work supported by NSF Award CCF-1320860: "Computer-Aided Grading, Feedback, and Assignment Creation in Massive Online Programming Courses" as well as an NSF Graduate Research Fellowship under Grant No. 1450681.

9. REFERENCES

[1] Google Code Jam. https://code.google.com/codejam.
[2] LeetCode. https://leetcode.com/.
[3] PC^2. http://www.ecs.csus.edu/pc2/.
[4] Project Euler. https://projecteuler.net/.
[5] Rosalind. http://rosalind.info/problems/.
[6] TopCoder. https://www.topcoder.com/.
[7] UVa. https://uva.onlinejudge.org/.
[8] A. Arcuri, M. Z. Iqbal, and L. Briand. Random testing: Theoretical results and practical implications. *Software Engineering, IEEE Transactions on*, 38(2):258–277, 2012.
[9] K. Beck. *Test-driven development: by example*. Addison-Wesley Professional, 2003.
[10] A. Belinfante, L. Frantzen, and C. Schallhart. 14 tools for test case generation. In *Model-Based Testing of Reactive Systems*, pages 391–438. Springer, 2005.
[11] T. Y. Chen and M. F. Lau. A new heuristic for test suite reduction. *Information and Software Technology*, 40(5):347–354, 1998.
[12] G. Fraser and A. Zeller. Mutation-driven generation of unit tests and oracles. *Software Engineering, IEEE Transactions on*, 38(2):278–292, 2012.
[13] A. Kittur. Crowdsourcing, collaboration and creativity. *ACM Crossroads*, 17(2):22–26, 2010.
[14] R. Kumar, S. Singh, and G. Gopal. Automatic test case generation using genetic algorithm. *International Journal of Scientific & Engineering Research (IJSER)*, 4(6):1135–1141, 2013.
[15] P. McMinn. Search-based software test data generation: a survey. *Software testing, Verification and reliability*, 14(2):105–156, 2004.
[16] S. M. Mohi-Aldeen, S. Deris, and R. Mohamad. Systematic mapping study in automatic test case generation. 2014.
[17] K. Muthyala and R. Naidu. A novel approach to test suite reduction using data mining. *Indian Journal of Computer Science and Engineering*, 2(3):500–505, 2011.
[18] S. Srikant and V. Aggarwal. A system to grade computer programming skills using machine learning. In *Proceedings of the 20th ACM SIGKDD international conference on Knowledge discovery and data mining*, pages 1887–1896. ACM, 2014.
[19] T. Tang, S. Rixner, and J. Warren. An environment for learning interactive programming. In *Proceedings of the 45th ACM technical symposium on Computer science education*, pages 671–676. ACM, 2014.
[20] L. Wu, B. Liu, Y. Jin, and X. Xie. Using back-propagation neural networks for functional software testing. In *Anti-counterfeiting, Security and Identification, 2008. ASID 2008. 2nd International Conference on*, pages 272–275. IEEE, 2008.
[21] S. Yoo and M. Harman. Regression testing minimization, selection and prioritization: a survey. *Software Testing, Verification and Reliability*, 22(2):67–120, 2012.
[22] Z. Zhang and Y. Zhou. A fuzzy logic based approach for software testing. *International journal of pattern recognition and artificial intelligence*, 21(04):709–722, 2007.

Integrating the Learning Objectives and Syllabus into a Domain Ontology for Data structures Course

Rekha Ramesh
IDP in Educational Technology
Indian Institute of Technology
Bombay
Mumbai, India
rekha.ramesh@iitb.ac.in

Sasikumar M.
CDAC Bombay,
Mumbai, India
the.little.sasi@gmail.com

Sridhar Iyer
Department of CSE,
Indian Institute of Technology
Bombay,
Mumbai, India
sri@iitb.ac.in

ABSTRACT

The design of an assessment instrument (AI) is one of the major components of assessment process. The teachers have to generate AI aligned with the course learning objectives (LOs) within the boundary of topics defined by the syllabus of that course. When the instrument covers the LO fairly, it covers the subject matter defined by the syllabus fairly. This paper discusses an approach towards integrating both the contents and cognitive level defined in the LOs into the domain ontology for a Data structures course. This forms the first step towards building an automated system to measure the alignment of AI to course LOs. In the proposed approach, the notion of domain ontology is introduced on which the LOs are overlaid. Concepts and cognitive levels from LOs are extracted using Natural Language Processing. Mapping these to the nodes of the ontology also involves complex processes to take decisions about selection of nodes and traversal of links. For each of these, issues and challenges are discussed in detail and a solution is proposed. We have done a prototype implementation of the system to test our design. The effectiveness of this framework was tested by comparing the manually generated results by the experienced teachers to the system generated results and obtained an average accuracy of 90%. The examples are taken from Data Structures course of second year engineering curriculum.

Keywords

Learning objectives; Syllabus; Domain ontology; Data structures; Assessment Instrument; Alignment; Ontology based knowledge Representation.

1. INTRODUCTION

Assessing students' performance means collecting students' information to measure the degree to which the student has achieved the learning objectives [8]. One of the most important stages of assessment process is the design of an assessment instrument (AI) . Most of the universities do not provide any guidelines for creating an AI. The freedom lies with the

ITiCSE '16, July 09-13, 2016, Arequipa, Peru
© 2016 ACM. ISBN 978-1-4503-4231-5/16/07...$15.00
DOI: http://dx.doi.org/10.1145/2899415.2899453

individual teacher given the syllabus and a set of LOs for the portion selected for the assessment. Although the general notion of quality is fairly well understood by teachers, formal mechanism for it is lacking. Hence the quality of the instrument is subjective to the individual teacher's experience and expertise.

To ensure the quality, the very first thing to check is whether the instrument is valid i.e. is it measuring what it is supposed to measure. What is to be measured is provided by the LOs of a course. LOs are clear statements that describe the competences that students should possess upon completion of a course. The AI should measure these competencies [1] [5]. So, the items in an AI should be properly aligned with the LOs. Today, teachers have to spend a lot of time and effort in manually ensuring this alignment. This brings forth the need for an automated system to measure the alignment of an AI of a course to the set of LOs of that course.

In order to build such a system, we need to capture the relevant knowledge from syllabus and LOs and map it into a knowledge representation which is in a machine parsable form. Ontology is one such mechanism. Ontology can be used to represent the domain knowledge and can capture the hierarchical structure among various concepts and also dependencies and relationships among them in a machine parsable way [7]. So, ontology is used to represent data structures domain in our system. The syllabus can be viewed as specifying a subset of this domain ontology as it contains list of concepts to be taught in a course. LOs are framed using natural language sentences. Every LO incorporates a set of topics/concepts and the level of competency expected to be achieved by students in those concepts. Cognitive levels defined using Bloom's taxonomy is used to represent competency [5]. Cognitive levels associated with LOs further indicate at what level these concepts should be taught and assessed. But these are not explicitly provided in the LOs. For example, in LO *"Students should be able to demonstrate and implement various operations on data structures"*, what are the concepts covered by this LO, which are nodes to be mapped in ontology and what is the cognitive level is not directly available. There are many issues and challenges that need to be addressed to extract this information.

This paper does a detailed analysis of all the issues and challenges in extracting the information embedded in the LOs and proposes a solution for this. An approach towards integrating both the contents and cognitive level defined in the LOs into a LO annotated ontology (LAO) is also discussed. When the knowledge from items in AI are also extracted and annotated into such an ontology, it can form as a representation mechanism for building an automated system to measure the alignment of AI to course LOs, to find how much part of the syllabus is covered by the AI [10], to check whether the items in AI are fairly distributed among the LOs as per their weightages assigned in the syllabus. Further, LAO can be used to check the adequacy of the LOs, for example, to find if there are any concepts in syllabus that is not addressed by any of the LOs. Such an ontology based knowledge representation mechanism can also be extended to guide and validate the constructive alignment between the content of instructional design and assessment instrument.

To capture the result of the mapping in LAO, color coding is introduced. This helps in effective visual representation of the LAO. The Data Structures course of second year engineering curriculum is chosen as the domain and all examples are taken from that. Data structures is considered to be one of the most important courses in computer science as it equips the students with fundamental building blocks for the development and design of complex systems. A prototype implementation of the system was done to test the design process. The effectiveness of this framework was tested by comparing the manually generated results by the experienced teachers to the system generated results and the findings are encouraging.

Section 2 discusses the related literature for our work in this area. The design approach is explained in section 3. The structure of domain ontology is described in section 4. The working of LO Annotator is explain in detail in section 5. Results of testing of the prototype implementation are given in section 5. Section 6 consists of discussion, conclusions and future scope of our work.

2. RELATED WORK

The literature survey was carried out in the area of alignment of assessment to LOs of the course and use of ontology for representing domain knowledge. LOs are clear statements that describe the competences that students should possess upon completion of a course [5] [9]. Effective LOs state what students should know and be able to demonstrate, as well as the depth of learning that is expected. LOs are usually framed in terms of (a) some subject matter content and (b) a description of what is to be done with that content [5]. As the learning objectives can span across all the cognitive levels, the assessment also should consist of questions of varying cognitive levels to achieve intended outcomes [8].

There are many research works that have reported the use of ontologies for representing the curriculum as well as syllabus contents. A case study to develop a tool for curriculum visualization using ontology was presented in [11] and concluded that ontologies are a good possibility to represent the structure and the dependencies between courses clearly and allow one to share, exchange, reuse, analyze and extend curricula. Chi Y. reports a study where an ontological mechanism is utilized in terms of a knowledge intensive approach to create general course sequence for planning the learning based on multiple textbooks [2]. The design of the integrated learning ontology conceptualizing multilevel knowledge structures, such as curriculum, syllabus, learning subject, and materials was proposed in [3][4]. A chapter by Fok and Ip in the book [4] addresses the issues and methodologies in the design and construction of education ontologies that can help in organizing, retrieving and recommending educational resources for personalized learning.

There is already a considerable research dealing with the application of ontology technology to education field. They are classified into curriculum or syllabus ontology creation, ontology-based learning object organization, and ontology-based learning content retrieval [7].

Even though the researchers have stressed the importance and benefits of aligning the AI to course LOs, to the best of our knowledge, none of them have reported attempts to formulate and automate this task. This motivated us to build such a system and as a first step towards it, integrate the course LOs and syllabus content into ontology based knowledge representation.

3. THE DESIGN OF OUR PROPOSED APPROACH

The problem we are focusing is on integrating both the contents and cognitive level specified in the LOs into the domain ontology to create LO annotated ontology (LAO). The proposed approach attempt towards achieving this and the overall process is shown in Figure 1. The main component of the system is the LO annotator which takes domain ontology, syllabus and LOs as input and outputs LAO.

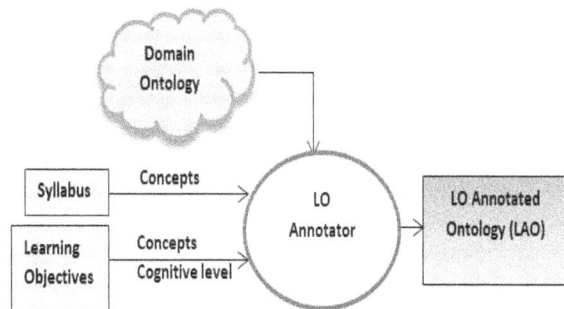

Figure 1. The overall process of generating LAO

The domain ontology contains all the concepts related to a particular domain and relationship between them. It forms the semantically connected network of concepts and also captures the hierarchical structure and also dependencies and relationships among them [9]. For example, for the domain of Data Structures, it will contain concepts relating to data structures including various known data structures, their representation and applications and operations on them [12]. Every university can have their own syllabus and LOs. The syllabus is viewed as a subset of domain ontology. Similarly, concepts and cognitive level information from LOs are mapped to the nodes of domain ontology. This information can be indicated in domain ontology using some color coding. This is called LAO. The annotator assumes that in initial ontology all the nodes are colored as white. When the syllabus is mapped to it, the matching nodes will be colored as black and when LOs are loaded, the matching nodes will be partially colored as red. Different cognitive levels will be indicated by varying shades of red. The shade/intensity of the red color is dependent on the cognitive level of LO involving those concepts. Higher the level, darker is the shade of the color.

Issues and challenges: In order to create LAO, there is a need to specify the structure of domain ontology, syllabus and LOs. Syllabus is considered as set of keywords which have a corresponding match to nodes of ontology. Similarly, LO statements contain concepts and cognitive levels which can also be mapped to the corresponding nodes of the domain ontology. LOs are mostly adopted from ACM computer science curriculum and later customized to suit the corresponding syllabus. Table 1 shows representative set of LOs for a data structures course. One of the major tasks is how these concepts and cognitive level can be identified from textual representation of LOs.

Table1. Representative LOs for data structure course

Students should be able to-------	
LO1	Model a given Data Structure as ADT
LO2	Describe how various data structures are represented in memory
LO3	Write programs that use data structures such as: arrays, linked lists, stacks, queues, trees, hash tables, and graphs.
LO4	Demonstrate and implement different methods for traversing trees.
LO5	Understand the working of multi-way search tree structures
LO6	Implement the Huffman coding algorithm using binary tree
LO7	Implement hash tables, including collision avoidance and resolution techniques
LO8	Implement various searching and sorting algorithms
LO9	Analyze a given problem and select the appropriate data structures required to solve the problem.
LO10	Demonstrate and implement various operations on data structures

Following are some of the issues and challenges that are identified in extracting concepts and cognitive level from LOs and mapping to the nodes of the ontology.

1. The concepts can be single or multiple worded. For example, in LO6, the concepts **Huffman coding algorithm** and **binary tree** are multi worded concept. So, how to identify a multi worded concept from an LO?

2. Teachers can frame the LOs in many ways. Hence, concepts from the LOs may not exactly match with the node names in the ontology. For example, in LO4, the concepts **methods of traversing trees** will not directly map with the node name **tree traversal operation** in the ontology. So, how to identify the concepts from LOs that are differently worded but synonyms of the node names in the ontology?

3. The concept that is identified may not be enough as it may be a higher level concept in the ontology tree. And the item in the AI may be from the sub tree under that. So, how to determine the alignment between the two is a major issue. For example, in LO8, does this means all the searching algorithms and sorting algorithms which forms the sub tree below these nodes also need to be mapped? Suppose there is a following item in the AI.
Que: Implement merge sort for a given set of numbers.

Is this item aligned with the above LO? So, apart from the concepts identified from LO which are other related nodes to be mapped in the ontology?

4. Sometimes we need to identify the relation names from LOs that correspond to links in ontology. These links is then traversed to find the associated nodes to the identified concepts that are to be mapped to node names in ontology. For example, consider an
LO: Students should be able to explain various operations on stack.
Here, **stack** is the only concept that is explicitly identified from LO. There are other implicit concepts to be mapped to ontology that are connected through **hasOperation** link. So how to identify relevant links from LO?

5. How to identify the cognitive level of LOs?

6. As the LOs are framed in natural language (English), there are some specific NLP related issues because of the inherent ambiguity present in the language. To solve this, extensive NLP techniques are required. How to handle such ambiguities? This is beyond the scope of the currently proposed system.

Following subsections explains the process of specifying the domain ontology, parsing the LOs to identify relevant concepts and cognitive level, mapping to nodes of ontology and traversing the links of ontology to mark related concepts.

4. STRUCTURE OF DOMAIN ONTOLOGY

The domain ontology captures a hierarchical structure of the domain. Figure 2 shows part of domain ontology.

The concepts in the domain are finalized by compiling the contents of various standard textbooks and also the data structures course contents of many different universities as well as consulting the opinion of expert teachers. Every node in the ontology represents a concept/topic from the domain. The root node of the ontology tree is the name of the domain itself i.e. Data Structures. All the major topics form the level 1 nodes in the ontology. The major topics can be further narrowed down to subtopics that form the subclasses in the ontology. The relationships include but are not restricted to hierarchy of

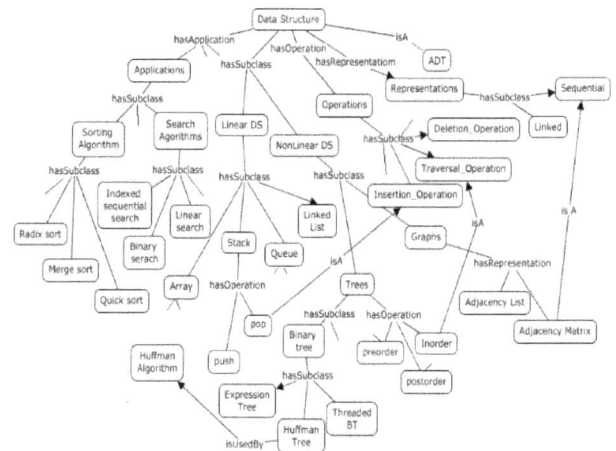

Figure 2. Part of Domain Ontology

concepts. The dependencies/ relationships between the concepts are shown using links.

In our ontology we are using following links.

- 'hasSubClass'--- indicates one concept is a subclass of another concepts
  – E.g. Queue is a *subClass* of Linear Data Structure.
- "hasRepresentation"--- indicate that every data structure has some type of representation either sequential or Linked or both.
  – E.g. Graph *hasRepresentation* 'Adjacency List' which is a *subClass* of Linked Representation
- "hasOperation"- indicate that every data structure has some operation defined on them such as insert, delete, search, etc.
  – E.g. Stack *hasOperation* Push.
- "hasApplication"--- indicate that every data structure has some applications in real world
  – E.g. Binary tree *hasApplication* in Heap sort.
- "isA"--- One concept is a type of another concept.
  – E.g. Every Data Structure *isA* ADT

The links are used to traverse the ontology to locate the neighborhood nodes which are relevant in the ontology. The type of links decides what nodes are to be included for mapping. For example, in LO10, annotator will include all the nodes that indicate various *data structures* as well as all the nodes that are connected by *hasOperation* link from every data structure.

Some links can be considered as connecting a node to a set of properties. All it subclasses can inherit the properties of its superclasses and can also override them by providing their own definitions of them. For example, various operations (*Insertion, deletion, display, traversal, and search*) can be considered as properties of *Data Structures* connected by *hasOperation* link. All the subclasses of it such as *stack*, queue, etc. can inherit those properties. Stack overrides insertion and deletion operation by providing its own definition of *push* and *pop* operation. Figure 3 depicts this scenario.

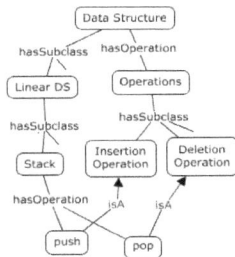

Figure 3. Property Overriding

The links can also have inverses. For example, in the statement "Heap sort uses binary tree" The *uses* link is an inverse link of *hasApplication*.

Figure 4.Inverse Links

There are many tools available for ontology development. Protégé is the most popularly used open source tool which can be considered as one of the options for developing Domain ontology.

5. LO ANNOTATOR

The annotator takes the input from the syllabus and LOs and annotates the domain ontology as described above. Syllabus is considered as set of keywords which have a corresponding match to nodes of ontology. The contents included in syllabus will be shaded in black in domain ontology which is shown in Figure 5.

Every course consists of a set of predefined LOs (l_1, l_2, l_3,.., l_n) covering the entire syllabus. Every LO contains 2 attributes: a set of topics/concepts (c_1, c_2, ..., c_l) from the syllabus addressed by that LO and cognitive level defined by Bloom's Taxonomy [5]. The key design element is how to automatically extract relevant information (concepts and cognitive level) from the LO text. The LO is first preprocessed using simple NLP techniques such as tokenization, lemmatization and POS Tagging. Basically, each LO text can be first parsed to separate into a set of words or tokens. All the punctuation marks are removed and the sentence is converted into lowercase. Then it is lemmatized to get the basic form of the word. Finally passes through a POS Tagger to get POS tagged words.

5.1 Extracting Concepts from LOs

Set of words or tokens from each LO is matched with the node names from the ontology. If the match is found the corresponding nodes are marked in the domain ontology. But the matching process is not direct. There are many issues and challenges that

need to be addressed as discussed earlier. This section attempts to provide solution to each of them.

1. To extract multiple worded concept N grams algorithm can be used. It can find N-grams (sequences of 1 to N words) from LO which is exactly matching with the node names in the ontology.
    For example, in LO6, *Huffman coding algorithm* and *binary tree* can be found using N =3 and N=2.

2. To identify the concepts from LOs that are differently worded but are synonyms of the node names in the ontology, every node in the ontology can be annotated with a set of synonyms. This can solve the problem to some extent. Synonyms form possible alternative names that the examiner may use in place of node names in the ontology while framing the LOs. For example, in LO4, the concept *methods of traversing trees* will be an annotation to the node *traversal operations* in the ontology.

3. To locate other related nodes to be mapped in the ontology apart from the concepts identified from LO, we have to explore neighborhood relations. For example, in LO8, the concepts *searching* and *sorting algorithms* is an umbrella term used for all the searching and sorting techniques mentioned in the syllabus and which forms the nodes in the subtree below them in the domain ontology. Such nodes can be reached by traversing a *hasSubclass* relation from the explicitly found nodes. So, in this case, in addition to the explicitly found nodes *searching algorithm* and *sorting algorithms*, we need to also map and color other related nodes in the ontology such as *Linear search, binary search, index sequential search, Hash search, Shell Sort, Radix sort, Insertion Sort, Quick Sort, Merge Sort, Heap Sort*.
    In such cases, the following decisions need to be taken by the system as it processes each LO i) Is there a need to find the related nodes? ii) What links to traverse in the ontology? iii) What depth it should be traversed? One of the ways to address the first issue can be to find hints from the LO text itself. After analyzing many such LOs, we found that there are some words typically associated with these LOs such as various, different, any, all, plural form of a concept etc. If these words are found in LO, they indicate that the associated concepts act like slot variables. Then annotator can find all the valid concepts that can be substituted for these slot variables. In the above example LO, the associated concepts to the word 'various' (**searching algorithms** and **sorting algorithms)** will act like slot variables and all the searching and sorting algorithms will form valid concepts that can be substituted for them. Mostly, it suffices to traverse the **hasSubClass** links in the ontology from these variables until you reach leaf nodes in that subtree.

4. In order to identify the relation names from LOs that correspond to links in ontology, the link names are annotated with associated synonyms. Tokens from LO are matched with the link names and its synonyms. If there is a match all the nodes connected to the identifying concept are considered for mapping by traversing the link. For example, in LO, "*Students should be able to explain various operations on stack.*", *hasOperation* link is traversed from *stack* and the nodes *push* and *pop* are included for mapping. If the concept from LO do not have the identified link connected to it, then each of the super classes can be traversed to see whether they have the link. If they have, then all the nodes connected to that link are considered for mapping by traversing that link.

5.2 Extracting Cognitive Levels from LOs

Revised Bloom's taxonomy forms the basis for cognitive level identification of an LO. Every level of Blooms taxonomy namely,

Recall, Understand, Apply, Analyze, Evaluate and Create is associated with an exhaustive set of keywords [5]. These keywords provide the guidelines that can be used to determine the cognitive level of LO. To determine the cognitive level information from LOs, we have stored these keywords into a dictionary. Apart from the list of keywords provided by Bloom's, we have added some domain specific keywords or phrases into the dictionary. The verbs from LOs identified using POS tagger are matched to the keywords in the dictionary and accordingly its cognitive level is identified. For example, in LO6, LO7 and LO8, 'Implement' is a keyword associated with Blooms level Apply. So the cognitive level of LO is identified as 'Apply'. Similarly the cognitive level of LO4 and LO5 is 'Understand' as they contain keywords 'explain' and 'demonstrate.

If two tokens match with the keywords of two or more different Bloom's level, then the higher level one is chosen as cognitive level of the complete question. For example, in LO4, the keyword '*Demonstrate*' is at Understand level and '*Implement*' is at Apply level. So the cognitive level of the LO4 is identified as Apply.

Table 2 summarizes the issues identified in section 3 and the proposed solutions in section 5.

5.3 Generating LO Annotated Ontology
The annotator identifies the relevant concepts and the cognitive level associated with them from each of the LOs as described in sections A and B. These concepts can then be then mapped to the nodes of the domain ontology and color coded to generate LAO. Figure 5 shows how the LAO will look after coloring all the relevant nodes. The nodes with black and red shades will indicate that the concept is within syllabus and is also addressed by an LO. And the nodes with white and red shades indicate that the concept is outside the scope of syllabus and is addressed by an LO. Nodes with only white color say that concept is in domain but not included in syllabus. Nodes with only black color say that concept is included in syllabus but there are no LOs addressing those concepts. Such information can be used subsequently when measuring alignment.

6. TESTING
A prototype implementation was done to validate the design process. The testing was primarily done to check whether the annotator is annotating correctly by giving the right color and right shade of color to the nodes. What is the right color was

Table 2. Issues identified to create LAO and corresponding proposed solution

Challenges and Issues	Proposed Solution
Identification of Multi worded concepts	N-Grams algorithm
Identification of differently worded concepts	Associating synonyms with the nodes in ontology
Finding other related nodes to be mapped in the ontology other than the identified concepts.	Introducing the concept of slot variable to decide whether to traverse the sublass hierarchy and include all the nodes in that.
Identification of differently worded links from LO	Links in ontology are associated with synonyms
Finding the nodes connected by links if the concept from LO do not have the identified link connected to it	Traverse the superclass hierarchy of concepts to find the connected link
Identification of cognitive level of LO	Matching of tokens or words in LO with keywords associated with Blooms level. If the LO has multiple concepts matching with keywords associated with different levels then it is resolved by considering the highest level among them.

decided by giving the domain ontology, syllabus and LOs to the three expert teachers who were manually told to create LAO. The teachers who have teaching experience of more than 5 years and have thorough domain knowledge were considered as expert teachers. The teacher generated LAOs were compared with the system generated LAO in terms of both concepts and cognitive levels. A confusion matrix was generated which classifies total number of concepts from all LOs into 4 classes: (a) number of concepts in which both the teacher and system have agreed that the concepts are covered by an LO. (b) number of concepts in which both the teacher and system have disagreed that the concepts are covered by an LO. So both did not color the nodes (c) the number of concepts in which only the system has agreed to color but teacher did not color and (d) the number of concepts in which only teacher has agreed to color but system did not color. The generated confusion matrix is shown in Table 3.

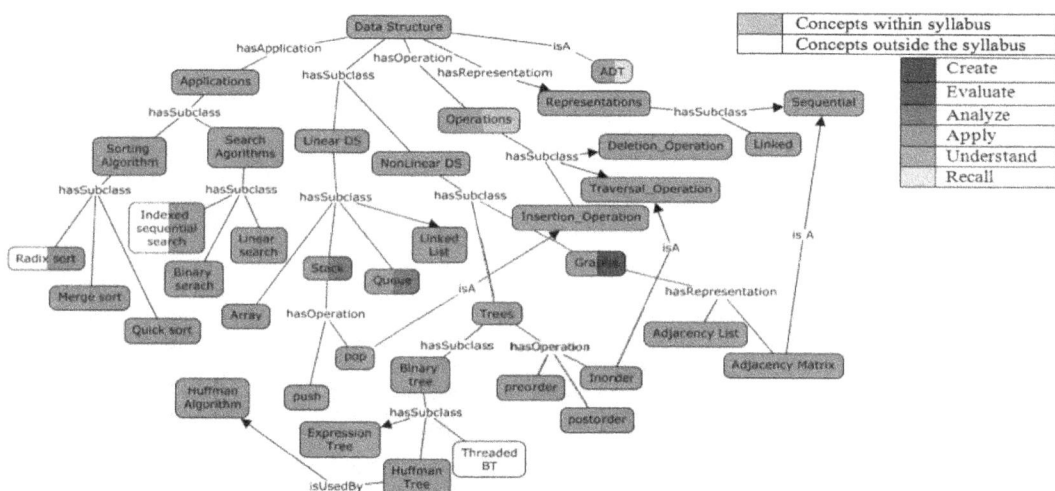

Figure 5. The Domain ontology with the example LOs mapped

There are total 88 concepts/nodes in the domain ontology.

Table 3. Confusion Matrix

	Both agree (a)	Both disagree (b)	Only system agree (c)	Only teacher agree (d)	% match (a+b)/ (a+b+c+d)
T1	70	8	6	4	88.6%
T2	76	5	3	4	92.04 %
T3	75	5	3	5	90.9%

From the table it can be seen that the teachers' notion of concepts covered by an LO and system extracted concept is matching with an average of 90%. It can be seen that there is no much variation among the teachers' agreement and disagreement. Each LO was further analyzed to determine which ones have contributed to False Positives (c) False Negatives (d) and what are the characteristics of such LOs. Sometimes the problem may be because of the framing the LOs in a particular way.

But as the LOs are framed in natural language (English), there are some specific issues that the algorithm cannot handle because of the inherent ambiguity present in the language. For example, in LO 7, the system will identify only two concepts **Hash search** and **Collision handling**. The word collision is actually connected to both handling and resolution because of the 'and' connective. The system is not able to find this.

Similarly, if there are multiple concepts after the slot indicator, then it gets associated to the nearest one as per our solution. But it may not be true always. For example, in LO 4, the algorithm identifies *'different'* as the slot indicator and *tree* and *traversal operations* as concepts. So the nearest one is *tree* and slot indicator gets associated to it. So *tree* gets expanded to all its subclass hierarchy. But, actually the LO is intending different **traversal methods** such as **inorder, preorder and postorder**. Such problems can be solved by using smarter NLP techniques which will require understanding the structure of the sentence itself. Currently, this is handled by manually modifying such LOs.

The teachers were in agreement with system for cognitive level also in most of the cases. The slight mismatch in cognitive level may be because of the inherent ambiguity at adjacent levels in Bloom's taxonomy. Further analysis can be done to find the degree of mismatch i.e. in how many levels of difference is there between the teacher and system generated results and accordingly weightages can be given.

7. CONCLUSION AND FUTURE WORK

The problem being focused is integrating both the contents and cognitive level defined in the LOs into ontology based knowledge representation. This can form a first step towards building an automated system to measure the alignment of AI to course LOs. This paper brings forth the need of such a system and proposes an approach to implementing such a system. In this paper only the part up to capturing the syllabus and LOs is discussed. Our proposed approach explains the process of extracting concepts and cognitive level from an LO using NLP techniques and the complex process of mapping these to the nodes of the ontology. For each of these, issues and challenges are discussed in detail and a solution is proposed.

We have built a prototype implementation of the system. The effectiveness of this framework was tested by comparing the manually generated results by three experienced teachers to the system generated results and was found to be satisfactory with an average accuracy of 90%. Motivated by the encouraging results, the real implementation of the system is in progress.

Some of the challenges are variability in which different teachers write LOs. So, we need to look at standardizing them. Adequately rich domain ontology is difficult to get. So, it needs to be created for different subjects. The concepts required for ontology can be finalized by referring to most of the standard text and reference books of Data Structures course offered by various universities across the globe. We are in the process of developing the complete system for measuring the alignment of AI to course LOs and thereby measuring the quality of AI.

8. REFERENCES

[1] Biggs, J. 2003. Aligning teaching and assessing to course objectives. In Proceedings of Conference on *Teaching and Learning in Higher Education: New Trends and Innovations*. 13-17.

[2] Chi, Y. 2010. Developing curriculum sequencing for managing multiple texts in e-learning system. In *Proceedings of International Conference on Engineering Education*.

[3] Chung, H. and Kim, J., An Ontological Approach for Semantic Modeling of Curriculum and Syllabus in Higher Education.

[4] Fok, A.W.P. and Ip, H.H.S., 2007. Educational ontologies construction for personalized learning on the web. In *Evolution of teaching and learning paradigms in intelligent environment*. 47-82. Springer Berlin Heidelberg.

[5] Krathwohl, D.R. 2002. A revision of Bloom's taxonomy: An overview. *Theory into practice*, *41*(4), 212-218.

[6] Kriglstein, S. and Motschnig-Pitrik, R., 2011, June. The Curriculum as an Ontology-A Human Centered Visualization Approach. In *World Conference on Educational Media and Technology* Vol. 2011, No. 1, 1343-1352.

[7] Mizoguchi, R. and Bourdeau, J., 2000. Using ontological engineering to overcome common AI-ED problems. *Journal of Artificial Intelligence and Education*, *11*, 107-121.

[8] Nitko, A.J. 2001. *Educational assessment of students*. Prentice-Hall. Inc. Des Moines. IA.

[9] Noy, N.F. 2001. Ontology Development 101: A Guide to Creating Your First Ontology: Knowldege Systems Laboratory, Stanford University. *Stanford Knowledge Systems Laboratory Technical Report KSL-01-05 and Stanford Medical Informatics Technical Report SMI-2001-0880.*

[10] Rekha, R., Angadi, A., Pathak, A., Kapur, A., Gosar, H., Ramanathan, M., Thatte, V. and Sasikumar, M. 2012, January. Ontology driven framework for assessing the syllabus fairness of a question paper. *International Conference in Technology Enhanced Education (ICTEE)*, *(January 2012)*, 1-5.

[11] Ronchetti, M. and Sant, J., 2007. Curriculum Management and Review: an ontology-based solution.

[12] Sahami, M., Roach, S., Cuadros-Vargas, E. and Reed, D. 2012. February. Computer science curriculum 2013: reviewing the strawman report from the ACM/IEEE-CS task force. In *Proceedings of the 43rd ACM technical symposium on Computer Science Education*, 3-4.

Students' Semantic Mistakes in Writing Seven Different Types of SQL Queries

Alireza Ahadi, Julia Prior, Vahid Behbood and Raymond Lister

University of Technology, Sydney, Australia

{Alireza.Ahadi, Julia.Prior, Vahid.Behbood, Raymond.Lister}@uts.edu.au

ABSTRACT

Computer science researchers have studied extensively the mistakes of novice programmers. In comparison, little attention has been given to studying the mistakes of people who are novices at writing database queries. This paper represents the first large scale analysis of students' semantic mistakes in writing different types of SQL SELECT statements. Over 160 thousand snapshots of SQL queries were collected from over 2300 students across nine years. We describe the most common semantic mistakes that these students made when writing different types of SQL statements, and suggest reasons behind those mistakes. We mapped the semantic mistakes we identified in our data to different semantic categories found in the literature. Our findings show that the majority of semantic mistakes are of the type "omission". Most of these omissions happen in queries that require a JOIN, a subquery, or a GROUP BY operator. We conclude that it is important to explicitly teach students techniques for choosing the appropriate type of query when designing a SQL query.

General Terms

Performance, Human Factors.

Keywords

Online assessment; databases; SQL queries.

1. INTRODUCTION

The Structured Query Language (SQL) is the standard language for relational and object-oriental databases, as well as the industry standard language for querying databases. As with other computer languages, SQL queries can be semantically or syntactically wrong. However, limited attention has been given to understanding novice programmers' challenges in writing correct

SQL queries [5]. A deep understanding of the common semantic mistakes that novices make when writing SQL queries will improve teaching and learning outcomes.

ITiCSE '16, July 09-13, 2016, Arequipa, Peru
© 2016 ACM. ISBN 978-1-4503-4231-5/16/07...$15.00
DOI: http://dx.doi.org/10.1145/2899415.2899464

In this paper, we use data collected over nine years from ~2300 students taking online SQL exams. One of the ways that we have analyzed this data is to qualitatively study the semantic mistakes committed by these students. We review these mistakes in seven different types of SQL queries and investigate the reasons behind them. More specifically, we map these mistakes to proposed mistake categories introduced in the literature, and explain why students are likely to make these mistakes.

In section 2, we review the literature on analysis of errors in SQL. In Section 3, we describe the data collection and analysis of the data to explore the types of SQL query errors made by students. In section 4, we review our findings on common semantic mistakes of novices in writing different SQL SELECT statements. Section 5 expands and discusses these findings, before our conclusions are given in Section 6.

2. RELATED WORK

Most computing education researchers who have studied database education have focused on tutoring and/or assessment tools. Most of that work has been concerned with the functionality of the tool itself, or on how the system supports a certain pedagogical model [1-4]. There has been relatively little work on novice errors and misconceptions when using SQL.

A few studies have investigated these challenges with programming in SQL. Reisner performed the first experimental study investigating SEQUEL, the predecessor of SQL [7]. In that study, a series of psychological experiments were conducted on college students to investigate learnability of the language, as well as the type and frequency of errors made by subjects. Reisner categorized students' mistakes into "intrusion", "omission", "prior-knowledge", "data-type", "consistency" and "over-generalization".

Welty and Stemple [8] explored users' difficulty in writing queries in SQL compared to TABLET. Their comparison revealed that constructing difficult queries in more procedurally-oriented languages was easier than less procedurally-oriented languages. They categorized SQL statements into "correct", "minor language error", "minor operand error", "minor substance error", "correctable", "major substance error", "major language error", "incomplete" and "unattempted", where the first four of those categories were considered *essentially correct* and the other five categories were classified as *incorrect*. Their categorization of the SQL statements was based on Reisner's categorization [7]. A few years later, Welty ran an experiment on a small group to test how assistance with error correction would affect user performance [9]. In that study, he categorized subject responses into "correct", "minor error in problem comprehension", "minor syntactic", "complex errors", "group by", "s-type error", "incorrect" and "unattempted".

Buitendijk [10] introduced a classification of natural language questions, as well as possible errors within each class which resulted in four general groups of logical errors including "existence", "comparison", "extension" and "complexity". This categorization is not only based on SQL anomalies, but also focuses on user mistakes.

Smelcer [11] developed a model of query writing that integrated a GOMS-type analysis of SQL query construction with the characteristics of human cognition. This model introduced four common cognitive causes of JOIN clause omission and resulted in the categorization of common mistakes in writing SQL queries to "omitting the join clause", "AND/OR difficulties", "omitting quotes", "omitting the FROM clause", "omitting qualifications", "misspellings" and "synonyms". Brass [12] reports an extensive list of conditions that are strong indications of semantic mistakes. However, none of these studies analysed student mistakes in large datasets.

3. METHOD

3.1 Snapshot Collection

The data collected in this study forms a total number of ~161000 SQL SELECT statement snapshots from ~2300 students. Each snapshot is of one student attempt at a particular test question. The students in this study were all novice undergraduate students enrolled in an introductory database course. The tool used to collect the data is a purpose-built online assessment system named AsseSQL. Further details on the tool and how it was used to test the students can be found in prior publications [5, 6]. These snapshots were generated during supervised 50 minute online tests in which students attempted to answer seven SQL questions based on a given case study database. Students were provided with the case study, which included the description of the database, the Entity Relationship Diagram (ERD), and the CREATE statements corresponding to the database tables. Each question tests a student's ability to design a SELECT statement that covers a specific concept. Table 1 shows the concepts covered in the online test and statistics of snapshots related to each concept. A more detailed explanation on the nature of these concepts and their relative difficulty levels can be found in an earlier publication [13].

Table 1. Different SQL concepts and the number of snapshots.

Concept	Snapshot count
Group by with having	~32k (20%)
Self-join	~27k (17%)
Group by	~25k (15%)
Natural join	~24k (15%)
Simple subquery	~19k (12%)
Simple, one table	~18k (11%)
Correlated subquery	~16k (10%)

3.2 Snapshot Categorization

In order to produce the execution result of the collected snapshots, all snapshot SQL statements were re-executed in PostgreSQL and the output of each snapshot was obtained. Depending on the output returned by the PostgreSQL and the marking results of

AsseSQL, each snapshot was tagged as *correct, syntactically wrong* or *semantically wrong*. We categorized each snapshot as a) correct if its result set was exactly the same as desired solution for the question corresponding to the snapshot, b) syntactically wrong when an error message was returned by the PostgreSQL, or c) semantically wrong when the execution of snapshot resulted in either an empty result set or a result set which was not exactly the same as the desired solution for the question corresponding to the snapshot. In this study, a student's snapshot is considered to be semantically incorrect if the output generated by the snapshot is different from the correct output. The categorization of the snapshots and its breakdown for each concept is shown in Table 2. While some of the snapshots in each level are correct, the majority of snapshots introduce an error (Figure 1). A detailed exploration of the reasons behind the syntactic errors is available in an earlier publication [14].

Table 2. Categorization of snapshots based on their output and their breakdown for different SQL concepts.

Concept	Correct	Syntactically wrong	Semantically wrong
Group by with having	4%	58%	37%
Self-join	2%	37%	61%
Group by	7%	63%	30%
Natural join	4%	64%	32%
Simple subquery	5%	61%	34%
Simple, one table	11%	48%	41%
Correlated subquery	6%	52%	42%
Among all snapshots	6%	54%	40%

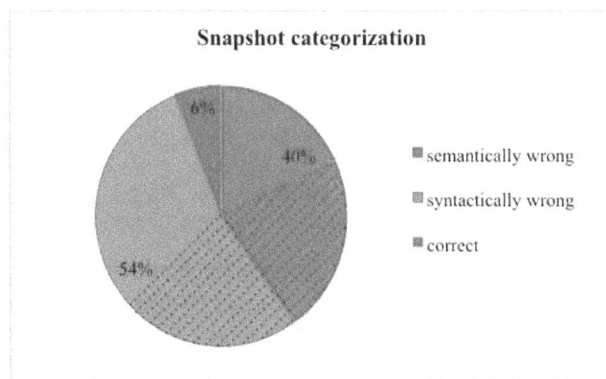

Figure 1. Categorization of collected SQL snapshots (N = ~161k). Snapshots in the hatched area were generated by students who subsequently fixed their error.

3.3 Semantic Mistake vs. Syntactic Error

As could be seen in Table 2 above, a considerable number of snapshots introduce an error, with the majority of snapshots falling into the syntactic error category. As the number of syntactic errors observed in students' attempts is higher than number of semantic mistakes, one could argue the importance of syntactic errors over semantic mistakes. However, in this study we chose to investigate the snapshots with semantic mistakes for the following reasons. Firstly, our analysis suggests that syntactic errors are more likely to be the result of lack of practice or carelessness. This is supported by the fact that among all syntactic error snapshots, ~69% of them are due to a typing errors in the SELECT statement (N = ~61000). These typing errors are due to wrong column names, wrong table names, or wrong syntax in one or more clauses of the SELECT statement. Excluding the syntax errors due to typing mistakes, the majority of mistakes made by novices are semantic. The second reason is related to the last snapshots generated by the unsuccessful students, which reflect the point where students stopped trying to get a query right. The number of students' last attempts with semantic mistakes is almost three times more than the number of last attempts that are syntactically incorrect (including typing mistakes). Another reason supporting our decision is that a SQL query that suffers from a syntactic error might already have a semantic mistake encapsulated in it. Our preliminary result suggests that a considerable number of *fixed* syntactic error snapshots are not correct as they include semantic mistakes (N = ~21000). Finally, the error code and the error message returned by PostgreSQL are usually enough to indicate the reason for a syntax error. In contrast, the output of a query that suffers from a semantic mistake is not as easily diagnosed as a syntactic error. This makes a semantic mistake much harder to fix.

3.4 Selection of Database Case Study

The set of ~161000 snapshots in this study are based on three different database case studies that are used in the online tests. The ERD structure as well as data complexity of these three databases are very similar. They consist of four to five tables, including one associate relation and three to four relationships, one of which is a unary relationship. The success rates of these case studies are only slightly different (Figure 2). The relative numbers of syntactic errors generated by students among these case studies are similar, however, the relative number of semantic mistakes made by students differs from one database case study to another. To make the result of our work less dependent on the comparative difficulty level of these case studies, we decided to limit our investigation dataset to the set of snapshots collected from only one database case study. We selected database case study 'Bicycle', which is based on a database from Post [15]. This database case study has the highest median success rate among different SQL query types, which reflects its lower level of difficulty relative to the other two case studies. For this case study we have ~45000 snapshots collected from ~700 students.

3.5 Primary Cause of Semantic Errors

According to Figure 1, the vast majority (94%) of snapshots do not generate the correct result, due to either a syntactic error or a semantic mistake. Almost half of these incorrect snapshots (46%) are from students who eventually were able to correct the errors and answer the question correctly. Figure 3 shows the frequency of incorrect snapshots **as a function of the attempt number** for these students who did eventually answer a question correctly. Among ~3200 cases where a student was able to answer a question correctly, 57% of students constructed at least one semantically incorrect SQL statement before they produced the correct SQL snapshot. Hence, we conclude that not all semantically wrong snapshots/student attempts are unfixable. This is also reported by Ogden *et al.* [16]. As a result, we elected to identify and investigate only those semantic mistakes that students were not able to correct. We limited our investigation to the set of snapshots (N = 551) that are final attempts with a semantic error. Those snapshots were generated by 321 students.

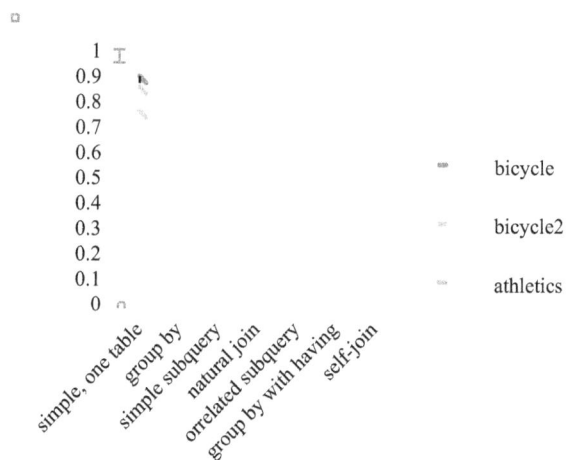

Figure 2. Success rates of different database case studies.

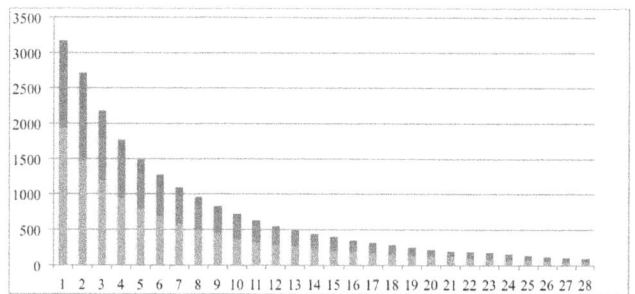

Figure 3. Distribution of correct (green), semantically incorrect (red) and syntactically incorrect (orange) snapshots, as a function of the number of attempts. X axis represents the nth attempt and Y axis represents number of snapshots.

A snapshot may contain multiple semantic mistakes. We focused upon the primary semantic mistake. Our process for manually identifying the primary semantic mistake in the 551 snapshots is illustrated in the following example:

List the given name, family name, address, the employee ID and the number of managers of those employees who are less than 25 years and have been managed by more than one manager.

The correct query for such a question could be:

SELECT *EMP_ID, FNAME, LNAME, ADDRESS* , COUNT(*EMPID*) AS *NUMBER_OF_MANAGERS FROM EMP_DETAILS* NATURAL JOIN *EMP_MANAGER* WHERE *EMP_AGE* < 25 GROUP BY *EMPID* HAVING COUNT(*EMP_ID*) > 1;

A student's attempt for this question might be:

SELECT * FROM *EMP_DETAILS* WHERE *EMPAGE* < 24;

This SELECT statement has multiple semantic mistakes; however, the most important mistake is the absence of the EMP_MANAGER relation in this query. Even if all other aspects of the given query related to EMP_DETAILS table are corrected, this query will not produce the correct result set unless the EMP_MANAGER table is included in the query. Thus the principle semantic error is the omission of the table.

4. RESULTS

Queries of type *self-join* have the highest number of semantically wrong last attempts (178 snapshots). Questions of type *natural join*, *group by with having* and *correlated subqueries* have the second highest frequency. The *simple with one table* and *group by* categories have the lowest frequencies. In all categories, the main reason behind the semantic mistake is students' lack of skill in identifying the required type of query (as listed in Table 2). Table 3 reviews different clauses of a SELECT statement and the mistakes allocated to those clauses.

Table 3. Clause based categorization of principle semantic mistakes.

Clause	Mistake/s	Concepts
where (46%)	Missing/wrong condition	Simple, self-join, correlated subquery, join
from (26%)	Self-join not used	Self-join
having (13%)	Missing group by or having clause, use of wrong column	Having
order by (5%)	Missing order by clause, incorrect/incomplete column	Simple, group by
select (5%)	Missing/extra column	Simple, group by
group by (5%)	Missing group by clause, use of wrong column	Group by, group by with having

4.1 Simple Query with One Table

Construction of simple queries with one table is the first concept that novices learn at the authors' institute. The students investigated in this study have the highest success ratio for questions of this type. However, snapshots that belong to this category also suffer from semantic mistakes. The most common mistakes observed for this query type includes missing/unnecessary columns in a SELECT clause or an ORDER BY clause. The absence of an appropriate condition or the presence of irrelevant condition in a WHERE clause is also a common mistake. In a few cases, the GROUP BY clause was irrelevantly used. The majority of these snapshots fall into Reisner's category of "essentially correct", as they are mostly the result of carelessness.

4.2 Group By

Four common mistakes were identified, including mistakes related to the GROUP BY clause, SELECT clause, WHERE clause or ORDER BY clause. The most frequent mistakes include missing the GROUP BY clause entirely or including unnecessary columns in the GROUP BY clause. Wrong conditions in the WHERE clause and a missing ORDER BY clause were also among the most frequent mistakes for GROUP BY queries. Also, a missing aggregate function in the SELECT clause was a common mistake, which has direct correlation with the absence of a signal word in the question (e.g. "average" or "sum"). This was originally observed in Reisner's experiments and further supported by the findings of Ahadi et al. [13].

4.3 Simple Subquery

More than 80% of the investigated snapshots in this category did not use a subquery at all. This could indicate that either students were not able to identify the skill required to answer these questions, or they did not have the skill required to construct such a query.

4.4 Correlated Subquery

More than 70% of snapshots in this category lacked the structure of a correlated subquery. In other words, the identification by students of the need for a correlated subquery was the most common problem. A further 13% of snapshots followed the syntax of a simple subquery. The rest of the snapshots included a wrong condition in the WHERE clause of the inner query.

4.5 Join

More than 80% of the snapshots in this category lacked the JOIN clause, that is, either the ON clause or the JOIN clause in the WHERE clause was missing. This is perhaps explained by the fact that the use of "NATURAL JOIN" in a SQL SELECT does not require the specification of the joining keys in the query. As a result, students who wrote the join queries may have forgotten that, unlike the NATURAL JOIN, the INNER JOIN requires the indication of the keys involved in the join. Unnecessary use of aggregate functions and incorrect joining conditions in the WHERE clause were also observed.

4.6 Group By with Having

Around 75% of the snapshots in this category lacked a HAVING clause and 15% of them did not even include the GROUP BY clause. Upon closer inspection, we noticed that the condition that is supposed to appear in the HAVING clause was often mistakenly written in the WHERE clause. Around 15% of the snapshots included the wrong conditions in the HAVING clause.

4.7 Self-join

Around 75% of the snapshots in this category demonstrated that students did not understand that they needed a self-join. While the remaining snapshots had a self-join, the self-join lacked a condition in the WHERE clause by which the result set is limited to non-overlapping sections of the main table and its replicate. In rare cases, unnecessary/incorrect conditions were included in the WHERE clause.

4.8 Mapping Semantic Mistakes

We mapped the 551 snapshots to the categorizations provided by Reisner, by Welty and Stemple, by Welty, and by Buitendijk [7-10]. Note, however that most error categorizations in the literature are a mix of semantic and syntactic mistakes.

4.8.1 Psychological experiments and error categorization

Reisner has done most of the work in experimental analysis of learnability of SQL [7]. She categorized students' mistakes into "intrusion", "omission", "prior-knowledge", "data-type", "consistency" and "over-generalization". More than half of the observed semantic mistakes in the snapshots analyzed in this study are of type omission. This error usually happens when a signal word such as "average" is not given in the question. Our results support Reisner's experiment. While omissions were reported by Reisner, her observations were limited to GROUP BY omission, and also AND clause omissions. Welty's "incomplete" category is (to some extent) similar to Reisner's omission error category. Table 4 reviews different omission errors observed among the set of 551 snapshots in our study.

Table 4. Omission errors in semantically incorrect snapshots. The second number in each row represents the percentage among all omission errors.

category	Frequency
Omitting JOIN clause	218 (48%)
Omitting SUBQUERY	115 (25%)
Omitting HAVING clause	58 (12%)
Omitting ORDER BY clause	23 (5%)
Omitting GROUP BY clause	17 (3%)
Omitting aggregate function	8 (1%)
Omitting WHERE clause	6 (1%)
Omitting column in SELECT	3 (<1%)
Omitting DISTINCT	3 (<1%)
Omitting column in ORDER BY	2 (<1%)

4.8.2 Categorization based on ease of error correction

Welty's experiment classified subject's responses into multiple categories according to the amount of effort needed to correct their mistakes [9]. In our data, snapshots with a semantic mistake of type "minor spelling errors" were frequent. Most of the time, in our data, a misspelling resulted in a syntactic error – e.g. typing "SELCT" instead of "SELECT" – but there are cases where a misspelling results in a semantic mistake, for example, using the string 'hawaii' instead of 'Hawaii' when referring to data stored in a table.

A similar error to Welty's "minor spelling error" is the "overgeneralization" error proposed by Reisner. For a given question "List the names of employees…", an overgeneralized solution would be:

SELECT *NAMES* FROM *EMPLOYEE … etc.*

The overgeneralization error happens when the information given in the question is directly extracted and used to construct the query, in the case above the *names* and *employees*. Reisner's overgeneralization category overlaps with Buitendijk's "comparisons" error category.

In some cases, snapshots of this type appeared immediately after a syntactically wrong attempt where the name of the columns or the tables were directly extracted from the question itself. Reisner classifies this kind of syntactic error as "intrusion error". The result of syntactic error analysis investigated by Ahadi *et al.*[14] reported that this type of mistake was common. In that study, syntactic errors due to prior knowledge – e.g. using AVERAGE instead of AVG – were also reported to be common.

Some semantic mistakes fall into Welty and Stemple's "major substance" error [8]. This error happens when the query is syntactically correct but the query answers a different question. Such errors are hard for students to detect and fix. Examples of these types of errors are a missing second column in an ORDER BY clause, an unnecessary condition in a WHERE clause, or the use of an incorrect aggregate function. This error was not common in our snapshots.

4.8.3 Natural Language based Categorization

Proposed by Buitendijk [10], this categorization of logical errors introduces "existence", "comparison", "extension" and "complexity" errors. Among our data, over one quarter of the semantic mistakes fall into the complexity category. An example of such cases is when more than one subquery needs to be included in the query.

Semantic mistakes due to the complexity of the written query are hard to detect. A query is regarded as complex if the translation the natural language question to the SQL answer is difficult. Interestingly, there is no relationship between the complexity of the given question and its corresponding answer. For example, longer questions do not necessarily require a complex query. However, longer queries are usually more complex and as a result more likely to contain errors.

5. DISCUSSION

Ogden *et al.* [16] categorized the knowledge of query writing into knowledge of the data, knowledge of the database structure and knowledge of the query language. The lack of knowledge of the first two categories is best reflected in syntactic errors, particularly those errors due to misspelling or referring to undefined columns or tables. On the other side, lack of knowledge of the query language is better reflected in semantic mistakes. Our findings suggest that the primary reason behind semantic mistakes is students' poor skill in selecting the right technique to design the query needed to answer the test question. The presence of a signal word such as "average" in the question seems to be helpful; however, students' dependency on a such "clue" in the question is not ideal.

Semantic mistakes also have implications for students' development in writing queries. Reisner's [7] model for the development of a query consists of three phases; generation of a template, transformation of English words to database terms, and insertion of database terms into the template. However, we noticed that the majority of our students who abandoned the question due to a semantic mistake had problems with the generation of the initial template. The first step in generating the template is to identify which technique – e.g. natural join, simple subquery, self-join, etc. – is most suitable. Our results suggest that there should be a greater emphasis on this matter when teaching students how to write SQL queries.

Our results show that the majority of semantic mistakes occur in the WHERE clause of the SELECT statement. This error may occur when the capacity of a student's working memory is surpassed [17]. For example, a high number of conditions in the WHERE clause could result in working memory overload, especially when many WHERE conditions are required to join two or more tables. This has been previously shown in the experiment performed by Smelcer [11]. This problem could perhaps be avoided by putting greater emphasis in teaching on following a systematic, step-by-step procedure in segmenting the question and formulating the correct answer in SQL.

6. CONCLUSION

This study attempts to both qualitatively and quantitatively investigate the semantic mistakes made by students. The results of our analysis show that syntactic mistakes are more common than semantic mistakes. However, semantic mistakes are much harder to correct, even among successful students. Our findings show that the majority of semantic mistakes are of type omission, indicating that students have difficulty with selecting the correct type of query, and they also lack a systematic approach to formulating the query.

The majority of omission errors happen in queries that require a JOIN, or a subquery, or a GROUP BY. This has implications for the way that we teach SQL query design, in that we should emphasize techniques that deal with the identification of the type of query necessary to return the requested information, e.g. a JOIN or a subquery. Furthermore, we believe that the selection of the right terminology by the teacher in articulating the question will decrease the chance of students' semantic mistakes that are due to complexity or the comprehension of the question. We are carrying out additional research to confirm this assertion.

7. REFERENCES

[1] Brusilovsky, P., Sosnovsky, S., Lee, D., Yudelson, M., Zadorozhny, V., and Zhou, X. (2008). *An open integrated exploratorium for database courses.* ITiCSE '08. pp. 22-26. http://doi.acm.org/10.1145/1384271.1384280.

[2] Brusilovsky, P., Sosnovsky, S., Yudelson, M. V., Lee, D. H., Zadorozhny, V., and Zhou, X. (2010) *Learning SQL programming with interactive tools: From integration to personalization.* Trans. Comput. Educ. 9, 4, Article 19 (January 2010). http://doi.acm.org/10.1145.1656255.1656257

[3] Mitrovic, A. (1998) *Learning SQL with a computerized tutor.* SIGCSE '98, pp. 307-311. http://doi.acm.org/10.1145/274790.274318

[4] Mitrovic, A. (2003) *An intelligent SQL tutor on the web.* Int. J. Artif. Intell. Ed. 13, 2-4 (April 2003), pp. 173-197.

[5] Prior, J., and Lister, R. (2004) *The Backwash Effect on SQL Skills Grading.* ITiCSE 2004, Leeds, UK. Pp. 32-36. http://doi.acm.org/10.1145/1007996.1008008

[6] Prior, J. (2014) *AsseSQL: an online, browser-based SQL Skills assessment tool.* ITiCSE 2014. Pp. 327-327. http://doi.acm.org/10.1145/2591708/2602682

[7] Reisner, P. (1977) *Use of psychological experimentation as an aid to development of a query language.* IEEE Trans. Softw. Eng. SE-3, 3, 218-229. http://doi.acm.org/10.1145/1103669.1103673

[8] Welty, C., and Stemple, D. W. (1981) *Human factors comparison of a procedural and a nonprocedural query language.* ACM Transactions on Database Systems (TODS) 6.4:626-649. http://doi.acm.org/10.1145/319628.319656

[9] Welty, C. (1985) *Correcting user errors in SQL.* International Journal of Man-Machine Studies 22(4): 463-477.

[10] Buitendijk, R. B. (1988) *Logical errors in database SQL retrieval queries.* computer Science in economics and management 1, 79-96. http://doi.acm.org/10.1007/BF00427157

[11] Smelcer, J. B. (1995) *User error in database query composition.* Int. J. Human-Computer Studies 42, 353-381. http://doi.acm.org/10.1006/ijhc.1995.1017

[12] Brass, S. and Goldberg, C. (2006) *Semantic error in SQL queries: A quite complete list.* The Journal of Systems and Software 79, 630–644. http://doi.acm.org/10.1016/j.jss.2005.06.028

[13] Ahadi, A., Prior, J., Behbood, V., and Lister, R. (2015) *A Quantitative Study of the Relative Difficulty for Novices of Writing Seven Different Types of SQL Queries.* In *Proceedings of the 2015 ACM Conference on Innovation and Technology in Computer Science Education*, pp. 201-206. ACM, 2015.

[14] Ahadi, A., Behbood, V., Vihavainen, A., Prior, J., & Lister, R. (2016, February). *Students' Syntactic Mistakes in Writing Seven Different Types of SQL Queries and its Application to Predicting Students' Success.* In *Proceedings of the 47th ACM Technical Symposium on Computing Science Education* (pp. 401-406). ACM.

[15] Post, G. V. (2001) *Database management systems: designing and building business applications.* McGraw-Hill.

[16] Ogden, W. D., Korenstein, R., Smelcer, J. B. (1986) *An Intelligent Front-End for SQL*, IBM, San Jose, CA.

[17] Miller, G. A. (1994). *The magical number seven, plus or minus two: Some limits on our capacity for processing information.* Psychological review, *101*(2), 343.

Introductory Programming: Let Us Cut through the Clutter!

[Extended Abstract]

Abhiram G. Ranade
Department of Computer Science and Engineering
IIT Bombay
Powai, Mumbai, India
ranade@cse.iitb.ac.in

ABSTRACT

Introductory programming courses often leave students unimpressed. We feel this is because teaching approaches (a) overemphasize the syntactic aspects of the programming language being taught instead of using programming to do interesting things, (b) do not respect the computational maturity/intellectual leanings of the students, and (c) are simply not fun enough.

We have developed an approach which we believe addresses these issues in the context of teaching introductory programming to college students majoring in science and engineering. We use the C++ programming language augmented with a graphics library and some linguistic devices we have developed. We believe that our approach enables interesting material to be handled from day one and generally garners more student interest.

Keywords

Introductory programming; C++; pedagogy; graphics.

1. INTRODUCTION

Computer programming is a unique skill which is at once deeply theoretical and strikingly hands-on/practical. It is its own science, but yet it can enable you to explore other subjects such as the sciences, engineering and even arts. Computer programming can be psychologically liberating in that a computer *obeys* the student, who for most of his/her life has deferred to elders. Computer programming thus has the potential to empower students and unleash their creative abilities.

And yet, introductory programming courses can appear boring. The most common reason given for this is that a lot of dull information must be conveyed before anything interesting can start. In the most popular languages such as C, C++ and Java your first program typically contains a lot of arcane mumbo jumbo, and even after that it barely prints "Hello world!". Even the rest of the course may convey the impression that computer programming is about getting the semicolons right and mastering obscure trivia ("What does i += ++i+k++; do?").

We believe that the introductory programming course should not only provide programming skills but also convey the power, the ex-

ITiCSE '16, July 09 - 13, 2016, Arequipa, Peru

© 2016 Copyright held by the owner/author(s). Publication rights licensed to ACM.
ISBN 978-1-4503-4231-5/16/07... $15.00

DOI: http://dx.doi.org/10.1145/2899415.2899430

citement and the pervasiveness of computer programming. Doing this is not easy. One of the major requirements is to use good programming examples: those which are exciting and challenging to the students, and yet not too hard. Another problem, ubiquitous in all education, is of providing the right motivation. Why should I learn inheritance? Why should I learn software engineering? We must either take the time to explain the motivation in a manner that can be appreciated by the student, or we must simply defer the topic to a later date. All this requires us to understand our student: what excites her, what she already knows on which we can build.

In this paper our goal is to design an introductory programming course for first year college students majoring in science and engineering. We begin in Section 2 by clarifying what we feel is of importance in introductory programming. In Section 3 we survey some of the major approaches to programming education. In Section 4 we present our approach. By being clear about the goals of the introductory programming course, by focussing the course on programming examples that are interesting to our target student, and by employing some linguistic devices that we have developed (based on preprocessor macros), we believe it is possible to design a course that enables interesting ideas to presented from day one, and generally make for efficient learning.

2. WHAT SHOULD WE TEACH?

For an introductory course, we believe that it is appropriate to define "programming" as "the act of expressing in a programming language the computations that you can perform manually". We mean the word "computation" in its widest sense: including not only arithmetic, but also algebra, geometry, calculus, physics, and even art. We want students to view computing as an extension of thinking – as pervasive and as powerful. By implicitly emphasizing the similarity between human computation and computer computation, we hope to inspire confidence in the student towards the subject.[1]

Programming involves three kinds of skills:

1. Expressing problems from different domains in terms of numbers and questions on those numbers.

2. Observing patterns in (manual) computation.

3. Expressing the patterns using appropriate language constructs.

Introductory programming courses and books often focus mostly on learning the language constructs. The first two skills are independent of the language, and more important and harder.

---

[1]Humans do not always think algorithmically, e.g. playing chess. But such exceptions really drive home the point about what humans indeed do algorithmically.

The first skill is about realizing that everything from calculus to games can be represented on a computer. It is not enough to merely give this infomation to the student; if the information is to sink in, we must get the student to write programs relating to diverse areas: geometry, symbolic computation, graphics. Students find this exhilarating and empowering.

By "observing patterns in computation" we mean something like: is some sequence of computations repeated? If so, how many times? We want students to introspect over how they compute/solve problems manually. They already know many interesting computations, starting from simple arithmetic on numbers with an arbitrary number of digits to linear algebra, calculus, and also calculations in physics. They have even seen recursion, e.g. taking the derivative of a sum simply involves adding the derivatives of the addends! Besides identifying the iteration or recursion present in their calculations, we also expect students to identify function abstraction and data abstraction – this is again a part of the idea of seeing patterns.

The last step is learning a programming language (though not all its idiosyncracies) and expressing the computation using that language. We are not suggesting that this step is easy. However, we believe that by focussing on appropiate computational examples we can motivate the syntax and semantics of language constructs.[2] This will help make the syntax/semantics appear natural and help learning. We will also show soon that we can use devices like *macros* to create more pedagogically convenient syntax for use in the early part of the course whereby we can plunge into interesting material right away.

3. APPROACHES

We will next survey some of the dominant approaches to programming education.

3.1 The C approach

The chronologically earliest, and perhaps the most dominant approach even today, is due to Kernighan and Ritchie[9]. Their little book has trained a huge number of programmers, and is lauded for its clarity. However, it nevertheless has to deal with the idiosyncracies of the C language in which the syntax often overwhelms the principles. A successor to this is perhaps the book on introductory programming through C++ by Stroustrup[16]. C++ is a clear improvement over C. But even in C++, there is serious danger of the syntax overwhelming the principles, especially for a beginner. The classic example of this is the introductory program:

```
#include <iostream> using
namespace std;

int main(){
  cout << "Hello world!" << endl;
}
```

To a beginner this must appear like some mysterious incantations – potentially leading to intimidation or to boredom. And on top of it, the program accomplishes precious little. Similar problems can appear quite often. For example, the student can get lost while understanding the details and syntactic aspects of a concept such as inheritance, or bored by the various tricky operators of C++.

This approach often draws programming examples mainly from operating systems or compiler viewpoints. These examples, concerning files and parsing, may not generate excitement among engineering and science students.

[2]Appealing to prior experience of the student in mathematics helps in motivating language constructs too: for example, the operator + is routinely "overloaded" in mathematics to mean many things.

3.2 The SICP approach

A strikingly different approach is offered by Abelson and Sussman, as documented in their book *The Structure and Interpretation of Computer programs* (SICP)[1]. SICP is a heady brew that you cannot put down, and Sussman's lectures on MIT OCW from 1986 are thrilling and give goosebumps. The appeal of the approach could be attributed to the simplicity of the Scheme language syntax which makes it possible to get to interesting topics very quickly. SICP does get quickly to interesting topics, e.g. the Babylonian algorithm for square roots, and representation and manipulation of (mathematical) functions symbolically. To see the computer doing tricky algorithms and "doing calculus" can raise the stature of the subject in the eyes of the learner.

However, overall it cannot be said that SICP is introductory. The Babylonian algorithm, for example, is compact but actually quite deep. Discussions about possible semantics of constructs, e.g. of assignments in the functional framework, are greatly exciting for experts, but difficult for novices. One indication of all this are the customer reviews of SICP on amazon.com. Of the 212 reviews listed at the time of writing this, 62 % reviews give it 5 stars, and it is clear that these are reviews from experienced programmers for whom SICP sketches out the grand panorama of programming to which they can relate. On the other hand 25 % of the reviews give it 1 star, and these are reviews from beginners who are frustrated because SICP purports to be introductory, but really demands considerable computational maturity.

3.3 The program derivation approach

Another approach is due to the Dijkstra school[5, 8]. They propose strategies using which programs and their proofs of correctness are generated ("derived") simultaneously. Dijkstra essentialy suggests that beginners should be kept away from computers before they master the logical calculus needed to argue correctness. However many of the "interesting" examples of program derivation are really about discovering new algorithms, e.g. an $O(n)$ time algorithm is derived for a problem that has an obvious $O(n^2)$ time algorithm. The techniques are often elegant and worth mastering; however in our opinion this should perhaps come in a later course.

On the other hand, discussion of program correctness, e.g. assertions and loop invariants is often neglected in introductory programming. These elementary ideas enable programmers to check that "corner cases" are correctly handled, and hence clearly have a place in introductory programming.

3.4 Logo

Logo[12, 6] was invented as a language for teaching programming to children. A major theme in Logo is *turtle graphics*: students get to program the on-screen movement of a symbolic animal, the turtle. The turtle has a pen which draws on the screen as the turtle moves; programs are to be written to draw interesting pictures on the screen. One of the important ideas in Logo pedagogy is to encourage students to "be the turtle". Student are encouraged to ask themselves "If you walk on the figure to be drawn, how much would you move and how much would you need to turn?". Such introspection enables students to make programming very personal and thus make a deep connection to it.

Logo has had many successors, one of the important ones is Scratch[15]. A popular genre of Scratch programming is *narrative* – the graphical objects in Scratch can be animated (along with audio) and a Scratch program is thus the story script. An analog of this in Logo is making the turtle write your name on the screen, or draw pictures without much symmetry. Logo and Scratch are often taught in schools, and often the syllabi focus on this narrative mode.

Less commonly, Logo and Scratch are used for drawing structured pictures, in which the programmer must understand the symmetries in the picture being drawn and implement them in the program by using suitable loops or recursion. In some sense, this *mathematical* mode of usage was the dream of the Logo inventors[6]. This resonates with our idea of "observing patterns in computation and expressing them using appropriate language constructs". We believe that adults with a greater background in mathematics are likely to be more excited about the mathematical mode.

3.5 Domain driven approaches

A class of approaches is motivated by the observation that we never write programs in a vacuum – programs are always written to solve problems. To help in this, one popular idea is to teach programming in conjuction with some application, e.g. robotics[10], or graphics. The Alice system[4] is is built around a 3 dimensional graphics package. We feel that three dimensional graphics is not entirely intuitive and produces a cognitive load which may distract students from the programming content. Several approaches use two dimensional graphics also. EZ windows is a two dimensional graphics system accompanying a well known textbook[3]. Like many such approaches, the book uses graphics as an add-on. It is not used as a pedagogic tool to help present concepts without clutter. Certainly not to help introduce programming on day 1. Programming education has also has been conceived to be given in the context of a geographical application[11]. These approaches are attractive also because they force the student to work alongside an existing system. This is useful because in the modern workplace programmers hardly develop programs for scratch, but rather work to enhance or modify existing programs. A drawback of the approach is that the domain chosen may not appeal to every student, or learning the domain (e.g. robotics principles, 3d graphics principles) may place additional learning burden on the student.

3.6 Paradigm based approaches

Introductory programming has been introduced in the context of specific paradigms, e.g. functional programming using ML[7], or approaches such as objects-first[2]. The Alice system[4] is motivated specifically by the desire to teach object oriented programming. Often the idea is, "let us teach students how to think correctly before other paradigms corrupt them".

From a pragmatic standpoint, we believe that important ideas (e.g. iteration, recursion, object orientation) from every paradigm need to be taught. Our preference is to introduce ideas in increasing order of cognitive complexity, motivated by the demands of the application problem being solved.

4. OUR APPROACH

We would like to have an approach which combines the best of all the approaches described above. Specifically, we would like to get to the heart of programming in the first lecture of the course, just as Logo does for children, and Abelson and Sussman[1] (seemingly) manage to do for adults. Like them, we would not like to be bogged down by syntax. We would like to go beyond basic arithmetic and text processing to provide programming examples and problems to our students without introducing the cognitive load of teaching a completely new topic such as robotics. We would like to teach difficult concepts such as recursion and object oriented programming, but with motivating examples that will appeal to our target audience. As to the choice of the language, we would like to use a mainstream language to improve the chance of our ideas getting accepted.

We use the C++ language, augmented with a library we developed, Simplecpp. Simplecpp supports two kinds of graphics: Logo style *turtle graphics* and more standard *coordinate based graphics* using which geometric shapes can be created and manipulated.

Another component of Simplecpp is a `repeat` statement, also inspired by Logo. The `repeat` statement has the form:

```
repeat (count) { statements to be repeated }
```

This causes the block of `statements to be repeated` to be executed as many times as the value of `count`. For this the statement is translated to a `for` loop using preprocessor macros which get loaded automatically; this is of course revealed to the student only towards the end of the course. The main reason for defining this statement is that it can be introduced in the very first lecture! You will see that with `repeat`, students can start writing interesting programs from day 1.

Our graphics library provides us with an additional domain for illustrating programming concepts and give interesting but challenging assignments. The turtle graphics as well as the two dimensional graphics are very intuitive, and learning them takes hardly any time. Indeed, it is possible to easily create reasonably exciting drawings and animations, e.g. Hilbert space filling curves, the *snake* game, bouncing balls, planets rotating around the sun and so on.

4.1 The first lecture in the course

The first lecture, if delivered well, can cause students to fall in love with the subject. Students tend to view it as setting the tone for the course: whether the course is going to be exciting, whether it will have interesting ideas, or whether it will just be lot of boring information. Our first lecture draws upon Logo/turtle geometry. Here is the first program that we show to students in the first lecture.

```
#include <simplecpp>
main_program{
  turtleSim();

  forward(100);   left(90);
  forward(100);   left(90);
  forward(100);   left(90);
  forward(100);

  wait(5);
}
```

As you can see, we only include the Simplecpp library, which in turn includes `iostream` and issues commands to use namespaces etc. Thus we only need to explain to the students that we need to include Simplecpp, other explanations can come later in the course. Next, we have a macro `main_program` which expands to `int main()`, so we dont need to explain what `int` means and why `main` has parentheses `()` following it. This will get explained after we discuss functions, when the students can understand everything.

The first statement `turtleSim()` in the body of the program opens the turtle simulator window, which already has a turtle at the center of the screen (a red triangle, as is customary). The command `forward(100)` causes the turtle to move forward 100 pixels. The command `left(90)` causes the turtle to turn left by 90 degrees. Thus the complete code causes the turtle to draw a square (because of the pen that drags on the screen as it moves). After that the program waits for 5 seconds, and then terminates.

Note that the first program is already providing a non-trivial ability to the students, and creates expectations in their minds, e.g. "Can I draw other kinds of polygons?". Some students might also ask if they need to write fifty `forward` statements if they wish to draw a fifty sided polygon. The `repeat` statement can be introduced immediately. Indeed the second program of the first lecture could be

```
main_program{          // will draw a decagon.
  turtleSim();
  repeat(10){
    forward(100); right(36);
  }
}
```

The turning angle, 36 degrees, is easily calculated from the high school geometry theorem "The exterior angles of a polygon add up to 360 degrees."

We have found that the students spontaneously understand nested repeat statements, as in the program below.

```
main_program{
  turtleSim();
  repeat(4){
    repeat(10){
      forward(5); penUp();
      forward(5); penDown();
    }
    left(90);
  }
}
```

Many students spontaneously infer that this will cause a square to be drawn, using dashed lines.

Notice that on the very first day we can accomplish many things. We can force students to think algorithmically. They need to figure out the turning angles; they also need to use `repeat` statements properly to draw more complex figures. This requires matching the pattern in the drawing with the pattern of `repeat` statements in the program. This is of course a very fundamental programming activity! And we have got to in on day 1.

4.2 Utility of repeat and graphics

The standard looping statements in C++ (and most languages) are fairly complex: they require you to understand variables, conditions, and of course issues about loop termination. Thus standard loop statements can be introduced only after a few weeks. We cannot go this long without interesting programming examples!

This vacuum is filled nicely by the `repeat` statement and graphics. Right after the first lecture students can be asked to draw intricate patterns involving lines and arcs (a circle after all is a limit of a polygon as the number of sides increase). These make for relevant, fun, and challenging programming exercises. After discussing data types and assignment statements (but still well before discussing `while`/`for`), we can write code such as the following

```
int i=1;
repeat(40){
  forward(i*10);
  left(90);
  i = i + 1;
}
```

As you might guess, this draws a spiral. Note further that the code contains *reassignment* of `i` to itself. This is a concept that several students find difficult. We believe that seeing `i` used graphically as above likely helps in understanding reassignment.

Graphics is useful in explaining difficult concepts such as recursion. A (botanical) tree has recursive structure – it consists of smaller trees on top of a trunk. Thus it can be easily drawn using a recursive function.

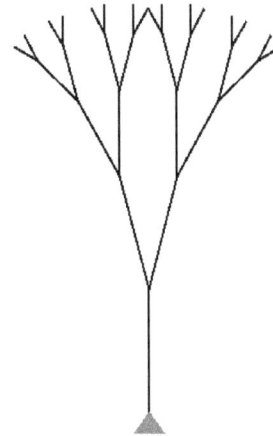

Figure 1: Tree drawn using recursion

```
void tree(int levels){
  if(levels > 0){
    forward(levels*10);
    left(15);
    tree(levels-1);
    right(30);
    tree(levels-1);
    left(15);
    forward(-levels*10);
  }
}
```

Figure 1 shows the picture produced when the above function is invoked by calling `tree(5)`. It should be noted that the tree does not appear instantaneously but is drawn by the turtle, one line at a time. Thus the recursion unfolds in real time in front of the students' eyes. We believe this helps in understanding recursion.

Coordinate based graphics can also be taught very early on. For example, here is the code for creating a rectangle and moving it.

```
Rectangle r(xc,yc,L,H);
  // center coordinates, Length, Height
r.move(deltax, deltay);
```

The astute reader will see that the first statement is really a constructor call, and the second a member function invocation. However, we explain this to students as: "the first statement creates a rectangle named `r`, the second statement moves it." Thus the students start using constructors and the dot notation well before object oriented programming is formally introduced.

Graphics can also provide a compelling motivation to learn inheritance. For drawing interesting pictures, it is necessary to compose the basic shapes together. For example, a car shape (Figure 2) might consist of a polygon shape representing the body, and two wheel shapes. A wheel might consist of a circle denoting the rim, and perhaps straight lines denoting the spokes. We would like to be able to define a car shape once, using wheel shapes defined earlier. Furthermore, it would be nice to be able to invoke member functions such as `move` on cars – this should cause all the contained shapes to move as a group. This precise functionality is provided by our `Composite` shape class.

Figure 2: A car constructed using the `Composite` **class**

A `Composite` class is a container class which automatically delegates operations such as `move` or `forward` or `rotate` to contained objects (`rotate` requires a bit more work than just delegation). A new composite shape such as a car or a wheel can be defined by inheriting from `Composite`.

Here is how a `Car` class can be defined.

```
class Car : public Composite{
  Polygon* body;
  Wheel *w1, *w2;
public:
  Car(double x, double y, Color c,
      Composite* owner=NULL)
    : Composite(x,y,owner){
    double bodyV[9][2]={{-150,0},
      {-150,-100}, {-100,-100}, {-75,-200},
      {50,-200}, {100,-100}, {150,-100},
      {150,0}, {-150,0}};
    body = new Polygon(0,0, bodyV, 9, this);
    body->setColor(c);
    body->setFill();
    w1 = new Wheel(-90,0,this);
    w2 = new Wheel(90,0,this);
  }
  void forward(double dx){
    Composite::forward(dx);
    // superclass forward function
    w1->rotate(dx/(RADIUS*getScale()));
    w2->rotate(dx/(RADIUS*getScale()));
  }
};
```

A car contains a polygonal `body`, and wheels `w1` and `w2` which are instances of a `Wheel` class which is another composite class. Thus composite classes can be nested. The definition of the `Wheel` class is omitted. This code also shows another interesting feature. We have overridden the `forward` function so that the wheels not only move forward, but also turn.

The `Composite` class thus provides considerable power for building interesting animations. But for this, you must understand and use inheritance. Isn't this compelling motivation?

We give two more examples of how graphics can be used to generate programming exercises that may interest our target student audience, i.e. students majoring in science and engineering.

The first example is shown in Figure 3. The goal in this is to trace the path of a ball as it bounces around in a box. In the simplest case (Figure 3), we consider a stationary, rigid box, with the collisions

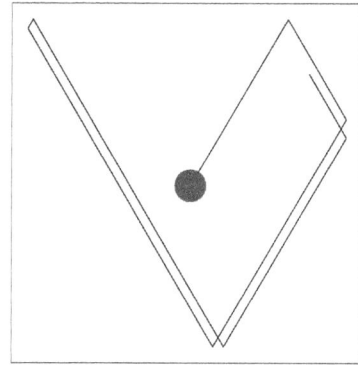

Figure 3: Path of ball bouncing in a box

being perfectly elastic. We can of course make the motion more complex, for example by involving gravity, or friction. Or we can have the box itself move due to the collisions. This can make up for progressively difficult (and interesting) assignments. Note however that even in the simple case above students might find something unexpected: usually the ball will overtrace its path after some time. This example is paradigmatic: it is an example of a *simulation* of a physical system.

Our second example concerns the processing of mathematical expressions. Can you create a library which enables you to represent mathematical expressions, and perform arithmetic or other operations on them? The expressions may or may not contain unknowns. Graphics comes in if you wish to typeset the expression in the standard manner, i.e. generate something like the following:

$$\cfrac{4}{1+\cfrac{1^2}{3+\cfrac{2^2}{5+\cfrac{3^2}{7+\cfrac{4^2}{9+\ddots}}}}}$$

The key problem in this is to determine the geometric positions of the various subexpressions and the sizes of the bars denoting division. Everyone can generate this layout "by hand", and yet it is an interesting challenge to introspect about how you do it and flesh out an algorithm. The recursion required is quite interesting. In general, since the representation of mathematical expressions is invariably heirarchical (e.g. an expression is a sum of other expressions), it provides fertile ground for using recursion. The problem also provides good motivation for using inheritance.

4.3 Overall pedagogical approach

Our general pedagogical approach is an extension of the ideas implied above. To motivate a new topic, we first find a problem which cannot be solved using what the students know so far. As far possible, we choose problems which are of interest to our students, and which also have a visual aspect, because we believe that pictures help learning. We then present the new topic, and develop complete programs required to solve the problem.

In addition, we believe it is useful to develop some larger paradigmatic case studies e.g. gravitational simulation, representation and solution of resistive circuits, and representation and manipulation of algebraic expressions. The basic theory of the case studies should be known to the student, although it is useful to review it. We believe that all this synergistically benefits the learning of computer programming and the other sciences, and such examples are better appreciated by students of science and engineering. Overall, we want to convey the impression that you are learning problem solving than just a language.

It may be interesting to note that many books on introductory programming discuss in some detail the historical development of computers. While this history is interesting, it can create the impression that computing began with computers. This is very far from the truth! Manual computation gave rise to many algorithms that are invaluable for computing even today, e.g. Euclid's GCD algorithm, the Babylonian square root algorithm, and even the basic notions of the positional number system and the related algorithms. Our approach attempts to connect to that tradition.

5. EXPERIENCE

A book based on the approach presented here was published by McGraw Hill Education[14]. The Simplecpp library is available from the author's webpage and the publisher's webpage. The book has now been used several times in the introductory programming course in IIT Bombay, and is also being used in Vishwakarma Institute of Technology, Pune. The book was also used in various offerings of a Massively Open Online Course (MOOC)[13].

The author is happy to report that the feedback has been very positive.

6. CONCLUDING REMARKS

We believe that computing must be presented to students as an extension to thought and intuition, as a *universal* skill that applies to all aspects of life. This must be conveyed as *active learning*, i.e. the students should be able to write programs that touch most subjects they have studied till then in their careers. In order to implement this plan, it is necessary to use classroom time efficiently, and ensure that the focus remains on important ideas. We believe that most courses in introductory programming in C++ (as well as several other languages) spend 2-3 initial weeks describing introductory material and without discussing any interesting programs. This we believe dissipates the excitement with which the students start a school term. By using the strategies suggested here (graphics and the `repeat` statement) we believe we can get to interesting material quickly and maintain focus on it.

It may seem that the agenda of getting to many applications in science and technology might conflict with the (primary?) goal of conveying the basic computer programming concepts. However, by choosing the examples carefully, we can in fact motivate even the programming concepts better. We believe our strategy makes for better integration of programming with the prior knowledge of the student.

While the `repeat` statement is present in Logo, we believe that using it in mainstream languages has not been tried before. Besides speeding up learning at the beginning of the course, we believe that students benefit from learning it before learning the standard looping constructs. We believe that many students have difficulty in managing the control variable and the termination condition in standard looping constructs. On the other hand, `repeats` are much easier to understand (even when nested) and thus provide a graded step towards learning the standard looping constructs.

Finally, several approaches use graphics. However we believe no approach (in adult education) has used graphics to start off an introduction to programming: by drawing mathematically interesting pictures. Even adults enjoy drawing; only we need to ask them to draw more intricate pictures than what children would be asked in Logo. We believe we have integrated graphics into basic programming education at a deeper level in general. In addition, note that graphics is very important for our target student group: graphics/visualization and geometric reasoning play a central role in science and technology. And last, but not the least, graphics is fun!

7. ACKNOWLEDGMENTS

The author is grateful to Om Damani for comments.

8. REFERENCES

[1] H. Abelson and G. J. Sussman. *Structure and Interpretation of Computer Programs*. MIT Press, Cambridge, MA, USA, 2nd edition, 1996.

[2] D. J. Barnes and M. Kolling. *Objects First With Java: A Practical Introduction Using BlueJ (3rd Edition)*. Prentice-Hall, Inc., Upper Saddle River, NJ, USA, 2006.

[3] J. Cohoon and J. Davidson. *C++ Program Design: An introduction to programming*. McGraw Hill, 2002.

[4] S. Cooper, W. Dann, and R. Pausch. Alice: A 3-d tool for introductory programming concepts. *J. Comput. Sci. Coll.*, 15(5):107–116, Apr. 2000.

[5] E. W. Dijkstra. On the cruelty of really teaching computing science, 1988. EWD-1036.

[6] A. diSessa and H. Abelson. *Turtle Geometry: the computer as a medium for exploring mathematics*. MIT Press, Cambridge, MA, USA, 1981.

[7] M. R. Hansen and H. Rischel. *Introduction to Programming Using SML*. Addison-Wesley Longman Publishing Co., Inc., Boston, MA, USA, 1st edition, 1999.

[8] A. Kaldewaij. *Programming: The Derivation of Algorithms*. Prentice-Hall, Inc., Upper Saddle River, NJ, USA, 1990.

[9] B. W. Kernighan and D. M. Ritchie. *The C Programming Language*. Prentice Hall Professional Technical Reference, 2nd edition, 1988.

[10] P. Lawhead, M. Duncan, C. Bland, M. Goldweber, M. Schep, D. Barnes, and R. Hollingsworth. A road map for teaching introductory programming using LEGO. In *ITiCSE-WGR '02 Working group reports from ITiCSE on Innovation and technology in computer science education*, pages 191–201. ACM, 2002.

[11] B. Meyer. The Outside-In Method of Teaching Introductory Programming. In *Ershov Memorial Conference, volume 2890 of Lecture Notes in Computer Science*, pages 66–78, 2003.

[12] S. Papert. *Mindstorms: Children, Computers, and Powerful Ideas*. Basic Books, Inc., New York, NY, USA, 1980.

[13] D. B. Phatak and S. Chakraborty. CS 101x Introduction to Computer Programming, 2016. https://iitbombayx.in/courses/IITBombayX/CS101.1xS16/2016_T1. Also 2015. Previous version at https://www.edx.org/course/programming-basics-iitbombayx-cs101-1x.

[14] A. Ranade. *An Introduction to Programming through C++*. McGraw Hill Education, 2014.

[15] M. Resnick, J. Maloney, A. Monroy-Hernández, N. Rusk, E. Eastmond, K. Brennan, A. Millner, E. Rosenbaum, J. Silver, B. Silverman, and Y. Kafai. Scratch: Programming for all. *Communications of the ACM*, 52(11):60–67, Nov. 2009.

[16] B. Stroustrup. *Programming: Principles and Practice Using C++*. Addison-Wesley Professional, 1st edition, 2008.

Learning to Program is Easy

Andrew Luxton-Reilly
Department of Computer Science
University of Auckland
Auckland, New Zealand
andrew@cs.auckland.ac.nz

ABSTRACT

The orthodox view that "programming is difficult to learn" leads to uncritical teaching practices and poor student outcomes. It may also impact negatively on diversity and equity within the Computer Science discipline. But learning to program is easy — so easy that children can do it. We make our introductory courses difficult by establishing unrealistic expectations for novice programming students. By revisiting the expected norms for introductory programming we may be able to substantially improve outcomes for novice programmers, address negative impressions of disciplinary practices and create a more equitable environment.

Keywords

novice; programming; computer science education; standards; expectations; learning outcomes; curriculum; CS1

1. INTRODUCTION

Learning to program is easy. Almost everyone can learn how to write their first computer program with minimal effort. Although the syntax of each programming language differs, producing a simple program that can print out a string of letters (such as that presented in Figure 1) is trivial to write, understand, reproduce and modify.

```
print('Hello World')
```

Figure 1: A simple Python program

Children have been successfully programming computers for more than 40 years [23], using a variety of programming languages and environments [16]. Recently, programming has been introduced into national curriculum for primary school children in both the UK [11], and Australia [13]. Other countries, such as New Zealand [4] and Denmark [12], have recently introduced programming at secondary school

ITiCSE '16, July 09 - 13, 2016, Arequipa, Peru

© 2016 Copyright held by the owner/author(s). Publication rights licensed to ACM.
ISBN 978-1-4503-4231-5/16/07... $15.00

DOI: http://dx.doi.org/10.1145/2899415.2899432

level. It is clear that children are capable of learning programming, and furthermore, that in several countries, it is expected that **all** children will learn programming as a standard part of their education.

In contrast, the commonly held belief of Computer Science educators and researchers at tertiary level is that programming is difficult to teach, and difficult to learn. In a 2003 review of the literature on teaching and learning programming, Robins summarizes the orthodox view:

> *Learning to program is hard however. Novice programmers suffer from a wide range of difficulties and deficits. Programming courses are generally regarded as difficult, and often have the highest dropout rates. [26]*

This view of computer programming as a difficult skill to learn may have implications for equity and diversity. It may encourage students to engage in activities that are not conducive to learning, it is potentially unfair to students and may also lead to research practices that focus on student shortcomings rather than curriculum deficiencies.

This paper challenges the orthodox view that computer programming is innately difficult to learn. Instead, an alternative explanation is proposed to explain the challenges faced by students as they learn to program.

2. STUDENT PERFORMANCE

The belief that learning to program is difficult appears to be widespread among teachers and researchers involved in Computer Science Education (e.g. see [5, 10, 26, 35]). Discussions about programming frequently begin with the **premise** that it is hard. Mark Guzdial noted in a 2010 blog post:

> *So what makes programming so hard to learn? Here's a possibility: It's inherently hard. Maybe the task of programming is innately one of the most complex cognitive tasks that humans have ever created.[14]*

So why do we think programming is hard? What is the evidence? In the following sections, we consider data from research studies of novice programmer ability, and course achievement data.

2.1 Failure rates

The conventional view of programming expressed in the Computer Science Education community is that:

...learning to program can be an incredibly diffi-cult task, to the point where the phrases "failure rate" and "programming course" are almost syn-onymous. [35]

Although it is often claimed that high failure rates are commonly observed in programming courses [6, 10, 26], there is little conclusive evidence to either support, or dispute, this view.

Bennedsen and Caspersen [5] conducted an empirical study to determine average pass rates among introductory programming courses. Instructors from 61 institutions contributed data, which revealed that an average of 67% of students passed their introductory programming course. Although the number of institutions was a relatively small sample of those teaching introductory programming, they concluded that it was hard to justify the claim that introductory programming courses have a high failure rate based on the data they collected. However, the authors note a significant risk of sample bias since those responding to the survey are active CS education researchers and more likely to be concerned and proactive in improving their teaching.

A subsequent study by Watson and Li [35] analysed data from 161 introductory programming courses across 15 countries. They found that an average of 67.7% of students passed, confirming the previous findings of Bennedsen and Caspersen [5]. An analysis of historical data revealed no significant differences in pass rates since the 1980's, suggesting that a pass rate of around 67% is typical and has remained so for more than 30 years.

Although the existing data seems to suggest that approximately a third of students in CS1 fail to learn how to program, it is not obvious whether this is particularly unusual for introductory courses.

It was not possible to obtain average pass rates for all courses taught internationally, but an analysis of national data from New Zealand revealed that the average pass rate across all degree-level courses was 82% [27]. Compared with this measure, the average introductory course appears to be substantially lower, which may explain why programming courses are perceived to be more difficult than other courses.

2.2 Novice programmer ability

There has been extensive research around novice programming capability, and overwhelming evidence that novice programmers cannot successfully complete the tasks we set. As early as the the 1980s, researchers such as Soloway and his colleagues showed that most novice programmers were unable to develop a working program for relatively simple problems, such the *Averaging Problem / Rainfall Problem* described below [30].

Write a program that repeatedly reads in positive integers, until it reads the integer 99999. After seeing 99999, it should print out the average.

The more recent multi-national, multi-institution studies such as those by McCracken et al. [22], Lister et al. [20], and Whalley et al. [36] provide further evidence that novice student programmers cannot perform at the level expected by researchers.

McCracken et al. [22] formed a ITiCSE Working Group out to answer the question: *Do students in introductory computing courses know how to program at the expected skill level?* The authors explicitly developed a set of learning objectives that described the expected level of skill for students at the end of their first year of study. Students were expected to be able to complete the following steps:

1. Abstract the problem from its description

2. Generate sub-problems

3. Transform sub-problems into sub-solutions

4. Re-compose the sub-solutions into a working program

5. Evaluate and iterate

Students in four universities were given programming tasks to solve. The vast majority of students were unable to develop correct solutions and many were unable to produce a solution that even compiled correctly. McCracken et al. [22] concluded that students in introductory courses did not know how to program at the expected skill level, and that the problem is fairly universal.

However, concerns were expressed that the tasks specified by McCracken et al. [22] were simply too difficult for students. This motivated a subsequent ITiCSE Working Group known as the "Leeds group", which investigated student performance on what was thought to be an easier task — the ability of students to trace code [20].

In the Leeds study, students from twelve universities were asked to answer a set of 12 multiple choice questions that required them to understand short samples of programming code. In general, students performed better than in the Mc-Cracken study with approximately half of the students correcting answering at least 2/3 of the questions. Although it is encouraging that some students can read and understand code, the bottom quartile answered less than 1/3 of the questions correctly. The authors express concern that a course with a pass rate of 75% would result in very weak students, who could correctly answer only 5 of 12 questions, potentially advancing to a typical CS2 course even though they demonstrated a very weak understanding of code.

Several multi-national, multi-institutional studies from the BRACElet group [36] investigated novice programmer performance through the analysis of student responses to exam questions. The SOLO taxonomy [8] was used to distinguish between students who could correctly determine the output of a piece of code by performing a code trace (i.e. multi-structural answers), and students who abstracted the meaning and could describe the purpose of a code segment in more general terms (i.e. relational answers). In one study that used the SOLO taxonomy to categorize student solutions to exam questions, only around one third of all students were able to produce an answer in relational terms. Even in the top quartile, less than half of the students responded in relational terms [21]. Lister et al. state that the ability to abstract the meaning of a set of instructions as a single "chunk" of code is a criticially important component of code writing. They claim:

... students who cannot read a short piece of code and describe it in relational terms are not intel-lectually well equipped to write similar code. [21]

In a study exploring the impact of different teaching approaches on novice programming understanding, Tew et al. [34] found that few students at the end of CS1 had a solid understanding of programming fundamentals. An average of only

42.29% of students who had completed CS1 answered introductory topic MCQs correctly. After completing a second course (CS2), an average of 61.53% of the students answered the introductory topic MCQs effectively.

2.3 Summary

The literature on failure rates (see section 2.1) and novice programmer ability (see section 2.2) have provided a substantial body of evidence that students are not able to program *at the level expected by instructors* by the end of an introductory programming course. Evidence suggests that the majority are unable to either read or write code typically covered in introductory programming courses. It is clear that it is difficult to master the content currently covered in typical CS1 courses in the available time. It is less clear that this means it is difficult to learn how to program.

3. EXPECTATIONS

In a post to the SIGCSE mailing list in 2014, Stephen Bloch recalled how he sometimes introduces the subject of programming in a CS course:

> *"Suppose I assigned you to write a fifteen-page paper, due two months from now, on Napoleon's invasion of Russia. [...] Now suppose I told you that the paper must be written in Swedish, using a quill pen. Now what would you need to know? [...] And if I expected you to learn all those things, from scratch, in one semester, you'd think I was nuts. That's what we'll be doing in CS1, trying to learn half a dozen different levels of knowledge at once."* [9]

Other teachers have compared learning programming to learning to write poetry in a foreign language. Anecdotally, such analogies are not uncommon among teachers describing programming — a subject in which students are typically expected to develop a mental model of a notional machine [31], understand a formal language, acquire technical expertise with a variety of software development tools, and to solve previously unseen problems using their knowledge of the machine and language.

The Computer Science Curricula 2013 [1] discusses the various tradeoffs between design decisions in first year courses, but is appropriately non-prescriptive with respect to first year curricula. Although there are exceptions, the expectations we have for a first programming course are reasonably similar across different institutions and across different countries. As a community, we have internalized what we think students should be able to achieve at the end of a novice programming course. Typically, students are expected to be able to write small programs that minimally use conditions, loops and arrays. They are frequently expected to solve problems using functional decomposition and write programs involving multiple methods. Although they are often not explicitly assessed, we also frequently expect students to acquire familiarity, if not expertise, with the systems and tools they use while programming on a given platform. We expect a lot, and the evidence indicates that many, if not most, students are unable to meet our lofty expectations.

3.1 Assessments

Not only do we expect many different kinds of learning within a CS1 course, it seems likely that the assessments we use to evaluate learning are simply too hard. Despite their working group consisting of international experts in the field, McCracken et al. [22] acknowledge that their expectations may have been too high. In other words, prior to the formal research project, a group of expert teachers who were also active Computer Science Education Researchers overestimated the capability of novice programmers. In a later study of exam questions, Whalley et al. [37] conclude that is likely programming educators are *systemically underestimating the cognitive difficulty* of their instruments for assessing programming skills of novice programmers.

The widespread use of assessment instruments that are more cognitively demanding than instructors expect have implications for our pass rates and grade distributions. Lister [19] expresses concern that the grade distributions we see in CS1 are not reflective of student ability, but rather the methods used to grade. He observes:

> *...if the computing education research community is going to have a productive discourse about CS1 grade distributions, then we must consider the validity of current approaches to grading. [19]*

Robins [25] suggests that concepts in programming are highly inter-related and proposes Learning Edge Momentum theory to explain how highly integrated concepts may result in the binomial distribution that is sometimes observed in CS1 courses. It is unclear whether or not programming *concepts* are more inter-related than other subjects that do not typically have binomial grade distributions. However, a study of exam questions by Petersen et al. [24] indicated that the *exam questions* used in CS1 were highly inter-related, and students were required to have knowledge of many different concepts before they were able to answer the questions successfully. Our *assessment practices* are a likely cause of binomial distributions. It is not necessarily the case that programming concepts are densely intertwined, but rather, our assessment instruments consist of questions that are densely intertwined and do not give students the opportunity to show which concepts they understand and which they do not.

4. UNREALISTIC EXPECTATIONS

Ultimately, the difficulty of any subject depends on the standards by which success in that subject is measured. For example, all primary school students are expected to learn basic mathematics skills such as addition. If success in year one mathematics was determined by performance of adding two single digit numbers together, then "learning to add numbers" would be considered to be easy. If instead, students were expected to add two 10 digit numbers together, then "learning to add numbers" would be described as extremely difficult. Learning to add numbers would have high failure rates and would be discouraging, perhaps leading to larger numbers of people avoiding mathematics in the future.

There is nothing intrinsic to the subject that makes it difficult to learn, but rather our subjective assessment of how much a student "should" be able to achieve by the end of the course that determines the difficulty. Learning to program is not difficult, as we have become accustomed to believing, but rather our expectations of what students "should" be able to do at the end of a first course are unrealistic.

It is time for the Computer Science Education community to undergo a paradigm shift. Rather than viewing the subject of programming as being intrinsically difficult to learn, we should be viewing our learning outcomes for novice programming courses as being unrealistic. The evidence that students are not meeting our expectations is overwhelming. In fact, research on novice programmers for at least 30 years has suggested that students have *never* met our expectations. This is not a problem with the students. This is (probably) not a problem with the way that we are delivering content. This is almost certainly a problem with the assessment of novice programming skills, derived from a mismatch between the progress that a novice programmer can realistically make in a single course and the established norms of expectation for what we *think* novice programmers *should* be able to achieve after a single course.

4.1 Consequences for Instructors

One potential problem that can occur if instructors have internalized an unachievable standard is that we assume the problem is with the students rather than the course, or we start to treat the subject itself as being difficult and one in which we now *expect* students to fail. As Bennedsen and Caspersen note:

> False views on failure and pass rates can have serious implications for the quality of introductory programming courses. A lecturer with a high failure rate might accept that "this is just the way programming courses are since all programming courses have high failure rates" and consequently not take action to improve the course in order to reduce the failure rate. [5]

4.2 Consequences for Students

If a course expects too much from students, then it is likely to result in higher rates of undesirable behavior, such as surface learning strategies and plagiarism [28]. The workload is likely to be too demanding for students and they are more likely to drop the course. Such issues have a greater impact on marginalized groups in the subject, perhaps contributing to the ongoing inequity between genders in Computer Science.

In Computer Science courses, drop rates of 30–40% are reported by several institutions [3]. A number of studies have identified excessive workload as being a significant factor in the decision of a student to drop out of a course, or to change majors. A recent study reported that "most incoming students appear to underestimate the number of hours of work that they are likely to be doing" [29]. In another study, students reported that the programming exercises took too much time and that the workload was higher than their other courses [18]. Students find that the workload in Computer Science courses is too high, the course is too difficult and takes too much time, so students drop out [17].

In an environment with such demanding expectations and excessive workload, students who are already familiar with the subject matter have a significant advantage. A study of factors contributing to the success of novice programmers found that prior programing experience was a significant factor [39]. A more recent study found that students who

entered novice programing courses with prior programming experience perform significantly better than those with no experience [15].

Given that more women than men are choosing to study Computer Science without any prior programming experience [29], this places women in novice programming courses at a severe disadvantage. A study of the reasons that women give for changing majors from Computer Science to another subject found that the excessive workload was a major factor, along with the low grades given in Computer Science courses [7]. The low grades awarded in particularly difficult courses appear to discourage women more significantly than men [40]. Students who believe that the pace and workload of novice programming courses is high, especially given their level of experience, are unlikely to pursue a Computer Science major [2].

As a community of educators, we have established unrealistically high expectations for the level of achievement that students can reach at the end of a single course. This has resulted in problematic rates of plagiarism, excessively high workload, high failure rates and high drop-out rates. These practices appear to have an especially high impact on women and may partially explain the gender inequity observed in the discipline of Computer Science.

5. ALTERNATIVES

Research on novice programmer ability has provided substantive evidence that students are not able to meet instructor expectations *within the time frame of a single course* (see section 2.2). However, it seems likely that students are capable of achieving the desired standards over a longer time frame. Tew et al. [34] provided evidence that less than half of the students at the end of a CS1 course could correctly answer questions about introductory programming topics. However, almost two thirds of the students at the end of a CS2 course were able to answer similar questions. This suggests that the introductory topics take most students longer to master than the time in a single course permits.

A longitudinal study by Teague and Lister [32, 33] provides further evidence that students may take longer than expected to acquire programming knowledge. One particular student was observed near the end of a typical introductory programming course attempting to understand code that used a loop to rotate all the elements in an array by one place to the right. The student was unable to clearly articular how the code worked and could not successfully rewrite the code to shift the elements in the array one place to the left. However, the same student was able to perform these tasks successfully one year later. Although the student struggled with basic concepts throughout their introductory course, he progressed to master that material a year later and eventually graduated with a high grade point average [32].

Although it is currently unknown how long it takes typical students to master basic programming skills, it appears to take longer than we expect. Introducing CS1 material at a slower pace has been reported positively, and may be a viable interim solution [38].

To truly establish reasonable and realistic expectations for student outcomes at the end of a novice programming course, we first need to know how long it takes students to master the various programming fundamentals. To this end, a challenge for the CS Education community is to determine an appropriate time frame for mastery of fundamental programming concepts and establishing appropriate expectations for the end of a introductory programming course — not based on historical norms, but rather on research based evidence.

6. CONCLUSION

Our current approach to teaching programming is to cover too much content too rapidly and expect students to be able to program at a higher level than they are capable of achieving at the end of an introductory programming course. The expectations we set for our students result in programming courses that are notoriously time-consuming and have high drop out and failure rates. These factors appear to have a greater impact on women and may be partially responsible for the gender inequity observed in the Computer Science discipline. This is not because programming is intrinsically difficult (at least not at novice level), but rather because we have collectively adopted disciplinary norms that are, and always have been, unrealistic. Learning to program is easy — all we need to do is collectively shift our view, and teach to achievable outcomes. The paper concludes with a challenge to the Computer Science Education community — collect research-based evidence of what novice programmer *can achieve* at the end of a first programming course and use evidence to derive realistic expectations for achievement.

7. REFERENCES

[1] ACM/IEEE-CS Joint Task Force on Computing Curricula. Computer science curricula 2013. Technical report, ACM Press and IEEE Computer Society Press, December 2013.

[2] L. J. Barker, C. McDowell, and K. Kalahar. Exploring factors that influence computer science introductory course students to persist in the major. In *Proceedings of the 40th ACM Technical Symposium on Computer Science Education*, SIGCSE '09, pages 153–157, New York, NY, USA, 2009. ACM.

[3] T. Beaubouef and J. Mason. Why the high attrition rate for computer science students: Some thoughts and observations. *SIGCSE Bull.*, 37(2):103–106, June 2005.

[4] T. Bell. Establishing a nationwide cs curriculum in new zealand high schools. *Commun. ACM*, 57(2):28–30, Feb. 2014.

[5] J. Bennedsen and M. E. Caspersen. Failure rates in introductory programming. *SIGCSE Bull.*, 39(2):32–36, June 2007.

[6] S. Bergin and R. Reilly. The influence of motivation and comfort-level on learning to program. In P. Romero, J. Good, E. A. Chaparro, and S. Bryant, editors, *Proceedings of 17th Workshop of the Psychology of Programming Interest Group*, pages 293–304, Sussex University, June 2005.

[7] M. Biggers, A. Brauer, and T. Yilmaz. Student perceptions of computer science: A retention study comparing graduating seniors with cs leavers. In *Proceedings of the 39th SIGCSE Technical Symposium on Computer Science Education*, SIGCSE '08, pages 402–406, New York, NY, USA, 2008. ACM.

[8] J. B. Biggs and K. F. Collis. *Evaluating the quality of learning: The SOLO taxonomy (Structure of the Observed Learning Outcome)*. Academic Press, New York, 1982.

[9] S. Bloch. Re: Motivating students: Was survey results. SIGCSE-members@listserv.acm.org, 14th October 2014.

[10] R. Bornat, S. Dehnadi, and Simon. Mental models, consistency and programming aptitude. In *Proceedings of the Tenth Conference on Australasian Computing Education - Volume 78*, ACE '08, pages 53–61, Darlinghurst, Australia, Australia, 2008. Australian Computer Society, Inc.

[11] N. C. C. Brown, S. Sentance, T. Crick, and S. Humphreys. Restart: The resurgence of computer science in uk schools. *Trans. Comput. Educ.*, 14(2):9:1–9:22, June 2014.

[12] M. E. Caspersen and P. Nowack. Computational thinking and practice: A generic approach to computing in danish high schools. In *Proceedings of the Fifteenth Australasian Computing Education Conference - Volume 136*, ACE '13, pages 137–143, Darlinghurst, Australia, Australia, 2013. Australian Computer Society, Inc.

[13] K. Falkner, R. Vivian, and N. Falkner. The australian digital technologies curriculum: Challenge and opportunity. In *Proceedings of the Sixteenth Australasian Computing Education Conference - Volume 148*, ACE '14, pages 3–12, Darlinghurst, Australia, Australia, 2014. Australian Computer Society, Inc.

[14] M. Guzdial. Is learning to program inherently hard? Retrieved from: https://computinged.wordpress.com/2010/04/14/is-learning-to-program-inherently-hard/, April 2010.

[15] D. Horton and M. Craig. Drop, fail, pass, continue: Persistence in cs1 and beyond in traditional and inverted delivery. In *Proceedings of the 46th ACM Technical Symposium on Computer Science Education*, SIGCSE '15, pages 235–240, New York, NY, USA, 2015. ACM.

[16] C. Kelleher and R. Pausch. Lowering the barriers to programming: A taxonomy of programming environments and languages for novice programmers. *ACM Comput. Surv.*, 37(2):83–137, June 2005.

[17] P. Kinnunen and L. Malmi. Why students drop out cs1 course? In *Proceedings of the Second International Workshop on Computing Education Research*, ICER '06, pages 97–108, New York, NY, USA, 2006. ACM.

[18] P. Kinnunen and L. Malmi. Cs minors in a cs1 course. In *Proceedings of the Fourth International Workshop on Computing Education Research*, ICER '08, pages 79–90, New York, NY, USA, 2008. ACM.

[19] R. Lister. Computing education research: Geek genes and bimodal grades. *ACM Inroads*, 1(3):16–17, Sept. 2011.

[20] R. Lister, E. S. Adams, S. Fitzgerald, W. Fone, J. Hamer, M. Lindholm, R. McCartney, J. E. Moström, K. Sanders, O. Seppälä, B. Simon, and L. Thomas. A multi-national study of reading and tracing skills in novice programmers. *SIGCSE Bull.*, 36(4):119–150, June 2004.

[21] R. Lister, B. Simon, E. Thompson, J. L. Whalley, and

C. Prasad. Not seeing the forest for the trees: Novice programmers and the solo taxonomy. *SIGCSE Bull.*, 38(3):118–122, June 2006.

[22] M. McCracken, V. Almstrum, D. Diaz, M. Guzdial, D. Hagan, Y. B.-D. Kolikant, C. Laxer, L. Thomas, I. Utting, and T. Wilusz. A multi-national, multi-institutional study of assessment of programming skills of first-year cs students. *SIGCSE Bull.*, 33(4):125–180, Dec. 2001.

[23] S. Papert. *Mindstorms: Children, Computers, and Powerful Ideas.* Basic Books, Inc., New York, NY, USA, 1980.

[24] A. Petersen, M. Craig, and D. Zingaro. Reviewing cs1 exam question content. In *Proceedings of the 42nd ACM Technical Symposium on Computer Science Education*, SIGCSE '11, pages 631–636, New York, NY, USA, 2011. ACM.

[25] A. Robins. Learning edge momentum: a new account of outcomes in cs1. *Computer Science Education*, 20(1):37–71, 2010.

[26] A. Robins, J. Rountree, and N. Rountree. Learning and teaching programming: A review and discussion. *Computer Science Education*, 13:137–172, 2003.

[27] D. J. Scott. A closer look at completion in higher education in new zealand. *Journal of Higher Education Policy and Management*, 31(2):101–108, 2009.

[28] J. Sheard and M. Dick. Directions and dimensions in managing cheating and plagiarism of it students. In *Proceedings of the Fourteenth Australasian Computing Education Conference - Volume 123*, ACE '12, pages 177–186, Darlinghurst, Australia, Australia, 2012. Australian Computer Society, Inc.

[29] J. Sinclair and S. Kalvala. Exploring societal factors affecting the experience and engagement of first year female computer science undergraduates. In *Proceedings of the 15th Koli Calling Conference on Computing Education Research*, Koli Calling '15, pages 107–116, New York, NY, USA, 2015. ACM.

[30] E. Soloway, J. Bonar, and K. Ehrlich. Cognitive strategies and looping constructs: An empirical study. *Commun. ACM*, 26(11):853–860, Nov. 1983.

[31] J. Sorva. Notional machines and introductory programming education. *Trans. Comput. Educ.*, 13(2):8:1–8:31, July 2013.

[32] D. Teague and R. Lister. Longitudinal think aloud study of a novice programmer. In *Proceedings of the Sixteenth Australasian Computing Education Conference - Volume 148*, ACE '14, pages 41–50, Darlinghurst, Australia, Australia, 2014. Australian Computer Society, Inc.

[33] D. Teague and R. Lister. Programming: Reading, writing and reversing. In *Proceedings of the 2014 Conference on Innovation & Technology in Computer Science Education*, ITiCSE '14, pages 285–290, New York, NY, USA, 2014. ACM.

[34] A. E. Tew, W. M. McCracken, and M. Guzdial. Impact of alternative introductory courses on programming concept understanding. In *Proceedings of the First International Workshop on Computing Education Research*, ICER '05, pages 25–35, New York, NY, USA, 2005. ACM.

[35] C. Watson and F. W. Li. Failure rates in introductory programming revisited. In *Proceedings of the 2014 Conference on Innovation & Technology in Computer Science Education*, ITiCSE '14, pages 39–44, New York, NY, USA, 2014. ACM.

[36] J. L. Whalley and R. Lister. The bracelet 2009.1 (wellington) specification. In *Proceedings of the Eleventh Australasian Conference on Computing Education - Volume 95*, ACE '09, pages 9–18, Darlinghurst, Australia, Australia, 2009. Australian Computer Society, Inc.

[37] J. L. Whalley, R. Lister, E. Thompson, T. Clear, P. Robbins, P. K. A. Kumar, and C. Prasad. An australasian study of reading and comprehension skills in novice programmers, using the bloom and solo taxonomies. In *Proceedings of the 8th Australasian Conference on Computing Education - Volume 52*, ACE '06, pages 243–252, Darlinghurst, Australia, Australia, 2006. Australian Computer Society, Inc.

[38] K. J. Whittington, D. P. Bills, and L. W. Hill. Implementation of alternative pacing in an introductory programming sequence. In *Proceedings of the 4th Conference on Information Technology Curriculum*, CITC4 '03, pages 47–53, New York, NY, USA, 2003. ACM.

[39] B. C. Wilson and S. Shrock. Contributing to success in an introductory computer science course: A study of twelve factors. In *Proceedings of the Thirty-second SIGCSE Technical Symposium on Computer Science Education*, SIGCSE '01, pages 184–188, New York, NY, USA, 2001. ACM.

[40] J. Wolfe and B. A. Powell. Not all curves are the same: Left-of-center grading and student motivation. In *2015 ASEE Annual Conference and Exposition*, number 10.18260/p.24527, Seattle, Washington, June 2015. ASEE Conferences. https://peer.asee.org/24527.

Developing a Rubric for a Creative CS Principles Lab

Veronica Cateté
NC State University
911 Oval Drive
Raleigh, NC 27606
vmcatete@ncsu.edu

Erin Snider
NC State University
911 Oval Drive
Raleigh, NC 27606
eesnider@ncsu.edu

Tiffany Barnes
NC State University
911 Oval Drive
Raleigh, NC 27606
tmbarnes@ncsu.edu

ABSTRACT

The "Beauty and Joy of Computing" Computer Science Principles class has inspired many new teachers to learn to teach creative computing classes in high schools. However, new computer science teachers feel under-prepared to grade open-ended programming assignments and support their students' successful learning. Rubrics have widely been used to help teaching assistants grade programs, and are a promising way to support new teachers to learn how to grade BJC programs. In this paper, we adapt general coding criteria from auto-graders to a lab where students write code to draw a brick wall. We tested the rubric on student assignments and showed that we can achieve high inter-rater agreement with the refined rubric.

CCS Concepts

•Social and professional topics → K-12 education;

Keywords

CS Principles, Rubrics, Assessment

1. INTRODUCTION

Beauty and Joy of Computing (BJC) is a version of Computer Science Principles (CSP), a new Advanced Placement course, created as an attractive and engaging introduction to computer science that can be taken in high school for college credit. BJC is a rigorous course that uses open-ended *Snap!* programming problems to teach the seven big ideas of CSP: creativity, abstraction, data and information, algorithms, programming, the internet, and global impact. With funding from the National Science Foundation, the BJC project has provided professional development for over 140 high school teachers nationwide. Teachers enjoy the course and it is well-received by students from diverse backgrounds [8], but teachers report that it is difficult to assess student work and provide students the detailed feedback they need to grow in their computing skills. Most BJC teachers do not

have a computer science background, and therefore have no experience evaluating code, or even in understanding how the complex, open-ended programming labs relate to the seven big ideas of the course. Therefore, it is critical that we help new teachers understand how the tasks students undertake in their labs can be assessed, and how their performance relates to the course's learning objectives.

To address this need, we are defining rubrics for BJC labs that teachers can use to grade student programs. We envision that these rubrics will be usable by new teachers for assessment, and for providing students with meaningful feedback that links to the course's important content. This paper represents the first step in our process - identifying common novice programming grading criteria, adapting them to a specific BJC lab, testing their application on student programs, and refining the rubric to obtain good inter-rater reliability. While grading student programs is straightforward for experienced computer scientists, inexperience with computing and the variety of student code makes this a difficult task for teachers. Less experienced graders must rely on the stated assignment objectives, which can be difficult to translate into numeric grades.

We used a three-phased approach to design and evaluate a rubric for the Brick Wall assignment. In Phase I, we first selected rubric criteria based on literature on automatic support for grading novice programming assignments, and wrote descriptions for 4 levels of performance for each criteria to create an initial rubric. Then, two raters applied the initial rubric to grade 9 student programs independently, and we measured inter-rater reliability. In Phase II, the raters compared their assessments, and refined the rubric and assessments of the initial 9 samples until they agreed upon the scores for each of these projects. Finally, the raters tested the robustness of the revised rubric on 10 additional college assignments, and computed Kappa to measure inter-rater reliability on the new assignments. We considered a Kappa value of 0.7 or higher to be reliable. In Phase III, we rated all of the projects to compare the results for students taught by an expert high school computer science (CS) teacher with those taught by novice undergraduates.

This work is important in demonstrating that it is possible to create a rubric based on computer science education literature, that can be reliably applied by people with no computing background, to programs that are actually created by novice programmers. Our results show that we can achieve high inter-rater reliability between a computer scientist and a science educator with no computing background, on diverse programs created in labs with teaching assistants

ITiCSE '16, July 09-13, 2016, Arequipa, Peru

© 2016 ACM. ISBN 978-1-4503-4231-5/16/07. . . $15.00

DOI: http://dx.doi.org/10.1145/2899415.2899449

with no prior programming experience. These results provide strong evidence that we can adapt a general rubric to help novice computing teachers evaluate student programs for particular BJC labs. In the remainder of Section 1, we present the Brick Wall assignment. In Section 2, we explain the development of the Brick Wall rubric. In Section 3, we describe the study methods and phases. In Sections 4 and 5, we present our results and conclusions.

1.1 Brick Wall Assignment

Surveys show that most high school BJC teachers from 2012-2014 used Brick Wall, so we chose it for rubric development. BJC's Brick Wall lab was designed to demonstrate abstraction and the value of creating a function that can be called to perform the same task multiple times, and with different parameters. The main objective of the Brick Wall lab is to create a brick wall with an alternating pattern of bricks. In the assignment, two row types A and B are defined, where an A row is made up of whole bricks, and a B row starts and ends with half-bricks. The assignment specifies that students should create a new block in *Snap!* that takes 'number of rows' as input and draws a brick wall that alternates A and B type rows accordingly, as shown in Figure 1. Students are instructed to create one method that generates a brick wall, two separate methods that draw the two row types, and a method that draws an individual brick. These specific instructions are explained as levels of abstraction for solving the problem. The visual nature of the task and the clear and simple repetitive structure of a brick wall are affordances that should help make iteration and functions seem to be natural solutions to the problem.

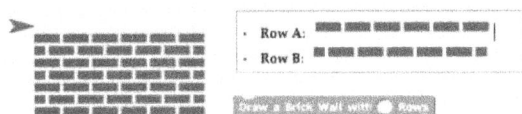

Figure 1: Levels of abstraction for the Brick Wall assignment

2. RUBRIC CREATION

To support new teachers to teach computer science, we would ideally build automated systems that could provide both students and teachers with feedback on student performance. Several such intelligent tutoring systems (ITS) have been used to teach programming to novice students. However, the new BJC course strives to inspire new and diverse students to explore computing with modern tools that can be used to express creativity, such as the *Snap!* programming language. To more quickly support teachers with these new environments, we determined it would be helpful to develop rubrics to help teachers understand the goals of each programming assignment. Our rubric development was strongly influenced by ITSs for programming, since we wish to make an objective system that can be used reliably by teachers with different backgrounds to accurately grade student work. In this section, we describe our process to create a rubric based on computer science education literature. We draw strongly from the literature in intelligent tutoring, where researchers have expended great effort to automate the processes needed to evaluate student code.

2.1 Rubrics in CS Ed

In education, rubrics are used as performance-based assessment for student projects. Rubrics use descriptive measures to separate levels of performance on a given task [10]. Then, each level of performance for a particular task is assigned a value. Values in rating scales on rubrics can be either holistic or analytic [2]. Holistic rubrics are quick and efficient, evaluating projects as a whole. Analytic rubrics take longer to design, but offer multiple dimensions that are evaluated separately. Since our goal was to enable teachers to provide more detailed feedback, we chose to design an analytic rubric.

Rubrics can effectively support teaching assistants, who are non-experts in computer science, to quickly, accurately, and consistently assess novice student programs for style, functionality, and design[1]. Researchers tend to agree on three levels of achievement ratings that denote shortcomings, meets expected outcomes, and goes beyond expectations [1, 3, 9]. Stegeman separates expected outcomes into two levels - almost there, and meets expectations [9], and we use this refinement to arrive at four levels. While there is agreement on the levels that programming rubrics should contain, McCauley highlights that it is important that rubrics have precise and consistent language [6]. Toward that end, we chose our rubric criteria from those developed for automated support for grading, as described in the next section.

2.2 Criteria Selection

The first step in designing a rubric is to identify a coherent set of criteria for evaluation [2]. When designing our rubric to help teachers evaluate student projects by hand, we wanted to focus on evidence that would be clearly observable in student programs. Since automated systems rely upon objective and observable criteria, they are a natural source for our rubric criteria: Accuracy (correctness), Efficiency (as measured by the number of times blocks are repeated in code), Reasoning (domain knowledge), and Readability (style). These criteria were inspired by Pillay, Zeller, Jackson and Usher as we discuss here.

In 2003, Pillay studied four separate programming tutors and identified four common ways they evaluate student code [7], including: accuracy or correctness of topic, efficiency of the code, adherence to style guidelines, and algorithmic domain knowledge. Domain knowledge is comprised of procedural knowledge on how to write programs and declarative knowledge on how to apply different programming concepts. Since these were common features, we included all four in our initial rubric design.

Jackson and Usher's ASSYST auto-grading system was built to alleviate the errors that people are prone to make when grading, while still keeping a human tutor involved [5]. ASSYST assesses student code for: correctness, efficiency, style, complexity, and test data adequacy. ASSYST measures correctness by how well the student program's output matches the output from a known correct program. Correctness, in BJC, corresponds to whether the program achieves the stated goal, and corresponds to the accuracy metric in Pillay's work and our rubric. ASSYST measures efficiency by keeping track of how often a particular block of code is executed. This assigns higher efficiency to a loop which runs a single command 10 times than code for the same task that uses 10 separate commands each executed once [4]. When

Table 1: Brick Wall rubric. Additions in italics were refinements to achieve the final rubric.

Category	4	3	2	1
Accuracy	At least 5-6 rows of bricks created *with alternating brick pattern but all rows same length*	Two rows of brick created with alternating patterns, *or 5-6 inaccurate rows*	1 brick created and repeated	1 brick created
Efficiency	Abstracted methods and loops used to repeat coding patterns	A few abstracted methods were created, but there is still a lot of repeated code	Code works but is repeated simple statements *(little abstraction)*	Abstraction of complex methods not identifiable
Reasoning	There is evidence of the use of mathematical and logical concepts **&** appropriate use of abstractions and algorithms.	There is evidence of the use of mathematical and logical concepts **or** appropriate use of abstractions and algorithms.	There is inappropriate use of abstractions and algorithms.	Little or no evidence of the use of mathematical and logical concepts exists
Readability	The source code has been commented and the source code is correct, logical, & easily readable.	The source code is correct, logical, and easily readable.	The source code is mostly correct, logical, and readable.	The source code is unclear, incorrect, or incomplete.

scoring code by hand, we estimate this by observing whether the projects contain identical code that is written more than once. Repetitive commands in code represent less efficient code, where a loop could have been used instead of copy-paste. ASSYST's style metric includes features such as indentation and variable naming. A similar metric can be found in Pillay's work, as well as in Zeller's readability metric, that refers to how easily another person can read and understand how the project code achieves the goals [7, 11]. We combined these to produce a single Readability criterion for our rubric.

2.3 Performance Descriptions

Once we identified the rubric criteria (Accuracy, Efficiency, Reasoning, and Readability), we used the Brick Wall assignment to write descriptions of observable behaviors for each level of performance for each criteria. Brookhart's guidelines suggest that performance level descriptions should be clear, descriptive, and cover the whole range of performance [2]. We started by identifying Level 3 for meets expectations, as described in the assignment. Level 1 descriptions were basically the opposite of these. We developed Level 2 descriptions by identifying how students might have just missed meeting expectations. To develop Level 4 descriptions, we added language about how students might enhance their programs along the lines of the given criteria. Table 1 lists our rubric, with initial descriptions in plain text and the refinements made to create the final rubric added in italics.

3. STUDY DESIGN AND METHODS

Our hypothesis was that we could develop a well-defined, analytic rubric, that raters can use to achieve an acceptable level of inter-rater reliability (with Kappa at least 0.7). The following sections describe our the context, data selection, and methods for rating and rubric refinement.

3.1 Context and Data Sources

Student code samples for rating were drawn randomly from three classes: two high school elective BJC classes taught by the same teacher in Fall 2013, and one college introductory non-majors computing course taught in Spring 2014. The high school data was from one high school teacher

teaching two sections of BJC in Fall 2014. Of the original 42 students, one joined the course halfway through and 2 were missing files, leaving a total of 39 high school submissions. In the Spring 2014 college course with 78 students, 57 files were submitted but 2 were unusable, leaving 55 college submissions. A total of nineteen projects were randomly chosen for analysis, with nine (three from each course) for the initial round, and 10 from the college course for the final round. These projects ranged from completely accurate walls, to one brick telling a joke to a circle.

The two high school classes were taught by an experienced AP Computer Science high school teacher. The college course had lectures by a Computer Science professor, but the seven lab sections were facilitated by five undergraduate teaching assistants (UTAs) with no prior experience in teaching or in BJC. This is similar to the preparation that new BJC high school teachers have, ranging from inexperienced teachers with no computing background to an expert with 20 years of experience teaching advanced computer science in high schools. The five UTA majors were: computer science, civil engineering, materials science, paper science, and textile technology. The UTAs had no prior teaching experience, and no similar computing course. The course professor led the UTAs through the lab the week before students did it, in much the same way that high school teachers keep one step ahead of their students when they teach a new class for the first time. We therefore felt that code from the college course would be representative of work we might expect from students taught by an inexperienced high school teacher with no computing background. Therefore, random samples were chosen from the college course for the evaluation of the final rubric.

3.2 Methods

In each phase, two raters worked independently using the rubric to grade each submission, and we computed Kappa for inter-rater reliability at the end of each phase. Rater1 has a Master's in Computer Science, and Rater2 has a PhD in Science Education. In Phase I, both raters rated nine samples from the three courses (three samples from each). To make the selections, we skimmed the programs and determined that the high school submissions were similar, so we selected three from each high school course at random. Since we wished to have programs demonstrating diverse performance levels, we made random selections from the college course but continued to make selections until we felt we had samples that were fair, good, and very good.

In Phase II, the raters compared their ratings of all nine samples, and when they did not agree, discussed the ratings, and refined the rubric, as shown in italics in Table 1, until they achieved 100 percent agreement on the ratings for the 9 samples. We will elaborate on some of the contentious coding samples in section 5.2. During this comparison, the raters realized that the quality of submissions from the high school course was higher and less variable. Therefore, the raters selected 10 projects from the college course to test the final, refined rubric for Phase II. As in Phase I, the college projects were selected randomly but samples were excluded if they were very similar to previously-selected samples.

Finally, in Phase III, we trained a third-year undergraduate computer science major to apply the final rubric to the Brick Wall assignment. Rater1 and the new undergraduate (UG) Rater3 applied the final rubric to all 94 Brick Wall assignments, and computed average composite scores for the high school and college projects to compare the performance between the classes. We hypothesized that the experienced high school teacher's students would outperform college students facilitated by university teaching assistants who were inexperienced at both teaching and CS.

4. RESULTS

In Phase I, three projects from each section (6 high school, 3 college) were rated using the initial rubric. We found very low agreement between our raters, with a Cohen's Kappa of 0.37. In Phase II, the raters discussed their ratings and refined the rubric, clarifying the descriptions, until they agreed on all ratings for all criteria on the 9 samples. The final rubric is shown in Table 1 with changes between initial and final in italics. In Phase II, the raters applied the resulting final rubric to rate 10 additional college coding samples, and achieved a high level of inter-rater agreement, with Kappa of 0.73. In Phase III, the newly-trained Rater3 achieved a Kappa of 0.735 with Rater1 and Rater 2 on the 19 projects rated in Phases I and II. Rater 1 and Rater3 then rated the remaining 75 projects and aggregated the rubric scores by high school and college. Results show a clear distinction in performance in labs between the students taught by novices versus the expert high school computer science teacher.

High school students taught by the "master" teacher averaged 3.60 on the Brick Wall assignment. College students taught by novice undergraduates scored an average of 2.79 on the assignment. Figure 2 shows the criteria scores for each class with 25 percent error bars, demonstrating that the high schoolers taught by a master teacher scored quite highly on accuracy and efficiency, and similarly to the college students taught by novices in readability. The largest difference occurs in the reasoning category, where high schoolers were more likely to use conditionals and mathematical expressions. This difference could be due to the teachers, but could also be due to a difference between the self-selection of high school students into a pre-college course, and students taking a low-level computing course as a general analytic elective in college. We present these results to show how the potential differences between novice and master BJC teachers may be impacting student performance in BJC courses.

To illustrate the application of the rubric to student code,

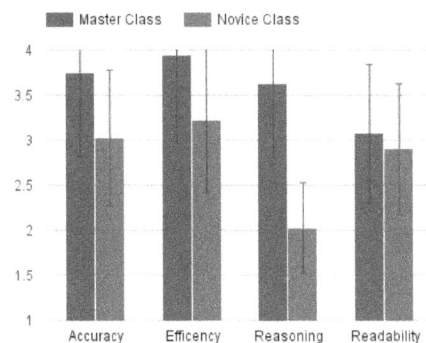

Figure 2: Rubric scores for master and novice teachers

we present sample projects that demonstrate low, medium, or high levels of overall performance, based on standard deviation (SD) away from the overall average for the 19 scored projects. Students more than one SD below average were ranked Low, students one SD above were ranked high. The remaining programs were ranked medium. Of the six high school projects, one was ranked Medium and five were ranked High for demonstrating appropriate abstraction, use of parameters, programming logic and mathematical reasoning. The 13 college class artifacts were rated with two High, seven Medium, and four Low.

4.1 Code Examples

In this section, we showcase one example at each performance level (low, medium, and high). Figure 3 shows an example of a low project with the average of all four ratings of 1.75. The Accuracy score was 3 for creating two rows of bricks with alternating lengths. The Efficiency score was 2, since the code works but consists of repeated simple statements. The Reasoning score was 1, as there is little or no evidence of the use of mathematical and logical concepts exists. Finally, the Readability score was 1, as the source code is unclear, incorrect, or incomplete.

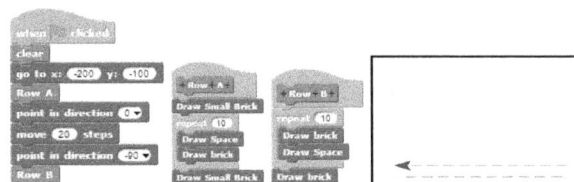

Figure 3: Low-level example, scored as: Accuracy = 3, Efficiency = 2, Reasoning = 1, and Readability = 1.

Figure 4 demonstrates medium performance, with an average score of 3.0. The Accuracy score was 4 for having at least 5-6 rows of bricks with alternating lengths. The Efficiency score was 3, since a few methods were created, but there is still a lot of repeated code. The Reasoning score was 2 since there is inappropriate use of abstractions and algorithms. Lastly, the Readability scored 3 since the code is correct, logical, and easily readable.

Figure 5 demonstrates high overall performance, with an average score of 3.75. The Accuracy score was 4 since the program creates at least 5-6 rows of bricks with alternating lengths. The Efficiency score was 4 for using methods and

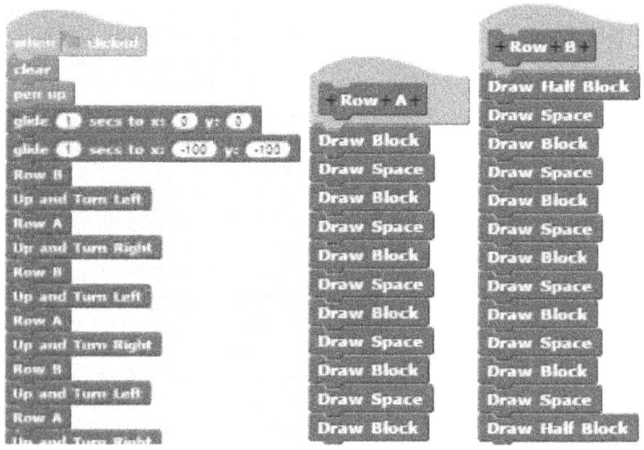

Figure 4: Medium-level example, scored as: Accuracy = 4, Efficiency = 3, Reasoning = 2, and Readability = 3. This program shows lack of loops and logic

loops to repeat coding patterns. Reasoning also scored 4 since there is evidence of the use of mathematical and logical concepts and appropriate use of abstractions and algorithms. Finally, the Readability scores 3 since the source code is correct, logical, and easily readable.

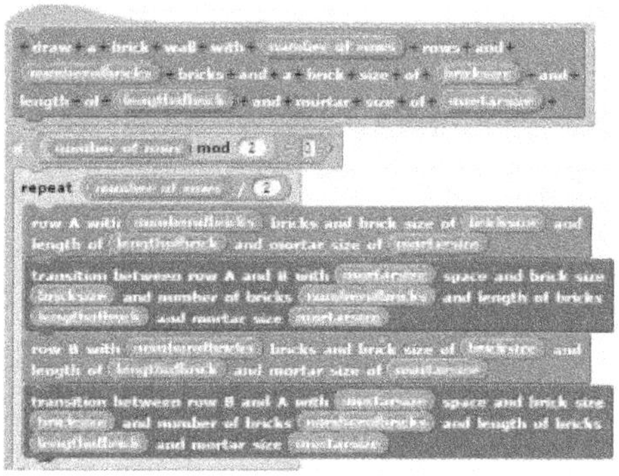

(a) First half of method to generate wall (even # of rows)

Figure 5: High-level example, scored as: Accuracy = 4, Efficiency = 4, Reasoning = 4, and Readability = 3. Program uses loops & math to generate correct output.

These three student code examples demonstrate the diverse ways students can complete an assignment. The low example uses a simple repeat loop, but only creates two rows. The medium example, forgoes loops, rather listing each row separately. The medium and high examples both draw a complete brick wall, but only the high example demonstrates how abstraction and parameters can be used to draw a brick wall customized to user input.

4.2 Rubric Refinement

There were four main areas where we edited the initial rubric to resolve rating differences, three in accuracy: misaligned row ends, parameter setting, and code needing edits to run properly; and one in reasoning, with student use of "magic numbers". The Accuracy criterion relies on matching the program's output to the lab assignment's objectives. The lab assignment was generally detailed enough

for the two raters to consistently score projects for Accuracy, but a few student programs demonstrated behaviors not accounted for on the rubric. Readability measures how well another person can read someone's code. This category was easily measurable by both raters and adjustments were not required. Efficiency is related to code length - shorter code with blocks that are executed more often than they appear in the program is more efficient. This difference can be seen between 4 which uses the 'Up and Turn Left' and 'Up and Turn Right' blocks each five times, versus 5 which uses each transition block once (it gets repetitively called using a loop). Since this was a straightforward measure, the raters agreed on scores. The Reasoning criterion describes use of logic and abstraction - such as having if or while blocks. The main difference in raters on this was that Rater1 could determine whether mathematical expressions logically matched the program requirements, or if a student inserted a parameter, we call a "magic number" to adjust program output to be correct, despite this number having no basis in logic.

The primary confusion between raters typically revolved around different interpretations of Accuracy. The first difference was in how to score Accuracy for code that correctly draws multiple rows of bricks but whose ends did not align, as shown in Figure 6. Originally, the rubric listed 5-6 rows as a 4 rating and 2 rows as a 3 rating, since we anticipated that some projects would not include loops to create multiple rows. Rater1 scored rows with alternating lengths with a 3, since they were not entirely accurate, while Rater2 scored them with a 4 since they had 5-6 rows. Therefore, we added the words "or 5-6 inaccurate rows" to the Accuracy level 3 description to settle this difference.

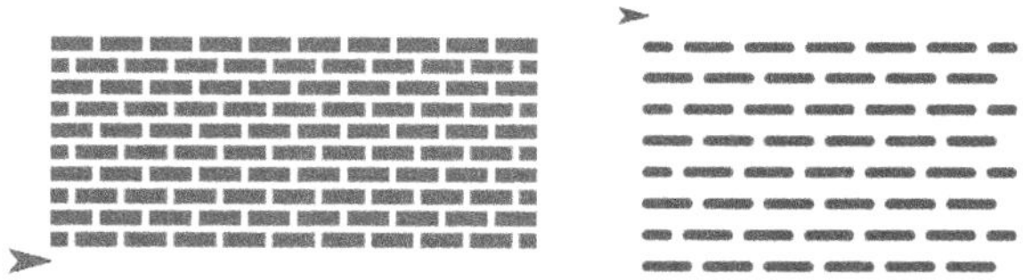

Figure 6: Two brick walls with differing row alignment on the right side.

A second difference between the raters was in judging Accuracy for programs that had adjustable parameters and inputs. In some student projects, the brick wall would not be drawn exactly right unless the rater modified a parameter or input before running the code. Rater1 (computer scientist) scored these higher than Rater2, since it is standard practice in computer science courses to test code with multiple input values. Rater2 was not familiar with this practice, so rated these projects as incorrect. Upon discussion, the raters agreed to count programs as correct if parameters could be easily adjusted to achieve the correct output, but this was not explicitly added to the rubric.

The raters discovered that some adjustment of the *Snap!* interface might be needed to fully observe some program behaviors. For a few projects, zooming out or re-centering the stage view made it possible to view the entire wall for evaluation. For a few others, the student had programmed fixed off-screen values for the start and end positions of the wall, relying on the *Snap!* interface to cut off the wall edges.

This did not require adjustment of the rubric, but rather adjustment in how the raters used *Snap!* to run programs.

(a) Wall drawn off screen (b) Code shows "magic numbers"

Figure 7: Blocks showing student misunderstandings.

The use of "magic numbers" was the source of confusion for both raters. It was apparent in one example that a student was having difficulty aligning the A and B-type rows and relied upon formulas or numbers to adjust the placement of bricks. However, these "magic numbers" were not applied systematically or in a way that appeared to have a logical reason (to either rater). In these cases, the brick walls looked good but it appeared that students applied a guess and check strategy to determine numbers to use to make the brick wall look correct. The intention of the assignment was for the students to discover a general solution to the brick wall problem, not one that is specific to a particular browser, screen resolution, or idiosyncrasies of student code. In this case, math and logic are clearly applied (since there are mathematical operators visible in the code), but, without a clear formula, it was unclear as to whether or not math and logic were being applied appropriately. This project was also one that had pre-programmed positions for the starting point, and attempts to center the brick wall on stage were difficult to make. It was resolved that there was in fact (inappropriate) use of magic numbers, and another field was added to Reasoning level 2 (Table 1).

5. CONCLUSIONS AND FUTURE WORK

In this study, we created an analytic rubric based on evaluation frameworks that automatically assist people in grading student programs, applied the rubric to a set of student work, refined the rubric, and applied it again, demonstrating a dramatic increase in inter-rater reliability. Our rubric rates BJC Brick Wall programs for accuracy, efficiency, reasoning, and readability. In Phase I, we observed that Rater2 (science education) initially had more difficulties with the rubric. In Phase II, after discussion and strategic updates to the rubric, this rater's scores aligned much more closely with those by Rater1 (computer scientist). One limitation of the study is that the raters' discussion likely informed the scoring of assignments in Phase II, so therefore do not represent the likely scores of novice teachers upon first application of the rubric. However, to help address this limitation, we have selected sample student programs that illustrates three levels of proficiency, and will provide these types of samples in our future studies of rubrics as they are used by novice BJC teachers. We also believe that teachers will learn, from the application of the rubric to student code, to differentiate programs according to the rubric criteria, promoting their learning of computer science and their skill in evaluating student programs. Eventually, we believe teachers can use the rubrics to guide students to create better programs.

Another limitation of this study was that the Brick Wall lab is relatively simple. This may be the reason that only minor changes were needed to achieve an acceptable rubric. For more complex assignments, it may not be as straightforward to map the assignment to the rubric criteria. We expect that the readability and efficiency criteria will not need much refinement, but accuracy criteria may need to be added for each program objective, and reasoning may also need individual criteria for each distinct objective.

In future work, we plan to align our rubric with essential knowledge components from the CS Principles course framework available at apcsprinciples.org. For example, Essential Knowledge component 4.1.1 D enumerates the learning goals for Mathematics; specifying iteration, loops, and using the modulus operator. Raters considered similar ideas within the Reasoning category of our rubric, but we could revise the rubric to be more focused on learning objectives, and this is better for providing students target learning goals [2]. By expanding the Reasoning section of our Brick Wall rubric to focus on learning goals and not just task completion, teachers will also be able to better identify what students should be learning and doing during a particular activity or lab.

6. REFERENCES

[1] K. Becker. Grading programming assignments using rubrics. In *ACM SIGCSE Bulletin*, volume 35, pages 253–253. ACM, 2003.

[2] S. M. Brookhart. *How to create and use rubrics for formative assessment and grading*. ASCD, 2013.

[3] S. Fitzgerald, B. Hanks, R. Lister, R. McCauley, and L. Murphy. What are we thinking when we grade programs? In *Proceeding of the 44th ACM technical symposium on Computer science education*, pages 471–476. ACM, 2013.

[4] A. Hicks. Bots: Harnessing player data and player effort to create and evaluate levels in a serious game. In *Educational Data Mining 2013*, 2013.

[5] D. Jackson and M. Usher. Grading student programs using assyst. *SIGCSE Bull.*, 29(1):335–339, Mar. 1997.

[6] R. McCauley. Rubrics as assessment guides. *ACM SIGCSE Bulletin*, 35(4):17–18, 2003.

[7] N. Pillay. Developing intelligent programming tutors for novice programmers. *ACM SIGCSE Bulletin*, 35(2):78–82, 2003.

[8] T. W. Price, J. Albert, V. Cateté, and T. Barnes. BJC in Action : Comparison of Student Perceptions of a Computer Science Principles Course. In *Proc. of the 1st Annual RESPECT Conference*, 2015.

[9] M. Stegeman, E. Barendsen, and S. Smetsers. Towards an empirically validated model for assessment of code quality. In *Proceedings of the 14th Koli Calling International Conference on Computing Education Research*, pages 99–108. ACM, 2014.

[10] D. D. Stevens and A. J. Levi. Introduction to rubrics. *Sterling, VA: Stylus*, 2005.

[11] A. Zeller. Making students read and review code. *SIGCSE Bull.*, 32(3):89–92, July 2000.

A New Metric to Quantify Repeated Compiler Errors for Novice Programmers

Brett A. Becker
School of Computer Science
University College Dublin
Belfield, Dublin 4, Ireland
brett.becker@ucd.ie

ABSTRACT

Encountering the same compiler error repeatedly, particularly several times consecutively, has been cited as a strong indicator that a student is struggling with important programming concepts. Despite this, there are relatively few studies which investigate repeated errors in isolation or in much depth. There are also few data-driven metrics for measuring programming performance, and fewer for measuring repeated errors. This paper makes two contributions. First we introduce a new metric to quantify repeated errors, the repeated error density (RED). We compare this to Jadud's Error Quotient (EQ), the most studied metric, and show that RED has advantages over EQ including being less context dependent, and being useful for short sessions. This allows us to answer two questions posited by Jadud in 2006 that have until now been unanswered. Second, we compare the EQ and RED scores using data from an empirical control/intervention group study involving an editor which enhances compiler error messages. This intervention group has been previously shown to have a reduced overall number of student errors, number of errors per student, and number of repeated student errors per compiler error message. In this research we find a reduction in EQ, providing further evidence that error message enhancement has positive effects. In addition we find a significant reduction in RED providing evidence that this metric is valid.

General Terms

Algorithms; Measurement; Human Factors; Languages

Keywords

Java; debugging; errors; syntax errors; error messages; compiler errors; repeated errors; consecutive errors; error quotient; EQ; feedback; novice; programming; CS1

1. INTRODUCTION

Many studies on novice programmer behavior analyze errors along with other facets of the programming experi-

ITiCSE '16, July 09-13, 2016, Arequipa, Peru

© 2016 ACM. ISBN 978-1-4503-4231-5/16/07. . . $15.00

DOI: http://dx.doi.org/10.1145/2899415.2899463

ence, with far fewer focusing extensively or exclusively on errors, particularly repeated errors. There are also few data-driven metrics to measure programming performance [15], and fewer for measuring repeated errors. This is despite the fact that the number and frequency of repeated errors has been cited as the best indicator of how well a programming student is progressing [11]. Most studies that focus on repeated errors investigate using metrics to predict student achievement, normally by correlating metrics with assessment marks. However, the quality and usefulness of these correlations have varied considerably. In addition, the metric normally used, Jadud's Error Quotient (EQ) [10, 11], has been recently shown to vary across groups, environments, and contexts, with further validation called for before the EQ can be used as a proxy for traditional measures of performance [12].

In that light, this paper introduces a new metric for measuring repeated errors, the *Repeated Error Density* (RED). We also demonstrate that this metric is less context dependent, useful for short sequences, and is significantly reduced by an editor that has previously been shown to result in significantly fewer compiler errors (including repeated errors). Being less context dependent is seen as important since being able to generalize on study results is a fundamental requirement for putting them into effective use [15]. The authors are not aware of any other study empirically comparing the number/frequency of repeated errors between control and intervention groups.

This paper is laid out as follows. In Section 2 we review related work involving repeated error metrics. In Section 3 we present a new metric, the *Repeated Error Density* (RED), and demonstrate that it has properties which enable it to answer some questions posited by Jadud in [11], which the Error Quotient cannot. In Section 4 we apply the RED to real-world data and compare it to the EQ. We show that RED is reduced in an empirical control/intervention study, providing evidence that this metric is valid. Reductions in EQ and RED also support the results of [3] and [4], providing further evidence that enhancing error messages is effective. We also discuss some threats to validity. In Section 5 we present concluding remarks and future work.

2. RELATED WORK

It has been shown that the majority of students spend the majority of their time on a minority of errors and that students spend more time solving certain kinds of syntax errors than others [9, 17]. In addition, repeating errors is common, and has been observed and studied for at least the last four decades, and across languages such as: assembly [8], C [15, 19], Java [3, 11, 15], LISP [14], Pascal [13] and Python [15]. In [10] it was found that when a student encounters certain high frequency errors in Java, there were often double-digit chances that the next error was the same error. Several reasons for students' frequently repeating errors have been postulated:

- Some students may be meticulous in their programming, and checking (possibly more often than necessary) that their code compiles, or that the state of play has not changed since their last thought [10].

- Some students may be sloppy in their interaction with the compiler. In some cases, interaction with the program source may cause the most recent error to disappear, requiring a recompile for a reminder [10].

- Some students may not trust the error message reported by the compiler, and are recompiling in a naive hope that the output will change [10].

- There is evidence that experienced programmers do not make as many repeated errors as novices [14], and that beginning students make more repeated errors than more advanced students [8].

- Students may be struggling with the nature of particular errors, a fundamental programming misconception [13], the actual compiler error message being presented to them, and/or the syntax of the language itself [11].

As early as 1984 repeated errors began to be noticed by those interested in novice programmer behavior. PROUST [13] analyzed Pascal programs written by novices, diagnosed non-syntactic bugs, and explained them to the programmer. When a bug was found, it was not initially known if it was for instance a typographical accident, or the result of a deep-rooted misconception. The authors of [13] noted that distinguishing between these two explanations required looking for the same bug being repeated; if a bug occurred just once it was most likely an accident, if it occurred repeatedly the case for a misconception being the cause was strengthened.

The authors of [14] studied a group of students programming in LISP. These students knew LISP 'reasonably well', in that their errors could be considered 'slips' as defined in [5]. These students were unlikely to repeat the same error within a single program or across different programs.

In [2], the authors analyzed over 37 million Java compilation events from the Blackbox data set [7]. In particular they analyzed the frequency of 18 errors also explored in [6]. They found that the number of times each of these errors was repeated by the same student (not necessarily consecutively), in the same file, varied between 1 and 7. On average it could be expected that a given student can expect to repeat an error that was previously committed in the same file a further 3.3 times.

The authors of [8] developed a model of students studying assembly language which included five stages: novice, advanced beginner, competent, proficient, and expert. Each stage was characterized by a number of debugging abilities and habits. The novice and advanced beginner stages were partly characterized by repeating the same types of error throughout a program *frequently* and *occasionally* respectively. Repeating errors was not listed as an ability/habit of the three more advanced stages.

In [19] a framework was proposed to support the education of novice programmers. Among many features, the framework sought to aid educators in helping students who kept repeating the same error(s) as these students in particular needed to be provided a long time for student support. In this framework when a student repeatedly made the same mistake, the identity of the student and the error were relayed to the instructor. This feature was seen to work well in a trial with students programming in C.

In [10], Jadud found that many Java errors were frequently repeated (consecutively) by novices. In particular he found that 21% of *; expected*, 17% of *unknown variable*, 20% of *bracketing* 30% of *illegal start of expression*, and 14% of *unknown class* errors were followed by the exact same error, representing consecutive repeats.

In [11], Jadud reported that the number of repeated errors was an indication of struggling students, and often the best indicator for how well (or poorly) a student was progressing. To measure this behavior, Jadud proposed the *Error Quotient* (EQ), a quantification for novice compilation behavior that provides an indication for how much a student is struggling with the language while programming [10, 11]. Specifically, the EQ is a value that is deterministically generated from observable (loggable) data. The EQ is normalized to between 0 and 1 inclusive, and averaged over a programming session. A low EQ indicates that a student is dealing with errors they encounter efficiently. A high EQ indicates that a student is struggling, making changes that do not rectify the error causing a particular compiler error message. Importantly, it was found that students with a low EQ generated relatively few compiler error messages while those with a high EQ generated many compiler error messages that were *repeated*, often in the same location and over many successive compilations. It was found that the EQ correlated significantly with traditional indicators of academic success such as coursework assessments and end-of-year exams. The EQ is determined by Algorithm *EQ* [11] which utilizes Figure 1.

Algorithm *EQ*

1. **Collate** Create consecutive pairs from all compilation events in a session, e.g. $(e_1, e_2), (e_2, e_3), ..., (e_{n-1}, e_n)$.

2. **Calculate** Score each pair according to Figure 1.

3. **Normalize** Divide the score assigned to each pair by 11 (the maximum value possible for each pair).

4. **Average** Sum the scores and divide by n, the number of pairs.

The EQ is very dependent on the amount of repeated errors. In fact if every compilation in a session ends with the generation of the exact same compiler error, the EQ for that session would be 1. If no errors are generated or all errors are fixed on the first attempt, the EQ would be 0. If there are repeated errors of differing types, the EQ would be somewhere between 0 and 1.

The penalties assigned in Figure 1 are not arbitrary. In fact the original EQ algorithm scored several more parameters including error and edit locality [11]. In an attempt to find the best parameters, Jadud sought to discover those which differentiated between students across the whole population by choosing the parameter set that had the greatest range for each student between the minimum and maximum

EQ values while minimizing the standard deviation of EQ values for each student.

In [10], Jadud found a distinct correlation between a student's error quotient and the grades they received on assignments. Despite the correlation being significant it was described as being of low quality ($R^2 = 0.11$). The correlation between error quotient and final exam grade was found to be more significant, but also of low quality ($R^2 = 0.25$).

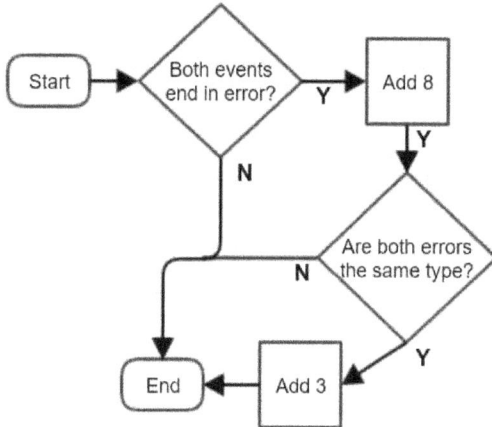

Figure 1: The error quotient event pairing algorithm. Values are then normalized and averaged according to Algorithm EQ.

In [11], Jadud noticed that the average error quotient dropped throughout the course of a year-long study, indicating that this population learned to deal with syntax errors more effectively with time. In trying to establish if the error quotient could be used to predict student assessment marks, a significant correlation between the error quotient and marks received on an exam given at the end of the first semester of observation was found, although of poor quality ($R^2 = 0.22$). Unfortunately there was no significant correlation found between the error quotient and an exam given at the end of the year.

Rodrigo et al. [16] asked if they could identify at-risk novice programmers and predict student achievement using the EQ metric. They found a moderate but significant correlation with mid-term exam scores. The authors of [18] also found a correlation between EQ scores and achievement on midterm exams, but their models could not accurately predict at-risk students.

In [15] the authors explored both versions of the EQ with data sets from four CS1 contexts involving different working practices, student backgrounds and languages: C, Python and Java. Using linear models the authors also explored a range of parameter values. These models relate average EQ to a measure of student performance, either a summative assessment or course mark. Overall they found that different contexts produced very different models. In fact the Python and Java data sets were best served by almost opposing models. The authors also found that the Java data set did not benefit from the additional EQ parameters, similar to conclusions reached by Jadud [10]. In addition their C data set did not yield a significant model. However the explanatory power of both Python data sets was improved. Nonetheless

even data drawn from two contexts with the same language (Python) resulted in extremely different models.

The authors concluded that context specific variables such as programming tools (IDEs, etc.), language, and type of work students are asked to perform while gathering data all greatly affect the EQ and its predictive power. Of course there are a multitude of other factors that may also have effects such as demographics, physical environment, etc. These results suggest that data-driven metrics such as the EQ need to be tuned for their specific contexts.

Watson et al. [20] also found a significant correlation between the EQ and the scores of students in their data ($r = 0.44$). They proposed an extended algorithm called Watwin which takes into account the time a student spends in overcoming a particular error. Like the EQ, the Watwin score is between 0 and 1 inclusive, with a score of 0 indicating that no errors were made over a session. A score of 1 indicates that every compilation ended in an error, and that the student spent longer than their peers between successive compilations. The closer the score is to 0, the stronger the student is deemed to be. With this improved algorithm the correlation improved to ($r = 0.51$).

The authors of [1] explored how the EQ and Watwin metrics perform for detecting high- and low-performing students. However they observed that the EQ and Watwin had relatively poor performance on the data at their disposal.

Finally, several avenues for putting the error quotient to further use are proposed in [11] including being used by tutors, students, peer groups, in interactive and passive tutorials, and as a real-time tool and formative evaluation mechanism. We have similar visions for the Repeated Error Density proposed in Section 3.

In this section we have reviewed that repeating errors is common among novices, the frequency with which errors are repeated is an indicator of how well a student is progressing, and that students require help with repeating errors. We also saw that the correlation between the EQ and traditional performance metrics is varied, and sometimes tenuous, and finally that the EQ itself is in need of further study and validation. Recent work [12] has gone a long way toward such, but specifically the impact of context on the EQ still leaves unanswered questions.

3. THE REPEATED ERROR DENSITY

In [11], Jadud asked "If one student fails to correct an 'illegal start of expression' error over the course of three compilations, and another over 10, is one student [about] three times worse than the other? What if the other student deals with a non-stop string of errors, and the repetition of this particular error is just one of many?" In these cases, both students would have an EQ equal to 1. Although the actual difference between these students is most likely forever debatable, is there a metric for repeated errors that does show a difference from which some meaning can be taken?

To answer this we must acknowledge that it is possible for repeated errors to manifest themselves in different ways. Let us start with the simplest case. Take student A, who logs two consecutive errors of type x, resulting in one repeated error r. Is it fair to say that student B who logs three consecutive errors of type x resulting in two repeated errors $2r$ is struggling with that error more, by a factor of two? What about student C who also logs $2r$, but not all in one string s (say across $2s$, by logging two consecutive errors of type x followed by some successful compiles, followed by two more consecutive errors of type x)? Assuming that no other errors are made, and all other variables among the three students are equal, the EQ will be equal to 1 in each case. Table 1 summarizes these three scenarios.

Table 1: Three students repeating error x in different scenarios. Student A repeats x once $(1r)$, while students B and C repeat x twice $(2r)$. Student B logs $2r$ in one string s, while Student C does so in $2s$. In all cases, EQ = 1.

student	sequence S	x	r	s	EQ
A	... x x ...	2	1	1	1
B	... x x x ...	3	2	1	1
C	... x x ... x x ...	4	2	2	1

In trying to answer Jadud's questions stated at the beginning of this section, Table 1 shows that the EQ is not of any help. What we are after is a metric that could tell us what seems intuitive - that student C is struggling twice as much as student A with error x (in as much as student C's sequence is two of Student A's strung together). Student B seems to be somewhere in the middle - having struggled with error x for longer than student A, but once it was overcome it did not recur as it did for student C. Then again, this student fought error x for a longer consecutive string of events than Student B. Does this indicate that this student had more trouble with error x overall?

The search for a new metric to give insight into the above went down many avenues. One involved looking at the amount of repeated error strings a student encounters. Another looked at the length of these strings. Ultimately a metric emerged which incorporates both the number of strings and their lengths. We call this metric the *Repeated Error Density* (RED). This entails summing a submetric calculated on each repeated error string encountered in a sequence of compilation events. This submetric is $r_i^2/|s_i|$ where $|s_i|$ is the length of string s_i containing r_i repeated errors. This can be expressed completely in terms of r_i as $r_i^2/(r_i + 1)$, since the length of a string s_i, containing r_i consecutive errors is always equal to $r_i + 1$.

The value of RED for a given sequence S of n repeated error strings is the sum of $r_i^2/(r_i + 1)$ for each string s_i in S, given by Equation 1, where r_i is the number of repeated errors in string s_i. Note that we define a repeated error r as a pair of events where each event results in the same error; in other words consecutively committing the same error. Table 2 shows the values of RED for all sequence combinations for which a total of 0-4 repeated errors occur.

$$RED = \sum_{i=1}^{n} \frac{r_i^2}{r_i + 1} \qquad (1)$$

The RED has properties which can help us answer Jadud's questions. The first question was "If one student fails to correct an 'illegal start of expression' error over the course of three compilations, and another over 10, is one student three times worse than the other?" Let us rephrase this to: If one student repeats error x once, and another repeats error x twice, is the latter student struggling two times more than the former? Sequence 3 in Table 2 is the only way that error x can be repeated once. A single occurrence of error x (sequence 1), or two occurrences separated by other activity (sequence 2), do not constitute any (consecutive) repeats.

Table 2: Values of RED for all sequence combinations for 0-4 repeated errors r. A, B, C correspond to students in Table 1.

no.	sequence S	r	RED
1	x	0	0
2	... x ... x ...		0
3 (A)	... x x ...	1	0.5
4 (C)	... x x ... x x ...	2	1
5 (B)	... x x x ...		$1.\overline{3}$
6	... x x ... x x ... x x ...	3	1.5
7	... x x x ... x x ...		$1.8\overline{3}$
8	... x x x x ...		2.25
9	... x x ... x x ... x x ... x x ...	4	2
10	... x x ... x x ... x x x ...		$2.\overline{3}$
11	... x x x ... x x x ...		$2.\overline{6}$
12	... x x ... x x x x ...		2.75
13	... x x x x x ...		3.2

There are however two ways that error x can be repeated twice consecutively, shown by sequences 4 and 5. Sequence 4 is the 'natural' choice for representing twice the struggle of sequence 3, as sequence 4 is exactly two sequences equal to sequence 3 strung together. Table 2 shows that RED = 1 for sequence 4, and 0.5 for sequence 3, a ratio of 2:1. This property applies to any two similarly related sequences; for example sequences 11 (RED = $2.\overline{6}$), and 5 (RED = $1.\overline{3}$), again a ratio of 2:1. Thus, according to the RED metric we can answer Jadud's first question affirmatively.

Jadud's second question was "What if the other student deals with a non-stop string of errors, and the repetition of this particular error is just one of many?" Table 2 shows that sequence 5, containing one 'long' string of two repeated errors has a RED = $1.\overline{3}$. Sequence 4 which also has two repeated errors but over two shorter strings has a RED = 1. In this case the RED metric assigns a penalty of 1/3 for encountering two repeated errors in one longer string, compared to the same amount of repeated errors in a greater number of shorter strings. Going back to our students in Table 1, we can say that according to the RED metric, student B is struggling more with error x than student C. Both have two repeated errors, but student B struggled with error x for a longer consecutive string of events than student C. This is reflected in a higher RED score.

Following is a non-exhaustive list of properties of the Repeated Error Density metric. RED...

1. specifically and exclusively measures repeated errors.

2. does not depend on parameter values, which must be matched to context and subject to debate, unlike the EQ.

3. accounts for the amount of repeated errors in a sequence.

4. accounts for the amount of repeated error strings a sequence.

5. accounts for the lengths of the repeated error strings in a sequence.

6. has a value of 0 for sequences with 0 repeated errors.

7. is additive: e.g. sequence 6 is sequence 3 + sequence 4, and RED for sequence 6 is equal to RED of sequence 3 + RED of sequence 4 - see Table 2.

8. is proportional: values of related sequences are proportional (e.g. sequences 3, 4; 3, 6; 5, 11 in Table 2).

9. assigns higher penalties for higher repeated error density (e.g. sequences 6, 7, 8 in Table 2).

10. $\in \mathbb{R}_{\geq 0}$, unlike EQ and Watwin which are both $\in [0, 1]$.

4. APPLICATION TO STUDENT DATA

To compare and contrast the Error Quotient and the Repeated Error Density, and to see how the RED behaves on real data, we applied each to a data set obtained with the methodology described in [4]. This data consists of 29,019 error events from two cohorts of programming novices (approximately 100 students each) who had compiler data logged for four weeks while using a custom Java editor. The control group experienced the normal JDK compiler errors while the intervention group experienced enhanced errors provided by the editor based on the JDK error and the student code. This editor was found, with the same data set, to significantly reduce the overall number of student errors, the number of errors per student, and the amount of repeated student errors per compiler error message [4].

Figure 2 shows a histogram of EQ values for the control and intervention groups. Shapiro-Wilk tests confirmed normal distributions for EQ of both groups. A Student's t-test (two-tail) showed that the mean EQ was reduced by approximately 15% for the intervention group ($M = 0.33$, $SD = 0.16$) compared to the control group ($M = 0.39$, $SD = 0.18$); $t(210) = 2.70$, $p = 0.008$.

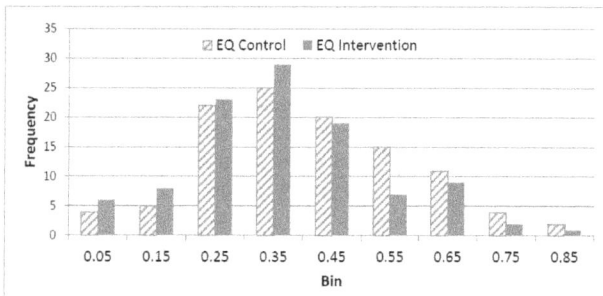

Figure 2: Histogram of EQ values for control and intervention groups.

Figure 3 shows a histogram of RED values for each group. A Shapiro-Wilk test confirmed that the control group was normal. However the intervention group was skewed right (skewness 0.76). A Mann-Whitney U test (two-tail) showed a 31% reduction in median RED for the intervention group ($Mdn = 34.0$) compared to the control group ($Mdn = 49.4$); $U = 3,638$, $p < 0.001$.

Of course RED is just one of many possible metrics that could be developed to measure repeated errors. However as RED takes into account not only the amount of repeated errors, but the number of strings in which they occur, and the lengths of these strings (the density), it allows us to answer Jadud's questions presented in Section 3.

As Jadud and Dorn pointed out in [12], the EQ has little predictive power with a small number of data points, which Table 1 confirms. On the other hand, the RED is very useful with a small number of data points, as Table 2

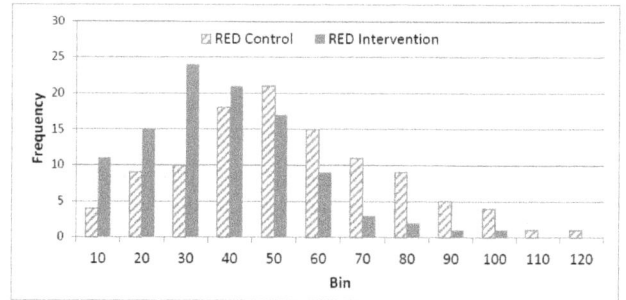

Figure 3: Histogram of RED values for control and intervention groups.

shows. However the unbounded nature of the RED brings some questions when a large number of data points are involved, as Figure 3 shows. Despite a significant reduction in RED, the presence of outliers, particularly toward the right, brings some questions. For instance it is evident that these outlying students did struggle with repeated errors, but how much of their RED scores is reflected simply by a large number of compilations? In other words, the more a student programs, the more errors that student is likely to make. This will, as repeated errors are encountered, increase the overall RED score. As mentioned in [12] and extensively explored in [15], the definition of a session can have a large impact on EQ, and on parameter choice. This could be the reason that our observed EQ scores (particularly for the control group) are slightly higher than in some other studies. We defined a single session to be the time a student is working on a single file. We observed that our students were not only working on lab assignments, but simply practicing their programming. Unlike some previous studies they were given no starter code. This could explain higher numbers of errors, including repeated errors compared to other studies. It is possible the the RED metric is more suitable for shorter sessions, while the EQ is more suitable for longer sessions.

We see it as a positive that the RED does not depend on parameter values unlike the EQ. Jadud spent considerable time exploring the EQ parameter space in [11], and in [15] it was found that useful parameter values are likely to be highly context dependent. This makes the RED metric attractive as it can be applied in any context without depending on parameter value selection.

We also see it as positive that the EQ and RED were reduced for the intervention group, adding to the evidence in [3] and [4] that enhancing compiler error messages can be effective.

Finally, the threats to validity discussed at length in [3] and [4] would also apply here. We feel that this work gives merit to the RED metric being worth further exploration, particularly where programming sessions are shorter, and when starter code is provided. It also shows theoretical promise, backed up with our initial experimental work here, as a less context dependent repeated error metric than the EQ.

5. CONCLUSIONS AND FUTURE WORK

Repeated errors, particularly those committed consecutively, have been shown to be a strong indicator of students struggling with programming. Several studies have investigated repeated errors, most of which utilize Jadud's Error Quotient (EQ). However the EQ has been shown to be context dependent and can have a large parameter space. Additionally, the EQ has limited use for short sessions with few errors. Recently, the predictive power of the EQ has been shown to be inconsistent and sometimes tenuous.

We have introduced an alternative metric to measure repeated errors which we call the Repeated Error Density (RED). This metric shows promise as a repeated error metric that is less context dependent due to being based only on the number of consecutively repeated errors and the number of repeated error strings in a compilation event sequence. Being less context dependent is seen as important since being able to generalize on study results is a fundamental requirement for putting them into effective use [15]. We have demonstrated that the RED is effective on short sequences and that it can answer two questions (which the EQ cannot) that Jadud asked when first proposing the EQ.

We applied the RED to existing control/intervention data and found that the RED is reduced by an editor that provides enhanced error messages, consistent with previous findings demonstrating that this editor also reduced overall errors, overall number of student errors, number of errors per student, and number of repeated student errors per compiler error message. This provides evidence that this metric is valid.

Finally, a reduction in the EQ and RED for the intervention group adds to the evidence in [3] and [4] that enhancing compiler error messages can be effective.

Future work involves investigating and validating the RED metric in greater detail, particularly in different contexts, including those involving short programming sessions and where starter/skeleton code is provided. We also plan on investigating if there is a correlation between RED and success in assessments.

6. REFERENCES

[1] A. Ahadi, R. Lister, H. Haapala, and A. Vihavainen. Exploring machine learning methods to automatically identify students in need of assistance. In *Proceedings of the Eleventh Annual International Conference on International Computing Education Research*, pages 121–130. ACM, 2015.

[2] A. Altadmri and N. C. Brown. 37 million compilations: Investigating novice programming mistakes in large-scale student data. In *Proceedings of the 46th ACM Technical Symposium on Computer Science Education*, pages 522–527. ACM, 2015.

[3] B. A. Becker. *An exploration of the effects of enhanced compiler error messages for computer programming novices*. Master's thesis, Dublin Institute of Technology, 2015.

[4] B. A. Becker. An effective approach to enhancing compiler error messages. In *Proceedings of the 47th ACM Technical Symposium on Computer Science Education*, pages 126–131. ACM, 2016.

[5] J. S. Brown and K. VanLehn. Repair theory: A generative theory of bugs in procedural skills. *Cognitive science*, 4(4):379–426, 1980.

[6] N. C. Brown and A. Altadmri. Investigating novice programming mistakes: Educator beliefs vs. student data. In *Proceedings of the tenth annual Conference on International Computing Education Research*, pages 43–50. ACM, 2014.

[7] N. C. C. Brown, M. Kölling, D. McCall, and I. Utting. Blackbox: A large scale repository of novice programmers' activity. In *Proceedings of the 45th ACM Technical Symposium on Computer Science Education*, pages 223–228. ACM, 2014.

[8] R. Chmiel and M. C. Loui. Debugging: from novice to expert. *ACM SIGCSE Bulletin*, 36(1):17–21, 2004.

[9] P. Denny, A. Luxton-Reilly, E. Tempero, and J. Hendrickx. Codewrite: supporting student-driven practice of java. In *Proceedings of the 42nd ACM Technical Symposium on Computer Science Education*, pages 471–476. ACM, 2011.

[10] M. C. Jadud. A first look at novice compilation behaviour using bluej. *Computer Science Education*, 15(1):25–40, 2005.

[11] M. C. Jadud. *An exploration of novice compilation behaviour in BlueJ*. PhD thesis, University of Kent, 2006.

[12] M. C. Jadud and B. Dorn. Aggregate compilation behavior: Findings and implications from 27,698 users. In *Proceedings of the eleventh annual International Conference on International Computing Education Research*, pages 131–139. ACM, 2015.

[13] W. L. Johnson. *Intention-based diagnosis of novice programming errors*. Morgan Kaufmann, 1986.

[14] I. R. Katz and J. R. Anderson. Debugging: An analysis of bug-location strategies. *Human-Computer Interaction*, 3(4):351–399, 1987.

[15] A. Petersen, J. Spacco, and A. Vihavainen. An exploration of error quotient in multiple contexts. In *Proceedings of the 15th Koli Calling Conference on Computing Education Research*, pages 77–86. ACM, 2015.

[16] M. M. T. Rodrigo, E. Tabanao, M. B. E. Lahoz, and M. C. Jadud. Analyzing online protocols to characterize novice java programmers. *Philippine Journal of Science*, 138(2):177–190, 2009.

[17] J. C. Spohrer and E. Soloway. Novice mistakes: Are the folk wisdoms correct? *Communications of the ACM*, 29(7):624–632, 1986.

[18] E. S. Tabanao, M. M. Rodrigo, and M. C. Jadud. Predicting at-risk novice java programmers through the analysis of online protocols. In *Proceedings of the seventh international workshop on Computing education research*, pages 85–92. ACM, 2011.

[19] H. Tamada, A. Ogino, and H. Ueda. A framework for programming process measurement and compiling error interpretation for novice programmers. In *Software Measurement, 2011 Joint Conference of the 21st Int'l Workshop on and 6th International Conference on Software Process and Product Measurement (IWSM-MENSURA)*, pages 233–238. IEEE, 2011.

[20] C. Watson, F. W. Li, and J. L. Godwin. Predicting performance in an introductory programming course by logging and analyzing student programming behavior. In *Advanced Learning Technologies (ICALT), 2013 IEEE 13th International Conference on*, pages 319–323. IEEE, 2013.

Reading Hierarchies in Code:
Assessment of a Basic Computational Skill

Thomas H. Park, Meen Chul Kim, Sukrit Chhabra, Brian Lee, Andrea Forte
College of Computing and Informatics
Drexel University
Philadelphia, PA, USA
{park, meenchul.kim, sukrit.chhabra, bl389, aforte}@drexel.edu

ABSTRACT

One of the skills that comprise computational thinking is the ability to read code and reason about the hierarchical relationships between different blocks, expressions, elements, or other types of nodes, depending on the language. In this study, we present three new instruments for assessing different aspects of reading hierarchies in code, including vocabulary, reasoning, and fluency. One of these instruments is Nester, an interactive tool we have designed to elicit mental models about the hierarchical structure of code in computing languages ranging from HTML, CSS, and LaTeX to JavaScript and Lisp. We describe a lab study in which we administered these instruments to 24 participants with varying degrees of web development experience. We report findings from this study, including participants' ability to define, reason about, and manipulate hierarchies in code, and the errors and misconceptions that relate to them. Finally, we discuss avenues for future work.

CCS Concepts

Social and professional topics → **Computational thinking** •
Social and professional topics → **Assessment**

Keywords

computational thinking; web development; assessment; program comprehension.

1. INTRODUCTION

Computation is increasingly recognized as a fundamental literacy alongside reading, writing, and arithmetic [2]. The term computational thinking was coined by Wing to describe "solving problems, designing systems, and understanding human behavior, by drawing on the concepts fundamental to computer science" [30]. In their work with Scratch, Brennan and Resnick expand on this notion by proposing a framework of concepts (*e.g.*, iteration, parallelism), practices (*e.g.*, debugging, remixing), and perspectives (*e.g.*, expressing, connecting) [1]. As their framework demonstrates, computational thinking can be thought of as a rich, multi-layered set of knowledge and skills.

ITiCSE '16, July 09 - 13, 2016, Arequipa, Peru
Copyright is held by the owner/author(s). Publication rights licensed to ACM.
ACM 978-1-4503-4231-5/16/07…$15.00
DOI: http://dx.doi.org/10.1145/2899415.2899435

Web development is one domain that reflects this rich and multi-layered quality, given the broad set of technologies and practices that it calls upon, as well as its role as the first major exposure to creative computation for many people [3, 22]. Multiple facets of web development have been examined through the lens of computational thinking. For example, Miller et al. [14] analyze the errors students make when using a tree representation of a filesystem to construct relative and absolute paths. Dorn and Guzdial [4] characterize the knowledge gained by web developers about fundamental programming concepts like assignment, scope, and recursion through their experience with languages like JavaScript and PHP, finding that participants often recognize but do not fully understand these concepts.

Previously we proposed that basic markup and style-sheet languages like HTML and CSS can also engage aspects of computational thinking, like notation, nesting, and parameters [15]. Our subsequent work has explored the common errors web developers make when writing HTML and CSS [17], identifying the deep nesting of code as a particularly troublesome area for beginners [16].

In this paper, we build on that work by focusing our attention on the knowledge and skills associated with reading deeply nested hierarchies in code. Navigating hierarchies in code involves multiple perceptual, cognitive, and motor processes, from parsing long strings of text by identifying delimiters and other features of the code, forming mental models that reflect the code's hierarchical structure, reasoning about relationships between different sections of the code based on this model, and editing the code to reflect a newly desired state.

Like many concepts found within computational thinking, hierarchies provide a way of managing complexity. By being able to move adroitly between different levels of nesting, one can view the same code at different levels of abstraction, focusing attention on a particular level or chunk of code while understanding its function in relation to the rest of the program. Moreover, this is a basic concept that can be applied to a wide range of computing languages. However, these abilities presumably must be learned over time and developed through practice.

To explore knowledge and skills related to navigating hierarchies in code, we pose the following research questions:

1. How familiar are web developers with the vocabulary of hierarchies?

2. How well do web developers apply rules and reason about navigating hierarchies?

3. How can we measure skills associated with fluently navigating hierarchies, and how do they transfer from familiar to unfamiliar computing languages?

2. RELATED WORK

The program comprehension literature describes several models of how programmers construct an understanding of code [23]. In early work, two fundamental approaches were proposed. The top-down model suggested that programmers start with the problem domain and program goals, relating them to elements of the code [25]. In the bottom-up model, programmers begin with elements of the code and map them to the program goals [19]. Since then, other models depict a more nuanced picture where programmers switch opportunistically between these approaches [11], depending on their present state of knowledge about the program and the programming task at hand [13].

During program comprehension, code can be read along multiple dimensions, with different features of the program becoming more relevant and providing alternate forms of information [7]. These dimensions facilitate different strategies that professional programmers use to understand code, like tracing the data flow and the control flow [10, 21]. Another dimension is spatial, referring to the code's order in the source, in contrast to its execution order [8]. In the present study, we consider a structural view in which programmers examine the hierarchical structure that is created by the nesting of code blocks in a program. This structural view is tied to both the logic underpinning the code's organization, as well as its spatial arrangement when formatted with indentation.

In expert program comprehension, researchers have found evidence for a reliance on beacons, which Wiedenbeck defines as "lines of code which serve as typical indicators of a particular structure or operation" [29]. Green has likewise found support for the indentation of nested code enabled by structured programming for acting as "redundant perceptual encoding... [that] provides a secondary clue to their logical structure" in improving program comprehension [6]. These empirical findings suggest that just as individual lines can serve as landmarks, reading hierarchies can help reveal the more general terrain of code during program comprehension.

Finally, several studies point to the design and practices of a language, such as its nesting syntax and use of whitespace, as having an effect on program comprehension. Like paired tags used in HTML and XML, the redundant labelling of "begin" and "end" statements used to mark a nested block of code in ALGOL was found to aid program comprehension among novices [24]. Stefik and Seibert conducted several studies that found the syntax of different program languages like Python, Ruby, and Java to have a significant effect on their understandability and ease of use [27]. If significant differences exist among imperative programming languages, then for drastically different languages like LaTeX, CSS, and Lisp, there is the question of the degree to which such differences exist, and how the basic skill of reading hierarchies in code may transfer across languages.

Despite distinct differences from reading code, the extensive research on reading comprehension as it relates to prose is also instructive [19]. Reading fluency—decoding and comprehending text accurately and with the appropriate rate and prosody—calls on a cascade of sub-processes and knowledge such as letter sound fluency and vocabulary [9]. Studies have found that lower-level skills like word decoding are a critical factor in reading ability [5]. We similarly consider reading hierarchies in code as a basic computational skill that can support higher-level programming activities.

3. METHODS

To address our research questions, we developed three instruments for measuring knowledge and skills about hierarchies in code. We then conducted a lab study in which we invited participants into the lab and had them complete tasks based on these instruments. We triangulate the data collected from these instruments for our analysis.

3.1 Data Collection

For our study, we sought participants who had prior experience in web development, ranging from beginner to expert. We posted on-campus flyers and announcements on mailing lists, and offered $25 for participation in the approximately hour-long session.

The participants were invited into a lab, where we provided them with a computer to be used for the study. After giving informed consent, participants were directed to complete a computer-based pre-questionnaire that collected information about their area of study and self-reported expertise with a variety of computing languages. Following this, they completed tasks based on the three instruments described in the next section. The study concluded with a post-questionnaire that asked participants to rate their perceived difficulty with the tasks, and provide demographic information such as age and gender. We delayed collection of demographic information until after the tasks in order to minimize the effect of stereotype threat [26].

24 participants volunteered to participate, 11 females and 13 males. All participants were either undergraduate or graduate students, with an average age of 22 years. Their areas of study emphasized design or technology, including majors in digital media, software engineering, computer science, and information systems. The sole exception was a chemical engineering student.

None of the participants practiced web development professionally, but all had some level of prior experience. Among the computing languages surveyed, participants were most familiar with HTML, followed by CSS and JavaScript. All 24 participants reported experience with HTML, with a mean of 2.1 on a scale 0 (no experience) to 4 (expert), 22 participants with CSS ($\mu = 1.7$), and 19 with JavaScript ($\mu = 1.3$).

3.2 Instruments

In this section, we present three instruments we have developed to assess knowledge and skills related to the concept of hierarchies in code. These include hierarchical vocabulary, hierarchical reasoning, and hierarchical fluency.

3.2.1 Hierarchical Vocabulary

The first instrument assesses basic understanding of vocabulary associated with hierarchies. Seven terms are presented:

- Parent
- Child
- Ancestor
- Descendant
- Sibling
- Root
- Leaf

For each term, participants are first asked to rate whether they know the definition in the context of hierarchies, recognize the term but do not know the definition, or are not familiar with the term. Next, they are prompted to define each of the terms in their own words.

3.2.2 Hierarchical Reasoning

In the second instrument, participants are presented with a code sample (Figure 1) and 14 items asking them to identify various nodes based on combinations of the aforementioned terms. For example, one item asks participants to identify the parent of the node present in line 2. This type of reasoning is frequently employed in activities like debugging HTML code, or navigating and selecting DOM nodes using CSS or JavaScript. The instrument provides definitions for the terms in case participants are not already familiar with them, and asks them to identify nodes by providing their element names and line numbers (*e.g.*, html in line 1).

The complete list of items is presented in Table 1. The first seven items apply the hierarchical terms individually, while the rest relate to more complex scenarios involving what we predict to be common misconceptions or pitfalls when reasoning about hierarchies. For example, item 10 assesses whether participants recognize nested nodes when formatted inline; Item 11 assesses whether participants mistake "cousins" for "siblings" when the cousins have no siblings of their own. The code sample is designed to support all of these items.

This instrument takes an approach that is similar to code tracing problems [12] in that participants must reason about a static representation of code. However, rather than predicting the program execution and output, they must determine hierarchical relationships between different parts of code.

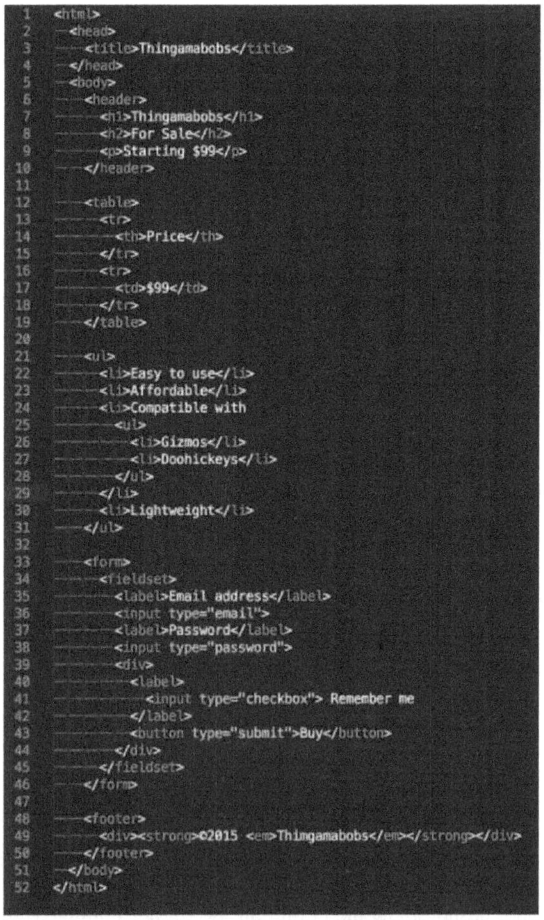

```
1  <html>
2    <head>
3      <title>Thingamabobs</title>
4    </head>
5    <body>
6      <header>
7        <h1>Thingamabobs</h1>
8        <h2>For Sale</h2>
9        <p>Starting $99</p>
10     </header>
11
12     <table>
13       <tr>
14         <th>Price</th>
15       </tr>
16       <tr>
17         <td>$99</td>
18       </tr>
19     </table>
20
21     <ul>
22       <li>Easy to use</li>
23       <li>Affordable</li>
24       <li>Compatible with
25         <ul>
26           <li>Gizmos</li>
27           <li>Doohickeys</li>
28         </ul>
29       </li>
30       <li>Lightweight</li>
31     </ul>
32
33     <form>
34       <fieldset>
35         <label>Email address</label>
36         <input type="email">
37         <label>Password</label>
38         <input type="password">
39         <div>
40           <label>
41             <input type="checkbox"> Remember me
42           </label>
43           <button type="submit">Buy</button>
44         </div>
45       </fieldset>
46     </form>
47
48     <footer>
49       <div><strong>©2015 <em>Thingamabobs</em></strong></div>
50     </footer>
51   </body>
52 </html>
```

Figure 1. The HTML code sample used in the hierarchical reasoning instrument.

Table 1. Items used in the hierarchical reasoning instrument.

Item	Principle	Instructions
1	Parent	List the parent of <head> (line 2)
2	Child	List all children of <header> (line 6)
3	Ancestor	List all ancestors of <h1> (line 7)
4	Descendant	List all descendants of <table> (line 12)
5	Sibling	List all siblings of <h1> (line 7)
6	Root	List the root element
7	Leaf	List all leaf elements contained in <table> (line 12)
8	Proximity	List the parent element of <button> (line 43)
9	Depth	List all leaf elements contained in <ul> (line 21)
10	Inline	List the parent element of <em> (line 49)
11	Cousins	List all sibling elements of <td> (line 17)
12	Filter	List all <input> elements that are descendants of any <div>
13	Compound	List all descendants of <body> (line 5) that are also ancestors of <td> (line 17)
14	Common Ancestor	List the closest ancestor that <input> (line 38) and <input> (line 41) share in common

3.2.3 Hierarchical Fluency

The third instrument assesses hierarchical rules as applied within an interactive coding environment. We developed a tool called Nester (Figure 2) that presents participants with unformatted snippets of code in various computing languages, with each line of code represented as a movable block. Participants are asked to indent the lines of code to reflect the nesting rules of the language, whether or not whitespace is significant in the given language. The purpose of Nester is to elicit observable representations of mental models that participants hold about the code.

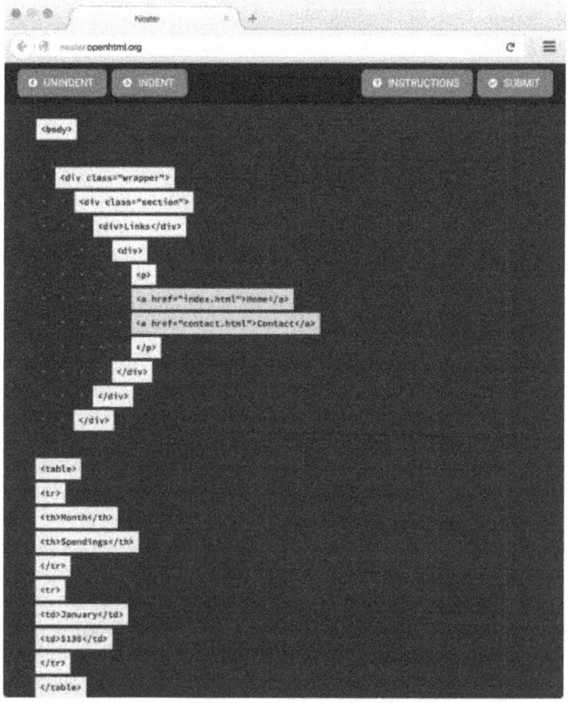

Figure 2. Nester, the interactive tool developed as the hierarchical fluency instrument, loaded with the HTML task.

In our previous work with HTML and CSS [17], we applied the skills-rules-knowledge framework [20] to differentiate rule-based errors that are rooted in misconceptions from skill-based errors that arise even when no misconceptions are held. While the previous two instruments are aimed at uncovering misconceptions or knowledge gaps, this instrument is designed to present more complex and interactive tasks that place a greater load on participants' working memory [28]. In short, it is designed to expose the fluency with which participants handle hierarchies in code.

Compared to a traditional code editor, Nester constrains the possible operations on code. Only the indentation of individual lines of code, not their contents, can be edited. Some programming environments offer auto-indent features that would render Nester's tasks trivial. However, although Nester does not provide an authentic experience that programmers would encounter in practice, like Parson's programming puzzles [18] they can be used to target assessment at a specific aspect of code comprehension.

The common operations for selecting, indenting, and unindenting lines of code are supported via key combinations and the graphical user interface. For example, the up and down arrow keys can be used to select different lines, and a selected line can be indented by using the tab or right arrow keys. Lines can also be selected by mouse by clicking specific blocks, and indent and unindent buttons are displayed prominently at the top of Nester. Multiple lines can also be added to a selection by holding down the shift or control modifier keys while selecting a new line, or by dragging a box with the mouse cursor (i.e., lassoing) around multiple blocks. Before the tasks, participants were given a freeform orientation task to familiarize themselves with the operations of Nester.

Nester is designed to support any number of languages and code samples, but for this study, we used Nester to present a single code sample for each of seven languages: HTML, XML, JSON, LaTeX, SCSS, JavaScript, and Lisp. These languages were selected to represent a broad range of syntaxes for delimiting nested blocks of code. For example, HTML, XML, and LaTeX as markup languages rely on start and end tags, JSON, JavaScript, and SCSS (an extension of CSS) on braces, and Lisp on parentheses. Additionally, we expected the languages to vary in terms of their familiarity among participants. This was confirmed in the pre-questionnaire where all 24 participants had prior exposure to HTML, but only 4 had exposure to Lisp.

The code samples used in the study were comprised of a root node and three sub-trees, each of which was designed to be isomorphic across languages in terms of their nested structure. This was to control for variables like lines of code and complexity in the code samples. For example, if an element in the HTML sample had two child elements, then the equivalent node in JavaScript had two statements in a nested block of code. The order of the sub-trees within a code sample was randomized for each task, and the order of the languages was randomized for each participant.

At the start of each task, instructions and an example are presented within Nester for how code should be formatted in case the participant was not familiar with the language. The instructions can also be invoked later on by clicking a button in the toolbar. After formatting the code, the participant was directed to click the Submit button, where Nester reports whether the task was solved correctly. If errors were present in the code, the opportunity is given to fix the errors and resubmit.

3.3 Data Analysis

For the hierarchical vocabulary instrument, self-reported familiarity with each term was converted to 0 (not familiar), 1 (recognize but do not know the definition), or 2 (can define). The definitions that participants provided were also graded as 0 (incorrect), 1 (partially correct), or 2 (correct). Summing these values resulted in a scale from 0 to 14 for each of the two parts.

For the hierarchical reasoning instrument, responses were rated similarly: 0 (incorrect), 1 (partially correct), and 2 (correct). This resulted in a scale from 0 to 28. Mistakes were examined qualitatively in further detail.

For the hierarchical fluency instrument, data logged by Nester for analysis included the total time spent on each task, the number of attempts per task, as well as the number and locations of errors per attempt.

4. FINDINGS

4.1.1 Hierarchical Vocabulary

In the hierarchical vocabulary instrument, participants' self-rated familiarity with the terms ranged the full scale from 0 to 14., with a mean of 10.7 ($\sigma = 3.8$). Five of the 24 participants had a score of 7 or less, indicating a low level of familiarity, with one participant reporting no familiarity at all. A breakdown of the items is provided in Figure 3, revealing that "leaf", "descendant", "ancestor", and "root" were the least familiar.

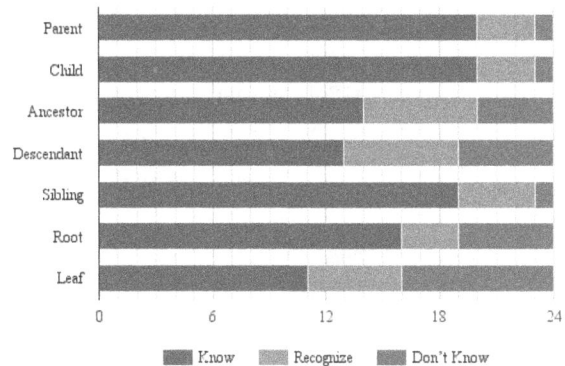

Figure 3. Count of participants' familiarity with terms.

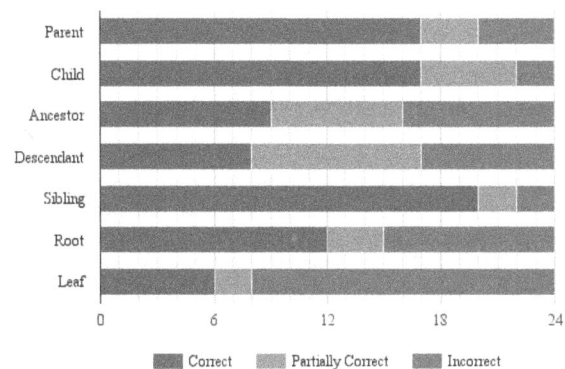

Figure 4. Count of participants' correctness of definitions.

In defining the terms in the participants' own words, scores again ranged from 0 to 14, with a mean of 8.7 ($\sigma = 4.1$). Seven participants had a score of 7 or less, with two participants not attempting any definitions. Correctness of each term's definition (Figure 4) was largely in line with the respective self-rating, with a correlation of $r = 0.81$, $p < 0.001$, though participants tended to overestimate their knowledge slightly.

Beyond the implicit metaphor of trees, a number of participants made references to families, object-oriented programming, and file systems in their definitions. Several had fuzzy notions of "leaf", confusing the term with nodes in general. Another common misconception was that "ancestors" excluded "parent" and "descendants" excluded "child" nodes.

4.1.2 Hierarchical Reasoning

For the hierarchical reasoning instrument, scores ranged from 2 to 28, with a mean of 23.1 ($\sigma = 5.9$). Performance on the term-centered items in the first half of the reasoning instrument (Table 1) was only moderately correlated with the equivalent items on the vocabulary instrument: $r = 0.72$, $p < 0.001$. However, this performance tended to be higher, suggesting participants were more comfortable applying the terms concretely in the context of code than they were expressing more abstract definitions.

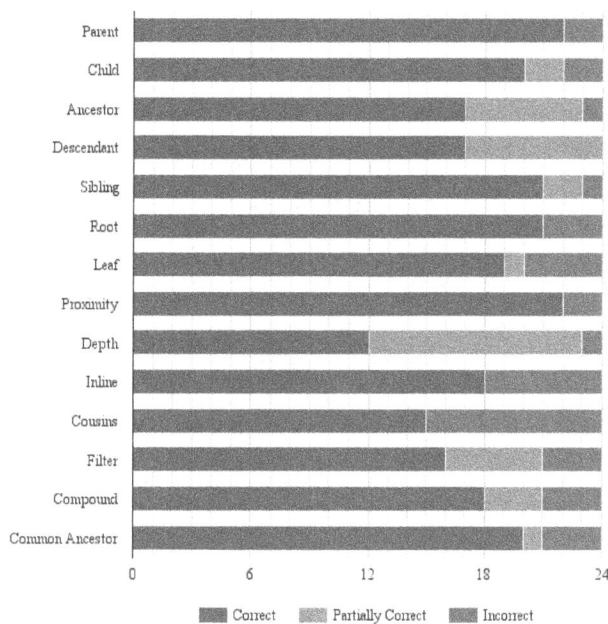

Figure 5. Count of participants' correctness in hierarchical reasoning instrument.

The second half of the instrument revolved around potential pitfalls or misconceptions, and participants did perform more poorly on several items including "depth", "cousins", and "inline". For "depth", a common error was to overlook more shallow leaf nodes when identifying leaf nodes deep within a hierarchy. For "cousins", a cousin node was mistaken for a sibling on several occasions. For "inline", three elements were nested within one another on a single line of code; the correct element, which was located in the middle of the line, was overlooked in favor of the element that was located most prominently at the start of the line.

4.1.3 Hierarchical Fluency

Hierarchical fluency was measured through seven tasks in Nester. Participants varied considerably in time on task, ranging from 6.2 to 64.3 minutes ($\mu = 16.7$, $\sigma = 11.9$). The cumulative attempts and errors averaged 12.8 ($\sigma = 4.5$) and 4.0 ($\sigma = 10.6$) respectively. Strong correlations were found between performance on the reasoning instrument and time ($r = -0.84$, $p < 0.001$) and attempts ($r = -0.70$, $p < 0.001$), but not errors ($r = -0.45$, $p < 0.01$).

The two programming languages Lisp and JavaScript had the greatest variability for time on task, with Lisp taking longest (Figure 6). Attempts (Figure 7) and errors (Figure 8) were highly skewed, with many tasks requiring just one attempt. No correlation was found between the participants' reported expertise with each language and performance on the corresponding task.

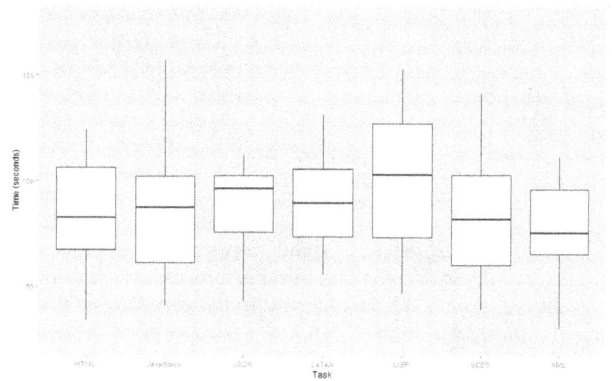

Figure 6. Time on each task.

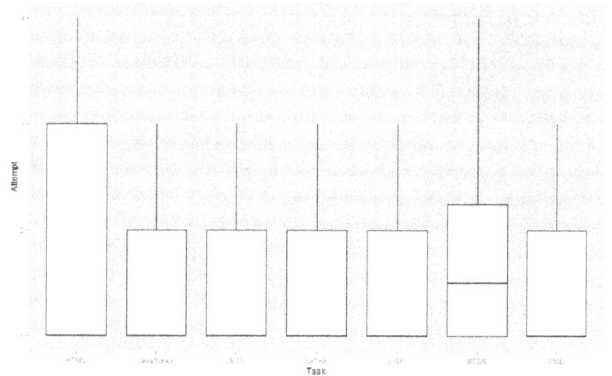

Figure 7. Number of attempts on each task.

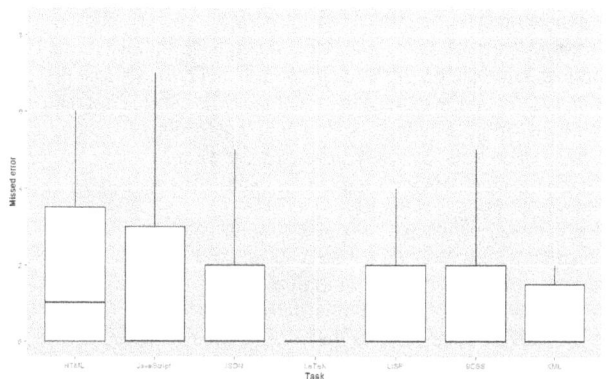

Figure 8. Cumulative number of errors on each task.

306

5. DISCUSSION

Overall, participants were generally found to be familiar with the vocabulary of hierarchies. However, they were more proficient in reasoning about these terms within the context of code than articulating formal definitions of them.

Contrary to expectations, familiarity with a language did not relate to better performance in the hierarchical fluency instrument. Learning effects with respect to Nester and the tasks themselves may be a factor here. In our analysis, we discovered steep changes in performance during the first three tasks that were administered, independent of language given that task order was randomized, before stabilizing for the rest of the tasks. To address this, a lengthier training session as well as greater quantity and variety in the code samples may be required.

Based on our experiences, we identified several opportunities to refine our instruments. For the vocabulary instrument, we plan to add a prompt for defining the concept of "hierarchy" itself. For the reasoning instrument, identifying nodes by element name and line number was cumbersome; an interactive format that allows nodes to be selected directly would improve usability. Finally, iterations on Nester could add features like syntax highlighting, providing a more familiar and authentic experience.

In future work, we plan to administer these in the context of introductory computing courses, gaining insight into the impact these courses have on student ability to read hierarchies in code.

6. ACKNOWLEDGMENTS

This work is supported by the National Science Foundation under CNS grant #1339344.

7. REFERENCES

[1] Brennan, K. and Resnick, M. 2012. New frameworks for studying and assessing the development of computational thinking. *Proc. AERA* (2012), 1–25.

[2] diSessa, A.A. 2001. *Changing Minds: Computers, Learning, and Literacy*. MIT Press.

[3] Dorn, B. and Guzdial, M. 2010. Discovering computing: Perspectives of web designers. *Proc. ICER* (2010), 23–29.

[4] Dorn, B. and Guzdial, M. 2010. Learning on the job: Characterizing the programming knowledge and learning strategies of web designers. *Proc. CHI* (2010), 703–712.

[5] Gough, P.B., Hoover, W.A. and Peterson, C.L. 1996. Some observations on a simple view of reading. *Reading Comprehension Difficulties Processes and Intervention*. C. Cornoldi and J.V. Oakhill, eds. 1–13.

[6] Green, T.R.G. 1977. Conditional program statements and their comprehensibility to professional programmers. *Journal of Occupational Psychology*. 50, 2 (1977), 93–109.

[7] Green, T.R.G. 1990. Programming languages as information structures. *Psychology of Programming*. J.-M. Hoc, T.R.G. Green, R. Samurçay, and D.J. Gilmore, eds. 117–137.

[8] Grigoreanu, V.I., Brundage, J., Bahna, E., Burnett, M.M., ElRif, P. and Snover, J. 2009. Males' and Females' Script Debugging Strategies. *Proc. IS-EUD* (2009), 205–224.

[9] Hudson, R.F., Pullen, P.C., Lane, H.B. and Torgesen, J.K. 2009. The complex nature of reading fluency: A multidimensional view. *Reading & Writing Quarterly*. 25, (2009), 4–32.

[10] Katz, I.R. and Anderson, J.R. 1987. Debugging: An analysis of bug-location strategies. *Human-Computer Interaction*. 3, 4 (1987), 351–399.

[11] Letovsky, S. 1987. Cognitive processes in program comprehension. *Journal of Systems and Software*. 7, 4 (1987), 325–339.

[12] Lister, R., Adams, E.S., Fitzgerald, S., Fone, W., Hamer, J., Lindholm, M., McCartney, R., Moström, J.E., Sanders, K., Seppälä, O., Simon, B. and Thomas, L. 2004. A multi-national study of reading and tracing skills in novice programmers. *ITiCSE-WGR* (2004), 119–150.

[13] Mayrhauser, A.V. and Vans, A.M. 1995. Program comprehension during software maintenance and evolution. *Computer*. 28, 8 (1995), 1–12.

[14] Miller, C.S., Perkovic, L. and Settle, A. 2010. File references, trees, and computational thinking. *Proc. ITiCSE* (2010), 132–136.

[15] Park, T.H. and Wiedenbeck, S. 2011. Learning web development: Challenges at an earlier stage of computing education. *Proc. ICER* (2011), 125–132.

[16] Park, T.H., Dorn, B. and Forte, A. 2015. An analysis of HTML and CSS syntax errors in a web development course. *ACM Transactions on Computing Education*. 15, 1 (Mar. 2015), 1–21.

[17] Park, T.H., Saxena, A., Jagannath, S., Wiedenbeck, S. and Forte, A. 2013. Towards a taxonomy of errors in HTML and CSS. *Proc. ICER* (2013), 75–82.

[18] Parsons, D. and Haden, P. 2006. Parson's Programming Puzzles: A fun and effective learning tool for first programming courses. *Proc. ACE* (2006), 157–163.

[19] Pennington, N. 1987. Stimulus structures and mental representations in expert comprehension of computer programs. *Cognitive Psychology*. 19, 3 (1987), 295–341.

[20] Rasmussen, J. 1983. Skills, rules, and knowledge; Signals, signs, and symbols, and other distinctions in human performance models. *IEEE Transactions on Systems, Man, and Cybernetics*. 13, 3 (1983), 257–266.

[21] Romero, P., Boulay, du, B., Cox, R., Lutz, R. and Bryant, S. 2007. Debugging strategies and tactics in a multi-representation software environment. *International Journal of Human-Computer Studies*. 65, 12 (Dec. 2007), 992–1009.

[22] Rosson, M.B., Ballin, J.F. and Nash, H. 2004. Everyday programming: Challenges and opportunities for informal web development. *Proc. VL/HCC* (2004), 123–130.

[23] Schulte, C., Clear, T., Taherkhani, A., Busjahn, T. and Paterson, J.H. 2010. An introduction to program comprehension for computer science educators. *ITiCSE-WGR* (2010), 65–86.

[24] Sime, M.E., Green, T.R.G. and Guest, D.J. 1977. Scope marking in computer conditionals: A psychological evaluation. *International Journal of Man-Machine Studies*. (1977), 107–118.

[25] Soloway, E. and Ehrlich, K. 1984. Empirical studies of programming knowledge. *IEEE Transactions on Software Engineering*. 10, 5 (1984), 1–15.

[26] Steele, C.M. 1997. A threat in the air: How stereotypes shape intellectual identity and performance. *American Psychologist*. 52, 6 (1997), 613–629.

[27] Stefik, A. and Siebert, S. 2013. An empirical investigation into programming language syntax. *ACM Transactions on Computing Education*. 13, 4 (2013), 1–40.

[28] Sweller, J. 2003. Cognitive load during problem solving: Effects on learning. *Cognitive Science*. 12, (Nov. 2003), 257–285.

[29] Wiedenbeck, S. 1986. Beacons in computer program comprehension. *International Journal of Man-Machine Studies*. 25, 6 (1986), 697–709.

[30] Wing, J.M. 2006. Computational thinking. *Communications of the ACM*. 49, 3 (2006), 33–35.

Programming Misconceptions in an Introductory Level Programming Course Exam

Einari Kurvinen, Niko Hellgren, Erkki Kaila, Mikko-Jussi Laakso, Tapio Salakoski
Department of Information Technology
University of Turku
Vesilinnantie 5, 20500 Turku, Finland
{emakur, nipehe, ertaka, milaak, tapio.salakoski}@utu.fi

ABSTRACT

Learning to program is known to be a difficult task, as the students typically lack the intrinsic motivation and find the new skills required difficult to master. It is hence typical for the educators to try to constantly improve their teaching methods to enhance the quality and outcome of the courses. We have developed an educational tool called ViLLE, which allows us to create interactive and automatically assessed programming exercises easily. In these exercises, the students have a near-to-authentic programming environment with compiler output and error messages provided. The same tool was used in our university's introductory programming course's final exam. In this paper, we analyze students' answers to three different coding exercises in this final exam. Since ViLLE automatically stores the program code when compiled, we have an access to previously unseen amounts of iterations of the exercise instead of just the final submission. The data is analyzed to identify typical misconceptions in programming exercises, and to show how the students gradually improve their answers based on the results and error messages. Finally, we discuss how the results of the analysis can be utilized to tackle these misconceptions during the course.

Keywords

Exams; misconceptions; automatic assessment; programming

1. INTRODUCTION

Learning the basics of programming is a complicated task. The basic concepts of programming are usually quite different from what the students have got accustomed to. Reaching the point of understanding the basic concepts of (object-oriented) programming takes time and the unique nature of the mindset needed causes most students to stumble upon the same misconceptions about the basic concepts.

Finding the common misconceptions students have in relation to programming would help teachers and lecturers address the main obstacles students face. Focusing on the common problematics and improving their teaching could help students overcome both the psychological and conceptual barriers hindering their learning.

ITiCSE '16, July 09-13, 2016, Arequipa, Peru
© 2016 ACM. ISBN 978-1-4503-4231-5/16/07...$15.00
DOI: http://dx.doi.org/10.1145/2899415.2899447

Misconceptions can reference to non-standard mental models and broader errors in thinking. In this paper we try to identify some of the most practical errors the students do during their first programming course. This data can help educators focus their attention better and improve their exercises.

For this study, development of students' answers in the exam of their first, 7-week-long programming course were analyzed commit-by-commit, tracking the evolution of their answers as they approached the final (and in most cases, correct) answer. Their solutions' issues were listed and analyzed in order to find the most common misconceptions present amongst entry-level programming students.

2. RELATED WORK

Various studies discussing and analyzing beginner programmers' misconceptions about basic programming concepts have been conducted. Even though the scopes of the studies have varied, the basic problematics seem to be quite similar across the board.

Ma et al. (2007) [1] studied the mental models of computer science students and found that even after completing their first year course, one third of students held non-viable mental models about the subject matter. Since programming holds such few parallels in the physical world, constructing viable mental models and avoiding thinking based on wrong presumptions or intuition is vital from the start. The sheer amount and diversity of these misconceptions make this a challenging task.

Goldman et al. (2008) [2] used a Delphi process to list the main misconceptions when it comes to Object-Oriented programming (OOP). According to the study, the main misconceptions amongst first year CS students concerned the scope and visibility of variables and objects, modularization and decomposition, general abstraction, testing and debugging, inheritance, and throwing and handling of exceptions. The more advanced aspects of OOP are out of this article's scope, but similar elementary level issues are found and discussed.

Based on the aforementioned study, Kaczmarczyk et al. (2010) [3] interviewed students about similar issues and found the main issues to divide into four main themes: misunderstanding the underlying memory and reference structure, misunderstanding the process of loops, lacking a basic concept of Objects and being unable to trace a given code. The difficult concepts found mainly agreed with the ones found in Goldman et al.'s Delphi study.

Both Hristova et al. (2003) [4] and Chen et al. (2013) [5] studied errors made by novice CS students in Java, and found problems not necessarily faced by students using other programming languages. The complex type system and verbose syntax of the language expose students to problems not present in more procedural-like programming languages. Especially special characters (brackets, semicolons) separating blocks and commands were found to cause problems with elementary students. The usage of available language libraries was also found to be problematic.

Asking students to simulate the state of the program instead of writing and executing it turns the situation upside down. Sirkiä & Sorva (2008) [6] examined the student-made solutions submitted to a Visual program simulation (VPS) system during a three-year period. This aspect brings out issues concerning the understanding of the states of the program and memory. They found that control structures (loops, conditional statements), logical statements and object references cause misconceptions among students. Similar visualization system is also used in ViLLE to practice program state simulation.

In his Master's thesis, Sirkiä [7] found that using a VPS has the advantage of first making students think about how the program's execution continues and then showing them what will actually happen, thus making them think about their possible misconceptions and what caused them. Nevertheless, successfully using a VPS as a teaching environment requires the user interface to be as operable as possible.

A survey conducted by Lahtinen et al. (2005) [8] showed that students' own views concerning their difficulties agree with the findings of aforementioned studies.

The consensus across the scientific community seems to be that same specific misconceptions about (OO) programming – scope, state, exception handling, inheritance, and underlying memory model – hinder students' learning when it comes to programming. Their identification and avoidance is an important task that should further the learning outcomes of entry-level programming courses.

According to Kaila et al. (2015) [9], using computers for teaching programming yielded far better results than using traditional pen and paper -based teaching methods. Instant feedback in form of points, output or stack trace enables students to pinpoint their own issues and misconceptions, and automatically collecting all student answers, regardless of whether they're wrong or right, gives teachers the possibility to find out exactly what their students' weak points and biggest misconceptions are.

In a study conducted by Malmi et al. (2002) [10], using automatically assessed exercises while learning to program gives students the possibility to test their code, get instant feedback about their solution, and find their personal problematics when it comes to writing code. The increase in motivation and self-esteem caused by positive feedback and expected results gives the possibility to focus on the essential parts of programming, thus preventing possible misconceptions.

3. VILLE

The data for this study was collected using an electronic learning environment called ViLLE. The environment is designed to automatically assess students' answers and give them immediate feedback based on their input. The system has been in development in-house since 2005. Originally made for programming visualization in university level CS courses, the system has since been extended for more generic teaching needs. Automatic assessment used gives students instant feedback and optionally shows the problems in their answers.

The system has approximately 100 different exercise types, with around 10% of them focused on programming. Some of the types included are:

- Coding exercise, in which students write a program with a given effect.

- Code sorting, a.k.a. Parson's puzzle [11], in which students are asked to sort given code lines to generate a program with a given output.
- Visualization exercise, in which students are asked to simulate the state (call stack, memory state) of a given program line by line.
- Robot exercise, in which students program a crane with simple programmatic commands to move boxes to given positions on a grid.

Other types cover general exercise types, e.g. multiple choice questions, sorting exercises, and mathematics exercises aimed at elementary school level and up.

The system also supports collaboration in two different levels: Firstly, it allows students to work together using a single computer, thus embracing the best practices of pair programming. Secondly, the system allows all teachers to utilize the exercises, courses and tutorials made by other teachers, enabling fast deployment of the system. For a complete description of ViLLE, see the technology paper [12] or ViLLE home page (http://villeteam.fi).

Members of the research group behind the system have participated in multiple studies concerning the teaching of programming to novice CS students, concentrating especially on program visualization (see e.g. [13] [14] [15]).

4. PROGRAMMING EXERCISES

The introductory level programming course discussed in this paper lasted for seven weeks. It's a compulsory part of both CS majors' and minors' studies. Most of the students are from the Faculty of Natural Sciences. Each course week consists of one lecture and one tutorial [9]. There are also four demonstration sessions, in which students present their solutions to simple programming exercises, and a small project, all of which are required to pass the course. The final exam of the course is done using ViLLE.

The final exam of the introductory programming course contained nine automatically assessed exercises. In this paper we analyze three of the exercises to grasp a more comprehensive idea of students' knowledge and abilities in Java programming. The exercises used for analysis are presented in this chapter.

Each of the three exercises requires the student to solve a problem by writing a small piece of code. The students are able to test their solution by submitting the answer and the solution is then compiled and tested against some random test cases. If there is a compilation error, the student receives the compiler error output and corresponding line numbers in their code. If the code compiles, the student sees the created output. There are always multiple test cases and they are different each time the code is executed. If the student decides to add any additional debug messages to the solutions, the result will automatically be zero, until the extra lines are removed. Every time the student executes their solution, the answer is saved as a submission in ViLLE.

4.1 Exercise 1

In the first exercise the students are asked to write a static method that takes a score value as a parameter and returns grade based on the score. Student is provided with a coding area that highlights Java syntax. The signature of the method is given in the instructions but otherwise the student has no other cues for the correct answer.

Table 1: Conversion Table for the Input Value

Score	Grade
0–10	0
11–20	1
21–30	2
31–40	3
41–50	4
51–	5

There are multiple ways of achieving the correct outcome. One possible solution is to use an else-if structure as shown here:

```
public static int countGrade(int score){
  if(score <= 10){
    return 0;
  } else if(score <= 20){
    return 1;
  } else if(score <= 30){
    return 2;
  } else if(score <= 40){
    return 3;
  } else if(score <= 50){
    return 4;
  } else {
    return 5;
  }
}
```

Every time the code is executed and it compiles, the student will be presented with the outputs of both their code and a correct code.

The example output shows only part of the output. The test case contains in total 40 random generated test cases for the score variable.

Example output of a correct solution for exercise 1:

```
Score:  13
Grade:  1
Score:  36
Grade:  3
Score:  1
Grade:  0
...
```

The typical and easy way to solve this problem at the introductory level is shown in the example solution. The students need to understand forming an if-else if -structure including the else branch.

4.2 Exercise 2

In the second exercise analyzed, the students were required to write a static method that takes a string variable as an argument and returns an integer. The returned integer should be formed by concatenating all the digits in the input string. For example if the string was "ab3cd2efghi89jkl6m", the method should return 32896. As opposed to the first exercise, students were asked to write the method signature themselves.

There are again numerous ways to achieve the outcome of the exercise description. One of the possible solutions is to loop through each character in the string and check whether the character is a digit or not. If the character is a digit, it is concatenated to a helper string. After all the characters have been checked, the helper string would contain only digits and it can be parsed into an integer, which is then returned.

The following method, utilizing a for-loop and the Java Character library is one possible way to accomplish the task given.

```
public static int parsiLuku(String s){
  String number = "";
  for(int i = 0; i < s.length(); i++){
    if(Character.isDigit(s.charAt(i))){
      number += s.charAt(i);
    }
  }
  return Integer.parseInt(number);
}
```

The test case contains ten randomly generated strings. The example output of a correct answer would look like this:

```
String: abcd16efg3hijk6lmnopq5rst2uvwxyz
Number: 163652
String: bc6def8gh8ijk3lm12n7o8p2qrstuvwxyz
Number: 688312782
String: ab5cdefghi1jk6lmnop94qrs7tuv5w4xyz
Number: 551694754
...
```

Compared to the first exercise, exercise 2 is way more demanding. The students need to be able to write the signature of the method and loop through each of the characters in a string and perform some sort of comparison to decide whether the character is a digit or not. This requires knowledge of primitive variable types in Java and their features. The second challenge is to parse the string into an integer.

4.3 Exercise 3

The last exercise asked students to write a static method that transposes the given matrix, swapping each row of the matrix with the corresponding column. The method does not have a return type; the changes are made straight to the matrix given as a parameter. The matrices are assumed to be complete.

The solution for this exercise requires knowledge of two-dimensional arrays and the usage of nested loops. The example code shows how to solve this problem without using a helper matrix.

```
public static void rotateMatrix(int[][] m){
  for(int i = 0; i < m.length; i++){
    for(int j = i; j < m[i].length; j++){
      int temp = m[i][j];
      m[i][j] = m[j][i];
      m[j][i] = temp;
    }
  }
}
```

The test case compared the solution against five randomly generated matrices, differing in sizes. Example output of a correct answer:

```
Matrix:
[9][6][4][8]
[6][0][9][0]
[0][4][9][1]
[5][8][2][7]
Rotated:
[9][6][0][5]
[6][0][4][8]
[4][9][9][2]
[8][0][1][7]
```

This exercise is relatively straightforward and does not require any deeper knowledge of Java API. It does, however, require some knowledge of two dimensional arrays and how to handle them in nested loops, which is not necessarily an easy task for a beginner programmer.

5. RESEARCH SETUP

Arranging an exam in an introductory level programming course that reflects the skill level of the students is almost impossible using traditional pen-and-paper methods. Therefore we use an electronic exam, which enables us to provide students with a near-to-authentic programming environment including compiler output and error messages. Java's API documentation is also provided. Other network access is restricted. This kind of setup allows us to create an exam with more complex problems than with traditional means, but the results also reflect the real life programming skills and problem solving skills of students better.

In this paper we analyze students' answers in three programming exercises from an introductory level programming course exam arranged in the fall of 2014. The course was about the basics of algorithmic programming in Java. Objects were not actually in the scope of the course but the nature of Java forced students to somewhat familiarize themselves with the concept. The course was taken by 148 students, 78 of which took the final exam in the first instance.

We chose nine students whose exam answers were analyzed submission by submission. The students were picked based on the submission counts for each of the three exercises observed. We wanted each of the selected students to have multiple submissions to make the comparison meaningful. Usually having only two submissions means that the students made a minor mistake in syntax and the error was easily fixed after compiler feedback. Therefore higher number of submissions were preferred. We also tried to find students from different skill groups. The students were divided into three groups based on their total score achieved from these three exercises. There are two students in the novice group, three in average performing group and four in the advanced group. The difference in group sizes is easily explained by the fact that the course mark average is not evenly distributed. [9]

All submissions made by the students were examined using a file comparison program (diff-tool). The diff-tool highlights any differences between two files, or submissions in this case. The difference was analyzed and marked down to describe changes made by the student. Subsequent submissions were compared to grasp a better idea of the problems students were struggling with before submitting their final version of the assignment. The answers were tagged by their characteristic misconceptions. Later on the changes were categorized into six different categories. Each student's submissions were then assigned into one or more categories. The categories are presented in subsections of section 6. The categories are not comparable in their scope but describe the difficulties students faced and mostly overcame. By scope we mean that for example try-catch-structures are broader and more complicated an issue than missing return statements.

We analyzed three programming exercises from an introductory level programming course's final exam. Nine students' answers were picked based on their submission count and performance. Subsequent submissions were compared to grasp a better idea of the problems students were struggling with before submitting their final solution and, in most cases, achieving some points from the exercise. The answers were tagged by their characteristic misconceptions.

6. RESULTS

In this chapter we discuss the findings from analyzing nine students' answers to an introductory level programming course's final exam. Three automatically assessed programming exercises' answers were analyzed, comparing the differences between subsequent submissions. With this comparison we hope to grasp a more comprehensive idea of students' understanding of basic programming concepts. Students were divided into three skill-groups (novice, average, and advanced) based on their overall scores from the final exam. First we present the points achieved and submissions used in the exercises observed. Then we explain the misconception categories the answers were divided to.

Table 2 presents the average scores achieved and the average number of submissions students made in each of the exercises before submitting a working version or giving up trying. The maximum score for each exercise was 10. The differences in submission counts can also be observed in Table 2. In exercise 1 there seem to be no substantial differences in submission counts, but in exercises 2 and 3 the novice group made remarkably more submission than the rest. In exercise 2 the advanced group achieved full score with half as many submissions as the novice group. The average group gave up on trying after on average 20 submissions and was on average satisfied in one third of the maximum score. In exercise 3 the difference between the novice and advanced groups grew larger. The advanced group achieved maximum scores with one third of the submissions of the novice group. The differences between the average group and the advanced group were minimal.

The answers were analyzed and categorized into six categories that emerged from the analyzed material. The categories are not in the same abstraction level or scope but they seem to describe the typical difficulties faced by the students.

Syntax

Problems initializing objects, difficulties to know when to read an array and when to pass a parameter to a function. This typically was visible on String object's `charAt`-function. The methods and fields representing strings' and arrays' sizes were also noticed to cause issues amongst students.

Indexing

Difficulties in understanding indices in loops and arrays. Typically students facing this issue tried randomly adding and subtracting the limits or values of array indices to achieve the wanted result.

Return statement

Missing the return statement in a method that has multiple different return values based on input.

Comparison

Different variable types caused some issues, especially in value comparisons. For example, the comparison of characters/strings and integers was found to cause a lot of issues. Java's anomalous string comparison caused problems in one case. In Java, primitive variables are compared using two equals signs, but since Strings are objects, they're compared with the `equals` method.

Table 2: The Average Submission Count and Average Score Achieved from the Exercises Observed

Skill-group	Exercise 1		Exercise 2		Exercise 3	
	Submissions (average)	Score (average)	Submissions (average)	Score (average)	Submissions (average)	Score (average)
Novice	2	10	44	10	36	2.5
Average	3.33	10	19.67	3.33	16	10
Advanced	3.25	10	20.25	10	13.25	10
Total	3	10	25.33	7.78	19.22	8.33

Table 3: The Overall Misconceptions and their Frequencies

Misconception	Syntax	Return statement	Indexing	Try-catch	Comparison	State and execution
Novice (2)	1 (50 %)	-	2 (100 %)	-	-	1 (50 %)
Average (3)	1 (33.3 %)	2 (66.7 %)	1 (33.3 %)	1 (33.3 %)	1 (33.3 %)	2 (66.7 %)
Advanced (4)	3 (75 %)	3 (75 %)	2 (50 %)	1 (25 %)	2 (50 %)	1 (25 %)
Total	5 (55.6 %)	5 (55.6 %)	5 (55.6 %)	2 (22.2 %)	3 (33.3 %)	4 (44.4 %)

Try-catch-structures

The usage of try-catch was not mandatory in any of the exercises. Two students tried this method for solving the number parsing problem. In both cases the try-catch structure was placed outside the loop and the function of the catch block seemed unclear.

State and execution

Some students had difficulties understanding the current state and execution order of the program code. In multiple cases this showed up as difficulties understanding how and when the value in a variable is changed. There were multiple instances of a student trying to swap two variables without using a helper variable. Nested loops also caused difficulties in understanding the execution order.

Table 3 describes the deviation of the misconceptions in skill groups and their total count in the observed nine cases. Many of the students seem to still struggle with the basic syntax and indexing. The return statement category is very detailed, but it seems to have been one of the hardest concepts to grasp. Strangely it's not found in the lowest level. Two students used a try-catch structure, even when it was not required. They also failed to use the structure correctly.

7. DISCUSSION

We analyzed nine students' answers in an introductory level programming course's final exam to better grasp the idea of what difficulties students face. The research was conducted as a pilot test to find out what can be learned by analyzing students' answers submission-by-submission. We found that students from all skill levels make mistakes and suffer from misconceptions in programming and, in this case, Java. The well performing students were able to overcome the misconceptions with the help of compiler and ViLLE output.

The misconception categories found in this study are solely based on the findings in students' answers. For example McCall et al. (2014) [16] have found a comprehensive list of errors made by novice programmers. This pilot study covers the answers from only nine students and therefore some of the categories remain very broad.

Many of the syntax errors were related to objects, which weren't in the scope of the course in question. Basic understanding of object creation and usage could be emphasized more during the lectures and tutorials [13]. Same difficulties were also found by other researchers [2] [3]. Indexing-related misconceptions were also common among the students analyzed. It is understandably somewhat counterintuitive to start counting from 0 instead of 1 and finding out the length of an array by getting the last index and incrementing it by one. To overcome these issues, the students need to gather more experience in handling arrays, lists and loops. This is already known by the teachers to be difficult and is addressed in a comprehensive manner in given time boundaries.

Issues in variable comparison fall into the same category as the previous two, being a very basic function in every program. Based on the problems student faced, they haven't completely digested the manner in which different variables are initialized. For example, character uses only a single quotation mark ('), whereas String initialization uses double quotation marks ("). Also the difference between comparing String-variables (objects) and primitive variables seems to cause confusion and should be emphasized at the end of the course again, when objects are lightly introduced.

Using a try-catch structure is a lot more complicated than the misconceptions mentioned earlier. None of the exercises required the usage of a try-catch-structure but two students decided to try it anyways. Issues surrounding the usage of a try-catch block were mainly present while using it together with other block structures, mainly loops. Both students who tried to implement a try-catch - based solution tried to use a loop inside the try-block. Neither of the students could solve the problem properly using try-catch and for the final answer, they used some other method of solving the problem

It should, however, be kept in mind that the nine cases were selected partly based on their submission count. This means there are students that could be described as iterators. Iterators tend to approach the problem via trial-and-error instead of planning and thinking. The sample size was also quite small and the division uneven. The final grades from the introductory level programming course in question tend to be unevenly distributed. In our courses there usually seem to be more good than poor grades. [13]

Based on the high average submission count and low average grade, exercise 2 was the hardest one of the sample. It required more comprehensive understanding of Java API than the rest. Surprisingly, only one student in the mediocre group gained any points from exercise 2.

As seen in Table 2, better performance does not automatically mean fewer misconceptions. The results could be described as follows: The better you can overcome your misconceptions, the better results you get.

8. CONCLUSIONS AND FUTURE WORK

Taking a deeper look into students' answers is a great way to get a more comprehensive idea of students' thinking and problem solving skills. Seeing students face and overcome the common pitfalls of programming could also help educators develop their teaching methods.

Even with such a small sample, some interesting results on students' thinking and problem solving skills were achieved. Based on the results of our pilot study, there is great potential in expanding this research setup to cover larger samples of students and include more exercises in to the comparison. There is also an interesting possibility to compare variations of misconceptions between different cohorts. Larger sample size would also enable greater precision in the list of common misconceptions and their frequencies. ViLLE offers a wide range of programming languages and comparing students' misconceptions between them would be interesting.

REFERENCES

[1] L. Ma, J. Ferguson, M. Roper and M. Wood, "Investigating the Viability of Mental Models Held by Novice Programmers," Covington, Kentucky, 2007.

[2] K. Goldman, P. Gross, C. Heeren, G. Herman, L. Kaczmarczyk, M. C. Loui and C. Zilles, "Identifying Important and Difficult Concepts in Introductory Computing Courses using a Delphi Process," in *SIGCSE*, Portland, Oregon, 2008.

[3] L. C. Kaczmarczyk, E. R. Petrick, J. P. East and G. L. Herman, "Identifying Student Misconceptions of Programming," in *SIGCSE*, Milwaukee, Wisconsin, 2010.

[4] M. Hristova, A. Misra, M. Rutter and R. Mercuri, "Identifying and Correcting Java Programming Errors," in *SIGCSE*, Reno, Nevada, 2003.

[5] C.-L. Chen, S.-Y. Cheng and J. M.-C. Lin, "A Study of Misconceptions and Missing Conceptions of Novice Java Programmers," Las Vegas, 2012.

[6] T. Sirkiä and J. Sorva, "Exploring Programming Misconceptions," in *Koli Calling*, Tahko, 2012.

[7] T. Sirkiä, "Recognizing Programming Misconceptions," Aalto University, Espoo, 2012.

[8] E. Lahtinen, K. Ala-Mutka and H.-M. Järvinen, "A Study of the Difficulties of Novice Programmers," in *ITiCSE*, Monte de Caparica, 2005.

[9] E. Kaila, T. Rajala, M.-J. Laakso, R. Lindén, E. Kurvinen, V. Karavirta and T. Salakoski, "Comparing student performance between traditional and technologically enhanced programming course," Sydney, 2015.

[10] L. Malmi, A. Korhonen and R. Saikkonen, "Experiences in Automatic Assessment on Mass Courses and Issues for Designing Virtual Courses," Aarhus, 2002.

[11] D. Parsons and P. Haden, "Parson's Programming Puzzles: A Fun and Effective Learning Tool for First Programming Courses," Hobart, 2006.

[12] M.-J. Laakso, E. Kaila and T. Rajala, *ViLLE: designing and utilizing a collaborative exercise-based education tool,* Sent to Computers & Education, 2014.

[13] E. Lokkila, E. Kaila, V. Karavirta, T. Salakoski and M.-J. Laakso, "Redesigning Introductory Computer Science Courses to Use Tutorial-Based Learning," Zagreb, 2015.

[14] S. Willman, R. Lindén, E. Kaila, T. Rajala, M.-J. Laakso and T. Salakoski, *On study habits on an introductory course on programming,* 2015.

[15] J. Holvitie, T. Rajala, R. Haavisto, E. Kaila, M.-J. Laakso and T. Salakoski, "Breaking the Programming Language Barrier: Using Program Visualizations to Transfer Programming Knowledge in One Programming Language to Another," Rome, 2012.

[16] D. McCall and M. Kölling, "Meaningful Categorisation of Novice Programmer Errors," in *IEEE Frontiers in Education Conference (FIE) Proceedings*, Madrid, Spain, 2014.

Design and Use of Static Scaffolding Techniques to Support Java Programming on a Mobile Phone

Chao Mbogo
Department of Computer Science
Kenya Methodist University
Nairobi, Kenya
chaombogho@gmail.com

Edwin Blake
Department of Computer Science
University of Cape Town
Cape Town, South Africa
edwin@cs.uct.ac.za

Hussein Suleman
Department of Computer Science
University of Cape Town
Cape Town, South Africa
hussein@cs.uct.ac.za

ABSTRACT

Most learners in resource-constrained environments own mobile phones that they could use to learn programming while outside the classroom. However, limitations of mobile phones, such as small screens and small keypads, impede their use as typical programming environments. This study proposed that programming environments on mobile phones could include scaffolding techniques specifically designed for mobile phones, and designed based on learners' needs. Scaffolding should be designed with some essential techniques that are mandatory for learners to use. Hence, one type of scaffolding technique that was designed to support programming on the mobile phone is static scaffolding that does not fade. Experiments were conducted with 64 learners of programming from three universities in Kenya and South Africa in order to investigate how they used the designed static scaffolding techniques to construct Java programs on a mobile phone. The results show that programming on mobile phones can be supported by providing scaffolding techniques that never fade, in order to address the limitations of mobile phones and to meet learners' needs.

Keywords

Mobile phone; Java; Programming; Static Scaffolding.

1. INTRODUCTION

The learning difficulties encountered in computer programming [23], especially by novice learners, indicate that some programming skills are beyond the novice learners' efforts. Scaffolding refers to support provided so that learners can engage in activities that would otherwise be beyond their unassisted efforts [24]. In order to contribute towards tackling learning difficulties in programming, novice learners can be supported to learn programming while they are outside the classroom. This makes any such support additional to the learner's classroom learning, and not a replacement.

Support to learners outside the classroom can be provided using PC-based applications. However, in many developing countries, people are much more likely to use computers at school or at work than to own them at home. For example, a survey conducted in Ghana and Kenya to investigate the ownership of information and communication technologies at home showed that only 10% of respondents in Ghana and 5% in Kenya have a computer at home [2]. The limited access to PCs outside the classroom aggravates the learning difficulties in the subject.

ITiCSE '16, July 09-13, 2016, Arequipa, Peru
© 2016 ACM. ISBN 978-1-4503-4231-5/16/07...$15.00
DOI: http://dx.doi.org/10.1145/2899415.2899456

The ubiquity of mobile devices provides an opportunity to use them as a resource to support learning of programming beyond the classroom. Mobile devices include laptops, tablets and mobile phones. Of these, mobile phones are the most widely used mobile devices among learners in developing countries [11]. Therefore, the mobile phone was selected as the resource that can be used for construction of programs outside the classroom. However, limitations of mobile phones, such as a small screen size and a small keypad, impede their use as typical programming environments. To deal with these limitations, and for handheld devices to become effective learning tools, the unique design challenges inherent in such a system must be understood [14]. In addition to addressing limitations of mobile phones, the challenges faced by learners of programming should be considered. This is because addressing these challenges maximizes the potential of meeting learners' needs. Consequently, this study proposed that programming environments on mobile phones could include scaffolding techniques that are specifically designed for mobile phones, and designed based on learners' needs.

One design recommendation is that scaffolding should be designed with some essential character that provides mandatory scaffolding to support learners [18]. For example, essential scaffolding was implemented in the design of a PC-based environment that provided a process wheel, which is a process map that visually described the space of possible science inquiry activities that learners could select from [17]. The design of such scaffolding that does not fade was encouraged because such scaffolds help to focus learners' attention and also ensure that a consistent, basic level of support is provided for every learner [20]. In this study, such scaffolds that do not fade are termed as static scaffolding.

Static scaffolding was designed as one of three types of scaffolding techniques to support Java programming on a mobile phone. The other two are: (i) automatic scaffolding that is automatically provided but fades with time or can be cancelled by the user; (ii) user-enabled scaffolding that is not automatically provided and the learner has to initiate its use. This paper focuses on static scaffolding. To implement the scaffolding techniques, an Android prototype was developed that supports the construction of Java programs on a mobile phone [15]. Android was selected as the platform of implementation because it is open source. Java was selected as the language for construction of programs because it was the common language taught across the institutions that participated in the study.

1.1 Designed Static Scaffolding Techniques

Static scaffolding techniques were designed using a theoretical scaffolding framework [16] that provides two strategies to support their design: (i) providing visual organizers in order to give access to functionality; and (ii) constraining the space of activities by using functional modes and by using ordered or unordered decomposition.

Providing visual organizers in order to give access to functionality was implemented by designing a program layout of the parts of a Java program. The order of the program layout was guided by standard Java coding guidelines [9], where a Java source file has the following ordering: beginning comments, package and import statements, and class and interface declarations. Figure 1 shows the designed main interface with parts of a Java program. This layout uses clickable buttons that provide: (i) collapsible and expandable views such as in Figure 1, where the main class button has been clicked to reveal some default code within the expanded area; and (ii) access to create individual parts of the program by clicking inside the expanded area. Such a collapsible and expandable interface was recommended for small screens [3].

Constraining the space of activities by using functional modes and decomposition was implemented by enabling construction of a program one part at a time. In the main interface (Figure 1) the learner clicks on the button that relates to the part they need to work on. Figure 1 shows only the main class as enabled and can be constructed at this stage. Until the learner correctly creates the main class the other parts of the program remain disabled. Thereafter, the learner is guided to create the header comments part then the main method part and so on. The program layout is retained even when learners progress to an advanced interface, where the order of program creation is not restricted. Thus, the program layout is a static scaffolding technique since it does not change or fade away with time.

On clicking each program part on the main interface another interface is opened with an editor that provides creation of only the selected program part. For example, Figure 2 shows creation of only the main method. The ability to work on one part of the program at a time could assist in working with the small screen. Because of the restriction of a small screen size, which remains unchanged, this scaffold is static and does not fade. Further, Figure 2 shows how working on a program one part at a time could assist in addressing the soft keypad on smartphones that takes up nearly half the screen.

For a learner to have a mental image of how the different parts of the program work together, learners should be able to inspect the task they are working on in multiple ways. In this case, while working on a program part (for example, while editing the main method in Figure 2), a learner could swipe to the full program interface and view the whole program at the state at which it was last saved (Figure 3). This ability to move between a program part and the whole promotes cognitive growth by keeping the learner connected to the program parts, while at the same time being able to appreciate existence of the whole problem [1].

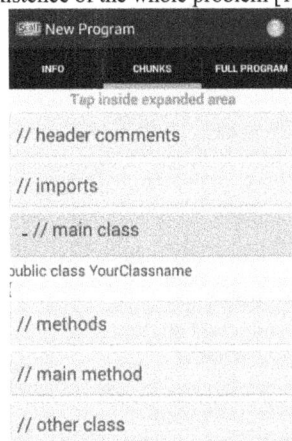

To compile the program at any time, the learner presses the button at the top right corner of Figure 1 and the full program is sent to the ideone online compiler and debugging tool [8]. The results and output are sent back to the mobile interface.

To evaluate the use of the static scaffolding techniques, an empirical evaluation was conducted where 64 learners from three universities in Kenya and South Africa attempted Java programming tasks using the application. Data was collected using computer logs and questionnaires.

The contribution of this study is fourfold: (i) an illustration of static scaffolding techniques that do not fade; (ii) how the static scaffolding techniques support the construction of Java programs on a mobile phone; (iii) feedback from learners on the use of static scaffolding techniques; and (iv) implications of the study.

2. RELATED WORK

Studies on supporting the learning of programing stress the importance of learning programming by doing, which is in line with the constructivist theory. Learning programing by doing requires access to computing resources such as PCs and laptops. Indeed, several studies have offered scaffolded environments on PC platforms targeting novice learners of programming, for example, 3D environments such as Alice [4], and teacher-learner assessment environments such as Test My Code [22]. However, most learners at institutions in parts of Africa are in resource-constrained environments where they have limited access to such resources, especially while they are outside the classroom. Even within the institutions, some schools have a limited number of desktop computers that could be shared among learners. For example, even in a relatively well-resourced developing country like South Africa, it is not uncommon for a school of 1,000 learners to have only one computer room with 30 PCs [20]. In fact, poor infrastructure and facilities is one of the major challenges faced by higher education in Africa [25]. This study was motivated by the resource constraints in a developing country's context.

The ubiquity and availability of mobile phones provides an opportunity to use them to support learning of programming outside the classroom. A study conducted in Kenya showed that most of the respondents studying for university degrees or higher own mobile phones [7]. However, mobile phones pose some limitations. The key limitation of handheld technology for the delivery of learning objects is the small screen that is available [3].

Figure 1. Main interface showing program overview with only the main class parts activated

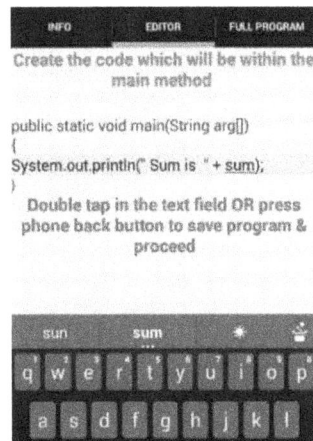

Figure 2. Editor interface showing construction of only the main method

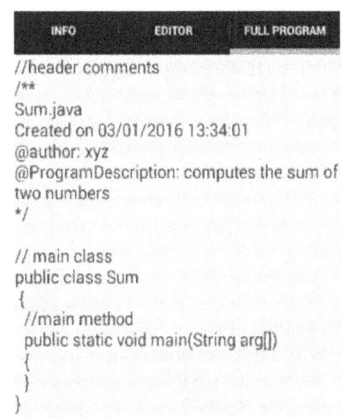

Figure 3. Full program as was last saved

One recommendation for designing scaffolds is by using activity decomposition that develops separate workspaces for each component task [13] to package contents in small program parts [5]. Such design recommendations were considered while designing the static scaffolding techniques discussed in this paper.

There are existing mobile programming environments that can be used by novice learners. Some, such as SAND IDE, can be used to create standard programs. However, mobile programming environments such as SAND IDE mostly mimic PC IDEs and do not address the limitations of mobile phones. A study by Microsoft enables development of applications using a new language - TouchDevelop - on the TouchDevelop programming environment where much of the code is created by tapping through menus [19]. TouchDevelop is a specialized language that was designed for a visual programming environment that creates mobile applications. In contrast, this study does not develop a specialized language. Further, it was not the aim of this study to support the creation of mobile applications, but to support the creation of standard programs that would typically be created in an introduction to programming class.

3. STUDY METHODOLOGY

3.1 Participants and Experiments

Table 1 shows the distribution of 64 learners of programming from one university in South Africa (University of Western Cape (UWC)) and two universities in Kenya (Jomo Kenyatta University of Agriculture and Technology (JKUAT) and Kenya Methodist University (KeMU)) who participated in two experiments. Participation in the experiments was voluntary. Experiment one was conducted with a group of learners different from the ones in Experiment two. Despite the geographical and background differences between South Africa and Kenya, all learners were taking an introductory course in programming using Java. The learners who took part in this study used desktop IDEs in their classroom learning. However, during the experiments they only used the mobile programming interface.

Each group of learners from each university took part in 2-hour experiment sessions. Each experiment session involved an introduction to the purpose of the research with learners signing consent forms, learners tackling the programming tasks, and completion of a post-experiment questionnaire. Learners who did not own Android phones were issued with such phones with the application pre-installed. The phones issued were the Samsung Galaxy Pocket S5300 phones that run Android version 2.3. The Samsung Galaxy Pocket has a display size of 2.8 inches.

3.2 Programming Tasks

The teachers were asked for a set of Java exercises relating to introductory topics that they had already taught in the course. Three sets of programming tasks were used during the two experiments: one set of questions for UWC in Experiment one; one set of questions for JKUAT in Experiment one; and one consolidated set of exercises for both KeMU and JKUAT in Experiment two. In the first Experiment, the exercises were obtained from the different teachers of the courses in their respective institutions. In the second Experiment, the teachers from both KeMU and JKUAT had taught similar topics in introduction to Java programming. Therefore, the exercises from the respective teachers were combined into one set. At the time of conducting the two experiments, all the teachers had covered the topics of Java syntax, input-output, loops, methods, and classes. The programming tasks attempted by learners in Experiment one are shown in Figure 4. The programming tasks attempted by learners in Experiment two are shown in Figure 5.

Table 1. Distribution of learners in two experiments

Experiment	Institution	Number of learners
One	UWC	14
	JKUAT	13
Two	KeMU	13
	JKUAT	24

Programming Task for UWC group in Experiment One

1. Write a program that calculates the total cost of an item that is R159.72 and incurs a VAT of 14%.
2. Write a program that uses a for-loop to calculate the sum of the numbers from 1 to 50 and displays the sum and average.
3. Write a program that uses a method name() to print out your name.
4. Write a program that uses the Scanner input to ask for the user's name and age, and prints
    "Hello " + name " your age is "+ age;
5. Write a program that uses a method input() to ask for height and width of a rectangle, and calculates and display the area using height x width.
6. Write a program that determines if a number that is input by a user is odd or even.

Programming Task for JKUAT group in Experiment One

1. Write a program that outputs 'Scaffolding at JKUAT'.
2. Write a program that computes the sum and average of the number 1-20.
3. Write a program that captures and displays the ages of two students.
4. Write a program that uses a method to capture two integers and outputs their sum.
5. Write a program that initialises default values of name and age in a constructor and outputs these in a main class.

Figure 4. Programming tasks attempted by learners in Experiment one at UWC and JKUAT

---

1. Write a program that initialises x to 10 and prints out its double value. Save this program as XValue.java
2. Using a for-loop print the first 10 natural numbers. Save this program as Natural.java
3. Write a program that accepts input from the user and displays this as
    "Your input is " + input. Save this program as Natural.java
4. Write a program that uses a method input() to capture and display the names of two students. Save this program as MethSt.java
5. Write a program that creates two classes. The second class contains the constructor below. Access this constructor from the main class
    Output() { System.out.println ("Constructor called"); }
6. Write a program that uses a for-loop within a method avg() to calculate the sum of the numbers 20-100 and displays the sum. Call this method from the main method.

Figure 5. Programming tasks attempted by learners in Experiment two

3.3 Data Collection

Google Analytics was used to collect logs of the learners' interaction with the application. At the end of the experiments the learners filled an online questionnaire that consisted of two parts: (i) demography; and (ii) reflections and perceptions on scaffolding techniques.

4. Evaluation

The CIAO model [10] and the micro and meso levels of the M3 evaluation framework [21] have outlined that while evaluating educational technology one should consider data about learners' interaction with the software and learners' attitudes and outcomes. Thus, in order to investigate the use of static scaffolding techniques, three criteria were considered: (i) task success; (ii) the use of the static scaffolding techniques to construct programs; and (iii) qualitative feedback from the learners.

4.1 Task Success

Each program was examined for the extent to which it was completed. A complete program is one that met all three criteria: (i) had all the required program parts completed; (ii) successfully compiled after completion of the required parts; and (iii) produced the required output. Four metrics measured task success: (i) which tasks were attempted; (ii) which tasks were not attempted; (iii) which tasks were incomplete; and (iv) which tasks were completed. Incomplete tasks are tasks that failed to meet at least one of the criteria for completeness. Attempted tasks are the combination of incomplete and completed tasks. Some tasks were not attempted.

4.2 Use of Static Scaffolding Techniques

Three metrics measured the use of static scaffolding techniques: (i) use of static scaffolding techniques in incomplete and complete programs; (ii) progression of use of static scaffolding techniques from one task to the next; and (iii) learners' characteristics while using the static scaffolding techniques.

4.3 Qualitative Feedback

Qualitative feedback was collected using self-reported data by learners reflectively indicating their perceptions on the use of static scaffolding to support construction of programs on a mobile phone.

5. Results and Discussion

This section presents results and discussion on the use of static scaffolding techniques, some characteristics displayed by learners while using the static scaffolding techniques, and representative learners' feedback. In the graphs, UWC-1 means the first experiment at UWC, KeMU-2 means the second experiment at KeMU, and so on.

5.1 Use of Static Scaffolding Techniques

Static scaffolding was provided using two techniques: (i) a program overview that also offered restricted program creation in the basic main interface; and (ii) editing of a program one part at a time while able to view the full program. Figure 6 shows a comparison of the use of static scaffolding techniques in complete and incomplete programs across the four experiment sessions in the first and second experiments. The average use per learner refers to the average number of times that each learner accesses the interfaces that provide each of the two static scaffolding techniques. Figure 6 shows that there was variation in use of the static scaffolding across the experiments. For example, in the first experiments at UWC and JKUAT, learners who completed programs edited the program parts more than the learners who did not complete programs. Whereas in the second experiment at KeMU, learners who did not complete programs edited the program parts more than the learners who completed programs. This variation in use could be because learners had to interact with the static scaffolds to construct the programs, whether or not they completed the programs successfully. In all the cases learners spent more time on average on the program overview than on editing the parts of a program. This could be because the program overview interface is the entry point to all the program

parts and a learner had to go back to this interface in order to access each program part. Conversely, the editing interface involved working on just one program part a time.

Additional analysis was conducted on the use of static scaffolding across the different tasks. The results from the second experiment at JKUAT are used to illustrate this because it is the group where the most number of tasks were attempted and completed (Table 2 shows the number of learners who attempted and completed each task at JKUAT in the second experiment). Figure 7 shows the progression of use of static scaffolding from the first program to the sixth program. Learners used the static scaffolding nearly two times less in the second program than in the first; meaning that learners spent less time both on the main interface and working on the program parts in the second program than in the first. The reduced use of the static scaffolding in the second program could be due to learners having familiarized themselves with the interface. Figure 7 also indicates that the static scaffolding was mostly used in the first program than in subsequent programs for both incomplete and complete programs. Some of the programs that were completed in the fourth task were constructed at the advanced interface. This explains the increased use of static scaffolding since learners encountered this interface for the first time. Further, all the tasks that were completed in the sixth program were completed within the advanced interface. These tasks required the construction of a method in addition to the main class, header and main method. This explains the increased use of static scaffolds at the sixth program. These results indicate that, indeed, learners were able to attempt and complete programming tasks using the static scaffolding techniques, which had to be used for all programs.

5.2 Learners' characteristics while using static scaffolding techniques

Further comparison of the use of static scaffolding with the use of automatic scaffolding (such as instructions and prompts for examples) and user-initiated scaffolding (such as hints on program parts) revealed that learners found static scaffolding alone sufficient to construct programs. Three examples will be used to illustrate this.

While creating a program part for the first time, some learners repeatedly went back to the editor on the same program part, before proceeding to the next one. For example, 7 learners in the first experiment at UWC exhibited this characteristic. In contrast, there were learners who initially worked on each program part just once or made at most two attempts before proceeding to the next program part. The common characteristic among such learners is that they mostly used only the static scaffolding techniques with partial use of some of the provided automatic scaffolding and very little use of the user-enabled scaffolding. This is evidence that the static scaffolding techniques are sufficient to support construction of programs on a mobile phone, even when the learners do not use scaffolding that they can choose (user-enabled) or that which fades.

Table 2. Number of learners who attempted and completed tasks at JKUAT in the second Experiment

	Attempted	Completed
Task 1	24	18
Task 2	19	17
Task 3	20	12
Task 4	12	7
Task 5	6	3
Task 6	5	3

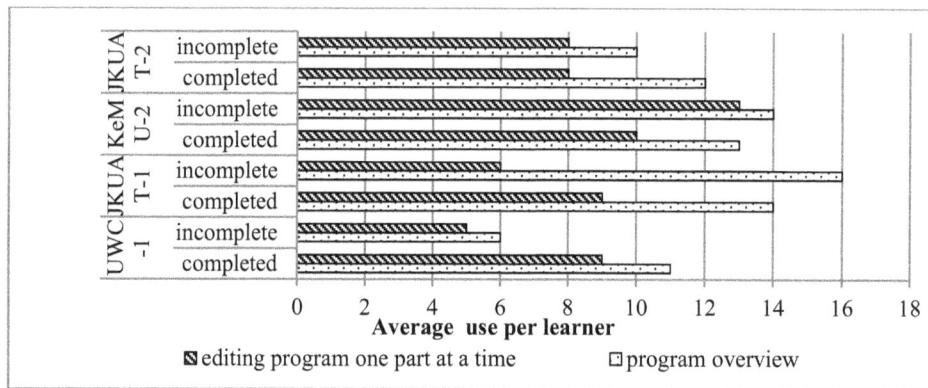

Figure 6. Comparison of use of static scaffolding techniques between incomplete and complete programs at UWC, KeMU and JKUAT in Experiments one and two

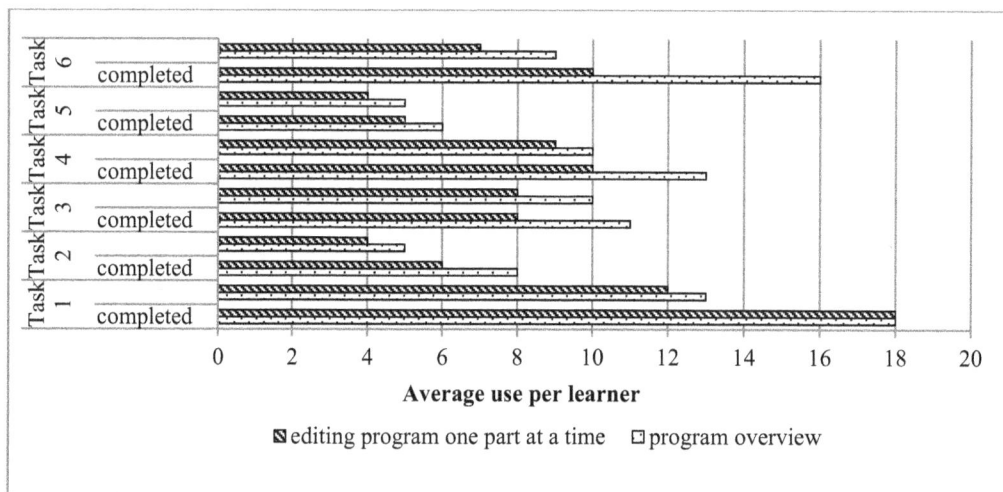

Figure 7. Progression of use of static scaffolding techniques in incomplete and complete programs at JKUAT Experiment two

Another illustration is when a learner was working on a program, where a suggestion to view a related example was provided (an option that a learner could accept or reject). These were automatic scaffolds. It was observed that several learners opted not to view these examples. For example, of the 24 learners in the second experiment at JKUAT, 18 rejected the use of one scaffolding technique or another, with 11 learners rejecting a suggestion to view an example. This suggests that learners may not have required extra support such as viewing of examples, but found it sufficient to use only the static scaffolding to create programs.

Further evidence that static scaffolding supports construction of programs on a mobile phone was observed by how learners edited programs after they encountered run-time errors. After learners encountered run-time errors, they were able to go directly to the part of the program that contained the erroneous code by easily accessing it through the program layout at the main interface.

5.3 Learners' feedback on the use of static scaffolding techniques

Learners found the two static scaffolding techniques useful as evidenced by the representative verbatim feedback: 'The application divides the program or code into sections then one can then track and write the code properly by following the sections.' 'The sections are well laid out.' 'The separate segments of program are useful.' 'How the codes are divided into chunks making the application easier to use.' 'The chunks made it easier to construct the program.'

The learners' representative positive feedback further indicates their usefulness in supporting programming on a mobile phone.

6. Conclusion

This study has presented two static scaffolding techniques: (i) a program layout at the main interface; and (ii) editing of a program one part at a time while able to view the full program. The results show that the program layout and constructing a program one part at a time enabled effective support and guidance towards correct creation of programs. Further, learners' verbatim feedback indicate that they found these static scaffolding techniques useful.

Desktop IDEs provide complex environments where a large amount of information is exposed to the learner at the same time, because this is possible on such large screens. This also means that it is possible to provide support to the learner all in one place without the learner having to leave the screen. However, providing all the functionality in one place does not work well on small screens. One technique that was used in this study to address the small screen is the static scaffolding technique of completing a program one part at a time. This way, the learner is able to focus on only the small part and correctly create it, hence learn it, before learning the next small part. This study has given an indication that the benefits of a static scaffolding technique such as completing a program one part at a time may not have been achieved if such as scaffolding technique was optional.

One of the main criticisms of the constructivist approach is that learners are expected to construct new knowledge with minimal guidance [12]. This criticism was discussed by Guzdial [6], where he posed the question: how then should programming be taught considering that the emphasis has been to learn programming by constructing programs? This study provides one possible answer.

The static scaffolding techniques designed in this study provide strong guides by ensuring that there is always support available that address the limitations of mobile phones and learners' needs. Thus, one possible answer to Guzdial's question is: learning programming on such small devices can be supported by providing some static scaffolding techniques that are always present. In addition, in resource-constrained environments where it may not be possible to easily acquire new desktops for learners that they could use outside the classroom, the solution could be to use the devices that the learners already have and design applications that consider both the limitations of the available devices and learners' needs. This study has shown that this is possible.

Future work from this study will include several aspects: (i) use of the scaffolding techniques to attempt more complex and larger programs than the ones presented in this paper, such as programs with multiple methods, controlled loops, or inheritance; (ii) the limitations of the interface encountered when tackling more complex and larger programs and if and how these might influence the design of additional scaffolding techniques; (iii) a comparative study with a desktop programming environment (with and without scaffolding); (iv) a study involving pre-test and post-test analysis in order to test if learners gained programming skills; and (v) a longitudinal study where learners use the static scaffolding over an extended period of time.

7. Acknowledgements

We thank the learners, teachers and institutions that participated in this study. We thank the Kenya Education Network (KENET) and Kenya Methodist University for travel grants to attend the conference.

REFERENCES

[1] Ackermann, E.K. 1996. Perspective-Taking and object Construction. *Constuctionism in Practice: Designing, Thinking, and Learning in a Digital World.* 25–37.

[2] Bowen, H. and Goldstein, P. 2010. *Radio , Mobile Phones Stand Out in Africa ' s Media Communication Landscape.*

[3] Churchill, D. and Hedberg, J. 2008. Learning object design considerations for small-screen handheld devices. *Computers & Education.* 50, 3 (Apr. 2008), 881–893.

[4] Dann, W.P. et al. 2011. Learning to Program with Alice. (Mar. 2011).

[5] Elias, T. 2011. Universal instructional design principles for mobile learning. *The International Review of Research in Open and Distributed Learning.*

[6] Guzdial, M. 2015. What's the best way to teach computer science to beginners? *Communications of the ACM.* 58, 2 (Jan. 2015), 12–13.

[7] Hannah, B. 2010. *Information at the Grassroots: Analyzing the media use and communication habits of Kenyans to support effective development.*

[8] Ideone ™ API: 2010. .

[9] Java Code Conventions: 1997. *http://www.oracle.com/technetwork/java/codeconventions-150003.pdf.* Accessed: 2015-01-19.

[10] Jones et al. 1999. Contexts for evaluating educational software. *Interacting with Computers.* 11, 5 (May 1999), 499–516.

[11] Kafyulilo, A. 2012. Access, use and perceptions of teachers and students towards mobile phones as a tool for teaching and learning in Tanzania. *Education and Information Technologies.* 19, 1 (Jul. 2012), 115–127.

[12] Kirschner, P.A. et al. 2006. Why Minimal Guidance During Instruction Does Not Work: An Analysis of the Failure of Constructivist, Discovery, Problem-Based, Experiential, and Inquiry-Based Teaching. *Educational Psychologist.* 41, 2 (Jun. 2006), 75–86.

[13] Luchini, K. et al. 2004. Design guidelines for learner-centered handheld tools. *Proceedings of the 2004 conference on Human factors in computing systems - CHI '04* (New York, New York, USA, Apr. 2004), 135–142.

[14] Luchini, K. et al. 2002. Supporting learning in context: extending learner-centered design to the development of handheld educational software. *Proceedings. IEEE International Workshop on Wireless and Mobile Technologies in Education* (2002), 107–111.

[15] Mbogo, C. et al. 2013. A mobile scaffolding application to support novice learners of computer programming. *Proceedings of the Sixth International Conference on Information and Communications Technologies and Development Notes - ICTD '13 - volume 2* (Cape Town, Dec. 2013), 84–87.

[16] Mbogo, C. et al. 2014. Initial Evaluation of a Mobile Scaffolding Application that seeks to Support Novice Learners of Programming. *To appear in Proceeding of Mobile Learning 2014 Conference* (Madrid, Spain, 2014).

[17] Quintana, C. et al. 2002. A Case Study to Distill Structural Scaffolding Guidelines for Scaffolded Software Environments. *Proceedings of the SIGCHI conference on Human factors in computing systems Changing our world, changing ourselves - CHI '02* (New York, New York, USA, Apr. 2002), 81.

[18] Quintana, C. et al. 2002. Scaffolding Design Guidelines for Learner-Centered Software Environments. (Mar. 2002).

[19] Tillmann, N. et al. 2011. TouchDevelop. *Proceedings of the 10th SIGPLAN symposium on New ideas, new paradigms, and reflections on programming and software - ONWARD '11* (New York, New York, USA, Oct. 2011), 49.

[20] Traxler, J. and Vosloo, S. 2014. Introduction: The prospects for mobile learning. *PROSPECTS.* 44, 1 (Apr. 2014), 13–28.

[21] Vavoula, G. and Sharples, M. 2009. Meeting the Challenges in Evaluating Mobile Learning: A 3-level Evaluation Framework. *International Journal of Mobile and Blended Learning.* 1, 2 (2009), 54–75.

[22] Vihavainen, A. et al. 2013. Scaffolding students' learning using test my code. *Proceedings of the 18th ACM conference on Innovation and technology in computer science education - ITiCSE '13* (Canterbury, England, Jul. 2013), 117.

[23] Watson, C. and Li, F.W.B. 2014. Failure rates in introductory programming revisited. *Proceedings of the 2014 conference on Innovation & technology in computer science education - ITiCSE '14* (New York, New York, USA, Jun. 2014), 39–44.

[24] Wood, D. et al. 1976. The Role of Tutoring in Problem Solving. *Journal of Child Psychology and Psychiatry.* 17, 2 (Apr. 1976), 89–100.

[25] Yizengaw, T. 2008. *Challenges of Higher Education in Africa and Lessons of Experience for the Africa-US Higher Education Collaboration Initiative.*

Factors for Success in Online CS1

Jennifer Campbell
Dept of Computer Science
University of Toronto
campbell@cs.toronto.edu

Diane Horton
Dept of Computer Science
University of Toronto
dianeh@cs.toronto.edu

Michelle Craig
Dept of Computer Science
University of Toronto
mcraig@cs.toronto.edu

ABSTRACT

Enrollment in post-secondary online courses has been increasing, but several studies have found that the drop rates in online courses are higher than in face-to-face. In our previous study comparing an online section of CS1 with a face-to-face flipped section, we also found the drop rate higher in the online section. Given that we plan to continue offering online options for our students, we aim to identify factors associated with success in online CS1. In this paper, we examine factors that are under students' own control such as how fully they participate in ungraded but important learning activities, and other factors that we may be able to manipulate and improve, such as students' skills for self-regulated learning, and their sense of community in the course. We found important differences between the online and flipped sections regarding what behaviours and attributes were associated with success. While completion of unmarked practice exercises was a factor for both sections, test anxiety and self-efficacy were factors only for the online section, and intrinsic goal orientation was a factor only for the flipped section.

Categories and Subject Descriptors

K.3.2 [**Computers and Education**]: Computer and Information Science Education—*Computer Science Education*

Keywords

online; CS1; novice programming; self-regulated learning

1. INTRODUCTION

Enrollment in online courses is increasing and, as of 2012, approximately 32% of post-secondary students in the United States took at least one online course [1]. In [12], we compare a CS1 course offered in two formats: online and face-to-face flipped. We found that the population of students who choose each section is different, with the online section attracting fewer CS majors, fewer first-year students and more beginners, retakers, and part-time students.

ITiCSE '16, July 09 - 13, 2016, Arequipa, Peru

ⓒ 2016 Copyright held by the owner/author(s). Publication rights licensed to ACM.
ISBN 978-1-4503-4231-5/16/07...$15.00

DOI: http://dx.doi.org/10.1145/2899415.2899457

Like others [5, 16], we found that online students were less likely to complete the course than face-to-face students. However, for the students who did write the final exam, exam scores in online and flipped were not significantly different. It is difficult to determine whether the poorer completion rate in the online section is due to differences in populations or to the course format. A number of studies have considered the factors leading students to drop out of online courses in multiple disciplines. For a survey of papers from 1999 to 2009, see [15].

In this paper, we explore possible success factors in both online and flipped offerings of CS1. There have been many previous studies of success in traditional, lecture-based CS1 courses, including explorations of demographics, study behaviours, previous academic experience or other computer experience, cognitive skills, and student beliefs. See [2] for a comprehensive survey of the pre-2006 work. Here we highlight results relevant to the factors we explore in this paper.

Rountree et al. [20] tested for associations between course outcomes and student demographics, background, and expectations. They found that desire to learn programming was the strongest influence on passing the course, and that grade expectations were a factor in the final grades. In a multi-institution study, Simon et al. [22, 8] reported that final course grades were more strongly correlated with students' shallow or deep approach to learning than with prior experience. Wilson and Shrock [24] found that the most important factors for success were students' comfort level in the course, math background, and attributing performance on the midterm to luck (which contributed negatively). Ventura [23] also considered comfort level, among other factors, and found that both comfort level and time spent in the lab had more predictive value than cognitive and academic factors such as critical thinking and SAT scores. In contrast, Chinn et al. [6] did not find that study time was a factor in their traditional CS1, but that lecture attendance and prior experience both positively correlated with final grades.

Another factor for student success is self-regulated learning (SRL). "Self-regulated learning and performance refers to the process whereby learners personally activate and sustain cognitions, affects, and behaviours that are systematically oriented toward the attainment of personal goals" [25, p. 1]. SRL has been studied extensively, and is an important source of differences in achievement between students. Furthermore, helping students to strengthen their self-regulatory processes can improve student achievement [25]. Pintrich and de Groot [17] note that definitions of SRL vary, but that three components are particularly important for classroom performance: cognitive strategies; metacognitive strategies such as monitoring cognition; and skills related to the management of effort, such as persistence. They emphasize that SRL skills are not sufficient for performance. Students must also possess the motivation to use those skills. They developed and validated a now widely-used instrument to assess SRL skills and motivational belief, the Motivated Strategies for Learning Questionnaire (MSLQ) [17, 18].

In an online gerontology course, Cho and Shen [7] used the MSLQ to study SRL motivations and behaviours. They found students' intrinsic goal orientation and academic self-efficacy to be important for academic achievements.

There has been little work on self-regulated learning in computer science. Falkner et al. [10] identify SRL strategies used by students in an introductory software development course, but they do not examine the relationship between SRL and course outcomes. Consistent with the literature on SRL, Bergin et al. [3] found that greater use of metacognitive and resource management strategies was linked to better performance in an introductory programming course. They also found that high intrinsic motivation and high task value are linked to better performance and to greater use of metacognitive and resource management strategies. Interestingly, they did not find the analogous relationships held for cognitive strategies.

2. METHODOLOGY

2.1 The Course

This study was conducted at the University of Toronto, a research-intensive North American university. We have been offering our CS1 in a face-to-face, flipped format since 2013 [4, 14, 13]. In [12], we described our first offering of an online CS1 in Fall 2014 and compared it to our flipped CS1.

Our online CS1 was modelled after the flipped CS1, with most face-to-face components replaced by online alternatives. For all students, flipped and online, course content was delivered through videos. The flipped students met face-to-face during lecture periods to complete exercises as described in [4], while the online students did analogous exercises asynchronously and online. In addition, to parallel the just-in-time teaching that occurred in the flipped lectures, the online students had access to explanatory videos in which an instructor solved the exercises and addressed anticipated misconceptions.

The online students completed their midterm online, while the flipped students wrote a traditional midterm on paper. The online midterm was limited to the question types available on our Learning Management System (Blackboard) and by the fact that online students could not be supervised during the test. Because of this, the midterm was worth only 5% of the course grade, compared to 14% for the flipped students. All students wrote the same final exam in-person and on paper, but the exam was worth 59% for online students and 50% for flipped students. The rest of the course work was the same for all students and was comprised of out-of-class weekly exercises and three larger assignments.

2.2 The Study

We wanted to determine how course outcomes were influenced by students' pre-course motivation and skills for self-regulated learning, and by their behaviour during the course. We therefore conducted a survey in the first week of

term that included the MSLQ [17][1] and a survey in the final week that asked students to report on behaviours of interest. We were also interested in how students' sense of community might differ in the online section, so in the final survey we included questions about interaction with each other and the instructor, as well as the Classroom scale of the Classroom and School Community Inventory (CSCI) [21].

855 students (118 online and 737 flipped) gave informed consent and completed at least one survey. Regardless of whether they consented to participate in our study, students who completed both the initial and final survey earned 1% towards their course grade.

We set a p-value of .05 for statistical significance. We report exact values for p, to three decimal places, unless it is < .001.

3. RESULTS AND DISCUSSION

3.1 Doing the unmarked exercises

Flipped students spent most of their lecture time solving unmarked exercises and online students worked on analogous exercises online. The exercises did not contribute to course grades for either group. Nevertheless, we consider these exercises to be important for learning, and want students to choose to do them. To measure whether students did, we asked online students on the final survey "How often did you complete the 'Rehearse' (not-for-credit) work on [the online system]?" For the flipped section, because the instructors did not record students' exercise work, we use lecture attendance as an approximation of participation in the in-class exercises. On the final survey we asked "Regardless of whether you were enrolled in the online or on-campus sections, how often did you attend lecture?"[2]

Figure 1 shows online students' self-reported completion of the Rehearse Exercises and flipped students' self-reported attendance at lectures.

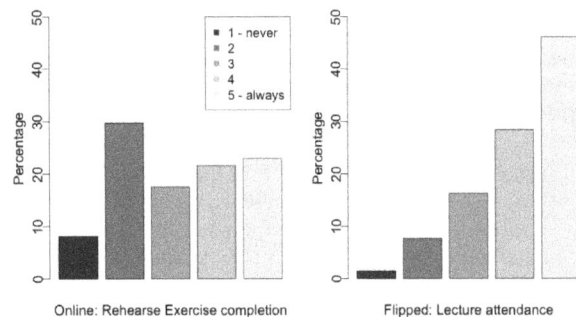

Figure 1: Self-reported Rehearse Exercise completion for online students and lecture attendance for flipped students

We hoped that online student participation in the unmarked Rehearse Exercises would be as good as attendance

---

[1]We used the 1990 version of the MSLQ. In the 1991 version [18] of the MSLQ, used by Bergin et al. [3], many questions assume that the survey is conducted once the course is well underway, rendering it unsuitable for our study.
[2]Because many online students were on campus and had access to lectures, we asked this question of both groups.

at lecture in the flipped section. This was not the case. The mean response for completion of Rehearse Exercises in the online section was 3.2 while the mean response for attendance in the flipped section was 4.1. A Welch two sample t-test finds this difference significant ($p < .001$).

To test our assumption that participating in the exercises is important for learning, we tested whether exercise participation correlated with exam grades. For online students, we did not find a significant correlation between exam grades and self-reported completion of Rehearse Exercises. Since prior programming experience is known to be a strong predictor of outcomes in CS1 [11], we performed a linear regression of exam grades modelled by prior experience[3] and completion of Rehearse Exercises as shown in Table 1. Once prior programming experience was factored out, completion of Rehearse Exercises was a statistically significant factor for exam grades.

	Estimate	Std. Error	t value	Pr(>|t|)
(Intercept)	32.2438	4.6398	6.95	0.0000
prior.exp	4.2878	1.5431	2.78	0.0071
rehearse	2.1966	0.9957	2.21	0.0308

Table 1: Statistical models: effect of prior experience and completion of Rehearse Exercises on exam grades for online students

The results are analogous for flipped students. There was no significant correlation between exam grades and self-reported lecture attendance, but once prior experience was factored out, lecture attendance was significant. Table 2 shows the result of a linear regression of exam grades modelled by prior experience and lecture attendance.

	Estimate	Std. Error	t value	Pr(>|t|)
(Intercept)	34.8040	2.3401	14.87	0.0000
prior.exp	3.7140	0.4913	7.56	0.0000
attend	1.7146	0.5041	3.40	0.0007

Table 2: Statistical models: effect of prior experience and lecture attendance on exam grades for flipped students

To summarize, for both online and flipped students, participation in the not-for-credit exercises is a factor for final-exam performance once prior experience is factored out. Students who participate more in the optional activities do better. We have no control over prior experience, but we can perhaps influence the students' participation rates once they enroll in the course. These results are consistent with the study by Chinn et al. [6], which found that prior experience and lecture attendance correlated with final grades.

There are several threats to the validity of these conclusions. Although the instructors report that flipped students who attended class participated well in the work, attendance may not be a good approximation of work on the exercises. Additionally, an online student who answered all the questions for a Rehearse Exercise, but did not get them correct,

[3]On the initial survey, we asked: "Many CSC108 students have no prior programming experience, while others have some. Rate the amount of prior programming experience that you have." on a scale from 1 (no experience) to 5 (a lot of experience).

may have reported that they did not "complete" the exercise while flipped students only had to report on their lecture attendance. Finally, both completion of Rehearse Exercises and attendance at lecture were self-reported.

3.2 Time spent on the course

In the end-of-term survey we asked "How much time did you spend on this course compared to other university courses you have taken?" This question addresses the amount of emphasis students placed on the course, rather than the absolute amount of time they invested.

In section 3.1, we saw that the completion rate of the optional Rehearse Exercises for online students was significantly lower than the lecture attendance of flipped students. However, students in online and flipped gave similar responses to our question about time. (Figure 2). The means were 3.2 for online and 3.4 for flipped.

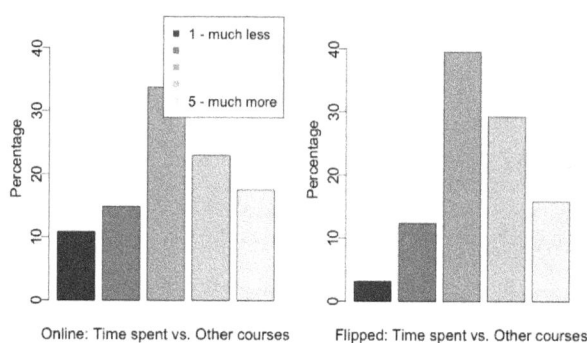

Figure 2: Time Spent vs. Other Courses

We tested for a correlation between exam grades and relative time spent for students in each section. In related work, Chinn et al. [6] did not find a correlation between study time and final results in a face-to-face CS1. For online students, we found a weak *negative* correlation (Pearson's product-moment correlation $p = .015$, $n = 70$, $r = -.29$). For flipped, there was no significant correlation between relative time spent and exam grades. Because our question asked about time spent relative to other courses rather than in absolute terms, as asked by Chinn et al., the results cannot be directly compared.

The negative correlation for online students between exam grades and relative time spent is surprising. To explore it, we examined the group of eight online students who reported spending "much less" time on the course than on their other courses. Their mean exam score was 81.2%, much higher than the 65.6% exam average for all online students. Their mean prior experience score was 2.1 (versus 1.6 for all online students), which may explain why these students could spend relatively less time on the course and still do well.

3.3 Sense of community

The online students were required to be physically present with each other and their instructor only once during the course, at the final exam. Despite this, the instructors hoped to create as strong a sense of community in the online section as the flipped section, by fostering substantial interaction in the online section, both among students, and between students and their instructor. Students in both the online and

Question	Online Average	F2F Average	p-value
How much did you interact (both online and face-to-face) with your instructor?	1.942	2.589	$< .001^*$
How satisfied were you with your sense of connection to your instructor?	3.371	3.543	$= .132$
How much did you interact (both online and face-to-face) with your classmates?	2.125	3.280	$< .001^*$
How satisfied were you with your sense of community with your classmates?	3.124	3.274	$= .227$
CSCI Inventory score (out of a possible 50)	24.22	24.21	$= .995$

Table 3: Average response to questions about interaction and sense of community, and CSCI Inventory score, by section. p-values are for a Welch two-sample t-test and an asterisk indicates statistical significance.

flipped sections were invited to participate in a shared on-line discussion forum and over 900 (of 1100) students joined. Students were extremely active in the forum, posting over 3600 times, and each reading, on average 141 posts. The instructors were also very active in the forum; they attempted to read all student posts, and themselves made over 950 posts. The TAs made an additional 1500 posts. In addition to the face-to-face office hours available to all students, the online instructor and a TA also held online office hours that were available to all. Unfortunately, the online office hours were poorly attended; the requirement to install additional software may have been a barrier.

To determine whether these efforts were successful in creating an equally strong sense of community, we asked four questions in the final survey about sense of community, and also administered the Classroom scale of the CSCI. Table 3 shows the results. Online students reported significantly less interaction with their instructor and their classmates, yet their sense of connection to their instructor and classmates was not significantly different, and their CSCI scores were nearly identical (mean 24.4 online; 24.2 flipped).

We wondered whether students with a stronger sense of community would do better in the course, so we examined the correlation between CSCI scores and exam grades. We found that this correlation was not statistically significant for either the online or flipped sections. Since the CSCI scale was administered at the end of the course, students who dropped earlier because they were dissatisfied with their sense of community would not be represented in these results. To determine whether sense of community was related to successful completion of the course, if not with exam grades, we examined the mean CSCI scores of students who passed and who failed the course; a Welch two-sample t-test showed that they were not significantly different. Our results are consistent with Drouin's findings that neither achievement nor retention is related to sense of community [9].

3.4 Motivational beliefs

The MSLQ [17] includes three scales about motivation: self-efficacy (the sense that one is able to perform a task), intrinsic value (being motivated by goals such as a desire for mastery, rather than by extrinsic goals such as grades) and test anxiety. For each, we compared scores between sections, and looked for evidence of a relationship to course outcomes.

Self-efficacy

Online and flipped students had nearly identical mean scores (rounding to 4.9 for both groups) for self-efficacy. However, we found evidence of a relationship between self-efficacy and outcomes only in the online section. For online students,

self-efficacy scores were positively correlated with final exam scores ($p = .009$, $n = 71$, $r = .30$). Not only did students with a weak sense of self-efficacy do more poorly on the exam, but they were also less likely to finish the course: the mean self-efficacy scores of those who dropped the course was 4.5 compared to 5.0 for those who completed the course (passed or failed). A Welch two sample t-test finds this difference significant ($p = .029$). Neither of these relationships held for the flipped students.

Our results suggest that one might improve outcomes for online students if we can boost their self-efficacy. Cho and Shen [7] emphasize that having a strong teaching presence contributes to students' sense of self-efficacy, as does encouraging students to set goals that are challenging but achievable so that they can experience success.

Intrinsic value

Students in the online and flipped sections also had nearly identical scores for intrinsic value (mean 5.4 online; 5.5 flipped). There was no correlation between exam grade and intrinsic-value score for the online or flipped sections. However, we found that once prior programming experience is controlled for, intrinsic value is a statistically significant factor for exam grades, but only for the flipped section (see Table 4).

	Estimate	Std. Error	t value	Pr($>$|t|)
(Intercept)	34.8479	3.7282	9.35	0.0000
prior.exp	3.1880	0.5060	6.30	0.0000
intrinsic.val	1.3976	0.6758	2.07	0.0391

Table 4: Statistical models: effect of prior experience and intrinsic value on exam grades for flipped students

Bergin et al. [3] found that, in their face-to-face course, students with high intrinsic motivation performed better in programming than those with low intrinsic motivation. This is consistent with our result for the flipped section. Other studies of online and face-to-face courses, have also shown that intrinsic motivation is positively related, directly or indirectly, to course outcomes [3, 7, 19].

Although we did not find a significant correlation between intrinsic motivation and exam scores for the online section, we hope that boosting intrinsic motivation may still help improve outcomes in not only flipped, but also online. Rakes and Dunn [19] survey the literature on increasing intrinsic motivation. They identify factors that they believe are particularly relevant to online courses, including creating a sense of community, projecting a supportive instructional style, encouraging a perception of competence, presenting challenges, and encouraging autonomy. In [7], they suggest introducing problem-based learning (PBL) and framing students' learning in terms of intrinsic goals.

Test anxiety

Scores on the test-anxiety scale were not significantly different for students in the two sections (mean 3.6 online; 3.8 flipped). We found a negative correlation between test anxiety and exam grade for the online section ($p < .001$, $n = 79$, $r = -.38$); students with greater test anxiety did worse on the exam. Surprisingly, in the flipped section there was no significant correlation between test anxiety and exam score.

Test anxiety was measured when the MSLQ was administered at the beginning of the course. It may be that the in-class, on-paper exercises that the flipped students complete during the term combat their anxiety prior to the paper-based exam, either by reducing anxiety or by increasing students' test-taking skills sufficiently to counteract the effect of their anxiety. Online students complete their analogous exercises online, so they get less practice working on paper.

3.5 SRL Strategies

Cognitive strategy use

Scores on the cognitive strategy scale were not significantly different across sections (mean 4.9 online; 5.0 flipped). We hypothesized that there would be a positive correlation between cognitive strategy and final exam scores. This hypothesis was not supported. The correlation was non-significant for the flipped section, and there was a weak negative correlation for the online section (Pearson's product-moment correlation $p = .025$, $n = 76$, $r = -.26$).

Bergin et al. [3] also failed to find a relationship between cognitive strategy and programming performance. They suggest that the strategies measured by the MSLQ may not be as useful in learning introductory object-oriented programming as in other academic areas. Indeed, the MSLQ (both the 1991 version that they used and the 1990 version that we used) places substantial emphasis on skills related to reading and studying, and little emphasis on mastering a skill, a key component of any CS1 course. An instrument that includes strategies related to mastering a skill, or to learning to program specifically, may be of greater value in predicting outcomes in CS1. Falkner's work [10] to identify discipline-specific cognitive and metacognitive skills used by students learning to program is a contribution towards this.

Self-regulation

The self-regulation scale assesses metacognitive strategies and management of effort. As for all the other MSLQ scales, scores were not significantly different between sections (mean 4.8 online; 4.9 flipped). We found no evidence that self-regulation, as measured by the MSLQ, is a factor for success for students in either section: for both the online and flipped sections, the correlation between self-regulation and exam score was not statistically significant, linear regression did not reveal a significant relationship to exam score even when prior-experience was accounted for, and there was no significant difference between the self-regulation scores of students who dropped the course and students who completed it.

In contrast, Bergin et al. [3] did find that both stronger metacognitive skills and better management of resources were associated with higher grades. Our failure to replicate this result may be due to differences between the versions of the MSLQ. However, as with the cognitive strategy scale, both versions of the MSLQ emphasize reading and studying, and neglect practise of skills.

4. CONCLUSIONS

Having observed a higher drop rate in our online CS1 than in the flipped section, we aimed to identify students' attributes and behaviours that may be factors for success in CS1 generally and for these formats in particular. We have identified several key differences between students in online and flipped. Because our online students choose to take the course in the online format, these results may not generalize to a context where online is the only format available. Several of our results suggest actions an instructor can take to improve an online course.

For both the online and flipped sections, once prior experience is controlled for, completion of the unmarked exercises is a statistically significant factor for exam scores. However, the completion rate of Rehearse Exercises by online students was significantly lower than the flipped students' rate of lecture attendance. In future offerings, we will try to boost Rehearse Exercise completion, for example by incorporating more reminders from the instructor and by following up with emails during the term to students who have not completed the exercises.

We found self-efficacy to be correlated with final exam scores for online, but not for flipped. For online students, the mean self-efficacy scores for those who dropped, passed, and failed were also significantly different. Cho and Shen report that instructor presence is key for increasing self-efficacy [7], so we will aim to increase instructor-student interactions in future offerings of the online course.

For our flipped students, once we control for prior programming experience, intrinsic value is a statistically significant factor for exam grades. Although we did not find the same for online, we feel it is still worthwhile to try to boost students' intrinsic value in both online and flipped. Based on the five factors [19] identified for encouraging intrinsic motivation, we plan to host informal get-togethers of the instructor and students, and include additional encouraging and supportive comments in communications with students.

For online students, there was a negative correlation between text anxiety and final exam scores, but there was no significant correlation between the two for flipped students. The difference may be explained by the fact that the exam is written on paper, but only flipped students were asked to regularly practice solving problems on paper. In future offerings, we plan to assign online students more unmarked exercises on paper in an effort to better prepare them for the final exam. One possibility is to assign a question each week from a past exam.

Online education will undoubtedly continue to grow, but much of what we know about teaching and learning comes from experience and research in face-to-face courses. If we are to provide effective learning environments for students in an online context, we must continue to research best practices and apply them in our teaching.

5. ACKNOWLEDGMENTS

The development of the online course was funded by the Ontario Ministry of Training, Colleges and Universities. We thank Hedieh Najafi for assistance with our literature search.

6. REFERENCES

[1] I. E. Allen and J. Seaman. *Changing Course: Ten Years of Tracking Online Education in the United States.* ERIC, 2013.

[2] S. Bergin and R. Reilly. Predicting introductory programming performance: A multi-institutional multivariate study. *Computer Science Education,* 16(4):303–323, 2006.

[3] S. Bergin, R. Reilly, and D. Traynor. Examining the role of self-regulated learning on introductory programming performance. In *Proceedings of the First International Workshop on Computing Education Research,* ICER '05, pages 81–86, 2005.

[4] J. Campbell, D. Horton, M. Craig, and P. Gries. Evaluating an inverted CS1. In *Proceeding of the 45th ACM Technical Symposium on Computer Science Education,* SIGCSE '14, pages 307–312, 2014.

[5] S. Carr. As distance education comes of age, the challenge is keeping the students. *Chronicle of higher education,* 46(23), 2000.

[6] D. Chinn, J. Sheard, A. Carbone, and M.-J. Laakso. Study habits of cs1 students: What do they do outside the classroom? In *Proceedings of the Twelfth Australasian Conference on Computing Education - Volume 103,* ACE '10, pages 53–62. Australian Computer Society, Inc., 2010.

[7] M.-H. Cho and D. Shen. Self-regulation in online learning. *Distance Education,* 34(3):290–301, 2013.

[8] M. de Raadt, M. Hamilton, R. Lister, J. Tutti, Simon, K. Sutton, B. Baker, I. Box, Q. Cutts, J. Hamer, M. Petre, and D. Tolhurst. Approaches to learning in computer programming students, and its effect on success. In *Proceedings of Higher Education in a Changing World, Higher Education Research and Development Society of Australia Conference,* pages 407–414, 2005.

[9] M. A. Drouin. The relationship between students' perceived sense of community and satisfaction, achievement, and retention in an online course. *Quarterly Review of Distance Education,* 9(3):267–284, 2008.

[10] K. Falkner, R. Vivian, and N. J. Falkner. Identifying computer science self-regulated learning strategies. In *Proceedings of the 2014 Conference on Innovation & Technology in Computer Science Education,* ITiCSE '14, pages 291–296, New York, NY, USA, 2014. ACM.

[11] D. Hagan and S. Markham. Does it help to have some programming experience before beginning a computing degree program? In *Proceedings of the 5th Annual ITiCSE Conference on Innovation and Technology in Computer Science Education,* ITiCSE '00, pages 25–28, 2000.

[12] D. Horton, J. Campbell, and M. Craig. Online cs1: Who enrols, why, and how do they do? In *Proceeding of the 47th ACM Technical Symposium on Computer Science Education,* SIGCSE '16, pages 323–328, 2016.

[13] D. Horton and M. Craig. Drop, fail, pass, continue: Persistence in cs1 and beyond in traditional and inverted delivery. In *Proceedings of the 46th ACM Technical Symposium on Computer Science Education,* SIGCSE '15, pages 235–240, 2015.

[14] D. Horton, M. Craig, J. Campbell, P. Gries, and D. Zingaro. Comparing outcomes in inverted and traditional cs1. In *Proceedings of the 2014 Conference on Innovation & Technology in Computer Science Education,* ITiCSE '14, pages 261–266, 2014.

[15] Y. Lee and J. Choi. A review of online course dropout research: implications for practice and future research. *Educational Technology Research and Development,* 59(5):593–618, 2011.

[16] Y. Levy. Comparing dropouts and persistence in e-learning courses. *Computers & education,* 48(2):185–204, 2007.

[17] P. R. Pintrich and E. V. De Groot. Motivational and self-regulated learning components of classroom academic performance. *Journal of educational psychology,* 82(1), Mar. 1990.

[18] P. R. Pintrich, D. Smith, T. Garcia, and W. McKeachie. A manual for the use of the motivated strategies for learning questionnaire. *technical report 91-b-004,* 1991.

[19] G. C. Rakes and K. E. Dunn. The impact of online graduate students' motivation and self-regulation on academic procrastination. *Journal of Interactive Online Learning,* 9(1):78–93, 2010.

[20] N. Rountree, J. Rountree, A. Robins, and R. Hannah. Interacting factors that predict success and failure in a cs1 course. In *Working Group Reports from ITiCSE on Innovation and Technology in Computer Science Education,* ITiCSE-WGR '04, pages 101–104, 2004.

[21] A. P. Rovai. The classroom and school community inventory: Development, refinement, and validation of a self-report measure for educational research. *The Internet and Higher Education,* 7(4):263–280, 2004.

[22] Simon, S. Fincher, A. Robins, B. Baker, I. Box, Q. Cutts, M. de Raadt, P. Haden, J. Hamer, M. Hamilton, R. Lister, M. Petre, K. Sutton, D. Tolhurst, and J. Tutty. Predictors of success in a first programming course. In *Proceedings of the 8th Australasian Conference on Computing Education - Volume 52,* ACE '06, pages 189–196, Darlinghurst, Australia, Australia, 2006. Australian Computer Society, Inc.

[23] P. R. Ventura. Identifying predictors of success for an objects-first cs1. *Computer Science Education,* 15(3):223–243, 2005.

[24] B. C. Wilson and S. Shrock. Contributing to success in an introductory computer science course: A study of twelve factors. *SIGCSE Bull.,* 33(1):184–188, Feb. 2001.

[25] B. J. Zimmerman and D. H. Schunk. Self-regulated learning and performance: An introduction and overview. In B. J. Zimmerman and D. H. Schunk, editors, *Handbook of Self-Regulation of Learning and Performance,* chapter 1, pages 1–12. Taylor and Francis, New York, 2011.

Applying Validated Pedagogy to MOOCs: An Introductory Programming Course with Media Computation

Katrina Falkner   Nickolas Falkner   Claudia Szabo   Rebecca Vivian

The School of Computer Science
The University of Adelaide
South Australia, Australia, 5005
{firstname.lastname}@adelaide.edu.au

ABSTRACT

Significant advances have been made in the learning and teaching of Introductory Programming, including the integration of active and contextualised learning pedagogy. However, Massively Open Online Courses (MOOCs), where Computer Science and, more specifically, introductory programming courses dominate, do not typically adopt such pedagogies or lessons learned from more traditional learning environments. Moreover, the improvement of learning within the MOOC context in terms of discipline-specific pedagogy, and the improvement of student learning outcomes and processes have not been studied in depth.

This paper reports findings from a foundation programming skills MOOC that supports the learning of fundamental Computer Science concepts and the development of programming skills through a media computation approach, based upon digital artworks and animations. In this paper, we explore the course activity data as well as a sample of students' source code submissions to investigate their engagement with the course and the quality and development of their programming skill over the six weeks of the course duration.

Keywords

Online learning; Massively Open Online Course (MOOC); Introductory Programming; CS101

1. INTRODUCTION

Massively Open Online Courses (MOOCs) have gained traction as a means to freely deliver course content online to the public [13]. Conventional MOOCs, such as those found on edX and Coursera, are typically delivered using short learning videos, and learning is evaluated using a number of automated assessment mechanisms including quizzes and peer-assessment among others. Although MOOCs present the potential to achieve learning at scale, participants struggle with the overwhelming abundance of information and the requirement of self-directed learning, common within MOOC environments [8]. While Computer Science courses dominate MOOC efforts, only a small number of

research studies have analysed introductory programming MOOCs [7, 9, 12, 26]. These studies have reported on course design considerations, student experience and performance, and participation demographics; important considerations in the development of a MOOC. However, there remains a need for further research that explores the translation of existing, validated, Computer Science pedagogy to this medium, and that provides analysis of student learning outcomes and student learning processes within large-scale, personalised learning environments.

In this paper, we explore our findings from an analysis of student engagement and learning within an introductory programming MOOC that adopts a *media computation* approach [19], exploring the development of digital artworks and animations with code. Learning to program can be challenging and a number of students struggle with introductory concepts and the development of programming skills. Novice computer science students are required to develop a diverse range of skills at an early stage, including problem analysis, problem solving, code development and testing. The students must then integrate those skills within the software development process. Advances over recent years in the teaching of introductory programming, including greater incorporation of active and contextualized learning approaches [2, 15] have reported improvements in both student achievement and retention. However, research indicates that students continue to struggle with introductory programming concepts. Lack of performance in programming has been seen to impact other facets of their study, including their overall program progression, confidence and study habits, all factors that affect engagement and retention [5].

This paper reports findings from a media-computation-based introductory programming MOOC, Code101x, with a student cohort of 20,511 students from 177 countries. We analyse the course with respect to student participation, satisfaction and engagement with materials, and student learning, as demonstrated by students' published artworks, created with code and shared in the community galleries. We analyse a sample of student programming submissions according to how they satisfy learning outcomes throughout the course. This analysis provides insights into difficulties that students have when learning introductory programming in the MOOC medium, prompting future research into the scaffolding of programming skill in online environments.

2. BACKGROUND

Learning to program involves both conceptual and skill development, with both novice and advanced students expressing concerns and reporting difficulties with the development of programming skills [21]. While recent research has found that students in introductory programming courses are able to construct working programs through incremental code development [11], there are many areas of difficulty that remain [20], presenting as *threshold concepts* for students. Threshold concepts in programming are fundamental to students' knowledge, in order to transform the way they understand the discipline, but are recognised as being significantly troublesome [3]. Once students have mastered the threshold concepts, their way of thinking about the discipline changes and they are more likely to be able to master the discipline. Threshold concepts in programming include the understanding of key concepts, such as variables, iteration and functions; and software development concepts, such as software usability and syntax errors [20]. Research identifies that students report difficulty with understanding the use of variables [11], specifically the concepts of variable scope and lifetime [20]. Iteration is in itself a difficult concept, with studies indicating students report confusion with the structure and purpose of loop constructs [25]. Further, students report persistent misconceptions regarding the role of variables in iteration constructs [22, 24]. Developing a good understanding of these fundamental concepts has wider impact as students who neglect usage of iterative constructs have been found to perform significantly worse overall in related studies [22].

In recent years, the teaching and learning of programming has undergone a significant transformation, with practices moving away from traditional, lecture-based methods to active and collaborative learning experiences, and contextualised learning environments [8, 18, 19] in order to address concerns of high attrition rates, low overall enrolments and to provide students with engaging learning experiences. In particular, the combination of pair programming, peer instruction and contextualised programming approaches has had significantly positive impact on engagement, motivation, and retention [9, 20].

Contextualised approaches [23], such as digital art creation and robotics, have been adopted to engage students in learning programming by providing a motivating context in which to apply the knowledge of computing. Such approaches have been found to have positive influences on student motivation and engagement when compared to traditional introductory programming approaches [6]. Contextualised courses that situate introductory programming within Media and the Arts have been found to be particularly effective in broadening participation [10] .

Media computation [19] is one such approach that involves the teaching of introductory programming concepts through the manipulation of digital media, such as photos, music, and video. This approach has been found to demonstrate the creativity of computing, increase relevancy, and produce a more supportive learning culture [7]. Media computation has been adopted within a number of introductory courses with significantly positive outcomes [9, 20]; increasing students' desire to continue programming (from a baseline less than 10% up to 60%), and improving both overall attitudes toward learning computer science [19] and pass rates [15].

3. MOTIVATION
Although the teaching and learning of programming on-campus has changed significantly, the application of innovative discipline-specific pedagogy has not been widely applied to online introductory courses [1], especially within the MOOC context [23]. A small number of studies regarding MOOC-based introductory programming courses have been published [7, 9, 12, 26]. However, these papers focus on course design considerations,

participant experiences, and student demographics and performance on tests and quizzes. There is limited research into the specific application of Computer Science discipline-specific pedagogy and the development of appropriate student learning processes and outcomes [23]. There is a clear need for research in this space that explores how existing good practice in learning and teaching of programming can be transferred from face-to-face to online MOOC formats, as well as research into the development of new MOOC-centric pedagogies. Finding ways to scale and adapt known successful strategies to this new environment is essential [23]. However, MOOCs provide a supportive environment for in-depth and informative education research due to the number of participants and the instrumented nature of the learning environment. A well-instrumented MOOC facilitates analysis of student engagement with learning resources, community development and discussion, as well as the effectiveness of learning outcomes.

This paper reports findings from a media-computation-based introductory programming MOOC that adopts Processing [18] as an approach to teach introductory programming constructs through the creation of digital artworks and animations. We present a quantitative and a qualitative assessment of submitted code projects to identify how students applied key concepts as well as areas for further improvement in the course design, specifically in how selection structures can be employed.

4. CONTEXT
4.1 The Code101x Course
The overall purposes of creating the MOOC was to promote the study of Computer Science at The University of Adelaide and develop a curriculum and online materials to be used for university blended learning in first-year introductory programming. Our approach was to design a MOOC that would support known CS pedagogy, specifically by incorporating media-computation and social learning opportunities. The course was developed within the edX on-line course framework.

The course learning goals were to develop learners' in the following areas:

- computational thinking skills;
- understanding of introductory programming concepts, such as sequencing, iteration and selection;
- skills and knowledge of how to create art and basic animations with Processing.JS; and
- preparation for study of computer science or other programming languages.

The course was run with Processing.JS [17]; a sister project of Processing, designed to allow users to write code in Processing in a browser without the need to install any software on their personal computers. Processing is a fully-featured programming language and environment built with the electronic arts, new media art, and visual design communities in mind, to facilitate the learning of fundamental introductory programming concepts within the context of art and design. Processing is suitable for introductory courses as learners can begin seeing visible outcomes with relative ease [6]. Using Processing.JS for a MOOC reduces barriers for online programming courses of the effort required to install software; the open source nature of the platform allows students to continue programming after the course finishes.

In addition, we introduced an open source *art gallery and exhibition* web-based environment where students could create and share artwork with peers, using Processing.JS. In this environment students could construct and share an online portfolio of their work throughout the course. They were able to comment on other student's artworks and code, integrate peer-based support, with social interaction extending beyond that of a typical MOOC environment.

The six-week course featured six core units, in addition to a preparation unit (Table 1). Within each week's activities, students were asked to create and share an artwork demonstrating their usage of new programming concepts, and their development of programming and algorithmic skill.

Table 1: Weekly course topics, content and artwork activities

Week/Topic	Content	Artwork Activity
0: Preparation	Overview of the learning environment	Introduction to community
1: Creative code: computational thinking	An introduction to Processing and algorithms; colour with code (RGB); creating lines and shapes; coordinates.	1) Create many different instances of a shape in a pattern. 2) Draw a face.
2: Building blocks breaking it down & building it up	Data attributes (strokeWeight & strokeCap); creating variables, using expressions; using variables to scale images.	1) Draw a house (the roof and fence must have thicker lines). 2) Create a pattern controlled by data. 3) Draw a car that is scaled to its position on the screen.
3: Repetition – creating & recognising patterns	Flowcharts as a tool for design; combining data and repetition to increase size or weight; loops to control image drawing.	1) Re-create one of the provided patterns. 2) Create an image of only lines and shapes, using loops. 3) Re-create one of the images.
4: Choice – which path to follow?	Introduction to decisions (branching); relational expressions; how data, expressions and choice can control program flow; logical operators and combining expressions.	1) Re-produce an image of repeating circles/squares on diagonal. 2) Find a pattern in your everyday environment and create it in code. 3) Find an image and reproduce that using shapes and lines.
5: Code with creative flair	Revisiting programming fundamentals; nested for loops and repetition in more than one dimension (using points to show structure); for loops and fill changes; other functions to improve look (smoothing, rotation, scale).	1) Create art that looks three-dimensional using nested loops. 2) Use nested loops to create a colourful drawing that changes slightly in colour using only one single fill statement. 3) Draw a shape with 8 vertices and/or recreate an image (rotation of shapes).
6: Animations & art – your online folio	Introduction to basic animations; frame rates; using setup function for image baseline; interactions with mouse; final summary.	Final assignment is an open-project where students put all skills and knowledge together to create a final "masterpiece" of choice.

An *exhibition space* was created for each week (Figure 1). Within the exhibition space, students could "vote up" ("like") other artworks. Artworks could then be sorted by vote frequency or most recent submissions. Learners could keep their own artworks private but could also select and share an artwork in the shared course exhibition space. Students were asked to share a minimum of one artwork per week.

Additionally, students were required to perform three peer reviews throughout the course, in addition to weekly, interactive quizzes that involved either multiple choice, drag and drop, or sequencing activities along the lines of Parson's Problems [14] (see example of sequencing activity in Figure 2).

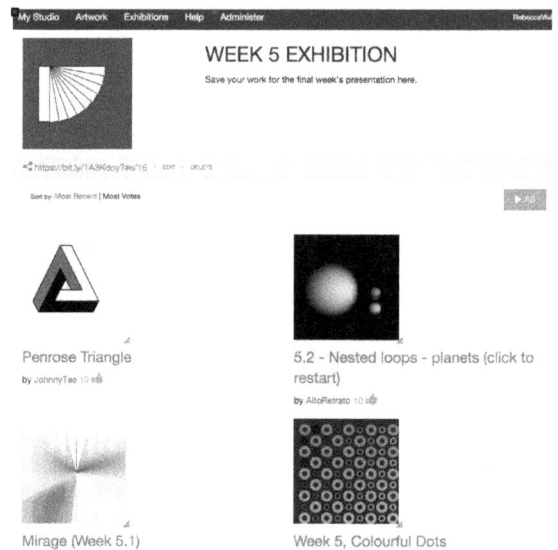

Figure 1. Example of the shared Weekly Exhibition with learner artworks

Figure 2. Example of Parson's Problem sequencing activity

5. METHODOLOGY

5.1 Ethics

This study was exempt from review under The University of Adelaide Human Research Ethics Committee guidelines, as the study has no foreseeable risk or harm to participants and as it involved the use of existing collections of data that contain non-identifiable data; including the artworks and pre- and post-survey data. An auditable record of exempt research was completed.

5.2 Data and Data Analysis

We obtained data from the anonymised edX platform metrics, additional anonymous pre- and post-surveys (non-edX) created by the course instructors, and artwork submissions submitted by users to the exhibition space. The data between each of these components were not linked and all data was presented in a way that individuals could not be identified.

The edX platform presents course metrics to instructors via their "edX insights" product. This includes information about: "Who are my students" (enrolments, demographics and background); "What are my students doing in my course" (interaction with content); and, "How are students doing on course assignments (grades)?". We used these metrics to support our course sample description and engagement in the course.

The course instructors released optional and anonymous pre- and post-surveys to gather information about participant motivations, experiences and satisfaction in the course. The surveys were included in the weekly email communication (the pre-survey in the first week and post-survey in the final email), as well as embedded in the course website "newsfeed". 5,428 learners responded to the pre-survey and 323 responded to the post-survey. We used the survey data to support our investigation into student engagement and experiences with the course content.

For this study, we analysed the artworks of 60 users, randomly selected from those users who submitted an artwork to the exhibition in the final week. This selection was made to support the analysis of skill development throughout the course. The analysis included questions about whether an artwork was submitted and if so, how many "votes" the user received for their work from peers. The researchers rated whether the overall design of the code was "missing or inappropriate" (1), "adequate with some limitations" (2) or "appropriate" (3). The researchers then had three further ratings about the use of variables, repetition, and selection structures according to the same scale, but focused on how adequate the concepts were used. For a code sample, an adequate use of: (i) variables requires assigning and employing variables for all data items; (ii) repetition structures requires loop boundaries to be properly defined, and for repetition to be used where needed (that is, not copying statements); (iii) selection structures requires conditionals to be correctly defined and branch statements to be logically different. The researchers were also asked to paste code samples. We present findings of the overall artwork analysis in the Results section. To ensure anonymity, we do not report student usernames.

5.3 Research Questions

In this study, we sought to investigate the following research questions: (1) *to what extent did participants engage with the MOOC and who were our audience?*, and (2) *do students' artworks align with learning and teaching goals over the weeks?*

6. RESULTS

6.1 Course Participants and Engagement

A total of 20,511 learners enrolled in the course by the closing date (12 June 2015), with 63 learners choosing to take edX's verified enrolment (0.32% of the total). Upon closing of the course, 832 certificates were issued to learners who had passed the course. This course received a 4% certification rate versus enrolment at course close. The optional survey instrument was completed by up 4,858 students but they did not complete all questions. For accuracy, each of the questions is shown with the number of students responding. Of 4,348 respondents, 86% (n= 3,735) of learners had previously enrolled in an online course. Of 4,379 respondents, 63% (n=2,777) reported completing an online course before; 37% had not. In response to the statement: "You are already very experienced at working with code", of 4,858 survey respondents, 23% (n=1,137) agreed, 56% (n=2,741) disagreed and 20% were neutral.

The course demographics differed from traditional enrolments in Computer Science in Australia, the United States and United Kingdom, with 57% (n=11,762) of learners identified as male and 30% (n=6,114) as female, with 13% (2.635) as 'other' or not reported, a much lower level of "declared" male enrolment than would usually be seen. Learners were from a total of 177 countries, with the United States (25%), India (13%), the United Kingdom (4%), Canada (3%) and Australia (3%) having the largest representation. The median age was 28 with 38% under the age of 25, 44% 26-40 years of age and 17.5%, 41 and over. 15% of participants chose to conceal their age and some ages had unlikely populations, such as 0 or 100, but not to a degree that influenced the statistics. In terms of highest level of education, 28% reported holding a High School Diploma or less, 42% reported having a college degree (Bachelor's/Associate) and 27% held some form of Advanced degree (Masters or above).

Student activity rose rapidly at the start of the course to a peak of 34.4% active students in the total number enrolled, where an active student viewed at least one web page. Within the cohort of active students, at the activity peak, 58.5% of students had watched a video and 26.8% had tried a quiz (Active student peak, n=7,097). As expected from the literature, student activity dropped over the six weeks of the course to a final active cohort of 2,217 students, 10.8% of total enrolment, with 53.2% watching a video and 41.3% trying a problem.

Videos for the course were hosted on YouTube.com, with 53 hosted videos contributing to the following statistics. On average, an active student watched 45 videos for 132.6 minutes in total, with an average view duration of 2:56 (90.6%). The most popular video was viewed 5,308 times. The short duration times agree with existing EdX analysis of views; the course in question was designed with short videos and average video length was under four minutes (3:56).

Across the active cohort, n=7,097, students generated a total of 14,593 artworks in their private practice galleries, 2,471 students submitted an artwork to the exhibition and 7,558 artworks were submitted to the gallery in total.

6.2 Code and Artwork Analysis

Our analysis of the weekly submissions of 60 students is summarized in Figure 4. As shown also in Table I, simple statements were introduced in week 1, variables in week 2, repetition in week 3, with selection introduced in week 4 and the use of Processing's animation mechanisms in weeks 5 and 6. Researchers assessed the weekly submitted artwork for each of these concepts, using a three-point scale as described in Section 5.2. In the following, we consider that a concept is poorly employed if the average weekly score (after the concept is introduced) is below 1.5, employed well with some limitations if the score is between 1.5 and 2.5, and well employed (within the analysed cohort) if the score is greater than 2.5. As can be seen in Figure 4, concepts are used in the week they are introduced, especially if the artwork submission specifically requires their use, but there is an immediate dip in usage in the following activity before students appear to be comfortable enough to employ the concept extensively. The most inconsistently employed concept was selection, with repetition the most consistently adopted. Recall that the Processing.JS environment is built on an animation idiom where a draw() is called through an infinite loop. Thus, while there is a drop in written repetition statements in week 6, all animations made implicit use of the redraw loop. In terms of usage, rather than written code, repetition remained the strongest and best-used structure.

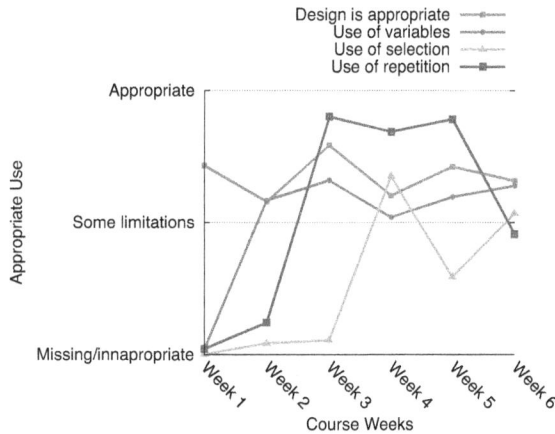

Figure 4. Analysis of student assignment activity.

The concept of *data attributes* and *variables* is introduced in Week 2, and as such it is initially missing from the Week 1 submission. Variable use was appropriate if assignment, updating and substitution were consistent in their replacement of the use of fixed values. The use of variables is generally appropriate with some limitations (with the weekly cohort score averaging between 2.08 to 2.32). We observe that variables tend to be used mostly only for key data attributes, with fixed values used elsewhere. The second most common mistake is re-declaring variables, as shown by the snippet in Figure 5.

```
// define relative coords based on car body
int x=0.125*width; // car body x start
int y=0.45*height; // car body y start
[...]

//first car with variables
int x=0.125*width;
int y=0.45*height;
[...]

//second car with new coords
int x=x+0.2*width;
int s=s+0.2*width;
```

Figure 5. Inappropriate use of variable re-declaration.

```
if(((a%100==0)&&(b%100==0))) {
    int x=50;
    int y=50;
    fill(0);
    quad(a,b,(a+x),b,(a+x),(b+y),a,(b+y));
    fill(255);
    quad((a+0.19*x),b,(a+x),(b+0.19*y),(a+0.8095*x),[...]);
    fill(0); [...]
}
else{
    int x=50;
    int y=50;
    fill(255);
    quad(a,b,(a+x),b,(a+x),(b+y),a,(b+y));
    fill(0);
    quad((a+0.19*x),b,(a+x),(b+0.19*y),(a+0.8095*x),[...]);
    fill(255); [...]
```

Figure 6. Example of duplicated code in selection, Week 4.

Repetition is introduced in Week 3 and is the most well-employed programming concept throughout (average quality between 2.69 to 2.80), with the caveat for week 6, as discussed above. Repetition use was appropriate if students could demonstrate understanding of the assignment, iteration and use of the loop variable, and successfully employ nesting. The artworks chosen

for examples often had innate symmetries and repetition (e.g. houses with multiple windows and faces with two eyes) and, having had to construct such examples without repetition in Week 1, the opportunity to reduce code length and simplify appears to have been attractive.

Selection is inconsistently applied, with the average weekly quality score for the analysed cohort ranging between 1.58 and 2.35. Our analysis shows that students either: (i) did not employ selection where it should be employed, (ii) had duplicate code in each selection branch (Figure 6) or (iii) made errors in the conditional statements.

6.3 Self-reported Learner Experiences

Learners' perceived experience in MOOCs is affected by their perceptions of their community involvement, the 'quality' of the course and how well it meets their requirements. Given that very few students were receiving anything approximating traditional grading feedback, the learner experience is not affected by penalty reaction but may be affected by other factors that do not affect the traditional classroom, such as time zone mismatch between student and teacher, or linguistic isolation. As such, a few post-survey responses from students expressed a desire for more immediate and direct communication with instructors.

The calculated broad agreement (BA) on self-reported confidence before and after the course shows a clear improvement in student perception of confidence. BA is calculated from those responses that are rated as being an explicit positive response, Likert items 5, 6 and 7. As expected, variables and expressions, fundamental concepts, have the highest initial self-reported level of confidence.

Table 2. Self-reported confidence with key learning areas in the surveys (7-point scale: 1= "poor", 7 ="excellent")

Key learning areas	Pre-(n=5,057)	BA	Post-(n= 317)	BA
ProcessingJS &algorithms	2.08	8.9%	5.54	83.9%
Variables & expressions	3.59	37.2%	5.82	88.0%
Repetition & data	3.24	29.3%	5.64	83.9%
Creative code & making choices	2.69	18.2%	5.38	78.5%
Animation & interaction in code	2.12	9.2%	5.11	69.9%

Post-survey respondents reported an average course satisfaction of 5.83 (n=278) of 7 and 96.2% (n=301) said they would recommend the course. Half of post-survey respondents had some form of previous experience in programming 51.8% (n=160), with only 21.4 (66) having no experience at all and others having limited experience (26.8%). 79.8% (n=249) said they would "definitely" continue programming and 17.3% (n=54) said "possibly".

7. Discussion and Limitations

Code101X presents an attempt to deliver an online introductory programming course that integrates social learning and media-computation pedagogy within a MOOC environment, based on evidence-based research and face-to-face practice. Reflecting on outcomes from more traditional learning environments, the course attracted a higher percentage of female students than that of typical Computer Science MOOCs, where participation is typically about 20%. Our analysis of student performance reflects outcomes from more traditional learning environments, specifically difficulties in the usage of data and variables despite initial positive perceptions, and difficulty in the correct usage of selection constructs. Students successfully employed variables in their exercises for Week 2, including appropriate analysis of data requirements, and update of variables throughout their program. However, in a pattern that repeated through the course, when first designing and using new constructs, students reverted to their more limited usage of previous concepts. These results support a hypothesis of the need to specifically scaffold the integration of concepts, beyond their mastery as individual concepts.

Repetition was consistently the most successfully applied construct, with students able to design and implement simple repetition constructs in their first exercises, progressing rapidly to the application of nested loops. Our interpretation is that the intuitive application of repetition within an image-based environment focused on patterns facilitates motivation and contextualization of this concept.

The teacher-assessed outputs indicate a clear demonstration of the concepts being taught, and the student-reported confidence data shows a clear improvement in student confidence. We interpret this, in conjunction, as an indication that learning design approaches can be successfully transferred to the massive, on-line scale, although we do note that the demographics of this self-selected student group means that we cannot generalize this result to pre-tertiary students and traditionally under-represented groups.

8. ACKNOWLEDGMENTS

We thank the University for funding the MOOC and for our development team for their design and data analysis support.

9. REFERENCES

[1] Ben-Ari, M. 2013. MOOCs on Introductory Programming: A Travelogue. *ACM Inroads*. 4, 2 (2013), 58–61.

[2] Butler, M., Morgan, M., Sheard, J., Simon, Falkner, K. and Weerasinghe, A. 2015. Initiatives to Increase Engagement in First-Year ICT. In *Proceedings of ITiCSE'15* (Vilnius, Lithuania, 2015), 308–313.

[3] Eckerdal, A., McCartney, R., Moström, J.E., Ratcliffe, M., Sanders, K. and Zander, C. 2006. Putting threshold concepts into context in computer science education. *ACM SIGCSE Bulletin*. 38, 3 (Jun. 2006), 103.

[4] Falkner, K. and Falkner, N. 2012. Supporting and structuring "contributing student pedagogy" in Computer Science curricula. *Computer Science Education*. 22, 4, 413–443.

[5] Falkner, K. and Munro, D.S. 2009. Easing the transition : A collaborative learning approach. *Australian Education Conference* (Wellington, New Zealand, 2009), 65–74.

[6] Greenberg, I., Kumar, D. and Xu, D. 2012. Creative coding and visual portfolios for CS1. In *Proceedings of SIGCSE'12* (Raleigh, 2012), 247.

[7] Ho, A., Reich, J., Nesterko, S., Seaton, D., Mullaney, T., Waldo, J. and Chuang, I. 2014. HarvardX and MITx: Fall 2012- summer 2013. *HarvardX and MITx: The first year of open online courses*. Social Science Electronic Publishing.

[8] Kop, R. 2011. The challenges to connectivist learning on open online networks: Learning experiences during a massive open online course. *Special Issue - Connectivism: Design and Delivery of Social Networked Learning*. 12, 3 (2011), 19–38.

[9] Liyanagunawardena, T Lundqvist, K., Micallef, L. and Williams, S. 2014. Teaching programming to beginners in a massive open online course. In *OER14* (Newcastle, 2014).

[10] Manaris, B., Mccauley, R., Mazzone, M. and Bares, W. 2014. Computing in the Arts: A Model Curriculum. *Proceedings of SIGCSE '14* (Atlana, 2014), 451–456.

[11] McCartney, R., Boustedt, J., Eckerdal, A., Sanders, K. and Zander, C. 2013. Can First-year Students Program Yet? A Study Revisited. In *Proceedings of ICER'13* (San Diego, 2013), 91–98.

[12] Miller, H., Haller, P., Rytz, L. and Odersky, M. 2014. Functional programming for all! scaling a MOOC for students and professionals alike. In *Proceedings of ICSE'14* (Hyderabad, 2014), 256–263.

[13] Siemens, G. 2012. MOOCs are really a platform, Available: *www.elearnspace.org/blog/2012/07/25/moocs-are-really-a-platform/*.

[14] Parsons, D. and Haden, P. 2006. Parson's programming puzzles: A fun and effective learning tool for first programming courses. In *Research and Practice in Information Technology Series* (Tasmania, 2006), 157–163.

[15] Porter, L., Guzdial, M., McDowell, C. and Simon, B. 2013. Success in introductory programming: what works? *Communications of the ACM*. 56, 8 (Aug. 2013), 34–36.

[16] Porter, L. and Simon, B. 2013. Retaining Nearly One-Third more Majors with a Trio of Instructional Best Practices in CS1. In *Proceedings of SIGCSE'13* (Denver, 2013), 165–170.

[17] Processing.js: 2008. Available: *http://processingjs.org/*.

[18] Reas, C. and Fry, B. 2006. Processing: Programming for the media arts. *AI and Society*. 20, 4 (Sep. 2006), 526–538.

[19] Rich, L., Perry, H. and Guzdial, M. 2004. A CS1 course designed to address interests of women. In *Proceedings of SIGCSE* (Norfolk, 2004), 190-194.

[20] Rodrigo, M., Andallaza, T., Castro, F., Armenta, M., Dy, T. and Jadud, M. 2013. An Analysis of JAVA Programming Behaviors, Affect, Perceptions, and Syntax Errors among Low-Achieving, Average, and High-Achieving Novice Programmers. *Journal of Educational Computing Research*. 49, 3 (Jan. 2013), 293–325.

[21] Sanders, K., Boustedt, J., Eckerdal, A., McCartney, R., Moström, J., Thomas, L. and Zander, C. 2012. Threshold concepts and threshold skills in computing. In *Proceedings of ICER'12* (Auckland, 2012).

[22] Sekiya, T. and Yamaguchi, K. 2013. Tracing quiz set to identify novices' programming misconceptions. In *Proceedings of Koli Calling* (Koli, Finland, 2013), 87–95.

[23] Settle, A., Vihavainen, A. and Miller, C. 2014. Research directions for teaching programming online. In *Proceedings of the International Conference on Frontiers in Education: CSCE* (Las Vegas, 2014).

[24] Sirkiä, T. and Sorva, J. 2012. Exploring programming misconceptions: An analysis of student mistakes in visual program simulation exercises. In *Proceedings of Koli Calling* (Koli, Finland, 2012), 19–28.

[25] Vainio, V. and Sajaniemi, J. 2007. Factors in Novice Programmers' Poor Tracing Skills. *SIGCSE Bulletin*. 39, 3 (Jun. 2007), 236–240.

[26] Warren, J., Rixner, S., Greiner, J. and Wong, S. 2014. Facilitating Human Interaction in an Online Programming Course. In *Proceedings of SIGCSE'14* (Atlanta, 2014), 665–670.

Enki: A Pedagogical Services Aggregator for Learning Programming Languages

José Carlos Paiva
CRACS & INESC-Porto LA &
DCC - Faculty of Sciences,
University of Porto
Porto, Portugal
up201200272@fc.up.pt

José Paulo Leal
CRACS & INESC-Porto LA &
DCC - Faculty of Sciences,
University of Porto
Porto, Portugal
zp@dcc.fc.up.pt

Ricardo Queirós
CRACS & INESC-Porto LA &
DI/ESEIG/IPP
Porto, Portugal
ricardoqueiros@eseig.ipp.pt

ABSTRACT

This paper presents Enki, a web-based IDE that integrates several pedagogical tools designed to engage students in learning programming languages. Enki achieves this goal (1) by sequencing educational resources, either expository or evaluative, (2) by using gamification services to entice students to solve activities, (3) by promoting social interaction and (4) by helping students with activities, providing feedback on submitted solutions. The paper describes Enki, its concept and architecture, details its design and implementation, and covers also its validation.

General Terms

Languages, Design, Experimentation

Keywords

E-Learning, Integration, Gamification, Educational Resources, Sequencing, Exercises, Programming Languages

1. INTRODUCTION

Engaging students with the subject is the constant challenge of every teacher. When the subject is computer programming this means conciliating many different things. To start with, it means creating appealing contents to explain programming concepts. It means adapting this content to the needs and preferences of individual students. It means selecting exercises that cover all the syllabus and make sure that they are graded, with the right amount of feedback, timely so that every student stays on track. It means also encouraging the students to work as a group, learning from each other, both by competing and by collaborating. Last but not least, it means selecting the right tools for teaching, and at the same time preparing the students to work with the tools of programming.

The approach presented in this paper sought inspiration in computer programming tools to design an effective web

ITiCSE '16, July 09-13, 2016, Arequipa, Peru

© 2016 ACM. ISBN 978-1-4503-4231-5/16/07. . . $15.00

DOI: http://dx.doi.org/10.1145/2899415.2899441

based learning environment. The result combines content presentation, automatic assessment, social and game-like features. Being a web tool it enables students to start learning how to program without having to install fairly complex tools, such as editors and compilers. Nevertheless, it prepares them to, later on, use more sophisticated tools such as Integrated Development Environments (IDE).

Enki is a web-based learning environment with an IDE inspired graphic user interface that integrates several kinds of tools. These tools include a Gamification Service (GS) to provide gamification features to students, an Educational Resources Sequencing Service (ERSS) to offer different learning paths, an Evaluator Engine (EE) to give automatic feedback to students' solutions, an Exercise Creator (EC) to allow teachers to create exercises and a Learning Objects Repository (LOR) to store those exercises. Apart from these tools, Enki also promotes social collaboration and can be integrated in an ecosystem of e-learning systems based on a Learning Management System (LMS).

The remainder of this paper is organized as follows. Section 2 reviews related work on the gamification and social collaboration in e-learning, sequencing of educational resources, automatic evaluation of exercises and interoperability. Section 3 introduces Enki, its architecture and graphical user interface. Section 4 describes its validation in a programming course. Finally, Section 5 summarizes the contributions of this research.

2. RELATED WORK

To the best of the authors' knowledge, there is no tool in the literature that provides all the features mentioned in the previous section, integrated in Enki. So, this section surveys systems with some of these features.

2.1 Gamification On E-Learning

Gamification aims to engage users by applying game principles (points, progression, competition), in non-game contexts. Gamification is currently being applied to e-learning environments with relative success, as it helps students to remain focused and thus to fulfill course goals.

In this context, the most widely used approach is to empower LMS with game mechanics such as badges, achievements, leaderboards in order to boost engagement and to improve knowledge retention. Some of the notable examples are Academy LMS, Axonify and Matrix. Despite the success of this approach, the concept of loser may adversely affect the motivation of students [27].

Peer 2 Peer University (P2PU) [1] is another environment defined as a social computing platform that promotes peer-created and peer-led online learning environments. In P2PU, learners can join, complete and leave challenges at any time. They can also earn badges, associated with learning tasks and courses, which are based on Mozilla Open Badges framework[1]. P2PU also promotes social collaboration by allowing any stakeholder to create a course.

2.2 Sequencing of Educational Resources

Most of the learning environments offer the same learning paths and resources to students, regardless of their prior knowledge, goals, progress or preferences which has a negative impact on their motivation [26].

Multibook [9] is a web-based adaptive hypermedia learning system for multimedia and communication technology, developed by the Technical University of Darmstadt and the University of Hagen. Multibook aims to offer different lessons to different users, by storing a huge number of compiled lessons or by dynamically generating lessons for each user. It uses four dimensions for each user. Firstly, Multibook fills the user's profile with his demands and preferences. The Multibook system also keeps track of the information that had been found and learned by users as well as the additional materials requested while users work with the system. The knowledge base of Multibook consists of two distinct concept spaces – Concept Space and Media Brick Space. Concept Space contains a networked model of learning topics and uses knowledge management approaches. Media Brick Space is used to store atomic information units (media bricks) of different multimedia formats which are interconnected via rhetoric relations. Media bricks use IEEE's LOM scheme and are described and treated as learning objects.

2.3 Social Collaboration On E-Learning

One of the main reasons that leads students to online course dropout is the lack of social interaction. Most students play a passive role on learning environments, often reduced to consult content provided by teachers which leads to an unstimulating environment [24]. The natural characteristics of online social networks, such as content sharing and comments, promote an active and stimulating learning environment[18].

SCALE (Supporting Collaboration and Adaptation in a Learning Environment) [11] is a web-based educational environment with learning and assessment content. It enables students to (1) work on individual or group activities proposed with respect to their knowledge, (2) participate in self-assessment, peer-assessment or collaborative-assessment activities, (3) work with embedded educational environments, (4) use synchronous and asynchronous communication tools and (5) have access to feedback components. Three studies [11] shown that this tool facilitates and supports learning and assessment.

2.4 Automatic Evaluation Of Exercises

The evaluation of exercises takes a large amount of time to teachers, and thus, many universities have invested in the development of automated assessment systems [3, 21]. Several of these systems are only prepared for the assessment of programming assignments [13, 20, 17, 5] and differ on the

extra features that they provide, such as multi-programming language support, evaluation type (static or dynamic), feedback, interoperability, learning context, security and plagiarism. However, there is also some work on automatic evaluation of other types of exercises such as UML, Mathematics and Physics [21, 4, 12].

Mooshak [17] is a web-based system to handle programming contests. It acts as a full contest manager and as an automatic judge for programming contests. Mooshak supports submissions of exercises written in several programming languages. The standard way of to evaluate a program is to compile it and then execute it with test cases input files, comparing the obtained output with the expected result (black-box approach). It also deals with non-determinism using special correctors, which are invoked after each test case execution. The feedback provided by this system consists of error status (e.g. wrong answer, compilation error, execution errors).

2.5 Interoperability

Most of the learning institutions have already adopted a Learning Management System (LMS) to organize and share their course resources, to deliver assignments and/or to report the performance of the students [8]. So, interoperability among e-learning content and components is increasingly becoming the key to the success of any e-learning environment.

Many approaches to couple LMS with other applications have been proposed, since defining LMS from scratch based on service-oriented architectures [2, 6], including web services layers within the LMS infrastructure [25, 7] or providing support for interoperability specifications [16].

The latter approach is primarily based on IMS specifications, namely the LTI (Learning Tools Interoperability) specification that facilitates the integration between LMS and external applications. The TSUGI framework [2] is a recent proposal to simplify the implementation of LTI tools.

3. ENKI

This section describes Enki, a web-based IDE for learning programming languages using gamification features. Enki blends assessment and learning, presenting content, from hypertext to video, as well as exercises, in an adaptive and engaging way.

The IDE makes use of gamification to engage students in the learning process, interacting with gamification services to support the creation of leaderboards, reward students for their achievements, among others. It also integrates a service for sequencing educational resources to provide different learning paces according to students' capabilities. The exercises and assessment are, typically, programming exercises. The system that hosts Enki includes also interfaces for teachers to author and manage both exercises and content, as well as to browse assessment results and student profiles.

The next subsections present the architecture of Enki and its main components, and describe its implementation.

3.1 Architecture

Enki is a part of the Mooshak 2.0, the new version of Mooshak [17], a web environment for automated assessment in computer science, both in competitive and pedagogical learning. The new version is a complete re-implementation

---

[1]http://openbadges.org/

[2]http://csev.github.io/tsugi/

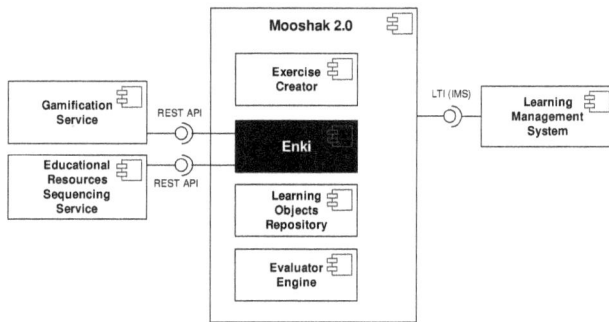

Figure 1: Components diagram of the network of Enki where Mooshak 2.0 acts as a tool provider for an LMS

of the code base with a wider variety of user interfaces for different use cases. It has interoperability features that enable it to interact with other e-learning tools such as LMSs.

Enki takes advantage of Mooshak 2.0 to have a pivotal role in a network of e-learning systems, coordinating the communication with all external components as depicted by the UML components diagram in Figure 1.

An important task for building the network of Enki is the choice of the systems that would play each role. The next sub-subsections describe the types of systems that compose the network presented in Figure 1, and introduce the selected system(s) for each of the components.

3.1.1 Learning Management System (LMS)

An LMS is a software application for the administration, documentation, tracking and reporting; used in training programs, classrooms and online events [10]. Typically it is used by two types of users' groups: learners and teachers. The learners can use the LMS to plan their learning experience and to collaborate with their colleagues; the teachers can deliver educational content and track, analyze and report the learner evolution within an organization.

Nowadays, an LMS plays a central role in any eLearning architecture. Still, the LMS cannot afford to be isolated from other systems in an educational institution. Thus, the potential for interoperability is an important, although frequently overlooked, aspect of an LMS system [15].

The purpose of Enki is to integrate an e-learning ecosystem based on an LMS. For this, Enki benefits from the interoperability mechanisms inherited from Mooshak 2.0 to provide authentication directly from the LMS and to submit exercises grades to the LMS, using the Learning Tools Interoperability (LTI) specification.

Although the majority of the LMSs support LTI communication [23], only Moodle and Sakai are able to fully integrate with Enki. Blackboard LMS is also capable of running Enki but it cannot receive grading results.

3.1.2 Gamification Service (GS)

A Game-Backend-as-a-Service (GBaaS), which is abbreviated here as Gamification Service (GS), is a subset of a Backend-as-a-Service (BaaS) - a cloud computing service model acting as a middleware component that allows developers to connect their applications to cloud services via application programming interfaces (API) and software development kits (SDK) - that includes cross-platform solu-

tions for the typical game concepts. These GBaaS that can leverage on their authentication services and massive user base already provide gamification features. However, gamification services that rely on external authentication are not adequate for a network of e-learning systems which already operates on a single sign-on ecosystem.

Since there was no service fulfilling the requirements of the network of Enki, a new gamification service was developed. This service – called Odin – [14] is inspired in the Google Play Game Service (GPGS) but with a different approach regarding authentication. Institutions, rather than end-users, are the ones that require authentication. The communication with Odin is made through its REST API, similar to the GPGS API[3].

3.1.3 Educational Resources Sequencing Service (ERSS)

The ERSS selected was Seqins [22]. Seqins is a sequencing tool of digital educational resources that includes a flexible sequencing model that fosters students to learn at different rhythms. Enki feds Seqins, through its REST API, with precedence among content units, assessment results and students' progress and Seqins provides an XML representation of the resources to present to the current student.

3.1.4 Evaluator Engine (EE)

The purpose of an EE is to mark and grade exercises. In this network, an EE should perform four tasks: (1) receive a reference to the exercise, an attempt to solve it (a program) and a reference to the student submitting the attempt, (2) load the exercise from the LOR (possibly itself) using the given reference, (3) compile the solution and run the tests, related to the exercise, against the attempt of the student and (4) produce an evaluation report with the classification, feedback and, possibly, corrections.

The EE system is provided by Mooshak 2.0. As in its previous version, the main feature is the automatic evaluation of exercises, adding support for different exercise types and better feedback. For the Enki purposes, this evaluator suffered some minor changes to be less strict.

3.1.5 Exercise Creator (EC)

An EC must allow teachers to create a complete exercise package, containing a statement, a solution, tests, skeletons, and a manifest file describing the contents of the package. This package must follow the same package specification as the LOR for programming exercises.

This kind of tool is offered by Mooshak 2.0, which also stores its exercises on its own repository.

3.1.6 Learning Objects Repository (LOR)

A Learning Objects Repository (LOR) is a system that stores educational resources and enables educators to share, manage and use them. These resources (or Learning Objects) are small, self-contained and reusable educational units which, typically, have additional metadata to catalog and search them. The system that plays the role of a LOR in the network of Enki is also Mooshak 2.0.

3.2 Graphical User Interface

Enki was developed using Google Web Toolkit (GWT), an open source software development framework that allows a

---

[3]https://developers.google.com/games/services/web/api

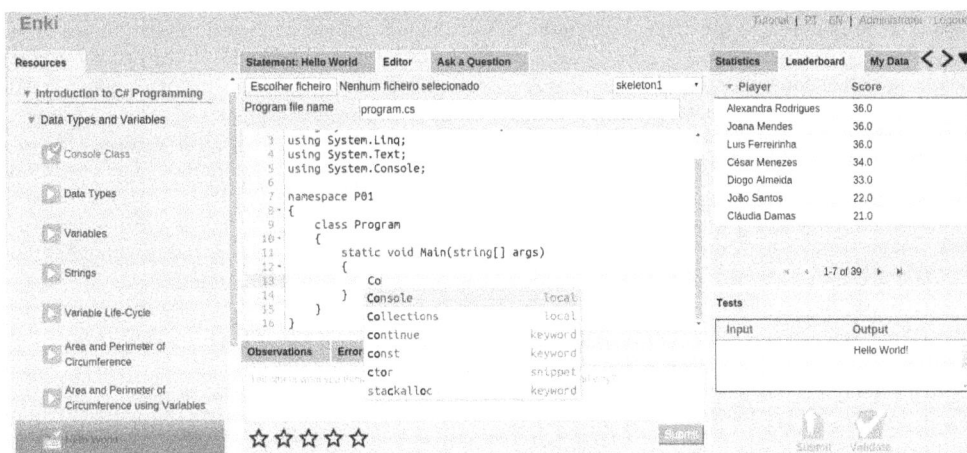

Figure 2: Interface of Enki for students

fast development of AJAX applications in Java. The GWT code is organized in two main packages, the server, which includes the service implementations triggered by the user interface, and the client, that includes the user interfaces.

A distinctive feature of Enki is its student interface, presented in Figure 2, which emulates an integrated development environment (IDE). It was designed for responsiveness, to be used in different resolutions and devices as well as to resize the browser window, keeping the panels' proportions or adjusting them to a better look and feel (in case of smaller resolutions). Students can rearrange panels and tabs to their needs with the drag-and-drop and resize features provided by the Enki's interface. These features rely on two free and open-source GWT libraries: GWT Bootstrap 3[4], for responsiveness and GwtQuery[5], for drag-and-drop.

The interface of Enki is composed of widgets in different panels which intercommunicate with each others – *gadgets*. These gadgets are independent components provided by Mooshak 2.0, although some of them were, in fact, developed having Enki in mind. The most important gadgets are the following:

Resources Tree – to browse and select the available course contents;

Leaderboard – a table with the players' name and score, sorted by decreasing score;

Problem Stats – a chart built using the Google Chart Tools API for GWT, that summarizes the submission statistics of a problem;

Achievements – contains the unlocked achievements;

Profile – summarizes information about the logged-in student;

Code Editor – based on the Ace Editor, allows students to code in most programming languages with syntax highlight and code completion, starting from a skeleton provided by the exercise author;

Test Cases – allows students to verify their programs with both public or their own tests;

PDF Viewer – shows both problem statements and static educational resources;

Video Viewer – allows the student to see and share video resources;

Ask Question – lists questions already answered and allows students to submit their own questions;

Resource Rating – enables students to give feedback on educational resources.

The resources tree mentioned above is particular important as it drives student interaction by presenting both the course structure and content. Every level may hold educational resources (the leaves of the tree), which can be of different types: text (HTML or PDF), multimedia and activities (exercises). Each resource presented in the cell tree has an icon reflecting its type and a color depending on its state relative to the student: available, solved/seen, unavailable or recommended.

The global system of Enki also contains two additional interfaces for teachers, to view the results of the submissions of the students and to author exercises.

4. VALIDATION

This section presents an acceptability evaluation of Enki. To carry out this evaluation an experiment was conducted with undergraduate students at *Escola Superior de Estudos Industriais e de Gestão (ESEIG)* - a school of the Polytechnic Institute of Porto - from the 4th to the 15th of January of 2016.

The experiment took the form of an Open Online Course entitled "Introduction to C# Programming", free of charge and without participation limits. It had an enrollment of 70 students, of which 28 were females. The course contains resources of two types: expository and evaluative. The expository resources are typically videos with working examples of exercises solving and a few theoretical resources. The evaluative resources are programming exercises that allow students to consolidate their knowledge. The videos were created with Camtasia[6], a software that records screen activity and voice, and deployed on YouTube. The design requirements of these videos where the following: (1) cover all the curricula (coverage); (2) have several difficulty levels (diversity); (3) have at most 5 minutes (fragmentation); and

---

[4]https://gwtbootstrap3.github.io/gwtbootstrap3-demo/
[5]http://code.google.com/p/gwtquery/

[6]https://www.techsmith.com/camtasia.html

(4) be composed by pictures, sound and subtitles (completeness).

The exercises comply with the Mooshak programming problem package specification. This package is an archive containing a problem description (typically an HTML file), a file with the solution, an XML file with the structure of the package, a folder with tests and their output, and optionally a folder with images and a folder with skeletons of the solution.

In the last day of this experiment, students were invited to take a final test with 5 questions covering all the syllabus. After the experiment they were also invited to fill-in an online questionnaire based on the Nielsen's model [19], using Google Forms. It includes questions on the usefulness of Enki, i.e. on its utility and usability. Utility is the capacity of the system to achieve a desired goal. Usability is defined by Nielsen as a qualitative attribute that estimates how easy is to use an user interface. The survey was completed by 25 students, of which 9 were females.

Figure 3 shows the results grouped by Nielsen's heuristics. The collected data is shown in a bar chart, with heuristics sorted in descending order of user satisfaction.

On the positive side the results showed that the consistence, recognition and aesthetic were the heuristics with higher satisfaction. The respondents selected the minimalist design as one of the strongest points of Enki. On the negative side the results highlighted deficiencies in three areas: speed and reliability, error prevention and users help and documentation. Students complained about the delay when they validate or submit their programs. This was due to a machine overload that was already solved. Other students stated that the messages of the system were scarce and difficult to interpret. The improvement of feedback is one of the major requirements for future versions of Enki. Finally, students complained of the lack of documentation while using Enki.

The questionnaire finalizes with an overall classification of Enki in a 5 values Likert-type scale (very good, good, adequate, bad, very bad). The majority of students (56%) classified Enki as an adequate tool and many of them (40%) stated Enki as a good or a very good tool. Very few students (4%) found it either bad or very bad.

5. CONCLUSIONS

This paper presents Enki, a web-based IDE for learning programming languages in an adaptive and engaging way. This IDE resorts to gamification services to support the creation of leaderboards, reward students for their achievements, among others, in order to engage the students in the learning process. It also mimics game levels by integrating with a service for sequencing educational resources in different rhythms to heterogeneous students.

The Open Online Course to introduce students to the C# programming language is a proof of the acceptability of Enki as a pedagogical tool to learn programming languages. Also, it has proven its ability to integrate in an e-learning environment based on a LMS.

Enki and its network will be subject to improvements. The students and teachers involved in the Open Online Course reported some minor issues, related to the user interface, which are already being solved for the next version.

Regarding new features, the evaluation feedback will be the major focus point in the next version. Currently, the feedback provided is only based on tests, which is not adequate to introduce students to programming. The next version will benefit of a new improvement to Mooshak 2.0, concerning the static analysis of code, to provide richer feedback to students. Also, the ERSS system will include a long-term recommendation component. This component will recommend resources to students with the final goal set to pass the final evaluation with the best score possible within the available time left to the end of the course and the personal characteristics of the student.

6. ACKNOWLEDGMENTS

This work is partially funded by the ERDF – European Regional Development Fund, through the Operational Programme for Competitiveness and Internationalisation – COMPETE 2020 Programme, with National Funds of FCT – Fundação para a Ciência e a Tecnologia (Portuguese Foundation for Science and Technology), within project POCI-01-0145-FEDER-006961; by the North Portugal Regional Operational Programme (NORTE 2020), under the PORTUGAL 2020 Partnership Agreement, and through the European Regional Development Fund (ERDF), within Project "NORTE-01-0145-FEDER-000020"; and by the Polytechnic Institute of Porto, by its Integration Research and Development Grants (BInt-ICD/IPP-BST/KMILT/01/2015).

7. REFERENCES

[1] J. Ahn, B. S. Butler, A. Alam, and S. A. Webster. Learner participation and engagement in open online courses: Insights from the peer 2 peer university. *MERLOT Journal of Online Learning and Teaching*, 9(2):160–171, 2013.

[2] M. Al-Smadi and C. Gütl. Soa-based architecture for a generic and flexible e-assessment system. In *Education Engineering (EDUCON), 2010 IEEE*, pages 493–500. IEEE, 2010.

[3] K. M. Ala-Mutka. A survey of automated assessment approaches for programming assignments. *Computer science education*, 15(2):83–102, 2005.

[4] N. H. Ali, Z. Shukur, and S. Idris. Assessment system for uml class diagram using notations extraction. *International Journal on Computer Science Network Security*, 7:181–187, 2007.

[5] M. Blumenstein, S. Green, A. Nguyen, and V. Muthukkumarasamy. An experimental analysis of game: a generic automated marking environment. In *ACM SIGCSE Bulletin*, volume 36, pages 67–71. ACM, 2004.

[6] O. Casquero, J. Portillo, R. Ovelar, M. Benito, and J. Romo. iple network: an integrated elearning 2.0 architecture from a university's perspective. *Interactive Learning Environments*, 18(3):293–308, 2010.

[7] M. Á. Conde, F. J. García, M. J. Casany, and M. Alier. Applying web services to define open learning environments. In *Database and Expert Systems Applications (DEXA), 2010 Workshop on*, pages 79–83. IEEE, 2010.

[8] D. Dagger, A. O'Connor, S. Lawless, E. Walsh, and V. P. Wade. Service-oriented e-learning platforms: From monolithic systems to flexible services. *Internet Computing, IEEE*, 11(3):28–35, 2007.

4. Consistence	26%	73%
6. Recognition	4% 29%	67%
8. Aesthetic	10% 30%	60%
3. Freedom	18% 22%	60%
2. Compatibility	6% 36%	59%
1. Visibility	20% 24%	56%
11. Ease of use	19% 29%	52%
10. Documentation	21% 32%	47%
7. Flexibility	25% 29%	45%
9. Users help	21% 34%	45%
5. Error prevention	26% 30%	44%
13. Reliability	37% 24%	39%
12. Speed	28% 37%	35%

0% 10% 20% 30% 40% 50% 60% 70% 80% 90% 100%

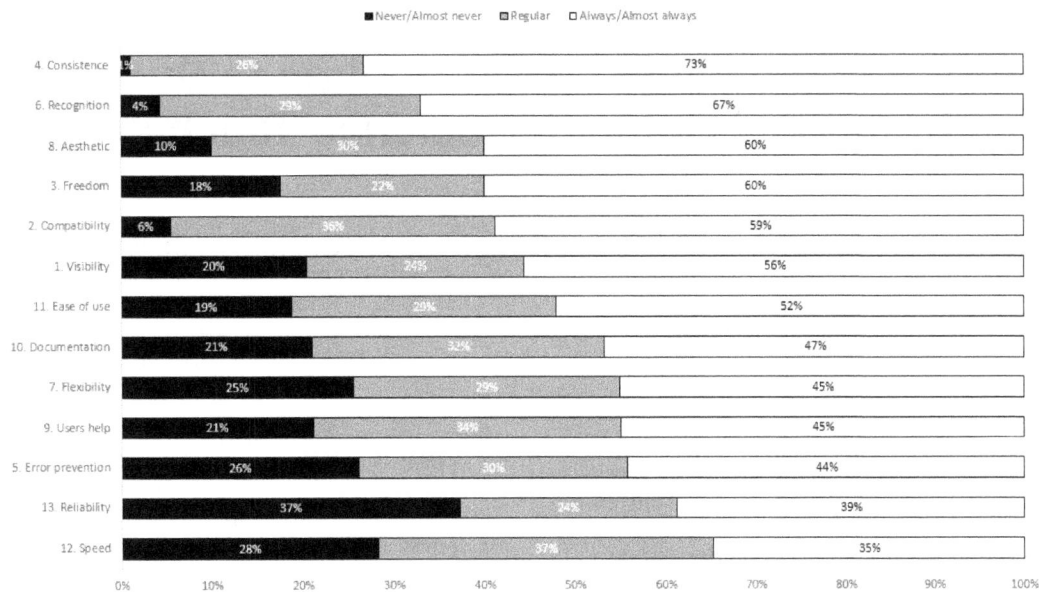

Figure 3: Enki acceptability evaluation

[9] A. El Saddik, S. Fischer, and R. Steinmetz. Reusable multimedia content in web-based learning systems. *IEEE Multimedia*, 8(3):30–38, 2001.

[10] R. K. Ellis. Field guide to learning management systems. 2009.

[11] A. Gogoulou, E. Gouli, M. Grigoriadou, M. Samarakou, and D. Chinou. A web-based educational setting supporting individualized learning, collaborative learning and assessment. *Educational Technology & Society*, 10(4):242–256, 2007.

[12] M. Harjula et al. Mathematics exercise system with automatic assessment. 2008.

[13] D. W. Juedes. Experiences in web-based grading. In *Frontiers in Education, 2003. FIE 2003 33rd Annual*, volume 3, pages S3F–27. IEEE, 2003.

[14] J. P. Leal, J. C. Paiva, and R. Queirós. Odin: A service for gamification of learning activities. In *to appear*, page to appear. Springer, 2015.

[15] J. P. Leal and R. Queirós. *A comparative study on LMS interoperability*. IGI-Global, 2011.

[16] J. P. Leal and R. Queirós. Using the learning tools interoperability framework for lms integration in service oriented architectures. 2011.

[17] J. P. Leal and F. Silva. Mooshak: a web-based multi-site programming contest system. *Software: Practice and Experience*, 33(6):567–581, 2003.

[18] M. Li and Z. Liu. The role of online social networks in students' e-learning experiences. In *Computational Intelligence and Software Engineering, 2009. CiSE 2009. International Conference on*, pages 1–4. IEEE, 2009.

[19] J. Nielsen and T. K. Landauer. A mathematical model of the finding of usability problems. In *Proceedings of the INTERACT'93 and CHI'93 conference on Human factors in computing systems*, pages 206–213. ACM, 1993.

[20] Y. Pisan, D. Richards, A. Sloane, H. Koncek, and S. Mitchell. Submit! a web-based system for automatic program critiquing. In *Proceedings of the fifth Australasian conference on Computing education-Volume 20*, pages 59–68. Australian Computer Society, Inc., 2003.

[21] F. Prados, I. Boada, J. Soler, and J. Poch. Automatic generation and correction of technical exercises. In *International Conference on Engineering and Computer Education: ICECE*, volume 5, 2005.

[22] R. Queirós, J. P. Leal, and J. Campos. Sequencing educational resources with seqins. 2014.

[23] R. Queirós, J. P. Leal, and J. C. Paiva. Integrating rich learning applications in lms. In *State-of-the-Art and Future Directions of Smart Learning*, pages 381–386. Springer, 2016.

[24] J. J. Rodrigues, F. M. Sabino, and L. Zhou. Enhancing e-learning experience with online social networks. *IET communications*, 5(8):1147–1154, 2011.

[25] C. Severance, J. Hardin, and A. Whyte. The coming functionality mash-up in personal learning environments. *Interactive Learning Environments*, 16(1):47–62, 2008.

[26] C. Stewart, A. I. Cristea, T. Brailsford, and H. Ashman. 'authoring once, delivering many': creating reusable adaptive courseware. 2005.

[27] M. Vansteenkiste and E. L. Deci. Competitively contingent rewards and intrinsic motivation: Can losers remain motivated? *Motivation and Emotion*, 27:273–299, 2003. 10.1023/A:1026259005264.

Towards a Technical Skills Curriculum to Supplement Traditional Computer Science Teaching

Craig Marais
Department of Computer Science
Rhodes University
Grahamstown, South Africa
g14m0023@campus.ru.ac.za

Karen Bradshaw
Department of Computer Science
Rhodes University
Grahamstown, South Africa
k.bradshaw@ru.ac.za

ABSTRACT

It is commonplace for students to enter university with skills deficiencies. However, this is cause for growing concern in the context of South Africa, as these 'deficient' students are becoming more numerous. Public secondary schools in South Africa are failing to create students with adequate skills for careers in the STEM fields.

This paper isolates these skills deficiencies to a subset of technical skills for prob lem-solving. The problem-solving skills are divided into content groups, which are then aligned to existing Computer Science content. A solution is proposed that demonstrates how the content can be presented without the need for extensive curriculum changes to established course content.

Categories and Subject Descriptors

K.3.2 [**Computers and Education**]: Computer and Information Science Education

Keywords

Computer Science education, curriculum development, problem-solving skills

1. INTRODUCTION

First-year university Computer Science courses (CS1) are structured to create a technical thinking ability in learners, who are required to both assimilate a large body of technical knowledge and to demonstrate this knowledge through the application thereof. Traditionally this content is taught through classes, tutorial sessions, and practical sessions.

However, growing disparity in the South African educational system is creating conditions where new university students are found to be lacking in these skills. This disparity is particularly evident between public and private sectors of high school education. As these conditions worsen, it is inevitable that a call for recurriculation will be made. This

ITiCSE '16, July 09 - 13, 2016, Arequipa, Peru

© 2016 Copyright held by the owner/author(s). Publication rights licensed to ACM.
ISBN 978-1-4503-4231-5/16/07. . . $15.00

DOI: http://dx.doi.org/10.1145/2899415.2899446

paper presents an alternative to widespread recurriculation of existing established university CS curricula.

Historically, these curricula were structured in accordance with international standards and expected secondary school outcomes. Previously this ensured that 'most' students were able to achieve satisfactory results without compromising standards. Unfortunately, the changing conditions in South Africa have resulted in a shift in the capabilities of the average student. These changes are the result not of a drop in intellectual ability of students, but rather the poor quality of education, particularly in STEM subjects, that the average South African secondary school learner receives.

Through the research presented herein, we detail how the abilities of new students are evaluated against our expectations, how these evaluations lead to the identification of specific technical skill deficiencies, and finally how we seek to instil these skills into students without extensive recurriculation.

2. EDUCATIONAL LANDSCAPE

The curriculum guidelines set out by the ACM-IEEE [1] provide an excellent foundation for any CS1 course; however, they do not (and naturally cannot) take into account all possible localised factors. Foresight of this fact is documented in the *Institutional Challenges* section identified by the ACM-IEEE joint task force [1, Chapter 6]. The challenge is thus, to achieve a balance between producing 'good' graduates who have the desired characteristics, and making allowances for localised institutional challenges.

Fischer and Scott [3] present a thorough summary of the disparity between the expected ability of a first time university entrant and the measured ability of said entrant. This disparity becomes more evident as university demographics shift to align with national demographics in South Africa.

At a national level there is a lack of resources available to schools. Many secondary schools lack qualified teachers for Mathematics and Science. It is commonplace to expect first time university entrants to have non-existent computing experience. Conversely, many schools are able to offer *Computer Applications Technology* (CAT). The CAT curriculum[1] is comparable to the ICDL certification, encompassing daily computer use and introductory workplace productivity with computers. However, the benefit provided by CAT at a tertiary level has not been proven academically.

Even if a school is able to provide adequate teaching of the Sciences, many students opt to take Mathematics Literacy

---

[1] www.education.gov.za/LinkClick.aspx?fileticket=MLRz54Uw5tk=

instead of traditional Mathematics. As the name implies, Mathematics Literacy is a simplified curriculum designed to teach everyday uses of Mathematics. Unfortunately, it fails to convey underlying principles usually associated with secondary school Mathematics.

The education landscape is further complicated by the discrepancy between public and private education. Private schools are able to provide excellent educational conditions for their learners, generally resulting in superior finishing results for these schools.

Ultimately it falls to the South African universities to accommodate students with educational deficiencies, and a critical challenge arises to maintain existing international standards while doing so.

The problems identified and discussed are not unique to South Africa; many of the social and economic problems have been found to exist in other developing countries such as India and Brazil [2, 5]. These papers highlight the far reaching importance of computational thinking and its associated problem-solving component. Additionally, these papers demonstrate the diverse approaches that are being investigated to improve the uptake of these skills.

2.1 SAQA qualification specifications

All qualifications offered at South African tertiary educational institutions are uniquely registered with the South African Qualification Authority (SAQA) and have a qualification ID. Pertinent to this research is the Bachelor of Science (BSc) qualification [11]. This qualification does not stipulate the content required for a BSc (Comp Sci), but rather defines broad assessment criteria for the scientific field. Thus, it falls to the individual universities to develop appropriate content for the specific scientific fields they wish to offer. In the case of CS, this content is readily available in the previously discussed ACM-IEEE guidelines.

Once again, the onus falls on the universities to align these guidelines with their own institutional challenges. In particular, the South African universities need to accommodate learners from the flawed public schooling system in South Africa.

2.2 South African secondary schools

South Africa is a country with a rich history, although much of this history is tainted with the exploitation of the local populus. For much of the latter half of the the 21st century, South Africa was governed by the National Party and its policy of *apartheid* (racial segregation). Today, South Africa is a fully democratic republic with equal rights for all, but the lasting effects of apartheid are still lingering.

Under apartheid, persons of color were given substandard education and restricted in many aspects of day-to-day life. One such restriction was the areas in which they were allowed to live. As a result, many parts of South Africa remain largely under-developed, especially when compared with the urban areas.

Many rural areas in South Africa find their schools understaffed, overcrowded and horribly underfunded. The result of this is that many schools simply cannot offer subjects such as Mathematics, Physics or CAT. Students from such schools may never have used any computing device more powerful that a cellular phone. However, students from these schools have the desire, the right, and the intellectual capability to pursue tertiary education. At the same time, South Africa

has many highly acclaimed private schools that provide a rich learning environment for their learners.

However, university entry requirements for a student to enter into a first-year BSc course require that they achieve sufficient results in their final secondary school year and specifically in Mathematics. This creates a dilemma where a student must demonstrate competency in a subject he/she was never offered.

Thus, it is common practice for university admissions to make special allowances for students who are identified as 'previously disadvantaged'. This results in great disparity in first-year skills; not based on a student's intellectual ability, but rather where he/she grew up.

2.3 Existing CS1 curriculum

Universities such as Rhodes University (RU) are facing a growing student population and a broadening range of first-year abilities. Lecturers at these universities must prepare to instruct students with varying capabilities. These universities have long established curricula structured according to international standards, such as is the case with CS1 at RU, which is structured to meet guidelines set out in the *Computer Science Curricula 2013* [1].

These guidelines describe a set of desirable characteristics of Computer Science graduates; through these characteristics and previous research conducted at RU [4, 8], a shortfall in student ability has been identified in the form of problem-solving ability in first-year students. Alongside this, CS1 experiences a high attrition rate (of the order of 30%) in the number of enrolled first-year Computer Science students within the first six months of the course [8]. These factors are not unique to RU, but are evident at other South African universities as well [3].

The immediate goal identified by this research is to produce a viable means of ensuring that students in CS1 develop good problem-solving skills. To achieve this goal, a curriculum incorporating problem-solving skills needs to be developed and matured.

2.4 Baseline ability

Prior to any structured intervention, students entering into universities fall into one of two categories: those likely to pass and those likely to fail. Failure here could be the result of insufficient intellectual ability of the students, or the lack of necessary skills that the students are deemed to possess when entering tertiary education. Since this research is concerned with the benefits derived from the inclusion of an intervention in the curriculum, the former group of 'failers' are excluded from the study as they will not likely benefit from the intervention. The ratio of those who do benefit to those who do not, is conceivably a future benchmark for the viability of the intervention.

The corollary is that we believe some students are able to achieve good results with or without the intervention. These are typically those students with above average intellectual ability and with the required skills. It is the intention of this research to target the middle group of students (those who can derive some benefit). Thus, the content produced should be tailored specifically for their needs.

3. A PROPOSED SOLUTION

As a solution to the skills deficiency in CS1 students, we have begun developing an intervention in the form of a set

	2014		2015	
	wrote	passed	wrote	passed
pre-test (Jan)	85	37	116	46
exam (June)	59	57	92	64
post-test (July)	45	33	60	36

of problem-solving tests, lectures, skills workshops, and exercises. This is the culmination of a number of years of research conducted by several researchers in the CS department. This research has taken many forms with much of its structure based on the guidelines of Johnson & Fuller [7] and Thompson, Luxton-Reilly, Whalley, Hu & Robbins [12].

3.1 Computational thinking test

At RU a longitudinal study has been conducted over three years (2013-2015), the purpose of which has been to assess the computational thinking ability of CS1 students via a pre- and post-test for the CS101 course. The pre-test is conducted prior to any instruction, while the post-test is conducted at the start of the subsequent semester, which represents a time delta of six months. Typically, a student would register for both semester courses at the same time; a student not attending the second course is assumed to have changed majors or dropped out entirely. The tests were designed to assess specific characteristics identified in the operational definition of CT [6], namely:

1. Enabling use of a computer (to solve problems)

2. Organising and analysing data

3. Models and simulations

4. Algorithmic thinking

5. Efficiency of solutions

6. Transference of solutions

An in-depth analysis of the results from these tests is available in a previous paper [8], but a summary of the 2014 & 2015 results is shown in Table 1. Notably, the number of students writing pre- and post-tests varies greatly, but for each year, the number who pass remains fairly consistent. The exam marks only reflect students that achieved sufficient aggregates to be allowed exam admittance. Based on a per-question analysis of these results, we found it possible to test for specific technical skills. These skills form the basis for the problem-solving model developed in conjunction with the CT tests. This model is divided into eight broad skills encompassing all components of problem-solving.

The skills can be further divided into three tiers; these are in order from the lowest to the highest tier:

Skills that are vital to meaningful communication:
Numeracy and Comprehension
Graphs and Figures

Skills that exhibit crucial techniques:
Logic and Inference
Simplification and Decomposition
Statistical Literacy & Analysis
Searching and Sorting

Skills that facilitate the resolution of the problem:
Prediction
Evaluation and Efficiency

It is assumed that a student entering university should possess adequate skills in the first tier. The subsequent two tiers of skills are those that students would improve on through the progression of the introductory CS courses. Students lacking a grounding in these second and third tier skills would not have a means to improve their abilities through the regular progression of the CS1 course.

3.2 Problem-solving skills

Problem-solving skills exist as a spectrum of abilities; for the purposes of this research they have been divided into key areas of interest. These divisions serve as focal points for the associated skills. The skills listed here are in a hierarchical order, and thus it is considered that *Graphs and Figures* should be covered before *Logic and Inference*, for example.

Numeracy and Comprehension (N&C) A student is expected to understand what is written within the context of the learning environment. An established foundation of Reading, Writing, and Mathematics forms the basis for all the other problem-solving skills.

Graphs and Figures (G&F) It is vital to ensure that students have a good understanding of the fundamentals of graphing; this skill enables the student to read and create visual representations of data.

Logic and Inference (L&I) This set of skills deals primarily with the field of logic and deductive reasoning, which are the basis of the scientific method.

Simplification and Decomposition (S&D) A key point to successfully accomplishing a difficult task is to 'break it up' into smaller more manageable parts. Learning to distinguish which parts of a problem can be completed in isolation is embodied by this skill and forms an integral component of problem-solving.

Statistical Literacy & Analysis (STA) A solid understanding of statistical methods, applications, and pitfalls is vital to all scientific fields. Without these skills a student has no basis for the actions he/she takes in an effort to understand data collected.

Searching and Sorting (S&S) Identifying when a problem can be solved by a search or a sort will facilitate quicker and more efficient problem-solving. Coupled with S&D, this skill can greatly reduce the amount of effort needed to solve a problem.

Prediction (PRD) When conducting experiments, a reasonable understanding of an expected outcome is necessary. This skill deals with determining aspects of the solution prior to attempting to solve the problem.

Evaluation and Efficiency(E&E) Understanding when a solution is 'good' or 'bad' and when it can or cannot be improved helps to develop more thorough solutions to problems.

Through this study certain of these skills have been found to be lacking in a significant percentage of students [8]. The motivation of this research is to produce supplementary (parallel) content to address these inadequacies.

3.3 Target students

In an ideal world, all learners would enter a course with all the prerequisite skills. However, the reality in South Africa is more likely that learners will have deficiencies in these expected skills.

In the identified 'middle group' in Section 2.4, the deficient students are expected to comprise a sizeable percentage of the class. Based on the figures presented in Table 1, this group could comprise up to 50% of the class. This has been calculated as the difference between the number of students that wrote the pre-test and those that wrote the post-test. Obviously not every student drops out for the same reason, and the number of students in the target group may be much lower than 50%; however, it is likely to be a significant portion of the class.

The lecturer is then faced with two possibilities: recurriculation of the course, or creation of supplementary parallel content for the course.

Each of these approaches has arguments both for and counter to its application to add content to an existing curriculum.

3.4 Content integration approaches

Parallel content would mean that all students would have equal access to the content, and would need to self-assess their own needs in terms of studying the given content. Thus, a student would be able to tailor his/her study plans according to his/her own needs. The onus is placed on the student to work independently in his/her own personal time.

The lecturer may find it difficult to motivate student investment without the pressure of the given work affecting term aggregate results. However, the lecturer need not invest class time in content that ideally does not belong in the course.

The alternative to this is the recurriculation of existing course content, which relies on the lecturer delivering the new content. This approach can be described as "one size fits all".

The inclusion of new topics in the curriculum in this manner would ensure that the lecturer has a better understanding of the capabilities of the class and he/she would be better able to address possible pitfalls as they develop.

However, this additional content may be repetitive for a student who already possesses the required skills, and may represent a significant investment of class time. This could lead to the point where a student describes the new class as boring. If the percentage of students who would not benefit from the new class outweighs those who would benefit, it becomes counter-productive to use this approach.

Finally, as is the case at RU, the existing curriculum is based on international standards, any major deviation from this standard would degrade the outcome degree.

The onus rests on the reader to discern the more desirable approach for his/her own circumstances. For the purposes of this research, the parallel approach was adopted.

4. PROPOSED CURRICULUM

The proposed curriculum would be 'parallel' to the existing CS1 curriculum. As shown in Figure 1, the *New Topic* forms an alternate path between existing topics (*Topic 2* and *Topic 3*). Students are encouraged to choose either the 'direct' path between topics if they feel they have already

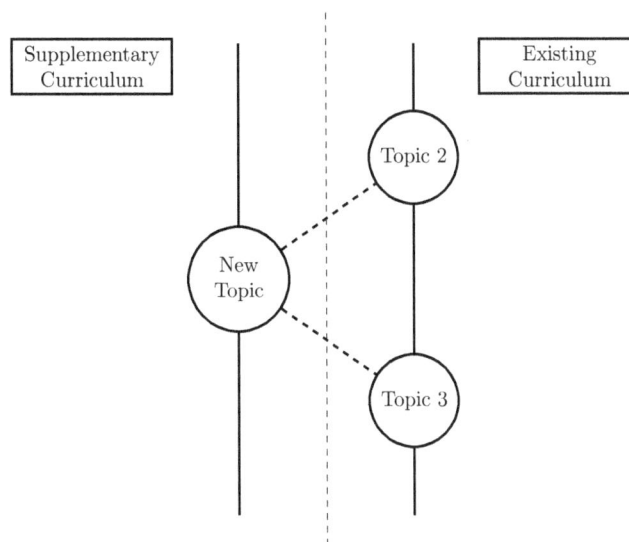

Figure 1: A subject with parallel supplementary content

Table 2: A sample CS1 curriculum skill breakdown

Typical CS1 Topic	N&C	G&F	L&I	S&D	STA	S&S	PRD	E&E
Algorithms (Design)			X	X				
Algorithms (Advanced)			X	X			X	X
Methods			X	X			X	X
Iteration	X		X			X	X	X
Data-types	X					X	X	X
Classes and Objects		X		X				
Events			X	X			X	X
I/O and Files				X		X		
Exceptions			X		X		X	
Recursion			X				X	X
Interfaces				X				

mastered the skill, or alternatively to review the extra topic offered in the parallel course.

4.1 Skills alignment with traditional content

Table 2 is an example of how the problem-solving skills can been aligned to topics covered in a sample CS1 curriculum. Each match indicates a point at which a student should possess a given skill in order to perform well in a given topic. The CS1 topics chosen are based on the course structure of the open-source CS1 textbook used at RU [13], while the problem-solving skills are those described in Section 3.2.

From this example it is evident that STA is less vital to the CS1 course than L&I. This is meaningful because it ensures that content can be tailored to emphasize important topics, and additional examples thereof can be provided to students. This does not imply that STA should be ignored entirely.

Content for each skill can be aligned with the most applicable CS1 topic, thus ensuring that content is tailored to what the students need, when they need it.

4.2 Supplementary Content

Table 2 indicates that initial focus of the problem-solving content must be on L&I followed by S&D, while the skills N&C and G&F should be considered pre-reading material. An initial determining test based on theses skills alone could be used to select students for supplementary content. The types of questions posed should be general logical puzzles.

The next significant portion of the content must focus on the S&S skills as this is considered vital to the topics of *Iteration* and *Data-types*. A jig-saw puzzle provides an excellent source of material for the S&S skill; solving a 1000 piece puzzle is no more difficult than solving a 100 piece puzzle, the same steps are applied. By logically dividing the puzzle, it becomes a matter of time and not skill to complete it.

The skills PRD and E&E must form part of the more advanced topics such as *Advanced Algorithms* and *Recursion*. These skills deal primarily with planning how a problem will be tackled and how to self assess a solution. In the context of CS they mark the difference between an adequate solution and a 'good' solution. It may be beneficial to review past questions with students; by analysing different techniques to solving a problem it is possible to demonstrate how to resolve the best solution.

Finally, the STA skill could be considered an addendum topic to the content. Statistical amusements could be used to demonstrate common misconceptions; an excellent example of this in a class environment is the birthday paradox[2].

It is important to provide a gradual learning curve that persists throughout all the skills content. As the skills are divided into tiers, it is reasonable to assume they should be presented in order of the tiers.

4.3 Delivery

As the content being presented is extracurricular, the lecturer may find it more appropriate to use less traditional delivery methods.

Many universities already make use of extensive blended learning tools, such as Moodle [9]. These tools provide an excellent platform for lecturers to share resources (compulsory or supplementary) with students. This is possibly the easiest (and quickest) delivery method a lecturer could use.

A workbook can be developed to provide students with a readily available resource of prepared content. This workbook would represent a significant investment of preparation (time) from the lecturer, but if published under a open-source license, could benefit many students at different institutions.

A lecturer may also choose to provide students with extra classes; however, care should be taken to ensure that students do not view the extra classes as compulsory towards their studies. These extra classes should be seen as a possible route to success for students who utilize them correctly.

The lecturer is encouraged to use whichever delivery vector they feel will be most applicable for the content. A combination of delivery methods may ultimately provide the best experience for the students, such as Moodle hosted content with recorded video lessons.

At RU we aim to take the middle ground, in the form of a

---

workbook, with a chapter dedicated to each problem-solving skill. Each chapter will have explanatory content followed by both worked examples and exercises for the students.

4.4 Assessment

The viability of the content provided is of little use if it does not improve the problem-solving ability of the students involved, and thus the intervention must be assessed to determine its effect on students.

In the case of RU, assessment takes the form of the CT tests, which have been revised over the years of the study. A few choice questions ensure that we can readily gauge a student's problem-solving ability.

A viable alternative to this would be for a lecturer to analyse existing exam papers to determine which questions best align with the skills in Section 3.2, or inclusion of a bonus question in an exam or test addressing specific skills. Merely attempting such a bonus question is indicative of a student's inherent problem-solving ability.

5. CONCLUSION

In this paper, we have established a view of the South African educational landscape through which a growing problem in the form of the problem-solving ability of first-year CS students has been identified. Based on the results of a longitudinal study over three years, this problem has been shown to be consistent.

Analysis of the data collected through this study has led to the development of an intervention in the form of a parallel curriculum for teaching problem-solving skills. This curriculum has been aligned to complement existing CS1 course material.

6. FUTURE WORK

It is the authors' intention to conduct a nationwide Delphi [10] study to create a unanimous view of the problem-solving skills described in this paper and other skills that may be identified as important to the problem-solving ability of students. The Delphi study is ideal for this task as it will be conducted amongst the primary course lecturers for the various first-year Computer Science courses offered at the different universities in South Africa. These lecturers have a broad base of first-hand experience specifically regarding the problems faced in the South African education system. The initial round of the Delphi study will focus on eliciting problem-solving skills from the Computer Science lecturers. The second round will be used to narrow the skills down via consensus. The third and subsequent rounds will target methods of disseminating these skills to learners. The completion of this Delphi study will be used to refine the course content to be used in the parallel problem-solving curriculum.

Once fully refined and peer-reviewed, the content will be made available to students at RU and other interested parties. It is our aim to provide first-year Computer Science lecturers with an extensive tool-kit of content and examples to aid them in teaching problem-solving skills.

7. REFERENCES

[1] ACM/IEEE-CS Joint Task Force on Computing Curricula. Computer Science curricula 2013. Technical

---

[2]This paradox identifies the likelihood of two individuals in a group of people sharing a birthday. As the group size grows, this likelihood grows far quicker than intuition would suggest.

report, ACM Press and IEEE Computer Society Press, December 2013.

[2] L. D. Almeida and C. A. Tacla. Supporting the development of computational thinking: A robotic platform controlled by smartphone. In *Learning and Collaboration Technologies: Second International Conference, LCT 2015, Held as Part of HCI International 2015, Los Angeles, CA, USA, August 2-7, 2015, Proceedings*, volume 9192, page 124. Springer, 2015.

[3] G. Fisher and I. Scott. The role of higher education in closing the skills gap in South Africa [White paper], 2011. http://www.glenfisher.ca/downloads/files/Higher Education in SA.pdf Retrieved December 2015.

[4] L. A. Gouws, K. Bradshaw, and P. Wentworth. First year student performance in a test for computational thinking. *Proceedings of the South African Institute for Computer Scientists and Information Technologists Conference*, pages 271–277, October 2013.

[5] S. Goyal, R. S. Vijay, C. Monga, and P. Kalita. Code bits: An inexpensive tangible computational thinking toolkit for K-12 curriculum. In *Proceedings of the TEI '16: Tenth International Conference on Tangible, Embedded, and Embodied Interaction*, TEI '16, pages 441–447, New York, NY, USA, 2016. ACM.

[6] ISTE. Operational definition of computational thinking for K-12 education, 2011. https://www.iste.org/learn/computational-thinking/ct-operational-definition Retrieved 10 April 2014.

[7] C. G. Johnson and U. Fuller. Is Bloom's taxonomy appropriate for Computer Science? *Koli Calling 2006*, 2006.

[8] C. Marais and K. Bradshaw. Problem-solving ability of first year CS students: A case study and intervention. In *Proceedings of the 44th Conference of the Southern African Computers Lecturers' Association*, 2015.

[9] Moodle Pty Ltd. The Moodle project, 2016. https://moodle.org/ Retrieved 14 January 2016.

[10] C. Okoli and S.D. Pawlowski The Delphi Method as a Research Tool:An Example, Design Considerations and Applications Information and Management 42 (1), 2004, pages 15–29,

[11] SAQA. Qualification 35954: Bachelor of Science. Digital, July 2015. http://regqs.saqa.org.za/viewQualification.php?id=35954 Retrieved December 2015.

[12] E. Thompson, A. Luxton-Reilly, J. L. Whalley, M. Hu, and P. Robbins. Bloom's taxonomy for CS assessment. In *Proceedings of the Tenth Conference on Australasian Computing Education - Volume 78*, ACE '08, pages 155–161, Darlinghurst, Australia, Australia, 2008. Australian Computer Society, Inc.

[13] P. Wentworth. Think sharply with C#: A workbook, December 2015. http://www.ict.ru.ac.za/resources/ThinkSharply/ThinkSharply/index.html Retrieved 14 January 2016.

Nifty with Data: Can a Business Intelligence Analysis Sourced from Open Data form a Nifty Assignment?

Matthew Love
Dept. of Computing
Sheffield Hallam University
Sheffield S1 1WB, UK
m.love@shu.ac.uk

Charles Boisvert
Dept. of Computing
Sheffield Hallam University
Sheffield S1 1WB, UK
c.boisvert@shu.ac.uk

Elizabeth Uruchurtu
Dept. of Computing
Sheffield Hallam University
Sheffield S1 1WB, UK
e.uruchurtu@shu.ac.uk

Ian Ibbotson
Better with Data Society
http://betterwithdata.co
ianibbo@gmail.com

ABSTRACT

This paper describes an assignment investigating the relationship between weather conditions and levels of air pollution. The case study illustrates aspects of finding and accessing Open Data, sections of the Extract-Transform-Load processes of data warehousing, building an analytic cube, and application of data mining tools. It is intended to aid tutors and students of databases by providing a study that gives a practical case example that gives an overview of how several topics in the area of data collection and analysis integrate together.

As well as being an interesting assignment in its own right, the case study raises a number of questions about what makes a good assignment for students learning to handle data (some of the usual nifty criteria have to be adapted), and about the use of Open Data in student assignments.

CCS Concepts

•Information systems → Information integration; Decision support systems; Data mining; •Social and professional topics → Student assessment;

Keywords

Nifty assignments; Open Data; Business Intelligence; Computer Science Education

1. INTRODUCTION

This paper proposes a *nifty assignment* in data mining. We consider the sources of data used, to study whether Open Data can form the basis of more such assignments, and if so how. We then discuss how assignments differ between databases and other domains in computer science, particu-

larly programming, and consequently how that affects criteria of quality or *niftiness*.

In the next sections, we describe the nifty assessment criteria and explain why use them as a standard for quality of assessment. We then propose an assignment which outlines a number of topics related to finding and accessing Open Data, merging sources, and analysing the data using self-service and data mining tools.

Once the assignment is clear, we will reconsider it against the nifty criteria, but also consider how the criteria themselves apply to the area of data mining which has few assignments proposed. Finally, we will consider whether the basis of this assignment, the use of Open Data as a source of data to analyse, can be extended to different cases and examples, and if so how.

2. QUALITY IN ASSIGNMENT

The notion and the need for the *nifty assignments* repository has been solidly defended by Nick Parlante [10]:

> Assignments play a crucial role in what my students take away from a course, but I'm always amazed at what an error prone and time consuming process it is to put together a good assignment.

Since 1999, Parlante has been maintaining a repository of assignments, coordinating regular additions at SIGCSE - most recently in [11]. The repository has become a reference, analysed for example by Layman et al. [8] to find the social context of scenarios, or by Fincher et al. [5] to evaluate repositories.

Given the popularity and established character of the nifty assignment repository, its criteria constitute a good framework to start evaluating assignments in areas cognate to computer science, including data mining. Here are the criteria as proposed on the Nifty Assignments website [9]:

- **Nifty** – Nifty Assignments often have a playful sort of "fun factor" to them. They are very visual, or they build a game, or they have entertaining output. The assignments invite the students to play around with the material. Of course we shouldn't regard this as a requirement. Not all CS fits into the "game with blinking lights" motif.

ITiCSE '16, July 09-13, 2016, Arequipa, Peru

© 2016 ACM. ISBN 978-1-4503-4231-5/16/07...$15.00

DOI: http://dx.doi.org/10.1145/2899415.2899431

- **Topical** – most Nifty Assignments fit into the curriculum and difficulty range that makes sense for most schools (typically CS0-CS2). This is just a practical bias, where we want to promote assignments that can work for the greatest number of students. Platform independence is also desirable, and we try to avoid dependencies on non-portable or non-standard libraries. At present, Java is a great language to make your Nifty Assignment adoptable by the widest audience.

- **Scalable** – many Nifty Assignments operate at two levels. First and most importantly, there's the mainstream part of the assignment that is nifty, meaningful, and effective for the average student. Beyond that, many Nifty Assignments have an open-ended aspect where advanced students can take the assignment beyond its original boundaries.

- **Adoptable** – for an ideal Nifty Assignment, the author has put together materials that make the assignment easy for another instructor to adopt: handouts (.rtf, .doc, or .html formats), starter source code, data files, and other ancillary materials. Here again, platform independence, use of open, vendor-neutral languages, libraries, etc., is a plus. Although they might lack glamour, high-quality materials are appreciated. It's easy to think of Tic-Tac-Toe or whatever as an assignment, but there's a big gap between the idea and having all the materials tested and ready to go. In this way, Nifty Assignments can complete that last step for the community, making the idea concretely available for the whole community.

- **Inspirational and thought provoking** – sometimes a Nifty Assignment is just thought provoking about what is possible in an assignment, inspiring people to work out their own assignments more than being something a lot of people adopt.

Some of these criteria apply straightforwardly to a data mining problem. But we will see that the peculiar process of procuring data, merging sources, and analyzing it, represents a large volume of work that may require to redefine what nifty means in the context of teaching and learning Business Intelligence.

3. CASE STUDY: AIR POLLUTION IN A MAJOR CITY

All the ancillary documents, data and scripts are available online[1].

Air pollution kills people. It is estimated that in the UK 29,000 people die early every year due to breathing difficulties at times of low air quality [1]. The UK government has imposed targets for reducing the quantities and/or frequencies of the main pollutants. Local Authorities are responsible for monitoring and publishing pollution levels in their areas.

Sheffield City Council uses two types of monitoring devices in the city: diffusion tubes and fully automated processing units. Both types of devices are illustrated in Fig. 1. There are around 160 diffusion tube devices and six fully automated processing stations. The diffusion tubes have the advantage of being spread throughout the city area. However,

Figure 1: Nitrogen Dioxide diffusion tube vs. 'Groundhog' pollution automated station

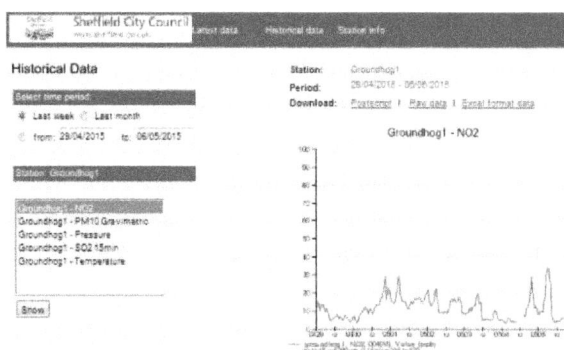

Figure 2: Council automated station results

they give data only when sent in for analysis, and typically this is once every six to eight weeks per tube. The results are aggregated to an annual level prior to publication.

The six automated processing stations, named 'Groundhogs', measure a variety of pollutants, and one also measures temperature and air pressure. Between three and eight readings are taken per hour. After a short delay, the public can access the log; the council occasionally may correct or delete readings from it. Although some of the stations have been operating since 2000, there are a number of gaps in the data logs. In addition, the stations are occasionally moved (usually to help investigate new pollution 'hot spot' concerns).

The council maintains a web site[2] that provides informative descriptions on pollutants commonly found in air, including relevant related images and additional information[3].

Readers (and their students) are invited to visit the latter website and then select 'Station info' (see Figure 2). This page illustrates a very common problem with data sourced from the Internet. The information is presented as textual descriptions, with no obvious way of automatically deriving further information. For example, readers are told that Groundhog1 is at 'Orphanage Road, Firhill' but it would take a human-based Web search to find the geographical location and then further searches to discover the nature of the location (residential or industrial area, proximity to main road, etc).

Tutors may use this to introduce a discussion on why data on the internet is not necessarily considered as *Open Data*. Moreover, if the user clicks on the 'latest data' tab, and then click on any of the Groundhogs (`Groundhog1` is often

[1]http://aces.shu.ac.uk/AirQuality

[2]https://www.sheffield.gov.uk/environment/air-quality/monitoring.html
[3]http://sheffieldairquality.gen2training.co.uk/sheffield/index.html

the best choice), they will notice that navigation to this page is not designed for automation. The user must click on a visual map to select the page. Notice too, that the URL for data pages does not reflect the name of the Groundhog being visited. These issues might be used to lead students to reflect on how, in an age of Internet-sourced data, URLs can and should be designed to allow for automated discovery by data harvesting tools.

The website, however, allows data (of any user-selected range) to be downloaded, in a choice of *PostScript*, *Raw* (i.e. comma separated values) or *Excel* formats. Students should — one 'hog', and one pollution type at a time — download `CSV` files. The Nitrogen Dioxide files (`NO2`) total about 15 MBytes. Downloads may be inspected using a text editor (avoiding Microsoft Notepad, as the `End of Lines` are not compatible), when it can be seen that there are date (`YYMMDD`), time (`HH:MM`) and `NO2` reading, roughly 3 to 8 readings per hour.

3.1 Integration of further data sources

One of the principles of Data Warehousing when used for analytic purposes (as opposed to 'data store housing' for safe custody of data) is to try to give added context to facts, through Dimension descriptors added from other sources.

`Groundhog1` lists temperature and air pressure readings. But other factors may influence pollution formation and/or dispersal as well. Obvious factors are wind strength and humidity. Wind direction is also a factor (a complex one: if the monitor is west of a pollution source then a strong west wind will increase measurement values; if the monitor was directly east of the source, then the same wind would remove the pollution from the area of the monitor).

Detailed historic weather data is commercially valuable, and rarely available for free download. Sheffield is fortunate in having a local enthusiast who had monitored and published readings at five-minute intervals for all the desired measures. Unfortunately the data is published in PDF format, with documents of around 200 pages per month of data. The tool *Bytescout PDF viewer*[4] can be used to extract all pages into one `CVS` file. Readers are requested to contact the data owner —details online— to get permissions to use the data for non-commercial purposes (any commercial use of the data could cause the site to be closed).

3.2 The Data Warehouse, and ETL processes

All data values are then uploaded into a Microsoft SQL Server with Business Intelligence database. This software is free (for academic use) to install from Microsoft Dreamspark[5] onto university teaching systems and student laptops. Alternatively, students can have 150-day free use of the same software from the *Microsoft Azure cloud platform*[6]. *Microsoft Azure* has convenient setup options for *SQL Server Business Intelligence*.

Once the data is loaded into tables on the *SQL Server* it needs to be transformed into formats suitable for data analysis. The case study demonstrates a realistic but manageable number of steps that can be found in many Extract-Transform-Load systems of Data Warehouses (the scripts used for ETL are available).

Tutors can use the ETL process to contrast the Server's menu-driven wizard approach for uploading files into tables, with SQL scripts that do the same tasks. Students are not always aware that SQL has commands that allow for manipulation of database structure (as opposed to manipulation of data values), but quickly start to see the value of relatively short scripts that can be reused across multiple uploads.

More complexity comes from the 'Sheffield Weather Page' data being at five minute frequency, while the Groundhog readings vary between twelve and twenty minute frequencies. Further SQL scripts first summarize the respective Groundhog and the Weather data into hourly readings (taking the means of readings within each hour, except for wind direction where the most frequent wind direction was taken), and then integrate these into a single observations table.

Students should open a second database on the same server, copy the observations table (via a short script command) into it, and create descriptive tables that give informative names and attributes for the Groundhogs, and descriptive category names range limits for each of the weather attributes (for example *dimWindSpeed*: No wind = 0 kph; very light breeze = 1-3 kph, through to strong winds 20 kph and over). A script then creates a data 'Star' based on Kimball's designs [7], with a single Facts table linked to relevant rows in each of the Dimension tables.

Having two databases on the same server, one for ETL data acquisition and preparation, and one for storage of the integrated Star of facts and dimension tables, helps students see for themselves the concept of a Data Staging area as described throughout Kimball's work. Just as Kimball describes, all the messy processes happen, hidden from end-user view, in the Staging area. Clean, usable, subject-structured data is then published to data marts.

3.3 Creation of Data Cube from Data Star

SQL Server with Business Intelligence provides a facility for defining Data Cubes for fast analytic processing. Cubes can source their data directly from the uploaded CVS files, but students quickly appreciate the simplicity of sourcing from the Star created in the previous step. Refreshes in the data values in the Star (or even alterations in the design of the Star) can quickly be pulled through into the Cube.

By default, when used for self-serve reporting (Figure 3) cubes automatically report totals (sums) of data value, aggregated over the user-selected timeframe (or geographic distribution, etc.). For example, selecting `NO2` (Nitrogen Dioxide) would automatically report on the total readings ever, or totals per year, or totals per month, or per day, or even per hour, depending on what date-range the use happened to select. Users usually start at the top level -the most aggregated- and then 'drill down' for more details.

In the current case study the averages of pollution values are much more relevant than the totals. It is a lot easier to compare calendar months of data if an averages are used, as this eliminates that some months are longer than others. Peak values within any selected time frame are also of 'headline' interest, but users need to treat information with caution as a peak may well be caused by a local factor such as a badly tuned lorry or tractor passing upwind of the monitor station).

The 'Calculated Measures' facility of the Data Cube was used to set formulas to report the means of each of the numeric measures. The formula for mean is as simple as 'Sum

---

[4]https://bytescout.com/products/pdfmultitool/index.html
[5]https://www.dreamspark.com
[6]http://azure.microsoft.com

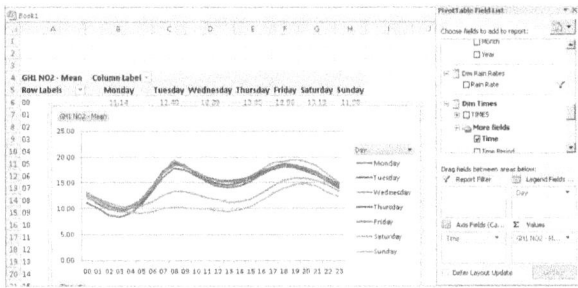

Figure 3: Self-service display of data: Nitrogen Dioxide levels per hour on days of week

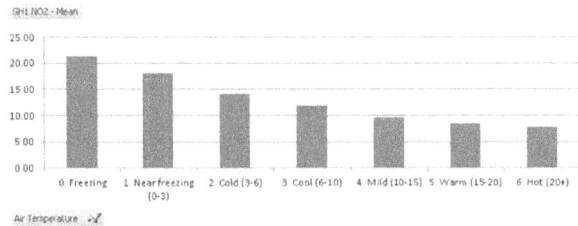

Figure 4: Average NO2 levels for categories of temperature

of NO2 divided by Count of NO2': the cube automatically applies the context of level of drilling for all selected dimensions. Setting up medians is beyond the scope of this simplified case study, but students can discuss how median values can be used to ignore the effect of outlier readings.

Many texts on Data Warehousing utilize Inmon's term of subject-oriented [6]. In simple case studies students often cannot see the difference between the data sources and the DW subject-orientation. One differentiator is that business rules can be encoded into the data or data presentation within the cubes. For NO2 air pollution, 40 mg is a threshold for concern, and 100 mg is a threshold for serious concern. Facilities within the Data Cube were used to encode these levels into colors of presentation. Key Performance Indicators, with 'traffic light' colors and 'trend' arrows could also be set up. The threshold values can usefully be explained to students as examples of Business Metadata, contrasting with Technical Metadata (such as field data types) more often seen in tutorials.

3.4 Self-Service Data Exploration

Microsoft's preferred self-service data exploration tool is Excel. Indeed, a single button click from within the cube development tool will open the cube in Excel. Data is presented via Pivot Tables (readers should note that the Azure cloud platform does not contain Excel. Users can set endpoints to allow their local copy of Excel to link to the cloud server. Alternatively users can simply install 30-day trial copies of Office onto Azure).

Students will very quickly (within minutes) start making discoveries about the data. For example, Fig. 3 shows NO2 pollution levels varying across time for each day of the week.

This image prompted a lot of discussion as to the timing of the apparent peak times for pollution (the effect of driving?) and the clear difference between Saturday and Sunday versus the rest of the week.

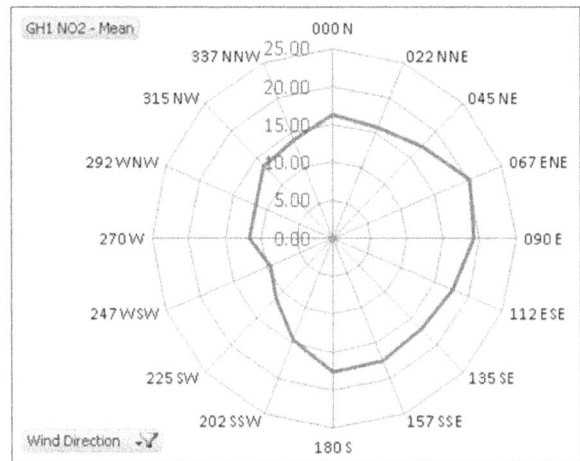

Figure 5: Average NO2 levels for source direction of wind (Groundhog 1 monitor)

It can also be discovered that freezing or near-freezing days are associated with high NO2 pollution levels (Fig. 4), and that low east winds measured by Groundhog1 coincide with worse pollution (Fig. 5).

Students can self-service discover other relationships between the data. Some are obvious (winter months tend to have colder days), but students do get to experience the concept of a data analyst exploring the data themselves. Many students do not know that displays other than line graphs and bar charts are available, and useful discussions can be held about using comparative percentages as a means of spotting patterns or exceptions.

3.5 Data mining

Many students of databases get a few introductory classes on Data Mining, but may not get to build and use a data mining facility for themselves. Having got the pollution and weather data into SQL Server, the same environment can be used to develop mining reports within a few minutes and with no further coding. For example, using the SQL Server Business Intelligence suite, a Clustering algorithm has identified ten clusters of weather data. The darker clusters, for example Cluster 9, contain a high proportion of bad pollution days, while the lighter ones (for example 3 and 6) contain hardly any bad pollution days (Figure 6).

Cluster 9, the cluster with a large proportion of High NO2 readings, can be understood by analyzing the characteristics of the cluster in more detail. An analysis shows that these are low pressure days, high/very high humidity but not actually raining, and cold or near freezing temperatures. In other words: murky, dry winter mornings. More plots are available including Association Rules, Decision Trees, Neural Nets, Regression and Naive Bayes.

The default settings for each of the analysis shown produce interpretable results quickly, then fine-tuning the parameters (controlling the number of clusters, for example) can improve data interpretation. Discussing with students what the parameters do can help students progress to more unsupervised learning. A frequent discussion point is whether Categories can then be fed back into the Data Warehouse, to fine-tune the Dimension attributes.

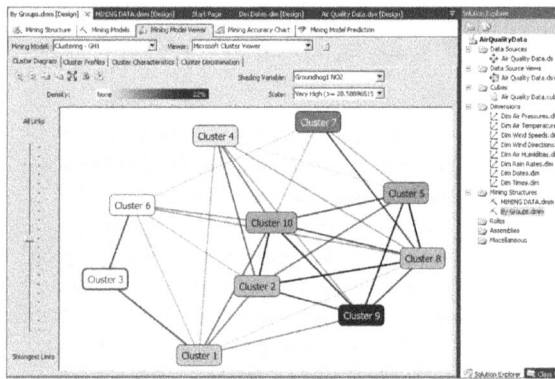

Figure 6: Result of running the Cluster data mining tool

4. EVALUATING NIFTINESS

This case study demonstrates the application of Data Warehousing and Data Mining tools, using data gathered from Internet sources. But it does not fit with the intended nifty assignment criteria straightaway. Let's consider the assignment against the *nifty* criteria:

- **Nifty**. Business intelligence doesn't lend itself easily to the 'game with blinking lights motif'. But the use of a local subject raises the students' interest.

- **Topical**. Most assignments in the nifty repository are about programming in one form or another. This one isn't, and so it may appear to ignore that criterion. However, it supports 'Data Management Systems', one of the core knowledge areas in the ACM computer science curriculum [12]. We would argue that Data Management quality assignments are, in fact, particularly difficult to produce, and that therefore there is a real need to provide examples and ideas in this area.

  It is also expected that the assignment discussed here will provide ideas to broaden the scope of nifty assignments. We could find only one other example of nifty assignment solely intended for Data Management, [3].

- **Scalable**. Frequently, Data Management assignments stay within reach of the 'average' student by radically limiting the scope of the problem and the data to study. One characteristic of this example is that rather than taking conveniently prepared datasets, it proposes to experience some of the common difficulties met by database professionals when collecting data from non-traditional sources.

  The present case study, and online support documentation, is intended so that tutors can use the resources described to give overview presentations of the topic without needing to overcome problematic barriers.

  The case study involves more data than might normally be used for overviews of the subject and is 'rich' enough in content to help highlight genuine issues, but remains sufficiently structured and simple as to not become overwhelming. This introduces and discusses a number of 'real-world' issues, particularly around the Extract-Transform-Load procedures of Data Warehousing, while keeping the study to a scale that is feasible for quick comprehension by students. Largely,

each of the steps can be done by taking default options of off-the-shelf tools, and mistakes in the design can be recovered simply by re-running relevant steps. Of course, there is a risk that students may ignore the alternatives to defaults. However, our experience is that it is very helpful to be able to see the 'end-to-end picture' at a relatively early stage. Better students are then able to revisit the pieces to see their connection with their mainstream database and data analysis studies, and develop a fuller mastery of the tools available.

- **Adoptable**. To make our work *adoptable*, all the tools used and data used, were selected to be available for free use in academic contexts; although note that the weather data could only be used with permission. Links and resources - assignment information, software tools and data are available online

- **Inspirational**. The theme of pollution in our city is one that interests and motivates our own local students. Many raise questions that the data might be of value in relation to public interests such as health or traffic. So the inspirational value of the assignment is in part due to the richness of this data set for local students. This of course will not apply to every potential user of this data.

The last point raises the question whether the ideas developed in this assignment would be adaptable to a wider range of students and of situations. To this end, we will return to the data sources of our assignment and consider whether we can exploit a movement to help increase the availability of public data: Open Data.

5. OPEN DATA: SELF-EVIDENT MATERIAL?

This time, Open Data (according to the *Open Data Handbook* [2], 'data that can be freely used, re-used and redistributed by anyone') provided a valuable case study. It might be expected that the data liberation movement offers many further examples, relevant to the locality and interests of our students at more institutions. As Atenas and Havemann [4] put it, in an educational context, Open Data becomes an Open Educational Resource by very definition.

5.1 How not to assess with Open Data

In practice however, Open Data is not a simple choice. Open data does not become usable for student assessment the moment it is publicly released. We may hope that its availability will lead to insightful analyses and applications; yet that process is anything but self-evident.

The release of Sheffield pollution data on a convenient, clear website is the result of several years lobbying local authorities to engage with liberating data. As part of this process, the *Better with Data Society*[7], a local Open Data group, welcomed students to apply their skills to the data released. The only result has been to show how unsuited that data was to student work. Only one student eventually pursued Open Data, and that was an investigation as to why *Better with Data* was making so little apparent progress!

The pollution data assignment presented above works precisely because a lot of work has been done to identify, cleanse

---

[7]http://betterwithdata.co/

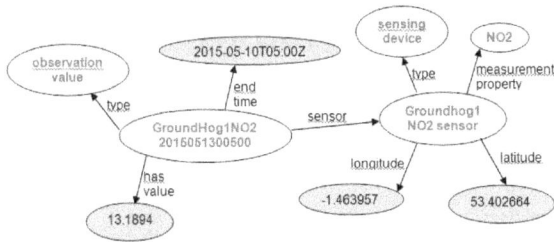

Figure 7: A subset of the *Sheffield Air Quality+* database. Data points in bold text are URIs

and ensure the availability of the data, with the result that the students are proposed a carefully chosen, set of sources, confusing enough to be challenging, yet within reach of the students in the time available.

All this highlights the need for better methods of publishing data for machine discovery and consumption.

5.2 How the Air Pollution assignment was born

Such a better method may form an alternative start for the assignment: to investigate the data in the machine-readable form of linked data. The impetus for the assignment presented here is actually the *Air Quality+* database, which allows over-the-web interrogation of the Sheffield pollution measurements as linked data.

Two of this paper's authors developed *Air Quality+* and an editor for SPARQL queries. The database holds each *Groundhog* and the sensor measurements for the *Groundhog* stations and diffusion tubes. For example, as figure 7 shows, the data about the Groundhog1 NO2 sensor records what it measures, its location, the type of device it is, and actual measured values with their date and time.

Educators interested in linked data could consider accessing the pollution data and sensor information via the the SPARQL editor[8]; this can be a worthwhile prequel to the assignment above. But our choice has been to not offer such a neat, ready-made, machine-readable access to the data for our students, precisely because the journey of discovering a set of open data and struggling to make the data into a usable form, is itself a learning experience.

As Sooriamurthi [13] said of his assignment: "it's not a calendar, it's a journey". Having traveled that journey, the path we map for our students is not shorter, but offers more opportunities for discovery.

6. CONCLUSIONS: NIFTINESS WITH DATA

The assignment discussed in this paper demonstrates the application of Data Warehousing and Data Mining tools, using data gathered from internet sources. Rather than taking conveniently prepared data sets, it shows some of the common difficulties met by database professionals when collecting data from non-traditional sources.

The same difficulties force us to redefine what nifty assignment might mean in a data mining context: the 'fun factor' is difficult to find, but the work of educators is in identifying and preparing data sets appropriate to the level and the interests of the students. At the same time, we show that there is value in not preparing data too carefully, because this is precisely the expertise that students need to develop.

---

[8]http://www.boisvert.me.uk/opendata

Finally, the reader should be aware that the opportunities offered by Open Data with students are not easily realised: providing an assignment which offers both an appropriate challenge for all students and open-ended opportunities for the better ones, requires discovering the data and considering its possibilities in detail before letting students investigate it.

7. REFERENCES

[1] Estimating local mortality burdens associated with particulate air pollution. public health england, 2014. https://www.gov.uk/government/uploads/system/uploads/attachment_data/file/332854/PHE_CRCE_010.pdf. Accessed: 2016-01-12.

[2] Open data handbook. http://opendatahandbook.org/en/what-is-open-data. Accessed: 2016-01-12.

[3] N. F. Angel, N. Young, and A. Dollman. Creating a database from scratch: Smarter solutions, inc. case study: nifty assignment. *Journal of Computing Sciences in Colleges*, 31(2):185–187, 2015.

[4] J. Atenas, L. Havemann, and E. Priego. Open data as open educational resources: Towards transversal skills and global citizenship. *Open Praxis*, 7(4):377–389, 2015.

[5] S. Fincher, M. Kölling, I. Utting, N. Brown, and P. Stevens. Repositories of teaching material and communities of use: nifty assignments and the greenroom. In *Proceedings of the 6th international workshop on Computing education research*, pages 107–114. ACM, 2010.

[6] W. H. Inmon. *Building the data warehouse*. John wiley & sons, 2005.

[7] R. Kimball. *The data warehouse lifecycle toolkit: expert methods for designing, developing, and deploying data warehouses*. John Wiley & Sons, 1998.

[8] L. Layman, L. Williams, and K. Slaten. Note to self: make assignments meaningful. *ACM SIGCSE Bulletin*, 39(1):459–463, 2007.

[9] N. Parlante. Nifty assignments. http://nifty.stanford.edu. Accessed: 2016-01-12.

[10] N. Parlante, J. Popyack, S. Reges, S. Weiss, S. Dexter, C. Gurwitz, J. Zachary, and G. Braught. Nifty assignments. In *ACM SIGCSE Bulletin*, volume 35, pages 353–354. ACM, 2003.

[11] N. Parlante, J. Zelenski, P.-M. Osera, M. Stepp, M. Sherriff, L. Tychonievich, R. Layer, S. J. Matthews, A. Obourn, D. R. Raymond, et al. Nifty assignments. In *Proceedings of the 46th ACM Technical Symposium on Computer Science Education*, pages 673–674. ACM, 2015.

[12] M. Sahami, S. Roach, E. Cuadros-Vargas, and D. Reed. Computer science curriculum 2013: reviewing the strawman report from the acm/ieee-cs task force. In *Proceedings of the 43rd ACM technical symposium on Computer Science Education*, pages 3–4. ACM, 2012.

[13] R. Sooriamurthi. Introducing abstraction and decomposition to novice programmers. In *ACM SIGCSE Bulletin*, volume 41, pages 196–200. ACM, 2009.

Multidisciplinary Minor in Forensics in a Small Liberal Arts University

Aparna Mahadev (CS)
Anne Falke (Chemistry)
Penny Martin (Criminal Justice)
Maura Pavao (Biology)
Worcester State University
Worcester, Massachusetts, USA
+1(508) 929-8715
{amahadev, afalke, pmartin1,
mpavao}@worcester.edu

ABSTRACT

Cyber security is an issue that has become important very quickly and that touches many different disciplines. Yet, many college students in non- technical fields lack the fundamentals of network security, cybercrime, and digital forensics concepts. There are many institutions that offer undergraduate and graduate programs in Forensics and Computer Security and there are many institutions that offer interdisciplinary minors in Forensics Studies. We have developed a multidisciplinary minor in Forensics that brings together the fields of Biology, Chemistry, Criminal Justice and Computer Science. This minor can be completed as a complement to a science or criminal justice degree or as a stand-alone minor. The minor introduces students to the multifaceted nature of criminal investigations. Students will gain knowledge in several disciplines that contribute to the forensic sciences.

Keywords
Digital Forensics; Cyber Security

1. BACKGROUND

Our campus is a liberal arts university with roughly 5500 students and is largely a commuter campus. The Computer Science department has approximately 140 students with 3 full-time faculty members. The department offers a major and a minor in Computer Science. Though we would like to offer a minor in computer security and digital forensics, we lack the manpower to do so.

Forensic evidence is a critical component of criminal investigations. Looking at one of the high-profile cases – the Boston Marathon bombing trial – the prosecutors used biological evidence (blood analysis), chemical evidence (explosive analysis) and computer evidence (cyber exploration of Tsarnaev's computer) in addition to witness testimony. As more and more forensic evidence is admitted in court, the demand for forensic scientists increases. According to Occupational Outlook Handbook, the growth in the field of digital forensics is expected to be 19% per year until 2024. A multidisciplinary minor in forensics will potentially increase the employability of our students. Additionally, students in non-science fields may find a minor in

ITiCSE '16, July 09-13, 2016, Arequipa, Peru
ACM 978-1-4503-4231-5/16/07.
http://dx.doi.org/10.1145/2899415.2925473

forensics provides interesting connections between their general education courses.

2. MOTIVATION

Anecdotal evidence shows that students are interested in learning about computer security related concepts. Implementing a forensics minor will draw students into sciences, or at least provide a context and a multi-disciplinary pathway for taking interesting Computer Science classes [2]. The majority of the courses in the minor will be designed as general education courses, providing a cross-disciplinary focus to student's general education program. Students who complete this minor will be able to: (1) integrate various disciplines as they apply to forensic sciences; (2) Apply scientific methods to analysis of evidence; (3) Make ethical decisions related to forensic science. We hope that students who choose to take CS courses as part of this minor will be drawn to the field and would continue to major or minor in Computer Science.

3. METHODOLOGY

The forensics minor comprises 6 courses with a common core. In addition to the two core courses (*Introduction to Forensics, Evidence Collection and Crime Scene Preservation*), students may take two courses in computer science to complete the minor: *Computer Networking, Security and Databases* and *Digital Forensics*. The minor has a capstone course that integrates knowledge from various disciplines. Students have the option of completing an internship as part of the minor with an opportunity to put learning into practice.

The minor has been approved by our university curriculum committee – the first cohort of students will start the minor in Fall 2016 semester. A faculty coordinator/advisor to be appointed by the provost will be responsible for student advising and course scheduling. The forensics science minor advisory board will be responsible for approving new courses in the minor, preparing marketing material for recruitment and for planning enrichment activities for students in the minor.

4. REFERENCES

[1] http://www.bls.gov/ooh/computer-and-information-technology/home.htm Accessed February 2,2016

[2] https://www.insidehighered.com/news/2016/02/23/liberal-arts-colleges-explore-interdisciplinary-pathways-computer-science Accessed February 25, 2016

Lab Activity Question Queue Software

Durell Bouchard
Roanoke College
bouchard@roanoke.edu

ABSTRACT

Lab activities in computer science courses provide instructors with opportunities to individually tutor students on concepts, problem solving, and techniques. Students who are stuck and in need of this assistance during a lab are sometimes too focused on attracting a lab instructor's attention. This time spent unproductively waiting is a missed opportunity to practice the skills and techniques of getting unstuck. This poster describes software developed for use during lab activities that allows students to put their name in a queue when they have a question. Using the software gives students the ability to focus on their lab activity and practice getting unstuck while waiting for lab instructor assistance.

CCS Concepts

•Applied computing → Interactive learning environments; Computer-assisted instruction;

Keywords

Lab queue; Lab software; Question queue

1. OVERVIEW

For students in introductory computer science courses, active learning activities, like programming labs, have been shown to promote positive learning outcomes [2]. There are many factors that contribute to this including providing opportunities for active learning, targeted tutoring, and developing community [1]. Lab activities also help reduce novice frustration by having an expert, the lab instructor or peer lab assistant, nearby to assist students who are stuck. A student is stuck trying to solve a problem when a misunderstanding of the problem, a concept, or the tools available prevents the student from making progress towards a solution. An expert can tutor students on techniques to get unstuck, such as problem solving, design, debugging, and testing.

At our institution, the recent computer science enrollment boom has led to lab sections of introductory computer science classes filling to or exceeding capacity. An unexpected consequence of this has been that during lab activities students may have to wait longer for instructor assistance. An obvious solution to this would be to hire more lab instructors, but having students wait for help could be advantageous to student learning. If students instantly receive instructor attention when they are stuck, they are given less incentive and opportunity to practice the skill of getting unstuck. However, we have observed that some students do not practice getting unstuck when waiting for instructor assistance. Instead, because the students do not want to wait too long for assistance, they will watch the lab instructors help other students so that they can attract a lab instructor's attention as soon as they are available.

In this poster, we describe lab question queue software developed to reduce the amount of time students invest in actively waiting for instructor attention so that they can better utilize the time to practicing getting unstuck. Students are able to press a button in online lab programming activities that enters their name into an online queue. Lab instructors use mobile phones to view and modify the queue to coordinate helping students in an efficient and fair manner that allows students to focus more on lab activities and increases time spent learning.

The software has been used by different instructors in both CS1 and CS0 classes. Anecdotally, we see fewer students paying attention to lab instructors when waiting for assistance. Some students also report that they find using the question queue software more fair. The queue provides a mechanism through which quieter students can be helped with the same priority as more demanding students. For future work, we would like to collect data on student time utilization, student learning, and student impressions of the software when used in different classes at several institutions. With larger and more diverse testing of the question queue software we hope to show that using it helps students learn how to get unstuck and solve difficult problems.

ITiCSE '16 July 09-13, 2016, Arequipa, Peru

© 2016 Copyright held by the owner/author(s).

ACM ISBN 978-1-4503-4231-5/16/07.

DOI: http://dx.doi.org/10.1145/2899415.2925474

2. REFERENCES

[1] N. Titterton, C. M. Lewis, and M. J. Clancy. Experiences with lab-centric instruction. *Computer Science Education*, 20(2):79–102, 2010.

[2] G. N. Walker. Experimentation in the computer programming lab. In *ACM SIGCSE Bulletin*, volume 36, pages 69–72. ACM, 2004.

Didactical Ideas in Computer Science

Beatriz Rabin
Universidad de la Empresa
Facultad de Ingeniería
bea.rabin@gmail.com

Sylvia da Rosa
Universidad de la República
Instituto de Computación
darosa@fing.edu.uy

ABSTRACT

In this poster, we present new didactical ideas for teaching recursion in introductory programming classes supported by Guy Brousseau's Theory of Situations [1], applying Jean Piaget´s epistemological theory[2]. We analyse students' responses in order to generate new teaching guidelines for this subject, not only in teaching this concept but also to enhance future assessments.

Keywords

Recursion; theory of situations; epistemological theory; computer programming; assessment.

1. INTRODUCTION

The aim of this work is to contribute to computer science education with an approach based on Guy Brousseau's Theory of Situations [1], developed for mathematics education. Taking Piaget´s epistemological theory[2] as its theoretical framework, Brousseau establishes that students produce knowledge by interacting with the environment of a problem and the students´ previous knowledge, without intervention of the teacher. This instance is called an a-didactical situation by Brousseau. In a second instance, termed a didactical situation, the teacher interacts with the students about the results of the a-didactical situation. One of the roles of the teacher then, is to develop appropriate a-didactical and didactical situations.

This special way of teaching recursion was done with all students in a computer programming class, in the second semester of 2015. This topic is mandatory and is followed by the use of inductive structures (lists and trees), that require recursion.

2. METHODS

In this work we present a study about learning recursion, applying Brousseau's main ideas for designing both types of situations. The a-didactical situation consists of several questions and small problems. The students solve the problems; reflect about how they did and why their solutions work (all without the intervention of a teacher). The students work individually.

The aim is to make them aware that:
- ✓ The problem is solved by repeating certain actions (inductive cases).
- ✓ Repetition stops when a special situation is reached (base cases).
- ✓ The objects over which the repeated actions are done change in each repetition (inductive structures).

ITiCSE '16, July 09-13, 2016, Arequipa, Peru
ACM 978-1-4503-4231-5/16/07.
http://dx.doi.org/10.1145/2899415.2925475

3. ANALYSIS

The analysis of the responses of the students provides the material that we use to design didactical situations aimed to help the students in surmounting the difficulties and correcting errors.

In the didactical situation all the solutions are combined to work out the best one. Then, a new a-didactical instance takes place in which the students are asked to solve another problem. This new problem is carefully selected, taking into account all the work done. In previous studies, we have gathered information about students´ behaviour facing new problems. Students tend to use methods that they already have understood, without considering the differences of the new problems. In a new didactic instance, they are helped to transform their knowledge to find new solutions for new problems. That process leads to a higher level of knowledge about the subject. For instance, once the students have found an element in a sorted list using binary search, they attempt to use the same method in any other search lists (sorted or not). The didactical situation helps them transform their knowledge to find other searching algorithms.

4. ASSESSMENT

Students were evaluated with common tests that were already being used with the classical approach to teaching recursion. We can see in students´ answers that they adopt a better understanding of recursion and they use it more easily for solving problems. The intention of this part of the work is two-fold, first to study different kinds of assessment strategies and establish if any adaptations to the existing tests are necessary and second, to study the results of the current students' tests and using a rubric, determine if this kind of assessment was good for this particular subject, and whether the results obtained from the students are as expected or different from other groups.

5. CONCLUSIONS

In conclusion, we have learnt to establish a direct connection between students' existing knowledge and the ways the concept can be introduced in class to help students attain a higher level of knowledge. The design of a-didactical and didactical situations helps us take as a starting point what students do, and encourage them to transform this into formal concepts.

6. REFERENCES

[1] La teoría de las Situaciones Didácticas: un marco para pensar y actuar la enseñanza de la Matemática. Patricia Sadovsky. https://www.fing.edu.uy/grupos/nifcc/material/2015/teoria_situaciones.pdf

[2] La Prise de Conscience, Jean Piaget, Presses Universitaires de France.

Industry Perspectives and the IT2017 Report

Barbara Viola

VioTech Solutions, Inc.
1111 Route 110, Suite 362
Farmingdale, New York 11735 USA
+1.631.630.4640
bviola@viotechsolutions.com

ABSTRACT

The term 'information technology' (IT) has many meanings for various stakeholders and it continues to evolve. This poster presents an overview of industry perspectives as they relate to information technology (IT), and in particular to the IT2017 report. This poster highlights the industry elements as they relate to IT.

1. INTRODUCTION

The field of information technology (IT) has truly developed, matured, and expanded throughout industry. IT professionals apply their skills in a broad range of diverse career sectors that include business, industry, government, services, organizations, and other structured entities that use computers to automate or drive their products or services efficiently.

2. ACADEMIC MYTH

Students who graduate from a four-year university program assume that the baccalaureate degree or a high GPA is a sufficient qualification to attain a position. This understanding is not necessarily true in information technology. In IT and other fields, a successful professional must be a good communicator, a strong team player, and a person with passion to succeed. Hence, having a degree is not sufficient to secure employment.

3. IT SKILLS AND PRACTICE

The poster highlight the skills needed for a practicing IT professional. These include soft skills, communication skills, teamwork skills, and technical skills. Soft skills "the character traits and interpersonal skills that characterize a person's relationships with other people" [Inv1]. By communication skills, we mean "the ability to convey information and ideas effectively" [Col1]. The idea of teamwork is the "cooperative or coordinated effort on the part of a group of persons acting together as a team or in the interests of a common cause" [Dic3]. From an industry perspective, hiring technically competent graduates is important, but with few exceptions, not as important as communication and team skills to ensure a competent hire. If a potential, new, or established employee lacks a particular technical skill, the employer usually allows him or her to enter a set of seminars or training sessions to achieve the missing skill. A survey conducted in 2015 contrasts the

IT skills faculty and industry professionals deem important as shown in the accompanying figure. It is also important to incorporate professional practice into the curriculum because graduates of IT programs will face real-world issues in the workplace such as the needs of employment sectors, the public's demand for high quality products, the increasing number of computing liability cases, and the need for lifelong learning.

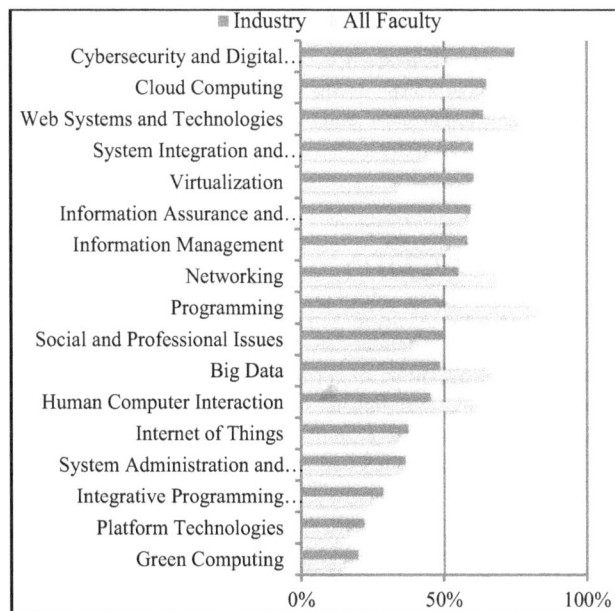

4. IT EXPERIENCE

Technical knowledge, even with the requisite soft, communication, and teamwork skills, may not be sufficient in certain industry environments without prior industry experience. Engaging in an internship or work-study program would not only allow students to gain practical experience, but it might also allow them to gain academic credit. Often, these experiences focus on the practicum and not just passing exams.

5. ACKNOWLEDGMENTS

Thanks go to the other IT2017 task group members. These include Hala Alrumaih, Brenda Byers, John Impagliazzo, Barry Lunt, William Newhouse, William Patterson, Svetlana Peltsverger Mihaela Sabin, Cara Tang, Gerrit van der Veer, Ming Zhang.

6. REFERENCES

[Col1] Collins Dictionary; http://www.collinsdictionary.com/dictionary/english/communication-skills. Accessed 2016 Mar 10.

[Dic3] Dictionary.com; http://dictionary.reference.com/browse/teamwork. Accessed 2016 Mar 10.

[Inv1] Investopedia; http://www.investopedia.com/terms/s/soft-skills.asp. Accessed 2016 Mar 10.

Influence of the Programming Environment on Programming Education

Daisuke Saito
Waseda University
Okubo, Shinjuku-Ku
Tokyo, Japan
d.saito@fuji.waseda.jp

Hironori Washizaki
Waseda University
Okubo, Shinjuku-Ku
Tokyo, Japan
washizaki@waseda.jp

Yoshiaki Fukazawa
Waseda University
Okubo, Shinjuku-Ku
Tokyo, Japan
fukazawa@waseda.jp

ABSTRACT
Although both visual and text environments have been used to teach programming, the most appropriate method for beginners is unknown. Herein we research the most suitable programming environment to introduce programming to beginners using Minecraft to provide different programming learning environments (Visual or Text) via ComputerCraftEdu as an extended function. The learning effects between these two environments are compared using a lecture course. The results show that a visual environment is more suitable to introduce programming to beginners.

Keywords
Programming language learning; Introductory education; Digital game-based learning; Minecraft

1. INTRODUCTION
Recently, programming education has become more important. However, when first learning to program, the programming environment is unfamiliar and must be introduced. This research examines one research question (RQ); "do visual-based and text-based programming environments induce different attitudes toward programming?" This RQ will be useful to optimize the environment for introductory education. We used Minecraft, which is an internationally popular sandbox game. Specifically, we used the ComputerCraftEdu (CCEdu) mod, which has two programming environments: text-based and visual-based (Fig. 1).

Fig. 1, Two programming environments by CCEdu

2. BACKGROUND
Previous works on programming education have used Minecraft [1] [2]. Reference [1], which compared text and visual programming education, found that these methods have similar relationships to programming languages, but their coding environments differ. Although both methods increase motivation, which method is better suited to educate beginning programmers has yet to be revealed. To resolve this, we investigate the effects of the

programming environment on learning by implementing two programming environments using the same format and level of abstraction.

3. EXPERIMENTS
We researched the suitability of two programming environments for introductory education using a comparison experiment. The subjects were 36 students, who were learning to program for the first time. The students were divided into the Visual (G1) and Text (G2) groups, which had 25 and 11 people, respectively. The participants, who ranged in age from 8 to 15 years, were recruited by a public offering. We implemented the same questionnaire on programming attitude before and after the lecture. Based on [1], we used five factors to assess attitude: Interest, Difficulty, Usefulness, Fun and Willingness. Each question was evaluated using a six stages of the Likert scale (1: Strongly disagree, 2: Disagree, 3: Somewhat disagree, 4: Somewhat agree, 5: Agree and 6: Strongly agree).

4. ANALYSIS AND RESULT
To address the RQ, we analyzed the amount of change in the before and after questionnaires using a simple averaged value. After the lecture, both groups showed increased interest, but thought that visual programming was more difficult. This increase in difficulty might be due to the 3D environment. Additionally, both groups felt that the lecture made programming more fun, but the change was statistically insignificant. However, G1 had an increased motivation to learn, whereas G2 did not, suggesting that the attitude toward programming improved for G1. That is, the visual environment is better suited for introductory programming learning. One limitation of our results is the population size. In the future, more experimental data should be accumulated.

5. CONCLUSION
We used the Mod of the ComputerCraftEdu with Minecraft, which adds methods for visual-based programming and text-based programming. Surveys designed to compare the learning effects by method inquired about students' attitudes toward programming. Visual programming had positive significant results with respect to interest and motivation to learn programming. In the future, we intend to survey more students to verify these findings.

6. ACKNOWLEDGMENT
We thank the ICT/Programming school TENTO teachers, MCEdu2015 Organizations Committee member who cooperate with the lecture.

7. REFERENCES
[1] Zorn, C., Wingrave, C. A., Charbonneau, E., & LaViola Jr, J. J, "Exploring Minecraft as a conduit for increasing interest in programming", The 8th International Conference on the Foundations of Digital Games, pp. 352-359, 2013

[2] Wilkinson, B., Williams, N., & Armstrong, P. Improving Student Understanding, Application and Synthesis of Computer Programming Concepts with Minecraft, The European Conference on Technology in the Classroom 2013

Reduction Patterns -
A Practical Tool for Proving Undecidability

Judith Gal-Ezer
The Open University of Israel
University Road 1,
Raanana 4353701, Israel
+972(9)7782244
galezer@openu.ac.il

Mark Trakhtenbrot
Holon Institute of Technology
Golomb St. 52,
Holon 5810201, Israel
+972(3)5026740
markt@hit.ac.il

Keywords

Theory of computation course; undecidable languages; reduction.

1. CHALLENGES IN PROVING UNDECIDABILITY OF LANGUAGES

In the theory of computation, Rice's Theorem states that any nontrivial property of languages recognized by Turing machines (e.g. being a regular language) is undecidable. This is a very general and highly abstract theorem; undergraduate students find it difficult to use it as a practical tool for problem solving.

Reduction, on the other hand, is a core technique that provides a more tangible way to prove that a certain language is undecidable or non-recognizable. However, this technique is based on creative steps such as construction of a mapping between two different languages. Hence, students tend to treat every reduction exercise as a completely new challenge that becomes even more severe when abstract objects such as Turing machines are involved.

2. REDUCTION PATTERNS

We have identified a number of patterns that address a variety of typical reduction problems, and that may be used by students as practical tools for solution of reduction exercises. Every pattern is a kind of "open source"; students can see how the mapping between two languages is defined and analyzed in cases similar to the investigated one, and learn to create such mappings themselves.

3. SAMPLE PATTERNS

In the sample patterns below, $P(s)$ is any computable predicate on words (e.g. "s is a palindrome"), and H_{TM} denotes the halting problem for Turing machines:

$$H_{TM} = \{<M,w> \mid \text{computation of Turing machine } M \text{ on input word } w \text{ terminates}\}$$

Pattern 1. The task is to prove that language L is undecidable:

$$L = \{<M> \mid M \text{ rejects no more than } k \geq 1 \text{ words } s \text{ satisfying } P(s)\}$$

ITiCSE'16, July 09–13, 2016, Arequipa, Peru
ACM 978-1-4503-4231-5/16/07.
http://dx.doi.org/10.1145/2899415.2925478

The proof is by establishing a reduction from H_{TM} to L :

Given $<M,w>$ (input to H_{TM}), a new Turing machine $N(s)$ is constructed (input to L):

$$N(s) \quad \{ \quad \text{if } (s = s_1 \vee s = s_2 \vee ... \vee s = s_k) \\ \text{then REJECT} \\ \text{else } \{ M(w); ACCEPT \} \\ \}$$

It is assumed that there exist at least $k+1$ words $s_1,...,s_{k+1}$ satisfying P (e.g. this is true when there are infinitely many such words). Computability of P is used to actually identify the words $s_1, s_2, ..., s_k$ needed for construction of machine N. Since $<M,w> \in H_{TM}$ if and only if $N \in L$, the described mapping indeed defines a reduction from H_{TM} to L. It is known that H_{TM} is undecidable; hence L is also undecidable.

Pattern 2. The task is to prove that language L is non-recognizable

$$L = \{<M> \mid M \text{ accepts all words } s \text{ satisfying } P(s), \\ \text{and only such words} \}$$

The proof is by establishing a reduction from $\overline{H}_{TM}$ (complement of H_{TM}) to L. Given $<M,w>$ (input to $\overline{H}_{TM}$), a new Turing machine $N(s)$ is constructed (input to L) :

$$N(s) \quad \{ \quad \text{if } P(s) \\ \text{then ACCEPT} \\ \text{else } \{ M(w); ACCEPT \} \\ \}$$

Computability of P is used to ensure that N is indeed a Turing machine. Since $<M,w> \in \overline{H}_{TM}$ if and only if $N \in L$, the described mapping indeed defines a reduction from $\overline{H}_{TM}$ to L. It is known that $\overline{H}_{TM}$ is non-recognizable; hence L is also non-recognizable.

4. OTHER PATTERNS

Other patterns address undecidable or non-recognizable languages that are defined in a similar way, but with different criteria - for example those that are obtained through replacing "rejects" by "accepts" / "terminates on" / "loops on", and/or through replacing "no more than" by "at least" / "all".

5. OBSERVATIONS

Our first experience with reduction patterns showed that they are a good (but of course not universal) practical tool that improves students' ability to cope with the reduction technique and its application in problem solving. Further research will include the gathering and analysis of relevant statistics, allowing the measurement of the degree of that improvement.

UNIXvisual: A Visualization Tool for Teaching the UNIX Permission Model

Man Wang, Jean Mayo,
Ching-Kuang Shene
Michigan Technological
University
{manw, jmayo,
shene}@mtu.edu

Steve Carr
Western Michigan University
steve.carr@wmich.edu

Chaoli Wang
University of Notre Dame
chaoli.wang@nd.edu

ABSTRACT

This paper describes UNIXvisual[1], which helps students learn access control in UNIX. UNIXvisual is aimed both at novice users, who need only to control access to their own files, and students of computer security, who need a deeper and more comprehensive understanding. UNIXvisual allows students to analyze permission settings without the need for a special environment. It allows a student to trace the value and effect of credentials within an executing process. It also provides a mechanism for instructors to give quizzes. UNIXvisual gives instructors flexibility in covering the material by supporting self-study, lowers the overhead required for teaching access control by running under an ordinary user account, and enhances learning by leveraging visualization. UNIXvisual is available for download [1] and runs on the Linux and MacOS platforms.

Categories and Subject Descriptors

k.3.2 [**Computers and Education**]: Computer and Information Science Education—*Computer science education, information systems education*

Keywords

Security, Visualization

1. OVERVIEW

UNIXvisual provides two perspectives on how decisions for granting or denying access to an object are made. It also supports visualization of access-related system calls in C programs to illustrate ideas in secure coding. The Query mode allows users to get answers to commonly-asked ques-

[1]The authors are supported by the National Science Foundation under grants DUE-1140512, DUE-1245310, IIS-1456763, IIS-1455886, and DGE-1523017.

tions and the Quiz mode provides instructors a subsystem to assign quizzes to students.

2. PERSPECTIVES

UNIXvisual provides two main views. The User and Group View allows a user to explore how access decisions are made. The Program Trace View allows a student to monitor process credentials within her running program.

The User and Group View illustrates the access allowed by a user or group through the file permission bits to objects under a user-specified directory. The view is based on permissions in the underlying system together with the permissions defined in a user-written specification file. The visualization includes several windows that demonstrate in detail the determination of access to objects. Objects can be arranged in a radial tree or a standard directory tree hierarchy. The owner, group and other permissions of an object of interest and all its parent directories up to the root directory are listed. The system steps a student from the root directory to the object, identifying in detail how access is determined at each step. The color of an object in the result shows whether the object can be accessed.

The Program Trace View is designed to help students understand initial assignment of credentials to a process, dynamic modification of credentials, and the effect of these credentials on an access request. This view allows the import of a custom C program and tracks process credentials across access control-related system calls, like open, fork, setresuid, read, write, etc. Different colors are used to indicate whether a call has been successful. A change of ID is highlighted as a hint for students to review the program for adherence to the principle of least privilege.

3. QUERY AND QUIZ

The Query mode includes a list of commonly-asked questions on the UNIX permission model. Animation is available to guide students through each step to the final answers. The Quiz mode provides an interactive environment for conducting quizzes. Text-based and visualization-based questions can be asked. Instructors can freely design the question file to accommodate their own teaching goals.

4. REFERENCES

[1] M. Wang, J. Mayo, C.-K. Shene, S. Carr, and C. Wang. UNIXvisual home page. http://acv.cs.mtu.edu/UNIXvisual.html.

ACM Undergraduate Curricular Guidance in Computer Science: The First Two Years

Cara Tang
Portland Community College
12000 SW 49th Avenue
Portland, OR USA
+1 971 722 4447
cara.tang@pcc.edu

Elizabeth K. Hawthorne
Union County College
1033 Springfield Avenue
Cranford, NJ USA
+1 908 510 5148
hawthorne@ucc.edu

Cindy S. Tucker
Bluegrass Comm. & Tech. College
500 Newtown Pike
Lexington, KY USA
+1 859 246 4634
cindy.tucker@kctcs.edu

ABSTRACT

Under the auspices of the ACM Education Board, the Committee for Computing Education in Community Colleges (CCECC) is updating the 2009 ACM associate-degree curricular guidance in computer science with inclusion of contemporary cybersecurity concepts. The CCECC convened a task force of community college educators to develop the initial draft of the updated guidance, called StrawDog, using CS2013 as a starting point. CS2013 includes a new knowledge unit on information assurance and security. To inform the work, a survey on CS2013 foundational knowledge deemed appropriate for the first two years of a computer science (CS) education was administered to a global audience of CS educators. Preliminary survey results are presented for feedback and critique by the international community.

CCS Concepts

• Social and professional topics~Model curricula   • Social and professional topics~Computer science education

Keywords

Junior College; Community College; Two-Year College; Technical School; Computer Science Education; Cybersecurity; Curriculum

1. BACKGROUND

Several driving factors motivated the ACM CCECC to update the *Computing Curricula 2009: Guidelines for Associate-Degree Transfer Curriculum in Computer Science* [2]: 1) the dated 2009 guidance; 2) the release of *ACM Computer Science Curricula 2013 for undergraduate programs* (CS2013) [1]; 3) tremendous need expressed by community college educators during a SIGCSE 2015 BoF session; 4) a projected multi-year global cybersecurity workforce shortfall [4], and 5) a top U.S. priority to build a highly capable cybersecurity workforce including computer science professionals [3].

The ACM CCECC formed a CS-Cyber task force in 2015 to update the 2009 associate-degree computer science guidance with infused cybersecurity concepts. The CCECC and the task force hosted community engagement workshops and administered a survey to capture input from an international audience of computer science and cybersecurity educators to create StrawDog. The survey collected recommendations of CS2013 foundational knowledge appropriate for the first two years of a computer science degree.

ITiCSE '16, July 09-13, 2016, Arequipa, Peru
ACM 978-1-4503-4231-5/16/07.
http://dx.doi.org/10.1145/2899415.2925480

2. CURRENT WORK

The *ACM Undergraduate Curricular Guidance in Computer Science: The First Two Years* poster provides an overview of the initial draft of the updated associate-degree curricular guidance in computer science with infused cybersecurity concepts. It reflects a summary of the CS 2013 knowledge unit survey, cybersecurity concepts, and provides sample learning outcomes and assessment metrics. The poster presents the following information:

(1) *Global input was solicited for StrawDog.* The survey was completed by educators in Australia, China, the United Kingdom, Peru, and the United States from institutions offering associate and baccalaureate degrees.

(2) *Portions of 15 of 18 CS2013 Knowledge Areas (KAs) are appropriately taught, at some level, in the first two years of computer science.* Three CS2013 KAs, Intelligent Systems, Platform-based Development, and Parallel and Distributed Computing, are not reflected in StrawDog.

(3) *Contemporary cybersecurity learning outcomes are included in StrawDog.* Faculty specialists in cybersecurity drafted these learning outcomes.

(4) *Sample learning outcomes and rubrics are illustrated.* The poster provides examples of computer science and cybersecurity learning outcomes and rubrics.

3. FOLLOW-ON OPPORTUNITIES

StrawDog is available for public review and critique by the global computing education community. Feedback from this review and the poster presentation will be collected and used to revise StrawDog producing a second draft, IronDog, which will also be released for public review and comment. If you are interested in reviewing StrawDog or IronDog or providing an exemplar for the curricular guidance, send a message to acm.ccecc@ccecc.acm.org. The final updated guidelines for associate-degree transfer curriculum in computer science are anticipated for release in 2017.

4. REFERENCES

[1] Association for Computing Machinery and IEEE Computer Society. *Computer Science Curricula 2013.* ACM, New York, NY. 2013.

[2] Hawthorne, E. et al. *Computing Curricula 2009: Guidelines for Associate-Degree Transfer Curriculum in Computer Science.* ACM, New York, NY. 2009.

[3] National Initiative for Cybersecurity Careers and Studies. *Draft National Cybersecurity Workforce Framework Version 2.0.* https://niccs.us-cert.gov/research/draft-national-cybersecurity-workforce-framework-version-20. Accessed February 2016.

[4] Suby, Michael. *The 2015 (ISC)² Global Information Security Workforce Study.* Frost and Sullivan. 2015.

Learning MMIX in Secondary School Through Conjecture, Critique, and Experimentation

Emma H. Wong
Carmel Institute
Carmel-by-the-Sea,CA USA
emma@carmelinstitute.org

Steven H. Hassani
Carmel Institute
Carmel-by-the-Sea, CA USA
steven@carmelinstitute.org

ABSTRACT

We report the early stages of our effort to introduce the mythical MMIX computer described in *The Art of Computer Programming* in an initial computer science course for secondary school students. Rather than starting students with a rigorous mathematical specification of the machine, we instead introduce an approach by which students conjecture their own explanations of machine instructions, and critique their explanations using experimentation. Students iteratively improve their explanations over time. When explanations reach a certain level of specificity, students are introduced to the mathematics required to describe the MMIX machine. Our preliminary work suggests that, when taught in this way, *The Art of Computer Programming* can be made both accessible and exciting to secondary school students without sacrificing rigor.

Keywords

K-12 education; Computer architecture.

1. INTRODUCTION

Like many educators, we have found that introducing students to high level programming often kindles interest in computer science. Yet, we have also observed that the majority of our students at the secondary school level express a desire to understand computing at a low level while they continue their high level course of study. High level programming sparks questions that only low level programming can address.

To address student interests, we have begun to teach low level programming using the mythical MMIX machine introduced in *The Art of Computer Programming* [2]. Often considered unsuitable for introductory courses, due to its presumed mathematical difficulty, we have found in our preliminary results that the book is perfectly appropriate for beginning students, if taught in a particular fashion.

Unlike other scientific fields of inquiry involving mathematical descriptions in which experimentation is relatively expensive, experimentation using the MMIX simulator is easy to conduct. Our approach leads students through a number of steps before they are ever expected to fully understand a mathematical description. First, students are assigned exercises to facilitate experimentation with various machine instructions using the MMIX simulator. Second, students are encouraged to offer explanations of machine features that are consistent with their experiments. While these early explanations are often loose, they provide a degree of working knowledge necessary for students to successfully use machine instructions for basic programming tasks. Third, students are encouraged to conduct further experiments in the simulator, which are designed to provide them with the opportunity to critique and test their early explanations. Fourth, students are asked to construct better explanations of the machine, given their findings.

Only after their explanations become sufficiently precise do we then encourage students to use the mathematical formalism in *The Art of Computer Programming* to describe their theories of the machine. We have observed that students tend to welcome the introduction of mathematical formalism at this point, because they find it provides a concise specification of the particular aspect of the MMIX machine they wish to describe.

The direct contribution of this pedagogical approach to computer science education is to make low level programming accessible, without compromising rigor and formality. Our students come away from their work with the MMIX machine with a deep appreciation for the benefits of formal modeling. Ultimately, this approach provides an excellent vehicle for introducing students to the very essence of science: conjecture, critique, and experimentation [1, 3].

2. REFERENCES

[1] D. Deutsch. *The Beginning of Infinity: Explanations That Transform the World.* Penguin, New York, 2012.

[2] D. Knuth. *The Art of Computer Programming, Volume 1, Fasicle 1: MMIX – A RISC Computer for the New Millennium.* Addison-Wesley Professional, Upper Saddle River, New Jersey, 2005.

[3] K. Popper. *Conjectures and Refutations: The Growth of Scientific Knowledge.* Routledge, New York, 2002.

ITiCSE '16 July 09-13, 2016, Arequipa, Peru

© 2016 Copyright held by the owner/author(s).

ACM ISBN 978-1-4503-4231-5/16/07.

DOI: http://dx.doi.org/10.1145/2899415.2925481

Challenges of Introducing Computer Science into the Traditional Grammar of K-12 Schooling

Maria Emilia Echeveste
Universidad Nacional de Cordoba
Medina Allende s/n
CONICET Argentina
meecheveste@gmail.com

ABSTRACT

Introducing CS (Computer Science) programming into the mandatory school curriculum, requires considering the effects and implications of adding a subject area with its own learning characteristics and dynamics into the preexisting and rigid structure of schooling. Based on classroom observations, this poster presents four classroom dynamics that resulted from introducing CS teaching into regular schools: 1) heterogeneous grouping 2) learning from practice 3) flexible blocks of times 4) inclusion of special ed. students. We argue these dynamics challenge the traditional school.

1. INTRODUCTION

There are some deep rooted regulations of the school organization. These rules have been identified as the "grammar of schools" [1]. The school grammar is characterized (among other traits) by: a division of knowledge into fragmented subject areas, the organization of time in short 80 minutes blocks, and homogeneous grouping of students. Teaching and learning programming requires classrooms dynamics that challenge the traditional grammar of schools. For example, most programming platforms provide immediate feedback to the programmer on their coding skills. In contrast, the majority of teachers provide summative assessments days after the activity was completed. Working hours are flexible for programmers who need to be on task uninterrupted. In opposition, school schedule forces students to change subjects every aproximately one hour.

Piloting CS programming teaching experiences in regular schools together with teachers during 2014 and 2015, we collected 47 primary and secondary school classroom observations in 26 schools that participated in a University program to introduce the teaching of CS in K-12 education. This poster presents emerging findings from these experiences.

2. PREVIOUS WORK

Following Cuban [2] in spite of great investment into computer technology in schools, teachers and students underused this technology because of the rigid grammar of schooling.

Cuban has studied creative mixes of the old and the new ways of teaching in schools and classrooms. The author argues that these hybrids of teacher-centered and student-centered instruction are the leading edge of a movement that will bring schools more in sync with the ways the larger society produce knowledge.

Heterogeneous teams that value differences, flexible working time, and encouragement of experimentation characterized today's work organization. Following Cuban's perspective, this poster presents findings on programming teaching experiences that represent a change in the traditional grammar of schooling.

3. FINDINGS

Based on lesson observations, we identified four innovative classroom dynamics where teachers and students are learning programming in regular schools. 1) Heterogeneous student grouping 2) learning CS concepts from practical knowledge 3) flexible and longer blocks of time where students remained on task, and 4) effective inclusion of special needs students.

The poster will describe each of the emerging themes and will present classroom observations excerpts as evidence. For example, in one fragment related to learning CS concepts from practical experience a tutor documented:

"*Sometimes I approached a group to see what the programming problem was and students told me: We already tried this and this, and this is the error we get. We checked for configuration, we checked for the code, but the robot is doing a different thing rather than what we coded for (Tutor in a Secondary School).*" This excerpt showed how programming a robot; contributed to students learning different programming commands.

On regards to heterogeneous groups an observation documented:

"*The teachers placed 2nd and 3rd grade together. Since the students from 2nd grade had already learned some programming, they played the role of teaching the 3er grade students*"

Besides participating teachers grouping students heterogeneously, we noticed that students labeled as special ed worked steadily on programming tasks performing sometimes better then their peers. In addition, most students systematically chose to skip breaks. These data indicates that teaching and learning programming could challenge the traditional grammar of schooling.

4. CONCLUSIONS

CS teaching and learning promoted teacher change in their pedagogical decisions and practices. Documenting what CS education can change in the classrooms, is important to inform research, educational programs, and policy makers on the effects of introducing CS in regular schools.

REFERENCES

[1]   D. Tyack and W. Tobin. The "Grammar" of schooling: Why has it
       been so hard to change? American Educational Research
       Journal, 31(3):453–479, 1994.

[2]   L. Cuban. Computers meet classroom: Classroom wins.
       The Teachers College Record, 95(2):185–210, 1993.

ITiCSE '16, July 09-13, 2016, Arequipa, Peru
ACM 978-1-4503-4231-5/16/07.
http://dx.doi.org/10.1145/2899415.2925482

Comparing Topics in CS Syllabus with Topics in CS Research

Julio Santisteban
Universidad Católica San Pablo
Arequipa, Peru
jsantisteban@ucsp.edu.pe

Danet Delgado-Castillo
Universidad Católica San Pablo
Arequipa, Peru
danet.delgado@ucsp.edu.pe

ABSTRACT

This study quantifies and compares the computer security themes found in the ACM Computer Science curricula with the themes addressed in top-ranked computer security research conferences over the past six years. On the understanding that current research should help set the agenda for course coverage, we use a strategic diagram to compare the research topics with the curriculum topics and identify specific future directions for the ACM CS curriculum and for computer security courses.

1. MOTIVATION

Computer Science is evolving rapidly, and the ACM CS curricula [1] will always lag somewhat behind the latest developments in various fields. Our objective is to analyze whether the computing security syllabus in the ACM curricula is in line with recent developments in the area.

2. METHOD

Examining the top computer security conferences according to the Qualis CAPES ranking [3], we identified 1,983 articles published between 2010 and 2015. From the abstracts of these articles we constructed and clustered an n-gram graph model, using the Leacock Chodorow measure to find keywords for the n-grams. Topics were then identified using paradigmatic clustering [4]. Thirty clusters were found and their centrality and density were calculated along with their average scores. These clusters were plotted on a strategic diagram [2], which plots density against centrality with the size of each bubble representing the combined frequency of the words in the cluster. The same process was applied to the keywords from the ACM CS computer security curricula, and the clusters plotted on the same graph (Figure 1). Topics on the strategic diagram fall into four quadrants [2]: motor or mainstream topics (top right); developed but isolated topics (top left); emerging or declining topics (bottom left); and basic and transversal topics (bottom right).

3. DISCUSSION

Figure 1 shows clusters from the research articles as light blue bubbles and clusters from the curricula as light red bub-

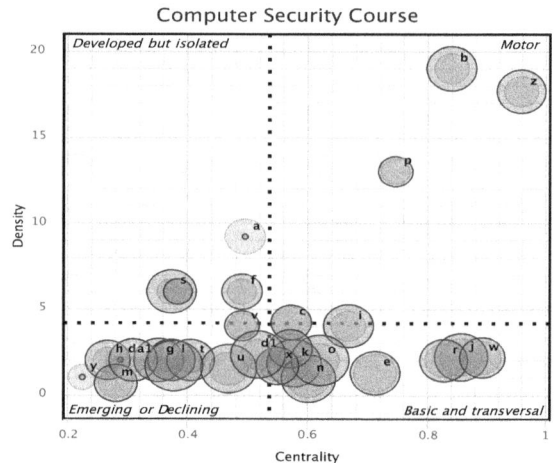

Figure 1: Strategic Diagram for Computer Science Topics

bles. Most of the research topics are transversal and emerging topics, as would be expected in an area that is evolving rapidly. Fewer research topics are found in the mainstream or motor quadrant, as research is seldom focused on the mainstream.

Most research clusters overlap with corresponding syllabus clusters, but there are three clear exceptions. Cluster *a* relates to *android* and *mobile programming*, which was not a major issue when the 2013 curricula were developed. Cluster *d* relates to *accuracy* and *data collection*, which appears to be a specialized research topic. Cluster *y* relates to *attack scenario* and *attack vector*, which is a declining topic as shown by its location on the far left bottom of the graph. This research will help educators to reorganize and reorient their curricula to follow cutting edge research. Current work includes comparison of the syllabus from prestigious universities with the relevant research topics.

4. REFERENCES

[1] ACM/IEEE-CS Joint Task Force on Computing Curricula. Computer science curricula 2013. Technical report, ACM Press and IEEE Computer Society Press, December 2013.

[2] T. Cahlik. Comparison of the maps of science. *Scientometrics*, 49(3):373–387, 2000.

[3] C. de Aperfeiçoamento de Pessoal de Nível Superior. http://www.capes.gov.br/. 2016 (acccessed Abril 15, 2016).

[4] J. Santisteban and J. Tejada-Carcamo. Paradigmatic clustering for nlp. In *2015 IEEE International Conference on Data Mining Workshop (ICDMW)*, pages 814–820, Nov 2015.

RoBlock: Programming Learning with Mobile Robotics

Pedro G. Feijóo
Systems and Computing Engineering Department
Universidad de los Andes, Colombia
pg.feijoo113@uniandes.edu.co

Fernando De la Rosa
Systems and Computing Engineering Department
Universidad de los Andes, Colombia
fde@uniandes.edu.co

ABSTRACT

One of the major challenges related to teaching programming and algorithms to novice students is the time spent on the language's syntax and how their attention is incorrectly focused on the syntax rather than the acquisition of concepts and the development of problem-solving and programming skills. This study focuses on the design and evaluation of a Web App (RoBlock) designed for autodidactic learning. It uses Visual Blocks Programming, and contains six interactive modules that cover programming concepts. The solution is presented as virtual scenarios for Mobile Robotics.

RoBlock is structured as a multi-layered architecture, delegating tasks and activities to specific software components. It was deployed in a hybrid manner, with the main system of Virtual Scenarios in Heroku as Cloud platform, and the Remote Laboratory sub-system in a local server configured at the laboratory. The GUI is user-friendly, designed for usability and interaction. It presents video-tutorials designed for self-learning.

Forty six novice Colombian students, divided in two groups, participated in the study of RoBlock. Experimental group students used RoBlock while control group students used Scratch [1]. They had to work on four modules: Variables, sensors and conditionals, cycles and iterations, and functions. They were evaluated before and after every session. Four experimental indexes were used to measure knowledge appropriation and software impact in every student during the study. In addition, students who worked with RoBlock were asked to fill out a quality assessment survey, which included questions on positive and negative aspects of the tool. The complete study consisted of five hours of experimental interaction, due to time limitations at the institutions that collaborated on the study.

The results on all four experimental indexes were satisfactory. The group exposed to RoBlock reported between 15% and 23% improvement in knowledge acquisition through all the modules (Figure 1). On the quality assessment survey (Figure 2), the students indicated that the designed application was interesting, friendly, and appropriate for autodidactic learning. At the end, the difference between RoBlock and Scratch groups was close, under 5% for the Global Index designed (Knowledge acquisition per module), showing that RoBlock offers an interesting learning environment. This is especially relevant since Scratch is the Visual Blocks Programming Tool most used at Colombian schools.

ITiCSE'16, July 09-13, 2016, Arequipa, Peru
ACM 978-1-4503-4231-5/16/07.
http://dx.doi.org/10.1145/2899415.2925484

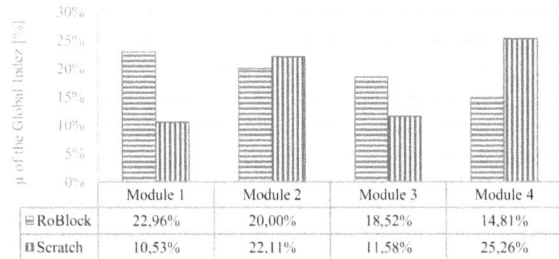

Figure 1. Results obtained for the Global Index per Module

	Module 1	Module 2	Module 3	Module 4
RoBlock	22,96%	20,00%	18,52%	14,81%
Scratch	10,53%	22,11%	11,58%	25,26%

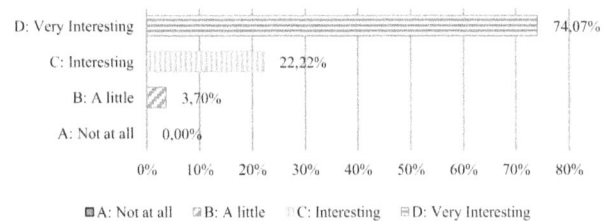

Figure 2. Quality Assessment Report

Even though the experimental time was short and some exercises were hard, this pilot study showed that it is possible for high school students to learn algorithms and programming concepts by using an autodidactic and scalable tool. The results obtained were successful, and we expect to extend this study in multiple ways.

There are several possibilities to evolve and extend this project, having shown that RoBlock fulfills the purpose for which it was designed: the tool could be improved, and so could the experimental methodology used, editing and adjusting the schema that was incorporated and followed within this first iteration.

Keywords

Interactive Learning; Visual Blocks Programming; E-Learning; Mobile Robotics; Web-based Technology.

REFERENCES

[1] Maloney, J., Resnick, M., Rusk, N., Silverman, B., and Eastmond, E. 2010. The Scratch programming language and environment. *ACM Transactions on Computing Education*, 10, 4, Article 16 (November 2010). DOI= http://dx.doi.org/10.1145/1868358.1868363

Broader and Earlier Access to Machine Learning

Thomas Way, Lillian Cassel, Paula Matuszek,
Mary-Angela Papalaskari, Divya Bonagiri and Aravinda Gaddam
Villanova University
800 Lancaster Avenue
Villanova, PA 19803, USA
+1 610-519-7307
thomas.way@villanova.edu

ABSTRACT

This poster presents the results of an ongoing project that has developed learning modules to provide access to the tools and techniques associated with machine learning to a broad category of undergraduate students. The changing nature of science and its reliance on massive data sets has led to the integral use of machine learning approaches in just about every discipline. Recognizing this shift, flexible teaching materials have been developed to provide educators and students in a wide variety of academic fields with relevant machine learning topics and discipline-ready activities. Goals, module design, example material, dissemination plans and evidence of student learning are presented.

CCS Concepts

• **Computing methodologies→ Machine learning • Social and professional topics→ Professional topics→ Education→ Digital libraries and archives.**

Keywords

Machine learning modules; Big data; Computer science education.

1. INTRODUCTION & GOALS

In this age of Big Data, the nature of science is changing [3] and machine learning is becoming an integral part of how science (and just about everything else) is done. The typical undergraduate is unlikely to see any introduction to machine learning though all can benefit [1]. This project addresses the need for broadly accessible machine learning content across the spectrum of disciplines.

The goals of the project are threefold: (1) identify machine learning topics and relevant presentation techniques for undergraduates and faculty across disciplines, (2) produce stand-alone modules that can be adapted for learning in a variety of fields, and (3) disseminate the knowledge to a wide audience.

2. RESULTS

To support broader and easier access to machine learning, we devised a structure for educational modules consisting of: a one page topic summary and lesson plan for an instructor, slides and accompanying notes, student learning exercises targeted to the topic, appropriate software tools for the topic, other resources as needed such as references, videos, visualizations and URLs.

For example, the starter module "Introduction to Classification and Clustering" can be done in half of a class meeting and consists of a summary, lesson plan, hands-on activity, slides, and a quiz. The more involved "Support Vector Machines" module assumes prior module experience and also includes data sets applicable to multiple disciplines and a tutorial for the popular and free WEKA software (www.cs.waikato.ac.nz/~ml/weka) to explore the topic using the provided data.

Modules are available, or in progress, for ten topics. Some are introductory and require no previous experience while others expect one or more of the other modules as background. Modules include: **Introduction to Machine Learning** (fundamental definitions, experimenting with the "Animal Game", prerequisite module for all others), **Classification and Clustering** (definitions, unplugged and paper-based activities, minimal slides), **Using WEKA** (illustrated step-by-step instructions on installation and basic use), **Evaluating Classifiers** (WEKA activities), **Decision Trees** (discussion, WEKA), **Naive Bayes** (paper-based and Python program-based activities), **Neural Networks** (WEKA or Simbrain activities), **Support Vector Machines (SVMs)** (slides, WEKA, data sets), **Dimensionality Reduction** (slides, hands-on activities), and **K Means Clustering** (WEKA or Python-based activities).

Module content is being disseminated via ComputingPortal.org, a digital archive created as part of the Ensemble Project [2]. The content is organized hierarchically with elements available for individual download or as a zipped package. Discipline-specific data sets are being gathered to cover a wide variety of relevancy.

Results of pre- and post-test evaluations of the Introduction to Classification and Clustering module were given two successive semesters and show that student understanding improved from 20% on the pre-test to 90% on the post-test. Follow-up discussions during class made it clear that students understood the concepts as well as the distinctions between the techniques.

3. ACKNOWLEDGMENTS

This project is funded in part by NSF DUE award 1141033. Thanks to Carol Weiss for assistance with learning measure design.

4. REFERENCES

[1] Domingos, P. "The Master Algorithm: How the Quest for the Ultimate Learning Machine Will Remake Our World." Basic Books, New York, NY, 2015.

[2] Hislop, Gregory W., et al. "Ensemble: creating a national digital library for computing education." Proceedings of the 10th ACM conference on SIG-information technology education. ACM, 2009.

[3] Tansley, S, and Tolle, K. M., eds. The fourth paradigm: data-intensive scientific discovery. Vol. 1. Redmond, WA: Microsoft Research, 2009.

A Parallel, Conjoined Approach to Interdisciplinary Computer Science Education

Thomas Way[1] and Seth Whidden[2]
Villanova University
Departments of [1]Computing Sciences and [2]Romance Languages & Literatures
800 Lancaster Avenue
Villanova, PA 19803, USA
+1 610-519-7307
thomas.way@villanova.edu

ABSTRACT

This poster presents the results of two full cycles of a novel approach to Computer Science education that simplifies many of the pedagogical, organizational and administrative challenges in reaching across disciplines. We introduce a *parallel, conjoined* approach to constructing interdisciplinary offerings between Computer Science and a wide variety of other disciplines in a loosely-coupled fashion. Cooperating courses run simultaneously in nearby classrooms and meet together to collaborate numerous times during a semester. We describe our approach, lessons learned, results of evaluations of the effectiveness of the approach, and ideas for replicating the approach in other disciplines and institutions.

CCS Concepts

• **Social and professional topics**→ **Computing education**→ **Computational thinking** • **Applied Computing**→ **Education**→ **Collaborative learning.**

Keywords

Interdisciplinary courses; distributed expertise; machine translation; natural language processing; writing; stylistics.

1. INTRODUCTION

The breathtaking pace of change in computing and technology, and its widespread adoption in virtually every human endeavor, has led us to the dawn of a never before seen era of interdisciplinarity where some understanding of computing is necessary to be an active member of society [2]. Many barriers exist within the academic world including siloed specialization, disciplinary differences to teaching and learning, differing emphasis on interdisciplinarity, and a host of institutional, administrative and logistic issues. Traditional approaches to interdisciplinary education often involve a merging of subjects into a single course, with two or more faculty members collaborating on the content, design and offering. Faculty can find the effort fulfilling, but also labor intensive and cumbersome. Administrators find the idea compelling, but wrestle with designating course categories, justifying faculty expenditures and assigning teaching credit. [1]

2. APPROACH

Our parallel, conjoined approach to interdisciplinary course design that uses a loosely-coupled structure [3] contrasts with the more common tightly-coupled approach as we rely on collaborating instructors offering simultaneous courses in nearby classrooms. After two successful iterations (and a third planned for Fall 2016) of collaboratively teaching previously independent offerings of *Machine Translation* (Computer Science) and *Writing and Stylistics in French* (French), we are confident this approach addresses many concerns regarding interdisciplinary computer science education pairings.

We first identified a desire to collaborate across disciplines and identified two courses that had cross-over potential. Prior to our offering, we identified seven to ten "join points" for our classes to meet and collaborate on learning and projects. The French course involved literature analysis and the Computer Science course devised tools and techniques for analyzing and transforming language, including ways that would benefit project goals of the French students. The courses met on the same days and times in adjacent classrooms. Departmental and college level buy-in was easy, as previous outcomes and objective for both courses remained in effect. Combined activities included accessible lecture materials from both disciplines, demonstrations of language analysis software by Computer Science students, descriptions of analysis goals by French students, and sessions where cross-discipline, team worked together to design, create and use software tools.

A measure of learning effectiveness and ample anecdotal evidence support the merits of our approach. Students and faculty report increased contextual and cross-disciplinary understanding. Benefits, lessons learned and future plans for implementation with other non-Computer Science disciplines are presented.

3. ACKNOWLEDGMENTS

This project was funded in part by NSF CPATH award IS-0829616 and a VITAL institutional course development grant.

4. REFERENCES

[1] Lori Carter. "Interdisciplinary computing classes: worth the effort." SIGCSE Technical Symposium (SIGCSE 2014), pp. 445-450, 2014.

[2] Lillian N. Cassel. "Interdisciplinary computing is the answer: now, what was the question?" ACM Inroads, vol. 2, no. 1, pp. 4-6, March 2011.

[3] Thomas Way and Seth Whidden. "A Loosely-Coupled Approach to Interdisciplinary Computer Science Education." Frontiers in Education: Computer Science and Computer Engineering, Las Vegas, Nevada, July, 2014.

A Web-Based Environment for Introductory Programming based on a Bi-Directional Layered Notional Machine

Li Sui
Massey University Palmerston
North, New Zealand
leesui0207@gmail.com

Jens Dietrich
Massey University Palmerston
North, New Zealand
j.b.dietrich@massey.ac.nz

Eva Heinrich
Massey University Palmerston
North, New Zealand
e.heinrich@massey.ac.nz

Manfred Meyer
Westphalian University of
Applied Sciences, Bocholt,Germany
manfred.meyer@w-hs.de

We present a novel browser-based environment to teach introductory programming. This platform combines gamification with peer-to-peer interaction. Students write programs (bots) that play simple board games on their behalf, and can exercise these bots by playing against the bots developed by their peers.

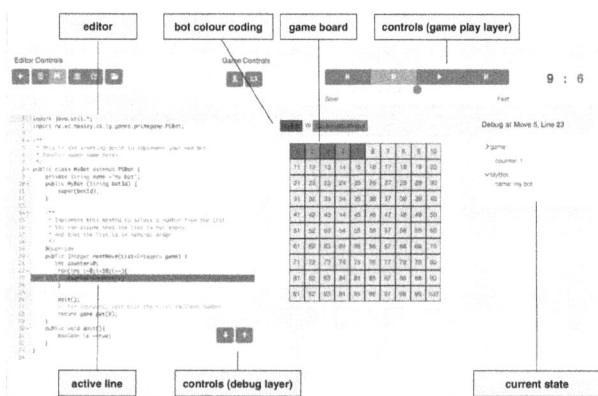

Figure 1: The debugger interface

The proof-of-concept implementation is based on the SoGaCo platform [1] and the PrimeGame using Java as the programming language. The PrimeGame is a turn-based game for two players on a simple board of natural numbers from which players take one number with each move while the opponent gets all its remaining factors - until all numbers are taken. The focus on board games facilitates a user interface design centred around a simple notional machine. This machine is based on the visualisation and the terminology of the board game used, displaying game states after each turn

---

[1] J. Dietrich, J. Tandler, L. Sui, and M. Meyer. The Primegame Revolutions: A cloud-based collaborative environment for teaching introductory programming. In *Proceedings ASWEC'15*. ACM, 2015.

ITiCSE '16 July 09-13, 2016, Arequipa, Peru

© 2016 Copyright held by the owner/author(s).

ACM ISBN 978-1-4503-4231-5/16/07.

DOI: http://dx.doi.org/10.1145/2899415.2925487

computed by a bot. This supports the student in understanding the semantics of the program developed. However, using only a visualisation of the board game is not sufficient as students also need to understand the program states (bot debugging layer) that lead to game states (game play layer).

The user interface (figure 1) provides unique tracing features based on a bi-directional layered notional machine. Students can seamlessly switch between levels and freely step forwards and backwards in either of two connected notional machines, one at game level, one at program level, allowing them to shift focus and repeat single steps as often as required to form understanding.

A critical feature is how state is represented and encoded (figure 2). The execution of a game consists of a series of invocations of the move(..) method to compute the next turn. The method itself performs multiple byte code instructions. After each instruction that alters state, a memory snapshot is created via instrumentation. This snapshot includes the stack and parts of the heap.

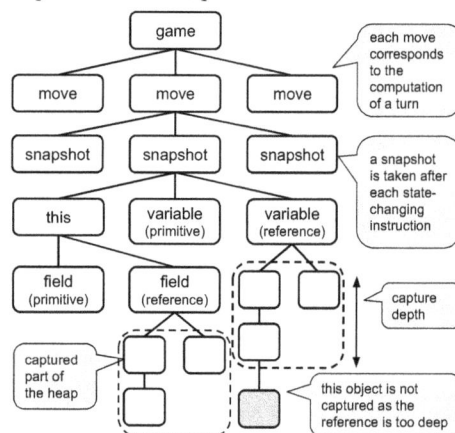

Figure 2: Structure of captured memory data

We executed several experiments to validate our various encoding strategies and also experimented with increasing the capture depth. The results indicate that the size of the data produced is very sensitive to both the complexity of the bot monitored and the method used to capture and encode state. However, with sensible choices, it is possible to encode the entire state and therefore to support reversible debugging on the client while facilitating a server architecture that supports high scalability.

Better Online Teaching Support Using Open-Source Web Applications

Dorian Voegeli
George Mason University
Fairfax, VA 22030, USA
+1-703-993-3682
dvoegeli@gmu.edu

Nicholas K. Clark
C4I & Cyber Center
George Mason University
Fairfax, VA 22030, USA
+1-703-993-1743
nclark1@c4i.gmu.edu

J. Mark Pullen
Dept. of Computer Science
George Mason University
Fairfax, VA 22030, USA
+1-703-993-1538
mpullen@cs.gmu.edu

ABSTRACT
This paper reports on combining emerging technologies for synchronous distance education in a student-implemented project. The goal is to realize, using latest web technologies, the MISTC open-source multimedia Internet client we developed earlier to support teaching in the classroom and online simultaneously. We summarize MISTC's capabilities, describe the development processes and tools utilized, and lessons learned.

Keywords
Open source, web application, Internet distance education.

1. INTRODUCTION
This poster summarizes a project enhancing a proven approach to distance education with Web applications. The project's goal is to realize, in technologies such as HTML5 and Web Real-Time Communications (WebRTC), the approach developed for the Moodle Integrated Synchronous Teaching/Conferencing (MISTC) system [1]. MISTC was designed to provide effective support for simultaneous classroom/online course delivery and provides facilities useful for both synchronous and asynchronous online teaching. The approach grew out of the continuation of an experimental course in web applications programming [2].

2. MISTC TO WEBMISTC
MISTC is a hybrid real-time multimedia Internet communication package, available as an integrated module for the Moodle open-source Learning Management System (LMS). For years, MISTC supported online distance education for the Masters Program in Computer Science at George Mason University. Available for Windows, Macintosh, and Linux as a native application, MISTC includes floor-controlled voice communication, shared whiteboard with slides and real-time annotations in real time, optional video capability, text chat, and recording/playback. WebMISTC re-implements MISTC in open source for execution in modern web browsers (see Figure 1), without plugins, to achieve portability across a wider variety of platforms and mobile devices.

The WebMISTC project applies emerging web development methodologies and tools. Most notable of these is a JavaScript web application framework, Meteor, which features a single code-base for the client and server that reduces redundancy and errors; templating engine and enforceable code structure; built-in

validation and testing components; and security authorization and authentication capabilities.

The Whiteboard is a core feature of MISTC that is re-implemented in WebMISTC. It supports importing pre-formatted slides and to annotate them in real-time with text, lines, arrows, rectangles, ellipses, and freehand drawing in a variety of colors and sizes; such slides are buffered to preserve annotations across slide navigation. Enhancements are thumbnail-based navigation, editable text notes, skeuomorphic eraser, integrated presentation controls, and WebRTC-enabled conferencing. WebMISTC applies responsive design for mobile devices, adapting to varying display sizes and touchscreen interfaces.

3. CONCLUSION
By embracing the open-source ecosystem of emerging JavaScript technologies, we found it possible to re-implement WebMISTC rapidly by integrating well-tested, dependable modules that the open-source community actively maintains and evolves. Additionally, we found that a modern web browser is well suited to deliver quality distance education web applications over all major hardware/operating system platforms.

4. ACKNOWLEDGMENTS
This work was supported in part by a NSF grant EEC#1408674 and its Principal Investigator Aditya Johri.

5. REFERENCES
[1] Clark, N., J. Pullen, P. McAndrews, and C. Snow, Moodle Integrated Synchronous Teaching/Conferencing: A Free Open-Source Synchronous Capability for Moodle, *Annual Conference on Distance Teaching and Learning 2010*, University of Wisconsin, Madison, WI, August 2010

[2] Clark, N, J. Pullen and C. Bashioum, An Experimental Project Course to Prepare Students for Agile Web Application Development , *ACM ITiCSE 2015*, Vilnius, Lithuania

Figure 1. WebMISTC Browser-based Interface

Make and Learn: A CS Principles Course Based on the Arduino Platform

Ingrid Russell
University of Hartford
200 Bloomfield Avenue,
West Hartford, Connecticut, USA
+1 860.768.4191
irussell@hartford.edu

Karen H. Jin
University of New Hampshire
88 Commercial Street, Manchester,
New Hampshire, USA
+1 603.641.4398
karen.jin@unh.edu

Mihaela Sabin
University of New Hampshire
88 Commercial Street, Manchester,
New Hampshire, USA
+1 603.641.4144
mihaela.sabin@unh.edu

ABSTRACT

We present preliminary experiences in designing a Computer Science Principles undergraduate course for all majors that is based on physical computing with the Arduino microprocessor platform. The course goal is to introduce students to fundamental computing concepts in the context of developing concrete products. This physical computing approach is different from other existing CS Principles courses. Students use the Arduino platform to design tangible interactive systems that are personally and socially relevant to them, while learning computing concepts and reflecting on their experiences. In a previous publication [1], we reported on assessment results of using the Arduino platform in an Introduction to Digital Design course. We have introduced this platform in an introductory computing course at the University of Hartford in the past year as well as in a Systems Fundamentals Discovery Course at the University of New Hampshire to satisfy the general education requirements in the Environment, Technology, and Society category. Our goal is to align the current curriculum with the CS Principles framework to design a course that engages a broader audience through a creative making and contextualized learning experience.

Keywords

Computer Science Principles curriculum framework; physical computing; broadening participation in computing

1. MOTIVATION

Physical computing has become increasingly popular in university classrooms as well as extracurricular computer science education [2]. Studies have shown that the choice of context or problem domain of assignments and examples used in class can have a dramatic impact on student motivation and in turn on the quality of their learning. Furthermore, research has shown that participatory or project-based learning methods can level the playing field for different types of students, especially for female and underrepresented minority students. A shift to a learning environment that values hands-on work, interactivity, and collaboration can result in a broader range of students who feel more engaged and, by extension, can lead to greater success.

ITiCSE '16, July 09-13, 2016, Arequipa, Peru
ACM 978-1-4503-4231-5/16/07.
DOI: http://dx.doi.org/10.1145/2899415.2925490

2. COURSE DESCRIPTION/OBJECTIVES

Our proposed introductory computing course is designed to meet the CS Principles curriculum framework and is based on our experiences introducing the Arduino platform in introductory courses. The main goal of CS Principles Courses is to introduce students to computational thinking and foster their creativity in developing computational artifacts. A physical computing curriculum provides the unique opportunity for a broader audience, including those often underrepresented in technologies, to design and implement innovative solutions that are tangible, creative and personally relevant. A variety of contexts and themes have been used in the physical computing curriculum. The Arduino platform provides a flexible and easy-to-learn environment for beginning learners. The proposed course provides an opportunity for students to become engaged with and understand the development of modern computing systems which have become part of our daily lives. In addition, the course provides an opportunity for students to have a hands on experience designing computing-based systems. Students will use microcomputer and microcontroller devices to design systems that they encounter routinely. Upon completion of the course, students should be able to (1) demonstrate knowledge of how the interaction of hardware components and low level software/firmware affects the operation of a modern computing system, (2) discover how an Engineering Design process functions and interacts with many other disciplines to yield new, useful and innovative products, (3) design a simple system that performs a meaningful and useful function using low cost, readily available computing modules and related software, (4) communicate and collaborate with peers of many backgrounds in the creation of computing based systems, and (5) connect computing systems with economic, social, and environmental contexts and with issues of diversity, inclusion, equity, and power.

3. EXPERIENCES

Preliminary results show that students had good experiences in the course. We found that the physical computing approach using the Arduino platform to be effective in teaching students computing concepts as well as engaging students in a creative making and learning process.

4. REFERENCES

[1] Mellodge, P. and Russell, I. Using the Arduino Platform to Enhance Student Learning Experiences In *Proceedings of the 2013 conference on Innovation & technology in computer science education* (ITiCSE'13).

[2] Przybylla, M. Physical Computing in Computer Science Education In *Proceedings of the 10th Annual Conference on International Computing Education Research* (ICER'14).

Improving Student Performance in a First Programming Course

Liliana Machuca
Universidad del Valle
Cali, Colombia
liliana.machuca@correounivalle.edu.co

Oswaldo Solarte P.
Universidad del Valle
Cali, Colombia
oswaldo.solarte@correounivalle.edu.co

ABSTRACT

Attending a computer programming course for the first time is a challenging task for many students who often fail or drop out. Moreover, this problem is not exclusive for computer science students, since students in other engineering programs must also take programming courses. In this poster, we propose a teaching approach for improving student's performance in a first programming course. This approach is based on four main features: the use of Python as first programming language, project-oriented and problem-based learning, multimedia resources, and rubrics for assessment. Our findings indicate that the proposed approach is valid and helps computer engineering schools and students to get better results in terms of both grades and retention rates.

1. Python as first programming language

Choosing an appropriate programming language is still challenging in first programming courses [1][4][5]. We replaced Java for Python because it offers a simpler syntax, higher-level programming structures and a friendlier programming environment. The most important learning goal here is the ability to understand basic programming concepts and develop problem-solving skills.

2. Project-oriented and problem-based learning

Our approach is grounded on constructivist theory of learning, specifically project-based and problem-based learning [2][3]. Through these approaches, students can achieve meaningful learning, critical thinking while developing computational skills as well. The learning activities are designed in order for students to build a collaborative project and solve real-life problems related to students' academic needs.

3. Multimedia Resources

Multimedia resources support learning activities. They comprise pictures, slideshows, videos, animations, and tutorials. We used them to strengthen further concepts and experiences in the learning of programming skills.

4. Rubrics for assessment

Providing detailed explanations of an assignment using a rubric can assist students in improving their performance because

students get a clearer picture of the kind of performance that is expected from them and the requirements under which they will be assessed. Therefore, in our approach rubrics for assessment of each project were presented and explained to the students in advance.

5. Results

The proposed approach has been implemented at the Faculty of Engineering at Universidad del Valle since 2015. To establish the impact of the approach, we report the analysis of the final grades in the programming courses from 2011 to 2015. In addition, we report results from a survey of student's preferences for programming language. Since the implementation of this approach in 2015, the percentage of students passing the first programming course has increased in 10 % (figure 1) as opposed to the 4-year period before its implementation in which no important variation can be observed. We expect that in the future this percentage will increase. In addition, the majority of students considered that using Python was easier than using Java.

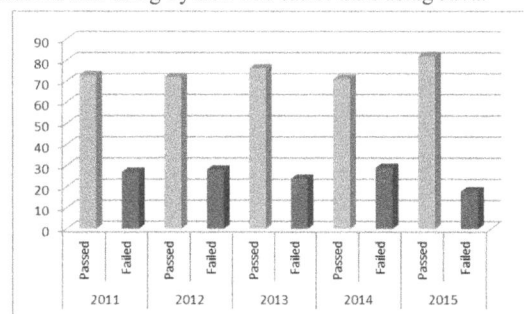

Fig. 1. Final marks of programming courses

6. Conclusions

The choice of a suitable programming language is a key element for the success of a first programming course; however, this is not enough. Professors should look for other strategies to improve the learning process. In our case, project-oriented and problem-based learning, evaluation rubrics and multimedia aids helped improve student performance.

7. REFERENCES

[1] Guo P., Python is Now the Most Popular Introductory Teaching Language at Top U.S. Universities (2014). Communications in ACM, Blogs

[2] Koneck M., Petrlić M. (2014) Main problems of programming novices and the right course of action Central European Conference on Information and Intelligent Systems: 116-123. Varazdin.

[3] Soares, A. (2011). Problem based learning in introduction to programming courses. Journal of Computing Sciences in Colleges, 27(1), 36-36.

[4] Vujosevic M., Tosic D. (2008) The Role of programming paradigms in the First Programming courses The Teaching of Mathematics Vol XI, 2, pp 63-68.

[5] Yading A. (2011)Reducing Dropout Rate in an Introductory Programming Course ACM Inroads. Vol 2. Pg.71-76

Potigol, a Programming Language for Beginners

Leonardo R Lucena
Department of Informatics
IFRN
leonardo.lucena@ifrn.edu.br

Márcia Lucena
Department of Informatics and Applied Mathematics
UFRN
marciaj@dimap.ufrn.br

ABSTRACT

Potigol is a new multi-paradigm programming language specially designed for beginners. Its main features are an agile syntax, which looks like dynamically-typed scripting languages, and a statically-typed semantics with limited side-effects. Both syntax and semantics encourage a functional programming style. It is an open-source project that can be freely used and modified.

Categories and Subject Descriptors

K.3.2 [**Computer and Education**]: Computer and Information Science Education – *Computer Science Education*

General Terms

Languages.

Keywords

Computing Education; CS1; Programming Language; Functional Programming.

1. INTRODUCTION

Potigol is a language specially designed for teaching and learning programming. It can be classified as an *uncommon teaching language,* according to Lewis et al [1]. Being so, it only has features that are appropriate for beginners. Its syntax is simple as scripting languages, like Ruby and Python, but with a static type system which makes it safer. Type inference (the type of a variable is inferred from the value attributed to it) makes it look like dynamically-typed languages. In terms of semantics, a functional style in contrast to an imperative style makes programs easier to understand and consequently easier to find errors.

Potigol language has been tested with small groups of students. Most of them reported that it was easier to write code in Potigol as compared to languages like Ruby and Java. Compared to Ruby, it was also easier to find errors. Potigol´s source code and documentation are available at [2].

ITiCSE '16, July 09-13, 2016, Arequipa, Peru
ACM 978-1-4503-4231-5/16/07.
http://dx.doi.org/10.1145/2899415.2925493

2. LANGUAGE FEATURES

The main objective of introductory programming courses is to enable students to express solutions to problems using a programming language. A programming language for beginners needs to be able to express algorithmic solutions in a natural way. The language must not be an obstacle. So it needs to be expressive and simple with an intuitive syntax. Potigol's syntax is inspired in dynamically-typed languages, which are well known for their simple syntax. Type inference makes statically-typed languages look like dynamically-typed languages. The programmer does not need to explicitly define the type of variables.

The process of developing a program is done by coding, executing, and finding errors. Statically-typed languages like Potigol can find type errors at compilation time, before execution. This assists students to automatically find many kinds of errors in their programs. It also provides error messages that are more relevant for beginners and suggestions to correct the code.

An element that makes programs hard to understand and fix are the side-effects. Side-effects, like changing a value of a variable, make code difficult to analyze since the student needs to execute the code in their brain. Programs without side-effects can be understood statically by just reading the code. A good thing about functional languages is that they have fewer side-effects than imperative languages. Programs can be written with only input and output side-effects.

To encourage a functional style, Potigol has a simpler notation for declaring values (constants) than for declaring variables. Declaring values is as simple as `x = 10,` while declaring variables must have a prefix modifier `var y := 20.`

In spite of having a simple syntax, Potigol has many features of modern programming languages, such as lambda expressions, high order functions, pattern matching, and immutable objects. These aspects may be explored by teachers. Further transition to well-established mainstream languages like Java 8, Scala, Haskell, C#, Swift, Ruby, and Python can be smooth.

3. REFERENCES

[1] Lewis, M.C., Blank, D., Bruce, K., and Osera, P.-M. 2016. Uncommon Teaching Language. SIGCSE 2016 (March, 2016), 492-493. DOI= http://doi.acm.org/10.475/123_4.

[2] Lucena, L. Potigol Language. http://potigol.github.io

Implementation of a Robotics and IoT Laboratory for Undergraduate Research in Computer Science Courses

Jorge Guerra Guerra
Laboratorio de Robótica e Internet de las Cosas
Facultad de Ingeniería de Sistemas e Informática
Universidad Nacional Mayor de San Marcos
jguerrag@unmsm.edu.pe

Armando Fermín Pérez
Laboratorio de Robótica e Internet de las Cosas Facultad de
Ingeniería de Sistemas e Informática
Universidad Nacional Mayor de San Marcos
fferminp@unmsm.edu.pe

ABSTRACT

This poster presents the results of implementing a Robotics and Internet of Things Laboratory to support the research activities of undergraduate students at the Faculty of Engineering Systems and Informatics in National University of San Marcos.

Keywords

Internet of Things, Robotics, Arduino, Computer Science Education

1. INTRODUCTION

Advances in technology have reduced the cost and increased the quality of small single-board computers like Arduino, communication shields, sensors, transducers and actuators [1]. This has made it possible for computer science students to research and develop more and better Robotics and Internet of Things applications using data taken directly from the physical world.

Physical computing covers the design and implementation of interactive objects that allows students to develop concrete, tangible products of the real world [2]. Therefore, physical computing can be useful in computer science education to motivate students in constructionist and creative learning environments. Furthermore, in computer science education, several strategies for effective teaching have been identified [3] and active learning is one of the ways to teach Computer Architecture topics, based on the interaction of students through oral presentation and self-preparation prior to addressing a topic of the subject. [4]

2. IMPLEMENTATION OF PROPOSAL

Based on initial achievements of "Big FISI Robotics" and "Internet of Things" students groups, the Faculty has created the Robotics and Internet of Things Lab, with following objectives:

- Improving the students' abilities to develop applications of Internet of Things and Robotics using open hardware and open software, and improving the high-level concurrent programming abilities of students using Arduino-based systems.
- Promote active participation of students in events, exhibits, conferences to showcase their projects and achievements.

To do this, the lab has several kits of Arduino, shields, sensors, transducers and actuators, with which the students have developed some initial projects, as follows:

- Drip irrigation with Arduino.

- Car movement control by avatar using Arduino
- Domotics in the web, using Arduino, Processing and Android.
- Safety Home: Using remote sensors in the web
- Measurement of heart rate data via GPRS and the web
- Controlling movements of robot arm with Arduino

3. ACHIEVED RESULTS

The lab has helped to introduce physical computing topics into the syllabus of several main courses at the Faculty: Digital Systems, Computer Architecture, Distributed Systems and Control Engineering, where the number of registered students attending these classes has increased by about 15. The average number of registered students was 40 and is now between 50 and 55. In addition, it has increased the number of theses being developed using Internet of Things by about 400%, from 1 per year to 4 per year.

The student teams' projects have been showcased in some events, exhibits and demonstrations, such as Arduino Day 2014, 2015 and 2016; in a national conference of engineering students in 2014; and in a national science fair called "Perú con Ciencia", by National Council for Science and Technology (Concytec) in 2014 and 2015. One of our articles about the Internet of Things was published in "Perspectivas" magazine. [5]

4. CONCLUSIONS

The implementation of a Robotics and Internet of Things Lab has been useful for teaching several aspects of computer science curricula including physical computing with sensing technologies, control mechanisms and the method of prototyping. Also, this way of developing applications using data taken from physical world and Arduino-based small computers is highly motivating for students.

5. REFERENCES

[1] Dopplick, R. 2015. Maker Movement and Innovation Labs. *ACM Inroads.* 6, 4. (Dec. 2015), 108. DOI: 10.1145/2829975.

[2] Przybylla, M. and Romeike, R. 2014. Physical Computing and its Scope–Towards a Constructionist Computer Science Curriculum with Physical Computing. *Informatics in Education.* 13, 2. 241-254. DOI: http://dx.doi.org/10.15388/infedu.2014.05

[3] Barba, E. and Chancellor, S., 2015.Tangible Media Approaches to Introductory Computer Science. *Proceedings of the 2015 ACM Conference on Innovation and Technology in Computer Science Education.* (Jul 2015). 207-212. DOI: 10.1145/2729094.2742612

[4] Arbelaitz, O., Martin, J., Muguerza, J. 2015. Analysis of Introducing Active Learning Methodologies in a Basic Computer Architecture Course. *IEEE Transactions on Education.* 58, 2. (May 2015). 110-116. DOI: 10.1109/TE.2014.2332448

[5] Fermin, F., Guerra, J. 2015. Internet de las Cosas. *Perspectivas. Revista de Tecnología e Información.* 10, 11. 45-49. ISSN: 1996-1952.

How Can We Improve Student Workflow Practices to Better Enable Student Success in CS1?

Anthony Estey
Department of Computer Science
University of Victoria
aestey@uvic.ca

Yvonne Coady
Department of Computer Science
University of Victoria
ycoady@uvic.ca

ABSTRACT

Recent research suggests that one-third of the students enrolled in CS1 courses typically end up failing [4]. Several studies have demonstrated how learning tools can assist struggling students [3]. We present an online, open-source, practice programming tool. *BitFit* was developed to (1) provide students with an environment to practice weekly material and receive support when needed; and (2) collect student usage data as students progress through programming exercises [2]. We present the core features of BitFit, as well as our qualitative and quantitative analysis of 652 students over three semesters of our CS1 course.

Our findings support recent studies that suggest that at-risk students can be identified as early as two weeks into the semester [1]; the metric used in our study was able to identify over 29% of the students who ended up failing with very high certainty. Our results also reveal that interaction patterns with BitFit, in particular with hint features requested by students, allow the identification of another 52% of students who eventually fail. Throughout the semester, students who failed the course used hint features four times as often as top students, while only attempting to compile code one third as often. The combination of early indicators and interaction patterns identify 81% of students who failed the course during our study.

Students were asked to reflect on their study habits and report on course progress in monthly surveys. Although workflow patterns on a per-question basis were very different between unsuccessful and successful students, students from both groups believed BitFit was effective in helping them learning the course material. Unfortunately, many students who ended up failing chose to learn course concepts by reading through hints and sample solutions. It appears that many of these students believed that memorizing a solution in BitFit was a more productive strategy than solving each problem and programming a solution on their own.

The quantitative data collected by BitFit suggests that there are identifiable differences in workflow patterns between unsuccessful and successful students. *Qualitative data collected through student surveys suggests that unsuccessful students do not know their study habits are unlikely to lead to success.* We are currently exploring intervention strategies to guide at-risk students towards more productive ways of learning course material.

Using a mixed-method approach combining qualitative BitFit data with quantitative survey data, we plan to continue to better analyze and understand where, when, and how our students exhibit ineffective study habits. We look forward to feedback and discussion about possible intervention techniques, and how to best evaluate the effectiveness of interventions focused on improving student study and learning habits using interactive learning environments.

In summary, the main contributions of this work are to (1) illustrate the differences between successful and unsuccessful student workflow patterns based on log data; (2) highlight the differences in survey responses between unsuccessful and successful students about the perceived effectiveness of their own study habits; and (3) overview a number of intervention techniques to potentially incorporate into upcoming course offerings. We believe that as we continue to learn more about the reasons certain students exhibit ineffective study habits, our efforts to support at-risk students will increasingly result in student success.

1. REFERENCES

[1] A. Ahadi, R. Lister, H. Haapala, and A. Vihavainen. Exploring machine learning methods to automatically identify students in need of assistance. In *Proceedings of the Eleventh Annual International Conference on International Computing Education Research*, ICER '15, New York, NY, USA, 2015. ACM.

[2] A. Estey, A. Russo Kennedy, and Y. Coady. Bitfit: If you build it, they will come! In *Proceedings of the 21st Western Canadian Conference on Computing Education*, WCCCE '16, New York, NY, USA, 2016. ACM.

[3] A. Papancea, J. Spacco, and D. Hovemeyer. An open platform for managing short programming exercises. In *Proceedings of the Ninth Annual International ACM Conference on International Computing Education Research*, ICER '13, New York, NY, USA, 2013. ACM.

[4] C. Watson and F. W. Li. Failure rates in introductory programming revisited. In *Proceedings of the 2014 Conference on Innovation & Technology in Computer Science Education*, ITiCSE '14, New York, NY, USA, 2014. ACM.

ITiCSE '16 July 09-13, 2016, Arequipa, Peru

© 2016 Copyright held by the owner/author(s).

ACM ISBN 978-1-4503-4231-5/16/07.

DOI: http://dx.doi.org/10.1145/2899415.2925495

Teaching High School Students Computational Thinking with Hands-on Activities

Wei-Lin Li
National Taiwan Normal University
162, Section 1, Heping E. Rd., Taipei City 106, Taiwan
+886-2-7734-3920
easycestlavie@gmail.com

Chiu-Fan Hu
National Taiwan Normal University
162, Section 1, Heping E. Rd., Taipei City 106, Taiwan
+886-2-7734-3920
chiufan@ntnu.edu.tw

Cheng-Chih Wu
National Taiwan Normal University
162, Section 1, Heping E. Rd., Taipei City 106, Taiwan
+886-2-7734-1012
chihwu@ntnu.edu.tw

ABSTRACT

In this study we developed three hands-on activities to teach high school students computational thinking (CT) and, specifically, the decomposition skills. The activities were designed to enable students to solve problems by using application tools. The computer science concepts utilized in the activities included binary search, quick sort and iteration. We evaluated the effect of the activities utilizing a post-activity questionnaire, a post-test, students' worksheets, and semi-structured interviews with the participating students. The results indicated that the hands-on activities developed in this study improved students' CT ability.

Keywords

Computational Thinking, Computer Science, Hands-on

1. INTRODUCTION

CT is an essential ability, as important as reading and writing, for students in 21st century. Traditional ways of teaching, such as programming or algorithm development may not interest high school students. The published research shows that CT is better acquired and understood when learning is enriched by hands-on exercises [1]. We designed three hands-on activities, along with three application tools, to facilitate students' CT ability and at the same time to solve problems in their daily lives. We used the concept of decomposition, defined as "breaking down data, processes, or problems into smaller, manageable parts" [2], to design our learning activities. After class, we use post-test to assess students' CT ability.

2. HANDS-ON ACTIVITIES

2.1 Activity 1: Looking out for the thief

The objective of the activity was for the students to identify the thief who stole the jewel case from an apartment. The apartment had a video surveillance system installed and students were allowed to screen the surveillance video to find the scene when the thief was stealing the jewelry. A video screening program was developed to facilitate this activity. Students had to develop a method to screen the video efficiently and were expected to apply Binary Search to solve the problem.

2.2 Activity 2: Weighing fruits

Students had to sort several different fruits by their weight. A virtual balance scale was offered to students for this purpose.

Students could drag the pictures of any two of the fruits onto the scale to determine which fruit was heavier. Students had to use the scale as few times as possible to sort all the fruits and were expected to apply Quick Sort to solve this problem.

2.3 Activity 3: Drawing geometric figures

In this activity, students had to decompose complex geometric figures and then develop algorithms to draw the figures by using Scratch. Students had to first learn how to use Scratch to draw simple geometric figures, and then familiarize themselves with the concept of iteration to repeat drawing similar structures to produce varied geometric figures. Students were expected to apply iteration concept to complete the activity.

3. METHOD

Our participants were 105 tenth grade high school students enrolled in an Introduction to Information Technology course. The study lasted four weeks in the following sequence of computer science themes: "Introduction to CT", "Binary Search", "Quick Sort" and "Iteration." In each theme, teachers integrated hands-on activities accordingly. Finally, we evaluated the impact utilizing a post-activity questionnaire, a post-test, worksheets, and semi-structured interviews with students.

4. RESULT AND CONCLUSION

The post-test results indicated that most of the students were capable of applying decomposition to solve problems. In the problem solving process, they applied the computer science concepts learned. Also, according to the analysis of post-activity questionnaire, students considered Activity 1 and 2 interesting and helpful for learning, whereas Activity 3 was helpful in learning decomposition but was reported as boring. The majority of the students indicated that the hands-on learning experiences enabled them to think clearly in decomposing complex problems. Approximately half of the students expressed their interest in taking computer science classes in the future. In general, traditional methods of teaching computer science or CT engage students in writing a computer program. This requires learners to master a certain programming language but does not offer more opportunities to focus on the thought process of problem solving. The hands-on activities provided students with the opportunities to engage in learning activities in real life contexts and to manipulate application tools to solve problems. This novel approach had a significant impact on facilitating students' CT ability.

5. REFERENCES

[1] Google. (2015). Google for Education. Retrieved from https://www.google.com/edu/resources/programs/exploring-computational-thinking/

[2] Rubinstein, A., & Chor, B. (2014). Computational Thinking in Life Science Education. PLoS Computational Biology, 10(11), e1003897. http://doi.org/10.1371/journal.pcbi.100389

Applying the Whole-Part-Whole Andragogy to Computing

Sarnath Ramnath
Department of CSIT; 320-308-4966
St Cloud State Univ., St Cloud MN
rsarnath@stcloudstate.edu

ABSTRACT
The Whole-Part-Whole approach for designing learning experiences has been found to be very effective for adult learners. This poster describes two experiences with applying this approach to design computing courses.

Keywords: Whole-Part-Whole, Andragogy, Course Design.

1. INTRODUCTION
Whole-Part-Whole (abbreviated WPW) was first proposed as a pedagogical (or rather, andragogical) approach by Knowles, Holton and Swanson in [1]. Their research showed that this approach was particularly effective for adult learners, since it provided a context within which the learning could occur. An adaptation of this approach, tailored to suit the content of typical computing courses, is described in **Table 1**.

Table 1 Structure of the WPW model

Whole	Parts	Description
		Stage1: Presentation of whole
		Stage2: Focus on individual parts that make up the whole
		Stage3: Return to whole, complete it and connect all the parts.

Each learning experience begins with a presentation of the whole as a black-box view. This allows the creation of a context within which the learning takes place. In the next stage learners works on mastering the parts that comprise the whole. The concepts learned are better retained, since they were learned in a context. The last stage gives a white-box view of the whole. This poster explains how these techniques have been employed and evaluated in two very different computing courses. Designing the entire course as a single "whole" experience is rarely suitable for most courses. Accordingly, a sequence of wholes was defined for each course. Student feedback from both courses has been very positive.

2. COURSES ADAPTED TO WPW
A Software Design Course. Based on the set of learning outcomes, three whole experiences were identified for this course:

Creating an object oriented database for a familiar application. Through this experience the students become familiar with the construction process, and the use of simple Design Patterns. The entire construction of a similar system is revealed to the students in stages, as they complete this.

Creating a GUI for the object oriented database. Here students learn the fundamentals of finite state modeling and the use of more sophisticated design patterns. Some pieces of the construction of a similar system are shown to students.

Adding new features to a drawing program. A complex system consisting of several classes, employing the Model-View-Controller architecture, is partially constructed and provided to students. They learn to add new features in a manner that is consistent with the existing architecture.

Instruction is mostly given through these experiences; guidance is progressively reduced, thus nurturing independent learners.

A CS1 Course. CS1 is a lower level course with a diverse student body. Experiences are simpler, with a smaller set of skills. The WPW approach was blended into the course material as required. Examples of the experiences developed are:

One-dimensional point location. Students explored the divide-and-conquer paradigm and were introduced to the problem solving stages of analysis, design and testing.

Comparison of square-root approximation algorithms. Two simple algorithms for finding the square-root were implemented using converging loops and experimentally compared.

Creating a simple business application. This is done with two wholes: (1) earlier on, a simple, batch-processing version of the project is implemented; (2) towards the end, an interactive version (also a capstone experience), using classes and lists, is created.

3. RESULTS
The effectiveness of these methods was evaluated both through descriptive comments, and by using a tool that measures student perception of relevance. Results show that methods are effective, but extensive adaption will be needed to validate them.

4. REFERENCES
[1] Knowles, M.S., Holton, E.F. III, and Swanson, R.A., 2011. The Adult Learner, Sixth Edition: The Definitive Classic in Adult Education and Human Resource Development, Taylor and Francis, seventh edition, 2011.

Towards an Open-Source Web Security Survey Applicable to University Students

Rafael I. Bonilla, Lenín Tenecela, Washington Vélez, Ruddy Moncayo
Escuela Superior Politécnica del Litoral, ESPOL
Campus Gustavo Galindo Km 30.5 Vía Perimetral, P.O. Box 09-01-5863, Guayaquil, Ecuador
{rabonilla,lhtenece,wjvelez,rmmoncay}@espol.edu.ec

ABSTRACT

This work makes two contributions: (1) we propose the novel idea of using an open-source approach to writing surveys, and (2) we give a first step towards applying this approach in the context of surveying students about their web security literacy. Questions that interest us include: Does taking a course in security help students be more aware of the risks and vulnerabilities in their web browsing practices? When presented with a security warning, do they make the right decision? We present our results in designing and applying a survey on web security at a large university. We have released our survey instrument to the public domain and are in the process of getting other institutions to help refine the questions. We envision the following advantages of open-sourcing surveys: questions can be re-used at different institutions, results can be compared between institutions, and a world-wide community can collaborate and improve the quality of the survey instrument over time.

CCS Concepts

•Applied computing → Digital libraries and archives;

Keywords

Open-source survey; collaborative survey; security

1. INTRODUCTION

Students interact with many web-based systems in their daily life. Usually these systems are protected using various security measures. Through this use, students are sometimes prompted with messages and asked to make a security decision; for example, accept an expired digital certificate. This can happen due to benign (yet risky) reasons, such as a misconfigured server, or it can be the result of an attack (e.g., a man-in-the-middle attack). Students should decide well what action to take, as the wrong one can lead to them being denied access to a service, or can lead to a security compromise (e.g., leaked credentials). Are they really prepared to make the right choice? Do they consider all the risks? How can we measure this?

While prior work has documented the security perception of people dealing with different types of online systems (e.g., e-learning systems [2, 1]), to the best of our knowledge, there are no studies showing either the security literacy level of university students or ways to measure it. We believe it would be beneficial to evaluate students on this subject using a collaborative survey, with a set of agreed questions, so that the results (and corrective measures) can be compared and shared between institutions. To this end, we propose the novel idea[1] of using an open-source, collaborative approach, to design the survey instrument. This approach can be extended to any kind of survey whose results are of interest to multiple institutions.

We designed a web security survey applicable to students and released it to the public domain. We have applied it to 349 students at ESPOL, and are in the process of collaborating with other institutions to improve and expand the survey questions.

2. OPEN-SOURCE SECURITY SURVEYS

Using a set of well-crafted questions, we can survey students to measure their responses to various critical security scenarios.

The questions can be open-sourced and published using versioning tools (`git`), to allow a world-wide community to agree on a set of useful questions to ask students. The community could contribute adding new questions, refining existing ones and sharing their experiences with using the survey instrument. As a result, the community can a agree on the best way to assess the students and use the same questions in their evaluations. This will facilitate comparison of results and possible corrective measures.

As a first step towards a web security survey suitable for university students, we designed a set of 4 questions that test their responses when presented with a web security message. We administered the survey to 349 students from ESPOL university. 85.1% of them correctly identify the error message as an expired certificate, but just 13.75% knew the exact meaning of that; and, only 31.11% of the 45 students that were in their last semester understood the risks of accepting an expired digital certificate.

After this trial run, we improved the questions, and are in the process of applying them at other Departments in ESPOL. We have released the questions using a "Attribution 4.0 International Creative Commons" license, and have published it in Github[2]. Over time, if people find this useful, we envision a more active collaboration that will allow us to agree on a good set of questions. We are also looking for parties interested in applying the open-source approach to other types of surveys.

3. REFERENCES

[1] Costinela and Nicoleta. E-learning security vulnerabilities. *Proc. - Soc. and Behav. Sci.*, 46, 2012.
[2] Zamzuri et al. Student perception on security requirement of e-learning services. *Proc. - Soc. and Behav. Sci.*, 90, 2013.

ITiCSE '16 July 09-13, 2016, Arequipa, Peru
© 2016 Copyright held by the owner/author(s).
ACM ISBN 978-1-4503-4231-5/16/07.
DOI: http://dx.doi.org/10.1145/2899415.2959087

---

[1] A thorough search in Google Scholar lead to no prior work on open-source surveys.
[2] In ENG and ESP: github.com/rbonillaa/Open-Source-Surveys.

Author Index